THE CAMBRIDGE HISTORY OF
LATIN AMERICA

VOLUME VIII

Latin America since 1930:
Spanish South America

THE CAMBRIDGE HISTORY OF
LATIN AMERICA

THE CAMBRIDGE HISTORY OF LATIN AMERICA

VOLUME VIII

Latin America since 1930
Spanish South America

edited by

LESLIE BETHELL
Professor of Latin American History
University of London

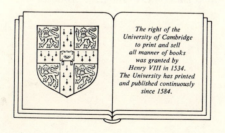

The right of the
University of Cambridge
to print and sell
all manner of books
was granted by
Henry VIII in 1534.
The University has printed
and published continuously
since 1584.

CAMBRIDGE UNIVERSITY PRESS

Cambridge

New York   Port Chester   Melbourne   Sydney

Published by the Press Syndicate of the University of Cambridge
The Pitt Building, Trumpington Street, Cambridge CB2 1RP
40 West 20th Street, New York, NY 10011, USA
10 Stamford Road, Oakleigh, Melbourne 3166, Australia

First published 1991

Printed in the United States of America

Library of Congress Cataloging-in-Publication Data

Latin America since 1930. Spanish South America / edited by Leslie
Bethell.
p.   cm. — (The Cambridge history of Latin America : v. 8)
Includes bibliographical references.
ISBN 0–521–26652–1 (hardcover)
1. South America – History – 20th century.   I. Bethell, Leslie.
II. Series.
F1410.C1834   1984 vol. 8
[F2237]
980.03'3–dc20   91–6743
                                                                      CIP

A catalogue record for this book is available from the British Library.

ISBN 0–521–26652–1 hardback

CONTENTS

MAPS

GENERAL PREFACE

For almost a hundred years multi-volume Cambridge Histories, planned and edited by historians of established reputation, with individual chapters written by leading specialists in their fields, have set the highest standards of collaborative international scholarship. *The Cambridge Modern History,* edited by Lord Acton, appeared in sixteen volumes between 1902 and 1912. It was followed by *The Cambridge Ancient History, The Cambridge Medieval History* and others. The *Modern History* has now been replaced by *The New Cambridge Modern History* in fourteen volumes, and *The Cambridge Economic History of Europe* has recently been completed. Cambridge Histories of Islam, of Iran and of Africa are published or near completion; in progress are Histories of China, of Judaism and of Japan.

In the early 1970s Cambridge University Press decided the time was ripe to embark on a Cambridge History of Latin America. Since the Second World War and particularly since 1960 research and writing on Latin American history had been developing, and have continued to develop, at an unprecedented rate – in the United States (by American historians in particular, but also by British, European and Latin American historians resident in the United States), in Britain and continental Europe, and increasingly in Latin America itself (where a new generation of young professional historians, many of them trained in the United States, Britain or continental Europe, had begun to emerge). Perspectives had changed as political, economic and social realities in Latin America – and Latin America's role in the world – had changed. Methodological innovations and new conceptual models drawn from the social sciences (economics, political science, historical demography, sociology, anthropology) as well as from other fields of historical research were increasingly being adopted by historians of Latin America. The Latin American Studies monograph series and the *Journal of Latin American Studies* had already been established by the Press and were beginning to publish the results of this new historical thinking and research.

Dr Leslie Bethell, then Reader in Hispanic American and Brazilian History at University College London, accepted an invitation to edit *The Cambridge History of Latin America*. For the first time a single editor was given responsibility for the planning, co-ordination and editing of an entire History. He began work on the project in the late 1970s.

The Cambridge History of Latin America, to be published in ten volumes, is the first large-scale, authoritative survey of Latin America's unique historical experience during the five centuries since the first contacts between the native American Indians and Europeans (and the beginnings of the African slave trade) in the late fifteenth and early sixteenth centuries. (The Press will publish separately a Cambridge History of the native peoples of the Americas – North, Middle and South – which will give proper consideration to the evolution of the region's peoples, societies and civilizations, in isolation from the rest of the world, during the several millennia before the arrival of the Europeans, as well as a fuller treatment than will be found here of the history of the indigenous peoples of Latin America under European colonial rule and during the national period to the present day.) Latin America is taken to comprise the predominantly Spanish- and Portuguese-speaking areas of continental America south of the United States – Mexico, Central America and South America – together with the Spanish-speaking Caribbean – Cuba, Puerto Rico, the Dominican Republic – and, by convention, Haiti. (The vast territories in North America lost to the United States by treaty and by war, first by Spain, then by Mexico, during the first half of the nineteenth century are for the most part excluded. Neither the British, French and Dutch Caribbean islands nor the Guianas are included, even though Jamaica and Trinidad, for example, have early Hispanic antecedents and are now members of the Organization of American States.) The aim is to produce a high-level synthesis of existing knowledge which will provide historians of Latin America with a solid base for future research, which students of Latin American history will find useful and which will be of interest to historians of other areas of the world. It is also hoped that the *History* will contribute more generally to a deeper understanding of Latin America through its history in the United States, Europe and elsewhere and, not least, to a greater awareness of its own history in Latin America.

For the first time the volumes of a Cambridge History have been published in chronological order: Volumes I and II (Colonial Latin America, with an introductory section on the native American peoples and civilizations on the eve of the European invasion) were published in 1984; Volume III (From Independence to *c.* 1870) in 1985; Volumes IV and V (*c.* 1870 to 1930) in 1986. Volumes VI–IX (1930 to the present) will be published between 1990 and 1992. Each volume or set of volumes examines a period in the economic, social, political, intellectual and cultural history of Latin America. While recognizing the decisive impact on Latin America of external forces, of developments within what is now called the capitalist world system, and the fundamental importance of its economic, political and cultural ties first with Spain and Portugal, then with Britain, France and Germany and finally with the United States, *The Cambridge History of Latin America* emphasizes the evolution of internal structures. Furthermore, the emphasis is clearly on the period since the establishment of all the independent Latin American states except Cuba at the beginning of the nineteenth century. Seven volumes are devoted to the nineteenth and twentieth centuries and consist of a mixture of general, comparative chapters built around major themes in Latin American history and chapters on the individual histories of the twenty independent Latin American countries (plus Puerto Rico), and especially the three major countries – Brazil, Mexico and Argentina.

An important feature of the *History* is the bibliographical essays which accompany each chapter. These give special emphasis to books and articles published during the past thirty years, and particularly since the publication of Charles C. Griffin (ed.), *Latin America: A Guide to the Historical Literature* (published for the Conference on Latin American History by the University of Texas Press, Austin, 1971), which was prepared during 1966–9 and included few works published after 1966. The essays from Volumes I–IX of the *History,* revised, expanded and updated, will be brought together in a single bibliographical Volume X, to be published in 1992.

PREFACE TO VOLUME VIII

Volumes I and II of *The Cambridge History of Latin America* were largely devoted to the economic, social, political, intellectual and cultural history of Latin America during the three centuries of Spanish and (in the case of Brazil) Portuguese colonial rule from the European 'discovery', conquest and settlement of the 'New World' in the late fifteenth and early sixteenth centuries to the late eighteenth and early nineteenth centuries, the eve of Latin American independence. Volume III examined the breakdown and overthrow of colonial rule throughout Latin America (except Cuba and Puerto Rico) during the first quarter of the nineteenth century and – the main focus of the volume – the economic, social and political history of the independent Spanish American republics and the independent Empire of Brazil during the half-century from independence to *c*. 1870, which was, for most of Spanish America at least, a period of relative economic stagnation and violent political and ideological conflict. Volumes IV and V concentrated on the half-century from *c*. 1870 to 1930. This was for most Latin American countries a 'Golden Age' of predominantly export-led economic growth as the region became more fully incorporated into the expanding international economy; material prosperity (at least for the dominant classes); political stability (with some notable exceptions such as Mexico during the revolution) despite rapid social change, both rural and urban; ideological consensus (at least until the 1920s); and, not least, notable achievements in intellectual and cultural life.

Latin America since 1930 is the subject of Volumes VI to IX. Volume VI brings together general essays on major themes in the economic, social and political history of Latin America from the crises of the 1930s to the crises of the 1980s. Volume VII is a history of Mexico, Central America and the Caribbean. Volume IX will have two distinct parts: a history of

Brazil since 1930 and general essays on the intellectual and cultural history of Latin America in the twentieth century.

Volume VIII is a history of the nine republics of Spanish South America since 1930. Part One consists of two chapters on the political, social and economic history of Argentina. The first covers the period from the onset of the depression and the revolution of 1930 to the Second World War, the revolution of 1943 and the rise of Perón; the second from the *peronista* decade (1946–55) to the military dictatorship of 1976–83, the transition to democracy and the administration of Alfonsín (1983–9). There are separate chapters on Uruguay and Paraguay.

Part Two is devoted to economic, social and political change in Chile. One chapter highlights the workings of Chilean democracy from the 1930s to the 1950s, especially under the governments of the Popular Front. A second concerns Chile under democratic governments of the Right (Alessandri), Centre (Frei) and Left (Allende) between 1958 and 1973 and under the military dictatorship of General Pinochet (1973–90).

Part Three covers Peru and Bolivia. There are two chapters on the economy, society and politics of Peru, first in the period from 1930 to 1960, and second in the 1960s and 1970s (especially from 1968 to 1975, when Peru was in the hands of a reformist military) and in the 1980s under the administrations of Belaúnde (1980–5) and García (1985–90). These are followed by a single chapter on economy, society and politics – and especially the problems of nation building – in Bolivia.

Part Four begins with two chapters on the economic, social and political history of Colombia, the first on the period from 1930 to the *violencia* of the 1950s, the second from the historic power sharing agreement between Liberals and Conservatives of 1958 and the *convivencia* of the 1960s and early 1970s to the violence and the challenge posed to democratic institutions by guerrillas and, more seriously, *narcotraficantes* in the 1980s. These are followed by separate chapters on Ecuador and on the economy, society and politics, especially democratic politics since 1958, of oil-rich Venezuela.

Many of the contributors to this volume – five British (one living in the United States), five Latin American, three North American and one from New Zealand – commented on the chapters of their colleagues. I am especially grateful in this respect to Christopher Abel, Alan Angell, Paul Drake and Laurence Whitehead. Malcolm Deas, James Dunkerley, Peter Klarén, Andrew Nickson and James Painter also provided valuable critical assessments of one or more of these chapters. I would like to thank

Malcolm Deas in particular for the help and encouragement he has generously offered since the beginning of this project.

James Dunkerley agreed to serve as an associate editor for both Volume VII and Volume VIII. His advice and support as well as his skills as an editor proved invaluable in the final preparation of these volumes for publication.

The New York office of the Cambridge University Press has responsibility for the production of the final volumes of *The Cambridge History of Latin America*. Katharita Lamoza was production editor and Mary Racine copy editor for Volume VIII. The index was prepared by Glorieux Dougherty. Secretarial assistance was provided by the staff of the Institute of Latin American Studies, University of London, and especially Hazel Aitken.

Part One

ARGENTINA, URUGUAY AND PARAGUAY

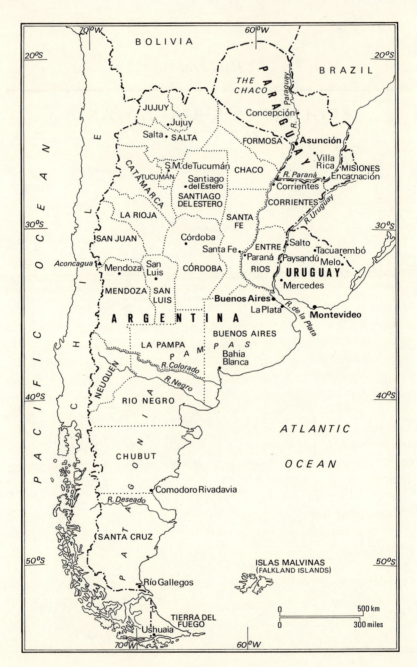

Argentina, Uruguay and Paraguay

1

ARGENTINA, 1930–46

The year 1930 opens the gateway into modern Argentina. The military coup of September 1930 brought the collapse of constitutional government and initiated the long sequence of weak democracies, punctuated by coups d'état and military dictatorships, that remained the cardinal feature of Argentine politics into the 1980s. The plunge into depression in 1930 permanently shifted the path of economic development. Hitherto Argentina had subsisted as an informal dependency of Great Britain, supplying Britain with meats and grains and serving as a leading British market for coal, manufactured goods and, at least till 1914, capital exports. Beginning in 1930 the Victorian structure, already under growing pressure since the outbreak of the First World War, began to totter. From the depression came a decline of agrarian exports and an expansion of manufacturing – conditions that impaired the stability of the Anglo-Argentine relationship as they transformed the components of the Argentine economy. Social change of equal magnitude, and with the same enduring consequences, paralleled the economic shifts. The population of Argentina grew from 11.8 million in 1930 to 15.3 million in 1946, but the rate of growth declined. Falling rates of growth were a consequence of a substantial decline in the birth-rate, from 31.5 per thousand in 1920 to 24.7 per thousand in 1935, which contemporaries conventionally blamed on the depression. (In contrast death-rates fell only slightly, from 14.7 per thousand in 1920 to 12.5 per thousand in 1935.) Declining population growth was also a result of the end of mass European immigration. Foreign-born men still represented 40 per cent of the male population in 1930, but only 26 per cent in 1946. It was no longer Spanish and Italian immigrants but internal immigrants who fed the continued expansion of Buenos Aires as mass migration from the land and the provinces greatly accelerated during the 1930s and 1940s.

3

The year 1930 also marked the acceleration of a profound ideological shift – the decline of liberalism and the rise of nationalism – that later coloured the texture of Argentine politics. A nationalist awareness began to emerge before 1930 among segments of the intelligentsia. But after 1930 nationalism evolved into a political movement, complementing and intensifying the other changes in government and institutions, economy and society and forming part of a complex, mutually reinforcing process of change.

In the 1930s echoes of the past combined with precursors of the future. In September 1930 'democracy' fell and 'oligarchy' returned, sustaining itself first through the army and then, for a decade or more, by electoral fraud. The conservative oligarchy of the 1930s marked a regression to the political system that had prevailed before the electoral reform of 1912 and the Radical victory of 1916, as successive governments again sought to exclude much of the eligible population from political activities. But as in 1900–12, the 1930s witnessed slow liberalization, and by early 1940 under President Roberto M. Ortiz politics seemed about to re-enter the democratic phase that began in 1912. In other ways, too, the 1930s recalled the past. At the centre of conservative economic policy during the depression stood the Roca–Runciman Treaty of 1933, an effort to protect the historic commercial and financial links with Britain that the nineteenth-century oligarchy had created. In other respects, however, conservative responses to the depression soon branched out in innovative directions. Led by the Central Bank in 1935, new institutions were established to manage the economy, and 'devaluation', 'exchange control' and 'deficit financing' entered the lexicon of economic policy-making, where they have remained ever since.

The conservative regime confronted the depression with striking success. Recovery commenced as early as 1934, and by the end of the decade Argentina had regained the prosperity of the 1920s. Yet oligarchical rule prevailed for a shorter period than the Radical rule which preceded it (1916–30), for in the early 1940s new political forces emerged and swiftly overwhelmed it. The collapse of conservatism in June 1943, following a second military coup, stemmed partly from the Second World War, which brought a crisis in international relations and economic policy after 1939. In mid-1940, as Nazi Germany swept through France and Belgium, the conservatives' attempt to revitalize the old European linkages ended in abrupt failure. Faced by a rapid fall in foreign trade, conservative leaders made vigourous efforts to create a new, yet essentially similar, relationship with the United States. But in treaty negotiations with the United States in 1940–1, Argentina failed to win its chief objective: the opening of the United States market to its meat and grain exports.

Internal conditions also strongly conditioned political change. After 1940 the rural sector underwent a major shift from farming to stock-raising, as cattle and pigs took over much of the land on which tenant farmers had once raised their crops and seasonal labourers harvested grains. Industry, meanwhile, was expanding and drawing the population displaced from the land into the cities. By the end of the war internal migration was radically changing the physical distribution and the occupations of a substantial part of the population. These changes helped to undermine the political base of conservatism by reducing the dominance of agrarian producers, while enhancing the weight of sectors dependent upon, or sympathetic towards, urban manufacturing.

If retrenchment and recovery became the keynote of the 1930s, revolution entered the agenda of the early 1940s. By 1942 the conservative regime, now under Ramón S. Castillo, who had reversed Ortiz's attempts at liberalization, stood divided and drifting. From abroad it faced growing U.S. opposition to its policy of neutrality in the war and its reluctance to join the pan-American alliance, stances it had taken, at least in part, in response to the reluctance of the United States to co-operate on trade. Domestically, the government faced similar opposition from a variety of interest groups and political organizations, some of them former conservative supporters. But its most serious challenge came from the ultra-right-wing *nacionalistas,* who were grouped in several different factions and enjoyed little popular support but who were becoming increasingly entrenched in the army.

The military coup of June 1943 unleashed the Nationalist Revolution: commitments to expunge all ties with 'imperialists', to pursue state-sponsored industrial development led by a new weapons industry and to establish an authoritarian political system to root out 'communism' and 'liberalism'. Led by the *nacionalistas,* Argentina embarked on radical reform and profound political change. Yet the corporatist military dictatorship sought by the *nacionalistas* of 1943 failed to materialize. By contrast, 1943–6 marked the rise of Juan Perón, culminating in his election as president. Backed by a newly created mass working-class movement, the *peronistas* swept into power on a programme of industrialization and social reform. Perón's victory in 1946 and the triumph of 'national populism' thus became the major consequence of the war, and Perón himself, the champion of 'economic sovereignty' and 'social justice' and the enemy of 'oligarchy', 'colonialism' and 'communism', embodied the ideological transition of the early 1940s.

POLITICS UNDER URIBURU AND JUSTO, 1930–8

The revolution of September 1930 sprang from deep personal animosities towards Hipólito Yrigoyen, president of the republic from 1916 to 1922 and again from 1928, on the part of conservatives. In 1930 few conservatives opposed 'democracy' as a political system. They remained more concerned with the way democracy had functioned under the Radicals. They analysed politics in Aristotelian categories: under Yrigoyen, 'democracy' had slid into 'demagogy' and 'tyranny'; the venality of the *yrigoyenista* party bosses and committees had stifled democracy's mission of achieving 'true representation'. Behind these perceptions stood a good deal of patrician snobbery. 'Obsequious cliques' and a 'low circle of inept flatterers' had dominated and eventually destroyed Yrigoyen's regime. The fallen president himself was 'low caste', the illegitimate son of an 'unknown Basque', who long ago embarked on his political career in the gambling halls and cockpits of the Balvanera District of Buenos Aires, where in the 1870s he had been chief of police. Yrigoyen's accomplices were men like himself, a 'low breed on the lookout for profit and self-enrichment' and responsible for democracy's other great failure, its 'flattening of due rank (*avasallamiento de las jerarquías*) at the caprice of the mob'.[1] In 1937, as he campaigned for the presidency, Roberto M. Ortiz declared that the 1930 revolution had 'terminated a system of misgovernment which substituted for the rule of law the arbitrary caprice of a demagogue, who subordinated the general interest of the nation to disorderly appetites stimulated by the pressure of the lowest of the masses'.[2]

Conservatives had long hated Yrigoyen. They had made every effort to destroy his reputation before the 1928 election, and soon after the election they began plotting to overthrow him. Their opportunity to do so arrived with the depression. *Yrigoyenismo* was built on patronage and held together by the flow of state spending. Controlling the middle class in this way worked well during periods of economic expansion, such as in 1928 and most of 1929, when revenues were growing. But it failed instantly in an

[1] See Carlos Ibarguren, *La historia que he vivido* (Buenos Aires, 1955), pp. 318, 368, 400, 428.
[2] Quoted in Felix Weil, *Argentine Riddle* (New York, 1944), p. 63.

economic crisis like that beginning in late 1929. At this point Yrigoyen fell victim to a contest for rapidly shrinking resources between the exporting and propertied interests, most of them conservatives, and the urban middle class, which was mostly Radical. As the depression struck, the former demanded drastic government spending cuts to reduce pressure on credit and interest rates and to enable the banks to respond more effectively to hard-pressed landowners and merchants. The middle class reacted by demanding still higher government spending to protect employment and to arrest the fall of urban incomes. In 1930 the government struggled desperately to surmount these conflicting pressures. Eventually it started to reduce spending, but not fast enough for conservatives and much too fast for Radicals. Thus, as opposition from the landed and commercial interests intensified, Yrigoyen's popular support also disintegrated.

Apologists for the 1930 coup commonly depicted the army as simply the instrument of the popular will, acting on the people's behalf: the revolution, declared Carlos Ibarguren, 'fue el ejército hecho pueblo, y el pueblo hecho ejército' (the army transformed into the people, and the people transformed into the army).[3] As Felix Weil later recalled:

Nobody . . . raised a hand to defend the legal government. The workers were disinterested, apathetic, no strike was called, no demonstration was held, no plant or shop closed. . . . With so many government employees, especially police and military officers, unpaid for some time, the military and civil bureaucracy did not mind exchanging the legal but insolvent, vitiated government of a senile, dreamy, insincere reformer for a general's government which could be expected to be favored by the banks, pay salaries on time and reward its followers handsomely.[4]

In this atmosphere it became easy to mount a coup with remarkably little organization and with a minimum of military force. The coup of 6 September 1930 was an almost exclusively military action. General José F. Uriburu, its leader, who had participated in the failed insurrection against Juárez Celman in July 1890, explicitly forbade civilian involvement on the grounds that civilians had caused defeat forty years before. Leaders of the ultra-conservative Liga Republicana, whose members had sporadically fought the *yrigoyenistas* in the streets during the past year, played a part in urging Uriburu to stage the revolution but no active role in the uprising itself. The function of civilians therefore consisted of laying the ground for

[3] Ibarguren, *La historia*, p. 380.
[4] Weil, *Argentine Riddle*, p. 39.

the coup through street demonstrations, inflammatory speeches and a massive onslaught by the opposition press during the weeks before.

The revolution itself entailed little more than a few hundred officer cadets marching from the military garrison at Campo de Mayo to take possession of the Casa Rosada, the seat of government, in the centre of Buenos Aires. Uriburu had made no effort to organize movements in the provinces or to make detailed plans to seize communications centres and major installations. Elaborate preparations proved quite unnecessary. Yrigoyen himself, having got wind of the insurrection, fled to La Plata. When troops there refused him support, he resigned and was placed under arrest. As they entered central Buenos Aires, the cadets were resisted by a handful of snipers, most of them firing from the roof of the Congress building; these exchanges produced a few casualties on both sides. But this opposition was quickly overcome, and the cadets proceeded down the Avenida de Mayo to the Casa Rosada. There the vice-president, Enrique Martínez, attempted to negotiate with the rebels, but having failed, he too resigned.

After seizing power, the revolutionaries proclaimed a provisional government with Uriburu as its head. The new regime consisted almost entirely of civilians, mostly ageing conservatives who had last served in office before 1916 under Roque Sáenz Peña or his successor, Victorino de la Plaza. The provisional government immediately began purging Radicals from the administration, the provincial governments and the universities, but it soon became apparent that the new regime was sharply divided into two factions and held together only through shared opposition to the *yrigoyenistas*. Uriburu himself led the first of the factions, supported by Matías Sánchez Sorondo, the minister of the interior, and by Carlos Ibarguren, who became 'intervenor' (*interventor*) of Córdoba. To many, Uriburu's faction comprised Argentina's 'fascists', those bent on imposing a system like Mussolini's. Uriburu not only persecuted the Radicals; he also coolly shot a pair of anarchists convicted on charges of sabotage. He encouraged the formation of the Legión Cívica Argentina, whose members wore Fascist-style uniforms and adopted the Fascist salute.

Yet Uriburu himself persistently rejected the label 'fascist' and dismissed fascism as a 'foreign doctrine' that was 'inappropriate' to Argentina. Instead he aimed for a 'true democracy', free of the *yrigoyenista* bosses and committees. Indeed, this aspiration appeared to make Uriburu not a fascist but a liberal, because 'democracy', as a right-wing critique charged, identified him with 'the language and the ideas of the French Revolution' – the foundation of modern liberalism.[5] In fact, neither fascism nor liberalism but Catholic scholasticism provided the chief inspiration for Uriburu's political ideas; his conception of democracy was closer to the ancient Greek idea than to its modern practice in the Americas or Western Europe. The scholastic foundations of Uriburu's ideas appeared most clearly in a manifesto he published in February 1932 which he described as the 'doctrine of the September Revolution'. This document – replete with ironies in view of Uriburu's conduct as president – echoed precepts of St Augustine, St Thomas Aquinas and their successors:

The supreme authority's reason for being. . . . is . . . the accomplishment of the collective welfare. . . . Any government that fails to serve that end, either through abuse of its authority or by abandoning its responsibilities, is a tyrannical government. . . . The tyrannical government is a seditious government because in sacrificing the common good it compromises the unity and tranquillity of society, which exists for the simple reason of ensuring the welfare of its members. . . . And every seditious government ceases, by definition, to be a government, so that an organized revolution which overthrows it by an act of force is quite legitimate as long as its objective is to restore the collective welfare.[6]

For Uriburu the whole purpose of the revolution was to establish a better system of representation, and thus to avoid the tyranny of an 'egotistical minority' like the *yrigoyenista* bosses, so that 'genuine representatives of real social interests may act within the State . . . and prevent electoral professionalism from monopolizing the government and imposing itself between the government and the living forces (*las fuerzas vivas*)'.[7] Drawing on current corporatist theory, Uriburu therefore suggested that associations (*gremios*), not parties, be represented in Congress. He and his supporters described this idea as *nacionalismo*, since it would, they claimed, unify and harmonize the constituent parts of the nation. The *uriburistas* therefore campaigned for constitutional reform, concentrating on changing Article 37 of the Constitution of 1853: the composition and functions of the Chamber of Deputies. Once he had achieved this reform, Uriburu appeared ready to call elections and retire. At least for a time he hoped to pass on the presidency not to a fascist but to Lisandro de la Torre, a veteran liberal-conservative who had been among his comrades during the 1890 revolution and his friend ever since.

[5] See Comisión de Estudios de la Sociedad Argentina de Defensa de la Tradición, Familia y Propiedad, *El nacionalismo: Una incógnita en constante evolución* (Buenos Aires, 1970), p. 29.
[6] *Crisol*, 14 February 1932.
[7] Quoted in Carlos Ibarguren, Jr., *Roberto de Laferrère (periodismo–política–historia)* (Buenos Aires, 1970), p. 32.

Uriburu failed both to accomplish constitutional reform and to stage his own succession. His supporters consisted mostly of conservative lawyers and academics. However, most of the army and the *fuerzas vivas,* the great ranchers and merchants who dominated the economy and provided the main civilian base for the revolution, supported the second faction in the provisional government. Led by General Agustín P. Justo, this faction aimed to create a popular conservative party of the type Sáenz Peña had envisaged in 1912 and that would keep the *yrigoyenistas* from regaining power. Its members wanted a conservative economic policy to protect the export economy, defending the linkages with Britain and Western Europe. The faction is thus best labelled 'liberal-conservative', and it differed from the *nacionalistas* led by Uriburu in opposing constitutional reform and corporate representation, which, like Uriburu's other opponents, it viewed as potentially fascist. At root the dispute between 'liberals' and 'nationalists' concerned the structure of the state. The former opposed the type of mediatory state set above society that the corporatist theoreticians envisaged. They wanted government by class, government controlled by themselves – the major producer and commercial interests.

The critical moment in the contest between the two factions came in April 1931 when Sánchez Sorondo as minister of the interior arranged an election in the province of Buenos Aires, intending to use it to demonstrate Uriburu's popular support and to strengthen him against Justo. The plan totally misfired when the election brought a large and quite unanticipated Radical victory, which observers attributed in part to a recent ill-advised increase in the price of postage stamps. From this time forward, as Uriburu's standing crumbled, the Justo group controlled the provisional government, which now set the date for presidential elections for November 1931, Uriburu's role being reduced to little more than that of keeping the Radicals in check. After defeating a Radical revolt in July 1931, the president arrested most of the leading Radicals, and in September he banned their candidates from appearing on the November ballot.

In this way Justo successfully manoeuvred his way towards the presidency. By November 1931, having carefully maintained his standing in the army and among the *fuerzas vivas,* he headed the newly formed 'Concordancia', a coalition of parties with three main branches: the old conservatives, who now called themselves the National Democrats, although they were mostly regional oligarchs; the Anti-Personalist Radicals, who had split from Yrigoyen in 1924; and the Independent Socialists, who had broken away from the Socialist Party in 1927. Justo's only opponents in

November 1931 consisted of a coalition between Lisandro de la Torre's Progressive Democrats and the orthodox Socialists led by Nicolás Repetto. Of an electorate of 2.1 million, 1.5 million voted. The Concordancia's vote totalled a little more than 900,000, and that of the Progressive Democrat–Socialist alliance a little less than 500,000. Three months later, in February 1932, Justo assumed the presidency, as Uriburu departed for Europe, where he died a victim of cancer a short time later.

The 1931 election restored the presidency to the same interests, in particular the pampas landowners and exporters, who had controlled the government before 1916. Justo had gained power thanks to the army's backing and that of the *fuerzas vivas* and because of the ban on the Radicals. Electoral fraud heavily tainted this election. Immediately after the poll, de la Torre, Repetto and the Radicals detailed cases of brazen fraud throughout the country. In some parts the police had robbed the opposition voters of their ballots as they waited in line to cast them; the records of those who had voted were shown to contain numerous falsified signatures, which meant that the Concordancia's vote contained many names of persons who had not actually voted. Opposition supporters had sometimes seen forged stamps and seals on ballot boxes, which suggested either that these boxes were bogus or that boxes had been opened before the official count, checked and 'adjusted' when necessary to ensure that their contents yielded the desired results. In numerable cases, fake ballots had been used, and in still more, dead men had voted.

Electoral fraud, endemic until the Sáenz Peña law of 1912, was no novelty in Argentina. Fraud had persisted under the Radicals, particularly in rural areas, although they had usually practised it in indirect ways, more through covert intimidation than by direct falsification. But in the 1930s, beginning in November 1931, fraud again became ubiquitous in politics and a practice conservatives sometimes openly admitted to: this, they claimed, was a 'patriotic fraud', an unhappy necessity to keep the Radicals at bay. Notorious examples included the election for governor in the province of Buenos Aires in 1935 in which the supporters of Manuel Fresco ensured victory by forcibly preventing the Radicals from voting, by switching ballot boxes and by replacing the real vote with another concocted in the conservative clubs. In an election in Corrientes in 1938 more men voted than were registered; in Mendoza in 1941 conservatives armed with rifles manned the voting booths and watched each ballot being cast. Among the many forms of electoral bribery during this period, one of the most common consisted in offering voters sealed voting envelopes containing already marked ballots, which the voter would then smuggle into the voting booth and use to cast his vote. To prove that he had accomplished the mission, he would emerge with the ballot card and the envelope he had been given inside; after handing it over, he would be paid for his services. In the 1930s the working-class city of Avellaneda, just outside the capital, had one of the worst reputations for political corruption. Here, in what some called the 'Argentine Chicago', conservative political bosses led by Alberto Barceló were alleged to be heavily involved in gambling, prostitution and racketeering, some of the profits of which were used to control elections. Throughout the 1920s the conservatives had complained repeatedly about the bosses, the committees and the corrupt patronage techniques the Radicals had used. Yet after they regained power in 1931, the conservatives themselves swiftly resorted to still cruder versions of the same methods.

The three parties that formed the Concordancia gradually fused, losing any separate identity. By 1934 the Independent Socialists and the Anti-Personalists had disappeared; the main function of both these parties had been to enable a small handful of political leaders to shift to the conservatives and to take office under the Justo government. From the Independent Socialists, for example, came Federico Pinedo, twice minister of finance during this period, who sponsored several of the Concordancia's major economic reforms.[8] A second prominent Independent Socialist was Antonio de Tomaso, a talented minister of agriculture, whose career ended on his death in 1934. But most of the Concordancia's leaders were Anti-Personalists: Justo himself; Roberto M. Ortiz, who became Justo's successor as president; and Leopoldo Melo, whom Yrigoyen had defeated in the 1928 election and who now served as Justo's minister of the interior. Throughout the 1930s the true conservatives remained a minority in the government. The most prominent was Ramón S. Castillo, the last of Justo's ministers of justice and public instruction, who in 1938 became Ortiz's vice-president and then president himself in 1940.

Thus, the more progressive figures substantially outnumbered the reactionaries in the government, and although for some time their preponderance did nothing to abate electoral fraud, it gave the Justo regime a relatively benign and tolerant quality that contrasted strongly with the repressive political atmosphere prevalent under Uriburu. Justo himself spent much of his time maintaining his position in the army, seeking to

---

[8] See below, pp. 20–1, 41–5.

isolate some diehard *uriburistas* led by Colonel Juan Bautista Molina, who were continually hatching plots to overthrow the government. Throughout the 1930s the army remained a critical political force that Justo kept firmly under control and out of politics through a skilful strategy of appointments and promotions.

On taking office in 1932 Justo lifted the state of siege that had prevailed since the 1930 revolution. He released and offered amnesty to Uriburu's political prisoners, among them Hipólito Yrigoyen, who until his death in July 1933 made feeble efforts to rally his supporters for a come-back. Justo reinstated the university professors whom Uriburu had dismissed because they were Radicals. He sharply curbed the activities of the Legión Cívica, the paramilitary organization sponsored by Uriburu. The legion, now under the leadership of retired general Emilio Kinkelín, commanded little significance after 1932, although it managed to survive into the early 1940s. The legion's fate illustrated the skill with which Justo repeatedly isolated and weakened his potential opponents. As Justo demilitarized the regime, he adopted a new technocratic style of government that entrusted certain areas of policy to the hands of specialists. The most famous of these specialists was the young Raúl Prebisch, who became a leading member of the team headed by Pinedo which conceived and implemented the major economic reforms of the 1930s.

Justo experienced few difficulties with organized labour since, at the height of the depression, workers struggled primarily to avoid unemployment. The government mediated a telephone workers' strike in 1932 and did the same in subsequent labour disputes. This approach contrasted with events under Uriburu, whose government at one point threatened to shoot three convicted taxi-drivers unless it obtained an obsequious statement of support from leading trade unionists. The Justo regime sponsored a substantial body of labour legislation that included indemnities for dismissal and curbs on Saturday afternoon working, a measure known as the 'English Saturday' (*sábado inglés*). Even so, this government never flinched from using repression against the unions, Justo continuing the deportations of 'agitators' that had begun after the Residence Law of 1901. The government increased the powers of the police, and it established a Special Section to deal with labour issues.

In 1930 the labour movement had formally united in the Confederación General del Trabajo (CGT), which fused the two leading confederations of the late 1920s, the Socialist Confederación Obrera Argentina (COA) with the syndicalist Unión Sindical Argentina (USA). Although printers for a time dominated the CGT's leadership, the sole union of any importance was the railwaymen's union, the Unión Ferroviaria, which provided about 40 per cent of the CGT's affiliates. Economic liberals led the Unión Ferroviaria; they supported free trade, renewed foreign investment and – their only departure from free-trade concepts – workers' protection against dismissal and redundancy. Throughout the 1930s fewer than one-fifth of the workers in Buenos Aires belonged to trade unions. Most unions at this point upheld at least informal links with the Socialist Party, although small anarchist and syndicalist groups survived. A syndicalist, Antonio Tramonti, headed the CGT until his overthrow in the union split of 1935, which left most of the unions under the dominance of José Domenech, a Socialist who guided the CGT into a more explicitly political, and specifically anti-fascist, stance. During the late 1930s the CGT directed most of its energies towards the defence of the Spanish Republic during the Civil War. Communist influence in the unions remained negligible until the creation in 1936 of a new construction workers' union, the Federación Obrera Nacional de la Construcción (FONC) in response to the Comintern's directive to Communists worldwide to erect an independent Communist-led trade union movement. By 1939 the FONC had become the second largest union in Argentina, and it led the way in unionizing the low-paid, unskilled workers, mostly of rural migrant origin. Despite the growth of the FONC during the late 1930s, the Communist Party had not developed much since its creation in 1920 and still consisted of little more than a handful of intellectuals and labour leaders whose political influence remained relatively small.

Persuasion and manipulation became the distinctive traits of the Justo regime. For a time it achieved political stability but at the cost of growing public disillusionment and indifference. The government never succeeded in freeing itself from the stigma of its origins, which lay in electoral fraud. Justo's apparent strength derived substantially from the weakness of the government's opponents, from the absence of an effective opposition presenting genuine alternatives to its policies. During the 1930s the old Socialist Party again failed to expand much beyond its traditional bulwark in the federal capital. The socialists never fully recovered from the defection of the Independent Socialists in 1927 and the death of the party's founder, Juan B. Justo, in 1928. Under an ageing leadership headed by Nicolás Repetto, the Socialist Party remained the largest party in the capital, where electoral fraud was less common than elsewhere, but its programme remained much the same as it had been twenty-five years before. As dedicated as ever to its constituency of working-class consumers, the party operated on much the same general liberal assumptions as the government. The appeal of the Socialists lay in their secular, hard-headed appraisals of public issues; what they now lacked was the energy and the evangelism they had displayed under Juan B. Justo in their earlier years as they challenged the old oligarchy. In mid-1936 a measure of the old style finally returned as the Socialists, side by side with the CGT, plunged into campaigns to support the beleaguered Spanish Republic, but by the time the republic finally succumbed to Franco's forces in early 1939, Argentine Socialism too was fast becoming a spent force.

Also in rapid decline was the Partido Demócrata Progresista, which by the mid-1930s amounted to scarcely more than the person of its leader, Lisandro de la Torre. At this point, de la Torre had been prominent in politics for more than forty years from his base in Rosario, where he had long served as a spokesman for the farmers and small ranchers of the littoral. Admired for his oratory, his integrity and his colourful, forceful personality, de la Torre upheld mostly conservative ideas. But throughout his career, which began in the 1890 rebellion against Juárez Celman, he had been a firm democrat who detested electoral fraud. Because of his outspoken support for democracy, de la Torre never commanded much support among more traditional conservatives, apart from Uriburu in 1930 (whose offer of the presidency he had rejected).

In 1935 de la Torre served as a member of a congressional commission investigating the meat trade, and in that capacity he provoked one of the greatest political scandals of the Justo presidency. During the early 1930s the British and American meat-packing plants reacted to falling prices by organizing a pricing pool to safeguard profits at the expense of their suppliers. Thus, whereas the prices the meat-packers paid to ranchers for livestock declined from an average of thirty-four cents per kilo in 1929 to only seventeen cents in 1933, between 1930 and 1934 meat-packers' profits ranged from between 11.5 and 14 per cent of capital investments. In 1935 the commission substantiated charges that an illegal pool had been created. But in a dissenting opinion de la Torre went far beyond his colleagues' somewhat muted criticisms and issued other accusations of numerous accounting and tax frauds by the meat-packers. One company, Vestey Brothers, had been discovered attempting to smuggle its accounts out of the country in a container labelled 'canned beef'. In addition, de la Torre declared, members of the government led by the minister of agriculture, Luis Duhau, had connived at these evasions and personally profited from them. Congress debated de la Torre's allegations, as each side traded insults, amidst bitter denials from members of the administration. As the tension rose, an unknown spectator attempted to shoot de la Torre, but succeeded in mortally wounding Enzo Bordabehere, his junior Senate colleague from Santa Fe. After this, de la Torre faded rapidly from politics, and within a few years he took his own life.

Throughout the 1930s, indeed almost till the eve of the 1946 election, Radicalism remained the largest of Argentina's political movements, and only proscription, fraud or internal dissent kept it from the presidency. Soon after the 1930 revolution much of the energy and élan the Radicals had displayed during the 1920s returned as they embarked on a sometimes violent attempt to regain supremacy. By April 1931 the Radicals had regained a popular majority in the province of Buenos Aires; in July they attempted armed rebellion, an adventure some of them repeated, again without success, in 1933. Following the coup d'état, Radicals incessantly denounced the imprisonment of Hipólito Yrigoyen, most of which took place on the island of Martín García in the middle of the Río de la Plata, and when Justo finally released Yrigoyen, scores of Radicals paid daily homage to him at his home in Buenos Aires. Yrigoyen's death in 1933 provoked a demonstration in Buenos Aires that ranked among the greatest in the city's history.

If at the time of his death Yrigoyen had regained much of the popularity he had enjoyed at the beginning of his second government five years before, after his overthrow, continually ailing, he had become little more than a nostalgic symbol. In April 1931 former president Marcelo T. de Alvear returned to Argentina from his second home in Paris and now became, with Yrigoyen's blessing and in spite of their past differences, the party's acknowledged leader, a position he retained until his death in 1942. Alvear, the scion of a great patrician family that to all outward appearances embodied the very 'oligarchy' Radicalism had pledged to destroy, had hitherto lacked a personal power base in the party. But his standing immediately rose in 1931 when he publicly repudiated Uriburu and then cheerfully submitted to arrest and imprisonment at the hands of the provisional government. In all likelihood had the Radicals escaped proscription and fraud during the election of November 1931, Alvear as their intended candidate would have regained the presidency.

Yet as party leader throughout the following decade, Alvear failed to maintain the momentum and energy of 1931. He now continued his attempts as president to bring the party committees and its bosses to heel and to mould the party, as the Anti-Personalists had sought to do, into a popular conservative movement around a clear set of programmes rather

than around the search for patronage or single issues like the oil nationalization campaign of 1927–30. In this quest Alvear again failed, and as
time passed he became an increasingly antiquated figure whose much-
rumoured secret deals with the government made him resented by many of
the party's rank and file. Nor did Radicalism change much after Alvear's
death when leadership passed to Honorio Pueyrredón, a man of similar
disposition and background.

Under colourless and uninspiring leadership, the Radicals therefore
drifted. Until 1935 they refused to contest any elections and readopted
'abstention', one of Yrigoyen's tactics from the party's early days that was
intended to highlight and protest electoral fraud. When abstention was
finally abandoned in 1935, the combination of fraud and the need to
rebuild the party organization left the Radicals electorally weak for several
years. Socialists dominated the capital into the early 1940s, and conservatives, under leaders like Alberto Barceló and Manuel Fresco, controlled
the province of Buenos Aires. The great stronghold of Radicalism now lay
in Córdoba under Amadeo Sabbatini, long Alvear's rival for control of the
national party. The Radicals, like the Socialists, appeared bereft of any
new ideas. Although they continued to demand oil nationalization (an
issue that Uriburu and Justo simply ignored), they too remained overwhelmingly liberal in outlook, nostalgic for the 1920s and, except for
fringe groups, the opponents of any major reform. The Radicals remained
long on moral imperatives but frequently short on substance, plagued by
incessant internal rivalries. In 1944 Felix Weil could discern no real
difference in outlook between Radicals and conservatives:

Dissension is even more prevalent among the Radicales [*sic*] today. They still have
no constructive platform, and their need for an authoritative leadership is greater
than ever since Alvear's death. Opposition to the conservatives is not a powerful
enough factor to unify a demoralised party, particularly since it is difficult to
distinguish between the glittering generalities of the Radicals and those of the
conservatives. The conservatives stand for 'moderate progress and honest government', and the Radicals a 'tempered program and clean government'. Neither of
them means it.[9]

ECONOMY AND SOCIETY IN THE 1930S

The revolution of September 1930 occurred as the Argentine economy was
hit by the world depression. In 1930–1 export earnings fell by one-third,

[9] Weil, *Argentine Riddle*, p. 6.

from an average of about a billion pesos during the late 1920s to only 600 million in 1931. Gross domestic product (GDP) slid 14 per cent between 1929 and 1932, with grain output declining by 20 per cent and manufacturing by 17 per cent. Following the suspension of the gold standard on the closure of the Caja de Conversión in late 1929, the peso depreciated by about 25 per cent by late 1931. Argentina escaped the worst afflictions of the depression, such as the 20 to 30 per cent unemployment rates among industrial workers in Germany and the United States and the catastrophe that struck Chile as foreign markets for copper disappeared almost completely. Even so, the crisis hit farming severely and provoked a wave of bankruptcies in the cities as manufacturing and commerce declined. By early 1931 bankruptcies were triple the rate of mid-1929, reaching a peak in the aftermath of the poor harvest of 1930. From 1929 to 1933 the wholesale prices of Argentina's major exports – grains, linseed and meat – declined by roughly half. Real wages fell by an estimated 10 per cent.

The provisional government of 1930–1 took immediate and energetic action on public spending and foreign trade. In 1930, after two years of rapidly growing government spending under Yrigoyen, the budget deficit had climbed to the high rate of 6.5 per cent of GDP. By 1931 the public debt had reached 1.3 billion pesos – an increase of more than 50 per cent since 1929. Rapidly falling revenues in the wake of the depression compounded the new government's difficulties in curbing the upward expansion of the public debt. The government responded with severe cuts in spending, which fell from 934 million pesos in 1930 to 648 million in 1932. Massive lay-offs among the personnel of the public administration – about twenty thousand in all – became the chief weapon in the fight to reduce spending, Radicals being the main victims. In a bid to contain the fall in revenues, the government raised taxes and in 1931 introduced an income tax that aimed to lessen dependence on tariff duties as a source of public finance. The budget deficit had fallen to 1.5 per cent of GDP by 1932.

In 1930 both the value of exports and, because of harvest failures, the volume of exports fell. Imports, however, contracted more slowly, and import prices fell much less steeply than export prices: terms of trade, taking 1937 as base 100, stood at 97.6 in 1928 but only 63.2 in 1931. The result was a severe balance-of-payments deficit which drained the country of its gold reserves and threatened its ability to service the foreign debt. In an effort to curb imports the Uriburu government raised tariffs, which now became more important as trade regulators than as instruments of taxation.

In October 1931, following the example of numerous other countries, Argentina imposed exchange controls. These measures proved at least temporarily successful, since by mid-1932 the balance-of-payments deficit had been eliminated. By 1932 imports by volume stood at scarcely 40 per cent of the 1929 figure.

Servicing the foreign debt in the early 1930s proved far less difficult than it had during the early 1890s. One reason was that the depreciation of the peso provoked a corresponding contraction in the gold or hard currency profits of foreign companies, many of which therefore ceased making remittances abroad in the hope that exchange rates would eventually improve. The British railway companies, for example, lost an estimated £6 million in this way between July 1930 and July 1932. Delayed remittances helped reduce the balance-of-payments deficits and the resources required to service the foreign debt. A second reason was that in the early 1930s public foreign indebtedness remained light by comparison with that in the early 1890s. Thus, out of a total foreign investment of 4.3 billion pesos in 1934, only 900 million constituted public debts. Although servicing the foreign debt absorbed around half the total gold reserves in 1930–1, Argentina was able to avoid a foreign debt default.

In Argentina the early depression years are better characterized as a period of dislocation than as one of collapse. Despite falling export prices, farm output and farm export volumes declined severely only in 1930 and then recovered to the levels of the late 1920s. In the cities the depression struck the food and drink, the metallurgical and the small-household-goods industries, but left construction and especially textiles unscathed. Visible unemployment remained remarkably light, at perhaps 5 to 6 per cent. In 1933 the British commercial attaché in Buenos Aires calculated unemployment at a mere 2.8 per cent. A year later his successor remarked that 'in comparison with the rest of the world, Argentina may be said to be free of any serious unemployment problem'.[10] Official statistics may have seriously underestimated real unemployment, however. They failed to take account of women workers, who made up perhaps one-fifth of the total, and they defined unemployment, quite misleadingly, as a percentage of the total population as opposed to the total labour force.

Apart from 1930, 1933 proved the most severe year of the depression, as world prices plummeted to their lowest levels in forty years and to

[10] H. O. Chalkley, in Department of Overseas Trade, Great Britain, *Economic Conditions in the Argentine Republic* (London, 1933), p. 146; Stanley G. Irving, in Department of Overseas Trade, Great Britain, *Economic Conditions in the Argentine Republic* (London, 1935), p. 174.

scarcely 50 per cent of those in 1929. This produced another serious balance-of-payments deficit that pushed the Justo government into taking new measures to deal with the crisis. In 1933, in an effort to promote exports and help farmers, the government encouraged the renewed depreciation of the peso, which by the following year had slipped to only 60 per cent of its 1929 value. A second measure of 1933 extended the income tax introduced two years before. As a result, import duties that had provided 54 per cent of revenues in 1930 accounted for only 39 per cent by 1934.

In 1933 the government also modified the system of exchange controls introduced in 1931. The original regulations were designed to check the depreciation of the peso and to ensure the availability of funds to service the foreign debt. At that point the government obliged exporters to sell to it the foreign exchange from their transactions, which it afterwards resold in open auction. The reforms of November 1933 established a review procedure for all remittances of foreign exchange by private parties and began classifying imports by a scale of priorities. The measures limited the number of possible purchasers of foreign exchange from the government by introducing permits. Those who lacked permits had to buy foreign exchange on a free market at much higher prices. With these changes the government could regulate not only the volume of imports, but their content and their source. Giving importers of British goods far more exchange-control permits than those who wished to import U.S. goods, for example, proved an effective means of channelling trade towards British goods.

After the exchange control reforms were introduced, the government began to make large profits from its foreign exchange dealings, which by 1940 totalled about 1 billion pesos. Some of these revenues helped service the foreign debt, but most were employed to subsidize rural producers. Regulatory boards, or juntas, were created to administer the subsidies. Starting with the *junta de cereales* in 1933, similar entities appeared soon after to deal with meat, cotton, milk and other products.

The economic reforms of late 1933 were accomplished under Federico Pinedo, who became minister of finance in succession to Alberto Hueyo, an orthodox figure who had been successful in controlling the balance-of-payments deficits, reining in public spending and avoiding default on the foreign debt. Pinedo, by contrast, proved imaginative and innovative, thanks largely to his team of technical advisers led by Raúl Prebisch. In 1934 Pinedo consolidated the public debt, a measure that fostered lower interest rates and shifted investment away from high-yield government bonds. But the Central Bank created in 1934 became the great monument of the Pinedo ministry. Hitherto the banking system had suffered from undue rigidity, with credit tight during harvest periods, banks competing for loans from the Banco de la Nación, a private entity that had some primitive central banking functions and with interest rates therefore tending to rise rather than fall during depressions. The Central Bank offered new methods for regulating the economy through control over the money supply: buying and selling government securities, rediscounting and changing reserve requirements. The Central Bank geared the supply of credit to the ebb and flow of business activity and gave the government greater control over exchange rates and foreign trade. Although it eventually became an instrument of deficit financing, this was not its original intention. Deficit spending, the Pinedo group believed, would intensify imports and therefore balance-of-payments deficits, while provoking inflation.

Pinedo's measures in 1933 and 1934 established many of the basic instruments that later governments refined and built upon in creating a centralized, directed economy. The Roca–Runciman Treaty of 1933 embodied the other, regressive side of conservative economic policy during the depression. The treaty followed Britain's adoption of imperial preference at the Ottawa Conference the year before. Under imperial preference, Britain would seek to import as much as it could from the Empire, while excluding imports from other countries in return for enjoying privileged access to imperial markets. Imperial preference threatened Argentina, because at Ottawa the British faced strong Australian and South African demands to import meat from these sources at the expense of supplies from Argentina. Rumours surfaced that Britain intended to apply 5 per cent monthly cuts on imports of Argentine meat, reducing purchases by as much as 65 per cent during the first year.

From the start it seemed unlikely that the British intended to carry through the proposal to this extent, since imperial suppliers appeared incapable of increasing production and exports fast enough to meet British demand. At the same time, cutting meat imports from Argentina posed a potential threat to Britain's exports to Argentina and risked retaliation against British investments and British companies. In 1933 the British were searching for bargaining power, seeking means to compel Argentina to buy more British and fewer American goods and to correct the trading pattern that had arisen during the 1920s when Argentina had sold large quantities of goods to Britain while continually increasing its imports from the United States, leaving Britain with a growing trade deficit.

During the early years of the depression, the British had also been irritated by the restraints on remittances by British companies in Argentina that arose from exchange controls and the depreciation of the peso.

The Argentine government responded to the threat against meat exports by despatching a negotiating team to London led by the vice-president, Julio A. Roca, Jr. In May 1933 Roca and Walter Runciman, president of the British Board of Trade, signed a trade treaty, which was followed in late September by a treaty protocol and an agreement on tariffs. The treaty specified that Britain would continue to import the same quantity of Argentine meat as it had from July 1931 to June 1932, unless a further substantial fall in consumer prices made it necessary to apply new restrictions to safeguard retailers' profits in Britain. Britain agreed that Argentine-owned meat-packing plants would supply 15 per cent of meat exports to Britain, a concession that sought to counter Argentine complaints about the foreign meat-packers' pool. Allowing exports from *frigoríficos* that were owned co-operatively by the cattle ranchers would, it was argued, help maintain cattlemen's profits. Finally, Britain undertook not to impose tariff duties on imported Argentine grains.

Since Britain did not import Argentine grains in large quantities, the treaty related principally to beef and amounted to an agreement to maintain beef imports at the relatively low levels of 1931–2. In return, however, Argentina agreed to reduce duties on almost 350 British imports to the level of 1930 before the Uriburu government's tariff increases and to refrain from imposing duties on goods such as coal that had so far escaped the tariff increases. In addition, Britain won an agreement that the remittances by British companies would now be paid by means of subtractions from Argentina's export earnings from its trade with Britain; any remittances that remained 'blocked' in Argentina would now be treated as interest-bearing loans. In the Roca–Runciman Treaty Argentina committed itself to the 'benevolent treatment' of British companies, granting them favourable terms to acquire imports under the exchange-control regulations. The treaty exempted the British railway companies from contributions to recently established pension schemes for their workers. The treaty made no specifications on shipping and therefore left the great bulk of Anglo-Argentine trade in the hands of British shippers, giving Britain an almost exclusive share of the invisible earnings from trade.

The Roca–Runciman Treaty enabled Argentina to maintain meat exports at the level of 1931–2, but little else. The concessions to the local meat-packing co-operatives proved meaningless, since British shippers avoided doing any business with them, and because they were unable to attract ships, the co-operatives could operate only in the domestic market. Britain, by contrast, regained the conditions for trade it had enjoyed before the depression. Since the British also gained preferential access to scarce foreign exchange, they won what amounted to the dominance in trade with Argentina, now protected by treaty, that they had enjoyed before 1914. The British won highly favourable terms for making remittances, including protection against the future devaluation of the peso. The Roca–Runciman Treaty also struck hard against the United States. Importers of American goods were now obliged to surmount the tariff wall created in 1930 and to purchase expensive foreign exchange on the parallel market.

Originally scheduled to be in force for three years, the Roca–Runciman Treaty was renewed and extended in 1936. On this occasion the British gained an authorization to levy new taxes on imported Argentine meat. In return for reducing freight rates, the British railways received still more favourable terms for making remittances. They gained an undertaking that the state railways would not be granted subsidized rates that undercut British rates, along with promises to curtail new road-building that took traffic away from the railways.

Despite all of Argentina's concessions in 1933 and 1936, Britain did little more than protect its existing trade in the 1930s. Although U.S. exports fell steeply, Britain's share, which stood at slightly less than 20 per cent in 1927, remained less than 24 per cent throughout the 1930s. Moreover, although Britain had gained better terms for remittances from Argentina, total earnings by British companies fell sharply during the depression, so that profits remained still far below the levels of the 1920s. In 1929–35 tonnages transported by the British railways fell by 23 per cent, but revenues fell by 40 per cent. Half of the British investors who held stocks in Argentine railways received no dividends during the 1930s; average share quotations of the railway companies in 1936, for example, stood at scarcely 10 per cent of those in the late 1920s. As an illustration of the financial distress of the British railways, in 1937 the Central Córdoba company volunteered its own expropriation by the government and its incorporation to the state lines.

The financial difficulties of the British railway companies resulted not only from the depression but from increasing competition from road transport. Throughout the 1920s Argentina had imported a large number of cars, buses and trucks, mostly from the United States. In 1932, despite bitter opposition from the railways, the Justo government inaugurated a road-building programme. Most of these new roads were constructed in the littoral, where they competed directly with the British railways. The growth of road transport became still more conspicuous in the cities, where the obsolescent British tramways faced an ever-growing challenge from the *colectivo* buses, which proved invariably cheaper, faster and more flexible. In 1929 the tramways earned 43 million pesos, but in 1934 only 23 million. In 1935, as preliminary negotiations began for the renewal of the Roca–Runciman Treaty – which it judged a propitious moment to act – the largest of the British tramway companies in Buenos Aires, the Anglo-Argentine, submitted a plan to the government to place the city's transportation services under a single entity, the Corporación de Transportes.

Establishing the Corporación de Transportes amounted to a thinly disguised plot to subject the *colectivos* to the control of the tramways, which would then try to destroy them. Under the scheme's provisions, all parties providing transport services in the city would be obliged to join the Corporación, receiving shares and voting power according to the size of their capital assets. Under this scheme the tramways would become dominant, since the *colectivos* were often shoe-string businesses operating heavily on credit. In 1935 the Anglo-Argentine Tramway Company further petitioned that the Corporación de Transportes receive a minimum 7 per cent profit guarantee, the type of subsidy that had been widely used before 1890 to attract British investment to Argentina. Since it feared retaliation against meat exports as the Roca–Runciman Treaty fell due for renewal, the Justo government felt obliged to agree to the creation of the Corporación, despite strong opposition from both the *colectiveros* and consumer interests led by the Socialist Party. But having done this, the government failed to follow up with the substance of the plan. It avoided any attempt to force the *colectivos* into the Corporación and repeatedly denied requests from the tramways to charge higher rates. On this score, the Justo government succeeded in outmanoeuvring the British, although simultaneously it was sustaining severe political damage on the issue of the meat-packers' pool at the hands of Lisandro de la Torre.

Economic growth had resumed in Argentina by 1934, and recovery continued at an accelerating pace throughout the late 1930s except for a recession in 1937–8 when the harvest failed. Grains led the recovery of the mid-1930s. In 1936–7 Argentina recorded its highest-ever volume of grain exports, as farmers gained a more than 20 per cent increase in prices over 1933. By 1937 Argentina remained the world's seventh-largest producer and second-largest exporter of wheat; it also produced half the world's linseed. The devaluation of the peso in 1933, which boosted grain exports during following years, triggered substantial inflation; the cost of living in Buenos Aires rose by about 25 per cent from mid-1934 to mid-1936, at which point inflation served as a symptom of economic recovery. Rising prices helped foster the construction boom in Buenos Aires during the late 1930s. In 1939, after several years of rising public spending and a 20 per cent rise in 1939 alone, Argentina had a budget deficit of 2 per cent of GDP.

During the early 1930s the manufacturing industry was depressed along with the rest of the economy, although the slide had been less severe than in other sectors. Manufacturing then recovered swiftly, and from the mid-1930s it began to outpace all other sectors, growing at more than double the rate of agriculture. Several conditions favoured industrial growth during the 1930s. Tariffs, bilateral trade, exchange controls and devaluations both restricted imports and distorted their composition, making local producers more competitive in the domestic market. Throughout the 1930s Argentine manufacturers could acquire second-hand machinery at knock-down prices from bankrupt industrial firms abroad. Cheap labour became increasingly plentiful as a result of migration from country to city.

The 1914 census had counted 383,000 'industrial' workers. In 1935 there were 544,000; by 1941 the number had climbed to 830,000; and by 1946 it was more than a million. In the early 1940s the manufacturing sector produced a variety of goods, of which textiles and processed foods, followed by chemicals, metals and cement, were most prominent. Most industries produced finished consumer goods. The absence of any heavy industry reflected limited local supplies of basic raw materials like coal and iron-ore and the unhelpful network of communications that remained heavily biased towards agricultural exporting. Credit shortages also constrained more diverse industrial development. Beyond all this, Argentina's manufacturers sometimes behaved more like speculators than entrepreneurs and long-term investors. They often appeared to believe that manufacturing might yield short-term profits with minimal investment, but it could not be relied on in the longer term except in a very few instances. Such attitudes derived in part from memories of the war and immediate post-war years; industry had flourished in 1914–18 but had then collapsed as imports resumed after the war. During the 1930s similar expectations prevailed; only the depression prevented the resumption of imports, and when it passed, foreign competition would again strangle local manufacturers. All these conditions helped preserve most industrial units as small-scale, low-investment concerns. Figures from 1939 showed that 60 per cent of 'industrial firms' had ten or fewer employees, and 75 per cent fewer than fifty. Two-thirds of industry in 1935 embraced food and drink and textiles. Side by side with these numerous small firms, however, stood a handful of very large concerns whose size derived from monopoly and from an abundant supply of cheap raw materials. Among them were the great Bemberg consortium, which dominated the brewing industry; Torcuato Di Tella, whose company, Sociedad Industrial Americana de Maquinarias (SIAM), produced a variety of appliances under licence from the United States; and Miguel Miranda, the rags-to-riches canned foods giant who in the late 1940s under Perón became Argentina's chief economic planner. Foreigners still occupied a prominent position in Argentine manufacturing as they had done before 1914. Part of the sudden surge in industrial growth at the end of the 1930s, for example, could be traced to the tide of Jewish refugees who arrived with whatever capital they could retrieve as the Nazis extended their grip over Central Europe. Another striking feature of the manufacturing sector in Argentina was its overwhelming concentration in the city of Buenos Aires and its immediate surroundings. The 1939 figures showed 60 per cent of industrial firms, 70 per cent of industrial workers and about 75 per cent of industrial wages in Buenos Aires.

Some of the expanding industries of the 1930s and 1940s, particularly textiles and manufactured foods, had been established for a generation or more. Among the industries that produced novel goods like electrical bulbs and rubber tyres stood several that sprang up as subsidiaries, mostly of North American companies. United States exporters set up operations in Buenos Aires because of the high tariffs and the discriminatory use of exchange controls after 1933. If U.S. investment as a whole was dwindling during the depression and war years, private investment in these manufacturing subsidiaries increased by U.S. $30 million between 1933 and 1940. By the later 1930s fourteen subsidiaries of U.S. companies appeared, employing a total work-force of fourteen thousand.

However, industry in the 1930s meant principally textiles, which continued to grow during the early 1930s, although manufacturing as a whole was contracting. The number of textile factories increased from twenty-five to thirty between 1929 and 1934, and the workers they employed from eight thousand to twelve thousand. In 1930 domestic textile producers provided only 9 per cent of total consumption. By 1940 the domestic producers' share of the market rose to almost half, and by 1943, as imports fell steeply during the war, it climbed to more than four-fifths. By the mid-1930s Argentina became self-sufficient in cotton knitted cloth and in the coarser counts of cotton yarn. A silk-weaving industry developed. During the 1930s and 1940s textiles achieved an annual growth rate of 11 per cent, compared with about 6 per cent in manufacturing as a whole.

Throughout this period textile producers enjoyed exceptionally favourable conditions. Foremost among them was an abundance of wool, as wool exports collapsed during the depression. Woollen textiles accounted for about three-quarters of total production until the late 1930s. As early as 1934 several wool manufacturers in Buenos Aires were working with twelve-month advance orders. Simultaneously, raw-cotton production was increasing rapidly, as cotton acreages grew from 258,000 acres in 1924 to 706,000 in 1934 and 832,000 by 1940. Small farmers in the province of Chaco in the Far North, most of them close to the city of Resistencia, supplied more than four-fifths of raw cotton. In 1933 the government introduced a subsidy for cotton growers financed by the profits of exchange control, and this *junta de algodón,* one of Pinedo's regulatory boards, helped maintain the upward expansion of cotton production.

Besides access to cheap raw materials, textiles enjoyed other advantages. Policies adoped during the depression – higher tariffs, exchange controls and devaluations – tended either to reduce imports of textiles or to change the relative prices of domestic goods and imports. The Roca–Runciman Treaty, for example, helped to reduce the inflow of cheaper textiles from countries like Japan and Italy in favour of relatively expensive British goods, in a way that increased the competitive edge of local producers. While supply conditions were changing, demand for textile products remained relatively constant and inelastic, and as imports fell the profits of local producers increased, boosting output. Like the rest of manufacturing, the textile industry benefited from the growing abundance of cheap labour, becoming perhaps the largest employer of women. The industry also benefited from the practice of requisitioning cheap second-hand machinery from abroad; the number of cotton spindles, for example, increased fivefold in 1930–6. Of all these favourable conditions, the ready supply of cheap raw materials was the most crucial. Other sectors of manufacturing, like metallurgy, which remained dependent on imported raw materials, grew at a slower rate during the 1930s than during the 1920s. The new textile industry displayed the same general features as industry at large. In 1936 some 225 firms were in operation, but the top 10 employed almost half the total labour force.

Mass migration from the land to the cities accompanied the rise of manufacturing. Internal migration did not begin during the 1930s, but the pace now rapidly increased. Having contributed an average of roughly 5 per cent to the growth of Buenos Aires and its suburbs between 1914 and 1935, the migrants' share rose to 37 per cent in 1937–47, reflecting also the much lower rate of foreign immigration during the 1930s and 1940s. Between 1937 and 1943 an average of 70,000 migrants entered the city of Buenos Aires and its suburbs each year, but in 1943–7 the rate climbed to 117,000. Migration played a major part in sustaining the expansion of Buenos Aires, whose population, 1.5 million in 1914 and 3.4 million by 1936, had grown to 4.7 million by 1947. Recent studies of internal migration have attempted to gauge movements out of the country-side, as opposed to additions to the urban population. These figures suggest not only that the rate of mobility was much higher than earlier estimates had indicated, but also that migration began to increase markedly during the early depression years rather than in the late 1930s. Nonetheless, the older view that migration intensified during the 1940s and after remains unchallenged. Alfredo E. Lattes' calculations, for example, show rural flight at about 185,000 during the quinquennium 1930–4, 221,000 between 1935 and 1939 and 446,000 during the years 1940–4. Throughout the 1930s and 1940s almost two-thirds of the migrants came from the pampas region, and mostly from the province of Buenos Aires, rather than from the interior. Lattes estimates that Greater Buenos Aires attracted 1.1 million migrants between 1935 and 1947, of whom two-thirds came from the pampas provinces and Mendoza. By the early 1950s the position changed substantially, but before then, it seemed, most migration occurred over relatively short distances and often consisted of first a movement from the land into adjacent small towns followed by a later shift into the metropolitan area.[11]

Manufacturing pulled population into the city; agricultural conditions expelled it from the land. The depression struck an agrarian society whose basic features had changed little during the past generation. In the pampas

[11] Alfredo E. Lattes, 'La Dinámica de la población rural en la Argentina', *Cuadernos del CENEP*, no. 9 (1979).

the rural population still consisted mostly of tenants and day-labourers who were employed on large estates on terms that often made their lives extremely insecure. Land tenure was hardly different from what it had been in 1914. In the province of Buenos Aires slightly more than 300 families owned one-fifth of the land, and only 3,500 families half the land. In both Buenos Aires and Santa Fe, the two leading pampas provinces, large farms of more than 1,000 hectares embraced two-thirds of the land area. An agricultural census in 1937 revealed that only 20,000 landowners, in a total rural population of about 1.5 million, owned 70 per cent of pampas land. During the early 1930s landowners who were threatened by the depression had incorporated their holdings to attract new capital and to prevent their alienation or subdivision.

During the early depression years, the government made some efforts to improve conditions for the farm population, particularly for the tenants. Legislation in 1932 established minimum five-year contracts for farm tenants and insisted that tenants be reimbursed for improvements they had made on the lands they farmed. In 1933, as farm prices on the international markets plummeted, the government imposed a moratorium on farmers' debts. Unless they found their rents increased, farmers also gained some protection from the depreciation of the peso after 1929 and from grain subsidies provided by the *junta de cereales*. From the standpoint of production at least, these measures helped to maintain agricultural output, which continued to climb up to the record harvests of 1937.

Yet there were other signs that the farmers remained unhappy and their position uncertain. In the 1930s farm tenants still suffered from the conditions that observers had criticized continually over the past fifty years: credit remained inadequate, and much of it still came from the often rapacious local storekeepers (*pulperos*) rather than from agricultural banks; farmers lacked storage facilities for their grains and therefore had to release their crops as they harvested them, forcing prices to fall; farmers remained in the hands of the railways for transportation and dependent on the goodwill of the monopolistic 'Big Four' grain exporters in Buenos Aires. Among the large grain exporters the biggest, Bunge y Born, now exported almost one-third of the total grain crop and served as broker in the financing of half the country's grain between harvesting and exporting. Only two firms handled almost three-quarters of all grain shipments. On the land the continuing practice of itinerant tenancy and reliance on a seasonal labour force fostered weak family structures, a low marriage-rate, a low birth-rate and a high rate of illegitimacy.

These adversities had plagued farmers for decades. But in the 1930s
came hints that conditions were deteriorating still further. As more and
more *estancias* underwent incorporation, landowner absenteeism – another
perennial complaint of farmers – grew. Relations between landlords and
tenants became still more impersonal, and the paternalistic links that had
sometimes bound them together diminished. Despite the 1932 legislation
most tenants continued to work without written contracts, and notwithstanding import shortages during the depression, farming continued to be
mechanized, the number of harvesters growing from 28,600 in 1930 to
about 42,000 by 1940. Increasing mechanization meant less need for
seasonal labourers, and it tended to force out marginal small farmers. In
1934 the British commercial attaché referred to 'the growing number of
tramps [who are] a matter of serious concern to owners of camp property
and to the railway companies'.[12] Farmers suffered their greatest blow after
mid-1940 with the collapse of agricultural exports during the war. But
even before 1940 at least fragmentary evidence suggested widening income differentials between countryside and city that may have spurred
internal migration.

THE RISE OF NATIONALISM

During the 1930s Argentine politics began to undergo the shifts and
realignments that were to culminate in Perón's rise to power. Of the new
political currents of this period, nationalism became the most central and
significant. Nationalism had complex roots that stretched back into the
early nineteenth century, but the sudden proliferation of nationalist ideas
after 1930 accompanied the depression. Nationalism emerged as a major
ideological force in 1934 with the publication of *La Argentina y el imperio
británico: Los eslabones de una cadena, 1806–1933* by Rodolfo and Julio
Irazusta. This book attacked the mentality of the liberal-conservative
ruling class that had conceded so much, the Irazustas claimed, in the
Roca–Runciman Treaty out of a misplaced sense of gratitude and loyalty
to Britain for British support during the struggle for independence. The
Irazustas dismissed this idea as myth: if Britain had ever supported the
independence movement, it had done so only to capture Argentina as a
commercial and investment market and to establish a new form of colonial
domination to replace that of Spain.

[12] See Chalkley, *Economic Conditions in the Argentine Republic* (1935), p. 174.

Within the nationalist movement at large there appeared two separate strands, which were ultimately united by Perón. The first was the popular nationalist thread that had first surfaced during the oil campaigns of the late 1920s. In seeking to extend state control over raw materials like oil and to exclude foreigners, the campaign aimed to stem the outflow of wealth that foreign control allegedly induced and to develop new areas of employment. In 1935 this *yrigoyenista* brand of nationalism re-emerged in a small organization of young Radicals known as the Fuerza de Orientación Radical de la Juventud Argentina (FORJA). The FORJA embodied two main principles: popular democracy ('Argentina's history', declared its first manifesto in June 1935, 'shows the existence of a permanent struggle by the people for popular sovereignty') and anti-imperialism ('We are a colony; we want a free Argentina').[13]

For a decade, until many of its members defected to join Perón in 1945, the FORJA became one of the chief irritants to Alvear within Radicalism. '*Forjistas*' intensified the anglophobia that the Irazustas had helped create. In his widely read *Ferrocarriles Argentinos,* published in 1940, Raúl Scalabrini Ortiz, a fringe member of the FORJA, depicted the British railway companies as corrupt exploiters and agents of British colonial domination. During the Second World War anti-imperialism led the FORJA into a staunch defence of neutrality against the pro-Allied position taken by Alvear and most other Radicals. But powerful and effective though its campaigns became, the FORJA had limitations as a full-blown anti-imperialist movement. Its overriding concerns and objectives lay in transferring property or resources controlled by foreigners to natives. Like the Radicals at large, the FORJA tended to ignore the deeper and ultimately more challenging issues like industry and social reform, and its chief role, fully in keeping with the Radical tradition, was to promote the interests of the 'statist' middle class that the Radicals represented.

Nacionalismo, a movement of the extreme Right of more complex origins and content than the FORJA, became the second nationalist current of the 1930s. The *nacionalistas* originally comprised Uriburu's small band of civilian supporters in 1930–2 who had supported his attempt to reform the system of congressional representation and created paramilitary groups like the legión Cívica. In some measure *nacionalismo* echoed nineteenth-century federalism. Its members detested Buenos Aires as an agent of internal

---

[13] Quoted in Arturo Jauretche, 'De FORJA y la década infame', in Alberto Ciria (ed.), *La decada infame* (Buenos Aires, 1969), p. 91.

domination over the provinces and as a symbol of 'corrupt materialism', while idealizing the provinces, rural areas and rural people as incarnations of virtues they regarded as characteristically hispanic and Argentine. Principally a literary movement in its formation period before 1930, *nacionalismo* had assimilated various ultra-conservative influences from Europe, of which the most important were Spanish clericalism and the doctrines of Charles Maurras, the French monarchist. These European influences shaped its basic ingredients of anti-liberalism and anti-communism. At the heart of *nacionalismo* lay a conviction that liberalism and popular democracy represented a mere prelude to communism. A liberal political system, declared Roberto de Laferrère, one the leading *nacionalistas* of the 1930s, 'allows all sorts of seditious propaganda. A powerful Communist organization has arisen among us. . . . Democracy hands us over unarmed to these forces of extreme socialism and anarchy'.[14]

Enemies of the *nacionalistas* attacked the unfounded exaggerations and the paranoia that underlay such claims and dismissed *nacionalistas* as 'creole fascists'. Indeed, the movement contained many fascist elements and imitations. Its members venerated dictatorship in the same terms as Mussolini ('to impel actions . . . [to] silence dissent, . . . [to] do constructive works'] and made a cult of will, intuition and virility, searching for the 'grandeur of life . . . through a leap into strenuous discipline'.[15] Like fascism, *nacionalismo* thrived on crusades against mythical anti-types. It regarded both liberalism and communism as Jewish in origin, contending that Jews simultaneously controlled world capitalism and the world revolutionary proletariat. Typical of *nacionalista* writing was the attack on the 'Jewish nihilist, the exploiter but also the secret director of the world proletariat . . . the God-less and nation-less Jew, who is infiltrating the minds of our young proletarians'.[16]

Throughout the 1930s the *nacionalistas* led muck-raking assaults against prominent Jewish families. Such attacks became closely associated with their dogmatic belief that in Argentina the city exploited the countryside, since in *nacionalista* propaganda urbanism often became synonymous with Jewry. Typical of their anti-Semitic campaigns were denunciations of the monopolistic grain export houses based in Buenos Aires, most of which were Jewish-owned. The *nacionalistas* were by no means alone in attacking the export houses, since they had long been a favourite target of

[14] Ibarguren, Jr., *Laferrère*, pp. 69–70.
[15] See Comisión de Estudios, *El nacionalismo*, pp. 110–11.
[16] Federico Ibarguren, *Orígenes del nacionalismo argentino, 1927–1937* (Buenos Aires, 1969), p. 398.

all who supported the farm interest. But the *nacionalistas* stood out on account of their violent racism. The Jewish Bemberg family became another of their major targets: its head, Otto Bemberg, the *nacionalistas* contended, had manoeuvred to secure a monopoly in the brewing industry and used his profits to buy up foreclosed lands from bankrupt farmers and ranchers.

Nacionalismo therefore contained echoes of Fascist Italy and some of Nazi Germany, coupled with a mystical ruralism and an aggressive defence of the smaller ranching interests and their peon dependants. In other respects *nacionalismo* developed as an offshoot of Spanish conservatism and as a weaker version of the Spanish nationalist movement that waged the Spanish civil war under Franco. In the early 1930s Argentina underwent a Catholic revival that reached a climax during the Congreso Eucarístico Internacional held in Buenos Aires in 1934. At this point militant priests and lay Catholics came to exercise a dominant role in the movement and to shape its central ideas. At the heart of *nacionalismo* lay an organic concept of society that was rooted in antiquity and Catholic scholasticism. Like Uriburu's 1932 manifesto, the *nacionalistas* regarded the purpose of government as that of serving the 'public' or 'common good', and they defined human society in the spiritual and corporatist terms that stood at the core of conservative Catholicism, rejecting liberalism because it treated humanity in falsely individualist terms and communism because of its atheism and materialism.

But the great peculiarity of *nacionalismo* that largely explains its importance after 1940 was its juxtaposition of the most reactionary attitudes with a commitment to progressive reform. Among the major influences on *nacionalismo* were the papal encyclicals of 1891 and 1931, *Rerum Novarum* and *Quadragesimo Anno*. Both documents contained bitter attacks on liberalism and socialism, but they also posed the issue of 'social justice', a better ordering of relations among the social classes to achieve the age-old Catholic quest for an organic, 'harmonious' society. By the mid-1930s, as they fulminated against 'liberals' and 'communists', the *nacionalistas* were proclaiming a concern for the working class and social reform. 'The lack of equity', declared La Voz Nacionalista, 'of welfare, of social justice, of morality, of humanity, has made the proletariat a beast of burden . . . unable to enjoy life or the advances of civilization'.[17] In 1937 one of the most stridently anti-Semitic groups, the Alianza de la Juventud Naciona-

---

[17] La Voz Nacionalista, *El nacionalismo argentino* (Buenos Aires, 1935), p. 5.

lista, coupled demands for a ban on Jewish immigration and the expulsion of Jews from public offices not only with 'social justice' but with what it described as 'revolutionary' land reform to destroy 'oligarchy'. The *nacionalistas* stood out among the first proponents of industrialization and the nationalization of foreign-owned public services. Proposals among them to develop a national steel industry appeared as early as 1931. In 1932 a *nacionalista* newspaper attacked the American-owned Unión Telefónica as a 'foreign firm that monopolizes a public service and that ought to have been nationalized some time ago'.[18]

Nacionalismo was not a political 'party', a designation its members totally rejected because 'party' implied the liberal proposition that a mere segment of the community could uphold an identity separate from society at large; 'parties', said the *nacionalistas,* 'split' an indivisible entity: the nation. Equally, the *nacionalistas* refused to take part in any elections, since they regarded electoral practices as another derivative of liberalism. Throughout the 1930s the movement consisted of a dozen or so factions, often competing and squabbling among themselves and headed by members of the intelligentsia, whose chief activities were disseminating propaganda, holding public meetings and staging occasional street demonstrations. By the end of the decade, in addition to the publication of numerous newspapers and periodicals, the *nacionalistas* had turned to 'historical revisionism', the rewriting of Argentine history to attack what they saw as the distorted historical vision of the liberal establishment, the heroes of liberal historiography, the British, and above all to rehabilitate the figure of Juan Manuel de Rosas as the great model of political leadership they aspired to. 'It's a foul lie', declared Marcelo Sánchez Sorondo, 'that we owe our historical being to liberalism. To liberalism we owe only the handover of our frontier lands, and the tutelage of foreigners'.[19] Rosas' governments, by contrast, exemplified the 'collaboration of each element of society: leader, enlightened minority and mass'.[20] Soon after after 1930 the *nacionalistas* had therefore renounced the *uriburista* aspiration for 'true democracy' in favour of a commitment to autocratic corporatism under a military leader. In spite of this shift, it remained the duty of the government to promote both the 'common good' and 'social justice'.

During the 1930s these right-wing sects began to achieve an influence

[18] *Crisol,* 21 February 1932.
[19] Marcelo Sánchez Sorondo, *La revolución que anunciamos* (Buenos Aires, 1945), p. 35.
[20] See Tulio Halperín Donghi, *El revisionismo histórico argentino* (Buenos Aires, 1971), p. 14.

that far outweighed their number — a few hundred activists. The *nacionalistas* played a major part in shaping the incipient anti-imperialist movement, as it gathered adherents not only from the Right but also the Left
and Centre. Anti-imperialism in Argentina developed on a web of conspiracy theories of the type that were fundamental to the political tactics and
techniques of the ultra-Right. In much anti-imperialist propaganda, for
example, the British, and later the North Americans, came to be viewed
in much the same terms as the *nacionalistas* painted the Jews, as covert and
malign conspiratorial forces. Thus, Raúl Scalabrini Ortiz, who was an
ostensible leftist, castigated the British in the same terms and language as
one of the *nacionalistas'* anti-Semitic tracts: 'We have in our midst an
enemy who has won world dominance through the astuteness and skill of
its indirect manoeuvres, through its acts of ill-faith, through its constant
lies'.[21]

In the 1930s the nationalist movement remained mostly civilian and,
despite the activities of Molina, Kinkelín and a handful of others, had as
yet failed to penetrate the army on a large scale.

ARGENTINA ON THE EVE OF THE SECOND WORLD WAR

On the eve of the Second World War Argentina was in much the same
prosperous and promising situation it had enjoyed on the eve of the first.
Only the recent expansion of industrial Buenos Aires and the growing
outward movement of population from the pampas suggested any striking
contrast with conditions thirty years before. The country upheld its regional diversity, along with the structural lopsidedness that concentrated a
disproportionate share of population, wealth and resources in and around
Buenos Aires. Since 1914 new regional growth centres, such as the Chaco
cotton belt, had emerged beyond the pampas, but in other respects the
interior remained largely unchanged: Patagonia as an empty land of vast
sheep farms, the Río Negro valley as an area of small-scale fruit farmers,
Mendoza and San Juan as wine producers and Tucumán as the source of
sugar. In the Far-North-east and Far North-west persisted the forced
labour practices that had long provoked the denunciations of reformers in
Buenos Aires. The interior remained extremely poor and largely bereft of

---

[21] Raúl Scalabrini Ortiz, 'De: Politica británica en el Río de la Plata', in Ciria (ed.), *La decada infame*,
p. 198.

population. In 1941 the combined incomes of nine interior provinces amounted to only 1 per cent of total taxable incomes throughout the nation, and the per capita incomes of Catamarca and Santiago del Estero, two of the poorest provinces, stood at only 10 per cent of those in the city of Buenos Aires. Diseases caused by malnutrition remained endemic in the interior, most of all among the Tucumán sugar workers, who continually fell victim to malaria, impetigo and even leprosy. In Tucumán, as in much of the interior, 50 per cent of births were illegitimate.

Despite recent industrial development the vast middle class of Buenos Aires had undergone little change during the past generation and remained heavily bunched in services, the professions, commerce and public administration. In 1944 Felix Weil described the middle class as

rather shapeless mass of independent handicraftsmen, merchants, general store owners, clerks and agents of export and import concerns, employees of public utilities, and innumerable beneficiaries of the political patronage system who live off salaries and stipends of all kinds. Since there was no large-scale industry until industrialization took an upward swing after 1930, there was no place for an independent middle class. What there was, were the remains of a colonial economy coupled with the political system of spoils. This mass is necessarily amorphous in politics and political philosophies. It easily becomes the object of manipulation by political machines.[22]

Throughout the 1930s successive conservative governments had deliberately cut the middle class's access to power and the spoils of office. Although the schools, academies and universities administered by the middle class upheld the city as a centre of high culture, they were often a breeding-ground for blocked social aspirations and cumulative frustrations. Observers in addition to Weil commented on the overcrowding of the professions and on the falling marriage- and birth-rates and rising suicide-rates of the middle class in this period. In a piece entitled 'Esplendor y decadencia de la raza blanca' (Splendour and decadence of the white race), published in 1940, the economist Alejandro E. Bunge urged his countrymen and countrywomen, 'particularly the more materially blessed ones', to practise 'Catholic marriages' and to rear large families. 'From now on', he declared, 'with all our vigour, our patriotism and with a selfless Christian spirit, we should seek to restore the acceptability of large families and the idea that children are a blessing'.[23]

[22] Weil, *Argentine Riddle*, p. 4.
[23] Alejandro E. Bunge, 'Esplendor y decadencia de la raza blanca', *Revista de Economia Argentina*, no. 259 (January 1940), pp. 9–23.

By early 1940 many observers were beginning to take note of the economic and social changes of recent years. But little of this was reflected in government policy. During the 1930s conservative leaders frequently acknowledged that the restrictions they had imposed on imports and their attempts to rechannel foreign trade would foster industrial growth, but they remained far from adopting a deliberate commitment to industrial development. By and large their outlook had changed little since the nineteenth century: some industrial growth, they argued, would strengthen the balance of payments and help stave off industrial unrest as it created new jobs. The American economist George Wythe exaggerated in 1937 when he declared, 'The new road of [industrialization] has been accepted from which there is no turning back.'[24] The Central Bank painted a more accurate picture in 1938: 'The country's capacity for industrialization is limited . . . and if we increase purchasing power by too much, production will fail to increase, and prices will rise . . . with all its unfortunate consequences on the cost of living'.[25]

Members of the government and bodies like the Central Bank wanted not to intensify industrial development, but to try to restore the conditions that had prevailed before 1930. Their policies thus favoured exporting interests and sought to revive foreign investment. Policy-makers emphasized repeatedly the obstacles to industrial development: the risk of inflation, meagre and inaccessible supplies of coal and iron-ore, inadequate power and transportation facilities, capital shortages and the restricted size of the domestic market, which impeded economies of scale. Outside the small band of economic nationalists, these views prevailed among other organized political groups, including a large majority of the Radicals.

By the late 1930s industrial expansion commanded greater interest among the trade unions as they perceived that new industry meant new jobs. Some, like the *nacionalistas,* argued that a policy of progressive income redistribution should accompany support for industry, since more money in the hands of wage-earners would widen markets and intensify industrial growth. However, ideas of this kind commanded little support among industrialists themselves, who continued to view low wages as the key to high profits. Typical of this outlook was that of the Federación Argentina de Entidades del Comercio y la Industria, which conducted an unrelenting war on trade unions for 'disrupting' labour markets. Some

[24] Quoted in Vernon L. Phelps, *The International Economic Position of Argentina* (Philadelphia, 1938), p. 7.
[25] Quoted in Eduardo F. Jorge, *Industria y concentración económica* (Buenos Aires, 1971), p. 172.

industrialists, however, had now begun to support protection. Protectionist ideas slowly gained favour after 1933, when the Unión Industrial
Argentina, the largest and most powerful of the urban employers' associations, led a campaign against foreign dumping. The union's later campaigns attacked anomalies in the existing tariff, which, it alleged, often
imposed higher duties on industrial raw materials than on finished goods.
But among all these groups, unions and employers alike, no concerted or
sustained effort had emerged to promote industrial development.

Early in 1938, Agustín P. Justo's six-year tenure as president came to an
end. At this point, in the Indian summer of pre-war prosperity, not only
were nationalist influences growing but sharp differences had emerged
within the ruling Concordancia between reformers and reactionaries. The
presidential election of 1937, which the Concordancia again won easily
thanks to extensive fraud, mirrored this cleavage: the presidency passed to
Roberto M. Ortiz, a reformer, but the vice-presidency went to Ramón S.
Castillo, leader of the conservatives.

As the self-made son of a Basque grocer, Ortiz became the first
president-elect whose background was among the urban middle class of
immigrant descent. Ortiz had made his living and his fortune chiefly as a
lawyer for several British railway companies and was therefore extremely
unpopular among the *nationalistas*. Having been a Radical deputy during
Yrigoyen's first term (1916–22), Ortiz joined the Anti-Personalists in
1924, serving as minister of public works under Alvear and then as
minister of finance under Justo. As his past career suggested, Ortiz was an
anti-*yrigoyenista* democrat with impeccable liberal-conservative credentials: 'liberal' because of his links with the British and his pledge to end
electoral fraud ('I am a sincere believer in the benefits of democracy', he
said on accepting the nomination for the presidency in July 1937), and
'conservative' because of his fear of *yrigoyenista* 'mob rule'. Castillo, by
contrast, came from Catamarca, one of the most underdeveloped western
provinces, the bastion of an oligarchy of *hacendados*. He had served many
years as dean of the law faculty of the University of Buenos Aires until
becoming Justo's minister of justice and public instruction.

With the accession of Ortiz, tension grew between the national government and Manuel Fresco, governor of the province of Buenos Aires. Fresco
was a former conservative, who like Ortiz himself had past ties with the
British railways but who now posed as a *nacionalista*. Fresco continually
attacked 'communism', persecuted those he saw as its adherents and
sought the friendship and patronage of Mussolini during a visit to Rome

in 1938. But he also emerged as a champion of social reform. Under Fresco the government of Buenos Aires Province organized large-scale public works that included public housing schemes and a large road-building programme. He sponsored labour legislation for both urban and rural workers, and he made some attempts to build a network of trade unions controlled by his administration. From the federal capital, Fresco was seen as a fascist.

The Ortiz administration began cutting federal funds and subsidies to the province, forcing Fresco into large budget deficits and eventually into curtailing his activities. Finally in March 1940 Ortiz decreed a federal intervention in Buenos Aires to unseat Fresco, whom he accused of plotting fraud in the forthcoming gubernatorial election. Soon afterwards Ortiz carried out interventions in other provinces, among them, to the extreme annoyance of his vice-president, Catamarca. In the congressional elections of May 1940 the Radicals scored their greatest victory of more than a decade and now regained a majority in the Chamber of Deputies. By early 1940 Argentine politics thus seemed to be following the same course as that after the election of Roque Sáenz Peña in 1910. Led by Ortiz, the Concordancia, like the conservatives of thirty years before, had pledged itself to restoring democracy. And, as before, democratization opened the door to the Radicals.

ECONOMY AND POLITICS, 1940–3

At the very time it appeared so strong, liberal Argentina stood on the brink of collapse. In May 1940 Germany invaded and occupied Western Europe, and after evacuating its battered forces from the beaches of Dunkirk, Britain imposed a naval blockade against the Continent. The German conquests and the blockade dealt a blow to the Argentine economy that was even more severe than that of 1929–30. Trade plummeted instantly: in 1940 exports shrank by 20 per cent. In 1938 40 per cent of Argentina's exports went to Western Europe, but by 1941 the proportion had fallen to only 6 per cent, nearly all to neutral Spain and Portugal. Britain imported most of Argentina's meat, and the British market remained open, but the Continent now became inaccessible to most of Argentina's grains, with the result that agriculture and farmers, rather than cattle and ranchers, suffered by far the more serious effects of the war. By late 1940 shipping in Argentine ports had fallen by half. Both exports and imports sank to levels below the low point of the depression.

The disruptive conditions that emerged in late 1940 persisted through-out the next four years of war. In 1937 Argentina had exported 17 million tons of grains, but managed only 6.5 million tons in 1942. Agricultural prices averaged only two-thirds of those of the late 1930s. Within agricul-ture as a whole the war damaged maize most severely, since before the war about 90 per cent of maize went to continental Europe. During the late 1930s maize exports averaged more than 6 million tons but in 1941–44 only 400,000 tons. By 1941 coal imports were only one-third those of 1939, and by 1943 they were one-sixth. By 1942 oil imports were half their 1939 level, and by 1943 half again.

Immediately before the war, Argentine importers had made few efforts to stockpile supplies of machinery, raw materials or spare parts, so that it now became necessary to improvise with existing materials. Denied their normal coal supplies, the railways resorted to burning quebracho logs, as they had in 1914–18, and then, as timber supplies dwindled, they turned to burning surplus maize. By 1944 grains provided about one-third of the country's energy needs. As imported oil supplies fell, Yacimientos Petrolíferos Fiscales (YPF) made great efforts to increase production and eventually managed to double output from the wells at Comodoro Rivadavia. Even so, oil shortages forced the widespread use of linseed as a substitute. Falling imports offered great new opportunities to Argentine manufacturers, and permanent shifts soon became common in the factories of Buenos Aires. Yet industrial growth occurred at a some-what lower rate during the war than in the late 1930s, since industrialists now fell foul of recurrent power shortages and of their inability to obtain needed supplies abroad. At the same time, urban unemployment re-mained all but non-existent as both manufacturing and services steadily absorbed new workers, including a large number of women. Repair work became the largest component of the new service sector, as an army of versatile mechanics sought to maintain ageing machinery, cars, lorries and thirty-year-old rolling stock.

The collapse of agricultural exports after mid-1940 had some beneficial effects on the urban economy, since it meant cheap bread and a relatively stable cost of living. But on the land, agriculture's decline produced turmoil. During the war two processes operated simultaneously: farming declined but ranching expanded as Britain steadily increased its meat imports. A massive shift from agriculture to cattle ensued as the cultivated area shrank by more than 3 million hectares during the war years. Land used for wheat declined by an estimated 8.4 per cent, but that for maize by more than 40 per cent. The maize surpluses helped to intensify the move into livestock, since they induced the growth of pig farming, an activity that doubled in size during the war. To some extent the growth of forage crops, alfalfa, barley and oats, which serviced the cattle economy, and some new industrial crops led by sunflowers compensated for the decline in the old grain staples. But the overriding trend was the move from grains to cattle. Between 1937 and 1947 the cattle population of the pampas increased by 25 per cent, or 3.5 million, whilst the human population fell by about half a million. Government attempts to arrest the outflow of population, such as the controlled tenant rents introduced in 1942, proved completely ineffectual in stemming the flight from the land.

By contrast, conditions in the interior now began to diverge from those in the pampas. Producers there responded to the rapidly expanding internal market centred in Buenos Aires by increasing production. Growth was especially marked in areas like the Chaco where virgin land remained available. Elsewhere in the settled peasant regions of the North-west and the North-east, increasing market production raised demand for labour and thus for a time helped draw population into the region. However, growth also increased demand for a relatively fixed supply of land and thus in the longer term provoked an expansion of the market-producing haciendas at the expense of subsistence-oriented peasant smallholdings. The final result was a process of peasant encirclement and the beginnings of an eventually acute latifundio–minifundio polarization that in the 1950s and afterwards provoked a second, still greater wave of flight from the land. In this way the interior, and no longer the pampas, eventually emerged as the main source of internal migrants.

In late 1940 the conservative government sought to respond to the fall in trade through a Plan de Reactivación Económica, better known as the Pinedo Plan, since its chief author was Federico Pinedo, serving a second term as finance minister. The plan was conceived on the assumption that in the following year, 1941, exports would remain at levels below those of the depression. If this happened, the result would be 'industrial crisis, unemployment and misery in the cities, a general collapse of all business, that would provoke social consequences of unforeseeable scope'.[26] Pinedo therefore proposed, New Deal style, to use government spending as a

---

[26] See 'El plan de reactivación económica ante el Honorable Senado', *Desarrollo Económico*, 19, no. 75 (1979), p. 404.

countercyclical device to revive demand, minimize inflation and safeguard employment. Above all the measure was concerned with the 'social consequences of unforeseeable scope', a phrase that would be readily understood as a reference to the labour unrest of the First World War that had climaxed in the 'revolutionary strike' of January 1919.

The Pinedo Plan marked Argentina's entrance into the field of comprehensive economic planning. First, it proposed to assist the farm sector by extending the crop-financing schemes administered by the juntas that Pinedo himself had created seven years before. The government would now expand its grain purchases from the farmers and offer higher prices, while urging landowners to show restraint on land rents in order to leave tenants with adequate profits. Second, the plan sought to foster faster industrial growth and to start exporting industrial products. It proposed a new state-backed credit fund for industry and the introduction of 'drawbacks' (*reintegros*), a scheme long sought by the Unión Industrial, that provided for the reimbursement of exporters of manufactures for the tariff duties they incurred when importing raw materials or capital goods. To complement these measures the government would attempt to conclude free-trade treaties with other nations in Latin America in order to create new markets for manufactures and assist producers in achieving economies of scale. Third, the plan proposed to finance the expansion of the construction industry, which the government believed capable of providing more than 200,000 new jobs. Through government-assisted construction schemes, cheap houses would be offered with long-term mortgages to workers and employees.

In 1940 the government remained extremely sensitive to the charge that it was leaning towards deficit financing and therefore risked inflation. The plan, Pinedo declared, would be financed not by printing money but from international loans, and expenditures would be directed into productive activities rather than into mere subsidies for the unemployed. The Pinedo Plan manifested far greater concern for agriculture than for industry since the sums allotted for credits to industry totalled only one-sixth of those destined for farmers. Thus, the shift towards industry remained relatively small. Government, Pinedo declared, would support only 'natural industries'. This phrase had been in common usage among liberals for the past seventy years, and it meant that only industries that employed a substantial quantity of local raw materials and could be expected to establish themselves competitively would receive government support. Pinedo expected that industry would continue to have a secondary role in the economy. When he argued the measure before Congress, he talked of farm exports as the 'master wheel' of the economy; manufacturing and construction would become 'lesser wheels' at their side.

The Pinedo Plan offered a formula for controlled change and a measure of diversification that would contain the effects of the war and minimize unrest and dislocation. But it remained only a plan, since by the time it appeared the country had fallen into political crisis. In July 1940 the diabetic president Ortiz, now a victim of bouts of blindness, was forced to leave office and to hand over power to the arch-conservative Castillo. For a year, until Ortiz finally resigned, Castillo was only acting president. But soon after taking over, he began reversing the policy of liberalization embarked upon earlier in the year. By September 1940 Castillo had partly reorganized the cabinet, and to the rising anger of the Radicals he began organizing elections in the provinces that Ortiz had placed under 'intervention'. Fraud heavily tainted several of these elections, most of which the conservatives won. Having so recently been convinced that they were at last on the road to regaining power, the Radicals now found themselves in danger of being cheated by Castillo. A bitter spate of party conflict followed, and the Pinedo Plan became its main victim. Although the conservative-dominated Senate accepted the plan, the Radical majority in the lower house prevented it from being brought to the floor. Radicals rejected Pinedo's appeal for a 'patriotic accord' to deal with the economic emergency until they gained redress for the recent elections.

The Pinedo Plan failed owing to the long feuds between Radicals and conservatives that Castillo had reignited. Yet even if politics had not prevailed, the plan contained certain assumptions and expectations that from the start made its success problematical. During the following months, executive decrees implemented many of its proposals for dealing with agriculture, but they did little to resolve the farm crisis or to halt the rising flood of migrants pouring into Buenos Aires.

The Pinedo Plan also raised the now-critical issue of relations with the United States. The plan's aim of promoting industry rested on the assumption that Argentina could continue to import the capital goods and raw materials that it lacked. Yet in order to import it had to export or, alternatively, secure a large, continuous flow of foreign loans and investment. Currently, with the closure of the European markets to its grains, only Britain survived among its largest markets. But as Britain mobilized for war, it ceased to be able to export to Argentina any of the goods useful to local industry. As a result throughout the war Argentina's export earnings accumulated in Britain as 'sterling balances'. By the end of 1942 the sterling balances had climbed to 295 million pesos, and a year later to 714 million. By December 1944 the balances were estimated to be more than a billion pesos, or some £80 million. The British undertook to protect the sterling balances from any future devaluation of the pound; but with the hope of repaying the debt in exports after the war, they kept the balances 'blocked' in Britain, completely beyond Argentina's reach. On several occasions the British refused Argentina's requests to use blocked funds to redeem part of its own debt to Britain or to exchange them for the assets of British-owned firms in Argentina; these companies, led by the railways, usually purchased most of their supplies in Britain and therefore helped British exports. Moreover, the British would never allow Argentina to convert its sterling balances into dollars, since this would mean a return to what in British eyes were the highly unfavourable trade practices of the 1920s, when Argentina's earnings on sales to Britain had been used to increase purchases in the United States. By 1940 Argentina found itself locked into the bilateral relationship with Britain that it had so eagerly sought in 1933, but in a way that was quite useless to Pinedo's goal of 'economic revival'.

In the plan of 1940 both Pinedo and Raúl Prebisch, still his chief adviser, anticipated the United States developing as a substitute supplier of the goods needed by local industry and as a new market for Argentina's exports. 'The great market of the United States', the plan declared, 'offers enormous opportunities. There is no logical reason why our producers should not take advantage of it'.[27] For a brief period in late 1940 Pinedo tried to orchestrate a pro-U.S. campaign in Argentina and to promote the idea that closer links with the United States would bring a flood of prosperity. Pinedo's calculations transcended purely short-term goals. To conservatives like Pinedo, Argentina now stood at a historical crossroads. The old link with Britain no longer functioned and indeed might collapse completely if, as now seemed very likely, Britain suffered invasion and defeat by Germany. A new relationship with the United States not only would resolve the trade issue, but in doing so would also safeguard the political dominance of the class of ranchers and merchants that underpinned liberal-conservatism. For these reasons Pinedo now pleaded for 'close and complete co-operation' with the United States.

However, at this critical moment Argentina again failed to surmount

[27] 'El plan de reactivación económica', p. 423.

the barriers that for almost a century had persistently impeded all efforts to create any stable and durable ties with the United States. During the past decade relations between the two countries had often been cool, as the United States extended its protectionist measures against goods from Argentina. In 1930 the Hawley–Smoot Act strengthened the restrictions on most meat and grain products from Argentina, raising tariffs on meat, corn and wool and imposing new duties on hides. In 1935 all imported farm goods that undersold American equivalents were banned completely. In 1936 came new duties on Argentine tallow. Throughout the 1930s the United States employed sanitary regulations, ostensibly directed against the spread of foot-and-mouth disease, to exclude other goods from Argentina. Both Uriburu and Justo made intermittent but unavailing protests against such policies, while the United States refused Justo's suggestion of a bilateral treaty between the two countries. In retaliation the conservatives, like the Radicals in the late 1920s, sometimes harassed American companies like Standard Oil, while employing exchange controls to exclude U.S. imports. Throughout the 1930s imports from the United States thus remained at a mere fraction of imports in the 1920s; at the same time, Argentina's exports to the United States halved.

The trade conflicts of the 1930s sharpened the latent anti-U.S. currents in Argentina. Argentines now ignored or attacked the Roosevelt administration's Good Neighbor policy, which renounced armed interventions by the United States in Latin America, and they saw the pan-American movement sponsored by the United States as an example of *maquiavelismo yanqui,* the real purpose of which was to promote U.S. control throughout the South American continent. After 1935 Argentina participated, at times reluctantly, in the succession of pan-American conferences sponsored by the United States, and when towards the outbreak of war the United States attempted to create a pan-American defence alliance, the Ortiz government gave the idea only half-hearted endorsement. Trade and diplomacy had become inextricably linked. By late 1939 at least some Americans were beginning to recognize the main source of Argentina's uncooperative behaviour. 'Winning the friendship of Argentina', declared John W. White, an American diplomat in Buenos Aires, 'is largely a matter of trade and economics'. 'We must reconcile ourselves', he continued, 'to some commercial sacrifices for the sake of our political and military safety, and permit the importation of Argentine products'.[28] But in

[28] John W. White, *Argentina: The Life Story of a Nation* (New York, 1942), pp. 21, 311.

1939–40, all Argentina gained from the United States was a credit from the Export–Import Bank of New York for the purchase of U.S. goods. Following the Lend-Lease act of January 1941, the United States began to provide arms to its Latin American allies led by Brazil, but it gave Argentina lowest priority, denying it military supplies almost completely because of its stance on hemispheric defence.

Against this discouraging background, but as part of the strategy of the Pinedo Plan, the Castillo government finally embarked on formal trade negotiations with the United States, seeking through a trade treaty – the first with the United States for almost a century – the concessions that had been so long denied. For a time members of the government, the political parties and even some of the trade unions became enthusiastic converts to pan-Americanism, as they contemplated a large flow of funds and goods from the United States. But when this treaty was concluded in October 1941, it proved a complete disappointment, since each side made only token concessions. The United States offered little more than to lower tariffs on the goods from Argentina it already imported, such as linseed and cattle hides. The only new goods to be admitted from Argentina were some rare minerals, such as tungsten, which was required by U.S. arms manufacturers, and some dairy products and wines that the United States had before imported from France and Italy. But the door remained shut to Argentina's great staples, its meats and grains. The United States thus gave the impression that this treaty was simply a wartime expedient that marked no major shift in traditional U.S. policy.

The failure of the October 1941 treaty with the United States signalled the approaching end of the liberal-conservative plan to achieve economic recovery and thus maintain political dominance. For more than a year, since Ortiz's forced leave of absence in July 1940, the balance of power in the Concordancia and the government had been changing. Early in 1941 Pinedo had resigned following accusations instigated by the *nacionalistas* of his involvement in corrupt dealings with the British railway companies. In March the liberal-conservative foreign minister, José Luis Cantilo, had also resigned, leaving the ultra-conservatives led by Castillo himself to dominate the government. But Castillo was becoming increasingly isolated, and he responded by bringing men with *nacionalista* sympathies into the government. Among them was the new minister of foreign affairs, Enrique Ruiz Guiñazú, who was widely known as a sympathizer with General Franco's Spain.

Nacionalismo was thus ceasing to be a movement on the fringe of politics. As fresh *nacionalista* organizations sprouted and their propaganda intensified, the *nacionalistas* began to pull the country in several new directions. The first was towards 'economic sovereignty', which meant principally greater industrialization and the nationalization of foreign companies that performed public services. The second became what was called 'active neutrality', which meant as one propagandist succinctly defined it in January 1941, 'We are not neutral, we are against everyone'.[29] The third was a new emphasis on 'social justice'. In late 1939 *nacionalistas* were complaining that

in Santiago del Estero the people lack water. [Elsewhere] there is no bread. In the south children fail to attend school for lack of clothing. But in Buenos Aires a committee made up of two ex-presidents, a vice-president, senators etc. . . . all of them Argentines collect funds for the war hospitals in France.[30]

By 1941 these sentiments had taken a more aggressive form. Now the *nacionalistas,* declared the Alianza Libertadora Nacionalista, aspired to 'the leadership of the proletarian masses, to bring them into harmony with other elements of society towards the conquest of justice and the grandeur of the Nation'.[31] A typical *nacionalista* program in 1941 listed the following demands: 'economic emancipation' to enable the country to regain 'all its sources of wealth' from foreign control; the creation of 'large markets of internal consumption' through 'industrialization'; the redistribution of 'uncultivated land so that it would be worked' (*para su trabajo*); 'functional representation'; 'just wages'; the reintroduction of Catholic education in the schools; defence against 'threats to national unity' (a euphemism for anti-Semitism and anti-communism); and measures to ensure the country's 'military preparedness'.[32] These ideas were commonly expressed in the slogans 'Sovereignty', 'Nationalization', 'Social Justice'.

Many observers viewed all this as symptomatic of the rise of Nazi-Fascism in Argentina. Years later Raúl Prebisch urged his audience not to underestimate Nazi influence in Argentina in the 1930s. 'I have seen it; I experienced it myself while in the Central Bank. The penetration of Nazism in the Army, in certain newspapers, aided by the resources of the German embassy was a highly disturbing element in Argentina'.[33] In-

[29] *El Fortín,* January 1941.
[30] *La Maroma,* October 1939.
[31] Quoted in Comisión de Estudios, *El nacionalismo,* p. 50.
[32] Estatutos del Consejo Superior del Nacionalismo (Buenos Aires, 1941).
[33] Raúl Prebisch, 'Argentine Economic Policies since the 1930s – Recollections', in Guido Di Tella and D. C. M. Platt (eds.), *The Political Economy of Argentina, 1880–1946* (London, 1986), p. 146.

deed, just as fascists lurked among the *nacionalistas* in the 1930s, so now did Nazi sympathizers, among them the staff of *El Pampero,* a new newspaper in Buenos Aires whose editor, Enrique Osés, received subsidies from the German Embassy in return for publishing Nazi war bulletins and some Nazi propaganda. Some looked to Germany in 1940–1 to provide the kind of relationship that the Pinedo group had sought with the United States. At the same time, many *nacionalistas* regarded Germany and Nazism with hostility. To the Catholic hispanophile groups, Nazism symbolized 'four hundred years of apostasy' that had begun with the Reformation, and local pro-Nazis reminded one *nacionalista* (referring to Carlos de Alvear, one of the leaders of the Argentine independence movement) 'of the posture of some of the men during the May Revolution [of 1810], who contributed towards our independence from Spain only to make us depend on the English'.[34] In September 1939 a Nazi diplomat in Buenos Aires remarked to his superiors in Berlin, 'The anti-British sentiment . . . must not be construed as pro-German. . . . The new Germany is viewed as anti-cultural [*sic*] . . . because of its supposed threat to the Catholic Church'.[35]

Rather than expressing an expansion of Nazi-German influence, *nacionalismo* emerged in the train of rising anti-U.S. sentiment and in the vacuum left by the defection of the liberal-conservatives from the Concordancia. At the end of 1941, following the failure of the approach to the United States, Argentina found itself starved of foreign markets and foreign supplies. Moreover, it faced what it perceived to be a military threat from Brazil, which the United States was now arming faster than any other country in the region. Prompted by the *nacionalistas,* Argentina's response grew increasingly spirited and recalcitrant. As it reaffirmed neutrality and refused to bend to U.S. pressure to join the pan-American alliance, it began seeking ways to conquer its economic and military isolation.

In late 1941 *nacionalista* influences became stronger and more entrenched within the army, where a growing fascination with a national arms industry emerged, which in turn provoked much stronger support than before for industrial development. The industrial promotion schemes of the past, such as those of the Pinedo Plan, had stressed *selective* industrialization, ventures that would aim for competitive efficiency and seek economies of scale through exporting. What was now taking shape was

---

[34] Ibarguren, Jr., *Laferrère,* p. 94.
[35] Quoted in Stewart Edward Sutin, 'The Impact of Nazism on Germans of Argentina' (Ph.D. dissertation, University of Texas, 1975), p. 68.

the commitment towards *total* industrialization that would be army- and state-directed. Under army pressure, the government created the Dirección General de Fabricaciones Militares to develop armaments. A year or so later Colonel Manuel S. Savio produced blueprints for a steel industry that he proposed would be state-financed and state-directed.

Throughout 1941 and 1942 Castillo clung to power despite his narrowing base of support and the steady growth of opposition led by the Radicals. Although some *nacionalistas* like Ruiz Guiñazú had been drawn into the government, a majority of *nacionalistas* rejected the regime as 'liberal', 'oligarchic' or 'electoralist'. With Congress controlled by the Radicals, the government began to rule almost exclusively by decree. The Japanese attack on Pearl Harbor in December 1941 was the pretext first for the imposition of a state of siege and then for the use of the police to stop (usually pro-Allied) demonstrations and to muzzle the press. But failing to staunch the opposition, Castillo was compelled to cultivate the army. At regular intervals he conducted lavish banquets attended by military chiefs. Crisis and an atmosphere of decay now pervaded the country. The American observer John W. White perceived the 'problems of 1942' as

reactionary government of force in the hands of a minority party, an over-specialized grain economy with an almost helpless dependence on foreign markets, an unhealthy concentration of population in the cities, an exploited farming class that was not settled on the land it worked, a falling birth rate, and a high rate of illegitimacy and illiteracy.[36]

To compound Castillo's difficulties, relations with the United States sharply deteriorated as Ruiz Guiñazú led an attempt to foster neutralism, at the expense of pan-Americanism, in other parts of Latin America. In January 1942, at the pan-American conference in Rio de Janeiro, the main purpose of which was to persuade the Latin American nations to break diplomatic relations with the Axis and Japan, Ruiz Guiñazú consistently opposed the United States, and although he failed to erect a 'southern bloc' outside the pan-American alliance, he did succeed in preventing an agreement to break relations. The resolution that emerged in Rio merely 'recommended' rupture, but left it to each country to determine its own course of action. Led by Secretary of State Cordell Hull, the United States retaliated by imposing on Argentina a total arms embargo, by halting credits from the Export–Import Bank and by cancelling supplies of oil tankers and machinery.

[36] White, *Argentina*, p. 292.

After the Rio conference, the United States began to label the Argentine government 'fascist' and 'pro-Axis'. In Buenos Aires there were recurrent rumours of an impending invasion by Brazil and of a planned occupation of Comodoro Rivadavia, the chief oil source, by U.S. marines. But as this pressure mounted throughout 1942, Castillo found unexpected support from Britain. In the early 1940s the United States and Britain had quite different objectives with regard to Argentina. The former was concerned chiefly with forging a united military and political front throughout Latin America, and it viewed Argentina as an obstacle to this end. Britain, however, became increasingly dependent on Argentine meat and resisted any course of action that threatened its meat shipments. In addition, Britain's extensive commercial and financial interests in Argentina made the British reluctant to allow Argentina to drift totally into the U.S. orbit, as seemed likely to happen if Argentina committed itself fully to pan-Americanism. Since 1940 Britain had been apprehensive of U.S. attempts to secure control of British companies in Argentina. A U.S. proposal that year, for example, suggested that Britain pay Argentina for its meat in the securities of British companies, which Argentina in turn would transfer to U.S. ownership to pay for imports from the United States. As a result opinion in Britain often favoured a neutral Argentina. If Argentina's neutrality risked allowing Axis spies to transmit intelligence on British shipping movements, it would help to protect the meat ships that sailed under the Argentine flag from German submarines.

From early 1942 the State Department pursued evidence to support its view that Argentina's neutrality merely masked an underlying support for the Axis. It exposed the subsidies to *El Pampero* from the German Embassy; it accused the government of favouring German propaganda against the Allies and of seeking to destroy pro-Allied organizations; it discovered that the government was dealing with German firms and that visas had been granted to persons suspected of being German spies. But the British Foreign Office often took a different line. It sometimes acknowledged the practical difficulties of administering neutrality in a country in which most of the belligerent powers possessed substantial business interests and sizeable expatriate communities. The British appeared to recognize the absence of a general commitment to the Allied cause in Argentina. By and large public opinion favoured democracy and feared totalitarianism, but clouding such sympathies were the lingering animosities towards Britain that stemmed from the Roca–Runciman Treaty and the deep-seated hostilities towards the United States. Throughout 1942 and early 1943 the

British view, if based on British self-interest, offered a more accurate picture of affairs in Argentina than that of the United States: rather than secretly supporting the Axis, Castillo in fact supported no one. He had no constructive foreign policy at all and aimed merely for a holding operation till the war ended, hoping, it seemed, that at that point Argentina could restore its pre-war relationship with Western Europe and that U.S. pressure would diminish.

In the middle of 1943 Castillo faced yet another domestic political crisis, and this time he failed to surmount it. In April Castillo's refusal to endorse the claims of Rodolfo Moreno, the governor of Buenos Aires Province, to succeed him split the Concordancia. A month or so later it became known that Castillo intended Robustiano Patrón Costas, a leading Tucumán sugar baron and an old-style conservative from the far interior like himself, to become the next president. Within days the news of Castillo's intentions had triggered a military coup d'état which, on 4 June 1943, swept the regime aside with the same ease that the army had dealt with the Radicals in 1930. Once again troops marched into the centre of Buenos Aires to occupy the Casa Rosada, while for a few hours Castillo made futile efforts at resistance from a naval destroyer in the Río de la Plata on which he had taken refuge.

THE RISE OF PERÓN, 1943–6

The coup of June 1943 differed from that of September 1930 in arriving unannounced, without the open civilian unrest that had foreshadowed the fall of Yrigoyen; the population at large appeared taken by surprise. Yet the coup had been in the wind for months. At the time of Castillo's fall, the Concordancia was only a shadow of its original form, and for some time the government had survived thanks only to the army. In two respects the 1943 coup resembled that of 1930: it was conceived and executed by the army alone, and its leaders were divided into 'liberals' and 'nationalists'. The former, initially more substantial in number and rank, aimed to re-create a government like Ortiz's, free of the fraud they expected would accompany the election of Patrón Costas and backed by the great liberal interest groups, or *'fuerzas vivas'*. The liberals could be expected to reach a speedy agreement with the United States, which now meant, before all else, breaking relations with the Axis. The *nacionalistas,* by contrast, were still committed to resisting the United States, to maintaining neutrality and to supporting the development of a national arms industry.

At the heart of the *nacionalista* faction was a secret association of military officers, the Grupo Obra de Unificación (GOU), consisting of only a score of active members, about half of them colonels or of lower rank. The GOU was obsessed with Communism. Before the June revolution, its members seemed less concerned at the prospect of another conservative government elected by fraud than with the possibility that a Communist-controlled popular front would emerge to contest the November elections. The election victory of a popular front, its members claimed, would bring disaster on the scale of the Russian Revolution or the Spanish civil war. The GOU considered it its duty to awaken the army at large to this danger: thus its 'task of unification'. Members of the GOU appeared to be *nacionalistas* in uniform, constantly discussing 'international conspiracies'. The international Masonic movement, for example, was 'a Jewish creation . . . a fearful secret organization, international in character . . . a kind of Mafia writ large. . . . Among its works were the French Revolution, the Spanish Civil War. . . . It is anti-Catholic, and therefore by definition anti-Argentine'. The Rotary Club was a 'network of international Jewish espionage and propaganda in the service of the United States'. And the Popular Front was 'a pseudo-democracy, a vulgar gathering of fellow-travellers (*comunizantes*) serving at the behest of Judaism . . . an openly revolutionary organization trying to repeat the pattern of Spain where the moderates fell and became Communist puppets'. The *nacionalistas,* by contrast, were 'the purest forces, those with the most spiritual awareness within the panorama of Argentine politics'.[37] The close links between the GOU and the *nacionalistas* can be illustrated by one remarkable statement purporting to justify the revolution of 1943 and the imposition of military dictatorship, which took the form of a lengthy quotation from St Augustine's *De libero arbitrarie:*

When a people is moderate and serious by custom . . . and esteems the interest of all above private interest, that law is just that allows it to elect its own magistrates. But when little by little it starts to place private interest above the common good, and if corrupted by ambitious men, it lapses into selling its votes and handing over government to the depraved, it is just that the man of goodwill, even though it be a single man possessing the influence or the necessary force, may take away the right of choosing government, and may submit the people to the authority of one man.[38]

[37] Quotations from Robert A. Potash (comp.), *Perón y el G.O.U.: Los documentos de una logia secreta* (Buenos Aires, 1984), pp. 101–2, 103, 199, 200.
[38] Quoted in ibid., p. 235.

The titular leader of the June coup d'état was General Arturo Rawson, popular and well connected in both the army and navy and able to unite the two forces against Castillo in a pledge to root out government corruption. But having assumed the presidency Rawson was immediately deposed by his military colleagues following wrangles over the composition of the new cabinet. Into Rawson's place stepped General Pedro Ramírez, who until just a few days before the coup had been Castillo's minister of war. The strength of Ramírez's claim lay in his secret links with the GOU, whose members had in fact sworn allegiance to him, but also in his appeal to liberals and Radicals: in months past there had been hints that the Radicals planned to make Ramírez their candidate in the November elections.

Ramírez's cabinet consisted almost exclusively of members of the armed forces, whose exact political affiliations remained as yet unclear but were in fact divided almost equally into liberals and *nacionalistas*. The one civilian member of the cabinet was Jorge Santamarina, the minister of finance, a liberal widely known as a scion of the *fuerzas vivas* or, as the GOU described him, 'one of them'.[39] At least outwardly the new government appeared to be under liberal control; the U.S. State Department quickly welcomed the coup and hastened to recognize Ramírez, while the German Embassy burnt its secret files the day after the coup. Certainly at this point the liberals controlled foreign policy through Admiral Segundo Storni, the foreign minister. Early in July Ramírez informed the United States that Argentina could be expected to break diplomatic relations with Germany in August. At this point, too, Ramírez, despite his links with the GOU, seemed ready to call early elections, apparently anticipating that he would become the candidate of a coalition headed by the Radicals.

Within a month of the coup, the two factions were engaged in a battle for full control of the military regime, the liberals campaigning to remove the *nacionalistas* from the government with the slogan 'Put the generals before the colonels', the *nacionalistas* counterattacking with their campaign to prevent Ramírez from naming a date for elections, which they argued would bring the Popular Front, and thus the Communists, into power. There were numerous disputes between the two sides over lower-level government appointments, as each struggled to stack the administration with its own appointees. Finally, in early September the liberals attempted to break the deadlock by enlisting the support of the United

[39] Ibid., p. 220.

States. In the celebrated 'Storni letter' the foreign minister, writing to Cordell Hull, intimated that the regime was now ready to break relations with the Axis, but he asked Hull first to lift the arms embargo. Storni argued that lifting the embargo would represent a goodwill gesture by the United States to demonstrate its willingness to restore the strategic balance in South America, removing what Argentina perceived as the military threat from Brazil. The obvious purpose of this request was to trigger a wave of pro-Americanism in the army, which the liberals could then exploit to outmanoeuvre and destroy the *nacionalistas*. But Hull ignored this crucial opportunity to intervene in ways that would further U.S. interests. Against the wishes of his senior advisers led by Sumner Welles, the under-secretary for Latin American affairs, he curtly rejected Storni's request, demanding that Argentina break relations with the Axis without any prior quid pro quo from the United States. In his reply Hull recalled Argentina's behaviour during the Rio de Janeiro conference eighteen months before, when it had systematically defied U.S. policies. The Storni letter thus did nothing to help the liberals; rather it vindicated the *nacionalistas,* strengthening the argument they had made persistently since 1941: the United States was hostile towards Argentina, and therefore Argentina's only recourse was to strike out alone. Within days of Hull's reply reaching Buenos Aires, all the liberals including Storni had resigned from the Ramírez government, to be replaced by *nacionalistas.* Among the new appointments the most significant were those of General Edelmiro Farrell as vice-president and of Gustavo Martínez Zuviría, the notorious anti-Semite novelist 'Hugo Wast', as minister of justice and public instruction. The stage was cleared for the *nacionalista* revolution and the rise of Perón.

Ysabel Rennie's comments on the coup d'état in June 1943, written soon after the event itself, amounted to a highly perceptive view of the future course of Argentina's politics:

When time has lent perspective, this event will be seen for what it was: economically, politically, socially, the most important event . . . since the [revolution of 1890]. For this blow, struck swiftly, and without warning, marked the end of a society, an economy and a way of life. With it were buried the Argentina that lived from beef alone, the Argentina of the Enlightened Oligarchy, liberal Argentina, the free trader, and the hopes, the power and the predominance of the landed aristocracy.[40]

[40] Ysabel Rennie, *The Argentine Republic* (New York, 1945), p. 344.

Her judgement was, however, more appropriate to the months immediately following the coup than the coup itself. It was in October, not June, that the most decisive political shift occurred before the final climax of February 1946 when Perón won election as president.

Once the *nacionalistas* had gained full control over the Ramírez junta in October 1943, they moved swiftly to consolidate themselves at home and abroad. They refused any further discussion with the United States on breaking relations with the Axis, and the United States replied by freezing the assets of Argentine banks in the United States. The *nacionalistas* reiterated 'active' neutrality and recommended the search for allies in Latin America. By late 1943 Argentina had built up a substantial export trade in manufactured goods in Latin America, which Ramírez sought to consolidate by concluding commercial treaties with several neighbouring Latin American states. The regime also began dabbling in its neighbours' politics; in an episode that again created serious friction between Argentina and the United States, a coup d'état in Bolivia in December 1943 brought a neutralist, pro-Argentine regime into power, to which for some time Argentina alone extended diplomatic recognition.

Internally the regime ceased to pretend that it would soon call elections. As a result it began to face growing opposition led by the Radicals. The regime responded with a blend of *nacionalista*-style enactments, repression, incipient populism and a growing flood of propaganda. A 20 per cent reduction in farm tenants' rents and a freeze on urban rents were imposed. The tramways in Buenos Aires, led by the Anglo-Argentine Tramway Company, were forced to cut fares, and the hated Corporación de Transportes was abolished. The regime nationalized the British-owned Primitiva Gas Company. The regime stepped up the drive against corruption and carried out a new wave of purges. It placed the provinces under military *interventores* and extended censorship of the press. At the end of 1944 it abolished all political parties, contending that they had failed to represent 'authentic public opinion' effectively. In the meantime members of the government delivered speech after speech replete with *nacionalista* slogans like 'Honesty, Justice, Duty'; Ramírez himself lauded, in particular, the rural working-class population, 'uncontaminated', as he put it, 'by the exotic ideas of the cities'.

Martínez Zuviría began his term as minister of justice with a speech urging measures to 'Christianize the country. . . . We should increase the birth-rate, not immigration; we must ensure labour's fair share of re-

wards, and put every household under a decent roof; we have to root out
doctrines based on class hatreds and atheism'.[41] To the Church's great
approval Martínez Zuviría reimposed religious teaching in the schools for
the first time in sixty years and then led a search for 'Communists' in the
universities, closing them when students replied with strikes. Anti-Semitic
policies were also pursued. Although rumours that the government had
set up concentration camps in Patagonia proved false, it suppressed several Jewish welfare associations, dismissed some Jewish teachers and cancelled the citizenship of some naturalized Jews. The *nacionalista* press
waged a long campaign against Bemberg, the brewing tycoon. In April
1944 the government took control of the grain export trade and nationalized grain elevators and warehouses, measures that some viewed as anti-
Semitic since they were directed against the Big Four grain export houses.
Finally, there was another spate of attacks on Communists, this time
among the trade unions. Immediately after taking power in June 1943
the government had dissolved a Communist-led faction of the CGT that
had succeeded in splitting the federation the previous March. At this
point too it destroyed the FONC, the Communist-dominated construction workers' unions. Strikes of meat-packing workers in Buenos Aires in
late 1943, denounced by the government as Communist-led, were met by
mass arrests. Several trade unions, including the railway organizations,
had already been placed under government control through the device of
intervención.

Much of this government behaviour manifested the negative and purely
reactionary face of *nacionalismo*, its exotic blend of prejudices against 'liberalism', 'capitalism', and 'communism', its habit of romanticizing rurality,
its blind antipathies towards the 'foreign' and its menacing anti-Semitic
impulses. Yet *nacionalismo* remained committed to 'social justice', the
purpose of which was to reconstruct the organic national community. This
other face of the movement also showed itself within less than a month of
the palace revolution of October 1943 with the appointment, on 28
October, of Colonel Juan Domingo Perón as head of the Departamento
Nacional del Trabajo. Those close to the regime immediately recognized
the great significance of his appointment. Perón, said *Cabildo,* now the
leading *nacionalista* daily newspaper, would bring 'weight and efficiency to
labour problems', because he knew the 'true needs of the workers' organizations', and would support the unity of the trade union movement, 'always

[41] *Cabildo*, 15 November 1943, 1 January 1944, 2 November 1943.

trying to avoid and solve [*sic*] conflict'. Perón's task was the 'organization of the trade unions'.[42]

Although not as yet a member of the cabinet, and quite unknown to the public, Perón thus emerged in the front ranks of the *nacionalista* regime. He had been among the founders and leaders of the GOU, active in the 'task of unification' campaign in the army, in the conspiracy against Castillo, as a supporter of Ramírez against Rawson in June and more lately as one of the chief figures in the battle between liberals and *nacionalistas*. Of Perón's past career, which since early adolescence he had spent in the army, the most striking feature was his long experience with military politics. Immediately before the 1930 revolution Perón had played a secondary role as an intermediary between the Uriburu and Justo factions, although he had avoided being identified with either of them. Immediately before and after the outbreak of war in 1939, on official missions in several European countries, he had become familiar with the Mussolini and Franco regimes and witnessed the fall of France. Perón enjoyed some standing in the army for his organizational talents and for his academic expertise on the subject of the role of the army in modern society. His views on this issue were typical of the *nacionalistas*. Unlike liberals, who regarded the army in a negative guardian role as a mere adjunct to the state, Perón and the *nacionalistas* saw it as the very epicentre of the national community, charged with leading and mobilizing society. As a member of the GOU Perón had avoided the anti-Semitic and crude xenophobic tirades of his fellow officers, but had distinguished himself as an extreme anti-Communist, apprehensive of Communist intrigues to fashion the Popular Front, and above all fearful of Communist influence in the trade unions. Perón's involvement in labour issues preceded his appointment to the Labour Department. He had been actively seeking contacts in the unions since the June coup d'état, especially in the 'intervened' Unión Ferroviaria, which was now administered by his close personal associate and friend Colonel Domingo Mercante.

By the end of 1943 the various sub-themes of 'social justice' had become subjects of almost daily debate in right-wing, Catholic and *nacionalista* circles in Argentina. For several years past the Alianza Libertadora Argentina had conceptualized social justice as a system of state-controlled trade unions. After the coup of June 1943, while in a typical vein demanding measures against 'Communists' and 'Jews', the Alianza urged the forma-

---

[42] Ibid., 28 October 1943, 30 October 1943.

tion of a 'state-protector of the Argentine working class'.[43] In 1943 the prestigious *Revista de Economía Argentina* devoted great attention to the recently issued Beveridge Plan in Britain and judged the formation of a 'welfare state' the best way to prevent a Communist revolution. Other *nacionalistas* perceived the working class under their control and tutelage as the instrument for carrying them to power: 'The conquest of the state begins with the conquest of the multitude', Marcelo Sánchez Sorondo had declared in May 1943.[44] Most of these ideas of mass mobilization and working-class tutelage sprang from European fascism. But the *nacionalistas* who looked for outside inspiration to create their programmes and strategies no longer had to focus on the now rapidly collapsing Fascist regime in Italy: a model lay much closer at hand in Getúlio Vargas' Brazil: 'Vargas has given an extraordinary impulse to workers' rights in Brazil. He started this activity with the creation of the ministry of labour. . . . The way they deal with this matter in Brazil . . . invites us to consider this as a basis for study and ideas'.[45]

Perón's take-over of the Labour Department in October 1943 could thus be seen as the execution of a long-established *nacionalista* strategy that Perón adopted with the full knowledge and support of his colleagues in the military junta. He made several quite explicit statements of his intentions and objectives, the first in an interview with a Chilean journalist, Abel Valdés, scarcely two weeks after he took office. Throughout this interview Perón made constant reference to *nacionalista* concepts that bore on working-class issues, as he also employed classic *nacionalista* phrasing and vocabulary:

Our revolution is essentially spiritual (*espiritualista*). In Argentina the wealth of the people [ought to stay] in our hands, so that each Argentine may receive the best return on his labours. I myself am a trade unionist (*sindicalista*), and as such I am anti-Communist, but I also believe that labour should be organized in trade union form, so that the workers themselves, and not the agitators who control them, are the ones to reap the benefits of their labours.

His aim, Perón declared, was to

improve the standard of living of the workers, but without tolerating social conflict. . . . I shall not allow free rein to the agents of destruction and agitation, who are often not even Argentines but foreigners. I have working class issues completely under control, and not by force but agreement (*conciliación*). . . .

[43] *La Razón*, 8 June 1943.
[44] Sánchez Sorondo, *La revolución que anunciamos*, p. 246.
[45] *La Razón*, 8 June 1943.

Don't believe we are anti-capitalist. Not at all. [But] international capitalism is quite mistaken if it believes it can conquer the national spirit in Argentina, which this government incarnates.[46]

Thus, in Perón's words the *nacionalistas* were attempting a *spiritual* revolution: the term, borrowed from Spanish conservatism, was among the most common in the lexicon of *nacionalismo*. The *nacionalista* revolution meant keeping the national wealth in the country and giving labour its due share; the purpose of trade union organization was to keep 'agitators' at bay and to improve living standards without provoking class conflict. Perón's remarks on 'international capitalism' also echoed the *nacionalistas*, and his hints that capitalists should make concessions to prevent labour from becoming revolutionary paraphrased the great papal encyclicals *Rerum Novarum* and *Quadragesimo Anno*. Again Perón had avoided explicit anti-Semitic remarks, but his simultaneous strictures against communism and 'international capitalism' adopted the general suppositions and the outlook on which anti-Semitism in Argentina was based.

The Valdés interview marked the first occasion on which Perón had exposed himself to the public at large. His air was one of confidence; his performance was appealing and provoked Valdés himself into making a memorable forecast: 'My general impression is that the present Argentine government is united, powerful and strong. . . . Another of my impressions is that . . . Colonel Juan Perón may very soon become the supreme chief (*el caudillo máximo*) in the Argentine Republic, and who knows for how long'.[47] Soon after, in an open letter to Ramírez, Perón modestly denied that he aspired to anything beyond his current position, but it was clear to all that he was rapidly gaining personal impetus and political stature.

At the end of November, in a decree signed by all eight members of the cabinet, the government replaced the Labour Department with the Secretaría de Trabajo y Bienestar Social, a measure which brought Perón, as its head, into the cabinet. In a lengthy preamble to the decree, Perón outlined his plans with respect to labour still more explicitly. The Secretaría de Trabajo, said the preamble, would serve as an 'organization that centralizes and controls', to produce 'greater harmony between the productive forces: to strengthen national unity through a greater measure of social and distributive justice . . . conceived in the Christian way in the

---

[46] *Cabildo,* 11 November 1943.
[47] Ibid., 11 November 1943.

light of the great encyclicals'. Speaking to a group of workers a few days after, Perón declared: 'I am a soldier in the most powerful unionized association (*gremie*) of all: the military. And I therefore advise you that to achieve the same cohesion and strength that we have, always remain united'.[48]

As Perón spelled out his intentions towards the unions, there were some immediate signs of labour's willingness to collaborate. In December 1943 the Secretaría de Trabajo reached an agreement on pay and fringe benefits with the Unión Ferroviaria, which amounted to conceding to the union virtually everything it had demanded but had been continually denied since 1929. Soon after this, union leaders led by the CGT's secretary, José Domenech, hailed Perón as 'Argentina's Number One Worker'. Perón ended the year with a public appeal to businessmen to volunteer a Christmas bonus to their workers in the shape of an extra month's wage. The campaign to further 'social justice' continued into 1944, as the *nacionalista* press, led by *Cabildo,* declaimed Perón's achievements as it fulminated against what it would characteristically describe as the pernicious canker (*ingerte*) of Manchester liberalism'.[49] In February 1944 Perón gained new prominence when he placed himself at the head of relief operations following a devastating earthquake that levelled the city of San Juan. At this point, too, Perón began his soon notorious relationship with the actress Eva Duarte, who was among a team of popular entertainers involved in the San Juan relief campaign.

Soon after the San Juan disaster, however, a new foreign affairs crisis suddenly overshadowed Perón's activities among the trade unions. Following the Storni letter affair the United States had intensified its economic boycott and renewed its propaganda campaign against Argentina, both of which had been briefly suspended since Castillo's overthrow. The campaign reached a climax in December 1943 following the coup d'état in Bolivia, amidst reports that Argentina was involved in a similar conspiracy to overthrow the government of Uruguay. The *nacionalista* regime now redoubled its efforts to create an arms industry, but in a desperate effort to relieve its immediate military weaknesses it began plotting to buy arms from Nazi Germany. This move proved a disastrous blunder, since Osmar Hellmuth, Ramírez's secret agent, was arrested by the British in Trinidad en route to Spain and Germany, and the British passed on information

---

[48] Ibid., 30 November 1943; *La Razón,* 10 December 1943.
[49] *Cabildo,* 12 January 1944.

about his activities to the State Department. The Hellmuth affair finally provided the United States with what appeared to be concrete proof of Argentina's collusion with the Axis, and armed with this evidence the State Department immediately threatened to make it public, placing Ramírez in an untenable position. He soon surrendered, and on 26 January decreed the break in diplomatic relations that the United States had demanded unsuccessfully since 1942.

Except to the handful of those familiar with the details of the Hellmuth case and its consequences, the diplomatic break lacked any rational explanation and seemed an unintelligible capitulation to U.S. pressures. The break in relations therefore precipitated an immediate political crisis that came to a head in the second week of February, as the government sought to silence a rising flood of criticism from the *nacionalistas* by suddenly dissolving and banning all the *nacionalista* associations. After the ban came a spate of cabinet resignations, which included that of Colonel Alberto Gilbert, who as foreign minister became the immediate scapegoat for the Hellmuth mission, and that of Martínez Zuviría, who left the government in protest against both the diplomatic break and the ban on the *nacionalistas*. But then as the *nacionalistas* fought back, Ramírez himself was ousted on 25 February by his critics, who forced him to take a temporary leave of the presidency that soon after they made permanent. The Hellmuth affair had thus brought down Ramírez and others, but left the *nacionalista* regime as a whole quite unshaken, as the United States acknowledged when it refused the new government diplomatic recognition. The episode marked another crucial stage in the rise of Perón. As Vice-president Farrell replaced Ramírez as president, he relinquished the position he had hitherto held as minister of war to Perón, at first temporarily but soon after permanently. Thanks to the fall of Ramírez, Perón now controlled two cabinet posts.

Under Farrell, Argentina continued to be estranged from the United States, and although meat shipments to Britain continued, the United States maintained a virtual blockade on supplies to Argentina. The regime replied to its forced isolation by launching a vast military mobilization of men and resources. By late 1945 it had tripled the size of the army, while increasing the military's share of government spending from 17 per cent in 1943 to 43 per cent in 1945. As the army grew, its personnel were deployed into road construction; new experimental industrial plants were formed under army control and supervision; the army led eager searches for industrial raw materials in the Andean region. In April 1944 the government established a Banco Industrial, charged with financing industries deemed of national interest, which meant primarily the state corporations producing armaments.

Rapid militarization in 1944, which started principally as a response to U.S. pressures, thus quickly became an instrument of economic policy, a means to funnel resources into industrialization. Militarization corresponded to the basic tenets of *nacionalismo,* which regarded the army as an instrument for reshaping society. But an overtly authoritarian structure was now taking shape. As it expanded the armed forces, the government imposed still more restrictions on the press and in April 1944 inflicted a five-day ban on *La Prensa.* At the end of July Farrell officiated over a great torchlit gathering in the Avenida Nueve de Julio in Buenos Aires. To an audience estimated to be a quarter of a million he issued a 'Declaration of Sovereignty':

Today . . . the entire people of the Republic . . . has understood the fundamental truths of nationalism (*nacionalismo*). . . . [This demonstration] reveals the existence of a powerful national movement (*fuerza*), seeking ends that are purely national, and which therefore cannot be a political party, because it does not defend the interests of any 'part' against any other part, but the grandeur of the whole nation.[50]

Still more *nacionalista* edicts flowed from the government, among them a 'peon's statute', which in setting minimum wages for rural workers exemplified the long-standing concern of the *nacionalistas* with the rural population. In mid-October Farrell presided over a ceremony that symbolically 'consecrated' the armed forces to 'the Virgin', an act meant to evoke the 'union of the Cross and the Sword' that formed the *nacionalista* vision of the Spanish conquest of the Americas.

Thus, despite the confusion of the Hellmuth affair, the *nacionalista* regime continued to gain momentum and to acquire an increasingly aggressive character. After the fall of Ramírez, Perón rededicated himself to his activities in the Secretaría de Trabajo and was now busily weeding out opponents in the unions, principally Socialists. By June, having eliminated its leader, Francisco Pérez Leiros, he had gained control of the large metal-workers' union, the Unión Obrera Metalúrgica. Unmistakeable signs now appeared that he had started to mobilize a vast popular constituency. In March 1944 a large number of railwaymen demonstrated on his behalf. For the first time ever the CGT joined the annual parade of 25 May

<hr />

[50] Ibid., 29 July 1944.

to commemorate the revolution of May 1810. Throughout this period Perón remained in constant touch with trade union leaders, promising, exhorting and if necessary threatening them. His message remained the same as in late 1943: he urged unity, and he constantly promulgated the classical Catholic precept of 'social justice':

> . . . the new social policy . . . is based on the need . . . to avoid a situation where some men are unduly rich and others unduly poor. The wisdom of the ancients '*in medio veritas*' continues to be valid. . . . Truth stands at the mean, at a due balance being maintained in the sharing of wealth so as to eliminate the absurd polarization . . . between the class of the wealthy and powerful and the class of beggars . . . a healthy balance . . . understanding and conciliation between the classes. . . . In his speech . . . Perón mentioned all the points that comprise the Christian concept of social justice contained in the great papal encyclicals.[51]

From his other position as minister of war, Perón actively supervised the expansion of the army, while increasing his own power and prestige within it. As minister he controlled communications between the government and the military, and he fully exploited his power over supplies, patronage and promotions at a time when the military budget was growing at an accelerating pace. Perón emerged as the foremost ideologue of the *nacionalista* proposition that the role of the army was to direct public policy and to construct a new society. On 11 June 1944 he delivered his most powerful speech to date, in which he advanced his concept of the 'nation in arms'. War, Perón declared, was an inevitable consequence of the human condition. But each nation's best deterrent against it was to become militarily strong, and military strength required the mobilization of all available resources; mobilization in turn meant industrialization and 'social justice'. 'Si vis pacem, para bellum', he proclaimed: 'If you wish peace, prepare for war'.[52]

In the United States Perón's speech was attacked as 'totalitarian', and it brought a further cooling of relations. Henceforth, the State Department referred frequently to the Argentine regime as 'Nazi'. But in Argentina itself the speech served to advance Perón's political standing. Thousands of trade unionists responded to the attacks on Perón in the United States with popular demonstrations. Capitalizing on his ever-growing stature, less than a month after the speech Perón provoked a conflict over spheres

[51] Ibid., 25 June, 1944.
[52] *La Prensa*, 11 June 1944.

of authority with General Luis Perlinger, who as minister of the interior had become his leading rival in the junta. In this conflict Perón proved irresistible, carrying the rest of the government along with him in a demand that Perlinger resign. When Perlinger did so, Perón acquired yet a third office, the vice-presidency, which had been vacant since the fall of Ramírez in February.

Within scarcely a year of the June 1943 coup d'état against Castillo, Perón had unquestionably become the leading figure in the military regime; Farrell retreated into the role of figurehead president. In the middle of 1944 Perón faced only two remaining adversaries: the U.S. State Department and an amorphous but large mass of domestic opponents, led by the Radicals and the *fuerzas vivas,* beneficiaries of the old liberal economy threatened by government policies of state-directed industrialization and social reform. For the rest of 1944 the State Department showed little interest in Argentina. The economic sanctions remained, but the United States proved unable to take further action against Argentina, mainly because of British opposition. By late 1944 domestic opposition to Perón was increasing, but it remained extremely disunited and unfocussed. The liberation of Paris in August provoked large street demonstrations in Buenos Aires which turned into an angry outburst against the regime for its 'Nazi sympathies'. Spokesmen for the still-banned political parties occasionally issued demands for elections, and the 'peon's statute' provoked a flood of criticisms from ranchers' and farmers' associations led by the Sociedad Rural Argentina. At the end of the year Perón became embroiled in a bitter dispute with the Unión Industrial Argentina, the chief industrial employers' organization, when he instituted an obligatory year-end workers' bonus, the *aguinaldo,* which the year before had been purely voluntary. But the nature of Argentine politics was being rapidly transformed: each time Perón's opponents, at home and abroad, struck out against him, his trade union and working-class followers immediately responded to support him.

As he erected his popular alliance, Perón benefited from various conditions that helped make labour responsive to his appeal. First, an industrialization policy that increased urban employment inevitably proved popular among a rapidly growing working class. Second, although between 1941 and 1945 the total number of *workers* affiliated in unions with the CGT increased relatively slowly from 441,000 to 528,000, or by 17.7 per cent, the number of *unions* affiliated with the CGT increased during the same period from 356 to 969, or by 285 per cent, a trend that illustrated the spread of trade unionism into the new small-scale manufacturing sectors. As a result, as it began its operations, the labour secretariat had a mass of potential contacts to which it could attach itself throughout the labour force. Employers, however, confronted by a sellers' labour market and separated from one another by enormous differences of scale, found it difficult to unite themselves in common resistance either to the unions or to Perón. Third, unlike the period 1914–19, which saw a steep decline in real wages, the years 1939–45 witnessed a slow increase in real wages, principally because of the growth of new industrial jobs and abundant cheap grains. In 1940 average real wages stood at roughly the same level as they had in 1929 and grew by 10 per cent by 1944. Strikes occurred much less frequently during the early 1940s than they had twenty-five years before. Between 1940 and 1944 the incidence of strikes, measured by man-hours lost, remained at only one-third that of 1915–19, although the labour force had roughly doubled between the two periods. Thus, during the Second World War, not only was labour less militant than it had been twenty-five years earlier, but the unions tended to be less concerned with wages than with fringe benefits such as sick pay, bonuses, paid vacations and accident compensation.

Fringe benefits were easier to deliver than wage increases, and were exactly the type of rewards the Secretaría de Trabajo could arrange. Equally, it proved much easier to deal with labour when the main issue concerned relatively superficial improvements to already fairly acceptable conditions, rather than the survival of desperate workers, often at the point of rebellion, as had been the case twenty-five years before. Perón's basic techniques were to enforce labour legislation that already existed, to support wage increases in sectors where unions were already organized and to promote new unions where none existed. Perón gained some advantage from the purge of Communist union leaders soon after the June 1943 coup. The Communists were the union leaders likely to have resisted him most tenaciously. Yet they remained few in number, and the government constantly exaggerated their influence. Nor was their standing among workers very secure, since throughout the war they had avoided militant stances that might affect the war effort. Although many union leaders in 1943–5 resisted dealing with Perón and attempted to keep their distance, rank-and-file pressures frequently forced them into contact with the Secretaría de Trabajo. By late 1944 the Secretaría had begun to deal only with unions that possessed *personería gremial,* or full legal standing conferred by the government. But to gain this status, unions had to be controlled by leaders acceptable to Perón, which meant those willing to follow his orders.

On the international front, after Cordell Hull's resignation as secretary of state in November 1944, responsibility for Latin American affairs in the State Department passed to Nelson Rockefeller, the new under-secretary. Supported by numerous manufacturing associations in the United States that regarded Argentina as a large potential post-war market, Rockefeller now led an attempt to win greater co-operation from Argentina through concessions. Soon after November the United States re-established diplomatic relations, lightened the trade and financial embargoes and hinted at its willingness to terminate the wartime ban on arms sales to Argentina. This new-style diplomacy had several, almost instant positive results. In February 1945 Argentina became a signatory to the Act of Chapultepec, which pledged inter-American co-operation on mutual defence and trade. Finally, towards the end of March Argentina declared war on Germany and Japan. At this point, with Germany's capitulation scarcely a month away, the declaration of war was only token, but in making the gesture Argentina ensured its admission to the United Nations, while suggesting a readiness for quite different future relations with the United States. For a fleeting period it thus seemed that the aspirations of the Pinedo Plan of late 1940 might ultimately be accomplished under the military junta.

However, the new approach to Argentina under Rockefeller ceased abruptly after mid-April when Truman replaced Roosevelt as president and the State Department underwent yet another reshuffle. Although Rockefeller remained at his post for some time, control over policy towards Argentina passed to Spruille Braden, one of the leading critics of Argentina's wartime neutrality and of the current Argentine government. As the war in Europe ended, the United States at last freed itself of British restraints, and led by Braden it now directed its energies into a campaign to sweep Perón and the *nacionalista* regime aside. In May Braden was designated ambassador to Argentina, and by June he was touring the country attacking the government and demanding immediate elections; he urged Washington to afford no further assistance to Argentina 'until such time as the Nazi militaristic control of this country has been replaced by a constitutional and cooperating [*sic*] democracy'.[53]

In the meantime, Perón had continued to expand and consolidate his

[53] Cable of 11 July 1945. Quoted in Bryce Wood, *The Dismantling of the Good Neighbor Policy* (Austin, Tex., 1985), p. 96.

alliance with the trade unions. In his most prominent speech of this period he defined his goal as the 'peaceful revolution of the masses':

If we fail to carry out the Peaceful Revolution, the People themselves will take the road of Violent Revolution. . . . And the solution to the whole problem is social justice towards the masses. . . . Naturally this is not a popular idea among rich men. . . . But they are their own worst enemies. Better to offer 30 per cent now, than within years, or perhaps even months, to risk losing all they have, including their ears.[54]

Indeed, the message was not popular among 'rich men', and in mid-1945 Spruille Braden's activities swiftly rekindled the opposition to Perón that for some months past had remained largely dormant. In June a 'Manifesto of the *Fuerzas Vivas*' attacked the government's social reforms, but this document was closely followed by a counter-manifesto from the trade unions 'in defence of the benefits won through the Secretaría de Trabajo y Bienestar Social'.

Finally, on 19 September, after three months of growing tension, thousands upon thousands of Perón's opponents gathered in the streets of Buenos Aires in a 'March of the Constitution and Liberty'. Five days later General Arturo Rawson, the one-day president of June 1943, led an unsuccessful coup d'état from Córdoba. At the end of September the navy pronounced in favour of a return to civilian rule. Soon after, the government itself split between the opponents of Perón led by General Eduardo Avalos and Perón's supporters. On 9 October Avalos succeeded in forcing Perón into resigning his multiple posts in the government. Three days later he was imprisoned on the island of Martín García. It seemed now that under challenge, *'peronismo'* had collapsed and that Farrell would soon concede the chief demands of the liberal 'constitutionalists': set a date for elections, while ceding control to a caretaker government headed by the justices of the Supreme Court.

Then came what Sir David Kelly, the British ambassador, described as an 'incredible comedy'. With victory in its grasp the movement to destroy Perón faltered. In the days that followed his fall, bickering within the liberal coalition delayed the efforts of Juan Alvarez, the chief justice of the Supreme Court, to organize a caretaker government. Other conflicts arose between the leaders of the coalition and the army. If the latter, led by Avalos, had eventually bent to pressure and sacrificed Perón, it stopped

[54] Quoted in Darío Cantón, 'El ejército en 1930: El antes y el después', in Haydée Gorosteguí de Torres (ed.), *Historia integral Argentina*, vol. 7 (Buenos Aires, 1970), p. 11.

short of further steps that would have meant the collapse and termination of the 1943 revolution. Within the army, partly out of concern for future reprisals but also because of an unwillingness to surrender its new powers in both the government and the economy, resistance quickly grew to the plan to hand over the government to the Supreme Court. As the deadlock continued, events suddenly took a decisive turn when on 17 October thousands of workers marched into the centre of Buenos Aires to demand Perón's release from imprisonment. Had the army wanted a new government dominated by the liberals, it might have acted quickly to prevent the workers' march. Not only did it permit the march, but it allowed Perón, who two days earlier had returned to Buenos Aires from Martín García, having convinced his captors that he required medical treatment, to address the vast crowds gathered in the Plaza de Mayo from the Casa Rosada. He proclaimed an 'indestructible union of brotherhood between the people [and] the army'.[55] After 17 October the Avalos faction in the Farrell government resigned; Perón and his supporters returned to power.

To all contemporary observers the workers' march occurred quite spontaneously. Yet Perón had obviously planned an event of this sort as part of his strategy for political survival. While taking leave of his staff on 10 October, he urged an attempt to rally popular support. After his fall, his leading associates led by Domingo Mercante toured the industrial and working-class areas of the city, urging action on his behalf. Many workers had already begun to strike by 13 October, after numerous employers had refused to observe Perón's enactment that the 12th, the 'Dia de la Raza', be treated as a workers' holiday. Attempts by workers to cross the Río Riachuelo, which divided the federal capital from the province of Buenos Aires, began on 16 October. The great march of 17 October owed virtually nothing to the CGT, whose leaders met only on the evening of the 16th as the demonstrations were reaching a crescendo. Even then the CGT voted to support action by the slender margin of 21 to 19. Above all the '*17 de octubre*' appeared to be an exhibition of established behaviour, since for the past year or more unions and workers had grown steadily accustomed to responding to threats against Perón through popular mobilization.

The events of September–October 1945 demonstrated the extent to which in only two years Perón had totally transformed Argentine politics: he had rendered the fifty-year-long feud between the Radicals and the

---

[55] The literal translation of this phrase reads 'brotherhood between the people, the army and the police'. See Felix Luna, *El '45* (Buenos Aires, 1971), p. 295.

conservatives an anachronism; he had precipitated the working class into politics, while virtually eliminating the traditional working-class parties, in particular the Socialists; he had divided the country into the *'peronista'* supporters of 'economic independence' and 'social justice' and 'anti-*peronista'* defenders of the old liberal order. In November, although it continued to resist making way to a government under the Supreme Court the junta announced elections for February 1946. By December 1945 Perón's opponents had finally overcome their internal differences and united in a Unión Democrática (UD) to contest the elections. The Radicals dominated this coalition, but alongside them stood a disparate mélange that included remnants of the conservative National Democratic Party, the Socialist Party and the Communist Party. The UD represented the closest analogue that appeared in Argentina to the Popular Front against which the GOU had mobilized in 1943. But the UD lacked the main ingredient of the Popular Front: the support of the organized working class. Behind its reformist façade, the coalition subsisted on little more than the impulse to oppose Perón. Nevertheless, led by José Tamborini, a former Radical with a political background similar to that of Roberto M. Ortiz, the UD remained confident of a sweeping electoral victory.

For Perón the crisis of September–October 1945 had ended in a nearby miraculous escape from political oblivion and yet, despite the *17 de octubre,* not in any final victory. He now faced the challenge of contesting an election against a coalition that comprised nearly all of the political parties with little organization of his own. He had the support of the unions in Buenos Aires, but almost none beyond. In less than five months he had to build a national coalition. First, Perón secured the support of the Partido Laborista, a new working-class party backed by the unions that was modelled roughly on the British Labour Party. Second, after numerous earlier failures during 1944 and 1945, Perón finally managed to win over a substantial minority of Radicals. Hortensio Quijano, the leader of the dissident Radical faction, the Unión Cívica Radical–Junta Renovadora, which now supported Perón, became his running mate and helped project the movement into the provinces. Among the other Radical defectors to join Perón in late 1945 were several leading members of the FORJA, along with some of the conservative *nacionalistas* led by the Alianza Libertadora Nacionalista. In the provinces Perón added further to his following by attracting a few conservative local political bosses who had last tasted power under Castillo and who remained opposed at all costs to the Radicals. Finally, Perón enjoyed support from the Church, as he undertook to retain the religious teaching in the schools that Martínez Zuviría had reintroduced in 1943 and continually reminded Church leaders that Communists formed part of the UD. In late 1945 'peronismo' thus mushroomed swiftly beyond its Buenos Aires trade union base into a heterogeneous movement with new sources of support in the provinces and the rural population.

As the election of February 1946 approached, having begun far behind his opponent Tamborini, Perón was gaining ground rapidly. Then only days before the election the U.S. State Department issued a 'Blue Book: A Memorandum of the United States Government [to other Latin American governments] With Respect to the Argentine Situation'. Spruille Braden, now assistant secretary of state, had instigated the preparation and distribution of this document, the aim of which was to show 'how Nazi agents in Argentina . . . had combined with totalitarian groups to create a Nazi-Fascist state'.[56] The report presented materials collected by the United States during the war that sought to show that members of successive governments in Argentina and senior military personnel, including Perón himself, had colluded with the Axis. It repeated the charges that Argentina had tolerated or encouraged German espionage and propaganda; it cited the pro-Axis speeches of military leaders, dealings between governments and German firms and loans by German banks to Argentine politicians.

The 'Blue Book' was received on almost all sides in Argentina as a crude foreign ploy to influence the elections. It instantly rekindled nationalist sympathies, crippled the UD and gave Perón a major issue with which to rally the electorate. In an interview with a Brazilian journalist, Perón sarcastically thanked Braden 'for the votes he has given me. If I carry two-thirds of the electorate, I shall owe one-third to Braden'.[57] In the run up to the election the *peronisto* campaign rang with the cry of 'Braden or Perón!': surrender to U.S. pressures or a bold commitment alongside Perón to a programme of revolutionary change. When the vote was counted, Perón had won 52.4 per cent against Tamborini's 42.5 per cent (1.49 million votes against 1.21 million), with the rest of the vote being won by minor parties. But having carried eleven of fifteen provinces, including the federal capital, Perón gained an overwhelming majority in the electoral college. He would now take office as president on 4 June 1946, the third anniversary of the 1943 coup.

[56] Quoted in Wood, *Dismantling of the Good Neighbor Policy,* p. 113.
[57] Quoted in Enrique Díaz Araujo, *La conspiración del '43* (Buenos Aires, 1971), p. 95.

The 1946 election showed that the bastions of *peronismo* lay in the capital and in two of the three principal littoral provinces, Buenos Aires and Santa Fe. In all three jurisdictions the *peronista* alliance captured more than 50 per cent of the popular vote. Within the littoral only Córdoba fell to the UD, thanks to a hastily arranged and fragile alliance between Radicals and conservatives. *Peronistas* gained a majority in Mendoza and Tucumán, the leading wine and sugar provinces, both of which had a large number of rural and urban workers, and in the most backward provinces of the West and North, which held large peasant communities: Catamarca, La Rioja and Santiago del Estero. In the eastern cities, above all Buenos Aires, the Partido Laborista won the vote of almost the entire working class, both the 'new' workers composed of migrants employed in new manufacturing and services and the 'old' proletariat that before had voted Socialist.[58] In the capital and its main suburbs led by Avellaneda, *peronismo* thus emerged as an overwhelmingly working-class movement, gathering support from only a small minority of other sectors. But elsewhere Perón's support was much more mixed and included numerous rural groups that had often supported conservative candidates. The dissident Radical Junta Renovadora faction supporting Perón played an important part in the election by taking votes from the orthodox Radical (Unión Cívica Radical) ticket.

In 1946 Argentina thus embarked on Perón's revised, popular version of the Nationalist Revolution. Until late in 1940 there had been few hints of the imminence of this great transition. That the shift occurred partly reflected the accident of Ortiz's retirement and early death, since if Ortiz had survived, the conflicts between Radicals and conservatives that undermined Castillo might have been much less acute. Yet the change of president alone did not release the forces that destroyed liberal-conservatism. Equally significant for its collapse were the Second World War and the failure to reach agreement with the United States, which provided the *nacionalistas* with the opportunity to spread their alternative vision of Argentina's future.

[58] The distinction between the 'old' and 'new' working classes and their contribution to Perón's electoral support in 1946 is documented and debated in Peter H. Smith, 'La base social del peronismo', and Gino Germani, 'El surgimiento del peronismo: El rol de los obreros y de los migrantes internos', in Manuel Mora y Araujo and Ignacio. Llorente (eds.), *El voto personista: Ensayos de sociología electoral argentina* (Buenos Aires, 1980), pp. 39–164.

2

ARGENTINA SINCE 1946

THE *PERONISTA* DECADE, 1946−55

On 24 February 1946 General Juan Domingo Perón was elected president of Argentina in an open poll. This victory was the culmination of his dizzying political rise, which had begun a few years earlier when the military revolution of June 1943 put an end to a decade of conservative governments and brought to power a clique of army colonels with fascist sympathies. The emerging military regime had been groping its way between the hostility that its authoritarian and clerical tendencies had awakened in the middle and upper classes and the diplomatic quarantine organized by the United States in reprisal for Argentina's neutral position in the Second World War. Through clever palace manoeuvring Perón became the regime's dominant figure and ended the political isolation of the military elite by launching a set of labour reforms that had a powerful impact on the working class, whose numbers had swelled with industrialization and urbanization since the mid-1930s. In Perón's vision, the function of these reforms was to prevent the radicalization of conflicts and the spread of Communism. But the Argentine bourgeoisie did not fear an imminent social revolution, a fear which, at other times and in other places, had facilitated the acceptance of similar reforms. As a result, they joined the anti-fascist front organized by the middle class, imbuing political cleavages with a visible class bias.

In 1945, the new climate created by the imminent triumph of the Allied forces led the military authorities to look for an institutional solution. Perón, after trying with limited success to obtain the backing of the tradi-

We would like to express our thanks to Guido di Tella, whose manuscript on the economic history of this period helped us greatly, although the final responsibility for this work is ours alone. The chapter was translated from the Spanish by Elizabeth Ladd.

tional parties, decided to launch his presidential candidacy by appealing to
the popular support he had developed when in office. In October 1945, this
mass following proved decisive when a military plot instigated by the
opposition was on the point of interrupting his political career. A popular
mobilization, organized by the unions and abetted by Perón's supporters in
the army and the police force, succeeded in releasing him from jail and
reinstating him in the electoral contest. Perón's candidacy was sustained by
the unions, which were the main force behind the newly established Labour
Party, together with dissidents from the Radical Party organized in the
Junta Renovadora. The opposition centred on the Unión Democrática, a
coalition of centrist and leftist parties which had considerable backing from
the business community and the U.S. government. Perón took full advantage of these circumstances to present himself as a champion of social justice
and national interests and to win the elections held in February 1946.

Formed over a relatively brief period from sectors of different origins,
the *peronista* coalition was on the verge of disintegration once the elections
were over. At the center of the conflict were the union leaders of the
Labour Party and the dissident radical politicians of the Junta Renovadora.
According to constitutional law, representatives to the Senate were elected
indirectly by the provincial legislatures. Before the elections, labour and
the junta had agreed to share the seats in the Senate equally, but after the
poll, the politicians used specious arguments and bribery in an effort to
oust the labour leaders in the Senate and the provincial cabinets. In this
conflict Perón decided to support more docile elements from the traditional parties and lessen the influence of labour. A few days before assuming the presidency in June, he ordered the dissolution of the parties of the
electoral alliance and called for the creation of a new party, invoking the
need for cohesive movement in order to govern with effectiveness and
unity. The leaders of the Labour Party, which was more insistent on its
own autonomy than was the Junta Renovadora, debated what course to
follow for several days. Finally, arguments in favour of unity won them
over. They were promised a representative place in the new party in
exchange for the renunciation of their old political ambitions. The potential benefits entailed in their inclusion in the official political order promised more than did the defence of independence, which would place them
on the margins of the nascent *peronista* Argentina.

Thus, labour's brief resistance ended in the middle of June 1946. Perón
appointed the organizers of the new party from among the recently elected
legislators. Although there were a few union men, the majority were

middle-class politicians. This tendency would become accentuated over time. There was no place in the scheme of the new organization for sectors which had a power base independent of the party itself.

In January 1947, when the organizers of the new party approached Perón to approve the name 'Partido Peronista', they explicitly sanctioned another and more decisive feature of the political structure of the movement. Personalism was an almost inevitable consequence of a movement formed in such a short period of time out of the convergence of heterogeneous forces. Moreover, Perón was careful to avoid being influenced by the forces that supported him. Article 31 of the statutes of the Partido Peronista, approved in December 1947, empowered him to modify all decisions made by the party as well as to review all candidacies. Although Perón owed an obvious ideological debt to the authoritarian tradition in which he had been trained, conflict within the triumphant bloc of 1946 also imposed a strong and centralized leadership role upon him. Anarchy was, in fact, the distinctive feature of the *peronista* movement during the first years. Only the constant exercise of authority by Perón himself neutralized the general lack of discipline among his followers.

Shortly after taking office Perón resolved local problems, beginning in the province of Catamarca, by replacing local authorities with an official appointed by the central administration. This mechanism of control, provided for in the constitution, was amply used during the first year – in Córdoba in 1947, La Rioja, Santiago del Estero and Catamarca again in 1948 and Santa Fe in 1949. Even Corrientes, the only province where the opposition had triumphed in 1946, was subjected to intervention in 1947.

Perón also attacked the last bastion of the survivors of the Labour Party. In November 1946 Luis Gay, former president of the party, was elected secretary-general of the Confederación General del Trabajo (CGT) and tried to follow an independent line. The controversial visit of a delegation of U.S. labour leaders gave Perón an opportunity to accuse Gay of plotting to withdraw CGT support from the government and joining the inter-American union movement promoted from the United States. The accusation unleashed a violent campaign against Gay in the official press, and he had to resign in January 1947. A few of his close associates resigned with him, but the majority chose to adapt to the new order. Led by figures of second rank, the CGT henceforth became an agency of official directives within the labour movement.

Step by step, Perón quelled those independent forces he had been obliged to tolerate during the election campaign. Besides the Partido Peronista and the CGT, the other fundamental pillar of the regime was the armed forces. The open breach between the military and the democratic opposition in 1945 had allowed Perón to pursue the presidency. After he was elected, he once again presented himself as a man of arms in an effort to gain the support of the military establishment. However, he sought to define his relations with the military on strictly institutional bases, and although many officers served in the government, the institution as a whole was not involved. Perón set as an objective the neutrality of the officer corps; to achieve this he addressed himself above all to the satisfaction of their professional demands.

These were the years of expansion and modernization in the armed forces. As a result of the boom in military investment following the 1943 coup, military spending represented 38.4 per cent of the national budget by 1945. The percentage decreased to 20.6 in 1951, but even this was well above the pre-war level of 18.2 per cent, and Argentina continued to earmark more of its budget for defence than did any other Latin American state. The enlargement of the officer corps at a faster rate than the increase in enlisted men (the number of generals doubled between 1946 and 1951) and the purchase of modern equipment permitted the armed forces to tolerate the regime during the early years.

This political exchange would not have been possible without some degree of identification by the military with the general principles of Perón's government. Nationalism, industrialization and social justice were congruent with deeply rooted beliefs among the officer corps. In addition, a prudent manipulation of internal rivalries and the distribution of favours helped to isolate the least trustworthy elements and reward the loyalty of the most faithful. Confined to a professional role that yielded tangible benefits, the armed forces were progressively integrated into the *peronista* regime.

The Church also contributed to the consolidation of the new regime. It had played a positive role even during Perón's election campaign of 1946. Harassed by anticlericalism among the traditional political forces, the ecclesiastical hierarchy, imbued with anti-liberal ideology, welcomed Perón's consistent homage to the social doctrine of the Church. On the eve of the election it circulated a flyer recommending that people not vote for candidates whose programmes and attitudes contradicted the Catholic message. This warning obviously applied to the Unión Democrática, which objected to the military government's 1943 decision to include religious instruction by decree in the schools. Once in power, Perón transformed the decree into law. Later, official activity in the field of social welfare and education cooled the bishops' enthusiasm, since they found it difficult to reconcile their support of Perón with their traditional links to the upper class. Nevertheless, they refrained from making these reservations public, in an effort to achieve peaceful coexistence with the new political order.

With the backing of the army and the Church, and the loyalty of a popular mass soon corralled under a centralized leadership, the new regime had established secure foundations. But Perón also decided to reinforce his government through bureaucratic and repressive mechanisms. The first victim was the Supreme Court, which had resisted Perón's social reforms from the beginning. In September 1946, its members were accused in Congress of, among other things, having recognized as legitimate the de facto governments that arose out of the military coups of 1930 and 1943. Eight months later they were dismissed as part of a general purge of the judicial power. Another stronghold of resistance in 1945, the university, went through a similar process with the expulsion of thousands of professors. In 1947 training schools run by opposition parties were closed, and economic groups linked to the regime began to buy up the national radio broadcasting system. In 1951 the expropriation of one of the most traditional papers, *La Prensa,* and its transfer to the CGT led to a virtual state monopoly over the mass media. Those who survived with a degree of independence took care not to challenge openly the proselytizing tone used by the official media to praise the policies of the regime.

With this gradual suppression of public freedoms, the political opposition found itself limited to the congressional sphere. However, the narrow margin of votes that had granted victory to the *peronista* coalition was transformed by electoral legislation into an overwhelming government majority. The application of the Sáenz Peña law, which awarded two-thirds of the electoral seats to the majority and the remaining third to the leading minority party, gave the *peronistas* control not only over executive power but also over the lower house, with 109 deputies out of 158. Furthermore, thirteen of the fourteen provincial governments went to the *peronistas,* and this gave them control of the Senate.

The psychological shock the opposition forces experienced following defeat in the elections was magnified when they realized that they had practically disappeared from the political map. The Partido Demócrata and the *antipersonalista* Unión Cívical Radical (UCR), which had governed between 1932 and 1943, were reduced to three deputies and two senators.

The Socialist Party, whose presence in Congress had been continuous since 1904, did not have a single representative; nor did the Communist Party. Only the Radicals had managed to survive, although they were reduced to forty-four deputies.

The regime's authoritarian tendencies hardly encouraged a reduction of political antagonisms. The small, militant opposition bloc would not declare a truce with the official movement, but its criticism did not extend beyond Congress, and even there it was silenced by the pressure of the large *peronista* majority. In the congressional elections of 1948, the 52 per cent obtained by the *peronista* coalition in 1946 rose to 57 per cent, concentrating political power even more.

Its legitimacy guaranteed on the internal front, the new government sought to re-establish relations with the United States. A few weeks after taking office, Perón sent Congress the Act of Chapultepec (March 1945) to be ratified, making official Argentina's re-entry into the inter-American community.

Simultaneously, he permitted himself a gesture of independence in renewing relations with the Soviet Union, which had been suspended since 1917. This was followed by the deportation of a number of Nazi spies and the state's acquisition of German- and Japanese-owned companies. In June 1947 President Truman announced his satisfaction with Argentina's conduct. At the long-delayed inter-American conference convened in Rio de Janeiro in September 1947, Perón's foreign minister, with a very different attitude than that of his predecessor at the previous conference in Rio in 1942, signed the Hemispheric Security Treaty. The reward was the lifting of the arms embargo by the United States.

At the end of the war, Argentina found itself free of external debt and in possession of substantial reserves of foreign currency, benefiting from high demand and high prices for its food exports and a growing industrial base. Within this framework, the *peronista* administration implemented an economic policy with three major objectives: the expansion of public spending, giving the state a stronger role in production and distribution; the alteration of relative prices to encourage a more egalitarian distribution of national income; and the progressive accumulation of a system of incentives that rewarded activities oriented towards the internal market and discouraged production destined for international markets.

This combination of state intervention, social justice and an inward-looking economy was not an isolated experience in Latin America in the 1940s. It is true that in the Argentine case, characterized by a tight internal labour market and a very active union movement, the egalitarian bias was more marked than in other countries of the area. Nevertheless, the leading role of the public sector in the accumulation of capital and the growing emphasis on the internal market constituted, almost without exception, a regional version of the Keynesianism in vogue in the countries of the Centre in the West.

The *peronista* economy was not the product of a deliberate economic strategy. The social bases of the regime influenced its economic choices. Between the project for industrialization for national defence, based on essential industries and sponsored by army officers during the war, and the continuation of light industrialization, Perón chose the latter alternative, which was more congruent with a progressive distribution of income. In only three years – between 1946 and the beginning of 1949 – real income increased more than 40 per cent. This alteration in relative prices, almost without national or even international precedent, led to a rapid expansion of consumption and an industrial growth that reached 10.3 per cent in 1946, 12.1 per cent in 1947 and 6.9 per cent in 1948. In this context optimism in the business community overcame the apprehension generated by the bold income policy and union power, paving the way for prolonged euphoria in the stock market and a wave of investment by private business. The idea that capitalist profit could increase at the same time that salaries were rising ceased to be a paradox extolled by the official line and became a widespread conviction.

The rapid growth of public stock and restrictions on the flow of foreign trade were not decisions rationally derived from an original economic strategy. It is true that from 1946 the *peronista* government carried out a policy of nationalization of public services (railroads, telephones, merchant marine, airlines, gasoline, etc.). These decisions, together with the growing share of the budget allocated for the social welfare policy, led to a progressive extension of state activity and to a leap of around 30 per cent in public spending. It is also true that due to the policy changes and the establishment of quantitative restrictions on imports – especially after 1948 – the economy was turning inwards and being exposed to a low level of international competition.

Nonetheless, there seemed to be no alternative to these developments, either from the government's point of view or from that of the main opposition. Both the government and the opposition were convinced of the imminent outbreak of World War III, which they expected to eradicate international trade. They also had a certain amount of distrust, common in Latin

America, for the leadership of private capital in the development process. From these premisses both sides agreed that the construction of a strong, extensive state and the protection of national enterprises – intrinsically weak in the face of foreign competition – were prerequisites for economic growth and, above all, for the maintenance of a high level of employment. Furthermore, the generalized statism in the majority of Western countries, the tense calm of the Cold War and the slow expansion of commercial opportunities in the world market for Argentine industry seemed to support the prevailing analysis.

The economic policy of *peronismo,* with its nationalist, Keynesian and distributionist features, was possible thanks to a combined set of favourable circumstances which would not be repeated in Argentine economic history. After nearly two decades of commercial crisis, the sudden improvement in the prices of agricultural exports and, consequently, in the exchange rate allowed the new prosperity to be financed with foreign currency and opened a channel for the redistribution policies needed to consolidate the *peronista* regime. The reserves of foreign funds accumulated during the war – a large proportion of which were not convertible – also permitted the financing of the nationalization of public services.

Moreover, the relative abundance of easily collected fiscal resources meant that the new level of public spending could be reached and maintained without major difficulties. The creation of the Instituto Argentino para la Promoción y el Intercambio (IAPI), an entity that had a virtual monopoly over foreign trade, provided the government with indirect access to the principal source of capital accumulation and permitted the diversion of the rise in export prices to benefit the public sector. To this end, IAPI bought grain from local producers at a price fixed by the authorities and sold it on the international market at higher prices. The resources obtained through this mechanism, together with the forced savings that came from a pensions system that had a large surplus and a broad battery of direct and indirect taxes that fell heavily on the highest income brackets, contributed to the justifiable image of a rich and generous state.

Finally, the nationalization of the finance system and the notable expansion of its deposits, which was due in good measure to the economic rise of small savers who benefited from the redistribution of income, permitted an increase in the flow of subsidized credit towards public and private enterprises. This credit policy was an important part of the *peronista* economy since it encouraged capital investment and reduced working capital, offsetting the effects of the higher cost of labour through financial profits.

Thus, the *peronista* economy was facilitated by the exceptional evolution of the international post-war market, growing fiscal income and the opening of institutionalized saving to the masses. This pattern of development, which was based on the purchasing power of the state and on high salaries, but which, since it was oriented towards the internal market, could ignore the inevitable costs in terms of efficiency and competitiveness, lasted barely three years. Nevertheless, these were the years that stamped an enduring profile of the economics of *peronismo* in the collective memory.

Between 1946 and 1948, Argentina had to face the obstacles to its foreign trade raised by boycott which the U.S. government had imposed as a consequence of Argentina's neutrality in the Second World War. It had begun as early as 1942, and until the end of the 1940s Argentina was treated under U.S. trade policy as an enemy nation. A partial fuel embargo was applied, and Argentina was denied other vital imports, over and beyond the restrictions imposed by the war. From 1946 to 1949, the focus of the boycott shifted from a deprivation of critical industrial inputs to an effort to reduce Argentine exports, which would force political concessions out of a regime perceived as unfriendly. When relations were normalized in 1947, the U.S. government's economic persecution of Argentina continued in a covert form, through the Economic Cooperation Administration (ECA). This powerful agency, which was in charge of distributing Marshall Plan funds to its European beneficiaries, discouraged purchases of Argentine foodstuffs while encouraging purchases from some of its competitors, such as Canada and Australia. This policy was against State Department guidelines, and its effects were sufficiently damaging to elicit the informal admission of U.S. officials that the agency's discrimination had contributed to Argentina's scarcity of dollars, paving the way for a future economic catastrophe. Because these obstacles to dollar-earning exports coincided with Great Britain's unilateral declaration of sterling inconvertibility in August 1947, the situation became progressively more difficult to manage.

Yet the Argentine landowners demonstrated considerable flexibility in the face of the new regime. Perón contributed to this by choosing a member of the Sociedad Rural as minister of agriculture. Furthermore, he made sure that the veiled threats of land appropriation made during the electoral campaign were soon shelved. The organization representing rural owners made peace with the new president and kept its institutional structure intact. The Unión Industrial met a different fate. The industrial entrepreneurs challenged the new administration by appointing an anti-collaborationist leadership to run the association. The price of their audacity was the government's decision to put an end to the Unión's independence. Little by little, however, businessmen accommodated themselves to the new situation when they realized that official policy would not go so far as to confiscate the profits of the economic boom, and their initial open resistance was transformed into enforced conformity.

The unions continued to recruit new members with official support. The 877,300 workers unionized in 1946 grew to 1,532,900 in 1948. In most sectors of the urban economy the rate of unionization climbed by 50 to 70 per cent. The greater union impact ran parallel to the extension and unification of the institutions that regulated labour relations. During previous years, labour laws had reflected great imbalances of strength within the labour movement; the working conditions enjoyed by, for example, railroad employees were unknown in other sectors. Perón's labour policy put an end to this type of union elitism. From 1946 collective bargaining penetrated deeply into the labour market; the retirement system was extended to employees and workers in industry and trade; and paid vacations and unemployment compensation were introduced. Official tolerance and a state of nearly full employment translated into a surge of union activism. In 1945 strikes in the city of Buenos Aires affected 50,000 workers; in 1946 the number of strikers increased to 335,000; and in the following year nearly 550,000 workers were involved.

The social climate that accompanied the development of the regime needed constant invigilation, for which Perón found the ideal partner in the person of his own wife. Eva Duarte had been born in a lower-middle-class household in the province of Buenos Aires, the illegitimate daughter of a rancher who refused to acknowledge either her or her brothers. At the age of fifteen she came to Buenos Aires, attracted by the glamour of the city, and played small roles in unmemorable radio plays and soap operas until she met Perón in 1944. Eva rapidly assimilated the rudiments of a political education given by the extroverted military officer who professed admiration for her. In 1946 Evita – as she was called – was twenty-seven years old, and it was soon obvious that she was hardly inclined to accept a decorative role as the first lady of the regime. While Perón concentrated on the tasks of government, Evita set out to champion the cause of the underprivileged, to whose service she brought a vibrant and deliberately brutal rhetoric that inflamed her followers and provoked fear and hatred among her enemies. As she wrote in her autobiography:

Because I know the personal tragedies of the poor, of the victims of the rich and the powerful exploiters of the people, because of that, my speeches often contain venom and bitterness. . . . And when I say that justice will be done inexorably, whatever it costs and whomever it may affect, I am sure that God will forgive me for insulting my listeners, because I have insulted out of love for my people! He will make them pay for all that the poor have suffered, down to the last drop of their blood![1]

Evita's meddling first became visible from her office in the Ministry of Labour, where she meted out rewards and punishment, teaching the union leaders the iron discipline of the new regime. Later she reached out to the most marginal sectors of the population, the urban sub-proletariat and the most backward classes of the provinces, for whom the new labour rights had only limited significance. She created a network of social and health services for them through the Eva Perón Foundation, which replaced and far surpassed the religious charitable organizations of the upper class. Developing into an effective instrument of proselytization among the poorest sectors, the foundation extended its activity to every corner of the country with shipments of sewing machines, bicycles and soccer balls. Evita later found another crusade to which she could dedicate her energies in the political condition of women: she led the campaign for women's suffrage and, once it was established by law in 1949, organized the women's branch of the official party. Through Evita's intervention, *peronismo* continued the political mobilization begun in 1945; new sectors were added to the regime's vast popular following, complementing and at the same time restricting the role of the unions within it.

Economic prosperity, popular support and authoritarianism combined to ensure the development of the regime, which sought to entrench itself through the constitutional reform of 1949. A constitutional assembly in which Perón's followers had a comfortable majority introduced modifications into the liberal charter of 1853. Some of these measures consolidated the advances in civil and workers' rights. An article based on the Mexican Constitution established state ownership of energy resources, but the most significant political modification was the repeal of the provision that prohibited the consecutive re-election of the president.

[1] Eva Perón, *La razón de mi vida* (Buenos Aires, 1951), p. 122; quoted in Marysa Navarro, 'Evita and Peronism', in F. Turner and J. E. Miguens (eds.), *Juan Perón and the Reshaping of Argentina* (Pittsburgh, Pa., 1983), pp. 15–32.

Once the reform was passed, a campaign was begun to re-elect Perón in 1951. The unions proposed that Evita join him on the presidential ticket, but the military commanders disliked the idea and advised Perón to refuse. The president yielded to the military veto, and Evita announced that she was withdrawing her candidacy. Perón's landslide victory in the elections of November 1951, with Hortensio Quijano as his running mate for a second time, dashed all hopes of overcoming *peronismo* through the electoral route. The official slate captured 4,580,000 votes, while the candidates of the Radical Party, Ricardo Balbín and Arturo Frondizi, who had been denied access to the mass media, received 2,300,000 votes.

In voting by a margin of 2 to 1 for Perón, the electorate effectively authorized him to continue along the authoritarian path. In 1952, Congress, in which the forty-four opposition deputies had been reduced to fourteen, raised *peronista* ideology to the status of national doctrine under the name of *justicialismo*. This 'new philosophy of life, simple, practical, popular and fundamentally Christian and humanist', had as its 'supreme goal' to 'guarantee the happiness of the people and the greatness of the Nation through Social Justice, Economic Independence and Political Sovereignty, harmonizing spiritual values and the rights of the individual with the rights of society'.[2] Its obligatory imposition on officials and citizens eliminated every trace of pluralism in political life and condemned the other parties to a virtually clandestine existence.

Once *peronismo* considered itself to be the only national movement, its relations with the rest of society were destined to change. One of the most important changes after the beginning of Perón's second term in June 1952 was the reorganization of the links between the state and the network of social interest groups. The corporatist order erected by Perón was congruent with his ideology; it promised a harmonious society free of class strife. The new equilibrium among social forces permitted the establishment of an 'organized community', the main competing components of which were brought together to operate as an organically independent whole under the state. After the 1951 elections, the incipient corporatist order was extended in successive steps. The CGT was joined by the Confederación General Económica (CGE), an umbrella organization for the economic establishment, and soon afterwards by the Confederación General de Profesionales, the Confederación General Universitaria and the Unión de Estudiantes Secundarios.

[2] See Alberto Ciria, *Política y cultura popular, la Argentina peronista* (Buenos Aires, 1983), p. 64.

Ideological motives were not the only factors that inspired the new architecture of the regime. There was also a desire to construct a political order that would be less centred on the working and popular sectors and would clearly assign the role of arbiter to the state. The creation of a new power structure also changed the position occupied by the armed forces, which had already begun to lose the relative autonomy they had enjoyed between 1946 and 1949. Perón had demanded increasing integration of military institutions into the official political movement, winning over high-ranking officers with new favours and privileges. Perón's electoral strength had convinced the political opposition that the ballot box held no future for them, and, supported by a number of retired military men who were victims of the 1945 purges, they made a number of vain attempts to overthrow the president. However, their luck appeared to change in 1951 due to military discontent in the face of clear evidence that Perón was preparing to be re-elected and that, even more serious, Evita would be his running mate on the presidential ticket. This threat helped to overcome the reluctance of the high military command, which began to discuss the removal of Perón. But first, tactical differences and personal rivalries, and then the withdrawal of Evita's candidacy, hindered the gestation of a co-ordinated uprising; the retired general Benjamín Menéndez launched an isolated attempt, which was rapidly suppressed. Perón's re-election by 62 per cent of the vote provoked a retreat by the conspirators and cleared the way for an intensification of political control over the armed forces. From 1952 onwards, attempts to replace constitutional subordination to the chief of state with loyalty to Perón's personal leadership became more overt. The military establishment yielded to the new demands, but their discontent remained alive, particularly in the middle ranks.

The reorientation of the military with respect to *peronismo* was part of a broader process. Because of their standard of living and social background, members of the officer corps shared the anxiety with which the middle class followed the overwhelming presence of the masses in public life. The speed with which social change had occurred dampened the traditionally progressive spirit of the urban middle class. Older countries had passed through structural changes similar to Argentina's with the intensification of industrialization, but these changes had been absorbed into the institutions more slowly, making the transition to mass democracy less abrupt. In Perón's Argentina everything seemed to happen at the same time: the growth of the working sectors, the development of the unions, the expansion of social welfare and, on a more profound level, the loss of the deference that the old order had expected from the lowest strata of society.

This subversion of traditional patterns of power and prestige was aggravated by a disquieting question: How far was *peronismo* going to go? When would Perón deem the historic reparation to the popular masses – a product of his intervention – to be complete? For the urban middle class to understand that behind such an aggressive policy lay a sincere respect for the bases of the existing order, it would have needed a perceptiveness of which, under the circumstances, it was scarcely capable. Motivated by a profound aversion to the plebeian tone that coloured the regime's accomplishments, the middle class became the moving force of the conservative opposition. A civil resistance movement began to take shape, at first surreptitiously, consisting of small, symbolic gestures of rebellion.

On 26 July 1952 Evita died, a victim of cancer. With her died the figure who best represented the *peronista* movement for the popular masses but also much of what was intolerable to its adversaries. The feeling of profound collective grief at her passing inaugurated, ominously, Perón's second term in office. With the key element of popular activism gone, the government now seemed to be a bureaucratic machine lacking the political attraction of the first years and exhibiting the vices associated with an over-confident power; at the beginning of 1953 Perón's intimate circle was involved in a scandalous case of corruption. They supported the president's efforts to rectify matters, but the resulting public trial ended dramatically with bombings that caused injuries and deaths. The immediate answer of the *peronistas* was to burn the Jockey Club, the traditional seat of the upper class, and to destroy the headquarters of the opposition parties. A wave of mass arrests followed these events, dealing a rude blow to the embryonic resistance movement.

Perón seemed to realize the need to dissipate the political tension. The doors of the presidential palace were opened to the opposition leaders. In the event, it was the Radicals who came to talk; ten years after the revolution of 1943, the electoral support of both the conservatives and the Socialists had practically disappeared. The Radicals, who had broadened their appeal by presenting their programme as the only alternative to *peronismo,* were little disposed to reach an entente that, if successful, would entail a retreat from their role as a zealous opposition. The government was also reluctant to compromise. Towards the end of 1953, an amnesty was declared, but its beneficiaries discovered that being out of jail made little difference, since the restrictions on political activity were maintained in full force.

By then the economic prosperity which had accompanied the establishment of the *peronista* regime was dissipating. The first signs of a deterioration in the economy were evident as early as 1949. After four consecutive years of surpluses, the trade deficit reached U.S. $160 million, due largely to a decline in the terms of trade. The index of the terms of trade (1935 = 100) was 133 in 1947 and 132 in 1948. By 1949 it slipped back to 110, and in 1950 to 93. At the same time, inflation, which had been 3.6 per cent in 1947, increased to 15.3 per cent in 1948 and 23.2 per cent in 1949. The expansion in public spending and the resulting growth in the fiscal deficit completed a picture of growing difficulties.

Although consciousness of the dawning crisis was growing among the members of the government, they did nothing beyond correcting relative prices, and lacking a policy of fiscal austerity, they vacillated for some time between continuity and change. For a growth model that had, from the beginning, been based on the leadership of the public sector and cheap credit to finance internal market expansion and high wages, stabilization had a very high cost for the level of internal market activity, employment and salary levels.

For these reasons, the first measures were partial and quite ineffective. Miguel Miranda, who had presided over economic affairs during the bonanza years, was replaced by Alfredo Gómez Morales, who was charged with taking a new direction. His first steps were a moderate devaluation of the currency and a rationing of credit for both the private and public sectors. Nonetheless, the interest rates charged by the Central Bank on special credit lines continued to be negative, and real wages were kept at the high levels of previous years. The results of this first stabilization trial, maintained from 1949 through 1950, were therefore ambiguous: the boom was interrupted as the economy entered a recessive phase, but relative prices and the existing distributive model were not modified.

The peak of the crisis came in 1951, endangering the survival of an economic strategy that had succeeded thanks to exceptional internal and external circumsances. During 1951 and 1952 the terms of trade continued to fall, placing the country in a situation of external strangulation that would later repeat itself frequently but which at this stage dashed official optimism about the evolution of international markets. The trade balance was U.S. $304 million in deficit in 1951 and $455 million in deficit in 1952. At the same time, inflation again accelerated, reaching a rate of more than 30 per cent in 1952. In that year the government decided on a turnabout in economic policy, revising its initial priorities. The new strategy favoured stability over the expansion of economic activity and consumption, agriculture over industry, private initiative and foreign capital over public sector growth.

Convinced that the distributionist struggle was the principal cause of inflation, the government imposed a social truce on business and the trade unions. The instrument for this was a wage and price freeze for two years, from May 1952 to May 1954, after wages were first readjusted. A Comisión de Precios y Salarios, formed by representatives of the CGT, business and the government, had the mission of controlling the progress of the social accord and studying wage increases based on labour productivity. The acceptance of wage restrictions by workers was facilitated by the control of prices and by subsidies granted to foodstuffs and public utility costs.

The priority given to the anti-inflation policy and the clear awareness of the social support that sustained the regime led Perón to dispense with the option of a new devaluation, although it represented a quick way to eliminate the balance-of-payments deficit. The exchange rate was kept constant in real terms, because devaluation would shift income to the farmers but at the cost of increasing food prices in the internal market. In order to manage the external disequilibrium, the authorities first resorted to a mechanism that had been selectively employed since 1948 – quantitative import restrictions. These restrictions had been used in December 1950, when the outbreak of the Korean War appeared to signal a third world war and led to the purchase of imported goods that could become scarce in the immediate future. In 1952 these had to be drastically reduced whilst a serious drought caused Argentina to import wheat for the first time in its history.

Once devaluation was ruled out as an option, agricultural production was stimulated by means of a reorientation of subsidies. The IAPI, which had hitherto served to transfer resources from the countryside to the urban centres, now subsidized the prices received by farmers for crops that were exported. The key to this operation was a more restrictive monetary policy towards industry and a fall in public investment.

This policy of adjustment and austerity had both benefits and costs. Inflation began to decline, reaching a low of 3.8 per cent in 1954. Imbalances in public finances were reduced to 9.8 per cent of GDP in 1949 and a little more than 5 per cent in 1952. At the same time, industrial production fell by 7 per cent in 1952 and by 2 per cent in 1953. Real wages fell by 25 per cent in two years. In spite of these costs the foundation for a rapid and surprising economic reactivation was laid. This recuperation also rested on a more moderate credit policy, greater financial assistance to the agricultural sector and a more restrictive incomes policy.

The reorientation of economic policy included a new role for foreign investment. At the time, Argentina was almost self-sufficient in finished manufactured goods. The demand for imports was concentrated on fuels and raw materials and capital goods required by a more diversified industrial sector than had existed before the war. The problems of supply and the obstacles to industrial modernization created by the hard-currency scarcity led Perón to call for foreign investment. This change in the statist and nationalist ideology for the regime began in 1953 with a new, more permissive foreign investment law that was followed by agreements with various companies, including Mercedes Benz and Kaiser Motors. The most audacious initiative occurred in the area of petroleum exploitation, a sacred bastion of Argentine nationalism, to which an attempt was made to attract a subsidiary of Standard Oil Company. Selling his new policy to a group of trade union leaders, Perón said:

And so, if they work for YPF [the state oil company] we lose absolutely nothing, because we even pay them with the same oil they take out. It is a good thing, then, that they come to give us all the petroleum we need. Before, no company would come if it weren't given the subsoil and all the oil it produced. Now for them to come, why shouldn't it be a business deal, a big one, if we are spending each year upwards of $350 million to buy the oil we need when we have it under the earth and it doesn't cost us a cent? How can we go on paying this? so that they will get profits? Of course they are not going to work for the love of the art. They will take their profits and we ours; that is just.[3]

The opening to foreign capital implied, if not an abandonment, at least a modification of many aspects of *peronista* foreign policy. This had been inspired by what came to be called the Third Position, an effort to find a place between the two rival blocks growing out of the Second World War. Influenced by the current of non-alignment among countries which had achieved independence in the post-war decolonization process, the Third Position was, above all, an instrument used by Perón to negotiate the price of his support to the United States on international issues. After

[3] *La Nación*, 17 September 1953; quoted in Robert Potash, *El ejército y la política en la Argentina, 1945–1962* (Buenos Aires, 1981), p. 225.

1953, this policy was progressively substituted by an open quest for good relations with the new Eisenhower administration.

The crisis that brought about the downfall of Perón had its origins less in the economic situation than in political conflicts that he himself unleashed. In fact, the Argentine economy from 1953 to 1955 was in good shape, compared with the emergency of 1952. The annual inflation rate, after having climbed to more than 30 per cent fell to 4 per cent in 1953 and to 3.8 per cent in 1954. After the abrupt decline of 1952, industrial real wages increased, although without regaining the level reached in 1950. The same occurred with company earnings. Economic activity recovered with a cumulative growth in gross domestic product (GDP) of 5 per cent between 1953 and 1955. The foreign trade balance was positive in 1953 and 1954, although it was in deficit at the end of 1955. Unresolved issues remained. Despite the excellent performance of 1953, agricultural production was unable to increase its volume of exportable surpluses. At the same time, the re-evaluation of the local currency and the lag in public utility prices constituted factors of repressed inflation. But the economic picture did not show signs of an imminent crisis. Moreover, the rapprochement in relations with the United States and the opening to foreign capital had galvanized the image of the *peronista* regime overseas.

The most direct cause of the military conspiracy that put an end to the *peronista* regime can be found in the government's confrontation with the Church. For the armed forces, the ecclesiastical hierarchy's support for official policies had provided confirmation of the culturally conservative character of *peronismo*. Yet at the end of 1954 a succession of governmental initiatives began to undermine the interests and the influence of the Church in national life. Among them were the elimination of state subsidies to private schools, the legalization of brothels and the suppression of religious teaching in public schools. What was behind this sudden offensive against the Church?

This issue has provoked innumerable questions, because Perón never clearly explained the causes of the conflict. It has been suggested that the reason might have been Perón's anger with the Catholic hierarchy's abandonment of political neutrality in deciding to support the creation of a Christian Democratic Party; others claim that the conflict lay in the search for a new element of cohesion in the *peronista* movement at a time when the regime had to shelve its economic nationalism. Whatever the explanation, it is certain that Perón set in motion a conflict that escalated beyond his control and precipitated the end of his regime.

The legal reforms were supported by a massive anticlerical campaign in the official press. Perón irritated the bishops by lavishing official attention on the clergy of other religious sects, even the spiritualists. During the first half of 1955 the confrontation took on a more threatening tone when a new constitutional reform was announced establishing the separation of church and state. In the face of these attacks the Church hierarchy opted for caution, but the militant Catholic sectors closed ranks and converted the churches into tribunals of moral and political protest. The most diverse groups of the anti-*peronista* opposition came to their aid, sensing that the conflict was an occasion for reviving the resistance movement. Flying new colours, the 1945 alliance of the middle class, conservative circles and students took over the streets once again. On 11 June 1955, the day of Corpus Christi in the Catholic calendar, a long procession made its way through the centre of Buenos Aires, challenging the police prohibitions.

The events of the next three months would reveal a new phenomenon: a Perón lacking the political brilliance that had previously enabled him to deal with the most difficult situations. The day after the procession of Corpus Christi, the government accused the Catholics of having burned a national flag and deported two clergymen, accusing them of anti-government agitation. A civil protest of 16 June was followed by an attempted coup d'état. Sections of the navy and the air force rose in rebellion, bombing and strafing the vicinity around the presidential palace and claiming numerous victims. That night, the uprising quelled, the principal churches in the city's centre were sacked and burned by *peronista* vigilantes.

The shock produced by these acts of violence, unprecedented in recent history, cast a shadow over Perón's victory. Furthermore, the CGT's intervention in supplying arms to the workers created justified alarm among the military leaders who remained loyal to the regime. A few days after these sombre events, on the advice of the high command, Perón initiated a policy of conciliation. The state of siege was lifted, the most abrasive members of the cabinet − in particular, the ministers of education and the interior, who were openly associated with the anticlerical campaign − were replaced and opposition leaders were invited to discuss a political truce. Perón declared to his followers that 'the *peronista* revolution is over' and promised to be, from then on, 'the president of all Argentines'.

But the call for pacification, which was aimed at isolating the resistance movement, did not have the desired effect. In fact, it further fuelled the civilian and military opposition. Political leaders, who were permitted access to radio broadcasting for the first time in twelve years, availed themselves of the government's concession to make it clear that they were unwilling to compromise. Arturo Frondizi, speaking in the name of the Radical Party, pledged to accomplish, in peace and liberty, the economic and social revolution that Peronism was renouncing and, with the confidence of a winner, promised a generous pardon to the regime's collaborators.

The failure of the truce prompted Perón to shift tactics. On 31 August, in a letter to the Partido Peronista and the CGT, he revealed his decision to leave the government in order to guarantee peace. Predictably, the unions organized a large demonstration of support. The Plaza de Mayo saw a new version of 17 October 1945. Following a prepared text, Perón told the crowd that he was withdrawing his resignation and then delivered the most violent speech of his political career. He began by saying that he had offered peace to his opponents but that they did not want it, and concluded by authorizing his followers to take the law into their own hands:

With our exaggerated tolerance, we have won the right to repress them violently. And from now on we establish as permanent rule for our movement: Whoever in any place tries to disturb order against the constituted authorities, or against the law and the Constitution, may be killed by any Argentine. . . . The watchword for every *peronista,* whether alone or within an organization, is to answer a violent act with another violent act. And whenever one of us falls five of them will fall.[4]

This unexpected declaration of war overcame the resistance of many undecided military officers. An initiative by the CGT also helped precipitate the dénouement. Shortly after Perón's harangue, it let the army know that it was placing the workers at the army's disposal so that together they could protect the regime. The military leaders, who had been uneasy for some time over the prospect of the creation of workers' militias, promptly rejected the offer. On 16 September, the decisive military revolt finally broke out. Rebel troops under General Eduardo Lonardi occupied the garrisons of Córdoba, and the rebellion spread through the rest of the country with various degrees of success. Superior in number, the forces loyal to the government nevertheless lacked the will to fight. For five days, the outcome of the conflict hung in the balance, until the loyal commanders received a message from Perón saying that he was ready to

---

[4] *La Nación,* 1 September 1955; quoted in Potash, *El ejército y la política,* p. 268.

negotiate a solution but that he refused to resign. The confusion was cleared up the next day when Perón sought refuge in the Paraguayan Embassy. On 23 September, while the CGT begged the workers to stay calm, a crowd thronged the Plaza de Mayo, this time to hasten the swearing in of General Lonardi as provisional president of the Argentine Republic.

THE *REVOLUCIÓN LIBERTADORA*, 1955–57

The members of the political and economic coalition who backed the armed movement in 1955 shared the objective of dismantling the system of authoritarian controls created by Perón. But there were few points of convergence when it came to the profile of the new social and economic order that would emerge from the urgent task of reconstruction.

The spokesmen for the old elite, who were linked to the countryside and the export economy, used the period of debate following Perón's fall to convey a crude and simple message: the origin of the country's problems lay in *peronismo*'s mistaken effort to subvert Argentina's 'natural' economy. They proposed a revision of the policies that had led to the creation of an over-protected industrial base, that discouraged rural producers and that fostered a premature and excessive incorporation of workers into the consumer market. In its place, they sought a return to the economic strategy based on free trade and its comparative advantages, which had stimulated Argentina's impressive growth until 1929. In the short run, it was a matter of adjusting the economy so as to offset the growing deficit in the balance of payments, using measures like large devaluations to reduce imports and promote agricultural exports, severe monetary and credit restrictions and a reduction in wages to bring internal consumption into line with the country's financial limitations. In the longer term, the aim was to re-create Argentina's pre-war economic structure and social balance of power.

After a decade of industrial growth and prosperity, social mobility and the extension of political participation, this was not a very viable alternative. The *peronista* experience had certainly not been able to modify the structural underpinnings established by the conservative political class in the 1930s: it was based on light industrialization, complementary to an agro-export country. However, by converting what had been a stopgap policy after the crisis of 1929 into a more permanent programme and by reorienting national resources towards the extensive substitution of imported manufactures, *peronismo* contributed to the deepening of differentiation within the existing economic and social structure. Alongside the landowning sectors, the large foreign and agrarian capitalists and the old commercial and bureaucratic middle class, a vast industrial world began to consolidate itself, weak in economic power, dependent in its productive capacities, but powerful in its impact on employment and urban life.

When the spokesmen for the old elite tried to promote their strategy in 1955, they met with resistance, not always co-ordinated but always disruptive, from this urban–industrial complex that had been nourished at their expense. If at the beginning of the 1950s it was evident that light industry oriented towards the internal market was losing its impetus for expansion, by 1955 it was equally clear that a return to pre-war Argentina was politically untenable. The transformations in society and the economy had not eradicated the old hierarchical order but had superimposed it on the new industrial, participatory order. Thus, landowners, businessmen, middle class, working class – every sector – nourished a compact knot of interests and managed to become entrenched in their own distinct institutions. Although no one of them by itself was able to steer the process of change, each was, nevertheless, powerful enough to prevent the others from doing so. After 1955, policy alternatives were played out against this background of negative pluralism.

The overthrow of Perón, far from being guided by a concerted military and political plan, was the result of isolated efforts by different and opposing military and political leaders. The crumbling of the anti-*peronista* offensive, which placed even the armed victory itself in jeopardy, led to a political crisis during the first days of the Revolución Libertadora. The unanimity with which the revolutionaries celebrated the end of the *peronista* regime vanished as soon as it became necessary to decide the political direction of the transitional period. Each of the leaders of the conspiracy desired to steer the new political process. The post-revolutionary stage was thus shaken by a silent internal struggle within the military establishment. The crucial bone of contention was what attitude to take towards the *peronista* movement.

One sector, that of nationalist affiliation, favoured a policy of co-optation. Under the slogan 'No winners, no losers', formulated by President Lonardi, they hoped to garner the political heritage of the deposed regime through co-operation with the leaders of *peronista* unionism. This policy was, from the beginning, resisted by another sector, which, in the name of democracy, declared itself adamantly against the enemies of democracy, whom they understandably identified as Perón's followers. The two factions had, nevertheless, one thing in common: the conviction that *peronismo* would not survive as a political force after the fall of the regime that had created it. For the nationalists this meant channelling the movement and purging its excesses under new leadership. In this spirit, President Lonardi named a *peronista* union lawyer to the Ministry of Labour. Those to whom gestures of conciliation were directed responded favourably and thereby managed to secure the survival of their organizations: to this end they exhorted their followers to avoid conflict and agreed to renew the union leadership through elections under the supervision of the Ministry of Labour.

The nationalists' political project never got off the ground. Everything about it aroused distrust in the majority of those who had gathered together to accomplish the Revolución Libertadora. Some of the nationalist military officers had remained loyal to the overthrown regime until the last minute; their political advisers were prominent Catholic intellectuals of anti-liberal sympathies. Attempts by a number of them to use the forces that had supported Perón for their own benefit understandably provoked suspicions of a return to the political situation that had just been brought to an end. Less than two months after the successful armed uprising, concerted pressure from within the military and from politicians led to the resignation on 13 November of President Lonardi, together with that of his nationalist entourage. The revolution would resume its course under the leadership of a new president, General Pedro Eugenio Aramburu, in pursuit of democratic regeneration.

The driving force behind this campaign was the conviction that Argentina had spent the past ten years in a totalitarian nightmare. Its mission was therefore to convince the masses who had been deceived by Perón's demagoguery to abandon their old loyalties and join, as individuals, the family of democratic parties. In the state of emergency, the Revolución Libertadora made use of repression and proscription to accomplish its task of political re-education. After an aborted attempt at a general strike, the CGT and the unions were placed under government control, the Partido Peronista was officially dissolved and a decree imposed to prohibit the use of *peronista* symbols or even the mention of the very name of the man who had been, and from exile continued to be, its undisputed leader.

The firm attitude shown in dealing with the *peronistas* was not extended to the economic problems inherited from the previous regime. During the last part of his government, Perón had already recognized the need to alter the country's economic course. The corrections he introduced in agrarian policy and in the area of foreign investment pointed to a new direction which his political commitments prevented him from pursuing. The Revolución Libertadora did not have any better luck. Hindered by internal conflict in the anti-*peronista* front, it too left the decision up to the future constitutional authorities. One of the Lonardi government's first measures was to ask Dr Raúl Prebisch to assess the economic situation and recommend a policy. Prebisch's report evaded the dilemma of agrarian versus industrial nation, which some nostalgic sectors wanted to reopen, and concentrated on continuing the process of industrialization. Nevertheless, in order to solve the problem of the balance-of-payments deficit, he advised a price policy favouring agricultural exports.

The less controversial measures of the programme were adopted without delay. The peso was devalued, bank deposits were denationalized, the country joined international financial organizations like the International Monetary Fund (IMF) and the World Bank and controls on foreign trade were eliminated at the same time that the IAPI was dissolved. Policy concerning foreign capital had been one of the most controversial issues under Perón. The political opposition that had criticized Perón for the more liberal attitude of his last few years was not inclined to abandon its nationalist bent, and it influenced the military government to cancel its negotiations with the California Petroleum Company. Consequently, foreign investment was negligible.

Policies to stimulate the rural economy collided with declining international prices for Argentine exports. In spite of a higher volume of exports, the dollar value increased by only 7 per cent between 1955 and 1958. In addition, the abolition of import controls caused an explosion in the demand for foreign currency, which had been repressed for a long time. This pressure was especially noticeable in the demand for imported motor vehicles, which doubled in volume between 1955 and 1957.

The military government's decision to call elections soon relieved it of the need to impose abrupt changes in the social equilibrium, which would have adversely affected the democratic regeneration of the *peronista* masses. The desire to avoid a serious deterioration in income levels limited the economic swing in favour of the rural sector and postponed the attack on the imbalances in the structure of production. Business responded to wage increases by raising prices. After a decline in the last years of Perón's regime, inflation accelerated again and in 1957 the cost of living rose by 25 per cent. That year saw another attempt at stabilization, which was moderately successful but did not prevent a decline in real income.

The contradiction between its economic objectives and its political objectives, the diversity of the views of the members of the cabinet, which included spokesmen for the business community as well as members of the Radical Party, set the Revolución Libertadora on a vague economic course which did not permit it to resolve the problems it had inherited.

General Aramburu's government did not suppress – as other military governments would in the future – union activity and collective bargaining. Its labour plan stressed, rather, the eradication of *peronista* influence in the labour movement. In April 1956 a decree was passed excluding from union affairs all leaders who had occupied posts between 1952 and 1955. Proscription and imprisonment were the measures by which the unions were purged, so as to return the unions and the exercise of their rights to the workers.

However, the union elections held at the end of 1956 and the beginning of 1957 witnessed the beginning of a return to *peronismo*. The decision to participate in these elections was the occasion for an outbreak of a conflict between Perón and the new generation of *peronista* union leaders. From exile, Perón ordered a boycott of the elections and the subordination of the old union leaders, some of whom had formed a clandestine organization. Ignoring these instructions, the new leaders who had emerged after 1955 chose to participate and gained control of a number of important industrial unions. Invoking their *peronista* identity first and foremost, the new leaders won the political support of the majority of workers. During 1957 the individual strikes typical of 1956 were followed by more concerted actions. In June and July two general strikes again brought the presence of *peronista* unionism to centre stage.

The political debut of the new labour leaders took place in the congress called by the government to normalize the CGT in August 1957. An alliance of *peronistas* and Communists won the majority of seats, which provoked the suspension of deliberations. The *peronista* delegates to the aborted congress then met at what was called the '62 Organizations', under which label they continued as a central entity of Argentine political life.

Significant though they were, the advances made by *peronista* unionism were still limited compared with the losses it had suffered. Its inclusion within the state had grown till 1955, but now an insurmountable breach opened between *peronista* unionism and government institutions. The only option that seemed viable was to fall back on its isolation, on the defence of its symbols and beliefs, and to radicalize its struggles. From exile in Paraguay, Panama and Venezuela, Perón initially shared this attitude. But there was another way, which began to take shape in the platform of the principal party of the anti-*peronista* coalition, the Radical Party.

Yrigoyen's old party had not survived the traumatic experience of 1946 undamaged. Since then, one of the internal factions, the intransigent wing, had repudiated the conservative bias of the Unión Democrática and, exploiting the crisis that followed the electoral defeat, progressively displaced the old moderate leadership. In 1954 the intransigents managed to elect one of their own as president of the National Committee: Arturo Frondizi, a lawyer who that year delivered in his book *Petróleo y política* a message of a strong nationalist and anti-imperialist tone. While the moderate faction openly rejected the *peronista* regime, the intransigents tried to position themselves to its left, questioning, not its objectives, but its weakness in addressing them, particularly in the field of policy towards foreign capital and international relations.

The success of the policy of de-Peronization conceived by the Revolución Libertadora depended on the ability of the democratic front to remain united behind the condemnation of Perón and his policies. Under these conditions there remained no alternative for Peron's followers but to join ranks with the traditional political parties. The elimination of General Lonardi left the political stage open for the Radical Party, which threw itself into the conquest of the *peronista* masses. This new attempt at co-optation designed by Frondizi broke the unity of the democratic front. From the first days of President Aramburu's government, the Radical Party stood on the side of the opposition in order to present itself as the new champion of national, popular interests. Thus, Frondizi denounced the regime's economic policy as a plan orchestrated by the oligarchy and imperialism, and seeking to gain the sympathy of *peronista* workers, he demanded an end to the persecutions and the continuance of the structure of one union for each branch of activity that had existed until Perón's overthrow. Frondizi's political strategy soon became obvious to all: to make himself the heir of the Revolución Libertadora and to be the politically viable alternative for the proscribed *peronista* masses.

To achieve this he first had to gain support for his positions within the Radical Party, where his attitudes aroused the justified suspicions of the moderate sectors. After a few months dominated by internal conflict, the party met in November 1956 to nominate candidates for the next presidential elections. The moderates and one faction of the intransigents decided to walk out of the assembly, but Frondizi managed to keep together the necessary quorum and was nominated candidate for president. Shortly afterwards the division was made official: in January 1957 the dissident sectors joined together as the Unión Cívica Radical del Pueblo (UCRP), while the sector victorious at the party convention renamed itself the Unión Cívica Radical Intransigents (UCRI).

This crisis had repercussions in the ranks of government, which continued to worry about Frondizi's political manoeuvres. In a gesture openly favourable to the UCRP, whose most important leader was Ricardo Balbín (once a leader of the intransigent wing, but now opposed to Frondizi's ambitions), President Aramburu offered Balbín three cabinet positions – among them the key portfolio of minister of the interior. President Aramburu's decision made it clear where the danger lay for the future of the Revolución Libertadora but was an implicit confession that he could not confront it with his own forces. The conservative political sectors, who best expressed the interests of the military government, carried no significant electoral weight. This phenomenon, which would be a constant in post-1955 Argentine political life, led the military to give its support to Balbín's party, with whose *yrigoyenista* rhetoric it had little in common. The *peronismo*–anti-*peronismo* conflict would thus be waged behind the men and traditions of the now-fragmented Radical Party.

The first instance of the confrontation for which Argentines were preparing themselves was the election for the Constitutional Assembly in July 1957. The military government called these elections to make official the repeal of the constitutional reform instituted by Perón in 1949, but its other objective was to measure the electoral importance of the various political forces before the coming presidential elections. During the electoral campaign Frondizi bent over backwards both to attract the *peronista* electorate and to neutralize the campaign for the casting of blank ballots mounted by local *peronista* leaders. The electoral results indicated that the number of blank ballots was larger than the number of votes received by any of the parties. The 2,100,000 blank ballots were, however, less than half the number the *peronistas* had obtained three years before. With a small difference, the UCRP came in second while Frondizi's party received 1,800,000 votes; the votes captured by the Conservative and Socialist parties barely exceeded half a million. In spite of having achieved considerable electoral support, the UCRI had to resign itself to having failed in its policy to co-opt the *peronista* electorate.

When the Constitutional Assembly began its deliberations, the representatives of the UCRI kept their promise to boycott it. Very soon they were followed by the representatives of other minority parties; even a

faction of the UCRP decided to leave. From the beginning mutual recrimi-
nations between Radicals and Conservatives dominated the Assembly's
sessions. In this atmosphere, the reforms to the charter of 1853, again in
force after the repeal of the *peronista* constitution of 1949, were few and
limited.

The Constitutional Assembly soon lost its importance, and the parties
got into the full swing of political campaigning for the upcoming presidential elections. Meanwhile, the economic situation had escaped the control
of the military government. One economic minister after another proved
unable to put a stop to rising prices or to attract foreign investment. One
obsession guided the behaviour of the leaders of the government: to hand
over power to the future constitutional authorities. But this did not
preclude the temptation to influence who those authorities would be.
Thus, official support was openly given to Balbín's candidacy; he was
summoned to play the role of the anti-*peronista,* in spite of his efforts to
present himself as a progressive politician.

Frondizi's political future, by contrast, could not have been more uncertain. The *peronista* electorate had not been responsive to his overtures,
while the anti-*peronista* sectors seemed to take him too seriously. In an
effort to break out of his isolation, Frondizi moved pragmatically in
several directions. The elections for the Constitutional Assembly had
clearly revealed the vitality of the proscribed movement: if the *peronista*
masses would not listen, it was necessary to negotiate with Perón.
Frondizi's emissaries left in great secrecy for Caracas, where the exiled
leader lived under the protection of Marcos Pérez Jiménez's dictatorship,
and promised him an end to political proscriptions and the restoration of
the union legislation that had been in force during the *peronista* regime, in
exchange for his support for UCRI's candidate.

While these negotiations were taking place, Frondizi maintained that
the Argentine dilemma was not *peronismo* versus anti-*peronismo,* as the
leaders of the Revolución Libertadora claimed, but industrialization versus
underdevelopment. Under this watchword, Frondizi called for the formation of a national popular front formed by the working sectors, the national bourgeoisie, the army and the Church. The ideology of this new
alliance of classes, convoked in the name of economic development and
political integration, was the invention of a group of dissident leftist
intellectuals, headed by Rogelio Frigerio, who gathered round the UCRI
candidate and relegated the party militants to secondary roles.

A novelty in Argentine political life, this convergence between intellectuals and political leaders was accentuated by Frondizi's own personality. More a teacher than a politician, he adopted a dry, technocratic language, making no concession to the traditional political rhetoric of which Balbín, his rival, was a master. This image of rationality, the very attempt to modify the terms of the political conflict that divided the country, made an impact on the modern middle class and captured the imagination of the new generation that had come of age after 1955. To these forces Frondizi tried to add more decisive sources of support. He appealed to the nationalist sector displaced in November 1955 in an effort to gain some influence in the army, and at the same time he tried to pacify conservative public opinion by coming out for the Church's position in favour of freedom of education and against divorce. The fundamental key to this complex political operation was, however, Perón, who, two and a half years after his fall, continued to be the arbiter of Argentine political equilibrium.

Finally, from the Dominican Republic, where General Trujillo extended him hospitality as the Venezuelan dictatorship of Pérez Jiménez was brought to an end, Perón withdrew his authorization to cast blank ballots and came out openly for a yes vote on Frondizi's candidacy. On 23 February 1958 the *peronista* masses went to the polls and followed Perón's instructions. Twelve years after 1946, they again sealed the fate of the elections, this time rewarding Frondizi's virtuoso politicking with 4,100,000 votes, as against 2,550,000 for Balbín. But 800,000 blank ballots were also counted, certifying the existence of alienation and political resistance that not even the exiled leader's own orders had been able to alter.

THE PRESIDENCY OF ARTURO FRONDIZI, 1958–62

Although Frondizi's victory had been a landslide, its significance was far from clear. The jubilation with which Perón's partisans celebrated the results of the election cleared up some of the questions, identifying the true artificer of the victory, but this only led to malaise in military circles. Sectors of the army and the navy insinuated the possibility of not recognizing the credentials of the candidate elected with the *peronista* vote. Rushing to congratulate Frondizi on the same day of his triumph, President Aramburu blocked this manoeuvre and sought the necessary support to honour the word of the 1955 revolutionaries to set the country on the road to democracy.

Given the electoral verdict, this would have to be, however, a tutelary democracy. The elections of 1958 ended the optimism with which the armed forces had launched into the dismantling of the structures of the *peronista* regime. In the face of a political reality that resisted change, they decided to respect it formally, regroup themselves in their headquarters and from there influence the future administration.

With the barely concealed resistance of the military and the open opposition of the UCRP, who had seen a sure victory vanish, the president-elect set about keeping the many promises made during the electoral campaign. If he perhaps had entertained the possibility of institutionalizing the winning coalition in a political movement that would transcend the old cleavages, this fantasy was short-lived. The contradictory nature of the aspirations of those who had voted for him were badly suited to such a project. But what really made it impossible was the distrust that surrounded Frondizi's person, which was shared by the temporary allies he had recruited during his ascent to power. Frondizi more than justified this distrust when he revealed the major outlines of his political plan, the true extent of which was not made known to his adversaries and his backers until 1 May.

The new president's first measures were aimed at paying back his debt to Perón: the repeal of the decree that prohibited *peronista* activities; the enactment of an amnesty law; the annulment of a decree (passed in the last moments of the military government) that had turned the CGT over to a group of non-*peronista* unions; the return of several important unions under state control to *peronista* leaders; the re-establishment of the monopoly union system in force until 1955; and a general wage increase. The revision of the Revolución Libertadora's anti-*peronista* policy stopped short, however, at one crucial aspect: the decree that dissolved the Partido Peronista was not revoked, so the *peronistas,* even though they could once again act and diffuse their ideas, remained unable to compete in elections.

The policy of conciliation towards *peronismo* carried out from May to July 1958 was accompanied by denouncements and accusations by anti-*peronista* civilian and military groups, who saw in it a confirmation of their worst fears. In August, there was an equally hostile reaction within the ranks of the winning coalition to the decision to authorize the granting of academic degrees by private universities. Conceived by the previous military administration but later abandoned to avoid conflict, the new legislation figured among the promises made by Frondizi to the Church. Allowing religious instruction in a field until then reserved to the state stirred up deep-rooted beliefs in the student movement and revived anticlerical sentiment in important segments of the middle class. Large crowds gathered in the streets to defend the lay tradition, while Catholic opinion took the same route to demand freedom of education. Congressional approval of the controversial initiative put an end to the conflict, but not to the hostility of the student movement towards the government.

The measure which had the greatest repercussions was revealed on 25 July when Frondizi announced the beginning of the 'oil battle'. The former nationalist intellectual told a surprised radio and television audience that he had signed several contracts with foreign companies for the mining and exploitation of oil:

The main obstacle to the advance of the country is its strict dependence on the importation of fuels and steel. This dependence weakens our capacity for self-determination and puts in danger our sovereignty, especially in the event of a worldwide armed crisis. Actually, Argentina imports about 65% of the fuel it consumes. Of 14 million cubic meters consumed in 1957, approximately 10 million came from abroad. Argentina has been forced to become simply an exporter of raw materials, which are exchanged for oil and coal. The country works to pay for imported oil, oil that we have under our feet. Argentina cannot continue on this road, which has been converted into a dangerous slope towards domination.[5]

Frondizi thus took up the policy which the *peronista* regime had attempted, with little conviction, in its last days. The goal was now, as then, to reduce the demand for imported fuel, capital goods and supplies that weighed so heavily in the balance-of-payments deficit. The 'oil battle' would be only the beginning of a new attempt at import substitution, which aimed to develop basic industry and build a more highly integrated industrial structure.

The leitmotif of Frondizi's principal adviser, Rogelio Frigerio, was a forced march towards industrialization, by any means and at any price. In spite of the growth of light industry since the mid-1930s, Argentina continued to be a food-producing country and an importer of fuel, machinery and supplies for local manufacture. The cause of Argentine underdevelopment and dependency lay, according to Frigerio, in the position the country occupied within the international division of labour. From this angle, industrialization, particularly the establishment of steel production, petrochemical complexes and oil refineries, would modify the pattern of development based on the export of primary materials and thus be the key to national liberation.

[5] Arturo Frondizi, *Mensajes presidenciales* (Buenos Aires, 1978), p. 133.

The old dream of economic autarchy encouraged by the military during the Second World War was reappearing in a new language. The necessary accumulation of capital had then conflicted with the political needs of the *peronista* regime, which chose a more limited course of industrialization compatible with the redistribution of income. Facing the same equation, Frondizi decided to finance the industrial effort with foreign capital. Argentina was able to take advantage of a novel phenomenon: investment by multinational companies in Latin American industry. To this end the Argentine government, like others on the subcontinent, offered to foreign investors a market closed by high protectionist barriers, with optimal possibilities for expansion, guaranteed by a pre-existing demand and an oligo-political control of its terms.

To justify this heterodox project without abandoning his espousal of nationalism, Frondizi maintained that the source of the capital was not important as long as it was used, with appropriate direction by the government, in areas of strategic importance for national development. The prejudice against foreign capital, he insisted, only consolidated the structure of underdevelopment by leaving the oil underground and postponing the integration of the industrial apparatus.

While the fruits of the new strategy ripened, Frondizi, aware of the fragility of the power he had been handed, launched a series of drastic and irreversible changes in the management of the country's economy. To appease the expectations and demands awakened in the electoral campaign he declared a general wage increase a few days after taking office. This was followed by more flexibility in monetary and fiscal policy, all of which aggravated the economic situation and prepared the stage for a serious crisis of inflation and in the balance of payments. The warning signals of the crisis did not seem to alarm either the president or his economic advisers, who felt confident that they were about to introduce major structural changes. Their attention was attracted more towards winning *peronista* goodwill for their overall economic strategy.

Even at this stage, to speak of *peronismo* was to speak of *peronista* union leaders. Perón's exile and the absence of a legal party created a situation in which the union organizations, in addition to their professional functions, were transformed into the natural spokesmen of the *peronista* masses. This displacement of representation of the political movement towards the union leaders had important consequences in the institutional life of Argentina. In the short run, it allowed the government to negotiate measures such as the new union law in exchange for a neutral attitude towards the abandonment of aspects of the program of 23 February which were, in any case, the very ones that the *peronista* regime had tried to jettison in its last days.

For the leaders of the 62 Organizations, the end of the military interregnum opened the possibility of recovering lost positions, both those of symbolic character associated with their full recognition in the political system and those of a more concrete character embodied in control over the resources of the union machine and the CGT. However, the rapprochement between *peronista* unionism and the government did not last very long. Eight months after Frondizi took office a crisis took place, in spite of efforts on both sides to prevent it.

Several factors contributed to this crisis. In September labour contracts were prorogued for another year, which implied a virtual freeze on wages, and it was made known that regulation of the right to strike was under study. This was more than the 62 Organizations were willing to tolerate in silence; in mid-October they demonstrated their discontent in what would be the first general strike of the constitutional period.

The government was under pressure from both directions. Every move that tended to pacify the *peronista* unions provoked the alarm of their civilian and military adversaries. In light of the attempt to attract foreign capital, this conciliatory attitude was even more contradictory. Frondizi believed he had found a way out of the dilemma by supplementing the search for compromise with the *peronista* labour leaders with exemplary gestures accompanied by political firmness. The oil workers' strike at Mendoza was the first test. Arguing that the conflict was part of an insurrectionary plot, Frondizi imposed martial law for thirty days and sent many union militants to jail. The 62 Organizations, in turn, called a new forty-eight-hour general strike. The government and the unions seemed to be marching towards a final confrontation. The rupture, however, was avoided. No doubt the willingness of the 62 Organizations to reach an agreement was influenced by fear of a breakdown in the order through which they hoped to consolidate their positions.

Frondizi's boldness was not limited to the abandonment of the ideological causes with which he had identified for such a long time. He also tried to change the relationship of the forces within the military establishment in an attempt to diminish the influence of sectors that were hostile to him. For this daring enterprise he sought the support of nationalist officers and those who had been excluded from active duty. At the beginning of September the president and his secretary of the air force tried to recommission an officer discharged by Aramburu in 1957. The resistance by the bulk of leaders and officers provoked a state of rebellion in the air force, which stopped only when the president withdrew his controversial decision and agreed to replace his secretary of the air force. At the price of a severe weakening of his authority, Frondizi had to acknowledge that the stability of the government was dependent on the maintenance of the inherited distribution of power.

For their part, Argentina's military leaders redoubled their vigilance over the government's activities. The spokesmen for these concerns was the former president, General Aramburu, who supported constitutional order but demanded the removal of Frondizi's *eminence gris,* Frigerio, from his position as secretary of socio-economic relations. Frigerio was deeply distrusted in military circles because of his leftist origins, his political rise on the fringes of the party structure and the role he was playing in the negotiations with the *peronistas.*

The president apparently acceded, and on 10 November he relieved Frigerio of his official functions but, demonstrating that duplicity which so infuriated his enemies, a little later let him in again through the back door as a member of his intimate circle.

Under these circumstances, strong rumours of a coup d'état began to circulate. The presumed existence of a secret pact between Frondizi and Perón, denounced by the opposition parties and denied with little success by the administration, engendered deep doubts about the stability of the government. Uncertainty about Frondizi's real intentions converted the hypothesis of a military uprising into a broadly debated possibility. The conspiratorial atmosphere the country had lived through on the eve of Perón's fall took over political life again. As before, one could hear, now in the voice of Balbín, the defence of revolution as the natural right of a society faced with a totalitarian threat. However, this campaign of the civil opposition collided with the scruples of the military, still undecided whether to put an end to the incipient constitutional experiment.

In this context, the leaders of the 62 Organizations decided to lift the November general strike. Although they only received promises from Frondizi, the *peronista* unionists decided to stop the workers' mobilization so as not to provide new excuses for a military take-over. The continuity of the truce between the government and the unions required that both be able to control their own decisions. It was soon evident that neither Frondizi nor the leaders of the 62 Organizations were in any state to do so.

On 29 December the stabilization plan reached with the IMF was announced. Its purpose was to obtain financial assistance to alleviate the balance-of-payments crisis inherited by Frondizi and made even more acute by his economic management. Its principal measures included an anti-inflationary monetary policy, stimuli to exports and new investment and the abolition of the system of controls and subsidies.

In the short run the consequences of the plan were predictable. Salaries fell by 25 per cent and GDP declined by 6.4 per cent. Exchange rates were unified and there was a 50 per cent devaluation, which spurred a rise in prices of such proportions that towards the end of 1959 the inflation rate was twice that of the previous year. The real devaluation amounted to 17 per cent, helping to transform the trade deficit of 1958 into a modest surplus in 1959.

The new economic policy left no room for negotiation with the unions. However, the confrontation took place long before its effects were fully felt. The incident that led to the rupture was Frondizi's decision to dislodge the workers by force from the Lisandro de la Torre meat-packing plant, which they had occupied in protest against its privatization. The policy of rapprochement with *peronista* unionism suffered a rude blow when Frondizi called in the army to neutralize the workers' protest. Having indebted himself to the military, the president was now obliged to respond to its disapproval of a policy that continued to restore the union structures to *peronismo*. In the following months the labour policy was revised, the minister of labour (a former labour leader and collaborator of Frigerio) resigned, the scheduled union elections were suspended and important unions which a short time before had been put in the charge of *peronista* leaders passed again into state control.

The new attitudes were not limited to labour policy. Frondizi mollified the military with other gestures: in April he prohibited the activities of the Communist Party, expelled several Soviet diplomats and replaced the government appointees most closely identified with Frigerio, who had to resign again. This did not save him from a serious political crisis in June 1959, when Perón, confirming the suspicions of many, gave the press in Santo Domingo copies of the alleged pre-election pact with Frondizi. Annoyed with his former ally, Perón thus offered a new excuse to anti-Frondizi and anti-Perón sectors to challenge the military's loyalty to the constitutional authorities. Frondizi's denials convinced no one. On the fourth anniversary of the anti-Perón uprising of 16 June 1955, a group of retired military men flew to Córdoba to lead a rebellion of local troops. But the attempt had no repercussions whatever. Although they were harshly critical of Frondizi's attitudes and policies, the high command still preferred to avoid extreme measures.

The crisis of June 1959 had a surprising outcome. In order to improve his deteriorating image in power circles, the president undertook a spectacular cabinet reorganization. On 24 June he offered Alvaro Alsogaray, a persistent critic of the government, the posts of Economy and Labour. A fervent defender of private enterprise and the market economy, Alsogaray seemed an impossible choice for Frondizi; but this decision was one more proof of the president's lack of political prejudice, which alarmed his supporters and surprised his enemies. Alsogaray's credentials were certainly the most apt for soothing the military and implementing the plan of austerity formulated with the IMF.

Under this program, 1959 was a year of sharp economic recession. Argentina had never before experienced such a strong effort to apply monetarist mechanisms. To the drastic decrease in the general liquidity of the economy was added the rapid rise in the cost of living provoked by the removal of price controls. In contrast to the experience of 1956, when negotiation allowed the unions to defend real wages successfully, the union offensive now collided with a solid defence of the official programme of capitalist modernization. The world of big business and the military establishment suppressed their reservations about the origins of the government, and at the moment of confrontation with the unions they gave it their full support.

Wages fell 30 per cent – it would take ten years for them to recover – and business regained the incentives suspended during the *peronista* decade of distributionism. Throughout 1959 labour conflicts were accompanied by a wave of terrorist attempts against businesses in an unprecedented exhibition of frustration and rage. The collapse of the strikes of 1959 brought the cycle of mobilizations begun in 1956 to a close. The man-days lost to strikes were more than 10 million in 1959, nearly 1.5 million in 1960 and only 268,000 in 1961. Under the impact of repression and economic hardship there began a process of demobilization and demoralization of the rank-and-file militants who had been the nucleus of the renaissance of *peronista* unionism.

The subjection of his economic policy to the orthodox monetarism recommended by Alsogaray did not relieve the president of new military anxieties. From the middle of 1959 until March 1962, Frondizi had to govern under the strict vigilance of the military chiefs. During this period, the armed forces acted according to their belief that the president could be pressured to adopt the policies they considered essential; it was neither necessary nor desirable to remove him from office. The most important figure in the exercise of this overbearing tutelage was General C. Toranzo Montero. Named commander-in-chief of the army after the crisis of June 1959, Toranzo Montero began to fill the high command with men he trusted and who, like himself, were convinced that the ideals of the Revolución Libertadora were at risk. When his plans were impeded by Frondizi's secretary of war, who ordered him to quit his post, Toranzo Montero declared himself in rebellion. On 3 and 4 September the country waited, expecting a battle between the tanks deployed throughout the centre of Buenos Aires. The clash was averted when Frondizi acceded to the rebel general's demands and sacrificed his secretary of war, an act which created acute reservations among his cabinet colleagues. To the consternation of the governing party, Frondizi henceforth had to coexist with a military caudillo whose authority emanated from a successful challenge to his presidential powers.

The preoccupations of the army led by Toranzo Montero closely reflected the new political climate provoked by the impact of the Cuban Revolution. The triumph of Fidel Castro in 1959 was initially interpreted by the anti-*peronista* press as being in line with the democratic crusade that had overthrown Perón. Then, following the rapid radicalization of the regime in Havana and the deterioration of relations with the United States, this positive attitude began to give way to a growing alarm about the new model of Latin American revolution. Because of his recent stay in Washington as Argentine delegate to the Inter-American Defense Board, Toranzo Montero was in an advantageous position to personify the anxiety of military circles throughout the continent. Accordingly, he began to reorganize the armed forces on the basis of an anticipated revolutionary war.

In March 1960 Frondizi capitulated to the wishes of the military and instituted the Conintes Plan, which assigned control of the anti-terrorist struggle to the armed forces, subordinated the provincial police to their control and authorized the trial of civilians by military courts. The intrusion of military power in areas of civil jurisdiction produced predictable conflict. Thus, the military commander of the region of Córdoba accused the local governor of complicity with terrorism and demanded his removal. Frondizi yielded to the demand and forced his followers in Congress to decree the intervention in the province of Córdoba.

This and other manifestations of a policy that increasingly reflected an attitude of capitulation on the part of the government led Toranzo Montero to challenge Frondizi's authority openly. In October 1960 the high command of the army circulated a memorandum accusing the government of tolerating the Communist presence in cultural and educational institutions, of exploiting the resentment of the *peronista* masses against the military and of administering state enterprises corruptly and inefficiently. The military's hard line created widespread fear that the precarious balance upon which Frondizi's government had survived would now collapse.

Such conflicts did not have exclusively negative consequences for political stability. Frondizi astutely found ways to exploit them in strengthening his ability to remain in office. His message was to persuade public opinion that the alternative was a slide towards civil war. To give some basis to his warnings he began to lift the restrictions that weighed on the unions, started negotiations to legalize the CGT and allowed more *peronista* activities. Frondizi hoped that this incipient threat would turn the anti-*peronista* sectors to his side and restore the backing he needed to resist the pressure of his civilian and military enemies.

At the beginning of 1961 the president took a step forwards in the search for greater autonomy by succeeding in removing Toranzo Montero, who resigned after failing to sway military opinion against official policy. Thus, after three difficult years in office, Frondizi now had greater liberty to set his government on course.

In addition, without offering any explanation, he removed Alsogaray, who had shown unexpected pragmatism but never been welcome in Frondizi's cabinet. Nevertheless, Alsogaray was replaced by another figure from the local financial establishment who did not substantially modify the policy established by the agreements with the IMF. After the sharp depression of 1959, the economy grew at a 7 per cent rate in 1960 and 1961. The key element in this reactivation was investment. Consumption remained stable because of salary containment and the austere fiscal policy, but this was more than compensated for by the mobilization of capital provoked by import substitution. Thanks to the increase in investment in the highly protected markets of automobiles, tractors, heavy chemicals, steel and oil, the expansion of global demand allowed a reduction of the extensive idle capacity created by the recession of 1959.

The success of the programme of reactivation was not independent of the backing of the international financial community. The financing of the investment push came from foreign savings, whether through short- or

long-term loans or direct investment. Foreign indebtedness helped overcome the restrictions on the capacity to import that derived from the
negative behaviour of exports. In spite of the devaluation of 1959, the
trade balance was negative again by about U.S. $200 million in 1960. The
flow of external funds helped to raise credit in the private sector without
compromising the goals of the monetary policy agreed on with the IMF.

In addition, the economic recovery was initially accompanied by a sharp
reduction in inflation. When Alsogaray was appointed, prices were rising
at an annual rate of 127 per cent; by April 1961, when he stepped down,
the rate had fallen to 9.5 per cent. His successor followed the same line,
but he could not prevent prices from rising by 21 per cent in January
1962, when, on the eve of the election, the government relaxed the
austerity policy. These fluctuations in both the economy and political life
took place in a very sensitive context. The central role of foreign capital in
the economic recovery had introduced an element of great instability in
the official programme. Keeping the confidence of the foreign investors
and bankers required a climate of political peace that Frondizi could not
ensure for long.

Foreign policy was the second front where Frondizi tried to take advantage of his increased freedom of action, following an independent line in his
treatment of the Cuban question. By August 1960, at a meeting of Latin
American foreign ministers held in Costa Rica, Frondizi had defined his
position on the new conditions created by the Cuban Revolution. On that
occasion, he instructed the Argentine delegation to call the attention of the
United States to the underdevelopment of the Latin American region at the
same time that it condemned the Communist threat. In Frondizi's view,
poverty and subversion went hand in hand, and so the fight against Communism went together with the fight against underdevelopment – a formula
that would be popularized by John Kennedy with the Alliance for Progress.
Frondizi appeared to it to ask for economic aid from the United States and to
justify an attitude of independence concerning the U.S. administration's
conflict with Fidel Castro.

In March 1961 Argentina offered its good offices to facilitate an understanding between the United States and Cuba. The offer was rejected, but
the opposition used it to accuse the government of protecting a Communist country. A month later, Frondizi gave new pretexts to his critics when
he signed a friendship treaty with Brazil. The open neutrality of Jânio
Quadros, the Brazilian president, on U.S.–Soviet rivalry and his sympathies towards Cuba jolted the relative calm that prevailed in the military

establishment. For the military the only acceptable posture was one of outright opposition to Fidel Castro. Given its suspicions concerning the ideological inclinations of Frondizi and his collaborators, the military greeted any official position that fell short of firm condemnation of the Cuban Revolution with alarm and outrage. Thus, after Frondizi held a secret interview with Ernesto 'Che' Guevara at the presidential residence in the middle of August, in a new attempt at mediation between Cuba and the United States, he was forced to remove his foreign minister and sign a joint declaration with the armed forces which ratified the condemnation of the communist experiment in Cuba.

The second and final chapter of the conflict between the military establishment and the government over the Cuban question took place at the conference of the Organization of American States (OAS) in January 1962. This meeting was sponsored by the United States, which wanted to apply sanctions against Cuba and expel it from the inter-American system. During the days preceding it the Inter-American Defense Board met in Washington for the same purpose, and the Argentine military delegate voted in favour of the motion to break relations with Fidel Castro's government. However, at the OAS conference, held in Punta del Este, the Argentine foreign minister, together with those of Brazil, Mexico, Chile, Bolivia and Ecuador, decided to abstain on the motion which, with fourteen countries voting, ordered the expulsion of Cuba from the OAS.

The refusal to side with the United States met with unanimous military disapproval. The chiefs of the three armed branches demanded that the president immediately break off relations with Cuba and put an end to the ambiguities in foreign policy. For several days Frondizi and the high command met round the clock, while unrest brewed in the garrisons. Finally, his arguments exhausted, the president had to yield to military pressure and sign the decree ordering the end of relations.

The outcome of the Cuban crisis was the prologue to another, more definitive crisis. In March 1962 elections had to be held in which control of the Chamber of Deputies and of several provincial governments was at stake. Frondizi looked to these for a victory that would permit him to shake loose the military supervision that had ruled his exercise of power, and to this end he made the most daring decision of his four years in government: he authorized the *peronistas* to vote. The risks were obvious. In the congressional elections of 1960 the banned *peronistas* had cast 2,176,864 blank ballots (24.6 per cent), followed by the UCRP with 2,109,948 (23.8 per cent). The official party, the UCRI, took third place with 1,813,455 votes (20.5 per cent). In order to change this picture, Frondizi had to surpass the UCRP vote and become the real alternative to the feared return of *peronismo*. Exploiting the comprehensible anxiety provoked by *peronista* propaganda, Frondizi hoped to transform the election into a plebiscite over who would emerge as the guarantor of peace and progress. Several pilot elections at the provincial level in December 1961 seemed to lend credibility to his hopes. Recovering the territory lost in the congressional elections of 1960, the official party grew at the cost of the UCRP, while the *peronistas,* competing outside their urban bastions, did not appear to be a force to be feared. On 18 March, however, the victory that would have retrospectively justified so many humiliations ended in defeat.

After seven years of political proscription, *peronismo* returned as the leading electoral force, with 32 per cent of the votes. The number of votes received by the various groups in which the *peronistas* participated — since the Partido Justicialista was still illegal — totaled 2,530,238; the UCRI received 2,422,516 votes, and the UCRP 1,802,483. Of the fourteen provincial elections, nine were won by the *peronistas,* including the most important district, the province of Buenos Aires, where the union leader Andrés Framini won the post of governor.

On 19 March the military obliged the president to annul by decree the elections in the districts where the *peronistas* had won. But this was not to be the only price of his lost electoral wager. In rejecting the election results, he apparently violated his constitutional oath to respect the law; his civilian and military enemies needed no other pretext to provoke his overthrow. Thus began ten days during which public opinion hung on secret negotiations in which the military and politicians laboured to find a formula to resolve the crisis. The time invested in this effort clearly illustrates the reluctance of important sectors of the armed forces to regard the democratic experience initiated in 1958 as finished. Finally, the high command prevailed, and on 29 March Frondizi was removed from the presidency.

Thus, in the midst of general indifference, a bold and innovative attempt to confront the problems of post-Perón Argentina came to an end. For four turbulent years, Frondizi tried to reincorporate the *peronista* masses into political life and inaugurate a new phase of import substitution with a view towards promoting economic development. His proposals did not gain the consensus necessary to secure a consolidation of democracy at the same time.

The economic programme was not well received, even in the business community. Although he promised the Argentine bourgeoisie much more than they had been offered in the immediate past, it was too ambiguous an experiment to be believed in. Very few politicians of the Right could discern the project hidden beneath Frondizi's rhetoric. The country was never closer to creating a modern conservative party, but it was a lost opportunity. In truth, the tortuous roads by which Frondizi chose to formulate his programme did nothing to facilitate it. The initiatives he launched from office began a process of great change. The industrialization effort modernized the country's economy and society. To complement foreign investment, the government had to generate additional savings in order to finance the construction of infrastructure and industrial subsidies. The alternative used by Perón – extracting savings from the agricultural sector – was no longer feasible. On the contrary, this sector had to be fortified by a policy of high prices. As a consequence, the government turned to wage reduction. This lowering of salaries was effective in two ways: in the public sector, spending decreased, leaving room for increases in investment; in the private sector, it permitted an expansion of profits. The belief was that greater profits, larger investment and more rapid growth in productivity would make it possible to restore wage levels later. In macro-economic terms this meant a translation of resources from consumption to investment. The ratio of investment to the GDP grew thus from 17.5 to 21.7 in 1961.

Foreign investment tended to concentrate in new areas, where it was guaranteed special protection, but very little was channelled into the modernization of existing sectors. A type of dualist industrial economy was being created in which a modern capital-intensive sector, with a strong presence of foreign companies, advanced technologies and high wages, began to coexist with a traditional sector, predominantly financed with national capital, which had obsolete equipment, was more labour intensive and paid lower wages.

Frondizi's policies encouraged import substitution and the development of the internal market. It was a paradox that the project of import substitution, conceived during the Second World War as an expression of nationalist sentiment, should end by increasing the influence of foreign capital in the economy. The modernization of the productive structure was a necessity, but it was carried out in an unbalanced manner. Limited to the internal market, it did not permit businesses to take advantage of economies of scale, as a greater emphasis on exports would have done. The new structure continued to depend on resources provided by traditional agricultural exports to obtain its critical supplies and capital goods – precisely the dependency that Frondizi's strategy was attempting to eradicate.

THE PRESIDENCY OF JOSÉ MARÍA GUIDO, 1962–3

The overthrow of Frondizi presented the military with the dilemma of how to fill the presidency. A military dictatorship was a solution favoured by only a few factions, and the international context was far from propitious for authoritarian experiments, as the failed intervention of President Kennedy's ambassador on behalf of Frondizi had demonstrated. The dilemma was finally resolved by the naming of the head of the Senate, Dr José María Guido, as president of the country in accordance with the legal provisions governing a vacancy in the office of head of state.

Once this institutional question was resolved, the new minister of the interior, Rodolfo Martínez, a key figure of the military faction opposed to a dictatorial solution, began to unfold a new political plan. In general terms, Martínez's plan resumed Frondizi's policy of very gradually reintegrating the *peronistas* into political life. But for this plan to be realized it was necessary for the legalistic faction of the military to prevail not only within the army but also within the navy and air force. This was the source of the first of a series of military crises that plagued Guido's administration. Within one month of Frondizi's overthrow, the powerful Campo de Mayo military base declared itself in opposition to the Martínez plan.

The navy also exerted its influence in defending the ideals of 1955. Under these circumstances, the minister of the interior resigned, and Guido was forced to sign decrees that annulled all the elections held in March, dissolved Congress and extended federal control also over those provinces where the *peronistas* had not won in the elections. Thus, the search for a political solution which would have included the *peronista* masses – even in a subordinate position – was abandoned.

Guido took charge of the economy in an extremely uncertain climate. In the months preceding the March elections, a flight of capital had been stimulated by signs of crisis in Frondizi's economic programme. The weaknesses of the 1960–1 recovery were becoming evident as the increases in economic activity and public and private investment came to an end, provoking a trade deficit at the end of 1961. The rise in imports stimulated by the great leap forward in industrialization was not matched by the volume of agricultural exports. In addition, the country had to face the large long- and short-term foreign debt contracted in previous years to finance the new investments. The deterioration of foreign currency reserves, aggravated by speculative manoeuvres, further complicated public finances. When the government found itself forced to resort to credit from the Central Bank to finance its running expenses, exceeding the limits agreed upon with the IMF, the international financial institution declared that Argentina had violated its commitments.

To cope with the inglorious finale of the *desarrollista* adventure, President Guido named Federico Pinedo as minister of economy. After twenty-two years, this founding father of liberal-conservatism took up the reins of the economy once more – an eloquent reminder of the permanence of that traditional Argentina against which Frondizi had tried to project his modernization program. Pinedo lasted only a few weeks in office, but this was long enough for him to do the job for which he had been summoned: he devalued the peso from 80 to 120 to the dollar. His replacement was A. Alsogaray, who returned to administer a new agreement with the IMF that incorporated extremely restrictive fiscal and monetary policies. Alsogaray's goal was nothing less than to balance the budget and purge the economy of the 'excess demand' incurred during the last years of Frondizi's term.

The severe monetary restriction provoked a sharp decline in activity. The GDP fell 4 per cent between 1962 and 1963 while business closures and unemployment increased. The crisis of liquidity meant that all payments – in the private as well as the public sectors – began to be postponed and that business checks and vouchers issued by the government circulated as substitutes for paper money. During this period the economy operated under the broadest free-market conditions known since 1930. Nevertheless, the shock therapy, in spite of the sharp recession, did not prevent inflation from accelerating until it reached an annual rate of 20 to 30 per cent. The positive note in this gloomy picture was the excellent crop of 1962, which made possible an improvement in the trade balance and a restocking of the country's foreign currency reserves. The economy, however, continued to be ruled by the uncertainty created by open dissidence among the military chiefs concerning the country's political future.

The outcome of the conflict of April 1962 did not solve the struggle for power within the military high command. In August, those who favoured the dictatorial solution staged another challenge, under the leadership of General Federico Toranzo Montero, the brother of former president Frondizi's most intransigent critic. The object of the uprising was the resignation of the secretary of war on the excuse that the internal promotion regulations of the army had been violated. With the secretary's resignation the search for a replacement was undertaken in a manner that clearly revealed the state of anarchy in the military. A genuine electoral process was set in motion which the country could follow in the press and in which the generals behaved like political bosses. When the ballots were counted and the fire power behind each vote evaluated, the election favoured the army's legalistic faction. President Guido named one of its members secretary of war, but his authority was ignored by the officers who had been defeated. Determined not to retreat, these men, still under Toranzo Montero's leadership, proposed their own candidate and deployed their troops in central Buenos Aires. The legalistic faction also entered the fray, and once again the country stood on the verge of armed confrontation. The military resources of the legalists were superior to those of Toranzo Montero's followers, but the president intervened to prevent open conflict. As in April, the most resolutely anti-*peronista* sectors emerged with a political victory despite the relative balance between the two sides.

Deprived of its military victory, the legalist faction was quick to react. Its spokesmen demanded the return of the constitution, the complete repudiation of dictatorship and the holding of regular elections. When they insisted on a changing of the guard, conflict once again broke out. The army base at Campo de Mayo assumed the leadership of the rebellion under the direction of General Juan Carlos Onganía, making appeals to public opinion over two radio stations in an effort to project the image of a democratic army: 'We're willing to fight for the people's right to vote.'

This time the military factions entered into combat. The legalists called themselves the 'blues' (*los azules*), while their adversaries were known as the 'reds' (*los colorados*). The *colorados* were always on the defensive, and posed no real challenge to the *azules,* who had not only the greater fire power but also the support of the air force, which threatened to bomb the concentrations of *colorado* troops, undermining their fighting spirit. The navy, although it sympathized with the *colorados,* stayed out of the fray. On 23 September 1962, General Onganía's troops obtained the surrender of their adversaries and proceeded to impose the peace of the victor over them. They took the principal army leaders prisoner and carried out a true purge, which put an end to the careers of 140 senior officers.

The victory of the *azul* faction in the army brought Dr Martínez back as minister of the interior, and he renewed the quest for a political formula that would permit the armed forces to return to their bases. The original decision to facilitate the incorporation of the *peronista* masses into institutional life was retained, as was the refusal to allow *peronista* leaders to occupy positions of power. To resolve the dilemma implicit in this dual objective an effort was made to form a broad political front, to which the *peronista* masses would bring their voting power whilst leadership would remain in the hands of other forces. This replay of the experience of 1958 seemed to elicit a favourable response from Perón: faced with the alternative of a military dictatorship, *peronismo* reconciled itself to accepting a slow and gradual return to the institutional system, meanwhile lending its support to the political formula sponsored by the dominant sector of the armed forces. The exiled leader accepted this compromise, entrusting the political moderate Dr Raúl Matera with the local leadership of the movement and removing Andrés Framini, the union leader who, after his frustrated attempt to become governor of Buenos Aires in 1962, had been adopting ever more intransigent positions and moving more towards the forces of the Left.

Under these conditions, the minister of the interior began to reassemble the scattered pieces of the complex political puzzle. Several small parties entered the competition for the coveted candidacy for president of the future electoral front. But Perón and Frondizi refused to give up their efforts to control the political outcome, and they manoeuvred to frustrate the aspirations of those who sought to become the saviours and heirs of the proscribed forces. At the same time, the minister of the interior extended official recognition to a neo-*peronista* party, the Unión Popúlar, which offered to channel the votes of Perón's followers.

This bold move by the minister of the interior provoked understandable unease in the anti-Perón camp, which tried to pressure President Guido into revoking his decision. In an effort to disarm this attempt, the organizers of the political front publicly announced their condemnation of the regime deposed in 1955. At the same time, they prepared another equally bold initiative that, in the end, would be the ruin of their plans. In March 1963 Dr Miguel Angel Zavala Ortiz, a fervently anti-*peronista* leader of the UCRP, refused an offer made by the minister of the interior to occupy second place on a presidential ticket that would be headed by General Onganía and have the backing of all the parties. His rejection and the indignation caused within the anti-*peronista* camp forced Martínez's resignation. Under pressure from his friends, among whom were numerous partisans of General Aramburu, Onganía had to deny that he was a candidate for the proposed alliance.

The divisions within the high command of the army encouraged a further military rebellion, this time centred in the navy, to be staged on 2 April in protest against the electoral policy of the government. After several days of bloody conflict, the army *azules,* with the help of the air force, forced the rebels to surrender. The defeat of the navy, where *colorado* sympathizers were in the majority, signalled its political decline; thirteen years would pass before it would recover its position in the military establishment. In the short term, the acute danger of institutional disintegration convinced the military leaders to abandon their political plans.

The government's change of direction surprised Perón, who was again allied with Frondizi and ready to play by the rules of the game established for the next elections, scheduled for 7 July. The government showed itself to be insensitive to these manifestations of goodwill. After a year of marches and countermarches, in which there had been five ministers of the interior, the new minister in charge of the government's political conduct put an end to ambiguity. Appointed in May 1963, General Osiris Villegas began by excluding the Unión Popular from the electoral race for executive posts, and he subsequently banned all those suspected of representing orthodox *peronismo* or being allied with it.

The endless number of legal obstacles and impediments that confronted the *peronista* front intensified the conflict within its ranks, which existed as a result of the difficulties encountered in trying to agree on a candidate for president. When Perón and Frondizi agreed to support Vicente Solano Lima, a conservative populist, the coalition fell apart. An important sector of the UCRI threw its support behind the candidacy of Oscar Alende despite Frondizi's effort to prevent it. Nor could Perón prevent the Christian Democrats from backing their own candidate, Raúl Matera. When, on the eve of the poll, the confusion provoked by these disagreements was deepened by the imposition of new legal obstacles, Perón and Frondizi called on their followers to cast blank ballots. Remaining in the race were Dr. Arturo Illia, a little known but respected provincial politician, for the UCRP; Alende for the dissident faction of the UCRI; and General Aramburu, the head of the Revolución Libertadora, sponsored by a new political group, the Unión del Pueblo Argentino, in the hope of attracting the anti-*peronista* vote. The effects of this strategy were counter-productive. Important sectors of the *peronista* electorate preferred not to express their protest with a blank ballot but to support the alternatives to Aramburu. The blank ballots totalled 19.2 per cent of the vote, which signified a retreat from the 24.3 per cent cast in 1957. Both sectors of Radicalism benefited from *peronista* support, but the winner, unexpectedly, was Illia, with 2,500,000 votes, followed by Alende, with 1,500,000, followed closely by the blank ballots, which in turn exceeded the 1,350,000 votes cast for General Aramburu.

THE PRESIDENCY OF ARTURO ILLIA, 1963–6

In 1963 Argentina embarked on a new constitutional experience in a climate of relative political relaxation epitomized by the personality of the president-elect. His parsimonious, provincial style seemed well suited to the mood of Argentine society, which, tired out by so much conflict, reacted to Illia without illusions, in sharp contrast to the fervour which had accompanied Frondizi's victory in 1958. Illia understood that the government's first task was to offer Argentina's citizens a moderate policy that would allow them to reconcile their differences. Where Frondizi had tried to innovate, Illia chose the security of the tried and true: respect for the law and periodic elections.

Illia and his party had traversed the changing landscape of post-war Argentina without themselves undergoing any great transformation. Perhaps the greatest change was in their attitude towards *peronismo*. Since 1946, the Radical Party had channelled the feelings of rejection that the movement led by Perón had awakened in the middle and upper classes. The anti-*peronista* reaction expressed resistance not only to the authoritarian tendency of Perón's regime, but also to the social changes that took place under his auspices. Anti-*peronismo* was identified, therefore, with a spirit of social restoration. However, the transformations that had taken place in the country were profound and irreversible. Argentina could not simply return to the past. *Peronismo* had modified the old order, but that order had also been corroded by, for example, industrial development, the modernization of labour relations and the expansion of mass culture. That this new reality was destined to endure was a painful discovery to those who wanted to turn the clock backwards. First Frondizi's attitude and later that of the military *azules* underscored this forced recognition of *peronismo*. The new Illia government, elected thanks to the proscription of the *peronistas,* also promised to make them legal again soon.

However, the Radical Party remained faithful to its traditions in its conception of economic policy. The party's platform since the middle of the 1940s – nationalism, income distribution, state interventionism – dictated some of the government's early measures. During the electoral campaign, the candidates of Radicalism had promised above all to revise

Frondizi's oil policy because it was detrimental to national sovereignty. Illia nullified the contracts signed by the international oil companies. The measure required the payment of important indemnifications, interrupted the oil industry's growth and earned the government the early antipathy of the business community and foreign investors.

The sharp recession of 1962–3 had caused GDP per capita to fall to its lowest level in ten years. The installed capacity of the manufacturing industry – sharply increased by the earlier wave of investment – was operating at about 50 per cent, while unemployment reached 9 per cent of the active population in Greater Buenos Aires and was even higher in the interior of the country. The Radical administration considered that its first objective was to reactivate production. The strategy chosen was to stimulate consumption through expansionist monetary, fiscal and wage policies. Here also the contrast with Frondizi's policies was evident. In 1963 the economy was at a low point in the economic cycle, comparable to that in 1959. Yet whereas in 1960–1 it was investment, financed with foreign resources, that impelled recovery, in 1964–5 the expansion was based on encouraging private consumption. Under the Radical government banking credit to the private sector was increased, which permitted improved financing of the sale of durable consumer goods; the Treasury proceeded to diminish the balance of unpaid debts to public employees and state suppliers and cleared the backlog of federal transfers to the provinces; salaries were also raised and a variable minimum wage law was passed.

The GDP grew 8 per cent in 1964 and 1965 – with annual increments in industry of 15 per cent and unemployment reduced by half – but growth still did not reach pre-recession levels. Moreover, the rapid expansion aroused fears that problems could develop in the balance of payments, not only because of higher demand for imports but also because of the need to confront the external debt obligations assumed during Frondizi's years in office. It was estimated at the end of 1963 public and private external debt service would cost U.S. $1,000 million during 1964 and 1965.

The initial fears about the balance of payments were subsequently reduced by the very good performance of exports, the Illia administration marking a turning point in the behaviour of the external sector. Exports grew from the previous plateau of U.S. $1,100 million that had prevailed since the 1950s to nearly $1,600 million, the level achieved nearly eighteen years before. The continuing rise in prices contributed to this (leading to an improvement of 12 per cent in the exchange rate between 1963 and 1966), but above all it was due to the increase in the volume of production. After remaining stagnant from 1953 to 1963, agricultural production increased by more than 50 per cent between 1963 and 1966. The traditional bottleneck in the Argentine economy – stagnation in agricultural exports – was therefore removed.

The early economic achievements of the government did not earn it greater acceptance among the population. Elected by less than a third of the voters, and lacking roots in the labour movement and in business organizations, the Radicals needed the collaboration of other forces to broaden their bases of support. However, they soon made it clear that they had no intention of sharing the government with other parties. Their rejection of a strategy of alliances provided poor preparation for that moment when the tactical truce that had accompanied their installation in office gave way to a level of conflict more in accordance with the country's recent past.

As for the Radicals' relations with the military, the situation could not have been more paradoxical. The defeat of the *colorado* military faction, with whom the Radicals were associated, had opened the way for elections and made possible Illia's unexpected victory. The marriage of convenience forged between the new government and the leaders of the blue army was, then, fraught with tension. The Radicals were too weak to impose a return of their own military allies and provoke a change in the chain of command of the armed forces. They had, therefore, to resign themselves to accepting the status quo, in which the figure of General Onganía, commander-in-chief of the army, was a key element. For their part, the military commanders had to adjust to the existence of a civilian administration for which they harboured no sympathy whatsoever. And they saw Illia's cautious response to the resurgence of union opposition as clear evidence of a lack of political authority.

Organized labour's opposition to Illia went back to the period before his election as president. In January 1963, the unions managed to reorganize the CGT and approved a campaign to force a return to constitutional order through a series of strikes. When at the eleventh hour the officers who surrounded President Guido decided to veto the participation of the Unión Popular, the CGT called off the scheduled mobilization and instructed its members to boycott the election and condemn its results, and thus Illia's presidency, as illegitimate. The government's positive moves on economic and social matters did not redeem it in the eyes of the unions. In spite of the passage of a minimum wage law – contrary to the wishes of business organizations – the CGT decided to carry out its original plan of action in

May 1964, alleging conditions of poverty which did not accord with the general indication of economic performance.

For several weeks the country watched a wave of occupations of factories which, in their scrupulous planning, resembled a military operation. This formidable demonstration of union power provoked alarm in business circles, but the peaceful nature of the plant occupations revealed their objective to be less a confrontation with business than a weakening of the government. Illia chose to ignore the challenge and did not call in troops, but his isolation was exposed to public view, and demands for a policy of law and order began to increase.

The mobilization of mid-1964 marked the entrance on the political stage of a new style of labour action. The unions were simultaneously agencies for wage negotiation and enterprises which provided their members with a broad network of social services, and as a result an extensive bureaucratic apparatus had been constructed. At the same time, union leaders had become accepted as elements of power in post-*peronista* Argentina. Between 1956 and 1959, when unionism was weak and marginal, it had launched an active protest of the working masses against the state. It now began to adopt a different strategy. Instead of stimulating mass action, it preferred to rely on general strikes, in which the intervention of the rank and file was eliminated in advance and priority was given to organizational efficiency. This strategy of strikes and negotiation went together with a search for allies among those discontented with the government. The person who best embodied this new style was Augusto Vandor, head of the metal-workers' union, a frequent go-between among businessmen, military officers and politicians; Vandor epitomized the leadership of the 62 Organizations.

A no less significant evolution was also taking place within the armed forces. At the risk of dividing the military establishment through involvement in political and sectarian conflicts, the leaders of the *azules* decided to bow to constitutional authority and return to the barracks. The consequent resumption of their institutional mission was intended to permit the armed forces to re-establish patterns of authority and improve the professionalism of their officers. In August 1964, in a speech given at West Point, General Onganía revealed a project to place the military above politics.[6] He said that the armed forces, 'the armed branch of the

---

[6] *La Nación*, 7 August 1964; quoted in M. Cavarozzi, *Autoritarismo y democracia, 1955–1983* (Buenos Aires, 1983), p. 100.

Constitution', could not be substituted for the popular will. He also pointed out, however, that their functions were 'to guarantee the sovereignty and territorial integrity of the nation, preserve the moral and spiritual values of western and Christian civilization, [and] ensure public order and internal peace'. In order to fulfil these functions, he added, it was necessary to reinforce the military as a corporation, as well as the economic and social development of the country.

In this broad vision of the role of the armed forces, their loyalty to the civil powers remained highly conditional. In the same speech, Onganía stressed that '[military] compliance refers ultimately to the Constitution and its laws, never to the men or the political parties who may temporarily hold public power'. Thus, due obedience could lapse 'if, taking shelter behind exotic ideologies, an excess of authority [was] produced' or if the exercise of the vast array of functions pertaining to the armed forces was hindered. The prevention and elimination of internal subversion occupied a central place in the new doctrine. In transforming economic development and the efficient running of the government into conditions necessary for national security, Onganía placed such objectives within the legitimate realm of military jurisdiction, completely erasing the line of demarcation between the military and the civilian. The scheme to place the armed forces above politics effectively eliminated politics itself.

The choice of West Point as the place to introduce General Onganía as the new crusader for the doctrine of national security was no coincidence. The United States was carrying on an active campaign to convert the armies of Latin America into its allies in the struggle against the internal enemy – Communist subversion. Popular mobilization and the crisis of authority in the Goulart administration brought the armed forces to power in Brazil in 1964 in the name of national security. In Argentina, President Illia continued to administer a legal government sharply aware of the fact that it was under close military surveillance. At the beginning of 1965, the military intervention of the United States in the Dominican Republic put the 'entente' between the Radical government and the armed forces to the test. Illia was trapped between the pressure of public opinion, which was hostile to the United States, and the demands of the armed forces, which favoured the intervention. His response was ambiguous: he proposed the creation of an inter-American military force which would re-establish order in Santo Domingo, but he refused to allow Argentine troops to be part of it. The president's refusal to follow the advice of the military chiefs aroused their bitter resentment.

Nor did Illia win the goodwill of the military by restoring legal status to the *peronista* movement, which enjoyed a freedom of action unknown until then. This greater tolerance was also intended to exploit the contradictions which were being created within the movement by Perón from his exile in Spain. Since the defeat of 1955, sharply distinct forces had grown up within *peronismo*. In the provinces least touched by modernization, it managed to preserve its multi-class profile under leaders from the conservative tradition who cultivated *peronista* rhetoric in order to retain Perón's political clientele while prudently submitting to the post-Perón order. Forced to act under new conditions, these local leaders chose to distance themselves from Perón's erratic tactics so as not to risk losing their laboriously reconstructed positions.

In the more modern and urban areas of the country, *peronismo* had lost its support outside the working class and the popular sectors but continued to exercise considerable influence in the union movement, since this was the only structure that had survived the political collapse of 1955. In the first phase, *peronista* unionism followed the instructions of the exiled leader with more discipline than the neo-*peronista* forces of the interior. With time, however, the labour leaders adopted the conservative logic of union institutions which were able to prosper only if they had the goodwill of the centres of national power. It became increasingly difficult for them to follow the strategies of Perón, who, proscribed from political life, had as his dominant objective the destabilization of the forms of government being laboriously erected by his enemies. In the end, then, the former president found himself at odds with the more conformist aspirations of the union leaders. While they sought a political order that would make room for them and allow them to consolidate, Perón waged a tireless war of attrition from exile.

After ten years of precarious existence on the margins of legality, the *peronista* movement began to consider the idea of emancipating itself from the political tutelage of Perón. Many union leaders concluded that disciplined obedience to Perón was preventing them from full inclusion in the prevailing power system. This rupture was not without difficulties. The faithfulness of the *peronista* masses to their absent leader was just as vigorous as ever; furthermore, they harboured the secret illusion of Perón's imminent return to the country, an illusion he encouraged in repeated messages from exile. The myth of Perón's return weakened the authority of the local leaders and conspired against their efforts to institutionalize the movement within the existing rules of the game. In order to remove this obstacle it was necessary to demonstrate that Perón's return was impossible.

At the end of 1964, the *peronista* unions led by Vandor organized the so-called Operation Return. Perón left Madrid by air on 2 December, but when he landed in Rio de Janeiro the Brazilian government, following instructions from Argentine authorities, forced him to go back. The reasons for Perón's participation in this dubious adventure have never been made clear. What is certain is that his prestige in the eyes of his loyal followers was not affected; the responsibility for failure fell squarely on the shoulders of the union leaders and the Radical government.

The calling of congressional elections for March 1965 postponed the resolution of the dispute over power among the *peronistas,* who decided to close ranks behind their candidates. The results yielded 3,400,000 votes for the different *peronista* groups and 2,600,000 votes for the government party. Since only half the seats of the Chamber of Deputies were at stake, the effects of the electoral defeat were attenuated; even so, the government lost its absolute majority and henceforth had to seek the support of other minority parties. Even more seriously the Radicals were further diminished in the eyes of conservatives and the military. Their latest failure to contain the electoral force of the *peronistas* and the government's performance in other areas did little to reduce the party's social and political isolation.

In the middle of 1965, the administration was obliged to admit that inflation, which was now approaching 30 per cent, had once again become a problem. The early expansionist policies now gave way to an anti-inflationary program, which began by reducing aid by the Central Bank to the banking system, especially in credit to the public sector. Efforts to reduce the fiscal deficit ran into difficulties, the government's electoral reverses making their efforts felt when the government failed to get Congress to pass a set of tax laws aimed at reforming public finances. In income policy the results were even worse: pressure from public and private wage-earners produced increases in excess of official guidelines. Finally, at the end of 1965 economic activity began to decline.

The economic policy of the Radical government did not earn the approval of the centres of economic power – especially in so far as this policy relied on a variety of controls and forms of state intervention to limit speculation and sectoral pressures. Accusations of *dirigismo económico, ineficiencia administrativa* and *demogogia fiscal* unified the principal corporations in industry, agriculture and finance in their attack on the government, an attack which was sharpened further still by the president's preferential treatment of small and medium-sized businesses.

In November 1965 an unforeseen confrontation between Onganía and the secretary of war led the former to resign his commission. The government, however, was in no position to alter the military balance of power: the new commander-in-chief, General Pascual Pistarini, came from that sector which regarded Onganía as its natural political leader. Furthermore, Onganía's star burned even more brightly when he left the army, attracting the sympathies of the constantly broadening band of those who were unhappy with the Radical administration.

Nevertheless, the political balance appeared to be most unstable within the *peronista* movement. Months after Perón's failed attempt to return to Argentina, Vandor and his friends believed the moment had arrived to do away with obedience to a person who came between them and the political order in which they sought acceptance. A party congress orchestrated by the unions approved a plan that aimed to substitute the voluble political will of the exiled leader with a structure more representative of the interests of local union chiefs.

His leadership challenged, Perón sent his third and current wife, María Estela Martínez, to Argentina on a mission to nip the rebellion in the bud. Isabel (the nickname by which she was known) began to gather followers among Vandor's rivals. The CGT itself went through a conflict of loyalties and split in two. However, Vandor managed to retain control of the bulk of the union machine as well as the support of the neo-*Peronista* politicians of the interior.

At the beginning of 1966 election for a new governor of the province of Mendoza was due to be held, providing an occasion on which to measure the balance of power between the supreme leader and the local *peronista* caudillos since Perón and his rivals nominated different candidates. A Radical–Conservative alliance prevailed in the elections, but of greater interest was the fact that the obscure candidate backed by Perón won more votes than the candidate backed by Vandor and the other rebels. This outcome was a severe blow to those within and without *peronismo* who were confident of the political decline of the exiled leader. The dissident faction was rapidly losing adherents. Everything pointed to the probability that *peronismo*, now united behind its leader, was on its way to a sure victory in the next elections scheduled for March 1967. It was clear to many that the political order that had arisen from Perón's overthrow would survive only if regular elections were suppressed. The possibility of a coup d'état began to be openly discussed in the media.

At the same time, the cultural and technical modernization of the country begun by Frondizi, paralleled by the economic changes brought about by the investment of foreign capital in industry, had begun to recast Argentina's social landscape. A new stratum composed of professionals, business managers and academics was gaining visibility. In this emerging sector, the values of liberal democracy that had galvanized the resistance to the *peronista* regime enjoyed little popularity. The mobilizing myths were now efficiency and economic dynamism. The new sensibility was expressed in the demand for 'structural change'. Under its auspices institutes were created to diffuse the methods of U.S. 'business schools' throughout the local executive population; weekly magazines reproducing the format of *Time* and *Newsweek* were published, generously supported by the advertising of large national and foreign corporations; a profusion of propaganda encouraged new aspirations and patterns of consumption.

In spite of its vagueness, the slogan of structural change was clear on one point: the biggest obstacle to Argentina's integration into the modern world was the archaism of its political parties. Illia, with his moderate style, was drawn by the caricaturists as a quiet figure with a dove of peace sitting on his head; at the end he had become a symbol of ineffectiveness and decadence.

The discrediting of the government was so intense and effective that public opinion rallied behind the increasingly explicit calls for a coup d'état. At a time when the Radical administration was being subjected to biting criticism, this campaign of psychological action aimed to create a new legitimacy through the exaltation of the armed forces, whose virtues of efficiency and professionalism – deemed absent in the politicians – were praised. Onganía emerged as the natural leader of this ideology of authoritarian modernization, which also found adherents in the labour movement. Many union leaders optimistically watched the rise of a military elite that shared their resentment towards the so-called *partidocracia*. Moreover, the suppression of the electoral system, which Perón was always in a position to influence, would remove some of the obstacles to their attempts to emancipate themselves from the caudillo's political tutelage.

The fate of the Radical government had been sealed for quite some time before the military uprising of 26 June 1966. On 29 May, General Pistarini, at an official ceremony in the presence of the president, delivered a defiant speech in which he expressed the dominant themes of the anti-government propaganda. Contrary to the expectations of the conspirators, who were waiting for an act of authority so they could declare their rebellion, Illia did nothing. Under a foolish pretext, Pistarini then arrested one of the few constitutionalist officers and ignored the orders of the secretary of war to release him. The president's response was to dismiss the commander-in-chief, finally provoking a decisive crisis. On 26 June, the army took over the radio, television and telephone systems and gave Illia six hours to resign. When the time was up, a police detachment expelled him from the presidential palace and sent him home. The search for a constitutional order begun in 1955 had come to a lame end.

On 28 June, the commanders of the three military branches formed a revolutionary junta, the first decisions of which were to dismiss the president and the vice-president, the members of the Supreme Court, the governors and the elected incumbents. Congress and the provincial legislatures were dissolved, all political parties banned and their assets transferred to the state. A proclamation, known as the Acta de la Revolución Argentina, informed the people that they would have a representative government again only after enlightened rule by the armed forces – for as long as was necessary – had dismantled the anachronistic structures and values that stood in the way of national greatness. The junta held power for twenty-four hours and then, predictably, named Onganía president of the new authoritarian government.

THE *REVOLUCIÓN ARGENTINA*, 1966–73

Onganía took over the presidency in 1966 with full powers. The coup d'état had already swept the political parties from the stage. The so-called Statute of the Argentine Revolution went a step further and excluded the armed forces from the responsibilities of government. This concentration of power was the natural corollary of the consensus that surrounded Illia's overthrow: to dismantle the system of *partidocracia,* and preserve the unity of the military, disconnecting it from public policy.

The direction of the new authoritarian regime remained, therefore, dependent on the ideological tastes of Onganía. Lacking personal appeal or rhetorical talent, he quickly surrounded himself with the pomp appropriate to a remote and self-sufficient power. From the heights of this unexpected absolutism, he informed the country of the key ingredients of his preferences. These were scarcely adapted to the image of champion of modernity carefully cultivated by his publicity agents. They were, in essence, those of a devout soldier, imprisoned by the narrowest of Catholic phobias in matters of sex, communism and art. An admirer of Franco's

Spain, Onganía saw in it an example to be imitated in order to restore morals and order to a people he considered licentious and undisciplined.

As had happened before with the rise to power of General Uriburu in 1930, the nationalist colonels in 1943 and, less emphatically, General Lonardi in 1955, the purest expressions of anti-liberal thought re-appeared. The country again witnessed the exaltation of corporatist schemes of government, and the state adopted a paternalistic style, extrava-gant with prohibitions and good advice in its feverish campaign of moral and ideological vigilance.

The first target of this crusade was the university. In July the public universities were deprived of their autonomy and were placed under the control of the Ministry of the Interior on the grounds that it was necessary to end Marxist infiltration and student unrest. In 1946, a month after Perón's electoral victory, a similar measure had been inflicted upon the Argentine universities. As had happened then, a considerable number of professors resigned to avoid becoming victims of the purge, many of them choosing to go into exile in Europe, the United States and other parts of Latin America.

The search for a new order was then aimed at public services. First came the Port of Buenos Aires. In October the prerogatives enjoyed by the union were abolished in order to place the docks in a competitive position with the rest of the world. In December it was the turn of the railroads, which Frondizi had already tried to modernize, at the cost of prolonged strikes. As in the port, the methods of rationalization ran up against worker protests; in both cases, however, an imposing military presence minimized union resistance. The northern province of Tucumán was a permanent centre of conflict and unrest due to the bankruptcy of the sugar mills, several of which were closed by the government under a somewhat improvised program to do away with the sugar monoculture of the region.

This series of forceful measures seemed to exhaust the repertory of responses of the new administration. It was generally thought that Onganía had stepped into office with a broad plan of action already prepared. However, during the first six months, outside of directing a number of coercive operations, he did nothing but announce grand policy objectives in which it was impossible to perceive any clear innovative economic programme. He had entrusted the Ministry of Economy to a newly rich and militantly Catholic entrepreneur, who failed to make any progress towards the declared objective of putting an end to the inflation-ary, nationalist and expansive policies of the immediate past. The difficulties that had plagued Illia's government intensified. The year 1966 ended with no growth in the national product, a decline in the level of investment, a squeeze in the balance of payments and an inflation rate that refused to decline. The government was slowly discredited among the large national and foreign firms that had applauded its installation. The major unions which had supported the new military regime soon faced the reality of a situation quite different from what they had imagined. On 1 December 1966, the CGT initiated a plan of agitation that would culminate in a national strike.

Thus the Argentine Revolution found itself on the defensive at the end of 1966. Onganía had alienated those who had supported him and was under pressure on the military front. In December came a turning point in the fate of the regime. The appointment of General Julio Alsogaray as commander-in-chief of the army marked the end of the days in which the positions of power were occupied by persons close to the president. Alsogaray was a critic of the nationalist Catholic current led by Organía and, through his brother, the former minister of economy, Alvaro Alsogaray, he was closely linked to the economic establishment. At the same time, Onganía appointed Adalbert Krieger Vasena to the Ministry of Economy. A minister during Aramburu's presidency and member of the boards of directors of important national and foreign companies closely connected with international financial institutions, Krieger Vasena enjoyed great prestige and was reputedly a liberal economist with pragmatic tendencies.

On political matters, however, Onganía was not prepared to compromise. His new minister of the interior shared his predecessor's view that the political reconstruction of Argentina must be sought through channels other than those of liberal, democratic constitutionalism. The attempt to substitute political pluralism with a community organized around a strong state continued to provoke irritation in liberal circles of the Right. These people knew that the electoral game condemned them to choose among political options all of which were unsatisfactory; lacking sufficient electoral power, they saluted the decision to replace politics with administration but they distrusted Onganía's corporatist nonsense. The president announced that the Argentine Revolution would unfold in three stages: the economic phase, destined to achieve stability and the modernization of the country; the social phase, which would allow for the distribution of the profits reaped during the initial stage; and finally the political phase, with which the revolution would culminate, by transferring power to authentically representative organizations. This grandiose plan, which would take at least ten years to carry out, clarified the role Onganía had reserved for Krieger Vasena and his team of liberal economists: to bring about the economic reorganization of the country so they could then be discarded when the social phase began. The new order pursued by Onganía was as alien to the kind of democracy desired by big business as it was to that sought by the masses. A critic of partyocracy, the president was also critical of capitalism, which was guilty, in his eyes, of a social egotism equally detrimental to the spiritual integration of the nation.

While Onganía was operating on the political and cultural plane with schemes that had become extinct thirty years before, Krieger Vasena launched a programme that differed significantly from earlier stabilization policies. He began by abandoning the 'crawling peg' with a devaluation of the peso of the order of 40 per cent, in a move to extinguish once and for all any speculation on future devaluations. But the real innovation was that this was the first attempt at fully compensated devaluation. Thus, taxes were levied on traditional exports at the same time that import duties were reduced. This meant that the *net* prices of exports and imports changed very little. The inflationary impact of the devaluation was thus minimized and, in the case of export taxes, the government availed itself of much-needed resources for public accounts.

Another central component of the stabilization programme was the establishment of an obligatory income policy. Wages, after being re-adjusted to average 1966 levels, were frozen for two years. Agreements were signed with the five hundred most important companies to ensure that prices would reflect increases only in basic costs. In exchange for the suspension of collective bargaining the unions merely received the promise that real wages would remain constant, while the incentives to get the companies to agree to the price controls were preferential access to bank credit and to government purchasing contracts. Coming from a minister with a background like Krieger Vasena's, the income policy was a complete innovation; it reflected the belief that the markets of goods and wages in a closed economy like Argentina's were far from competitive — a more realistic view than that of other traditional programmes with liberal roots.

The attack on the fiscal deficit was accomplished by improving tax collection, raising charges for public services and reducing public employment and losses in state enterprises. This helped the public sector to play a major role in the rapid expansion of investment, which nearly reached the levels of the boom of 1960–1, this time financed basically by internal savings. Rejecting the opinion of orthodox monetarists, Krieger Vasena opted for an expansive monetary policy to avoid the risks of recession. Banking credit to the private sector grew significantly, in part because the severe fiscal policy permitted a reduction in loans to the state by the Central Bank.

Furthermore, Krieger Vasena succeeded in winning the confidence of the economic community by eliminating exchange controls, renewing contracts with the foreign oil companies and signing a new agreement with the IMF. Conceived as a global economic adjustment to address the needs of the most dynamic and concentrated groups, the programme required other sectoral interests to contribute. Rural producers ceded part of the extraordinary profits derived from the devaluation in the form of taxes on exports; industry had to compete with cheaper imported goods; the unions were deprived of collective bargaining; state enterprises and public administration had to go through a process of rationalization.

The launching of this programme in March 1967 coincided with a great defeat for the unions. The Plan of Action they announced had elicited a severe response from the government. By way of warning, the bank accounts of several unions were frozen; the juridical recognition which was indispensable for them to function was withdrawn from others, and the regime threatened to dissolve the CGT. On 6 March the workers' confederation decided to cancel its protest. A few days later it received the coup de grace when Krieger Vasena suspended collective negotiations, reserving the ability to fix wages to the state for two years.

The collapse of the tactic of strike first, negotiate later, by which the unions had acted until then, provoked a serious crisis of leadership. The majority of the labour leaders chose to take a step backwards, taking refuge in prudent passivity. A smaller but still significant group approached the government in the hope of receiving the small favours that Onganía occasionally handed out to compensate for the oppressiveness of his policies. The president's ambiguous relationship with the liberal economists who surrounded Krieger Vasena awakened, in certain leaders, hopes of re-creating the old nationalist alliance between the armed forces and the unions. The labour movement entered into a long period of political retreat. Thus, the government could boast that in 1967 the man-days lost to strikes were only 242,953 as against 1,664,800 in 1966.

In the meantime, Krieger Vasena's economic programme was bearing fruit. Towards the end of 1968, the annual inflation rate had fallen from

30 per cent to less than 10 per cent, and the economy was beginning to achieve sustained growth. Although the economic reactivation of 1967 and 1968 was fuelled primarily by state investment, especially in public works, the entrance of short-term foreign capital strengthened net reserves of foreign currency and compensated for the unsatisfactory performance of the trade balance. In both 1967 and 1968 the growth of agricultural production did not prevent the net value of exports from falling below the 1963 level due to the deterioration in the terms of trade which had begun in 1964 and would continue until 1972. Moreover, other problems that would deepen over time were coming to light as the strategy of import substitution, based on an internal market protected by tariff barriers, was reaching its limit.

The economic successes of these two years, however, did not broaden the popularity of the military regime. Krieger Vasena's policy, backed by the most powerful factions in the business community, entailed heavy costs for many sectors. The complaints with which rural producers had greeted the export taxes became more shrill when there was an attempt to institute a tax on land in order to stimulate productivity and combat fiscal evasion. Small and medium-sized companies saw their access to cheap credit closed and the tariff protection they had enjoyed in the immediate past eliminated, and they accused the minister of trying to weaken them to the end of concentrating and de-nationalizing the economy. Although wage losses were not very large, the unions were unhappy with the freezing of their power to exert pressure. This accumulation of tension in a variety of sectors nourished growing discontent.

The suppression of the political system had allowed Onganía to protect the state from the play of pressures that had in the past paralysed more than one government. But, inevitably, a dangerous rift was opening up between the forces of civilian society and a state power that was becoming increasingly remote and authoritarian. In an attempt to isolate himself from the exigencies of the economic groups, Onganía undertook little innovation. But while previous presidents had also tried this to safeguard their policies, he made a philosophy of government out of what for others had only been a defensive attitude. Thus, his disdain and arrogance made interest groups feel that all he expected from them was unquestioning adherence to the official line.

Onganía's autocratic style also affected his relations with the military establishment. Repeating on every occasion that presented itself that 'the armed forces neither govern nor co-govern', he was deaf to anxieties in the military hierarchy about the way the revolution was going. In August 1968 this conflictive coexistence finally reached a crisis, and Onganía fired the commanders-in-chief of all three military branches. Stepping down, General Alsogaray explicitly criticized the 'absolutist and personal conception of authority' held by the president, at the same time denouncing the government's 'unclear orientation in political matters'. His successor as head of the army, General Alejandro Lanusse, shared these points of view, and as a result Onganía became progressively more isolated from his comrades at arms.

The fateful year of 1969 began with promising signs for the economy. The level of activity continued to rise, the year closing with an exceptional increase in GDP of 8.9 per cent; the annual inflation rate was about 7 per cent in May; while in the month before the launching of Krieger Vasena's programme net reserves of foreign currency were U.S. $176 million, in April they were $694 million. These successes were the product of the social and political truce imposed by the government. The question was whether these achievements could become permanent.

In spite of the success of the anti-inflation policy, exchange rates had fallen to levels below the devaluation of March 1967. To compensate for inflation, Krieger Vasena kept reducing export taxes, but without being able to avoid a deterioration in the relative prices of agricultural products. Real income, frozen at 1966 levels, also declined. These incipient difficulties, however, did not alter the regime's smugness about the healthy performance of the economy and the solid order imposed on society. The sporadic conflicts that flared up tended to die out rapidly, and it seemed as if political life had been reduced to a domestic quarrel in which Onganía opposed his liberal critics of the Right about the future of the revolution. Nevertheless, there was evidence of the high potential for protest that lay beneath the surface of this authoritarian 'peace'.

In March 1968 a congress was convened to elect officers to the CGT, which had been leaderless since the resignation of those responsible for the great defeat of March 1967. A new, highly radicalized leadership emerged with the backing of the unions most affected by the government's policies. The traditional, more moderate wing of the union movement, represented by Augusto Vandor, then decided to call another congress and create an alternative confederation. The militant CGT issued calls to battle that initially had some response but then lost power, in part due to repression but above all because of defections to Vandor's side. More important in the long run were the series of conflicts at the plant level that began to break out in the industrial zones of the interior, where a new generation of union leaders was beginning to appear at the head of workers' committees imbued with leftist ideology.

In March 1969, in protest against the university authorities, students in the city of Corrientes took to the streets, and on the 15th one of them was killed by the police. The protest extended to the rest of the universities, particularly in Rosario, where another student died and the city was the scene of a vast popular uprising. The governor of Córdoba added a new stimulus to the protest by withholding some fringe benefits enjoyed by the workers of his province, the second most highly industrialized in the country. On 15 May there were sharp confrontations with the police and on the next day a general strike was declared. A few days later came the event which would be called '*el cordobazo*': on 29 and 30 May, workers and students occupied the centre of the city. Overwhelmed by the angry crowd and attacked by snipers, the police retreated. With the city in their hands for several hours, the mob turned to burning and sacking government offices and the property of foreign firms. The rebellion was quelled only when the city was occupied by troops.

The events of May provoked astonishment and alarm. The violence in the streets, which amounted to popular insurrection, were expressions of protest that had few antecedents in recent history. It was true that since 1955 political struggle had not taken place only within the legal framework, but the political and labour leaders had always managed to avoid being overwhelmed by their supporters. In fact, they appealed to mass mobilization only as a tactic of compromise. In 1966 Onganía closed off the legal and extra-legal mechanisms within which this political game had been played. The result was the rapid loss of authority by the leaders of the popular movement. The parties fell into a state of paralysis, the labour leaders had to retreat and Perón himself became little more than a political corpse when he lost the electoral stage from which he had managed to undermine both civil and military governments.

In this way, Onganía paved the way for the acts of spontaneous rebellion that were to come. In spite of the repressive measures, the events of May had set an example. Popular uprisings in the cities of the interior now proliferated, wildcat strikes multiplied in open defiance of national union leadership and student unrest took over the universities. Finally, urban guerrilla warfare made its appearance.

The extent and nature of this emerging opposition alarmed the ranks of the Argentine Revolution and opened up a debate about what path to take. General Aramburu, who had remained on the sidelines of the government, began to advocate a retreat negotiated on the basis of the rehabilitation of the political parties. It would be incumbent on them to accomplish the double task of channelling the protest and placing their votes at the service of a presidential candidate acceptable to the armed forces. The proposal did not gain favour: the return of the political class which had so recently been guilty of the crisis of governance was hardly an attractive option. New reverses would be necessary before the idea would finally be approved by the military establishment.

Under the psychological impact of the wave of protest, solidarity initially prevailed within the military, the officer corps closing ranks behind Onganía. The president took advantage of this situation to remove Krieger Vasena, install a *tecnico* with no political background as minister of economy and breathe new life into his corporatist project. In this context, there was a sudden worsening of the economic situation. Uncertainty over the stability of the peso following Krieger Vasena's resignation gave way to a massive flight of capital. Both the economic expansion and the prevailing speculative climate led to a heavy increase in imports. In sum, the reduction of foreign currency reserves was so sudden that the new authorities were forced to impose a more restrictive monetary policy. The recent favourable expectations had turned, by the end of 1969, to a generalized scepticism. Prices began to rise again, affecting the fixed rate of exchange, which the Ministry of Economy obstinately insisted on maintaining as a symbol of continuity. Weakness in the balance of payments together with inflationary tensions created irresistible pressure for a new devaluation.

The optimistic outlook of members of the economic establishment also came to an end with Krieger Vasena's resignation. Their discontent increased proportionately as Onganía announced the imminent arrival of the social phase of the revolution in an effort to contain the proliferation of conflicts. A promise to restore collective bargaining and a law granting labour leaders control of the vast resources of social union funds were gestures in this direction. But the labour leaders were in no condition to dampen popular activism. Even the police were not able to secure the tottering authoritarian order. The armed forces were increasingly obliged to resort to repression, and this led them to press for greater say in policy. But Onganía defended his autocratic prerogatives, and when in June 1970 he refused to share the responsibilities of leadership, the junta decided to depose him.

The Argentina that Onganía left behind was not the same one he had found. His regime had proposed to eradicate political conflict forever, but in the end exacerbated it severely. In his search for a new order, Onganía had eroded the very bases of the modus vivendi within which, at the price of a high level of institutional volatility, the Argentine people had previously resolved their differences. The shattering of this fragile and almost underground system of political coexistence freed forces animated by a violence hitherto unknown. Born in the heart of the middle class, the armed resistance movement left the military and politicians facing a formidable challenge. The attempt to exorcise this simultaneously bewildering and threatening presence would inflict on Argentina its deepest and most lasting wounds.

The guerrilla groups were evolving along the classical model of full-time clandestine militants common in Latin America at this time and similar to those witnessed in Argentina in 1959 and 1964. With the passage of time, they managed to create true organizations of the masses, whose members participated in armed violence to differing extents. It was the broad acceptance the guerrillas achieved among middle-class youth that lent the Argentine experience its most distinctive feature. The two most important guerrilla groups were the Ejército Revolucionario del Pueblo (ERP) of Trotskyist leanings, and the *peronista* Montoneros, so called in memory of the irregular armies of gauchos who fought in the North against Spanish troops during the wars of independence. While the Trotskyist guerrillas saw their acts as an extension of the social struggle, the armed branch of the *peronista* youth wanted to intervene in the political conflicts, including those of the *peronista* movement itself. Its objective was to neutralize any chance of a political resolution of the military crisis, to punish every manifestation of collaboration; thus, the Montoneros took responsibility for kidnapping and later assassinating General Aramburu and for murdering prominent union leaders, among them Vandor.

After Onganía was ousted, the first act of the junta was to reorganize the structure of military power. To avoid a repetition of recent experience, the chiefs of the three branches required the president to consult them on all important decisions. General Rodolfo Levingston, an almost unknown officer who the commanders believed to be above all factional military disputes, was appointed as head of state and entrusted with the task of constructing an efficient, stable and democratic political system.

At least this was the belief of General Lanusse, the army commander who was the real architect of the change of direction and who decisively influenced the composition of the new cabinet, the majority of which was associated with the so-called liberal current within the armed forces. The Ministry of Economy was assigned to a former colleague of Krieger Vasena, Carlos Moyano Llerena. In the emergency, Moyano resorted to measures similar to those taken in March 1967: he devalued the peso from 350 to 400 to the dollar, enabling the government to appropriate funds by imposing new taxes on exports; he lowered import tariffs and called for voluntary price agreements. However, this formula failed to repeat its earlier success, because the political context had changed radically. The devaluation was interpreted as a signal of future changes in parity of the currency, and the acceleration of the inflation rate to more than 20 per cent in 1970 generated heavy pressure on wages. The government was no longer in any condition to turn a deaf ear to the demands of the unions; in September it had to concede a general raise of 7 per cent and promise another 6 per cent at the beginning of 1971. The previous administration's policy of monetary contraction became untenable in the face of rising prices and salaries, so that the money supply had to expand at the same rate as the rise in prices in the second half of 1970. From January 1971 the dollar was also adjusted in small monthly increments. At this point, the eclipse of the policy of stabilization was total.

The result was that the new direction of the military regime was also put in jeopardy. Levingston seemed unwilling to settle for the mission entrusted to him and took upon himself a more elevated role: that of preparing a 'new model for Argentina' based on a more 'hierarchical and orderly' democracy than that associated with the return of the old parties. For this it would be necessary to 'deepen the revolution', an enigmatic slogan the extent of which was revealed in October 1970, when Levingston reorganized the cabinet and prepared to leave his mark on the already convulsed history of the Argentine Revolution.

He named as minister of economy Aldo Ferrer, an economist with ideas diametrically opposed to those of his predecessors, linked to the ideology of the UN Economic Commission for Latin America (ECLA) and favourable to the fortification of state and national industry. The nationalist rhetoric that coloured Ferrer's term appealed to the sentiments of the middle sectors of the Argentine bourgeoisie and the officer corps, which had been alienated by Krieger Vasena's policies favouring big business and foreign capital. The new direction involved a return to protectionism with a rise in import duties, restrictions on foreign investment and the enactment of a law which obliged state enterprises to give priority in their purchases to local supplies. In the short run, Ferrer, besieged by a wave of sectoral demands, prudently limited himself to administrating inflationary pressures through a gradual indexing of the economy.

Prudence, however, was not a characteristic of Levingston's political conduct. After getting rid of the ministers imposed on him by the junta, he sought the support of political figures who had been deprived of nearly all popular following during the vicissitudes of recent times. With their help and the use of nationalist and populist slogans, he attempted to create a new political movement, and this awoke the traditional parties from their lethargy. In November 1970, *peronistas,* Radicals and other minority groups gave birth to the 'Hora del Pueblo', a coalition designed to force the holding of elections. The years spent under military rule had brought the former rivals together in the common demand for a return to democracy. This was particularly striking because since 1955 one side or the other had participated in military coups, hoping either to win influence in the government (the *peronistas* in 1966) or to be its electoral heirs (the Radicals in the Revolución Libertadora).

The reappearance of the parties dealt a rude blow to Levingston's ambitions. His nationalist and populist line, while it antagonized conservative circles, made little impact on those to whom it was directed. Both the unions and the middle class preferred to align themselves with the new opposition than to associate themselves with a president who was growing increasingly isolated. The power structure erected by the military commanders had slipped out of their hands, but they vacillated in the face of their failure. Eventually, Levingston's audacious indiscretions facilitated matters for them. In February 1971 he appointed to the unsettled province of Córdoba a governor whose outlook was close to the fascist conservatism of the 1930s and who began his term with a defiant speech in which he announced exceptionally punitive measures. The response was a new popular uprising, no less violent and widespread than the one of 1969. This second '*cordobazo*' precipitated a national crisis, and on 22 March the junta removed Levingston and assumed the reins of power again.

Thus began the last phase of the military regime, directed at the re-establishment of the democratic institutions. Lacking the cohesion and the capacity for repression necessary to restore the original objectives of 1966, the armed forces began a search for a political solution that would enable them to control the wave of popular protest and return to their barracks. General Lanusse was appointed president and immediately unfolded the new strategy, legalizing the parties and calling for a broad agreement between the military and the political forces to draw up the rules of institutional transition.

The novelty of this initiative was that it included *peronismo*. For the first time since 1955, the armed forces were ready to accept *peronismo,* admitting that any political solution that excluded Perón was illusory and short-sighted. 'Perón is a reality, whether we like it or not', Lanusse recognized publicly,[7] putting an end to one of the most costly taboos of the Argentine military. Perhaps no other officer could have dared to say it. As a young lieutenant, Lanusse had been imprisoned under Perón's first presidency. Moreover, his credentials as a representative of the liberal wing of the army were impeccable, and his family ties linked him to the economic establishment. This background and the prestige he enjoyed among his colleagues, thanks to a style quite distinct from the gruff arrogance of Onganía and Levingston, made him a trustworthy leader for the daring political manoeuvre that lay before him.

What brought the military to negotiate with Perón was not its traditional reluctance to come to terms with the role of the working class in national politics but the threat posed by the middle-class youth movement. The youth radicalized at the end of the 1960s in the struggle against the military regime had adopted *peronismo* as a way of identifying themselves with the people. In a historical twist, the sons of those who most firmly opposed Perón turned their backs on their parents to embrace the very cause they had fought against. Under the spell of the ideas of Che Guevara and Franz Fanon and the theology of liberation, the protagonists of this political patricide transformed Perón and *peronismo* into the militant embodiment of a national socialism. Lanusse's idea was that, once included in the political system, Perón would withdraw ideological support for the revolutionary movement that was invoking his name. A curious paradox of history became apparent: he who once had been identified with one-half of the country came to be everything to everyone. Perón was now called upon to apply his remarkable skills to the rescue of a drifting polity. In 1972 the very governability of the country was at stake.

Lanusse's strategy was close to that which inspired the conservative elite in the first decade of the century, when it resolved to guarantee free, secret elections in order to allow the participation of the Radical Party. Then, too, it was judged less dangerous to incorporate the Radicals into the

[7] *Clarín,* 28 July 1972; quoted in L. de Riz, *Retorno y derrumbe, el último gobierno peronista* (Buenos Aires, 1987), p. 46.

system than to leave them out and exposed to revolutionary temptations. However, the conservative elite lost control of the process it launched and the Radicals, led by Yrigoyen, instead of occupying the subordinate position reserved for them, ended up by taking over the government. As time passed, this historical parallel would become much more direct than Lanusse was initially willing to admit.

Lanusse's proposal was aimed at ensuring the participation of *peronismo* under controlled conditions. The *peronistas* would be able to run for any elective office except the presidency. Furthermore, Perón was to disavow publicly the Peronist guerrillas. This proposal, negotiated in secret by agents sent by Lanusse to talk with Perón in Madrid, was part of a broader agreement in which all the major political forces were invited to give their support to a common presidential candidate acceptable to the armed forces. Lanusse received a favourable response from the *peronista* politicians and even the union leaders, for whom a return to democracy promised positions of greater influence. The unknown factor was the attitude Perón himself would take after years of sabotaging the political arrangements painstakingly engineered by those who had overthrown and banned him.

Beyond the historical reparation the negotiation itself implied, Perón was offered the cancellation of all the penalties that had been pending against him since 1955 and something else that was particularly symbolic. In September 1971, the military delivered to him the embalmed body of Evita, which fifteen years earlier had been transported secretly to Europe and buried in an Italian cemetery under another name. Nevertheless, Perón side-stepped the commitments being asked of him. Determined to exploit the initiative given to him by the military crisis, he followed an ambiguous course, leaving open all the possibilities the situation offered. Furthermore, even he, like so many others, could not be absolutely certain about the final outcome.

In October 1971 a military uprising was led by officers sympathetic to Onganía and Levingston, who accused Lanusse of betraying the goals of the revolution and of handing the country over to the old politicians. The rebellion was easily put down, but it changed the conditions of negotiation. Lanusse was so identified with the election that if it failed it was not certain whether he could maintain his leadership of the armed forces. Perón took advantage of this to continue encouraging the guerrillas and to reduce his concessions to a minimum; he made things more tense by forcing the elections to be held on his own terms rather than on terms that were supposedly being imposed on him. In the process he also took into account the widespread repudiation that surrounded the military domination and encouraged the increasingly bold actions of the guerrillas to be viewed with a certain benevolence. The repressive measures, both brutal and ineffective, that were employed against the guerrilla involvement contributed to the military's loss of face, both at home and abroad.

The military government found itself obliged simply to follow the dynamic of the process which it itself had unleashed. Less dramatic circumstances had led to the coup d'état of 1966. This time, however, nothing was done to interrupt the elections scheduled for March 1973. Fear of an explosive fusion between popular discontent and the guerrilla movement strengthened the decision to institutionalize the country. As had occurred every time the prospect of an election was reopened, Perón became a pole of attraction, and he easily manipulated his renewed popularity to build up a network of alliances. Thus, without ceasing to praise the guerrillas, he began to move in two other directions. First, towards the Radicals, with whom he forged a pact of mutual guarantees in which he declared himself respectful of the rights of minority parties at the same time as he demanded that his old enemies promise to hold elections with no vetoes or proscriptions. Second, he began to approach interest groups through Frondizi, whom he included in a political-electoral alliance which proposed nothing that could alarm the landowners and businessmen.

Time worked against Lanusse, who was unable to display the promised fruits of his strategy before his comrades. The Radical Party was not willing to play the role assigned to it. Although it did not oppose official policy so as not to provoke a coup d'état, neither did it wish to support the plans of those who had defeated it in 1966. Lanusse's situation became even more complicated in the middle of 1972, when Perón, in Madrid, revealed the hitherto secret contacts with his emissaries. The furor this produced in official circles could be calmed only when Lanusse publicly announced that he was withdrawing his candidacy for president. This decision was followed by another, obviously directed at Perón, whereby a time limit was set for all candidates to establish residence in the country. Although protesting, the exiled caudillo carefully avoided challenging the outer limits of the now restless military government's tolerance. When the deadline arrived in November 1972, Perón returned to Argentina after an absence of seventeen years, and remained for several weeks. 'I have no hatred or rancour. It is not a time for revenge. I return as a pacifier of spirits'[8] were his words to the Argentine people, who welcomed him with a mixture of amazement and disbelief.

During his stay Perón sealed his reconciliation with the leader of the Radicals, Ricardo Balbín, and lay the cornerstone of the electoral front that would unite the *peronistas,* the Partido Conservador Popular, the followers of Frondizi, the Partido Popular Cristiano and some Socialists. Back in Madrid he named Hector Cámpora, a minor politician known for his dogged fidelity to the populist leader and his recent close links with militant *peronista* youth, as the front's presidential candidate – a decision which provoked visible resentment among union leaders and the moderate politicians in the movement, who felt unjustly passed over. Cámpora, furthermore, came under the electoral restrictions imposed by the government, and many suspected that Perón wanted his candidate to be disqualified, in a new twist of his changing political tactics. Lanusse decided not to respond to this last-minute challenge by Perón. On 11 March 1973, the *peronista* coalition obtained 49 per cent of the votes, the Radicals 21 per cent, the parties of the Right 15 per cent and a leftist front 7 per cent. After the ostentatious failure of Lanusse's strategy, the military abandoned the government, taking as their consolation a vision of the old caudillo facing the titanic task that they had not been able to accomplish: that of constructing a political order capable of maintaining control over the expectations and passions unleashed by nearly two decades of frustration and discord.

THE RETURN AND FALL OF PERÓN 1973 – 6

Once the votes had been counted and Cámpora's government installed, the political situation rapidly evolved towards an institutional crisis. Encouraged by the backing received from Perón, radical elements accompanied the new president into office and began to practice the politics of mass mobilization. Under Cámpora's complacent gaze, worker revolts in defiance of the union leadership occurred on a daily basis, and many public buildings were occupied by bands of *peronista* youth. The objective that unified this militant offensive was to regain both the government and the movement for the new generation of socialist *peronismo*. Under these conditions, the conflicts that had hitherto been latent within the conglomeration of forces which had supported the return of *peronismo* to power now broke out into the open.

[8] Quoted in L. de Riz, *Retorno y derrumbe*, p. 63.

The union chiefs – who had been ignored in the operation that led to the military's defeat – manifested their alarm over a political process that shunned traditional values. This preoccupation was already bothering Perón as well and the members of the intimate circle that accompanied him in exile, notably José López Rega, his secretary, a former chief of police and *aficionado* of the occult sciences. Scarcely forty-nine days after having been sworn in as president, Cámpora was forced to resign, and new elections placed Perón himself in the presidency, with his wife, Isabel, as vice-president. The balloting, held in September 1973, gave the victory to the Perón–Perón ticket with 62 per cent of the votes cast. The magnitude of the electoral triumph was a clear indication that many of his former enemies had decided to vote for the old caudillo in the hope that he would now impose control on his young followers. Two days after the elections, even before the celebrations were over, Perón received an ominous warning when the secretary-general of the CGT, José Rucci, one of his most loyal adherents, was assassinated by the guerrillas.

The tactical shift that would alienate Perón from his young admirers of the Left had been announced on 20 June, the day he returned to live permanently in Argentina. Nearly 2 million people were waiting for him at Ezeiza Airport, most of them under the banners of the revolutionary tendencies of *peronismo*. What should have been a great popular celebration turned into a pitched battle, with many deaths and injuries, when armed bands of the Right and the Left confronted one another. The aeroplane in which Perón was flying was diverted to another airport.

That night, Perón gave a speech revealing the political project with which he was returning.[9] He began with a call for demobilization: 'We have a revolution to make, but for it to be valid it must be a peaceful reconstruction. We are in no condition to keep destroying in the face of a destiny pregnant with ambushes and dangers. It is necessary to return to what in its time was our maxim: from work to home and from home to work'. His new vision of the political community was reflected in this announcement: '*Justicialismo* was never sectarian or exclusive and today it calls upon all Argentines without distinction so that all of us, with solidarity, will join together in the task of national reconstruction'. Later, this summons was more explicit, when he replaced the slogan 'Nothing is better for a *peronista* than another *peronista*', which had divided the country during his first two presidencies, with a new one, 'Nothing is better for an

---

[9] *La Nación,* 21 June 1974; quoted in L. de Riz, *Retorno y derrumbe,* p. 90.

Argentine than another Argentine'. His final words were dedicated to dashing the hopes for a doctrinaire renewal which he himself had stimulated during his last years in exile. 'We are *justicialistas*. We fly a flag that is as distant from one of the dominant imperialisms as from the other. . . . There are no new labels that qualify our doctrine. Those who naïvely think they can corner our movement or take away the power that the people have reconquered are mistaken'.

With this message, Perón validated the bold decision that Lanusse had made two years earlier. To the bewilderment of the young *peronistas,* Perón now set about reversing the shift to the left that marked the struggle against the military regime and that Cámpora erroneously converted into government policy. After the electoral triumph, the ERP ratified its subversive strategy, but the Montoneros suspended their activities, indicating that their future conduct would depend on the new government keeping to its revolutionary promises. Thus, the head of the Montoneros, Mario Firmenich, when asked whether they were abandoning the use of force, answered:

By no means; political power comes out of the mouth of the rifle. If we have come up to this point, it is because we had rifles and we used them. If we abandoned them we would suffer a setback in our political position. In war there are moments of confrontation, such as those which we have gone through, and there are moments of truce, in which preparations are made for the next confrontation.[10]

The change observed in Perón's attitude confronted the young *peronistas* with an agonizing alternative between breaking with him and being excluded from the popular coalition united around his leadership.

The dissidence of the young did not exhaust the questions raised by *peronismo*'s return to power. If Perón now seemed able to change the policies that he had advocated from the opposition, could the same flexibility be expected from a movement that had remained formidable over the previous eighteen years and hardly felt committed to an institutional system in which its participation could at any time be curtailed? How could Perón impress the need for political coexistence on those who had been led into an undisguised sectarianism by constant proscriptions? How could he convince those who had seen the relentless diminution of their share of income that it was prudent to make the demands of labour compatible with the stability of the economy? Finally, how could Perón

---

[10] *El Descamisado,* 11 September 1973; quoted in Guido Di Tella, *Perón–Perón 1973–1976* (Buenos Aires, 1983), p. 55.

wrest a commitment to peace from those whose violence he had previously endorsed?

The old caudillo's call for conciliation had a more favourable reception among his enemies than among his followers. In Perón's message the former saw a promise for political order in an Argentina shaken by conflict and violence; the latter, by contrast, wanted the electoral triumph to herald their historical vindication. When he came into power in 1946, Perón had faced a similar challenge. But then there had been an energetic and ambitious caudillo in the center of the populist coalition; the Perón who now returned to tame the hopes and passions unleashed by his return was a man of seventy-eight years, in poor health.

During the remaining ten months of his life, Perón invested the still vigorous powers of his charisma in channelling the diffuse and virulent aspirations of his followers and in reconstructing the battered political system he had inherited. The two instruments of his institutional project were the political agreement between the major parties represented in Congress (*peronistas* and Radicals) and the Social Pact between business and the unions. His goal was an 'integrated democracy' in which the old organic model of the organized community was expanded to place the interest groups and the political parties on an equal footing. The attitude towards the armed forces was, in turn, another expression of the new times. During Cámpora's brief administration, the command of the army was exercised by General Jorge Carcagno, who strongly advocated the unity of the armed forces with the people in a pathetic attempt to accommodate himself to the complex situation created by the *peronista* victory. When he became president, Perón ordered changes in the military hierarchy. An apolitical commander-in-chief was appointed to replace Carcagno, who by his overtures to the government had alienated himself from the sentiments dominant among his comrades. With this gesture, Perón meant to underline the professional and non-political role he had reserved for the armed forces during his third presidential term.

Cámpora's original cabinet was purged of its leftist elements, who were replaced by trusted veterans. The two most important figures who survived the purge were López Rega, in the Ministry of Social Welfare, and José Gelbard, in the Ministry of Economy. President of the Confederación General Económica (CGE), the association representing the national bourgeoisie, Gelbard was linked to Perón from the years of his second presidency. His economic programme was mildly nationalist and redistributionist, with a strong accent on state intervention in the economy. The key

component was an incomes policy based on a tripartite agreement among
the government, business and the unions, with which Gelbard tried to
contain the inflationary pressures that dominated the last years of the
military regime. In 1971 and 1972, the rise in price levels was 39.2 and
64.2 per cent, respectively, moving up in the first five months of 1973 to
an annual rate of 100 per cent.

Together with rising inflation, Gelbard also faced a growing economy.
After the peak reached in the year of the *cordobazo* – 8.5 per cent in
1969 – the rate of economic growth continued at 5.4 per cent in 1970,
4.8 per cent in 1971, descending to 3.2 per cent in 1972 and rising again
to 5.1 per cent in the first quarter of 1973. This growth had begun in
1964; during the ten years since then, the economy had been growing at
an average annual rate of 4 per cent. However, this remarkable performance, which was fuelled by sustained growth in exports and the maturation of investments since the Frondizi era, was clouded by the persistence
of conflict and the instability of prices. The new administration, therefore,
was concerned about a gloomy future that current economic indicators did
not reflect.

The political movement galvanized by nostalgia for Perón's earlier presidencies naturally exhibited a dominant preoccupation with the standard of
living of the workers. The decline in real wages in 1972 reflected a real fall
in the contribution of wage-earners to national income: from the 46.5 per
cent it had reached in 1952 it had tumbled to less than 38 per cent in June
1973. The memory of one of Frondizi's first decisions after being elected
with the *peronista* vote – a general salary increase of 60 per cent –
encouraged optimistic forecasts by many union leaders, including Minister of Labour Ricardo Otero, a member of the metal-workers' union. The
increase granted under the Social Pact, however, was only 20 per cent, and
it was accompanied by the suspension of collective bargaining for two
years as well as a price freeze.

The signing of the price and wage agreement did not meet with much
resistance in the business community, many members of which had anticipated it and already increased their prices. Moreover, the general moderation of the measures facilitated acceptance by those who feared more
demagogic policies. In order to obtain the consent of the unions, Perón
had to explore all his political authority. The unions grudgingly gave up
the freedom to negotiate – a permanent demand under the military
regime – since their weak political position within the *peronista* movement
left them no alternative. However, by signing the Social Pact, the union

leaders reverted to *peronista* orthodoxy, from which they had been alienated so many times in the past. This allowed them to regain Perón's approval; with his backing they led the offensive against the radicalized youth and got from Congress a law that further suppressed internal union democracy and protected their positions from the anti-bureaucratic rebellion that had been under way since the *cordobazo*.

The change in expectations provoked by the Social Pact was impressive. While in the first five months of 1973 the cost of living had risen by about 37 per cent, from July to December it rose by only 4 per cent. Furthermore, with exports 65 per cent higher than those of the previous year and imports that had increased in value about 36 per cent, the trade balance by the end of 1973 was 30 per cent higher than in 1972. But it was in the external sector that the first negative signs appeared to cast a shadow over this optimistic picture. By December the effects of the oil crisis reached the Argentine economy, provoking a sharp increase in the price of imports. Given the freeze on prices, the higher cost of imported goods began to erode business profit margins; some companies interrupted or cut down production, and all joined the clamour against the rigid price policy. Gelbard tried to sanction a resolution authorizing companies to pass on higher costs in the form of higher prices, but Perón forbade this at the demand of the unions, which threatened to withdraw from the Social Pact.

The unions' refusal to approve a rise in prices without a simultaneous rise in wages was fully understandable. While the signing of the Social Pact had frozen their institutional power, labour mobilization had been given new vigour by the electoral triumph. After the *peronista* government took office, conflict at the plant level multiplied, fuelled by disputes over working conditions, disciplinary regulations, dismissals, etc.; the rank and file were in a general state of rebellion. Harassed by the flourishing leftist elements that viewed the Social Pact as a betrayal, the union chiefs blocked Gelbard's proposal, which favoured business. The emergency solution was to resort to the foreign currency reserves built up by the excellent external balance in order to subsidize the purchase of critical supplies with a preferential exchange rate.

However, confidence in the income policy now began to collapse, as was demonstrated by the proliferation of the black market. In addition to the pressure exerted by business for greater price flexibility, at a plant level workers' delegates obtained, through the device of job reclassification or increased bonuses for productivity, hidden salary increases. Meanwhile, an obvious incongruity was becoming apparent between the rigid price policy and the permissive monetary policy adopted to manage a fiscal deficit that exceeded 6 per cent of the GNP.

At the beginning of 1974 the need to revise the price and wage agreements became imperative, and in February Gelbard convened the CGE and the CGT. After several weeks, the parties had to admit that compromise was impossible and Perón was obliged to intercede between them. The arbitration handed down on 28 March established a salary increase 5 to 6 per cent greater than the deterioration in real wages and authorized the companies to raise prices by an amount to be decided by the government. Although the leaders of the CGT were hoping for a greater increase, the decision was interpreted as favourable to the workers. When price levels were announced in April, profit margins were fixed at less than the level demanded by business, which began to launch a systematic and generalized violation of the Social Pact. Between April and May the cost of living rose 7.7 per cent, whereas in January it had increased only 2.8 per cent. The resumption of the income struggle soon converted zero inflation into a thing of the past.

Perón's last public appearance, a month before his death, was also the most dramatic. On 12 June he stepped onto the scene of his past triumphs, the balcony of the Casa Rosada, and threatened to resign before a crowd hastily assembled in an effort to regain the political initiative over a society that in recent weeks had slipped from his command.

On 1 May, the traditional Labour Day celebrations had culminated spectacularly in a confrontation between the radical youth and Perón. Harassed by criticism and chanting that interrupted his speech, Perón accused the youth of being 'mercenaries paid by foreigners' and called for the expulsion of the 'infiltrators' of the *peronista* movement. The rupture had been brewing since the beginning of the year, when the initial exhortations for moderation were followed by a drastic offensive against those positions still held by the radical *peronista* wing. The removal of the governor of the province of Buenos Aires after armed action by the ERP at a military base, the overthrow by force of the governor of Córdoba – both left-wing politicians – an assault on the offices of the *peronista* youth and the suppression of their publications formed part of a campaign that left no doubts about the incompatibility of the two currents that had converged with the return of *peronismo* to power: that which headed the wave of popular mobilization and aimed at the breakdown of the political order in the name of revolutionary populism and that which, based on the party and the unions, corresponded to the traditional ideals of Perón.

Against the background of this confrontation, labour conflict continued with redoubled intensity. The period between March and June registered the highest average number of strikes per month in the three years of *peronista* government. The outcome of the conflict was ensured in large part by a change in attitude on the part of business. The decision of 28 March weakened its already reluctant willingness to compromise on the incomes policy. Wage demands were now accepted only to be translated immediately into higher prices without government authorization. Alarmed by the situation, the CGT leaders went to Perón at the beginning of June to ask for some official reaction that would ease the pressure they were under. On 12 June Perón tried to fill the vacuum that surrounded his government project with his own political authority. But he did not have time to harvest the fruits of this final effort, since he died on 1 July.

Perón had been clearly aware that even the impressive electoral majority of 62 per cent obtained in 1973 was insufficient to keep him in power. A *peronista* government resting solely on its own bases could rapidly become vulnerable to pressures from the opposition, which, although politically defeated, had the powerful backing of big business and the military hierarchy. In order to avoid the predictable risks of political isolation, Perón had sought to build a network of agreements, such as the Social Pact and the convergence with the Radical Party in Congress. With his death, Perón's goals of political reconciliation and social collaboration, which had already suffered appreciable reverses, were abandoned by his successors. Inspired more by sectarianism than by the politics of conciliation, Isabel Perón and her entourage and the union leaders – the two influential groups in the new power structure – dedicated themselves to dismantling the agreements they had inherited. The hour of *peronismo,* they announced, had arrived.

The first step in this direction was taken against Gelbard, who, once the brief armistice that followed Perón's death was over, submitted his resignation in October. With his departure, the links that tied the CGE to the government were weakened. A similar fate befell the inter-party accords. After taking over the presidency, Perón's wife reorganized the cabinet, replacing representatives of the parties who had formed the electoral front with members of her intimate circle. She also brought an end to the special relations with the Radical Party, which was no longer consulted about major government decisions. While this operation of political homogenization was taking place, the violence entered a new phase. At the end of 1974 the Montoneros announced that they were going under-

ground to continue their struggle, now against the government of Isabel
Perón. At the same time there emerged a right-wing terrorist group
known as the Triple A (Alianza Argentina Anticomunista) armed and
commanded by López Rega, the president's minister of social welfare and
her private secretary.

Within a few months, the political scene was reduced to the arcane
palace manoeuvrings of the presidential entourage and the macabre routines of the practitioners of violence. Worker protest, in turn, declined,
partly because of the ruling climate of insecurity and partly because the
repression was eliminating, step by step, the bastions of the leftist union
opposition. Eventually, the palace clique clustered around Isabel Perón
and the union leaders were left face to face. The last contest that led to the
downfall of *peronismo* was played out around the aspirations of these two
rival sectors.

In spite of the encouraging picture painted by Gelbard when he left
office – a 7 per cent growth in GDP in 1974 and a decline in unemployment from 6 per cent in April 1973 to 2.5 per cent in November 1974 –
the immediate economic prospects looked dismal. In July the European
Economic Community had prohibited the importation of Argentine meat,
sharply affecting the volume and value of exports. Meanwhile, the prices
of imports continued to rise. Fearful of the effects it might have on real
wages and inflationary trends, Gelbard had not readjusted the exchange
rate and thereby stimulated a current of speculative importing. The surplus of U.S. $704 million accumulated in 1973 reverted to a deficit of
$216 million in the second half of 1974. The first task of the new minister
of economy, Alfredo Gómez Morales, was to adjust an economy that was
'overheated' – nearly full employment, a growing money supply and a
rising inflation rate – to the unfavourable situation in the external sector.

A central figure in the adoption of the successful stabilization programme of 1952, Gómez Morales had occupied the presidency of the
Central Bank during Gelbard's administration, a job he abandoned after
disagreement over the permissive fiscal policy. He first attempted to
change course through greater control over public spending, reduction of
monetary expansion and selective price increases. While necessary, the
adjustments were too moderate and did not include the exchange rate,
which continued to rise in real terms, with a consequent loss of foreign
funds. In March 1975 there was another devaluation, which reduced but
did not eliminate the overvaluation of the currency. Consonant with
Gómez Morales' gradualist focus, salaries were also increased. This hesi-

tant shift of economic policy collided, in addition, with an unexpected obstacle: the new minister did not belong to the president's intimate circle. Thus, throughout the 241 days of his incumbency, he waited in vain for official endorsement to adopt stricter measures while he contemplated the deterioration of the economic situation.

In this climate of drift, collective bargaining sessions were held as scheduled in February. Very soon, however, discussion of the new wage contracts was stalled by the absence of guidelines for negotiation from the government. The unions had been anxiously waiting for the opening of direct bargaining with the companies so they could rehabilitate their battered leadership after nearly two years of incomes policy. But the president, under the powerful influence of López Rega, paid no attention to their concerns, busy as she was preparing a drastic realignment of the government's political and social bases.

In essence, this policy entailed gaining the confidence of the armed forces and the economic establishment through the suppression of subversion by using the terrorist bands of the Triple A, which would avoid the direct involvement of the military; the eradication of the Left in its last refuge, the university; a return to foreign capital investment and a market economy, with a reduction in wages and the re-establishment of industrial discipline; and finally, the removal of the union movement from the structure of power. In the name of these ambitious goals the military was asked to abandon its political neutrality, which had been maintained since General Carcagno's resignation. This seemed to be achieved when, in May, the new commander-in-chief of the army, General Alberto Numa Laplane, advocated tactical support to the government. Isabel and López Rega then believed that their bold shift to the right, combined with the manipulation of *peronista* symbols, was ready to be launched.

When the day fixed for concluding the wage negotiations — 31 May — arrived without any official effort to facilitate new contracts, worker protest escaped union control in the form of street demonstrations and occupations of factories. On that very day Gómez Morales' resignation was accepted and Celestino Rodrigo, a conspicuous member of the presidential entourage, replaced him. Rodrigo announced a programme of measures that entailed an increase of the order of 100 per cent in the exchange rate and the cost of public services, at the same time recommending an increase of 40 per cent as a guideline in salary negotiations. A readjustment of relative prices was predictable, after a period of repressed inflation and currency overvaluation.

However, both the magnitude of the readjustment and the timing of the announcement seemed to indicate that the president wanted to create an untenable situation for the union leaders relative to the rank and file, thus clipping their political influence. Suddenly, they found themselves struggling not only for a wage increase but also for their own political survival. During the two succeeding weeks they mobilized to obtain the annulment of the restrictions on free wage negotiation. Thus, after a series of stormy meetings, facing businessmen who finally set aside all resistance, they negotiated wage increases amounting on average to 160 per cent.

Isabel Perón's response was equally forceful. On 24 June she nullified the agreements reached between the companies and the unions and offered a wage increase of 50 per cent to be followed by two more increases of 15 per cent in August and October. The union leaders found themselves faced with a dilemma they had desperately tried to avoid: either to continue the confrontation, with the risk of precipitating the fall of the government, or to accept the official offer, resigning themselves to political defeat and the collapse of their prestige before the rank and file. The spontaneous reaction of the workers to the president's announcement paralysed the country. For one week no one went to work. The CGT had no alternative but to ratify this fait accompli and call for a general strike of forty-eight hours on 7 July. This decision, unprecedented in the history of *peronismo,* brought an aggressive crowd before the Casa Rosada to demand the resignations of the president's entourage and the approval of the wage agreements. Contrary to expectations in official circles, the military stayed out of the conflict. Left to their fate, López Rega and Rodrigo tendered their resignations, and Isabel had to retrace her steps and accede to the labour demands. The political crisis concluded with the victory of the union leaders, who, although they renewed their support for Perón's wife, had effectively frustrated the political operation through which she sought to dislodge them from power.

After this dramatic episode, the *peronista* administration was never able to restore its credibility. It survived eight more months, during which the threat of a military coup dogged its every step and deepened the political crisis. After López Rega's resignation, the president temporarily withdrew from her duties on leave of absence, and a coalition of union men and old *peronista* politicians took over the government under the leadership of the president of the Senate, Italo Luder. General Numa Laplane was also forced to resign by the military high command; the new commander-in-chief, General Jorge Videla, again distanced the armed forces from the government, although their involvement in anti-subversive operations became more direct under Luder's instructions.

The immediate consequence of the measures taken by Rodrigo and the union counter-offensive was a violent acceleration in the inflation rate. In the months of June, July and August consumer prices rose 102 per cent, closer to a monthly rate of 7 to 10 per cent than to the 2 to 3 per cent that had been the average over the past thirty years. For the post of minister of economy, the unions proposed Antonio Cafiero, whose policy consisted of a gradual indexing of prices, salaries and the exchange rate. This tactic had the virtue of avoiding major serious distortions in relative prices, but it also implied an admission that it was impossible to reduce inflationary pressures. In all events, it permitted a reversal of the unfavourable trends in the external sector, assisted by the devalued currency that had been inherited and some short-term financing obtained from the IMF and other public and private organisms. The effects would be felt above all during the first quarter of 1976 when the balance of trade would show its first surplus in fifteen months.

Unable to check the high and fluctuating inflation rate, Cafiero had to live with one of its predictable consequences, the dizzying expansion of financial speculation. In the face of the depreciation of the value of goods and salaries, people found it more profitable to engage in feverish manipulation of the differences between the official dollar and the black market dollar, between posted interest rates and the rate of inflation. The voracious speculation attracted capital from the whole economy, from large corporations down to small savers. Under the impact of the acceleration of prices, the economy began a rapid slide from the 'overheated' situation in April, with strong pressures on the side of demand and a low rate of unemployment, to a situation close to recession in July and August. In Buenos Aires unemployment rose from 2.3 per cent to 6 per cent and in Córdoba it reached 7 per cent. The reduction in industrial production was 5.6 per cent in the third quarter of the year and 8.9 per cent in the last quarter. The declining economic situation did not, however, attenuate the level of labour conflicts; instead, the new situation prolonged them and made their resolution more difficult to achieve.

In this context, there was increased activity by the guerrillas, who kidnapped and assassinated plant managers in order to force acceptance of worker demands. These actions unleashed equally violent reprisals from paramilitary groups against union activists. The factories thus became one more site for the wave of violence that provided a tragic backdrop for the critical economic situation. In the second half of 1975 the guerrillas decided to step up their operations; in addition to kidnappings, assassinations and bombings, the Montoneros and the ERP launched more ambitious actions against military targets. The pressure of the security forces, however, obliged them to revert to more rudimentary terrorism, which increased their already irreversible isolation from the movements of popular protest. Dazed by the daily acts of violence, vast sectors of the population began to contemplate the possibility of military intervention. But the military commanders did not seem anxious to act, apparently allowing the crisis to deepen so that their final move would have the broadest support.

The coalition of unionists and politicians that sustained Luder in the presidency failed to fulfil the expectations of stability that they had encouraged. The exaggerated demands of the unions made coexistence with the moderate politicians difficult while at the same time causing alarm in traditional circles. A new business organization, Asamblea Permanente de Asociaciónes Gremiales (APEGE), led by big agrarian and industrial capital, took over the place left vacant by the CGE to assume an openly rebellious stance against the government. In January 1976 Isabel returned to the presidential palace and reorganized the cabinet, getting rid of the ministers linked to the alliance of union leaders and politicians and surrounding herself with figures who were outside the *peronista* movement. Some of them were survivors of the López Rega clique, others were unknown functionaries, but all were ready to follow this lone woman, heir to the ideals of a movement in whose history she had not taken part, a movement whose natural leaders she hated and whose followers inspired only her distrust. The initial reaction of those who had been ousted was indignation; they went so far as to discuss the possibility of filing suit against the president, under charges of misuse of public funds. Very soon, however, they yielded to the inevitable, realizing that her downfall, foreshadowed by an aborted military uprising in December, was imminent.

During these troubled days, the Radical Party tried to regain the role as principal opposition party that had been denied it in the past three years as *peronismo* became both the government and its opposition. Marginalized from the conflicts in which the movement created by Perón was being torn apart, the Radicals had till then centred their discourse on the defence of the institutional order, an attitude that led them to unaccustomed extremes in their tolerance for the conduct of the veteran populist leader and his followers. They now proposed the erection of a government without Isabel. Their call went unheeded. Already looking ahead to the period that would begin after the inevitable coup d'état, the unionists and *peronista* politicians decided to close ranks behind Perón's wife. She, in turn, dedicated her last days to launching a series of economic measures that she imagined were responsive to the needs of the military hierarchy and big business.

During the first days of March a new minister of economy tried to address the economic calamity with another abrupt change in relative prices. The exchange rate and the prices of public services were raised by between 90 and 100 per cent while salaries were increased by 20 per cent. Like Rodrigo's earlier measure, this new readjustment explicitly included a decline in real wages. A wave of strikes began to paralyse the principal centres in heated protest against the economic measures. When everything looked as if it were leading to a confrontation similar to that of June 1975, the military overthrew the government – without opposition.

THE PROCESS OF NATIONAL REORGANIZATION, 1976–83

For a country with a long history of military interventions, the coup d'état of 1976 held no surprises. Accustomed to reading the warning signs, the majority of Argentines saw it as the inevitable outcome of the ongoing political crisis. The armed forces had patiently waited for the deepening of the crisis in order to legitimize their intervention. When they decided to act, many people shared their sombre assessment of the state of the country:

All constitutional measures having been exhausted, all possibilities of rectification through institutional means having been exceeded, and with the irrefutable demonstration of the impossibility of restoring the government process by natural means, a situation resulted which oppressed the nation and compromised its future. . . . Faced with a tremendous power vacuum, capable of overwhelming us with dissolution and anarchy, with the lack of capacity for dialogue that the national government has demonstrated, with the lack of an overall strategy . . . to confront subversion, with the lack of a solution to the basic problems of the nation, the result of which has been a permanent increase of all extremist movements, with the total absence of ethical and moral example by the leaders of the state, with the manifest irresponsibility in managing the economy . . . the armed forces, in the fulfilment of a permanent obligation, have assumed the leadership of the state.[11]

[11] Quoted in C. Floria and C. García Belsunce, *Historia política de la Argentina contemporánea* (Madrid, 1988), p. 238.

The commanders-in-chief of the three armed services installed themselves as the supreme power and named General Jorge Videla, the army chief, as president. However, the privileges accorded to the army as the oldest and traditionally pre-eminent branch ended there. Governmental administration was divided equally between the army, the navy and the air force. This institutional innovation owed much to the strong leadership of Admiral Emilio Massera, who managed to regain for the navy the positions lost during the intra-military confrontations of 1962. In initiating a 'process of national reorganization' it was predictable that the military regime would put a policy of repression into practice, but the scale and nature of the violence to which it resorted were unprecedented. The initial measures followed a familiar pattern: the prohibition of political activities, censorship of the press, the arrest of labour leaders and intervention in the unions. To this was added the death penalty, administrated in a form which was different from anything ever known before.

First, there were the victims. Although the goal of the military was to do away with subversion, the repressive measures were not limited to the guerrillas. Videla himself said that 'a terrorist is not only one who carries a bomb or a pistol, but also one who spreads ideas contrary to Western Christian civilization'. Thus, the enemy included all kinds of dissidents; together with the guerrillas and those who aided them by giving them food and refuge, politicians, union members and intellectuals fell within the orbit of repression. For the military, the Communist threat it had intermittently denounced over the past twenty years had finally taken bodily form and dared, furthermore, to defy it with arms.

Second, there was the method of violence. Councils of war were created and given the power to inflict death sentences for a great variety of crimes. But it was not primarily through them that the summary justice of the military operated. The repressive infrastructure was based, rather, on officially authorized but clandestine detention centres and in special units of the three military branches and the police, the mission of which was to kidnap, interrogate, torture and, in the majority of cases, kill. This infrastructure was highly decentralized; the real authority was invested in the regional commanders, who in their own territory were the supreme power and reported only to their immediate superiors. This decentralization and autonomy granted the shock forces enormous impunity. This mechanism had several advantages: it was a difficult network to infiltrate, it was immune to the influence of well-connected relatives of the victims and it allowed the government to deny any responsibility for the violation of human rights.

Between 1976 and 1979 a wave of terror swept the country. The activities of the repressive apparatus were basically secret, making it difficult to establish the number of victims. They were part of a group for which Argentina became tragically famous: *los desaparecidos* (the missing ones), those about whom nothing was ever heard again. At first, the violence was not entirely one-sided. In the nine months that followed the coup d'état, the guerrillas carried out acts of terrorism against military targets. The response of the armed forces was explosive and crushing. Hundreds of guerrillas were killed in the streets while they mounted a desperate resistance. But the main cause of the defeat of the guerrillas were the kidnappings and their consequences. Over time, the majority of those kidnapped had their spirits broken. Driven by the physical pain of torture, without hope for the future of a struggle that was only suffering defeats, the victims ended by informing on their comrades and thus increasing the number of victims. Many innocent people met the same fate, trapped in the vast net of counter-insurgency operations.

The policy of extermination launched by the armed forces fed on the culture of violence that flourished in Argentina after the *cordobazo* of 1969. Public opinion had been subjected to an intense propaganda campaign aimed at making the use of violence acceptable. First came the rebellion of the youth, who in the name of revolution postulated the need to resort to arms. Then the terrorist bands of the Right took the same course, with the result that the military regime's repression was imposed on a country where the cult of violence was already deeply rooted. All the moral obstacles were removed when Argentina became submerged in what the military itself called the 'dirty war'.

The resort to violence initially relied on a certain tolerance on the part of politicians and intellectuals. When the armed utopia of the youth movement materialized in the early 1970s, many saw it as an understandable reaction to military authoritarianism. During the dramatic years of the *peronista* return to power, violence became an everyday occurrence to which public opinion resigned itself. Now, the moral collapse of a defenceless society opened the doors to a repression that was implacable, clandestine and indifferent to basic human rights. The panic of those who had encouraged the guerrilla movement was silenced by the attitude of the majority of Argentines, who, tired and afraid, opted to ignore the bloody experience that they knew was taking place behind their backs.

This atmosphere of collective debility enabled the military regime to mount its ideological crusade, couched in a language rich in medical imagery. For the new rulers, civil society was seriously ill. The disease that afflicted the country came from below and had to be met by decisive surgery from above. There was, however, something new in the message. The ideologues of the Catholic Right, who ten years earlier had accompanied General Onganía in his advocacy of a corporatist system, had no influence whatsoever in 1976, when the ideas of liberal-conservatism enjoyed a dominant position within the military regime.

Traditionally, the military had been in conflict with this ideology prevalent in the economic establishment. Although the armed forces shared its disdain for political parties and universal suffrage, they never fully accepted the liberal critique of nationalist and interventionist state policies, of the inward-looking model of industrialization or of the excesses of labour legislation. As a result of the lessons of the recent *peronista* experience, the liberals were able to show that the policies and practices they were criticizing had created the conditions for social subversion. To preserve national security meant not only to destroy the guerrilla movement but also to eradicate the model of development that was its breeding ground. Thus, the liberals managed to impose their ideological stamp – although the high-ranking military chiefs did not renounce their own obsessions and set limits and conditions. The man who personified the ideals of liberal-conservativism was the minister of economy, José Martínez de Hoz, member of a traditional landowning family and president of the largest private steel company, who had held the same office during Guido's precarious presidency in 1962.

The critical state of the external sector was at the top of the new minister's agenda. Available reserves of foreign currency were practically exhausted. Thanks to his access to international financial sources, Martínez de Hoz was able to run the risk of stopping payments. In August a stand-by agreement was signed with the IMF which supplied U.S. $300 million and facilitated a loan of $1,000 million by a pool of banks led by Chase Manhattan. Inflation next claimed the minister's attention. The anti-inflationary policy, of orthodox inspiration, was helped by a number of decisions made by the previous administration. A short time before the coup, there was a final shock to relative prices as a result of adjustments in the cost of public services and the exchange rate to levels above the growth in wages. Martínez de Hoz took advantage of this to freeze wages, at the same time eliminating existing price controls. As a consequence, real wages fell sharply. Five months later, when the purchasing power of wages was less than 40 per cent of what it had been in 1972, nominal remuneration was periodically adjusted to inflation. The fiscal deficit was, in turn, reduced by half, to about 8.4 per cent of the GDP during the last part of 1976, by means of a real increase in collections and a fall in the wages of public employees. After an initial spurt in prices when controls were lifted, the inflation rate stood at 4.3 per cent in July. This success was offset by a decline in economic activity due to lower demand deriving from the decrease in real wages. But the reduction in labour costs provoked expansion in investment and exports. All in all, the government believed that it had found a quick solution to the crisis. The drop in real wages was not considered a negative factor but rather the inevitable price of reorganizing the economy.

This formula, which combined growth with a regressive redistribution of income, had already been used at the beginning of the 1960s. Martínez de Hoz thought the moment had come to launch his more ambitious outward-looking project. This strategy tried to break the pattern of the past fifty years, during which Argentine industry had been protected by high tariff barriers. In the official view, this model of semi-autarchic development had created the conditions for state intervention and, by discouraging competition, was the cause of Argentine industry's lack of efficiency. The first measure in the new direction was a plan to reduce ad valorem rates on imports over a five-year period.

The government's optimism did not last long. Inflation failed to come down further. On the contrary, in early 1977 prices rose at between 7 and 10 per cent each month and exposed the new economic behaviour induced by the inflationary acceleration of 1975. Since then it had become a general practice amongst entrepreneurs to make rapid adjustments in their prices in response to changes in the economic environment. Contracts were short term, salaries were revised every three months and the absence of price controls allowed companies to react quickly to variations in public sector charges, the exchange rate or salaries. The economy became increasingly indexed, fortifying the extraordinary resilience of the inflation rate.

The persistent rise in prices began to unsettle the military junta, which had made the taming of inflation one of its immediate objectives. In April 1977 Martínez de Hoz asked business for a 120-day truce, but this was carried out with so little conviction that its effects were negligible. In the middle of the year, the economic team made its own diagnosis: inflation was a monetary phenomenon, and failure to curb it was due to the fact that the money supply had not been strictly controlled. Consequently, the new attempt to control inflation lay in a restrictive monetary policy, implemented within the framework of a major financial reform.

The reform changed the system imposed by the previous *peronista* administration and fixed the capacity of banks to grant loans in direct relation to the deposits they could attract from the public. This led to the liberation of interest rates to facilitate competition. However, the military opposed eliminating the Central Bank guarantee on deposits. Thus, a dangerous hybrid system developed in which uncontrolled interest rates and guaranteed deposits coexisted, making competition for funds among financial entities very easy and risk-free. This led to over-expansion of the financial system, which became populated with speculators and fortune-seekers.

Interest rates increased substantially in real terms and prejudiced the economic reactivation begun at the end of 1976. Nevertheless, after two years of contraction, 1977 ended with a positive growth rate of 4.9 per cent. There was also a trade surplus of U.S. $1,500 million, and the fiscal deficit continued to decline (3.3 per cent of the GNP). But the annual rise in consumer prices reached the extraordinary rate of 180 per cent.

The successes promised by the restrictive monetary policy were slow to materialize, and the armed forces were not willing to face the social and political consequences of a prolonged recession. In contrast to the case in Chile, the military junta had vetoed resorting to unemployment.

In March 1978, against the backdrop of a monthly inflation rate of 11.1 per cent and the lowest level of activity since 1973, Martínez de Hoz again changed his policy. Inflation was now conceived as an expression of the expectations of economic agents who, in a climate of uncertainty, adopted defensive measures. He thus decided to defer the increases in public charges and the exchange rate in relation to past inflation. In December 1978 this decision became formal policy through a program that determined future increases in the exchange rate and public charges and fixed guidelines for the increase in the volume of internal credit. In January 1979 the increases forecast for these economic variables were established at much lower levels than the indexes of inflation registered at the end of 1978.

While this daring economic experiment was being launched, Argentina was moving towards a serious conflict with Chile. A year earlier the military junta had rejected the verdict of the arbitration entrusted to Great Britain in a long dispute with Chile over the control of the Beagle Channel in the extreme south of Argentina. By December 1978 bilateral talks with Pinochet's government had reached an impasse. The Argentine armed forces were ready to take action. Only the last-minute intervention of the Vatican averted the imminent war. The principal economic consequence of this incident was the refurbishing of the armed forces. In 1979, 1980 and 1981 military spending reached unprecedented levels and was largely responsible for the deterioration of fiscal deficit and the increase in foreign debt because of arms purchases abroad.

In 1979 repression was eased. Its objectives had been reached. The guerrilla movement had been destroyed; those who escaped with their lives secretly left the country. A majority of leftist intellectuals were also forced into exile. The oppressive atmosphere of the first years of military rule was relaxed. General Roberto Viola, who replaced Videla as army commander-in-chief after the latter had been confirmed as president for another three years in the middle of 1978, presented a less sullen and authoritarian image than his predecessor.

The first signs, albeit weak, of a liberalization of the regime put the hard-line sectors of the army on guard. At the end of 1979 General Luciano Menéndez tried to stage a rebellion from Córdoba, calling for the re-establishment of the total prohibition on political activity and the silencing of the increasingly loud demands for an official explanation of missing persons. The attempt failed, but it was a revealing symptom of the conflicts that were brewing in the military corporation. In contrast to Menéndez's attitude, Admiral Massera, who was responsible for one of the bloodiest chapters of the repression before stepping down from the leadership of the navy in 1978, began to dissociate himself publicly from the dirty war.

The upper class and the economic establishment which had backed Videla did not conceal their disgruntlement over Argentina's international isolation. In spite of the self-assigned mission of the military junta – the defence of Western values at the dawn of a third world war – they had garnered little sympathy. Relations with the United States were extremely tense, owing to the conflict between the methods being used by the military junta to carry out its mission and the human rights policy of President Carter. The good relations with the international financial community were, perhaps, the only positive aspect in a very unfriendly climate. Hostility towards the military regime was symbolically manifested when a little known but tenacious human rights militant, Adolfo Pérez Esquivel, won the Nobel Peace Prize in 1980.

The program of de-indexing launched by Martínez de Hoz in December 1978 was based on a daring gamble. Given the decreasing rate of devaluation, the economic authorities hoped that the growth rate of internal prices would eventually coincide with the sum of the predetermined rate of devaluation and the international inflation rate. This exchange rate policy was supported by the surge in exports provoked by a sharp increase in agricultural production. Income from exports went from U.S. $3,000–4,000 million in 1976–7 to $6,000–8,000 million in 1979–80. These increases reflected a certain lag in the exchange rate, which was the key tool of the programme. The immediate consequence of this policy was the anger of rural producers and the resignation of some members of the economic team who were linked to this sector.

In an effort to accelerate the convergence of the inflation rate with the official exchange rate policy, the level of exposure of the economy to international competition was increased. Convinced that if the industrial firms did not discipline themselves, there would be no success in the battle against inflation, Martínez de Hoz intensified the reduction of tariffs. This would allow price increases to be fixed by competition with imported goods, while simultaneously helping to eliminate inefficient enterprises. This challenge to a highly protected structure opened a new focus of conflict, this time with the industrial sector.

The anti-inflationary programme turned out to be more problematic than expected. During the first eight months of the regime, the growth rate of domestic prices was nearly double the guideline for the devaluation rate. Following this, inflation tended to decelerate, from 175 per cent in 1978 to 160 per cent in 1979 to 100 per cent in 1980. However, the lag in exchange rate required to decelerate inflation generated a growing deficit on the current account; in turn, higher domestic interest rates were needed to close the gap with the external sector. In a context of repressed inflation, higher interest rates became impossible for the productive sectors, and the growing unpaid debts of business pushed the financial system into crisis.

Reviewing the sequence followed by Martínez de Hoz's experiment, it can be seen that the decline of inflation was achieved at the cost of an enormous devaluation of the peso: between 40 and 50 per cent more than the average of the previous thirty years. The trade surplus of U.S. $2,000 million in 1978 turned into a deficit – a modest one in 1979 and a not so modest $2,500 million in 1980. Through the 1970s, the trade balance had been a surplus, except in 1975. But while the 1975 deficit was produced by strong increases in domestic activity, the deficits of 1979 and 1980 occurred in a context of recession, where the increase in spending on imports – induced by the exchange rate lag and the lowering of tariffs – was oriented towards goods that competed with local production.

Martínez de Hoz endeavoured to cover imbalances in the current account by encouraging the entry of foreign capital. As a result, the deregulation of the financial system undertaken in 1977, the progressive lifting of restrictions on obtaining foreign credit and the domestic policy of expensive money led to a growing process of a foreign debt. This process acquired a new impulse after December 1978, when the peso was progressively revalued by making the real interest rate negative in local money and thus stimulating an intense demand for foreign capital. Net foreign debt went from U.S. $6,459 million at the end of 1978 to $19,478 million in 1980, tripling in only two years.

As the external sector began to deteriorate and the Banco Central lost the reserves it had accumulated, doubts arose about the economic authorities' promise to maintain the predetermined devaluation rate. This uncertainty, in turn, drove up the cost of money, and by the end of 1979 interest rates had become strongly positive. Businesses entered into a crisis of liquidity, harassed by more expensive credit and declining sales. Many went bankrupt, immobilizing the active portfolios of the banks. In March 1980 there was a financial panic when the Banco de Intercambio Regional, the most important private bank, could not meet its obligations and was closed, along with twenty-seven others which successively declared bankruptcy, by the Central Bank, which had to inject an enormous quantity of liquid funds in order to pay off the closed banks' depositors.

Public confidence in the official exchange rate policy was severely affected. Many took advantage of what seemed to be the last months of a free financial market to get their capital out of the country. By this time, the bleeding of reserves could not be stopped. The economic authorities sought to compensate for the outflow of capital by forcing public enterprises to incur foreign debt. The pressure on the exchange rate market continued to rise; in February 1981, Martínez de Hoz abandoned the guideline policy, deciding on a devaluation of 10 per cent, which was, however, insignificant in the face of a lag of about 50 per cent. The economic experiment begun in December 1978 had come to an end.

This disheartening picture formed the backdrop to the presidential succession. In accordance with the political timetable fixed by the military junta, the new president had to take over from Videla in March 1981. The natural candidate was General Roberto Viola, commander-in-chief of the army, but his candidacy awoke significant resistance in the navy and important sectors of the army, which feared that he would attempt a process of political liberalization. After several months of negotiation, Viola's appointment was finally made official in October 1980, but over the six months before he took office there was a notable increase in concern over the already uncertain course of the economy. The 10 per cent devaluation decreed by Martínez de Hoz was not enough to quiet speculation over future devaluations, particularly because Viola's economic advisers were known critics of the policy in force. In addition, the hard-liners in the armed forces, led by General Leopoldo Galtieri and Admiral Jorge Anaya, the commanders-in-chief of the army and the navy, respectively, distrusted the political opening the new president was attempting.

The project of Videla's successor recalled General Lanusse's attempt in 1971, but circumstances were not equally favourable. Ten years earlier, Lanusse was able to justify a return to open politics to his colleagues by invoking the need to contain a strong social opposition. Now, the protest against the military regime lacked the destabilizing potential it had then. For Viola's critics in the military establishment the step he was ready to take was hasty. The ominous memory of the final outcome of Lanusse's attempt condemned any pretence at repeating a similar project. Outside the conservative groups, the military leaders of 1976 had not developed a significant political following. *Peronismo* and Radicalism continued to be the most popular political forces. A rapprochement with them would lead to free elections and a return to the rule of law. From the perspective of the military hard-liners, this meant shelving the goals of the coup of 1975 in favour of the same politicians they had dislodged from power.

Hence, General Viola took office in March 1981 representing one sector of the armed forces but under the watchful eye of the other. Nine months later he was removed and his open policy brought to a close. During this brief interregnum, critics of Martínez de Hoz's policy joined the cabinet and made official contacts with the unions and political parties. In July 1981 the so-called Multipartidaria was created which, like the Hora del Pueblo in 1971, was a coalition of parties whose majority sectors were *peronista* and Radical. Its objectives were the same as ever: to negotiate a political transition and prevent the uncontrolled growth of a radicalized opposition. The cautious advances of General Viola and the moderate proposals of the Multipartidaria ran in the same direction. Neither wanted to antagonize the rigid sectors of the military junta, which were issuing repeated warnings against a populist detour and were discouraging any hope of rapid institutionalization. Their prudence was in vain.

The crisis of credibility that accompanied Viola's brief presidency did not assist management of the critical economic situation that had been inherited. Viola's minister of economy began in April with a devaluation of 30 per cent in order to tackle the collapse of Martínez de Hoz's exchange rate policy. But he could not cool the markets, and in July he had to announce another devaluation of 30 per cent. The real exchange rate was fortified, although at the price of accentuating the recession and the decline in real wages. Later, Viola had to introduce restrictions in the exchange markets in order to block the flight of capital. In turn, the devaluations further complicated the situation of companies that had borrowed short-term credit from abroad. The government then offered them guarantees and subsidies that tended to stimulate the renewal of the debts, with the goal of averting pressures on the exhausted reserves of foreign currency. At the cost of significant fiscal weakening, the transfer of private debt to the public sector thus began.

In December 1981 the leadership of the military regime was entrusted to General Galtieri, who combined three posts: president, member of the junta and commander-in-chief of the army. Under his direction, the Argentine military reverted to the regime's original stance, re-establishing authoritarian control over political life. The rise of the new strong man owed a great deal to the change in the international context. The arrival of Ronald Reagan in the White House put an end to the regime's isolation. Galtieri had travelled twice to the United States during 1981 and gained the sympathies of the Republican administration, which was quick to set aside Carter's human rights policy. The future Argentine president repaid these attentions, offering to lend military support to the U.S. counterinsurgency operations in Central America. Argentine experts in intelligence and anti-subversive operations were sent to El Salvador, Guatemala and Honduras. The lessons learned during the years of the dirty war were also used to train former Somoza supporters in actions against the Nicaraguan government.

With the backing of his hosts in Washington, whom this tall, uncouth and rough-spoken man had amused with imitations of General Patton, Galtieri reintroduced the liberal economists into the Ministry of Economy. They were led by Roberto Alemán, who had been minister in 1961 and was highly respected in financial circles for his orthodoxy. Alemán tried to reproduce the liberal political economy of the first years of the regime, endeavouring to control inflation by reducing the role of the state. Although public spending did decrease, this was not due to a reform of the state – which was never undertaken – but because government employees' salaries and the cost of public services were frozen. Both measures helped to slow down inflation in the short run. Alemán also lifted the controls on the exchange market imposed by his predecessor and allowed the peso to float freely. This implied a devaluation of about 30 per cent, which, added to the successive devaluations since April 1981, improved the trade balance. The goal was to generate a strong surplus with which to confront foreign payments, since access to international financial markets was closed.

Galtieri's minister of economy tried to assuage the financial community's anxiety about Argentina's growing crisis of payments. But the uncertainty did not disappear. The exchange rate began to move in an erratic pattern, and Alemán had to back away from his policy of a free-floating exchange in a retreat that was also clearly related to developments on the political scene. The return of economic orthodoxy had caused widespread discontent, which took a more militant form than in the recent past. This growing protest seemed to conspire against the idea largely shared among military leaders of reducing their isolation and preparing for the political succession of the regime. Although not all senior officers admitted it openly, they were aware that they were passing through one of those familiar moments in Argentine history when pressure for an institutional solution was irreversible. Admiral Massera was already engaged in the creation of his own party and had made contact with some *peronista* sectors. Against this backdrop, Galtieri launched a daring operation to shore up the battered legitimacy of the regime and keep it in power: the occupation of the Islas Malvinas (Falkland Islands), which had been a British possession since 1833.

The issue of the Falklands had always been present on the military's international policy agenda. In December 1976 Argentina had persuaded the UN Assembly to urge Great Britain, for the third time, to open talks on the de-colonization of the islands. The British chose to continue their procrastinating tactics for the next four years, while frustration and irritation mounted in Buenos Aires. The Argentine navy began to prepare a plan of invasion. At the end of 1981 London decided to reduce its presence in the South Atlantic, and the Argentine government made a new effort to unlock the negotiations. When General Galtieri took office, after the failure of diplomatic overtures, he gave permission to Admiral Anaya, who had played a key role in his rise to power, to begin operations. On 2 April 1982 the first Argentine sailors disembarked on the Falkland Islands.

General Galtieri's political expectations were immediately satisfied. Widespread nationalistic fervour swept the country, and the regime was provided with much-needed popular backing. The Plaza de Mayo, which four days earlier had been the scene of a labour mobilization that had been violently repressed by police, was now filled with an enthusiastic crowd cheering the military. Confident that once its prestige was restored the military would be less reluctant to leave office, the political parties also lent their support. In the end, however, this patriotic wave carried the armed forces beyond their original plans. The invasion had been conceived to exert pressure on Britain. It was expected that, in light of the Argentine government's decision, the international community would oblige the British prime minister, Margaret Thatcher, to enter into negotiations; as soon as these began, the Argentine troops, after a short stay on the islands, would return to their bases. But the triumphant tone of the official propaganda caused the military junta to lose control over events. Moreover, Mrs Thatcher was unwilling to compromise. The United States, upon whose neutrality the Argentine military had been counting, remained loyal to its traditional ally. Argentina found itself at war with a major power. By 4 June 1982, the Falklands were again in British hands.

The political aftermath of the defeat in the South Atlantic war precipitated the disintegration of the Argentine military regime, just as the defeat by the Turks in the war for Cyprus had put an end to the government of the Greek Colonels in 1974. The military survived in power for one more long year, during which the conflicts which divided it rose shamelessly to the surface. The military junta was dissolved with the departure of the navy and the air force. The army remained in charge of the government and appointed General Reynaldo Bignone to the presidency with the mission of transferring power as quickly as possible. While the three services settled their accounts in public, accusing each other of responsibility for the military defeat, the administration had to confront the immediate economic problems.

With the reserves of the Banco Central virtually exhausted, exchange controls were imposed and external payments were suspended. The external debt now exceeded U.S. $35 billion, half of which fell due at the end of 1982. Until 1981 it had been possible to make the scheduled repayments by taking new short-term loans. Now, however, Argentina's credibility in international financial circles was destroyed. Bignone also found that he could not negotiate freely with creditors, since some elements of the military were trying to maintain a state of financial hostility. A middle line was established, and negotiations began with the IMF and the commercial banks in an attempt to settle the past due amounts and postpone new payments.

In January 1983 a new stand-by agreement was approved with the IMF, whereby the government promised to correct an economic crisis characterized by a fiscal deficit of 14 per cent of the GNP, an annual inflation rate of 310 per cent and a deficit in the balance of payments of U.S. $6,700 million. The economic programme agreed on reflected the traditional view of the IMF that the external deficit was attributable to excess internal spending. However, while Argentina's external imbalances had in the past been expressed by a deficit in the balance of trade, the trade account now had a surplus, and the imbalance was provoked by the payment of interest on the external debt and by the rise in international interest rates. The stand-by agreement with the IMF and the subsequent negotiation of the debt with commercial banks allowed the amassing of the $3,700 million needed to take care of the external situation in the short term.

In parallel developments, the administration embarked on a financial reform designed to aid the private sector. The existing internal debt was extended obligatorily for five years at low interest rates fixed by the Central Bank, which also provided the funds. The basic idea in this respect was to reactivate the stagnant economy through a liquidation of the private sector's debt, which had reached dangerous levels due to high interest rates and the enormous devaluation of the peso – 800 per cent over the increase in prices in the past eighteen months. Equally serious was the debt contracted by the government in local markets. The intention of the government was to unleash a once-and-for-all jump in prices that would reduce public and private debt in real terms through a permanent transfer of resources from depositors to debtors; consequently, prices rose at a new monthly level of between 15 and 20 per cent. The administration also continued to be generous with the external debt of the private sector, taking new steps to transfer the majority of external obligations to the public sector. Camouflaged by the collapse of the military regime, this shock of heterodox measures for the business community's benefit provoked strong public discontent. Bignone had to reorganize the Ministry of Economy, naming as its new head Jorge Whebe, who had already occupied the position during the last part of Lanusse's presidency in 1973. This symbolic choice was a clear sign that the military was about to withdraw.

The economic situation it left behind was hardly healthy. Between 1976 and 1982 the global GDP showed a negative cumulative annual rate of 0.2

per cent. During four of the seven years of military administration, GDP decreased in absolute terms (1976, 1978, 1981, 1982). The level of global activity in 1982 was 1.3 per cent lower than that in 1975, when the long period of growth that began in 1964 was interrupted. The fall was even more acute in industry and trade: manufacturing output was 20 per cent lower than that in 1975, while trade activity was 16.4 per cent lower. The negative growth of the economy was associated with a decline in internal demand, as well as with the substitution of domestic production by imports. This went along with a decline in industry, which fell to 22.3 per cent of the GDP in 1982 from 27.8 per cent in 1975. During the same period the number of industrial workers fell 35 per cent.

The only positive development had been in exports, although an increase of 8.1 per cent between 1976 and 1982 did not offset the flooding of imports into local markets. A paradoxical effect of the liberal policies was the growth of public investment over total investment. The uncertainty dominant during these years turned state investment projects into a hedge against stagnation, attracting private businessmen to public contracts.

One predictable result of these policies was a contraction in the real income of wage-earners; this can be estimated at between 30 and 50 per cent in the period from 1976 to 1982, accelerating a regressive redistribution of income. Thus, the 5 per cent of the population who received the highest incomes saw their share of the total income grow from 17.2 per cent in 1974 to 22.2 per cent in 1982. To this concentration of income must be added the flight of capital, which converted a significant number of upper-middle-class investors into holders of thousands of millions of dollars in foreign financial centres. At the end of 1982 the external debt was U.S. $43,600 million. In contrast to the situation in other indebted nations, the growth of the external debt was not accompanied by growth of the GDP but was generated to sustain a policy that led to de-industrialization and stagnation.

The other legacy of the military was the sequel to the policy of repression. During the final phase of its period in power, the military had made a fruitless effort to obtain assurances from the parties that they would not be punished for the violation of human rights. The armed forces therefore had to transfer power without having reached any agreement on how to deal with its profoundly divisive heritage. This was a conspicuous difference between the Argentine situation and the processes under way in Brazil and Uruguay, where the military was in a position to influence the dynamics of the political transition. Elections were scheduled for October 1983, the parties competing in distancing themselves from the military regime. Of the two most important forces – the *peronistas* and the Radicals – it was the latter, contrary to expectations, which succeeded best in this regard.

Since 1946 the *peronistas* had come first every time the population was able to express its political preferences freely through elections. The Radical Party faced this challenge with an internal reorganization, from which the new leadership of Raúl Alfonsín emerged. In order to confront the revival of the old populist rhetoric of the *peronistas,* Alfonsín formulated an original platform. He defined the electoral competition in terms of democracy versus authoritarianism and announced that his party was best equipped to reconstruct a democratic system in Argentina. In this manner, he won over the voters who wanted to leave a long decade of political violence behind them. *Peronismo* was unable to present itself as a credible representative of this collective aspiration, which was much more moderate than the one that had handed it victory in 1973. Furthermore, during the campaign Alfonsín made an explicit and convincing connection between the *peronistas* and the military by warning of the existence of a 'union–military pact' and alleging that the high command of the armed forces had decided to support a future *peronista* government, in exchange for which the *peronista* union leaders would promote a pardon for the military's violation of human rights.

The results of the elections of 30 October 1983 gave the Radicals 7,725,873 votes (50 per cent) and the *peronistas* 5,994,406 (39 per cent). The contrast with the percentages from 1973, when the Radicals won 26 per cent and the *peronistas* 65 per cent, could not have been greater. In addition to those traditionally loyal to Radicalism, the triumphant coalition gained the support of the Centre–Right electorate, the votes of small groups of leftists and a significant percentage of *peronista* adherents; it also received a majority of the female and youth vote. In the context of a grave economic crisis and with the wounds of repression still open, a new democratic experiment began in Argentina.

THE ALFONSÍN PRESIDENCY AND THE TRANSITION TO
DEMOCRACY, 1983 – 9

Once surprise over the outcome of the election had dissipated, Raúl Alfonsín's assumption of the presidency was received, both in Argentina and abroad, with widespread relief and hope. The new government emerged out of the ruins of two experiences that, marked by violence and crisis, had profoundly affected the collective consciousness: the return and fall of the *peronista* government and the collapse of the military dictatorship. Indeed, the democratic experiment that was initiated at the end of 1983 was invested with a desire for a new beginning after forty years of political instability and economic failure.

However, the same conditions that had made this seem possible also raised difficult challenges. First, the authoritarian regime left power without establishing a political pact. While in Brazil and Uruguay the military explicitly or implicitly entered into an agreement with civilians on the return to constitutionality, in Argentina their rapid loss of power prevented the armed forces from fixing the terms under which they abandoned control of the state. The democratic leaders were, as a result, free of commitments but, at the same time, weighed down by a grave responsibility in deciding how to manage the unresolved military question. The memory of recent human rights violations complicated the future even more.

Second, the first *peronista* electoral defeat in free elections had unexpected consequences. The outcome could be interpreted as the end of one political era and the beginning of another; this was the dominant perception among the Radicals, in spite of the important number of votes given to the Partido Justicialista. The Radicals thought that the *peronista* defeat, as well as the crisis that broke out among its rank and file, forecast the disintegration of this formerly powerful political force. Confident of this interpretation, they prepared to form a new political movement, centralized around the leadership of Alfonsín and enlarged by the collapse of *peronismo*. This vision encouraged attitudes that made it very difficult to arrive at agreements with the *peronistas* on crucial questions about the democratic transition. The 1983 electoral defeat was an unexpected and damaging shock indeed to the *peronistas,* who were accustomed to thinking of themselves as the natural governing party. The electoral results added fuel to the continuing internal crisis experienced by the party since Perón's death. Afraid of losing their identity in the political offensive launched by the new government, the *peronistas* accentuated their role as the party of the opposition. This strategy kept them united but, at the same time, it led them to act according to the logic of adversarial politics, which did not facilitate the search for accord. As a result, the two principal political forces entered the post-authoritarian period in open competition.

The consequences of the political polarization between Radicals and *peronistas* were magnified by the distribution of institutional power that resulted from the 1983 elections. The Radical Party won the presidency but was deprived of a clear majority in Congress. The Radicals achieved a slight majority in the Chamber of Deputies: 129 seats out of a total of 254. The Partido Justicialista won 111 seats, thus maintaining an important position from which to assert pressure that was supplemented by their strength in the Senate, where they won 21 out of 46 seats while the Radicals held 18. (The remaining 7 were distributed among provincial parties.)

Despite the magnitude of the problems he inherited, Alfonsín, galvanized by the success, domestically and internationally, of his democratizing crusade, approached the tasks of government in a daring and decisive manner. His first measures were dictated by the message of justice that had captured the imagination of so many Argentines during the campaign. Three days after assuming office, the government dictated two decrees. The first ordered the arrest and criminal prosecution of the members of the three military juntas that had governed the country between 1976 and 1983. The second ordered the criminal prosecution of the surviving guerrilla leaders.

With respect to the military institutions, Alfonsín's strategy had two objectives: the punishment of military officers who had committed human rights violations and the incorporation of the armed forces into the new democratic order. For this reason, a legal process was undertaken that should have resulted in the military passing judgement on itself. A successful self-purification, Alfonsín was convinced, would permit the punishment of those with primary responsibility for the repression without antagonizing the military institution as a whole. He therefore sent to Congress a project amending the Code of Military Justice that gave the Supreme Council of the Armed Forces initial jurisdiction over military personnel. With the aim of obtaining a prompt judgement, this measure established that if, after six months from the beginning of the legal process, the military tribunal had not handed down a decision, the case would be judged by civilian courts. The amendment also limited the number of military personnel incriminated. During the electoral campaign Alfonsín had distinguished three groups of personnel with differing levels of responsibility: those who had given orders of repression, those who had committed excesses in carrying out orders and those who had done no more than carry out orders. The weight of punishment would fall on the first two groups, while the third would be pardoned for having acting according to the norms of military discipline.

While Alfonsín unfolded his strategy, the human rights organizations exerted pressure for the formation of a congressional commission to investigate the disappearance of individuals. This was an initiative loaded with risk for the government's objectives. Alfonsín instead created the Comisión Nacional de Desaparecidos (CONADEP), composed of independent figures whose only mission was to receive and verify accusations within a period of six months. However, during its period of activity, CONADEP served to sensitize public consciousness, which, after both forced and voluntary ignorance, was awakening to the extent of the military repression through testimonies given by relatives of the victims, the discovery of clandestine torture centres and cemeteries where unidentified persons were buried.

Congressional consideration of the amendment to the Code of Military Justice upset the delicate balance on which Alfonsín's strategy rested. Following a proposal by a *peronista* senator, Congress modified the concept of due obedience, excluding from its benefits those who had committed aberrant or atrocious acts. This new version frustrated the government's intention to limit the number of accused, given that a majority of the cases to be judged could fall into this vague category. The success of the official policy came to depend more than ever on the collaboration of the military tribunals: if these failed to complete the mission assigned them by Alfonsín, the entire strategy would be endangered because the cases would pass to the civilian courts and these, jealous of their recovered independence in the new democratic climate, would be unlikely to collaborate with the government.

At the end of September 1984, with the proscribed period of its jurisdiction ended, the Supreme Council of the Armed Forces issued a declaration supporting the procedures used in the war against subversion. On 22 April 1985 the public trial of senior military officers therefore began. After three and a half months of great tension, General Videla and Admiral Massera were, by unanimous decision, condemned to life sentences, while General Viola was sentenced to seventeen years in prison, Admiral Armando Lambruschini to nine years, and Brigadier Osvaldo Agosti to four and a half years. The members of the third military junta were released for lack of sufficient evidence but General Galtieri, as well as Admiral Anaya and Brigadier Basilio Lami Doza, had to stand trial by courts martial for the defeat in the Malvinas War. The sentences against Videla and Massera were received with satisfaction by democratic sectors, although they would have preferred stiffer sentences for the other military leaders. In contrast, in circles associated with the military, the sentences were judged to be a political manoeuvre to erode the prestige of the armed forces. For some, the violation of human rights had not been sufficiently castigated; for others, the officers who had been punished were men who, in defeating subversion, had saved the nation.

Alfonsín's policy towards the trade unions encountered similar difficulties. Together with the military, the unions had been the preferred targets of Radical Party propaganda in the 1983 campaign. The old Radicals who returned to the government with Alfonsín had not forgotten the hostility of the *peronista* trade unions towards President Illia between 1964 and 1966. This memory and the more recent suspicion of a union–military pact led the new government to give priority to a change in union leadership. As it had been necessary for political leaders to revalidate their legitimacy in the 1983 elections, so now came the turn of the union leaders. At the beginning of 1984 Alfonsín sent Congress a proposed law for organizing union elections which, due to a lack of political competition, many leaders won year after year.

The government's draft law proposed a very liberal structure for the selection of candidates and voter qualification with the objective of facilitating the rise of new leaders. It also charged the Ministry of Labour with supervising the elections. This placed union leaders on a war footing since they had always enjoyed unrestricted control over the political life of their organizations. The undisguised official offensive had the effect of unifying the *peronista* movement. The same union leaders who had, until then, been seen as responsible for the electoral defeat now mobilized the support of *peronista* congressmen. In spite of having been approved by the Chamber of Deputies, the law was defeated by the vote in the Senate.

Following the failure of the initiative, Alfonsín's labour minister had to resign; his successor managed to achieve union democratization but, to do so, he had to make compromises with union leaders. A new law, with more restrictive conditions and less government intervention, was approved by Congress after an agreement was reached between Radicals and *peronistas*. The union elections, which took place at the end of 1984, did not, however, produce many surprises. The government's hope for a renovation of the union leadership was to a large degree disappointed. This failed attempt was early evidence of the limits placed on the new government's aspirations by the distribution of institutional power.

The resolution of the controversy with Chile over the small islands in the Beagle Channel was more successful. After the near confrontation of 1978, both countries agreed to submit the matter to arbitration by the pope. In 1983 the military government and the political parties decided jointly that a response to the arbitration award would be made by the incoming elected government. In January 1984 Argentina and Chile signed a Declaration of Peace and Friendship in Rome, which gave Chile possession of the islands in dispute. Despite the reaction of nationalist sectors, Alfonsín strongly endorsed the award and set 25 November 1984 as the date for a national referendum to decide on the issue. The intent of this popular consultation, the first in Argentina, was to put pressure on Congress, where the *peronista* opposition threatened to use its power to deny ratification of the treaty. In a large turn-out, more than 80 per cent voted to accept the terms of the treaty, which was later ratified by Congress, although by a small majority. Not much progress was made on the other central issue of foreign policy, the dealings with Great Britain on the Islas Malvinas (Falkland Islands). Mrs Thatcher was unwilling to discuss sovereignty over the islands or to dismantle new defence installations, and Alfonsín could not resort to step-by-step diplomacy because of the military intransigency of the *peronistas* and the military.

In the management of the economy, Alfonsín initially underestimated the magnitude of the crisis. First, the new government inherited an economy which in 1983 had a GDP equal to that of 1974. Second, the Argentine economy was characterized by the highest inflation in the world; by 1983 the consumer price index had registered annual increases of three digits during nine consecutive years. Third, Alfonsín inherited a public sector with deficit of the order of 14 per cent of GDP in 1983. Finally, the new government took over a highly indebted economy. Service payments to foreign creditors rose from 2.2 per cent of GDP in 1980 to 9.9 per cent in the first year of the constitutional government. The total foreign debt of U.S. $45 billion required interest payments of $5.4 billion in 1984, or $3 billion less than the trade balance.

The new government lacked a proper diagnosis of the economy. It had only the analytical tools and the economic policies the Radicals had successfully implemented twenty years before. On the one hand, it was thought that economic stagnation could be attacked by a Keynesian redistributionist strategy while maintaining a high level of public spending; on the other hand, there was the view that inflation could be defeated by implementing a gradualist incomes policy, without substantially reducing the fiscal deficit. Finally, it was assumed that the establishment of a democratic regime would in itself open the way to a favourable renegotiation of the foreign debt. The initial economic policy barely lasted eight months, and its results were clearly discouraging for a government that expected simultaneously to reactivate the economy, increase real wages and slow down inflation. In fact, real wages grew by more than 35 per cent compared with the previous year, mainly as a consequence of an acceleration in the revaluation of the domestic currency. But other indicators quickly showed how brittle the government's programme was: the GDP growth rate slowed down; the annual inflation rate went from 626 per cent during the last quarter of 1983 to 1,080 per cent during the third quarter of 1984.

In June 1985, after a brief and failed attempt to stop inflation with the traditional instruments of demand management, Alfonsín's government launched a heterodox anti-inflationary plan – the so-called Austral Plan – that contained the basic requirement for a shock stabilization: an instantaneous shift towards fiscal–monetary balance, a rigid incomes policy (the freezing of wages, prices, the exchange rate and public utility rates) and monetary reform.

The fiscal–monetary balance was to be achieved by means of a dramatic increase in public sector resources through higher taxes on foreign trade, a tax reform and, particularly, a higher real tax collection rate due to the effect of falling inflation. The new fiscal deficit estimated for the second semester of 1985 would not exceed 2.5 per cent of GDP (including servicing of the foreign debt) and would be financed with foreign credit. The freeze – decided after careful adjustment in the exchange rate and public utility rates that accelerated inflation before the shock – was to meet the essential goal of breaking inflationary inertia and establishing a visible mechanism for the coordination of the many micro-economic decisions that would otherwise have tended to reproduce inflation. Finally, the monetary reform was aimed at avoiding the large transfers of wealth from debtors to creditors that could have resulted from the sudden drop in the inflation rate. The reform included a change in the currency (from the Argentine peso to the austral) and the establishment of a scale for converting from the old currency to the new one to honour the real terms of those contracts – agreed to before but cancelled after the reform – while preserving distributional neutrality.

Even though some sectors refused to accept the plan – particularly the trade unions, which staged a general strike – the general public placed their trust in it, as was shown by the renewal of bank deposits, the falling exchange rate of the U.S. dollar on the black market and acceptance of the price freeze, although there were no major bureaucratic controls. Within ninety days after the launching of the Austral Plan, most of the population felt that inflation had been beaten and that the country was finally facing a period of economic stability. In July wholesale prices had already dropped below their nominal terms, something that had not occurred since November 1973; consumer prices, which had increased 30.5 per cent in June, rose only 6.2 per cent in July, 3.1 per cent in August and 2 per cent in September. The demand for money, which had touched a historic low in the days before the stabilization plan's announcement, began to rise after a brief initial period during which firms reduced their inventory; production and private investment picked up, the purchasing power of wages was improved by the sudden drop in inflation and, finally, the imbalance in public accounts was significantly improved. Consequently, at the end of 1985, President Alfonsín's government seemed to have gained control over the economic situation. With these credits under its belt, the Radical Party passed its first electoral test. In November's partial elections for the Chamber of Deputies, Alfonsín's party received 43 per cent of the vote, while the *peronistas,* fragmented by internal conflicts, managed to capture only 34 per cent.

Galvanized by his domestic successes and by the recognition he received when travelling abroad, where he was hailed as the embodiment of the new Argentine democracy, Alfonsín attempted to govern on his own terms. This implied a relative marginalization of the Radical Party, which, although proven as a vote-winning machine, did not offer Alfónsin the skilled cadre needed to run the administration. The presidential cabinet was progressively staffed with professionals and independents more attuned to the modernizing spirit that marked the government. These new faces, best exemplified by the economic team led by Juan V. Sourrouille, were not always welcomed by veteran party members. But the UCR that took over in 1983, having doubled its historical following and overwhelmed by the new experience, was far from being able to create a well-defined party identity. Many Radicals claimed to know where they came from but few were certain as to where they were heading. In fact, 'alfonsinismo', as the new style of political action was called, developed mainly as a consequence of the exercise of power. Confined to a supporting role, the Radical Party followed Alfonsín's initiatives, although sometimes with little conviction and after manifesting its resistance.

Alfonsín's inclination to govern autonomously could not fail to upset

the sensibilities of sectors and institutions accustomed to exercising informal leverage over public policies. The Church, for example, reacted with
undisguised displeasure over the policies of a president who, confident of
his democratic legitimacy, encouraged the most diverse expressions of
pluralism and cultural modernization without consulting its opinion. The
ecclesiastical hierarchy, perhaps the most conservative in South America,
was uneasy with the re-establishment of freedom of expression and innovations in education. In 1986 the proposed divorce law put the Church on a
war footing, which led to a call for a popular mobilization against congressional approval. The response was slight. The question of divorce did not
divide the country or awaken great passions. When Congress finally
passed the law, Argentina ceased sharing with Ireland the anachronistic
status of being the only countries without legal divorce, thereby granting
delayed sanction to a reform that public opinion had accepted long before.
The Church never abandoned its attitude of mistrust towards the government of Alfonsín.

The Austral Plan permitted Alfonsín a bridge to the business community. For the first time, the government of a party suspicious of business
could forge a modus vivendi with a corporate sector that had traditionally
reciprocated its prejudices. This was a development laden with implications. For many years the prevalent conviction among the largest companies had been that in order to achieve the stability and predictability
necessary for managing the economy it was convenient to suppress the
arenas of policy negotiation characteristic of democratic life. This had led
them to support military governments and restrictions on the activity of
political parties and trade unions. Such a conviction was severely shaken
by the manifest failure of the recent military regime; now businessmen
appeared more disposed to reconcile themselves to the new democratic
order. Alfonsín's conversion to a more austere and rigorous economic
policy facilitated this process, which, although never translated into manifest sympathy for the government, at least contributed to neutralizing the
traditional animosity of the world of big business. At the same time, the
favourable attitude of the United States towards the Argentine democratic
transition contributed to this process.

By 1986, only three sectors were explicitly excluded from the consensus
that surrounded Alfonsín. First were important groups within the armed
forces, resentful over what they understood to be a campaign of slander
towards the military orchestrated from within governing circles and over
financial belt-tightening after a reduction by half of defence spending,

which in 1983 represented 4 per cent of GDP. Next were the trade union leaders, particularly those of the CGT, which since 1984 had chosen open confrontation with the government by means of repeated general strikes. Finally, the Partido Peronista, which, in the midst of an internal crisis it could not overcome, contested Alfonsín's policies with populist and nationalist slogans that were its trademark in Argentine political life.

The central role played by the president in a situation of crisis and economic emergency such as gripped Argentina was a normal and predictable phenomenon. But those in the circles that surrounded Alfonsín went beyond this and succumbed to the temptation, always present in the national political culture, to claim a hegemonic position. There was talk about a 'Third Historical Movement' that, resuscitating the broad popular coalitions which had been raised first around Yrigoyen and later Perón, would now be articulated around the leadership of Alfonsín. There were grand schemes to found a 'Second Republic', such as moving the capital of the country to the South and reforming the constitution, ostensibly with the intention of effecting Alfonsín's re-election as president for a second term.

Consumed by a vision of a Radical hegemony over Argentine political life and convinced that *peronismo* was incapable of overcoming the crisis that followed its 1983 defeat, the Alfonsín team did not correctly evaluate the gradual change in leadership that had begun to take place among the followers of Perón. In the 1985 elections, those who had given birth to what was called the *peronista* Renovation made important advances. In provinces like Buenos Aires and Córdoba they broke with the party leadership and presented their own tickets. Their relative triumphs in the midst of the party's debacle opened a new stage in its development. The construction of a democratic *peronismo* was the banner of the new current. In contrast with the pejorative tone used by Perón when speaking of politics and '*partidocracia*', the new figures, such as Antonio Cafiero, Manuel de la Sota and Carlos Grosso, spoke in very positive terms of democracy and political parties. The institutionalist message, while an effect of the new political spirit motivated by Alfonsín, also pointed towards a questioning of the Radical democratic monopoly. The aim of the 'Renovators' was to distance themselves from Alfonsín and his policies. They tended to characterize the Austral Plan as a continuation of the economic policies of the military government: it reflected submission to the IMF and the interests of creditor banks, while being ineffective in reactivating the economy.

The Austral Plan did not open the new economic era promised by the

government in 1985. Hyperinflation was avoided, but various structural
and institutional factors — seasonal scarcity of foodstuffs, the continuation
of indexation in labour contracts and an increase in the price of private
personal services, all omitted from the freeze — combined to complicate a
reduction in inflation. As a result, consumer prices rose at 3.8 per cent per
month in the third quarter of 1985, at 2.5 per cent in the final quarter and
3.1 per cent in the first quarter of 1986. This level of inflation created
obvious difficulties, and early in 1986 it was necessary to end the freeze on
prices and wages. This shift towards a short-term policy of greater flexibility occurred, however, within the context of diminished attention to
securing stability. The government was harried by the unions, the *peronista*
opposition and some industrial sectors which insisted that the country had
entered a deep recession. Although the facts did not support this claim, it
weakened the will of the ruling party. Seeking respite from pressure, the
government relaxed restrictions on the terms of agreements between companies and unions. Day by day it became more evident that this was
conducive not to strengthening the programme of stability but to reviving
the traditional distributive conflicts of the Argentine economy.

Contrary to the initial policies of the minister of economy, during 1986
wages rose by a monthly rate of 5 per cent whilst public prices increased
by 3.9 per cent and the official exchange rate by 3.5 per cent. As a
consequence of this disparity, the economic programme became imbalanced. At the same time, monetary policy followed an expansionist course
in an effort to palliate, through credit, constant demands for greater
support for production and employment. The instrumental success of the
Austral Plan was not paralleled at an ideological level: the notion of
stability rapidly retreated in the face of the more attractive slogans encouraging growth and reactivation.

This weakness was mirrored in the unstable character of fiscal adjustments. As time passed the emergency measures applied to decrease public
expenditure and increase revenues were abandoned without being replaced
by new policies of comparable strength. The fiscal deficit, which stood at
14 per cent of GDP in 1983, fell to 12 per cent in 1984, the first year of
the Alfonsín administration. As a result of the Austral Plan it was further
reduced to 6 per cent in 1985 and 4.3 per cent in 1986. This was achieved
on the expenditure side through adjustment of items more vulnerable to
administrative manipulation: pensions, public sector wages and small
public works. In contrast, by virtue of protection through specific legislation, tax subsidies for private companies, large public works and holders

of state contracts were not affected and suffered only slightly from the fiscal adjustments. Neither the provinces nor the state-owned companies supported the economic effort of the central government. The provinces, which were permanently seeking larger transfers from the federal administration, actually managed to avoid the cuts that had to be borne by other sectors of the state. The state-owned companies had to reduce investments, but were at least able for some time to defend a privileged position within the wage structure of the public sector.

Initial advances on the revenue side were also stalled. Giving priority to the success of their policy of shock, the government directed its attention to those resources that were transitory by definition (windfall tax on high incomes and companies) or were a one-off result of the decrease in inflation (reduced losses incurred between the formal date of tax payments and their actual receipt by the state) or were exceptionally blessed by the temporary high agricultural prices on the world market.

The fragility and unevenness of the fiscal adjustment showed clearly the difficulty of imposing a stabilization plan when only a few, even within the ruling party, had the fight against inflation as their priority. With most of the provinces in the hands of the opposition, with only partial control of the legislature and with a public administration in which indifference prevailed, the day-to-day operation of the Austral Plan suffered from obstructionism and compromise. The external environment was also unfavourable to the plan. Throughout 1985, 1986, and 1987 international cereal prices fell sharply. In 1987 they were 35 per cent lower than in 1984, resulting in a major loss of export revenue. Moreover, while the government upheld an exchange rate designed to control inflation in 1985 and 1986, the fall in dollar prices was followed by a reduction in the revenue of agricultural production for the internal market. In order to compensate for this, export taxes were lowered with a predictably adverse effect on public finances.

The reduction in international prices of agricultural products – which during the first four years of the Alfonsín administration produced a fall in the terms of trade of 40 per cent – dramatized the effects of another burden that hampered the stabilization program: the external debt. In 1983 the external debt was 77.3 per cent of GDP and remained around this level during subsequent years. If all the interest due had been paid, the transfers of resources abroad would have been, on average, 6.5 per cent of GDP. The government was able to reduce the transfers of resources through negotiations with the creditors to half of this amount, but the

interest that was not paid increased the total debt from U.S. $45.9 billion
in 1983 to $56.8 billion in 1987. Not only was the external debt a
constraint on growth; it also had a domestic dimension. Because the debt
was nationalized during 1981–3, most external indebtedness was in the
public sector. As a result, the responsibility for its servicing fell mainly on
the government, which had to purchase the private trade surplus to meet
these obligations. Thus, the interest payments added 5.1 per cent of GDP
between 1984 and 1987 to the fiscal deficit, creating more obstacles for
the stabilization plan.

The Austral Plan was already a falling star at the beginning of 1987,
when the country entered a crucial electoral year, with half the lower
house and all the provincial governments to be renewed in September. In
February, the government introduced a new wage and price freeze in a
desperate attempt to break a potentially inflationary spiral. The economic
authorities were afraid of an acceleration in prices as a consequence of a
generalized push by most interest groups at a time when the ruling party
would give in to pressures. The freeze was intended to hold the line until
September, after which a more serious stabilization programme would be
implemented.

The approaching elections dictated another official initiative that added
a new source of instability to the management of the economy. Alfonsín
appointed Carlos Alderete, a trade union leader, as minister of labour.
This was the culmination of negotiations begun between government
officials and an important group of trade unions. By this step, the former
were looking to weaken the CGT, obtain a labour truce and deprive the
Partido Justicialista of union support in the coming elections. The initial
motivation of the union leaders was their discontent with the CGT's
policy of confrontation, which had been an obstacle to changing the
system of labour relations. After three years of democracy, labour legislation was the same as it had been under the previous military government.
This impeded collective bargaining, the re-election of union leaders by
their organizations and the independent management of the considerable
resources of the union's social and health programmes. Moreover, the
politicians of the *peronista* Renovation, with the aim of capturing independent voters, had opted for conducting an electoral campaign without the
irritating presence of the unionists. Resentful of their marginalization,
they sought to draw closer to the government in order to dispute power
within the *peronista* movement subsequently.

In the short run, the government objective of diminishing labour conflict was achieved, but at a high price. To a large degree, the conflicts were transferred inside the government. The daily confrontation between the minister of economy and the minister of labour complicated the adoption of policies and forced Alfonsín into a position of permanent arbitration. At the same time, the government postponed the project to decentralize collective bargaining and regulate the right to strike. In its place, the new labour minister managed to gain congressional approval of free collective bargaining and a legal framework similar to that put into place under the last *peronista* government in 1974, which operated under the direct influence of the trade unions.

At the beginning of 1987 the military also dramatically reappeared on the scene. Once the leaders of the military juntas had been condemned in 1985, the civil courts had proceeded with other trials. Every time an officer was summoned to appear before the courts, progressively less disguised expressions of unrest emerged from within the military. Despite the growing official concern, Alfonsín did not act, because he had little support from the *peronista* opposition and faced resistance by some sectors of his own party. Finally on 5 December 1986 he submitted to Congress the so-called *Punto Final* law whereby, following enactment, a sixty-day term was fixed for the filing of legal actions; once the term expired, there would be no further chance to initiate claims against military personnel. Congress passed the bill swiftly, though not easily: *peronistas* chose not to take part in the Chamber of Deputy sessions, and Alfonsín had to employ all of his influence to persuade his own people to vote favourably. The law was enacted on 24 December, but the official initiative backfired. Judges decided to interrupt their annual vacation period, which normally took place in January, and stood by to accept all the cases presented in the sixty days set by the law. On 23 February 1987, when the period was to end, legal action had been taken against more than three hundred top-ranking officers.

A period of high tension ensued. On 16 April in Córdoba a military officer due in court on charges of human rights violations became a fugitive from justice and took refuge in a local regiment. At the Campo de Mayo garrison in Buenos Aires, Lieutenant Colonel Aldo Rico rallied a hundred officers, who pressed the government for a 'political solution' to the trials and the removal of the army's high command for having subordinated the interests of the institution to Alfonsín's political convenience. The president issued the order to end the revolt; no military unit obeyed. As massive civilian protest erupted and a crowd estimated at 400,000 gathered in the Plaza de Mayo, Alfonsín went to the rebel stronghold and convinced the rebels to lay down their arms. On 13 May, bowing to the rebels' demands and after replacing the army high commander, the government submitted to Congress a bill that clearly specified the scope of due obedience in order to protect the middle levels of the armed forces, but now in much broader terms than Alfonsín originally intended and the Congress had later stipulated. On 4 June the official party once again had to enact a law against the solid opposition of the *peronista* deputies.

The Due Obedience Law fulfilled one of the objectives included in the government's agenda since the very beginning: to limit the sentences for human rights violations to a small number of top-ranking officers. However, the circumstances surrounding its approval led it to be perceived as a capitulation, thus weakening Alfonsín's credibility weeks before the September 1987 elections. At the same time, inflation again accelerated as a result of the government's policies. The February freeze did not last more than three months; inflation reached 13.7 per cent, the highest since 1985, one month before the elections. Although official efforts to prevent the economy from spiralling into hyperinflation had hitherto been quite successful, this was too modest a conquest for a society that had been promised much more four years before.

The government, as well as the opposition, converted the September elections into a referendum. Thanks to the Renovators, *peronismo* managed to recover legitimacy as a democratic alternative, depriving the Radicals of one of their principal banners. The *peronistas* won 41 per cent, compared with 34 per cent in 1985, whilst the Radical vote declined from 43 to 37 per cent. The outcome was even more adverse for the governing party at the gubernatorial level. The Partido Justicialista not only kept the provinces it had won in 1985 but also added five of the seven provinces that had been in the hands of the Radicals, thus controlling seventeen of twenty-two provinces. Within this overall picture, the defeat of the Radical candidate in Buenos Aires Province was particularly important, since the two candidates, Antonio Cafiero and Juan Manuel Casella, were potential candidates for the presidency in 1989. The electoral results had special significance for the *peronista* Renovators, which later took Cafiero to the presidency of the party; they won without the explicit support of the trade unions.

The fact that the elections were broadly seen as a plebiscite compounded the effects of defeat on the government's legitimacy. In a parliamentary system Alfonsín would have been obliged to resign, but under the constitution the president still had two years of his term to serve. This anomalous position was eased somewhat by an improvement in relations between Alfonsín and Cafiero and by the fact that the opposition's strengthened representation allowed it to drop its confrontational approach in favour of negotiating on behalf of its constituency. In this light, Congress regained its importance – hitherto diminished by the executive's use of decree laws – and long-delayed legislation, such as the National Defence Law and the statute to regulate financial relations between the republic and the provinces, was finally approved. Discussions over reform of the constitution were also renewed with a view to establishing a semi-parliamentary system. However, this process of increased collaboration and the attendant notion of co-government were short-lived and always restricted by enduring suspicion on both sides. In the second half of 1988 Radicals and *peronistas* began to select their presidential candidates for the elections of 1989, and the logic of political competition reopened traditional hostilities.

At Alfonsín's direct injunction, the Radical Party nominated the governor of Córdoba, Eduardo Angeloz, whose efficient administration had enabled him to survive the recent electoral defeats suffered by the governing party. Alfonsín's decision cut short the internal debate engendered by this set-back, and the official candidate was grudgingly accepted by militants who would have preferred an ideologically less moderate figure. After the experience of 1987 political realism demanded a search for votes in the centre of the political spectrum, and this became even more imperative once the *peronistas* elected their presidential candidate.

In July 1988 the supporters of *peronismo* were able for the first time in their history to elect their presidential slate. As a consequence the heterogeneity latent in the *peronista* revival was brought out into the open. The victory of Carlos Menem, with 53 per cent of the votes against 47 per cent for Cafiero, represented a distinctive current within the new *peronismo*. As governor of La Rioja, a small and underdeveloped northern province which he ruled as if it were his personal fiefdom, Menem incarnated the antipolitical traditions of *peronismo*. Cafiero was much more closely associated with republican institutions and the party system. Menem's victory owed much to the support of the poorest sectors of society and trade union leaders who reacted to the brusque treatment they had received at the hands of Cafiero in 1987.

The election campaigns of Menem and Angeloz presented Argentines with two clearly contrasting visions of the country's problems and the means by which they should be solved. The *justicialista* candidate toured the cities and countryside making promises of large wage increases and a moratorium on the external debt, but above all he called for confidence in his own person. Angeloz's message, by contrast, placed more emphasis on an austere and efficient state and an economy more open to world trade. Both sought to distance themselves from Alfonsín, whose prestige was now badly eroded. Menem did this directly, attacking the president as responsible for the economic crisis; Angeloz was more moderate, accusing Alfonsín of demonstrating a lack of will in confronting the crisis.

In the meantime Alfonsín himself had to preside over a government that had little time left to serve and yet was being subjected to rising pressure. In December 1988 there was a further military revolt led by Colonel Mohamed Seneildin, who returned to the country from Panama, where he had been training General Noriega's forces, to direct an insurrection with the objective of restoring political legitimacy to the war against subversion. The uprising did not last long, but it highlighted another conflict wracking the military. The rebels, largely members of elite units, accused the high command of corruption and lack of martial spirit, which they held responsible for the army's growing problems since the Malvinas War. A month later an unexpected and rapidly suppressed attack on a barracks by a small left-wing group reawakened memories of the recent past that were exploited by the armed forces to justify their previous actions and cast aspersions on the weak pacifism of the Alfonsín government.

The Alfonsín government was also confronted by growing economic difficulties as inflation and fiscal disequilibrium continued despite the October 1987 renewal of wage and price freezes and accompanying emergency taxes. In an effort to regain the initiative, and out of frustration at the failure of the Austral Plan, the government introduced a new programme of economic reforms aimed at correcting structural weaknesses in the public sector and progressively opening the economy to international trade. These measures were an attempt to strike at the causes of inflation from a position much closer to that of economic liberalism than had been the case in 1983–4. A policy of deregulation was introduced for public services in order to eliminate the legal obstacles to private investment in them; 40 per cent of the state airline and the public telephone system was put up for sale; the system of industrial support was reformed with a limited reduction in public subsidy to the private sector; the domestic price of petrol was brought towards the international level and encouragement given to private investment in the oil industry; progress was made in deregulating certain basic industries – paper, steel, petrochemicals – that had traditionally been protected by high tariffs; and a start was made in the progressive diminution of quantitative restrictions on imports.

These policies were introduced not by a strong government, such as that which had launched the Austral Plan in 1986, but by one weakened by recent electoral defeat, and the reform programme yielded uneven results. The policy of privatization, which had to be approved by Congress, did not come to fruition because of *peronista* obstructionism and because many Radicals were in two minds about it, whilst others saw it as a surrender of the party's programme. The measures for commercial and industrial deregulation and reductions in public subsidies were strongly resisted by private firms and had to be moderated as a result. The reform policies were intended to correct structural faults in the economy that encouraged inflation, but there was little to suggest that they could in themselves guarantee short-term stability. The first part of 1988 saw a test of the imbalance between the policy of stabilization and that of reform. Under the argument that it was necessary to halt Treasury financing of public corporations, the government began to increase public sector prices sharply. At the same time wage negotiations were freed and controls on private prices relaxed, further accelerating inflation, which reached a monthly rate of 25 per cent by July, its highest level since 1985.

In these circumstances and in the face of widespread public scepticism, the government felt obliged to make a final effort to avoid the hyperinflationary crisis which had hovered over it since 1984. In August 1988 the Plan Primavera was introduced with the aim of controlling the economy until the presidential poll of May 1989. But the Alfonsín administration now lacked the political resources upon which it had been able to rely in the past. A wage and price freeze was no longer possible, since Congress had approved the free collective bargaining long demanded by the unions. Moreover, fiscal adjustments could not be carried out through new taxes, since it was unlikely that the congressional opposition would consent to them. Export taxes were similarly excluded because Alfonsín had promised the rural sector that, following the Plan Austral, they would not be reimposed. Finally, support from the international financial community was constrained by the fact that in April, as a result of a fall in reserves, the government had ceased paying interest on the external debt and had silently introduced a moratorium.

As the presidential campaign got under way Menem's populist campaign engendered disquiet amongst business sectors, and this in turn prompted co-operation among the government, the Unión Industrial and the Cámara Argentina de Comercio in an agreement to sustain free collective bargaining whilst maintaining controlled prices. However, rural interests were not included in this concordat. One of the main means for improving public finances was the development of an exchange rate mechanism that effectively imposed an export tax, which, it had formally been agreed, would not be levied. The state thereby appropriated the higher international prices currently prevailing for agricultural produce as a result of the U.S. drought, and these funds were used to finance the fiscal deficit. This produced an open conflict with the Sociedad Rural. Externally the IMF refused to support Alfonsín's anti-inflationary programme, but the World Bank, acting in accord with the U.S. Treasury, broke ranks and released an important set of credits to assist the country's reserves. With this combination of domestic and foreign backing, the plan achieved some initial success; the monthly inflation rate fell from 27.6 per cent in August to 6.8 per cent in December. Nevertheless, behind this apparently favourable result there was a growing disequilibrium caused by a programme that was designed to reduce price increases by relying on periodic adjustments below those of past inflation with consequent lags in the exchange rate and public prices. But the Plan Primavera faced a still greater threat from the uncertainty surrounding the election campaign, which kept alive the dangers of a run on the austral. The government kept interest rates high, while clinging to the hope (in the event, unfulfilled) that Angeloz would at least keep pace with the *peronista* candidate, whose platform frightened the business community. At the end of January 1989 the World Bank notified the government informally that it would not release a significant portion of the credit it had promised on the grounds that the conditions for payment had not been met. This was indeed the case, but the decision also reflected an unexpected result of the inauguration of the Bush administration: the replacement in the Treasury Department of those officials who had been favourably disposed towards the Plan Primavera by others who opposed it. A little later the creditor banks renewed their pressure for payment of overdue interest, and the IMF confirmed its refusal to offer support. These decisions were carefully leaked to the press and immediately unleashed the feared run on the austral.

An important sector of financiers, including local branches of the creditor banks, began to sell off their holdings of australes and buy dollars from the Central Bank. On 6 February, with reserves almost exhausted, the government was forced to halt its sale of dollars. This confirmed the worst fears of the populace, provoking a rise of 45 per cent in the price of the dollar on the free market in just six days. At the same time, the Central Bank was shown to be powerless to stop the loss of reserves, because the grain exporters were now able to take their revenge and refused to release hard currency. This weakness was further emphasized when, despite a series of devaluations, the exporters continued their refusal to come to the government's aid. As a result, savers became convinced that a major external blockade was being imposed, and in March there was a massive withdrawal of dollar deposits from the banks.

The political foundation of the Plan Primavera also disintegrated. The Unión Industrial and the Cámara de Comercio distanced themselves from both the government and the failure of its economic programme in an effort to gain a more favourable position for what now seemed an inevitable *peronista* election victory. At the end of March the minister of economy and his team resigned. The Alfonsín administration slid from a state of impotence to one of complete prostration whilst the country finally entered full hyperinflation.

The crisis in the exchange rate, which increased the price of the dollar by 400 per cent between February and April, affected consumer prices, deepened the fiscal deficit, severely destabilized the banking system and drove the population back to a range of defensive reactions. Confronted by the threat of the dissolution of their capital, businessmen resorted to preemptive price increases and reduced supply; workers demanded advances on their wages up to three times per month; exporters continued to withhold goods despite the record exchange rates; generalized speculation was fuelled by the retention of taxes and failure to pay public bills.

It was in this context that, on 14 May, the electorate voted for the Partido Justicialista's presidential candidate. Menem received 49 per cent of the vote, while Angeloz obtained 37 per cent. But it was no time for celebration. At the end of May food riots broke out, reflecting growing social unrest. In mid-June and after a failed attempt to gain Menem's support for a joint economic action, Alfonsín announced that he would resign in order to shorten his mandate due to end in December 1989. On 8 July, as Argentines learned that the inflation rate of the previous month had been 114 per cent, Alfonsín transferred power to Menem. For the first time in sixty years an elected president was succeeded by one who had also been democratically elected. This remarkable achievement of the democratic transition was clouded, however, by the general atmosphere of crisis.

The distribution of institutional power resulting from the elections gave Menem more favourable leverage than Alfonsín had had in 1983; *peronistas* had a majority in the lower house, the Senate was under full *peronista* control and seventeen of twenty-two governors were *peronistas*. Sensing the unavoidable weight of extra-institutional power, however, Menem made a bold decision that took everyone by surprise: he made overtures to the economic establishment and, with the enthusiasm of the newly converted, gave full support to a programme of fiscal austerity, privatization and economic liberalization. Later, yielding to the demands of the military, he granted a presidential pardon to high-ranking officers accused of human rights abuses and those who had been involved in the rebellions against Alfonsín. With his new allies in the business community, with backing from the armed forces and confident of his charisma, Menem led *peronismo,* reeling from the political U-turn, into a new experience in governing a society in conflict.

The first stage on the democratization process initiated in 1983 having been completed, the balance remained uncertain. Institutions had managed to survive the challenges posed by a serious economic crisis. Hyperinflation had not prevented the transfer of power in 1989 from one democratically elected president to another. Thus, it had been possible to dissociate the legitimacy of democratic institutions from the negative evaluation of their economic and social performance. However, though a catastrophic outcome had been averted, the reality was that many of the hopes raised by the new political cycle had been disappointed.

Throughout the period after 1983, the stagnant condition of the Argentine economy persisted: between 1984 and 1988 GDP increased at an annual rate of only 0.3 per cent. The unemployment rate, which in October 1983 was 3.9 per cent, by the end of 1988 had reached 6.2 per cent. Nor was the process of deindustrialization begun during the previous military administration reversed. The level of industrial employment, which in 1983 was 69 per cent of that of 1970, at the end of 1988 was 59 per cent. As for industrial wages, the last quarter of 1988 found them at the same level as they had been in 1983. All of these indicators worsened drastically when hyperinflation broke out in 1989.

The political parties and their leaders paid a high price in popularity and credibility for the economy's deterioration. In fact, Menem's ascent to power was due in large part to his ability to portray himself as a popular leader far removed from the discredited political class. The open involvement of the major economic corporations in the polity was still another sign of the current weakness of the traditional seats of the representative system: Congress, the parties and the presidency. Furthermore, the successive amnesties granted, under military pressure, to officers on trial for human rights violations revealed that force endured as a means of attaining political objectives.

Neither Argentina's economic decline nor its tendencies towards political praetorianism appeared to have changed during the years of the restoration of democracy. As the 1990s began, the search for an alternative to the economic and political order born in 1946 continued amid the recurrent but failed attempts to change it.

3

URUGUAY SINCE 1930

'In no other country do people live as we do . . . no other people on earth currently enjoy achievements such as ours'.[1] Thus, in the course of a speech in 1949, did President Luis Batlle Berres express euphoric sentiments of satisfaction with the state of the Uruguayan nation. They were not necessarily shared by all his listeners, but during the following decade the notion that 'como el Uruguay no hay' (there's nowhere like Uruguay) was quickly absorbed into national mythology. As late as the mid-1960s Uruguayans might still cling to the belief that they were citizens of an exceptional country, blessed (unlike their neighbours) with the capacity to achieve political stability, as well as prosperity and social justice. Such an optimistic and complacent view was generally shared by external observers. But in reality Batlle Berres' statement had lost all meaning, except perhaps in an ironic sense. At mid-century Uruguay had fully recovered from the authoritarianism of Gabriel Terra in the 1930s and was now engaged, in the new age of import-substitution industrialization, in an attempt to re-establish and extend the political and social institutions of the *batllista* system of the pre-1930 period. The nation turned inwards, as if it preferred to live on the strength of a legend, choosing to enjoy a comfortable present rather than to contemplate an uncertain future. The consolidation of the new ideology, neo-*batllismo,* was facilitated by international changes of which Uruguay was a passive and, in the short term, favoured beneficiary. But by the mid-1950s the neo-*batllista* system had become a debased imitation of its predecessor, and a decade later its economic basis had collapsed. Events and policies after 1968 undermined the 'Uruguay *feliz*' of tradition, paving the way for twelve bitter years of

[1] 'Puedo asegurarles que no hay país en el que se viva como vivimos nosotros . . . conquistas como las nuestras, no las vive, en estos momentos, ningún pueblo de la tierra'. Luis Batlle, *Pensamiento y acción,* vol. 2 (Montevideo, 1966), p. 72.

military rule (1973–85). In 1985 Uruguay returned to democracy with profound relief but in a mood of anxiety which the events of succeeding years did not wholly dispel.

The factors which had made Uruguay a special case by 1930 were its favourable natural endowment and its social structure, as well as the political and legislative achievements of the first two decades of the century. Indeed, it may be that these achievements not only were made possible by underlying economic and social conditions, but were prompted by them. Because of the sparse population of the country – about 1.2 million in 1920 – relative to the vast area of natural pasture, Uruguay had high levels of exports and income per capita. However, the tide of immigrants drawn to the country, especially in the decade before the First World War, did not find employment in the rural sector, which had in fact released surplus labour in the preceding decades, but instead remained in the city of Montevideo. This influx served not only to accelerate the development of the urban economy, but also to accentuate the political tensions of an export-oriented but substantially urbanized society.

It was the management of these tensions which marked the outstanding achievement of the presidencies of José Batlle y Ordóñez (1903–7, 1911–15). The beginning of his term of office coincided with the abortive rebellion of Aparicio Saravia in 1904, a final echo of the civil wars of the nineteenth century and a demonstration of the deep division within the landowning class between modernizing *estancieros* and traditional caudillos. Batlle's success in imposing the authority of central government conclusively ended the era of regional *caudillismo,* and that success, together with the under-representation of the landowning class within the governing Colorado Party, enhanced his capacity to mediate between the demands of the landowning class, on the one hand, and the strengthening urban working and middle classes, on the other. Thus, policies of industrial protection, expansion of the state sector and of educational provision promoted enterprise and social mobility. At the same time, the political process showed itself responsive to the requirements of the urban working class, within which trade unions and left-wing political groups were establishing a base among the immigrant population. The preservation of a political system dominated by the two traditional multi-class parties, Colorado and Blanco (or National), required a body of legislation in support of labour and the socially disadvantaged, which served to appropriate for the Colorados the potential mass support of class-based organizations.

Batlle thus promoted the role of the state as mediator between conflict-

ing social classes and secured relative social stability by measures to redistribute income during a period of economic prosperity. The deployment of
redistributive techniques, the prominence of the political process and of
politics as a full-time career and the high social value placed on compromise as the proper solution to conflict all became part of the meaning of
batllismo. In this general sense, *batllismo* refers to a national style or ideology, rather than to the actual achievement of Batlle y Ordóñez or to the
political programme of the *batllista* wing of the Colorado Party. But if
Batlle's settlement was achieved in the context of a buoyant economy, it
remained to be seen how it would adapt to conditions of economic decline.
During the generally prosperous conditions of the 1920s, Batlle was out of
office but remained an enormously influential figure, though increasingly
within the ranks of the *batllista* Colorados rather than nationally. In October 1929 he died; and in the following year the effects of the world
depression began to reach Uruguay.

DEPRESSION AND *TERRISMO*, 1930–42

In Uruguay, as elsewhere in Latin America, the depression signified the
end of the era of export-led growth, even though its political sequel
resulted in power being held by interests which were closely linked to the
export sector. The impact of the depression was certainly severe. Compared with the peak year of 1930, the value of exports fell by 22 per cent
in 1931 and a further 20 per cent in 1932. Of the principal commodities,
meat was more severely affected than wool, which partly reflected the
dependence of beef exports on the British market. Indeed, chilled beef,
Uruguay's leading meat export product, was consigned exclusively to
Britain, although Uruguay's position in the British market was that of a
marginal producer. The crisis in the export trades had effects throughout
the economy, with a decline in the supply of imports by 30 per cent
between 1930 and 1932 and a marked increase in the level of unemployment. The destabilizing effects of the depression were increased in turn by
the reduction of government revenue, heavily dependent on export and
import taxes.

Under the constitution of 1919, responsibility for the management of
the economy (and thus for coping with the crisis) resided with the nine
members of the Consejo Nacional de Administración (CNA), while the
president's share of executive authority was confined to internal security
and foreign affairs. In 1930 Gabriel Terra was elected to the presidency as

a *batllista* candidate, but nonetheless almost immediately began a campaign of criticism against the CNA (and therefore of its main supporters, the *batllistas*) which culminated in its abolition in Terra's coup of 31 March 1933. The campaign was based on demands for the reform of the allegedly inefficient and ineffective CNA, the attempts of which to deal with an unprecedented and deepening economic crisis provided obvious ammunition for the attack. A paradoxical aspect of this episode is the extent to which the *batllista*-led CNA implemented quite severe measures of fiscal orthodoxy and conservatism, while after 1933 public expenditure was allowed to rise and indeed the interventionist policies of the CNA in the external sector were maintained, albeit in modified form. In fact, the coup had little to do with the inadequacies of the CNA as an institution and is better explained by Terra's personal ambition and the reaction of the property-owning class at a time of severe crisis against traditional *batllista* policies.

There is no doubt that even at the time of his election Terra was widely regarded within the *batllista* faction as dangerously ambitious. He was also liable to act inconsistently and impulsively. But the split with his former colleagues was precipitated late in 1931 by an agreement between the *batllista* Colorados and the majority faction of the National (Blanco) Party, which was soon labelled the Pacto del Chinchulín (Pork-barrel Pact). The agreement secured Nationalist support for a long-standing *batllista* objective, the creation of a new public corporation, Administración Nacional de Combustibles, Alcohol y Portland (ANCAP), which would manufacture or distribute petroleum products, alcohol and cement. The price of this support was a concession to the principle of co-participation by the minority party in government, since it was now agreed that the boards of public corporations should reflect the political composition of the CNA. The pact unquestionably represented a major step towards the politicization of public administration and the consequent growth of patronage, although there was no immediate major increase in the level of public employment before 1933, as is sometimes alleged. But the pact did not go unopposed within the National Party, and Terra was able to find a valuable ally in the leader of its non-participating faction, Luis Alberto de Herrera.

Underlying the divisions within the parties and the executive was the long-standing and growing discontent of the propertied class, and of the British-owned public utility companies, with the unhelpful or hostile attitude of the *batllista* Colorados. The landowning and commercial sectors were hard hit by the collapse of world markets, and their immediate grievance was the trade and exchange control policy introduced by the CNA in 1931–2 which limited the rate of depreciation of the peso. A greater fear, however, was that in the forthcoming Anglo-Uruguayan trade negotiations following the Ottawa Agreements of 1932, the old antagonisms between the British Foreign Office and the *batllistas,* and between the *batllistas* and the landowners, would combine to wreck the country's principal export market. If the interests of the conservative classes were to be preserved in the new circumstances of the 1930s, it was imperative that the *batllistas* be replaced.

The coup of 1933 aroused almost no active resistance. The required show of force was provided by the police, the armed forces remaining passive. It had the support of Herrera's Blancos as well as the anti-*batllista* Colorados and the large landowners. The Foreign Office was delighted, and Terra received the immediate congratulations of the British minister in Montevideo. British companies made loans to the new regime, in the expectation that the antipathy of the *batllistas* to British capital would be replaced by a more congenial attitude. To a limited extent this proved to be the case, and yet an important aspect of the 1933 regime was the degree to which it resembled its predecessor, in both its mode of government and its economic policies.

The authoritarian and illiberal nature of Terra's rule (1933–8) cannot be questioned: press censorship was introduced, opposition political groups persecuted and political leaders exiled. But the repression was in general as mild as opposition to the coup had been muted. It was said to be a *dictablanda* rather than *dictadura.* The element of political continuity between the two regimes lay in the survival of co-participation after 1933 as the basis of political support for the government, although its application was now restricted to the supporters of Terra and Herrera. The growth of public employment during the 1930s testified to the traditional manner in which political support was consolidated. In economic policy, the ousting of the *batllistas* was reflected in an interruption of the programme of social and labour legislation, and the 'firmness' of the regime on labour questions resulted in depressed real wage levels. But while the representation of the capitalist class as a whole was strengthened, and the beginning of a historic age was promised for the rural sector in which the wrongs imposed by the *batllistas* would be redressed, the reality was disenchanting. It was impossible for the new regime to reverse the changes brought about by the depression. In the

short term there was more favourable exchange rate treatment for exports, the burden of land mortgage payments was relieved and the fiscal
burden was lightened somewhat. Agreement was reached with the British government in 1935, which ensured continued if much reduced
access to the British beef market. But against this, the new era of
dirigismo (interventionism) in economic policy persisted. The structure of
trade and exchange controls, introduced as emergency measures in 1931,
was institutionalized by the 1933 regime, and indeed as exports began to
recover after 1935 it was policy to resist too rapid an upward revaluation
of the peso. The fact was that the preceding decades of urban growth had
created an economy which in 1930 was, proportionate to its size, one of
the most highly industrialized in Latin America. It was not possible for
the new government to disregard the claims of manufacturing industry
for higher protection and access to imports of necessary intermediate
goods. In spite of its public commitment to the rural sector, therefore, it
was the urban sector which by the late 1930s was showing the greater
dynamism, especially following the commissioning of ANCAP's oil refinery in 1937.

The regime installed by coup in 1933 legitimized itself by a new
constitution in 1934. The regime was constructed on an alliance of the
Terra and Herrera factions of the two parties, and this was reflected in the
composition of the new Senate, which was reserved for the two majority
party factions. Indeed, changes in the electoral laws in 1934 gave them
exclusive use of the Colorado and Blanco party names (*lemas*). The new
constitution was approved by little more than half the electorate, the
opposition factions of both parties abstaining. During 1935–6 some of
these factions participated with the parties of the Left in attempts to form
a popular front, but the initiative did not succeed. Nonetheless, both
traditional parties were profoundly split into pro-regime and opposition
groups, and to guard against any such future schism, the *ley de lemas* was
again modified and given the basis of its modern form in 1939 whereby
the opposition factions might have access to the *lema* and accumulate their
votes within it. Alliances (and factionalization) were thus to be encouraged
within parties, and not between them.

Terra's presidency ended in 1938, by which time the influence of the
herreristas was already waning. In a massive Colorado victory Alfredo
Baldomir, a relatively liberal figure, was elected to succeed him. There was
soon speculation about constitutional reform, and the collapse of the
terrista–herrerista alliance in 1941 opened the way for the overthrow of the
constitution of 1934 the following year. Although domestic factors (in

particular the dynamics of the urban economy) were instrumental in producing this transformation, the changing international context after 1933 also had great significance. The rise of Italian Fascism had certainly impressed Terra. Nevertheless, the strength of the two-party (or two-faction) tradition in Uruguayan government confined its influence to superficial aspects of the regime, and attempts to construct a corporatist state were half-hearted. German influence grew markedly with commercial bilateralism and the award of contracts for the hydroelectricity projects on the Río Negro to a German consortium. Moreover, diplomatic relations with the Soviet Union were severed in 1935 and with the Republican government in Spain the following year. However, the Republican cause in the Spanish civil war aroused widespread popular support and thus demonstrated the strength of opposition to Terra.

The outbreak of the Second World War further weakened the alliance of the governing Colorado and Blanco factions and emphasized the isolation of the *herreristas*. Although Uruguay formally declared neutrality, public sentiment was strongly against the Axis powers, particularly after evidence of Nazi activity in the country was made public, and Alfredo Baldomir's government gave all possible assistance to the Allies. While Britain had every reason to be satisfied with this attitude, relations with the United States grew particularly close. In 1940 it was proposed that the United States be allowed to establish a naval air base on Uruguayan territory, a plan which was revived in the later stages of the war though never in fact approved. At the Rio de Janeiro conference in January 1942 Uruguay strongly backed Brazil's position in support of the United States, leaving only Argentina and Chile to maintain diplomatic relations with the Axis powers. For the *herreristas*, the sympathy of the 1930s with fascism was modified to strict wartime neutrality; besides international Communism, Uruguay was threatened by the hegemonic designs of the United States under the cloak of pan-Americanism.

The political base of the 1933 regime was therefore eroded by its inability either to reflect the popular consensus at home or to maintain its coherence in the face of a rapidly changing international situation. That, and the more favourable conditions for the growth of manufacturing industry, under which *batllismo* had traditionally flourished, made change inevitable. By 1940 constitutional reform was under discussion, the following year the *herreristas* withdrew from the cabinet and in February 1942 the legislature was dissolved and a Consejo de Estado formed. It was ironic that President Baldomir, brother-in-law of Gabriel Terra and his chief of police in 1933, should instigate the *golpe bueno*.

THE *BATLLISTAS* RESTORED, 1942–51

The immediate need to replace the 1934 constitution arose out of the capacity of the *herrerista* Blancos, having an equal share of seats in the '15 + 15' Senate with Baldomir's Colorados, to obstruct reform proposals. This two-faction control of the Senate was eliminated under the new constitution. Among other complex changes, the politicization of the state corporations was checked, and the legislation governing the use of party *lemas* was consolidated. The new constitution was approved by plebiscite in November 1942, and the Colorados won a substantial victory in the elections held simultaneously. The de facto regime established in February 1942, necessary to permit the reincorporation of all political groups, was thus brief.

The presidency of the neutral Colorado Juan José Amézaga (1943–7) represented in general a tranquillizing interval, threatening no expectations, endangering no established interest. In international relations, the period was marked by a growing coolness towards Argentina, a trend not reversed until the overthrow of Perón; but there was also a closer association with the United States, which had been a traditional Colorado counterweight to British influence but was now more a function of the economic, political and military dominance of the United States in the region and Uruguay's briefly held ambition to take a prominent role in the inter-American system. The United States increased its importance to a great extent as a commercial partner during the 1940s. Loans were received from the Export–Import Bank in 1942 for the completion of the Río Negro hydroelectricity works and in 1943 for public works including the airport at Carrasco, though little of this credit line was in fact used. The Blanco Party was successful in blocking the creation of a military base for the United States, even though plans were well advanced by 1944, but it failed to reverse the decision to declare war on the Axis in February 1945 by which Uruguay secured its place at the San Francisco conference of the United Nations in April. Nor could it nullify government support for the multi-lateral agreements on hemispheric defence sponsored by the United States in the Act of Chapultepec in 1945 and at Rio de Janeiro in 1947. Late in 1945, indeed, Eduardo Rodríguez Larreta as foreign minister proposed a policy of collective intervention in the affairs of erring American nations as the basis of security in the hemisphere, but the response of the rest of Latin America to this doctrine was as cold as it was enthusiastic in Washington.

Domestically, the broader changes occurring in the economy and society contributed to the revival of the *batllistas*. These changes were partly a reaction to the new international economic environment and partly an attempt to return to the main themes of Uruguayan development following the disruption of Terra. During the late 1930s the process of industrialization, interrupted by the depression, was resumed. The effect of restrictions on trade during the Second World War was to slow down the rate of growth and diversification of the industrial sector, though some industries such as textiles continued to expand. Still, by 1945 the contribution of manufacturing industry to the gross domestic product (GDP) had increased to 19 per cent, compared with 15 per cent a decade earlier, while industrial employment in the same period had increased from about 60,000 to almost 100,000.[2] The continued growth of the urban economy and the changed national and international political climate encouraged a resurgence of the trade union movement following its almost total eclipse under the 1933 regime. Concern about working-class living standards also received expression in the 1941 report of a commission of the House of Representatives, which revealed widespread poverty and economic insecurity.

The short-term result of these changes was a revival of legislative activity in the areas of labour and social security. The most important enactment was the regime of *consejos de salarios* (wages councils), which was introduced in 1943 and which represented state intervention in the process of wage bargaining alongside labour and capital. Other legislation concerned compensation for industrial injuries, compensation on dismissal, regulation of rural labour and limited unemployment benefits for export industry workers. In social security, provision for family allowances in 1943 was an innovation, but the main task was to extend to other workers on a gradual and unsystematic basis the benefits of pension schemes similar to those established in the period before 1930 for major occupational groups. By 1954 all workers were entitled to retirement pensions from one of the various pension funds. The proportion of the population that was dependent on the state was increased by extensions of the state sector, either by the creation of new public corporations (the national airline PLUNA in 1944) or the acquisition of British-owned assets (railways, tramways, water supply in 1948–9).

---

[2] Julio Millot, Carlos Silva and Lindor Silva, *El desarrollo industrial del Uruguay* (Montevideo, 1973), Tables 7, 23.

Plainly these developments were in line with traditional *batllista* ideology, but they were not the product merely of increasing *batllista* influence. The *consejos de salarios,* for example, were supported by all political parties and by the employers' associations as well as the trade unions, even though the declared intention was to use them to bid up real wages. The long-term significance of the new labour and social legislation was essentially that it laid the basis for an implicit alliance between industrial capital and the urban working class which was to dominate Uruguayan politics until the late 1950s and survived, though with increasing strains, until the end of the 1960s. Manufacturing industry was entirely dependent on the heavily protected domestic market, and a return to the redistributive policies of the earlier *batllista* period provided it with an expanding demand. Competition from the informal sector was undermined by the enforcement of industry-wide wage awards, while trade union militancy was absorbed by the new institutional structure, and the allegiance of the working class to the two traditional parties was confirmed. The trade union movement itself did not easily escape the ideological schisms which had kept it divided. But these began to assume less importance as unions acquired mass memberships and became more concerned with wage bargaining, and as political ideology was replaced by economism. Left-wing political parties continued to receive only a small percentage of the popular vote. The main political beneficiary of the new alignment of forces, and in turn a principal proponent of post-war import-substitution industrialization, was Luis Batlle Berres, nephew of Batlle y Ordóñez.

Luis Batlle became president in 1947, following the death of Tomás Berreta, Amézaga's successor elected in 1946, shortly after he had assumed office. With a brief interruption in the early 1950s, Batlle remained the commanding figure in the governing Colorado Party until the electoral defeat of 1958. With his ascent, the restoration of *batllismo* was complete; but in important respects the new version was very different from the old. First, whereas Batlle y Ordóñez had sought to establish an equilibrium between contending social forces based on economic diversification and concessions to the middle and lower classes which combined egalitarianism with a high level of social mobility, neo-*batllismo* was based on the aggressive promotion of particular sectors, especially manufacturing industry and arable agriculture. It was no coincidence, however, that one of the basic conditions for the success of the earlier model had been the growth of the livestock sector before and during the First World War, and that the same conditions of high export values and rural prosperity applied during and after the Second World War. Scope for redistributive policy was thus enhanced, while opposition from the landowning class was reduced.

Secondly, the new *batllismo* differed from the old in its political bases. Batlle y Ordóñez was unquestionably the dominant political figure of his time, and in order to attract working-class support away from the left-wing parties his style sometimes approached that of a populist leader. But in recognizing the legitimacy of working-class demands but not the separateness of a working class, Batlle y Ordóñez was more paternalist than populist. Luis Batlle also dominated the political stage, and he constructed around himself a powerful political apparatus. Neo-*batllismo* sought to integrate what had become an organized and active working class and employed elements of corporatism and populism. Batlle's demagogic style showed little of the social vision which had informed the old *batllista* party. Indeed, by the time of the elections in 1950, Luis Batlle's faction of the Colorado Party, the 'List 15' faction, had separated itself from the traditional and increasingly conservative *batllistas,* 'List 14', led by the two sons of Batlle y Ordóñez, who still controlled the newspaper *El Día,* which Batlle y Ordóñez had edited.

The adoption of a strategy of import substitution after the war did not go unopposed. As relations with the United States grew close during the early 1940s, this held out the promise to some (and the fear to others) of substantial reductions in the structure of exchange controls and protection on which industry depended, in line with the commercial and financial interests of the United States. Nonetheless, at the end of the war the traditional dependence on European markets was re-established, while the prosperity of the export sector and the flood of imports muted the opposition to increased interventionism. The export price index rose from 36 in 1938–40 to 119 in 1948–50 (1961 = 100), while the participation of consumer durable goods in imports during 1948–50 was at its highest level since the 1920s.[3] Of more significance were the accelerated decline in imports of consumer non-durables, the category most directly competitive with national production, and the surge of capital goods imports. This restructuring of imports was achieved from 1947 through discriminatory exchange allocations and from 1949 by a multiple exchange rate system geared mainly to the requirements of manufacturing industry.

The rapid growth of exports, industry and arable agriculture benefiting

[3] Instituto de Economía, *Uruguay: Estadísticas básicas* (Montevideo, 1969), Table 64; M. H. J. Finch, *A Political Economy of Uruguay since 1870* (London, 1981), Table 6.3.

from large subsidies engendered a new wave of euphoria in the country in the late 1940s. This was not lessened by the state's purchase of British-owned public utility companies, in particular the Central Uruguay Railway, although on economic grounds there was a more compelling case for their being sold by their existing owners than for being acquired by their new. The prosperity of the period was to a considerable extent fortuitous, since it derived from a favourable but temporary international conjuncture, but it was on this basis that Luis Batlle established his political ambition. The following decade would reveal the shallow foundations of both the prosperity and the nation's new caudillo.

THE SECOND *COLEGIADO* AND ECONOMIC CRISIS, 1951–9

Although Luis Batlle was constitutionally ineligible for the presidential election of 1950, the result nonetheless appeared to be highly satisfactory for his cause. Herrera was the candidate with the most votes, but the total Colorado vote exceeded that of the Blanco *lema,* and victory therefore went to the *sub-lema* of Colorados with the most votes, which was that of the List 15 candidate Andrés Martínez Trueba. The victory over the List 14 *batllistas* and over the Independent Colorado list, which united the Colorados who had opposed Batlle y Ordóñez in the 1920s and those who had followed Terra, was narrow but decisive. It was evident that Luis Batlle would remain an influential figure and would seek the presidency again in 1954. The decision of Martínez Trueba to seek to reform the constitution by substituting a collegiate executive for the office of president, a reform unenthusiastically approved by plebiscite in 1951 and made operative in 1952, came therefore as a major surprise.

Not only did the constitutional change of 1952 directly reduce the power of the List 15 faction; it also required a change of heart among those who had in the past opposed the *colegiado.* For all *batllistas* the *colegiado* had been an article of faith since the time of Batlle y Ordóñez, but Martínez Trueba's decision aroused ill-concealed dismay among followers of Batlle. The List 14 *batllistas* were also delighted at the prospect of curbing the personal influence of Luis Batlle. Herrera's support for the reform was crucial, and his was the outstanding *volte face.* Having participated in the regime which ended the first *colegiado* and ousted the *batllistas,* he now entered a pact with the *batllistas* to introduce the second *colegiado.* Herrera's electoral failures were doubtless part of the explanation, but even more enticing was the prospect of co-participation in government. The doctrine of co-participation, implying representation of the minority party in government and a share in the patronage, was as basic to the philosophy of the Blancos as was belief in one-party rule to the Colorados. Critics of the reform, notably the Independent Colorados and small non-traditional parties, observed the convenience to the major political groups of a measure which would consolidate their political power. In terms of their electoral showing the previous year, the supporters of the reform should have produced a massive majority in the plebiscite. In fact, the majority in favour was minute; only 20 per cent of qualified voters expressed their support, while 17 per cent were opposed.

The Consejo Nacional de Gobierno (CNG) was thus greeted with scepticism and viewed in the main with cynicism until its demise in 1966. Six of its members were to be drawn from the majority party, and the remaining three from the minority. The directorates of the public corporations were composed of nominees of the majority and minority parties, in the ratio of three plus two. It was as if the most damaging features of the 1931 Pork-barrel Pact had been written into the constitution. Precisely because the mode of operation of the new constitution had obvious antecedents in early decades and because the economic situation deteriorated within a very few years of its initiation, it would be quite wrong to associate the characteristic forms of political activity in the 1950s and 1960s in any simple way with the evident deficiencies of the collegiate executive. The mechanisms by which the two traditional parties kept themselves in power were fortified by the new system, but their roots lay deeper. One was electoral – the *lema* system, which permitted Colorados and Nationalists to split into a multiplicity of factions without jeopardizing the electoral strength of the two *lemas* and which made the formation of governments a product of inter-party alliances. Another was the clientelistic basis of political support which thrived on political intervention in the administration and public sector. The growth of the bureaucracy, the decline of administrative efficiency and the conversion of surpluses in the public corporations to massive deficits were especially marked in the 1950s and early 1960s. The particular contribution of the CNG to this process was to deny the country a unified and effective political leadership. It was overburdened with matters of administrative detail and tended to become a third debating chamber from which a sense of urgency and final responsibility was largely absent.

By the mid-1950s the process of import-substitution industrialization had run its course, and the economy then entered an extended period of stagnation. In the decade from 1945 to 1955 industrial growth averaged nearly 9 per cent annually, and although traditional manufacturing activities continued to dominate the sector, there was also some industrial diversification. However, the favourable factors underlying this period of relatively dynamic growth were short-lived, and their removal revealed the limitations of the post-war industrialization process in Uruguay. The most important reverse came with the down-turn of wool prices after the exceptionally high levels of 1951. This, together with the increasing domestic consumption of exportable beef and the depletion of foreign exchange reserves accumulated during the Second World War, imposed a severe foreign exchange constraint on an industrial sector that was largely dependent on imports for its supply of energy and raw materials and wholly dependent for its supplies of equipment. These adverse features of the 1950s were superimposed on a stagnating supply of exportable livestock products, a trend rooted mainly in the failure to shift from an extensive land-use pattern employing unimproved natural pasture to an intensive system permitting an increase in the total number of livestock. This failure, so damaging to the long-run performance of the economy, was related to the greater risks and more skilled management entailed in artificial pasture technologies and their inadequate adaptation to local conditions, resulting in a low financial rate of return for most products. Continued industrial growth was constrained on the supply side by inadequate foreign exchange. On the demand side – despite income distribution which was relatively equitable by Latin American standards and a per capita income of approximately U.S. $900 (1960 purchasing power) – a total population of only 2.25 million imposed evident limitations on a manufacturing sector producing exclusively for the domestic market. In spite of the fall in wool prices which brought to an end the euphoric phase of post-war Uruguayan history, there were few signs that the members of the first new collegiate government, drawn from the principal political groups in the 1950 elections, were aware of the impending economic problems.

The elections of 1954 proved a triumph for Luis Batlle's List 15. Denied a second presidency by the new constitution, he was nonetheless the outstanding figure in the new government. But the deterioration of the economy, and more specifically the exhaustion of the industrial strategy initiated in the late 1940s, posed problems which the institutional structures of government and the political parties were ill-equipped to solve. The personalist nature of political leadership and the divided executive impeded the process of policy formulation, while the control of the political groups over access to the bureaucracy, state corporations and pensions funds enabled the parties to defend their political clienteles. During the late 1950s policy effectively intensified interventionism, more in the hope of mitigating the effects of economic stagnation than in the expectation of solving its causes. The multiple exchange rate system became enormously complex. Trade controls were strengthened. Subsidies were increased on a range of consumer goods and on some traditional exports. The consequence was accelerating inflation and a worsening balance of payments as exports were withheld from the market in reaction to the overvalued export exchange rates or made illicitly across the border with Brazil. Strikes became more frequent and more damaging. Attempts to secure external financial assistance were unsuccessful. It was in this context of economic decline and the inability of government to arrest the decline that in 1958 the Nationalists inflicted their first electoral defeat on the Colorado Party.

THE NATIONALISTS IN POWER, 1959–67

The coming to power of the first Blanco administration for more than ninety years was in part, it is true, the result of intense rural dissatisfaction with the contradictions and failure of economic interventionism under the Colorados. Yet the Blancos had shared office with the Colorados through co-participation, and their victory in 1958 owed little to the quality of their policy proposals. It was based primarily on a realignment of party faction loyalties. The crucial development was the formation of an uneasy alliance in 1956 between Herrera and Benito Nardone, leader of the Liga Federal de Acción Ruralista. The phenomenon of *ruralismo* dated from the 1940s but acquired political significance only in the 1950s, when it had shed its links with the conservative landowning sector and developed a political base in the rural middle class, Nardone himself projecting a demagogic appeal. In 1954 he had supported Luis Batlle, but subsequently found sufficient common ground with Herrera to lead the *herrerista* list in the 1958 elections alongside Eduardo Víctor Haedo. The political opportunism of the alliance and the fascist antecedents of its leaders aroused the mistrust of urban and moderate Nationalists, and a new National Party faction emerged, the Unión Blanca Democrática. Both factions polled more votes than the List 15 Colorados, but victory went to the *herrerista–ruralista* alliance.

To the inherent deficiencies of the CNG as a policy-making body were now added the further complications that the ruling group within it was deeply divided; this group had little coherent policy to offer anyway since it had not expected to win the election. In such circumstances, and with the strong backing of the rural export sector, the decision to dismantle the inherited structure of trade and exchange controls and enlist the support of the International Monetary Fund (IMF) was almost inevitable. Within a few months of its inauguration the new government received a mission from the IMF, and at the end of 1959 the Monetary and Exchange Reform Law was promulgated.

The economic context in which the reform was introduced was very severe. Per capita incomes reached a plateau in 1954–7, but thereafter began a long period of almost uninterrupted decline. Contraction was particularly marked in the primary and secondary sectors of the economy. The crisis was accentuated in 1959 by heavy flooding, such that the recorded volume of exports that year was probably the lowest of any peacetime year in the twentieth century. While the trade gap widened, inflation increased to 40 per cent in 1959 and investment declined. The monetary and exchange reform may be regarded as a classic IMF stabilization measure, identifying excess demand as the origin of the disequilibria in the economy and advocating the elimination of price distortions as the appropriate means of promoting development. Thus, the exchange rate was unified at a substantially devalued level, trade controls were lifted and the supply of credit restricted. In what was intended to be a transitional measure, differential export taxes, variable import surcharges and advance deposits were introduced, such that an essential feature of the old system, discriminatory treatment of export commodities and import categories, was retained in the new.

Although the reform had little long-term relevance to the problems of the Uruguayan economy, which lay fundamentally in the technical backwardness of the livestock sector and the exhaustion of the import-substitution process, in other respects it was highly significant. The recovery of the pastures from the floods permitted modest rates of economic growth to be achieved in 1960–1, and trade liberalization increased the supply of investment goods and consumer durables to satisfy the demand of upper-income groups. But in spite of the fact that the reform did not produce the recession with which IMF measures in Latin America were generally associated, it was responsible for a heightened popular discontent with government policy and was a factor in the radicalization of opposition to traditional forms of political authority. It would be wrong to suppose that such opposition was wholly new in the 1960s, that it had immediate repercussions or that the reform was alone responsible. Rather, the prominence of the landowning class in the economic strategy implicit in the reform, following long periods in which its existence had been disguised by the pursuit of *batllista* objectives, led intellectuals in particular to look at the kind of political alternative now exemplified by the Cuban Revolution. The divergence was made more pointed by the visits to Uruguay of Nixon and Eisenhower (1958 and 1960), on the one hand, and Castro and Guevara (1959 and 1961), on the other. The radicalization of the weekly journal *Marcha* after 1960 and the increasing willingness of the Left to identify imperialism as the root cause of the nation's problems were characteristic of the period.

While industrial conflict had intensified during the 1950s – as early as 1952 emergency security measures had been adopted by the CNG to suppress industrial unrest – massive strikes became still more frequent during the 1960s in response to the withdrawal of food subsidies, increases in public sector prices and the shortage of meat. The rise of economism in the trade union movement was reflected in the growth of mass memberships and the emergence of strong white-collar unions. At the same time anti-imperialism and demands for structural reform in the face of economic stagnation permitted a much greater degree of ideological unity than in earlier decades, and this, together with the greater militancy of the student movement, contributed to the formation of the first unified trade union central, the Convención Nacional de Trabajadores (CNT), in 1964.

If the early 1960s saw an increasing mobilization of the trade union movement and intellectual disaffection, there was as yet little evidence of widespread dissatisfaction with a political system dominated by Blancos and Colorados. The combined vote of the Socialist, Communist and Christian Democrat parties was still only 9 per cent in the elections of 1962, again won (though narrowly) by the Blancos. The prestige of the traditional parties was diminishing in line with their tendency to legislate in their own interest – the self-awarded pension privileges of Article 383 of the 1961 budget were particularly notorious. But the resources of the state continued to be manipulated in the interests of electoral clienteles, so that the higher the level of unemployment and the longer the waiting list for authorization of a pension, the more important it became to secure the protection of a political leader. The size of the bureaucracy expanded no less rapidly in the early 1960s than in the late 1950s, indicating the limited control which the rural sector could exercise over the Nationalist administration. The survival of the political system by the enlargement of public expenditure was necessarily at the expense of short-term stability and the long-term strategy based on the increased profitability of exports. Particularly during 1963–5, it became impossible to comply with IMF norms on trade and exchange.

The attempt to stabilize the economy was the most important policy commitment of the Blanco government, but efforts to introduce economic planning were no less significant. The Comisión de Inversiones y Desarrollo Económico (CIDE) was set up initially in 1960 to coordinate public sector investment proposals, but its functions were subsequently extended to the preparation of a national plan. In 1963 a comprehensive diagnosis of the problems of the Uruguayan economy was published, and in 1965 an economic plan covering the years 1965–74 was produced. Without minimizing the gravity of Uruguay's problems, the tone of CIDE's reports was optimistic. The diagnosis made was fundamentally 'developmentalist', based on the belief that by agrarian, fiscal and administrative reform it would be possible to resume the interrupted process of economic growth. Moreover, these reforms and the plan itself were presented as technical instruments for achieving development. The area of political decision was confined to the adoption of planning and the securing of the private sector's collaboration. This exercise had two significant results. First, it became clear that there was no serious intent within the political system or the private sector to implement any kind of economic planning or reform programme. The appearance of a commitment to planning was required partly to secure external assistance under the terms of the Alliance for Progress and partly to conceal the limitations of the government's long-term economic strategy. Second, although 'developmentalism' was abortive, the preparation of the plan had a profound educative value not only for those directly involved in CIDE, but also in spreading a wider, better informed and more fundamental understanding of the nation's problems. The first population census since 1908 and the introduction of national income accounting exemplify one aspect of the change; another was a marked increase in the 1960s in the volume of published material dealing with aspects of the national crisis.

The final years of the second *colegiado* were marked by the deaths of outstanding political figures – Herrera (1959), Nardone (1963), Luis Batlle (1964) and Daniel Fernández Crespo (1964), leader of the victorious Nationalist faction in the 1962 elections. Their departure and the lack of new leaders of comparable stature emphasized still further the shortcomings of the collegiate executive. The principal issue of the election of 1966 was constitutional reform, the *colegiado* being identified as the cause of all problems by most groups. Though the new one-man presidential constitution which came into force in 1967 did embody some of the institutional reforms indicated by CIDE – the creation of a Central Bank in place of the issue department of the Banco de la República, a Social Security Bank to regulate the operations of the pensions funds and an Office of Planning and Budget – its fundamental objective (approved by the U.S. State Department) was to restore a strong executive. The new caudillo, who brought conservative tendencies and a rare reputation for honest administration to the refashioned presidency, was retired army general Oscar Gestido. One of the three Colorado candidates, Gestido led the Unión Colorada y Batllista (UCB) faction, which had been formed in 1959. His vice-president, a third choice for the office, was Jorge Pacheco Areco, a boxing enthusiast, briefly a journalist with *El Día* and almost completely unknown to the people of Uruguay.

PACHEQUISMO, 1967–72

The Gestido administration was at first indecisive in its choice of economic strategy. Initially there were signs of continued interventionism, especially in an attempt to maintain an official exchange rate which was substantially overvalued and to remain independent of the IMF. But by the time of Gestido's sudden death in December 1967, there were already indications of the policy lines which would be followed by his successor. In October a rift developed between Gestido and the ministers then in charge of economic affairs, and in November, following the appointment as finance minister of César Charlone, who had held the same post under Gabriel Terra in the 1930s, the peso was devalued in the official market by 100 per cent. The following four years under the presidency of Pacheco were a period of intense social conflict and unprecedented bitterness, which many regarded as marking the end of traditional *batllista* Uruguay.

The economic background of the years 1967–8, during which the new orientation took shape, was increasingly unfavourable. The long-run economic stagnation returned after 1961 with the average per capita income steadily declining. The rate of inflation, which had fallen to 10 per cent in 1961, increased to 90 per cent in 1967. In spite of generally favourable world prices, exports showed no sustained tendency to increase, and in

1967 an adverse price movement coincided with heavy rain to depress the value and volume of exports. This accentuated difficulties in servicing the foreign debt, which had increased sharply during the Blanco administration. More orthodox economic policy was a condition of IMF assistance, and the main surprise was that its adoption had been so long delayed under Gestido.

The instability of the economy had important implications for the traditional political system, which had sustained itself during the economic crisis fundamentally because its control over the resources of the state enabled it to reduce the social conflict inherent in an inflating and stagnating economy and, in doing so, to consolidate its electoral support. This role attracted some support from urban–industrial capital, which had most to lose from an intensification of conflict. Moreover, economic instability did not necessarily imply low financial rates of return. A variety of new employments for capital developed in the early 1960s, of which the most outstanding was the growth of the banking system, a process marked by serious bank failures in 1965 and later in 1971. Currency, land and building speculation also attracted funds. Nonetheless, by the late 1960s these short-term methods of reducing the impact of the crisis were no longer satisfactory. In the first place, economic disequilibrium and the strengthening of radical and revolutionary political movements were threatening the stability of the capitalist system, such that the traditional political process could no longer command the support of the capitalist class as a whole. Second, the capacity of the traditional parties to secure a sufficient degree of social consensus was limited by the extent to which the state could command a share of the nation's resources. The increasing social tension in the late 1960s did not encourage the capitalist class to accede either to further fiscal impositions or to the inflationary implications of an enlarged public sector deficit. The result was initially the curtailment of the power of the traditional political groups, a process which led subsequently to the collapse of the institutional structure within which they operated.

Thus, Pacheco's administration (1967–72) was characterized to a far greater extent than earlier governments by the presence of representatives of the private sector and technically qualified individuals. There was no sustained effort to construct an alliance with majority elements in the legislature. Apart from the political loyalty of some members of his own UCB faction, Pacheco's most significant support came from another Colorado group, Unidad y Reforma, led by Jorge Batlle (son of Luis Batlle).

But the frequently expressed hostility of the legislature to Pacheco's ministers was rarely pressed to a vote of censure for fear of dissolution and new elections.

The institutional device which enabled Pacheco to govern so implacably was the almost continuous imposition of emergency security measures from June 1968. The right of the executive to assume emergency powers was not an innovation of the 1966 constitution, and they had from time to time been invoked. What was exceptional under Pacheco was their use as the normal mode of government. Having closed two newspapers and suppressed certain left-wing political groups (other than the Communist Party) within a few days of taking office, from mid-1968 Pacheco employed emergency measures to arrest trade union leaders, prohibit assemblies and censor the press. In 1970 and 1971 Congress voted to lift the measures, but Pacheco's immediate reaction was to reimpose them. The hard-line policies were directed most intensively at student and working-class dissent. In July 1968 workers in essential services were placed under military jurisdiction. Street demonstrations were prohibited and put down with violence when they occurred. The independence of the judiciary was infringed by the practice of re-arresting those facing charges whose provisional freedom had been declared by the courts.

The economic strategy underlying the arbitrary and repressive political regime began to take shape late in 1967 when negotiations with the IMF were reopened. In February 1968 a stand-by credit was approved and a letter of intent signed. The stabilization policy received full expression in the decree of a wage and price freeze in June 1968 and the tightly controlled relaxation of the freeze, which was administered by the Comisión de Precios e Ingresos (COPRIN). The effect of the freeze, and of the accompanying monetary and fiscal measures, was a remarkable reduction in the annual rate of inflation, from 125 per cent in 1968 to 21 per cent in 1969. The effect on wage-earners, corresponding to the attack on the trade union movement, was an average fall of 10 per cent in real wages between 1967 and 1968. However, the commitment of the regime to the liberalization proposals of the IMF was ambivalent. Although salutary as a short-term measure, price controls could not be justified as a regular policy instrument, but in practice they were to become a device for holding down inflationary pressures. Even more startling in its departure from orthodoxy was Pacheco's decision to maintain the exchange value of the peso at its April 1968 level in the face of pressure from the IMF to devalue. The reason for this was perhaps as much an attempt to legitimize the policy of the regime by showing its independence from its international creditors as it was an integral part of the economic design. It was certainly facilitated by an improved export performance and favourable terms of trade after 1968. Although the credit restrictions of 1968–70 resulted in a large number of business failures, the stabilization did not induce further recession in an already depressed economy. On the contrary, in 1969–70 output achieved the highest rates of growth since the early 1950s, while real wages recovered the loss sustained in 1968 in spite of the continued attack on organized labour. During 1971 it became clear that Pacheco proposed to seek a constitutional amendment in the elections at the end of the year which would permit him to retain the presidency for a second term and that he would use increased public expenditures as the basis of an electoral campaign. The economy reacted badly during 1971. Faced with a ratio of public spending to GDP at record high levels, and an unrealistic official exchange rate, the private sector lost confidence in the government's economic management. Of more lasting significance, however, was its loss of confidence in the capacity of the political system to resist the radical challenges of the Tupamaros and the Frente Amplio.

The origins of the Movimiento de Liberación Nacional–Tupamaros (MLN-T) may be traced to the attempts of its acknowledged leader Raúl Sendic to organize the sugar-cane workers in north-western Uruguay at the beginning of the 1960s. Disillusioned by the limited results achieved and by the ineffectiveness of the electoral process as a vehicle for radical politics, Sendic had by 1963 initiated a movement which by the end of the decade was probably the best organized and most successful guerrilla force in Latin America and which transformed the nature of guerrilla warfare by demonstrating the potentialities of urban operations. During the mid-1960s Tupamaro activity was sporadic rather than sustained, but from August 1968, during the period of popular (and especially student) reaction against Pacheco's economic and political measures, it was intensified. The Tupamaros continued to secure arms and cash to strengthen the movement; but more publicity was secured (in spite of a prohibition on press reporting of the Tupamaros) by the revelation of financial scandals, by the temporary seizure of radio stations and by the kidnapping of public figures associated with Pacheco. In this period the movement's most potent subversive weapon was probably the ridicule aroused by the established authority's incompetence and revelations of corruption among the interests which the authorities tried in vain to defend.

The Tupamaro threat served as a justification for Pacheco's use of emergency powers, although their original target was organized labour. Anti-subversive actions quickly came to rely on violent interrogation techniques. In 1970 a Senate commission investigating denunciations found that the use of torture was 'normal, frequent and habitual', and the Tupamaro campaign entered a new stage with operations against those responsible for the use of torture, including the execution of a U.S. agent. The kidnapping and prolonged detention of foreign officials emphasized the inefficiency of the police and the obduracy of Pacheco, who resisted external pressure to negotiate with the guerrillas. The success of the Tupamaros against the police – especially the mass escapes of Tupamaro prisoners – resulted in the displacement of the police by the armed forces in matters of internal security and coincided with a cessation of guerrilla operations to permit the Frente Amplio to contest the elections of November 1971. When operations were resumed in 1972, they resulted in an overwhelming defeat for the Tupamaros.

The Frente Amplio in 1971 represented the maximum organization and deployment of left-wing political groups achieved in any election. Ideologically based parties had consistently failed to establish themselves as an important electoral force in the face of both the traditional parties' monopoly of state patronage and the electoral legislation which allowed them to split into *sub-lemas* while aggregating the votes of the *lema* as a whole. The combined votes of the Socialist and Communist parties had not reached 7 per cent of the poll since 1946. The Frente Amplio was a coalition of Marxist and non-Marxist groups (made possible by the *lema* laws) based on the Socialist, Communist and Christian Democrat parties with the support of dissident former members of both traditional parties. The coalition was led by a retired general, Líber Seregni, who had resigned his army command in 1966 in protest against the repressive policies of the government. The electoral campaign produced impressive displays of support, but while the total vote for Frente Amplio – 18 per cent of the official count – represented an unprecedented mobilization by the Left, it was insufficient to challenge the domination of the traditional parties. Allegations of ballot-rigging were widespread, but the victim was less the Frente Amplio than one of the Blanco candidates, Wilson Ferreira Aldunate. Ferreira was the presidential candidate with the largest number of votes, but since in accordance with electoral law victory went to the candidate of the *lema* with the most votes, the presidency was bestowed on Juan María Bordaberry, whose Colorado *lema* received thirteen thousand highly disputed votes more than the Blancos. Pacheco's re-election required a majority of votes cast and was therefore defeated. Bordaberry, whose political origins lay with the *ruralistas* rather than the Colorados, was nonetheless Pacheco's running mate, and his accession appeared to signify a degree of continuity with the previous regime. In the event, the deterioration of the political crisis wrested the initiative from Bordaberry. From 1972 onwards it lay with the armed forces.

MILITARY RULE, 1972–85

Among the characteristics which in earlier periods appeared to differentiate Uruguay from other Latin American republics, the lack of an interventionist, politically active military was one of the most striking. Even in the two coups of the first half of this century, the military's role was passive. The fundamental explanations of the political passivity of the armed forces are probably to be found in their traditional loyalty to the Colorados and in the long period of dominance of the Colorado Party and the achievement of peace between the parties early in the twentieth century, which enabled the military to develop along professional and bureaucratic rather than political lines. The factors which progressively altered the character of the armed forces were the election results of 1958 and consequent elevation of Blanco officers, the growing emphasis in U.S. policy on counter-insurgency techniques in Latin America and the much increased deployment of the armed forces to suppress social and labour unrest during the period of economic crisis, particularly, of course, in the late 1960s. The role of the armed forces as 'neutral' guardians of an open political system was, however, a short-lived phenomenon, given the fragility of the system itself by the end of the 1960s.

Late in 1971 the Tupamaros had declared a truce during the election period, an interval which the armed forces employed to prepare themselves for a more effective anti-subversive campaign. In April 1972, when the guerrillas renewed their operations, they were met by a fierce counter-attack from the military, whose powers were reinforced by the declaration of a state of internal war. Interrogation under torture, betrayal and the superior resources of the military had weakened the Tupamaros irreparably by the end of 1972. Nonetheless, the contacts maintained by the movement with the political system and a degree of sympathy with some of its objectives among the officer ranks gave it significance even in defeat. Evidence of the corruption of leading political figures, passed by the Tupamaros to the military, served to discredit the political process and strengthened the position of those officers who sought to displace the politicians. The coup itself came in 1973, but by stages. In February the power of the president to make ministerial appointments which did not have military approval was denied; a military-controlled Consejo de Seguridad Nacional (COSENA) was set up to advise the president, and Bordaberry lost political support by his acquiescence in this infringement of civilian authority. In April certain state corporations were brought under military administration. The armed forces then moved against the legislature by demanding the right to bring charges against one of its members. Fearful of the precedent this would set, the legislature denied the right and was dissolved in June, a nominated Consejo de Estado being established in its place.

Widespread repression was then unleashed, with the arrest of leading political figures of all parties, trade unionists and members of the university, which was occupied by the military in October. The pattern of arrests, newspaper closures and the banning of the Communist Party in December 1973 revealed the ideological basis of the military at this stage to be anti-Marxism and the doctrine of national security. Individual political figures were investigated for corruption, but the political system as a whole was held to have been compromised by Marxism. The prisons were filled and new prisons were prepared to house Tupamaros, radical political dissidents and trade union militants. At the height of the repression, in the mid-1970s, the regime held more than seven thousand political prisoners; it was claimed that Uruguay had the highest ratio of prisoners of conscience to total population of any country in the world. In addition, those suspected of left-wing sympathies lost their jobs in the public sector, state bureaucracy and educational system. The brutal practices of the regime and its contravention of human rights became an important factor in relations with the United States, particularly during the Carter presidency, and military aid was temporarily suspended. The severity of the repression may be explained in part by the isolation of the armed forces within the social system before the coup and the low social prestige attaching to a military career. Nonetheless, mainly because of the regime's success in extinguishing political activity, the scale of its violence was less than was experienced in Argentina and Chile in the 1970s; by mid-1985 some two hundred cases of 'disappearances' (mostly of Uruguayan exiles in Argentina) had been denounced to an investigating commission.

The regime formally designated itself 'civilian-military'. President Bordaberry was retained in office until 1976 and was succeeded by civilian presidents until 1981. Civilians were also appointed to head ministries and to the Consejo de Estado. In practice, the key contribution made by non-military members of the government came in the formulation and implementation of economic policy at the Ministry of Economy and Finance and the Central Bank. Middle-ranking officers were also appointed to ministries and public corporations, and COSENA functioned as the main decision-making body of the armed forces. But authority in the regime indisputably lay with the commanders-in-chief, amongst whom the army commander was pre-eminent, although the system of annual postings succeeded in preventing the emergence of a single strong man or self-perpetuating junta. The sequence of figurehead civilian presidents (Bordaberry, Alberto Demichelli, Aparicio Méndez) was not broken until 1981, when General Gregorio Alvarez was appointed for the final three years of the regime. But by then the transition to civilian government was under way, and despite Alvarez's political ambitions, his appointment did not imply any concentration of personal or military authority.

The economic orientation of the new regime was not clarified until August 1973. In February two military communiqués had been issued which stated the need for land reform, reduction of foreign debt, full employment and the maintenance of living standards. It appeared briefly that reformists, influenced by the example of the Peruvian military, held the ascendancy, but there was to be no further evidence of reformist zeal. The economic strategy of Bordaberry's government was published in April 1973 in the form of a new five-year plan, and this document was adopted by the new regime at a week-long civilian–military conclave at San Miguel in August. The eclipse of the reformists had much to do with the fact that their proposals resembled the ideas of political radicals and Marxists and were not the coherent foundation of an elaborated economic strategy. The April plan, by contrast, was avowedly neo-liberal in inspiration. It proposed to revitalize market forces and incentives to enterprise, reducing the role of government in the economy and the long-established practice of interventionist economic policy. In its place a market-determined price structure would guide resource allocation, and the economy was to become more open through reduced barriers to international trade, with an enhanced export performance led by agro-industrial exports. Inflation, diagnosed as a transitional obstacle to improved economic performance, was attributed to wage pressure and excessive monetary expansion. The strategy outlined in the plan was generally consistent with the central tendency in economic policy after 1968; in spite of the radically changed economic and political context of the 1970s, there was considerable continuity between the programmes of the military regime and its predecessor.

One such change was the marked deterioration in the already adverse economic situation which resulted from the rise in oil prices at the end of 1973. Although export prices were high during 1972–3, the brief revival of the economy in 1969–70 was not sustained, and inflation accelerated to 77 per cent in 1972 and 100 per cent in 1973. To manage this crisis and superintend the implementation of the plan strategy, Alejandro Végh Villegas was appointed minister of economy in mid-1974. Végh had strong connections with the banking system and brief ministerial experience in Pacheco's administration. Although he resigned as minister in 1976, apparently in disagreement with the political proposals of the regime, and in particular its extension of executive control over the judiciary, Végh's influence was dominant in the first phase of the regime's economic policy.

During this period, from 1974 to late 1978, the policy objective was to restructure the economy while seeking economic stabilization through the elimination of internal and external disequilibria. Stabilization proved elusive, with the rate of inflation declining only to 46 per cent in 1978, but in other respects the strategy had considerable success, albeit at a severe social cost. Between 1973 and 1980 GDP grew without interruption, after nearly two decades of almost total economic stagnation. Following the distortions of the import-substitution era, long-term restructuring entailed bringing domestic prices more closely in line with world prices, while depressing private consumption in order to stimulate export activities and increase the rate of accumulation. In spite of the liberal inspiration of the programme, which benefited mainly the financial sector, the principal results were achieved, ironically, by illiberal or interventionist measures. The rapid expansion of non-traditional exports, overcoming 'export pessimism', was promoted by subsidies and selective price controls. Livestock producers and exporters of traditional products found themselves forced to subsidize a variety of processing and manufacturing activities, especially in textiles and leather goods. The abolition of free collective wage bargaining reduced labour costs and resulted in a 50 per cent decline in real wages during the period of the regime. Investment increased largely as a result of an expanded public sector programme of infrastructural expenditure. Private sector investment grew only very modestly. Although special privileges were available to it, foreign enterprise showed as little interest in investing in Uruguay as it had in the period of industrial growth in the 1950s. External support was confined largely to foreign loans. Manufacturing industry producing for the domestic market was hard hit by the decline in consumption and the reduction of protectionist barriers behind which it had grown up.

A central feature of this first phase of the new regime's economic policy was therefore a combination of liberal ideology and pragmatic interventionism. In the second phase, which ran from late 1978 to the end of 1982, the principal objectives and techniques of policy changed, and the gains of the earlier years were lost. The emphasis on a restructured, dynamic economy promoted by incentives to exporters gave way to an economic stabilization effort to be achieved primarily by the manipulation of the exchange rate. In place of the sequence of mini-devaluations, the exchange rate that would apply in future months was pre-announced in a schedule (the *tablita*), which implied a progressively greater overvaluation of the peso. At the same time, liberalization of financial and commodity markets was extended. With the availability of foreign loans, balance-of-payments adjustment was left to occur automatically. The results of this experiment with an imported doctrine were disastrous, although they were initially disguised by a construction boom financed by capital seeking refuge from Argentina and by a fall in the rate of inflation to 21 per cent in 1982. But at the end of that year the *tablita* was abandoned and the peso devalued, leaving a legacy of external and internal indebtedness which expressed the dominance of the financial over the productive sectors of the economy. Sustained economic growth during 1973–80 gave way to stagnation in 1981 and a fall in GDP of 14 per cent in 1982–3. The years of cheap dollars caused a huge rise in the level of imports, whereas export growth faltered in the face of adverse exchange rate policy, inadequate domestic raw material supplies, countervailing duties in the U.S. market and eventually international recession.

Between the abandonment of the *tablita* in November 1982 and the installation of democratic government in March 1985, the economic crisis intensified without any coherent attempt by the regime to achieve defined objectives beyond minimizing the economic disequilibria. At the end of 1983 Végh was restored to the Ministry of Economy, but this appointment was primarily a holding operation, and expectations of a new initiative to revitalize the economy were disappointed. During 1984 GDP fell by a further 2 per cent while inflation reached 66 per cent. Real wages continued to fall, and open unemployment in Montevideo exceeded 13 per cent. The profitability of capital in both urban and rural sectors was depressed by the burden of bank debt. Foreign debt totalled U.S. $4.6 billion at the end of 1984, equivalent to three-quarters of GDP, or more than four times the annual value of exports. The burden of servicing this debt was accommodated by halving the level of imports between 1981 and 1983–4; exports remained depressed. The new civilian government thus inherited an economy afflicted by paralysis and overwhelming popular frustration. Following its real gains in export growth and diversification achieved, if painfully, in the 1970s, the neo-liberal model ended its career entirely discredited.

The political project of the armed forces was even more unclear than its economic strategy in the early years of the new regime. At first the threat of subversion gave it legitimacy, but since the Tupamaros were a defeated force by the time of the coup and the trade unions were suppressed immediately after it, the emphasis on national security and social discipline would be hard to sustain unless the alleged threat to the social order was broadened. The journal of the Centro Militar published material which identified liberalism, no less than Marxism, as the enemy of society, and some evidence of anti-Semitism also appeared. However, the central problem for the regime concerned the role that the traditional political parties should be permitted to play in the future institutional order, given their alleged complicity in the breakdown of democracy.

The issue was not resolved until 1976–7, when the definition of the regime's political project was precipitated by President Bordaberry's own proposals. These envisaged the abolition of the Blanco and Colorado parties, their substitution by 'currents of opinion' and the holding of occasional referenda in place of regular elections. The military rejected these proposals, describing them as 'bonapartist', and removed Bordaberry from office in June 1976. Opposition was based on the reduced role of the military in government implied in Bordaberry's plan, but mainly on a fundamental disagreement concerning the future role of political parties. Bordaberry envisaged an institutional structure dominated by a strong civilian executive, with no place for the parties as instruments of policy formulation or popular adhesion. The armed forces, by contrast, defended the institutional role of the parties in terms of national tradition and implicitly because, as multi-class groupings, they operated as an effective defence against class politics. Accordingly, it was the leadership and hierarchies of the parties in the pre-coup period, not the parties themselves, which should bear the blame for permitting subversion, corruption and chaos to flourish. In September 1976 a military decree deprived all political figures involved as candidates or in the party structures in the elections of 1966 as well as 1971 of their political rights, including in the case of left-wing parties the right to vote, for a period of fifteen years. Thousands of Uruguayans were involved, including former presidents Pacheco and (briefly) Bordaberry. In addition to the cleansing of the parties, a 'reform' of the judiciary and the elimination from public administration of those regarded as politically unsafe were decreed. The plan for political reconstruction was completed in August 1977 with the announcement of a gradual return to elected government. A new constitution was to be prepared, without the participation of the parties, and submitted to the nation for its approval in a referendum in 1980. The two traditional parties would then bring forward an agreed-upon candidate for the office of president, who must be approved by the military, for uncontested elections in 1981. Finally, contested but still controlled elections would be permitted in 1986. The legitimation of the regime was thus to be accomplished by a transition period in which political and institutional structures would be sanitized and reshaped, followed by the restoration of a form of representative government as political activity was gradually permitted to resume.

However, this political strategy failed at its first test and in a remarkable manner. When the new constitution, which institutionalized the role of the armed forces in government, was submitted to a plebiscite in 1980, the profound popular dislike of the military resulted in its rejection by 57 per cent of the electorate. This defeat was the major turning point in the history of the regime. After 1980, popular opposition to the de facto government was open and incontrovertible; this was even more the case after 1982, when in internal party elections 77 per cent of voters supported party factions opposed to the regime. Thereafter, legitimacy could be claimed only through implementation of a revised timetable for democratization. In that sense the fundamental reason for the withdrawal of the military from power was the continuing strength of Uruguay's democratic tradition and the acquiescence of the military itself to the authority of the ballot box. But there were other reasons as well. The political reversal of 1980 was accompanied by a rapidly deteriorating economic situation, aspects of which, such as the escalating foreign debt and extension of foreign ownership of the banking system, did not match the nationalist rhetoric of the armed forces. Thus, the tensions of the 1970s between the military and civilian components of the regime, over such questions as the level of military expenditure and the impact of neo-liberal policy on sectors of the national economy, were now heightened by the failure of the neo-liberal programme itself and the absence of any new policy initiative. At the same time, political developments in Brazil and Argentina threatened to leave a Uruguayan military regime alone in the region, and the Argentine experience in particular showed the perils of returning to the barracks defeated and in disarray. Attention turned therefore to achieving an abdication on terms which would safeguard the interests of the armed forces under an elected civilian government.

Negotiations on the transfer of power between the military high command and leaders of the two traditional parties (and the tiny Unión Cívica Party) opened in 1983 but were abandoned after three months without agreement. When they were resumed in May 1984 – with elections due to be held in November but still far from certain – the tactics of the armed forces changed. Some of their demands regarding participation in government and jurisdiction over civilians were scaled down, but they now sought to influence the framework of the elections in order to promote the result likely to be most favourable (or least damaging) to themselves. A victory for the centrist majority faction of the Colorados led by Julio María Sanguinetti, as the least radical of the serious contenders, was the preferred outcome (a judgement endorsed by the U.S. State Department). The principal challenge to a Colorado victory was the personal following of Wilson Ferreira Aldunate, a formidable critic in exile of the regime, whose radical Por la Patria faction now dominated the Blanco Party. In June 1984 Ferreira returned from exile and was immediately arrested. The Blancos, deprived of their principal electoral asset, withdrew from the negotiations in protest. In July the left-wing coalition Frente Amplio was rehabilitated (though its leader Líber Seregni was not) and joined the negotiations. The Naval Club Pact in August between the military and the parties (minus the Blancos) settled the terms of the transfer of power, reinstating the 1967 constitution and reserving only an advisory role for COSENA. The regime was thus successful in breaking the common front of the political parties in the negotiations and in reducing electoral support for the Blanco Party by jailing its leader and by reinstating the Frente Amplio.

In spite of this interference, the result of the November 1984 elections was accepted by all contenders. The Colorado Party won a clear victory with 41 per cent of the total (the same share as in 1971), and within the Colorado *lema* the vote for Sanguinetti overwhelmed the right-wing UCB *sub-lema* of former president Pacheco Areco. Without Ferreira, and perhaps also in mistrust of the new radicalism of the traditionally more conservative of the two main parties, the Blanco share of the poll fell to 35 per cent, 5 per cent less than in 1971. The Frente Amplio with 22 per cent achieved a modest gain, but its electoral appeal remained largely restricted to Montevideo. The elections were conducted within the complex and highly criticized framework of the double simultaneous vote, which allowed parties to fragment into *sub-lemas* without weakening the electoral strength of the *lema*. However, a notable feature of the 1984 elections was the extent to which the largest fractions of the traditional parties dominated the *lema:* 75 per cent of Colorados voted for Sanguinetti, compared with 56 per cent for Bordaberry in 1971, while the Por la Patria *sub-lema* increased its share of the Blanco vote from 66 to 83 per cent. Such a degree of unanimity within the main parties was unlikely to prove permanent. But since the voting system was fundamental to the electoral strength of all three major parties, reform of the traditional *lema* laws did not seem probable. Indeed, in spite of the long interruption of Uruguayan democracy during which major changes occurred in the structure of the economy and the distribution of incomes, as well as the repression of formal political activity and the emigration of some 10 per cent of the total population, a remarkable aspect of the 1984 elections was the extent to which they represented continuity with the pre-1973 period. Not only was the electoral system unchanged, but the party hierarchies were also little altered except by the passage of time and residual military interference.

The electoral process therefore took the form of a resumption rather than renewal, perhaps because arguments for reconstruction of the political system might have implied disloyalty to the democratic tradition. Certainly there was a clear element of conservatism in the election results. Indeed, since the complete rejection of the military regime was a universally shared sentiment, it might seem perverse that the electorate awarded victory to the party evidently favoured by the armed forces, whose programme of government was far more orthodox than the radical proposals concerning landed property and bank assets of the other parties and whose economic philosophy had elements in common with the constructive phase of neo-liberalism before 1978. It is likely that for many the attraction of Sanguinetti's Colorado faction was that, precisely as the most conservative option seriously being offered, it was the party least likely to incite the military to return to power. The margin of victory was in the event more clear-cut than opinion polls had predicted, suggesting that indecisive voters sought stability and reassurance rather than the less predictable programmes of reform offered by the other parties.

Sanguinetti therefore assumed the presidency on 1 March 1985 with 31 per cent of the total vote, a figure which nonetheless represented greater personal authority and electoral support than that of any of his predecessors under the 1967 constitution. Even so, since his faction had only minority representation in the legislature, the formation and conduct of government required inter-party agreement. Before the elections, negotiations had begun among the political parties, trade unions, employers' associations and other organizations in an attempt to secure agreement on a framework of policy to be implemented by the new government. It was hoped that this would limit the extent of political and social conflict during the transition period which might destabilize the new democracy and encourage the military to plan a return to power. By February 1985 this process of Concertación Nacional Programática (CONAPRO) had been successful on a range of issues, but not on central aspects of economic policy or on the terms of an amnesty for Tupamaros still in jail. Immediately following his election victory Sanguinetti announced that he proposed to form a government of national unity through the inclusion in his cabinet of leading members of the other parties. However, neither Ferreira's Blanco faction nor the Frente Amplio was willing to accept ministerial appointments (though they were represented in the administration of the state sector), and Sanguinetti therefore looked to minority factions or parties or to distinguished figures with tenuous party links to head key ministries, including Defence and Foreign Affairs. These appointments were on the whole well received, and the new government took office with the general, though far from unconditional, support of all parties.

DEMOCRACY RESTORED

The five years which followed Sanguinetti's election in 1984 revealed many of the strengths and the weaknesses of the Uruguayan system. Neither the euphoria experienced by many at the time of redemocratization nor the forebodings of those who feared for the stability of democracy proved justified. Instead, Uruguay experienced a modest economic revival with relative stability, promoted more by fortuitous external conditions than by domestic economic reconstruction. The threat of further military intervention in politics receded as the human rights issue was settled, though on terms which gave satisfaction to few outside the armed forces. As the 1989 election approached, the overwhelming impression was that, in spite of some modest realignments, neither the military dictatorship nor the transition to democracy had fundamentally affected the functioning of the Uruguayan political system or its personnel. And underlying the customary frantic political activity was a strong sense of frustration over the inability of the system to give expression to demands for change and reform.

Sanguinetti's own political standing reflected the ambiguity of what had been achieved. Hailed by outsiders (especially from neighbouring countries) for its moderation in the interests of stability and consolidation, the Sanguinetti administration experienced a steady decline in prestige at home. Future judgements may well be kinder. The first years of Sanguinetti's presidency demonstrated that, in spite of the prior attempt to achieve consensus on critical policy questions and to form an administration with a broad political base, the support it could command rested more on a common fear that the price of failure might be another military coup than on a shared positive perception of how the nation's problems might be solved. A balance had initially to be struck between the threat from the military, on the one hand, and the demands of the political parties and other social forces, on the other. But as the short-term prospect of renewed military intervention began to recede, so divisions and conflicts emerged more clearly. The restoration of democracy, which appeared to be an aim in itself as long as the dictatorship lasted, began to be perceived as providing the framework within which sectional interests suppressed by the regime could now be expressed. This was particularly true for the working class and marginalized population, for whom the abstract value of democracy could have meant little compared with the opportunity to recover some part of the devastating fall in living standards experienced over the previous decade. The danger for economic and political stability represented by strong wage pressure emphasized that the threat to democracy came not only from the military presence, but also from the legacy of a profoundly depressed economy. Even before the new government took office, there was a significant increase in labour disputes and strike activity, which intensified during 1985–6.

Nonetheless, the management of the economy represented a considerable achievement for the administration, until recession tarnished the image after 1988. In spite of pressure within the CONAPRO process to revive the economy on the basis of increased domestic demand, the eco-

nomic strategy gave priority to export-led growth. Following the accumulated fall in GDP of 17 per cent in the last three years of the dictatorship,
growth in 1986–7 totalled more than 13 per cent. Visible exports experienced sustained growth at almost 20 per cent per annum after 1985,
contributing to a positive trade balance. Real wages improved sharply in
1985–6 while open unemployment fell in Montevideo, though progress
in these basic social indicators was much less certain thereafter. The annual
rate of inflation, 77 per cent in April 1985, rose a few percentage points at
the end of the year but declined to a low of 54 per cent in early 1988. This
achievement, which fell short of current aspirations and left open the
question of its continuation, owed much at various times to the good
fortune of dynamic conditions in the Brazilian market, falling oil prices
and lower interest rates. The government exercised its wage policy
through a resurrection of the *consejos de salarios* introduced in 1943, seeking to contain pressure for higher wages while minimizing social conflict
and relying on excess capacity in manufacturing industry to meet increased demand for consumer goods. A telling indicator of the lack of
confidence on the part of the private sector, in spite of the dramatic
economic recovery from the collapse at the beginning of the 1980s, was
the extremely low level of investment, which continued the downward
trend initiated in the mid-1950s.

Although the Naval Club Pact laid down the terms of the transition
from military to civilian rule, it left open – unless, as some alleged, it
contained secret clauses – the question of the criminal liability of military
personnel for human rights abuses committed during the dictatorship.
The issue was sharpened in 1985 by the administration's decision to
release 250 former Tupamaro guerrillas still held in jail. Their release, and
the rehabilitation of the MLN-T (which in 1989 entered the Frente
Amplio) as a political movement following its defeat as a military force,
were both remarkable and inevitably disturbing to the military hierarchy.
The terms of the 1985 amnesty specifically excluded members of the
armed forces involved in the violation of human rights; and while indictments were prepared against named individuals accused of the worst
abuses, the military establishment remained determined to deny the jurisdiction of civilian courts over military personnel. In December 1986,
facing a constitutional crisis over the issue, the administration secured a
law which exonerated the military for offences committed during the
dictatorship. Since the Colorados did not have a majority in Congress, the
law could be passed only with the support of the Blanco leader (and

principal critic of the military while in exile), Wilson Ferreira Aldunate, who invoked the need to ensure the governability of the country to explain his *volte face*. The popular response to the amnesty was a successful campaign to secure the signatures of 25 per cent of the electorate needed to invoke the constitutional right to hold a referendum on the law. In the referendum of April 1989, however, 57.5 per cent of the voters approved the amnesty.

The realignment of political forces after 1985 was undramatic, tending to confirm rather than qualify the view that Uruguayan democracy was merely restored, not renewed. The Blanco Party strengthened its popular support, to such an extent that it defeated the Colorados in the 1989 elections. More significant, however, were developments within each party. The Colorados continued to occupy a political space to the right of Centre, with Jorge Pacheco Areco (a supporter of the military constitution in the 1980 referendum) and Jorge Batlle (a defeated presidential candidate in 1966 and 1971 and neo-liberal in economic philosophy) as the two main Colorado candidates for the presidency in 1989. In the Blanco Party, the Por la Patria faction was weakened by both the military amnesty issue and the death of Ferreira Aldunate in 1988. Beneficiaries of this decline were in part the reformist Movimiento Nacional de Rocha, but mainly the conservative *herrerista* faction led by Luis Alberto Lacalle, grandson of Luis Alberto de Herrera. Within the Frente Amplio, tensions between the Marxist and non-Marxist Left resulted in the departure of the Christian Democrat Party and the Partido por el Gobierno del Pueblo (PGP), which had won considerable support in 1984. The traditional aim of the Left, to unify its electoral forces and challenge the domination of the traditional parties, appeared, therefore, to have failed.

The outcome of these changes, revealed in the results of the 1989 elections, indicated continuing developments in Uruguay's political structure. The victory of the Blanco Party, its first since 1962 and, in the election of Lacalle, its first non-collegiate president in the twentieth century, was clear-cut. Yet the significance of this shift in electoral loyalties was overshadowed by the decline in the combined vote of the two traditional parties to 67 per cent of the poll, compared with 76 per cent in 1984, while the Frente Amplio's vote (in spite of the defection of the PGP and Christian Democrats) remained firm at 21 per cent. To that extent the two-party character of the political system, scarcely challenged before 1971, had come to an end. In two other respects the country's political life showed signs of developing a dual nature. First, although the performance of the traditional parties remained strong in the interior, with 81 per cent of the poll, their failure to secure even half the vote in Montevideo suggested that urban voters were developing new bases for their party allegiances. Certainly the very different socio-economic composition of the rural and urban electorates, masked for so long by the particular character of the traditional parties, received more direct expression in 1989 than in previous elections. Second, the convergence towards conservative, market-oriented policies in the dominant factions of both traditional parties during the election campaign, combined with the victory of the Frente Amplio in Montevideo, which gave the Left executive authority (in the municipal government) for the first time, suggested that an .opposition between conservative and left-wing forces might be more important than formerly as an organizing principle of Uruguayan politics. Such a view was strengthened by the nature and composition of Lacalle's administration in 1990, a government of 'national agreement' rather than a coalition but containing cabinet ministers drawn from the Colorado Party. Its programme of government, which secured unprecedented agreement from all factions of the traditional parties, envisaged legislation on trade unions, reform of the social security system, privatization of much of the public sector and the de-indexation of wages. The first major decision of the new legislature, an emergency budget designed to slow an accelerating inflation by reducing the public sector deficit, was opposed only by representatives of the non-traditional parties.

It would be unwise to press the case either that these political developments were likely to be sustained in future years or that the modernization of Uruguay's institutional structure would be readily achieved. In spite of the trauma of the military dictatorship, it was the forces of tradition and continuity which best characterized the political system. The constancy of political leaderships and political families in Uruguay was not accidental. It reflected a system in which political profiles were determined not essentially by programme but by family connection and what leaders were thought to stand for within the infinitely flexible and divisible traditions of the two main parties. At the beginning of the 1990s Uruguay perhaps continued to deserve its long-standing reputation as the most democratic country in Latin America, on the basis of its high level of political participation and the skill of its leaders in finding agreement through procedures of negotiation and transaction. Yet it was impossible to sustain the view that the collapse of democratic institutions in 1973 had been the product of the outside intervention of Tupamaro guerrillas and politically ambitious generals, with the political system itself helpless and blameless. Uruguay's political tradition was directed not at solving problems but at dividing and sub-dividing the spoils of patronage, and by the 1960s this was no longer appropriate. The relative prosperity created by the expansion of livestock production during the first *batllista* period up to 1929, and by import-substitution industrialization during the years of neo-*batllismo* after the Second World War, gave rise subsequently, in less favourable periods, to the myth of a former 'golden age'. But before 1960 economic growth was achieved comparatively easily, on the basis of passive adaptation rather than active change and with no great sacrifice of present consumption to finance capital formation. The characteristic conservatism and nostalgia of Uruguayans were therefore understandable but, like the functioning of the political system, did not give grounds for optimism that the country's economic and social problems – in particular its long-run economic stagnation – would be easily resolved.

4

PARAGUAY SINCE 1930

In 1930 Paraguay, despite the appearance of calm, was on the verge of a major upheaval. In 1928 the governing Liberal Party had won the right to rule in the first freely contested election in the country's history, and after years of sullen abstentionism the opposition Colorado Party had been induced to accept minority status in Congress. Moreover, political progress was matched by relative economic stability. Outside Asunción, the nation's capital and only real city, the effects of the world depression were little felt by the predominantly self-sufficient agrarian population of some 750,000. Beneath the surface, however, lay explosive tensions.

Popular discontent with President José P. Guggiari stemmed from a growing impatience with his failure to take a firm stand against Bolivia over conflicting claims to the Chaco, a large wasteland of desert and jungle lying between the Andes Mountains and the Paraguay River. Despite his efforts to lead an honest and progressive administration, Guggiari was to leave office in 1932 a very unpopular man. His government was most severely damaged by a notorious incident on 23 October 1931, in which his guards attacked a student rally protesting his apparent weakness in the face of Bolivian aggression. Eleven people were killed and many more wounded. Although Guggiari was later exonerated by a congressional investigation, the Colorados resigned their legislative seats and Paraguay's young intellectuals turned away from Liberalism to embrace new movements such as the Liga Nacional Independiente, which called for massive war preparations. The election in 1932 of a new Liberal president, Eusebio Ayala, in a one-man race, did little to reverse the party's growing political isolation.

THE CHACO WAR AND ITS POLITICAL IMPACT

Paraguay and Bolivia went to war in July 1932, a month before Ayala took office. The conflict lasted until June 1935, during which time more than 56,000 Bolivians and 36,000 Paraguayans were killed. The Chaco War was the bloodiest war in modern Latin American history. Moreover, it left both sides financially exhausted. Bolivia was eventually defeated, even though it fielded more than 250,000 men to Paraguay's 140,000 and began the war with the advantages of superior equipment, a German-trained officer corps and fortified positions deep inside the disputed territory. Beginning with the Battle of Boquerón in September 1932, the Paraguayans took the offensive and inflicted one surprising defeat after another on the demoralized Bolivians. General José Félix Estigarribia proved to be a sounder strategist than General Hans Kundt, the Prussian general hired by the Bolivians. Moreover, Paraguay's soldiers had more fighting spirit and were better adapted to the Chaco's torrid climate than were the hapless Bolivian Indian conscripts, who had been taken from their villages in the cold *altiplano* and sent to fight for a cause they scarcely understood. Thus, by mid-1935, Paraguay had expelled the Bolivian forces from most of the Chaco and won control of almost all the disputed land.

It might be supposed that President Ayala's victorious government would have basked in popularity, but that was not the case. Seven months after the armistice, Ayala was toppled by a military revolt. He and General Estigarribia were jailed, branded as traitors and sent into exile. To some extent this was the result of wartime passions, which Ayala ignored in offering Bolivia moderate peace terms. But the military's anger, and that of its many civilian supporters, went beyond this. Three decades of Liberal Party rule had produced many enemies, and the war had been a catalyst in bringing them together. Nationalists in the army accused the Liberals of weak diplomacy and failing to prepare the country for war. Populist politicians and reformist intellectuals accused the party of neglecting social reform. Foreigners owned the country, it was alleged, and Liberalism's doctrinaire loyalty to laissez-faire had failed to protect the people from exploitation. For Colorados, as well as for the dissident factions of the Liberal Party, the government was an authoritarian oligarchy that cloaked itself in democratic rhetoric and fraudulent elections.

Although much of this criticism was exaggerated, it contained an element of truth. Even the politically cautious General Estigarribia had complained of the Liberals' neglect of the country's defences and commented in his memoirs about the 'pitiful negligence' he found during an inspection tour of the Chaco in 1931.[1] Ayala was involved in the blame, for as Paraguay's diplomatic representative during the negotiations for a boundary treaty in 1913 he had deliberately overlooked some of Bolivia's violations of an earlier agreement. Although he later claimed that he was only trying to buy time for Paraguay, he acquired the reputation of wanting peace at any price. Nationalist suspicions about his half-hearted patriotism were apparently confirmed when, immediately upon assuming the presidency, Ayala proposed a cessation of hostilities and the creation of a demilitarized zone to be policed by an international commission. Not until May 1933, eleven months after the fighting began and ten months after Ayala was inaugurated, did Paraguay actually declare war on Bolivia. 'If I opposed the army further', Ayala told the U.S. ambassador, 'I should have no army'.[2] After the armistice of June 1935 Ayala provoked more criticism by agreeing to exchange all prisoners, even though there were 17,000 captured Bolivians to only 2,500 Paraguayans. By failing to keep the exchange on a man-for-man basis, as the army wished, he precipitated his downfall.

Discontent with the government revolved around the popular but hot-tempered Colonel Rafael Franco, who had nearly started the war as early as 1928 when, acting without orders, he had destroyed a Bolivian fort that had just been built deep inside territory claimed by Paraguay. Although he had been relieved of his command, he immediately became a national hero, a status he exploited to attack the government. Franco was later implicated in a coup attempt and sent into exile, but he was called back at the outbreak of the war and given command of the Second Army. His dashing tactics and concern for the men under him added greatly to his popularity. Although he was quickly brought back from the front after the armistice and given the innocuous task of heading the Military College, Franco continued to enjoy a large political following as president of the 100,000-member National War Veterans' Association.

There was much discontent among the veterans because the Liberal-dominated Congress, pleading an exhausted treasury, had voted down

[1] In an article for *El Liberal* (6 December 1934), p. 1, Estigarribia claimed that at Boquerón, the war's first major battle, his men fought without adequate arms, ammunition, medical supplies or food. Oxen, not trucks, were used for transport; and his men fought on empty stomachs. Quoted in Alfredo M. Seiferheld, *Estiquagibia: Veinte años de política paraguaya* (Asunción, 1982).
[2] David H. Zook, Jr., *The Conduct of the Chaco War* (New York, 1960), p. 79.

pensions for the disabled. At the same time, however, it voted General Estigarribia a lifetime pension of 1,500 gold pesos per year. The rumour began to spread that Ayala was plotting to keep himself in office and wanted to buy Estigarribia's support. The veterans' association also demanded a land reform to reward the victorious peasant-soldiers. Franco and his supporters pointed out that only 5 per cent of Paraguay's predominantly agricultural population owned farms, while the rest of the land was held in large — usually foreign-owned — latifundios. Was it right to send the nation's veterans back to their former poverty and servitude?

Ayala and Estigarribia initially tried to ignore Franco, but rumours of plotting finally led to his arrest and exile to Argentina on 6 February 1936. However, this only spurred on the other conspirators, who were able to win over the key Campo Grande cavalry base, just outside Asunción. During the night of 16 February troops began to move by train towards the capital, and in the morning Ayala awoke to find the rebels in control of the city. Although he managed to escape arrest and take refuge aboard a gunboat in the harbour, he soon surrendered. Estigarribia, having flown back from his headquarters in the Chaco to try to save the situation, was arrested as soon as he stepped off the aeroplane. In the meantime the triumphant revolutionaries wired Colonel Franco in Buenos Aires to come back and head the new government. He arrived on 19 February, to be installed by a 'Plebiscitary Decree' issued in the name of the armed forces.

THE FEBRUARY REVOLUTION, 1936–7

Franco promised that his government would institute sweeping changes favouring the popular classes, ignored for so long by the Liberal governments. The revolution would not be communist — or fascist, despite the regime's military origins. Paraguay, Franco insisted, was a 'natural democracy' in the sense that all segments of the society had a strong feeling of national solidarity. The new laws and institutions would reflect this unity. However, these were never properly put into effect and tested since the government of the February Revolution was overthrown by a Liberal-inspired counter-revolution within eighteen months. Moreover, during its brief existence, the revolutionary government was riven by factions whose quarrelling prevented it from following any well-defined course. Nevertheless, the *febreristas* — as the revolutionaries later came to call themselves — could claim to have broken with the past in at least three important areas.

First, they replaced the formerly dominant liberal ideas with a cult of nationalism, to which all subsequent governments had to pay at least lip service. Second, they launched the country's first serious land reform. Third, they gave official recognition to the rights of labour.

The new nationalism revolved around the symbol of Marshal Francisco Solano López, Paraguay's president and commander-in-chief during the War of the Triple Alliance, or Paraguayan War (1865–70). During the Liberal era, he was branded in all the school textbooks as a brutal despot whose megalomania had brought the country to disaster. Probing deeper, the Liberals argued that such unchecked power was the inevitable result of his regime's state socialism, to which individualism and free enterprise were the proper antidotes. Franco changed all that. 'El Mariscal' was now proclaimed a patriot, and a commission was sent to the site of his last battle to find his unmarked grave. His remains were exhumed and carried back to Asunción, where, along with the body of his father, Carlos Antonio López, and mementoes of Dr. José Gaspar Rodríguez de Francia, Paraguay's first dictator, they were deposited in a reconverted chapel that was christened the 'Pantheon of Heroes'. Popular nationalism now had its shrine.

Less lasting in its consequences, but more practical in content, was the Agrarian Reform Law of May 1936. This provided for the expropriation of up to 5 million acres, with indemnification for the owners, and the creation of small and medium-sized farms of between 25 and 250 acres. Tenants and squatters already on the land were to have first choice of properties which the government would sell on easy terms. The law discouraged speculation by requiring that the new owners personally work their land and forbidding them to sell, lease or subdivide their holdings. By the time Franco fell in August 1937 more than half a million acres had been redistributed to about ten thousand families. Franco's successors drastically slowed the pace of land reform. Although some land from the public domain was given out to peasants from time to time, no further attempt was made to tackle the latifundio problem.

Franco's attitudes towards the small but growing labour movement reflected a mixture of sympathy, suspicion and paternalism. In June 1936 a presidential decree created the country's first Department of Labour and its first Labour Code. Many of the reforms workers had long demanded were conceded: an eight-hour day, annual paid vacations, a weekly rest day and the right to form and join unions. The Department of Labour declared its intention to enforce the code and to make sure that all work-places were sanitary and safe. Existing unions were given official status and protection while workers in other areas were encouraged to unionize; the Confederación Paraguaya de Trabajadores (CPT) was set up to consolidate the labour movement. These gains had their price, however, in the form of more official control. The *febreristas* were concerned about Communist influence, which had been growing in the unions since 1928, and to combat this they required that all labour organizations obtain legal recognition from the Department of Labour. Failure to do so meant that a union could not hold meetings, publish its views, own property, sign labour contracts, collect dues, go to court or represent its members before management or the government. A legal union could do all those things. Indeed, the government would collect dues for it through automatic payroll deductions. If, however, a legal union challenged the government's policies, it could be 'intervened'. If this happened, it might lose its legal status, have its assets frozen or suffer the replacement of its officers by government intervenors. Thus, the revolutionary government's labour reforms were double-edged. The unions could blossom under a benign regime like Franco's, but their dependence on the government left them impotent under Franco's conservative successors.

The February Revolution might have accomplished more had it not been weakened by factionalism. Franco's cabinet was a hodge-podge of political interests and ideologies held together only by a common hatred of the Liberal Party. The minister of justice and education, Anselmo Jover Peralta, was a Socialist and pacifist; the brothers Gómez and Luis Freire Esteves, the ministers of interior and finance, respectively, were admirers of Mussolini's corporate state; Bernardino Caballero, the agriculture minister, was the grandson of the Colorado Party's founder and saw the revolution from that partisan perspective; the foreign affairs minister, Juan Stefanich, was head of the Liga Nacional Independiente, which he hoped to make the nucleus of a new official party of the revolution.

Conflict within the government was matched by chaos outside it. In the period immediately after the revolution, students, labour leaders and radical populists of every kind were exalted by the revolutionary atmosphere and impatient with the government's slow approach to reform. While strikes and street demonstrations disrupted the capital, agitators travelled around the countryside urging the peasants to seize the land. The spirit of rebellion even spread to the enlisted men in the army. On 10 March 1936, to impose order, Gómez Freire Esteves had persuaded Franco to sign a decree abolishing all political parties and public associations.

This infamous Decree-Law 152 identified the February Revolution as the same 'type as the totalitarian social transformations of contemporary Europe' and authorized the interior minister to form a 'committee of civil mobilization' whose powers would be unlimited.[3] Since this would have threatened the existence of the Colorado Party, the Liga Nacional Independiente, the National War Veterans' Association, the CPT and various student clubs supporting the revolution, the other cabinet ministers threatened to resign unless Franco rescinded the decree and dismissed the Freire Esteves brothers. Faced by such a revolt, he gave in. But this failed to put an end to the ministerial infighting.

As the original cabinet ministers fell from power, Stefanich, who had emerged as the new *eminence gris,* manipulated the politically naïve Franco into appointing members of the Liga Nacional Independiente to take their place. To do this, he counted on the support of the National War Veterans' Association, whose acting president, Elpidio Yegros, was his former student. In November 1936 Stefanich and Yegros formed the Unión Nacional Revolucionaria (UNR) as the official vehicle of the revolution. Although the Liga Nacional Revolucionaria dissolved itself afterwards, most of the UNR officers were Liga men. As a result, Bernardino Caballero left the government and the Colorado Party withdrew its support from the revolution.

Stefanich's ascendancy was short-lived. Despite Yegros' campaign, only a minority of the war veterans joined the UNR, and by the end of 1936 the Franco government had lost almost all of its original supporters. The Liga proved to be too narrow a base, and Stefanich's position was soon in doubt. After months of tense diplomatic negotiations at the Chaco Peace Conference, he had agreed finally to some minor concessions, which gave the government's critics the issue they needed. Chief among them was Colonel Ramón Paredes, head of the Chaco troops, who owed his position largely to the fact that he was godfather of one of Franco's children. Through his brother, a prominent Liberal, Paredes had been in touch with exiled party leaders, and he now saw an opportunity to play the role of king-maker. On 13 August 1937 Paredes ordered his soldiers to occupy Asunción and demanded the cabinet's resignation. It was necessary, he said, to save Franco from the bad advisers surrounding him.

The government had no time to defend itself. Franco had refused to

---

[3] The text of this law is reprinted in Policarpo Artaza, *Ayala, Estigarribia, y el Partido Liberal* (Buenos Aires, 1946), pp. 155–7.

believe any rumours of an impending coup, saying that Paredes was a *compadre* and would never betray him. Realizing too late that he had been deceived, Franco refused to see Paredes or accept his terms. Paredes therefore had him arrested and exiled along with the other *febreristas*. The revolution was over.

COUNTER-REVOLUTION

Like the revolutionary regime it replaced, the provisional government was a coalition of antagonistic elements. There were the old Liberal Party politicians, who hoped to turn back the clock. There were also many nationalist army officers who, although disillusioned with Franco, still wanted reforms. Between these two groups was a third, the so-called New Liberals, composed of younger men who wanted the party to drop its traditional laissez-faire position and put itself at the head of social change. The 'New Liberals' tended to look for support in the military in their struggle to wrest control of the party from the 'Old Liberals'. Positions in the new government had to be allocated carefully in order to preserve a balance. The two chief power brokers were Colonel Paredes and Major Damaso Sosa Valdes, who commanded the Campo Grande Cavalry. To please the Old Liberals they chose Félix Paíva, an elderly Supreme Court judge, as president. The new police chief, Colonel Arturo Bray, was an army man but also a militant Old Liberal. The nationalist wing's representative was Colonel Higinio Moriníngo, head of the Army General Staff, who was named minister of interior. The other cabinet ministers were little-known men with no close identification with any particular faction. The New Liberals had no representation in the senior levels of government, and they pinned their hopes on General Estigarribia, who still had great popularity as a military leader. The Old Liberals, distrusting Estigarribia, sent him out of the country as ambassador to the United States. Later, as the Chaco peace negotiations reached their crucial phase, he was called back to head Paraguay's delegation.

For two years the Paíva government struggled to keep order, but it was increasingly clear that the February Revolution, for all its mistakes, had stirred up expectations that could not be ignored. Strikes, student riots and attempted coups by *febrerista* military officers kept the situation volatile. The government's sole achievement was to sign a definitive peace treaty with Bolivia, and even this was highly controversial. Although Paraguay got most of the disputed Chaco territory, critics pointed out that the boundaries were drawn somewhat behind the Paraguayan army's final battle lines, which meant that some 110,000 square kilometres of territory originally claimed by the Franco government had been surrendered. Both the *febreristas* and the Colorados repudiated the treaty, and when the government called a plebiscite to approve the agreement, it prohibited any public debate on the issue. The opposition, certain that the votes would not be counted fairly, boycotted the polls. Officially, the treaty was approved by 135,385 votes to 13,204.

With this important issue settled, the Paíva government scheduled elections for a president and Congress. This brought the struggle inside the Liberal Party into the open, since the Old Liberals wanted Gerónimo Zubizarreta to head the ticket, while the New Liberals insisted on running General Estigarribia. In a passionate campaign that almost split the party's convention, the New Liberals managed to bring enough military pressure to bear to force their rivals to concede.[4] Estigarribia received the support of all but a few Old Liberal die-hards. He ran unopposed and took office in August 1939.

Despite his great prestige, the new president was no more able than Paíva to pacify the country. Plotting was rife within the army, even after the dismissal of Paredes, Bray and Morínigo from their posts. Estigarribia's plan to coax the Colorados back to open participation by giving them seats in Congress alarmed the Old Liberals, while the *febreristas,* who were still outlawed, continued to agitate against the regime. Moreover, international rivalries among the great powers significantly influenced domestic politics. Germany's strategy in Paraguay, as elsewhere in the region, was to play on resentments towards U.S. imperialism, especially strong in the army. Many officers also admired Germany for its military prowess. In addition, Nazi influence and propaganda were disseminated among the many German immigrants in Paraguay, as well as those from neighbouring Argentina, where there was a strong pro-German element in the government.

Despite the military nationalists' preference for Germany, Estigarribia was friendly towards the United States and hoped to use U.S. aid as a counterweight to Argentine economic power. The Argentines therefore decided to finance opposition to him. With their encouragement, an alliance was formed in 1939 between the *febreristas* and a new movement of

[4] On the Liberal Party's factions and Estigarribia's controversial candidacy, see Seiferheld, *Estigarribia,* pp. 343–76.

conservative Catholic intellectuals called the *'tiempistas'*, after their news-paper, *El Tiempo*. Estigarribia was attacked as an agent of Yankee imperial-ism, and various members of his cabinet were accused of graft. The Febrerista Youth, which at that time was the largest group in the univer-sity, organized anti-government demonstrations that eventually resulted in troops being sent in to restore order. Students and *tiempista* leaders were jailed. This invasion of the campus touched off protests from the Colo-rados, who broke off their negotiations with Estigarribia. On 14 February 1940, a coup was attempted at Campo Grande by officers sympathetic to the opposition.

Faced with a rapidly deteriorating situation, Estigarribia declared a state of emergency. On the same day that the Campo Grande coup was put down he called Gustavo Riart, the Liberal Party president, into his office and told him that only a temporary dictatorship could save the country from anarchy. Riart demurred, but asked for time to sound out the party about such a proposal. Two days later Estigarribia raised the issue again at a morning meeting of his cabinet. That same afternoon the Liberal Party's executive committee debated the matter, with the New Liberals, led by Justo Pastor Benítez, calling for the dissolution of Congress and the transfer of full power to the president. Riart and the Old Liberals insisted that the party remain faithful to its liberal political principles, but they found themselves in a minority of 3 against 13 and immediately resigned. With this endorsement from the Liberals, Estigarribia proclaimed himself dictator on 18 February 1940. He justified himself by insisting that the political institutions set up by the constitution of 1870 were no longer capable of functioning, but he promised to restore orderly government by appointing a team of jurists to write a more realistic constitution.[5]

The new constitution was published on 10 July 1940 and was ratified by a plebiscite on 4 August. Unlike its predecessor, it rejected such concepts as limited government, the absolute rights of property and indi-vidualism. Instead, it granted the state important new powers to regulate economic and political behaviour. 'In no case', it proclaimed, 'will private interests prevail over the nation's general interests'. Private property would be respected only if it served a useful social function. Congress was made unicameral and stripped of most of its former powers, while the president's role was greatly expanded. In an effort to emulate Fascist

---

[5] Estigarribia's justification can be found in an essay following the text of the 1940 constitution in Amos J. Peaslee, *Constitutions of Nations*, vol. 2 (The Hague, 1956).

Italy's 'corporate state', a Council of State, representing farmers, cattle-men, businessmen, the armed forces, the university and the Catholic Church, was created to advise on policy.

Less than a month after the 1940 constitution was promulgated, Estigarribia was killed in an aeroplane accident. The top military officers immediately met to choose a successor, completely ignoring the Old and New Liberals. Colonel Paredes, who was director of the Military School, and Colonel Sosa Valdes, who was still Campo Grande commander, were once again at the centre of affairs. This time they chose as president General Higinio Morínigo, a seemingly genial and unambitious officer who was popular with the nationalist faction. Estigarribia had not trusted Morínigo and sent him to the Chaco after taking office, but in the midst of his troubles he had brought him back and installed him in the cabinet as minister of the army in order to win support from the pro-German offi-cers. Paredes and Sosa Valdes thought Morínigo could be easily controlled, and for a while he encouraged this belief. He appointed Paredes minister of interior and allowed him to exile the New Liberals. Over the next few months, however, Morínigo carefully lined up his own support in the barracks. On 4 February 1941 Paredes was suddenly dismissed and re-placed by Colonel Vicente Machuca, a popular officer of the nationalist faction. A few days later a revolt at Campo Grande removed Sosa Valdes in favour of a regimental commander, Major Victoriano Benítez Vera, also a nationalist. These changes made Morínigo's position much more secure. The Old Liberals were not dealt with until the following year, when Morínigo, seizing upon a published account of the Chaco Peace Confer-ence, accused the Liberals of conspiring with the Bolivians while in exile to overthrow the Franco government. On 25 April 1942, he branded them traitors, proscribed the party and sent its leaders into exile.

THE MORÍNIGO ERA

With the Liberals and *febreristas* in exile, and the Colorados withdrawn once more into sullen non-participation, Morínigo was obliged to rely primarily on the military. His overtures to the *febreristas* were rebuffed: Franco would have nothing to do with any Paraguayan government he did not head. Indeed, the *febreristas* provoked a great deal of trouble in the form of labour strikes, student protests and even a brief uprising in the southern garrison of Pilar on 16 April 1941. The Colorados were equally intransigent. Although they would talk with the government, they always raised the price for their collaboration. By June 1941 Morínigo decided to write them off, which left the *tiempistas* as the only civilian group willing to work with the regime. Although they were only a handful, Morínigo used them as bait to other groups, treating them lavishly by giving them several ministries and the presidency of the Central Bank. For the next three years *tiempismo* had considerable influence, although it never became a popular movement. Real power lay with the military, and especially with a pro-Nazi faction called the Frente de Guerra led by Colonel Victoriano Benítez Vera, the Campo Grande commander; Colonel Bernardo Aranda, the army chief of staff; and Major Pablo Stagni, head of the air force.

Lack of organized civilian support and an extreme right-wing bias were not serious disadvantages to Morínigo at first. Himself the son of peasants, he had a populist touch that appealed to Paraguay's rural population. Moreover, the war years were a time of unprecedented prosperity. Despite grumbling from extreme nationalist officers and the Argentine Embassy, Morínigo was willing to accept generous U.S. aid, most of which was processed honestly and put to good use. New roads were built, farmers were able to get loans easily, small industries were encouraged, the military was re-equipped and a modern airport was built. Although he was unwilling to touch the issue of land reform, Morínigo experimented with creating peasant co-operatives on state property. Nevertheless, the government's inability to win over any leaders from the major parties meant that it could not afford to relax political controls. Although Morínigo won election, unopposed, to a second term in February 1943, the jails remained full of political opponents. The most dangerous were kept either at military outposts in the Chaco or in concentration camps in the jungles of the northern Paraguay River. Police spies abounded in the capital, and the press was tightly censored.

Tensions increased inside Morínigo's cabinet as the war in Europe turned against the Axis. Though hardly pro-Allied, the more pragmatic *tiempistas* favoured a break with Germany in order to curry favour with the United States. This brought them into conflict with the Frente de Guerra, which, urged on by the Argentine Embassy, was determined not to permit any liberalizing U.S. influence in Paraguay. As the dispute became more heated, Morínigo bowed to his key officers and dismissed the *tiempistas* in March 1944. However, the Frente's victory was short-lived, because in August a new U.S. ambassador arrived in Asunción and bluntly informed Morínigo that future U.S. aid would depend on his restoring freedom of the press, lifting the ban on political parties and holding honest elections. By this time it was obvious that the Axis was going to lose the war and many officers were anxious to have Paraguay on the winning side. Their main spokesman, Defence Minister Vicente Machuca, demanded that Paraguay declare war on the Axis, and he was supported in this by Major Enrique Giménez, a regimental commander at Campo de Mayo who was believed to be expressing Morínigo's own views.[6] Machuca was known to have *febrerista* contacts, while Giménez had once acted as Morínigo's go-between with the Colorados. Both men were now busy trying to sound out those parties about their willingness to participate in the government. The Frente seems not to have been aware that a decisive switch in official policy was in the making until the blow actually fell in June 1946. Then, taking advantage of Colonel Benítez Vera's temporary absence from the country, Morínigo put Giménez in charge of Campo Grande and arrested the other Frente officers. Over the next few weeks the government ended press censorship and relaxed its prohibitions on political party activities. Finally, on 23 July, Morínigo announced that he was forming a coalition government with equal representation for the *febreristas* and Colorados. Its purpose, he said, would be to prepare the country for a return to democracy, first by organizing elections for a constitutional convention, since it was widely agreed that the 1940 constitution was an authoritarian document and could hardly serve the future democratic system. After the constitution had been changed, there would be general elections open to all parties, even the Liberals and the Communists. Once a new government was elected, Morínigo would step down, perhaps to retire to his ranch, or even go abroad so as to remove any doubt about his intentions.

COALITION GOVERNMENT AND CIVIL WAR, 1946−7

During the second half of 1946 under the coalition government, Paraguayan politics were intoxicating. Exiles returned to their friends and families. The press was free. There were public meetings, marches and rallies. Yet behind all the talk about democracy were signs that the major political forces were not prepared to countenance an authentically democratic regime. The Catholic clergy demanded that the government suppress the Communist Party. The *febreristas,* knowing that Franco still had

---

[6] Nevertheless, Paraguay did not declare war on Germany until 9 February 1945, some six months later.

many highly placed admirers in the military, were plotting a coup in the event of losing the elections. Liberal Party newspapers excoriated Morínigo and called for his immediate overthrow by the army. The Colorados were split between the 'democratic' faction, which was led by Federico Cháves and attempted to uphold the coalition government, and a violent opposition group known as the Guión Rojo, or 'Red Banner Faction'. Led by Juan Natalicio González, an extreme nationalist and Liberal-baiter, the *guionistas* attacked the *democráticos* as traitors for accepting parity with the *febreristas* in the cabinet. They organized themselves as shock troops to drive their opponents off the streets. Guión Rojo thugs broke up meetings of other parties, student groups and labour unions. They attacked the offices of the Liberal newspaper *El País* and blew up its presses. Meanwhile, González was approaching an understanding with Morínigo by which the former would succeed to the presidency and the latter would hold on to power as the army's commander-in-chief.

Under such circumstances it was not surprising that the police did nothing to stop Guión Rojo violence. Nor was there any sign that elections were about to be held, despite *febrerista* demands that a date be set. Morínigo created a new Labour Ministry and turned it over to the *guionistas*, making the *febreristas'* strong base in the unions vulnerable to hostile intervention. On 11 January 1947 the *febreristas* resigned from the cabinet and called on the army to take over. Morínigo responded by declaring a state of siege, rounding up all the *febrerista*, Liberal, and Communist leaders he could find and sending them across the border. *Guionista* Colorados were appointed to fill the vacant cabinet posts.

The opposition was thrown into confusion, and it appeared that Morínigo was once more in control. But on 7 March a gang of *febrerista* youths attacked the central police station in Asunción. After a fierce gun battle they took possession of it, only to be dislodged a few hours later by cadets rushed to the scene from the nearby Military School. On the following day, the army garrison in Concepción, a river town about 130 miles to the north of Asunción, declared itself in revolt. Within a few days most of the army units in the Chaco and eastern Paraguay joined the rebellion. As the news spread, Liberals, *febreristas* and Communists seized any weapons they could find. Some headed for Concepción to fight for Morínigo's overthrow, while others formed an underground movement in the capital to sabotage the government's defences. Hope soared further when it was learned that Colonel Franco had flown back from Argentina to take command of the rebel forces.

If the rebels had marched directly on Asunción, they might have won easily, for the government was shaken by the desertion of such a large part of the army. Instead, they waited for the important cavalry, infantry and artillery bases in or near the capital to declare themselves, hoping that a fight could be avoided. As a result, Morínigo was given time to organize his defences. In this the Colorado Party played a pivotal role, for it had a large peasant following – the *py nandí,* or 'barefoot ones' – who could be formed into an irregular militia. At the same time, the Guión Rojo were allowed to enter any home without a warrant and arrest any suspicious persons in order to uproot 'fifth columnists'. More than a thousand people were rounded up in the first weeks of the revolt, while many thousands more fled the country. Finally, Morínigo was able to secure support from the Argentine president, Juan Perón. Anxious to reduce U.S. influence and pull Paraguay back into the Argentine orbit, Perón supplied Morínigo with enough arms, ammunition, trucks and medical supplies to tip the military balance in his favour.

The rebels' dilatory tactics thus lost them the advantage. Heavy rains throughout April flooded the roads and low areas between Concepción and Asunción, making it impossible to attack. Rebel sympathizers in the navy, however, chose this moment to revolt against Morínigo. Since the naval yard was near downtown Asunción, the revolt probably would have been fatal to the government if there had been a supporting land attack. However, the Concepción troops were unable to move, so the naval revolt got no further than occupying several city blocks of a workers' district near the shipyards before it was checked by cavalry, police and *py nandí* units. For the next three days there was fierce fighting in the capital, until finally Morínigo called in the artillery and destroyed the naval base with heavy bombardment. The few survivors were shown no mercy.

By the time the weather cleared in June, the government forces were ready to take the offensive. The rebel army was gradually forced to retreat until on 31 July, after a bitter siege, Concepción fell. When the news reached him, a jubilant Morínigo ordered church bells rung throughout the capital to celebrate the triumph. His joy was cut short, however, when he learned that the rebels had abandoned Concepción the previous night, leaving behind only a skeleton force of the sick and wounded, and were now proceeding downriver on a fleet of boats to attack Asunción. Morínigo's army was stranded 130 miles away. At the same time, another threat was closing in from the south. Two of Paraguay's gunboats had been taken over by mutinous crews while taking on supplies in Buenos Aires. Now they were heading upstream to join the revolution.

While panic began to grip Asunción, Morínigo and the Colorado leaders assembled another rag-tag army of volunteers and began to throw up defensive works around the city. To stop the gunboats Morínigo sent Lieutenant Colonel Alfredo Stroessner with some artillery to take possession of the fort of Humaitá, whose heights command the river's passage. The civil war had reached a climax. The fighting was ferocious as Franco's men circled the capital in the face of a surprisingly tenacious Colorado defence. In the meantime, a rumour spread that the gunboats had broken through the blockade and were closing in on the city. Government officials and supporters, fearing rebel revenge, began commandeering every available boat to carry them across the river to Argentina. Instead of running, however, Morínigo personally visited the front lines to exhort the *py nandí* to stand firm. The rumours were false, he claimed. It was necessary to hold on and give the regular army time to double back from Concepción and raise the siege.

Morínigo was right. After two days and nights of an artillery duel, the rebel gunboats had been knocked out of combat. At the same time, the *py nandí,* aided by new airborne shipments of weapons from Perón, stopped Franco's forces in the suburbs of the city. By 14 August the rebels themselves were besieged by regular government forces. Unwilling to surrender so near their goal, the rebels fought on for another five days before those who could flee headed for the Argentine border, while the rest surrendered.

THE COLORADOS IN POWER, 1947–54

Since Morínigo had survived by relying on the Colorados, they now became masters of the situation. They immediately launched a street-by-street, house-by-house search for any opponents who might have gone into hiding. Hundreds were seized and sent to join their comrades being held in soccer stadiums turned into makeshift concentration camps. Some were executed; most were sent to camps in the jungle. Thousands of Paraguayans escaped to Argentina or Brazil over the next few months.

It was obvious that the Colorados would take over the government after going through the formality of elections. But which faction would dominate the new regime: Cháves' *democráticos* or González's Guión Rojo? That issue was to be decided at the November 1947 party convention. The party elections that preceded the convention gave rise to many charges of fraud as each side tried its utmost to ensure a majority. Although Cháves claimed most of the delegates, the *guionistas* challenged their credentials, and Morínigo and González continued to work closely together. The convention was opened on 17 November and soon degenerated into a brawl. Immediately after the *democráticos* won the balloting for convention chairman, the *guionistas* began pelting them from the galleries with stones; as the *democráticos* fled the hall, they ran into the arms of Morínigo's police. After this coup d'état, the elections of 15 February 1948 were an anti-climax, since no one was allowed to run against González.

Nevertheless, new conspiracies were afoot, this time inside the Guión Rojo itself. The unsuspecting González had a rival, Felipe Molas López, his minister of education. Since Molas López's brother was a high-ranking cavalry officer, he had good connections inside the military. He also enjoyed a personal following among the *guionistas,* for while González had cultivated support from the United States and Brazil, Molas López had spent many years in exile in Argentina and was an admirer of Perón. An ambitious man with a proclivity for conspiracy, Molas López saw his route to the presidency blocked by the alliance between González and Morínigo. His first step was to eliminate Morínigo by stirring up suspicion among the Colorados that the dictator could not be trusted to hand over power to González. Molas' brother-in-law, who was chief of police, began to marshal 'evidence' of plotting in the presidential palace. As a result, Morínigo was deposed by a bloodless coup on 3 June, thus bringing to an end one of the most turbulent administrations in Paraguay's history.

González had not been informed of any of these moves until Molas was able to present him with a fait accompli. Morínigo's fall took him by surprise, and a provisional government, staffed mainly by Molas supporters, was formed to govern the country until his inauguration. Thus, when González came to power, on 15 August, he was forced to accept most of the incumbent ministers in his new cabinet. On 25 October 1948 the expected coup took place under the leadership of Colonel Alfredo Stroessner and his artillery regiment. The attempt misfired, however, because of a last-minute switch in the loyalties of the cavalry commander, Colonel Adalberto Canata. Much of the credit for this must be granted to President González, who drove in his own car to Campo Grande to demand the officers' loyalty. His courage in doing so swayed the waverers among them. The cavalry's switch to the loyalist side forced Stroessner to abandon his attack and flee to the Brazilian Embassy in the trunk of a car to avoid arrest. Although many officers were jailed, Molas López had the protection of powerful friends and could not be implicated directly in the coup. The fact that González had to keep him in the cabinet reflected the weakness of his position.

Molas' set-back did not deter him. He was ready for another attempt a few months later when rumours that González was intriguing to bring Morínigo back from exile caused Colonel Canata to switch sides again. On 29 January 1949 a smoothly executed coup removed González from office and sent him permanently into exile, but instead of replacing him with Molas López the army turned to the defence minister, General Raimundo Rolón. Rolón announced that he would try to bring peace to Paraguay by a general amnesty and the calling of elections. The army, tired of squabbling civilian politicians, began to tout Rolón as the ideal non-partisan president.

The prospect of losing their hold on power brought the Colorado factions together. While the *guionistas* and *democráticos* agreed to set aside their differences, Colonel Emilio Díaz de Vivar, a regimental commander at Campo Grande, promised to back a revolt. At the same time, Colonel Stroessner was to slip across the border and raise his old artillery regiment. This plan proved successful. On 26 February 1949, while top government officials were at Molas López's house attending a wake for the highly revered archbishop of Paraguay, rebel troops occupied the capital. Only at the last minute, when the house was surrounded, did Molas López inform his guests that they were under arrest.

Molas was president at last, but like González he came to office without real power. To secure the support of the *democráticos* he agreed to give them key military and government posts. Colonel Díaz de Vivar commanded at Campo Grande, Federico Cháves presided over Congress and the police were placed under a rising young *democrático* named Epifanio Méndez Fleitas. Rather than await the inevitable coup, Molas decided to move first. A group of his followers were to seize control of Campo Grande and then attack other army units with the help of Stroessner's artillery. But instead of joining the plot, Stroessner informed Díaz de Vivar and Méndez Fleitas. On 10 September 1949 the main conspirators were rounded up and the Colorado Party's executive committee demanded, and got, Molas' resignation. As he was being taken into custody and conducted towards the border, Federico Cháves was sworn in as president.

Although reputed to be a democrat, Cháves soon fell into the same authoritarian style as his predecessors. He had little choice, for he was beset by plots from every quarter: Liberals, *febreristas,* rival Colorado factions and former president Rolón. Furthermore, he had inherited an economy that was badly damaged by the civil war. Exports were declining, with shipments of cotton, Paraguay's main cash crop, down by a quarter from their 1946 level. Cattle herds were diminished, and the production of rice, a local staple, had also fallen. Nearly a third of the population, especially skilled workers, professionals and entrepreneurs, had emigrated. Inflation was climbing at an alarming rate, capital had fled the country, the currency (guaraní) was practically valueless and in most areas production was stagnant. Only a firm government could provide the order necessary to lure investment back to Paraguay.

Yet if Cháves was a dictator, he was no reactionary. He lifted most of the restrictions on the labour unions and tried to maintain the workers' purchasing power through generous periodic wage increases. Price controls were applied to a wide range of consumer goods, and the government bought articles of prime necessity for resale to the public at cost.

Such measures were of little avail; indeed, they probably impeded economic recovery. The per capita gross domestic product (GDP) fell from U.S. $203 in 1949 to $201 by 1954 (figured in constant 1970 prices), while the cost of living soared from an annual increase of 35 per cent to more than 117 per cent by 1952, before tapering off at around 71 percent. The effort to hold down inflation through price controls only encouraged evasion. Smuggling and black marketeering were further stimulated when the government, to save foreign exchange, placed high tariffs on luxury imports. The fall in value of the guaraní, from 8.9 to 50 to the dollar, reflected the loss of public confidence in the government. When Cháves tried to fix the exchange rate at 15 to the dollar, he only encouraged the brisk black market in dollars. Meanwhile, stagnant production, high inflation, economic controls and doubtful political stability caused international investors and lenders to consider Paraguay a bad risk. After 1951, when Cháves declared a moratorium on his country's debt payments, Paraguay was unable to get long-term loans. Without some $5.8 million in direct grants from the United States between 1951 and 1955, it would have been impossible to import basic goods.

Although Cháves had presided over an unusual period of political stability and manipulated his re-election, unopposed, in 1953, it was clear that the government was drifting. Its backers were divided between those who believed in lifting most economic controls and those who wanted to take even more radically populist measures. Prominent among the latter was Epifanio Méndez Fleitas, who now headed the Central Bank and had considerable influence over the president. An admirer of Perón, Méndez advocated closer economic ties with Argentina, and although forced by powerful economic pressure groups to drop Méndez from the government, Cháves signed a treaty in August 1953 establishing a customs union with Argentina. This cost him much support, but he might have survived had he not made the mistake of trying to build up the police force as a counterweight to the army. General Stroessner, who was now commander-in-chief, looked on with misgiving as police units were expanded and armed with heavy weapons. Soon he was plotting with Méndez Fleitas, who had a large number of personal supporters and coveted the presidency.

On 3 May 1954 a 'command crisis' at Campo Grande brought Cháves and Stroessner into direct conflict. Some of Stroessner's supporters tried to take control of the base and were arrested by its loyalist commander. When Cháves approved of the arrest orders, Stroessner claimed that the military's 'honour' had been insulted by civilian interference and declared himself in revolt. There was bitter fighting in downtown Asunción throughout the night of 4 May and throughout most of the following day before Stroessner prevailed and Cháves was removed from office.

A provisional president from the Colorado Party, Tomás Romero Pereira, took over until the victors could agree on whether Stroessner or Méndez Fleitas would occupy the presidential palace. Eventually a compromise was worked out by which the Colorados would nominate Stroessner for president and Méndez would regain his control over the distribution of favours as head of the Central Bank. So began the rule of Alfredo Stroessner, which Paraguayans came to call the *stronato.*

STATE AND PARTY UNDER THE *STRONATO*

Alfredo Stroessner was inaugurated president on 15 August 1954 and was to retain power for more than thirty-four years − the most durable dictator in Paraguay's history. His success lay in controlling two key institutions, the army and the Colorado Party. The former gave him the raw power that dictators require, while the latter provided him with the mass base that few military governments enjoy. In order to gain control of them he was obliged to divide and eliminate his opponents by stages.

The Colorado Party was Stroessner's chief problem, because neither the supporters of former president Cháves nor those of Méndez Fleitas, known as *epifanistas,* would accept his presidency as more than a temporary compromise. Had they combined against him, he might not have survived, but the *democráticos* would not forgive Méndez Fleitas for betraying their chief. Thus, when Stroessner moved against Méndez at the end of December 1955, the *democráticos* stood on the sidelines. First, *epifanista* cavalry and artillery officers were deposed from their commands, after which Méndez was removed as president of the Central Bank. Over the next few weeks any officer suspected of harbouring sympathy for the *epifanistas* was separated from the control of troops, sometimes receiving a nominal promotion, only to be arrested a few days later. By the first week of February 1956 Stroessner was strong enough to have Méndez and the top men in his clique exiled. Lesser figures were sent to detention camps.

Cháves *democráticos* were the next group to be purged. Once Méndez was eliminated, they turned on Stroessner, criticizing him for adopting an IMF-sponsored austerity program that, with its wage and credit controls, bore down hard on businessmen, farmers and workers. In August 1958 the CPT called a general strike, but Stroessner retaliated by alleging Communist infiltration in the CPT and sending in the police to break it.

The atmosphere was tense, therefore, when Stroessner ran (unopposed) for a second term in 1958. Although he received the Colorado Party's nomination, the *democráticos* were only biding their time. Their position seemed strengthened by events outside the country, especially the overthrow of the dictatorships of Venezuela and Cuba. The former brought to power a democratic regime dedicated to supporting other anti-dictatorial movements around Latin America, including the opposition to Stroessner. The latter led to the financing of guerrilla groups just across the Paraguayan border with Argentina, under the tolerant eye of the civilian government of Arturo Frondizi. Over the next two years there were several invasions by young militant exiles hoping to rouse the Paraguayan peasantry to revolt.

To counter such attacks Stroessner ordered the imprisonment of relatives and friends of known guerrillas, and any invaders who were unlucky enough to be taken prisoner were usually tortured and executed on the spot. The guerrilla strategy failed because the peasants refused to cooperate and also because the army – well trained, well equipped and convinced that it was saving Paraguay from Communism – snuffed out every incursion with grim efficiency.

Nevertheless, many officers, as well as civilians, were beginning to question whether social reforms were not necessary in order to avoid a Cuban-type revolution. Eventually, on 1 April 1959, Stroessner bowed to pressure and proclaimed that he was lifting the state of siege and offering an amnesty to all political exiles. Euphoria prevailed for almost two months, with talk of holding free elections and rewriting the constitution. However, Stroessner's opponents overestimated their strength. Impatience with the government's attempts to keep order at public rallies transformed a student demonstration on 28 May into a riot. The police were called in and several demonstrators, including two *democrático* congressmen, were arrested. The *democráticos,* who held a majority in Congress, passed a motion of censure against Stroessner and his police chief, which was tantamount to calling for the army to remove them. Stroessner responded by dissolving Congress, reimposing the state of siege, ordering the arrest of all *democrático* leaders and purging their supporters in the armed forces.

By 1960, therefore, Stroessner had eliminated two of the three most important Colorado factions. Only the remnants of the Guión Rojo, led by Edgar Ynsfrán, the interior minister, remained more or less autonomous. Ynsfrán was generally regarded as the second most powerful man in the country and Stroessner's most likely successor. Although he was a loyal and efficient aide, Ynsfrán's growing influence was his eventual undoing, for Stroessner would tolerate no potential rivals. Taking advantage of a police scandal in May 1966, the president purged all of Ynsfrán's close associates in the police force, his main base of power, and six months later Ynsfrán himself was forced to resign.

Stroessner was now free to undertake a complete reorganization of the Colorado Party. He decided to impose a military-type discipline on it, centralizing all authority and constructing a clear chain of command from himself, through his hand-picked executive committee, to the smallest village and neighbourhood organizations. Every rural hamlet and every city block had its party committee, and each of these was linked by an adviser appointed by the National Executive Committee to the central organization. In addition to these geographical units, the party's ancillary organs reached out to women, veterans, university and high school students, peasants, workers, lawyers, doctors and journalists. They, too, were supervised by advisers from the party's executive.[7]

The result was a monolithic party that bore a close resemblance to those found in totalitarian regimes. And, like them, its functions were closely intertwined with those of the government. Cabinet ministers, ambassadors, senators, deputies and high administrators usually sat on the Colorado Executive Committee as well. Even at the lower levels it was often necessary to belong to one of the party's organizations in order to be

---

[7] On the Colorado Party's reorganization, see César R. Gagliardone, *Plan de organización política del Partido Colorado* (Buenos Aires, 1968).

appointed as a teacher, judge, doctor at a public hospital or minor functionary in the bureaucracy. In return for such patronage the Colorado faithful were expected to return part of their salary to the party treasury, to attend public rallies and to help the government root out its enemies. Thus, Stroessner was able to fill the streets with cheering demonstrators, supplement police surveillance with a vast network of volunteer spies and amass huge majorities at election time.

The military was the other main pillar of the regime. By 1967 Stroessner's friends were in firm control, after successive purges. Moreover, unlike civilian presidents, Stroessner directly commanded his own armed forces, devoting a large part of every week to inspecting military installations, reviewing equipment purchases and deciding on promotions and assignments. During the course of a year he would visit every garrison at least once, and he ended each day by going to all the bases close to the capital to make sure that nothing unusual was happening. And to raise the stakes of any attempted coup he created a hand-picked, and heavily armed, Presidential Escort Battalion.

Stroessner also secured the support of the military by improving its pay and upgrading its equipment. Officers were permitted to import cars or appliances duty-free, could shop at subsidized stores and were eligible for low-interest loans at the bank. Those favourites put in charge of military purchasing were able to acquire substantial incomes through corruption. Retired officers managed various state enterprises, collecting both their pension and an executive's salary. Others were hired by private firms because of their political contacts. Beyond such ordinary graft and influence-peddling lay an underworld of smuggling, gambling, prostitution and drug-running, all made possible by Paraguay's location in the heart of the continent, its poorly patrolled borders and an acquiescent government. Such trade was organized into a system of rackets, each headed by a powerful military officer who parcelled out franchises. Tempted by large rewards and facing enormous risks involved in plotting, the vast majority of military men predictably opted for conformity. Thus, the armed forces and the Colorado Party, linked by a system of checks and balances, provided Stroessner's regime with an exceptional degree of stability.

OPPOSITION UNDER THE *STRONATO*

During the first decade of his rule, when his hold on power was not yet firm, Stroessner offered no quarter to his enemies. At his urging, Congress in October 1955 passed the Law for the Defence of Democracy, which allowed the police to search homes and arrest 'Communists' without a warrant, reserving for the government to decide who was a 'Communist'. Congress also extended indefinitely the state of siege, which allowed the executive to suspend habeas corpus, prevent the holding of political meetings and censor the press.

Stroessner's survival depended directly on this toughness. The exiles who fled Paraguay after the civil war had gradually recovered from their defeat and were trying to regroup. Moderate Liberals and *febreristas* had formed the Unión Nacional Paraguaya (UNP), which sought to bring international pressure on the regime. More youthful exiles favoured direct action. Early in 1958 militant Liberals formed the '14th of May' guerrilla movement, soon to be followed by the 'Vanguardia Febrerista'. Both launched invasions with the discreet backing of Argentina and Venezuela, but all of them failed. They were then superseded by the Cuban-backed Frente Unida de Liberación Nacional (FULNA), which was denounced both by Stroessner and by the UNP as Communist-dominated. FULNA had no more success than its predecessors. All three of its invasions in the latter half of 1960 were quickly crushed as the peasants, instead of welcoming their 'liberators', turned them in to the authorities.

Guerrilla tactics lost their appeal as it became clear that Paraguay was not to become another Cuba, and spokesmen for a more conciliatory line began to gain popularity. In 1963 two young Liberals, Carlos and Fernando Levi Ruffinelli, organized a splinter Movimiento Renovacionista. Breaking with the more intransigent party leaders, they petitioned Stroessner for legal recognition. This initiative was taken at a time when Stroessner was considering a change of strategy towards the opposition because he was under pressure from the United States to liberalize the regime and had been warned by the Kennedy administration that unless he did so he might have to forgo aid under the Alliance for Progress. Consequently, Stroessner accepted the Levi Ruffinellis' proposal as a way of providing him with a tame opposition to run against in the forthcoming presidential elections. The *renovacionistas* now officially recognized as the 'Liberal Party', were granted one-third of the seats in Congress, which allowed Stroessner to show his U.S. critics that he now had a two-party system.

At first the so-called Levi-Liberals were castigated by the other exiles as mere renegades and were expelled from the Liberal Party by its Executive Committee in exile. But as it became clear that Stroessner was willing to allow them to hold meetings, publish their newspaper and criticize govern-

ment policies (though not Stroessner himself, nor any top regime officials), pressure built within other opposition groups to follow suit. The
febreristas applied for amnesty in 1964. Wracked by internal feuds and cut
off from their old bases of support among labourers and students by long
years of exile, this once-powerful movement had dwindled to a mere
skeleton. Since it was no longer a serious threat, Stroessner accorded it
legal recognition as well. This left in exile the Communist Party, a coalition of *epifanista* and *democrático* Colorados known as the Movimiento
Popular Colorado (MOPOCO) and the parent body of the Liberal Party.
Stroessner refused to have any dealings with the first two groups but was
willing to negotiate an amnesty for the Liberals. In 1967 they came to
terms: in return for legal recognition, the Liberals agreed to disown the
left wing of their party and accept the regime's legitimacy. Since the
renovacionistas already had the title of 'Liberal Party', the mainstream
Liberals renamed themselves the Radical Liberal Party.

Thus, beginning in 1963 the *stronato* went through a phase of relative
'liberalization' which lasted about a decade. Although the opposition
parties were not allowed to win any elections and were restricted in their
criticism of the regime, they could recruit members, hold meetings,
campaign and publish their opinions. Their followers were able to return
from exile, get jobs, open businesses and raise their families. Although
this still left Paraguay far short of being a democracy, such gains were not
considered insignificant by most older activists who had spent nearly a
generation in exile. However, the younger generation of Liberals and
febreristas thought differently. They chafed at the narrow limits set upon
the opposition and grew frustrated at Stroessner's seemingly endless rule.

A left wing soon emerged inside the *febrerista* party, and by 1969 it
controlled a majority of the Executive Committee, albeit at the cost of
driving many moderates out of the party. A similar split appeared among
the Radical Liberals at their 1972 convention. Led by the fiery Domingo
Laíno, the left wing finally won control in 1975. Laíno's strategy was to
create a united opposition. In 1977 he succeeded in reuniting the Levi-
Liberals with the parent party to form the Partido Liberal Unido, and in
1979 he was instrumental in forging the Acuerdo Nacional, a broad
coalition composed of the Partido Liberal Unido, the *febreristas*, the
MOPOCOs, and the Partido Democrático Christiano – a small, Centre-
Left reform party that lacked official recognition. Before long, however,
the young militants learned what their moderate colleagues had long
maintained: that Stroessner would never permit opposition to go beyond

certain bounds and that he was prepared to impose unlimited repression in order to retain power. The most prominent Acuerdo Nacional leaders were exiled; the Partido Liberal Unido was declared illegal, and since it lacked official recognition all its assets, including its newspaper, were seized.

In the meantime, Stroessner faced a challenge from another source: the Roman Catholic clergy. During the 1960s a new generation of socially conscious priests had emerged. The opening of the Catholic University in 1960 led to the hiring of many European-educated Jesuits, who brought with them reformist ideas attacking social inequality, capitalism and traditional political practices. This approach soon influenced the Catholic Youth Movement and, through it, the peasants and trade unions. A Catholic labour federation was formed to rival the government-controlled CPT, while in the countryside radical priests attempted to organize the peasants into Christian Agrarian Leagues for the purpose of achieving land reform. The tactics they employed – church-sponsored entertainment, literacy campaigns, charities and a weekly magazine called *Comunidad* – were aimed at *concientización,* the creation of an anti-regime, anticapitalist consciousness among the lower classes. The clergy advocated a Christian communal society in which all land and other forms of capital would be shared equally, formal hierarchies of authority would be abolished and 'personal egoism' would disappear.

By the late 1960s these opinions had filtered up to the Paraguayan bishops' Episcopal Conference, although they were not endorsed by the ageing head of the Church, Archbishop Anibal Mena Porta. There was increasing friction between the clergy and the government as the former protested against the rewriting of the constitution so as to permit Stroessner to run for additional terms, demanded the release of all political prisoners, accused the government of torture and called for far-reaching social reforms. In 1970 Archbishop Mena Porta finally stepped down, to be replaced by the more reform-minded Monseñor Ismael Blas Rolón, despite Stroessner's attempts to prevent his appointment.

Rolón's promotion was followed by renewed efforts by the militant clergy to organize the peasants and workers and an equally determined resistance on the government's part. Catholic protest demonstrations were broken up, foreign priests were expelled from the country, others were arrested or forced to flee for safety and *Comunidad* was closed. In 1972 plain-clothes policemen and Colorado thugs raided the Catholic University's campus during an anti-government rally, beat the participants and smashed the buildings. In the countryside the Colorado *py nandí* attacked meetings of the Christian Agrarian Leagues, while soldiers were sent to disperse two experimental colonies set up by the leagues. Official violence did not even spare the offices of the Episcopal Conference, which were raided by the police on the excuse that they were searching for evidence of support by the bishops for guerrilla groups.

By the end of the 1970s Stroessner had succeeded in discrediting *concientización* as foreign-inspired and 'communistic'. The Church abandoned tactics of confrontation as more moderate clergymen gained the upper hand in the Episcopal Conference. In part, the government's victory was due to the *py nandí*'s loyalty to the Colorado Party; in part it was because the Church had never been very strong in modern Paraguay. Above all, however, it was the *stronato*'s record of material progress in the 1970s that tended to marginalize all opposition.

STROESSNER'S ECONOMIC POLICIES

Stroessner's long rule was not based solely on force; the regime also sought legitimacy through economic progress. It should be remembered that Stroessner inherited a disordered economy in 1954. Years of unstable government had prevented any real attempt to repair the damage done by the 1947 civil war. And not until the fall of Méndez Fleitas, early in 1956, was it possible to make a concerted attack on inflation by agreeing to a stabilization plan with the IMF under which Stroessner restricted credit, held wages in line with productivity, eliminated subsidies and price controls and devalued the guaraní. Such a policy was unpopular and involved high political risks. Farmers and businessmen, and even loyal Colorados, were unable to get loans. Only a determined dictator like Stroessner could have carried the plan through, especially since the benefits were not immediately apparent. Although the inflation rate fell sharply, from 71 per cent to only 6 per cent by 1958, production was slow to recover, largely because of the scarcity of credit. The rise in per capita GDP was less than 2 per cent during the regime's first five years. Exports were sluggish, which required restrictions on imports, and foreign exchange reserves dwindled to their lowest point in 1960. The only bright spot, besides the much-diminished inflation rate, was the gradual restoration of Paraguay's international credit. There was a sharp rise in long-term loans and direct grants from foreign sources, which helped Stroessner to survive this period of austerity.

The stabilization plan also included a program of internal improvements to encourage investment. During the 1960s the government spent large sums on transportation, schools, port facilities, merchant ships and energy projects. Stroessner was particularly quick to boast about his extension of the country's road network, from only 1,166 kilometres, of which only 95 kilometres were paved when he first took office, to 1,814 kilometres – including 261 kilometres paved – by 1968. Most importantly, a new highway linked Asunción to Brazil, which gave Paraguay an alternative trade route to the Atlantic and freed it from its former dependence on Argentina. In the area of electric power, Paraguay entered a joint project with Argentina to build a dam on the Upper Paraná. The plant opened in 1969, the first of similar and larger projects.

Such projects required heavy foreign borrowing, because government revenues were always insufficient. Even Stroessner did not dare to levy steep income or property taxes on the wealthy, or higher sales taxes on the poor. Import and export duties were easily evaded by smuggling, so there was never enough in the Treasury to cover all state projects. Private domestic savings, though on the rise at an annual rate of 12 per cent, were likewise inadequate. Consequently, foreign capital acquired a crucial role. New laws guaranteeing low taxes and easy repatriation of profits brought direct investment from the United States to record levels in 1966 and 1967. Most went into construction and factories that processed local primary products. More important, however, were foreign loans to the government. During the 1960s, total fixed capital doubled, mainly because of state development projects, while the foreign debt rose from U.S. $22 million to $81.7 million. At the same time, the GDP rose, averaging 4.6 per cent for the decade.[8]

The growth rate accelerated during the next decade. During the 1970s Paraguay registered some of the highest annual increases in Latin America, reaching an average of almost 11 per cent between 1977 and 1980 (with per capita growth at about 8 per cent). Nevertheless, this encouraged inflation, which, despite government austerity measures, reached 28 per cent by 1979.[9]

A key factor in both the high growth and high inflation rates was the construction of the world's largest hydroelectric dam at Itaipú, in co-operation with Brazil. This project caused a great deal of criticism in Paraguay

[8] James Wilkie (ed.), *Statistical Abstract of Latin America*, UCLA Latin American Center Publications, vol. 17 (Los Angeles, 1976), p. 333; and ibid., vol. 27 (1989), p. 961.
[9] On the economic boom of the 1970s, see Carlos Fletschner et al., *Economía del Paraguay contemporáneo*, 2 vols. (Asunción, 1984).

because, according to the opposition, the contracts stipulated the sale to Brazil of much of Paraguay's share of the energy at a fixed rate over fifty years. Assuming that inflation continued, this meant that Brazil would be buying increasingly cheap energy and that Paraguay's profits would drop. In its defence, the government argued that the abundance of cheap energy produced by Itaipú would more than meet Paraguay's own needs and would provide the basis for unprecedented economic growth. In any case, the opportunities for employment created by Itaipú, and the construction contracts that resulted, pumped large sums into Paraguay's modest economy. This coincided with a rise in exports and a boom in the tourist industry, which led to a decade of prosperity. Asunción, once a sleepy colonial town, became a bustling capital replete with skyscrapers, new hotels and restaurants. Its port hummed with an ever-increasing volume of trade, while the country's foreign exchange reserves rose from only $18 million in 1970 to $462 million by 1980.[10]

It was an optimistic time and Stroessner was quick to claim credit for it. A neon sign in downtown Asunción proclaimed proudly, 'Paz, Trabajo, y Bienestar con Stroessner'. Some disputed the claim about welfare; property owners, investors and high government officials were getting rich, but the working class was suffering a serious erosion of its living standards. As part of its anti-inflation strategy the government consistently kept wage increases below the rise in prices.

At the same time, the government's revenues lagged ever further behind its expenditures. Although Stroessner finally pushed an income tax law through Congress in 1971 after a rare show of legislative resistance, the rates were so modest and there were so many loopholes that it failed to raise much revenue. Foreign investors also continued to enjoy liberal tax relief. Meanwhile, the government spent heavily, and thus had to resort increasingly to foreign borrowing. The external debt, which stood at U.S. $144 million in 1970, rose to more than $1 billion by 1980, at which time it represented nearly one-fourth of the GNP. Also, while the government was pumping money into the economy it loosened its controls on private lending, thus capitulating to the clamour of upper- and middle-class Paraguayans who wanted to join the new consumer society. With so much money in circulation, together with rising oil prices and the higher cost of imported foreign goods, inflation increased rapidly.

The *stronato* had a mixed economic record: success in promoting

---

[10] *Statistical Abstract of Latin America*, vol. 27 (Los Angeles, 1989), p. 723.

growth, failure in distributing the benefits equitably and in managing the problems created by growth. The government defended itself, of course, by arguing that 'social justice' had to be postponed in order to encourage capital formation. Moreover, Stroessner could point to the large number of schools built under his rule; impressive gains in the literacy rate; a steady improvement in the ratio of physicians to the general population; a significant drop in infant mortality; the network of army-run rural clinics; and such showcase projects as the capital's water purification system. But if education and health were not entirely neglected, spending in those areas was among the lowest in all Latin American countries.

As long as Paraguay's economy was expanding and physical improvements were clearly visible, Stroessner was able to play on national pride and appear before the public as the indispensable bringer of progress. All this changed in the 1980s. The economic 'boom' was followed by a disastrous slump. The president's popularity waned, the opposition grew and finally in 1989 Stroessner was overthrown.

THE END OF THE *STRONATO*

During the early hours of 3 February 1989, only three months before the thirty-fifth anniversary of the *stronato,* Stroessner (who had been elected in 1983 for a seventh and in 1988, at the age of seventy-five, for an eighth presidential term) was overthrown in a bloody coup led by his second in command, General Andrés Rodríguez, head of the First Army Corps. The following day Stroessner signed his resignation and departed with his family for Brazil. At the airport crowds jeered him, crying, 'Death to the tyrant! Death to the assassin!' It was a humiliating reversal of fortune from the previous decade, when even some of Stroessner's enemies were forced to concede his popularity. What had happened to bring down, so suddenly and unexpectedly, this seemingly indestructible regime?

Stroessner's success in presiding over two decades of economic growth had resulted in a far more complex society than that which had produced him. It was also a society more difficult to manage. From 1.3 million inhabitants in 1950, Paraguay's population had grown to more than 4 million by the late 1980s. The urban sector, which was only a third of the total in 1950, was more than 40 per cent in 1980. Asunción had been transformed into a bustling capital of more than 600,000, while once-sleepy backwaters like Encarnación, Concepción, Villarica, Coronel Oviedo and Pedro Juan Caballero were active regional centres with tens of thousands of inhabitants. Puerto Presidente Stroessner, near the site of Itaipú, had grown practically overnight from a muddy village to a city of more than 100,000.

Urbanization brought an increase in commercial and industrial activities. Agriculture, which employed about 55 per cent of the economically active population in 1962, accounted for just over 40 per cent in 1988. The greatest expansion was registered in the commercial and service sectors, but industry also grew. The great economic surge of the 1970s increased the number of industrial establishments from about 5,800 to more than 18,000, and although most were small scale they nevertheless employed some 130,000 workers, as opposed to only 35,000 two decades earlier. In short, Paraguay had acquired a sizeable urban working class, both blue and white collar, as well as a much larger urban middle class. This meant that Stroessner was faced with a more sophisticated and less docile public: one that no longer lived off of subsistence agriculture, but depended on government action to protect jobs and satisfy rising expectations. In 1954, when the bulk of the population consisted of small peasants, it mattered little whether prices rose or trade balances were unfavourable. Now it mattered a great deal, and it mattered to people who were more likely to make their views known.

It was a serious problem, therefore, when the economic boom of the 1970s ended with the completion of the Itaipú dam. With no new investment coming in, by 1982 Paraguay was in the grip of a severe economic recession, coupled with an annual inflation rate of about 30 per cent. This coincided with sharp down-turns in the Argentine and Brazilian economies, upon which Paraguay depended so heavily for export revenues. The recession was felt especially in the urban sector, as tourist hotels stood empty, commerce stagnated and much of industry's installed capacity lay idle.

Farmers and businessmen, once Stroessner's strong supporters, were angered by his refusal to devalue the guaraní and furnish easy credit to stimulate domestic production and exports. Nor did he heed the demand to end the flourishing black market in cheap contraband imports. Discouraging contraband would undercut his support in the military, and devaluation would raise the prices of goods for urban consumers. Stroessner was anxious to avoid squeezing labour's living standards, because his grip on the unions was becoming increasingly difficult to maintain. His minions at the head of the CPT were forced to rig elections to stay in office in 1982 and subsequently the CPT had suffered a split. Though denied legal recognition, the rebel unions' Movimiento Intersindical de Trabajadores (MIT) grew in strength and enjoyed the backing of the international democratic trade union movement. As the decade wore on and the economic recession deepened, there were an increasing number of strikes, which often enlisted the support of students and white-collar employees.

In the countryside, too, economic modernization proved to be destabilizing. Although in the early 1960s the government had begun settling peasants on public lands as a means of reducing social tension, during the next decade it abandoned this in favour of selling off large parcels to army officers and Colorado Party leaders, who in turn sold them to land-hungry Brazilian colonists and multinational agro-businesses. The result was to introduce modern capitalist agriculture into a society previously characterized by subsistence farming. This was especially the case in the regions bordering on Brazil, where squatters and Indian communities, which once had occupied unmolested the empty land, were suddenly driven off. Some of the peasant colonies also broke up. Discouraged by the lack of government assistance, they sold out to the Brazilians or multinationals, or else became victims of land-grabbing. Where there was resistance to the foreign newcomers, the army was called in to suppress it. In December 1980 the Movimiento Campesino Paraguayo (MCP) was founded to defend smallholders and the landless. By 1987 the MCP claimed the support of ten thousand families, which made it the largest mass organization in Paraguay.[11]

As the social environment grew more hostile and the economy worsened, the regime began to blunder. Those in high places inevitably grew concerned about what would happen when Stroessner, who was seventy-five at the time of his re-election in 1988, departed from the scene. As early as August 1984 at their party convention, the Colorados, who continued to control two-thirds of the seats in both houses of Congress, had begun positioning themselves for the inevitable power struggle to succeed the general. One faction, the '*tradicionalistas*' took the view that the party must prepare itself for the future by improving the regime's public image, eliminating corruption and removing the more brutal elements. A more radical faction, based in the party's youth organization, which came to be known as the '*éticos*', even dared to denounce the government in public. The *éticos*, however, went beyond what Stroessner would tolerate and were

[11] R. Andrew Nickson, 'Tyranny and Longevity: Stroessner's Paraguay', *Third World Quarterly*, 10, no. 1 (1988), p. 256.

purged. The *tradicionalistas* and *éticos* were opposed by the 'militants'. Drawn from the palace *camarilla* whose leaders were Mario Abdo Benítez, Stroessner's secretary, and Sabino Montanaro, his minister of interior, this faction placed personal loyalty to Stroessner ahead of loyalty to the party. The militants were prepared, in the event of Stroessner's death, to support his elder son, Gustavo, so as to maintain the continuity of the *stronato*.

Afraid of losing its grip on power, this inner circle of militants became increasingly high-handed. The country's leading newspaper, *ABC Color*, was suppressed in 1984 after it published articles exposing corruption in the government and attacking undue Brazilian influence in Paraguay's affairs. In 1987 the independent Radio Nandutí was shut down, as was the *febrerista* paper *El Pueblo*. The climax came at the Colorados' convention in May 1987 when the *tradicionalistas* were barred from the hall and deprived afterwards of any representation on the party's Executive Committee. Although they appealed to Stroessner, he professed himself unable to act in the party's internal affairs.

This piece of hypocrisy was a serious mistake that undermined one of the two basic pillars of his regime, for the militants had little support outside the presidential palace. Alienating the *tradicionalistas* cost the regime much of its former mass base. That might not have been fatal but for the fact that Stroessner then proceeded to undermine his support in the military as well. Here, too, the succession question proved to be a volatile issue. For some time General Andrés Rodríguez, who was second only to Stroessner in the army hierarchy, had coveted the presidency. Stroessner had kept him under control, first by mobilizing mass demonstrations of Colorado supporters every time Rodríguez expressed any doubts about public policy, and second by marrying his younger son, Hugo, to Rodríguez's daughter. Rodríguez also was allowed to grew very wealthy through the illegal drug trade. Unappeased, Rodríguez suddenly saw his chance when Stroessner and the militants began to scheme for Gustavo to succeed to the presidency in 1993.

As an air force colonel, it might be supposed that Gustavo Stroessner had the right credentials for claiming the military's crucial support; but he had the fatal flaw of being a homosexual. La Coronela, as he was known in the barracks, was an unacceptable choice.[12] When General Stroessner, in his usual ham-fisted way, sought to impose his decision on the military, he quickly brought about his own downfall. Aware that Rodríguez was orga-

[12] 'El futuro colorado', *Somos*, 8 February 1989, p. 52.

nizing the resistance to Gustavo, Stroessner tried to remove him from command of the pivotal First Army by forcing his retirement. Instead, however, the soldiers rallied behind Rodríguez and brought the *stronato* to an inglorious end on 3 February 1989.

Installed as provisional president, General Rodríguez placed the militant leaders under arrest, restored the *tradicionalistas* to their former places in the party and government and called for elections to be held on 1 May. Although the opposition Authentic Radical Liberals, *febreristas,* and Christian Democrats complained that this did not leave them enough time to prepare, they agreed to participate when given guarantees of a fair count. The Colorados, meanwhile, nominated Rodríguez as their presidential candidate, in return for his promise not to seek re-election. They also set about reincorporating formerly disaffected elements such as the MOPOCO, the *éticos* and Edgar Ynsfrán's right-wing Movimiento de Integración Colorado (MIC).

The elections, while hardly a model of democracy, especially in the rural districts, were nevertheless an improvement over those conducted by Stroessner. Moreover, they took place in an atmosphere of relative openness. The opposition press was allowed to function freely, radio and television were open to differing viewpoints and political exiles were allowed to return. Rodríguez and the Colorados won, as expected, so that by no means was there a great break with the past. Whether the process of liberalization would continue, and result eventually in a genuine democracy, or whether the old system would now try to entrench itself in a new guise, was still very much an open question.

Part Two

CHILE

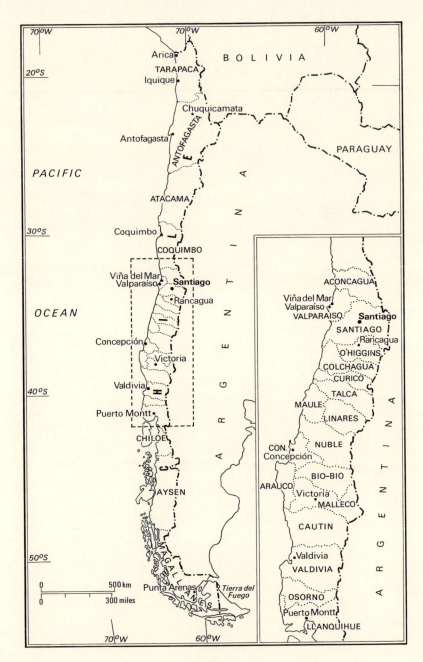

Chile

5

CHILE, 1930–58

During the three decades after 1930 – and indeed until the coup which brought down the government of Salvador Allende in 1973 – Chilean politics were unique in Latin America. Only Chile sustained in this period an electoral democracy including major Marxist parties. And for almost fifteen years, between 1938 and 1952, Radical presidents held power through the support, erratic but persistent, of both the Socialists and the Communists, with lasting consequences for the nation's political development. These multi-party governments based on multi-class alliances simultaneously pursued industrial growth and social reform. They failed, however, to attack the roots of Chilean underdevelopment in either the latifundia-dominated rural sector or the United States-dominated external sector.

From the 1930s Chilean reformers criticized the excessive national dependence on the foreign sector that had been highlighted by the world depression. After that crisis, Chile gradually achieved greater self-sufficiency: between the 1920s and the 1940s the estimated share of gross domestic product (GDP) being sold abroad declined from approximately 40 to 20 per cent, as did foreign capital as a proportion of the total capital in Chile.[1] By contrast, direct U.S. investments grew by 80 per cent from 1940 to 1960, the vast majority of this foreign capital going to the mining sector. Overwhelmingly controlled by U.S. companies from the 1920s to the 1960s, copper came to account for some 50 per cent of Chilean exports, copper and nitrates nearly 80 per cent. Not only was the United States the leading foreign investor in Chile; it also regained its position as Chile's premier trading partner after a spurt of German competition in the 1930s. Chile consistently relied on the United States for

---

[1] Aníbal Pinto Santa Cruz (ed.), *Antecedentes sobre el desarrollo de la economía chilena, 1925–1952* (Santiago, 1954), pp. 78–82.

manufactured consumer goods and, increasingly after the Second World War, for food and capital goods.

The foreign sector contracted as a proportion of GDP as domestic industry expanded. The proportion of the economically active population working in industry climbed from 15 per cent in 1930 to 20 per cent by 1952, while the proportion in agriculture and fishing, which together constituted the largest single employment sector, fell from 39 to 31 per cent. Between 1940 and 1954 industrial production increased 246 per cent and agriculture only 35 per cent. This trend continued into the early 1960s, when urban industry, construction and services came to account for 78 per cent of GDP, compared with 12 per cent for agriculture, fishing and forestry. As a result, manufactured goods shrank from 50 per cent of the value of Chilean imports in 1925 to 16 per cent by 1969. Most of this import-substitution industrialization took the form of consumer items, which accounted for 95 per cent of Chilean manufacturing output at the end of the 1940s. Yet although manufactured consumer products declined as a percentage of imports, Chilean industry remained heavily dependent on foreign raw materials, semi-processed goods, parts, capital and technology; more than one-fourth of the primary products used by domestic industry came from abroad.

The service sector expanded more than any other area of the economy: from 36 per cent of the active population in 1940 to 41 per cent by 1960, mainly thanks to an increase in those engaged in government services from 5 to 8 per cent. The growth of the bureaucracy slowed in the 1950s, but that of public investment did not. Indeed, the public sector already accounted for more than half of domestic investment capital in the 1940s. Measured in 1950 pesos, total government expenditure nearly doubled from 1940 to 1954 and continued to spiral upwards thereafter. Allocations for economic development climbed from less than one-fourth of the total government budget in 1940 to more than one-third by 1954. Although foreshadowed in the 1920s, it was during and after the depression that Chileans began increasingly to look to the state for solutions to the problems of underdevelopment.

Increasing population growth as well as the expansion in manufacturing and services swelled the urban areas (which, among other consequences, enlarged the potential constituency for the Left). The total population rose from 4.3 million in 1930 to 5.9 million in 1950 and 7.4 million in 1960. Low by Latin American standards, Chile's average annual population growth rate of 1.5 per cent (1925–52) did not generate unmanageable pressures for expanded governmental services. However, the rate increased from 1.3 per cent in the 1930s to nearly 1.8 per cent in the 1940s, while per capita income grew at an annual average of only 2 per cent. Thanks to declining mortality, Chile's population growth rate had by the 1960s reached 2.5 per cent – close to the Latin American average. From 1940 to 1952, the urban population increased 42 per cent, the rural barely 3 per cent. According to national censuses, the total population shifted from 49 per cent urban in 1930 to 53 per cent in 1940, 60 per cent in 1952, 68 per cent in 1960 (and more than 70 per cent by the 1970s).

Urbanization accentuated the traditional dominance of central Chile over the peripheral regions. Santiago Province's share of the national population grew from 16 per cent in 1930 to 30 per cent in 1952, after which it continued to account for about one-third. In the same years, its proportion of national industry rose from 37 to 65 per cent. The outlying regions complained about internal colonialism, under which their mining and agricultural reports paid for the growth of manufacturing, bureaucracy and wealth in and around the capital city. While the North and South produced more than 80 per cent of all exports, Santiago and its port of Valparaíso consumed more than 50 per cent of all imports. Benefiting from popular resentment of exploitation by the urban and rural elites of the central region, the Left's presidential candidates – Pedro Aguirre Cerda in 1938, Gabriel González Videla in 1946 and Salvador Allende de Gossens in 1958 – registered their highest percentages of the ballots in the distant northern and southern provinces. In office, however, they tended to ignore regional grievances and, by expanding industry and the state apparatus in the cities of the Centre, further compacted power and prosperity in the country's historic nucleus.

Chile's interlocking upper class, which owned the great estates (*fundos*), factories, mines and banks, probably accounted for less than 10 per cent of the population. Middle-class white-collar employees, small proprietors and merchants, intellectuals and professionals probably accounted for some 15 per cent and the lower class, increasingly urban, comprised around 75 per cent. Most of the population classified as illiterate – nearly 25 per cent – belonged, of course, to the lower strata.

The rural and urban upper class – often interconnected through families and portfolios – dominated oligopolistic means of production in all economic sectors. According to the 1930 census, 7 per cent of all farms surveyed accounted for 81 per cent of the value of rural property. Fewer than six hundred families owned 1 percent of all farms but 62 per cent of all agricultural land, while 82 per cent of owners possessed only 5 per cent of all farm-land. The Radical governments, usually backed by the two Marxist parties, ignored this inequitable distribution of rural property so as not to antagonize *latifundistas* and inflate food prices. An estimate for the 1950s revealed that 10 per cent of landowners still held 86 per cent of the arable land, while 75 per cent of the country's farmers claimed only 5 per cent of the soil. While retaining their control over land and labour, the rural elite endured a shift in government favouritism to the urban sectors as national trade, credit, currency and price policies all encouraged industry and construction.

These rural and urban elites excercised political influence through such institutions as the Sociedad Nacional de Agricultura (SNA) and the Sociedad de Fomento Fabrie (SFF), the latter being the less antagonistic of the two towards the Popular Front. They also exerted influence through the Roman Catholic Church and the armed forces. They operated politically mainly through the Conservative and Liberal parties, whose leaders came from equally aristocratic, landowning backgrounds and therefore set aside their nineteenth-century squabbles over the role of the Church to unite against the threats of populism and socialism; both parties relied heavily on the support of intimidated peasants, especially in the central provinces.

The Chilean upper class and the Right were frequently intractable and repressive, but they distinguished themselves in this era by coping with new contenders for power principally through minimal concessions and co-optation. At least compared with their counterparts in most other Latin American countries, they seldom resorted to overt violence as a means of social control. Gradually and reluctantly they surrendered direct political domination to challengers representing the middle and lower classes. However, the upper class retained significant veto power, imposed firm limits on reform and continued to hold economic privileges and social status. In the 1930s and 1940s, their accommodation of Popular Front politics did not cost them dearly; on the contrary, many elements among the elite made substantial economic gains. By the end of the 1950s, 9 per cent of the active population still received at least 43 per cent of national income.

Serving as brokers between the upper and lower strata, the middle groups were politically strengthened in the inter-war years. Never a tightly knit social sector, the urban middle class asserted itself through professional organizations, student associations, intellectual societies, the secretive Masonic order, the military, the bureaucracy, unions and, above all, reformist parties. It identified most closely with the Radical Party, which enrolled professionals, merchants, teachers, white-collar employees, bureaucrats, small-mine owners and even dissident members of the elite, especially in the outlying provinces. Although numerous Radical leaders issued from the same exclusive social circles as the Conservatives and Liberals, their commitment to industrialization and state interventionism in order to dilute middle- and working-class discontent established tenuous links with the Left. At the same time, the middle sectors played a prominent role in new parties, notably the Partido Socialista (PS) and the Falange. During the 1930s and 1940s, these middle groups, simultaneously seeking support from beneath and acceptance from above, usually rallied the workers as allies in order to gain ground within the system. Through Popular Front politics, the *capas medias* benefited more than the lower classes. As in other regional populist movements, they became increasingly defensive about their gains through the growth of the state, education and industry and decreasingly enthusiastic about coalitions with labour. Always divided – normally between the upper middle class more in tune with the Right and the lower middle class more sympathetic to the Left – some middle-sector Chileans, especially professionals and small businessmen, applauded the Radical government's switch to conservative policies in alignment with the United States at the end of the 1940s.

The majority of workers toiled in the countryside. The term peasants, or *campesinos,* consisted loosely of three main groups of agricultural labourers: *inquilinos,* about half the rural work-force, who were tied to the great estates; *afuerinos,* migratory labourers who suffered even worse poverty than the *inquilinos;* and *minifundistas,* small-property owners. Rural workers, who became more independent of conservative landowners during these years and sometimes protested against their squalid living conditions, still lagged far behind urban labourers as an electoral force for the Left. The Radical governments of the 1940s neglected their plight and impeded their unionization; miners received roughly four times and industrial labourers three times the income of farm workers, who saw their real wages decline by nearly 20 per cent. Similar to patterns elsewhere in the hemisphere, this bargain between urban reformers and rural oligarchs traded peasant poverty and subordination for upper-class toleration of populist participation in national politics.

During the Popular Front years, the minority of politically active workers lived mainly in the cities and mining towns, venting their grievances primarily through trade unions and the Socialist and Communist parties. One reason for their unusually vigorous record of mobilization and militancy was that a relatively slow rate of population growth created a smaller labour surplus than in much of Latin America. Moreover, the strongest proletarian concentrations emerged in the under-populated and isolated mining zones, where labour's struggles against foreign companies controlling a crucial enclave acquired exceptional strategic and national importance. The political dedication and skill of the Marxist parties channelled those protests into the most dynamic radical electoral movement in the hemisphere.

Despite impressive gains, labour remained weak, partly because of the small size of the industrial proletariat. The artisan sector – those in enterprises of four or fewer workers – still accounted for approximately 60 per cent of the industrial labour force in the 1930s, at least 50 per cent in the 1940s and 46 per cent in 1960. The labour code permitted industrial unions only in factories with at least twenty-five workers and prohibited national labour federations, which therefore arose outside the legal framework. Moreover, agricultural unions remained virtually outlawed until the 1960s. Given such restrictions on labour activities, workers had to rely on the interventionist state and thus on political parties for assistance with job security, wages, working conditions and welfare benefits. At the same time, the Popular Front coalitions encouraged unionization. The number of legal unions more than quadrupled between the early 1930s and the early 1940s, but they still represented only a tiny fraction of the workforce, rising from 8 per cent in 1932 to nearly 13 per cent by 1952, and then falling back to 10 per cent in 1959 under less favourable administrations and economic conditions. This slow growth of unionization – and of the electorate – kept stable political institutionalization well ahead of disruptive mobilization.

From 1932 to 1958 Chile's political system remained adaptable and resilient despite fundamental conflicts between traditional parties and avowedly revolutionary groups. Like their adversaries, the Left accepted the inherited rules of the game whereby all political forces joined heterogeneous coalitions in order to win elections and function effectively in Congress. Among and within the parties of the Left – the Socialists and the Communists – battles raged over tactical issues of leadership, coalition partners and details of programmes, but until the Cuban Revolution of 1959 these groups rarely questioned the strategic necessity and desirability of immersion in the multi-party, polyclass electoral and bargaining system. In particular, both Marxist parties muffled their ideological objectives to facilitate alliances with the moderate Radical Party.

The narrow scope of the electorate also reduced the impact of workers and their parties, since only literate males of at least twenty-one years of age could vote in most elections in this period. Women received the franchise first in the municipal elections of 1935, then in the 1949 congressional elections and finally in the 1952 presidential election. Despite leftist support for their suffrage rights, women voted disproportionately against Marxists; together with factionalism and repression, this contributed to the decline of the Left in the late 1940s and early 1950s. The exclusion of women and illiterate men from most elections until the 1950s reduced potential voters to some 20 per cent of the population. Among those eligible to vote, fewer than half usually registered. Out of those inscribed on the electoral rolls, close to 80 per cent normally cast ballots in presidential contests. In other words, between 7 and 9 per cent of the total population voted for presidential candidates from 1932 until the beginning of the rapid expansion of the electorate in 1952. For example, less than 5 per cent of the national population gave Aguirre Cerda's Popular Front its victory in 1938. Until the 1950s populist politics in Chile, in contrast to some other Latin American countries, did not involve any major expansion in electoral participation. Despite the under-representation of workers at the ballot box, the Left, realizing the limits of rightist toleration for political change, made no significant effort to enfranchise illiterates or to employ non-electoral means to power. The durability of Chile's circumscribed political system required extraordinary restraint by both reformers and conservatives.

DEPRESSION AND CRISIS, 1929–32

Chile was more profoundly affected by the world depression than any other country in the Western world. Foreign trade collapsed: by 1932 exports had tumbled to less than 12 per cent and imports to less than 20 per cent of their 1929 value. (The dollar value of exports in 1929 was not reached again until 1955.) Loans from the United States, which had created a veneer of prosperity in the late 1920s, plummeted from 682 million pesos in 1930 to 54 million in 1931 and then to zero in 1933. The heavily indebted government's budget shrank correspondingly, falling by roughly 50 per cent from 1929 to 1932, when it registered a resounding deficit of 189 million pesos.

Of all Chile's economic sectors, the depression struck mining earliest and hardest. The value of copper and nitrate exports dropped 89 per cent from 1927–9 to 1932. As world prices for farm goods plunged and consumption of food from central Chile by the northern mining provinces dwindled, the depression reverberated from the mineral into the agricultural sector. From 1929 to 1931, prices for farm products in Chile fell by nearly 50 per cent. Manufacturing suffered from the depression only belatedly and briefly: the index of industrial production (1927–9 = 100) fell from 117 in 1930 to 87 in 1931 but then rebounded to 99 in 1932, 109 in 1933 and 119 in 1934. Only one foreign and two domestic commercial banks collapsed, but bank reserves, deposits and loans shrank until mid-1931. By 1932, national unemployment had soared to more than 200,000, with nearly half of the jobs lost being in mining, where production dropped by more than 50 per cent. Throughout Chile, real salaries plunged some 40 per cent from 1929 to 1932. The sight of unemployed, hungry and angry workers demonstrating, begging and forming bread lines frightened the upper and middle classes.

As foreign exchange, savings and investment evaporated, landowners and industrialists bemoaned government inaction, although advocating different solutions to the crisis. Chile's dictator, Carlos Ibáñez del Campo, who since coming to power in 1927 had thrived on the mystique of his efficient management of the economy, at first clung to orthodox laissez-faire policies, maintaining the gold standard, pursuing a balanced budget, increasing taxes and pruning expenditure, which alienated bureaucrats, the armed forces and those employed in the public sector. Then in mid-1931, service on the foreign debt was suspended and exchange controls were imposed. These measures, however, did not go far enough to stem the economic collapse. In July, middle-class university students (both Catholics and Marxists), professionals and public employees took their protest to the streets. Such opposition, which could be silenced only with massive armed force, convinced Ibáñez to resign. Whereas in most of Latin America the depression destroyed civilian governments, in Chile it discredited military rule.

A wave of anti-militarism swept the country as a provisional government prepared for presidential elections. In September 1931 a mutiny by radicalized sailors in the northern naval squadron sharpened fears of revolutionary upheaval and further convinced the Chilean elites that a firm civilian administration would be more effective than the armed forces at preserving order. The short-lived naval uprising also persuaded many officers that the military should steer clear of political entanglements.

The fall of Ibáñez had left a vacuum in which traditional political parties splintered and scores of new contenders for power sprang up. Minuscule corporatist movements arose, but it was the Left that was most active as the Communists split decisively into Stalinist and Trotskyist branches and many tiny Socialist parties were established. Broadly speaking, the multi-party political spectrum was recast in 1931–2 into Left (Socialists and Communists), Centre (Radicals and *falangistas*/Christian Democrats) and Right (Liberals and Conservatives). To show solidarity against the threats of both militarism and Socialism, the Right and the Centre – representing most of the upper and middle classes – coalesced behind Juan Esteban Montero Rodríguez, a cautious Radical lawyer closely related to land-owning and banking interests. The convulsions of the depression moved the Conservatives and Liberals to prefer their old political enemies as insulation against more ominous alternatives. At a convention of the Left, disaffected Liberals and Radicals, the artisan-based Democrats and a handful of new Socialist groups nominated the populist paladin of 1920, and president of the republic from 1920 to 1925, Arturo Alessandri Palma, who, once again, campaigned as champion of the middle and working classes. Both the Stalinist and Trotskyist Communist parties also fielded candidates – Elías Lafertte Gaviño and Manuel Hidalgo Plaza, respectively – appealing to labour. Despite the depression, however, there was no evidence of dra-matic voter radicalization in the 1931 election. Even after five years in hibernation under Ibáñez, the traditional parties easily dominated the con-test: Montero won a landslide victory with 64 per cent of the votes – the first member of the Radical Party to be elected president. Thirty-five per cent went to Alessandri and only 1 per cent to the two Communist candi-dates combined.

The return of the established ruling groups to power, however, failed to remedy the economic disaster, calm the turmoil among leftists or dispel the general climate of fear. During the Tragic Christmas of 1931, clashes between rioting workers and panicky police and soldiers in two small northern towns ended in a massacre of the protestors. This violence in-creased elite fears of working-class insurrection and confirmed leftist be-liefs that Montero's government represented only the gilded oligarchy. While the plodding president (nicknamed 'Don One-Step') dedicated him-self to respecting the constitution and preaching austerity, production and employment sank to new depths.

In June 1932 Air Force Commander Marmaduke Grove Vallejo over-threw Montero and installed a putative Socialist Republic, which the rest of the armed forces scrapped after only twelve days. Although confused ideologically and ineffectual administratively, the ephemeral republic gave birth to the Socialist Party of Chile and anointed the dashing Grove as 'the Socialist caudillo' for the next decade. For one hundred days after Grove's ouster, Ibáñez's former ambassador to the United States, Carlos Dávila Espinoza, a journalist, presided over a second version of a Socialist repub-lic, which came closer to corporatism and state capitalism. The armed forces then ousted Dávila in September and called new presidential and congressional elections for October.

While the president of the Supreme Court presided over an interim government, Alessandri emerged as the leading candidate in the 1932 campaign. As in previous elections, the Radicals and Democrats provided his official support, but many Liberals and neophyte Socialists also flocked to his banner. He now appealed to all social strata as a reformist strong man who could restore order after the exhaustion of other alternatives, although he attracted more elite elements and fewer workers than in past contests. He posed as the embodiment of national unity with the slogan 'The triumph of Alessandri is the triumph of civilian rule'.

Recovery of the economy and reconstitution of civilian authority were the dominant issues at the end of 1932. In response to the depression, most Chileans looked to state intervention, industrialization and moderate eco-nomic nationalism. Many on the Right argued for corporatist state regula-tion to control dissatisfied workers, while many on the Left pressed for socialist state action to relieve the suffering masses. Import-substitution industrialization protected by tariffs and accompanied by modest welfare measures superficially blended these desires without endangering domestic or foreign capitalists. Rightists, worried that military disruptions of consti-tutional order opened the way for leftist uprisings, set up paramilitary Republican Militias to defend civilian government. Most leaders of the armed forces, resenting such hostility and fearing divisions within the ranks, now repudiated open political involvement. To avoid new nemeses on the Left, many on the Right were willing in 1932 to support their former adversary Alessandri. The 'Lion of Tarapacá' emerged victorious with 55 per cent of the vote. Demonstrating that socialism was now an option for the future, Grove leapt from obscurity to finish second with 18 per cent. In April 1933 he founded the Socialist Party of Chile – an uneasy populist grouping of Marxists, Trotskyists, Social Democrats and anarchist/anarcho-syndicalists bridging the middle and working classes. Trailing the field in the poll were the president of the Conservative Party, Héctor Rodríguez de la Sotta with 14 per cent, the Liberal Enrique Zañartu Prieto with 12 per cent and the Communist Elías Lafertte with a mere 1 per cent. The president-elect had changed little from his days following the First World War as a liberal reformer. But the leftward slide of the electorate found him straddling the middle and therefore acceptable to the Right. Once in office, Alessandri governed with the Conservatives, Liberals, and the right wing of the Radical Party.

The 1932 congressional elections reflected the new tripolar alignment of the electorate, which persisted for four decades thereafter. The vote for the Right – mainly Conservatives and Liberals – which had been 76 per cent in 1912 and 52 per cent in 1925 had fallen to 37 per cent in 1932. Meanwhile, the Radicals and like-minded centrist groups won slightly more than 20 per cent of the 1932 vote, and the Democrats, Socialists, Communists and other leftists secured some 33 per cent. Chile's leading newspaper *El Mercurio* placed the transformed political landscape in the following perspective:

The Socialists of today are the Radicals of yesterday and the Liberals of the day before yesterday. The vanguard has changed in name, but its nature is the same. As much can be said of those stigmatized today as oligarchs; they are the same ones that yesterday were Conservatives and the day before yesterday Ultramontanes. Between them both is the centre, which today is Radical and yesterday was Liberal. The names change: humanity does not.[2]

From the 1930s to the 1950s, it was the question of which forces the intermediate Radicals would accept as allies that provided the critical variable in Chilean politics.

THE SECOND PRESIDENCY OF ARTURO ALESSANDRI, 1932 – 8

President Alessandri's personal authority, electoral mandate and economic success reinvigorated constitutional legitimacy in Chile after 1932. At his inauguration, he pointedly refused to review the troops, although he stressed that a majority of the officers were honourable and deserved praise. He brought the military under control by rotating commands, retiring conspirators and rewarding loyalists. Scarred by public condemna-

---

[2] *El Mercurio*, 9 June 1932.

tion of their role in the dictatorship and the depression, most of the armed forces preferred to abstain from open politics. They snuffed out an attempted coup in 1933 and remained loyal to the constitution for the next four decades. Alessandri also re-established order by wielding extraordinary executive powers against rightist and leftist agitators. He briefly jailed Grove, and between 1933 and 1936 he used the heavily armed Republican Militia as a bulwark against military or socialist adventurers. As the decade wore on, he increasingly relied on the parties of the Right and the economic elite as the mainstays of his government.

Economic reconstruction benefited from the gradual revival of the international market, especially the demand for copper and, to a lesser extent, nitrates. The inadvertent Keynesianism of the short-lived governments between Ibáñez and Alessandri, which had abandoned the gold standard and fanned inflation, also facilitated recovery. By 1932, the peso had fallen to one-fifth of its 1929 value. Although monetary depreciation slowed under Alessandri, the amount of money in circulation more than doubled from 1933 to 1940. His government tried to strike a balance between growth and stability. Exchange controls, protective tariffs, tax incentives and credit expansion by the Banco Central encouraged urban enterprises to lead Chile out of the depression. Despite the generally orthodox beliefs and policies of Gustavo Ross Santa María, the finance minister, the Alessandri administration favoured manufacturing, construction and mining, which lowered the number of unemployed from nearly 300,000 in 1932 to less than 15,000 in 1935. After slashing public works expenditures during 1932–4, the government launched new construction programs during 1936–8. By 1939, Chilean factories produced nearly 60 per cent more goods than in 1930.

Despite renewed growth, issues of economic nationalism as well as social justice continued to fuel leftist opposition to the Alessandri administration. Although the president dissolved Ibáñez's controversial nitrate cartel, he left majority control of the industry in the hands of the Guggenheims. He also disappointed nationalists by using the government's earnings from nitrates to resume partial service on the burdensome foreign debt (suspended from 1932 to 1935) and by refusing to take over the U.S.-owned and mismanaged Chilean Electric Company. Leftist nationalists – including many left-wing Radicals – urged the government to hold out for further reductions of repayment rates in its protracted negotiations with U.S. bondholders over the 1920s debt, to complain more vociferously about high tariff barriers in the United States and to defend exchange discrimination in favour of import-substitution domestic industries and against U.S. interests eager to extract dollars from Chile. Despite some disagreements and pressure from the emerging Popular Front for more energetic anti-imperialist actions, Alessandri maintained good relations with the United States, even as Great Britain and Europe (especially Germany) recaptured a larger portion of Chilean trade. Both Left and Right shared his desire for expanded commerce with the Colossus of the North, and Roosevelt's Good Neighbor policy improved attitudes towards the United States across the political spectrum. On the other controversial foreign policy issue in the 1930s – the Spanish civil war and the rise of conflict in Europe – Radicals, Socialists and Communists excoriated the administration for adopting a posture of neutrality towards the Spanish conflagration that was biased in favour of Franco. Although most Chileans probably shared the Left's sympathy with the Spanish Loyalists, they also endorsed Alessandri's desire to avoid involvement in European conflicts, in accord with long-standing foreign policy principles.

Critics also attacked Alessandri's conservative programmes as prejudicial to the workers, whose wages and salaries trailed behind the cost of living. Social security policies gave white-collar employees benefits far superior to those delivered to manual workers. Alessandri did institutionalize labour–industrial relations through implementation of the legal code of 1924, but he accepted landowner demands for the restriction of union rights to the cities. While holding down the price of basic foodstuffs to quell urban labour discontent, the government compensated landed elites with continued dominion over the rural work-force.

Despite dissatisfaction with restrictions on food prices and exports, many *latifundistas* tolerated Alessandri's support for urban industry because they also possessed economic interests in the cities. The more sophisticated agriculturalists realized that urban expansion would gradually increase consumption of foodstuffs, raw materials and excess labour in the countryside, which they hoped would curtail pressures for land reform. At the same time, agrarian elites retained special access to public credits and railways, extremely low taxes (always beneath 2 per cent of total government revenues), influence over government agencies concerned with farming and numerous seats in Congress thanks to the compliant peasant electorate. Naturally, urban industrialists and financiers exuded even greater enthusiasm for Alessandri's administration, which presaged many of the sectoral preferences of future Popular Front governments. Recognizing the erosion of the rightist parties, the Chilean upper class relied increasingly on its corporate organizations and their links with the state. While the SNA and the SFF became more active, the founding in 1933 of the Confederación de la Producción y del Comercio epitomized this capitalist assertiveness. It co-ordinated all the elite economic interest groups in opposition to the new Left and in favour of low taxes and ample credits from the government.

The political parties representing the upper class sought to hang on to power mainly through gradual liberalization and endorsement of increasingly statist measures. The Conservatives now joined with the Liberals against the new spectre of populism and socialism in the hope that greater employer and governmental paternalism would preserve social peace and thus undercut the Left. Within the Conservative Party, young reformers – notably Manuel Garretón Walker, Bernardo Leighton Guzmán and Eduardo Frei Montalva – wanted to go even farther with semi-corporatist programmes for social welfare to outbid the Marxists for the loyalty of the masses. Inspired by reformist Catholic thought from Europe, they created the Falange, which became an independent centrist party in the 1940s and was transformed into the Christian Democrat Party in the 1950s. In the 1930s and 1940s, many Liberals also moved beyond Manchester individualism towards more reformist positions consonant with state capitalism.

A rash of minor right-wing parties also sought a path between the tarnished laissez-faire past and a dreaded socialist future. These corporatist and regionalist movements included the Agrarian Party, the Popular Corporative Party, the Republican Union, National Action and, most significant, the Movimiento Nacional Socialista (MNS) led by Jorge González von Marées. The MNS spliced together reformist ideas – such as administrative decentralization and land redistribution – from European fascists and Latin American populists, notably Peru's *apristas*. These 'creole Nazis' clashed with the Marxists in the streets and competed unsuccessfully with the Socialists for middle-class allegiance. Neither the MNS nor the more democratic and reformist Falange ever captured more than 4 per cent of the votes in national congressional elections.

Both the Right and the Left courted the middle class. Heavily dependent on government programmes and employment, the middle sectors supported state expansion. In an oligopolistic economy with few industrial openings and many executive posts filled by foreigners, the middle groups sought mobility and security by taking charge of the bureaucracy and political parties.

In the 1930s the Radical Party, like the middle class as a whole, debated whether to become the progressive wing of the Right or the moderate wing of the Left. Far more than the rightist parties, the Radicals, although always divided and opportunist, converted from classic liberalism to welfare state interventionism, officially recognizing the class struggle generated by capitalism and vowing to ameliorate it. After initially supporting Alessandri, they gravitated to the Popular Front, which allowed them to become senior rather than junior partners in a multiparty coalition. Their inclusion also blurred polarization and provided a safety valve for class conflict.

The depression and its aftermath enhanced the attractiveness of multiclass coalitions for workers in the cities and mines. At the beginning of the 1930s, the few existing unions were feeble and wallowing in internecine feuds. From more than 100,000 members (or so it was claimed) in the early 1920s, the Communist-led Federación Obrera de Chile (FOCh) had shrunk by nearly 90 per cent, leaving a residue mainly among nitrate and coal miners. As the mines revived, so did the Partido Comunista Chileno (PCCh), adding unions of transportation and dock workers as well as a few industrial labourers. The anarcho-syndicalist Confederación General de Trabajadores (CGT) was even more devastated than the FOCh and failed to revive, maintaining fewer than six thousand members by the early 1930s. Erstwhile CGT supporters in construction, printing, leather, maritime and a few industrial trades for the most part drifted to the Socialist Party, as did legal unions surviving Ibáñez's regime and new associations, which gathered into the rising Confederación Nacional Sindical (CNS). Dominated by the Socialists, the CNS attracted principally industrial labourers and white-collar employees. Significant nonaligned unions, such as the railroad workers and bakers, also recovered from the damage wrought first by Ibáñez and then by the depression. Fledgling Catholic unions, however, experienced little success.

In the 1930s this fragmented urban labour movement gained strength and unity. Thanks to the lack of opposition of Alessandri and encouragement from the Popular Front, the number of unions and their members more than tripled from 1930 to 1940. Although monitored by the government, this growth took place independently of it as unions obtained firmer legal standing through more intimate collaboration with state agencies and leftist political parties. The older Democrat Party, which had nurtured many of the Communist and Socialist leaders, gradually lost its worker and artisan clientele to the advancing Marxists. Increasingly opportunist, the Democrats split between the Right and the Popular Front. Their share of the congressional votes shrivelled from 14 per cent in 1932 to 6 per cent by 1941 and subsequently vanished.

By combining the combative slogans of Marxism with the charismatic populism of Grove, the PS became the leading party of labour in the 1930s. It also developed a strong following among urban professionals, intellectuals and students, who came to dominate an organization based on the working class. The Socialists appealed to the workers with revolutionary imagery and to the middle strata with an evolutionary approach. Although committed to class struggle in theory, in practice the party increasingly emphasized nationalist, reformist, electoral and coalition politics. Outdistanced by the Socialists in the labour movement and at the polls, the Communists began to change their strategy and broaden their base. They edged away from sectarian demands for an immediate proletarian revolution, a combative stance dictated by the Comintern from 1928 to 1935. The PCCh also accepted more members from the middle class, symbolized by Carlos Contreras Labarca, a lawyer, who served as secretary-general of the party from 1931 to 1946. Meanwhile, most of the Trotskyist rebels had by 1937 joined the Socialist Party.

Despite sporadic Marxist recruitment, incipient unionization and occasional outbursts of discontent, rural workers remained largely isolated from the ferment on the Left. The most violent instance of agrarian unrest occurred in 1934 at Ránquil, where the national police (*carabineros*) defended traditional landowners by slaughtering scores of protesting *campesinos*. The Marxists' failure to capitalize on oppression in the countryside and to galvanize rural labour kept the Left reliant on coalitions with centrist groups. The Right preserved its dominance over the rural electorate.

In 1934–5 the Socialists had anticipated what became the Popular Front by assembling a congressional Bloc of the Left, which included left-wing Democrats, Trotskyists and a handful of maverick Radicals. For their part, the Communists had already begun to tone down their doctrinaire, proletarian revolutionary positions when late in 1935 the Comintern endorsed the Popular Front strategy. The PCCh now stressed electoral over insurrectionary tactics, class coalitions (even with 'the petty bourgeoisie and the progressive national bourgeoisie') over conflict, industrialization over socialization, nationalism over internationalism. As a result the party's electoral base grew from barely 2,000 voters in 1931 to more than 53,000 by 1941. As Alessandri increasingly shifted to the right, the PCCh began winning converts to the idea of a popular front. In 1935–6 the Communists concentrated on wooing the Radical Party, convincing many of its wavering leaders by delivering enough votes in a 1936 by-election to capture a senatorial seat for a Radical millionaire landowner. Supplying the Popular Front with crucial respectability, organization, voters and money, the Radicals argued that their party, 'within the Left, is called upon to discharge the role of a regulating force, one which makes possible the desired transformation by means that preserve democratic rights and avoid social explosion'.[3] The Communists' success with the Radicals left the Socialists little choice. Left-wing Socialists feared that the Popular Front would deceive the workers with bourgeois demagoguery, but party leaders concluded that the pact was necessary both to avoid fascism and to acquire power. Inspired by similar experiments in Spain and France, the Socialists, like the Communists, now expanded their following by diluting their ideological zeal.

The new Confederación de Trabajadores de Chile (CTCh) also enlisted in the Popular Front. Founded in 1936 as a result of new leftist unity, the CTCh banded together middle- and working-class unions, incorporating the FOCh, the CNS, the Association of Chilean Employees, most independents and even a few peasants, although the shrinking CGT spurned affiliation. Like the Marxist parties, the CTCh improved labour solidarity but restrained militancy. It curbed worker demands in order to facilitate Popular Front electoral victories, as politicians who owed first loyalty to their party came to dominate the confederation. Among the members, the Socialists held a slim majority and the secretary-generalship. Through the CTCh, workers helped launch and sustain the Popular Front, beginning with a major strike in 1936 by railroad labourers that provoked government reprisals against the leftist press and parties as well as the workers, thus cementing the coalition.

Largely representing the middle class, the Masonic lodges also helped to weld the Popular Front together. Eminent leaders of the Radicals, Socialists and Communists found common ground through their membership in the Masons, whose grand master promoted prudent reform coalitions as an antidote to revolutionary or reactionary dangers. At the same time, the national student federation and many intellectuals lent support to the Popular Front. Outstanding writers active in the campaign included Pablo Neruda, Vicente Huidobro, Volodia Teitelboim, Ricardo Latcham, Luis Galdames and Ricardo Donoso.

[3] *Hoy*, no. 278 (18 March 1937), p. 10.

As the largest member party, the Radicals assumed leadership of the Popular Front. They dominated its national executive committee and its platform, which bore the redistributive populist slogan of 'Bread, roof, and Overcoat', coined by the 1932 Socialist Republic. The Popular Front's program promised to enhance democratic freedoms, generate economic modernization under state guidance, promote economic and cultural nationalism and ensure social welfare for the middle and working classes. It pledged to respect and improve electoral rights and civil liberties. It advocated protection for industrialization and redistribution of under-utilized agricultural lands. Demanding 'Chile for the Chileans', the coalition suggested scaling down payments on the foreign debt and nationalizing some foreign-owned mines, industries and public utilities. Phrased in vague terms, the platform offered disadvantaged groups better incomes, housing, health, education and representation. Since this social democratic program differed more in tone than in substance from the public pronouncements of the Right, the actual policies of the Popular Front would obviously be determined by which members of the coalition carried them out. Most observers agreed with the U.S. Embassy's evaluation that 'the platform of the Popular Front is sufficiently vague so that the Conservative Party itself could operate under it and later point with pride to its well-kept promises.'[4]

In the 1937 congressional elections, the political extremes scored impressive gains. The Conservatives and Liberals combined won 42 per cent of the vote; together with minor party collaborators and a few renegades from the Radicals this gave the Right a thin electoral and congressional majority. At the same time, both the Socialists (11 per cent) and the Communists (4 per cent) approximately doubled their 1932 share of the vote, while the Radicals once again won about 18 per cent. Thereafter, the disappointed Popular Front redoubled its efforts to build an electoral majority.

Following a bruising battle with the Socialists, the Radicals installed their candidate as the Popular Front's presidential nominee. Pedro Aguirre Cerda, a teacher, lawyer, wealthy wine grower and Mason, came from the right wing of the Radical Party, which had resisted the formation of the Popular Front. His advocacy of industrialization was one of the few policy objectives he shared with the left of the party. His moderate appeal

[4] U.S. Department of State Archives, Record Group 59 (hereafter cited as USDOS), Santiago, 29 October 1938, 825.00/1085.

mellowed the reformist content of the coalition at the same time as it brightened its electoral prospects, illustrating the inescapable dilemmas of such evolutionary coalitions for the revolutionary Marxists.

In his campaign Aguirre Cerda succeeded by appealing to the middle and working classes without unduly frightening the wealthy. His bland, compromising character also served to hold the quarrelsome Popular Front together. The diminutive candidate's dark complexion prompted the Right to scorn him as 'El Negro' and the Left to embrace him as 'Don Tinto'. The key to his eventual victory, however, came from the Marxists' ability to mobilize the workers against the traditional ruling parties, raising the consciousness of labourers and convincing them not to sell their votes to the Right. Although the Radicals supplied the largest single block of votes for the Popular Front, it was the growing identification of the workers with the Socialists and Communists which transformed the political scene in Chile.

The Right contributed to the Popular Front's momentum by nominating as its candidate Alessandri's stern minister of finance, Gustavo Ross, to the dismay of moderate Liberals and the Falange. Whereas Aguirre Cerda represented the moderate face of the Popular Front, Ross exemplified the rapacious image of the propertied class. The Popular Front branded him the 'Minister of Hunger' and the 'last Pirate of the Pacific'. In addition to the Conservatives and Liberals, the SNA, the SFF, the Chamber of Commerce, the leading banks and corporations and many clergy openly worked and prayed for his election. U.S. businessmen in Chile also preferred Ross, who sounded the campaign theme of 'order and work'. Although issuing no formal platform, the Right differed from the Popular Front mainly in its emphasis on production over redistribution, efficiency over import substitution and control of foreign investors over nationalization. The conservative forces tried to lure the middle class and timid Radicals away from the Popular Front by warning that the Marxists would destroy religion, family, property and social harmony. While the Right hammered away at the atrocities of communism, the Left drummed up the horrors of fascism. Ross and Aguirre Cerda each vowed to save Chilean democracy from the other.

Rather than rely on programmes or oratory, the Right expected to triumph through its seasoned party machinery. One of Ross's campaign managers assured the U.S. ambassador that the parties would buy enough working-class votes to vanquish the Popular Front, even though he conceded that Aguirre Cerda would win handily in an honest election. At least in the cities, however, Popular Front vigilance and rising working-class political consciousness complicated such customary bribery.

Even more than the Right's tactics, the existence of a third alternative obstructed the Popular Front's path to the presidency. The personalist campaign of former dictator Ibáñez had no chance of success but withheld potential supporters — especially in the middle class — from Aguirre Cerda. Ibáñez's platform echoed the Popular Front's by trumpeting state planning, economic nationalism and social welfare, but his ambition and his support from González von Marées' MNS rendered the two reform movements irreconcilable. However, a few weeks before the balloting, youthful Nazis staged a foolhardy putsch against the Alessandri government. The botched coup shocked public opinion less than did the administration's massacre of the perpetrators. Discredited by the incident and alienated from the Right, the *ibañistas* switched their support to Aguirre Cerda. The incongruous alignment of Nazis behind the anti-Fascist Popular Front showed again the need of Chilean politicians, like those elsewhere, to subordinate ideological to electoral considerations.

The Popular Front won a narrow victory over the Right in 1938 with 50.3 per cent of the vote. When Aguirre Cerda beat Ross in the far northern and southern provinces and in the cities, the conservative forces learned that votes from the central latifundia zones could no longer guarantee supremacy. As in every other Chilean electoral victory by reformist or left-wing presidential aspirants — Alessandri in 1920, González Videla in 1946, Allende in 1970 — tense days passed between the counting of the ballots and the ratification of the results by Congress. Many rightist leaders grudgingly accepted the defeat because of assurances of moderation from the victors, but others, warning that Aguirre Cerda would become the 'Kerensky of Chile', conspired to overturn the result through charges of electoral corruption and by inciting a take-over by the armed forces.

The Popular Front legitimized its claim to the presidency by restraining its jubilant followers and discrediting rightist rumours of impending anarchy. It simultaneously encouraged the view that it would merely introduce a Chilean 'New Deal' if allowed to take office but that it could unleash effective mass resistance if denied: 'Chile will not be a second Spain. We will scotch fascism here before it can lift its head.'[5] As Aguirre Cerda warned the opposition, 'I am the second Chilean President from the Radical Party. . . . I will be the second and the last if those of the other

[5] Ibid.

side do not know enough to listen to reason and to make concessions, as the great leaders of their own group have advised. . . . Either I open a regulating channel for the desires of the people or after me comes the flood.'[6] Those arguments convinced a minority of leaders of the Conservatives, Falange and Liberals to acknowledge his right to the presidency. These rightists calculated that the social and political costs of reversing the Popular Front's fortunes might exceed the price of bowing to its victory: 'Since we cannot count on either the masses or the armed forces,' it was argued, 'it suits us [the Conservatives], even more than our adversaries, to maintain constitutional democracy.'[7]

Three public announcements from establishment groups were critical at this juncture. First, although the Alessandri government abstained from official recognition until the Right's charges of electoral irregularities could be adjudicated, the minister of the interior, Aguirre Cerda's godfather, acknowledged the Popular Front victory when the results first came in, and this declaration was communicated to Chilean legations abroad by the minister of foreign affairs. Second, a northern bishop sent Aguirre Cerda a congratulatory telegram and, in subsequently becoming archbishop, eased relations between the Church and the Popular Front. Third, and most important, the commanders-in-chief of the army and the national police proclaimed that the Popular Front's election had already been accepted by the military and public opinion and that denying the coalition office would ignite more civil violence than they were prepared to confront. Implying that they opposed communism but not reformism, the armed forces thus convinced most recalcitrant rightists to combat the Popular Front through the regular channels – Congress and the bureaucracy – which they still dominated. Thus, at the end of 1938 Arturo Alessandri peacefully transferred the presidential sash to Pedro Aguirre Cerda of the Popular Front.

THE POPULAR FRONT, 1938–41

With the Popular Front victory in the 1938 elections, the Radicals realized their long-standing dream of taking all key government positions away from the Right. At the same time the centrist domination of the incoming administration reassured the upper and middle classes. The Left obtained only minimal representation: the Socialists were given a few minor cabinet

---

[6] USDOS, Santiago, 9 November 1938, 825.00/1093.
[7] Rafael Luis Gumucio, *Me defiendo* (Santiago, 1939), p. 65.

posts – Health, Development, and Lands and Colonization – the Communists, in order to shield the government from rightists' charges of Marxist control, none. Although capturing few patronage plums, the Communists, Socialists and the CTCh reaped a large number of new recruits during the Popular Front period. In a clientelist political system, many middle- and working-class Chileans eagerly clambered aboard the bandwagon; the CTCh reportedly doubled its membership in the year following Aguirre Cerda's victory.

Through the Popular Front, the Marxist forces claimed a regular place in the political system. The Socialists and Communists had progressed from participation in elections in 1932 to participation in government six years later. Yet a decade of intense leftist mobilization of the middle and working classes had produced an administration far less advanced and daring than its composition and rhetoric implied. The very coalition politics which had allowed the Marxists to gain influence in high national offices also inhibited the enactment of the programmes for which they had sought those offices. Predictably, the inauguration of a Popular Front president did not herald sweeping structural transformations. Rather, it ushered in a new political era with the Socialist and, to a lesser extent, Communist forces institutionalized as part of the established bargaining system, with government legitimacy based on support from the urban masses through the brokerage of the centrist groups and with state capitalism accelerated in the name of industrialization.

Like Alessandri, indeed, like all Chilean presidents in the 1930s and 1940s, Aguirre Cerda essentially pursued a model of paternalistic state capitalism in which government collaborated with private enterprise in the construction of a mixed economy. Aiming to catch up with the more industrialized West, Chile's Popular Front mobilized the labour movement behind national economic development more than working-class social conquests. Compared with the Right, however, it placed greater emphasis on state intervention, industrialization and the needs of labour. Economic policy was in any event influenced more by international than by internal factors. As elsewhere in Latin America, the onset of the Second World War accelerated domestic production of manufactured consumer items, widened the scope of the central state and augmented dependence on the United States instead of Europe. All these trends dampened Marxist campaigns for bold redistributive measures at the expense of domestic and foreign capitalists.

The Popular Front's primary economic instrument became the new

Corporación de Fomento de la Producción (CORFO), fashioned originally to promote recovery from the earthquake of 1939. CORFO allocated public credits to all sectors of the economy, but especially industry and construction. From the end of the 1930s to the early 1950s, this quasi-autonomous agency accounted for nearly one-third of total investment in capital equipment and nearly one-fourth of total domestic investment. While supplied mainly from national sources, almost one-third of its investment funds flowed from abroad, principally the U.S. Export–Import Bank. When those loans, which had to be spent on imports from the United States, were extended in 1940, Chile dropped retrospective tax claims against the North American telephone and copper companies.

Although hailed by the Popular Front as a breakthrough for state socialism and economic nationalism, CORFO evolved into a vehicle for state capitalism linked to private and foreign vested interests. In a trade-off between the twin goals of industrialization and social reform, the Popular Front sided with the former. The elites were initially suspicious of this leap forward in state activism, but they soon became the primary beneficiaries. At the same time, Chile's dependence on U.S. capital increased. Under the Popular Front government, the United States nearly doubled its Chilean sales and tripled its purchases, as British and German commerce dwindled; discussions between Chile and the United States about lowering trade barriers, however, made little headway.

Under Alessandri, the government had counted on credit inflation from the Central Bank to spark economic recovery and full employment. Under Aguirre Cerda, credit expansion to fund import-substitution industrialization pushed inflation still further, as did the war. During 1939–42, the cost of living jumped 83 per cent, surpassing the entire price rise from 1931 to 1939. By imposing ceilings on prices of agricultural produce, the government effectively transferred income to the urban sector. The index of industrial production rose over 25 per cent while agricultural output virtually stagnated, a pattern which persisted throughout the 1940s.

While the right-wing parties fought tenaciously against the Popular Front mainly because it jeopardized their political livelihood, other elite groups tried to conciliate, co-opt or neutralize the Radical governments of the 1940s. One traditional institution which reached a modus vivendi with the Popular Front was the Roman Catholic Church. The Vatican replaced the reactionary archbishop of Santiago with José María Caro, the northern bishop who had congratulated Aguirre Cerda on his election. In his new office, Caro advocated reformist positions close to those of the indigenous Falange, bestowing upon the Chilean Church a reputation as the most progressive in Latin America. The archbishop even stunned the landed elite by urging unionization, higher wages, profit-sharing and better living conditions for rural labourers. Such an enlightened stance was designed to revive clerical influence among the working classes and counter the spread of Marxism. At the close of the 1930s, some 98 per cent of Chileans still baptized their children, but barely 10 per cent attended mass on Sundays and only some 50 per cent were married in the Church.

The landowners in the SNA also sought a truce with the more conservative elements in the Popular Front. The president of the SNA and of the Confederación de la Producción y el Commercio, Jaime Larraín García Moreno, encouraged the rural elites to provide better treatment for their workers in order to pre-empt Marxist proposals for agrarian reform: 'It is impossible to stop social evolution. We must put ourselves on the side of social evolution in order to channel it'.[8] Many landed Radicals now joined the SNA for the first time, which facilitated co-operation with the Popular Front government. Cristóbal Sáenz Cerda, the Radical landowner who had won the first by-election for the Popular Front in 1936, became vice-president of the SNA and a spokesman against agrarian reform in Aguirre Cerda's cabinet. As a fellow large landowner, the president also helped to bury reforms for the peasants through his own cordial relations with the rural upper class.

During the first year of Aguirre Cerda's administration, Marxist unionization of farm workers threatened to disrupt the tacit agreement between landowners and the Popular Front. Although no precise and reliable statistics are available for either rural or urban unions, in late 1939 the Communists boasted nearly four hundred rural associations with almost sixty thousand members and growing daily. The CTCh gave *campesino* organization a high priority and enrolled thousands, and the Federación Nacional del Campesinado, led by Emilio Zapata, a Socialist, superseded the smaller Liga Nacional de Defensa de los Campesinos Pobres (1935) and escalated rural mobilization and strikes. In former conservative strongholds the Popular Front began winning rural by-elections, both by Marxists rallying agricultural workers and by Radicals buying up estates.

[8] Erico Hott Kinderman, *Les sociedades agrícolas nacionales y su influencia en la agricultura de Chile* (Santiago, 1944), pp. 21–2.

Aguirre Cerda made a critical concession to the landlords by establishing a moratorium on peasant unionization and strikes, even though some 35 per cent of the active population worked in the countryside compared with less than 20 per cent in urban industry. In terms of political economy, the government, despite its ideological affinities, chose to favour least the group least able to put pressure on it. Marginalizing rural workers in order to reduce demands on limited resources appeared especially necessary to politicians when wartime shortages restricted the government's campaign for industrialization and benefits for the urban middle and working classes. The suppression of *campesino* activism also averted disruptions of food supplies to the mines and cities, which would have further accelerated agricultural imports. Holding down the cost of basic foodstuffs and peasant demands slowed inflation and mollified urban constituents, whereas higher food prices would have engendered more urban strikes and thus hindered industrialization.

In spite of protests by the Left, all of the Popular Front parties and the CTCh acquiesced in the government's suspension of agricultural unionization. The Communists and Socialists deplored this surrender to the SNA but bent to the administration's wishes to cool conflicts with the Right. By co-operating with the Radicals at the cost of leaving the workers largely unorganized, the Marxists remained dependent on segments of the middle groups. Consequently, the compromises and dilemmas inherent in populist multi-class coalitions and policies persisted.

The industrialists and the SFF welcomed CORFO and Aguirre Cerda's support for their tepid brand of economic nationalism. Although still apprehensive about state intervention, most manufacturers came to realize that the Popular Front's activism boosted private enterprise. As the Radical Party boasted, 'Never have industry and commerce had larger profits than during the government of the Left'.[9] The more far-sighted industrialists saw that better organization, representation, health, housing and education for workers defused social conflict. Moderate reforms for workers increased their productivity and consumer capacity more than their cost to employers, while inflationary credit policies also kept wages from rising commensurately with productivity. Since Chile had relatively cheap but not proportionately inefficient labour, the Popular Front's guarantee of social peace made welfarism and industrialism compatible.

The middle class was another leading beneficiary of the Radical govern-

[9] Isauro Torres and Pedro Opitz, *Defensa de los gobiernos de izquierda* (Santiago, 1942), p. 3.

ments in the 1940s. The gap between white-collar employees and manual workers widened as the middle sectors received more employment, income, health, housing, education, social security and other benefits than did the lower strata. They also accumulated many new political offices, partly thanks to the decline of bribery at the ballot box. Bureaucratic expansion mainly benefited followers of the Radical Party, which came to represent a majority of public employees. Although criticized by the elites, this growth of central government assuaged middle-class aspirations without impinging on the fundamental privileges of the upper class.

Continuing working-class support for the Popular Front and its successors in the 1940s was not easily explained by material gains or class consciousness. Through inflation and increasingly indirect taxes, the subordinated classes paid for the government's pumping up the bureaucracy and industry. The few labourers who experienced real wage gains were concentrated in urban, skilled and unionized occupations; most workers saw their standard of living stagnate or deteriorate in the 1940s, as income distribution became more regressive.

Organizational advances for labourers exceeded their material progress, as the number of legal unions nearly tripled during the administration of Aguirre Cerda. From 1941 to 1949, the total number of union members increased more than 40 per cent. Nevertheless, most union stalwarts were still miners, artisans or middle-class employees, because manufacturing growth did not foster as large an industrial proletariat as the Marxist parties had hoped. From 1940 to 1954 the percentage of the economically active population grew twice as much in services as in industry. The CTCh reined in worker militancy in order to provide support and tranquillity for Aguirre Cerda, and the government, in turn, ensured that a rising number of labour–management disputes were settled in favour of workers (from 184 in 1938 to 266 in 1939). The Popular Front argued cogently that backing the administration was at least preferable to a rightist government and, in the long run, more in the best interests of labour than were destabilizing demands for immediate payoffs.

In contrast to the generally accommodationist approach of the upper-class interest groups, the right-wing parties opposed the Popular Front implacably, erecting a congressional barricade against nearly all of Aguirre Cerda's initiatives. Rightist legislators and newspapers constantly charged the regime with incompetence, corruption, extremism, illegality and illegitimacy. Amidst such political polarization, only the tiny Falange sustained a compromising centrist position. In August 1939 extreme right-ists and *ibañistas* convinced General Ariosto Herrera Ramírez, an anti-Communist and admirer of Mussolini, to pronounce against the Popular Front, but loyal military officers, backed by Popular Front party militias and union cadres, suppressed the uprising. The abortive coup persuaded many of the Right and Left to modulate their rhetoric and retreat from the brink of armed conflict.

Aguirre Cerda laboured constantly to hold the squabbling coalition together. In the tussle for advantage, the Radicals entrenched themselves in the state apparatus and laid the groundwork for a decade of domination. Even the left wing of their own party complained about the Radicals' bureaucratic feast, favouritism for wealthier party members (especially from the right wing and the capital city) and lack of interest in social reforms.

All of the Popular Front parties grew, but the Communist Party did so most spectacularly by pursuing moderate policies and muzzling worker discontent. It temporarily revived the rhetorical radicalism of the early depression years during the period of the Nazi–Soviet pact when Popular Front co-operation in the cause of anti-fascism received less emphasis. However, Germany's attack on the Soviet Union quickly bought the PCCh back into full collaboration with its coalition partners opposed to the Axis. Despite such deviations, Communist involvement in the coalition government generally furthered the harnessing of the Left and labour as non-revolutionary and subordinate participants in electoral, congressional and bureaucratic politics.

The Socialists acquired sinecures in the government hierarchy at the cost of postponing worker mobilization and structural reforms. For example, they disbanded the Socialist militia and downplayed peasant unionization. Dissidents, who soon broke away from the party, complained that the PS was becoming an employment agency devoted to electoral and bureaucratic advancement as an end in itself. The Socialists grappled with a trickier dilemma than did their allies. The Radicals could concentrate on pragmatic administration with fewer ideological qualms and less erosion of their social base, blunting the Socialists' initiatives in the executive branch and outbidding them for middle-class allegiance. Conversely, the Communists could dedicate themselves to recruiting the working class with less responsibility for a mediocre administrative performance. Not surprisingly, the PS never resolved the paradox of how to lead the masses towards socialism through the bourgeois democratic state without succumbing to reactionary resistance or getting stuck in the half-way house of incremental reformism.

Early in 1941 the Socialists withdrew from the Popular Front party coalition while remaining in Aguirre Cerda's cabinet. They shattered the original coalition not so much because of discontent with the paucity of social reforms introduced by the Radicals but largely because of discord with the Communists. The Socialists resented Communist competition over unions and opposed the Stalin–Hitler pact. Their increasingly negative posture toward the PCCh reflected a correspondingly positive attitude towards the United States. This rapprochement resulted from the Socialists' animosity towards fascism, their participation in the national government, desire for industrialization and quest for better economic relations with the United States under the stringencies of wartime. Many Socialist leaders came to appreciate the limited choices available to policy-makers in a highly dependent economy, and they became more eager to acquire credits from the Export–Import Bank than to nationalize foreign enterprises or press worker demands. When they berated the Communists for obstructing co-operation with the United States, consorting with Fascists externally and fomenting labour unrest internally, the PCCh retorted with charges that the Socialists were selling out to North American imperialism. Unable to convince the Radicals to break with the Communists, the PS and a majority of the CTCh left the Popular Front and ran independently in the 1941 congressional race.

Although Aguirre Cerda compiled a laudable record of reform compared with past administrations, his achievements fell far short of his campaign promises. The Popular Front – especially the Marxists – determined finally to put through its program by breaking the conservative control of Congress in the 1941 mid-term elections. Fearing substantial losses and hoping to curtail leftist mobilization by other means, the Conservatives and Liberals threatened to undermine the legitimacy of the balloting by abstaining. To ensure rightist participation, Aguirre Cerda's administration temporarily restricted union political and strike activities, muffled the leftist press, banned Marxist militias and called out the armed forces to prevent intimidation, violence or corruption at the polls. As the original Popular Front parties swept into control of both houses of Congress with 59 per cent of the votes, both the Radicals and Socialists secured more than 20 per cent while the Communists significantly increased their vote from 4 per cent in 1937 to almost 12 per cent. The Conservatives and Liberals together now accounted for only 31 per cent. Most dramatic were the Popular

Front's gains in rural zones, which showed that the Right's fears of Marxist activism in the countryside and of the continuing leftward movement of the electorate had been well founded.

Even following the Popular Front's congressional victories, wartime economic constraints still discouraged substantial reforms. Marxist desires for a broad consensus against fascism also favoured compromises rather than conquests. More importantly, Aguirre Cerda died from tuberculosis in November 1941, nine months after the elections, having observed at one of his last cabinet meetings:

We promised the people to pull them out of misery, to raise their social, economic, and moral level. Apart from the intelligent and constructive action of some of my ministers, we have wasted time here with long debates and discussions, without ever arriving at practical and effective solutions for the great problems. It burdens my soul with profound sorrow, because I imagine that the people, whom I love so much, could think that I have deceived them.[10]

THE CONTINUATION OF RADICAL RULE, 1942–52

Although not now based on a formal alliance among the reformist parties, Popular Front politics endured after the death of Aguirre Cerda for another decade on an informal basis. The Radical Party nominated Juan Antonio Ríos Morales, a businessman identified with the anti-Communist right wing of the party, as Aguirre Cerda's successor without constructing or consulting any multi-party coalition. Nevertheless, to avert the return of the Right behind the irrepressible Ibáñez, Communists, Socialists, members of the CTCh, Democrats, Falangists and even some renegade Liberals, including Alessandri, gave their support to Ríos. His Alianza Democrática (AD) secured 56 per cent of the vote in the extraordinary 1942 election.

Ríos devoted his government to national unity, social stability and economic growth. He perpetuated the late president's emphasis on industrialization but soft-pedalled his accompanying concern with social welfare and reforms for urban labour. Whereas his predecessor's slogan had been 'To govern is to educate', Ríos proclaimed, 'To govern is to produce'.

In response to wartime scarcities, especially of capital goods (total imports fell to 13 per cent of national income), Ríos gave priority to maintaining economic productivity. The general index of production rose

[10] Arturo Olavarría Bravo, *Chile entre dos Alessandri*, 4 vols. (Santiago, 1962, 1965), vol. 1, p. 555.

from a base of 100 in 1938 to 108 in 1942 and 112 in 1945, while
industry went from an index of 112 in 1942 to 130 in 1945. Between
1940 and 1945, industrial output increased by more than 9 per cent
annually. The upper and middle classes constituted the major beneficiaries
of Ríos's policies, since the cost of living galloped ahead of workers'
wages. The general price index climbed roughly three times as much from
1942 through 1945 as it had between 1938 and 1941. During 1940–5
monetary national income soared by 120 per cent while real national
income inched up only 8 per cent.

As the Socialists and Communists had demanded, Chile finally broke
relations with the Axis powers in January 1943. Following Pearl Harbor,
Chile had hesitated to back the Allies strongly because the United States
could not guarantee its security against a Japanese attack. At the same
time, Alessandri and many other rightists had lobbied effectively for
maintaining Chile's neutral stance. Pressures and inducements from the
United States as well as the ground swell of domestic public opinion
against the Axis, however, finally overcame traditional reluctance to become embroiled in conflicts outside South America. Even after severing
relations, Chile was never satisfied with the amount of aid and lend-lease
military equipment it received, and neither was the United States content
with the extent of Chilean action against Axis agents and firms operating
there. Nevertheless, Chile subsidized the Allied cause by accepting an
artificially low price for its copper exports to the United States while
paying increasingly higher prices for its imports. The war gradually
boosted Chile's mineral exports and foreign exchange accumulation, while
U.S. trade, credits and advisers facilitated state support for capitalist
enterprises. For example, U.S. loans were granted to CORFO projects in
steel, oil and fishing. Not unlike that of Ibáñez in the 1920s, Ríos's basic
policy was to develop the Chilean economy through external alignment
with the United States.

Ríos' wartime cabinets included Socialists, Democrats, Radicals and
Liberals (including the president of the SNA). Dismay over shared responsibility for an increasingly conservative administration further ruptured
the PS, while the PCCh again abstained from taking cabinet seats and
continued its expansion in the unions. Yet under the banner of anti-fascist
unity, both Marxist parties renounced strikes and held back labour demands. Even with a majority in Congress from 1941 to 1945, the original
Popular Front parties passed very little of the social legislation long promised to urban and rural workers.

The governing coalition's diminishing ardour for reform coincided with declining electoral support. Between the 1941 and 1945 congressional elections, the Radical vote fell from 21 to 20 per cent while the increasingly dispirited and divided Socialists saw their share reduced from 21 to 13 per cent, and that of the Communists fall from 12 to 10 per cent. Meanwhile the combined Conservative–Liberal share of the vote increased from 31 to 44 per cent, demonstrating the resilience of traditional party strength.

Because of the failing health of Ríos, another right-wing Radical, Alfredo Duhalde Vásquez, took over as interim chief executive at the end of 1945. Duhalde overreacted to Communist-led strikes in the nitrate and coal mines, supported by solidarity rallies in Santiago. His marshalling of troops against the strikers and demonstrators produced bloodshed, widespread opposition to his shaky stewardship and unusually bitter battles between Socialist and Communist unions.

The same Marxist parties which had forged labour unity in 1936 demolished it in 1946, when the end of the Second World War and the onset of the Cold War unleashed pent-up hostilities between them. The Communists had acquired a majority in the CTCh and refused any longer to obey a Socialist secretary-general. As the PCCh seized control of most of the confederation, the PS seceded with its followers, so that organized labour, still dependent on party leadership, was weaker at the end of the 1940s than at the start of the decade.

Both Moscow and Washington contributed to this division. In accord with a harsher line from the Soviet Union, the Communists tried to tighten their grip over unions even at the cost of splitting the national federation. They set out to crush the Socialists, who, by the same token, became determined to drive the PCCh out of the Chilean and Latin American labour movement. Having drawn closer to the United States during the war, the PS now aligned with the AFL–CIO and its international crusade against Communism. Even with support from U.S. government and U.S. labour officials for the remainder of the 1940s, the Socialist's smaller branch of the CTCh lost ground to the Communists. The PS retained the greatest strength among copper, public transportation, railroad, textile and chemical workers, while the PCCh dominated nitrate, coal, construction, port, baking and scattered industrial unions.

The extraordinary presidential election of 1946 to replace Ríos demonstrated the political metamorphosis from ideological and social struggles in the 1930s to opportunist manoeuvring for party advantage in the 1940s. A left-wing Radical, long considered a firebrand and a friend of the

PCCh, Gabriel González Videla, revived, it is true, in the optimistic post-war atmosphere the reformist promises and expectations of 1938. The Communists enthusiastically joined his campaign, and most Socialists, although officially endorsing their secretary-general Bernardo Ibáñez Aguila to avoid a formal alliance with the rival PCCh, also ended up voting for González Videla. The Conservatives countered with Social Christian representative Eduardo Cruz-Coke, backed by the reformist Falange, while the Liberals tried to capitalize on Chile's most durable political family name by nominating Arturo's son, Fernando Alessandri Rodríguez.

A sense of political malaise, however, was reflected not only in party fragmentation and the dearth of fresh options but also in reduced turn-out at the polls. Whereas 88 per cent of the registered voters cast ballots in 1938 and 80 per cent in 1942, only 76 per cent bothered to do so in 1946. The dwindling appeal of Popular Front politics was also evidenced when González Videla eked out only a 40 per cent plurality over Cruz-Coke (30 per cent), Alessandri (27 per cent) and Ibáñez (3 per cent). If the Conservatives, Liberals and Falange had put up a single candidate, the Right would probably have won. As in 1938, the candidate of the Left had to walk a tightrope from election to inauguration. González Videla ensured his congressional certification by granting the Liberals, who were just as likely as the Conservatives to be large landowners, new legal restrictions on peasant unionization, which lasted until 1967. He also pasted together the most bizarre administration in Chilean history, seating Liberals in the cabinet alongside Communists and Radicals.

As a result of these political compromises, González Videla shelved his campaign pledge to transform Chile from a 'political democracy' into an 'economic democracy'. Instead, he promoted industrialization, technological modernization in agriculture and improved transportation, all through increased state intervention and the expansion of the public sector. The government's share of national income and expenditures grew even more under González Videla than it had under Aguirre Cerda and Ríos, rising from 16 per cent of GDP in 1945 to 18 per cent in 1950. Nevertheless, the pace of industrial expansion slowed down, and the general growth rates of real production and real per capita income slid below wartime levels. From a base of 100 in 1938, the general price index climbed to 238 by 1946 and then accelerated to 417 by 1949, intensifying the siphoning of real national income away from wage-earners. This inflation was fuelled by inadequate output from agriculture as well as by deficit spending from government for manufacturers and the middle class.

Economic ties with the United States tightened as productivity in the mining sector and prices for minerals, especially copper, scaled new heights. Total export revenues rose from U.S. $329 million in 1938 to $406 million in 1945 and $547 million in 1952, while total import expenditures went from U.S. $240 million to $187 million and $430 million. Chile's foreign trade had almost recovered from the impact of the depression by the end of the Radical era. Foreign investment – nearly 70 per cent from the United States – also increased during the post-war period, rising from $847 million in 1945 to $1,025 million in 1952; foreign loans to CORFO continued to foster industrialization.

Chile's deepening dependence on the United States – now pressuring Latin America to enlist in a global cold war – helped to turn González Videla against his Communist and labour allies. The shift away from the Left also reflected growing conservatism among the middle class and the Radical Party. The middle sectors increasingly preferred to use the bureaucratic state rather than multi-class coalitions and co-operation with labour to pursue their interest and provide protection against inflation. Many in the middle strata – particularly in the wealthier and professional levels – came to look more favourably on co-operation with the traditional elites, the Right and the United States.

The Radical governments of the 1940s, especially the González Videla administration, continued to benefit the middle class far more than the workers. Although precise figures vary, the best estimates for the Radical era agree on the increasingly regressive distribution of income. According to one calculation, real national income rose some 40 per cent from 1940 to 1953, while the real income of the upper class went up 60 per cent, that of the middle class 46 per cent and that of the workers only 7 per cent. Another estimate for the period from 1940 to 1957 concluded that the per capita income of the upper class climbed from twelve to fourteen times that of the workers, and the per capita income of the middle class rose from four to five times that of the workers. The Radical Party itself estimated that the average daily wage of a factory worker would buy 9 kilos of bread in 1938 and 11 kilos in 1950, while the average monthly salary of a white-collar employee would purchase 292 kilos in 1938 and 633 in 1950. Indeed, average real wages for industrial workers, measured in 1950 escudos, improved only slightly between the First World War and the 1960s: 30.4 escudos in 1914–16; 26.9 in 1938–40; 32.3 in 1951–3; and 34.0 in 1960–1. Despite minimal gains, labourers in the factories and mines fared much better than their counterparts in services or farming, who saw their wages plunge after the Second World War. Average annual real wages per manual worker in 1940 pesos rose from 4,451 pesos in 1940 to 6,304 in 1952 in industry and from 9,024 to 10,499 in mining, while those in services fell from 3,489 to 2,613 and those in agriculture from 3,422 to 2,824, making the total average wage increase per worker a paltry rise from 4,353 pesos in 1940 to 4,361 in 1952. During the same period the average salary for white-collar employees climbed from 11,011 pesos to 16,811. By the end of the 1940s, approximately 70 per cent of the active population still received less than the minimum income defined as necessary for survival by the government.[11]

In order to continue subsidizing the middle class and high-cost industry, González Videla clamped down on the mounting post-war protests of the Marxist parties and of organized labour. During their initial months in the administration, the Communists made rapid progress on the labour front, spearheading union demands and renewing organization of *campesinos*. They also secured 17 per cent of the vote in the 1947 municipal elections, which compared with 10 per cent in the 1945 congressional elections and was triple their tally in the municipal elections of 1944. The conservative political and economic groups now brought to a head their incessant campaign to convince the Radicals to jettison their Marxist partners. Each government in the 1940s had tilted farther to the right than the one before it. The Radicals finally caved in completely to rightist pressures because they were losing votes while the PCCh was gaining and because they wanted to pre-empt any military plot against the government by ejecting the Communists. Moreover, years of state involvement in the growth of the modern sector had woven a web of common interests between rich property owners and Radical leaders, many of whom had always been apprehensive about collaboration with the Communists. The decision was made to outlaw the PCCh and to stifle urban and rural labour demands in a period of economic uncertainty. Particularly during the 1947 recession, it became attractive to the government to quash labour interference with a policy of industrialization dependent upon U.S. co-

[11] Most of these figures are taken from Héctor Varela Carmona, 'Distribución del ingreso nacional en Chile a través de las diversas clases sociales', *Panorama Económico*, 12, no. 199 (1959), pp. 61–70; idem, 'Distribución del ingreso nacional', *Panorama Económico*, 13, no. 207 (1959), p. 405; Flavián Levine B. and Juan Crocco Ferrari, 'La población chilena', *Economía*, 5 nos. 10–11 (1944), pp. 31–68; Partido Radical, *14 años de progreso, 1938–1952* (Santiago, 1952), esp. pp. 37–47; Corporación de Fomento de la Producción, *Geografía económico de Chile*, 4 vols. (Santiago, 1950, 1962), vol. 2, pp. 224–324; idem, *Cuentas nacionales de Chile: 1940–1954* (Santiago, 1957); Markos J. Mamalakis, *Historical Statistics of Chile*, 2 vols. (Westport, Conn., 1979, 1980), vol. 2, p. 315; Aníbal Pinto Santa Cruz, *Chile, un caso de desarrollo frustrado* (Santiago, 1962), pp. 136–9, 185–198.

operation. It also enabled the government to control inflationary pressures at the expense of the workers.

In April 1947 the Communists were expelled from the cabinet, and the final break between González Videla and the Communists came in August. They retaliated with protests and strikes, notably in the coal mines, which the government countered by deploying troops. When rightist groups, particularly the paramilitary Acción Chilena Anticomunista, called for sterner measures, González Videla in April 1948 banned the PCCh under the newly enacted Law for the Defence of Democracy and then severed relations with the Soviet Union, Yugoslavia and Czechoslavakia. Although González Videla turned against the Communist Party mainly because of domestic political and economic considerations, Cold War ideological pressures and financial incentives from the United States significantly contributed to that decision. After the Communist Party was declared illegal, an appreciative U.S. government stepped up its loans, investments and technical missions and also signed a military assistance pact with Chile.

While the Communists went underground – where they were to operate for a decade – the splintered Socialists continued to flounder, seeking fresh leadership, strategies and popularity under the guidance of new Secretary-General Raúl Ampuero Díaz, who rekindled the party's ideological commitment to revolutionary Marxism. In the 1949 congressional elections, however, in which women voted for the first time, the combined fractions of the PS netted only 9 per cent of the ballots; the Radicals mustered 28 per cent and the Right 42 per cent. A host of minor parties accounted for the remainder of the vote.

By the end of the Radical era, most Chileans were disenchanted with Popular Front politics. The contradictions of the 1940s had peaked with the González Videla administration, when a president promising to elevate the workers and secure 'economic independence' had ended up suppressing labour and embracing the United States. Disillusioned with shop-worn party programmes and slogans, Chileans groped for fresh political options at the outset of the 1950s.

Populist developmental strategies had proved tenable during the 1930s and 1940s. Import-substitution industrialization satisfied industrialists with protection and credit. Although penalized, agriculturalists welcomed expanding urban markets, low taxes and controls over rural labour. The middle class and the armed forces appreciated state growth and moderate nationalism, while the more skilled and organized urban workers received consumer, welfare and union benefits superior to those accorded other lower-class groups. These allocations postponed any show-down over limited resources and temporarily made Right and Left willing to compromise. Political institutionalization and accommodation stayed ahead of mobilization and polarization because the unorganized urban and especially rural poor remained effectively excluded. None of the reformist coalition governments ever mounted any assault on the fundamental privileges of domestic or foreign oligopolists, and severe obstacles to later development were left intact. Although operating through distinctive party mechanisms, Chilean politics produced few economic or social changes at variance with general patterns in Latin America. In the twilight of the Radical era, however, populist development strategies and Popular Front politics lost their dynamism. They came to be seen by the Right as an impediment to non-inflationary economic growth and by the Left as a diversion from essential structural change.

THE RETURN OF IBÁÑEZ, 1952 – 8

In the 1950s new battle-lines were being drawn up among seemingly incompatible ideological and social alternatives. On the Left, resurgent Marxists presented more militant projects for the construction of socialism and disdained alliances with centrist parties. Equally zealous Christian Democrats displaced the Radicals in the Centre and offered proposals for 'communitarian' reforms that bisected the poles of communism and capitalism. And the Right gradually closed ranks in defence of neo-capitalist and semi-corporatist visions of reconstruction. All three alternatives used the hiatus of the personalist presidency of Carlos Ibáñez (1952–8) to stake out firm new positions for future electoral combat, which would result in a victory for the Right in 1958, for the Centre in 1964 and for the Left in 1970, after which the military would brush aside all democratic competition. The second presidency of Ibáñez, then, served as the last gasp of the politics of the past and the seed-bed for the politics of the future.

The new directions taken by the parties in the 1950s corresponded to significant changes in the economic, social and political terrain. Under Ibáñez it became evident that import-substitution industrialization was hard pressed to transcend the stage of replacing light consumer goods from abroad or to provide the employment, productivity and national independence expected of it. As the growth of population and the cities increased, rural-to-urban migrants, agricultural workers and women emerged as social and political forces of greater consequence. The previously narrow electorate expanded enormously, mainly because the enfranchisement of women breathed new life into rightist and centrist parties. The percentage of the population registered to vote in presidential contests rose from approximately 10 per cent in the 1930s and 1940s to 18 per cent in 1952 and 21 per cent in 1958. This increase was also a result of improving literacy and the electoral reforms of 1958, which introduced an official secret ballot as well as stiff penalties for abstention or fraud. As elsewhere in Latin America, escalating and intensely politicized competition over indequate resources reduced the likelihood of broad populist coalitions, overloaded delicate political institutions and apparently pushed Chile towards a zero-sum game. Like the Radicals before him, Ibáñez entered office as a reformer governing with leftist parties and departed from it as a conservative surrounded by rightist groups, jettisoning his programme for economic nationalism and social justice along the way. Although the crises from 1958 on were not inevitable, the lack of attention by President Ibáñez to festering problems rendered subsequent demands for overdue changes less manageable.

In the 1952 presidential campaign, the old warhorse Ibáñez posed as a personalist alternative to the politics of spoils practised by the existing parties. Wielding the symbol of a broom, he promised to sweep out the rascals, represent all Chileans above petty partisanship, halt inflation and defend economic sovereignty. Thus, the 'General of Victory' attracted a ground swell from the discontented middle and working classes. His only firm party support, however, came from the tiny Agrarian Labour Party and Ampuero's fraction of the Socialists, which was attracted to the Argentine *peronista* model and hoped to use Ibáñez's mystical, nationalist appeal to recapture the masses for the Left. On his own momentum, the former dictator drew support from all points on the political spectrum and finished first with 47 per cent of the vote. His most surprising source of electoral support came from rural workers and Marxists, as the Left gathered new converts in the countryside with calls for land reform.

Ibáñez was trailed in the poll by the Conservative–Liberal candidate Arturo Matte Larraín (28 per cent), Pedro Enrique Alfonso Barrios for the Radicals (20 per cent) and the dissident Socialist Salvador Allende Gossens (5 per cent), formerly minister of health under Aguirre Cerda. Allende's token effort unfurled the banner of Socialist and Communist unity against centrist reformers that would become the strategy of the Left after infatuation with Ibáñez faded and the prohibition of the Communist Party was rescinded. Instead of heterogeneous coalitions of the middle and working classes behind programmes of industrialization, the Marxists began emphasizing mobilization of urban and rural labourers behind concerted demands for collectivist social and economic changes.

The rejuvenation of the Left was fed by President Ibáñez's failure to remedy economic dependence, stagnation, inflation and working-class poverty. Although posturing as an economic nationalist in tune with rising public resentment against U.S. influence, Ibáñez tried mainly to liberalize trade and stem inflation. Faced with declining export revenues and rising domestic prices, he began the return to economic orthodoxy that would be accelerated under his successor, Jorge Alessandri. He tried to reduce the emphasis on industry and restore some incentives to mining and agriculture. Although copper prices shot up briefly during the Korean War, after 1946 the general trend in mineral production and employment was downwards, the share of the labour force engaged in mining dropping from 6 per cent in 1940 to 4 per cent by 1960. In the 1950s, imports grew more rapidly than exports, paving the way to subsequent deficits and indebtedness. Ibáñez tried to resuscitate the mines by reversing the discriminatory government policies of the previous fifteen years and entering into a 'New Deal' with the copper companies in 1955 that lowered tax rates on the U.S. firms in order to stimulate investments and sales. During the remainder of the decade, however, copper exports rose only slightly, few new investments materialized and the primary result was higher profits for the U.S. copper firms, Anaconda and Kennecott. Ibáñez made similar attempts to reinvigorate the nitrate industry. Continuing severe dependence on the mining sector was also spotlighted by friction with the United States over possible copper tariffs and by the fact that in 1958 every one-cent fall in the world price of copper reduced Chilean foreign earnings by some $7 million.

Agriculture also remained in the doldrums. Productivity per worker declined 20 per cent under Ibáñez as farming came to account for barely 12 per cent of the GDP. The resultant gap between supply and demand boosted food imports and prices. The proportion of the active population in agriculture fell from 37 per cent in 1940 to 31 per cent in 1960, when farm workers received only 11 per cent of total wages paid in Chile. After sinking by 18 per cent from 1940 to 1952, real wages for agricultural labourers plummeted by another 38 per cent between 1953 and 1960. Many of those workers who had finally broken the grip of the landowners to vote for Ibáñez in 1952 thereafter switched to the Marxists or the

Christian Democrats, who promised to recast rural property and power relationships.

Stagflation also afflicted industry. Whereas industrial production per inhabitant had increased 6 per cent annually during 1946–52, it rose by less than 1 per cent annually during 1953–9. Import-substitution industrialization stalled as Ibáñez gave manufacturers less support for their efforts to move beyond the replacement of light consumer goods. When this dynamic sector of the economy lost its momentum, Chileans noted that it had brought neither the promised prosperity nor economic independence, especially given the manufacturers' heavy reliance on imported raw materials, equipment, technology and capital. Import substitution had also failed to absorb the burgeoning work-force – industrial employment only crept up from 17 per cent of the active population in 1940 to 18 per cent in 1960. Consequently, many Chilean intellectuals began advocating nationalization and redistribution – to transform ownership and income patterns – instead of merely the subsidization of domestic manufacturing. These critics observed that per capita income had grown by only 1.4 per cent annually during 1940–60 and that the gap with the industrial powers was not being narrowed. Per capita income in 1954 in Chile was still less than $150 compared with nearly $2,000 in the United States. They also criticized support for high-cost, oligopolistic industry on the grounds that it contributed to inflation.

A key reason for the industrial slow-down under Ibáñez was in fact the attack on inflation. Based on recommendations from the U.S. Klein–Saks mission, the administration restricted public spending, credit and currency emissions and imposed ceilings on prices, wages and salaries. It also lifted some controls on foreign exchange and trade. These drastic measures reduced the rise in the cost of living from 88 per cent in 1955 to 38 per cent in 1956. They also triggered the worst recession since the depression, convincing many Chilean economists that inflation was a necessary concomitant of growth and that orthodox stabilization medicines were inimical to national development. This controversy heated up the debate between 'structuralists', who blamed endemic inflation mainly on foreign trade dependency, archaic modes of production (especially in agriculture) and political struggles over government largesse among entrenched vested interests, and 'monetarists', who attributed rising prices principally to classic financial causes such as currency expansion and deficit spending. Whereas the former, with greater influence among Christian Democrats and Marxists, argued for the transformation of backward economic structures rather than financial belt-tightening, the latter, who held more influence with Ibáñez and the Right, contended that development would have to be delayed and distorted until financial practices were sanitized and monetary and wage–price increases were checked. Although the rate of inflation dipped to 17 per cent in 1957, it rebounded to 33 per cent in 1958, whilst economic growth and per capita income continued to sag. Amidst the debate as to whether stability and growth were compatible or conflictual, Chile was enjoying neither.

The resounding failure of Ibáñez's economic policies produced mounting social discontent and friction. According to one estimate for the years from 1953 to 1959, slower economic growth dragged the workers' portion of national income down from 30 to 26 per cent and that of the middle strata from 26 to 25 per cent, while the share of property-owners, financiers and top executives rose from 44 per cent to 49 per cent. In response to their shrinking purchasing power and rising unemployment (which leapt from 4 to 10 per cent in Santiago during 1952–8), workers manifested their discontent through the ballot box, demonstrations and agitation. Mainly in protest against the widening chasm between workers' incomes and the cost of living, strikes escalated from an average of 85 per year in the period 1939–46 to 136 per year in 1946–52 to 205 per year during the Ibáñez years. Although still concentrated in the cities and mines, such labour activism increasingly penetrated the countryside. At the same time, squatter slums proliferated as rural–urban migrants poured into the metropolitan areas, especially Santiago, creating mounting pressures for political representation, employment and housing. The unsatisfied demand, from both the working and middle classes, for dwellings led Ibáñez to create a government housing corporation, but an estimate for 1960 still placed the housing deficit at more than 500,000 units. A reasonably scientific poll of Santiago residents in 1957 turned up a shortage of housing and money as the chief worries of the inhabitants, a majority of whom felt their standard of living was deteriorating and unlikely to improve.[12] Thus, Ibáñez left the presidency with accumulated and compounded social ills, inequalities and complaints unattended to and crying out for attention from new political contenders.

There had, of course, also been considerable progress in the decades since the depression. For example, life expectancy at birth had increased

---

[12] Information on the sample survey as well as other aspects of the second Ibáñez period can be found in Federico G. Gil, *The Political System of Chile* (Boston, 1966), pp. 28–31.

from forty-one years in 1932 to fifty-seven years in 1960, while daily per capita protein intake had risen from sixty-nine grams before the Second World War to eighty grams by the end of the 1950s. Literacy among those fifteen years or older had risen from 75 per cent in 1930 to 80 per cent in 1952 and 84 per cent in 1960, and school enrollment from the primary grades through the universities had climbed from 743,125 in 1940 to 958,958 in 1950 to 1,506,287 by 1960. Chileans in the 1950s took justifiable pride in having one of the best-educated and healthiest populations in one of the most democratic countries in the hemisphere. They also, however, gazed with apprehension on the millions of workers and peasants whom decades of unfulfilled promises had left mired in poverty. Out of the urban slums and rural shanties were emerging renewed and intensified pressures on the inherited political order. The disappointments of the Radical years and of the return of Ibáñez convinced many Chileans that more comprehensive and dramatic cures would be required. As a result, electoral support flowed away from Ibáñez to the advancing Christian Democrats and the revivified Marxists, who offered competing concepts of reform to the masses.

Two splinter groups from the Conservative Party, the Falange and the Social Christians, fused to found the Partido Demócrata Cristiano (PDC) in 1957. Exuding youth and dynamism, they attracted new followers with their innovative wedding of Catholic and reformist appeals. Energized by the personal magnetism of Eduardo Frei, the Christian Democrats began dislodging the Radicals as the dominant centrist party. Their rise reflected the changing contours of Chilean society, as they carved out significant constituencies among the middle class, urban squatters, rural workers and women.

The Marxists achieved greater success, as they had in the 1930s, with a unified national trade union movement. Inspired by the ravages of inflation, the major labour unions replaced the defunct CTCh with the Central Unica de Trabajadores Chilenos (CUTCh) in 1953. Within this conglomeration of white- and blue-collar, Marxist and non-Marxist unions, the Socialists and especially the Communists quickly took command, primarily on the basis of their enduring support in older unions in mining, construction and manufacturing. In 1956–7 the Socialists and Communists formed an electoral alliance known as the Frente de Acción Popular (FRAP). This new approach grew out of the experimental Allende presidential campaign of 1952 and the subsequent Socialist call for a workers' front. FRAP rejected coalitions dominated by the upper or middle class, the Right or the Centre, and instead emphasized more intense dedication to urban and rural workers and to socialist programmes for radical national-ization and redistribution.

The stage was set for the 1958 presidential contest by the congressional elections in 1957. The various Socialist factions increased their share of the poll from 10 per cent in 1953 to 11 per cent while the Christian Demo-crats' vote jumped from 3 to 9 per cent. With the waning of Ibáñez's popularity, the Radicals saw their share of the vote increase from 14 to 22 per cent, the Conservatives from 10 to 18 per cent and the Liberals from 10 to 15 per cent. Following the reunification of the Socialists and the re-legalization of the Communists immediately after the 1957 elections, the Left joined the Centre and the Right in harbouring high expectations for 1958. The Conservatives and Liberals banked on the family reputation of the austere businessman Jorge Alessandri Rodríguez, son of the deceased Arturo. In the Centre, the Radicals nominated Luis Bossay Leyva and the Christian Democrats Eduardo Frei. The FRAP, supported by some smaller parties and *ibañistas,* campaigned for Allende.

Alessandri won the 1958 presidential election with 31.2 per cent of the vote. Advocating more draconian state intervention to restructure the national economy and society than any previous major candidate in Chil-ean history, Allende with 28.5 per cent came within a hair's breadth of victory. Had not Antonio Zamorano, a former priest and FRAP deputy with a following among the poor, taken 3.3 per cent of the vote, and had not only 22 per cent of women compared with 32 per cent of men voted for the FRAP, Allende might easily have won. The leftists' impressive showing, including major inroads in rural districts, convinced them to maintain their independent approach and awakened the United States to the possibility of a democratically elected Marxist president in the Ameri-cas. The 1958 election also set patterns for the future by more clearly defining electoral options in three main ideological camps, by revealing a strong class bias behind those three positions and by establishing the Christian Democrats, whose candidate, Frei, collected 20.5 per cent of the vote, as the successors to the centrist Radicals, who secured only 15.4 per cent. For the first time since 1932, it was the historic parties of the Right which occupied the presidency. The era of Popular Front politics and populism was over. Beginning in 1958 Chile became a laboratory for contemporary developmental models, with each of the three political camps – Right, Centre and Left – taking its turn in power until, in 1973, the armed forces imposed their own solution to Chile's economic, social and political problems.

6

CHILE SINCE 1958

Since 1958, Chile has been ruled by four administrations (three elected, the fourth and longest imposed by a military coup), profoundly different in their ideologies and political aims, social basis and economic policies. The government of Jorge Alessandri, elected in 1958, was conservative and pro-business. Its support came from the private sector of the economy, from landowners (and the substantial peasant vote they still controlled), from sectors of the urban poor still ignored by the Marxist parties (Socialist and Communist) and by the Christian Democrats, and from the urban middle class, disillusioned with the Radicals, who had dominated political life from the Popular Front of 1938 to the election of Ibáñez in 1952, and not yet won over to the Christian Democrats. Alessandri proved incapable of dealing with Chile's persistent and increasing economic and social problems, and in 1964 Eduardo Frei, a Christian Democrat, was elected president.

Promising a 'revolution in liberty' the Partido Demócrata Cristiano (PDC) offered economic modernization combined with social justice and reform and the pursuit of class harmony. Even though the PDC enjoyed almost unprecedented electoral and congressional support (though without a majority in the Senate), the contradictions produced by trying to secure all those objectives, coupled with increasing ideological conflict and political strife, proved too much even for the able technocrats brought into the state apparatus. The threat of further reform and the electoral collapse of the Right in 1965 pushed the divided right-wing parties, Liberals and Conservatives, into the new and influential National Party. At the same time, mounting social conflict and the challenge posed by the PDC pushed the frequently discordant Socialist and Communist parties into strengthening – and broadening – their fragile alliance; the Frente de Acción Popular (FRAP) formed the axis of a new coalition of six parties of the Left, Unidad Popular (UP). The PDC, caught between the now stronger Right and Left, and weakened by small but damaging defections from its own ranks, offered a profound self-criticism in its electoral programme of 1970 and chose as its candidate the radical Radomiro Tomic, who pledged to accelerate the reforms partially implemented by the outgoing PDC administration. The National Party nominated former president Alessandri on a platform emphasizing authority, law and order. The UP coalition chose, though not without some unseemly public wrangling, Senator Salvador Allende to face his fourth presidential campaign on a programme of profound economic, political and social change. Allende was elected by a very narrow margin over Alessandri. The tasks Allende faced were more formidable than those of his predecessors, and the support he had was far less firm. Allende's government was by no means unique in its inability to deal with Chile's economic problems, especially inflation. However, political and ideological polarization and conflict reached levels of intensity which no constitutional political system could survive. Interference by the United States compounded Allende's problems, and no doubt there were grave errors of political leadership. The breakdown of democracy took place on 11 September 1973 with a brutal military coup.

A military junta in which General Augusto Pinochet, the last commander-in-chief of the armed forces in the UP government, soon took the leadership, combined political authoritarianism with an economy guided by the precepts of the monetarist school of economists—a return to the rule of market forces after a long period of state direction of the economy. Like the previous experiments, this one faced the obstacles that had plagued previous governments – over-dependence on earnings from copper exports, too high a level of external indebtedness, too low a level of new investment in productive activities and too low a level of productivity in agriculture. The economy did recover in the late 1980s, thanks to careful macro-economic management and favourable international prices. This recovery, however, has to be seen in the light of two severe recessions, and the social cost was great. Even economic recovery could not counteract the loss of popular support and an increasingly mobilized and active opposition. In a plebiscite held in October 1988, only 43 percent of the electorate voted for President Pinochet to remain in office for another eight years, while 55 percent opposed him.

SOCIAL CHANGE AND ECONOMIC INSTABILITY

In 1960 Chile had a population of 7.6 million; it had risen to 11.7 million by 1983 and to 12.5 million by 1987. Most of this population increase was absorbed by the cities, the urban population increasing from 68 to 82 percent. The population of Santiago doubled between 1952 and 1970, when it reached 2.8 million inhabitants; it had risen to more than 4 million by 1983.

Agriculture contributed 13.2 per cent to gross domestic product (GDP) in 1950, 10.1 per cent in 1960, a low of 7.1 per cent in 1981 and 8.6 per cent in 1986. Whereas 25.7 per cent of the economically active population was employed in agriculture in 1967, by 1980 this figure had fallen to 16.3 per cent, although it rose to 20.6 per cent by 1987 as the expansion of export agriculture generated more rural employment.[1] The political power of the traditional landowners declined sharply as the agrarian reform process, begun in a very mild way under Alessandri, accelerated with a new law and the legalization of rural unions under Frei. Virtually all large estates were expropriated under the UP government. The struggle of landowners to block reform and increasing peasant demand for land redistribution transformed a generally peaceful rural world into one of sharp class and political conflicts between 1967 and 1973.

Although the social structure of Chile became increasingly urban, employment in modern manufacturing enterprises generated only a relatively small proportion of total employment. Manufacturing, which contributed 21.9 per cent of GDP in 1950, increased its share to 24.7 per cent in 1970 but fell to 20.6 per cent in 1986; and the proportion of the economically active population engaged in manufacturing declined from 18.0 per cent in the mid-1960s to 16 per cent in 1980 and to 13.6 per cent in 1987. Moreover, most workers were not employed in large factories. Excluding the large artisanal sector, in 1978 21.2 per cent of the manufacturing work-force was employed in small-scale industry (10 to 49 workers), 30.2 per cent in medium-size industry (50 to 99 workers) and only 48 per cent

[1] Chilean statistics are a political minefield. This chapter relies heavily on the World Bank Report, *Chile: An Economy in Transition* (Washington, D.C., 1980), Markos Mamalakis, *The Growth and Structure of the Chilean Economy* (New Haven, Conn., 1980) and, especially, *Estudios CIEPLAN*. It is difficult to construct series becauses of changes in official methods of calculation – not least for price increases. Moreover, the official planning agency, ODEPLAN, from time to time revises its past estimates.

in large-scale industry (more than 100 workers).[2] In 1950, mining occupied 5.1 per cent of the work-force and in 1980, 3 per cent; the service sector (including government services), 23.8 per cent in 1960 and 28.1 per cent in 1980; and commerce 10.5 per cent in 1960 and 14.9 per cent in 1980.[3]

The relatively large size of the Chilean 'middle class' has often been noted; and though the term 'middle class' is very imprecise, it is not without meaning. White-collar workers (*empleados*), for example, considered themselves members of the middle class, and they were distinguished from blue-collar workers by separate legal codes, special privileges and higher earnings. This was a large group in 1970; it accounted for 24 per cent of the work-force in manufacturing, 49 per cent of the service sector and 29 per cent of the commercial sector. However, a much wider range of occupations fall into the category of middle class – small businessmen, professional groups, teachers, shopkeepers, managers and so on. Some groups were powerful, others were not; some formed part of the state sector, others worked in private enterprises. These middle-class sectors constituted a very influential segment of society; the political allegiance of the more Catholic sectors tended towards the PDC and the Right, whilst more secular elements provided the basis for the Radical Party and an important source of support for the Socialist Party. Others were attracted by the independent image of Alessandri in two presidential elections (1958 and 1970). In many ways the key political struggle in Chile was for the support of this sector of society.

One reason for the proliferation of political parties in Chile was the fragmentation of the electorate into a variety of social groups. Their perception of distinct interests and their increasing ability to make organized demands on the economic system help to account both for the way in which economic issues became highly politicized and for a general feeling that the economy was in serious difficulty. Yet poor economic performance should not be exaggerated. The overall annual growth rate per capita from 1960 to 1970 was 2.6 per cent, and there were periods of high growth thereafter despite a decline in the overall rate. In 1983 GDP per capita was lower than in 1970. Only by 1988 was it higher (by 10 per cent).

All four administrations in the period after 1958 pursued very distinct

[2] Guillermo Campero and Jose A. Valenzuela, *El movimiento sindical chileno en el capitalismo autoritario* (Santiago, 1981), p. 44.
[3] See Ricardo Lagos and Victor Tokman, 'Global Monetarism, Employment, and Social Stratification', *World Development* 12, no. 1 (1984), pp. 43–66.

economic policies to deal with problems that recurred with monotonous regularity. Each government tried to implement a growth model that avoided excessive inflation or foreign indebtedness. In this there was nothing new. Chile has had a long history of what Aníbal Pinto has called 'frustrated development'.[4] All these governments hoped to maximize earnings from the basic export mining sector, but found themselves victims of fluctuating international prices. Each government sought to attract new investment into the manufacturing sector and to increase the productivity of the neglected agricultural sector. Each government achieved some success in its efforts to stabilize the economy, but that success was only temporary and obtained at high cost. Alessandri's price stabilization of 1960–1 was financed by reckless foreign borrowing. The PDC found that its social reforms intensified demands and cost too much for the early economic achievement to be maintained. The Allende government achieved stabilization and growth for only a short period. The limited success of the military government before the sustained recovery after 1985, reflected in the high growth rates between 1977 and 1980, was based on massive foreign borrowing and by the use of the recession of 1975 as base year for calculations.

Nothing indicates more clearly the instability of the Chilean economy than the fluctuating rate of inflation. The rate in Alessandri's first year was 33.1 per cent; this was reduced to 5.4 and 9.4 per cent in the two succeeding years, but it accelerated again to 45.9 per cent in 1963. The Frei government gradually brought it down to a low of 17.9 per cent in 1966, but it rose again in 1970 to 34.9 per cent. Under Allende, although the rate fell to 22.1 per cent in 1971, thereafter it accelerated sharply and rose to 605.9 per cent in 1973. Only by 1977 did it fall below three figures, to 84.2 per cent and in 1978 to 37.2 per cent.[5] Inflation reached a low point of 9.5 per cent in 1981, rose again to 20.7 per cent in 1982 and then fell to 12.7 per cent in 1988.

The persistence of inflation in Chile was clearly much more than an economic phenomenon. In 1950 an International Monetary Fund (IMF) mission pointed out the non-monetary causes of inflation: 'Ideally the Chilean inflation could be ended by cutting off its sources one by one. Individual acts of investment, the Government budget, foreign transac-

[4] Aníbal Pinto, *Chile, un caso de desarrollo frustrado* (Santiago, 1962).

[5] Calculating the real rise in the consumer price index is very difficult when price movements are so erratic. However, the question is important since it affects politically sensitive issues such as the level of real wages. The most careful and accurate estimates are those of René Cortázar and Jorge Marshall, *Indice de precios al consumidor,* in *Estudios CIEPLAN,* no. 4 (1980), pp. 159–201.

tions, proposed wage increases and price increases could all be investigated and any plans inconsistent with a stable price level nipped in the bud. But this is a counsel of perfection'.[6] The reasons that these painful choices were not made in the competitive political world of Chile were analyzed and the gravity of the problem outlined by President Frei in his outgoing speech in 1970:

The country is destined to tackle inflation either by consensus which is the democratic approach or by coercion: but an inflationary process like that which Chile has been experiencing over recent decades will lead inevitably to a grave social and economic crisis. The problem is more than merely technical. From the technical point of view the procedures for containing inflation are well known. But what happens here is that the patient calls the doctor and then he doesn't want to take the medicine. The problem is mainly political. . . . Everyone wants the sacrifices to be made by others than themselves. Every year I presented laws which would have enabled us to control inflation and every year they were rejected. Then the very people who had rejected these laws and fomented conflicts were the very ones who said that the government was to blame for inflation. It is a game with sinister overtones.[7]

One reason for the political importance of inflation was the central role of the state in almost every aspect of economic activity. The state came to control a growing share of the GDP in this period, rising from 38 per cent under Alessandri to 43 per cent under Frei and 53 per cent under Allende. The state's share of investment was even higher. There were, of course, differences in emphasis. Under Alessandri state activity was intended largely to support business; under Frei it was more actively concerned with the modernization of the economy; under Allende it emphasized redistribution and nationalization; and under Pinochet its role in theory was to be subsidiary to an economy shaped by market forces. Nevertheless, even under the military government, a very important part of economic activity continued to be controlled by the state; the top eight firms in Chile in 1980 were still in state lands, even though they were expected to operate as private firms, and much of the financial system was taken over by the government during the recession of 1982–3.

There were, however, limitations on the ability of the state to control the economy. One obvious factor which complicated economic planning in

---

[6] Quoted in Oscar Landerretche, 'Inflation and Socio-political Conflicts in Chile, 1955–1970' (Dissertation, Oxford University, 1983), pp. 33–4.

[7] Quoted by Laurence Whitehead in Rosemary Thorp and Laurence Whitehead (eds.), *Inflation and Stabilisation in Latin America* (London, 1979), p. 68. Whitehead adds, 'Needless to say, between 1970 and 1973 Frei's party adopted exactly the strategy he criticised in his opponents'.

Chile was the external vulnerability of the economy. Any economy in which imports were so crucial, and exports so unstable, would tend towards instability unless changes in international prices could be absorbed into the domestic price structure, but the absence of sufficient resources for subsidies (e.g., to agriculture) and the oligopolistic character of much of the economy did not permit such flexibility in relative prices. Between a quarter and a third of total tax revenue came from the copper sector and from imports. After being very unstable in the 1950s, copper prices rose throughout the 1960s only to fall sharply in 1971–2. They rose briefly in 1973–4 but then fell sharply to real values well below those of the 1950s. Only in the late 1980s did prices rise substantially – even to record heights in 1988.

The problem of fluctuating export revenues was patched over by heavy foreign debt, which was in itself to become a major burden on the Chilean economy. The foreign debt grew rapidly from Alessandri's period onwards, especially from the raising of foreign loans to cover the fiscal deficit. The proportion of export revenues taken up by servicing the foreign debt was already varying between 40 and 60 per cent of export revenues by the late 1960s. The level of public and private foreign debt rose from U.S. $598 million in 1960 to $3 billion in 1970 and to an estimated $20 billion by 1986. Chile's per capita indebtedness was estimated in the early 1970s to be one of the highest in the world. Debt equity swaps helped to reduce the Chilean debt – in sharp contrast to the rest of Latin America – but it was still around $18.5 billion in 1988.

Chile was economically dependent on the United States, and this was to cause serious difficulties for the Allende government. Almost 40 per cent of Chilean imports came from the United States (including 90 per cent of supplies for copper mining). Most of the overseas credits that Chile obtained came from the United States. And the United States was Chile's main international public creditor, accounting for 50 per cent of the Chilean debt in 1970. The United States was by far the largest source of foreign investment in the Chilean economy—largely in mining until Frei's 'Chileanization' and Allende's nationalization and then increasingly in other sectors, though not on the scale of Mexico or Brazil. The United States also provided large loans from AID and extensive military aid.

Although Chile's economic relationship with the external world created problems for policy-makers, other countries had similar economic relationships without suffering from the same degree of persistent inflation and instability. The factors propagating inflation – disequilibria in the public finances, expansion of banking credit, excessive wage and salary increases and so on – reflected the national, as well as the international, political economy of Chile. The state of public finances in Chile has been referred to as 'fiscal anarchy'.[8] Throughout the period of civilian government there was the wide-spread practice of approving budgets that ignored important costs foreseen at the outset of the fiscal year. These costs, often the result of pressure from a powerful group, were then passed on by the printing of more money and an increase in the rate of inflation. Moreover, the fiscal budget did not include the autonomous and semi-autonomous agencies that sent their budgets to the Ministry of Finance, which approved and modified them without discussion in Congress. In effect, these agencies, which accounted for half of total public expenditure, were free to determine the size of the deficit which the state would have to finance.

One of the major bottlenecks in the Chilean economy was the inadequate rate of capital formation. Chile's disappointing growth rate was due in large measure to the low rate of savings, normally about 12 per cent of GDP when other Latin American countries achieved rates of more than 20 per cent. Even following the economic recovery of the late 1980s, savings rose to only 17 per cent of GDP. Most investment in Chile, even during the Pinochet years, was public. The share of total public investment in gross domestic capital formation rose from 46.6 per cent in 1961 to 74.8 per cent in 1969, while private direct investment grew at an annual cumulative rate of only 3.2 per cent. All three civilian governments tried different methods to stimulate private investment. Alessandri offered substantial benefits to the private sector, but the response was lukewarm; Frei tried a forced savings scheme from workers' contributions, but union resistance undermined his plans, aided by opposition from employers who were also expected to contribute; and Allende faced a virtual private investment boycott.

Various factors explain the private sector's reluctance to invest. The small size of the market set limits on the extent of industrialization possible in an economy like that of Chile. Industrialists imported a large proportion of their inputs and faced problems of price variation and supply difficulties. It is often noted that the concentration in most industrial sectors permitted large profits with only limited new investment. Another

[8] Ricardo Ffrench-Davis, *Políticas económicas en Chile, 1952–1970* (Santiago, 1973), p. 199.

explanation stresses entrepreneurs' lack of expectation of stable growth: quick profits from speculation looked more secure than investment in long-term growth or reinvestment in land. The absence of a well-organized capital market and frequently erratic interest rates discouraged long-term investment and encouraged reliance on borrowing from abroad. Bank credit was highly concentrated, and those who enjoyed access to it in effect received a substantial subsidy. Such a high level of concentration led to an inefficient use of resources, permitted enormous speculative gains and discriminated against small enterprises, and the low real cost of credit under civilian governments generated inflationary pressures.

As agricultural development lagged behind population growth, Chile became an increasingly heavy importer of food. The cost of food imports rose from an equivalent of 9 per cent of the value of non-agricultural exports in 1956 to 22.2 per cent in 1965 and to more than 30 per cent by 1972. There are many reasons for this dismal performance of agriculture, some of them contradictory. One argument is that urban food prices were kept low by means of controls that suppressed income and profits for farmers and reduced the incentive and the possibility of investing. A counter-argument suggests that food prices rose faster than the costs of agricultural inputs and that the real reason for the dismal performance of agriculture was the grossly unequal distribution of land tenure.[9] Exchange rates were generally overvalued, making food imports relatively cheap and Chilean food exports relatively expensive. Government policy towards agriculture was divided among competing agencies. Like the industrial sector, credit was concentrated in a very few hands and marketing facilities were inadequate. Until the Agrarian Reform Law was passed by the PDC government, the land tenure system concentrated the best agricultural lands in large, inefficient estates. But simple redistribution of land alone could not increase productivity, which depended on a series of other measures that civilian governments could not afford in either political or financial terms. In any case, the process of reform lasted only a relatively short time before it was ended by the military coup. Though agriculture suffered initially under the military regime, increased investment, a more realistic exchange rate after 1983, government help and protection and low agricultural wages eventually led to growth, especially in the export sector.

---

[9] This is the argument of the classic article by Osvaldo Sunkel, 'La inflación chilena: Un enfoque heterodoxo', *El Trimestre Económico* (Mexico), (October 1958).

The economy exhibited features of concentration other than that of income and credit even before the process intensified after 1973. The industrial and construction sectors were highly concentrated, and overlapping membership and ownership confined economic power to a relatively small circle. This pattern of a small number of large firms and a huge number of small enterprises and artisanal workshops (as late as 1963 almost half of industrial employment was in some seventy thousand artisanal firms) was not efficient. Industry needed a high level of protection, charged high prices and was heavily dependent upon imports while having a poor export performance. The removal of protection by the Pinochet government did not lead to a notably more efficient industrial structure— though it did lead to a record number of bankruptcies.

Although not excessively inequitable by international standards, Chile's income distribution pattern was still sufficiently imbalanced to supply ample ammunition to reformers. Income differentials did narrow in the post-war years: between 1954 and 1968 the share of the poorest 20 per cent rose from 1.5 to 4.9 per cent of total incomes and that of the richest 10 per cent fell from 49 to 35 per cent. Although this trend was initially accelerated under the Allende government, the gains were eroded first by inflation and thereafter by government policy under the military. Unemployment fell from 7.3 per cent in 1960 to a low of 3 per cent in 1972. But it was consistently in double figures during the military government, rising to a high of about 30 per cent in 1983. Unemployment fell sharply in the late 1980s, but low wages and a decrease in state provision of basic services meant that some three to four million Chileans were living below the poverty line.

The Chilean economy was a battle-ground between economists of the structuralist and the monetarist persuasions, both of which had an opportunity to apply their theories. Monetarists first experimented in a mild way in 1956–7 and then in a very extreme way between 1975 and 1983. Structuralist ideas informed the Frei government in 1965–7 and influenced the analysis of UP policy-makers as well. The costs of the monetarist experiment were reflected in a decline in economic activity, recession and unemployment. The economic and social costs of the structuralist reforms proved to be incompatible with the need for short- and medium-term stabilization. Even with strong authoritarian government, those bearing the social cost of the monetarist experiment were not permanently passive, and the Pinochet government was incapable of permanently repressing discontent.

THE CRISIS OF CONSTITUTIONAL POLITICS

Since the election of Arturo Alessandri in 1932, Chile had experienced a long period of constitutional government. However, political conflicts frequently entered the institutional arena in the form of clashes between president and Congress. These clashes were not simply the product of a reforming president facing a hostile Congress: Jorge Alessandri's conservative administration (1958–64) had to resort to measures to by-pass Congress. The system of proportional representation used for elections made it virtually impossible for a president to have a majority in both chambers of Congress; the fact that elections were staggered rather than simultaneous compounded the problem; and since presidents could not offer themselves for immediate re-election, there was inevitably a lame duck period towards the end of a presidential term of office.

Although the major problem of political management for the executive lay in the party system, the administrative system itself was an obstacle to effective rule: it was fragmented; it exhibited marked degrees of independence, especially in the decentralized agencies; and it often developed close links with the sector it was supposed to oversee to the detriment of overall planning. The fifty or so decentralized or autonomous agencies employed almost 40 per cent of public employees in Chile, and in many ways they were a law unto themselves. The PDC, for example, constantly found its housing policies undermined by the activities of these agencies.

The party system permeated all layers of political life, from the remote *municipio* to the national Congress. Trade unions of all sorts enjoyed close and often traditional links with the political parties: with the Socialist and Communist parties in the case of blue-collar workers, with the Radicals and PDC in the case of white-collar workers. Employers associations, associations of landowners, university student movements, neighbourhood associations and even football clubs were subject to competition for support from the political parties. In a remote coal-mining area like Lota, for example, the municipality and the trade union seemed to be extensions of the Communist Party, and the only alternative forms of social organization were the evangelical chapels.[10] Such a party system could function only as long as ideological commitment was qualified by compromise. It needed a basic political consensus – or else the inability of those who did not accept

[10] See Penelope Pollitt, 'Religion and Politics in a Coal Mining Community in Southern Chile' (Dissertation, Cambridge University, 1981).

Table 6.1. *Percentage of votes for major parties in congressional elections (deputies), 1957–73*

Party	1957	1961	1965	1969	1973
Conservative	17.6	14.3	5.2	20.0	21.3
Liberal	15.4	16.1	7.3		
Radicals	22.1	21.4	13.3	13.0	3.7
PDC	9.4	15.4	42.3	29.8	29.1
Socialist	10.7	10.7	10.3	12.2	18.7
Communist	–	11.4	12.4	15.9	16.2
Others	24.8	10.7	9.2	9.1	11.0

Source: Adapted from Arturo Valenzuela, *The Breakdown of Democratic Regimes: Chile* (Baltimore, 1978), p. 35. The Conservatives and Liberals formed the National Party in 1966. The Communist Party was illegal until 1958.

the consensus to disrupt the political system. During the period from 1958 to 1973 the consensus weakened while the capacity for disruption increased.

The Chilean party system had a number of unusual features. Electoral competition was intense, and apart from the 42.3 and the 35.6 per cent for the PDC in the congressional election of 1965 and the municipal election of 1967, no party gained more than 30 per cent of the popular vote in any election under the 1925 constitution. Moreover, despite the huge increase in the size of the electorate, it was divided into three relatively stable blocs – Right, Centre and Left – as the distribution of support for the major parties in five congressional elections held over twenty years shows (Table 6.1). Of course, this tells us nothing about the relations of the parties and movements inside those blocs, nor about the nature of competition between them. And it begs the question about the definition of the 'Centre'. But it does show how difficult it was to create majority government.

It is not possible to establish a simple correlation between social class and support for a particular party. In the first place, the existence of so many parties undermined the claim of any one of them to represent a particular class. The organized working class, for example, was divided between Socialists and Communists, with a not inconsiderable number supporting the PDC. The urban poor, not subject to the politicizing influence of trade union membership, spread its vote (or abstention) quite widely, including support for parties of the Right. Moreover, the Socialist Party received considerable support from middle-class groups, especially university-trained professionals. Middle-class groups were at home in the PDC, Radical Party or the National Party. This distribution of social class amongst political parties was by no means unique to Chile. Nor was it peculiar that the ideological inflexibility of the party militants and party elites increased quite markedly after 1964. There were, after all, enough deep social cleavages in Chile to provide the basis for the politics of class confrontation.

One change that did take place in this period was the reduction in the number and importance of minor parties. The percentage of the vote received by the five largest parties increased from 52.5 per cent in 1957 to 78.6 per cent in 1961, to 85.6 per cent in 1965 and to 90.9 per cent in 1969, although there was a small decline in 1973 to 87.8 per cent.[11] It would, however, be an exaggeration to attribute this process of concentration solely to an increase in ideological hostility among the parties; there were also changes in the electoral laws which made it virtually impossible for small parties to win seats in Congress.

It would also be an exaggeration to trace a simple development in Chile during this period from the politics of compromise and clientelism to the politics of exclusion and polarization. Yet it is undeniable that from the mid-1960s onwards political parties in Chile became more ideologically dogmatic and intransigent and that party relationships deteriorated. One element in this process was the replacement of a pragmatic party, the Radical Party, from the central position in Chilean politics by an ideological party, the PDC. The PDC had a much more coherent project of national transformation than the Radical Party, and it attempted to exclude other parties from power rather than construct alliances. On the Left, the Socialist Party adopted a much more intransigent line at its congress in 1967, which expressed a preference, if not for the *via armada,* at least for the *via insurreccional.* This line was never the choice of Allende, but represented the victory of pro-Cuban groups in that divided and factional political party. Yet at the same time, the party elected a moderate, Aniceto Rodríguez, as secretary-general. Although the Communist Party was less intransigent that the Socialist Party, by its very nature it could not be other than opposed to the PDC and the Right. The days of

[11] Arturo Valenzuela, 'Origins and Characteristics of the Chilean Party System: A Proposal for a Parliamentary Form of Government', mimeo (1984), Table 3. This section on parties owes a great deal to the insights of Valenzuela.

Eurocommunism had not yet dawned. On the Right, the rise of the technocrats of the Chicago school saw the growing influence of a political dogma which was more doctrinaire than that of the PDC. The traditional politicians of the Right saw their influence decline with the growth of both the technocrats and the neo-fascist groups organized in movements like Patria y Libertad.

The evolution of the Chilean political system up to the coup of 1973 supports Linz's proposition that 'the conditions leading to semi-loyalty or even suspicion of semi-loyalty by leading participants in the political game, opposition and government parties alike, account for the break-down process almost as much as the role of the disloyal oppositions'.[12] It was the combination of the growth of extremism with the 'semi-loyalty' of the major parties that was to create the conditions for the breakdown of the democratic system in 1973.

THE CONSERVATIVE AS TECHNOCRAT: THE PRESIDENCY OF JORGE ALESSANDRI, 1958–1964

Although his candidacy was backed by the parties of the Right (Conservative and Liberal), Jorge Alessandri was elected president in 1958 as an independent. One reason for this was tactical. The combined Liberal and Conservative vote was unlikely to win a plurality. By presenting himself as an independent, Alessandri would draw on the multi-class support of those who identified party politics as corrupt and narrowly sectoral. The traditional Right in Chile was to face this dilemma in subsequent presidential elections: by itself it could not hope to win, and yet alliance with the Centre (now represented more by the PDC than the Radicals) was very uncomfortable. However, Alessandri's stance as an independent also represented his genuine belief in the virtues of technocracy over party politics. He hoped in government to avoid the political compromises and concessions of previous administrations.

Alessandri was a prominent businessman who held important positions in a number of firms, including a monopoly on paper processing, and was closely associated through the Alessandri–Matte economic conglomerate with three large private banks. Before becoming a senator in 1957 he was the president for fifteen years of Chile's major business association, the Confederación de la Producción y el Comercio. His father had twice been

---

[12] Juan Linz and Alfred Stepan (eds.), *The Breakdown of Democratic Regimes: Crisis, Breakdown and Reequilibration* (Baltimore, 1978), p. 38.

president of the republic. His two brothers were senators (both Liberals), and one had been a presidential candidate in 1946. Alessandri had served as finance minister in the last Radical administration and had been forced to resign in 1950 when white-collar unions opposed his proposed wage freeze.

Alessandri's proposals in the 1958 campaign were far less specific than those of major rivals – Allende (FRAP, Socialist–Communist), Frei (PDC, Christian Democrat), Bossay (Radical) – but his general stance was in favour of economic liberalism. His electoral platform advocated less government control over the economy, including the suppression of controls over prices, credits and foreign exchange and a policy of price stabilization. An essential part of his strategy was the opening of the economy to foreign economic interests by making the conditions for foreign investment more attractive. However, Alessandri and his economic team were not monetarists. He rejected a policy of credit restriction and saw no need for a reduction in economic activity or an increase in unemployment in order to combat inflation. His policy was to create the right conditions for the private sector to develop the economy. Since this could not be achieved overnight, the government was initially prepared to increase state investment and to try to attract foreign capital and loans both to finance government expenditure and to assist the process of domestic capital formation. In effect, the short-term economic policy of Alessandri was a mixture of liberalization and reflation of the economy, with public investment playing an important role. Wage and salary increases were to be held down to prevent inflation (redistribute income to profits). Tax increases could be avoided by foreign borrowing.

In spite of the initial support that Alessandri received from the dominant economic sectors, his position was not an easy one. The economy he inherited from the previous administration was weak: the balance of payments was in deficit, unemployment had risen to 9 per cent in the cities, there was a large fiscal deficit in spite of a low level of investment and the economy had suffered a long period of stagnation. Nor was his political position very strong. He had gained less than one-third of the popular vote (see Table 6.2), and his supporters controlled only about one-third of the seats in Congress. So he eventually had no alternative but to seek coalition allies, especially since some of his measures proved to be very unpopular with the FRAP and the PDC.

Alessandri's attempt to reactivate the economy enjoyed initial success but soon ran into difficulties. Overall growth rates were quite positive. In

Table 6.2. *The 1958 presidential election*

Candidate	Vote	Percentage
Alessandri (Conservative–Liberal)	389,909	31.2
Allende (Socialist–Communist)	356,493	28.5
Frei (Christian Democrat)	255,769	20.5
Bossay (Radical)	192,077	15.4
Zamorano (Independent)	41,304	3.3
Blank/void	14,798	1.1
Total	1,250,350	100

Source: Arturo Valenzuela, *The Breakdown of Democratic Regimes: Chile* (Baltimore, 1978), p. 40. The abstention rate was 16.5%.

fact, the annual increase in GDP per capita of 2.7 per cent for the period from 1959 to 1964 was far more impressive than the 0.3 per cent of the previous period, or even the 2.0 per cent of the next five years.[13] But inflation, which declined from 33.3 per cent in 1958 to 7.7 per cent in 1961, rose sharply to 44.3 per cent in 1963. Nevertheless, unemployment fell from 9.0 per cent in 1959 to 5.5 per cent in 1963, and industrial output rose steadily throughout the period. There was also substantial investment in the road network and in housing construction for the working and middle classes.

The breakdown of economic policy came on the external front. By 1961 the fiscal deficit had risen to 5 per cent of the GDP, and this growing deficit was financed by foreign loans. Exports did not rise as anticipated, and the deficit on the current account balance of payments rose to 55 per cent of the value of exports in 1961. Most of the foreign loans were short-term financial loans, and the policy of freezing the exchange rate could not be sustained. The result was a massive devaluation of 33 per cent in 1962. The period of stabilization was over, and one of the major legacies of the Alessandri administration was a crippling level of debt. In 1960 total public debt was U.S. $589 million, equivalent to 20 per cent of GDP. Over the next five years the level rose to just over U.S. $1 billion, or 26 per cent of GDP, though only a modest amount went into long-term investment. If paid, the total servicing of foreign capital (including profit remittances) would have amounted to 70 per cent of exports in 1965.

[13] World Bank Report, *Chile,* p. 11. The government seems to have absorbed the effects of the 1960 earthquakes even though they destroyed an estimated 9% of GDP, mostly in buildings.

Foreign financing of private sector activities to expand working capital also grew rapidly during this period – from $63 million in 1960 to $219 million by the end of 1965.

Alessandri's policies soon ran into political difficulties. The attempt to hold down wages led to union protests, culminating in a series of strikes in 1960. In November there was a national strike and a series of demonstrations all over the country, in which two workers were killed. Many of the strikers were white-collar workers and government employees, and this discontent was translated into adverse results in the March 1961 congressional elections, even though Alessandri softened his policy on wage restraint.

The 1961 elections were the first to be held after significant changes in the electoral law. For the first time there was a single official ballot and increased penalties for electoral fraud and bribery. Landowners could no longer manipulate peasant voters by ensuring that they took the correct party list along with them to the ballot box, although, of course, the political influence of landowners over peasants was not ended overnight. The vote was also made compulsory. The results were a set-back for the Right: for the first time, the PDC polled more than the combined vote of the Conservatives and Liberals and – just as troublesome – the FRAP won nearly a third of the seats in the lower house and elected thirteen out of forty-five senators.

The illusion of technocratic administration was replaced by the realities of party politics as the Radicals were brought into the cabinet. Moreover, influenced by the newly founded Alliance for Progress, the government took several reformist measures that, although modest in themselves, paved the way for further and more drastic remedies. Reform of its relationship with the (largely U.S.-owned) copper companies was placed firmly on the political agenda, even though this was partly a device of the landlords to deflect attention away from the issue of agrarian reform. Taxes on the copper industry rose by 10 to 15 per cent, and there were moves to increase drastically the amount of copper refined in Chile to 90 per cent and to increase overall production. Although Alessandri replaced the Conservative minister of mines who made these proposals, it was clear that the pressure for nationalization would grow. The first steps towards land reforms were also taken, under pressure from the United States, which was anxious to avoid another Cuba in Latin America. Law 15020 was a modest measure, and very little land was expropriated. But it did establish two agencies that were to play a crucial role in transforming the countryside, the Corporación de Reforma Agrícola (CORA) and the Instituto de Desarrollo Agropecuario (INDAP).

Alessandri's economic policies were no doubt in the long-term interests of the economic elite, which certainly benefited from them. But for its part the elite failed to transform itself into a modernizing autonomous sector: it preferred protection and monopoly profits to the bracing effects of competition. The political consequence of this was the continued dominance of traditional conservatism and the maintenance of the Right in an essentially defensive posture. This left the way open for the PDC to adopt the task of modernizing capitalism and reforming the traditional land structure, a measure bitterly opposed by the Right. Morever, the Right had failed to free itself from reliance on a candidate who made a personal appeal above parties; in 1970 it was to turn again to Alessandri.

Although Alessandri remained personally popular with the entrepreneurial sectors, their support for the government declined. And as inflation started to accelerate after the 1962 devaluation, popular opposition mounted. The strikes called that year by the Central Unica de Trabajadores (CUT) were widely supported, especially in the shanty towns that surrounded Santiago. In the demonstrations against the government, six people were killed and many were wounded and arrested. The government once more gave in to the striker's demands, thus accelerating inflation and reaffirming the Left's new-found strength and confidence. In the 1963 municipal elections the real victors were the PDC, whose vote rose from 15.4 per cent in the 1961 congressional elections to 22 per cent in 1963; both Communists and Socialists registered small gains.

The scene was now set for the 1964 presidential election. The Right could not hope to do well. Inflation was running at nearly 50 per cent; the balance of payments was still critical; real wages and salaries had fallen, especially those of government employees and the poorest members of the work-force, who received little more than the government minimum wage, which fell by 14.2 per cent in 1963. The announced right-wing presidential candidate, Julio Durán, saw his alliance (Radicals, Liberals and Conservatives) come a poor third in a by-election in the rural and normally Conservative province of Curicó. The election was unexpectedly won by the FRAP candidate, with 40 per cent of the vote to the PDC's 27 per cent. The forthcoming presidential election began to look like a contest between those two forces. In such circumstances the Liberals and Conservatives reluctantly supported the least undesirable candidate, Eduardo Frei, who won with 56 per cent of the vote (Table 6.3). The shadow of Cuba loomed large over the

Table 6.3. *The 1964 presidential election*

Candidate	Vote	Percentage
Frei	1,409,012	55.7
Allende	977,902	38.6
Durán	125,233	5.0
Blank/void	18,550	0.7
Total	2,530,697	100

Source: Arturo Valenzuela, *The Breakdown of Democratic Regimes: Chile* (Baltimore, 1978), p. 40. Abstention was 13.2%.

subsequent electoral campaign, and the United States provided considerable financial and technical support for the PDC.[14]

THE REVOLUTION IN LIBERTY: THE PRESIDENCY OF EDUARDO FREI, 1964–70

I am convinced that the failure of the 'revolution in liberty' was inevitable, essentially because of the contradiction between its *programme for economic development* based on and reinforcing the capitalist structure of the Chilean economy and its *programme for social development*. The latter, mobilizing the people in defense of their interests, increased the many contradictions in Chilean society, particularly those related to the functioning of capitalist economy in an underdeveloped country. (Radomiro Tomic, PDC presidential candidate in 1970)[15]

Tomic's statement reflects the judgment of hindsight. It is far removed from the sense of excitement that swept the PDC when its triumph in the 1964 presidential elections was announced. The electoral euphoria of 1964 was reinforced by the results of the congressional elections of March 1965, when the honeymoon with the new administration had not yet worn off. The PDC gained 42.3 per cent of the vote, a massive increase compared with its last congressional election showing in 1961, when it gained only 15.4 per cent. The PDC took 82 of the 147 seats in the lower house; and

[14] According to the U.S. congressional report, 'The CIA spent more than $2.6 million in support of the PDC candidate. . . . More than half of the PDC's candidate's campaign was financed by the United States, although he was not informed of this assistance.' Staff Report of the Select Committee to Study Governmental Operations with Respect to Intelligence Activities, *Covert Action in Chile, 1963–1973* (U.S. Senate, Washington D.C., 1975), p. 9.

[15] Radomiro Tomic, 'Christian Democracy and the Government of the Unidad Popular', in Federico Gil, Ricardo Lagos and Henry Landsberger (eds.), *Chile at the Turning Point: Lessons on the Socialist Years, 1970–1973* (Philadelphia, 1979), p. 214.

in the Senate (where only half the seats were up for re-election) it increased its number from 12 to 21, although it lacked an overall majority.

The PDC's historical roots dated from the break of the Falange from the Conservative Party in the 1930s. At first a party of socially committed students from Chile's Catholic University, it remained a small, though sometimes influential, body until the 1950s, when it started to gain popular support. Hierarchical in structure and led by men from the upper and middle classes, it nevertheless began to attract considerable support from the urban poor, neglected by the Socialist and Communist parties, which concentrated on trade unions, as well as backing from large sectors of the middle class, disenchanted with the Radicals.

Naturally a party which enjoyed such widespread support across the social spectrum, and whose growth had been so rapid and so recent, contained several divergent groups. Even before the divisions assumed a more solid form in the splits between the *Oficialistas, terceristas* and *rebeldes,* there were differences in the pace and direction of social and economic change. The most conservative group was concerned to modernize the capitalist system and intensify the process of industrialization. A second group emphasized income redistribution and the organization of the poor. The most radical group, the *rebeldes,* was more concerned with profound transformations of such areas as the agrarian landowning system and the concentration of economic power, especially in the banking and financial system, and with the development of communitarian forms of ownership. Frei's presidency saw a constant struggle among these sectors.

Even so, for a multi-class party with such divisions over policy, the degree of unity was surprisingly high – much higher than that in the Socialist or Radical Party. This was due in part to a common sense of ideological purpose, not unlike that of the other relatively united ideological force in Chilean politics, the Communist Party. Perhaps it had something to do with the mores of obedience and hierarchy that came from its identification with the Catholic Church. Perhaps it also derived from the feeling that the electorate had entrusted the party with a mission that was not to be diluted with alliances with other parties. There is little doubt that many members felt that they had become the natural governing party of Chile – which gave rise to a degree of sectarianism that many Christian Democrats came later to regret.[16]

---

[16] Thus, according to Andrés Zaldivar, a leading member of the PDC and a former finance minister, 'We are guilty of a great deal of sectarianism . . . we made a fundamental error in not having sought alliances with the Radicals, and others of social-democratic tendencies'. Florencia Varas, *Exilio en Madrid* (Santiago, 1983), p. 56.

The U.S. government, also hoping that the PDC would become the natural governing party, gave consistent support to Frei's government. It should not be assumed that policy was unduly influenced by the United States. Frei pursued an independent foreign policy, marked by several important initiatives towards Latin American unity, and he was one of the few Chilean politicians to emerge as a statesman of world repute. Yet between 1962 and 1969 Chile received well over a billion dollars in direct, overt U.S. aid – more aid per capita than that to any other country in the hemisphere. Such help reinforced economic dependence on the United States and partly explains the favourable terms offered to U.S. multinationals, including, initially at least, the copper companies. But it was also to prove a source of internal dispute within the PDC.

In contrast with the two previous administrations, the PDC did not propose a policy of price stabilization as top priority. Rather, the emphasis was on stabilization through structural reform to encourage both economic growth and income redistribution. This would lead to the eventual creation of a communitarian society in which class conflict would be eliminated. Three reforms were regarded as of utmost priority. The first was the 'Chileanization' of the copper sector – a project of partnership between the state and the U.S. companies. Massive investment in copper was needed to provide the revenue for imports. The second was an agrarian reform combined with rural unionization and organization. The old large estates would be replaced initially by communally run farms which would increase production and secure a base for the PDC in the countryside. The third was a programme of organization of the popular sectors, especially shanty town dwellers, and of women. This programme of *promoción popular* would end the marginalization of these sectors. Of lesser urgency, but no less important, were measures to 'democratize' the union movement and break the hold of the Marxist parties, a massive educational reform and a constitutional reform to strengthen the executive branch.

The Frei government benefited from very high copper prices, although this was due partly to a change in the pricing policy by the government itself. Tax revenues from the large foreign companies averaged U.S. $195 million per year from 1966 to 1970 – a considerable increase over the level of $80 million under Alessandri's administration. Exports rose from $676 million in 1964 to $1,139 million in 1969, and although imports rose quickly too, a deficit of more than $4 million in 1964 was converted into a surplus of $183 million by 1969. GDP growth, however, was slightly lower than in the Alessandri period, at an annual per capita increase of 2 per cent. The external debt doubled during the period of PDC rule to reach a little more than $2 billion in 1969. Perhaps the greatest disappointment was the failure to curb inflation. The rate did come down from 40.4 per cent in 1964 to 17.9 per cent in 1966 but it thereafter rose gradually to 34.9 per cent in 1970.

Real progress was made in dealing with the problems of poverty. Compared with the end of the Alessandri period, when the figure was about 42 per cent of GNP, the wage and salaried sector received closer to 51 per cent at the end of the Frei presidency. Government policy encouraged this transfer, especially in the rural sector, where real wages rose by 40 per cent. Total enrollment in education rose by 46 per cent from 1964. A quarter of a million new houses were built, mostly for the poorest sectors of society. The PDC administration also increased the efficiency of the state apparatus. Taxes rose as a percentage of the GNP from 12.8 per cent in 1964 to 21.2 per cent in 1970. The government introduced a wealth tax and carried out a property tax reassessment.

The PDC period is notable for an impressive growth in state participation in the economy. Public expenditure as a proportion of the GNP rose from 35.7 per cent in 1965 to 46.9 per cent in 1970. The share of the state in public investment and in the banking sector also grew rapidly. As in the Alessandri period, however, this increase in public investment reflected the weakness of private sector investment and an overall failure to improve the level of new investment in productive sectors of the economy. The PDC spent more on social reforms than was justified by the increases in state revenue. Tax revenue continued to finance only about three-quarters of total government spending in 1965. Expenditures on housing, agriculture and education increased sharply: on housing alone they rose by 70 per cent in real terms in 1965. Once the process of expansion had started, it became difficult to restrain, especially as initial expenditures aroused popular enthusiasm for more. Fiscal problems were also caused by large salary and wage increases, especially for civil servants. But this enthusiasm was not shared by the private sector. Private sector investment fell, as investors feared the extension of the redistributive reforms of the PDC. The two greatest obstacles to the achievement of successful stabilization were the failure to raise the level of national savings and the increases in remunerations over the planned level. The former aspiration of the union movement – readjustments in line with inflation – now became the starting point for negotiations.

The 'Chileanization' of copper was regarded as the keystone of the government's policy. The objectives were to double the production of copper in the Gran Minería by 1972, to set up a series of joint ventures between the Chilean government and the U.S. companies, to increase the amount of copper refined in Chile, to integrate the copper industry into the Chilean economy and to give the Chilean government a more active role in international marketing. The Kennecott Company, whose Chilean holdings represented only a small part of its international operations, took the initiative in order to push the government into a quick deal; the government, anxious to show a successful initiative, responded quickly. The agreement proved to be a triumph for a firm that had a poor record of investment in Chile. The company secured an estimate for the value of the 51 per cent share in the El Teniente mine purchased by the government that was far higher than the book value (the real value was assessed at U.S. $160 million, compared with the book value of $66 million). Moreover, tax on sales was reduced, providing the company with a considerable increase in profits. This, combined with an underestimation of the price of copper, meant that the profits on the 49 per cent of the shares owned by the company were higher in 1967 and 1968 than they had been for the complete holdings in the preceding six years. It was agreed that the Chilean government would invest $110 million obtained from the U.S. Export–Import Bank; CODELCO, the Chilean copper corporation, would invest $27 million; and the company would invest $92 million, just $12 million more than it received as compensation. Moreover, Kennecott maintained management control as a condition of the Export–Import Bank loan to Chile.

The political outcry at the leniency of the deal with Kennecott, and the reluctance of the Anaconda Corporation, whose Chuquicamata and other mines were an important part of its overall operations, led to a more prolonged and difficult negotiation – 'nacionalización pactada'. Anaconda, which had also made record profits from its limited agreements with the government, agreed in 1969 to transfer 51 per cent of its assets to the government at once and the remainder over three years; and a new agreement over prices increased government revenue. The initial compensation was based on the book value, but the rather less favourable agreements for transferring the remainder were overtaken by the nationalization of the Gran Minería under the Allende government. The Anaconda deal was still regarded as too favourable to the company – not least by important sectors of the PDC itself.

The main benefit of these agreements with the U.S. mining companies was a considerable increase in productive capacity. The process was not as rapid as anticipated, but by the end of the 1970s, the production of copper had doubled, thanks in part to the investments made during this period. Moreover, the Chilean government gained considerable experience in the marketing, pricing, and control of the product. The local economy bene-fited as the value retained in Chile rose from an annual average (in constant 1979 prices) of U.S. $513 million in 1960–4 to $953 million in 1965–9 and as companies made more local purchases in Chile. Fiscal revenue rose from an annual average, in the earlier period of $225 million to $511 million.

Many factors made agrarian reform an urgent priority, although propos-als had existed since the 1940s. The Catholic Church became an advocate of land distribution. The U.S. government, through the Alliance for Progress, advocated reform as a way of countering the possible growth of rural guerrilla movements. The political power of landowners had been eroded by social, demographic and economic changes. The level of food imports was far too high for a country with Chile's agricultural potential. The traditional agrarian structure was seen as a bottleneck on industrial production.

The PDC put great emphasis on land reform. In the words of a leading PDC theoretician, it was to be 'drastic, massive and rapid'. The major problem was seen as the highly inequitable distribution of land. In the agricultural provinces of Chile between Coquimbo and Llanquihue, where 92 per cent of Chilean farms were located, latifundia occupied more than half (55.3 per cent) of the land area in 1965; minifundia, making up a total of 82 per cent of farms, occupied only 9.7 per cent of arable land. Concentration of credit and resources was similarly inequitable. But the original proposals for expropriation were diluted by Congress. The land-owners, organized in the Sociedad Nacional de Agricultura (SNA) were no longer such a powerful political group, but they still exercised influence and could count on support from other sectors of the propertied classes. The basic unit guaranteed to efficient landowners was to be eighty irri-gated hectares, and depending on local conditions, as much as four times that amount could be held. There were a number of favourable conditions regarding retention of animals and equipment, as well as compensation for improvement, all of which the Left considered far too generous. Although the law allowed for the creation of collective *asentamientos* on expropriated properties, this was seen as a transitional form to the preferred PDC solution – a large number of efficient medium-sized and small family farms. Little would be done under these proposals for the *minifundistas* or landless labourers, the most numerous groups in the countryside.

The reform proceeded more slowly than the government expected, but nevertheless by 1969 substantial advances had been made. More than 1,300 farms had been expropriated, with a land area of more than 3 million hectares, representing about 6 per cent of all arable land in Chile and including about 12 per cent of all irrigated land. About 650 *asentamientos* were created to incorporate some twenty thousand families, and another two thousand families were given land directly. The problem was not so much that the results were poor, but rather that the initial target was set too high – reflecting perhaps the over-enthusiasm of an inexperienced team.

Perhaps of equal political significance was the encouragement the government gave to rural unions with the law of 1967. In 1964 rural unions barely existed. By 1969 there were more than 400, with 100,000 members. In addition, there were 22 rural co-operatives with 30,000 members and 59 committees of small producers with 37,000 members. However, it was not only the rural poor who organized. The 1967 law allowed for employers' unions, and with the help of the SNA there were by 1970 nearly 10,000 members organized in local and provincial groups; at the national level the Confederación Nacional de Empleadores Agrícolas (CONSEMACH) brought together a third of the large and medium landowners in the country. The scene was set for organized conflict.

Agricultural production grew at a reasonable rate during the PDC years, even though crops were badly hit by the severe drought of 1968. The production of field crops rose at an annual average rate of 5 per cent from 1965 to 1970 (compared with 2.3 per cent for the preceding period). Livestock production reached an annual average of 5.5 per cent growth compared with a historical rate of less than 2 per cent. But imported foodstuffs still constituted a heavy drain on the balance of payments (accounting for a little less than 20 per cent of the value of exports for the 1965–70 period), in spite of an increase in agricultural exports of 40 per cent. The historical neglect of Chilean agriculture would take more than one presidency to put right, especially when two harvests were badly affected by drought.

The Frei government could not sustain its early pace of reform and began to lose the political initiative. In an attempt to restrain inflation, it tried to claw back some of what it viewed as excessive wage payments through a forced savings scheme to which both employers and workers would contribute. It was intended that the resulting funds would be used to establish worker-run industries, increase savings and restrain consumer demand. However, the proposal, put forward in 1967, brought the government into headlong collision with both the unions and the Right, and the plan had to be withdrawn. The PDC was dismayed that despite rises in industrial profits and wages neither employers nor workers gave institutional support to the government (although as voters, sections of the working class gave considerable backing to the party). Industrialists, always mistrustful of PDC rhetoric about the communitarian society, became increasingly alarmed after the *oficialistas* lost control of the party apparatus in 1967. They were also concerned about possible alterations in the constitutional status of property after this had been redefined in 1967 in order to allow the Agrarian Reform Law to be implemented: they feared that once large farms had been expropriated, the same might happen to large firms. Moreover, they were worried that in the competition for scarce investment resources, an increasing share would go to the state to the detriment of the private sector.

Relations between the PDC and the unions were never good. The trade union movement, mostly dominated by the FRAP parties (though the PDC had made inroads into the white-collar sector at the expense of the Radical Party), resented proposals to do away with the closed-shop and single-plant union system, and eventually the CUT. These proposals were seen, not unreasonably, as an attempt to divide the union movement. The PDC government increased the number and importance of unions quite considerably, but then tried to control them, which was not at all popular amongst the more radical wing of the PDC. This group had gained control of the party apparatus in July 1967 and, alarmed at the decline in the party's vote in the municipal elections of that year to 35.6 per cent (from 42.3 per cent in 1965 congressional elections), was urging an intensification of the reform process.

The urban labour force in unions doubled in the six years of the PDC government. Peasant unions grew rapidly to include more than 120,000 members by 1970. Shanty towns became organized and increasingly militant in this period. The number of strikes increased from 564 in 1964 to 977 in 1969 (and to 2,474 in 1972). In the countryside where there had been only 3 strikes in 1960 and 39 in 1964, there were 648 strikes in 1968 and 1,580 in 1970. Seizures of farms, urban land sites for housing and factories also increased. In 1968, 16 farms were invaded by their workers; in 1970 there were 368 invasions. In the same period the number of urban land seizures rose from 15 to 352, and the number of factory seizures from 5 to 133.

Former Conservatives and Liberals, and some distinctly undemocratic members of the nationalist Right, united in the National Party and began to take the offensive. In the 1967 municipal elections the National Party gained an impressive 14.3 per cent of the vote, and this rose to 20 per cent in the 1969 congressional elections. In 1969, however, the Marxist parties took 28.1 per cent of the vote, and the Radical Party, now in political alliance with them, another 13 per cent. Within the PDC itself, the defeat of the Left in 1968 after an active campaign by the president, returned an executive of the party loyal to Frei. But even this was insufficient guarantee to the Right that the now-divided and uncertain PDC could stop the Marxists.

Political activity became increasingly bitter as the PDC government came to an end. The Right was infuriated with the administration's reforms, especially with the agrarian reform, and having little positive policy of its own to offer, increasingly emphasized authoritarian, non-democratic solutions to the political stalemate. The Left had been profoundly affected by the Cuban Revolution, and its attachment to Marxism was, in the case of some sectors of the Socialist Party, increasingly couched in the language of the guerrilla struggle and popular insurrection.

The victory of President Frei's supporters in the internal party elections in 1968 can also be seen as a turning point. Although the margin of victory was by no means large, a section of the party youth, a small but influential group of congressmen and the party theoretician of agrarian reform, Jacques Conchol, left the party to set up the Movimiento de Acción Popular Unitario (MAPU). Whatever chance there might have been of an agreement between the PDC and the FRAP in the forthcoming presidential elections was clearly no longer possible. Perhaps it was never feasible, given both the PDC's opposition to coalitions and the hostility of the Marxist Left to Christian Democracy. Indeed, it has been argued that by presenting itself as the natural governing party, by eschewing the usual bargaining politics employed by Centre parties and by undermining the power of Congress (in the reform of 1970), the PDC helped to undermine the consensus that made party agreement possible in a multi-party system.

The period preceding the 1970 elections was marred by increasing polarization and violence, the worst example of which occurred when police fired on a group of squatters in the southern town of Puerto Montt, killing nine people. The seizure of urban land sites and farms increased. A revolutionary break-away group from the Socialist Party, the Movimiento de Izquierda Revolucionario (MIR), went underground and began to incite subversion. Even the military began to reflect the uneasy atmosphere with an uprising of the Tacna regiment – the so-called *tacnazo*. The object of the uprising was unclear, but it seemed to be a combination of economic grievances of the military and a warning to the government not to let the process of 'subversion' continue.

The presidential campaign of 1970 was fought among three evenly balanced movements. Former President Alessandri was the first to announce his candidacy, backed by the National Party and a group of dissident Radicals. At first he seemed to take the political initiative and was well ahead in the polls, which was a factor in discouraging the Right from repeating its tactic of 1964. But Alenssandri's age (seventy-four) showed in the campaign, especially on television, and he had little new to offer in terms of policy or programme. His strength was his personal standing above party politics – though no one doubted his commitment to the economic ideas of the powerful groups associated with the National Party.

Radomiro Tomic, the candidate of the PDC, had been the former ambassador to Washington and was identified with the leftist segment of the party. Tomic's programme was not noticeably less radical than that of Allende. He promised, for example, to complete the agrarian reform by expropriating all the large estates 'from the Andes to the sea'. His attacks were directed at the National Party and the Right, rather than at the parties of the Left united in the UP.

Salvador Allende, a senator and at sixty-two the presidential candidate of the Left for the fourth time, only narrowly secured the nomination of the Socialist Party – a foretaste of the difficulties he was to have with his party in government – for the Socialist Party had changed over the decade. It was more hostile to political alliances and deals and more concerned with doctrinal purity. It was more Leninist in its conception of the role of the party, less committed to a gradual process of building socialism and more to a vision of a permanent popular revolution. But it was still divided internally over many issues, and it had to work within a political coalition that covered a wide spectrum of political positions.

Allende's victory with 36 per cent of the vote (Table 6.4) did not represent a great swing to the left or any radicalization of the electorate. It was more the product of party relationships and hostilities than a great shift in opinion. Nevertheless, the UP government set itself the task of

Table 6.4. *The 1970 presidential election*

Candidate	Vote	Percentage
Allende	1,070,334	36.2
Alessandri	1,031,159	34.9
Tomic	821,801	27.8
Blank/void	31,505	1.1
Total	2,954,799	100

Source: Arturo Valenzuela, *The Breakdown of Democratic Regimes: Chile* (Baltimore, 1978), p. 40. Abstention was 16.5%.

producing the shift in public opinion necessary for it to transform its programme into practice.

The pace of politics during the next three years was prefigured by the frenzied activity that occurred before Allende could assume the presidency. In order to secure the congressional ratification necessary for a candidate who had not achieved a majority of the votes, Allende agreed to sign a Statute of Democratic Guarantees proposed by the PDC.[17] At least one major U.S. corporation, the International Telegraph and Telephone Company (ITT), tried to 'destabilize' the incoming administration and to persuade the PDC not to support Allende's ratification. An attempt was made by the extreme Right, encouraged by the CIA, to kidnap the commander-in-chief of the armed forces, General René Schneider, in order to spread panic. The plan went tragically wrong when Schneider resisted and was killed. Capital flight heralded the difficulties the incoming government was to have with the business sector.

THE 'VIA CHILENA AL SOCIALISMO': THE PRESIDENCY
OF SALVADOR ALLENDE, 1970−3

I won't be just another president. I will be the first president of the first really democratic, popular, national and revolutionary government in the history of Chile. (From Salvador Allende's victory speech)

[17] The statute called upon Allende to respect political and civil liberties and to guarantee the existence of political parties, freedom of the press, freedom of education, freedom of the unions from state control and freedom of the armed forces from political interference. As Arturo Valenzuela points out, the very need to ask the president-elect to guarantee that he would, in effect, respect the constitution was a measure of how far political trust had eroded. Valenzuela, *The Breakdown of Democratic Regimes: Chile* (Baltimore, 1978), p. 49.

The central policy objective of the Unidad Popular forces will be the search for a replacement of the present economic structure, doing away with the power of foreign and national monopoly capital and of the latifundio in order to initiate the construction of socialism. (From the programme of the Unidad Popular)

The UP government led by Salvador Allende transformed the atmosphere of public life in Chile. Old concepts, like party membership, changed from being seen as a simple expression of party preference to a position in the class war. The general consensus about the validity of the constitutional system was broken. Political violence, until then rare in Chile, grew in intensity and frequency. New movements, loosely identified as *poder popular,* expressed an intensification of popular demands that not only alarmed the opposition, but also weakened the political authority of the government. All aspects of life became politicized, and politics became polarized – it was impossible not to be either for or against the government. The terrible brutality with which the government was overthrown on 11 September 1973 is sad testimony to the level which political passion had reached.

The UP government promised to nationalize the economy, to implement a massive programme of income redistribution, to end the dominance of the latifundia, to transform the political system through the creation of a unicameral legislature, to develop popular participation in the running of the economy, in the making of political decisions and in the administration of justice and to pursue a genuinely independent foreign policy. Although this programme was little short of revolutionary, the government intended to implement it within the bounds of a pre-existing constitutional system. That system would, of course, be modified, but for the majority of the UP coalition there was no question of revolutionary illegality or insurrection. The government argued that the implementation of the programme would adversely affect only a tiny minority of landowners and only a small fraction of the highly concentrated economic elite. In the industrial sector, for example, the government initially intended to nationalize 76 companies. These crucial companies accounted for about 44 per cent of total manufacturing sales, but even added to those the state already owned or controlled, the nationalized sector was to consist of only about 130 out of 30,500 industrial firms.

There was considerable vagueness about the methods of implementing such a sweeping set of policies within the existing institutional framework. How were they to be implemented and over how long a period, and how were the short-, medium- and long-term measures to be related?[18] The implementation of UP policies depended on a number of interrelated assumptions about the success of its economic policies, about the firmness of political support for the government and about the behaviour of the opposition. The assumptions turned out to be unrealistic.

The UP government was a coalition of six parties, and the programme itself was a compromise document drawn up to accommodate the distinct tendencies within the coalition, from the social democratic moderation of the Radical Party to the Leninism of the leftist segment of the Socialist Party. Most important were the differences between the Socialists and the Communists over the speed of implementation of the programme and the political balance between popular mobilization on the one hand, and the need to assure middle-class sectors, on the other.[19] The endless debate on the way to create the Chilean road to socialism produced uncertainty about policies and fuelled suspicions on the Right that the road to socialism would prove to be a Marxist cul de sac from which there would be no return.

The difficulties Allende faced as president were compounded by the lack of discipline and the factionalism of his own Socialist Party. Ever since the party had declared in its 1967 congress that 'revolutionary violence is inevitable and necessary', there were important sections of the party that supported, in theory at least, the *vía insurreccional* rather than the *vía pacífica*. And there were groups outside the Socialist Party, notably the MIR, which practised what some of the leftist Socialists preached. The ambivalent attitude of some leading Socialist politicians towards the activities of the MIR and the legitimacy of revolutionary violence embarrassed the Allende government and gave an opportunity to the Right to create fears about the intentions of the UP as a whole. Such fears were not allayed by the tone of the propaganda of either the Left or the Right. The murder of Edmundo Pérez Zujovic, a leading Christian Democratic politician, by an extreme leftist group in June 1971 sharply intensified the climate of political fear and hostility.

[18] The question that defeated the UP, according to the left-wing Socialist senator Carlos Altamirano, was not what to do, but how to do it. This is not very different from the point made by Sergio Bitar, a minister of mining in the UP government, that one of the major defects of the government was its inability to implement a clear strategy. Carlos Altamirano, *Dialéctica de una derrota* (Mexico, 1977), p. 44, and Sergio Bitar, *Transición, socialismo y democracia: La experiencia chilena* (Mexico, 1979), p. 15.

[19] Joan Garcés, one of Allende's close political advisers, strongly criticized the lack of 'confidence, respect and discipline' of the parties towards each other, towards the government and towards Allende himself. Garcés, *Allende y la experiencia chilena* (Barcelona, 1976), pp. 228, 455–5.

The Socialist Party never shed its suspicions of the Partido Comunista Chileno (PCCh) The PCCh was a long-established party in Chile, firmly rooted in the labour movement, very disciplined, a strong supporter of Moscow on international issues, but not without flexibility on domestic issues. Its moderation and caution were not acceptable to sectors of the Socialist Party. There appeared to be a dual leadership at the core of the UP. The Radical Party tended to side with the caution of the Communists, but it split three ways and lost its political significance. The other two ideological parties of the UP, the MAPU and the Izquierda Cristiana (IC), also suffered losses and the MAPU split into two separate parties. The Acción Popular Independiente (API) of Senator Rafael Tarud was a personalist party of little political significance.

One major problem caused by the existence of so many parties was the imposition of a quota system in apportioning government posts. Places were to be distributed according to a more or less fixed schedule, favouring the smaller parties; but subordinates were to be of different parties than their immediate superior. This system was designed to stop any one party from colonizing a ministry. In practice the results were damaging. Party authority superseded administrative authority; the control of the executive over the governmental machine was weakened; and the effect on the professional civil service, whose co-operation was essential if such an ambitious reform programme was to be successfully carried out, was very adverse.

These divisions would have been damaging enough if the UP had enjoyed a majority in Congress, but it was a minority. As a result of the 1969 elections, the UP had eighteen Senate seats; the opposition thirty-two. The PDC had twenty senators; the largest UP party, that of the Communists, only six. In the lower house the government had fifty-seven seats; the opposition ninety-three. The PDC had forty-seven seats and the National Party thirty-three, whereas the Communists had twenty-two and the Socialists fourteen. The gains that the UP made in the 1973 elections only slightly reduced the opposition majority. Thus, the UP government faced a congress that became increasingly hostile. Unless an agreement could be reached with the PDC, the only hope for the UP was that its economic policies would be so successful that there would be a massive swing in its favour. But after a year of initial success, the economy began to deteriorate.

The initial action of the government on the economic front was a massive wage and salary increase. Although the rate of inflation in 1970 was 35 per cent, the wage increase averaged 55 per cent. There were differential increases for the poorest sectors, but in effect there was a wage explosion rather than a redistribution of income from the rich to the poor. The poor did better, relatively, than the rich; but the top income-earners did not suffer. Price controls were established, and the government set up an elaborate system of distribution networks through various agencies, including local committees on supply and prices (Juntas de Abastecimientos y Precios – JAPs) to make sure local shopkeepers were following the rules.

The copper mines were nationalized, with support from the opposition, by July 1971; and during the first year more than eighty enterprises from important commercial and industrial sectors were taken over. Land reform was also accelerated, but the government had to work within the confines of the law passed by the preceding government. Almost as many farms were expropriated in the first year as in the whole period of PDC government, many as a result of land seizures. By late 1971 virtually all of the financial sector was under government control, transferred to the Area de Propriedad Social (APS).

Government-led expansion produced a high rate of economic growth in 1971. Because of unused capacity in industry, stockpiles, rapid growth in imports and a high level of international reserves, the government achieved a lower rate of inflation than the previous year. The GDP in 1971 grew by 7.7 per cent overall, gross industrial production went up 11 per cent and a good harvest increased agriculture's share of GDP by 7 per cent. Unemployment fell from 8.3 per cent in 1970 to 3.8 per cent by the end of 1971. Wages and salaries rose to 61.7 per cent of income in 1971, as compared with 52.2 per cent in 1970 and an average of 48.4 per cent for the decade of the 1960s.

On the external front the government announced its intention to maintain a fixed exchange rate. The Left had been a fierce critic of the crawling peg system of devaluation of the Frei government, arguing that it increased costs and fuelled inflation. But as a result the escudo started to become increasingly overvalued. Other warning signs were beginning to appear before the end of Allende's first year in office. Central government expenditures rose sharply, more than 66 per cent in nominal terms in 1971 over the previous year, from 21 to 27 per cent of GDP, but government current revenue declined from 20 to 18.5 per cent of GDP. The fiscal deficit rose to 8 per cent of GDP compared with 4 per cent in the preceding year. The money supply more than doubled, and the huge expansion of credit went mostly to the public sector. During 1971 the average price of copper fell by 27 per cent, and since production also fell slightly in the three major mines, the value of copper exports fell by 16.5 per cent. Although international reserves were high, so was the outstanding debt. The trade balance turned from a U.S. $95 million surplus in 1970 to a deficit of $90 million in 1971. Traditional sources of external finance in the United States virtually dried up, and the government was forced to turn to other sources – Europe, Latin America and the USSR. Chile's reserves fell by three-quarters in 1971, and in November the government was forced to announce the suspension of debt service, pending renegotiation.

All of the problems already visible in 1971 – capacity limits in industrial and other sectors, breakdowns in the distribution system, industrial conflict, the growth of a black market, the decline in private investment, uncontrolled monetary expansion, the exhaustion of international reserves – accumulated and multiplied with terrible force in 1972 and 1973. By the time the UP government came to an end, real GDP per capita and real wages were falling, agricultural output was down sharply (perhaps to the levels of the early 1960s, though the workings of the black market make calculation difficult), inflation was out of control, several years of debt service had to be rescheduled, net international reserves were more than U.S. $200 million in the red and the balance of payments was heavily in deficit. Government revenue fell sharply while expenditure grew. With the growth of the black market and congressional obstacles to tax changes, the central government deficit rose to record heights: 22 per cent of GDP in 1973. The money supply grew by 576 per cent from the end of 1971 to August 1973; total expansion of the money supply under the UP government was 1,345 per cent.

Although the government devalued in December 1971, and at intervals thereafter, such a high rate of inflation kept the escudo seriously overvalued. After a fall in export revenues with declining copper prices in 1972, there was a recovery in 1973. But imports continued to grow faster; total food import costs were almost four times what they had been in 1970 (and accounted for more than one-third of total imports as compared with only 14 per cent three years earlier). This reflects rising international prices as well as the result of rising incomes of the poor and declining production.

Agrarian reform accelerated during 1972. More than 60 per cent of irrigated land had been taken into the hands of the state for redistribution. There was, for such a massive process, remarkably little violence and destruction of property. But there was also a giant disincentive to invest and serious decapitalization, leading to a decline in production in 1972 and 1973. In the industrial sector, the take-overs by the state continued, and the threat of expropriation as well as spontaneous take-overs by workers led to the virtual cessation of investment by the private sector.

Analysis of the economic policy of the UP government tends to concern itself with what went wrong, why things turned out so badly. However, one of the major and enduring achievements of the UP government was the nationalization of the large copper mines. The decision to transfer these assets to the nation needed a constitutional amendment, and this was passed with the support in Congress of all the parties. The UP government promised compensation to the companies at the book value of their assets but warned that they would be penalized for earning excessive profits in the past. After some complicated legal wrangling, the government decided that the amount owed by a number of companies exceeded book values. Some payment for certain mines was offered, but nationalization was fiercely contested by the companies and created difficulties for Chile's international trade. Although there were initial problems in the transition, and though unit costs did rise appreciably, overall production did increase; the combination of the measures taken by the PDC and UP governments helped to ensure both a considerable expansion of copper production in the 1970s and that earnings from copper remained in Chile and were not exported.

Other reforms of the UP period, such as the distribution of free milk to schoolchildren, were admirable on many grounds. There was a positive attempt to reform the tax system although it was left rather late and faced too much hostility in Congress. The schemes for worker participation in industry and for co-operative ventures in agriculture were imaginative and in less troubled times might have made a positive contribution both to production and to a genuine extension of participation. But the times were troubled, and the reforms were caught up in a political controversy that destroyed them.

The strength of the opposition was not enough by itself to explain the economic reversal. There was a lack of co-ordination between the economic team and the politicians, between the political strategy of gradual change and consensus and the radical economic strategy of redistribution. The apparent lack of concern of the government about the gathering

economic storm denoted an unjustified optimism about long-term prospects and an unjustified lack of concern about short-term management.

The strategy of Pedro Vuskovic, the minister of the economy, was based
on the reflationary effects of a massive redistribution of income. Vuskovic
was the key economic strategist and exercised considerable influence over
Allende. The major intention of his strategy was to widen the political
base of the UP, and the vote in the 1973 election showed that the political
base was indeed remarkably firm, although the strategy had not increased
support dramatically (and it had intensified the opposition to the government). Consumption demand, however, was not held down to a level
consistent with foreign exchange earnings or the desired level of investment. The huge increase in purchasing power soon ran up against supply
limitations, resulting in the growth of the black market, hoarding and
inflation. Redistribution did not affect the upper income-earners – except
by reducing the relativities – and everyone benefited in terms of increased
purchasing power. It has been argued that the income explosion was the
principal factor behind the economic crisis.[20]

The government's policy would have had more chance of success if a
policy of wage restraint had been possible, but this was in practice very
difficult: in 1971 wages and salaries already accounted for that share of
GNP that they were supposed to reach in 1976. The government's attitude towards wage demands was generally supportive. After all, this was a
government supported by, and working in the interests of, the working
class. Parties of the UP jostling for influence sought in some cases to
increase their support by encouraging wage claims; and opposition parties
desiring to increase the government's economic difficulties also promoted
excessive wage demands. How could the government contain these pressures? The use of repressive measures that had been implemented in the
past was completely unacceptable on political grounds. But the result was
disastrous. The large unplanned deficit of both traditional state enterprises
and recently nationalized ones was due mainly to the combination of wage
increases and price controls. In 1972 the government proposed a wage and

---

[20] José Serra and Arturo León, *La redistribución del ingreso en Chile durante el gobierno de la Unidad Popular*
Documento de Trabajo no. 70, FLACSO (Santiago, July 1978), p. 61. They also criticize the
unjustified confidence on the external front that led to a year's delay in seeking debt renegotiation;
an erroneous policy of maintaining a fixed exchange rate; and excessive permissiveness in relation to
social expenditures. The extent to which income redistribution based on wage increases really
benefits the very poor (many of whom do not receive wages) is open to question. See the perceptive
discussion of Alejandro Foxley and Oscar Muñoz, 'Income Redistribution, Economic Growth and
Social Structure', *Oxford Bulletin of Economics and Statistics* 36, no. 1 (1974), pp. 21–4.

Table 6.5. *Strikes in 1971 and 1972*

	Number of strikes	Total days of strike	Total workers involved	Total man-days lost
Private sector				
1964	564	–	138,476	–
1969	977	– 275,405	972,382	
1971	2,377	18,153	251,966	1,281,834
1972	2,474	11,097	262,105	1,177,186
Public sector				
1971	322	1,088	50,431	132,479
1972	815	2,881	135,037	476,965

Source: H. Landsberger and T. McDaniel, 'Hypermobilisation in Chile', *World Politics* 28 (July 1976), p. 520, using the official figures in the annual presidential address to Congress.

salary increase of 22 per cent for the public sector; the average of the actual increases obtained was 47.7 per cent (and the private sector level was not far short).

Wage and salary increases were not obtained without a struggle in the private or even the public sector, and the period saw a sharp increase in the number of strikes (Table 6.5). Many of these strikes in 1971 and 1972 were preludes to take-overs of factories or farms by the workers and enjoyed the active support of local government officials even if central government became increasingly worried.

The incorporation of enterprises into the APS, the state sector of the economy (Table 6.6), created many problems. Many more firms were taken over than intended (though some twenty-five that were planned to be nationalized managed to escape). By 1973 the manufacturing enterprises of the APS accounted for more than 40 per cent of total industrial production and employed 30 per cent of the industrial labour force. In addition, the state sector accounted for 93 per cent of total bank credit, 90 per cent of mining production and 28 per cent of food distribution. Intended to be run jointly by representatives of workers and managers, they were not meant to represent a threat to small and medium-sized enterprises, though that was how they were in fact perceived.

Apart from the question of worker participation, which had mixed results, the major function of the APS according to Vuskovic was to generate a surplus and increase capital accumulation. But independent

Table 6.6. *State sector, 1970–3*

	Number of firms			
	Nov. 1970	Dec. 1971	Dec. 1972	May 1973
State ownership[a]	31	62	103	165
Under intervention or requisition	–	39	99	120
Total	31	101	202	285

[a]Includes both social and mixed areas (i.e., jointly run by state and private sectors) and six new industries created after 1970.

Source: Stefan de Vylder, *Allende's Chile: The Political Economy of the Rise and Fall of the Popular Unity* (Cambridge, 1976), p. 149.

action by the workers, following from the worker take-over of the major Yarur textile plant in April 1971, meant the dominance of political rather than economic criteria in the process of nationalization. Many of the firms taken over were small or medium enterprises, and these nationalizations often occurred against Allende's wishes.

In spite of government appeals for restraint, workers in the APS began to demand special benefits, such as discounts on produce and wage increases well above the rate of inflation. Management of the APS was divided according to party lines, and considerations of party policy often overrode those of economic efficiency. Different parties had distinct strategies and used their control over certain enterprises to implement the strategies they believed in. Rather than provide a surplus for the economy, the state sector as a whole was responsible for a large part of the huge fiscal deficit, although this was a product of running the traditional state enterprises rather than the newly nationalized concerns.

The UP government abandoned the strategy of Vuskovic in July 1972 when he was replaced as minister of the economy by Carlos Matus, an Allende Socialist, and Orlando Millas, a Communist, became minister of finance. Matus and Millas tried a more coherent strategy in order to reduce the gap between supply and demand. But relaxation of price controls and devaluation sent inflation spiralling upwards. The government lost any capacity for long-term planning: survival on a day-to-day basis was all that could be achieved.

The opposition did its utmost to sabotage the UP's economic plans and undoubtedly contributed decisively to its economic difficulties. The opposition in Congress refused to accept tax reforms and readjustments, and in 1972 substantially increased the fiscal deficit by its refusal to finance the budget. Nor did the opposition confine itself to congressional activities. There was sabotage of production, massive strikes such as the so-called bosses strikes of October 1972 and June 1973, which severely damaged the economy.

The question of North American interference is controversial. The CIA was authorized to spend U.S. $8 million to secure the overthrow of Allende; and given the black market price of dollars this was probably worth closer to $40 million. In addition, U.S. loans were cut off; the United States used its influence to block loans from the World Bank and Inter-American Development Bank; it tried to obstruct renegotiation of the Chilean debt; short-term credits from U.S. banks dried up; and the North American copper companies took legal action against Chile to block exports of copper to Europe. There was, of course, substantial borrowing, particularly from other Latin American countries, and important financial aid was given by the USSR and other Communist countries in 1972 and early 1973. But the credits for long-term development, including a total of U.S. $500 million from the Soviet bloc, were nearly all unspent at the time of the coup. There may not have been a blockade by the United States, but there was a virtual boycott, and the effect on an economy so tied to the U.S. economic system could not but produce serious dislocation.

The political centre disappeared in Allende's Chile. The Radical Party disintegrated into three factions. Under electoral pressure, pushed by its own right wing and with the defection of several progressive congressmen to form the IC, the PDC moved, in 1972, into a working relationship with the National Party. His own moderation made Allende increasingly isolated as his supporters developed new forms of political organization, outside the control of the executive, in the so-called *poder popular.*

Why could the conflict not have been contained inside the institutional system? Probably because neither side was sufficiently committed to that system and because the expectations of all the parties were too high. The opposition indulged in a series of measures designed to obstruct the executive, which, if not illegal, certainly violated the conventions of the congressional system. The government, for its part, employed measures of dubious legality. There was intensive use of constitutional censures of ministers in an attempt to create administrative confusion and conflict among the branches of government. Restrictions on legislative initiatives were avoided by turning proposed laws into projects to amend the constitution. The major conflict there was over the proposal by two PDC senators, Juan Hamilton and Renán Fuentealba, to restrict the executive's powers to take firms into the APS beyond those agreed between the executive and Congress. The opposition tried to devise measures to blunt the executive's long-established powers of veto over congressional proposals. This culminated in the famous debate on 22 Augusst 1973 in which the Chamber of Deputies declared unconstitutional and illegal the policies of the president and, by a vote of 81 to 47, invited the military to defend the constitution.

The government, for its part, used some unorthodox measures to implement its policies – such as the use of a 1932 decree to facilitate the takeover of enterprises. Whatever the rights and wrongs of these questions of interpretation of the constitution, the effect was to politicize the judicial system by seeking legal arbitration of disputes that had previously been decided by agreement among the politicians. This did nothing to help solve issues of principle or to ensure the impartiality of administrative procedures.

If the UP's project of social transformation was possible only with the support of the majority of the people, it could have come about through elections, a plebiscite on constitutional reform or an agreement with the PDC. The municipal elections of April 1971 gave a total of 48.6 per cent of the vote to the UP, 48.2 per cent to the opposition and the rest blank or void. However, the municipal elections did not alter the balance of political power. In some ways it was a bad result for the UP. It gave the government no new power, but it helped to create a sense of false confidence, and it bolstered arguments against a deal with the PDC. The congressional elections of March 1973 were also to some degree inconclusive. The UP obtained 44.2 per cent of the vote (the Socialists 18.4 per cent and the Communists 16.2 per cent) and the opposition parties 54.2 per cent (the PDC 28.5 and the National Party 21.1 percent) with 1.6 per cent blank or void. Such a result could not resolve the political impasse one way or the other. But it did show that the opposition could not get the two-thirds majority in Congress it needed to impeach Allende – a conclusion not lost on those favouring a coup.

A plebiscite on the constitution, dissolving the existing chambers and re-electing a unicameral people's assembly, was debated several times in the UP coalition. It was considered immediately after the municipal elections of 1971, but rejected by Allende and the Communists on the grounds that it would force the opposition to unite. It was considered again in the last months of the government, but although now favoured by Allende, it was rejected by the parties, some of which sought cooperation with the PDC, others of which anticipated conflict and wanted time to prepare.

There were always members of both the PDC, not least of all Tomic, and the UP who argued for co-operation. There were frequent attempts to come to agreement on a common programme right up to an attempt at mediation by the cardinal-archbishop of Santiago in mid-August 1973. But attempts at co-operation always broke down. The Socialist Party opposed such agreements on the grounds that they would be betraying the central objectives of the UP and would alienate its supporters. Patricio Aylwin, a leading PDC senator, similarly felt that to co-operate with the UP would be a betrayal, unless there were concrete concessions to the PDC.[21] Indeed, hostility of some PDC leaders towards co-operation with the UP actuary led them to welcome a military coup. The tragedy is that at certain stages, when, for example, the agreements were reached in June and July 1973, there was acceptance of so many substantive points previously in dispute that little remained apart from an act of political will by both sides to put these agreements into practice. One continuing element working against co-operation was the press of both Left and Right. Violent attacks on politicians of both camps and wildly exaggerated reports of plots and counterplots all contributed to the creation of a siege mentality. Agreement between the PDC and UP became increasingly unlikely as social and political developments pushed them into antagonistic positions. The UP found it easier to accept a military presence in the cabinet to resolve the October 1972 crisis than to revive talks with the PDC.

Although UP theorists speculated on the problems of winning over the middle class, it seemed to be assumed that the loyalty of the working class could be taken for granted. This was not the case. There were substantial elements of the working class whose political allegiance was elsewhere; and those sectors of the working class whose loyalty to the ends of the UP government was firm nevertheless developed organizations and undertook actions that further reduced the possibility of an institutional and constitutional resolution of the political crisis.

The difficulties experienced by the government in retraining wage in-

---

[21] According to Tomic, 'The strategy of the UP was never to collaborate with the Christian Democrats but to divide and destroy them'. According to Altamirano, the PDC only appeared to want to negotiate in order to confuse the UP and to keep the democratic senators of the UP quiet. Tomic, 'Christian Democracy', p. 190. Altamirano, *Dialética,* p. 98. See also Garcés, *Allende,* p. 213.

Table 6.7. *The CUT national election, 1972*

	Votes	Percentage
Manual workers		
Communists	113,000	38
Socialists	95,900	32
Christian Democrats	47,400	16
MAPU members	22,000	7
FTR[a] members	5,800	1
Radicals	5,600	1
Total	291,400[b]	
White-collar workers		
Christian Democrats	61,000	41
Communists	33,000	22
Socialists	29,000	19
Radicals	11,000	7
Total	146,000[c]	

[a]An MIR group.
[b]Includes votes for other small parties and invalid votes.
[c]Includes minor parties' votes and invalid votes.

Source: Official CUT figures. Slightly different figures are published by Manuel Castells, *La lucha de clases en Chile* (Buenos Aires, 1974), p. 427. But since the counting took about six weeks and was disputed, it is not surprising that such discrepancies exist.

creases demonstrate the extent to which the CUT was unable to restrain its constituent unions. Much more than before, the CUT became part of the system of government, but its weaknesses remained an impediment to the exercise of central control. The Chilean trade union movement had always been a very decentralized one; federations and even plant unions had a tradition of robust independence which they were not willing to surrender. And a substantial proportion of union members belonged to parties of the opposition, as the results of the 1972 elections to the executive of the CUT show (Table 6.7).

Although the parties of the UP took about 70 per cent of the total vote, the PDC had a plurality in central Santiago with 35,000 votes against about 30,000 for the Communists and 25,000 for the Socialists, and the PDC controlled the regional branch of the CUT for Santiago Province. Many PDC unionists were to the left of their party leadership, and some collaborated with the UP unionists in the participation schemes. But they were obviously not going to be more modest than UP unionists in demanding wage increases and other benefits for workers, and this led to damaging strikes such as the El Teniente copper mine dispute of April 1973, which not only meant an unwelcome loss of export earnings but was also a blow to the government's authority.

Even if the unions had been solidly behind the UP, they would still have been only a minority of the total work-force. Women workers, for example, were largely unorganized, and their electoral behavior showed them to be more opposed to the UP than men. The participation of women in the electorate had grown more rapidly than men, and by 1970 they constituted half of the electorate. While it is clear that the UP was closing the gap between the electoral behaviour of men and women in urban working-class areas, in the 1973 elections 61 per cent of women's votes went to the opposition compared with 51 per cent of men's.

The political allegiance of shanty town dwellers was always something of a problem for the UP. Only a small proportion were organized in unions; the extreme Left MIR had more support here than amongst other social sectors; the PDC also had strong backing; and normal mechanisms of government control were much weaker in these areas. By mid-1973 there were 275 *campamentos* in Santiago, in which about one-sixth of the capital's population lived. Many of the *campamentos* had been established by seizures of land; such activities were expected of the urban poor in a political climate for once sympathetic to their aspirations, but the *tomas* contributed to loss of governmental authority. Very few of these inhabitants would benefit, for example, from participation in the work-force of the APS: according to government figures, only about a quarter of the economically active labour force was employed in the state sector. The government, therefore, had to deal with the grievances of those outside the state sector in other ways – price controls and state distribution agencies, for example, and subsidized transport. The problem was that the UP did not have enough resources to deal with all these pressing demands at the same time.

The countryside presented a different set of problems for the government. As it stood, the reform law could do little for substantial sectors of the poor – the landless labourers and the *minifundistas*. In the late 1960s *minifundistas* held 80 per cent of all land holdings, but these made up only 10 per cent of total arable rural land, even though they employed 40 per cent of the work-force. The major beneficiaries from the reform process were the resident labourers on expropriated estates. The problems facing the government were immense. In the first place there were a large number of land seizures (*tomas de tierra*) – perhaps 1,700 during the first year and a half of the UP government. Many were directed at the medium-sized properties that the government was pledged to defend, and whilst the MIR was active in the *tomas,* the parties of the UP did not encourage land seizures. The proportion of the rural labour force involved was relatively small – perhaps 20 per cent – but the opposition press seized on the *tomas* to wage a propaganda war against the government. Second, many of the beneficiaries of the reform, the *asentados,* had no desire to see their benefits diluted and became strong supporters of the PDC. Third, the government's alternative organizations, Centros de Reforma Agraria (CERAs) and the *consejos campesinos* did not really take root amongst the peasantry. They were essentially state-promoted agencies, and many of them indeed were taken over by the opposition. Social conflict in the countryside was complex. The process of agrarian reform and peasant unionization had not eliminated conflict but rather transferred it to a different level from the simple *hacendado*–peon conflict. In any case the period was too short, and the pressures too great, for the reforms either to increase productivity or to resolve the remaining inequalities in the countryside.

Thus, the opposition counted on the support of many urban and rural workers – most obviously white-collar workers and the beneficiaries of the reform process in the countryside. Pro-government supporters in the working class were increasingly taking their own initiative, decreasingly controlled by central party or union bureaucrats, increasingly mobilized and militant. Activities such as farm and factory seizures created problems for a government anxious to preserve its image as constitutional and hopeful of winning majority support for its policies.

Popular power and popular participation were fundamental aims of the UP, but the exact form that participation was to take was never entirely clear, and there were differences of emphasis between the Socialists and Communists. The local UP committees, for example, never really developed. A People's Assembly held in Concepción in July 1972 was opposed by the Communist Party and did not have Allende's approval. The more successful forms of participation were those that responded to local pressures and involved community and work-force. The most radical expression of *poder popular* developed in the *cordones industriales* that developed dramatically in response to the 'bosses' strike' in October 1972.

'*Poder popular*' was the name given to the host of organizations – *comandos comunales, comandos campesinos, cordones industriales* – that grew up to defend local communities, farms and factories. They organized the defence of their communities and undertook the tasks of maintaining production and supplies. But *'poder popular'* was a misleading name, for the movement included only a minority of the work-force, was defensive in character and was not co-ordinated above the local level. Nevertheless, it was an impressive demonstration of determination to defend the gains made by workers under the UP government.

The maximum expressions of *poder popular* were the *cordones* in the working-class belt surrounding Santiago that brought together local inhabitants and workers in a joint effort to run the enterprises and administer services in the area. As economic paralysis threatened Chile with the October 1972 truckers' strike, these organizations sprang up, on the basis of a number of existing organizations, in defence of the government. In October 1972 perhaps 100,000 people were active in the Santiago *cordones*. They rejected party affiliations; they were not supported initially by nor were they responsive to, the CUT; and they alarmed not just the opposition but also the Communist Party and the government. These were short-lived, crisis-based organizations, and their decline after October 1972 was not reversed, except in response to another opposition strike in June 1973, when in a single day they took over about 250 factories. This time the take-overs had the support of the government and the CUT. But this only served to intensify opposition accusations that the government was acting illegally; and further accusations that arms were being distributed to the workers (though there is no evidence of this) led to clashes between workers and the army and police in their search for arms. It was far too late to construct a parallel *poder popular* movement in order to take over state power, even if this was envisaged by the government. The general slide into anarchy continued.

In some ways as impressive as the growth of the popular sectors and their organizations was the parallel expansion of the *gremios*. These were associations of non-manual employees and professional groups, ranging from doctors, lawyers and architects to lorry owners, small shopkeepers and taxi-drivers. Small shopkeepers organized a *gremio* of some 160,000 members (claimed to be close to 90 per cent of the national total). Lorry owners, many of them running only one vehicle, could call on 25,000 members. The twenty or so professional associations, or *colegios*, including such large organizations as those of the 20,000 accountants or the 7,000 doctors, formed a confederation during the UP period. These groups were led by men associated with, or members of, right-wing parties or the PDC, and some of them, such as León Villarín of the truckers, became prominent opponents of the Allende government. These groups were not passive instruments of the dominant industrial and business circles. They enjoyed a robust independence and actively sought to further their members' interests by putting pressure on the government of the day. The Frente Nacional del Area Privada (FRENAP) became a major co-ordinating body of large and small businesses. Some anti-Marxist unions, like the Confederación Marítima backed the *gremialistas*. In 1973 a Comando Nacional de Defensa Gremial was formed to co-ordinate the activities of various groups. More than a thousand *gremios* were in active opposition to the UP in 1973, and some of them could count on generous funding from the United States.

The UP hoped to win at least some of these groups to its side. Allende himself, in speech after speech, emphasized that small and medium-sized entrepreneurs and farmers had nothing to fear from the UP. But these groups had never given much electoral support to the parties that made up the UP, apart from the declining Radical Party. Although many of them benefited materially during the first two years of the UP, the fear of loss of privileges, of worker lack of discipline, of a Communist take-over and a situation like that in Cuba (Castro's prolonged visit to Chile in 1971 did nothing to reassure them) was more real than any attractions the UP offered. And whatever Allende said, there was little reassurance from the speeches and writings of other UP politicians. UP rhetoric stressed its Socialist and popular character; little attempt was made to construct proposals in a way that would attract these sectors. The press and radio, controlled largely by the opposition, played an active, sometimes hysterical, role in spreading fear of the long-term aims of the UP.

The major confrontation with the government came in October 1972 after a proposal was made to increase state control over supplies to the trucking companies. The importance of this sector is obvious in a country with a geography like Chile's. The vital transport sector was virtually paralysed for a month, and there were powerful solidarity strikes by other professional and petty bourgeois sectors. More than one hundred *gremios* went on strike, in a movement that shook the government and that received the support of the PDC and National Party. As a result of the strike, the armed forces were incorporated into the cabinet, but it was too late to arrest the process of polarization.

With government and opposition now lined up against one another in bitter confrontation, with the economy out of control, with the commander-in-chief of the armed forces, General Carlos Prats, resigning his command in acceptance of his failure to mediate the crisis and control the officer corps, with the Church unable to bring the sides together and with growing violence and an increasing number of assassinations, there was little prospect of a peaceful solution. The end came with a violent military coup on 11 September 1973, in which La Moneda, the presidential palace, was bombed, President Allende was killed and thousands of Chileans were murdered.

Before 1973 the Chilean military had intervened only intermittently in the political process, and the political views of its officers corps were not generally made public. The military tended to be ignored by civilian politicians, though there were signs that this neglect could be dangerous, as in the minor uprising that occurred in 1969. But it was generally believed that the military would not depart dramatically from its accustomed political neutrality. General Prats, who had succeeded the assassinated General Schneider as commander-in-chief of the armed forces, adhered to the same strict constitutional interpretation of the role of the armed forces. Allende was consistent in his policy of not interfering in the institutional concerns of the military. Officers' salaries were improved. Spending on arms increased. Some officers were involved in the administration of public services, but they were very few, not in command of troops and obviously did not include those whose sympathies were alien to the UP. Allende abstained from interfering in the army hierarchy, and those few members of the UP who wished to appeal over the heads of the officers to the rank and file received no encouragement.

The military, however, could hardly have remained aloof from the intensifying polarization and violence that marred the last year of the Allende government. Politicians of the Right were calling for a coup and were constantly trying to instigate military plots.[22] Even the PDC, by its support for the strike of October 1972, by its backing of the congressional declaration of illegality in 1973 and through the increasing violence of its

---

[22] The direct involvement of the United States in the coup remains a matter of dispute. What is certain, however, is the long and close relationship between the United States and the Chilean military. Between 1950 and 1972 Chile received U.S. $43 million in U.S. arms and military supplies; between 1973 and 1976, it received $143 million. Allende's foreign minister, Clodomiro Almeyda, alleges that the U.S. armed forces, especially the Naval Intelligence Service, participated in the technical planning of the coup. Almeyda, 'The Foreign Policy of the UP government', in S. Sideri (ed.), *Chile, 1970–1973: Economic Development and Its International Setting* (The Hague, 1979), p. 116. This, however, is denied in the account of U.S. Ambassador Nathaniel Davis, *The Last Two Years of Salvador Allende*.

attacks on the government, seemed to point to a military coup as the only way to resolve the conflict.[23] Indeed, several prominent PDC leaders openly welcomed the coup, though many did not.

Various incidents contributed to the deterioration of relations between the government and the military. The military was notably unenthusiastic about Castro's long visit to Chile in 1971. The army and police resented the existence of Allende's personal bodyguard, the Grupo de Amigos del Presidente, which was drawn from the ranks of the extreme left wing of the UP. They grew uneasy at rumours of workers being armed and at the presence in Chile of many revolutionaries from other Latin American countries, especially Cuba. Resentment was publicly expressed at the proposal to set up an Escuela Nacional Unida (ENU). Although educational reform was overdue and the proposed reform itself progressive in many respects, the draft proposal employed a Marxist vocabulary that alarmed many sectors, and it was seen by the Church as a threat to its own private schools and to the teaching of religion in state schools. The Catholic Church as a whole had remained relatively neutral in the political battles of the period, though individual priests were active on both sides. But the ENU proposal was condemned by the bishops, and the army also made known its opposition.

It became impossible for the armed forces to maintain a united neutrality towards the political process once they entered the cabinet in November 1972 in an effort to restore some degree of political calm. But if their involvement in the cabinet produced temporary political solutions, it increased tensions within the army between those who supported Prats's constitutionalist stand and those who came to hate the UP and all it stood for. As the military officers in the cabinet refused to sign decrees of insistence that would have authorized more factory take-overs, they also increased the resentment of the left wing of the UP towards the military. The military became a direct participant in politics.

The military remained in the cabinet to oversee the March 1973 elections, but the inconclusive results convinced those military officers already plotting that a coup was the only solution. A premature coup attempt on 29 June, the so-called *tancazo,* had the support of an armoured regiment, but General Prats was able to contain the threat. Although the amount of overt support given to the rebels was limited, the *tancazo* had serious

---

[23] These points are made by Radomiro Tomic. Quoted from an article by Tomic in Gil et al. (eds.), *Chile at the Turning Point,* p. 273.

consequences. The government's call for workers to take over factories worsened relations with the military, which saw this as a prelude to worker resistance to the armed forces and even to the formation of workers' militias. When Allende met the army generals to seek their backing, only four of fourteen offered full support. For those military men concerned over the response of the workers, the lesson they drew was that the response was very limited: there was no march to the centre of Santiago. The military plotters concluded that a coup would meet only limited resistance.

The prelude to the coup itself was a confused period of increasing violence, rumours and counter-rumours. A final attempt by the cardinal-archbishop to bring together the PDC and the UP failed. Mutual suspicion was too great. When three armed forces chiefs were removed from their positions in the air force, army and navy, the plot could be consolidated. The most crucial removal was that of Prats. Although he had entered the cabinet again in August, he was increasingly isolated within the army. He resigned after a bizarre incident in which officers' wives staged a hostile demonstration outside his house.

By now the slide into anarchy was irreversible. The forcible searching of factories for arms by the military led to bitter clashes with the workers. Protests against alleged brutality by naval officers against conscripts who were resisting being used for anti-UP activities led to a call for an insurrection of naval conscripts against officers by the Socialist senator Carlos Altamirano and the MIR leader Miguel Enríquez. The officer corps was furious at such interference, and its resolve to go ahead with the coup and get rid of the naval chief, Admiral Montero, was stiffened. The last obstacle to the coup was dissolved with the removal of Admiral Montero on 7 September. The allegiance of General Augusto Pinochet to the plot came, it seems, very late but, once given, signalled the beginning of the final arrangements. On 11 September 1973, the armed forces rose and overthrew the government of Salvador Allende, the democratic system and the rule of law.

PINOCHET'S CHILE: LAISSEZ-FAIRE ECONOMY AND AUTHORITARIAN STATE

The unity of the Armed Forces is the unity of Chile. (Official statement, 11 September 1973)[24]

---

[24] Taken from the pamphlet issued by the Press Department of the Government entitled *September 11th, 1973: The Day of National Liberation*, p. 10. The propaganda agencies of the military

Although Chilean political life had seen outbreaks of violence, there had been nothing to compare with the intense repression that took place after the coup of September 1973. Thousands of Chileans were killed. The exact number will never be known, but estimates range between three thousand and thirty thousand. In the first six months after the coup, as many as eighty thousand political prisoners were taken. This scale of repression did not continue, but torture of political suspects, imprisonment, exile and even assassination continued to be part of the system of political control, centralized in the Dirección de Inteligencia Nacional (DINA).

Why was the coup so brutal? There was nothing in Chile to compare, for example, with the powerful urban guerrilla movements in Argentina or Uruguay. Talk of arming the workers was mostly talk, and whilst some political militants undoubtedly possessed weapons, the scale was tiny. However, the scale of social disintegration and polarization was very great. The feeling of civil war was in the air. In these circumstances, the members of the UP were defined as the enemy, not as mere political opponents.

The military in Chile had delayed intervention. A more interventionist military, as in Argentina or Brazil, would probably have taken action much earlier when the political temperature was lower. The brutality of the coup owes something to the feeling that army involvement in politics as had occurred with the UP government was a grave mistake. Solutions had to be, initially at least, military and not political; the coup was a move against all politicians and not just those of the Left. The aim of the plotters was to abolish political parties, not to make a deal with right-wing parties, however much those parties supported them. Finally, the intention of the military was to eliminate whole political and social movements from Chilean life. The military did not assume that the parties of the Left were creatures of a small political class.

Whatever explanations are offered for such terrible violence, it seems inconceivable that such barbarities could have been committed in a country like Chile. Yet very little is known about the way the military saw political life or why men who were not psychopaths acquiesed to the government's use of torture. Although many politicians foresaw the coup

government produced a flow of documents designed to prove the sinister intentions of the UP government, including a 'Plan Zeta' to assassinate leading political and military figures. This 'plan' and other imaginative inventions are contained in the *'White Book'* of the government published shortly after the coup. Other documents emphasize the national and patriotic character of the armed forces; see, e.g., the *Declaración de principios del gobierno de Chile* (Santiago, March 1974).

in 1973, only those of the extreme Right and Left expected such a high level of repression and such a prolonged period of military rule.

It is an error to attribute too uniform a degree of ideological conviction to the military or a very clear vision of its long-term aims once the initial destruction of the old regime had been accomplished, which was in itself seen as a long-term task. It was obvious that urgent measures of economic stabilization were necessary and that the coup could be legitimized only by the adoption of a dramatically new economic and political model. The lack of consensus on a basic programme helps to explain why power became so personalized. The cohesion of armed forces stemmed from the command structure rather than agreement on policy measures.

The doctrines with which the military were most familiar were those of 'national security'. These have been defined as a belief in the concept of the nation as an 'essence', 'tradition', or 'spirit' that has been ruined by political demagogy and menaced by antinational aggression, in the acceptance of social inequalities as the natural order, in the idea of government as authoritarian, and in the definition of Marxism as the principal enemy of society.[25] Vague as these authoritarian ideas are, they help to explain why the military accepted not simply the task of overthrowing Allende, but also the construction of a new society in which political divisions would be superseded by common action for national greatness. General Pinochet, fifty-eight at the time of the coup and with a record of forty years of service in the army, was a specialist in geo-politics.[26]

The Chilean military, having rejected its constitutional tradition, fell back on a direct transference to the political arena of military values – hierarchy, discipline and respect for order. This, like the lack of agreement on policy, helps to explain the personalization of authority of the regime under Pinochet – in contrast to the corporate rule of the Brazilian military after 1964, or the hostility towards personalism that developed in Argentina, Uruguay and Peru in the 1970s. Pinochet showed considerable political skill in outmanoeuvring his potential opponents in the officer corps (such as General Gustavo Leigh) and appointing loyal subordinates to all command posts in the armed forces. As head of state and commander-in-chief of the armed forces, Pinochet wielded immense

[25] Manuel Antonio Garretón, *El proceso político chileno* (Santiago, 1983).
[26] The other members of the ruling military junta were Admiral José Toribio Merino, aged 57, another specialist in geo-politics; General Gustavo Leigh, head of the air force, at first identified with the neo-fascist elements of the government but later dismissed by Pinochet for his criticisms on policy matters; and General César Mendoza, chief of the Carabineros.

power. After ratification of the new constitution, he appropriated much of the symbolic authority of the presidency.[27]

Belief in authoritarian doctrines such as national security is normally associated with an increase in the economic activities and role of the state, whereas Pinochet's Chile took the opposite course. However, conversion to the economic doctrines of the Chicago school of monetarism did not come immediately. Many officers were attracted initially to a kind of catholic integralism, or corporate state ideology. Their rejection of the values of socialism and their admiration for the role of the *gremios* led to a strong vein of nationalist corporatism, as expressed by the influence of reactionary theorists like Jaime Guzmán. Such ideas received political expression in institutions like the Council of State, which was set up in December 1975 on the pattern of a similar organization in Franco's Spain and included political notables and representatives of the *gremios*.

These ideas, however, were not an appropriate basis for legitimizing the regime. In the first place, the Church was not sympathetic to such reactionary doctrines (though it did not emerge as an outspoken opponent of the regime until 1975). Second, these ideas would not find favour with the external actors with which the regime wanted to ally itself, that is to say, the United States and the international banks. The regime wanted international approval, financial support and investment. Flirtation with fascist ideas – as distinct from militant anti-communism – was not likely to gain support. Third, corporatism might be used by the pre-existing political groups to manoeuvre their way back to power and dilute the military's monopoly on power. But most important of all, these doctrines offered little specific advice on how to deal with economic problems. The initial measures of the government – removal of price controls and subsidies, cutting of real wages, reduction of the fiscal deficit – had not convinced the country that inflation could be controlled. Inflation in 1974 was 376 per cent and in 1975 was 341 per cent.

A group of economists trained in the Catholic University and in Chicago, with considerable experience in the world of Chilean business, commerce and politics (several had been advisers to Alessandri in 1970), had been meeting since 1972 to prepare a policy for a new right-wing government. However, it was not until July 1974 that they started to

---

[27] The legislative function was exercised by the junta, serviced by a series of committees. These committees were staffed by civilians who played a crucial part in shaping and determining policy. But Pinochet maintained his own band of civilian advisers, conducting his affairs with great secrecy.

influence policy through the appointment as finance minister of Jorge Cauas, although he himself was a PDC adviser rather than a 'Chicago boy', as they were called. At the Economics Ministry Fernando Léniz (a business-man) was first advised and then, in April 1975, replaced by Sergio de Castro, a convinced monetarist. The dominance of the neo-liberal school of economists was complete.

The project that the Chicago economists offered the military involved a complete restructuring of the economy, society and the political system. The whole legacy of Chilean politics since the 1930s, and not just the UP period, would be changed. Such a transformation could be achieved only through strict authoritarian controls to eliminate the distortions brought about by populism and to create the right conditions in which market forces could operate. Reducing the size of the public sector would remove the basis for popular or sectoral pressures for concessions from the govern-ment; redirecting the surplus to the private capital market would strengthen those forces supportive of the military's policies and penalize those who were likely to be against them; opening the economy to free trade would provide the means for growth without having to give state support to uncompetitive sectors; allowing market forces to regulate wage rates would undermine the political bargaining strength of the labour movement. All of these would combine to eliminate that greatest propaga-tor of social unrest – inflation. And the beauty of the solution was that the regulatory mechanism would be that most liberal of concepts – the operation of free-market forces.[28] At the same time the old forms of political allegiance would be eroded, and new forms, classless and na-tional, would develop.

Monetarism offered a new utopia in contrast to the failures of the past, and the offer of a utopia could 'justify' the brutal suppression that followed the military coup. The new economic orthodoxy was attractive to the military because it offered coherence and discipline, and it was seen as technical and scientific and therefore ideologically neutral. Once under way, the process was to be irreversible and, as necessary means for national salvation, its premises were not to be questioned.

Many sectors were to find the new measures unpleasant. But entrepre-neurial groups accepted austerity and competition as the price to pay to

[28] The most sustained and informed critique of the government's economic policy comes from the economists at CIEPLAN. This section relies heavily on Ricardo Ffrench-Davis, 'El experimento monetarista en Chile', *Estudios CIEPLAN* no. 9 (1982); and Alejandro Foxley, *Latin American Experiments in Neo-Conservative Economics* (Berkeley, Calif., 1983).

avoid a repetition of the past. Many middle sectors welcomed any measures that would restore discipline and order. And the long-term promises
of the Chicago boys were attractive. General Pinochet's rule was based not
only on the army and repression, but also on support from influential
groups in civil society.

The first economic decisions made by the government had already
reversed the direction of economic policy of previous decades. Tariffs were
reduced and prices were unfrozen. The process of 'privatization' of the
state began. The exchange rate was devalued and unified. A new investment code was promulgated in an effort to attract foreign capital. But
these measures did not halt the deterioration of the economy. Copper
prices fell from 93.4 U.S. cents per pound in 1974 to 56.1 cents per
pound in 1975, and export earnings fell by half. Moreover, the rise in oil
prices was very detrimental to the economy. The deterioration in terms of
trade was equal to a loss of 5.6 per cent of GDP in 1975.

One major problem for the policy-makers in Chile in this initial period
was the difficulty of obtaining foreign funds to back a stabilization effort.
Chile was to some extent an international pariah, although substantial
help was given by the United States. In 1975, Chile received U.S. $93
million from AID and the Food for Peace programme, compared with
$6.9 milion in 1973. In the first three years of the Pinochet government,
Chile received loans of $141.8 million from the U.S. Export–Import
Bank and other U.S. agencies (only $4.7 million went to Allende) and
$304.3 million from the World Bank and the Inter-American Develop-
ment Bank (compared with $11.6 million to Allende). But the volume of
private bank lending fell sharply (it did not reach significant levels until
1976), and huge debt repayments had to be made.

It was in these circumstances that the doctrinaire monetarists took over
and in April 1975, with Pinochet's full support, applied a 'shock' treatment. In effect this meant the president's long-term support for the
Chicago boys; any retreat from the measures initiated in 1975 would have
implied a confession that the severity of the measures then imposed was a
mistake. And the measures taken were indeed severe. Real government
expenditure was cut by 27 per cent in 1975, and the fiscal deficit from
8.9 per cent of GNP to 2.9 per cent. Tariffs on imports fell from an
average of 70 per cent in mid-1974 to 33 per cent by mid-1976. Credit
was severely restricted, and annual real interest rates rose from an already
high 49.9 per cent to 178 per cent by the end of 1975. Public investment
fell by half. The GDP fell by almost 15 per cent compared with the 1974

value. Industrial production fell by 25 per cent. Real wages fell yet again; by 1975 they reached their lowest point at 62.9 per cent of their 1970 value. Unemployment rose from 9.7 per cent of the labour force in December 1974 to 18.7 per cent in December 1975. Yet inflation was slow to respond and remained at 341 per cent in 1975. In spite of the worst recession in more than forty years, recovery was slow. The shock treatment needed more time to work and had to be applied with unbending rigour.

The Chicago boys completely dominated the scene until the exit of Sergio de Castro from the Finance Ministry in April 1982, and even then they continued to be influential and to occupy leading economic posts. The technocrats in charge of the economy were convinced that the state occupied far too important a role. Their intention was to reduce the state's involvement as much as possible by the sale of public enterprises. Apart from those companies in which the UP government had intervened, the state owned, through the Corporación de Fomento de la Producción (CORFO), some three hundred enterprises in 1973. By 1980 this number had declined to twenty-four, and half of those companies were in the process of being transferred. There were another dozen or so state enterprises that depended on governmental agencies other than CORFO – amongst them the state copper and petroleum corporations. The sale of assets took place in extremely favourable conditions for the new owners. Given the recession and the high domestic rates, those able to purchase state assets were the large conglomerates (*los grupos*) in the private sector with access to foreign funds at interest rates significantly lower than the domestic ones. In effect the state paid a substantial subsidy to the rich and the powerful to take over state assets – a subsidy that had been calculated as equivalent to up to 40 or 50 per cent of the purchase price. But the military resisted the sale of state assets it deemed to be strategic. Including the copper corporation CODELCO, the current revenue of state companies in 1982 still amounted to about 25 per cent of GDP. The Chicago boys were opposed by a sector of the military that still considered government control over certain vital services and sectors necessary for the maintenance of national security.

The adherents of free-market economies encouraged an intensification of economic concentration in Chile. A handful of multi-sectoral groups dominated the banking, financial, industrial and export-agriculture sectors. Two conglomerates, the Cruzat–Larrain and Javier Vial groups, were particularly important and dominated the private banking system until the economic collapse of 1982–3. Their access to international finance gave them immense advantages and benefits. The major groups made an estimated U.S. $800 million in profit between 1977 and 1980 simply by borrowing abroad and relending domestically at interest rates that varied from 100 per cent in 1976 to 30 per cent in 1978 above international rates. These profits were rather more than the cost of the state firms and banks sold back to the private sector between 1973 and 1978.

It has been calculated that by the end of 1978 five economic conglomerates controlled 53 per cent of the total assets of Chile's 250 largest private enterprises. These five, plus another four, controlled 82 per cent of the assets in the Chilean banking system, 60 per cent total bank credits and 64 per cent of loans made by financial institutions.[29] The conglomerates grew at dizzying pace and made windfall profits, as overseas banks attracted by high interest rates in Chile were prepared to make short-term loans, knowing that the government's economic fortunes were so bound up with the Chicago model that honouring international commitments would be top priority even if there was recession. Abolition of strict control over banking and over foreign exchange led to a process of concentration and of indebtedness that would destroy the foundations of the Chicago-inspired economic 'miracle'.

A similar process of privatization occurred in the agrarian sector. About a third of the land was returned to its former owners. Although something like 40 per cent of land was assigned to the peasants who worked it, lack of access to credit and technical assistance forced some 60 per cent to sell out. Unemployment in agriculture was significantly higher than it had been in previous decades, and by 1980 wage rates had declined to about their 1965 level. State support to agriculture was drastically reduced, apart from the profitable export sector.

The state retreated from many areas where previously it had played an important role. Fiscal expenditure as a percentage of GDP dropped from 29.1 per cent in 1972 to 19.7 per cent in 1978. There were significant reductions in social expenditure per capita in education, health, social security and housing. Government investment fell drastically, by almost one-half between 1970 and 1978. Pension funds were transferred to the private sector in a massive influx of liquidity to companies that were largely owned by the conglomerates. The political intention of this proposal, of course, was that the fortunes of workers would be tied to the

---

[29] Fernando Dahse, *El mapa de la extrema riqueza* (Santiago, 1979). The share of financial resources deposited in private institutions rose from 11% in 1970 to 64.7% in 1979.

fortunes of the private sector — 'socialism' would become a threat to pension rights. At the same time, labour legislation introduced in 1979 strictly limited the effectiveness of union collective bargaining. Unions lost much of their former power.

Government statistics tended to use the recession of 1975 as a base year and so give a somewhat distorted picture of the progress of the economy, following the 'shock' administered by the Chicago boys. But the government could point to a number of achievements. High growth rates were recorded in the period from 1977 to 1980, although the overall annual rate of growth of GNP between 1974 and 1980 was only 4 per cent; on a per capita basis, 2 per cent, lower than the rate of the 1960s.[30] The rate of inflation at last began to fall and in 1981 was 9.5 per cent. The fiscal deficit had been eliminated by 1979. Non-traditional exports tripled between 1974 and 1980. There was a balance-of-payments surplus in the period from 1978 to 1980 as a result of the accumulation of international reserves, based on a huge inflow of foreign capital that reached more than U.S. $16 billion annually in the 1978–80 period.

But there were negative features as well. The inflation rate was brought down by the application of a fixed exchange rate in 1979. This led to a severe balance-of-payments problem as cheap imports flooded the Chilean market and exports were made expensive. The trade gap was met by higher levels of foreign borrowing; but this borrowing was for short-term loans to the financial sector. The government was forced into a series of hasty, ill-timed devaluations of more than 70 per cent between June and October 1982. The rate of investment, whether private, state or foreign, remained well below past levels. Real interest rates at the high levels that prevailed in Pinochet's Chile discouraged investment and encouraged speculation. Even the vital copper sector was starved of new investment for expansion above existing levels of production. The lowering of tariffs hit national industry hard, and bankruptcies reached record heights. Most new imports were consumption goods of the luxury variety, and not the capital goods and machinery that were needed to maintain the level of industrial production. Although non-traditional exports grew, the rate was not fast enough to match the growth in imports.

The social costs of the experiment were also very high. Real wages in the 1974–81 period scarcely reached three-quarters of their 1970 level.

---

[30] These figures have been subject to careful revision which suggests that the growth rate was 20% *lower* for 1976–81 than claimed by the government. Patricio Meller et al., '¿Milagro económico o milagro estadístico?', *Mensaje* (May 1985), pp. 145–9.

Even by 1982 the level was lower than that in 1970. Unemployment rose to record heights: it was never lower than an annual rate of 16.5 per cent after the 1975 shock and rose to more than 30 per cent in 1982–3 (compared with 5.7 per cent in 1970). Income distribution worsened appreciably. The average monthly consumption of the poorest 20 per cent of households fell by 31.1 per cent between 1969 and 1978, while that of the highest 20 per cent rose by 15.6 per cent. The structure of employment also changed. The number of blue-collar workers fell by 22 per cent between 1970 and 1980 – a not unwelcome development to a government that opposed a strong union movement. The 'informal' sector of employment grew by 13.3 per cent in the same period.

Although the warning signs were there in 1980 for those who chose to read them, the regime remained confident and there was talk of an economic miracle. The international isolation of Chile was lessening as the memory of the coup faded. Moreover, the domestic political front was tranquil. A new constitution and a plebiscite in 1980 expressed the determination of the government to carry on as long as necessary to secure the success of its reforms.

A number of factors help to explain the consolidation of the Pinochet regime's power. First, there was support for the coup from wide sectors of society, and fear of a return to the disorder of the UP years kept many loyal to the new government even when promised benefits did not materialize. Second, the government was exceptionally ruthless. The development of a powerful secret police, DINA, made opposition to the government a crime, the consequences of which could easily be torture, exile or death. At least three prominent Chileans were victims of assassination attempts abroad by DINA agents. Two succeeded, those of General Prats in Buenos Aires in 1974 and Orlando Letelier, an effective and respected leader of the opposition in exile, in Washington in 1976; one failed, against the respected and moderate PDC leader Bernardo Leighton. Third, the process of economic concentration gave the government powerful backers. Fourth, although many foreign governments shunned Chile, international banks did not, and the external finance needed to run the economy was, after the mid-1970s, always available. Fifth, the way that Pinochet personalized power and concentrated authority in his own hands gave a dictatorial solidity to the regime. Pinochet's manipulation of the military and of civilian groups showed considerable political cunning. Potential military challengers did not last long. The military as such had no policy-making function, but it was well rewarded materially. Civilians were involved in government as individuals and not as representatives of powerful groups. Pinochet divided and ruled.

On the other side, the opposition was divided and hounded. Many of the prominent leaders of the UP parties and unions were killed or exiled after the coup. Although the PDC suffered less, it was soon suspended, and some of its leaders were forced into exile. Legislation made political actitivity virtually impossible. The opposition spent much time trying to analyse what went wrong in 1973, but the process of attributing blame did not help to unite it. Not until 1975 did the Church come out against the government. The press and the mass media were not only strictly controlled but also used to convey government propaganda. Universities were placed under military control, certain disciplines prohibited and many lecturers and students dismissed. Unions were similarly 'intervened', divided and controlled.

Two plebiscites were used to create the appearance of consultation. In 1978 Chileans were asked whether they supported General Pinochet in the face of international aggression. According to official sources, 75 per cent did. In 1980 the country was asked to approve a new constitution of markedly authoritarian form, with a transition period of eight years in which Pinochet was to exercise unconstrained executive power and with the possibility of his re-election for a further eight years after that. The 1980 constitution created a system of presidential rule with few limitations. A substantial part of the Senate was to be nominated rather than elected. The Chamber of Deputies lost any effective power of scrutiny over the executive. The constitution institutionalized the power of the armed forces in a Council of National Security, which was given a role in almost all important matters and a decisive role in constitutional affairs. The principle of civilian control over the military was effectively abolished. The government claimed that the results of the plebiscite on the constitution, in which 93.1 per cent of the total electorate participated, were 67 per cent in favour, 30 per cent against and the rest null or void. However, the absence of registers, complete government control over the electoral process, massive official propaganda, tiny opposition protests and, undoubtedly, fraud, intimidation and fear of expressing opposition in what might not be so secret a ballot cast considerable doubt on these figures.

General Pinochet's centralization of power owed a great deal to this control over the DINA (later renamed the Central Nacional de Informaciónes [CNI] in an attempt to introduce some cosmetic changes).

Pinochet had established a secret police system under his personal control, independent of any military structure. It became an instrument of surveillance not only over the civilian population but also over other intelligence agencies and the military itself. At the height of its power in 1977, the head of DINA, General Manuel Contreras, commanded a small army of more than nine thousand agents and a network of paid volunteer informants several times as large, pervading all aspects of life. The DINA obtained funds from illicit control over several firms nationalized under the UP government, and there was occasional evidence of corruption and extortion involving DINA officials. The DINA suffered a set-back as a result of the international scandal that followed the assassination of Letelier in Washington in 1976; Pinochet was eventually forced to dismiss Contreras and agree to the extradition of the U.S. citizen Michael Townley, who, while working for the DINA, had carried out the assassination. The newly named CNI essentially performed the same functions as the old DINA and was active in repressing the popular movements that broke out in opposition to the government in 1983.

Pinochet was politically astute in building on the strong tradition of loyalty and hierarchy in the Chilean armed forces. Neither the army as an institution nor individual officers had never been the recipients of such lavish expenditure: the military budget almost doubled in real terms between 1973 and 1981. A disproportionate amount went to the army, police and security services – those sectors directly involved in internal repression. Chile was amongst the highest spenders on the armed forces in Latin America, with no less than 6 per cent of the GDP going to the military in 1980. The personnel of the armed forces had every material reason for identifying their futures with that of Pinochet. Yet Pinochet was careful to avoid giving the armed forces any institutional role in the political process. Generals who became cabinet ministers did so in a personal capacity and were strictly accountable to Pinochet. The number of generals increased from twenty-five in 1973 to forty-two in 1980 and to fifty-four in 1984; all were appointed by Pinochet and manipulated to remain loyal to him, not simply as president of the republic, but also as *capitán general* of the armed forces.

The most significant opposition to Pinochet came from the Catholic Church and its cardinal in Santiago. The Catholic Church and other denominations quickly became involved in relief agencies and in helping those who suffered from the massive repression of 1973. But the Church was slower to take a stand against the government's policies as opposed to its abuses. Indeed, the general tenor of ecclesiastical pronouncements was to praise the generals for having saved the country from Marxism. It took three and a half years before the hierarchy cast doubt on the legitimacy of the government. One of the reasons for this change in attitude was the suppression of the PDC and increasing repression directed at party members and at radical Catholics, both priests and laity. Once embarked on a process of criticizing the government, the Church became increasingly important. This was a grave source of embarrassment to a government that saw itself as the saviour of Christian civilization. The Church kept attention focussed on the continuing violation of human rights. It provided a forum within which trade unions and popular organizations could manage a precarious existence. And it provided shelter to those who would criticize the regime.

The development of unions in this period show how difficult it is, even for an authoritarian regime, to control trade unions if they are allowed even minimal rights. Class and political consciousness could not be abolished by decree. The copper workers, for example, rejected the leaders imposed by the government and played a crucial role in breaking the political deadlock in 1982–3. And there were many earlier examples of union members standing up against the regime, notably in the Coordinadora Nacional Sindical. But the trade union movement was seriously weakened by the years of military government. Union leaders considered threatening to the regime were persecuted, exiled and even killed. The murder of the prominent leader of Agrupación Nacional de Empleados Fiscales (ANEF), Tucapel Jiménez, a Radical and formerly a fierce opponent of the UP, showed that even politically moderate union leaders ran grave risks. Only 10 per cent of the labour force was unionized in 1983 compared with more than 30 per cent in the days of the Allende government. Union leaders, mostly unemployed themselves, realized how difficult it was to bring the employed out on strike, especially in the state sector, where the government's response was instant dismissal. Strikes were, in practice, demonstrations of the unemployed, who hoped to paralyse economic activity by impeding public transport and forcing shops to close. Although the Comando Nacional de Trabajadores, formed in June 1983, was the most representative national movement to emerge since the coup, it could only exhort and persuade. In view of the repression of the labour movement and the high level of unemployment, traditional industrial conflict had to give way to protest in the streets, to riots and demonstrations of the poor and unemployed.

The financial crisis that threatened Chile in 1981 broke with severity in 1982 and 1983. Chile was not alone in facing enormous problems of debt repayment; Argentina, Brazil, Mexico, Venezuela and even Cuba were facing similar problems. Indeed, the military's explanation of the crisis as the effect of the international recession was not without force. Copper prices were depressed, oil prices were still high and interest rates rose sharply on the international markets. Although other countries suffered from the recession, Chile was particularly hard hit.

The crisis developed rapidly. By 1981 the deficit on the current account of the balance of payments was 20 per cent larger than total exports and amounted to almost 15 per cent of GDP. International bankers became nervous, the enormous amounts of money that Chile needed were no longer so readily available and interest rates were higher. A squeeze on domestic credit and refusal to change the overvalued exchange rate led to a series of bankruptcies. Of the unprecedented 431 firms which went into liquidation in 1981, the most important was the sugar refinery Compañía Refinadora de Azúcar de Viña del Mar (CRAV), one of Chile's largest enterprises. In November 1981 the state was forced to intervene in four banks and four *financieras*. The government's failure to regulate the banking system was to have disastrous consequences, especially after it rescued the Banco Osorno from collapse in 1977, fearing that bankruptcy would damage internal and foreign confidence. As a consequence, depositors, domestic and foreign, felt that their loans to the private sector were effectively guaranteed by the state. This, as well as the failure to maintain a stable exchange rate and the international recession, led to huge increases in non-performing assets in the banking system: these rose from 11 per cent of the capital and reserves of the banking system in 1980 to 47 per cent in 1982 and to 113 per cent by mid-1983.

In 1982 GNP fell by 14.1 per cent and investment by nearly 40 per cent. The peso was devalued, contrary to government promises, and by the end of 1982 was down to 40 per cent of its previous parity; foreign exchange reserves fell by 40 per cent. The economic team began to change as rapidly as it had under any previous civilian government. In 1983 the government took over most of the private financial system and so acquired a large number of firms whose assets had passed to the banks. The fiscal deficit reappeared and the rate of inflation rose to 20 per cent in 1982. The major groups were broken up, and hostility between their former owners and the government replaced the formerly close working relationship. Monetarist policies of the kind applied in Chile were shown to be inapplicable in an economy with such a heterogeneous structure, segmented markets and sectoral and regional differences. The costs of economic adjustment were not only excessively high in social terms, but also extremely damaging to the very economy they were supposed to benefit. The heaviest cost fell to the poor. In mid-1983, 10.9 per cent of the economically active population (380,529 men and women) were working for the government Programa de Empleo Mínimo (PEM), receiving a monthly income of two thousand pesos, equivalent to the price of 1.3 kilograms of bread per day. The government also ended the linking of wage increases to the increase in the cost of living.

Opening the economy to international forces came to mean in practice the accumulation of an enormous short-term debt, mostly in private hands, as well as a process of de-industrialization. Between 1973 and 1979 the traditional foreign debt (public sector plus the private sector debt guaranteed by the government) fell by 35 per cent, but the private sector debt rose by 91.3 per cent. Even in 1978 Chile's debt service ratio was 45.3 per cent, one of the highest in the world, and it was to rise sharply. The debt constituted an immense burden on the Chilean economy.

After ten years of military rule, Chile was no advertisement for monetarism. Per capita income was 3.5 per cent lower than in 1970, and increasing inequality and unemployment meant that the poor were worse off than they had been twenty years ago. Industrial production was 25 per cent lower than in 1970. The foreign debt was equal to 80 per cent of GNP, compared with 8.2 per cent in 1970. And ironically in view of its aims, the state owned most of the financial sector and thereby much of national industry. International banks forced the government, against its will, to include private sector debt in its renegotiation.

Demonstrations organized on a monthly basis from May 1983 rocked the regime. It was in the shanty towns, above all in Santiago, that popular protest took its most potent form. At least a third of the population of the capital city lived in such areas, or urban slums, not notably better. Unemployment was rife – a level of 80 per cent was not uncommon – and many of the youth of the shanty towns never knew stable employment. Days of protest and struggles with the army and police in the shanty towns saw them converted into veritable battle-grounds. Not all shanty towns expressed their opposition in such militant fashion as La Victoria, where the French priest André Jarland was killed in early September 1984, but social deprivation and hostility to the regime were so widespread that they constituted the government's main political problem. As a result, the police and army staged a brutal repressive operation in the shanty towns in late October and in November 1984.

Opposition party activity was resumed in a more open form in 1983. The opposition parties of the Centre, led by the Christian Democrats and a faction of the Socialist Party, formed the Alianza Democrática (AD). They called for Pinochet's resignation, a properly elected constituent assembly and a broad social pact to oversee the return to democracy. But as it became clear that the government would make no more than token gestures and would not even discuss the question of Pinochet's resignation, the left-wing opposition parties, led by the Communist Party and another wing of the Socialists, formed the Movimiento Democrático Popular (MDP) and pressed for a policy of mass mobilization and confrontation. The Communist Party, much to the discomfort of the centrist AD, refused to renounce the right to use violence as a method of ridding the country of the dictatorship.

Given the unpopularity of the regime, it may seem paradoxical that the opposition was so divided, but it was extremely difficult to organize opposition in Chile. Opposition parties and movements had been denied means of communicating with their supporters for more than eleven years. They had no regular access to radio, television or the popular press, had not been able to organize internal elections and enjoyed only a brief period of relatively open activity after the protests began in May 1983. Politics was practised in a vacuum. No one really knew how much support any party, or internal faction of a party, enjoyed, and if there was no test of support, any group could claim to be representative. For the first decade of the dictatorship, parties had to concentrate on surviving and maintaining some degree of internal organization. This led, inevitably, to emphasis on immediate party tasks rather than initiatives to oppose the regime, but it also made the parties slow to recognize how many changes had taken place in Chile and how many ideas and policies had to be formulated.

A cycle of violence, protest and repression marked the years after 1983. The government's survival depended on the unity of the armed forces. The opposition's prospects depended on the extent to which it could create a broad agreement on the transition to democracy. At a time when most other military regimes – those in Argentina, Uruguay, Brazil, Peru and Ecuador – had returned power to civilians, General Pinochet demonstrated very effectively how dictatorial authority could be established in a society with even as long a tradition of democratic government as Chile. The key to Pinochet's power lay in his control over an army that was disciplined, loyal to its commander-in-chief and contemptuous of civilian politicians. Another element of his survival was the inability of the opposition to unite and offer a credible alternative. It seemed as if the opposition might do this with the Church-inspired Acuerdo Nacional para la Transición Hacia la Plena Democracia in 1985, but the exclusion of the Communist Party created one major problem outside the Acuerdo Nacional and party sectarianism created another within it.

If domestic politicians seemed unsure of how to confront their president, international politicians suffered the same fate. President Pinochet was unmoved, even defiant, in the face of international hostility. Although President Carter shunned the regime, Chile was a low priority for the United States, and unless the opposition could produce an effective alternative, there was always the fear that the Marxists might return if the general were overthrown. President Reagan was far more preoccupied with Central America than with Chile, and although the United States became noticeably cooler towards the Pinochet regime after 1985, it was no more effective in influencing the government, though it did help the opposition.

With economic recovery, the government was able to reward some of its followers and restore business confidence. At least some groups of the Right wanted to see Pinochet himself remain in power until 1997, and most supported a continuation of the authoritarian political system and free-market economy, even if not under the same leadership.

Recovery from the recession of 1982–3 was steady and sustained. Growth increased to about 5 per cent annually from 1986 to 1988, inflation remained contained, unemployment dropped to approximately 12 per cent and higher copper prices and good export earnings from non-traditional exports provided a favourable external financial position. Although political protests continued with the creation of the Asamblea de la Civilidad, the opposition did not seem to be making significant inroads into the government's authority. A failed assassination attempt against General Pinochet in September 1986 reinforced his prestige and lent credence to his claim that the opposition could not control those who were prepared to use violence. Although details of the assassination attempt are obscure, it seems almost certain that it was the work of the Frente Patriótico Manuel Rodríguez, a group created with the blessing and support of the Communist Party. The opposition had called 1986 the 'decisive year'; but if anything, it seemed to show that Pinochet could run rings around a still divided and relatively weak opposition.

Certainly, the president and his closest advisers assumed that they enjoyed the support of the majority of the population, and they looked forward with confidence to the outcome of a plebiscite that would be held no later than January 1989 to decide upon the first elected president to take power under the 1980 constitution. Pinochet himself would have preferred a sixteen-year presidency from 1980 but was persuaded that his rule would be more legitimate if he were to present himself to the electorate for a renewal of his mandate in 1988 or 1989. It was assumed that the military junta would in fact nominate Pinochet as the sole candidate of the plebiscite, and although air force, police and navy representatives made it clear on several occasions that they would have preferred a younger, civilian candidate, in the end they bowed to pressure from the army; Pinochet received their nomination in late August 1988. The immediate protests that greeted this decision should have been a warning that electoral victory was by no means a certainty, but the president's advisers, above all Minister of the Interior Sergio Fernández, the architect of the constitution, were confident of victory on 5 October 1988.

Such confidence in Pinochet's triumph was not unrealistic. Chile was at the time a highly efficient police state with the government exercising enormous power. A whole range of tactics from intimidation to persuasion could be used to secure votes for the '*sí*' option. Pinochet still enjoyed the undoubted support of the army, and the army governed Chile, especially at the regional level. Regional governors, provincial authorities and city mayors were expected to do their utmost to secure a majority for the government. Moreover, the government had virtually complete control of television, most radio stations and newspapers. The opposition was granted a fifteen-minute television 'spot' each day for three weeks before the vote, but that hardly offset fifteen years of sustained government propaganda. Chile was also enjoying an economic recovery, and pointed references were made to the political uncertainty and economic crises of neighbouring states.

Pinochet despised politicians and firmly believed that they were incapable of making a united and effective attack against his authority. There was evidence to the contrary, especially in February 1988, when the opposition signed a pact to organize the '*no*' vote in the plebiscite. But dictators tend to be told what it is expected they would like to hear, and Pinochet was no exception. The politicians of the Right were excluded from the campaign, which was firmly in the hands of a few top military advisers and Sergio Fernández. Even before the results were known, politicians of such parties as Renovación Nacional, the largest party of the

Right, were making it obvious that they felt the official campaign was poorly organized. The plebiscite was a fair and free choice, with massive participation. Of the potential electorate, some 93 per cent were registered to vote; and of the registered electorate of 7.4 million voters, 97 per cent voted. The result was 55 per cent for the '*no*' option and 43 per cent for the '*sí*', and 2 per cent null or void.

Many Chileans still felt excluded from the benefits of economic recovery. Income distribution remained grossly inequitable, and opposition claims that 5 million Chileans (40 per cent of the population) lived in poverty were not convincingly refuted by the government. Average wages in 1987 were 13 per cent less than in 1981 and still less than in 1970. Reduced expenditures on health and education were strong grievances amongst many Chileans. The privatized social security system provided excellent benefits for those who could afford to join. But more than 50 per cent of the population was excluded and had to endure an increasingly deficient state system. Such grievances help to explain support for the opposition. The government also suffered from its human rights record. Against expectations that this would be a minority preoccupation, the poll showed that a majority of the population was well aware of the widespread abuse of human rights and firmly condemned those abuses. Perhaps the strongest long-term factor working against the government, however, was the desire to resume democratic, competitive politics. This did not necessarily represent a rejection of the free-market economic model, or even of the main features of the 1980 constitution. It did, however, reflect popular support for a return to the predominant mode of political activity over the past hundred years in Chile. In the end, the plebiscite was not about the economy, but about politics – the freedom to choose and the right to vote. Even some admirers of General Pinochet felt that fifteen years had been enough and that it was time for him to step down.

The impact of the campaign itself was enormous, as was shown by the extraordinarily high level of participation. It was, after all, the first political campaign of this sort since 1973. There is little doubt that the government's negative and backward-looking campaign was inferior to that of the opposition. Pinochet was not a great success as a democratic politician seeking votes, and the efforts of his advisers to create such an image were often destroyed when Pinochet threw away his prepared speeches, recalled the crudest assaults on Communism and launched bitter attacks on former collaborators. Sweeping economic gestures to win support were ruled out by the very nature of the economic model he had constructed. An economy emphasizing fiscal restraint and sound management cannot suddenly make grand populist gestures without running the risk of undermining confidence.

By contrast, the opposition campaign was professional and forward looking, was aimed at youth and stressed reconciliation and political moderation. In February 1988, the opposition had at last reached an agreement to unite against the candidacy of Pinochet, and although the Communist Party was initially very hostile to playing the game by the general's rules and never officially formed part of the sixteen-party coalition, it lent important support. The opposition campaign would not have had the impact it had without months of careful political work persuading the electorate that the vote would be secret and that there would be no adverse consequences in voting '*no*'. The Church played an important role in this process with its Cruzada Cívica. Funding from the United States and Europe allowed the opposition parties to organize throughout the country and to count the vote with its own computer systems, thus minimizing the possibility of government fraud. A new 'instrumental' party created by Socialist leader Ricardo Lagos played an important role in bringing into political activity previously passive or independent citizens and focussed attention on the single issue of defeating the general. The presence of more than a thousand international observers was a support to the opposition and an indication to the government that the significance of the plebiscite was a matter of concern to the international community and not just to Chile.

Opposition politicians were surprised by the way in which powerful sectors of the Right immediately accepted the verdict. There was fear of a coup or some kind of interference with the voting or with the results. The Chilean armed forces, however, did not see the rejection of Pinochet as a rejection of the military as an institution, nor of the constitution of 1980, nor of the free-market economic model. Neither the armed forces nor the political Right, let alone the business sectors, would have welcomed the political violence that would inevitably have followed any attempt to interfere with the results of the plebiscite. Moreover, there remained more than a year before the presidential and congressional elections which had to be held following the rejection of Pinochet, and the Right expected in that period to build upon the 43 per cent vote gained by President Pinochet. For his part, Pinochet was determined to pass a series of laws that would make any future alteration of his constitution and economic model as difficult as possible.

From October 1988 until December 1989 Chile lived in a state of permanent electoral campaign. The opposition made few political errors. The man who had led the opposition in the plebiscite, former senator and PDC politician Patricio Aylwin, was chosen as its presidential candidate. Once chosen, Aylwin behaved with the confidence of a president-elect and assembled a political team of considerable experience and authority. Even the difficult task of selecting the candidates to represent the seventeen-party coalition, the Concertación de los Partidos por la Democracia, in the congressional electoral campaign was resolved without damaging public disputes. The Concertación was firm in its rejection of the Communist Party, which though it did present a few candidates in a separate coalition, in effect lent its support to Aylwin. The opposition also extracted two major concessions from Pinochet. In July 1990 a plebiscite approved major constitutional reforms which made further reform somewhat easier and also reduced the power of the military in the new post-Pinochet system. Just before the December elections, Pinochet accepted a formula which meant that the executive of the powerful Central Bank would be composed equally of representatives of the government and of the opposition, and not, as he originally wanted, members exclusively loyal to him.

By contrast, the campaign of the Right was disorganised and unimpressive. The chosen candidate, Hernan Buchi, who had been minister of finance since 1985, proved far less capable as a presidential candidate than as an economic technocrat. The two major parties of the Right, Renovación Nacional (RN), a moderate party which included politicians who had been active in right-wing politics before the coup, and the Unión Democrática Independiente (UDI), a combination of free-market technocrats and unconditional supporters of Pinochet, demonstrated much less unity than the opposition alliance, and it frequently appeared that they were more concerned with fighting each other than with opposing the coalition led by Aylwin.

President Pinochet kept aloof from the electoral campaign. Instead, his major concern was to press ahead with a series of measures that would reduce the power of the incoming government. The process of privatization of the econoomy, already well advanced, was accelerated. An electoral law was devised that at the congressional level would give substantial over-representation to the Right. An armed forces law was passed that would make presidential control over the military very difficult: the president, for example, would have no power to dismiss the commanders-in-chief of the various services. The composition of the Supreme Court was altered. A series of restrictions was imposed on the future Congress that would make it almost impossible to investigate the activities of the Pinochet government. The opposition protested against these measures, sometimes with success, as with the plebiscite on constitutional reform and with the composition of the executive of the Central Bank. But there was little doubt that the political agenda of the future government would be concerned largely with trying to amend the restrictions on its activities imposed by the government of Pinochet.

The results of the presidential election on 14 December 1989 resembles those of the October plebiscite. Aylwin won 55 per cent of the vote. The vote of the Right was divided between Buchi, who took 30 per cent, and a populist businessman, Francisco Javier Errázuriz, who gained 15 per cent. The results of the congressional elections gave a majority to the opposition alliance. However, although the Concertación won twenty-two seats in the Senate compared with sixteen for the Right, the presence of nine senators designated by the outgoing Pinochet government meant that the Aylwin government would lack the majority necessary for important measures of constitutional and political reform. In the election for the lower house the Concertación won seventy-two seats to the forty-eight of the Right. The most popular political party was clearly the PDC, which elected thirteen senators and thirty-eight deputies, followed within the opposition alliance by the PPD, which elected four senators and seventeen deputies. On the Right, RN did much better than the UDI, electing six senators to the two of the UDI; and most of the eight independent senators were close to RN.

The government of Patricio Aylwin, which took power in March 1990, faced a Chile that had changed in many respects since the 1973 coup. There was now much more agreement about economic policy: almost all parties accepted that the market and the private sector had a fundamental role in economic development. The former project of the Left to nationalize the commanding heights of the economy was now seen to be as irrelevant as the former PDC claim to establish a communitarian society. The Aylwin government promised to improve income distribution and to spend more on social services, but not at the expense of careful macroeconomic management. The ruthless policies of the Pinochet government had created a smaller and more efficient state apparatus, and there was little desire to inflate the role of the state to its previous dominant role in the economy. The incoming government wanted to maintain the successful export economy and welcomed the co-operation of foreign investment, even if it also intended to increase tax revenues.

This consensus in the field of economic policy was reflected more generally in attitudes towards the political system. There was widespread agreement about the need to make concessions in order to sustain a democratic system. On the Left, the popularity and influence of the Communist Party had been reduced by mistaken policies, by its toleration of political violence during the Pinochet years and by the crisis of international Communism. The Socialist Party, once more united, was more moderate than it had been in the past: the old sectarianism and admiration for the Cuban Revolution had disappeared. The PDC had abandoned its belief in the party as the natural governing party without allies and was more open to dialogue and negotiation than before. The political Right in Chile was not disturbed by the electoral results. It had the power to block reforms in Congress, and it had sufficient electoral backing to make it hopeful about future electoral victories. It was not alarmed by the government's economic policy.

The legacy of the Pinochet years had its harsh side as well. The problem of poverty was acute and challenging. Income distribution had worsened appreciably in Chile, and some 3 to 4 million Chileans were living in poverty. Moreover, many of the services that were necessary to alleviate poverty – health, education, social security – had been neglected by the Pinochet government and were badly underfunded. Sustaining economic growth and dealing with social inequality would be a challenge to governments for years to come.

One other legacy of the Pinochet government was the unresolved issue of justice for victims of human rights abuses. There is little doubt that human rights had been violated on a massive and unprecedented scale in Pinochet's Chile. Future governments would have to try to deal with those seeking redress and yet at the same time not provoke the military to withdraw its support from the democratic order. The fact that the commander-in-chief of the army under the Aylwin government remained General Pinochet indicated the nature of the problem the new government faced in trying to consolidate a fully democratic political system.

Yet the plebiscite of 1988 and the elections of 1989 were remarkable affirmations of popular desire to re-establish democracy in Chile. In both cases participation was massive, involving more than 90 percent of the registered electorate. Both elections were free and fair, neither produced significant political violence or conflict, and in the 1989 elections the vote for parties of the Left and Right that could be considered extreme or anti-democratic was insignificant. This popular affirmation of democracy gave a firm base for future governments to consolidate a stable constitutional order. The responsibility of the political parties was to design a democratic political system which did not repeat the errors that led to the overthrow of the constitutional order in 1973.

Part Three

PERU AND BOLIVIA

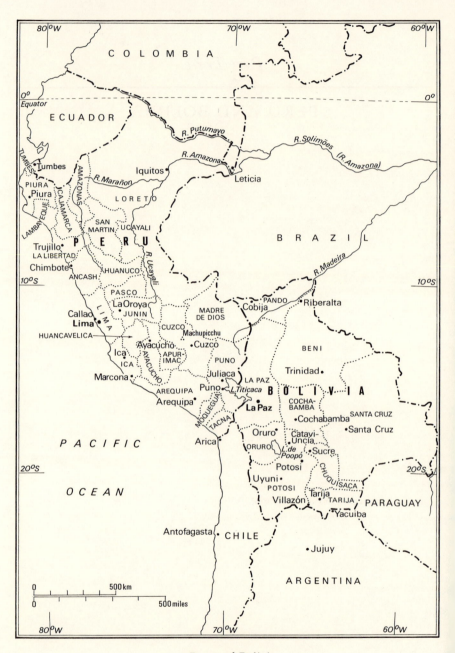

Peru and Bolivia

7

PERU, 1930–60

During the period from 1890 to 1930 Peru had been characterized by an export-led economy, a strong oligarchy-dominated state known as the Aristocratic Republic, and a hierarchical social order with strong roots in agrarian institutions – the hacienda in the Sierra and the plantation on the Coast. After 1960 the country entered into a crisis of political hegemony (with the military playing an increasingly important role), a belated quest for industrialization and economic autonomy, and a struggle to come to terms with the breakdown of the old mechanisms of social control, manifest in the collapse of the hacienda and the emergence of a political Left. The thirty years from 1930 to 1960 were a period of transition, with a ramshackle ancien regime surviving almost by default as the country drifted with the tides of history. Economic development was dominated by spurts of activity within the old framework of laissez-faire export-led growth. In contrast to several other Latin American countries, Peru undertook no new departures such as a deliberate shift to protected industrialization or an attempt to construct state capitalism. The social and economic predominance of the country's established ruling class (commonly described as the 'oligarchy' or 'grand bourgeoisie') was not challenged or even much diluted by any rising new national bourgeoisie. Equally, no organized challenge to oligarchic hegemony was mounted by the working class (still weak and divided, and with most of its leadership co-opted into the status quo), or by the peasantry (whose concerns remained focussed at the local level, in a successful struggle with the hacienda and a debilitating process of intra-class division), or by the middle class (although the professional stratum occasionally stumbled onto the political stage, more by accident than by design).

Politics after 1930 remained faction-ridden and personalist. Very few politicians or statesmen of major stature emerged. The most notable individuals were Víctor Raúl Haya de la Torre and Fernando Belaúnde Terry, neither of whom achieved the presidency during this period. Since no social class had a clear political project to promote against the status quo, the struggle for control of the state apparatus was reduced to a struggle for shares in the spoils of export-led growth and foreign borrowing. The only major political party to survive throughout the thirty years – Haya's Alianza Popular Revolucionaria Americana (APRA), founded in 1924 – was conspicuously and consistently unsuccessful either in winning majority electoral support or in mounting any serious armed challenge to the state. In fact, the party's leaders generally pursued a course which seemed calculated to keep them permanently involved in national politics but never in command of them.

It was military intervention, not civilian politics, which produced the two most stable and effective administrations of the period: those of President Oscar Benavides (1933–9) and, after the post-war democratic interlude, President Manuel A. Odría (1948–56). Both could be described as authoritarian modernizers, seeking to defuse social problems by economic growth and some judicious social engineering, while using repression to maintain stability in the short run. Both clearly felt themselves to be acting in the best interests of the civilian ruling class, but both fell foul of factional feuding within that class. Indeed, given the political weakness of other social groups, the oligarchy's internal squabbles set the tone for political life.

Of the two main political factions within the oligarchy, that headed by the Prado family succeeded in capturing the presidency by electoral means on two occasions (in 1939 and 1956), and on each occasion Manuel Prado occupied the presidency for a full six-year term. The distinguishing feature of Prado's politics was a relatively conciliatory stance towards APRA, to whose support (covert or explicit) he owed his electoral successes. The other main faction of the oligarchy, which can be described as the Right, was distinguished both by unrelenting hostility towards APRA and by its inability to secure an electoral majority except in the extraordinary circumstances of 1931 (with Luis M. Sánchez Cerro as the candidate). The Right's other major political success during this period was the coup of 1948, in which General Odría seized power.

Although the full fruits were not to be seen until after 1960, major economic and social forces were at work during the middle three decades of the twentieth century. Two trends in particular stand out: the post-depression recovery of export-led growth and the emergence of large-scale

unemployment and under-employment. In 1930 Peru had a severely depressed export economy but very little open unemployment; in 1960 the
country was at the peak of an export-led growth boom with a huge reserve
army of labour. Thus, the long-term cyclical upswing from depression to
prosperity (in response to forces at work in the world economy) was
accompanied by a transition from labour scarcity to labour surplus, symptomatic of the internal dynamics of Peru's response to capitalist development and population growth. These two trends, which are discussed in
more detail later, respectively strengthened and weakened the position of
the country's ruling class. The recovery of the dependent export economy
facilitated political and economic stabilization on the oligarchy's terms,
but at the same time the emergence of powerful mass interests, which had
to be appeased or repressed, posed a problem for oligarchic hegemony.

ECONOMY AND SOCIETY

The Peruvian economy has been heavily dependent on export performance
throughout the twentieth century. During periods of export-led growth
from 1890 to around 1924, and from 1949 to 1963, the Peruvian owners
of the means of production in the export sectors, together with the top
strata of the commercial, professional and financial systems, formed an
effective ruling class with a strong hold over the broad outlines of national
government policy. Stability and conservatism were the keynotes of political life. Economic policy consisted of free trade and 'sound finance'; social
policy revolved around the defence of vested interests and resistance to
reforms; political life was dominated by factional squabbles within the
ruling class, while challenges to their hegemony were relatively easily
neutralized by co-option and paternalism. During the periods of crisis in
the export economy, from 1925 to 1948 and from 1963 to the 1980s,
competition for shares in the slowly growing economic cake was more
difficult to defuse, and the problems of economic and social management
were more severe. These were periods of relative political instability,
characterized by a weakening of the ruling class's control over policy
formation and by the emergence of social forces which were kept in check
during the growth phases. The period covered by this chapter spans an
entire cycle of collapse and upswing in the export economy.

Despite considerable short-run fluctuations, Peru experienced a virtual
stagnation of the volume of exports from the outset of the world depression in 1930 until the late 1940s. The value of total exports in U.S.

dollars fell by 68 per cent between 1929 and 1932 and recovered to the 1929 level again only in 1946, before falling again during the economic crisis of 1947–8.[1] This stagnation of total export earnings, however, masked a major shift from foreign to local control. In 1930, 60 per cent of exports by value were produced by large foreign firms, which took most of their profits out of the country. By the end of the 1940s, the share of these foreign firms had dropped to 30 per cent of export sales and their place had been taken by expanding, locally controlled sectors – especially medium-scale lead and zinc mining, sugar, fishmeal and cotton. The expansion of locally controlled export enterprises did not result from take-overs of foreign-controlled activities; rather, foreign-controlled enterprises declined while Peruvian enterprises expanded. Thus, although there was virtually no rise in aggregate export revenues over the twenty years after 1929, there were gains for local capitalists and some growth in the economy's net foreign-exchange income as the proportion of total export earnings lost through repatriated profits fell. As a result, the upper echelon of agricultural and financial capitalists retained their long-standing belief in the viability of the export-led open economy. They continued to invest in export-oriented ventures and set their faces against a switch to a strategy of inward-directed growth. Consequently, there was no basis for an alliance between the grand bourgeoisie and small industrial capitalists to put new economic policies into effect.[2]

If the crisis of the export economy after 1929 was less acute in Peru than in several other Latin American economies, so also the strength of export-led growth after 1949 was spectacular by continental standards. Between 1950 and 1960, export volume trebled and the dollar value of exports more than doubled. Real growth of GNP was 65 per cent over the decade – an annual average growth rate of more than 5 per cent. The balance-of-payments impact of the rapid growth of export earnings was supplemented by a strong inflow of foreign investment. From 30 per cent in 1950, the share of Peru's exports produced by foreign firms rose again to 45 per cent by 1960 and continued to rise thereafter.[3]

Not all Peruvians shared in the bonanza of the 1950s. Approximately one-quarter of the total population, at the bottom of the Sierra rural economy, experienced stagnant or worsening standards of living, and overall

[1] R. Thorp and G. Bertram, *Peru, 1890–1977: Growth and Policy in an Open Economy* (London, 1978).
[2] For a contrary view, see B. Caravedo Molinari, *Burguesía e industria en el Perú, 1933–1945* (Lima, 1976), chaps. 1 and 2.
[3] Thorp and Bertram, *Peru 1890–1977*, p. 295.

income inequality increased sharply.[4] The boom, however, provided urban workers and the middle class with enough material benefits to forestall any major radicalization of national politics. The relative impoverishment of Sierra agriculture in this period produced not a political movement, but a process of massive social mobilization – first in the form of large-scale rural–urban migration and subsequently (in the late 1950s and early 1960s) in a series of land occupations and confrontations between peasants and police, which heralded the end of the era of the hacienda in the Peruvian Sierra.

Industrial development came late to Peru, having been stifled after a promising beginning in the 1890s. In the 1950s, however, the effects of rapid export expansion, combined with the emergence of a mass urban market in Lima, set off a new growth phase. The share of manufacturing in GNP rose from 14 per cent in 1950 to 17 per cent by 1960, making it the most rapidly growing sector of the national economy; and by the second half of the 1950s import substitution had become the focus of industrial growth – a process which developed spontaneously rather than as a result of any deliberate government policy. Between 1950 and 1960 the share of consumer goods in total imports dropped from 24 to 22 per cent while capital goods moved up from 20 to 22 per cent. The proportion of the local market for manufactures supplied from Peruvian factories (which had briefly been as high as 77 per cent in 1945 under the pressure of wartime restrictions and exchange control) hit a low of 59 per cent in 1952 and rose through the later 1950s to reach 65–70 per cent by the early 1960s.[5] These figures indicate a definite swing from the mid-1950s towards import substitution, although the process in Peru was limited by the standards of other Latin American economies at that time. The surge of new investment in manufacturing industry altered the economic base of the established oligarchy and opened the way to a new generation of industrial capitalists whose influence was to be felt in succeeding decades.

In 1930 the population of Peru was between 5 and 6 million, of which two-thirds was concentrated in the Andean Sierra and less than one-

[4] R. C. Webb, *The Distribution of Income in Peru*, Princeton University, Woodrow Wilson School Research Program in Economic Development, Discussion Paper no. 26 (Princton, N.J., 1972); idem, *Trends in Real Income in Peru*, Princeton University, Woodrow Wilson School Research Program in Economic Development, Discussion Paper no. 41 (Princeton, N.J., 1974); R. Vandendries, 'Income Distribution in Peru after World War II', *Journal of Developing Areas*, 8, no. 3 (1974), pp. 421–36; Thorp and Bertram, *Peru, 1890–1977*, pp. 275–8.
[5] Thorp and Bertram, *Peru, 1890–1977*, pp. 261–74.; I. G. Bertram, *End-Use Classification of Peruvian Imports, 1891–1972*, Microfiche St Antony's College Latin American Centre (Oxford, 1976), table 6.5; Thorp and Bertram, *Peru, 1890–1977*, p. 407.

quarter on the Coast. By 1960 the population had grown to more than 10 million, with just over half in the Sierra and 40 per cent on the Coast, the increased concentration of population on the Coast reflecting the strongly regional character of capitalist economic growth. The Andean Sierra constituted the traditional heartland of Peru. But it was the arid plain of the Coast, crossed by fertile river valleys and containing the three major cities of Lima, Trujillo and Arequipa, which was the setting for most of the economic growth of the twentieth century. Of the economy's leading sectors during the period from 1930 to 1960 – cotton, sugar, mining, oil, fishmeal, urban services and manufacturing – only mining had a strong presence in the Sierra, especially in the central part of the country. But the mining camps, for all their local economic impact, functioned more as enclave extensions of the coastal economy than as integral parts of the Sierra economy.

Events in the Sierra during the middle decades of the twentieth century were dominated by the changing demographic balance, the failure of attempts at the capitalist modernization of Sierra agriculture and a change in the relationship of the Sierra with the developing capitalist economy of the Coast and the mining camps. This last change has been characterized as a switch from 'functional dualism' to 'disfunctional dualism', involving an increasing separation of the Sierra economy from the country's growth poles, as a permanent proletariat replaced temporary migrant workers in the mining camps of the central Sierra by about 1945 and similar changes occurred on the plantations of the Coast.[6]

The Sierra's demographic history from the sixteenth to the twentieth centuries is one of recovery from catastrophe. War, social dislocation and disease at the time of the Spanish Conquest had dramatically reduced the population and left Peru a land-abundant and labour-scarce society until population densities in the Sierra returned to something approaching their fifteenth-century levels. Thereafter, continued population growth implied growing strain on limited land resources (in the absence of major technological advances in agriculture) and the emergence of surplus la-

[6] C. F. Oman, 'The Formation of Capitalist Society in Peru: "Dualism" and Underdevelopment' (Ph.D. dissertation, University of California, Berkeley, 1978), chaps. 11 and 12; see also A. DeWind, 'Peasants Become Miners: The Evolution of Industrial Mining Systems in Peru' (Ph.D. dissertation, Columbia University, 1977). F. E. Mallon *The Defense of Community in Peru's Central Highlands: Peasant Struggle and Capitalist Transition, 1860–1940* (Princeton, N.J., 1983), chap. 7, dates the key changes somewhat earlier, noting that the *enganche* labour recruitment for the mines ended with the 1920s and that following lay-offs during the depression the Cerro de Pasco Corporation operated in a buyers' market for wage labour.

bour. This turning-point was reached during the first half of the twentieth century, with dramatic effects on the national labour market by the 1950s.

The transition from labour scarcity to labour surplus was clearly visible in the experience of the modern sector of the economy. For any large-scale enterprise launched in Peru during the nineteenth century the mobilization of a labour force had been a crucial problem. To extract guano, grow sugar and cotton, build railways or operate mines, employers were obliged to resort to non-local sources of labour (negro slaves, Chilean *rotos*, Chinese coolies) until the 1880s. Thereafter for several decades it became gradually easier to recruit temporary migrant labour from among the Sierra peasantry by means of debt peonage (*enganche*) or the manipulation of the traditional service-tenure institutions of the haciendas.

However, a continued expansion of labour supply from the turn of the century permitted the development of fully capitalist relations of wage labour over a widening range of economic activity. By 1930 a settled proletariat had emerged in the plantations and cities of the Coast, although the Coast itself was not yet an area of labour surplus. Cotton and sugar production remained dependent on the availability of seasonal migrant workers from the Sierra, and in Lima migrants (who were predominantly from the Coast, not the Sierra, at that time)[7] had no difficulty finding employment during the 1920s. The depression brought only moderate open unemployment to the Peruvian economy; most workers laid off from factories and mines simply disappeared back into the ranks of the peasantry or the casual self-employed. As usual in a largely pre-capitalist economy, the impact of the depression was felt in intensified poverty rather than open unemployment. The 1931 census of Lima reported that 37,089 males, or one-quarter of all males aged fifteen to sixty-nine in Lima, were unemployed; but only 19,000 of these were registered, the remainder having resorted to casual self-employment in the informal economy.[8] By the 1950s, however, the picture was transformed. A flood of migrants from the Sierra was pressing into the coastal cities, permanent wage labour was displacing seasonal migrants from most of their previous employment opportunities on the plantations and the old problem of labour recruitment had given way to the problems of

---

[7] S. Stein, *Populism in Peru* (Madison, Wisc., 1980), chap. 3, suggests that between a quarter and a third of migrant workers in Lima in 1931 were from the Sierra. A further third or so were from the (mainly coastal) Far South.

[8] Census of Lima, 1931 (Junto Pro-Desocupados de Lima, n.d., pp. 248–9).

housing and feeding the new reserve army of labour in the barriadas of the coastal cities.

While population growth provides the basic explanation for the transition from labour scarcity to surplus at the national level, the timing and nature of this transition were rooted in the evolving social structure of the Sierra. Through much of the nineteenth century the Sierra had been economically irrelevant to the guano-based export economy, and haciendas had been in a state of decay, which permitted de facto occupation of much of their land by the peasantry (both the collectively structured Indian communities and the nominal tenants of the haciendas). The subsistence peasantry was thus well endowed with resources and consequently unavailable for employment elsewhere in the economy. During the last two decades of the nineteenth century (following the collapse of guano), the Sierra recovered to play a central role in national economic life. Railways connected the central and southern Sierra with external markets for wool, hides and foodstuffs; the revival of gold, silver and copper mining brought a strong demand for pack animals, timber and food; and the new cocaine industry brought profits to coca growers in La Libertad. Agricultural and livestock production had abruptly become more profitable, and the result was a revival and expansion of the hacienda as the dominant institution in Sierra society, laying claim to land long occupied by the peasantry and reimposing labour obligations on the hacienda tenants. This rise of the commercial economy and of the hacienda proceeded for some forty years, from 1880 to about 1920, and was reflected in the degree to which Sierra landowning interests shared in political power at the national level during the Aristocratic Republic (1895–1919).

If the spur of profit had brought the hacienda back to life, the same applied to the Sierra peasantry. 'Indian' herders found themselves able to sell their wool and other products through newly established merchant buyers in the Centre and South, while throughout the Sierra the owners of mules and llamas found their services in steady demand for transport purposes. At the same time imported consumer goods became more freely available in the Sierra, strengthening the incentives towards monetization of the peasant economy and threatening local artisan production. Peasant groups were increasingly embroiled both in conflicts with the haciendas over access to land and in competition among themselves. This has been identified as the period when the 'Indian community' began to dissolve into a privatized, internally differentiated peasantry, and this change (accompanied as it was by the emergence of individual indebtedness and impoverishment in place of communally shared burdens) was a key factor in the opening up of the national labour market around the turn of the century.[9]

In the first two decades of the twentieth century, parts of the Sierra ceased to have spare land available to support further extensive expansion of livestock and crop production. Indigenous communities could no longer endow all their members with adequate subsistence plots, and haciendas could not expand further without triggering off peasant revolts on a scale which threatened to disrupt the fabric of society. At this stage many large landowners tried to intensify their operations by modernizing their properties; but this movement towards enclosures and investment was successfully opposed by the peasantry, aided by merchants whose profits were derived from the peasant economy. The strength of peasant opposition to encroachment and enclosures made it impossible to switch to capitalist relations or to invest heavily in improvements to raise productivity.

The struggle over hacienda expansion, enclosures and peasant opposition to capitalist modernization peaked in a wave of revolts in the early 1920s and inspired the ideology of *indigenismo* among coastal intellectuals. This was a romantic vision of the *comunidad* as a collective institution, which would be 'liberated' by the elimination of feudal relations of production in the haciendas. Politically the main fruits were two early measures during the *oncenio* of Augusto B. Leguía (1919–1930): provisions in the 1920 constitution which recognized the *comunidad* as a legal entity and protected its lands from alienation; and the establishment in 1922 of the Patronato de la Raza Indígena to provide an institutional channel for the expression of Indian grievances. The 'Indian question' remained politically sensitive until the end of the 1920s, when both Haya de la Torre's APRA and José Carlos Mariátegui's fledgling Partido Comunista produced programmatic statements in favour of agrarian reform and the 'redemption' of the Indian.

By 1930, however, the tide had turned. The hacienda as an institution had passed its peak, and the following half-century was to witness its decline throughout Peru, as the balance of class power in the Sierra shifted decisively from *hacendados* to peasantry. Only a very few large landowners in the central and southern Sierra persisted with the attempt to modernize livestock production. In the northern Sierra, where social tensions were

---

[9] Oman, 'The Formation of Capitalist Society', pp. 248–50; Mallon, *The Defence of Community*, pp. 144–64.

less formidable, there was a greater push towards the modernization of livestock haciendas in the 1930s and 1950s, but even there the writing was on the wall by the 1960s. In both livestock and agricultural production, furthermore, the incentive to modernize haciendas was steadily eroded by the national government's determination to maintain social peace in Lima by keeping down the prices of foodstuffs. Between 1920 and 1970 the rural—urban terms of trade moved dramatically against farm products, except for a brief recovery in 1943–7 (a recovery which, significantly, coincided with the emergence of peasant unions in the central Sierra).[10]

As large landowners' interest in achieving capitalist transformation in the Sierra faded, so did the political visibility of the Sierra and the agrarian problem. After Leguía's 1922 Patronato law it was to be forty years before the next major law concerning Sierra society was passed – the 1962 agrarian reform for La Convención. In national terms, the Sierra was a sideshow between 1930 and 1960, with its politics focussed inwards on local issues and its problems largely ignored by coastal politicians. In so far as debates on the 'Indian question' continued in Lima, they were confined to stereotypes established in the 1920s; and the participation of the Sierra population in national politics became reduced very largely to visits by village deputations to congressmen, seeking redress on specific issues.

The expanding road network constructed in the 1920s and 1930s facilitated temporary migration to the Coast for those in pursuit of employment and provided peasants as well as haciendas with improved access to coastal markets for their products; but these benefits were offset by the increased penetration of Sierra rural markets by coastal products, the worsening rural—urban terms of trade and the growing difficulty of obtaining seasonal employment on the Coast as the labour shortage came to an end. Meanwhile, the internal fragmentation of the *comunidad* proceeded, with income and wealth becoming steadily more inequitable in their distribution. Few communities succeeded in becoming affluent; in most, the better-off members became exploiters of their fellows (both through their activities as small merchants and truckers and as the main local employers of labour), without becoming a class of progressive small capitalist farmers. Cash earnings came less from agricultural activity than from labour migration. However, by the 1940s the era of national labour shortage had ended, and the leading sectors of the coastal capitalist economy were switching from the use of unskilled

<hr>

[10] Thorp and Bertram, *Peru, 1890–1977*, fig. 13.1.

temporary labour towards the employment of permanent skilled workers. Growing competition for work made it increasingly difficult for Sierra peasants to supplement their income by short-term migration, and a large number of them began to opt for longer-term migration to the coastal cities, in the hope of acquiring skills and higher-paid employment.

At the same time there was some revival of agrarian activism, stimulated not so much by a clash between rising peasant aspirations and the expanding hacienda (as had produced the conflagrations of the 1910s and 1920s) as by the steady relative impoverishment of a large part of the Sierra peasantry. (This is not to say that rising aspirations, especially of successful individuals within the peasantry, were altogether absent from the new activism.) The movements began with the formation of peasant unions on many haciendas in the central Sierra during the administrations of Manuel Prado (1939–45) and José Luis Bustamante (1945–8), were suppressed during the regime of Manuel Odría (1948–56), when rural–urban migration was the only outlet for the social pressures in the Sierra, and reappeared in a wave of strikes and land occupations at the end of the 1950s and in the early 1960s. Only one of the movements of the late 1950s – the celebrated La Convención tenants' unions – arising from the increased economic strength of both peasantry and haciendas in a booming coffee-growing region, reproduced the pattern of the revolts of the 1920s. The others resulted from the growing weaknesses of both components of rural society – unprofitable haciendas, willingly abandoned to their fate by a national elite which saw the Sierra as an irrelevance; and the economically deprived peasants faced with worsening terms of trade for both their products and their labour as population growth put inexorable pressure on the stagnant productive base. That the peasantry carried the day is a tribute not to its strength, but to the weakness of the hacienda. Long before the haciendas of the Sierra were parcelled out or expropriated in the 1960s and 1970s, the real social problem in the Sierra had ceased to be the hacienda–community division and had become the internal inequalities and divisions among the peasants themselves.

The failing economic fortunes of the Sierra had their political counterpart. Nineteenth-century civil wars had been decided, to a great extent, in the Sierra by armies made up of peasant recruits; the last such occasion was the conflict which brought Nicolás de Piérola to power in 1895. The subsequent 'Aristocratic Republic' had established the hold of the coastal elite over the presidency, but left the dignitaries (*gamonales*) of the Sierra with substantial political influence through the Congress, in which Sierra electorates controlled by the ruling groups had a clear majority of seats. The last generation of Sierra caudillos – Cáceres, Durand, Piérola – were still alive and politically active until the 1920s, but as that generation vanished and as Leguía's centralism took its toll on the regions, the ability of ruling groups in the Sierra to influence national policy declined. (The short-lived interim presidency of David Sámanez Ocampo in 1930–1 was the last time a Sierra-based political figure held the presidency.) The coherence of these ruling groups declined after 1930, as key members of provincial elite families moved down to the coastal cities to further their careers and education.

The declining importance of the Sierra was encouraged by the political stance of the ostensible parties of reform – APRA and the Partido Comunista. Although both included *indígenista* planks in their programmes, neither saw the mobilization of the Sierra peasantry as part of its political strategy. The Communists, once Mariátegui's influence had been removed, concentrated almost exclusively on organizing urban and mining workers, although the party became accidentally involved with the peasant movement in La Convención at the end of the 1950s. APRA focussed its attention on the lower middle class and organized labour, especially in Lima and on the northern coast; the party's involvement in the Sierra was restricted to individual proselytizing by *aprista* lawyers and schoolteachers, which certainly contributed to local mobilization of peasant communities and made possible some successful individual careers in Congress, but did not make the peasantry a national foundation of APRA strength. This organizational vacuum was exploited in the 1962 and 1963 campaigns of Fernando Belaúnde, the first presidential aspirant after Sánchez Cerro in 1931 to take seriously the benefits of campaigning in Sierra villages.

The rise of the Coast was the counterpart of the Sierra's decline. Dominating the evolution of coastal society during the period 1930–60 was the rapid growth of the cities. Between 1940 and 1961 the proportion of Peru's population living in cities of more than 2,500 rose from 18 to 39 per cent. Lima alone went from half a million inhabitants to more than 2 million. Lima's rapid expansion, especially during the 1950s, meant a corresponding increase in the demand for products and services meeting urban needs – especially housing, transport, manufactured consumer goods, administration and education. In turn, the social and political weight of industrial workers and white-collar middle-class professionals rose, with APRA providing the main political vehicle for the first and Acción Popular (AP) for the second by the late 1950s.

In contrast to the Sierra, where rural society was locked in a defensive struggle against capitalist transformation, coastal agriculture exhibited strong trends towards commercialization. Major irrigation projects contributed to a 66 per cent increase in the cultivated area on the Coast between 1929 and 1961, despite the loss of agricultural land as the cities spread.[11] Much of this increase was in the rice-growing North, where improved irrigation and the impetus from growing urban demand brought prosperity in the 1950s. Within coastal agriculture, there was a clear evolutionary divergence between the sugar plantations and the rest. In the growing and milling of sugar, economies of scale combined with the emerging labour surplus from 1930, and the periodic repression of APRA and its unions enabled a fully capitalist mode of production to become consolidated in the form of huge 'agro-industrial complexes' with permanent wage labour. In cotton and rice growing areas, systems of share tenancy (*yanaconaje*) remained the norm through the 1930s and 1940s. Some landowners managed to evict tenants and move to direct cultivation with wage labour; this process encountered strong opposition from tenants, organized by APRA and (in the Far North) the Partido Socialista. Long, and eventually successful, campaigns were organized by tenants seeking written contracts, security of tenure and the transformation of rentals from labour service or crop shares to straightforward cash rentals. A milestone in this struggle was the 1947 Ley de Yanaconaje, pushed through Congress by APRA during the Bustamante regime. The non-sugar-producing large properties of the Coast thus served as a seed-bed for a class of small rural capitalists as landowner control over the means of production was weakened; the agrarian reforms of 1964 and 1969 were later to transfer formal ownership of substantial areas of coastal non-sugar-growing lands to the former tenants, while leaving the large sugar plantations intact as producing units.

Export sectors led the growth of the Peruvian economy throughout the period 1930–60. Until fishmeal processing plants began to proliferate in Callao at the end of the 1950s, all export production was located outside the main cities, although the provincial cities of the Coast had their fortunes clearly linked to production of regional staples: Trujillo with sugar, Ica and Piura with cotton, Chimbote with fishmeal, Arequipa with wool. Lima's pre-eminence, based on its role as the country's financial and

[11] Ibid., table 12.1.

administrative centre, was already established by 1930 and had been
greatly strengthened by centralist policies under Leguía in the 1920s. The
explosive growth of Lima as a mass market, however, started in the late
1930s and was stimulated by the subsidization of urban living standards
during the 1940s by the Prado and Bustamante regimes, both of which
used exchange-rate policy and price controls to hold down food prices.
Government patronage of the urban lower class continued under Odría in
the 1950s as *barriadas* began to spread out from the old centre of the
capital, with infrastructural support provided by governmental housing
and public works programmes.

The combination of rising government spending and centralized accumulation of export sector profits through the banking system provided the
driving force for Lima's growth until the 1950s. During that decade,
manufacturing development began to gain momentum, and with most of
the new manufacturing activity located in Lima, the city began to be less
parasitic on the national economy than hitherto.

SOCIETY AND POLITICS

The existence of a clearly defined upper class of large capitalists and
rentiers – the 'oligarchy' – is widely accepted in the literature on republican Peruvian society and politics. In so far as this group constituted a
ruling class, its political power, as we have seen, was not altogether
secure, and rested crucially on the success of export-led growth. The
hegemony of the oligarchy was sustained through most of the period
1930–60, but not without difficulty.

In the 1930s the main challenge to the oligarchy's position came from
the combination of economic crisis and the emergence of political mass
movements such as APRA and Unión Revolucionaria. In the 1940s the
rise of a strong middle-class–professional political movement headed by
Arequipa interests fortified opposition to the oligarchy; and in the 1950s
came the steady spread of a modernizing ideology among the military,
which made the armed forces both less willing to underwrite ruling-class
priorities and increasingly committed to reformist ideas. By the time of
the 1962 elections these three elements of challenge to the ancien
regime – embodied in APRA, Acción Popular and the army – had moved
to the centre of Peruvian political life.

Many Latin American ruling classes exhibited political divisions, but
these were commonly institutionalized in a two-way balance between

established political parties — Liberals versus Conservatives, for example, in Colombia and Ecuador. In Peru, the lines of division were too fluid and complex to result in a stable party system. Once internal tensions had torn apart and destroyed the old Partido Civilista, it proved impossible to consolidate any durable new political vehicle controlled by and sympathetic to the oligarchy's interests. In contrast, political parties linked to organized labour (APRA and the Partido Comunista) became firmly established during and after the depression, and middle-class parties such as Acción Popular finally took root in the 1950s. To some extent, the consistently conservative stance of the Church throughout this period reduced the need for any separate ruling-class ideology or party; but the Church's influence in Peruvian politics was not as strong as in some other South American countries.

The nature of the divisions within the old Peruvian ruling class remains the subject of research and debate. One suggestion has been that there was a conflict of interest between coastal and Sierra elites, arising from the contrast between rapid capitalist development on the Coast and slow growth in the Sierra.[12] Leguía's strong anti-feudal rhetoric of the 1920s is then explicable in terms of an alleged desire of coastal capitalists to enforce the modernization of the backward, feudal Sierra, against the wishes of the Sierra elite, in order to shake labour out of traditional agriculture and widen the domestic market.

While it would be rash to dismiss the idea of such a conflict, the available evidence does not support the view that the attitudes of landowners were primarily to blame for the Sierra's economic backwardness. On the contrary, among the large landowners of the Sierra were to be found several of the most prominent and successful of the coastal capitalist elite, and if any group stood in the way of 'modernization' in the region it was the peasantry rather than the *latifundistas*. Furthermore, Coast–Sierra divisions within the ruling class, in so far as they existed, do not contribute much to an understanding of national politics during the period 1930–60. Members of the Sierra elite who failed to establish firm footholds on the Coast or in mining by the 1930s were effectively excluded from the national ruling class in both political and economic terms. If there was any regionally determined conflict of interest with major repercussions at the national level, it was the division between southern Peru and the rest, discussed more fully later in the chapter.

[12] Oman, 'The Formation of Capitalist Society', 214–15.

Other studies have claimed that over time a 'national bourgeois' element emerged within the ruling class, supporting industrialization and protectionism and producing thereby a split between industrialists and agro-exporters.[13] Although the growth of investment in manufacturing from the mid-1950s provides a grain of truth to such an interpretation of the 1960s, attempts to document the existence of a national bourgeois fraction in earlier periods have been unconvincing. Certainly, successful entrepreneurs from humble origins, including one or two industrialists, were recruited into the oligarchy's ranks; but it does not appear that they formed any sort of separate group. When established oligarchic families invested in manufacturing, those investments were never more than peripheral to their basic interests until the late 1950s, when changing economic opportunities brought a surge of oligarchic interest in industry.

It is nevertheless interesting and significant that part of the Peruvian ruling class sought to identify themselves as a rising 'industrial' class opposed to the landed interest. In the 1920s, President Leguía distinguished himself by a rhetorical commitment to the ideal of bourgeois revolution: '*Leguiismo* . . . is Peru's reaction against the feudal classes, . . . it is the seizure by the bourgeoisie of the posts formerly held by privilege'.[14] This was language typical of the oligarchy's factional feuding not only during the Aristocratic Republic and *oncenio* but also through the 1930s, 1940s and 1950s. In interpreting such statements, it is important not to confuse this self-declared 'bourgeoisie' with an industrial class, in the sense of a class committed to manufacturing. The distinction in practice lay between urban mercantile capital and export producers in the agricultural and mining sectors of the economy. A study of the histories of three oligarchic families with clearly specialized interests has documented the differences between urban financiers such as the Prados and agro-exporters such as the Aspíllagas.[15] Part of the ruling class had its primary base in urban finance, commerce, utilities and other services and liked to define itself by attacking as 'feudal' other groups whose base was in the production of agricultural

[13] See, e.g., W. Bollinger, 'The Bourgeois Revolution in Peru: A Conception of Peruvian History', *Latin American Perspectives*, 4, no. 3 (1977), pp. 18–56; A. Ferner, 'The Dominant Class and Industrial Development in Peru', *Journal of Development Studies*, 15, no. 4 (1979), pp. 268–88; Caravedo, *Burguesía e industria*.

[14] Cited in G. R. Garrett, 'The Oncenio of Augusto B. Leguía: Middle Sector Government and Leadership in Peru' (Ph.D. dissertation, University of New Mexico, 1973), p. 84. Leguía's anti-feudal speeches bear strong similarities to some passages of J. C. Mariátegui's *Siete ensay sobre la realidad peruana* (Lima, 1928).

[15] D. Gilbert, *The Oligarchy and the Old Regime in Peru*, Cornell University, Latin American Studies Program Dissertation Series no. 69 (Ithaca, N.Y., 1977).

commodities for export or the control of large properties in the Sierra. Some of the landed segment of the ruling class reciprocated by claiming aristocratic superiority over the interests of urban trade. Each group would happily denounce its rivals as 'the oligarchy'.

In practice, business alliances spanned the urban–rural and mercantile–productive divides, and the distinction between these two fractions of the oligarchy was always blurred. Many leading families spread their interests across export production, commerce, finance, the professions and (when circumstances were favourable) manufacturing enterprise. Chameleon-like, they could choose to be seen as aristocrats, bourgeoisie, members of the 'middle class', or *gamonales*. (Leguía, who rose through trade to become involved in sugar, insurance, banking, mining and politics, epitomized this ambiguity.)

There was nevertheless a tendency for the ruling class to divide along broad rural–urban (or mercantile–productive) lines over certain major issues of economic policy, although the composition of the contending factions changed over time. One key economic issue dividing the country's economic elite during the period was the exchange rate of the sol. Bankers and importers opposed devaluation and profited from exchange crises; export producers pressed for early devaluation when export markets fell. The oligarchy divided on these lines in 1931–2, 1942–7, 1952–4 and 1957–8 (as they had previously in 1897 and would again in 1966–7); on all four occasions the anti-devaluation lobby was in command at the start of the balance-of-payments crisis, and the pro-devaluation lobby at the end.

The question of whether to appease or confront organized labour raised a similar conflict of interest between that section of the ruling class which was in a position to pass on rising wage costs (finance, trade, urban services) and that which was not (especially direct export producers). The urban-based Prado family led a faction which was committed to reaching an accommodation with the APRA-controlled segment of the labour force (and the electorate), while agro-exporters tended to support harder-line regimes such as those of Sánchez Cerro and Odría. On neither this nor the devaluation issue, however, were the lines of intra-class division clear or permanent. Disputes over these matters resulted in disunity, but not in a sufficient polarization of views and interests to produce established political parties.

Although no new 'national bourgeoisie' arose to challenge the grand bourgeois elite, there was a large and growing stratum of people in Peru with professional, managerial and commercial interests. These interests took political shape most clearly in the provinces, where they were influential in local politics. Their political stronghold was the southern city of Arequipa, and their potential electoral strength at the national level was indicated by Fernando Belaúnde's strong bid in the 1956 presidential election.

The southern region, dominated by Arequipa, had a long history of separatism within republican Peru, and the regional upper class retained in the twentieth century a distinctive identity. Arequipa's opposition to political and economic centralization led naturally to a 'constitutionalist' position in the 1930s and the subsequent adoption of Christian-democratic ideologies in the 1940s and 1950s. Lawyers and the Church had a strong influence on Arequipa politics, and as the relative economic fortunes of the South declined, the regional elite in the South became 'middle class' both in attitudes and in relation to the national class structure.

Arequipa had been peripheral to the national politics of the half-century before 1930 (although it had provided one of the sugar-planter presidents, Eduardo López de Romaña). The city enjoyed a boom around the turn of the century as a commercial centre, based on the wool trade and the Southern Railway. By 1930 both of these economic pillars were in serious decay. For this and other reasons, Arequipa was to produce a series of political leaders for Peru's ill-defined but growing middle class of professionals, intellectuals and technocrats – people who had a stake in democratic legality and economic stability. Two of these leaders – V. A. Belaúnde and José Luis Bustamante y Rivero – made their mark as strong-minded constitutionalists in the early 1930s, and from 1945 to 1948 Bustamante y Rivero served as president of the republic. In 1950 the lawyer Francisco Mostajo (a prominent Arequipa liberal since 1901) headed an Arequipa revolt against Odría; in 1956 the *arequipeño* Fernando Belaúnde Terry captured a large block of middle-class votes and by 1962–3 Belaúnde's Acción Popular, supported by another party originating in Arequipa, Democracia Cristiana, was strong enough to capture the presidency.

With its one-third of the electorate allied with the APRA constituency, the Arequipa lobby and its supporters in Lima and elsewhere were electorally invincible in 1945. Then as later, however, the interests and ideology of these Centre–Left democrats differed sharply from those of APRA, and the 1945 alliance quickly and permanently collapsed. Nevertheless, the Bustamante regime of 1945–8 remained by far the most interesting and revealing political episode of the period – a brief interval when both the oligarchy and the military stood aside and opened the way for an experiment in middle-class rule.

In addition to their electoral strength the Arequipa constitutionalists mounted the most serious and effective civilian insurrectionary movements of the period. In March 1931, only six months after supporting Sánchez Cerro's military coup against Leguía, they forced him out of the presidency again when he sought to be elected president while still occupying the office. This revolt, which installed the veteran Cuzco *gamonal* David Sámanez Ocampo as provisional president, was headed by Sámanez himself and by Manuel Bustamante de la Fuente, supported by Francisco Mostajo and several other southern landowners and Arequipa professionals. Again in 1950, in opposition to Odría's repetition of Sánchez Cerro's 1931 plans, Francisco Mostajo was at the head of an insurrection which was contained only with the greatest difficulty; and in 1956, when Odría tried to block Belaúnde Terry from standing in the presidential elections. Belaúnde was able to mount a credible threat of a civilian uprising in his support. None of the numerous *aprista* insurrections of the three decades, including that in Trujillo in 1932, secured as much political leverage as these three Arequipa-based movements.

If Arequipa was the heartland of liberalism, other regions of Peru promoted their interests through ideologies of their own. Piura, for example, was the home of the Partido Socialista and La Libertad of the APRA. Histories of APRA abound, and too many have accepted APRA's claim to speak for 'the masses' in the 1930s and 1940s. In fact APRA's mass following was concentrated among the unionized workers and employees of Lima and Trujillo. Since these groups were a minority of the labour force, APRA was and remained the party of a privileged minority of 'the masses', and from the outset its central objective was to protect their vested interests — modern sector wages and salaries and security of employment. While insurrectionary violence was a recurrent theme of APRA tactics of the 1930s and 1940s, at no time did the party mobilize mass forces on anything like the scale that would have been required to capture power. Indeed, it is a mistake to take APRA's insurrections seriously as threats to the established order — their purpose was to dramatize particular issues and reinforce party solidarity. Nor did APRA ever command a clear majority of the Peruvian electorate (securing only 40 per cent of the vote even in 1945). It was, however, notably more successful than its rival among organized labour — the Partido Comunista — partly no doubt because the greater autonomy of the APRA leadership enabled it to negotiate advantageous deals with ruling-class politicians and hence to deliver patronage to its followers.

APRA's high profile probably owed more to the strength of anti-*aprismo* than to APRA's own real strength. APRA attracted ferocious criticism and repression from the Church, from the intransigent right wing of the civilian oligarchy and from the military establishment. In the case of the last two, antagonism was inflamed by APRA's alleged involvement in acts of violence against members of those two groups. The issue of how to cope with APRA split the upper class more deeply than any other political issue of the period.

APRA arose originally out of Haya de la Torre's personal role, as a student leader, in negotiating on behalf of the workers in the 1919 strikes for the eight-hour day. Haya subsequently set up 'popular universities' to train union leaders and built a political movement which was very much his own personal following. The strategy of these early labour unions, combining intransigent threats (strikes, demonstrations, street violence) with a tacit acceptance of the legitimacy of the existing order, was replicated in APRA's approach to political action. A study of mass politics in Peru in the early 1930s sums up APRA's character as follows:

Class distinctions were replaced by identification with the person-to-person relations of trust, dependency and obedience between a charismatic upper-middle-class leader and his mass following. As it stepped on the political stage in 1930–31, Aprismo did not represent, as many terrified members of the elites thought at the time, the beginning of the class struggle in Peru or even an attempt at structural change, but instead an attempt on the part of certain sectors of the urban masses to gain more desirable lifestyles by tying themselves to a man whom they considered their protector and benefactor.[16]

APRA, in other words, fell into the familiar mould of Latin American populism; but it enjoyed substantially less success than the contemporaneous movements in Argentina, Brazil or Venezuela. APRA's mass appeal remained limited by the existence of other competing mass movements, as well as by particular dynamics of the relationship between the leadership and the rank and file.

APRA's political activities were dominated from the outset by tension between the quasi-religious fervour of the party's mass following, which spilled over in continual insurrectionary violence, and the self-interested

[16] Stein, *Populism in Peru*, pp. 156–7.

manoeuvring of the leadership. Repeatedly, *apristas* with a strong commitment to the party's ideals felt themselves betrayed by unprincipled leaders. The leadership, for its part, saw grass-roots militancy as the basis of its political bargaining strength, and it used the party's principles as rallying cries for that militancy; but it did not translate those principles into concrete policy proposals, either in opposition or in brief periods of power-sharing during 1946 and 1956–9. APRA's radical rhetoric enabled it to hold political ground which might otherwise have been occupied by the Communists while the opportunism of its leadership enabled it always to catch the prevailing political wind. As a result, it was Peru's most durable political party, and the general climate of political opinion was heavily conditioned by the speeches and writings of Haya de la Torre.

In 1928 President Leguía had permitted the return from exile of Colonel Luis M. Sánchez Cerro, an officer of humble origins who had been embroiled in two ineffectual attempted coups during the early years of Leguía's rule. Sánchez Cerro had no following or influence in Peru, and on his own he posed no threat. He was, however, given command of an army battalion stationed in Arequipa. As Leguía's power crumbled in 1929–30 under the impact of corruption, the depression and an unsustainable foreign debt burden, credible successors were lacking. The main opposition politicians and anti-Leguía military officers were in exile, the Partido Civilista in ruins and APRA still in its nascent underground stage. The collapse of the *oncenio* left a vacuum into which Sánchez Cerro stepped with the boldness of a political and social outsider. On 22 August 1930 he issued a manifesto to the nation and called on the rest of the armed forces to join his troops in revolt against the government. On 24 August Legúia resigned the presidency and handed over power to a hastily organized junta headed by his chief of staff, General Manuel Ponce. Efforts by Ponce to rally support in the armed forces for a campaign to stop Sánchez Cerro were unsuccessful, and on 27 August Sánchez Cerro flew to Lima and made himself provisional president of Peru.

The popular reception which greeted the new president elevated him overnight to the status of a charismatic caudillo in the eyes of the unemployed artisans and unskilled labourers of Lima. The bonds of loyalty forged on that day, and assiduously cultivated thereafter by Sánchez Cerro, introduced to the political scene an entirely new urban mass movement with a structure which paralleled that of APRA. At the top was the caudillo, the patriarchal protector and benefactor, while at the bottom was the mass of his loyal dependants.

APRA's leader, Haya de la Torre, had been building up a clientelistic following among the organized workers in factories, plantations, mines and offices, with their union leadership trained in Haya's 'popular universities' of 1921–4. Now Sánchez Cerro, at a stroke, had captured a mass following among the larger mass of unorganized workers outside the formal unionized labour market. The urban lower class had thus become politically polarized on lines which reflected the division between the corporate and the non-corporate economy; and this separation between organized and unorganized labour meant that 'mass politics' in Peru henceforth had two competing expressions of lower-class interests, organized in vertical coalitions whose leaders manoeuvred for position in endless intrigues while their loyal followers voted or fought as they were directed.

The existence of these competing populist movements resulted in a particularly Peruvian parallel to the conflicts between Conservatives and Liberals in Colombia and Ecuador. What was distinctive in Peru was that there were no such strongly constituted elite parties to polarize the political scene. The polarization was therefore organized and led by newly emergent personalist leaders over whom ruling-class factions exercised only tenuous influence.

Sánchez Cerro's support extended well beyond the unskilled workers of Lima, as was to become evident when he swept the southern and central Sierra in the 1931 presidential election. One of his first acts as provisional president in August 1930 was the abolition of Leguía's hated *conscripción vial* (use of *corvée* forced labour for road construction). This, plus his dark complexion and his willingness to campaign in the provinces, made Sánchez Cerro the hero of the peasantry. In the election, he won 51 per cent of the votes at a time when 44 per cent of registered voters were in rural occupations and 25 per cent were recorded as 'Indians'.[17]

Since Sánchez Cerro had come to embody the aspirations of an enormous mass of the population by accident, it was necessary to give some political substance to the resulting movement. After only a brief flirtation with APRA and the Arequipa constitutionalists, Sánchez Cerro was drawn into alliance with the anti-Leguía right wing of the oligarchy and with the large foreign firms which dominated the export economy. During the

[17] C. F. Herbold, 'Developments in the Peruvian Administration System, 1919–1930: Modern and Traditional Qualities of Authoritarian Regimes' (Ph.D. dissertation, Yale University, 1973), pp. 128, 322.

following three years Sánchez Cerro's mass following was used against APRA, creating a bitter hostility which lasted for most of the following thirty years.

Sánchez Cerro was assassinated in 1933, leaving his followers politically adrift to be appropriated by other would-be paternalistic caudillos of the Right, such as Luis A. Flores and his quasi-fascist Unión Revolucionaria in the mid-1930s and General Odría in the late 1940s. No durable organized political party emerged to channel this current, but its separation from APRA remained definitive. The hostilities of 1930–3 between *sanchez-cerristas* and *apristas*, combined with the conflicts of interest between organized labour and the remainder of the lower class, permanently blocked APRA from recruiting a majority following among the Peruvian population. However, the *sanchezcerrista* coalition won a clear electoral majority only in the single open election fought by the caudillo himself (in 1931). After his death, it subsided to roughly one-third of the electorate (still evident in Odría's showing in the 1962 elections).[18]

The Peruvian military formed a third political corporation alongside *aprismo* and *sanchezcerrismo*, although it was distinguished from them by the possession of weapons, which were decisive in any outright confrontation, and by the institutional character of the military leadership, with a steady turn-over of personnel and frequent political disagreements within the officer corps. The presidency was in military hands for roughly seventeen years in the period between the fall of Leguía in 1930 and the elections of 1962.

All three military presidents of the period (Sánchez Cerro, Benavides and Odría) were strong personalist leaders who used the military as their stepping-stone to power rather than embodying the aspirations of the military institution as such. Political consciousness among junior officers, however, became steadily more important during the period. *Aprista* sympathies in both army and navy posed problems of discipline and led to several abortive revolts during the 1930s and 1940s, culminating in the Callao insurrection of 1948. The military establishment responded by developing its own institutional ideology and indoctrination programme, operated through the Centro de Altos Estudios Militares (CAEM), which in the 1950s trained a generation of officers who in the 1960s and 1970s were to give the military a radically different political role. Odría was the

[18] E. Chirinos Soto, *Cuenta y balance de las elecciones de 1962* (Lima, 1962), pp. 46–7.

last of the old-style military caudillos; subsequent military leaders were to represent their institution more than their own personal interests.

The emerging military ideology can be traced back to the programmes of Leguía in the 1920s and Benavides in the 1930s, combining maintenance of social order with a desire for rapid national modernization and an attempt to defuse explosive social issues by judicious measures of limited reform. Such a political alignment invites comparison between the military and APRA; and indeed the early leadership and inspiration for the CAEM came from former *apristas* within the military. Such similarities, however, did not prevent a growing institutional hostility between the two, fed by APRA's attempts to suborn the military, and recurrent episodes of military repression of *apristas*.

The labour movement in Peru by 1930 had come through two decades of fluctuating fortunes: first a wave of militancy in the 1910s and then a period of repression and co-option during Leguía's *ocenio*. At the end of the 1920s there had emerged two new political parties aspiring to lead the working class: José Carlos Mariátegui's Partido Comunista and Haya de la Torre's APRA. Communist union organizers made rapid headway in the mining camps in 1930, and as Communist-linked unions spread, a national federation, the Confederación General de Trabajadores Peruanos (CGTP) was formed. APRA began with a strong foothold among the workers of Lima and the northern sugar plantations, and its Confederación de Trabajadores Peruanos (CTP) was the dominant force in organized labour during most of the period to 1960. APRA's union strength went hand in hand with the party's success in building a mass political movement; the Partido Comunista enjoyed less success on both counts.

The existence of the two competing labour organizations enabled governments to play one off against the other and diverted a good deal of working-class energy into internecine struggles. The competition with the Partido Comunista however, contributed to APRA's solidarity; and since the former never figured at the level of national politics, APRA virtually monopolized the role of political representative for organized labour.

The political problem for the Peruvian oligarchy was how to install and replace civilian governments sympathetic to ruling-class interests. Military regimes provided a fall-back option, but from the oligarchy's point of view, they had disadvantages; it was difficult to maintain control over a military president once he was installed, and civilian politicians were often excluded from office and spoils.

The last civilian to gain the presidency by means of a coup was Sámanez Ocampo in March 1931. Thereafter, the military was occasionally prepared to install one of its own in the presidential palace, but never a civilian. Civilian candidates were therefore required to pass some sort of electoral test. As the electorate expanded steadily, from 4 per cent of the population in 1919 to 7 per cent in 1939, 14 per cent in 1956 (when Odría extended the vote to women) and 17 per cent in 1962,[19] the difficulty of securing a majority of votes in a system without a solidly established conservative party became steadily more daunting. The disintegration of the Partido Civilista between 1912 and 1935 left the ruling class with no solid political vehicle of its own, and hence no possibility of a return to the virtual one-party state of the Aristocratic Republic. The Partido Democrático-Reformista – Leguía's faction of the *civilistas,* which monopolized power by means of rigged elections throughout the 1920s – collapsed when its founder and patron fell. The oligarchy's own factionalism and the rise of the populist movements thereafter made authentic electoral competition inescapable.

Politics in Peru from 1930 to 1960 was thus dominated by a series of experiments in which competing factions of the ruling class toyed with alternative strategies for gaining and retaining control over the executive and/or the Congress. One such strategy was to build an alliance between the oligarchy's right wing (with such leaders as the Miró Quesada family and Pedro Beltrán) and the *sanchezcerrista* following of peasant, lumpenproletarian and petty bourgeois groups sufficiently large to carry the day in an open election. This strategy won Sánchez Cerro the presidency in October 1931 under rather special circumstances, but consistently failed thereafter. Political alliances constructed on these lines nevertheless cornered large shares (generally about one-third) of the vote in the elections of 1936, 1939, 1945, 1956, and 1962. The Right faced three problems: first, the existence of a literacy restriction on the franchise (abolished only in 1978) which removed much of the peasantry and unorganized labour force from contention; second, the lack of any ideology or shared class interest to bind these disparate groups together; third, the solid one-third or so of the national vote commanded by APRA, which provided the core for a perennial blocking coalition against the Right.

---

[19] For the two years for which census data are available, 1940 and 1962, the voting proportion of the population aged twenty and over was 14 and 36 per cent, respectively.

Not surprisingly, hostility towards APRA was the hallmark of the Right. A more conciliatory attitude marked the other main group of elite politicians, whose strategy for gaining and holding power rested upon co-option of the organized working class and educated middle class into an alliance dominated by themselves but founded on mutual self-interest. From 1935, the Prado family headed this 'collaborationist' wing of the oligarchy, seeking to enlist or neutralize APRA and similar working-class organizations by offering material benefits for organized labour in return for elite control of the state. The resulting political constellation – mockingly known as the 'convivencia' in the late 1950s – was the key to two electoral successes, in 1939 and 1956, but failed in 1936 when APRA missed its cue. The 1962 election saw the demise of this alliance.

With the ruling class fundamentally split over the question of political strategy and with the electorate settled into an extraordinarily stable three-way split among *apristas,* conservatives and Arequipa-style liberals, attitudes for and against APRA loomed larger in political discussion than substantive policy questions. From time to time this resulted in stalemates which opened the way to military intervention or (in 1945) to success for a non-elite-dominated political coalition. In the last analysis, however, the oligarchy was not confronted by any direct challenge to its position which could not be defused by co-option or repression. The real strength of lower-class and regional movements in Peru lay in their ability to block central government policy rather than in any threat of a take-over of power.[20] The major trends in rural society described earlier proceeded in virtually complete isolation from central government policy, as did the evolution of the informal economy and the *barriadas* in Lima. The weakness of class formation in a regionally fragmented society made it possible for the Peruvian oligarchy to achieve with relative ease its primary aim: to block from control of state power any class or organization which might attack the export-led model of economic growth.

POLITICS AND ECONOMIC POLICY

The Sánchez Cerro Years, 1930–3

Peru was one of many Latin American countries in which the government fell in 1930. Augusto B. Leguía's hold on power had seemed secure until

---

[20] On this point, see A. Angell, 'The Difficulties of Policy Making and Implementation in Peru', *Bulletin of Latin American Research,* 3, no. 1 (1984), pp. 26 and 40.

U.S. bankers cut off loans late in 1929. Thereafter, as Leguía's personal popularity and power faded, the debility of Peruvian elite politics quickly became apparent. Upper-class opinion was becoming hostile to Leguía because of the corruption of his inner clique, his policies on irrigation rights and conciliatory border treaties with Colombia and Chile. The government's retrenchment of public works spending in 1930 brought to an end the Lima construction boom, throwing a large number of un-skilled workers out of employment, while the depression brought hard-ship to many white-collar employees of commercial firms in the capital. Yet there was a conspicuous lack of organized opposition. The military was still mostly loyal; the anti-Leguía elite was leaderless; organized workers were relatively unaffected by the rising unemployment among unorganized labour; and the latter, by definition, had no structured chan-nels for political activity. It was into this vacuum that Luis M. Sánchez Cerro stepped.

Following Leguía's resignation on 24 August and Sánchez Cerro's trium-phal entry into Lima three days later the anti-Leguía *civilista* leaders, hungry for power and revenge, returned from exile. Out from under-ground came the organized cadres of APRA. Into the streets of Lima came delighted mobs to loot the homes of *leguiistas*. In factories, plantations and mines, labour unions emerged. Sánchez Cerro found himself in the presi-dency with great spontaneous popular support among the lower classes, but with no structured political machine of his own. The army command was uneasy; the civil service and the police were staffed with Leguía's appointees; APRA was feverishly recruiting support; and government finances were sliding towards collapse, as revenues from the taxes on exports and imports fell with the depression.

After a brief initial alliance with APRA against the *leguiistas,* Sánchez Cerro was quickly boxed in by the large foreign firms which dominated the export economy of 1930. In September and October 1930, workers in the mining camps of the Cerro de Pasco Corporation were organized into a union by the Partido Comunista and strikes were called. When Sánchez Cerro and his APRA-leaning minister of government, Colonel Gustavo Jiménez, were slow to respond to the company's demands for government support, a strong concerted campaign of pressure was launched by the foreign mining and oil firms, together with the British and U.S. embas-sies, to have the strikes repressed and Jiménez dismissed for his pro-worker sympathies. A clash between police and strikers at Malpaso, near Oroya, left a number of workers dead and triggered riots, which gave

Cerro Corporation an excuse to close down its operations, lay off fifteen thousand workers and dictate terms to the government.

In the midst of the depression, Sánchez Cerro had little option but to fall into line. His treasury was heavily dependent on export taxes, and the Cerro Corporation was one of the dominant export enterprises. From this point on Sánchez Cerro was committed to repressing the organized labour movement (in other words, APRA and Partido Comunista) as well as the *leguiistas*. His mass base of popularity remained, but political realities as well as his own inclinations dictated an alliance with foreign capital and conservative elite interests. Foreign firms helped to finance his government with informal loans, while the right-wing faction of the elite manoeuvred to appropriate Sánchez Cerro for their own purposes, a goal in which they had largely succeeded by November 1930.

Sánchez Cerro was determined to secure the presidency on a longer-term basis, and at the end of 1930 he announced his intention of standing for election in March 1931 without stepping down from the provisional presidency. Opposition among both middle and upper classes was quick to emerge, swelling into a constitutionalist rising in Arequipa in February 1931 which forced Sánchez Cerro to abandon his election plans. On 1 March he resigned and went into voluntary exile, vowing to return to stand for election at a later date. He left behind a tottering economy and a government riven by factional squabbling. The head of the Supreme Court, Ricardo Leoncio Elias, who took over the provisional presidency, was overthrown on 5 March by Colonel Jiménez, who in turn was replaced on 10 March by David Sámanez Ocampo, one of the leaders of the Arequipa uprising.

Constitutional and economic problems were now acute; in 1931 the desperate struggle by government and business to weather the depression was intricately interwoven with the struggle for political power. The country's elite was deeply divided between *civilista* and *leguiista* factions, with the *civilistas* on the offensive. Control of the Central Bank and Finance Ministry had passed into *civilista* hands, and several key economic policy decisions had a strong political flavour. The country's largest bank, the *leguiista*-controlled Banco del Perú y Londres, which had failed in the face of a run on its reserves in December 1930, was refused support and forced into liquidation in mid-1931; the foreign debts incurred by Leguía were defaulted in April (making Peru the second Latin American country to default, after Bolivia); and a purge of *leguiistas* from the upper ranks of the civil service helped to cut the government payroll.

The Sámanez Ocampo junta approved a new electoral law in May 1931. The property qualification was removed from the franchise, the vote thus being extended to all literate adult males (although the change in the size of the electorate resulting from this was surprisingly small, from 203,882 in 1919 to 323,623 in 1931).[21] The secret ballot was introduced, and responsibility for supervising national elections was removed from the provincial to the departmental authorities. These changes reduced the ability of *gamonales* to dominate election results and increased the prospects for mass-based parties. The changes may have been designed to improve APRA's chances of winning the presidency. Colonel Jiménez was again minister of government in this junta and tried in May 1931 to engineer a ban on Sánchez Cerro's candidacy in the elections scheduled for October 1931, which would probably have given victory by default to APRA. However, Sánchez Cerro's allies among the *civilista* elite ensured that the ban was lifted, and he returned to Peru on 7 July to launch his campaign. Shortly afterwards Haya de la Torre also returned from exile.

The 1931 contest between the two populist caudillos was reminiscent of the 1894–5 confrontation between Nicolas de Piérola and Andrés A. Cáceres. This time, however, the issue was to be decided by votes rather than guns. Both candidacies represented tactical alliances between factions of the oligarchy and politicians capable of commanding loyalty among the lower classes: the displaced *leguiistas* with Haya, the *civilistas* with Sánchez Cerro. Both candidates issued policy programmes appealing to the same principles: nationalism, social reform, *indigenismo* and the need for 'sound' finance. Neither offered any strategy for coping with the depression other than the orthodox prescription of deflation. Programmatic differences were matters of emphasis rather than fundamental disagreements. Haya, for example, made more public mileage out of anti-imperialism while appealing to Latin American internationalism as the best alternative (and covertly wooing support from the U.S. Embassy in Lima). Sánchez Cerro took a more chauvinistic line. APRA was more inclined towards state intervention to make up for perceived deficiencies in the 'national bourgeoisie', whereas Sánchez Cerro adopted a more private-enterprise line (which appealed, of course, to the petty bourgeois segment of his constituency as well as to many large capitalists).

The October 1931 election did not, however, turn on policy. Sánchez Cerro emerged the winner with 51 per cent and clear majorities in his

---

[21] Herbold, 'Developments in the Peruvian Administration System', p. 128.

home department of Piura in the far northern coast, in the South, where
his various revolutionary enterprises had been launched, and, most significantly, in the centre of the country including Lima-Callao (which accounted for 28.2 per cent of the national vote in 1931, compared with
only 9.7 per cent in 1919).[22] Haya won in his native mid-northern coast
and in Loreto (where the cession of Leticia to Colombia in August 1930
was still a live issue). APRA's strength among organized labour and
white-collar groups was outweighed by Sánchez Cerro's support from
small shopkeepers, artisans, unskilled urban workers and literate 'Indians'
in the Sierra. This division of the masses into groupings of Left and Right,
with the Right occupying generally lower socio-economic positions than
the Left, remained a feature of Peruvian electoral politics until the 1960s.

The rejection of APRA by a clear majority of the electorate in 1931 was
highly significant, since the political loyalties established at that time
tended to remain thereafter. Even at the height of its electoral strength in
the 1940s, APRA never commanded a clear majority of the voters, and the
party was thus reduced to a status of one power broker among others – it
could command the balance in three-way national elections but not
emerge as a clear winner. APRA's main strength was therefore its ability
to block other contenders from gaining a clear electoral majority, *provided*
that there were at least two other candidates in any election; the lesson of
1931 was that a unified anti-APRA candidacy could win easily. APRA
tactics after 1931 were therefore aimed at promoting the fragmentation of
competing political groups by harassing governments and conspiring with
opposition groups.

Installed again as president on 8 December 1931, Sánchez Cerro proceeded at once to launch a sustained campaign against *apristas* and
leguiistas in the armed forces, the civil service, the unions, the Constituent
Assembly and the streets. In January 1932 virtual martial law was declared; in February the twenty-three *aprista* deputies in the assembly were
deported, together with Colonel Jiménez. In March an *aprista* assassination attempt on Sánchez Cerro failed; in May there was an abortive *aprista*
mutiny at Callao, and Haya was arrested; in July a planned *aprista* insurrection was prematurely triggered in Trujillo and bloodily repressed. In the
meantime, government finances grew steadily more desperate, and pressure on the exchange reserves forced Peru off the gold standard in April.

On 1 September 1932, without warning, a band of armed Peruvians

[22] Ibid., p. 129.

seized control of the Amazon part of Leticia from Colombia and presented Sánchez Cerro with his chance to play patriot. The invaders were organized by rubber and sugar entrepreneurs who had lost land in territory recently ceded to Colombia. Their action was in clear contravention of international law, but since they were supported by Peruvian military units in the Oriente, there was no quick way to repair the damage. Sánchez Cerro opted for a bellicose defence of the invaders against the Colombian army and took the opportunity to replenish the government's coffers with a large internal war loan. Militarily, however, little was done. Colombia had time to sail a naval flotilla around via the Atlantic and the Amazon, reaching the disputed territory in February 1933 and recapturing most of it without difficulty from Peruvian troops.

In March 1933 an attempted coup by Colonel Jiménez in Cajamarca was easily defeated; in April General Oscar Benavides (behind the scenes a long-standing patron of Sánchez Cerro) was brought back from Europe to take charge of the war effort; and when, on 30 April, Sánchez Cerro was assassinated, Benavides took over as president to complete Sánchez Cerro's term (until 1936).

The Benavides Regime, 1933–9

By 1933 the worst of the depression was past. The world cotton market had turned the corner, export-led recovery was beginning and the devaluations of 1930 and 1932 were stimulating investment in production both for export and for the domestic market. Benavides thus took power at an ideal time for a moderate conservative restoration. Politically, he had ample room for manoeuvre as a result of the bitter polarization of mass politics under Sánchez Cerro. APRA had been fought to a standstill and was counterbalanced by the new Unión Revolucionaria (originally set up as a vehicle for Sánchez Cerro, but now modelling itself on European Fascism under its new leader, Luis A. Flores). There was a widespread desire for political stability after the turbulent Sánchez Cerro era, and the Benavides slogan 'Paz, orden, trabajo' was well fitted to the political moment.

The new president had a record which made him the obvious choice to stabilize Peru in 1933. His military reputation was founded upon his success as a commander of the Peruvian forces which defeated the Colombians in the Putumayo region in 1911 – precisely the ground over which the Leticia war was in progress in 1933. He could therefore move quickly to negotiate peace on Colombia's terms without facing a credible challenge to his nationalist credentials. His political reputation arose from a term as provisional president in 1914–15 when as leader of Peru's first 'institutional' military coup he had steered the country out of Guillermo Billinghurst's populist experiment (1913–14). Then, as in 1933, he had faced the need to pacify a militant labour movement, handle the aftermath of an economic crisis and re-establish the political position of the civilian political elite. As president in 1914, furthermore, Benavides had established some reputation as an economic nationalist by taking steps to enforce the application of normal tax laws to the International Petroleum Company, one of the pet hates of anti-imperialists in the 1930s. Finally, his anti-Leguía credentials were impeccable; he had opposed Leguía's 1919 coup, supported insurrectionary movements against Leguía during the early 1920s and spent the entire *oncenio* in exile.

Benavides initially adopted a conciliatory stance towards APRA while he took steps to end the Leticia War. Repression was eased, and by November 1933 a political alliance of APRA and the ephemeral new Partido Social Demócrata (led by Lima mayor Luis A. Eguiguren) had been formed to fight the anticipated elections. But Benavides responded by installing an anti-APRA cabinet, and in May 1934 (following the final settlement of the Leticia issue) the promised elections were cancelled. Subsequent *leguiista–aprista* uprisings in the Sierra in November 1934 provided grounds for outlawing both APRA and the Partido Comunista and imposing new emergency laws in early 1935.

During the intervening months the improving economic climate, combined with the ending of Sánchez Cerro's style of repression, had increased the incidence of strikes, many of which were organized or assisted by APRA's CTP, formed in 1934. Benavides dealt with this resurgent labour movement by a combination of repression and paternalism (the familiar tactics of Leguía). Minimum wage legislation in 1933 was followed by a law providing compensation for workers made redundant. The Welfare Ministry was set up in 1935, and in August 1936 a social insurance law provided pensions and other social security benefits for workers in the corporate sector, funded by contributions from employers, workers and government. With full employment in the corporate sector being maintained by the buoyant state of the export economy after 1934, these measures were accepted by employers with little opposition and served (together with judicious doses of repression) to keep organized labour quiet throughout the second half of the decade, at minimal cost to the government. Benavides also took steps to reduce unemployment by an expansion of the tax-financed public works programme, which employed between thirty thousand and forty thousand workers in the later 1930s.

The timing of the social insurance law, with its strong overtones of paternalistic patronage, was not at all fortuitous. It was a key element in Benavides' unsuccessful attempt to return the country to elite civilian rule by means of national elections held in October 1936. The elections were scheduled for the end of Sánchez Cerro's five-year term, then being served out by Benavides, and were intended to be a replay of 1915 (when Benavides had persuaded the *civilistas* and other elite parties to declare a truce in their customary factional infighting in order to secure the election of José Pardo to the presidency). In preparation for the orderly transfer of power to an acceptable civilian, Benavides promoted the formation of a Frente Nacional to back the candidacy of Jorge Prado. The Frente was pieced together from a number of small political parties of elite and upper-middle-class leadership, which were apparently felt to command the political 'Centre' and which therefore might attract votes from all sides. The Democratic and Liberal parties were vestiges of the Aristocratic Republic; the leader of the latter, Amadeo de Piérola (a son of the caudillo), became Prado's vice-presidential running mate. To these were added Leguía's Partido Democrático-Reformista and Eguiguren's Partido Social Demócrata (both allies of APRA as recently as 1934) and the Arequipa-based Partido Descentralista (which had fought hard but in vain in the Constituent Assembly debates of 1931–3 for an anti-centralist constitution). This motley collection was united only by opportunism and by a vague commitment to liberal democracy.

That Benavides expected to achieve a peaceful transfer of power without more effectively neutralizing APRA, Unión Revolucionaria and the *civilista* Right suggests a degree of political naïveté surprising in one with so much previous experience in Peruvian politics. He may have hoped for tacit support from APRA and abstention by the Right, but hope alone was insufficient. Haya de la Torre and Luis Flores entered the contest, while the oligarchic Right promoted the candidacy of Manuel Vincente Villarán, accompanied by two prominent landowners (Clemente Revilla from the Sierra and Salvador del Solar from the Chancay Valley). The Villarán campaign was supported by prominent right-wingers such as Pedro Beltrán and José de la Riva Agüero and also had the tacit support of Flores.

The outstanding feature of the 1936 election campaign was the political fragmentation of those interests Benavides had sought to unite behind Prado. The Frente Nacional's moderate paternalism, despite wide-spread support from the urban elite and some of the intelligentsia, was of no avail in the absence of a machine to garner the mass vote, without which elections could no longer be won in Peru. Unión Revolucionaria supported the Villarán candidacy, while the Frente Nacional had failed to tie down APRA support on the Left. A strong charismatic caudillo figure might have won the mass vote for the Frente, but Prado was not such a figure.

The 1936 situation illustrates the complexity of Peruvian politics throughout this period. This was not a system in which the will of a unified ruling class prevailed without difficulty. The oligarchy was not united, and no reliable means had been found to control electoral out-comes in the new era of mass politics. The key issue dividing the civilian ruling class in 1936 was how to cope with the masses: would elite interests be better served by paternalistic reformism incorporating the new social forces, or by intransigent reaction dedicated to excluding APRA and similar parties from power? In this strategic disagreement over the means to be used to sustain hegemony, Benavides and the Prado family came to stand for the first option while Pedro Beltrán and Miró Quesada clan embodied the second. Benavides himself, alternating his cabinets between the two factions during 1933–6, was a president acceptable to both sides; but elite conservatives were increasingly worried that he might be soft on APRA – especially after he failed to arrange the death penalty for Carlos Steer, an *aprista* who assassinated Antonio Miró Quesada in 1935.

APRA, meanwhile, was in a typically ambiguous position: the party underground and its leader in hiding whilst candidates were announced for the election. The party's subsequent actions were no less contorted. Although continuing its campaign in Peru, APRA conducted secret nego-tiations with President Toro in neighbouring Bolivia, seeking his support for armed insurrection in exchange for promises of subsequent APRA backing for Bolivia's claims to a Pacific port. Strong diplomatic pressure aborted the plot,[23] and on 5 September APRA was barred from participat-ing in the Peruvian election.

This did not, however, solve Benavides's problem. With only a month remaining until polling day, Eguiguren and his Social Democrats broke with the official Frente Nacional and made a bid for APRA's share of the mass vote. And on 11 October Eguiguren gained about 40 per cent of the

[23] See D. M. Masterson, 'The Peruvian Armed Forces in Transition, 1939–1963: The Impact of National Politics and Changing Professional Perspectives' (Ph.D. dissertation, Michigan State University, 1976), p. 62; and V. Villanueva, *El APRA en busca del poder* (Lima, 1975), pp. 174–5.

total votes cast, which put him comfortably ahead of the other contenders. Benavides arranged to have the election annulled and his own term of office extended to 1939, thus restoring the status quo ante; at the same time he dissolved the Assembly and installed an all-military cabinet. This outcome was received with apparent relief by all concerned. APRA mounted a token uprising at Ancón, but thereafter was content to keep its head down. Unión Revolucionaria also maintained its insurrectionary credentials when Luis Flores and alleged co-conspirators were arrested and deported in November.

During the following three years, Benavides did nothing to contribute to a resolution of the 1936 stalemate. If he hoped to remain dictator indefinitely, he signally failed to lay the necessary groundwork. His short-term political position was bolstered by the strong performance of major export sectors (cotton, oil, minerals) during 1937 and 1938; but in the meantime his support within the military faded, making the government vulnerable to a coup for the first time since 1931. The labour front remained relatively quiescent. Benavides provided employment for un-skilled workers in large-scale public works (especially road-building and housing), and the healthy state of the economy kept both the self-employed and the corporate sector workers occupied. The growing body of well-educated aspirants to white-collar employment, however, posed a greater problem and provided new recruits for APRA's vision of a rapidly expanding state sector dedicated to social engineering and economic planning. At the same time, the elite conservatives were unhappy with the growing tax burden imposed by Benavides to finance his paternalistic programmes of public works, health and education.

In February 1939 Benavides was confronted with a serious challenge from within the military, in the form of an attempted coup by his minister of government, General Antonio Rodríguez Ramírez. Rodríguez's conspiracy incorporated both the mass parties (Unión Revolucionaria and APRA), but failed because of indecisive leadership and a quick counter-coup by the minister of war, General Ernesto Montagne Markholtz. Having lost military support, and despite his failure to close the breach with the oligarchy's conservative faction, Benavides decided to replay his 1936 experiment. In March 1939 he announced that elections for a new president and Congress would be held in October, preceded in June by a plebiscite to extend the presidential term from five to six years and strengthen the constitutional position of the executive. In April Manuel Prado (Jorge's brother) was brought into the cabinet and a Concentración Nacional, on lines similar to the 1936 Frente Nacional, was set up.

The anti-Prado faction of the elite again put up a right-wing challenger, José Quesada Larrea, with Luis Flores as his running mate. Benavides's opponents in the oligarchy thus revived the 1931 winning formula (but without Sánchez Cerro). To carry the election, Prado would require not only the centrist votes of the middle class, but also the APRA vote to act as a counterweight to Unión Revolucionaria's mass strength. APRA itself was kept firmly out of the running, and although Prado was unable to reach a clear public alliance with the APRA leadership, financial blandishments and the expectation that Prado would expand the state payroll helped to bring *aprista* votes behind him.

In the event, government repression of the Quesada camp, and careful supervision of the vote itself, secured Prado 55 per cent of the votes cast – under the circumstances, a far from overwhelming victory. Even after the results were declared, Benavides was obliged to take further steps to ensure that Prado could be inaugurated in December: on 16 November, military pay was raised and on 19 November the usual APRA insurrection (this time in Trujillo) was suppressed.

Economic Policy in the 1930s

The dominant theme in Peruvian economic policy-making during the 1930s was monetarist orthodoxy. The Central Bank, firmly controlled throughout the period by conservative elite figures, successfully enforced a deflationary response to the depression by refusing to lend to the government to finance any fiscal deficit. In any case, the ministers of finance under Sámanez Ocampo, Sánchez Cerro and Benavides, were unanimous on the need for balanced budgets and maintenance of free trade. These policy attitudes were strongly reinforced by an advisory mission headed by Dr. Walter Kemmerer, the conservative U.S. economist, who was invited to Peru in November 1930 to advise on stabilization policy and whose reports were published in April 1931.[24]

Consequently, when tax revenues fell by more than 30 per cent between 1930 and 1932, government spending was cut by very nearly an equal amount. Expenditure cuts were the central preoccupation of the Finance Ministry. Civil service salaries were cut 10 per cent by the Sámanez junta in 1931, and thereafter salaries were often paid in arrears. The biggest threat to balancing the budget was proposals to provide some relief for the

---

[24] H. W. Kemmerer et al., *Report on the Public Credit of Peru* (Banco Central de Reserva, Lima, 1931).

Lima unemployed. When in March 1931 a relief programme was agreed upon, its cost was fully covered by new taxes on trade, postage, incomes, gambling and motor vehicles.[25]

Nevertheless, the government's floating debt crept up during 1931 and 1932, and on two occasions the government resorted to paying its creditors with tax-credit coupons. Both developments were attacked on all sides as fiscal irresponsibility. When an emaciated budget was sent to the Constituent Assembly for debate in January 1932, APRA delegates demanded further spending cuts and insisted on the need to avoid any deficit. Later that year, confronted with the need to finance war preparations over Leticia, the government imposed additional taxes on lotteries, salaries and property income, raised an internal loan of 20 million soles and also called for voluntary public donations. In the end, the 1932 fiscal year (the worst of the depression) resulted in a deficit of only S/4 million on a budget of S/95 million; in 1933 the government moved back into surplus and paid off the previous year's floating debt. For the remainder of the 1930s, under Benavides, budget surpluses were the norm.

On the monetary front, there was less unanimity on policy. In 1931 Kemmerer and the Central Bank insisted on the defence of the gold standard as the top priority – a task made easier by Leguía's 16 per cent devaluation of the gold standard exchange rate in 1930. All elite interests agreed that exchange controls were to be avoided, but there was a conflict of interest over whether the exchange rate should be defended. The conflict had two aspects. First, there was the desirability or otherwise of devaluation itself; export producers (especially sugar planters) were in favour of it, while bankers and the urban business community tended to favour a 'strong currency'. Second, there were the monetary consequences of the Central Bank's determination to defend the exchange rate. Monetary expansion tended to cause depreciation, and monetary contraction tended to drive the rate up. To offset the downward pressure on the rate resulting from the collapse of export earnings, the bank embarked upon a ferocious credit squeeze, which quickly aroused opposition among capitalists large and small. Agricultural export producers, who in any case were unenthusiastic about a strong exchange rate, were united in demanding more credit to keep them from bankruptcy; and since Sánchez Cerro's ministers were themselves linked to agro-exporting interests, a number of measures were devised to circumvent the squeeze for their benefit. The

[25] *West Coast Leader,* 14 April 1931, p. 1.

government ran down its equity capital in the Central Bank from S/26 million in 1931 to S/10 million by mid-1932, using the proceeds to fund an expansion of credit through other state-controlled financial institutions, especially the Banco Agrícola.

The Central Bank's tight stance was reinforced by a run on Peru's gold reserves, which worsened early in 1932, and a growing number of elite and small-business voices were raised against the bank's policy. In September 1931 Benjamín Roca, chairman of the Budget Commission, called for 'judicious inflation', and in February 1932 the finance minister echoed this plea.[26] The Consejo Económico del Sur in Arequipa (representing southern chambers of commerce) strongly attacked the monetary and exchange-rate policy in early 1932 and was supported by some of the Lima press.[27] By May gold reserves were down by one-third, and the Central Bank admitted defeat; the gold standard was abandoned, the exchange rate promptly fell and credit conditions began to ease, though not until a year later did the Central Bank agree to monetary expansion as export earnings recovered.

Peruvian management of the world depression was thus rigidly orthodox. Sánchez Cerro's response was soup kitchens and a balanced budget. Sámanez Ocampo and APRA backed the gold standard, balanced budgets, a credit squeeze and tax-financed public works. Benavides from 1933 to 1939 continued to preach 'sound finance', although in practice monetary conditions were eased during his regime. The only serious debate during the 1930s was over the gold standard, abandonment of which served certain strong interests within the oligarchy. 'Peru reacted, rather than moved', a study on the effects of the depression on Peru and Colombia concluded, and 'let recovery come of its own accord via international prices'.[28] Certainly there was no deliberate attempt to reorient the direction of the country's development towards more autonomy or import substitution.

The First Prado Administration, 1939–45

At the outset of his term of office, Manuel Prado was faced with many conflicting pressures, and his political survival was due largely to the

[26] Ibid., 8 September 1931, p. 30; 16 February 1932, p. 7.
[27] Ciccarelli, O., 'Sánchez Cerro and the Depression in Peru', *Southern Quarterly*, 9, no. 3 (1971), pp. 231–52.
[28] R. Thorp and C. Londoño, 'The Effect of the Great Depression on the Economics of Peru and Colombia', in R. Thorp (ed.), *Latin America in the 1930s: The Role of the Periphery in World Crisis* (London, 1948), pp. 81–116.

Second World War, although one should not underestimate his considerable political abilities. First, the war brought high prices for sugar, which took the edge off right-wing discontent as the planters' economic position strengthened. Second, it brought in 1941–2 an excuse for the government to expropriate all property owned by the Japanese in Peru and distribute it to political friends. (German property remained sacrosanct.) Third, it induced APRA and (after Germany attacked the Soviet Union) the Partido Comunista to declare a truce in labour relations, as a result of which real wage rates were allowed to drift downwards during the first half of the 1940s to the satisfaction of employers. In turn, the rising profitability of industry, commerce and certain export activities enabled Prado to increase tax rates without encountering serious opposition. Fourth, the war brought a revival of U.S. interest in Peru, with support for the Prado regime as an ally and several U.S. investment projects which the government could portray as a development programme. Special bilateral deals under which the U.S. government guaranteed to buy Peruvian cotton and minerals at fixed prices rebounded to Prado's credit. Also on the positive side, from Prado's point of view, was the composition of the Congress, elected under tight control by Benavides. With no *apristas* and only a few hard-line right-wingers, the Congress was composed mainly of placemen without strong party affiliations. It therefore gave Prado little trouble and enabled executive dominance of government (established by Leguía in 1919) to continue.

On the negative side was the fact that Benavides bequeathed a divided military, with opponents of Prado well placed among the officer corps. Fortunately, there was no high-ranking officer with strong political ambitions, and during his first two years in power Prado was able to placate the military by taking a strong patriotic line, by supplementing military finances through his family connections in the banking world and by allowing the high command to proceed with preparations for a war with Ecuador – a cherished dream of the Peruvian military since its humiliation by Colombia in 1932–3. In May 1941 there were a series of border incidents between Peru and Ecuador, and in June the Peruvian commander in the North, General Eloy G. Ureta, offered Prado the choice of approving an attack on Ecuador or being overthrown by military coup. On 5 July, ignoring Prado's wishes, Ureta proceeded to launch his offensive against Ecuador. The fact that it took the Peruvian armed forces a further month to secure the collapse of the outnumbered and incompetent Ecuadorean army caused Prado considerable diplomatic embarrassment, as international demands for a cease-fire had to be evaded. However, the Peruvian military was eventually satisfied, and Prado was allowed to negotiate an end to the war.

More important even than the issue of military loyalty was the question of civilian support for Prado, who shared Benavides' perception of the need to buy off mass discontent with judicious concessions, while seeking to co-opt potential opposition leaders. APRA remained illegal, but was allowed to operate informally, provided that it refrain from attacking the government directly; other civilian opponents received a political amnesty in June 1940. Prado's overriding aim was to avoid urban mass discontent. By 1940 this meant, above all, providing employment for the educated lower middle class. Prado's response was a rapid expansion of state employment, especially in the education sector (whose expansion had been begun by Benavides). Probably the most important social legacy of the Prado years was the spread of schools through the Peruvian Sierra, often staffed by young city-educated teachers who had been exposed to APRA ideas in the universities. (In the 1940s rural schoolteachers seem to have played a leading role in peasant mobilization, especially in the central and northern Sierra.) While some downward tendency of real wages was politically permissible during the war because of the tolerance of labour leaders, it was most important to be seen to be fighting any rise in the cost-of-living index. Politically visible inflation, as measured by that index, was 12 per cent in 1942, 9 per cent in 1943, 14 per cent in 1944 and 11 per cent in 1945; inflation was thus kept from accelerating, and labour unrest was held in check.

However, Prado's supporters among the oligarchy became increasingly alarmed at his departure from the principles of 'sound finance', and a steady drumbeat of criticism began to sound in the business press and the Club Nacional. From 1942, the moderate faction of the oligarchy became increasingly estranged from the government, while the Right set about its preparations for the 1945 elections.

In 1943 the Miró Quesadas persuaded General Ureta (still a serving officer) to stand for president in 1945 against the widely expected candidacy of Benavides. Prado was torn between trying for re-election or backing Benavides, who in December 1943 made a private bid for support from APRA. The prospect of two military figures standing against one another for election to the presidency was alarming not only to many civilian politicians but also to a large group within the military. In 1944 new groupings emerged in both quarters; in both cases the initiative came from middle-class elements. In June 1944 the Frente Democrático Nacional (FDN) was set up in Arequipa by groups similar to those which had been junior partners in the Benavides front organizations of 1936 and 1939. The declared intention of the Frente was to present a civilian alternative to Ureta and Benavides, and it apparently had tacit support from APRA. The desertion of an important part of his 1939 political coalition to the Frente left Prado with few options. It also deprived Benavides of any hope of success; in January 1945 he formally announced his decision not to stand and his support for a civilian succession. In the meantime, within the army, junior officers headed by Major Víctor Villanueva were calling for an end to political competition within the military and a programme of social and institutional reforms. In July 1944 they formed the Comité Revolucionario de Oficiales del Ejército (CROE), which quickly became involved in intrigues with APRA's civilian leadership.

The byzantine intricacies of Peruvian electoral politics ran their familiar course through the first half of 1945. In March Ureta formally announced his candidacy, while the Frente persuaded José Luis Bustamante y Rivero to stand. CROE mounted an insurrection at Ancón, which their ally APRA failed to support (having already privately agreed to work with Bustamante). Bustamante reached a private deal with Prado to secure legalization of APRA in May, opening the way for Bustamante to be elected by essentially the same coalition that had voted for Prado in 1939, with the important difference that formal participation by APRA (and continued growth of the urban middle class and organized labour) raised Bustamante's winning margin to 66 per cent of the total vote.

The election of June 1945 marked a low point in the political hegemony of the Peruvian oligarchy. The conservative faction, derived from the anti-Leguía element of the old Partido Civilista, via the Sánchez Cerro coalition of 1931, had three times since 1931 failed to construct a viable electoral vehicle for its interests, even when it found in General Ureta another popular military figure to act as figurehead. It had altogether failed to build a middle-class constituency, and its claim on the mass vote formerly commanded by Unión Revolucionaria had faltered as the latter's machine disintegrated in the 1940s. By 1945 the unskilled workers and peasantry were once again (as in 1930) a floating vote, but APRA was still making only very limited inroads into this segment of the electorate.

At the same time, the more moderate ruling-class faction had no new leader to replace Prado and by 1945 had retired to the sidelines, leaving the political field clear for their junior partners and APRA to confront the

Right. The FDN victory thus brought to power a new group of middle-class politicians, many of whom had little experience with national government and were poorly equipped to confront the multiple crises looming over the horizon as the Second World War drew to a close.

In the elections for Congress, politicians associated with the FDN (28 of them *apristas*) won 35 of the 46 seats in the Senate. In the Chamber of Deputies the FDN held 73 of the 101 seats, of which 46 were *aprista*. With three-quarters of the seats in both houses, the Bustamante coalition started out with an apparently strong position; but neither the APRA nor the non-APRA group held a clear majority in either house, and any split between Bustamante and APRA held the threat that the president might lose control of Congress.

The Bustamante Administration, 1945–8

President José Luis Bustamante had a solid electoral mandate for social and political reforms within a democratic parliamentary framework. Furthermore, the conservative forces had been placed on the defensive. However, Bustamante also inherited problems on several fronts. Economically, Peru had low foreign exchange reserves and poor external credit, while the monetary expansion and repressed inflation of the Prado years had left a backlog of unsatisfied demands, which was putting pressure on both the balance of payments and prices. On the labour front, the union movement had rapidly built up its strength during 1944, in which year the CTP had been re-established and successful strikes had been organized in textile factories, bakeries and breweries for higher wages. Attempts by Prado to rein in the labour movement had been greeted by a general strike in late 1944. Following the 1945 elections, both APRA and the Partido Comunista encouraged strikes for higher wages, with considerable success since the government was in no position to use open repression to defend employer interests. The unions' goal of restoring real wages to their pre-war levels was achieved in 1946–7 despite the worsening economic crisis.[29] Politically, Bustamante lacked the contacts and experience to deal effectively with the established elite, none of whom served in his government. Benavides, who might have proved a political asset, had died in June 1945, and Prado had departed to live in France. Meantime General

---

[29] J. Payne, *Labour in Politics in Peru* (New Haven, Conn., 1965), p. 20; W. Warren, *Inflation and Real Wages in Underdeveloped Countries: India, Peru and Turkey* (London, 1976).

Ureta, Bustamante's opponent in the election, remained a high-ranking officer in the military (and would in 1948 play an important role in the military coup which overthrew Bustamante's government).

Bustamante started badly by failing to include any *apristas* in his first cabinet. APRA responded by asserting an increased role for Congress. On the first day of the 1945 session Congress gave itself the power to override a presidential veto by simple majority vote. APRA then embarked on a legislative programme of its own, as though the party controlled full state power rather than merely a foothold in the legislature. Bustamante was powerless to prevent this, since he did not have direct control over the FDN's non-APRA members of Congress and was committed to maintaining the authority of the presidency without resorting to repression against APRA. (His 1945 decision to abolish the secret police and their network of informers was unprecedented before or since in republican Peru.)

Faced with worsening inflation and balance-of-payments trouble, Bustamante's first finance minister, the non-*aprista* technocrat Rómulo Ferrero, struggled in vain during the second half of 1945 to persuade the APRA delegates in Congress to accept cuts in government expenditure and increased taxation in order to reduce the fiscal deficit. In January 1946 the non-*aprista* cabinet led by Rafael Belaúnde was forced to resign by a congressional no-confidence vote, and in the new cabinet led by Julio Ernesto Portugal *apristas* were put in charge of the portfolios of Finance, Development and Agriculture. Since APRA now shared responsibility for government policy, it was possible for Bustamante to raise taxes, restrain wage increases and embark on new development initiatives without being blocked in Congress. Furthermore, the economic pressures on the government eased off during 1946 (due to a combination of rising export earnings and world shortages of goods for import), opening the possibility of implementing far-reaching structural reforms.

Many APRA members and supporters saw the party as a vehicle for anti-imperialism, agrarian reform and economic planning. Neither in Congress nor in the cabinet, however, did APRA initiate any such programme. Early in 1946 the *aprista* minister of development signed an agreement with the International Petroleum Company (the chief target of anti-imperialist sentiment in Peru) for the exploration of the Sechura Desert for oil; and the Sechura Contract was readily approved by the Chamber of Deputies on 8 June with full APRA support. Indeed, from 1945 Haya de la Torre repeatedly called for more foreign investment to develop Peru and insisted on a revisionist reading of his writings of the

1920s and early 1930s so as to remove any suggestion that imperialism should be opposed per se.

APRA also had little new to offer on the agrarian front. The only new agrarian legislation of the Bustamante years was the 1947 Ley de Yanaconaje, regulating tenancy contracts on the Coast. No agrarian reform bill was proposed or even drafted, and if APRA made any contribution to the long-run emancipation of the Sierra peasantry it was at the lower level of clientelistic patronage. Equally, in the management of the Finance portfolio APRA brought no new approach to fiscal and monetary policy. Economic policy guidelines inherited from Prado – a fixed exchange rate and price control – were retained, and the main addition was a tightening up of fiscal policy to reduce the government deficit and assist in defending the exchange rate. Only feeble attempts were made during 1946 to ratio-nalize the administration of import licences, and the regressive impact of low food prices on rural incomes was entirely ignored.

APRA's participation in the cabinet lasted for only a year and was ended by a series of incidents reminiscent of the political battles of the early 1930s. In December 1945 *apristas* broke up a conservative rally, and in April 1946 they stormed the offices of the newspapers *La Prensa* and *El Comercio*. Violence against APRA's political opponents continued through the rest of the year, culminating in an assassination attempt on the minis-ter of government (General Rodríguez) in December 1946 and the killing of the director of *La Prensa,* Francisco Graña Garland, in January 1947. At this point Bustamante forced the resignation of the *apristas* and appointed a new cabinet in which the Ministry of Government and Police was headed by General Manuel Odría, a hard-line anti-*aprista* with a distinguished record in the 1941 war against Ecuador. The presence in the cabinet of General José del Carmen María Marín (a sympathizer, though not a mem-ber, of APRA) as minister of war provided some check on Odría's power, but did not prevent the new minister of government from reconstructing the repressive apparatus previously dismantled by Bustamante and turning it against APRA and the labour movement.

As a result, the Right began to gain ground politically from January 1947, with APRA on the defensive and Bustamante clinging desperately to democratic principles in the middle. By mid-year the APRA-leaning prefects in six major cities had been replaced by military men, and in March 1948 the APRA-dominated municipal councils (elected following Bustamante's victory in 1945) were disbanded and replaced with new councils appointed from Lima (as had been the usual practice since 1919).

Most damagingly, in July 1947 Congress was prevented from opening its annual session by a conservative boycott of the Senate, which left the Senate without a quorum and rendered unconstitutional any meeting of the deputies. APRA's earlier tactic of using its congressional bloc to dictate terms to Bustamante was thus vitiated; the party was isolated from all formal levels of power and left with only its political machine and its strong hold over the organized labour movement. The second half of 1947, in consequence, witnessed a severe worsening of industrial relations, including a general strike in Lima at the end of August. Squeezed between the APRA-led labour movement and the Right, Bustamante tried to placate the latter without mounting a head-on attack on the former. He persistently refused to outlaw APRA or to give a free hand to the Odría faction of the military, and he successfully resisted for an extraordinarily long time the extreme demands of the Right.

The survival of the Bustamante regime for fifteen months after the Senate boycott of July 1947 indicates the limits to the power of the oligarchy in mid-century Peru. Accounts which condemn Bustamante as a weak and inept president seriously underestimate not only his personal obstinacy in defence of what he conceived to be vital democratic principles, but also the strength of support for his position among important, albeit disparate, segments of Peruvian society. His support among professionals and in his home town of Arequipa remained solid. For the organized labour movement, the real enemy was the Right, and the government appeared reasonably benevolent; Bustamante continued to decree periodic wage and salary increases, and he refused to push unions underground. For white-collar employees, even those involved with APRA, Bustamante remained a sympathetic figure, and his defence of the fixed exchange rate appealed to their economic interests.

Within the military, the Odría group was merely one faction among many. There was a strong middle group of officers opposed to political involvement and anxious for the establishment of a stable civilian constitutional order (which of necessity implied some accommodation with APRA); and there was also a strong *aprista* faction, particularly among junior officers. Within the oligarchy, opinion was far from unanimously in support of the Right and its newly formed political party, the Alianza Nacional, headed by Pedro Beltrán and the Conservatives' Senate leader, Hector Boza. (Beltrán had been dismissed from his post as Peruvian ambassador in Washington for orchestrating U.S. pressure on Bustamante to devalue the sol. Back in Peru, he assumed the editorship of *La Prensa* and became intimately involved in attempts by leading figures in the oligarchy to destabilize the government.) Although elite opposition to Bustamante's economic policies was hardening steadily, in 1947 this did not yet imply a general desire for an Odría coup. Exporting interests were actively subverting the government's exchange controls and hoping that the chronic balance-of-payments crisis would eventually force Bustamante to devalue the official exchange rate and attack wage inflation head-on; but they were not unanimously committed to destroying the government itself.

However, Bustamante could not orchestrate a coherent basis of support from classes with clear-cut economic interests to defend. His own group, the professional middle class, was worried by inflation and committed to legality, but its members were not a 'national bourgeoisie' of the type that might have provided clear strategic guidelines for policy formation – nor, indeed, did such a national bourgeoisie exist as a political creature apart from the oligarchy. The Bustamante group was in government by default, as long as neither a popular insurrection nor a rightist military coup materialized.

That the conditions for a popular seizure of power did not exist is evident from several abortive APRA insurrections during 1948. *Aprista* plots to overthrow Bustamante by force had begun in November 1947, when Major Víctor Villanueva returned from semi-exile in the United States and took over the task of organizing APRA's chaotic militant wing into an insurrectionary force. Villanueva's efforts were rewarded most strongly among junior officers in the army and enlisted men in the air force, navy and police. Conscripts in the army (the military group most representative of the civilian 'masses') were indifferent. The civilian wing of the APRA conspiracy was confined to a few dozen party militants, and the leadership (with good reason) consistently refused to test the strength of its civilian support by means of a call for insurrection. Soundings taken in Arequipa in December by Haya's aide Luis Barrios Llona revealed no civilian support for an uprising, and at the end of January 1948 a serious split developed between the Villanueva-led activists and the party leaders over whether the conditions existed for a successful rising.

When Villanueva, on the basis of calculations concerned solely with his narrow base of support within the military, ordered the insurrection to proceed, the civilian APRA leaders had no difficulty in aborting the exercise at such an early stage that the entire story remained unknown to the public for some time. On 3 October 1948 the militant faction tried

again to spark off a general insurrection, when five hundred naval personnel seized control of key installations in Callao early in the morning. The
plan could have succeeded only if it was immediately supported by mass
civilian demonstrations in Lima; but the APRA leadership gave no such
orders, and there was no sign of spontaneous civilian support for the
military rebels. It has been estimated that only a hundred civilians were
involved in the fighting.[30] Subsequent student demonstrations at San
Marcos University, although noisy, were equally isolated from popular
sentiment. Far from believing in any possibility of removing Bustamante
by mass civilian action, Haya clearly felt in 1948 that the most productive
approach was likely to be a military coup and lent his support to a
proposed (but never realized) plot by the minister of war, General Marín,
in August–September. As the civilian Right began to press openly for a
military coup against Bustamante, APRA's unwillingness to engage in an
uncompromising defence of the constitutional system opened the door to
Odría's ambition.

The outcome was not a foregone conclusion, however. Hard-line military men had gained cabinet posts in increasing numbers, but found
themselves obliged to operate within limits set by Bustamante. In October 1947 and January 1948 Bustamante refused demands that he outlaw
APRA, although on each occasion he reorganized the cabinet membership
to accommodate the Odría military faction. In June 1948 he stood firm
against Odría's demand for all-out repression and forced the resignation of
the entire cabinet, Odría included.

In July 1948 a planned coup involving Odría in Lima and Colonel
Alfonso Llosa in Juliaca quickly collapsed when Llosa moved prematurely;
neither the Arequipa nor the Cuzco garrison commanders hesitated to
move their troops against Llosa. (Links with the civilian Right were
indicated by the fact that Llosa's manifesto was written for him by Carlos
Miró Quesada of *El Comercio*.)[31] Only a few of the Lima commanders were
sympathetic, and probably a majority of the officer corps either was opposed to a coup at that stage or sought nothing more than a brief military
intervention followed by new elections. The aborted *aprista* rising of February 1948 had provided Odría with an excuse to remove several APRA
sympathizers from key military posts, but did not secure right-wing
domination of the military institution.

[30] Masterson, 'The Peruvian Armed Forces', p. 190.
[31] Ibid., pp. 177–8.

After disposing of his right-wing cabinet in June 1948, Bustamante granted a 20 per cent salary increase to public sector employees in August, brought in a new 'exchange certificate' scheme in September (in an attempt to make exchange control workable again) and proposed the holding of elections to add 107 new members to Congress, convert it into a Constituent Assembly and thus break the Right's boycott on proceedings. (The elections would almost certainly have reduced APRA's strength in the Assembly, and the party joined the Right in condemning Bustamante's proposal.) The government was once again on the offensive against its opponents, and in retrospect it seems possible that had Bustamante managed to coax respected members of the elite into his cabinet, he might have survived politically until the economy was rescued by the export boom which began at the end of 1949.

The Callao uprising in October, however, changed the atmosphere within the military. The revolt had been a military, not a civilian affair; it had dramatized the effect of factionalism within the military and threatened the whole structure of military discipline. A large number of formerly moderate officers became convinced at this stage of the need to do something about APRA, not because of the party's civilian activities but because of its subversive influence on the morale and cohesion of the armed forces. Odría now went to the South to repeat the strategy used by Sánchez Cerro in 1930: a seizure of control in Arequipa, followed by an ultimatum to the high command in Lima to join the movement or face a bloody confrontation which would divide the military yet again. He arrived in Arequipa on 25 October, and the revolt by local units was launched on the 27th. The following day the other garrisons in the South joined the rebels, leaving the decision to the high command in Lima. It was only late on the 29th that the Lima commanders moved against the government, after intense debate in which Bustamante's supporters were finally deterred by the threat of civil war. Odría arrived by plane to take over on the 30th, a few hours after Bustamante had been sent into exile in Argentina.

Economic Policy in the 1940s

In the 1940s, the ground rules for economic policy shifted away from the orthodoxy of the 1930s. In part, this reflected the exigencies of wartime economics and the international popularity of Keynesian ideas. More important, however, was the steady growth of the Peruvian state as an employer and provider of social services. This growth had begun with

Benavides' paternalistic policies in the second half of the 1930s and had initially been financed out of rising current revenues. However, Prado faced much stronger pressures to increase the state payroll and was not as well placed to resist those pressures as Benavides had been. The emergence of a growing budget deficit which was translated into monetary expansion coincided with inflationary pressures created by the Second World War.

The pressure of events, rather than any consciously developed strategy, forced Prado and then Bustamante into the policy dilemmas of the mid-1940s. Neither felt politically able to reduce the momentum of state expenditure on what seemed to be the urgent needs of Peruvian society – education, social services, employment creation. Prado, in addition, became committed to a grandiose plan to build a state-run iron and steel complex at Chimbote. Yet despite tax increases in the early 1940s, revenues fell steadily behind expenditure. Prado resorted to borrowing on a growing scale. A 1940 defence loan was followed by an S/150 million public works loan from the local banks and in January 1942 an S/25 million loan was obtained from the U.S. Export–Import Bank to finance public works and replenish foreign exchange reserves. Other internal loans followed, including a growing amount of Central Bank credit to cover subsidies on food prices and general government expenditures; this in turn expanded the money supply and led to the accumulation of large idle balances in the local banks. Since orthodox criticisms of the deficit focussed on the proposition that monetary expansion would cause inflation, Prado (and later Bustamante) set out to repress inflation by direct controls on internal prices and the exchange rate.

These controls developed in an unco-ordinated fashion in response to a series of mini-crises. Although by 1946–8 economic policy in Peru had become unorthodox and interventionist by the standards of the 1930s, this neither implied abandonment of the basic perception of Peru as an open, export-led economy nor generated any attempt to create a more autonomous economic structure. The one apparent exception – Prado's iron and steel project – was a pale imitation of contemporary state projects in Brazil and Argentina, promoted for political rather than economic reasons, and never the centre-piece of a coherent alternative development strategy.

Prado's main weapon against inflation was a fixed exchange rate of S/6.50 to the U.S. dollar, established in mid-1940 and defended by an informal version of exchange control agreed upon with the banks and the export producers.[32] In addition, price controls on consumer goods and fuel, first imposed by Benavides at the outbreak of the war in September 1939, were retained and extended, and laws were passed obliging commercial agriculture to devote a fixed minimum proportion of productive land to food crops in an attempt to hold down the price of urban wage goods.

The problems with this policy mix began to come into clear focus during 1944–5, Prado's last year in office. As the informal exchange-control system devised in 1941 came under severe pressure from surging imports and speculation, Prado announced his intention to introduce import control in July 1944, only to be forced into retreat by fierce opposition from commercial interests. With capital flight and greater ease of obtaining supplies of goods for imports on world markets, foreign exchange reserves fell to desperate levels by the end of 1944, and in January 1945 Prado finally resorted to a system of what amounted to import control.

By the middle of 1945 when Bustamante took over, this system had already degenerated into chaos, with waiting lists of up to two months for applications to be even considered and more import licences outstanding than there was foreign exchange available. Only a recovery of exports after the end of the war enabled the government to get through 1945 and 1946 without abandoning the fixed exchange rate of S/6.50 to the dollar, which was regarded as vital to retaining worker and middle-class urban support. (Exporting and some commercial elite interests were generally pressing for devaluation.) At the end of 1946 renewed pressure on the exchange reserves became unmanageable, and a dual exchange market was introduced, retaining the fixed official rate for 'essential' imports ('essential' being understood to mean politically sensitive) while other transactions were relegated to a free market in which the sol immediately depreciated 50 per cent.[33]

In the following year, inflation broke through the controls. During 1947 the wholesale price index abruptly rose 35 per cent and retail prices rose 29 per cent as the price control system broke down and the repressed inflation of previous years surfaced. Across most economic sectors serving the local market, producers tried to restore their profit margins via price rises, and real wages fell back. This was rapidly perceived by workers, since food prices led the 1947 price inflation, and nominal wage claims were stepped up accordingly.

[32] J. Dragisic, 'Peruvian Stabilization Policies, 1939–1968' (Ph.D. dissertation, University of Wisconsin, 1971), p. 38.

[33] Ibid., p. 55.

Rising real wages, continuing price controls, the rising cost of materials imported at the free-market exchange rate and the losses to exporters (which were implicit in their having to sell their foreign exchange earnings to the Central Bank at the low official rate) contributed to a squeeze on profitability in the private capitalist sector. In February 1946, in addition, Congress approved increases in direct taxes. These pressures might have been acceptable to private capital in a context of rapid growth, or if the government was felt to be under elite control (as had been the case when Prado raised taxes in the early 1940s). By 1947, however, neither of these conditions obtained. Growth in that year slowed down to 2 per cent even on an optimistic reckoning, and investment was down by 25 per cent. A poor sugar crop had cut foreign earnings back towards the end of 1946, and in 1947 part of the rice crop failed, forcing the government to resort to heavy food imports. The struggle to keep food prices down led to heavy subsidies financed by Central Bank credits, and in an attempt to prevent these from feeding inflation, the government imposed tight credit controls, which worsened the position of private business. At this stage the Peruvian business sector turned definitively against the Bustamante regime and set about subverting its economic policies. It was a sign of the changing times that the oligarchy should resort to economic pressures rather than the traditional coup. The anti-Bustamante campaign was the first of several similar uses of economic muscle to pressure Peruvian governments in the following thirty years.

In an attempt to moderate the monetary expansion Bustamante agreed to the removal of subsidies on foodstuffs (except wheat) in January 1948. Both inflationary pressures and labour unrest eased during the first half of 1948, but the balance of payments continued to worsen. By 1948 it was broadly accepted that the official exchange rate was overvalued; the adoption in late 1946 of a dual exchange rate had merely brought new distortions and encouraged speculation against the sol. Anyone with foreign exchange to sell naturally tried to do so in the free market or the black market, rather than through the Central Bank as regulations required. In April 1948 Augusto Gildemeister led a move among export producers to use their foreign exchange to bring in imports themselves, rather than sell the exchange to the Central Bank to finance 'essential' imports. The government's response was an exchange certificate scheme, which in effect compelled exporters to surrender 65 per cent of their export earnings to the Central Bank at the official rate.[34]

---

[34] Ibid., p. 62.

Bustamante was thus moving into head-on confrontation with the oligarchy, continuing policies which were strongly biased against exporters and in favour of urban consumers. Advice from the newly established International Monetary Fund (IMF) at this stage was supportive of Bustamante's policies, although the IMF viewed exchange controls as a transitional strategy until the exchange rate could be brought down in an orderly way. Also on IMF advice, Bustamante moved in September 1948 to authorize the raising of reserve ratios for the commercial banks, a measure which was designed to squeeze monetary growth and hinder capital flight, but which naturally alienated financial interests (including the Prado family).

Although the IMF was sympathetic towards Bustamante's problems, no such sympathy marked the work of a visiting U.S. economic team known as the Klein mission, which operated in close collaboration with the Gildemeister–Beltrán clique of the Right and which in 1948 came out strongly for total deregulation of the economy, including the floating of the exchange rate.[35] The Klein mission formed part of the emerging strategy of economic pressure on the government. Exporters were deferring the receipt of foreign exchange earnings, and importers were bringing payments forward, in anticipation of an eventual devaluation. To meet this speculative pressure Bustamante imposed exchange surcharges on imports, which made the regulations more complex without solving the basic problem of shortages. Pressures for a free-market solution from the Klein mission and Beltrán began to attract support from many other groups who were finding that the disadvantages of perpetual shortages outweighed the benefits of the cheap official exchange rate.

The overthrow of Bustamante put an end to this era of experimentation with controls and rationing as a means of stabilizing Peru's economy. It should, however, be emphasized that the exchange-control strategy was never designed to provide a climate for import-substitution industrialization; the government's objectives were to hold down the cost of living rather than to promote an alternative model of development. Manufacturers had to queue with everyone else for the cheap 'official' foreign exchange, or else had to resort to the expensive free market; there was no priority assigned to imports of essential intermediate or capital goods, and in 1945 Prado had tied the structure of import controls to the 1944

[35] M. J. Frankman, 'Export Promotion and Development Priorities in Peru, 1946–1965' (Ph. D. dissertation, University of Texas, 1968), p. 186; R. Thorp, 'The Klein Correspondence', mimeo (Oxford, 1974).

structure of actual imports, which blocked any shift towards import substitution of consumer goods. In so far as Bustamante relaxed this, it was in the direction of increased exchange allocations for imported foodstuffs rather than industrial materials. The sole consistent aim of policy throughout the period was to subsidize urban consumption.[36]

The Odría Dictatorship, 1948–56

General Manuel Odría came to power with strong support from the civilian Right and with the acquiescence of most of the military establishment. The Right clearly hoped to be able to repeat the experience of 1930–3, with Odría devoting himself to the repression of APRA and the labour movement, while civilian conservatives took over the management of the economy and eliminated the anti-export bias of the previous two regimes. In the early months, this indeed seemed to be happening. Pedro Beltrán was appointed to head the Central Bank within a week of the coup; a major drive against APRA was launched, the Partido Comunista was outlawed, import licensing and exchange surcharges were abolished and the exchange-control system was liberalized. By early 1949 APRA had disappeared underground and Haya was besieged in the Colombian Embassy (where he was obliged to remain until April 1954). 'Business confidence' had revived in anticipation of pro-elite policies, and political stability had been restored.

The following year, however, brought a series of rude shocks. Odría was in agreement with the civilian Right on the need for repression, but his objectives went beyond simply destroying APRA. The death penalty for political terrorism, decreed in March 1949, and the draconian Internal Security Law of 5 July 1949 were used to intimidate the president's opponents regardless of their political colour. At the beginning of the year Odría had announced that elections for president and Congress would be held in July, and a centrist organization, the Liga Nacional Democrática, was accordingly formed by non-*odriistas* to promote the candidacy of General Ernesto Montagne Markholtz – who had crushed General Rodríguez's attempted rightist coup in 1939, and who was now backed by the moderate Prado faction of the oligarchy.

It quickly became apparent, however, that Odría's commitment to democratic principles did not extend to the surrender of power. On 19

---

[36] On this point, see Thorp and Bertram, *Peru, 1890–1977*, pp. 187–90.

May he announced that (as expected) he himself would run for president with the conservative civilian leader Hector Boza as his running mate. Shortly thereafter Odría arranged for the Junta Nacional Electoral to invalidate Montagne's candidacy, leaving himself unopposed. Not since Leguía's notorious elections of 1924 and 1929 had expected standards of political conduct been thus flouted. Inevitably, the strongest reaction came from Arequipa, where on 13 June the students drove out the (evidently demoralized) army garrison, took over the city and proclaimed the *arequipeño* Francisco Mostajo (Montagne's running mate) as president. The city was recaptured only after heavy fighting on 16 June, and the subsequent token election of Odría and a tame Congress on 2 July occurred under a cloud of resentment and suspicion which afflicted the military as much as the civilian elite and middle class.

The Right was also finding Odría an unsatisfactory puppet in terms of economic policy. After the first round of economic liberalization in December 1948, he continued for nearly a year to cling to the dual exchange rate system, with its implicit subsidies on imported goods for urban popular consumption. To defend this, Odría maintained a contractionary fiscal stance, backed up from mid-1949 by a credit squeeze on the commercial banks – a continuation of policies adopted by Bustamante during 1948 and with the same aim of placating urban labour and the middle class. Odría had begun to cultivate mass political support and had recognized that this required the provision of material benefits for the lower class. The mid-1949 credit squeeze was therefore accompanied by a general salary increase, while a large-scale programme of public works in and around Lima provided employment (and encouraged the growing flood of rural–urban migration).

By 1950 the resources were at last available to buy a respite in Peru's economic conflicts of interest. The Korean War was under way, and world markets for the main Peruvian exports were rising at a rate not seen since 1919–20. Foreign exchange was suddenly plentiful, exporters' incomes were rising, and government revenues with them, and imports were in unrestricted supply. None of this was to be attributed to Odría's policies, but the effect was to render his political position secure. The new economic and political climate also brought a renewed surge of foreign investment. Odría's reaction was to relax, rather than tighten, the terms imposed on foreign firms in Peru, with two immediate results: the capital inflow rose to truly dramatic heights, and Peru became locked into policies that heavily favoured foreign investors and would in the following decade become serious political embarrassments (notably the mining developments at Toquepala and Marcona).

Behind the façade of prosperity, the original twin props of the regime – the army and the Right – had by 1953–4 become alienated from Odría: the army because of widespread distaste among the officers for their role as the repressive apparatus of a conspicuously corrupt dictatorship, and the Right because of its loss of control over Odría's economic policy. (Conversely, the moderate wing of the oligarchy – headed by the Prado and Ayulo families – became more closely associated with Odría at this time.)

Odría's loss of support within the military was a measure of the degree to which his caudillo style of rule had become a political anachronism in Peru. A growing body of opinion within the officer corps was opposed to the idea of military leaders behaving as traditional politicians and was attracted to a new view of the military as an institution committed to social engineering. The new ideas were developed from 1950 at the CAEM under the control of the former APRA sympathizer General Marín; but APRA doctrines had very little influence on the new technocratic military ideology. More important was the idea, stemming from the Second World War, that military preparedness must rest on a solid economic and social foundation and that Peruvian society (especially the backward Sierra, from which most of the army's conscript manpower was obtained) was in need of restructuring and modernizing. Odría, while wooing mass favour with public works and welfare schemes, took no interest in more fundamental social change and ignored the problems of the Sierra, despite serious crop failures in 1952–3, which contributed to the flood of migrants streaming down to the coastal cities.

Military discontent was reinforced by the problems of repression. Support for the destruction of APRA had been reasonably strong within the officer corps in October 1948, but after the extensive purge of November 1948, anti-APRA operations were confined to minor mopping up and the containment of Haya in the Colombian Embassy. The principal security problem for the regime after 1949 was not APRA, but Arequipa. In June 1950 the army found itself shooting down students and citizens in this, the least *aprista* of Peruvian cities. In 1952 the situation in Arequipa again became tense, with student strikes and growing labour unrest. In January 1953 a general strike paralysed the city and the military prefect (General Ricardo Pérez Godoy, later to become provisional president in 1962) faced the task of restoring order – a task made the more difficult by rising unemployment, since Odría's government undertook few employment-generating projects in Arequipa.

The Right's worries about the government stemmed mainly from Odría's attachment to a stable exchange rate and his willingness to pass on some of the benefits from the export bonanza to the workers via rising real wages.[37] There was more 'trickle-down' than the agro-export sector capitalists wanted. However, an export recession beginning in late 1952 put heavy pressure on the exchange rate, and the government reluctantly allowed the sol to fall in April 1953. But this in turn led to worker mobilization in defence of real wages. Strikes resulted in a 20 per cent salary increase for bank clerks in April and government employees the following May. And pressure swelled into a general strike later in the year. Besides his evident inability to control the labour movement, Odría had not convinced the Right that he had fully accepted a return to orthodox fiscal policies; he had come to heel on depreciation, but with obvious reluctance. In April 1954 he enraged the Right by allowing Haya to leave the country in exile – a move probably calculated to appease organized labour as the strikes spread but which earned Odría the same hostility from the Miró Quesada clan as Benavides had suffered in the wake of the 1935 Steer Affair.

In August 1954 the first direct attempt from within the government to unseat Odría was made by the minister of war, General Zenón Noriega, who led an abortive coup in Lima. From exile, Noriega proceeded to develop plans for another revolt in Arequipa, in concert with the Miró Quesadas and other prominent members of the Right. This conspiracy was broken up in December 1954, but its central aim of preventing Odría from remaining in power beyond the end of his 'constitutional' term in 1956 was revived in July 1955 by the prominent conservative Pedro Beltrán, whose newspaper *La Prensa* began a sustained campaign with a wide spectrum of political support (including several Arequipa liberals) calling for the lifting of repression and the calling of free elections. Pressure on Odría from this civilian coalition was reinforced in February 1956 by a military revolt in Iquitos headed by the garrison commander, General Marcial Merinos Pereyra, in protest against the repressive role assigned to the military.

Odría responded in a way which again offended the Right: the Iquitos

---

[37] 'Odría, like Benavides, was anti-union but not anti-worker. While he gave employers what amounted to complete liberty to destroy the unions, he would give startling wage and social benefits to the workers' (R. B. Marett, *Peru* [London, 1969], p. 176).

rebellion was crushed, the leaders of the Coalición Nacional, including Beltrán, were imprisoned and Odría granted de facto legality to APRA by permitting the party to hold its Third National Congress in March 1956. In April Odría declared his support for Hernando de Lavalle (a lawyer who was vice-chairman of the Ayulos' Banco de Crédito) as candidate for president; it was clear that he hoped for APRA support, and the APRA leaders entered into negotiations with Lavalle, indicating that they would deliver the party's block vote in exchange for legalization.

In the meantime, the emergence of two other candidates posed a problem for Odría. One was Fernando Belaúnde, at the head of the ramshackle new Frente Nacional de Juventudes Democráticos (later renamed Acción Popular), with an ill-defined base of middle-class support. Odría arranged for his candidacy to be annulled by the Junta Nacional Electoral in May. The other was the former president Manuel Prado, who suddenly reappeared from France and declared his candidacy. (Prado's decision to stand appears to have been taken against the wishes of his family.)[38] Had Lavalle managed to cement his alliance with APRA, neither challenger would have stood a chance. APRA, however, now chose to bargain with all three contenders, and Odría's calculations were upset by a series of demonstrations that showed Belaúnde's popularity and forced the Junta Electoral to restore him as a candidate on 1 June, only two days before the date originally set for the election. With the poll delayed for two weeks, intense negotiations proceeded until Prado and APRA announced the 'pact of Monterrico' (reached in negotiations at Odría's home). Prado would legalize APRA; in return the party would support his government and expect to win power in 1962. With APRA's block vote and considerable support from sections of the oligarchy and the property-owning middle class, Prado won 45 per cent of the vote (substantially less than his 1939 winning margin) and was inaugurated as President on 28 July. Odría's last act as president was to secure an informal undertaking from Prado to refrain from any investigation into corruption during Odría's period in office.

The atmosphere of intrigue and cynical calculation which surrounded the 1956 election did nothing to mitigate the factional infighting of the elite. The Miró Quesadas, as always, were opposed to any government connected with APRA. Beltrán, despite having backed Prado's candidacy, distrusted his ability to handle economic policy, on the basis of experience

---

[38] Gilbert, *The Oligarchy and the Old Regime*, pp. 248–9.

in the 1940s. However, all the established groups, including APRA, were now looking over their shoulders at the phenomenon of a new political machine, led by Belaúnde and representing the interests of middle-class professionals and technocrats. Beláunde had garnered a respectable 36 per cent of the vote in 1956 and was already running hard for 1962. His ideology was well judged to appeal to the new spirit abroad in the military (which from 1956 to 1962 stood scrupulously aside from political affairs but then moved decisively in Beláunde's favour), and his party, Acción Popular, provided at last a stable repository for the interests and ideas which Bustamante had represented in 1945.

The Second Prado Administration, 1956–62

The second administration of Manuel Prado provided the basis for much subsequent commentary which claimed that Peru was ruled directly by an 'oligarchy'. This period was a throw-back to something approaching the Aristocratic Republic of the early twentieth century, with direct elite participation in government, the military firmly out of politics and a Congress majority held by the governing coalition. The period was extraordinary for its political stability; until 1960 Prado faced only one insignificant and bungled coup (in January 1958), and labour unrest was muted since APRA kept its unions in line (though not without exception – there were serious clashes over manning levels and new technology on the northern sugar plantations in 1956–7, and a country-wide wave of strikes in 1958).

President Prado took more interest in international diplomacy than in internal affairs, and with both APRA and the military quiescent there was little pressure on the government to take action on social or structural issues. The travails of rural society in the Sierra were passed to a commission of conservative landowners headed by Pedro Beltrán, which succeeded in burying the issue of agrarian reform for the duration of Prado's term; and the rapidly expanding *barriadas* of Lima were left to their own devices, except for the usual clientelistic recruitment of support by APRA, which as a partner in government was able to deliver local benefits such as water supply and street lighting.

The economic predominance of the elite was also more evident during the Prado years, as the export-led growth process of the 1950s matured. In sugar, cotton, medium-scale mining, petroleum and even a couple of fishmeal ventures, elite capital was well to the fore. The elite, in addition, were moving into manufacturing on an unprecedented scale, constructing the integrated 'industrial groups' of Peruvian and foreign capital which controlled much of the country's corporate manufacturing activity in the 1960s.

The solid establishment façade of the second Prado regime, however, concealed a fragile structure which depended on a delicate balancing act between the interests of the oligarchy and those of mass consumers. Prado (like Odría and Bustamante before him) was obliged to take account of the explosive urban unrest which could be triggered by any increase in the cost of living or in the level of modern sector unemployment. He was also constrained by the knowledge that the military, though anxious to live down the repressive Odría era, was hostile to the transparent political ambitions of APRA. During his first year in power, Prado pursued relaxed economic policies that permitted rapid expansion of credit and a consumption-led boom, which quickly led to rising imports. More ominously, the credit expansion also financed a surge of capital flight as part of the elite's new wealth was shifted out of Peru.

The Peruvian boom did not run its course, however, for in 1957 there was a sharp recession in the United States. The Eisenhower government imposed tariff restrictions on mineral imports to the U.S. market and began unloading some of the commodity stockpiles which the U.S. had built up earlier in the decade – most importantly cotton, the world market for which fell catastrophically in 1957 as a result of U.S. dumping. Prado reacted with two years of deflationary monetary and fiscal policy which drove his government into head-on collision with organized labour and showed that in the final analysis, Prado lacked either the will or the strength to 'stabilize' the economy on the IMF's terms. The impossibility of smashing the labour movement was crucial: APRA's ability to rein in the unions did not extend to major cuts in real wages, while the military had no taste for massive repression after its experience with Odría. The oligarchy's profits could therefore not be protected through the recession by means of a squeeze on wages and salaries. The oligarchy responded by capital flight, which the government allowed to proceed unchecked. The imposition of direct exchange controls was rejected by Prado, and the continuing injection of money into the economy through the unfunded government deficit meant that the worsening balance-of-payments position could not be addressed by tight monetary policy. The mounting economic and political crisis culminated in the fall of Prado's cabinet in July 1959. Prado at this stage embarked on a political opening to the

Right, bringing Pedro Beltrán into the government as his new prime minister.

Beltrán effectively ran Peru from July 1959 until December 1961, when he resigned to prepare to stand for president in 1962 (although in the event his bid for the presidency failed to get off the ground and he withdrew). Like Benavides in 1933, he took control at the ideal moment for a conservative, just as an export boom in fishmeal got under way and triggered a new era of prosperity for the Peruvian export economy. To the surge of growth in fishmeal was added a jump in export earnings (and government revenues) from copper as the giant new Toquepala mine entered production, and new horizons for Peruvian sugar producers as the Cuban Revolution removed their strongest competitor from the U.S. market.

Against this background of a strengthening balance of payments, Beltrán was able to use creative accounting techniques and an internal bond issue to stop the monetary expansion. The prices for oil products were raised and subsidies on meat and bread removed. These three years, 1959–61, were the high tide of elite hegemony in the post–Second World War growth cycle: both the export economy and the conservative government seemed to be riding high. The impression of stability, however, was illusory. In the Sierra, La Convención Valley was already seething, and peasant land invasions had begun in the central zone. In the political arena, APRA and Acción Popular were limbering up for an electoral contest over which the oligarchy would have only the most tenuous influence. In the economy, despite the rapid growth of indicators such as GNP or export earnings, the rate of capital accumulation had begun an inexorable decline that was to continue through the next decade.[39] Peru's ancien regime had not quite ended by 1960, but the signs of its impending demise were evident.

Economic Policy in the 1950s

The replacement of Bustamante by Odría in 1948 is usually taken as a turning-point in Peruvian economic policy: from a period of controls and rationing to 'orthodox'. It is important, however, not to overstate the speed of this transition. Not until November 1949 (a year after the coup) did Odría accept a unified and floating exchange rate, at the urging of the

[39] E. V. K. Fitzgerald, *The Political Economy of Peru, 1956–78* (Cambridge, 1979), pp. 147–52; Thorp and Bertram, *Peru, 1890–1977*, pp. 288–9.

Klein mission, and even then he sweetened the pill by decreeing a new social security scheme for white-collar workers and by using tight credit controls to hold up the free-market exchange rate, against strong protests from export producers and from Pedro Beltrán, who resigned from the Central Bank in March 1950 after failing to persuade the government to relax monetary conditions and thereby allow the exchange rate to fall.

The Korean War boom enabled Odría to adopt expansionary policies without threatening the exchange rate, but when export markets turned down again in 1952 and the trade surplus faded, Odría was faced with the familiar dilemma which had confronted Prado and Bustamante. To protect the exchange rate would require either internal deflation of demand or the imposition of direct controls. If neither of these was adopted, the weakening balance of payments would force down the exchange rate. Exchange depreciation was still very unpopular with organized workers and employees. It was also opposed by manufacturers and by the booming urban construction industry (both increasingly dependent on imported materials and equipment). Controls were universally unpopular after the disastrous experience under Prado and Bustamante. Deflation ran the obvious medium-term risk of increased unemployment, but for Odría it was the path of least resistance, and in December 1952 the government instituted a series of measures to damp down internal demand, while looking (without much success) for foreign loans to boost the exchange reserves. By April 1953, exchange rate depreciation had become inevitable, but the government still tried to minimize it by a fiscal and monetary squeeze to cut back imports and capital flight. Continuing export recession, plus speculative pressure from the commercial sector and the exporting elite, pushed the exchange rate down steadily, resulting in a 20 per cent depreciation over the two years 1953–4, while the government's restrictive policies ran into the usual problems of IMF-type stabilization.[40] Fortunately for Odría, the export recession did not last beyond 1953, and renewed rapid growth began to bring the exchange rate back up again in 1954. At this stage the government (advised now by Prado and Ayulo banking interests) took the opportunity to reintroduce a fixed exchange rate, making inevitable a replay of the entire familiar devaluation battle on the next down-swing three years later, in 1957–9.

The 'orthodoxy' of Odría's economic policies was thus orthodoxy of a particular kind, corresponding to the IMF's prescription for defence of the

---

[40] See Dragisic, 'Peruvian Stabilization Policies', chap. 3

exchange rate in times of crises by means of domestic deflation.[41] The case made by the Klein mission and Pedro Beltrán in the late 1940s and early 1950s for leaving balance-of-payments adjustment to a freely floating exchange rate, while keeping the domestic economy buoyant by means of monetary policy, represented an alternative conception of economic orthodoxy. This debate of the 1950s revived the issues which had split the oligarchy during the depression, pitting defenders of a strong currency against proponents of price flexibility.

Within a year of Prado's election in 1956, the international recession produced a crisis of confidence and a down-turn in the Peruvian economy. Cotton earnings, one of the mainstays of popular consumption spending, fell, while at the same time speculation against the exchange rate produced capital flight, which cut the domestic money supply and accentuated the recession. To defend the exchange rate without resorting to controls, the government adopted a tight fiscal stance. Only loyal support from APRA prevented a serious outburst of labour unrest in the last quarter of 1957. In the meantime, drought resulted in crop failures in the Sierra and a poor sugar harvest on the Coast. The IMF, brought in to advise at the end of 1957, told Prado to batten down the hatches and wait for exports to recover. A large stand-by credit was provided to defend the sol on the understanding that the budget deficit, the money supply and real wages would all be squeezed. The exchange rate nevertheless began to drop in the face of capital flight. Over the following year the government's deflationary policies drove the economy into a deepening recession, without succeeding in preventing the continuing depreciation of the exchange rate. Organized labour managed to defend living standards by securing periodic increases in wages and salaries decreed by the government in order to compensate for the higher prices resulting from exchange depreciation; these increases kept the squeeze on export producers' profits, while forcing the government into deficit financing to pay its rising salary bill. The resulting monetary expansion financed additional capital flight, which the government facilitated by borrowing abroad and by refraining from any form of exchange controls. Seeking to achieve a reduction in the deficit, the government cut its investment spending heavily and tried (in April 1959) to raise new taxes, but APRA balked at these, and congressional approval could not be obtained. The banks eventually engineered a

---

[41] S. C. Tsiang, 'An Experiment with Flexible Exchange Rates: Peru, 1950–54', *IMF Staff Papers*, February 1957.

credit explosion in May–June 1959, while strikes succeeded in securing a new round of wage and salary increases.[42]

Thus by 1959 all the ingredients for a full-blown economic crisis were present. As in 1949 and 1953, however, the underlying strength of the Peruvian export economy defused the government's problems once the short-run recession in the world economy had passed. From 1959 to 1962 export volumes grew 21 per cent annually and real GNP grew at nearly 9 per cent.[43] Fishmeal and copper exports rescued Prado and his newly appointed prime minister, Beltrán, from the explosive urban unrest and consequent political vunerability which could have followed from continued imposition of severe stabilization measures.

CONCLUSION

Between 1930 and 1960 the Peruvian oligarchy remained hegemonic in the sense that it (together with foreign capital) controlled the commanding heights of the economy and was generally able to cope with political challenges to its position by co-option and/or repression. As a ruling class, however, it produced neither an outstanding leader nor a durable political party to act as a vehicle for its interests. Its control over the state apparatus was consequently tenuous and heavily dependent on military tolerance or goodwill. At the same time, there was an absence in Peru of other national political factors able to articulate new economic and social strategies in the interests of any coherent class or group of classes. This was especially striking during the 1930s. While other countries of the continent experimented with import substitution, exchange controls, populist redistributive policies and various forms of planning, Peru stumbled into these things (if at all) late and on an ad hoc basis. The dismal record of economic management under Bustamante from 1945 to 1948 is the most striking case of this, since a clear political opening existed in 1945 for the promotion of new policies by the APRA–FDN alliance. Instead, the role which APRA chose for itself in those years seemed designed more to precipitate the breakdown of Bustamante's administration than to wield effective power in positive policy formation. This abstention in turn contributed powerfully to the strength and success of the Odría-led reaction of 1948, since no viable

[42] J. Santistevan and A. Delgado, *La Huelga en el Perú* (Lima, 1981), pp. 179–81; DeWind, 'Peasants Become Miners', pp. 358–60.
[43] Thorp and Bertram, *Peru, 1890–1977*, p. 205.

alternative to orthodox conservatism seemed by then to exist for politically conscious Peruvians.

APRA's approach to state power was primarily instrumental, aimed at securing access to influence and patronage at lower levels of the state apparatus rather than at taking command of the system at the top. In the local-level politics of organizing peasant community conflicts with landlords, or *barrida* residents' campaigns for public utilities, or labour unionists' attempts to play off the state against their employers, APRA performed well. The party possessed a large cadre of professional people, especially lawyers and teachers, who were deployed to good effect in rural and suburban Peru during the 1940s and 1950s; it had many active members among the employees of the state apparatus (including quite a number in the armed forces); and it had its strong-arm group, the *bufalos*, to keep the upper hand in the political underground of local protection rackets and competition for union posts. It was the successful operation of this grass-roots patronage machine which kept the party large and powerful – not its ideological stance or the pronouncements of its congressmen or presidential candidates.

The detailed political history of the period reveals a fluid world of opportunistic manoeuvring, with an 'oligarchy' divided both by factional feuds and by sectoral conflicts. As suggested earlier, if elite hegemony survived, this was due not so much to any intrinsic strength of the 'oligarchy' as to the fragmentation and weakness of other possible contenders for power. Nevertheless, the imperatives of political survival (quite apart from any long-run role of the state in protecting the capitalist mode of production) obliged politicians and administrators to heed the demands of working-class and white-collar groups, regional interests, foreign firms and even on rare occasions the Sierra peasantry. Generally the response of the state was to accommodate such groups if possible by providing a share of the spoils from export-led growth, but to combine such co-option, if necessary, with some degree of repression.

Of the non-elite contenders for power, the most consistent and effective were the professional middle class of Arequipa, whose staunch (if not altogether disinterested) defence of constitutional principles made it a permanent threat and repeatedly brought its representatives within reach of national power (without providing the degree of class support and political organization that would have been necessary to sustain it in control of the state). Also effective, but less consistent, was the military, which from the 1930s began to exhibit a growing independence from the civilian elite and which passed through a long process of internal political debate and conflict before emerging finally as a group of technocratic social engineers in their own right.

It may be noted that this chapter has not presented the familiar interpretations of Peruvian history in the middle decades of the twentieth century as some sort of epic struggle between APRA and the oligarchy, or between military and civilian rule. Such themes have been overplayed in the writing about Peru and have obscured the real character and dynamics of Peruvian political life. In the manoeuvring and infighting of *la política criolla,* APRA was only one of several actors, and seldom the most important (though often the most vocal). The key to political history in this period was the difficulty of cementing *any* viable political coalition, rather than some mythical contest between clearly defined and well-entrenched adversaries. The issue of whether the president was of military or civilian origin was far less important than the question of how different presidents handled the perennial balancing act between the determinate power of the elite (in the sense that they could generally bring down a government once they set their minds to the task) and the unavoidable need to placate mass unrest by material concessions (wage increases, public works, subsidies on foodstuffs). Even control of the state, of course, by no means conferred control over events. The ruling class thus had only limited capacity to shape the direction which Peruvian society took. Economic policy was successful in maintaining a strong commitment to laissez-faire and the export economy; but key elements in the historical story could not be controlled in the long run – especially the world economy and the Sierra peasantry. A great deal of Peru's history, in other words, was made outside the sphere of formal national politics.

8

PERU SINCE 1960

Peru after 1960 experienced significant changes in its social structure, a notable expansion and intensification of political participation and important advances in the national integration of the peasants, as well as the urban middle and working classes, which were traditionally characterized by fragmentation and a marginal political status. At the same time, Peru underwent a series of changes in its political regime, shifting from an oligarchic system to a relatively broad-based democratic polity. Yet the relations between state and society acquired a conflictive character in so far as political 'inclusion' was accompanied by 'exclusionary' policies in the socio-economic arena which impeded the democratization and nationalization of Peruvian society and politics. The resulting tension produced a high level of political conflict and violence, contributing to the disintegration of the state.

After the Second World War, Peru had experienced a short period of democratic transition that ended in 1948 with a military coup headed by General Manuel A. Odría. The Odría dictatorship (1948–56) paved the way for increased participation by U.S. capital in the economy as a result of which traditional exports expanded and high rates of growth in gross domestic product (GDP) were achieved. (During the period from 1950 to 1967, exports grew 7 per cent annually – as against 4 per cent in Latin America as a whole – and GDP rose 6 per cent annually. In 1965, 47 per cent of the country's exports were produced by U.S. corporations, and 62 per cent of the financial capital was controlled by U.S. banks.) Odría sought to win the support of the lower and middle urban classes in an attempt to undermine the social base of Alianza Popular Revolucionaria

This chapter was translated from the Spanish by Elizabeth Ladd.

Americana (APRA), the traditional enemy of the oligarchic coalition. With the fiscal resources that the government obtained from exports, the regime encouraged public spending for urban development and public employment and, at the same time, controlled food prices and subsidized food imports, enhancing urban demand and the development of import-substitution industrialization. The agricultural policies eroded the traditional landowners' control of the indigenous peasant population and shed light on the anachronistic character of their domination. Finally, as capitalist development was centred mainly in the urban and coastal regions, especially Lima, it drastically increased regional economic and social differences and opportunities. Together with demographic pressures, these factors promoted two processes that transformed the social fabric. First, there emerged a broad indigenous peasant movement, centred in the Sierra, that was determined both to recover the property that landowners had pillaged from the Indian communities and to put an end to their traditional exploitation and political domination. This movement spread throughout the country, ending the isolation of the peasants, who irrupted into the political scene and shattered the clientelistic-oligarchic framework of state organization. Second, these changes produced an intensification of migration from the highlands to the coast and from the rural and urban areas of this region towards Lima. Though the migrants initially consisted of landowners and members of the traditional provincial middle class, they later included peasants. This internal migration modified the demographic profile of the country: while the population settled in urban centres with more than five thousand inhabitants comprised 21 per cent of the total population in 1940, it reached 38 per cent in 1961, 49 per cent in 1972, and 65 per cent in 1990. While the average annual growth of the rural population was 1.3 per cent between 1940 and 1961, it dropped to 0.72 per cent between 1961 and 1972, whereas urban growth was 4.1 and 5.6 per cent during the same periods.

As economic growth and the policies of the Odría government began to change the social structure, they opened a new path for the political development of Peruvian society. Odría tried to become politically independent of his original supporters and to develop a kind of populism similar to that of Perón of Argentina. The backers of the 1948 coup that had brought him to power attacked the dictator and demanded a return to the 'rule of law', which would make it possible to form a constitutional government under which they would regain full control of the state. The daily *La Prensa,* defender of exporters' interests, mobilized the opposition and with the approval of the clandestine Aprista Party forced Odría to call elections in 1956. Simultaneously, the various oligarchic factions entered into negotiations with the leaders of APRA, who decided to support Manuel Prado for the presidency in return for the establishment of what came to be known as 'political coexistence'. As a result, Prado won the 1956 elections with the *apristas'* votes.

The implicit rules of the new constitutional regime were that APRA would abandon its radical position and become a 'loyal opposition', while the governing group promised to concede some social benefits to the urban sectors organized by APRA, thus establishing a policy of 'segmentary incorporation'. For the dominant group that supported this experiment, the survival of the regime of oligarchic domination in a situation of rapid urbanization and mobilization could be achieved only by co-opting the *aprista* leaders, who were put in charge of controlling the social demands and containing the rise of Communism. There was an implicit threat that the army would be called in once again to repress APRA if the party jeopardized the new political rules of the game.

For its part, APRA, and in particular its leader Víctor Raúl Haya de la Torre, became convinced of the need to consolidate an institutional system that would permit them to complete and eventually win office in the next elections. Haya felt that it was not possible to maintain, as he had in the 1930s, that 'only APRA will save Peru', since this position had merely led to clandestine political status and ineffectiveness. Furthermore, Haya thought that urbanization and industrialization would eliminate the 'feudal' character of society and facilitate the emergence of a new ruling class that would give him the opportunity to join elites and masses in a coalition. The 'popularization of capitalism' would eliminate any radical tendencies present in the party itself and in society.

However, from the beginning of the coexistence pact, new political forces openly rejected the *aprista* policy, which contradicted its traditional anti-oligarchic and anti-imperialist position. The Peruvian population was becoming increasingly organized. New channels for social and political participation were being created. Peasant movements demanded agrarian reform, credits and public services from the government. Migrants to the coastal cities, especially Lima, occupied public and private lands on which to build homes and exerted pressure on the authorities to supply water, electricity, transportation, health, education and employment. An expanded and better organized working class demanded that the government recognize its rights to greater participation in the economy and to access to social services provided by the state. Members of the rapidly growing middle class added their voices to these demands, insisting on the expansion of educational facilities to enable them to obtain newly created jobs in the public sector. The emerging industrial capitalists sought state protection through higher tariffs and broader credit facilities. These new social groups all sought to satisfy their needs through state intervention and an increase in public spending. Political life was focussed on the central role of the state.

Attempts were made to integrate the mobilized peasants, the working class and the professional middle class, as well as the new industrialists around a nationalist and reformist platform by the Partido Demócrata Cristiano, the Movimiento Social Progresista and Acción Popular (AP). Within a few months, AP won the support of one-third of the electorate. In the following years, a group of radical *apristas,* who argued for the need to bring about the anti-imperialist, anti-feudal revolution that Haya had once proposed, split off and, following the example of the Cuban Revolution, formed the Movimiento de Izquierda Revolucionaria (MIR), which joined other new leftist groups. During this process, APRA began to lose its political control in the unions and the universities. In fact, the political mobilisation of Peruvian society during the 1960s favoured the association of the working class and university population with reformist and leftist groups, making them champions of 'structural change'.

The reformist platform was based on a diagnosis that, in general terms, was the same one that Haya de la Torre had offered in 1930. Underdevelopment and the extreme poverty of the majority were attributed to the persistence of an archaic agrarian structure, the excessive opening of the economy to foreign capital and the monopolistic control of credit – all of which was the result of the concentration of power among 'forty families' in alliance with a number of North American companies engaged in mining and agriculture. Any correction of this situation would have to include a redistribution of wealth and income in order to broaden the internal market and to develop an independent capitalism, a position being advocated by the influential Comisión Económica Para América Latina (CEPAL) of the United Nations. To attain this goal, structural reforms were necessary: agricultural property was to be restructured and based on co-operatives, indigenous communities as well as small and medium-sized pieces of property. Through the active participation of the state in industrial development, workers were to be granted a share of company profits. Furthermore, the functions and capacities of the state were to be enhanced to cover the exploitation of natural resources and the control of banking and to displace foreign interests. Finally, economic activity was to be organized around a development plan designed to harmonize different social interests. Only in this way would the state be in a position to assign social resources in accordance with national interests and to incorporate the new classes peacefully into the political system, culminating in the long-awaited national and political integration of Peruvian society.

The emergence of new social and political forces divided the traditional property-owning class and the institutions that supported the oligarchic regime – the Church and the army. Since the oligarchy had not been politically organized since 1919, its divisions were identifiable only from the positions adopted by the country's two most important dailies. While *La Prensa,* the mouthpiece of the exporters, recommended the reinforcement of a market economy, which was supposed to cause Peru to experience a 'German miracle', *El Comercio* expounded the urgency of a reformist, nationalist policy which was at the same time anti-*aprista*. On this issue, *El Comercio* was ideologically associated with the new political parties, since it supported the need for substantive reforms in order to overcome the two basic contradictions inherent in Peruvian society: the persistence of non-capitalism in the face of the industrial development of the country and the growing subordination of national capital and the Peruvian state to U.S. government and business.

The urgency of these reforms, according to *El Comercio,* was based on national security – a position which fully coincided with new tendencies emerging within the armed forces. Externally, the country faced the danger of 'international Communism' and, at the same time, the supposed expansionist policy of Chile. Internally, popular discontent encouraged the diffusion and implantation of extremist ideologies and organizations. Therefore, without a redistributionist policy that would resolve the differences between capital and labour, without a state that would be in a position to manage the economy and transfer the control held by foreign capital back to the Peruvians, the nation's precarious existence was in serious danger. But these changes could be carried out only 'from above', by 'enlightened' persons, with the collaboration of the army. This is why *El Comercio* consistently attacked the 'coexistence' between the oligarchy and APRA.

Since the end of the 1950s, a reformist school of thought had also been developing within the Church which proclaimed the need for 'structural changes' aimed at improving living conditions for the masses; this trend was later supported by the Second Vatican Council and episcopal meetings

both in Peru and throughout Latin America. One of the principal consequences of this new position was the involvement of priests with peasant
movements, poor neighbourhoods, labour unions, and universities, building up organizations that were based on the ideas which later were to be
manifested in the Theology of Liberation. Through 'courses in Christian-
ity', other Church groups were directing their activities towards the emerging technocratic sectors of the middle class – the military and professional
managers. In both cases the interest of the Church in fostering social
change was aimed at smoothing the rough edges within Peruvian society
and promoting a sense of solidarity and community in national life.

Institutional and ideological changes took place in the army which
favoured its independence from the dominant coalition and the strengthening of a reformist and nationalist orientation. After the Second World War
and with the beginning of the Cold War, the Peruvian army, like those of
other countries of the region, established close links with the U.S. military
in order to contain the advance of international Communism. The technical
relations between the Peruvian armed forces and the U.S. military involved
material support and assistance in logistical organization which made it
necessary to upgrade the professional training of the military. The modernization of the institution involved a new strategic perspective, especially
with regard to 'total war', which required an analysis of Peruvian realities
and led to the rejection of much that had hitherto been taken from French
textbooks. In this context, the Centro de Altos Estudios Militares (CAEM)
was created. From its inception, CAEM, which brought together high-
ranking officers and executive personnel from the public and private sectors,
embarked on an analysis of the country's resources. The resulting studies,
increasingly directed by technocrats with reformist orientations, revealed
that Peru, compared with other countries of the region – mainly Chile –
was in an alarming state of underdevelopment. This gave rise to military
demands for planned development.

At the beginning of the 1960s, a CAEM document declared, 'The sad
and depressing reality is that in Peru real power is not held by the
executive, legislative, judicial or electoral branch of government, but by
the large landowners, exporters, bankers and North American companies'.
The obvious conclusion was that 'nationalization' and the reorganization of
production had become indispensable to enhancing the country's potential
and that it was necessary to plan the economy in order to secure national
sovereignty.

At the end of the 1950s, the army underwent a series of organizational changes aimed at rationalizing the military apparatus. One of the key features of this reorganization was the strengthening of the military intelligence service, which expanded its traditional functions after analysing the wars in Algeria and Vietnam, the Cuban Revolution and the construction of the state of Israel and its conflicts with neighbouring countries. At the same time, in internal matters it paid special attention to the social movement in the cities and in the rural areas. The study of these situations, along with the academic analyses of insurgency and counter-insurgency developed by the United States, led to the conclusion that national defence had to be seen not only as an external problem, but also as an internal issue. While the United States was considered responsible for containing the Soviet threat on an international level, the Peruvian army had to deal with the countries on its borders – Chile and Ecuador – and the possible development of subversive centres aided by the USSR, which, under the pretext of injustice, might try to attack the rear guard of the 'free world'.

The intelligence services reached the conclusion that the social movement was developing because of ownership of large areas of land by a relatively small number of families, as well as poverty among the peasants, urban unemployment, a lack of political participation and political alienation. Thus, not only was the country too underdeveloped to engage in 'total war', but the population had no 'national' identity. As one officer noted, the country had 10 million inhabitants but very few Peruvians. This diagnosis required that the army actively participate in changing the conditions in which the majority of the population lived. Only then would the population identify itself with the nation, grant legitimacy to the state and resist subversion.

Thus, a nationalist and reformist consciousness was created within the upper echelons of the army which was similar to the stance taken by *El Comercio,* the Church and the new reformist parties and in opposition to the coexistence between APRA and the oligarchic bloc.

The redefinition of the military's functions was accelerated at the end of the 1950s when the political scene was dominated by an open nationalist and anti-oligarchic struggle. Representatives of the new reformist parties attacked the International Petroleum Company (IPC) with the full support of *El Comercio* for illegally exploiting the national resources of the country. (The U.S. Embassy and IPC, in co-ordination with other U.S. corporations, organized through *La Prensa* a campaign against reformist trends, associating them with Communism.) At the same time, a powerful peasant movement emerged and occupied landholdings of the Cerro de Pasco

Copper Corporation in the central Sierra, while workers went on strike in the coastal plantations of the Grace Corporation. At the beginning of the 1960s, a peasant mobilization in Cuzco, led by Hugo Blanco, sent shock waves through the country and caused *La Prensa* to launch a violent anti-Communist and anti-reformist campaign in an effort to get the army to take on the task of repressing the peasants in particular and all social movements in general. The army, although it took charge of dismantling the peasant movement was increasingly convinced that generalized and violent mobilization would ensue unless an attempt was made to deal with Peru's social problems.

THE ELECTIONS OF 1962−3 AND THE FIRST
BELAÚNDE PRESIDENCY, 1963−8

Six candidates contested the presidential elections of 1962. The most important were Haya de la Torre (APRA), in his first presidential bid since 1931, the former dictator general Manuel Odría (Unión Nacional Odriísta, UNO) and Fernando Belaúnde Terry (AP). It was the first open and intense electoral struggle for many years. All the candidates proclaimed their willingness to promote substantive social change. Furthermore, Belaúnde insisted on the need to readjust the conditions under which foreign capital entered Peru and, in particular, to nationalize IPC, the symbol of nationalist vindication.

In the face of a possible victory by Haya de la Torre, who had the open support of the U.S. ambassador, *El Comercio* launched an intense campaign for the benefit of the army, denouncing the fraudulent nature of the elections due to government aid to APRA under the 'coexistence' pact. Although no candidate obtained a clear one-third of the votes, Haya narrowly won the election and APRA commanded enough congressional strength to secure him the presidency. The military high command made it clear that it would not allow Haya's inauguration, forcing him to give his support to Odría. But Odría was now equally unacceptable to the military. On 18 July 1962, a few days before President Prado finished his term, the military deposed him and installed the first 'institutional' military government in Peru and Latin America.

The military junta attempted to put the army's new philosophy into practice and proclaimed its autonomy from oligarchic forces: it carried out an agrarian reform in La Convención (Cuzco), the centre of the largest peasant mobilization; it created the Instituto Nacional de Planificación, the objective of which was to organize economic development, and announced the imminent nationalization of IPC. At the same time, the armed forces attempted to demobilize the social movement by jailing hundreds of its leaders and confining workers, peasants, employees, students, intellectuals, journalists and politicians in prison camps.

During the junta's year in government, open opposition to its 'Nasserism' was expressed by the oligarchy and APRA, by the U.S. government and by the new leftist movement. The isolation of the government and the division this produced, especially the threat of an end to U.S. military assistance, obliged it to call elections in June 1963. Nevertheless, the declared autonomy of the military from society changed the expected political alliances of the principal groups. The oligarchic bloc and U.S. companies felt no longer confident that the army would safeguard their interests as it had done previously. Reformist groups, however, discovered that they could organize the 'revolution from above' with the help of the military. For its part, the military realized that, if it were again to take over the government, it would have to take far more radical steps to destroy the dominant groups and thus gain the support of the lower- and middle-classes.

In the 1963 elections, the Partido Democrático Cristiano (PDC) and other small reformist groups joined in an alliance with AP, enabling Belaúnde to win a narrow victory over Haya and Odría, which met with a euphoric response in many sectors of society, the Church and the armed forces. The peasants took agrarian reform into their hands and occupied large property holdings; organized workers embarked on a wave of strikes in order to improve their standard of living; students were organized in 'Cooperación Popular' and went by the thousands to assist peasants in 'community development', allowing AP to penetrate the country side politically; the government called on experts, professionals and intellectuals to help achieve 'the conquest of Peru by the Peruvians', in the words of President Belaúnde. After six months in government, Balaúnde called municipal elections, for the first time in fifty years, and the AP–PDC alliance made considerable advances. Everything seemed auspicious for the realization of reformist hopes and the satisfaction of the needs of the peasants, the workers, the middle class and the new entrepreneurial class.

The reformist project, however, faced a formidable – and eventually insurmountable – obstacle due to the resistance of the oligarchic coalition. Moreover, APRA and UNO had a majority in Congress, with the government alliance ranking second, and President Belaúnde had difficulty forming alliances and negotiating congressional support for his government. From the beginning, Manuel Seoane, APRA's second-ranking leader, along with several AP leaders, stressed the need to establish an accord between the two organizations, which had similar political programmes and together represented 70 per cent of the electorate. The internal and external barriers to an alliance between AP and APRA were, however, substantial. If AP cast its lot with the *apristas,* it had to expect to be rejected by the Army and *El Comercio.* Moreover, the radical sector of the party believed that the *aprista* leadership had 'sold out' to the oligarchy and imperialism. From APRA's point of view, AP was a disloyal competitor that had joined forces with its traditional enemies, the army and *El Comercio,* in order to block Haya's election to the presidency; moreover, the *apristas* believed that the *acciopopulistas* were seeking to rob them of their traditional banners and their activists. Finally, Haya de la Torre refused to recognize Belaúnde as the leader of a mass movement capable of competing with him.

Thus, political co-operation between the reformist parties, APRA and AP, and the establishment of constructive relations between the executive and legislative branches, failed to materialize, making it difficult for the democratic regime to consolidate. Instead, APRA allied itself with *odriismo,* its former enemy, and formed the 'Coalición' that came to control Congress following the 'coexistence' pact that APRA had formed with the oligarchic bloc during the Prado government. This new arrangement provoked another split in APRA: its youth leadership joined the new reformist groups and the embryonic groups of the Left. From now on, the new generations of the working and middle classes no longer saw APRA as a revolutionary, or even a reformist, party and began to embrace the radical positions of the Left.

The formation of the Coalición resulted in a permanent congressional obstacle to the reformist proposals of the executive, especially the Agrarian Reform Law and the solution of the IPC issue. The ability of Congress to block executive initiatives was derived from the powers granted to it by the 1933 constitution: it had the right to approve and modify financial measures and censure ministers, powers which the APRA–UNO coalition used and abused during the Belaúnde government. As a result, over a period of five years, Belaúnde appointed 178 ministers, 94 of whom were replaced, seriously altering the composition of six cabinets. The constitution denied the president the power to call new elections, which might have changed the distribution of representation in the legislature; he did not even have the power of presidential veto.

Belaúnde found himself chained to the will of the Coalición, which developed a strategy aimed at the unconditional surrender of the executive. The President had, in fact, no viable alternatives. Closing down the legislature – the first power as Haya called it – with military help, as some leaders of AP and army officers suggested, would have meant breaking the law and being a prisoner of the army. The other possibility – mobilizing the masses in order to force the Coalición to yield, as the young radical leadership of his party demanded – was unacceptable to the armed forces and *El Comercio,* because it would have provoked disorder and would have inhibited the development of gradual reforms 'from above'. In any case, such methods went against the grain of Belaúnde's legalistic and aristocratic character and style.

Thus, it was clear that the government was incapable of satisfying the demands of the peasantry, as well as of the working and middle classes. The remaining solution was to repress the demands for structural change and, at the same time, to increase government spending. Indeed, the Belaúnde administration resorted to repressing the peasant and worker movements that were developing outside of APRA's party machine and sphere of control, reinforcing the radical leftist tendencies among the university students, who in 1965 organized four *focos* in an abortive effort to imitate the Cuban revolutionary campaign.

Yet both Congress and the executive independently approved growing social expenditures, against fierce opposition by *La Prensa,* thus underlining the independence of the political forces of the Coalición from the propertied classes. Belaúnde's government began by spending 11.5 per cent of GDP, one of the lowest figures in Latin America, but by 1968 this share had risen to 16 per cent, one of the highest in the region, especially in education, allowing for an unprecedented growth of the student population. Between 1965 and 1967, the budget deficit grew at an average annual rate of 95 per cent, measured against that of 1964, because the Coalición systematically opposed tax reforms. At the same time, new tax exemptions were decreed in favour of import substitution and urban employment was developed – ultimately encouraging peasant migration to the cities and reinforcing the acutely regressive character of the tax system and the distribution of income, which made Peru an exception even in Latin America.

Furthermore, the volume of exports, which had begun to grow in the 1950s, stagnated in 1965 as a result of the withdrawal of U.S. investment. One of the central motifs of the electoral campaigns in 1962 and 1963 was the nationalization of IPC, which Belaúnde had promised to resolve in the first three months of his term. In response to this, the U.S. government cut Alliance for Progress aid and blocked public and private U.S. capital investment until an agreement could be reached that the company considered advantageous. Meanwhile, despite angry protests by exporters, the rate of exchange was kept unchanged in an effort to support industrial development and subsidized food prices, thus causing a further deterioration of the peasants' conditions and pushing them to urban areas. This in turn caused a rise in imports, which the government financed by increasing its external debt from U.S. $235 million to $680 million between 1963 and 1968; while in 1965 the debt represented 8 per cent of the total value of exports, by 1967 it had reached 18 per cent.

In 1967 the government was forced to declare a 44 per cent devaluation, causing general confusion and tarnishing the government's credibility, since Belaúnde had repeatedly assured the country that he would not resort to devaluation (which, he said, would be a 'betrayal of our country'). Two months later the government lost a seat in the department of Lima to the Coalición in a by-election in which the candidate of the Left won 17 per cent of the vote at a time when the labour unions were detaching themselves from the *aprista*-controlled Confederación de Trabajadores del Peru (CTP) and the Communist Party had gained control of them in the Confederación General de Trabajadores del Peru (CGTP).

As the Belaúnde government and the political system as a whole progressively lost their legitimacy within AP and among reformist groups, there was a growing tendency to regard the democratic parliamentary system as a barrier to the achievement of structural change, which could be realized only through revolutionary action, or rather through the installation of a 'strong' government that would not be fettered by parliamentary restrictions. Thus, as soon as the guerrilla defeat became evident, prospects for change became associated with a military government capable of radicalizing the measures carried out during the 1962–3 period.

The economic crises, the growing trend amongst workers, peasants, students and intellectuals to join together in a leftist front and the menace of *aprista* interference in the armed forces caused anxiety within the army over the loss of its autonomy and general political disintegration. Moreover, the decision of the air force to purchase modern jet fighters from

France, given the unwillingness of the United States to sell these aircraft to Peru even though they had already been sold to Chile, gave rise to new tensions and increased nationalism in the armed forces.

The military's apprehension was deepened by successive ministerial crises, the last of which arose in June 1968 and was to be the final event in the breakdown of Belaúnde's government and of oligarchic rule. Under unprecedented pressure, the president turned to a cabinet composed of 'independents' approved by Haya de la Torre, who, after five years of obstruction, now detached himself from *odriísmo* and joined forces with AP in granting the new cabinet 'extraordinary powers' for a sixty-day period. The governability problem forced both Belaúnde and Haya to adopt this risky position.

As had been foreseen in 1963, the agreement between the executive and APRA provoked a sharp realignment of political alliances. Odría's group split, with one faction, supported by *La Prensa,* attacking the new government, whilst the leadership of AP itself split from Belaúnde and joined forces with *El Comercio* and the army in rejecting this 'infamous' pact.

As a result of the extraordinary powers he was given by the new majority in Congress, Manuel Ulloa, the minister of economics, was able to develop a 'structural adjustment' programme and a series of economic reforms that infuriated the owners of land and capital. He enforced tax reforms denied by the opposition during the previous five years, restricted foreign activity in banking, strengthened the role of the state and domestic industrialists in companies considered strategic for the national economy and 'nationalized' the Central Bank, which had hitherto been controlled by private capital. The minister also tried to control and reduce military spending, enraging the high command.

Manuel Ulloa refinanced the external debt, securing a U.S.-capital-financed multimillion-dollar investment in mining exploitation which would provide for the recovery of export growth. This measure reflected an agreement with IPC, which in July 1968 suddenly modified its unyielding opposition to the terms the president had proposed five years earlier. In his message to the nation, Belaúnde announced that the problem between the state and IPC had been resolved, and he pledged to congressional leaders and military chiefs that the oil wells held by IPC would be handed over. In the midst of so many failures, this seemed to be the beginning, albeit belatedly, of concrete governmental achievements.

However, a series of political scandals soon brought the government down. The pledge signed by the president provided that IPC would hand over the half-exhausted oil wells which it had been exploiting illegally for more than fifty years and for which it owed about U.S. $200 million, according to some sources, or $600 million, according to others. In return for this transfer, the government agreed to remit the corporation's debts. In addition, the refinery would remain in the hands of IPC, with the understanding that it would be enlarged and modernized. Furthermore, the company would continue to exercise its monopoly on gasoline for a forty-year period, with the option of renewing the concession for another forty years, or until the year 2048. The government also granted the corporation a concession on 1 million hectares of forest land for exploration and oil exploitation. When the agreement was made public, it was unanimously repudiated and had the effect of increasing nationalist and reformist demands for a drastic and definitive solution to the IPC problem as well as the problems caused by other foreign companies.

In addition, a few days after the 'Acta de Talara' was signed, the manager of the State Petroleum Company publicly denounced the fact that page 11 of the agreement, which stipulated the price IPC was obliged to pay to the state-owned company for oil, had been withdrawn. This news destroyed a government whose situation was already precarious. APRA refused to accept the arrangement and left Belaúnde to his own fate. *El Comercio* launched a furious assault on the government and called for the army to take charge of the situation. At the end of September, the cabinet was forced to resign, and it was only after several attempts that the president was able, on 2 October, to assemble a new administration. The following day, a military coup, which had been in gestation since February, had no trouble deposing a president who had lost all semblance of public support, and put an end – 'sin pena ni gloria' – to the last experiment aimed at transforming the oligarchic regime by institutional means. It was now clear that it was necessary to change the political structure in order to introduce structural changes in society and the economy.

MILITARY GOVERNMENT AND 'REVOLUTION FROM
ABOVE', 1968 – 75

The inability of the Belaúnde government to reform Peru's social and political structure and the development of a new reformist ideology in the high military command contributed to the coup d'état of 3 October 1968 and the formation of the Revolutionary Government of the Armed Forces under the leadership of General Juan Velasco Alvarado. Those in charge of the military take-over were determined to heed the lessons of the short-lived experiment of 1962–3 as well as Belaúnde's failure. First, the armed forces were transformed into autonomous pillars of the state, monopolizing governmental activities and seeking to transform policy into a purely administrative process with the advice of technical experts and intellectuals who were frustrated by the political parties and the parliamentary system. Second, the Revolutionary Government of the Armed Forces decreed a series of changes of a clearly authoritarian, nationalist, anti-oligarchic nature, which shook the foundations of society. Within six days of its installation, the military took over the IPC oil complex and embarked on a series of nationalizations which turned the state into Peru's main financial agent; the production of minerals and hydrocarbons, electricity, transportation, fishing and foreign trade were all taken over by the state.

In June 1969, the government decreed a radical agrarian reform which eliminated the rural declining sector of the oligarchy, encouraging the formation of various types of agricultural co-operatives that benefited one-fourth of the agrarian population. This reform met with strong approval at home, as well as abroad, since it was consistent with the propositions of the Alliance for Progress. In parallel with these drastic changes in the distribution of property, the state created the 'labour community', which was to enable workers to share in the management and profits of their respective companies and allowed for an unprecedented increase in the number of officially recognized unions. The Revolutionary Government of the Armed Forces also embarked on a number of new initiatives in foreign policy. From the beginning this policy was characterized by 'third worldism' and 'non-alignment', aiming to reduce Peru's external dependence on the U.S. government and private corporations. To this end, the military government firmly supported regional economic integration in the Andean Pact and the accords that regulated foreign capital; and it promoted the diversification of the country's markets and sources of finance and support. It broke with the U.S. blockade of Cuba, opened relations with China and expanded Peru's trade with the socialist bloc. By 1975, about 20 per cent of Peruvian exports went to these countries. At the same time, the military government managed to avoid a confrontation with the U.S. government and international capital. Thus, in 1974 the two governments signed agreements by which the United States granted a loan to Peru to enable it to pay for the nationalization of U.S. companies, and U.S. capital was able to engage in the exploitation of oil and copper. In the same vein, Peru obtained loans from private banks.

The long-awaited nationalist structural reform dislodged the traditional oligarchic bloc from power and paved the way for the development of national capitalism and the Peruvian state, which, after having been one of the least interventionist in Latin America, quickly acquired substantial importance in the country's economy.

The government tried to design an original development model that would be 'neither capitalist nor communist', in the hope that social conflict would be eliminated and society's sense of solidarity would be enhanced. The government energetically propagated its ideology, developed by intellectuals who had been members of APRA and the Left, attacking the bases of the old regime and recognizing the legitimacy of the demands of the lower and middle classes. In that sense, they proclaimed themselves standard-bearers of the 'second independence' of Peru; they called themselves Christians, socialists, humanists, 'libertarians' and 'pluralists' and affirmed their 'originality and conceptual autonomy'. Later they drew up the 'Plan Inca', in which they presented the government's actions as part of a project the military had supposedly prepared in advance of its seizure of power.

Both the reforms and the ideology of the government initially attracted surprise, then drew attention and finally met with acceptance by the masses. At the same time, the Soviet bloc and leftist and nationalist governments and organizations of Latin America and Europe gave their support. The military persecuted and deported a small number of officials of the preceding government, but it was careful not to repress either the political parties or the unions, so as to avoid a confrontation with these organized sectors, which, as in 1962, could have tried to isolate the regime. Instead, the military and its advisers systematically attempted to humiliate the leaders of AP and APRA, accusing them of having 'sold out' their ideals for personal political reasons.

In this way, the government hoped to undermine the bases of party support and facilitate the co-optation of their constituency, culminating in a massive transfer of loyalty of the politically active population. In other words, the military planned a process of passive integration into the state apparatus of the social classes that had been entering national political life since 1930, especially intellectuals and the leaders of mass organizations. But contrary to the expectations of the political—military strategists, the structural reforms and the radical ideology of the regime encouraged the active participation of new sectors of the peasantry and the working and middle classes in the political life of the country. True to its military character, however, the regime failed to exploit the possibility of establishing political mechanisms for mediation, negotiation and arbitration in order to control and, eventually, absorb the mass movement that was developing. Instead, it tried to silence political activism, increasingly by means of physical repression.

The union movement, which at the end of the 1960s had begun to distance itself from APRA in both organizational and ideological terms, came under the influence of the Partido Comunista (PC) through the CGTP. These organizations, which were tolerated by the government as long as they lent it their 'critical support', controlled social pressures by securing sectoral advantages for their affiliates – as the *aprista* CTP had done in the past – and continued to isolate APRA, which, in Haya de la Torre's words, remained in a 'wait-and-see phase'. However, neither the PC's control over the CGTP leadership nor the backing the government obtained from the USSR, China, Cuba and a number of progressive Latin American movements helped to curb the strikes, marches and protests of the mass organizations or the many groups of the Left. Notwithstanding their Maoist or Castroist affiliations, these groups supported the peasant, worker, student, teacher, employee and neighbourhood movements in their pursuit of the complete enforcement of the government's new legislation, the radicalization of its scope and the elimination of its authoritarian, bureaucratic-military character. The convergence of the diverse political organizations of the Left with the urban protest and peasant movements encouraged the development of new and important channels of mass participation which were independent of the CGTP and PC. The accusations of being 'ultra-leftist' or of being 'accomplices of counter-revolution' that government officials and the PC launched against the leaders of these movements and the 'new' Left had little or no effect.

The development of a mass movement independent of, and in conflict with, the military government led the regime to accede, albeit very reluctantly, to the proposal of a group of its political advisers to promote a 'Sistema Nacional de Movilización Social', or SINAMOS (acronym also meant 'without masters'), which would pave the way for the promotion of a 'social democracy of full participation'. This system would be composed of organizations covering different 'sectors' of the population into which they would channel official policies and popular demands. The idea of forming a 'revolutionary party' representing different sectors of society, as in the Mexican PRI, was rejected. This would have invalidated the strictly military character of the government and would have encouraged military officials to engage in party activities, which would have jeopardized institutional integration. Moreover, the military, as well as its civilian advisers, was against parties because these organizations 'expropriated power from the people'. The political incorporation of society into the state would be ensured by its integration in a corporatist manner.

Thus, between 1971 and 1975 the regime created and recognized a variety of peasant, labour, student and neighbourhood organizations whose aim was to capture politically strategic sectors of the population and ensure their co-operation in achieving the goals of the military revolution. However, this corporatist project failed completely due to resistance and opposition as well as the antagonism it caused among officials and bureaucrats. The bureaucratic way in which these organizations managed the relationship between state authority and the different sectors of society, and the limited political benefits these sectors obtained from the relationship, which denied them representation, enhanced the traditional distrust and hostility of the population towards the state and particularly towards the military, which is why the workers developed an effective opposition to official attempts to marginalize or invalidate their own independent organizations. Furthermore, several of the organizations that were created under SINAMOS succeeded in freeing themselves from official directives and joined the independent social movements.

The efforts of these organizations and the Left to achieve autonomy and political representation at the decision-making level engendered different political responses by the sponsors of SINAMOS, state officials and the military apparatus, especially the intelligence service. Bureaucratic competition, ideological differences and suspicions of the presence of 'infiltrators' generated a complex web of contradictions that prevented the state from implementing its proclaimed commitment to SINAMOS, which, as a consequence, failed to develop into a viable structure, either for realizing the government's programmes or for providing the regime with social support.

At the other end of society, both capitalists and foreign firms felt seriously threatened, even if the government insisted on securing their collaboration and granting them cheap credits, tax exemptions and other benefits. The changes in property ownership, the 'labour community', the government's apparent backing of the expansion of the union and peasant movements with the support of the PC, the official quasi-socialist rhetoric, including support for 'economic democracy' and taking Yugoslavia as a model, were all repudiated as manifestations of an arbitrary dictatorship with a communist tinge, which could be corrected only by the retreat of the military to its traditional functions. In spite of the economic benefits provided to the capitalists, they refrained from collaborating with the government on its economic project.

The monopoly which the military was determined to maintain over state and political activities, and the energy it directed towards shaping the country in accordance with its own will, were accompanied by an economic policy that sought but failed to satisfy conflicting social interests. Economic policies in general, and the changes in the structure of property ownership in particular, were designed to promote import-substitution industrialization. The government maintained an exchange-rate level which resulted in a spectacular increase in imports, while the value of Peru's export earnings remained stable thanks to a significant rise in international prices for minerals that offset the fall in the volume of exports. The growth of internal demand was reinforced by wage rises, which reached a historical peak in 1974, by the doubling of the number of public employees and the increase in public spending. As the private sector refrained from investing, the government promoted a large capital investment programme which in the majority of cases could produce returns only over the long term. Some increased expenditure was for military purposes. The Peruvian armed forces felt seriously threatened by the 1973 military coup in Chile and embarked on a high-cost programme of arms purchases, mainly in the Soviet market, thus creating new difficulties in its relations with the U.S. government. Between 1970 and 1974, military purchases represented 4 per cent of GDP, while between 1975 and 1978 the average had gone up to 6 per cent, one of the highest figures in Latin America.

Despite the U.S. financial blockade during the first years of the military government, these investments and the growing expenditure on government consumption were made possible by the credit facilities of the Euro-dollar market stimulated by the hope of finding important new oil fields. In 1974, 45 per cent of current expenditures were financed by external debt. In order to sustain the economic plan that favoured the organized urban population, the military government continued to pursue the traditional policy of subsidizing fuel and food imports, whilst simultaneously maintaining control over the prices of domestic agricultural products. These measures accelerated the growth of the fiscal deficit and the fall of already low peasant incomes, perpetuating the process of pauperization of the rural population and enhancing the continuous wave of political mobilization. By 1974 the policies of the regime had produced increasingly serious economic problems. In order to combat them, a select group of technocrats sought to 'adjust' prices, restrict imports and reduce arms purchases, but the proposal was rejected by the ailing Velasco, who decided to persist with established policy, trusting that, in a race against time, oil would be found and these temporary difficulties would be resolved. Besides, his economic measures were aimed at securing mass support for the government and realigning the 'internal front' against any presumed confrontation with Chilean troops.

Under these conditions, the increasingly well organized lower and middle classes presented lists of urgent demands, some of which were for the first time related to regional issues. While these petitions were selectively repressed or ignored, the government designed new and radical initiatives such as the creation of a 'social property' sector. This 'sector' was to introduce collective property in industry assisted by public funding, thus expanding the scope of the Plan Inca. This latest proposal provoked a vehement reaction from the capitalists, who launched a campaign through the mass media against government economic policies which, they argued, would lead to a totalitarian communist regime. In response, in June 1974 General Velasco, against the opposition of important members of the government and the armed forces, seized the media. When the navy openly opposed these measures, Velasco retired a number of its senior officers.

This situation produced the first serious political schism in both the government and the armed forces. It became evident that Velasco and the group around him were determined to act without taking into account the interests of the military establishment. The offensive that was launched against the press illustrated the increasingly personalistic character of the military government: Velasco appointed to the highest government posts and army ranks people who were committed to him, personally, contrary to the original institutional arrangements under which the regime had been established. The political division of the armed forces was aggravated when the police joined the wave of strikes in February 1975 and demanded both salary increases and the inclusion of its commanders in the government as an independent branch of the armed forces.[1] The ab-

---

[1] According to the revolutionary statute passed by the leaders of the coup, the military junta which headed the government was made up of the commanders-in-chief of the three branches of the armed forces, who appointed the head of state. In 1970, General Velasco reached his retirement age and would have had to leave the government, but as leader of the revolution he managed to retain his post. However, neither the length of his term nor the manner of his succession was specified. Thus, when he became ill in 1973, an open struggle over his succession broke out. This situation and the ever more personalistic conduct of government and the armed forces gave rise to an institutional crisis which increased in intensity with the seizure of the media and the police strike.

sence of the 'guardians of order' from the streets of Lima provoked wide-spread rioting and looting – with accusations of APRA's involvement – which was only stopped by army tanks. Now it was clear that the Peruvian Revolution had no defenders except the Armored Division and the expropriated press. The seizure of the newspapers and the radio and television stations had silenced the opposition of the capitalists and the traditional parties, whose political voice was replaced by news media that covered the 'ideological parameters of the Peruvian Revolution'. The papers were handed over to persons who represented different interests within the government, sponsored by different generals in the regime. Competition was limited to the presentation of different interpretations of the signifi-cance and scope of revolution. Yet the existence of different interests in the government, including some leaning towards the radicalization of the revolutionary process and therefore seeking to win mass support, led to an expansion of the press coverage of social demands. And some of the media began to adopt political perspectives that were relatively independent of the government's views and even those of the armed forces, further encour-aging the growth of various social movements, and especially the PC- and Maoist-led working-class organizations. The Velasco group decided that the time had now come to silence and tame social protest. On the one hand, they created the Movimiento Laboral Revolucionario (MLR). On the other, in August 1975 they deported thirty leaders of the union movement, leftist party leaders and news reporters of the opposition. The friction between the state and society had reached unprecedented levels. At this point General Velasco, without consultation, suddenly decided to expropriate a U.S. mining company in an effort to compensate for his increasingly unpopular image and as a new expression of the revolutionary character of the government. Moreover, Velasco made this move in spite of the fact that in 1974 his minister of foreign affairs and the U.S. Depart-ment of State had signed an agreement in which the issue of compensation to U.S. companies that had been nationalized by Peru was considered to have been settled. Velasco thus produced another international dispute that failed to help him resolve his internal problems. Moreover, an agree-ment between the presidents of the military governments of Chile and Bolivia, Augusto Pinochet and Hugo Banzer, concerning Bolivia's access to the sea further strained relations between these governments and Peru, nearly setting off a war with Chile in August 1975 in a situation of internal social disarray and military divisions that were a reminder of 1879 and the disaster that followed.

The solution to these problems demanded an end to Velasco's personalism and improvisatory style and immediate readjustments in domestic and foreign policy. At the end of August, after military ceremonies related to the War of the Pacific, the chiefs of the military regions deposed General Velasco and appointed the minister of war, Francisco Morales Bermúdez, the new head of state. In his first speech, Morales proclaimed the installation of the 'second phase' of the Peruvian Revolution, in which the military high command would recover its leadership in government and adapt the economic reforms on the basis of experience gained in the past seven years.

THE 'SECOND PHASE' OF MILITARY GOVERNMENT AND
THE TRANSFER TO CIVILIAN RULE, 1975–80

The 'second phase' of the military revolution began with the transfer of state control to the military junta, composed of the chiefs of the armed forces. The junta sought to legitimate itself with the military establishment by keeping the officer corps informed, consulting it on the problems facing the government and trying to harmonize different points of view. The new structure of the government reduced the power held by the head of state and isolated those members of the military group and their ideological advisers who had initially led the revolution, to the point of ignoring their status as delegates of the armed forces. Likewise, the governmental reorganization allowed the high command to reaffirm the original motives of its revolution and focus on problems of defence and national security, especially as the possibility of a Chilean attack became more acute. To this effect, the new government came to be more representative of the armed forces and less representative of society at large.

The removal of Velasco raised hopes in all social circles. The capitalists and political parties thought that it marked an end to the era of arbitrariness and the beginning of a return to constitutional government. The lower-class organizations and leftist groups also breathed a sigh of relief, since the change in government was followed by the dismantling of the MLR, the return of deportees and an end to the censorship of the journals and magazines of the opposition. Thus, the government of the second phase started with unanimous acceptance.

These different expectations reflected the 'pluralism' that existed inside the new government. If Velasco had built up a strong image of himself as the 'undisputed and undisputable chief of the revolution', as the official propaganda presented it, the image of Morales Bermúdez was one of a weak man wavering between the different interests within the regime. This was reflected in the way in which the government approached a variety of serious problems, such as the economic crisis, the opposition to government policy and the need of the military to arm in the face of what it perceived as the Chilean threat.

The mass opposition inherited by Morales Bermúdez's government was aggravated by the implementation of two economic readjustment 'packages' introduced during the first six months of 1975. In response, the regime resorted to the official rhetoric of the 'first phase', but this was plainly insufficient to placate anti-government sentiments, especially among urban workers, public employees and the underemployed residents of the shanty towns, whose incomes continued to fall. Consequently, the protest could not be contained by the PC and the CGTP, whose leadership kept stressing the need to support the 'progressive' sectors of the government and the military revolution during this economic crisis.

The government in turn accentuated its policy of 'selective repression' but kept channels of communication and negotiation open in order to avoid overt and total confrontation and isolation. At the same time, the second phase marked the opening of the government to capitalist interests and APRA as the regime sought to establish alliances that would counteract the strength of the mass movement and attract support for an economic recovery programme. In its first steps towards liberalization, the regime allowed the capitalists and political parties to denounce the mistakes and 'excesses' of the first phase, especially the pampering and 'politicization' of the union movement as central factors in the country's economic and political crisis. Moreover, it allowed these forces to demand a purge of the remaining elements of the first phase from the government, the restoration of freedom of the press, the reduction of the state's economic role and the broadening of the role of the market. That is, the return of the country to constitutional rule had to go hand in hand with the re-establishment of a liberal economy as a prerequisite for economic recovery and subsequent political disengagement.

In January 1976, in conjunction with the first of a total of nine economic packages imposed by the government of the second phase, the regime deported a group of generals who had held key positions in the Velasco government for denouncing the 'counter-revolutionary' character of the new regime. In the following month, however, contrary to all expectations, General Jorge Fernández Maldonado, one of the leading radical figures since 1968, was promoted to the rank of commander in chief of the army and for that reason was appointed as minister of war and prime minister. But instead of making the widely expected about face which had raised hopes and fears in different sectors of society, the government dismissed the state-appointed directors of the mass media that had maintained a certain level of autonomy. And at the end of March 1976 in a message broadcast to the country, Morales Bermúdez asked the population to make a 'temporary' sacrifice and agree to a political truce for the sake of avoiding a military dictatorship like those in the Southern Cone. A month later, he gave a speech in Trujillo, the home base of Haya de la Torre and of APRA, where he asked that the old conflicts and ill will between APRA and the army be forgotten and proposed the establishment of a political accord in view of the fact that both organizations shared a nationalist outlook.

The long wait of the leader of APRA seemed to have been successful in so far as the Revolutionary Government of the Armed Forces was finally admitting its political isolation and recognizing Haya de la Torre as the spokesman of society, inviting him to contribute to a political consensus. Morales was looking for APRA's support, isolating and dividing the opposition, both on the Right and on the Left. For his part, Haya replied by affirming that the 'unfinished symphony' offered by Morales could be completed only if general elections were held and the country returned to constitutional rule. This dialogue marked the re-emergence of party politics in the country, and Haya's message served to rally the support of individuals and groups who were in favour of a return to democracy and gave him a renewed importance that went beyond his own party. Soon after, Belaúnde returned to the country from exile and added his voice to that of Haya de la Torre. The rejection of each new step taken by Morales Bermúdez and Fernández Maldonado to find partners with whom they could negotiate a truce and establish a consensus between military and political forces tended to strengthen rightist elements inside the government who were inclined to enter into a 'third phase'. This, they felt, would do away with Morales Bermúdez's indecision in the face of the Left and persistent mass protests in the form of strikes, marches and land invasions. Their model was the military dictatorship in Argentina.

In March 1976 the regime decided to take the first steps towards solving its problems with the international banking community and confronting the growing balance-of-payments deficit by securing international loans. The leading U.S. banks sent a commission which demanded that the government take radical measures: to declare a 44 per cent devaluation, to put an end to price controls, to open the country to foreign investment, to make changes in labour legislation and to return to the system of private property in the sectors now monopolized by the state. In addition, Peru was required to settle outstanding accounts with the banks in question and to accept fiscal supervision by a commission that would be appointed by the banks.

In April 1976 the government declared that all strikes in sectors that produced foreign exchange income – especially mining and fishing – were illegal under a legal provision dating from 1913. This measure encouraged the unification of unions and leftist groups with the aim of calling a national strike. The response of the government was to declare a state of national emergency and impose a curfew – measures which remained in force for eleven months – and to close down the independent newspapers and radio stations which had re-emerged since the policy of liberalization had been initiated. With these measures, repression was intensified against workers, peasants and student organizations associated with the Left. In June the government imposed a second set of economic measures required by the international banking community in an attempt to solve the problem of servicing Peru's debt of U.S. $4 billion.

In July 1976, in a major challenge to the regime, General Carlos Bobbio led a military uprising in Lima, demanding the resignation of General Fernández Maldonado and other *velasquista* generals of the first phase who had remained in government, as well as the definition of a new political course in the military's interests, that is, a firm decision to crush social resistance by the establishment of an emergency war situation and at the same time the preparation for the transfer of power to civilian rule. In response, the military command decided to remove both rebel generals and *velasquista* officers. As a result, the political leadership of the regime took on a more consistent character in its efforts to repress popular opposition and impose its terms on the capitalists and the political parties.

Meanwhile the Left and the social movement continued to grow through the proliferation of organizations, protests, meetings, demonstrations, publications and rallies which strengthened the awareness that 'civil society' was at complete odds with the government. The capitalists and political parties did not miss a single opportunity to demand a return to constitutional rule, accusing the military of creating an atmosphere of class struggle that might culminate in an uncontrollable situation. Faced with such a formidable opposition, General Morales Bermúdez tried to revive the exhausted revolutionary rhetoric of the first phase of the regime, which no longer convinced anyone on the Left, while trying at the same time to pacify the capitalists and win their support for the economic recovery by modifying the legislation on labour communities and job stability. He returned the fishing industry to private enterprise and authorized lifting the ban on the independent press that had consented to a 'gentleman's agreement' with the government.

The government's promise to fulfil the requirements of the U.S. banks yielded a U.S. $400 million loan to alleviate its immediate financial problems. Soon after, however, news that Peru had purchased Soviet military aircraft led the banks to insist on intervention by the International Monetary Fund (IMF) before negotiations would be resumed, and the government was obliged to accede to this demand in November 1976. As might have been expected, the IMF insisted on a shock policy that was rejected by both the officials of the Central Bank and the military high command. The former proposed a gradual policy of stabilization to reduce the serious 'social and political costs' which would otherwise be incurred.

The position of the regime could scarcely have been more difficult. The country faced the possibility of having to declare itself unable to meet its international liabilities, while social conflicts were escalating so rapidly that even the state of emergency could no longer guarantee basic public order. The dangers arising from internal struggles inside the regime and the pressures it faced from both the domestic opposition and the international banks threatened to destroy the precarious institutional order. Conflicts between the leaders of the armed forces over how to cope with the opposition and the pervasive economic crisis consequently increased. There were those officers who proposed an authoritarian repressive solution 'à la Argentina', whilst others tended towards a renewed populist initiative. The divisions within the armed forces, their isolation and the general rejection of their government made it absolutely clear that their situation was now untenable.

In this context, Morales Bermúdez proposed an institutional solution that would permit the transfer of government to civilian rule, withdraw the armed forces from the political conflict and allow them to concentrate on problems of defence. This proposal won the support of a majority of the officers corps, and in February 1977 the government presented the Plan Tupac Amaru, which stated that on an as yet undetermined date, elections would be held for a constitutional assembly, which would draw up a new charter to legitimize the reforms dictated by the military government. In June 1977 President Carter's wife visited Peru and made it clear that the U.S. government would provide support to the Peruvian military only in return for the implementation of measures that would restore political democracy and economically sound policies.

Under these new conditions, talks were resumed, albeit in a cautious and guarded manner, between the government, APRA and Partido Popular Cristiano (PPC). These negotiations were designed to determine the mechanisms of the transfer of power. Belaúnde, however, stubbornly insisted that general elections be called immediately. In the light of Belaúnde's refusal to accept the conditions of those who had deposed him in the 1968 coup, it was clear that the military would look for a valid deal only with Haya's APRA, which, as Morales Bermúdez would say, was capable of controlling the demands of the masses and thus of establishinging some entente between the state and society. This power of APRA, which hitherto had been the main reason for the military's opposition to it, was now seen as a virtue. Furthermore, APRA shared the government's intention to revise, rather than abolish, the reforms that had been introduced since 1968. While the parties and capitalists focussed their demands on the return to democracy, the labour movement and leftist leaders mobilized the population and exerted pressure on the government to abolish the increasing number of economic measures that were harmful to the lower and middle classes. Thus, due to its 'bourgeois' nature, the problem of democracy was entirely abandoned by the Left. For the political leaders of the Left, the country was going through a pre-revolutionary phase which would culminate in a new political order opposed to class-based domination – in short, socialism. APRA and the PPC therefore monopolized the campaign for political democracy, winning the support of broad sectors of society that were tired of and hostile to military authoritarianism and economic and political turmoil.

The expectation of an immediate transfer of political power to civilian rule was, however, premature. The government tried to postpone the transfer, in order to provide time for further rearmament and for further economic recovery so that the armed forces could retire with a 'mission-accomplished' image.

In May 1977 the minister of economics resigned over the authorities' unwillingness to stick to a rigid stabilization plan and was replaced by Walter Piazza, a prominent businessman. Piazza opened the regime to the private sector and with bravado promised prompt economic recovery as a result of a third package of 'readjustment' measures prescribed entirely by the IMF. However, after one month Piazza's inability to discipline the military ministers was evident; like his predecessor, he was unable either to reduce the purchases of military equipment or to rationalize the ministries' budgets.

However important those issues may have been, they were soon dwarfed by mass mobilization, which now reached a scale that altered the entire political panorama. In both Lima and the interior, the incidence of localized strikes and protests had been growing for some time. As a result of the economic measures imposed by Piazza, these isolated movements had rapidly gathered force and culminated in the successful general strike of 19 July 1977 organized by a variety of unions and leftist forces. The strike had the tacit approval of APRA and even of sectors of the business community, although they used the workers' mobilization as a way of accusing the military of allowing the unions and the Left to disrupt the country at a time of severe economic crisis. The government's first reaction was to decree that employers could fire workers who had led or participated in the strike, issuing a legal provision that eliminated job stability. The capitalists gleefully took advantage of this to get rid of union activists, firing nearly five thousands workers, whilst the labour force was placed on the defensive under conditions of sharply increasing unemployment.

Having sanctioned this important resurgence of entrepreneurial authority with the approval of APRA, the government duly called elections of a constitutional assembly in May 1978.

The call for elections encouraged political mobilization, party competition and the division of the opposition to the military government. At first, it looked as if the military's initiative might be sabotaged by the abstention of Belaúnde and leftist groups. But the new access given to the political parties to the government-controlled media, the debates between old and new public figures with different approaches and alternatives for dealing with Peru's problems and the proliferation of magazines caused the population to take an increasing interest in elections and constitutional forms of political representation.

Under Luis Bedoya Reyes, the PPC presented itself as a proven and able representative of the business community. The emphasis on the re-establishment of order and the Pinochet-style economic measures that Bedoya espoused with the advice of the 'Chicago boys' sealed his rightist image. At the other extreme, leftist groups engaged in sharp competition among themselves, proposing alternatives that varied from a return to the nationalist-populist route of the first phase of the military revolution to the sovietization of both the army and the means of production. Between these two poles, Haya de la Torre presented himself as a focus of conciliation, ready to seek formulas for coexistence between civilians and the military on the basis of a constitutional charter, which would enhance the state's role in integrating different social interests. Furthermore, Haya accepted the military's conditions for the transfer of power, restricting debate to the legal formulas of the new constitutional order and postponing solution of the economic and social problems. To this effect, he actually allied himself with the government, isolating the unions and the Left. However, this alliance still had serious deficiencies in so far as it did not establish a policy for economic stabilization. The government had only managed to weaken the opposition front, and although it was no longer alone in accusing the mass movement and the Left of wanting to thwart the transition to democracy, this did not suffice to ensure agreement within the political alliance on how to manage an extremely unstable economy.

After a series of conversations between General Morales Bermúdez and the U.S. Treasury Department, the United States agreed to negotiate with the IMF in order to help re-establish its relations with Peru on the condition that the government would keep its promise to provide for a political transition. As a result, an agreement was signed with the IMF in October 1977 in which the Peruvian government promised to take stabilizing measures and to start repaying its external debt. In return, the IMF granted a U.S. $100 million credit to the military government.[2]

In January 1978 the government dictated the fourth 'package' of measures, which again provoked mass mobilization and general unrest, including a call for a national strike to protest this assault on the livelihood of the masses and to demand the rehiring of workers who had been dismissed

---

[2] The Morales Bermúdez government sought to 'normalize' relations with the United States, playing down Peru's relations with the non-aligned countries. Peru's international conduct and the steps taken towards the transfer of power captured the Carter administration's interest in Peru because it offered an alternative model to the dictatorships of the Southern Cone for the resolution of political polarization. Thus, each step taken by Morales Bermúdez's government to transfer power met with a positive response from the United States through increases in assistance from AID, government loans and political support. To this effect, the U.S. Embassy in Lima had explicit orders to reject insistent suggestions of army officers and distinguished representatives of the haute bourgeoisie that a military coup be undertaken to install a strong government similar to those of the Southern Cone. Furthermore, the Embassy let it be known that a new government which closed off the possibility of a transfer of power would be explicitly repudiated by the United States, as happened later in the case of Bolivia.

after the national strike of July 1977. However, in view of the build-up of military tension on the Ecuadorean border, the two-day national strike, which received broad support, was postponed until February. In the same month, the IMF representative charged with verifying the national accounts left the country in disgust, declaring not only that the government had failed to meet its liabilities but that, over and above this, it had been doctoring the figures with the deliberate intent of misleading the IMF. In fact, since the country was on the eve of elections, the government had considered it unwise to reduce public spending to the levels demanded by the IMF, which would have produced a sharp recession and radicalization of social and political forces.

The economic situation continued to deteriorate to the point where it was considered very likely that the government would have to admit its inability to meet its international liabilities and declare a halt to debt payments. A few weeks before the May elections, when the Treasury was in fact on the verge of bankruptcy, a delegation composed of the foreign minister, businessmen and public officials went to Washington to re-establish negotiations with the IMF. As a result of this meeting, a provisional agreement was prepared by Javier Silva Ruete and Manuel Moreyra, who were later to be appointed as minister of economics and president of the Central Bank, respectively. But before accepting these positions, they demanded that the Morales Bermúdez government impose yet another package of measures, its fifth, as proof of its intention to stabilize the economy.

The new adjustment policies of May 1978 had the greatest impact since those imposed in July 1976, provoking another two-day national strike on 22 and 23 May, which was successful throughout the country. The government responded by deporting a group of union leaders, journalists and politicians – some of whom were candidates for the the Constitutional Assembly – to Argentina. In addition, it postponed elections until June 18. APRA and PPC justified the new economic measures as necessary for the stabilization of the country after the 'excesses' and mistakes committed by Velasco and 'his allies, the Communists'.

In spite of the turbulent events between May and June 1978, and in an atmosphere of increased social and political conflict, the elections were held for the one hundred representatives who would draw up the new constitution that would replace that of 1933. The elections illustrated the political changes that had taken place in the country since 1968: APRA obtained 35 per cent and PPC, which captured that sector of the middle class which naturally supported AP, got 24 per cent of the vote. The different leftist organizations showed unprecedented strength, with a total of about 30 per cent, while the 'parties' of Odría and Prado disappeared from the political map.

As soon as the initial results became known, the military junta declared that it would recognize the people's will. In spite of the army's traditional animosity towards APRA, it felt that under current conditions the party was a suitable successor to the armed forces. Haya was elected president of the Constituent Assembly since he had obtained the largest number of votes and sought to confine its activities to the formulation of the new constitutional document, trying to reach agreements with what he called the 'responsible Left'. The Left, however, refused to work with Haya or APRA or to restrict its work to the writing of the charter; instead, it encouraged discussion of the multiple social problems that had arisen from the economic crisis. Moreover, some of the leftist groups demanded that the military junta be ignored, thus creating a situation of 'dual power'. The majority systematically rejected this position and joined the government in accusing the Left of trying to disrupt the incipient legal process through a wave of strikes in order to 'aggravate the contradictions' and develop the supposed revolutionary situation. So in drawing up the new constitution, APRA was at the mercy of PPC.

Since the progress of the Constitutional Assembly was impeded by the issues raised by the Left, its president decided that the drafting of the charter would be handled by committees, whose proposals would be discussed in specific plenary sessions. As a matter of fact, this division of parliamentary labour silenced the demands and accusations leveled by the Left, but it tarnished the public image of the Assembly, and allowed the leftist representatives to take advantage of their parliamentary immunity and encourage the mobilization of social organizations. Contrary to the hopes of the government and its allies, the Assembly was not an effective arena for the political struggles that were being carried on outside its doors. APRA's dependence on PPC meant that it had to minimize the state's economic role, which frustrated the hopes that Haya de la Torre had been entertaining for many years in terms of forming a corporatist body called the 'Congreso Económico Nacional'. However, APRA had the backing of the Left in its efforts to establish job stability and the right to strike, universal suffrage and support of human rights as constitutional principles. The final outcome was a semi-presidential system, because it granted 'executive' privileges to Congress and 'legislative' privileges to the executive.

In July 1979, after the work of the Constitutional Assembly had been completed, Luis Alberto Sánchez, who had replaced Haya de la Torre as president because of the latter's illness, demanded that the government call general elections immediately and put the new constitution into force. The military government rejected both petitions, suggesting that the National Electoral Board needed several months both to inscribe illiterate voters and to revise the register. The elections were scheduled for May 1980; the new government was to be installed in July and would be responsible for introducing the constitution. In the meantime, the military government would continue to rule under the Statute of 1968, and it refused to approve four of the transitional clauses, one of which related to human rights. Furthermore, the government asked the Assembly to modify some constitutional paragraphs that restricted military jurisdiction over the social order – a request that the Assembly unanimously rejected. With the signing of the constitution by Haya de la Torre on his deathbed and the refusal of the leftist representatives to do so, the duties of the Constitutional Assembly were brought to an end in a tense atmosphere. The manifest frustrations of APRA and PPC members, on the one hand, and those of the military, on the other, again gave rise to fears that the transfer of government to civilian rule might still be suspended.

The postponement of the elections and the dissolution of the Constituent Assembly raised the question as to what steps would now be taken towards the transition. Sánchez proposed the creation of a multi-party committee that would take charge of negotiating with the military. But Bedoya Reyes of PPC and Armando Villanueva of APRA rejected this idea, arguing that he was trying to take advantage of it for personal ends. The military also ignored Sánchez's proposal, since it wanted to keep control of the political transition until the elections were held. The pro-APRA elements in the government, led by Morales Bermúdez, wanted to give Villanueva time to secure his presidential candidacy before the imminent demise of Haya de la Torre, because, as Haya's successor, he would support the consolidation of reforms and establish a 'social democratic' regime which would channel popular demands and restrict the role of the Left. For the anti-*aprista* officers concentrated in the navy and the air force, Bedoya and Belaúnde also needed time to allow for APRA's internal conflicts to come to light after Haya's death and to present themselves as a clear alternative for power. Finally, the military found it necessary to postpone the elections until July 1980, not only with a view to commemorating the centennial of the War of the Pacific and remaining alert to any

Chilean provocation, but also because it was their hope that economic recovery would dispel the military's poor image and the unprecedented political advances made by the Left would be brought to a halt.

Between May 1978 and July 1980 Silva Ruete and Moreyra decreed four economic adjustment packages, which stimulated the recovery of profits at the expense of wages, while the rise in international mineral prices allowed the Treasury to recover substantial levels of foreign exchange reserves. The application of this economic policy and its apparent success permitted the government to reschedule the payment of the external debt. Nevertheless, inflation and recession continued to wreak havoc in medium-sized industry and to lower the standard of living of the working population as well as of the middle class, culminating in general strikes in January and July 1979. In the face of these pressures, the economic team adopted a policy of differential wage increases in various labour sectors in a move to complement its 'selective repression' of leading politicians of the Left and the union movement. Generalized discontent with economic policy was carried into the electoral campaign, pending the inauguration of a democratic regime which could be expected to satisfy the neglected needs of the lower and middle classes.

In addition to mass opposition, Silva Ruete and Moreyra had to face continual pressure from inside the government and the armed forces, which, on various occasions, seemed ready to abandon their monetarist plan. First, they had to contend with the continual scrambling for funds by generals and admirals who were determined to increase defence expenditures since there were dollars in the vaults of the Central Bank. Second, some military authorities thought that the drastic measures taken by Silva Ruete and Moreyra were intended only for coping with an emergency situation. Thus, as soon as the problem of the 'external gap' had been resolved, a 'heterodox' policy was proposed by the minister of industry reactivating internal demand through state intervention with the goal of attacking inflation and the growing unemployment problem, thus demonstrating the persistence of reformist and nationalist orientations in the army and government. This political struggle was also resolved in favour of Silva Ruete and Moreyra by virtue of the support they got from the international financial community and from the fact that when they threatened to resign if their proposals concerning economic management were not accepted, it was the minister of industry who left the government. Silva Ruete and Moreyra insisted on the link between democracy and the development of a market economy. In this highly unstable and conflictive atmosphere, Morales Bermúdez, Silva Ruete and Moreyra managed to overcome the obstacles surrounding the elections and the transfer of the government to civilian rule.

THE 1980 ELECTIONS AND THE SECOND BELAÚNDE PRESIDENCY, 1980–5

A few days after the dissolution of the Constitutional Assembly, Víctor Raúl Haya de la Torre died. The armed forces – in one of history's ironies – bestowed the highest honours on him, and General Morales Bermúdez posthumously decorated him with the highest order in the country. With Haya's death, APRA lost its only leader capable of influencing broad sectors of society. Owing to the vertical structure of the party and the cult around Haya's personality, the remaining *aprista* leaders were no more than 'satellites who orbited around the star, illuminated by his light and his strength', as was stated at his funeral. Thus, the man who had forged and preserved the unity of the most important mass party as if it were his own property left a legacy that was difficult to preserve. Before his death, personal and ideological conflicts inside the party had surfaced and there were no institutional mechanisms for solving them. As one of the 'satellites' remarked, the party faced the problem of passing 'from absolute monarchy to a republic'.

A few days after Haya's burial, the *aprista* command met to elect its presidential candidate. Armando Villanueva defeated Andrés Townsend thanks to his control of the party machine and the support of radical youth leaders. Townsend, who had gathered around him a group of elderly experts with parliamentary skills, and who was openly willing to make a pact with the capitalists, was reluctant to accept the results, foreshadowing the future division of the hitherto monolithic Aprista Party. In the hope of saving the deteriorating image and precarious unity of the party on the eve of the election, Villanueva made Townsend accept the candidacy for the office of first vice-president and chose Luis Negreiros, a labour leader of the unpopular *aprista* bureaucracy that ran the Confederación de Trabajadores del Perú, as a candidate for the office of second vice-president. APRA launched a multimillion-dollar campaign presenting Villanueva as Haya's heir who was capable of solving social problems by democratic means, who would serve as a mediator between different class interests, and between national and foreign interests, and who would readjust and reorganize the reforms that had been introduced by the military government. This image contrasted with the one he had had for years, both inside and outside the party, which his opponents did their best to revive, since Villanueva had made his career in close association with the APRA 'shock troops', the *'bufalos'*. The slogan that the party had chosen for the election campaign, 'Armando is forceful', which was supposed to depict him as a leader capable of achieving the reorganization the country needed, backfired on the man who had habitually relied on force to suppress his opponents. Another aspect that hurt his image, especially with regard to the commemoration of the centenary of the War of the Pacific, was the fact that Villanueva's wife was of Chilean origin. For many, it was unthinkable for a 'first lady' to have links with the country's traditional enemy.

Luis Bedoya Reyes and the PPC entered the electoral contest in fierce competition with APRA, but also seeking to make electoral inroads into Belaúnde's territory. Bedoya confirmed the image he had projected in 1978, presenting himself as a leader who would manage state business with a qualified team of experts in a tough managerial style without falling prey to the indecision and weakness displayed by Belaúnde during his term of office. In contrast, Fernando Belaúnde for AP conducted his campaign while touring the interior of the country, calling attention to the work which had been accomplished there during his administration but which had been suspended over the past ten years. He presented himself as a man with a talent for public works who understood the problems and potential of the country's rural and provincial society. But his main asset was that he placed special emphasis on a pluralist approach in terms of 'work and let work', contrary to his opponents' image as intolerant and inflexible. To this effect, he built up an authentic image of a 'gentleman', benevolent and able to respond reasonably and positively to the different requests of diverse social interest groups. At the same time, Belaúnde stressed his independence from the military in refusing to accept its conditions for participating in the Constitutional Assembly, although he also emphasized his support of the professionalization and modernization of the armed forces – which had overthrown him eleven years earlier – displaying his 'gallantry' in treating them with fairness.

The leftist groups staged demonstrations attacking the military dictatorship for its repressiveness, and they denounced the collusion of the 'bourgeois parties' with the military, accusing them of hoping to prolong the capitalist dictatorship in the pseudo-democratic disguise. Even if they participated in the elections 'for tactical reasons', they still believed, with

Mao, that power came from guns. They failed to present a convincing alternative and were unable to present a united bloc. Efforts to form an electoral alliance consisted of endless meetings among leaders of the Marxist, Christian and *velasquista* groups to discuss two items. The first, and most relevant, concerned the number of candidates each organization should have and the place they should be assigned on the united slate of the Alianza Revolucionaria de Izquierda (ARI) so as to maximize their chances to win the elections. But their inability to compromise and form partial agreements – a characteristic feature of the political system – prevented them from reaching any general accord. The second issue, the minimum program that ARI should present to the electorate, was therefore rendered redundant, and the Left entered the elections divided into five slates.

Against all expectations Belaúnde won the 1980 elections overwhelmingly with 45 per cent of the vote. APRA, which had won 35 per cent of the vote in 1978, saw its share drop to 27 per cent; the PPC's share declined from 24 to 15 per cent; and the Left, which had won a combined total of about 30 per cent in 1978 suffered a spectacular defeat, obtaining only 14 per cent of the vote. The shift of large sectors of the population from APRA in 1978 to AP in 1980 was due to the death of Haya de la Torre and their rejection of Villanueva's coercive and sectarian image and behaviour; the reduction in Bedoya's vote could be explained by his close identification with a government that exclusively upheld the interests of the ruling class. Those who had voted for the Left in 1978 and shifted their preference to Belaúnde in 1980 were reacting to the inability of the leaders of its diverse factions to formulate an effective alternative policy. With Belaúnde they chose the 'lesser evil' as a means of blocking APRA, dreaded for its supposed capacity to engineer the destruction of the mass movement controlled by the Left.

As soon as the election results were known, a process of moderation and co-operation, which was unique in the political history of Peru, began to take shape and seemed to mark the inauguration of a process of democratic consolidation of the country. The military accepted the will of the people, even though they had voted for the man it had deposed twelve years before, and established committees composed of representatives of the old and the new governments with a view to co-ordinating the process of setting up ministerial teams. The political parties publicly recognized the election results and offered to give their support to the consolidation of the constitutional regime. Belaúnde invited APRA and PPC to participate in the government, hoping to draw broad-based social support. Villanueva and APRA, chastened by their electoral defeat and internal dissension, offered to form a 'loyal opposition' to the government. PPC accepted the proposal to form a coalition with AP, which established a majority in both houses of Congress. Various unions, peasant and shanty town organizations associated with the Left were received by the president-elect, who, together with his future ministers, offered to satisfy their demands. Regional, professional and labour delegations paraded before Belaúnde to offer their collaboration.

The most difficult problem concerned future relations between the executive and the armed forces. Despite the fact that the general command of the armed forces was presided over by Rafael Hoyos Rubio, the man who had personally been responsible for expelling Belaúnde from the president's palace in 1968, an agreement was reached to leave the command structures unaltered, thus respecting the internal arrangements of the military organization. In return for this, the ministries of the three branches of the armed forces were assigned to retired officers who had been loyal to the government at the time of the coup of 1968.

On 28 July 1980 General Morales Bermúdez divested himself of his powers, and Fernando Belaúnde was inaugurated as president. It appeared as though a new chapter in the history of Peru had begun. The crisis of the oligarchic regime had been resolved in part by the military government's reforms, which had encouraged a process of relative social democratization by an authoritarian route. Now, with the transfer of power to an elected civilian president, it was a matter of completing the cycle and democratizing politics and the state.

With the alliance between Belaúnde and Bedoya – the leaders of AP and PPC – the government was in control of Congress and was in a position to pursue an economic policy that was diametrically opposed to what the president had proposed in his election campaign – namely, that his government would initiate a policy of economic expansion and create 1 million new jobs, the resources of which would be channelled primarily into the country's provinces. Since the prices of its exports had been rising between 1978 and 1980, it seemed that Peru would be able to solve its balance-of-payments problem and that the new government would thus be in a position to renew deals with the international banking community and service its external debt. However, the new government decided to follow the adjustment programme which had been in force during the two last years of the military regime. This, together with the impact of worldwide recession in 1982 had a devastating effect on the Peruvian economy and the living conditions of the people.

Between 1980 and 1985, while Peru's external debt grew from U.S. $6 billion to $10.5 billion, GDP decreased by 11.3 per cent. Unemployment, which was 8 per cent in 1980, reached 18 per cent five years later, in parallel with an explosive growth of underemployment and the so-called informal sector. The annual rate of inflation – 44 per cent during the 1975–9 period – increased to an average of 66 per cent during the first two years of the democratic government and, after rising to 110 per cent in 1984, reached 250 per cent in the government's last year. Real wages fell by 31 per cent and the average per capita income declined to 1960 levels. The indices of social welfare, which were already very low compared with those of other countries of the region, continued to fall and eventually reached critical levels. While 50 per cent of the population was reduced to extreme poverty, the concentration of wealth in the hands of a few, which had always been considered excessive, reached an unprecedented level. Measures which had been implemented in the Southern Cone only after the mass movement had suffered defeat at the hands of a brutal military dictatorship were taken in Peru by a newly elected democratic government.

As if he were a patrimonial *seigneur,* Fernando Belaúnde re-established the traditional political practices of favouritism and patronage, despite expectations that he would democratize politics. To his loyal friends and relatives he delegated the job of administrating the economy and selecting experts whose experience and international prestige would ensure the application of liberal-style measures and thus the backing of U.S. and European governments and financing agencies. In this way, he dissociated himself from the political responsibilities of economic management. Under the new constitution, Prime Minister Manuel Ulloa, who had been minister of economics during the last phase of Belaúnde's first administration, issued 240 decrees aimed at reorganizing the economy, which the legislative majority ratified without any discussion or consideration of the opposition or public opinion. Not only were AP provincial legislators excluded from decision-making about economic policy, but also the technocrats in charge of formulating and applying policy neither owed loyalty to the party and its provincial leaders nor identified themselves with their social and political interests. Worst of all, they did not place any significance on the political consequences of their measures, which benefited the interests of big business, centred in Lima, but precluded regional development – another of Belaúnde's broken promises – affecting the social bases of AP.

Thus, antagonism developed between the 'Lima people' and the 'provincials' inside AP. Belaúnde tried to solve this through a 'division of labour' in which Ulloa and his 'Chicago boys' dictated macro-economic measures, while others controlled patronage, which allowed them to broaden their clientelistic networks, swelling public spending and increasing corruption. Furthermore, with Belaúnde himself persistently refusing to abandon his grandiose public works project, his stabilization policy fell apart at the end of 1982.

From the very beginning, the economic adjustment measures prompted a hostile reaction by the middle and lower classes, and this was soon echoed by industrialists. Initial surprise soon developed into protest and heated public debate, with the active participation of a broad spectrum of politicians, union members, professionals, intellectuals and businessmen, whilst renewed union mobilization led to four general strikes. All of this failed, however, to change the government's approach. Owing to his personal control of the representatives of AP, the support of PPC and the media – which the president had returned to their former owners – Belaúnde was in control of the situation. Ulloa and his team relied on both the Peruvian and international media and on the international banking system, with a view to discrediting and ridiculing the opposition, which often was neither coherent nor consistent in its criticism. At the same time, the administration managed to convince people that its actions, although unpopular, were necessary and the only feasible options in view of the disastrous legacy of twelve years of military rule.

The technocratic arrogance of the Ulloa administration was revealed by its disdain for the opinions and concerns of the 'inept' and 'ignorant' opposition, which developed into what was to become a characteristic trait of the regime: outright rejection of the discontent, criticism and opposition evidenced by the increasing number of strikes and the results of opinion polls, many of which had been commissioned by the government itself.

In 1982, the world recession aggravated the impact of the economic policy: raw-material prices fell so low that the value of Peru's export earnings was reduced to 50 per cent of the 1979 level. This situation evoked sharp opposition in AP and society at large, and Ulloa was finally obliged to resign. The following year, Peru was hit hard by the combined

effects of continued world recession, the devastation produced by the El
Niño and the government's economic policy, resulting in a 12 per cent fall
in GDP. Belaúnde tried to blame external factors and the forces of nature,
but these accounted for only 5 per cent of the decrease. It was then that
Pablo Macera, a well-known and prestigious intellectual declared that
Peru was undergoing the worst crisis in its history after the defeat suffered
in the War of the Pacific. The Belaúnde government lost all semblance of
coherence, bouncing from one crisis to another and finally producing a
three-digit inflation rate.

In the municipal elections of 1983, Alfonso Barrantes, who headed the
slate of the recently created Izquierda Unida (IU), was elected the first
Marxist mayor of Lima in a demonstration of the widespread rejection of
Belaúnde's policy and the growing political unification of the Left. The
president, however, continued to behave, as one journalist commented, as if
his election victory meant he had been given a blank check which he could
use indiscriminately, without any accountability to the voters. The proposal
of Alfonso Grados Bertorini, the Minister of Labour, to conclude a pact
between capital, labour and the state proved useless, since the technocrats
were not willing to recognize the expectations of the general population. In
fact it was clear that the state had come to represent the IMF and the
interests of the propertied classes more than society as a whole. Prospects of
a social pact between the different social actors and political forces, which
had been a top item on the agenda for the consolidation of democracy,
rapidly began to vanish. Although the growing conflict in society and
between society and the state did not yet go beyond institutional channels,
there were clear signs that this might indeed happen.

Labour strikes, which had been a key factor in the transition to democracy during the late 1970s, were no longer effective. The job stability law
decreed by General Velasco had been weakened by Morales Bermúdez in
response to employers' demands and became meaningless under Belaúnde.
While internal demand fell by 17 per cent, industry tried to adjust to the
new situation by laying off workers and relying on temporary workers and
subcontractors, which led to an unprecedented growth of the 'informal'
sector. Union organization was eroded and the work force was fragmented.
In the meantime, the radicalization of the workers became increasingly
apparent, as was shown by the continuing wave of long wild cat strikes, by
workers taking over their factories and by the occupation of churches and
public places, hunger strikes and violent confrontations with the police.

Public employees, not only administrative personnel but also professionals, such as doctors, nurses, and even the police joined the wave of strikes,
some of which lasted for months. This trend consolidated a political
culture that was increasingly based on the exertion of violent pressure as
the only way to achieve results. Furthermore, there was a clear increase in
a variety of extra-legal and illegal activities – delinquency and drug-
trafficking – which were further indications of the state's inability to
respond to social demands. The likelihood of a military coup that would
put an end to this situation of ungovernability, as would have traditionally
been the case, was lessened by new factors which complicated the political
panorama, especially the emergence and development of Sendero Luminoso (SL).

Founded in 1970 by a Maoist university professor, Abimael Guzmán,
Sendero Luminoso started its terrorist actions in 1980 on election day in a
small Ayacucho village. At first it was given little importance, but soon
the assassination of police and local authorities in Ayacucho demonstrated
the determination of this group to realize the revolutionary objectives the
Left had proposed in the 1970s. From the very beginning, it was evident
to all political actors that the strategy of SL was aimed at provoking a coup
which would eliminate the institutional channels of democratic participation and representation. The armed forces, however, came to the conclusion that any direct political intervention aimed at overthrowing the
constitutional order and starting a generalized campaign of repression was
contrary to their own interests. The institutional frustrations and divisions
caused by their participation in government were still fresh. Moreover, the
international climate was unfavourable for authoritarian and repressive
governments, and such intervention would have encouraged political polarization and the eventual unleashing of a civil war, which was precisely
what the insurrectionary groups were seeking. Thus, the armed forces
reluctantly accepted restrictions on their repressive actions in conformity
with the law.

Nonetheless, growing terrorist activities against the authorities, and
especially against the police and the armed forces, produced a reaction
which distanced the military from the Left, the Church and the peasant
population. In December 1982, when it was already evident that SL was
not simply a gang of common criminals but a very cohesive military and
political group that was committed to destroying the political system, the
president declared Ayacucho an 'emergency zone' and placed it under the

political control of the armed forces. By December 1984, the president
had empowered the armed forces command to carry out anti-subversive
operations throughout the country, sealing his effective abdication of
power to the military in this critical area.

The army's campaign of repression against the peasantry and the supposed accomplices of subversion provoked heated accusations and protests
by leftist representatives, the Church, international and national human
rights organizations, mass organizations and the media, especially after
several journalists were killed. The campaign culminated in a broad national debate on the human rights issue, which henceforth became a
central political theme and included the issues of racism and the traditional ethnic and social exploitation of the country's indigenous peasants.
This reduced the autonomy of the military by exposing its operations to
public scrutiny, despite the support of Belaúnde, his allies in Congress and
sections of the media.

Relations between the government and the armed forces became increasingly conflictive, however, partly because Belaúnde succeeded in stopping
a military confrontation with Ecuador in 1981 when that country's army
occupied Peruvian territory along their common border but, more importantly, because of differences over anti-subversive strategy. In the view of
the military establishment, national security could be only through social
participation and economic development. In the long term only when the
peasantry rejected the insurgents and accepted the rule of law would it be
possible to isolate and politically destroy SL. In the meantime the armed
forces had to pursue the war against the insurgency, concealing the facts
from the civilian leaders and preventing the media and political organizations from publicizing events that occurred in the emergency zone.

The need perceived by the military to improve the living conditions of
the peasants of the Sierra in order to win them over to the constitutional
order produced a new sphere of political tension which was politically
exploited by the opposition – APRA and IU – thus contributing to a
further erosion of Belaúnde's legitimacy. In 1984 an open conflict broke
out with the commander of the emergency zone, General Felix Huaman
Ceuteno, when he complained that he had not received the funds he had
been promised to help the population and that, therefore, the military was
unable to combat the enemy. At the same time the military continued to
display dissatisfaction with the government's economic policy. The result
was a sea of internal contradictions and inefficient action by the govern-

ment, whose legitimacy continued to decline. Public demoralization grew and ministerial turn-over increased dramatically.

Political party mobilization for the 1985 presidential elections raised new hopes that the winner would be able to bring an end to disorder and terrorism, although there were now many reasons to doubt the effectiveness of a democratic government in Peru. An increasing number of the poor and the young were feeling alienated from the political system and were turning to radicalism and messianic ideologies. But the strong and growing presence of the leftists and the Church in lower- and middle-class organizations – among peasants, urban workers, the unemployed, students, professionals and intellectuals – which alone were capable of politically confronting SL, raised hopes for new avenues of political development. In this context, the restructuring of IU and APRA's renewal opened a political avenue for those who were looking for a democratic alternative to the Belaúnde government.

THE 1985 ELECTION AND THE GARCÍA PRESIDENCY, 1985–90

Interest in the 1985 elections was focussed on two political fronts, IU and APRA, and two new figures who had redefined the representation of the political interests of the country's middle and lower classes: Alfonso Barrantes of IU and Alan García of APRA.

The various national elections held since 1978 had created favourable conditions in which the national, regional and local leaders of the IU were able to mobilize the population and extend their influence at different levels of the state and society. The groups of the ultra-Left, among them SL, characterized by their lack of influence or roots in mass organizations, accused IU of 'reformism' and 'election-mongering'. But IU refused to 'sharpen the contradictions', to the extent of risking political suicide. Whilst continuing to oppose the Belaúnde government and the actions of the military, IU had stuck to democratic rules and procedures to ensure its survival and the possibility of growth. In addition, the danger that IU would be accused of complicity with subversives, and therefore subject to repression, contributed to the change in its traditional rhetoric and its rejection of insurgency. And the precarious integration of IU was also a decisive factor in strengthening its democratic position, despite the intentions of some of its members. It had been founded with the aim of unifying the electoral and broader political interests of the leadership of various groups – Moscouvites, Maoists, Guevarists, Christians – whose size and importance varied, and it was focussed on the pivotal role of Alfonso Barrantes, the only person who was able to bring them together. However, conflicts between the party leaders and Barrantes soon surfaced, since his personal popularity, which increased after his election as mayor of Lima, gave him new and greater political resources and made him more independent of them. Thus, party and personal loyalties impeded the integration of the different groups of the Left, which continued to suffer from political fragmentation and doubts about its capacity to govern.

APRA's defeat in the 1980 elections had revived the unsettled conflict over its ideology and its leadership. Haya de la Torre's authoritarianism, APRA's opposition to the political changes that had taken place between the mid-1950s and mid-1970s and the party's failure to address new social demands had had a detrimental effect on membership recruitment. From the 1960s, APRA had been successfully challenged by the labour unions and shanty town and peasant organizations of the Left. In addition, it had suffered ideological blows during the revolutionary phase of the military government and was alienated from university students, teachers and the new intellectuals, who felt suffocated by the party's gerontocracy and its obsolete political machine, which was unable to adjust to the new currents sweeping the country. In these difficult circumstances, more than one critic of the party predicted the final decline of APRA.

With Haya de la Torre dead and posthumously decorated as a national patriarch, his legacy was of little use to Armando Villanueva in the 1980 elections, and he failed to reconcile the divisions between the conservative and nationalist-populist mass-oriented wings of the party. After 1980, however, the young activist Alan García, who had held important positions in the last years of Haya's leadership and had distinguished himself by leading the *aprista* opposition against the Belaúnde government, attempted to unite and renew APRA. The first step was to hold internal elections; procedures were established which, for the first time, were to ensure the democratic participation of party members. García was elected secretary-general of APRA after waging a national campaign that extended beyond the confines of the party. While the other parties remained anchored in anachronistic leadership patterns that resembled those found in parties of 'notables', substantial sectors of the middle and lower classes, which had left the party, now came to regard it again as representative of their interests. APRA regained ground both in society at large and in politics, at a time when President Belaúnde was rapidly losing it. The party campaign also brought Alan García a national reputation that later helped him win the nomination as presidential candidate for APRA in the 1985 elections. García endeavoured to eradicate the sectarian image of the party which had caused its 1980 defeat. In his platform he included issues that were of concern to the nation at large, while reviving the nationalist-populist rhetoric that Haya de la Torre had used in the 1930s. He established links with prestigious figures from different social, business, professional, military and intellectual circles and avoided confrontations that might have rekindled anti-*aprista* sentiments. García tightened the ties between the party's leadership and its grass-roots members and substantially broadened the social base of the party, projecting an image of a national leader.

Two phenomena were decisive in defining García's orientation and style as a candidate and, later, as president: the victory of Alfonso Barrantes and IU in the municipal elections in Lima in 1983 and the emergence of the SL insurgency. Barrantes succeeded in overcoming the problems caused by continuous tensions in IU by appealing directly to the masses and championing the cause of the poor population of Lima, focussing especially on young migrants from the Sierra. He used a broad range of social and political symbols reminiscent of Haya de la Torre's career at its peak. García was obliged to respond to this challenge, whilst simultaneously offering a solution to the SL issue, which he interpreted as having arisen from a long history of social and regional exploitation and ethnic-racial discrimination against the Andean population. Thus, in order to win the election, García had to identify with and express the interests of the poor masses in both the city and the countryside, especially in the Sierra. As he himself acknowledged, APRA had never really taken into account the indigenous population of the Andes and had been unable, for decades, to overcome its pro-urban, coastal and 'criollo' bias.

Yet in contrast to Barrantes and the Left, García recognized that focussing exclusively on the poor while keeping aloof from the middle class and the business community would result in the further social isolation of APRA. His slogan – 'My commitment is to all Peruvians' – emphasized his goal of integrating different social interests in a 'nationalist, broad-based and democratic' platform that was aimed at coming to terms with the common enemy – the IMF and its demands for recessive adjustments and the payment of the external debt. García flatly rejected the conservative slogan so dear to the *aprista* gerontocracy, 'Politics is the art of the possible', which cautioned prudence, discretion and accommodation. Instead, he repeatedly insisted that the time had come to demonstrate the 'political will' to transform the Peruvian reality radically and change the pattern of the centralist, bureaucratic development that had marked the history of the country for the past thirty years. García insisted that the changes under his youthful leadership would benefit everyone equally, without harming anyone. The message had a therapeutic effect; the different classes of society perceived García as a leader who inspired confidence, optimism and the certainty of a secure future, which would reverse the demoralization and political alienation of the Belaúnde years. Persistent terrorist attacks and assassinations by SL led to increased pressure to seek a political solution to Peru's social conflicts. The overwhelming participation of the voters in the 1985 election constituted, in fact, a decisive political defeat for SL, which had urged people to abstain from voting.

García, and APRA, won the 1985 election with 53 per cent of the votes cast, which included support in the southern Sierra and urban shanty towns. Barrantes and IU won 25 per cent of the vote. With a combined share of almost four-fifths of the vote, these two political groups were in a position to contemplate a broad mass-based alliance of unprecedented strength. As for the other parties, AP's candidate Javier Alva Orlandini obtained only 7 per cent – compared with 45 per cent which Belaúnde had obtained in 1980 – and Luis Bedoya, who had run for PPC, only 12 per cent. This reduction in the number of votes cast for the Right to only 19 per cent clearly illustrated the shift that had taken place in the minds of the electorate.

The success of García in the elections reflected the efficacy of his approach in presenting APRA as a force that represented different social classes and different regions. As a result of this success, the nature of the government was to be closely determined by Alan García's will; it became an *"alanista"* rather than an *aprista* government. As the president of the republic and later as the president of his party, García decreed a number of ambitious measures with a clear populist tinge that helped boost his popularity to remarkable levels during his first year in office. His constant direct communication with the urban masses – the *'balconazos'* – as well as the rural population and his denunciations of the state bureaucracy for causing social inequality and exploitation went hand in hand with an intensive personal involvement in virtually all of the country's problems outside established administrative channels.

In response to rising inflation, economic speculation and recession in the manufacturing industry, a 'nationalistic' and 'anti-imperialistic' plan was drawn up that ran counter to the recommendations of international organizations. The nationalistic element consisted of a 'heterodoxy' with a clear distributive intent in terms of employment, incomes and subsidies, and the provision for indiscriminant support of industry; this made it possible to increase GDP growth by 8.5 per cent in 1986 and 9 per cent in 1987 while at the same time reducing inflation. The anti-imperialistic orientation of the plan was focussed on denouncing the developed countries' exploitation of the Third World in terms of the repayment of the foreign debt, which was turning these countries into net exporters of capital. Distancing himself from Fidel Castro's proposal simply to reject the debt, García decided to pay only the equivalent of 10 per cent of export earnings.

Both aspects of the plan caused Peru's relations with international lending agencies and private banks to deteriorate. Simultaneously, García relaunched a Third World-oriented foreign policy and gave his firm support to the *sandinista* government in Nicaragua and the Contadora initiative to negotiate a peace settlement in Central America. At the same time García attacked drug-trafficking, not least in order to balance his anti-American policy. He also restructured the police forces, which were widely accused of corruption, and took the unprecedented measure of retiring high-ranking army officers who had been involved in covering up the killing of peasants in the emergency zones, thus reaffirming the president's constitutional powers as supreme commander of the armed forces.

These policies received warm popular approval and forced the opposition, albeit reluctantly, to subscribe to them, or at least to keep silent. After the lacklustre performance of the Belaúnde administration, García's dynamism heightened the hopes of different sectors for changing the social order via democratic channels. However, the president's voluntarism and his populistic caudillo style soon caused alienation and provoked confrontation first with IU and later with APRA's own party machine. These problems were followed by sharp conflict with the business community and the middle class. After two years in office, García's image as a pluralist and conciliator was in disarray.

In June 1986, the killing of some 250 prisoners accused of terrorism marked the intensification of human rights violations that had begun to grow during Belaúnde's term. But while a military court passed judgement on a few policemen, APRA representatives in Congress aligned themselves with the president and, temporarily, with the armed forces. The delay in the appointment of a Senate committee of investigation, which did not become active until a year later, enraged the Left. Then in the 1986 municipal election campaign García strongly supported the *aprista* candidates, thus breaking a tradition of presidential abstention from local campaigning and causing a narrow defeat of the Left in Lima. Meanwhile, García took up secret negotiations with the top leaders of the large capitalist groups, the so-called twelve apostles, passing over the formal organizations of the business community. These negotiations were aimed at guaranteeing the concessions granted to large capital interests, with a view to enhancing the effectiveness of the heterodox economic policy. For their part the 'apostles' took advantage of the favourable rate of exchange the government granted them by exporting capital and depleting the country's foreign exchange reserves. The workers, whose incomes had not been improved, manifested discontent with both the distribution of sacrifices and their exclusion from the negotiations between the president and the large enterprises.

García had neutralized the Right – AP and PPC – but exacerbated the conflict with the parties of the Left and their constituencies. This led to a relatively successful general strike called by the CGTP in May 1987, which was followed by a number of partial strikes, especially in the public services. Furthermore, IU leaders and their most radicalized political cadres demanded of Alfonso Barrantes that he challenge the validity of the 1986 election results; that he head a campaign against the government's dubious practices in the elections; that he put a stop to his talks with García, which were being carried on surreptitiously and without previous consultation; and that he enter into open confrontation with APRA and the president. Barrantes refused to comply with these demands, however, and his repeated absence from the meetings of the IU executive committee restricted the efficacy of its opposition and eventually paralysed it. His refusal to challenge the election results, even though they had been unfavourable for him and his persistent adherence to the established rules and procedures unleashed furious opposition in some groups inside IU and caused him to resign from its leadership, although his personal popularity was undiminished. Thereafter, IU experienced a protracted crisis that culminated in a split in January 1989 at its first national convention. At the same time, SL was stepping up its attacks, which were no longer solely directed against public authorities, but also included the killing of political leaders of the Left, labour unions, peasant organizations and of university professors.

A constitutional amendment in favour of the re-election of the president for a second term prompted a revolt against García inside APRA, because it blocked the emergence of new candidates and their respective clienteles and because it also provoked popular opposition to such an extent that it jeopardized the future of the party, which, in one minister's view, was to govern the country for the next fifty years. For these reasons the constitutional amendment was rejected.

This confrontation made it evident that the party machine was discontented with the president's overt lack of interest and refusal to heed their opinions and recommendations on numerous political initiatives. This discontent also stemmed from García's close relations with Barrantes and the 'twelve apostles' about which he had never consulted the party's leaders. At the same time, it derived from his failure to provide activists, who had been waiting patiently for this opportunity for decades, with a sufficient number of executive positions; these were often assigned to 'Alan's friends', who did not always have the necessary *aprista* credentials. García's populist style and behaviour were conducive to the formation of political alliances around him, without addressing the bureaucratic interests of the party machine, which he considered a nuisance, or even an obstacle, to his own 'national, popular and democratic' project. The old *aprista* leadership, for its part, reacted by openly challenging the young president's growing independence.

The severity of the tensions that had been building up between García and his followers and the party machine was bluntly demonstrated when Luis Alva Castro, the second vice-president, prime minister and minister of economics, decided to resign from his cabinet posts and run as a candidate for the presidency of the Chamber of Deputies with a view to launching his candidacy for the office of president of the republic in 1990. García's rejection of this initiative paralysed public administration during the first half of 1987 and caused an indefinite delay in adjusting the heterodox economic policy, thus provoking the reappearance of inflation. These factors were decisive in prompting the decline of both García's popularity and his capacity to determine the course of events. The president was finally obliged to acquiesce in Luis Alva's resignation from the cabinet posts he had still been nominally holding. He also had to accept that Alva would win the nomination as a candidate for the presidency of the Chamber of Deputies with the backing of the APRA majority in Congress. In July 1987 García was forced to appoint a new cabinet whose prime minister was a member of the party machine who sought to resume negotiations with the IMF and face up to the looming economic crisis.

At a moment that seemed to mark the start of his removal from the centre of political power, García decided to stage a typical *fuite en avant*. In his presidential message of 28 July 1987, he addressed Congress with a proposal – which had not been discussed either in the government or with the party – for the nationalization of the private banks. The rationale for this proposal was that, notwithstanding the subsidized rate of exchange, reduced interest rates, income tax incentives and other facilities, the large capitalist groups had not only failed to invest their growing profits but also had stepped up the flight of capital and further added to the country's economic ills. In this sense García argued that breaking the 'financial circuits' was a necessary precondition for the democratic consolidation of Peruvian society.

The sudden presentation of such a proposal produced a political earthquake. On the one hand, García was breaking his links with the business community and the party's conservative leaders, whilst, on the other, attempting to restore links with its radical grass-roots constituency and forcing the Left and its social constituency to rally around him. In this, he was playing a dangerous game, breaking social and political coalitions with the aim of realigning them around himself. He elicited a rapid and determined response from AP, PPC and big business, which embarked on a massive public relations offensive. This succeeded in gaining the support of substantial sectors of the middle class, intellectuals and professionals for a liberal and anti-statist counter-platform aimed at preventing the country from supposedly falling into totalitarianism. Its main promoters and mobilizers were Hernando de Soto and Mario Vargas Llosa.[3]

Faced with this opposition, the president waged a solitary campaign in defence of the nationalization of the financial system. However, this was

[3] At the beginning of the 1980s, Hernando de Soto had developed a neo-liberal approach to Peru's problems which, broadly speaking, explained the stagnation and the distortions of the economy and society by the 'blockade' of the the market by 'mercantilistic' interference exerted by 'distributivistic coalitions' with privileged access to the state – somewhat in line with Mancur Olson's reasoning in *The Rise and Decline of Nations: Economic Growth, Stagflation and Social Rigidities* (New Haven, Conn., 1982). This blockade caused a boom in the 'informal sector', which comprised those poor sectors of the population that were not in a position to develop within a legal framework. This approach was expounded by de Soto in *The Other Path: The Invisible Revolution in the Third World* (New York, 1983), which, with a preface written by Mario Vargas Llosa, was widely disseminated in Peru and other countries, and even came to be quoted by Presidents Reagan and Bush.

Henceforth, this anti-statist conception came to be perceived as 'common sense' by the Peruvian people. Paradoxically, García's discourse against bureaucratic centralism further enhanced this effect. Likewise, the leftist conceptions with regard to the rentier outlook of the propertied classes in Peru also helped the popularization of these ideas. The result was a widespread conviction that it would be necessary to restrict the economic intervention of the state and to reform its apparatus so as to enable the market to develop.

systematically silenced by the media, which, in turn, launched unrelenting attacks on García, demanding his resignation. Luis Bedoya Reyes went so far as to appeal to the armed forces to intervene.

Bank employees, whose leadership had traditionally belonged to the Left and who had been demanding the nationalization of the banking sector since the Velasco era, aligned themselves with the bankers, impeding the enforcement of García's measures. Their position was backed by important professional and intellectual groups who defended the private sector and attacked state interference in the economy and society. The president's proposition thus provoked the first politically organized reaction ever to have been launched against the redistributive role of the state which the lower and middle classes had been demanding since the 1960s.

The liberal opposition appealed to the population at large for support and especially the poorest sectors that were hardest hit by inflation. It presented itself as a democratic alternative, seeking to enhance freedom – that is to say the market – against 'collectivism', 'statism' and communism.

APRA's leadership was taken by surprise. The political confusion that García had provoked threw the party into uncertainty and threatened to return the party to the marginal political status it had struggled so hard to overcome during the previous sixty years. Yet circumstances obliged the APRA apparatus to side with García, albeit with open reluctance and expressions of resentment at his personalistic presidential style. However, while the APRA majority in the Chamber of Deputies quickly passed the law, the Senate debate dragged on for months, thus dooming the presidential initiative to end in fiasco.[4]

Alan García's repeated populist attempts to rally around him different political forces and social actors not only had been unsuccessful during his first two years in office, but had effectively created new sources of conflict and political fragmentation. From July 1987 onwards, the political crisis caused by his proposal to nationalize the financial sector combined with various other economic and political factors to produce a proliferation of centrifugal forces that encouraged the disintegration of state and society, a process that was dubbed by various commentators as the 'Lebanization' of Peru. Even though it was evident by the end of 1986 that the govern-

---

[4] APRA's youth organization, where radical trends were rampant, at first gave decided support to Alan García, but when he later announced the government's backing down following the institution of legal proceedings by the bankers, the young militants withdrew their support. By contrast, IU's representatives turned out to be the most effective and determined defenders of the presidential proposition.

ment's heterodox economic policies were no longer effective, the president persisted over the next two years with his personalistic and erratic management of the economy. The effect on production and income was disastrous: between 1987 and 1989, GDP fell 15 per cent and average real wages and salaries by 60 per cent. Meanwhile the rate of inflation rose to 100 per cent in 1987, 1,000 per cent in 1988 and 2,500 per cent in 1989. In June, October and December 1987 the government's attempt to fix prices and wages proved inadequate. New measures were taken in March, May, June and August 1988. A *'paquetazo'* in September ('Black September') failed to produce the promised stabilization and recovery of the economy. These measures and their results prompted many demonstrations and prolonged strikes in such sectors as public health, education, the judiciary, agriculture, communications and mining and fisheries, as well as regional movements. However, unlike previous protest movements, these mobilizations were not interconnected – a fact that revealed how far the efforts of the union confederations to secure political centralization of the demands of the lower and middle classes had been weakened by so many fruitless struggles.

The results of García's economic policy also produced dissent inside APRA, evoking strong criticism during the party's December 1988 convention that led to some cabinet reshuffling. Veteran APRA members dislodged the group of 'Alan's friends', who in the party's view were to blame for the economic policy. Moreover, some allies of both APRA and García withdrew their support and joined the opposition. The capitalists, who were now politically represented by the Movimiento Libertad – later the Frente Democrático – launched a series of bitter attacks on the president aimed at forcing his resignation and creating a situation close to a constitutional crisis. In the Cuzco region, the opposition joined forces with APRA and leftist members of both houses of Congress in order to prevent foreign companies from investing in natural gas exploitation; the fishing contracts with Soviet companies were sharply disputed; and new presidential proposals for the regionalization of the country, which had been presented with the hope of shifting the focus of the political agenda, stood to be stopped or, at best, modified. When Peru was declared 'ineligible' by the international financial agencies and was in danger of being expelled from the IMF and the World Bank for defaulting on its foreign debt payments, García's nationalistic and Third World policies finally collapsed. Albeit reluctantly, García was forced to resume negotiations with these organizations in order to obtain the funds the country needed for its 'reintegration' into the international economic system. In short, from July 1987 political life became highly complex and controversial and García was increasingly isolated, his credibility reduced to an unprecedented extent; according to different opinion polls, he had enjoyed the support of nearly 90 per cent of the population during the first few months of his term, but his support had now dropped to less than 10 per cent.

The novel and dangerous aspect of this situation lay in the fact that the failure of García and APRA raised for the first time the question of Peru's 'governability'. The country's democratic institutions had demonstrated their inability to solve the old problem of nation-building. This was illustrated by the aloofness of the 'political class' from the problems and requirements of society. Politics and politicians were increasingly looked upon with disdain – a fact which favoured the 'independents' and the movement headed by Vargas Llosa. At the same time, subversion persisted and intensified, as was manifested by the increasing number of assassinations not only of state officials, policemen, and members of the armed forces but also of peasants who failed to obey SL's orders. SL's campaign was pursued through the destruction of co-operatives, the slaughter of cattle, the assassination of union leaders and leftist leaders, as well as of national and foreign technicians, and the regular cutting off of the supply of electricity to the country's main cities, including Lima. This offensive was stepped up on the eve of the 1989 municipal elections, when SL increased its threats against and assassinations of candidates and local officials of different political affiliations in and beyond the emergency zones – Ayacucho, Huancavelica, Huanuco, Pasco – creating power vacuums with the intention of establishing SL as the undisputed occupying force. Notwithstanding the set-backs it suffered, the SL repeatedly proved able to recover and continued to recruit young people. Most numerous among these were the educated sons and daughters of '*mistis*' and migrants from the Sierra Highlands who felt alienated from a political system that they justifiably perceived as denying their economic, cultural and political needs. Having obtained control of large rural areas and many urban centres in the southern and central Sierra highlands, where the police and the armed forces were forced to retreat to their barracks in the main cities, SL decreed 'armed strikes' in various cities of the southern Sierra. These proved to be successful at intimidating the authorities and the population at large. SL later ventured into the coastal areas, but its success there was uneven.

In 1983 the Movimiento Revolucionario Tupac Amaru (MRTA) had emerged as another force dedicated to armed struggle. Its members were recruited from the urban and coastal young populations, as well from the Left and APRA. This movement bore a certain strategic and programmatic resemblance to the guerrilla movements of the 1960s, while SL related more closely to the example of Mao. Their competition over revolutionary leadership and the financial resources to be obtained from controlling the production and marketing of coca led to bloody confrontrations.[5]

Alan García's anti-subversion policy suffered an early failure when SL rejected his proposals for talks. The possibility of negotiation was further diminished by the 1986 killing of prisoners, the responsibility for which was attributed to the president and his minister of the interior by the minority report of the Senate compiled by representatives of the Left. García suffered a second set-back when it was revealed that a former *aprista,* a member of a family historically linked with the party and a former friend who had shared the president's bohemian life in Paris, was a commander of MRTA. As a consequence, anti-subversion policy fell firmly under the control of the military high command – a fact that exacerbated violations of human rights. As a result of subversion and efforts to counteract it, approximately eighteen thousand people lost their lives in the 1980s. Furthermore, it was publicly known that the 'death squads' – called the Rodrigo Franco Command in homage to an APRA activist murdered by SL – originated in the Ministry of the Interior. These groups operated in parallel with the subversive groups, terrorizing the emergency zones and deepening the destabilization and destruction of social organizations and state institutions.

The breakdown of state and society was reflected in disputes over competence between and within governmental institutions and between the army and the police. It was evident in the permanent tensions within the armed forces and police over their budget, which caused the police to strike on more than one occasion. It could be seen in the incessant advance of delinquency which jeopardized the movement of people and goods across the country and in the growing corruption of the magistracy, the police and the army with regard to drug-trafficking, smuggling and subversion. (Accusations were even brought against high-ranking state officials.) The crisis was sharpened by the impunity of officers accused of

---

[5] Differences in the social recruitment, socialization, alliances, revolutionary ideas and geographic location between SL and the MRTA showed that the segmentation of Peruvian society reached even these levels.

assassinations or of being responsible for 'disappearances' and by the desertion of soldiers and policemen who refused to risk their lives in the struggle against subversion, as well as by the large number of military officers who applied for retirement. The economic bankruptcy of the state involved the dismantling of a whole range of services such as social security, the postal services, public health, education and public transportation in addition to the continuous interruption of the electricity supply by terrorist attacks. As a result there was a mass emigration of hundreds of thousands of Peruvians of different social backgrounds.

Despite this disastrous state of affairs, municipal elections were held in November 1989, and the general elections of April 1990 gave rise to new – albeit timid – hopes for a government capable of finding solid and democratic solutions to the sundry crises endured by the country. Although the 'political class' and the state organization were widely criticized, broad sectors continued to demonstrate commitment to democracy, since there was no alternative other than increased violence through subversion and/or a military coup d'état. At the same time various political realignments took place before the elections. APRA was discredited not only by its disastrous record in government but also by widespread accusations of favouritism and corruption both from within and outside the party. Luis Alva Castro, APRA's candidate for the presidency, initially attempted to maintain that everything had been going well when he was prime minister and minister of economics, indirectly blaming García for subsequent disasters. But the president's campaign to defend his measures and attack his opponents prompted accusations that he was waging a political campaign as though he were a candidate himself, and this dwarfed Alva Castro's role.

In IU, tensions between Barrantes, the most radical sectors and the moderates exploded at the first national convention in January 1989, which had been organized to institutionalize IU. However, these divisions had been present since the constituent parties of the alliance had joined together in 1980 for electoral purposes, and they had already been an issue of public debate for almost a year. The dispute that arose in the convention was between those groups which postulated the need to organize an 'armed wing' for the purpose of self-defence against state terrorism and Barrantes and others, who maintained that IU must wage a 'struggle for the democratic revolution'. The PC and the radical Christians – who had joined forces in the Movimiento de Afirmación al Socialismo (MAS) – found themselves caught in a tug of war between

the different interests, but finally opted for Henry Pease, a member of
MAS, as its candidate for the presidency, while the opposing groups
withdrew and merged, first in Acuerdo Socialista and later in Izquierda
Socialista, with Alfonso Barrantes as their presidential candidate. However, the increase in terrorist actions, even against the radical groups,
together with the impact of international events, such as the massacre in
Tiananmen Square, perestroika in the Soviet Union and the breakdown
of Communist rule in Eastern Europe, plunged IU into ideological confusion and strengthened moderate, 'social democratic' currents within it.

In marked contrast to the trends towards disintegration in APRA and
the Left, Vargas Llosa succeeded in integrating AP and PPC and his own
Movimiento Libertad into the Frente Democrático (FREDEMO). This was
not achieved without difficulty. Indeed the obstacles erected by the leaders
of these parties – Belaúnde and Bedoya – even prompted him to resign as
a presidential candidate in June 1989. However, this ultimatum caused
the parties to accept Vargas Llosa's conditions and acknowledge him as
FREDEMO's undisputed leader, while reserving the right both to nominate their respective candidates for the office of vice-president and to have
a preferential say in the designation of candidates for the congressional
elections. As a result, the front won new affiliates among small political
groups and some well-known individuals. Vargas Llosa's neo-liberal
programme – market liberalization, privatization, opening the economy
to foreign investment – quickly came to dominate the country's political
agenda. This success was above all due to Vargas Llosa's international
renown as a writer and liberal essayist, which helped him to win support
amongst domestic and international business organizations and the media;
this enabled him to wage a costly and increasingly strident campaign with
the assistance of well-known and successful international PR agencies. In
addition, he gained the backing of the new intellectual liberal school that
was gaining ground in Peru as a result of the collapse of Peruvian populism as well as the crisis of Marxism throughout the world. Vargas Llosa's
ability to mobilize the high-income sectors and to rally mass support
became evident after the victory of the 'independents' in the November
1989 municipal elections. It also illustrated the yearning for a 'saviour'
who would initiate a new era.

However, the 'transparent' liberal stance that Vargas Llosa adopted in
order to obtain an unequivocal electoral mandate was likely to provoke a
new earthquake that would undermine the very fragile foundations of

society. While there seemed to be no imminent possibilities of reconstruction, there were widespread fears that the floodgates would be opened and the violence that had been contained thus far would be unleashed. Whatever the outcome of the 1990 presidential elections, the incoming government would be faced with a critical situation that would force it to take radical measures.[6]

6 The first round of the elections (8 April) was won by Mario Vargas Llosa (FREDEMO) with 27.6% of the vote. A political outsider, Alberto Fujimori (Cambio 90), a Japanese-Peruvian, came second with 24.6%. Luis Alva Castro (APRA) secured 19.1%, Henry Pease (Izquierda Unida) 6.9% and Alfonso Barrantes (Izquierda Socialista) 4%. In the second round (10 June) Fujimori (56.5%) defeated Vargas Llosa (33.9%) to become president of Peru.

Part Two

9

BOLIVIA SINCE 1930

The history of Bolivia could be viewed as the history of a rather small elite (or cluster of political, economic and bureaucratic elites) whose members were frequently on first-name terms with one another and whose alliances and divisions often had as much to do with private as with public life. Membership might be achieved through family background, education or success in one of a limited range of (essentially urban) careers, but the qualifications did not have to be particularly high to exclude the great majority of the population. Fluency in spoken and written Spanish, access to a town and a means of livelihood sufficiently secure to leave a margin above individual subsistence disqualified the great majority of adult males, at least until well into the second half of the twentieth century.

Nevertheless, the internal affairs of these elites could be highly complex and arouse great passion, and their divisions could have important consequences for the population as a whole (as in the Federal Revolution of 1898, when an armed conflict between Conservatives and Liberals – or perhaps between the elites of La Paz and Sucre – raised the peasant masses of the *altiplano* into collective action on a massive scale). The Bolivian elites were by no means homogeneous, or even coherent. The country's geography, the centripetal tendencies of its pattern of economic development (aptly symbolized by the external orientation of its railway system) and the colonial character of its social structure conspired against the emergence of a socially unified elite and contributed to the complexity and instability of its 'traditional' history.

However, the half-century after 1930 was dominated by a series of social convulsions that can hardly be encompassed, and certainly not adequately explained, by an account based on the preoccupations of the Bolivian elites.

Over these fifty years Bolivia's social structure was transformed almost beyond recognition. Perhaps the most fundamental change was the consolidation of a nation-state, with much denser and more complex interrelationships between the disparate social and linguistic groups, classes and regions that comprised Bolivian civil society. This consolidation was not an entirely spontaneous process. In fact, it was actively (at times almost desperately) promoted from above. Many of the activities of government that commentators and historians have tried to classify as 'socialist', 'corporatist', 'fascist' or 'revolutionary' may best be interpreted as efforts to create a modern nation-state in Bolivia before it was too late. Defeat in the Chaco War (1935) crystallized the fear that, unless the process of nation-building was accelerated, the dynamic tendencies of neighbouring countries would produce the final disintegration of this landlocked and impoverished buffer state. The eventual outcome of these various governmental efforts was to establish a more geographically unified society with a wider popular participation and a greater sense of national identity. Over half a century Bolivia acquired a much more integrated market network, a more homogeneous and mobile labour force and a much larger and more complex state apparatus, modelled essentially on military lines. Although this process had not produced what might be termed a 'modern nation-state' by 1980, it is evident that 'nationalism' played a dominant role in shaping Bolivian society from 1930 and that it operated powerfully enough to produce a profound transformation.

During this period, the Bolivian elites only briefly, and with great effort, achieved a degree of unity and solidity against the challenges always implicitly presented to them by the unsatisfied aspirations of the great majority of the population: the mostly illiterate and often non-Spanish-speaking rural labour force; the 'proletarian' work-force in the highland mining camps; the petty traders of the towns and villages; and newer occupational groups who also found themselves living in extremely precarious economic conditions – schoolteachers, transport workers, minor bureaucrats and so on. For the elites, unity and solidity required a willingness not only to repress threatening mass movements from below, but also to discipline those within their own ranks who identified with any movement for change or who believed that their sectional position might be advanced by mass mobilization. But such elite unity against real or imagined threats from below was achieved only briefly and partially, in 1931–2, in the early part of the Second World War (1940–2) and perhaps in the period before the National Revolution (1949–51). A strategy of blind repression failed to avert the National Revolution of 1952, which turned into total collapse of elite authority and inevitably paved the way for a social upheaval of far-reaching proportions — one which many of its instigators soon found uncomfortably radical and beyond control. The phase of maximum radicalization lasted no more than four years (1952–6) and left the country economically vulnerable and politically disoriented. Piece by piece the leaders of the revolutionary movement sought to assemble the elements of a new political order that would both express and contain the aspirations of the new social forces that had acquired a taste of power in the aftermath of 1952. But although many ingredients seemed to resemble (perhaps even to imitate) those used so effectively in the Mexican formula for 'institutionalizing' a social revolution, it proved impossible to combine them in the right proportions. The disintegration of the revolutionary coalition proceeded apace in the early 1960s, and this paved the way for the 1964 restoration both of military government and of political dominance by the most privileged minorities. Thereafter, the period from 1974 to 1977 could be characterized as one of sustained and relatively successful elite unity, associated with tightened political discipline and fierce exclusion of most pressures from below. The military coup of July 1980 and the resulting temporary annulment of electoral politics appeared to represent yet another, and even fiercer, reassertion of exclusionary politics, which ended in bankruptcy. The anti-democratic content of these episodes became progressively more explicit in each episode after 1964. However, after 1980 the extreme Right and the radical Left were deeply discredited, with the result that a range of more centrist parties reappeared to compete for electoral support from an insecure and disillusioned, but no longer totally excluded, mass of subjects. In fact, the return to democracy in 1982 allowed the political leaders of the 1950s to stage an encore in the 1980s.

THE 1930S

Exactly ten years elapsed between the overthrow of the Liberal Party in June 1920 and the downfall in June 1930 of President Hernando Siles, who, pleading the economic crisis induced by the world depression and the need to avert a war in the Chaco, attempted to extend his term of office beyond the constitutional limit. During that turbulent decade, major new social groups had entered the political arena, and exotic ideological currents such as Marxism and fascism had begun to make an impact in educated circles. Patiño Mines and Enterprises had risen from its former

status as an outstandingly successful Bolivian mining company to a position of strategic dominance in the world tin market. The rival colonizing
efforts of the Bolivians and Paraguayans in the Chaco hinterland had
finally reached the stage of contact, and therefore of conflict. Efforts to
devise a system of government that would secure political stability and
economic expansion without reverting to pre-1920 conditions of Liberal
oligarchy and mining company pre-eminence had failed, just when the
liberal economic system was itself entering into crisis. These are indispensable considerations for judging the 1930 revolution and the constitutional
presidency of Daniel Salamanca (1931–4) that resulted from it.

   In the opinion of most contemporaries the revolution was staged by a
very broad alliance of political groups, uniting to block an attempt by
President Siles and his party to circumvent the constitutional ban on
immediate re-election. Although the Liberals captured an unexpectedly
large proportion of seats in the Congress elected in January 1931, and
reoccupied such key positions as the presidency of the Central Bank, other
groups also obtained important advantages: the students, who had played
a leading part in the street demonstrations of June 1930, won a constitutional guarantee of university autonomy in the 1931 referendum; the
teaching profession was released from political controls; and the press
would no longer be subject to censorship or official manipulation. The
cornerstone of the new regime was to be strict respect for constitutional
norms, so that no one group or interest would be in a position to dominate
the others, as had been the tendency during the 1920s. Such at least was
the initial rhetoric,[1] and possibly the conviction, of adherents to the new
regime. But this is not how it was judged in retrospect. President Siles
himself never accomplished a political comeback, but the more aggressive
nationalists of the next generation included quite a few young men who
acquired political experience under Siles's government in the late 1920s.
And it was one of the president's own sons (Hernán Siles Suazo, president

---

[1] Although most contemporary commentators saw the change of regime in strictly political terms,
the young Víctor Paz Estenssoro was a significant exception. 'Nowadays', wrote Bolivia's first
technocrat, 'it is economic phenomena, such as production, foreign trade, etc., which in reality, and
beyond apparent causes, regulate the life of nations'. He considered that parliaments were not suited
to the new tasks of economic management. These were better performed by organizations composed
of representatives of the major functional interests in society, which he apparently believed could all
share power harmoniously under the new regime, guided only by the principles of economic
rationality. In his view Bolivia had been engaged throughout the 1920s in public spending beyond
its means, so that the fall in tin prices would have the healthy effect of eliminating the 25% of
profligate and unnecessary spending that had created an artificial illusion of prosperity. See his
articles in *El Diario* (La Paz), 17 May 1930 and 6 July 1930.

1956–60, 1982–85) who organized the revolutionary insurrection of April 1952 and thereby in a sense reversed the verdict of June 1930, which was now seen as a triumph of reaction.

The 1930 coup was undoubtedly favourable to Patiño's interests, and it was welcomed by landlords, bureaucrats and Liberal oligarchs who all saw the need to reassert social discipline in a semi-colonial society which faced acute economic crisis. The officer corps also regarded 1930 as an opportunity to increase the prestige and cohesion of the military establishment after the disruptions of the 1920s. In June 1930 the army established a transitional military junta and appointed army officers as prefects; it also exerted influence over the ensuing elections, marginalizing the popular former president Bautista Saavedra and bolstering the old order. One should not underestimate the extent to which dominant interests had felt threatened by the political experiments of the 1920s; now they had a chance to redress the balance. With the prospect of severe budget cuts, the need for unity must have been apparent to them, even before they could appreciate the depth of social discontent that would be occasioned by the depression or perceive the imminence of a protracted foreign war. Thus, despite initial constitutional reforms the early 1930s were years of social repression.

Nevertheless, the idea that Salamanca's government represented the triumph of reaction must be qualified in two respects. The attitudes of his predecessor towards the various proposals for social reform can only be described as ambiguous; and the reactionary features of Salamanca's own administration must be judged in the context of almost unprecedented internal and international crisis. His reputation as a militant reactionary derived from the obsessive fear of social dissolution that he expressed from 1931 onwards. Salamanca was in fact an old-fashioned provincial land-owner, wedded to a legalistic version of liberal doctrines, who was forced by circumstances to rely mostly on *palo* in the absence of *pan*.

The impact of the economic crisis was felt unevenly in a productive system so lately and imperfectly integrated into the world economy.[2] Without a sea coast or navigable rivers, the railways provided almost the sole modern means of communication in a vast and very unevenly populated territory. With a population of perhaps 2.5 million in a territory twice the size of France, Bolivia in 1929 had fewer than 1,200 motor cars,

---

[2] See L. Whitehead, 'El impacto de la Gran Depresión en Bolivia', *Desarrollo Economico* 12 (1972), pp. 49–80. Bolivia was the first South American republic to default on debt servicing, in December 1930, followed by Peru in March 1931 and Chile in July 1931.

fewer than 1,000 trucks, 54 buses and just 6 aeroplanes. The Pacific rail route had confirmed the urban primacy of La Paz with its productive hinterland and had condemned the formal capital, Sucre, to irrelevance and decline. The densely populated valleys of Cochabamba and some of the windswept settlements of Potosí were also closely linked to world markets, but in 1931 the money ran out before a rail link could be completed to the lowland city of Santa Cruz. (Some claimed later that Bolivia would have won the Chaco War if only this project had reached fruition.) Even among the urban population, regional loyalties posed a serious challenge to any popular sentiment of 'nationhood'. The rural majority, officially classified as 'Indian' and treated accordingly, still lacked either fluency in Spanish or any mechanized means of transport; their horizons remained inescapably parochial.

Nevertheless, in the forty years since the opening of the first railway a sustained process of economic 'modernization' had powerfully affected a substantial sector of the *altiplano* population. Those most closely engaged with the international economy were naturally to feel the strongest impact of the depression. Probably the most severely affected area was the railhead and mining centre of Oruro, where the authorities were soon overwhelmed by the demands of the unemployed. These problems had become unmanageable even before Salamanca took office, for not only were Bolivian mining enterprises laying off workers, but the Chilean nitrate industry was also entering into the final phase of its collapse. The trains from the coast were packed with the families of impoverished Bolivian workers expelled from the nitrate zone, returning to a home country from which they had often been absent for more than a decade. By mid-1932 desperation had become far more widespread as declining tax revenues, tightening credit and diminished allocations of foreign exchange through the import quota system added many public employees, small entrepreneurs and shopkeepers to the ranks of the destitute. Nor were landlords and mine-owners sheltered from the impact of the recession. The British vice-consul in Cochabamba reported that many landlords accustomed to selling their agricultural surpluses to the miners had been unable to service their mortgages and that the banks were in some cases selling off estates acquired by default in small parcels to peasants and small traders.[3]

At the heart of the economic crisis were the problems of the mining sector. Tin had displaced silver as Bolivia's principal export at the turn of

---

[3] T. O'Connor, in *British Consular Reports: Economic Conditions in Bolivia* (London, May 1931), p. 19.

the century. It accounted for more than 72 per cent of all export earnings in the 1920s, a ratio which held more or less constant until the end of the Korean War (after which tin's pre-eminence gradually declined, falling at last below a half at the beginning of the 1970s). For at least half a century, therefore, tin was the export staple of Bolivia; other products which also earned significant amounts of foreign exchange – minerals such as silver, gold, wolfram and antimony – were produced mainly by the same enterprises that controlled the tin sector. In 1929–33 (before the New Deal in the United States raised gold and silver prices) tin constituted 75 per cent of Bolivia's exports, and 68 per cent was dispatched to the United Kingdom, where Simón I. Patiño, Bolivia's largest tin producer, owned a smelter. Although the statistics must be treated warily, it seems likely that in 1929 Bolivia's tin production reached the never to be repeated peak of more than 47,000 long tons, just less than one-quarter of world output. By 1933 output was down to 14,400 long tons, just below one-sixth of the world total. In terms of dollar values the blow was more severe, for in 1932 world tin prices were less than half the levels attained at the height of wartime demand in 1918. In June 1929, four months before the Wall Street crash, major producers had become sufficiently concerned about the record levels of unsold tin stocks to form an international association aimed at reducing excess supply either by financing stockpiles or by limiting production. It has been argued that it was not so much over-expansion of production as a rapid decline in consumption that caused most of the trouble, a decline heavily concentrated in the United States.[4] Whether or not they had over-expanded before 1929, Bolivia's producers were badly exposed when prices collapsed. In contrast to the alluvial mining prevalent in Malaya, the Bolivians were dependent on underground mines that seemed far more vulnerable to rapid exhaustion or cost escalation. Patiño's biographer goes so far as to suggest that by the end of 1929

it looked as if history was going to repeat itself and that the Bolivian tin mining, just when it had reached full development, would suffer the fate of its rubber and quinine industries and decline almost to the point of disappearing. . . . production costs in the Orient in 1930 were about £70 per fine ton cheaper than in Bolivia.[5]

---

[4] The United States, which produced almost no tin of its own, consumed 44% of world output in 1929, but only 34% in 1932. 'Over the eight years 1925–32 U.S. consumption fell by 41,000 tons per annum but the consumption of the rest of the world fell by only 12,000 tons'. William Fox, *The Working of a Commodity Agreement: Tin* (London, 1974), p. 118.

[5] Charles F. Geddes, *Patiño: The Tin King* (London, 1972), pp. 221–5. In the absence of a smelter within Bolivia, the companies had to transport a heavy weight of worthless mineral all the way to Europe before the tin content could be extracted. All imports for the mines also bore heavy freight charges.

In fact, Bolivia was to remain a major tin exporter for a further half-century, but there are some grounds for thinking that the mining magnates may have genuinely feared an early and total collapse of their Bolivian enterprises even before the world depression produced generalized alarm. Dewett C. Deringer, the U.S. manager of Patiño's Catavi plant, later wrote:

Shortly after Patiño Mines was organized, in 1924, the New York firm Yateman and Barry estimated its probable life at 5 years. . . . In 1927, with the exhaustion of the then commercial bodies of mineral – 3% in content – the firm made a heavy capital investment [enabling it] to increase production on the basis of minerals with an average tin content of 2.25% . . . no-one in their right minds would have foreseen in 1929 that mineral bodies containing 0.8% tin would ever become commercial.[6]

Under Patiño's leadership, and with the full backing of the Bolivian government, the tin-mining companies of the world responded to the fall off in demand by putting ever tighter restraints on production, enforced after March 1931 through an international body, the semi-governmental Tin Producers Association. While the largest companies generally secured satisfactory shares of the officially allocated production quotas and had the financial strength to ride out a period of heavy losses, Bolivia's small mining entrepreneurs were not so fortunate. The greatest test of endurance began in mid-1932, when the association set production quotas at only 33 per cent of the levels achieved in 1929, a cut-back that was maintained until the end of 1933. By early 1933 the tin price had rebounded to the level of late 1929, with the result that the private interests financing buffer stocks of tin made a healthy profit. However, both producers and consumers suffered from the disciplines that were imposed by the cartel and contributed to the hostile climate of opinion in which Patiño mines would henceforth operate. During his presidency, Salamanca maintained a correspondence with Simón Patiño in Europe, securing assistance with military procurements and advice on financial matters. The president wrote on 16 May 1933 thanking Patiño for his 'daring and risky efforts to

[6] Deringer, Letter to *El Diario* (La Paz), 10 January 1960. He added that 'In 1938 certain improvements in domestic and international transport, plus new techniques . . . enabled us to keep up the volume of output although the ore grade was now below 2%. . . . However by 1947 the reserves economically useable on the basis of existing technical processes were barely sufficient for another four years of production. . . . We recruited the services of specialists . . . and at the end of 1947 we were able to develop and try out the method of Block Caving [and other major innovations] which permitted the profitable mining of ore grading 1.0%'. By 1980 the *average* tin content of Bolivia's commercially viable ore was below 0.6%.

maintain and to push up the price of tin'. However, a week later Salamanca added the following warning: 'I have noticed that on the slightest pretext a tidal wave of jealousy threatens to engulf the mining industry'.[7] In fact, after Salamanca's presidency, the conduct of Bolivian governments towards the mining industry began to vary markedly. To Patiño himself this seemed very unjust, since he was proud of his patriotic achievements in expelling Chilean capital and assisting the war efforts. It was hardly surprising, however, considering the good shape in which the major mining enterprises (now dubbed the '*rosca*', or the 'mining superstate') emerged from the economic crisis of the early 1930s, and the contrast between their prosperity and the general immiseration of Bolivian-based producers, employees and workers.

The financial and economic crisis only contributed to a much more generalized social and political crisis that was already in embryonic form before 1929 and was greatly exacerbated by the experience of the Chaco War – three years of desperate fighting capped by a bitter and humiliating defeat. Although pre-1930 radical currents aiming, in Tristan Marof's phrase, at 'tierras al indio, minas al estado' lacked an organizational focus and were socially dispersed and ideologically confused, their explosive potential was apparent both to left-wing militants and to defenders of the status quo. By 1931 both Salamanca and the economic elite were thoroughly alarmed both by the social consequences of the economic crisis and by the unsettling effects that experiences of violent political change might have on the minds of the masses. However, although the president and his single-party (*Partido Republicano Genuino*) cabinet experienced continuous friction with the resurgent Liberal Party (which held the majority in Congress, controlled the Central Bank and upheld propertied interest and laissez-faire economic doctrines), both groups could be relied upon to unite against the political leader with most support among the lower middle class and the disenfranchised poor – former president Saavedra. In March 1932 Saavedra, anxious to maintain his position at a time of increased lower-class strikes and protests, changed the programme of his *Republicano* party and added 'Socialista' to its title.

More threatening to Salamanca's political position, however, was increasing bellicosity over relations with Paraguay. For thirty years in opposi-

---

[7] Quoted in Geddes, *Patiño*, pp. 255–6. Further extracts from this correspondence are published in David Alvestequi, *Salamanca*, Vol. 3 (Buénos Aires, 1963), pp. 284–9. For testimony that even in Salamanca's cabinet Patiño's privileges were resisted, see also Benigno Carrasco, *Hernando Siles* (La Paz, 1961), p. 312.

tion, Salamanca had presented himself as the most intransigent upholder of the nation's territorial rights, but after eighteen months in office he had to recognize that 'even a hasty glance at our "economic situation" showed it would be madness . . . to provoke international disturbances'. For the most part, however, Salamanca continued to speak in warlike terms, perhaps influenced by the fear that his old rival Saavedra would otherwise denounce him for 'appeasement'.[8] Indeed, by the time he stumbled into war in the middle of 1932, Salamanca had lost virtually all room for manoeuvring; he had either to achieve international success or to acknowledge the bankruptcy of his policies and the collapse of his authority.

It seems that the war was not, however, deliberately planned to distract attention from the depression or the political difficulties of the president. Rather, it was the culmination of a process of militarily backed land occupations that had for a generation or more threatened to end in war. The terrain in dispute was remote, inhospitable and, as it turned out, of little economic value, although hopes of its oil potential may have influenced some political decisions.[9] The root of the conflict was that the rival republics had long since adopted mutually incompatible stances on the principles which should govern boundary demarcation between them. Bolivia, with its larger population and more formidable armed forces, underestimated the enormous geographical disadvantages that would frustrate an offensive war. But once the country's political and military leaders had misled one another into setting up a strategic fort at a point previously occupied by the Paraguayans, and once the fort was seized back from them (mid-July 1932), the only choices left were a resort to diplomacy from a position of weakness or a major reprisal for which Bolivia would be labelled the aggressor. To an ill-informed public opinion hypersensitive after the territorial losses of 1879 (to Chile) and 1899 (to Brazil), the issues were presented quite differently. Paraguay had launched an unprovoked attack which demanded retaliation in strength. Salamanca personally propagated this version, whilst the military command, which he considered had done much to lead him so far into the morass, suddenly faced the implications and cast around for some way out. No line of retreat with dignity remained, and so the president chose to go forward, no

[8] See Herbert Klein, *Parties and Political Change in Bolivia, 1880–1952* (Cambridge, 1969), pp. 136, 145.

[9] Standard Oil had wells in production on the Bolivian fringes of the Chaco throughout the 1920s. During the war, the Paraguayans declared that Standard Oil had prompted Bolivian aggression, because the Chaco was oil-rich. Standard Oil stated that the Chaco contained no oil before the war, and none has been found since.

longer so sure of victory but apparently gambling on a national regeneration through suffering.

After three years of bitter fighting against a smaller and supposedly weaker enemy, the Bolivians had been driven out of the Chaco and obliged to accept a cease-fire (June 1935) that signified conceding to Paraguay control over approximately one-fifth of the area previously claimed by the republic.[10] Bolivia's third successive loss of territory through military defeat was much the most costly in terms of both military equipment and casualties. During the course of the war, well over 200,000 men had served in Bolivia's armed forces – a substantial proportion of the nation's eligible males. Over 50,000 died – more from sickness, hunger and dehydration than from battle. Although in the last few months before the cease-fire Bolivia had some success in driving the Paraguayans back from their most advanced positions, the overall balance of the fighting was clearly revealed in the statistics on prisoners of war. Bolivia held about 2,500 Paraguayans captive, whereas Paraguay had taken about 23,000 Bolivian prisoners of war. Even after La Paz had paid out half a million dollars in what amounted to ransom money for the release of imprisoned soldiers, Asunción still exercised control over the main international highway linking Bolivia to Argentina and used this until the end of 1937 in bargaining over the definitive peace treaty. Although the fighting stopped in June 1935, it was another three years before peace was formally re-established and national energies could be fully transferred to the task of post-war reconstruction. Indeed, Bolivia proceeded throughout 1937 and early 1938 with a costly programme of rearmament, and by May 1938 it had rebuilt its military strength to 35,000–40,000 men, far above the level agreed upon. It was only the imminent threat of a resumption of the war, this time on a greater scale, that finally convinced Paraguay and its *porteño* backers[11] to ratify in July 1938 a compromise peace treaty, which, however, contained no more than marginal improvements in the Bolivian position. Thus, the Chaco conflict dominated all other considerations not just for three years, but for six, or, in an even broader sense, for the whole decade from 1928 to 1938.

After such a disaster, the first priority of successive governments was to

[10] Auguste Céspedes has described the Chaco War as 'a colonial campaign conducted by a semi-colonial country without the benefit of foreign assistance'. In military terms it was for Bolivia 'a three year long retreat which eventually proved to be strategic since it enabled our army to reach terrain where it had the advantage over the enemy'. *El dictador suicida* (Santiago, 1956), p. 127.

[11] Argentina had economic interests in the Chaco and needed Paraguay as an ally against Brazil.

deflect responsibility from themselves and to curb or co-opt their critics. None of the post-war experiments with 'military socialism', nationalization, 'corporatism' or even constitutional forms of government can be understood unless this motive is taken into account. The November 1934 military coup that ended the career of President Salamanca was symptomatic of much that was to follow. Placed under arrest by a rebellious high command, the embittered Salamanca observed sardonically that this was the first military operation they had executed effectively. Confirmation that this low opinion of their performance was widespread came in July 1935 when the high command slowed the process of demobilization for fear of the mutinous mood of many units. Although the military exercised sufficient internal control to protect itself from frontal attack for the debacle, it lacked the unity and prestige to establish a stable regime. In consequence, a succession of military-based governments lurched from one policy stance to another, seeking strength first from alliance with Salamanca's traditional political opponents, then from the renascent labour movement, then from an upsurge of nationalist feeling against Standard Oil and finally from an attempt to lay blame for the disaster on the mining industry.

By the outbreak of the Second World War, all of these expedients had been tried with only passing success. The bitterness of defeat had not been fully exorcised, and no firm relationship had been established between military-based governments and the various new forms of popular movement which had emerged in the aftermath of the Chaco War, notably the Veterans – the first modern movement to establish a nation-wide presence in the Bolivian countryside. Nor had the cost of the war been apportioned in an acceptable way amongst the various economic sectors. The war inflated public expenditure and accelerated the shift, already taking place as a result of the depression, from economic liberalism to interventionism. The resulting inflation and currency depreciation acquired a momentum that would continue for many years to feed distributional conflicts and erode the basis for political compromise. Above all, the mining industry required new guarantees and less onerous operating conditions or future Bolivian governments would have to face the consequences of progressive decapitalization. Until the late 1930s these underlying problems were masked by the Chaco issue. Through much of the 1940s they were obscured by the disruptions of the Second World War, which focussed attention on security of supply in the provision of strategic minerals, provided a temporary bonanza for the mining companies and generated paranoia about real and invented Nazi influences. Yet these essentially internal processes, unresolved sources of social instability, were to persist as the shocks derived from external warfare faded. Exacerbated by the Chaco War (although they already existed in embryonic form before the fighting with Paraguay became unstoppable), they are rightly regarded as the main source of the 1952 National Revolution.

The years 1935–9 represent a relatively compact period in which these unresolved problems can be observed. The Liberal Party had never really granted carte blanche to Salamanca in his conduct of the war. Its nominees controlled a majority in Congress, headed the Central Bank and occupied the vice-presidency. Vice-President José Luis Tejada Sorzano contributed to successive cabinet crises that undermined Salamanca's executive authority. When in November 1934 the high command arrested the president, Tejada assumed the presidency and arranged to have his term in office and that of the Congress extended until August 1936, under the pretext of maintaining continuity during the last phase of the war and the peace negotiations. For his party and its associated business interests, the main priorities were to stop the war, to demobilize the armed forces and to re-create as quickly as possible the economic and legal bases for a return to the status quo ante. But Tejada Sorzano headed a precarious de facto government, and his party could neither credibly dissociate itself from the war nor deliver tangible benefits from the peace. It had nothing to offer the military except demotion and a return to the bad old rituals of party politics.

Nevertheless, the high command hesitated to break entirely with constitutional forms, the restoration of which had been the purpose of the 1930 coup. It was not until the trade unionists of La Paz took the initiative, calling a general strike to regain the real income workers had lost during the depression and the war, that the military was propelled into an outright seizure of power. The president declared the strike illegal, subjecting strikers to military law, but this produced more stress than the fragile structure of Bolivian constitutionalism could withstand. On 17 May 1936 he was obliged to resign, and the strikers hastened to make their peace with the new military junta (the first explicit assumption of power by the armed forces since 1880). This was headed by Colonel David Toro, whose record in the Chaco War left something to be desired but who had served as minister of interior in the final weeks of the Siles presidency. In more than one sense, then, the verdict of 1930 was about to be reversed.

Toro lasted in office only fourteen months, but during that time many initiatives were begun that would foreshadow the future. His first task was to strike a bargain with the labour organizations that had helped bring him to power. A Department of Labour was created in June 1936; the first congress of a new labour confederation, the Confederación Sindical de Trabajadores Bolivianos (CSTB) was held in December; and in February 1937 the junta decreed that at least 85 per cent of each firm's payroll must go to Bolivian nationals. The following month Standard Oil was nationalized, and minimum wage and salary rates were decreed. Such measures should have generated an upsurge of political support, at least in the short run, even if they aggravated the problems of government in the long run. However, distrust of Toro was such that there was no resistance on 13 July 1937 when the military withdrew its support from him and appointed the thirty-five-year-old Lt. Col. Germán Busch as his successor. Military government was still unpopular, the army was still divided and groups as disparate as the large mine-owners, the students, and former president Saavedra's Republican Socialists all welcomed Toro's departure. The labour movement felt little loyalty to the outgoing president, and the nationalists quickly transferred their attention from the wily and cynical Toro to the inexperienced and idealistic Busch. One factor contributing to the ease of the transition from Toro to Busch was the hope that Bolivia would now be governed by an authentic war hero and one whose credentials as a populist were at least as respectable as those of his former mentor turned rival.

Busch held office for little more than two years before his death (apparently by suicide) in August 1939. The myths that subsequently surrounded him reflected both his tragic death and his tragic life; and they served as a powerful weapon in mobilizing nationalist opinion against the mining oligarchy. His scant education and terrible wartime experiences provided little preparation for the tasks of government. He could, however, attract desperately needed popular support: the lower ranks, labour activists, former servicemen and rural schoolteachers responded to his appeals, as they would to no one else. While he lived, senior officers, employees, landowners and conventional politicians all disguised their doubts and pursued their separate aims through apparent collaboration with his government. But Busch's own doubts and confusion often broke through the surface, expressing themselves in startling denunciations and high-handed threats of military retribution against those who incurred his disfavour.

The economic situation confronting the new president would have alarmed a far more seasoned statesman. Another recession had begun in the United States, less serious than that of 1930–2, but demoralizing enough as the demand for minerals fell off steeply, and the post-Chaco disruption left Bolivian mine-owners unable even to fill the quotas allocated to them by the international cartel. The prospect loomed of a reduction in the national quota that would signal diminished exchange earnings for many years ahead. Those companies whose assets were entirely within Bolivia therefore intensified their lobbying against Patiño Mines, which was the main culprit in the production shortfall, the most powerful element in the cartel and the enterprise most highly protected from adverse developments in Bolivia because of its international resources. The second and third largest mine-owners, Aramayo and Hochschild, apparently went so far as to finance an attempted restoration of Colonel Toro. If these problems were not sufficient, the effort to rearm imposed further strains, complicated by conflicts with Standard Oil and U.S. bondholders over compensation claims. On the internal front, former soldiers and returned prisoners were beginning to spend the incomes they had accumulated during the war, and the wage increases conceded by Toro were also working their way through the economy. Consequently, inflation accelerated, public finances remained in disarray and an overvalued exchange rate stimulated capital flight.

Economic hardship affected the population unevenly. The biggest losers, in terms of real income, were probably the urban *cholos,* who lacked real property or foreign trade connections to defend them from the currency depreciation.[12] (Between the end of the Chaco War and the beginning of the Second World War the boliviano depreciated about fourfold, providing a focus of resentment against the mining barons.) At the same time, parts of the rural population, for example in the Cochabamba Valley, may actually have benefited from increased urban demand for basic foodstuffs, from transfer payments and from government campaigns to promote peasant education. Some import-substitution industrialization also took place, creating new enterprises (producing soap, candles, stockings, hats, canned goods and liquors) that were dependent on government protection and favouritism.

On the one hand, therefore, the mining companies, owners of real estate and major trading houses needed to restore the influence they had traditionally enjoyed within Bolivian governments and hoped that Busch could be

---

[12] Merwin Bohan [U.S. commercial attaché in Santiago], 'Economic Conditions in Bolivia', 10 June 1937, U.S. National Archives, 824.50/8, Washington, D.C.

brought round to their points of view. On the other hand, new organizations and new social interests were emerging to compete with them for influence. These new forces were not necessarily very cohesive or clear about their objectives, but they could claim to be more authentically national and patriotic than the established groups held responsible for the Chaco defeat. This became Busch's formula for government. Whatever the contradictions of his record, his June 1939 attack on the mining companies followed by his violent death ensured him first place in the pantheon of Bolivia's revolutionary nationalism. Although the young president had first restored the 1931 constitution and then held elections for the Constituent Assembly, which elected him to the presidency for a constitutional term of four years (1938–42), these measures were superseded in April 1939 by his declaration of a dictatorship. When the confirmation of peace and the ratification of a progressive labour code had proved insufficient to stabilize his government, Busch took all power into his hands. He used this concentration of executive authority to promulgate a decree requiring the mining industry to deposit all of its foreign exchange proceeds with the Central Bank, which he placed under state control, excluding the private shareholders. A parliamentary or collegial form of government would not have generated such legislation, it was claimed. Only a heroic dictator could overcome the obstructionism of the 'mining superstate' to channel all of Bolivia's foreign exchange through the institutions of the national government. Thus, tax evasion and capital flight could be monitored, and the country's wealth turned to domestic development rather than foreign enrichment. The mining companies responded with a suspension of exports until the terms of the decree were clarified. They had objections of principle, but it sufficed simply to emphasize the impracticalities of the decree of 7 June. Drafted without consultation, it was found to be unworkable, a testimony of the dictator's lack of administrative skill as well as his heroism. Busch's death in August dramatized this impasse. By the end of the 1930s two irreconcilable views of Bolivian reality had crystallized: that of the mine-owners and that of the national revolutionaries. Each side was capable of mobilizing numerous allies to its views. The 1940s were to be dominated by the unfolding of this confrontation.

1939–46

Just as the Chaco War shaped most of the major developments of the 1930s, so, despite Bolivia's geographical remoteness, the Second World

War heavily influenced its internal evolution between 1939 and 1946. Bolivian political conflicts were judged through the prism of international alignments, which meant equating the incipient nationalists with the Axis powers, the Marxists with the USSR and the traditional right with Anglo-American democracy. The year 1946 witnessed the culmination of this trend, with Marxists and conservatives allying against the nationalists to replicate the international events of 1945, by 'liberating' Bolivia from alleged Nazism. Although political groupings that owed their origins mainly to internal factors took sides in the world conflict, borrowed from the competing ideological models, and saw the various fortunes of the war reflected in their own, the strength of these international influences was easily exaggerated. In reality, the three main groupings that crystallized into organized forces during the war originated from local circumstances and continued their rivalries long after the Allied victory. Indeed, it would not be long before the 'Nazis' were being reclassified as Communist revolutionaries, after which the 'democrats' would be reclassified as feudalistic landowners only concerned to resist agrarian reform.

It was the British government that was most sensitive to German influences in Bolivia and to the danger that 'Fifth Column' activities there could cut off the supplies of tin-ore for the Liverpool smelters. (By 1945 Bolivia was supplying about half the world's total output of tin, a metal essential for war purposes.) Several months before Busch proclaimed his dictatorship, the British ambassador was already warning of the influence of 'a small body of men who have lived for a considerable time in Germany and all are deeply impressed by the Nazi regime . . . it is rumored [that] the German Minister is giving his assistance and advice.'[13] The ambassador included the name of General Carlos Quintanilla, who became provisional president following Busch's suicide. Quintanilla's conduct in office, however, was not unfavourable to British and U.S. interests. On the contrary, his top priority was to obtain U.S. credit, without which he feared serious food shortages in the cities. 'More through economic necessity than changed ideas', as the U.S. ambassador explained it, he strove to restore the confidence of foreign interests, rescinding the June 1939 decree and inviting a Patiño lawyer to submit proposals for reform of the mining laws.[14]

Quintanilla's constitutional successor, General Enrique Peñaranda,

[13] A 9011, 3 November 1938, Public Record Office (London).
[14] 20 September 1939, U.S. National Archives, 824.50/11, Washington, D.C.

elected in March 1940, had a more satisfactory reputation from the viewpoint of the mine-owners and the Allies. Nevertheless, the British in
particular remained highly concerned about German influence, and in
1941 the British Intelligence Service went so far as to concoct a false
message supposedly sent from Germany, implicating leading Bolivians
(including Víctor Paz Estenssoro, the leader of the newly formed Movimiento Nacional Revolucionario, or MNR) in an alleged Nazi plot to seize
power.[15] Foreign Office sensitivity about possible Nazi activities in Bolivia persisted throughout Peñaranda's presidency. Whatever assurances of
loyalty might be given by the head of state, London remained convinced of
the pro-Nazi currents under the surface, and it was in this light that the
nationalist coup of December 1943 was instantly judged. German and
Italian training of the Bolivian officer corps provided a major motive for
the suspicion. Another factor was highlighted in an October 1942 report
to London, which identified Cochabamba as both the logical capital for
Bolivia and the main centre of Nazi activity. 'The Germans found themselves thoroughly at home there. . . . the military connection (most provincial authorities being army officers) and the air network were used to
their full value and a close knit and well-organised politico-commercial
domination of almost the whole Eastern part of Bolivia was built up with
Cochabamba at the centre of the web'.[16] Major Gualberto Villarroel, who
became president as a result of the December 1943 coup, was a
Cochabambino.

[15] Cole Blasier unravelled this plot. See his 'The U.S., Germany and the Bolivian Revolutionaries,
1941–6', *Hispanic American Historical Review* (February 1972). The British agent
concerned admitted the forgery. See H. Montgomery Hyde, *Secret Intelligence Agent: British Espionage
in America and the Creation of the O.S.S.* (New York, 1982), pp. 159–60. Paz Estenssoro came from a
distinguished conservative family in the southern province of Tarija. A Chaco veteran qualified as
an economist, he had been employed by Patiño Mines before entering Congress and supporting
Busch. In January 1941 he became founder–leader of the MNR, and he briefly served as economy
minister under Peñaranda, before the forged letter cast him as a German agent. His priorities were
to diversify the economy, promote neglected regions and neutralize 'the enormous political power
of the mining industry'.

[16] Memo to UK ambassador from Mr. Howell, second secretary at the British Embassy in La Paz, 20
October 1942, which reached foreign-secretary level. Howell added that 'there are many influential
elements that are friendly to our cause and would readily respond to a little "pressure" or encouragement. These even include some of the most respected Germans themselves, besides the numerous
and wealthy Yugoslav colony; large numbers of refugees; a Francophile section of educated Bolivians; and quite a lot of decent Bolivians . . . [but] . . . the Palestinians and Syrians, a very high
proportion of whom are disloyal and an easy tool for the Nazis must be made to toe the line "or else"
(A 1069/3017/5 P.R.O. London). To illustrate the significance of the ethnic categories for Bolivian
internal political alignments, it is worth recalling that one leading mine-owner, Mauricio
Hochschild, was Jewish and from Austria. The miners' leader, Juan Lechín, was sometimes
classified as a Syrian.

However, the nationalist movement in Bolivia was far from being just a direct product of Axis influence. In fact, Berlin took only a distant interest in Bolivian affairs, and such pro-Axis influence as did reach Bolivia was mainly filtered through Argentina, which had objectives of its own to promote. Viewed from the *altiplano,* it was possible to believe that Germany and Italy had found a formula for national reconstruction after the collapse of liberalism that was also applicable to post-Chaco Bolivia. Senior officers like Peñaranda, who spoke of democracy and kept Bolivia on the path laid down by the Allies, were resented by those below them. The next generation of officers had served in the front line of the Chaco and their secret societies (like Villarroel's Razón de Patria, RADEPA) bore some resemblance to the SS and Perón's Grupo Obra de Unificación (GOU). Similar mimicry of Franco's Spain gave birth to the Falange Partido Socialista in 1938. And in 1942 the MNR went public with a Nazi-style policy statement when Hitler looked likely to win the European war. But the driving force of nationalism came from else-where – hostility to the so-called *rosca* of large mining companies, who profited from tying Bolivia as tightly as possible into the Allied war effort. Nationalist struggles against the power of the mine-owners com-bined with their competition with the Marxists of the Partido de la Izquierda Revolucionaria (PIR) for labour support progressively radical-ized some of these groups, especially the increasingly effective movement led by Paz Estenssoro.

The PIR drew inspiration, of course, from the Soviet Union, but it was not subject to much Comintern control. The main international influences on Bolivian Marxism filtered through the Chilean Left, and since this was the period of Popular Front tactics Bolivia's Marxists attempted a similar approach. They had established positions in the student and labour move-ments, and indeed had enjoyed state patronage (in the Labour and Educa-tion ministries at least) for a short time during Toro's presidency. Neverthe-less, their opposition to the Chaco War had created deep enmities. Under Busch, all Communist and anarchist activities had been prohibited, but in the 1940 election the PIR had succeeded in fielding a last-minute presiden-tial candidate, José Antonio Arze. The only civilian candidate in a country weary of militarism, Arze obtained nearly 19 per cent of the vote, with a much stronger showing in the main mining departments of Oruro and Potosí. The PIR took the lead in organizing trade unions in the mining camps, but this headstart was eroded in 1942, when the MNR proved itself more effective as the mine-workers' champion in Congress than its

Marxist rivals. The problems faced by PIR tacticians at this point are usually overlooked. The mining companies were reaping a bonanza from the insatiable Allied demand for strategic minerals, and the benefits were not passing through to the labour force. On the contrary, mine-workers suffered overcrowding, inflation and intensified labour discipline as a consequence of the emergency created by the war. All this pointed to a campaign for labour militancy, but the PIR felt it must do nothing that would detract from the war effort, since the survival of the Soviet Union was now at stake. Moreover, the leaders of the PIR must have feared that intensified social conflict might precipitate another military dictatorship, advantageous to the nationalists but of no interest to the Marxist Left. So the party restrained its fire against the mining companies, in marked contrast to the virulence of its eventual attacks upon the Villarroel regime. Dissident Marxists, perhaps closer to the aspirations of Bolivian workers, therefore gained significant influence and established a tradition of Trotskyism more ineradicable than elsewhere in Latin America.

It is generally said that the Peñaranda government was destroyed by its complicity in the Catavi massacre of 1942, in which troops killed workers protesting against Patiño Mines. That episode indeed severely damaged the government, but another year elapsed before its overthrow. This year gave more time for evidence to accumulate that the economic opportunities presented by the war were not being turned to national advantage. The main impressions conveyed by Peñaranda's presidency were of servility towards the mine-owners (who were prospering from the war) and the Allies (Standard Oil was generously compensated and the United States contracted to buy all Bolivia's tin, wolfram and quinine at fixed and relatively favourable prices) and of cynicism and brutality in regard to domestic dissent. It also gave more time for the rival factions within the military to organize themselves in anticipation of the expiration of Peñaranda's four-year term of office.

Until the coup of 20 December 1943 the MNR was no more than a very small grouping of middle-class graduates and Chaco veterans confined to the four or five largest cities. Congressional leadership was provided by a handful of deputies from La Paz and one deputy from Tarija – their *jefe*, Paz Estenssoro. The party program of June 1942 was nationalistic in tone, unspecific in content and recognized at the time for its National Socialist sources of inspiration. The associated newspaper *La Calle* was already an effective instrument of agitation which focussed its attacks on the overweening mining companies. But although this gave the party a base of appeal somewhat broader than its basic membership, the movement was still incipient. The best available study of the MNR's early years is almost certainly too generous in describing the 1943 membership as 'not higher than a few thousands'.[17] A few hundred members and a few thousand voters or newspaper readers would seem the limit of the party's strength before it obtained access to the state machine. That access was obtained through the skilful manoeuvring and good military contacts of the party leadership rather than through mass support.

Paz Estenssoro certainly strengthened his party's claim for support by his forceful condemnation of the Peñaranda government's subservience to the mining companies in the August 1943 congressional debate on the Catavi massacre. This speech also contained a direct appeal to the army to distance itself from the mining *rosca* and turn towards the people. Parallel with this public appeal went private negotiations which brought the MNR into alliance with the secret military lodge RADEPA led by Villarroel. Such contacts must have boosted Paz Estenssoro's confidence quite considerably, for in November 1943, six weeks before the coup, he virtually announced 'the revolution' in advance. He addressed Congress on the forthcoming elections as follows:

In the next presidential election it will not be possible to repeat the frauds of 1940. . . . But there are many signs that an apparatus of electoral fraud is being erected . . . if the governing class, instead of resolving social problems, reinforces the defences of the privileged, and seeks by violence and fraud to hold on to power . . . inevitably, revolutionary action will triumph.[18]

Like the military government which came to power in Argentina in 1943, the Villarroel regime was not well understood at the time, and when viewed retrospectively it is also open to misinterpretation because of the myths which subsequently grew up about the period. The coup, which was directed principally against the mining companies, occurred one day before the first anniversary of the Catavi massacre. Even before Villarroel came to power, the Bolivian government was under great pressure to act

[17] Christopher Mitchell, *The Legacy of Populism in Bolivia: From the MNR to Military Rule* (New York, 1977), pp. 17–33. The party's organization secretary, Luis Peñaloza, in his *Historia del MNR* (La Paz, 1961), suggests a membership of fifty before the 1942 elections, rising perhaps to several hundred during 1943. See also Luis Antezana's massive but confusing *Historia secreta del MNR*, 6 vols. (La Paz, 1984–7). There were three main nuclei – the economics faculty of La Paz University, sons of elite families in Cochabamba and the customs house at Oruro. According to one informant, party membership cards were numbered starting at 501. This informant joined when the coup was imminent, and his number was in the nine hundreds.

[18] Víctor Paz Estenssoro, *Discursos parlamentarios* (La Paz, 1955), pp. 167–75.

more effectively in defence of the country's mine-workers. Such pressure came both from domestic opinion and (especially after Pearl Harbor and the cut-off of Far Eastern tin supplies) from the United States in the form of a mission headed by Judge Calvert Magruder in February 1943 to enquire into mining conditions, following which the U.S. Board of Economic Warfare wrote labour clauses into its contracts to purchase minerals from Bolivia and a labour attaché was appointed to the U.S. Embassy in La Paz. Nevertheless, the U.S. government did not welcome the installation of the Villarroel government, which it viewed as an extension of Axis and *peronista* influence that might put the supply of strategic raw materials for the war effort in jeopardy. The mining companies also retained some influence in Washington (particularly in the U.S. Bureau of Mines, where many engineers formerly employed in Bolivia could be found). Faced by both international hostility, which took the form of six months of non-recognition, and internal resistance from the mine-owners, the Villarroel government was inescapably driven to mobilize new bases of popular support. A key position in this strategy was naturally occupied by the mine-workers, now at the peak of their numerical strength and better placed than at any other time since the First World War to exert economic pressure in defence of their living conditions, which had deteriorated under the pressure of inflation, overcrowding and shortages that accompanied the war. The establishment of the national Federación Sindical de Trabajadores Mineros Bolivianos (FSTMB) in June 1944 should be viewed in the context of this national situation, so exceptional in its political, economic and social characteristics. The similarities with *peronismo* naturally attract attention, but in Bolivia it was a political party allied to the military, the MNR, that took the lead in mobilizing mass support, rather than a military conspirator, as in the case of Perón.

Under Villarroel, there came to the fore a cohort of military officers who had experienced the miseries of front-line action in the Chaco War and who had in consequence developed a sense of inward solidarity and outward distrust. Their hostility was directed against senior officers like Peñaranda, who had given the orders of war but escaped the consequences and who were thought to have 'sold out' to mining companies tied into a foreign imperialism. They also seem to have resented the landowning class, whose neglect and oppression of the peasantry bequeathed such unprepared conscripts to the army. Indeed, although conflicts with the mine-owners commanded most public attention, the Villarroel government's frictions with the landowners played an important part in determining its fate. Military attitudes towards the peasantry were in fact highly condescending and at best paternalistic, and the only timid proposals for land reform came from the civilian political parties rather than the armed forces. Nevertheless, rural elites were provoked to unprecedented mobilization against the military government. The Indian Congress of 1945 and the formal abolition of unpaid labour services were rightly seen as very serious threats to social order in the countryside. Civilian-led peasant movements were relatively manageable, but when it seemed that local military officialdom might begin to usurp the functions of the rural elites, that was another matter. It became an issue of considerable urgency to reestablish a more traditional role for the military, and Bolivian landed society still possessed the social resources (including the presence of family members in the officer corps itself) to retaliate against RADEPA and isolate the Villarroel clique. From this standpoint the worldwide repudiation of 'Nazism' of 1945 provided a convenient disguise for a sectionally based counter-attack.

It would be misleading, however, to attribute too much clarity of purpose to the military nationalists of 1943–6. Even with regard to rural issues, their positions were mostly confused and reactive, although they clearly had some sense that this was one realm in which hierarchy and discipline might produce effective results. In relation to non-peasant social forces and political movements, they were soon out of their depth. Nationalism and anti-imperialism directed them against the mining companies and in favour of extended state control. But for the implementation of policy they needed to build alliances and work through intermediaries, and this proved sorely trying. They were unclear about the type of relationship to seek with the United States and undecided for a while on their attitude towards the Marxist PIR. In the end they found themselves bitterly attacked by both groups. (In March 1946, President Villarroel told the North Americans that 'his program was to cut the ground from communism by granting the working class the very things that communism offered them.'[19] Four months later the U.S. government joined the Communists in approving his overthrow.)

At the same time, the military nationalists worked uneasily with their civilian allies in the MNR, and became wary when they found that mobilization of the mine-workers served to strengthen and radicalize the party. It

[19] U.S. Embassy cable dated 7 March 1946, U.S. National Archives 824.00/3-746, Washington, D.C.

was by no means clear that the military government would remain allied to the MNR, nor could that party rely on its influence in official circles to secure it favourable electoral results. Just as the Villarroel government required some form of popular mobilization as a reinforcement against its internal and external enemies, so the MNR needed to demonstrate its support in order to retain its influence with the military regime. The June 1944 congressional elections were therefore a genuine trial of political strength as important in their own way as elections in well-established democracies. Under the electoral system then in force, the mine-workers were a decisive proportion of the electorate, and it was the MNR that succeeded, by means of vigorous and possibly even demagogic campaigning, in gaining the great majority of the mine-workers' support.[20] The founding congress of the FSTMB at Huanuni on 10 June, attended by delegates from twenty-three *sindicatos* claiming to represent 45,000 to 60,000 miners, was the culmination of the MNR's election campaign. The FSTMB was clearly identified with the MNR, and viewed accordingly by the PIR and the unions it controlled.

The outcome of the election campaign was essentially to strengthen the MNR's hold on the national government, even though the MNR leaders had left the cabinet in May as the price for U.S recognition. The result also intensified the hostility and resistance of their rival for working-class support, the PIR, especially since its leader Arze was severely injured in an attempted assassination the week after the elections. To make matters worse, RADEPA members kidnapped Mauricio Hochschild at the end of July and only reluctantly released him a fortnight later under pressure from the president.

When an attempted counter-revolution on 19 November failed, members of RADEPA executed a number of dignitaries implicated in the plot. The resulting scandal left Villarroel's government so demoralized and discredited that some MNR leaders opposed the proposal that their party lend its support by rejoining the cabinet. Paz Estenssoro, however, imposed only a single condition, one that was accepted by Villarroel: the Busch decree of June 1939 requiring the mining companies to hand over 100 per cent of their foreign exchange from exports to the Central Bank must finally be activated. With this pledge, on 1 January 1945, the MNR rejoined the government and infused it with a new element of political

[20] Laurence Whitehead, 'Miners as Voters: The Electoral Process in Bolivia's Mining Camps', *Journal of Latin American Studies*, 13, pt. 2 (November 1981), pp. 313–46.

competence. Among the appointments was Germán Monroy Block as minister of labour, the first time a party member had occupied this post.

The mobilization of the mine-workers naturally elicited intense hostility from the mine-owners. The Compagnie Aramayo des Mines en Bolivie (CAMB) argued that the unions employed violence and that the cost of social benefits had been raised by the regime to 58.7 per cent of the average mine-worker's wage, that a worker received a higher income when on sick pay than when at work.[21] The influence exerted by the mining companies over urban public opinion can be deduced from the fact that the circulation of the La Paz daily press totalled about a hundred thousand, of which more than eighty thousand was divided between the three anti-Villarroel newspapers – *La Razón* (owned by Carlos Victor Aramayo), *El Diario* (in which Patiño held a majority of shares) and *Ultima Hora* (linked to Mauricio Hochschild). The leading pro-government paper, *La Calle,* sold only about eight thousand copies.[22]

The Villarroel government therefore saw itself as waging an unequal struggle against an 'anti-*patria*', which was headed by the mining barons using the charge of 'Nazism' as black propaganda to cover their narrow economic motives. Having brought free trade unionism into the mining camps, having confiscated the property of Axis nationals and sent many prominent German and Japanese residents to the United States for internment, having endured continuous attacks from the establishment press, having diligently supplied the Allies with all the strategic raw materials the country could produce at what most Bolivians considered to be subsidized prices, and having played an active part in the creation of the United Nations, how could the Bolivian government continue to be classified by any impartial observer as 'Nazi'? In 1946, however, there were few impartial observers to be found when the charge was sympathy with defeated powers. And in truth, there were many in the Villarroel regime (and in the MNR) whose private enthusiasm for Hitler far outstripped their public actions, and as the government as a whole headed for destruction, its capacity for self-defence was fatally impaired by its 'pro-Nazi' reputation.

By the end of 1945 both Argentina and Brazil had undergone political upheavals occasioned by pressures for a post-war realignment of forces. In Bolivia, by contrast, the government became more rigid and the opposi-

[21] Compagnie Aramayo des Mines en Bolivie, *Sinopsis de su economía en el ultimo quinquenio* (1944–8) (La Paz, 1949), pp. 38–40.
[22] José Fellman Velarde, *Víctor Paz Estenssoro* (La Paz, 1955), p. 139. See also Jerry W. Knudson, *Bolivia: Press and Revolution, 1932–64* (Lanham, Md., 1986).

tion more inflamed. Troubles mounted in Washington, where the establishment of peace signified a drastic change in the demand for strategic
minerals. For the U.S. government the purchase of tin at a fixed price was
no longer a military necessity; on the contrary, it now seemed an act of
charity. Villarroel's ambassador in Washington, Víctor Andrade, believed
that the mine-owners, together with Assistant Secretary of State Spruille
Braden, used their negotiations in an attempt to weaken or overthrow the
regime.[23] However, Washington's major contribution to the destruction
of Villarroel came as a side effect of Braden's counter-productive campaign
against Perón. On 13 February 1946, two weeks before the democratic
election that was to elevate Perón to the presidency of Argentina, the State
Department published a Blue Book labelling Perón and his associates Nazi
accomplices, charging them with creating a totalitarian state in Argentina
and posing a threat to neighbouring countries. Part II of the Blue Book
publicly implicated Paz Estenssoro (then finance minister as well as MNR
chief) in the Nazi–Argentine plot. The British forgery of 1941 was apparently taken at face value. A State Department memorandum of 12 February 1946 commented on this aspect of the Blue Book as follows:

What the reaction will be in Bolivia to the publication of this information can
only be speculated upon. The following three alternatives are suggested:

(1) The overthrow of the Villarroel government by revolution.
(2) The present regime made up of the Army and MNR continuing in power by
     turning the Junta into a "fortress" ready to take on all comers in "a battle to
     the death" and prepared to suppress any opposition to it by every means at its
     disposal, including violence and bloodshed.
(3) The reforming of the government . . . with the elimination of the
     MNR . . .[24]

In the event, the threat of a revolution produced a certain degree of
tactical reconciliation between the MNR and the army, so that the immediate outcome was fairly close to the second alternative. However, the
'fortress' was not of very solid construction, and the ensuing measures of
repression only heightened the passions of the opposition. The Frente
Democrático Anti-Fascista (FDA) was established as an umbrella organization uniting opponents of the regime from Left to Right, and it proceeded

---

[23] Víctor Andrade, *My Missions for Revolutionary Bolivia, 1944–62* (Pittsburgh, 1975), pp. 56–73,
113–22. State Department memos of 13 July and 23 July 1946 indicate that Washington was at
least discussing the use of the tin contract as a political lever, both before and after the death of
Villarroel.

[24] U.S. National Archives, 824.00/2-1246, Washington, D.C. The memo was non-committal on the
relative likelihood of the three outcomes.

to boycott the elections of May 1946. In June the FDA taunted the regime into confiscating *La Razón* and *Ultima Hora,* and it organized a series of revolts and strikes that culminated in violent revolution on 20 July. The following day a street mob burst into the presidential palace, and the corpse of Villarroel was hung from a lamp post in the Plaza Murillo, in apparent imitation of the death of Mussolini. This was the last, perhaps most unworthy, Allied victory of the Second World War.

1946–52

After the traumatic events of July 1946, it was hard to believe that there could be an overwhelming 'reversal of verdicts' in fewer than six years. Even on the assumption that the socio-economic structure of Bolivia made a popular revolution inescapable in the near future (a plausible view, but not widely held at the outset of the *sexenio* of 1946–52), it was far from obvious that the fleeing remnants of the MNR could still possess either the aptitude or the resources, let alone the inclination, for effective leadership. Furthermore, political tendencies in the other Andean republics were deeply discouraging to Bolivian radicals: Chile's government turned against the Left in 1947; Colombia's leading social reformer, Jorge Eliécer Gaitán, was assassinated in April 1948, nearly leading to civil war; and in Peru and Venezuela reformist parties were displaced by reactionary military dictatorships later the same year. However, on the morrow of Villarroel's overthrow it was not apparent that Bolivian political life was about to acquire a deeply reactionary character. On the contrary, the first stage of the *sexenio* seemed to offer a prospect of liberalization.

Six months elapsed between the overthrow of Villarroel and the election, in January 1947, of a constitutional government under the presidency of Enrique Hertzog with Mamerto Urriolagoitía serving as vice-president. During that six months the army was drastically purged, a second round of lynchings occurred and the contradictions within the FDA were sharpened. It was the Marxist PIR that seemed in the ascendant in these early months, but already there were signs that its advantage would not last long. The PIR was initially regarded with some sympathy by U.S. officials, but this quickly evaporated as the Cold War intensified. The PIR commanded a considerable following among organized labour (outside the mines) and the student population, and since the military was temporarily too highly discredited to maintain public order, PIR-organized militias controlled the streets and meted out revenge. But, like the Communist parties of Western

Europe, the PIR held back from bidding for full power, judging that it needed the tolerance of Washington and the co-operation of all democratic (i.e., anti-Axis) forces. The support of the United States was especially vital to the new authorities, since only Washington could provide the wheat imports required to avert bread riots once Perón reacted to the July 1946 revolution by cutting off Argentine supplies. Consequently, with the MNR outlawed and the PIR stymied, Bolivia's mine-owners and landowners seized the chance to reverse Villarroel's social reforms. Within a couple of years, U.S. officials would be lamenting the social instability of Bolivia, but such commentators never recognized the extent to which Washington's own policies of commission and omission had created these very conditions. No friendly and stable Bolivia was possible once the Cold War induced the United States to follow its ideological war against the MNR with a second (and in local terms contradictory) offensive against the only other major source of political leadership, the PIR, least of all when tentative and long-overdue social reforms were being withdrawn.

The requirements of the mining companies were incompatible with any non-authoritarian political settlement. If the privately owned mines were to survive in post-war conditions, they would have to reverse the wage and organizational gains made by the FSTMB since 1944. The mine-workers had not supported the July 1946 revolution, and their organizations re-mained intact during the democratic phase of the *sexenio*. Indeed, they had been radicalized by the overthrow of Villarroel, which they attributed with some reason to the machinations of the mining magnates and the U.S. government. U.S. mining engineers began complaining of threats to their physical security, and mine-workers threatened to occupy any enter-prise that the owners attempted to close. This clash of economic interests occurring at a time when the unions were also in political opposition led to episodes of violent confrontation, notably in Potosí in January 1947 and in Catavi in May and September 1949.

From the standpoint of the mine-owners there seemed an overwhelming economic case for rescinding the trade union and tax reforms of the Villarroel–Paz government. The ending of the war signified both a dimi-nution of demand for strategic minerals and the restoration of supplies from Bolivia's low-cost competitors in the Far East. If Bolivia's most vital industry was to have any future in this new environment, there would have to be ruthless cost-cutting, the closing of non-viable or exhausted units and a major programme of new investments. But Bolivia's main mining enterprises were international in scope. Simón Patiño died in New

York in 1947, and his successors could be counted on to invest wherever the rate of return seemed highest and most secure. Unless the Bolivian authorities could provide incentives and reassurances that compared favourably with the opportunities available in, say, Canada, Patiño Mines would simply 'milk' their Bolivian investment until it ran dry. Even Hochschild had the alternative of developing his Chilean mining properties, and by 1948 the government in Santiago seemed to offer far more assurance to investors than the authorities in La Paz.

The governments of the *sexenio* were actually more ambivalent towards the *rosca minera* than MNR propaganda would lead one to suppose. During 1947 the PIR retained substantial influence and harboured the vain hope of wooing the mine-workers away from their allegiance to the supposedly 'Nazi' MNR. In due course the PIR was forced to disown its minister of labour when he condoned a plan by the Patiño management to lay off all its employees and rehire only non-trouble-makers. With the main left-wing party thus discredited and then driven into opposition, the Hertzog government was stigmatized as no more than an agent of the mining companies, but this was not how either the cabinet or the mining management perceived the relationship. As the political challenge from the MNR intensified and the Cold War eliminated international pressure for the maintenance of a democratic façade, the mining enterprises focussed their hopes on the establishment of a tough government prepared to take effective action against subversion, labour agitation and what they considered to be irreparable reforms. They therefore welcomed the enforced transfer of power in 1949 from the cautious Hertzog to his aggressive vice-president, Urriolagoitía. However, this change only aggravated political polarization and insecurity without providing the physical and economic support the enterprises felt they required. On 5 September 1949, Dewett C. Deringer, Patiño's general manager in Bolivia, wrote to the head office of the impact of an attempted MNR uprising at the end of August, which led to a week of virtual civil war across the country before government control was reasserted. In Catavi the violence caused '100–200' dead and 'disorganization and destroyed morale'. In order to recover from this upheaval:

As a permanent measure it is recommended that for police work a new 'elite guard' be formed of young, capable men, training them thoroughly in modern methods of mob control. For this training, two or more experts could be brought in from the F.B.I. and/or other well-known police organisation. A first class regiment should and must be stationed within three or four kilometres of the company's mining camps but only brought into action on request of the commander of the 'elite guard' or the management. Without some such arrangement the top level staff, both foreign and national, will not remain. . . . All this will cost the company considerably, and there will be some capital expenditure for troop quarters.[25]

Bolivian *latifundistas* were equally adamant on the need for tightened discipline and the abandonment of Villarroel's reforms. Although according to the Agricultural Census of 1950 two-thirds of all the land in cultivation was held in units of two hundred hectares and above, it could be argued that the figures show that probably less than half the land under cultivation was in fact owned by *hacendados,* and a significant proportion of this land may in practice have escaped landlord control. There is in any case no dispute that indigenous communities retained title to more than a quarter of the cultivated land and exercised a significant degree of influence over the use of more. From the standpoint of national politics, however, what counted were the several thousand *latifundista* families whose limited control over a complex and alien rural society was nevertheless sufficient to give them economic privileges, local political authority and a dominant position within Bolivia's restricted elite. These families were closely interconnected with the legal profession, the clergy (still a pillar of reaction at the time) and the officer corps. They viewed themselves as a seignorial, Catholic elite in a country largely populated by ignorant and potentially dangerous Indians. Within the landowning class many distinctions could be made, of course. A minority of very large landowners knew that they were in a most exposed position, whilst many smaller owners hoped there might be some gains for themselves in the event of an MNR victory. (Smaller landowners constituted a significant element in the composition of the MNR in Cochabamba, for example.) Indeed, landowning members of the MNR in the Oriente actually did secure major economic advantages for themselves after the revolution, since cheap credit was extended and there were few peasant claimants to land in their area. Nevertheless, as a class, represented by the Sociedad Rural Boliviana, Bolivia's landowners constituted one of the most stubborn obstacles to gradualistic reform and therefore one of the greatest provocations to radical upheaval. Even Villarroel's mild paternalism and hesitant efforts to spread basic rural education were viewed as mortal threats to the ascendancy of this narrow privileged class.

[25] The U.S. Embassy, expressing approval, forwarded a copy of Deringer's letter to the State Department. 14 September 1949, U.S. National Archives, 824.00 (8-2749), Washington, D.C.

A great surge of peasant unrest in 1947 was apparently triggered by the withdrawal of Villarroel's modest reforms and henceforth any signs of rural protest were met with exemplary punishment. From the very beginning of a supposedly 'democratic' regime the view that 'Indians have rights' was liable to be considered rank subversion. (Similarly, for this elite it was almost unthinkable to respect the outcome of the May 1951 election, just because a majority of the voters had been so irresponsible as to vote for the MNR, which as a result of shared persecution had at last acquired a peasant following.) This 'bunker' mentality in *latifundista* circles also coloured the attitudes of many in the urban upper class and in the officer corps, and it coincided with the interests and outlook of senior management in the mines. It explains how a regime founded in the name of democracy and constitutionalism evolved into a military dictatorship so isolated, incompetent and discredited that it provoked, and fell victim to, a popular revolution.

The various elements that came together to make the April 1952 revolution began as largely uncoordinated currents of resistance that surfaced at different moments during the *sexenio*. Rural unrest died down after 1947, although latent rural tensions never disappeared and were quick to resurface once the old order collapsed in the cities.[26] After defeat in the 1949 civil war a similar quiescence affected the FSTMB, although since many of the members had votes they helped greatly to inflict a surprise defeat on the regime in the May 1951 presidential elections. The urban working class (largely Marxist in leadership) suffered severe repression in May 1950 following the general strike in La Paz, after which the Korean War ensured continued political harassment. Reformist and radical politicians and their middle-class allies saw their moment of electoral triumph stolen from them on 16 May 1951 when outgoing President Urriolagoitía responded to the MNR's unexpectedly strong electoral showing of 6 May by closing Congress and handing power to the armed forces 'in order to preserve democracy and the future of republican institutions'. The new junta promised to preserve 'our democratic-Christian institutions', to block 'Sovietizing' forces and to 'control sub-soil resources'. Its initial project to convoke a constituent assembly was soon abandoned, and by March 1952 President Hugo Ballivián was pledging the army to suppress all manifestations of party politics.

[26] Silvia Rivera, *Oprimidos pero no vencidos* (Geneva, 1986). Chapter 4 gives a good account of the rural unrest of 1947, although Rivera perhaps overstates the absence of convergence between urban nationalists, organized labour and 'Indian' rebels.

The establishment of the military junta in 1951 and resulting polarization culminating in the revolution of April 1952 bore some superficial resemblances to the revolution of 1946, but the political context was very different. A number of groups which might have made a revolution did not do so. In the first place, the PIR was no longer in a position to take the leadership of a radical insurrectionary movement. The Cold War, followed by the Korean War, combined with errors of leadership, had effectively destroyed the party. For example, when in 1950 the Catholic Church announced the excommunication of Communists, the PIR split between those who went on to found the Partido Comunista Boliviano (PCB), and those – the majority – who bowed their heads. In the 1951 election, with the threat that Bolivian soldiers might be sent to Korea, the incipient PCB lent its electoral support to Víctor Paz, thus weakening the appeal of the PIR's candidate, who came in sixth. Nevertheless, the PIR possessed a following in the labour movement, including the strategic rail union, the leader of which reportedly delayed until 6 a.m. on 9 April 1952, the day of the revolution, before taking the MNR's oath of allegiance. The Trotskyists of the Partido Obrero Revolucionario (POR) were always a weaker force, but at least for a while after 1946 they had enrolled the support of the miners' leader, Juan Lechín. In April 1952, however, Lechín made the revolution with his former protectors in the MNR. At this time the POR was too caught up in the turmoils of the Fourth International in Europe to play a decisive role.

Another candidate for power at this stage was the junta's minister of labour, Lt. Col. Sergio Sánchez, who was trying to imitate Perón and conducting his own conspiratorial campaign. Sánchez was in Catavi helping the Marxists re-establish their *sindicato* when the revolution broke out, and when the fighting became bitter, union leaders had to protect him from their rank and file. The *falangistas* were given the opportunity to participate in the insurrection of 9 April, even though they had initially co-operated with the military junta. In a fateful decision, for reasons that are still uncertain, Oscar Unzaga de la Vega, the leader of the movement, decided not to commit his forces. It is possible that he thought FSB would receive insufficient reward from the MNR; in all events, it was later alleged that he alerted the army high command to the conspiracy that was afoot. Unzaga subsequently led his party into radical opposition to the National Revolution, which lasted until he and his closest associates were killed in an abortive uprising in 1959 – one of several attempts by the FSB to remove the MNR by force during the early years of the revolution.

General Antonio Seleme, interior minister of the overthrown military junta, might well have become president in April 1952 if the rebellion had run according to plan, which depended upon an initial coup against Ballivián led by the police under Seleme's command. It was only after most of the military establishment decided against participation in the revolt that Seleme lost heart and the more radical civilian forces took over control of the movement.[27] In order to understand why such determined civilian support was available to the MNR, it is necessary to take into account the effects of six years of bitter struggle (including the 'White Massacre', or mass lay-off of sympathetic mine-workers in 1947, and the party's painful defeat in the civil war of 1949) which had transformed its social base and radicalized its membership. Moreover, Seleme gravely misjudged the intensely factional and demoralized state of the military. The Chaco defeat had been followed by extensive and traumatic political purges in 1946 and 1949 so that an officer corps which proclaimed its commitment to democracy had become implicated in a directionless military dictatorship. Not even the propertied classes expressed any confidence in the junta, and internationally it was isolated from Washington by a dispute over the terms of mineral sales during the Korean War.

A number of conspiracies came together on 9 April 1952 to launch the revolution. According to some accounts they were all co-ordinated by the deputy chief of the MNR, Hernán Siles, who together with Lechín directed the three-day civilian insurrection in La Paz. (Paz Estenssoro remained in exile in Buenos Aires.) Their fortunes took several twists before the revolutionaries emerged triumphant. Indeed, on the second day the army could have crushed the revolution, since the rebels had exhausted their initial supplies of ammunition. What decided the issue this time – in contrast to 1949 – was the fact that the military high command lost control in La Paz, where the police force supported Seleme and only the cadets of the Colegio Militar (who had been forbidden to participate in previous confrontations such as that of 1946) made any sustained military

[27] For his apologia see General Antonio Seleme Vargas, *Mi actuación en la junta militar de gobierno con el pronunciamiento revolucionario del 9 de Abril de 1952* (La Paz, 1969). Seleme alleges (p. 86) that it was a last-minute *falangista* betrayal of his coup that caused the confrontation between army and populace. He suggests (p. 77) that Siles, the deputy leader of the MNR, offended the *falangistas* by offering only 'two or three portfolios' if they joined the conspiracy. Paz Estenssoro served under Seleme in the Chaco War, and Lechín had access to him through the 'Syrian' network. Seleme's verdict on the junta is as follows: 'Without mincing words I must state that various members of the Military Junta were incompetent' (p. 64).

effort. The conscript soldiers lacked training and often simply deserted to their families in La Paz. The regular forces met determined resistance from snipers, factory workers and a detachment of miners. Three days and nights of street fighting in which some 1,500 died brought the MNR and Víctor Paz Estenssoro to power.

THE NATIONAL REVOLUTION, 1952–64

The April 1952 National Revolution has been overshadowed by the subsequent social revolutions in Cuba and Nicaragua and the more successful democratic revolutions in Colombia and Venezuela. Even before the late 1950s its significance was often underestimated, because it took place in landlocked and impoverished Bolivia (not viewed as a potential 'model' to follow in any neighbouring states); because its leadership was often viewed as tainted by fascist and/or Marxist associations; because within a very few years the regime became acutely dependent upon U.S. aid; and because all this took place at the height of the Cold War, with Korea, Dien Bien Phu, McCarthyism and the CIA's successful operation in Guatemala as a backdrop. Nevertheless, April 1952 was a profound upheaval, the watershed event in the history of independent Bolivia and a highly significant development in the Latin American–wide struggle for mass participation in politics and for socio-economic modernization.

The most obvious analogy is with the Mexican Revolution, which was undoubtedly a major source of inspiration for the MNR. (Mexico sent advisers to help with the land reform and the administration of the state oil corporation, Yacimientos Petrolíferos Fiscales Bolivianos [YPFB], and in June 1964 President Paz Estenssoro made the misguided assertion that 'the revolution has institutionalized itself, as in Mexico'.) But the measures adopted in 1952–3 were far more drastic than the legal and constitutional reforms envisaged for Mexico by Madero in 1910. Whereas Mexico's constitutionalist army prevailed and the 'red battalions' were dissolved into a state-controlled trade union movement, Bolivia's armed forces were purged, confined to barracks and substantially disarmed while worker and peasant militias flourished. Bolivia's nationalized mines may bear some resemblance to the Mexican oil nationalization of 1938, but in this case state ownership was accompanied by the establishment of 'Controles Obreros', a more radical form of workers' control than Cárdenas ever attempted. The scale of economic interventionism attempted in Bolivia between 1952 and 1956 was unprecedented in Latin America until that undertaken in Cuba in the 1960s, as was the sweeping agrarian reform, implemented a decade before the Alliance for Progress legitimized such initiatives. Recent scholarship has tended to emphasize the limitations and deformations of the Bolivian agrarian reform, contrasting the intentions of the reform programme with the realities of its execution. But it should not be forgotten that in 1953 only Mexico, the USSR and China had attempted anything of the kind, in each case at a tremendous cost in bloodshed and protracted internal strife. The Guatemalan government was about to be crushed, at least partly because of its commitment to a much milder variety of land reform. Landowners and capitalists in neighbouring countries such as Peru and Chile reacted to the Bolivian Revolution with quite as much horror and detestation as similarly placed groups have always expressed towards social revolutions, whether in France, Mexico or Central America.

In contrast to those in Mexico and Cuba, the Bolivian revolutionaries failed to consolidate their power into a permanent ('institutionalized') regime. Consequently, the conflicts that rent the revolutionary leadership were aired more openly, and little remains hidden about the contradictions and deficiencies of the four successive MNR governments. As with the more entrenched regimes, the National Revolution developed a legitimizing mythology, but it failed to stick in Bolivia, where the main leaders of the MNR were obliged by subsequent events to repudiate (or at least to reinterpret radically) some of their earlier ideological doctrines. But even without consolidating their power, institutionalizing their regime or creating a legitimizing mythology, the revolutionary leaders of Bolivia achieved such a profound impact on their society that a third of a century later political conflict and political allegiances still revolved around the same key personalities (Paz Estenssoro, Siles Suazo and Juan Lechín) and consisted of distorted re-enactments of the dramas of the 1952–64 period.

The conventional historiography of the revolution contains an important degree of truth.[28] Between 1952 and 1956 a spate of measures were enacted that cumulatively amounted to a profound social transformation. Viewed in isolation, universal suffrage (enfranchising illiterates, women and even soldiers) might not be so significant; but in Bolivia it was compelled by mass mobilization at a time when nationalization affected nearly all the major enterprises in the private sector, and when weaponry was being redistributed from the army to the police and from both to popularly organized worker and peasant militias. Paz Estenssoro's first

[28] See, e.g., Robert Alexander, *The Bolivian National Revolution* (New Brunswick, N.J., 1958).

term as president was the heroic age of the National Revolution, and it marked the national consciousness as no earlier, or subsequent, period of government would do.

Nevertheless, viewed with almost forty years of hindsight, it can be seen that many of the truths of the conventional historiography were extremely selective. If the tin mines had not been nationalized in October 1952, the private owners would surely have reacted to the revolution and the ending of the Korean War with mass dismissals and the withdrawal of capital. If an agrarian reform law had not been promulgated in August 1953, most landlords would in any case have been dispossessed by extra-legal local initiatives. Four years of de facto government followed the introduction of universal suffrage, and when elections were eventually held in 1956 they were designed to ratify rather than to regulate the MNR regime. Although the MNR emerged as the sole party of government, the exclusive proprietor of the revolution, this formula obscures more than it reveals. The leadership of the party, its composition, its strategy and its 'right to rule' were all relatively open questions in April 1952, and they remained subjects of controversy for the next twelve years.

Víctor Paz Estenssoro had been designated *jefe* since the party's inception in 1941 and had run as its presidential candidate in 1951. Between 1952 and 1956 he encouraged something of a personality cult, and after his return to office in 1960 he convinced himself and many others that the party was his personal vehicle. But in fact his authority within the movement was always conditional, and even at times precarious.[29] When Paz returned from exile in Argentina and assumed the presidency (for a four-year term) on 15 April 1952 it was because his vice-presidential running mate, who had organized the revolution and appointed the first cabinet, resisted contrary pressures and chose to wait his turn under the constitution. (Siles, not Paz, was the first president elected by universal suffrage.) During his six years of exile, many former allies had abandoned his party and many more newcomers had been recruited. It was uncertain how strong an allegiance was owed to the new president by those who had joined and perhaps suffered persecution while he was abroad. (Indeed, with the disappearance of the PIR many late-comers to the MNR came

---

[29] 'He preferred the game of dividing and balancing forces to the exercise of authority, an indication of a subtle vein of insecurity which was somewhat surprising in a man whose wish for power was so evident' (José Fellman Velarde, *Historia de Bolivia, vol. 3: La Bolivianidad semicolonial* [La Paz, 1970], p. 373). Fellman was a close associate who had formerly contributed to the 'personality cult'; see his *Víctor Paz Estenssoro: El hombre y la revolución* (La Paz, 1955), esp. pp. 268–70.

from unions that had previously denounced Paz as a Nazi.) Within the MNR rival factions immediately crystallized, especially on the Left, where the labour unions came together in the Central Obrera Boliviana (COB) to create a well-structured alternative focus of power within the ruling party. Under its leader, Juan Lechín (who owed no special loyalty to Paz and who had indeed been passed up as his vice-presidential running mate in 1951), the COB even secured the right to nominate and dismiss three members of the new president's cabinet.

For the first year of the revolution, the party was divided between Paz and Lechín over the question of whether to reopen the Colegio Militar; and Lechín, a hero in the street battles of 1952, was backed by armed militias that could give his arguments additional weight. The party was also deeply divided over other critical issues: how quickly to requisition the major mines, whether to pay a compensation for them, and what role to assign to the unions in their management; whether to accelerate or slow down a partly spontaneous process of agrarian revolution; what bridges to build with the United States; whether to grant new oil concessions to foreign companies; and perhaps most important of all, how to manage an increasingly severe economic crisis.

In 1945–6 Paz had served Villarroel as an orthodox minister of finance, balancing the budget, curbing credit, restraining inflation and quite possibly contributing as a consequence to the social discontent that helped destroy the government. After 1952 he took a very close interest in economic issues, but in the first phase of the revolution he gave priority to the consolidation of popular support and the implementation of drastic reforms. Only subsequently would he design unpopular measures for economic retrenchment, which he adroitly left to his successor Siles. The redistribution of assets was bound to produce a degree of economic disruption, and the revolutionaries could only expect that for a time they would face production difficulties while experimenting with a new structure of ownership and administration. Undoubtedly many of them (not necessarily Paz himself) overestimated the gains to be obtained from 'capturing the surplus' formerly creamed off by the Big Three companies and by the associated oligarchy. In practice the new state mining corporation, Corporación Minera de Bolivia (COMIBOL), acquired assets that were already quite worn out. Moreover, as the Korean War wound down, world demand for tin and wolfram entered a phase of depression that was to last almost until the end of the MNR's twelve years in office. Given this broad context, it can be argued that for some years the nationalized mines performed relatively well, generating a surplus which was largely squandered by other state enterprises – in particular by the state oil corporation YPFB (which invested $100 million in unproductive exploration) and by the Corporacíon Boliviana de Fomento (CBF), a state holding company engaged mainly in poorly supervised ventures in the eastern lowlands. At the time few Bolivians seem to have understood the complex and disguised resource transfers that took place in these years of artificial exchange rates, severe shortages, subsidized credit and looming hyperinflation. On a machiavellian view Víctor Paz may have judged that the mines had little future, but the balance of political forces precluded open recognition of this fact, since it clearly implied a period of economic disorder with resources reallocated covertly through inflationary interventionism until the new power structure had been consolidated. It is hardly surprising, given the disorganized state of Bolivian public administration even before the revolution, that this attempt to replace private initiative by public enterprise ran into acute problems of inefficiency and corruption. (The joke that the MNR had democratized corruption reflected a bitter truth.) While the Left could make a strong case for the revolutionary achievements of the labour movement and for the new system of worker participation in management, in practice these changes further diminished the chances of successful management of the state's enlarged patrimony. Although not perhaps the main authors of the economic crisis of 1955–6, the labour unions were the main losers from the fact that it occurred after they had secured the great bulk of their demands. Certainly, by 1956 Lechín seemed at a loss for viable left-wing economic policies.

Despite this profound economic crisis the MNR regime achieved a degree of political consolidation during Paz's first term. For almost four years (until the amnesty of 1 April 1956) the MNR governed as an arbitrary de facto regime. There was no congress (other than the COB) and no local government (other than the party and *sindicato* militias). In January 1953 the first serious revolt (supposedly to free Paz from dependence on 'the Communists') was met with harsh repression by the MNR's security police, the Control Político. Perhaps the turning point in this explicitly 'dictatorial' phase of the revolution came in 1955 when an attempt by both the MNR and the COB to 'intervene' in the universities met with unexpectedly strong and broad-based resistance. (It may also be that the violent overthrow of Perón in neighbouring Argentina in 1955 caused reflection among MNR leaders about how to stabilize their regime.) In any event, President Paz inaugurated the 'institutional stage' of the regime in August 1956, although he continued to stress socio-economic change rather than elections as the essential source of the revolution's legitimacy. He told the first Bolivian Congress elected under universal suffrage: 'The political struggle is polarized between the MNR, the legitimate representative of the Revolution, of the great national majority, a product of current historical necessity, and the forces of reaction embodied in an aggressive oligarchic vanguard which aims to restore landlord-mining domination.'[30]

Like the Mexican Partido Revolucionario Institutional (PRI), the MNR clearly envisaged an unbroken succession of electoral victories for the indefinite future. It recognized no democratic or constitutional restraint capable of overriding revolutionary legitimacy, and it therefore offered the opposition only a stark choice between ineffective tokenism and violent conspiracy. The *falangistas* assessed the 1956 electoral code as follows: 'Thus the illiteracy of the countryside swamped the true spirit of citizenship rooted in the cities and provincial capitals. Where indian obedience is blind everything was fixed with specially coloured voting papers.'[31] Between 1956 and 1964 the MNR consistently secured about 85 per cent of the vote in what its opponents denounced as fraudulent elections. On the other side of the political divide, Communists and Trotskyists faced the problem that many of their policies, and even their preferred forms of organization, were being purloined by a revolutionary movement whose leadership they knew to be profoundly hostile to many of their most cherished ideas. Within the national leadership of the victorious MNR, there was, of course, a great diversity of views and aspirations. What kept the government together for twelve years was less a shared ideology than a shared interest in monopolizing political power and a willingness to improvise ruthlessly with that end in view.

The COB, whose backbone was the FSTMB, provided the ideological and organizational axis of MNR's radical faction, which embraced labour unions, peasant organizations and student activists and which claimed authority over 'worker ministers' and workers' militias.[32] Juan Lechín

---

[30] *Mensaje del Presidente de la República*, 5 August 1956, p. 142. The 1956 electorate was almost five times larger than that of 1951. The MNR received 787,202 votes and the *falangistas* 130,669. But in the cities, and especially in middle-class areas, the large vote for the FSB shocked the governing party.

[31] Benjamin I. Cordeiro, *Tragedia en Indo-America* (Córdoba, 1964), p. 286.

[32] On the MNR's left wing during the radical phase of the revolution, see Guillermo Lora, *A History of the Bolivian Labour Movement* (Cambridge, 1977), and James Dunkerley, *Rebellion in the Veins* (London, 1984).

served as the general secretary of the COB from its inception in April 1952 until 1987, and for more than thirty years its political fortunes remained inextricably bound up with his own personal career. Until 1957 the COB flourished as its programs gained ascendancy within the MNR, and as it largely occupied the space left vacant by the absence of an elected congress. Even in its heyday, however, some critical weaknesses were visible. During 1953, when Paz seemed both under serious threat from the Right and willing to accept many suggestions from the Left, Lechín became more co-operative. He backed down over closure of the Colegio Militar, although the COB tried to set up its own national labour militia, which collaborated, often uneasily, with Colonel Claudio San Román's Control Político and the paid _milicianos_ of the MNR's paramilitary forces. According to General Gary Prado's well-informed account, after consultations with President Paz, the army high command decided to send senior officers as advisers, who in practice often exercised control over the _milicianos_.[33] These officers were enthusiastically welcomed by the COB; thus the danger that the _milicianos_ might become a parallel army was headed off. According to Paz's own testimony, the worker ministers were also relatively unthreatening, not least because Lechín (when in the cabinet) seemed incapable of attending to administrative work or systematic plan. Despite the tone of his discourse, Lechín was no Lenin, and during the heroic phase of the revolution he fell under the spell of the MNR _jefe_.

The fragility of Lechín's power base became apparent as soon as Siles assumed the presidency after the 1956 elections. Lechín's close ally, Nuflo Chávez Ortiz, was elected vice-president. As minister of peasant affairs, Chávez had promoted radical land reform and was viewed as the leader of the peasantry, in the same way that Lechín led the workers. But President Siles soon contrived the resignation of his vice-president in circumstances which demonstrated that the beneficiaries of land reform owed their loyalty to the government rather than to any individual politician. In the short run this benefited Siles, who split the peasantry away from the COB and then went on to launch an initially effective attack on Lechín's working-class support as well. But Lechín's hold over the COB proved more tenacious than Chávez's hold over the peasantry, and in due course Paz Estenssoro came to Lechín's rescue, offering him the vice-presidency in 1960 on condition that the Left back Paz for a second term. In the long run these rivalries between the main victors of 1952 taught the army how

---

[33] Gary Prado Salmón, _Poder y fuerzas armadas, 1949–82_ (Cochabamba, 1984), p. 54.

to wean the peasantry away from the MNR altogether, and showed that an isolated COB could be defeated.

In all elections held between 1956 and 1966 the newly enfranchised peasantry delivered a massive and apparently uncritical vote of support to the officially approved or incumbent candidate. Despite an attempted veto from the right wing of the MNR, Lechín benefited from this support as vice-presidential running mate to Paz in 1960. (The same applied at the other end of the political spectrum to General René Barrientos in 1966, even though he had overthrown the authors of the 1953 Agrarian Reform Law.) It was not until a generation after that upheaval in landownership that rural voters began to divide their allegiance between rival parties and to vote in large numbers for opposition candidates.

Just as students of the Mexican Revolution were for many years unduly influenced by Zapata's exceptionally intense and effective agrarian struggle in Morelos, so generalizations about Bolivia may have been over-influenced by the highly visible but unrepresentative processes of peasant mobilization in the valleys adjoining Cochabamba. In reality there was great regional heterogeneity. In some places landlord dominance quickly collapsed with the disappearance of the reactionary army; elsewhere, landlords retained considerable local power despite the hostility of the MNR. In between there were important cases of selective accommodation between the authorities and some elements of the rural elite. But in general the *latifundistas* as a class were driven out of the countryside by the time the Agrarian Reform Law was enacted. A long time often elapsed before the de facto beneficiaries of land redistribution received their individual titles. (Until Barrientos came to power in 1964, each document required the personal signature of the president.) It was not until the late 1960s that the fear of landlord dominance through counter-revolution really subsided. In the meantime, peasant beneficiaries felt a strong motive for maintaining solidarity, collective defence and self-protection through their MNR-created and -controlled *sindicatos*. Whoever was in government had access to this machinery for the delivery of votes in return for local favours – provided only that the pledge against counter-revolution was maintained.

Eventually about one-quarter of Bolivia's cultivable land was legally distributed through agrarian reform. The *sindicato* system also incorporated many rural producers who were not recipients of redistributed land but who relied on their local leaders to protect their pre-revolutionary holdings during a period of great insecurity. It was not only landownership, but also market access, credit provision and the administration of local justice that were channelled through the *sindicatos*. In some cases these provided 'Indian' communities with a long overdue means of redress against *mestizo* oppressors in the nearby small towns. Whatever the local circumstances, these arrangements drastically shifted the balance of power in national politics. According to one study:

The peasantry became a subject of its own history, capable of imposing its own terms on the state for participating in the new structure of power. This almost voluntary act of loyalty to the new state, far from being a mechanical consequence of the parcellization of peasant plots, should be viewed rather as the acceptance and defence of a manner of insertion into the market system and the power structure that could not subsequently be easily dismantled even by the state itself.[34]

The emergence, and then the curbing, of new social forces of the Left (the COB and the peasantry) was mirrored by the apparent eclipse, and subsequent reorganization, of the old sources of social power. The major mining enterprises passed into state hands. And by 1953 few members of the traditional landlord class felt it safe to journey to their estates, whatever their legal rights. In the first year of the revolution, the armed forces were drastically purged and reorganized; from mid-1953 officers were allowed to join the MNR, and thereafter membership in a 'military cell' within the governing party became a major route to preferment (as Generals Ovando and Barrientos, for example, well understood). Immediately after the revolution, Aramayo's *La Razón* was permanently closed, and in November 1953 *Los Tiempos* of Cochabamba was closed after it had conducted a fierce rearguard action against the agrarian reform. (The middle classes, however, were still allowed to read cautiously conservative newspapers like *El Diario,* which took over *La Razón*'s leading position in La Paz.) The traditional parties of the Right lost all raison d'être, and counter-revolutionary activists therefore flocked to the FSB, which demonstrated its urban strength in the elections of 1956 despite having operated underground for much of the previous period.

---

[34] Rivera, *Oprimidos pero no vencidos,* pp. 104–5. These generalizations are backed up by a series of regional case studies which bring out the diversity. Rivera belongs to a modern school of interpretation which views the MNR as engaging in an urban-based liberal-style project of 'incorporating' the peasantry, without taking into account much of their traditions or aspirations. She also insists on using the term '*Indian* peasantry' to emphasize the ethnic separation that the nationalists tried to deny. However, she may underestimate both the extent to which the 1952 reform fitted the circumstances of the Cochabamba valley (no measure would fit all regional conditions) and the party's success in politically 'incorporating' so much of the 'Indian' population.

As its name suggests, the Falange was not interested primarily in electoral politics despite the overwhelming support of the urban middle class, not least because the combination of universal suffrage and radical land reform gave the MNR an unbeatable advantage in any purely electoral contest. The *falangistas* used electoral opportunities to further their conspiratorial opposition in much the same way that the MNR had done after 1946. This phase of their activities came to a bloody culmination in 1958 (when they effectively captured the leadership of a militant regionalist movement in Santa Cruz, which was eventually put down by the army, reinforced by peasant militias brought down from the highlands) and 1959 (when most of the party's high command, including its founder-leader Unzaga de la Vega, was wiped out in the course of a conspiracy in La Paz). Thereafter, the *falangistas* generally avoided open confrontations with the constituted authorities (and especially with the army), but until the late 1970s they remained a major political force, deeply hostile to many consequences of the revolution, and in particular willing to use the most violent methods to suppress working-class and peasant ('Indian') radicalism.

The Falange expressed the desperation – the psychological trauma – that the radical phase of the revolution inflicted on many in the 'middle strata' of Bolivian society. They saw their meagre credentials and precarious privileges being swamped by a mobilization of those even worse off than themselves, at a time of acute severity and economic insecurity. There was also a racial element in this backlash, which may explain why the supposedly 'white' inhabitants of the eastern lowlands were particularly attracted to the movement, as were the petty oppressors of the Indians who inhabited small *mestizo* towns in the provinces. In fact, the revolution posed profound issues of national and personal identity that went beyond the mere distribution of material resources. It was of more than folkloric significance to many people when segregation of buses and cinemas was abolished in the cities, or when President Paz instructed his ministers to disguise their reluctance and dance with the *cholas* from the central market. Although the cultural manifestations of the revolution were meagre and although huge social inequalities continued to exist, it would be wrong to underestimate the significance of the barriers that were torn down. Certainly many followers of the Falange felt this as an irreparable loss which left them with no future.

In the second half of the MNR's twelve years of rule, other forces gradually began to coalesce on the Right, forces that were more in tune with the new order and therefore more capable of reshaping it to their needs. In the 1960 elections, for example, the Partido Revolucionario Auténtico (PRA), a break-away faction from the MNR opposed to Lechín's vice-presidency and a resurgence of the COB, briefly displaced the Falange as the largest opposition party, winning 14.1 per cent of the national vote and achieving striking results in the departments of Cochabamba and Oruro. Outside the electoral arena, more important alignments were under way. A new stratum of mine-owners began to prosper with the help of the government and U.S. AID; a regional agricultural bourgeoisie re-formed, based initially on the processing of sugar and rice in the east (*Oriente*); and private banking reappeared. All of this followed from the remarkably successful stabilization programme of 1956, backed by the International Monetary Fund (IMF) and U.S. government, which abruptly halted inflation, rolled back state controls and restored exchange rate stability.

From 1958 to 1972 Bolivia's currency was pegged to the dollar and freely convertible. This was the country's longest period of monetary stability and economic liberalism. However, the transition from one model of economic management to another was fraught with risks and difficulties. It was made possible only by President Paz's success in neutralizing the internal opposition and cementing a strong relationship with Washington in his first term; and that in turn was possible only because of the authority he derived from the radical phase of his government. In addition to these pre-conditions, the shift also required all the outgoing president's skill, cynicism and commitment.

In fact, by 1956, with inflation out of control and the rationing system in chaos, Paz Estenssoro the revolutionary had reverted to type, becoming once again a sober economist. Extreme dependence on U.S. aid (without which there might well have been famine in La Paz in 1955) certainly accelerated this transformation and made it easier to sell to the party as a whole. But in the light of his whole career, it is easy to see that in any case this shift in direction would have been Paz Estenssoro's personal choice. It was first signalled by the decision in 1955 to invite U.S. oil companies to explore where YPFB had failed – a decision which involved allowing U.S. advisers to draft the so-called Davenport Code in English, and then to legislate the Spanish translation without debate. The IMF's drastically anti-statist stabilization plan of 1956 was negotiated when Paz was still president, although from his standpoint it had the great merit of burdening his successor, Hernán Siles, with all the heavy responsibilities of implementation.

At first the MNR's acute dependence on U.S. aid took the form of receiving emergency relief, perhaps aimed at staving off Communism and/or *peronismo,* and possibly also motivated by the wish to demonstrate that, notwithstanding Guatemala, Washington could support revolutionary social change. But the reconstruction of a conventional army became an explicit objective of U.S. aid-givers well before the stabilization plan of 1956. Lechín and his workers' militias were viewed with dismay in Washington from the very first day (not only for abstract ideological reasons, but also because of the deaths of some U.S. mining engineers at the hands of miners during the 1949 civil war). After 1956 the objectives of U.S. economic leverage were simultaneously to reduce the size and the organizational strength of COMIBOL's work-force and to increase the size, firepower and autonomy of the armed forces. It was only a matter of time before this policy came to fruition, with the army invading and reestablishing military control over the mining camps from 1964 onwards. In short, notwithstanding endless assurances of non-intervention in internal political affairs, one enduring effect of U.S. aid was to reinforce those factions which can best be labelled 'thermidorean' and to isolate and disarm the radicals. Perhaps this did more to determine the fate of the MNR regime than any internal process of realignment of the Right. It powerfully influenced, if not determined, the strategic choices of the party's leaders.

Any assessment of the strengths and failings of the Siles administration (1956–60) must take into account the fact that until 1957 the cities were desperately short of food. In conditions of hyperinflation and uncertainty about the desirability of the revolution, many land reform beneficiaries may have chosen simply to eat better and not to trade. The startling success of the stabilization programme may be attributed in large degree to the delayed benefits of the land reform, together with improved communications to the Oriente. Starting in 1957 urban food supplies became readily available at mostly unsubsidized prices. Such a development clearly affected the MNR's success in splitting the peasantry (now pro-regime) from the COB (now increasingly isolated as the standard-bearer of left-wing opposition).

With hindsight (and with knowledge of the second Siles presidency of 1982–5), the period 1956–60 looks rather better than it seemed at the time. In very adverse economic conditions and under severe pressure from various strategic groups, Siles implemented the stabilization policy and the agrarian reform and fended off serious challenges from both the COB and the Falange. He governed with less repression than his predecessor and tolerated a substantial degree of harassment from within his own party, including a choice of successor that was not at all to his liking.

When Paz returned to the presidency in 1960, he had no intention of reverting to what he viewed as the failed economic policies of 1952–6. Lechín was elected as his vice-president and was charged with drawing up a ten-year economic plan. But a further confrontation with the labour Left over central issues of economic management was almost inevitable. Initially the aid to public enterprises and land reform promised by the Alliance for Progress may have raised hopes that this conflict could somehow be circumvented, but with the unveiling of the 'Triangular Plan' in 1961 for rehabilitating COMIBOL, the underlying tensions resurfaced with a vengeance. Just as Paz had acted ruthlessly towards the Right in 1952–6, he now acted forcefully to overcome resistance to his economic plans from the Left (a pattern he repeated again in 1971–2 and in his fourth term as president, which started in 1985). By 1964 (as in 1946) he faced a range of enemies from both Left and Right, united only in their determination to destroy his personal power. The military coup of November 1964 can be understood only in relation to the decomposition of the MNR after the 'heroic phase' of the revolution. Whereas the PRI in Mexico was able to head off both types of threat, the MNR succumbed within twelve years. At a superficial level one can say that Paz Estenssoro's decision to return for a second term of office in 1960–4, and his still more grave decision to purge the party and change the constitution in order to succeed himself in office in 1964, account for much of the contrast. Yet the founder of the MNR opted for re-electionism in response to deep-rooted contradictions within the movement he had launched. These contradictions concerned political nationalism, social revolution and economic management. The best explanation of why he chose to personalize power within the MNR and thus secure his own re-election in 1964 is probably that only by those means could he expect to achieve a continuation of his new economic policies until they achieved results. (In a rare expression of self-criticism he subsequently commented about this period, 'Tal vez caí un poco en el error del desarrollismo'.)[35]

Thus, issues of economic management played a critical part in the disintegration of the MNR regime, but they do not provide the entire explanation. The social revolution of the early 1950s unleashed new forces

[35] Author's interview with Víctor Paz Estenssoro, Lima, 26 June 1968.

that subsequently proved very difficult to control. From the mid-1960s onwards it became clear that military repression would be a major component of the Bolivian state's response. Between the late 1950s and the early 1960s, as alternative, more political strategies of management failed, the MNR gradually ceded political hegemony to the reorganized armed forces. The nomination of air force General René Barrientos as Paz Estenssoro's running mate (and therefore as deputy leader of the MNR) in the 1964 elections represented the culmination of this process. However, there is another part of the story which is of at least equal importance. Although the United States created strong economic incentives for the armed forces to suppress the radicalism of the miners, the MNR was not a merely passive instrument for implementing this policy. A succession of party leaders – Paz, Siles, and Walter Guevara Arze – bent their ingenuity to the task of containing or deflecting working-class unrest without ultimate resort to the military. If the mines had posed the sole problem of disorder, the MNR might well have remained in control. It was the need to control the peasantry of Cochabamba and the regionalist politicians of Santa Cruz that caused the MNR to deploy miltary force to solve political problems. The outbreak of a virtual war between rival peasant militias in the Cochabamba Valley in 1959–60 led to the first imposition of military control over the supposed beneficiaries of the revolution; General Barrientos, a *cochabambino* and Quechua-speaker, derived his electoral strength from a peasant base that the MNR had handed him on a plate. The 'Military–Peasant Pact', which was to underpin army rule for a dozen years after the fall of the MNR, derived its origin from this experience in Cochabamba, where the armed forces acquired the power to exclude undesirable civilians from a densely populated rural area and to reorganize the peasant *sindicatos* in accordance with instructions from the local barracks.

Thus, the MNR regime collapsed over issues of both economic management and social control. The third contributory factor is more intangible but of equal importance. In its ideology and mystique the MNR was a movement of national pride and regeneration. Its nationalist claims gave it a critical edge over the Marxist revolutionaries and enabled it to assemble a very broad coalition of potentially antagonistic interests. In the heroic phase of the revolution the MNR was still able to capitalize on a nationalist sense of assertiveness even though it was forced into what some regarded as undignified transactions with the IMF, Gulf Oil and the Pentagon. The Cuban Revolution marked a watershed in this process. After 1959 Fidel Castro overshadowed Bolivia's tepid radicals, and from 1961 pressure from Washington to dissociate Bolivia from the Cuban example destroyed the MNR's revolutionary nationalist mystique. It was transparently under U.S. pressure that Bolivia acquiesced in Cuba's expulsion from the Organization of American States in 1963. Whatever other factors may have caused President Paz to seek his re-election and to accept General René Barrientos as his running mate, many Bolivians saw this as another step dictated by Washington. (Vice-President Lechín had supposedly been promised the party's nomination for the presidency in 1964, but was allegedly vetoed by the United States because of his sympathy for Cuba.) There is some evidence that at this time even President Paz himself viewed a majority of his cabinet as untrustworthy because they were at the service of the Americans in general, and of Gulf Oil in particular. A revolutionary nationalist movement so patently unable to defend national autonomy was almost bound to fragment into its antagonistic constituent parts.

In 1964 under irresistible provocation, Juan Lechín had no choice but to break away and found his own party – the left-wing Partido Revolucionario de la Izquierda Nacional (PRIN) – and he then joined with his old enemies from the MNR's right, Siles and Guevara Arze, to bring down Paz, re-elected in August 1964. Paz, for his part, was forced into ever greater dependence on his military allies. This, however, was an unsustainable solution. By November 1964 it no longer served the officer corps to preserve the fiction of subordination to a civilian party that had destroyed itself. At the start of the month the flamboyant Barrientos declared himself in revolt, and once he received the support of the calculating army commander Alfredo Ovando, the MNR's fate was sealed.

MILITARY GOVERNMENT, 1964–78

The Barrientos regime (1964–9) has been given a number of contradictory characterizations, each of which contains an element of truth. Because he rallied support from many peasants (especially in his home department of Cochabamba), who saw him as a guarantee against any reversal of the MNR's land reform, the air force general has been described as a typical 'bonapartist'. To the leading figures of the Paz Estenssoro administration – including General Ovando, who stayed on as army chief during the Barrientos presidency – the 'bonapartist' label would have seemed grandiose in view of the new ruler's patent unsuitability for high office. (Barrientos had seemed a safe choice for the vice-presidency. After his first term as president, Paz – like Perón – preferred running mates who were not credible successors.) Because he relied heavily on the reconstituted military, strongly backed by the U.S. Embassy, and sought to reassure domestic and foreign capitalists, Barrientos has also been viewed as a representative Latin American military *entreguista* on the Batista model. (Che Guevara may have been unduly impressed by this analogy before staging his abortive guerrilla campaign of 1966–67.)

Barrientos had received military training in the Canal Zone and in Texas, and he was the pilot who flew Paz Estenssoro back from exile in 1952. When, in August 1961 President Paz declared Santa Cruz a military zone, the Santa Cruz section of the MNR was placed under the control of an official appointed by the national party – namely, General René Barrientos. Although he occupied this position for only a couple of weeks, and in spite of the semi-literate quality of his public statements, the young general was considered a great success and was subsequently given a similar assignment in Cochabamba. The establishment of military control over one area of strong peasant organization set the pattern that was later extended throughout the country. In each department the commander of the local garrison became a key figure in determining which of the rival peasant leaders would be recognized by the authorities and how much latitude the peasant organizations would be allowed.

Thus, by the time a weakened President Paz bowed to military pressure and accepted Barrientos as his vice-presidential running mate in March 1964, the general had secured substantial backing from the North Americans, from within the party, from two important cities where he had placed his protégés, and from far-flung rural areas where the civic action budget had purchased him a local following.[36] Paz must have realized the danger, but he had so weakened his party that he had little choice; he appears to have hoped that the army would not be involved in a conspiracy that might bring disproportionate power to the head of the air force. In the event, many of the most important former leaders of the MNR sought to obstruct its election campaign, and when they failed to defeat Paz at the

[36] U.S. support for Bolivian civic action programmes began in the late 1950s with local currency accumulated from Food for Peace sales. 'By 1958, with U.S. aid . . . in several areas the government had turned all projects over to the military. These were road construction and maintenance . . . school construction; land clearing and cultivation; house building; community development . . . and the provision of medical treatment and air transportation for remote areas'. In 1965 alone 156 schools were scheduled for construction under this civic aid budget. Barrientos 'used the dedication of such schools as opportunities to build a political following among the Campesinos' and consolidated his personal control over all such projects. (Gary J. Ewell, 'Effects of U.S. Military Aid on Military Intervention in Bolivia and Chile' [Ph.D. dissertation, University of Santa Clara, 1970], p. 18).

ballot box, they proceeded to conspire against him in the garrisons. It was due to agitation by a large coalition of elements detached from the original MNR alliance, including labour unions and student activists, that the rump loyal to President Paz was brought down. A power-sharing pact between air force leader Barrientos and the reluctant commander of the army, General Ovando, removed the last obstacle upon which Paz may have relied: inter-service rivalry.

Although the COB had indirectly assisted the November 1964 coup, organized labour soon came to view the Barrientos government as the most implacable and repressive since before the revolution. Lechín and his followers had experienced considerable harassment from the *paz estenssoristas* since 1961, and they hoped to benefit from the abolition of the Control Político and the release of jailed union leaders following the coup. Although the remaining peasant militias were quickly domesticated by the new military regime, the workers retained their weapons and their organizational autonomy, particularly in the mines. Consequently, there was a stand-off for the first six months, until the Barrientos regime felt secure enough to impose on the miners the same formula that had neutralized the peasantry. In May 1965 Lechín was arrested and deported, and the ensuing general strike was rapidly broken. Trade union leaders were dismissed en masse, and wage levels were 'rationalized' drastically downwards. Military detachments were stationed in all the main mining camps, and local commanders were given unlimited powers of political control. This system (reminiscent of Deringer's 1949 proposal) was maintained in place for over three years, during which a number of massacres took place in the mines.

Military unity was essential for this purpose, so General Ovando as army commander joined Barrientos in a joint presidency. Lechín's half-brother, Colonel Juan Lechín Suarez, was placed in charge of COMIBOL. In fact, military appointees invaded all levels of the public administration, leaving few remunerative posts for civilian collaborators. By January 1966 the regime felt sufficiently solid to convoke elections, and Barrientos ceded all presidential functions to Ovando for six months while he embarked on a vigorous campaign of electioneering and junketing.

The July 1966 election overwhelmingly ratified Barrientos' seizure of power and was described by reasonably independent observers as perhaps the freest and most representative in Bolivian history (a defensible proposition, but less impressive than it sounds). He roundly defeated an ageing *falangista* opponent, with little resistance from some splinters of the MNR or a divided Left. After this victory Barrientos counted among his ministerial collaborators distinguished figures from the MNR and the PIR, together with future military politicians ranging from Juan José Torres of the Left to Hugo Banzer of the Right.

Thus, at the high point of his brief career General Barrientos had apparently outwitted his most brilliant rivals, defeated a challenge from Latin America's foremost exponent of guerrilla warfare (Che Guevara) and seemed on the verge of consolidating a personalist political and paramilitary apparatus that would free him from dependence on any of his original sources of support. Then, quite simply, in April 1969 his helicopter crashed and he was killed. With him died his entire political formula, his only heritage being a large number of illegitimate children and some slow-burning scandals concerning bribes paid by Gulf Oil, suspicious arms deals and the intrusive presence of the CIA in the highest echelons of government.

The MNR regime had disintegrated because of its own internal failings. It was unable to resolve the social conflicts it had unleashed, without resort to repression. It suffered deep internal divisions on policy, which were complicated by heavy pressure from the United States and an inability to resolve peacefully the problem of succession. Each of these problems forced the government into greater reliance on the military sector within the party. The party cells established within the armed forces did not check the authority of senior officers; rather, it reinforced them. Membership in the governing party conferred various privileges, and these were distributed from the top down. Thus, military leaders like General Ovando and General Barrientos became active promoters of party organization within the armed forces. The party enabled them to achieve institution-wide pre-eminence without threatening the military hierarchy. Moreover, as leading members of the governing party, they had acquired privileged access to the civilian authorities and a licence to make contacts with civilian local organizations that would otherwise have seemed beyond the proper scope of senior officers. Indeed, as factional divisions intensified within the MNR, party leaders became increasingly dependent upon the military section of their organization to re-establish central control when local branches of the party were tempted into dissidence. Furthermore, the social changes brought about by the MNR reduced various obstacles that had previously stood in the way of effective military control over national life. For example, rather like the Mexican PRI, the MNR had developed a nationalistic rhetoric, which justified repression of both 'extreme Left' and 'extreme Right' while drawing attention away from the less than wholly nationalistic content of its actual policies. From within the MNR, senior officers learned the techniques involved. Subsequently these were appropriated as an aid to military rule. Likewise, by expanding the role of the bureaucracy and increasing state control over the levers of economic management, the MNR forged instruments of political patronage that would also be available to successor military regimes.

In a sense, then, Barrientos was the chance legatee of the MNR's failure and was obliged to govern by piecing together fragments left over from that collapsed experiment. He was not engaged in anything as coherent as a reversal of the previous philosophy of government (the *falangistas* who advocated that became a tolerated opposition within his regime), nor – as he himself tried to argue – did he attempt a restoration of the original purposes of the revolution. His government embraced the Johnson administration as Paz Estenssoro had embraced Kennedy, but the United States was no longer promoting the reformist vision laid out in the Alliance for Progress. All Washington required from its military protégés in La Paz was anti-Communism and good housekeeping, whereas a coherent policy for the post-revolutionary era would have to address a host of internal issues with which the U.S. Embassy was incapable of dealing.

Although the Military–Peasant Pact, which provided the cornerstone of Barrientos' approach to internal order, drew some inspiration from U.S. counter-insurgency doctrines, it was essentially another *movimientista* conception that had escaped the control of its inventors. Similarly, the use of military force to crush the miners' union can be attributed in part to the urgings of U.S. aid-givers from as far back as 1956, but this too was just a culmination of tendencies that had been gestating within the leadership of the MNR ever since the Colegio Militar was reopened and the COB militias were pushed back from their positions of urban dominance in the mid-1950s. The corruption and gangsterism that accompanied this presidency were not alien to the preceding MNR regime; they were all the more inevitable in an administration that lacked any overarching justification for its existence and that depended for its survival upon the accommodation of mutually antagonistic cliques and factions. With the Bolivian Left in disarray and with conventional party politics confined to a handful of the largest cities, it was not difficult for such a regime to 'win' a 'clean' election to the satisfaction of pro-American foreign observers.

But other foreign observers, of a different ideological persuasion, drew

very different conclusions from constitutionalization of the military dictatorship. Che Guevera arrived clandestinely in Bolivia in October 1966.
The existence of his small guerrilla force became known in April 1967,
and it was crushed by October. The celebrated Argentine–Cuban revolutionary was captured and executed by units of the Bolivian army who were
closely supervised by their U.S. Special Forces 'advisers'. He never succeeded in breaking out from the extremely isolated and unfriendly terrain
between Cochabamba and Santa Cruz where the operations began, he
enlisted almost no peasant support and the number of those under his
command never exceeded fifty (of whom eighteen were Cubans). The pro-
Moscow PCB channelled a minimum of resources to the quixotic venture.
The rest of the Bolivian Left was marginalized and could offer no significant support. The episode naturally attracted worldwide press attention
and produced extensive repercussions within the military regime.

The guerrilla campaign of 1967 may have ended in spectacular – and
all too foreseeable – failure, but the analysis of Bolivian politics on which
it rested was not so mistaken, as is often supposed. The popular expectations aroused in the 1950s had not been satisfied or diverted by 1967; they
had merely been suppressed. The distribution of spoils among the military
was too recent to have yet created a solid structure of interests committed
to the survival of the regime, especially considering that the officer corps
had only just begun to recover from the humiliations of the 1930s and the
early 1950s. Although private mine-owners and agro-exporters were beginning to prosper once more, Bolivia still lacked anything like a 'national
bourgeoisie', and in consequence the U.S. Embassy found itself almost
directly in charge of many administrative and executive tasks. Hence, of
all the partial truths proposed as interpretations of the Barrientos regime
the analogy with Batista probably stands up best. However, this was the
young Batista, and those who defied him therefore experienced the fate of
Guiteras rather than of Castro.

After the death of Guevera, the Barrientos government became increasingly erratic. Radicalized students declared La Paz university a '*teritorio
libre*', and others followed suit, bringing bitter political conflict to the
heart of the cities. A whole class of Bolivian student activists imitated
Che's guerrilla adventure in the Treponte campaign of 1970, and met the
same fate. Junior officers, passed over for promotion by Barrientos, became restless over the privileges he had conceded to Gulf Oil and expressed shock when his interior minister defected to Cuba, exposing deep
CIA penetration of the government. An anti-American military coup in

neighbouring Peru in October 1968 offered them an alternative political model, which they began to urge on army commander Ovando. Barrientos responded by recruiting a paramilitary force answerable only to himself. Thereafter, the armed forces found themselves increasingly torn between Ovando's emerging presidential candidacy (new elections were due in 1970, and the 1966 constitution barred re-election) and Barrientos' growing determination not to step down.

The death of Barrientos (probably an accident, although the timing was bound to arouse suspicions that cannot be disproved) inaugurated a two and a half year cycle of instability, during which two major attempts were made – by General Ovando and General Torres – to reassemble fragments left over from the disintegration of the MNR. Both attempts failed through a combination of internal disunity and fierce resistance, thus paving the way for a sustained period of right-wing authoritarian government under the leadership of Colonel Hugo Banzer.

General Ovando's presidency lasted just over one year (1969–70). Ovando aimed to establish a military variant of populist revolution, nationalizing Gulf Oil and shaking off the excessive North American interference that had characterized his predecessor's administration. The example set by the Velasco experiment in Peru obviously provided encouragement, but Ovando had been piecing together a formula along these lines virtually since the fall of Paz Estenssoro (whose overthrow he always regretted). The formula had numerous antecedents in Bolivian history, but all of them dated from before the 1952 revolution. The task of reconstituting this type of government *after* the more radical experiments of the 1950s was far more difficult than that in Peru, where Velasco had little difficulty in outflanking all of his critics of the Left. Ovando, by contrast, found himself from the very beginning engaged in slowing down a process that threatened to escape from his control into the hands of more intransigent radicals. The least he could do to establish his progressive credentials was to withdraw the army from the mines and to authorize the return of exiles and the re-establishment of the COB. But once these steps were taken, he faced a series of demands that threatened the basis of his power. Would the crimes of the Barrientos regime be thoroughly investigated? Would the corrupt deals be nullified, the perpetrators punished? More than just amends for the past, his radical critics demanded assurances for the future, and not just personal promises or paper guarantees. Nothing short of a return to the distribution of power as it had existed in the mid-1950s could placate them; but Ovando's position within the military establishment (and his bargaining power with the civilian Right) depended on his ability to protect most of the vested interests that had been built up during the 1960s. This balancing act soon proved impossible, and the military high command therefore withdrew its support from him, endorsing instead a conservative junta dedicated to the restoration of order.

October 1970 was an unpropitious moment to attempt such a step. General Juan Carlos Onganía's efforts in the same direction had just brought Argentina to the brink of a civil war, from which the military had drawn back with considerable loss of face; the 'Peruvian experiment' was still gathering momentum; Allende had just been elected in Chile; and U.S. prestige was at a low point because of Vietnam. Moreover, in La Paz important factions within the Ovando administration would rather make common cause with the reviving civilian Left than quietly accept a restoration of *barrientismo*. The inept timing and bad tactics of the Right provided an opportunity for the very thing it was most eager to prevent – a weak military government largely captive of the radical Left.

It is perhaps too charitable to credit the ten-month administration of General Torres with a coherent set of principles, since from the beginning its energies were devoted almost entirely to the herculean task of survival. Nevertheless, both supporters and opponents were perfectly clear about the kind of regime that would result if Torres could stabilize his position. The language, the personnel, the methods of mobilization were recognizable from the experiences of the mid-1950s, with what conservatives saw as an even more alarming element contributed by the student radicals who drew their inspiration from Che Guevara. The Torres administration tolerated the People's Assembly (essentially the COB wearing a legislative hat), which called for popular militias and aimed to recapture the popular enthusiasm that had once been the patrimony of the MNR without using the historical leaders of the party (other than Lechín) as its intermediaries.

By this time all of the main functionaries of the MNR had been out of office for a full six years, and with no spoils to distribute, their hold over their followers was rapidly dwindling. To optimists of the Left, and to those who rated the appeal of ideology above that of machine politics, this seemed to offer an opportunity for a return to the best days of the revolution, without the encumbrance of the MNR's cynical and opportunist leaders. But in reality it was always quixotic to imagine that the prestige of April 1952 could be regained and made the basis of a new regime in defiance of that revolution's living figureheads. The only way that Torres might have succeeded in stabilizing his position was by striking a deal with either Paz or Siles. By this time the price might not have been exorbitant. Neither option was pursued, however, in part because of ideological objections from the Left, but above all from fear that once an old fox like Paz regained a foothold in the state apparatus everyone else would suffer the fate of the proverbial chickens.

In the event, it was the enemies of Torres who took the risk of striking a deal with Víctor Paz. In August 1971, with support from Brazil, the *falangistas* and the new rich of the Oriente, Colonel Banzer launched an uprising against 'Communism' that soon rallied the bulk of the military and secured the backing of the 'historic' wing of the MNR. The Siles faction stayed on the sidelines, hoping at least to demonstrate the truth of its claim that Paz belonged with the Right whereas this faction recently renamed MNR de la Izquierda could be counted with the Left. For the radicals of the Torres period the defeat of August 1971 was a crushing experience which foreshadowed, on a small scale, the fate that would befall Allende's followers in Chile two years later. They had expected the military to split and the masses to rise, as in 1952, or at least in 1970. But by this time most of the military was ready to abandon Torres, and the popular pressure that might have counteracted this tendency was insufficiently strong. In retrospect it is not difficult to explain why so few officers were prepared to distribute arms to civilians, or why the civilian supporters were relatively reluctant to engage in an unequal fight.[37] In addition to all of the reasons conventionally rehearsed in left-wing discussions of this issue, the 'nationalist' reason given by Víctor Paz for excusing his alignment with the Right probably deserves some attention. At best, he argued, the Left might hold the *altiplano*, relying on support from Santiago. With Brazil backing a rebellion that was strongly rooted in the Oriente, the result would be partition (*polonización*) or even an international war. This, claimed Paz, was the danger that all patriots must avert.

When Hugo Banzer arrived in La Paz, few observers imagined that he would serve the longest continuous term of office of any twentieth-century Bolivian president or that he would oversee a period of remarkable political stability and economic success. Moreover, only those well versed in the intricacies of the Bolivian underworld could have foreseen the 'Paraguayan'

[37] Jorge Gallardo Lozada, *De Torres a Banzer* (Buenos Aires, 1972) analyses in detail the balance of forces both in October 1970 and in August 1971. Gallardo was the interior minister charged with defending the regime, and this self-justificatory memoir is rather harsh on Torres. Clearly his government was living on borrowed time and Gallardo's radicalism was the gambler's last throw.

style that would accompany this appearance of success, as high-level complicity in the production and export of illegal narcotics (cocaine derived from the indigenous coca leaf) came to dwarf all other aspects of public life. In the end, this evil legacy of the Banzer administration outweighed the positive accomplishments, which were paraded as a 'modernizing' and 'technocratic' veneer.

Three phases can be distinguished in the Banzer regime. The period from 1971 to 1974 saw a gradual definition and consolidation of the government; 1974–6 marked the height of Banzer's authoritarian success; while 1976–8 witnessed a surprisingly rapid process of decomposition. This led to yet another prolonged period of indefinition and instability, finally cut short by the García Meza coup of July 1980, which inaugurated a period of 'all power to the drug traffickers'. By the time constitutional government was finally restored with Hernán Siles's return to office in September 1982, the economic and social basis of the country were almost irreparably damaged.

Colonel Banzer was not an outstanding public figure at the moment of his accession to power. His father was a German military adviser who had taken Bolivian nationality and acquired land and dependants in Santa Cruz. A lieutenant at the time of the 1952 revolution, Banzer was one of the few not purged, but instead sent to the Canal Zone for further training. He served under Barrientos as an undistinguished education minister, and by 1971 had risen to the post of commander of the Colegio Militar. Caught in a clumsy conspiracy against Torres, he was exiled to Argentina, where he naturally became involved in successive negotiations to create an anti-Marxist front. The breakthrough came in June 1971, when Paz Estenssoro joined with his old enemies of the Falange in a front against Torres. Banzer was in a position to make a double contribution through his contacts with the Santa Cruz oligarchy and his seniority in the military. Even so, it took him some time to secure his leadership after the ousting of Torres. Initially he was one of a triumvirate, and it was not until December 1971 that he decisively outmanoeuvred his rival in the Interior Ministry. His presidency began with a power-sharing agreement conceding key ministries to the two civilian parties allied in the conspiracy. Banzer promised to hold elections in 1972 and to respect the professional autonomy of the military (i.e., not to repeat the behaviour of Barrientos). Most of the initial urban repression was carried out by *movimentistas* and *falangistas,* not by the army.

After the relatively easy and swiftly completed task of suppressing the Left, President Banzer faced the far trickier and slower assignment of outmanoeuvring the supporters of Paz – an essential step if he was to consolidate his power and to impose his own priorities. Paz and his followers had been out of office for seven years, and in desperation they had offered their services to Banzer's conspiracy on very modest terms. With one-third of the spoils of office, they hoped that their superior skills and capacity to mobilize popular support would enable them to outmanoeuvre the dominant military faction and claim the strategic initiative. But with the promise of an election soon forgotten, the army firmly denied them access to the peasantry, where their following had once been most solid, so that their mobilizing efforts were confined largely to the cities. For example, in February 1972 it was announced that Paz would be visiting Cochabamba, seeking to renew contact with his old supporters. On hearing this news, the Federación Campesina of Cochabamba held a special meeting at which it ratified the Military–Peasant Pact and instructed its supporters to boycott the visit of the man who had signed the Agrarian Reform Law. The meeting was sponsored by the *coordinador agrario* of the pact, Colonel Víctor Lora, and held at the base Aérea Militar, which he commanded. Paz took the hint and dropped all attempts to develop support amongst the peasantry.

Attention focussed on the Ministry of Labour, where the MNR attempted to regain its old popularity with the labour movement. But it proved impossible for the party to live down its complicity in Banzer's pro-business and anti-labour administration – especially after the devaluation of October 1972, which entailed a reduction of 10 per cent in the real earnings of the average wage-earner. This devaluation was an especially severe blow to the popularity of the MNR – in charge of the economic ministries – since it brought to an end fourteen years of currency stability. The party's efforts were therefore soon concentrated on the rapidly expanding public administration, but here, of course, President Banzer was well placed to use his ultimate control over patronage to outmanoeuvre the party leaders. *Paceños* were shocked at the number of public positions assigned to (often ill-qualified) *cruceños*. It soon became apparent that with his 'revolutionary' credentials discredited and his leadership of the MNR under challenge, Paz Estenssoro could not afford to keep his party in government through the odium of two successive periods of economic austerity. He had been obliged to endorse the 1972 devaluation, but announced the MNR's withdrawal from the government in November 1973 when he saw that the confidence of the Right had been boosted by events in neighbouring Chile and that another batch of unpopular price rises was imminent. For the MNR's ministers, however, and for those party members who had secured jobs in the administration by virtue of their party affiliations, withdrawal was not so easy. Thus, when Paz was exiled in January 1974, the rump of his party clung to its bureaucratic privileges and surrendered its autonomy. The most dangerous ally on Banzer's left had been very effectively neutralized.

In January 1974 Banzer authorized big increases in the prices of rice, sugar and other lowland products, while the prices of Cochabamba's products were left unchanged. The ensuing regionalist protest encompassed both urban and rural workers, but it was a new experience for the Cochabamba peasantry to bear the brunt of the repression. An unnecessary display of force was mounted and more than one hundred peasants were killed. The Military–Peasant Pact formally survived, but in the wake of this massacre Banzer could no longer rely on it to deliver him an easy electoral victory, like that attained by Barrientos in 1966.

By 1974, however, an electoral challenge was looming for Banzer. Constitutional presidents transfer power after four years, and in Bolivia ad hoc rulers have always been expected either to step down or to legitimize their rule after a shorter time span. By 1974 it was thought that there might be elections soon, and at the least that there would be some redistribution of spoils so that those with strategic support could advance their careers, their ideals or both. Various military leaders felt that they were as well qualified for the presidency as Banzer; and even if they forswore the supreme prize, their support had become sufficiently vital to command a good price. Well-entrenched regional army commanders could exercise considerable influence over candidates' access to the peasant voters of their zones in the pre-electoral period. As a result, the merest hint of forthcoming elections produced a ferment of political agitation throughout the military.

As the candidate of the established regime, with control over the peasant *sindicatos,* Banzer could probably have secured his re-election despite the opposition of both the MNR and the FSB, but the campaign would have been risky and costly. Worse still was the precedent established by Barrientos in 1966 – that an incumbent president running for a second term in office must step down for the six months of the campaign; this would mean temporarily ceding crucial positions to a potential rival. Throughout most of 1974, Banzer dithered in the face of this obstacle. He was almost ousted in June 1974, when young officers allied with a segment of the MNR attempted to enforce a 'return to barracks', which they hoped would preserve military solidarity and allow a relatively open election campaign. The conspirators nearly carried the day, but then accepted a compromise formula that gave Banzer time to stage a comeback by greatly raising officers' pay and lobbying the garrisons. He finally managed to convince enough officers that any attempt to constitutionalize the regime would put all the country's political and economic gains at risk, and would expose the military to a process of internal decomposition like the ordeal it had experienced only three years before. In November 1974 the planned elections were abruptly cancelled; an all-military cabinet was established; all political parties, trade unions and most other interest associations were virtually suspended. The military proceeded to rule alone.

General Hugo Banzer lacked the demagogic appeal of Barrientos or the administrative talents of Ovando, his main predecessors in office. A man of limited vision and no great natural authority, his success must be attributed not only to luck and to his intermittent bursts of bold and unpredictable assertiveness, but also to the substantial economic interests he served especially in the Oriente, and the shrewd advisers he attracted. Moreover, between 1971 and 1976 the Bolivian gross domestic product (GDP) grew at an average annual rate of 5.7 per cent, and the foreign trade sector flourished. Some even called this the Bolivian 'economic miracle', although the improvement was, in fact, patchy and relative. After 1976 economic performance deteriorated, with petroleum production falling and the surplus available for export dwindling rapidly.

During the middle period of Banzer's government (from the *autogolpe* of November 1974 until November 1977) power was effectively concentrated in the presidency and in the leader's immediate circle of technocrats and business associates. During these three years Banzer presided over an all-military cabinet and ruled without the collaboration of organized political parties. However, below cabinet level there were far fewer military officers in positions of authority than there had been in the 1960s; many civilians initially recruited through their political parties stayed on as servants of the regime. During this period private business interests, which had lacked much direct means of political expression during the period of MNR government and mass mobilization, gained a new self-confidence and capacity for collective action. To some extent, therefore, it would be correct to argue that the propertied elite within the civilian population had displaced the political parties. Whereas between 1964 and 1974 successive military regimes relied on their civilian party allies to stabilize their power and give a coherent direction to their policies, from

November 1974 to 1977 that role was more directly assumed by the increasingly flourishing business community. But even at the height of the Banzer dictatorship, Bolivia's business interests were still far from being homogeneous, let alone hegemonic. The interests of private mine-owners were significantly different from those of the landowners of the Oriente or the mushrooming banking community. Furthermore, the greatest upsurge in prosperity occurred in parts of the publicly owned sector of the economy, most notably YPFB. Thus, 'private enterprise' remained largely an abstraction referring to a relatively small number of individual property-owners, each of whom might feel he owed his security and prosperity to a political clan or faction. In short, the Bolivian business community was still capable of acting only as a subordinate partner to the authoritarian regime. It was not strong in itself nor farsighted, but merely flourished in comparison with the other sectors of society that were disorganized by systematic repression.

In the pattern established during Banzer's seizure of power, popular protest was repeatedly suppressed (La Paz factory workers in October 1972; Cochabamba peasants in January 1974; highland miners in June 1976), although none of these apparent successes enabled the regime to enlist new social bases or decisively block off the subterranean currents of opposition. The regime's basis of ideological legitimation was also unsteady. Initial promises of democratization were mixed with the rhetoric of an anti-Communist national security state; later, Banzer placed more emphasis on national unity to secure economic development.

Even the *autogolpe* of November 1974, through which Banzer consolidated his personal power, contained flagrant contradictions. On the one hand, representative organizations were outlawed, the political parties were sent into recess, elected labour leaders were replaced with government-appointed 'co-ordinators' and the government even provided for the conscription of citizens in 'strategic' occupations. On the other hand, pre-existing constitutional conventions were not completely forsworn. Thus, Banzer still acknowledged the limitation of a fixed term, simply changing the starting date from August 1971 to November 1974. He again pledged elections at the end of his term, now postponed to 1980. Between 1974 and 1976, even this degree of dictatorship seemed relatively benign compared with the political and economic disasters befalling various neighbouring countries, but from 1976 onwards, as economic performance waned, the contrast between Bolivia and its neighbours lost its power to impress.

1978–89

In November 1977, when President Banzer embarked on a process of electoral transition, he had no sense of possible defeat. This was one more improvisation, no more dangerous than many of his successful earlier moves. Popular demands for change had certainly mounted, and the international setting had also changed in ways that required adaptation, particularly as a result of Jimmy Carter's victory in the U.S. elections. The decisive impetus for change probably came from Banzer's soundings of opinion within the leading army garrisons, the only real form of political consultation allowed at that time. The ostensible focus of concern was Bolivia's claim to an outlet to the Pacific. Banzer had for a while benefited from this issue when he re-established diplomatic relations with Santiago and opened negotiations with Pinochet for a territorial exchange, but the Chileans had manoeuvred skilfully, trying to shift the blame onto Peru for any failure to resolve the question before the hundredth anniversary of the War of the Pacific (1979). With this symbolic deadline approaching and no prospect of demonstrable gains from his policy, Banzer seemed somewhat vulnerable before his military and civilian critics. A democratic opening that could be arranged on Banzer's own terms would deprive these dissidents of the excuse to conspire and might enable the government to deflect possible disappointment over the Pacific Coast issue from the executive to an array of squabbling and ineffective political parties.

A calculation such as this seemed plausible enough at the time, even to leading strategists of the opposition. With the Military–Peasant Pact still in operation and the Ministry of Labour more or less in control of organized labour, only the Church and the incipient human rights movement (neither of which seemed very formidable opponents) retained a capacity for autonomous organization. It appeared that Banzer could conduct an election on very favourable terms and might well succeed in prolonging his personal ascendancy by 'constitutionalizing' his rule. This was, after all, the course adopted by General Barrientos in 1966, transforming a junta in which Banzer himself had initially served. The president's confidence in his strategy probably rested on an underestimation of the grievances of the opposition – a misperception rulers often suffer from when they deny their rivals any open means of expression.

The fact that the candidate with the least influence among the military turned out to have been most strengthened by the contest lends some weight to opposition claims for the effectiveness of their resistance work, if not during the dictatorship, then during the run up to the election. Hernán Siles Suazo (president from 1956 to 1960) had, from the outset, opposed the Banzer coup of August 1971. His 1978 election campaign rallied student, worker and peasant support around a coalition that ranged from progressive churchmen to Communist trade unionists, endorsing a platform that was unmistakably anti-militarist. Perhaps the most dynamic element in the coalition was provided by the Movimiento Izquierdista Revolucionario (MIR), which was founded in 1971 and subsequently developed a strong following among students and youth. The MIR claimed the heritage of the 1952 revolution and condemned those older civilian leaders (like Paz Estenssoro) who had compromised with the military in exchange for a fragment of patronage. This party used militant language and provided enthusiastic activists, but its leaders were in practice rather pragmatic and capable of appealing to some significant military and business interests. Another vigorous new force of the Left, Marcelo Quiroga Santa Cruz's Partido Socialista, spoke the same language but with less inclination to compromise.

Despite manifest electoral fraud, Siles officially obtained 24.6 per cent of the vote, registering particular strength in the *altiplano,* especially in La Paz and the mining zones. Paz Estenssoro was credited with 10.8 per cent of the vote, and the official candidate – former Interior Minister General Juan Pereda Asbún – with a suspiciously precise 50 per cent (just the amount needed for outright victory in the first round). The upsurge of support for Siles was largely an expression of the strong hostility towards the dictatorship felt in working-class areas and a consequence of effective organization by the Unión Democrática y Popular (UDP) coalition, both in the urban areas and among the aymará-speaking peasant population around Lake Titicaca. A majority of the electorate were still rural cultivators, most of whom had benefited from the agrarian reform twenty-five years earlier.

Both Paz Estenssoro and Siles Suazo could claim credit for the land distribution of the 1950s. But since the death of General Barrientos there had been no military candidate who could appeal to the peasantry as a benefactor. A younger generation of more highly educated peasant organizers had since emerged and had found that the complex post-reform needs of the rural sector were not being well attended to by the military. Once independent labour unions had been re-established in the cities, the example of autonomous organizations overthrowing government-protected leaders soon spread to the countryside, and the twenty-year-old rift between

worker and peasant organizations began to close. Thus, in 1978 military
control over the rural vote was far more tenuous than it had been in the
previous electoral contest of 1966, and the electoral campaign caused a
crisis for the already discredited Military–Peasant Pact. In short, the 1978
election undermined military discipline, dissolved the Military–Peasant
Pact and created a climate of uncertainty in which radical mobilization
might be rewarded by political success. What began as a 'controlled'
liberalization slipped out of control, as long-repressed social demands
surfaced and the authoritarian regime split into warring factions.

As the election results were announced, denunciations of fraud came
pouring in. The electoral process had been launched to promote national
unity against Chile and to head off complaints by the human rights lobby.
Instead, it had aggravated internal disunity and confirmed some of the
worst fears of the regime's international critics. General Banzer and General Pereda each sought to shift blame for this debacle onto the other.
Pereda called for the annulment of his own election, hoping to try again
with less tainted results. Siles proclaimed himself president-elect. Banzer
declared that, when his term ended on 6 August, power would devolve on
the armed forces, given the absence of a clear electoral mandate. On 21
July 1978, with support from Banzer's traditional stronghold of Santa
Cruz, Pereda seized power, promising new elections within six months.

In the ensuing two-year interregnum, rival civilian factions intensified
their bid for military support, successive generals attempted to hold the
reins of power and two further elections failed to produce a stable constitutional government. The military found itself unable to resolve its internal
problems by once again suppressing civilian political life. Civilian political groups were unable to construct a united front against the military, at
least in part because they lacked an electoral verdict which measured the
true weight of each party against its rivals. A series of precarious interim
governments faced a cascade of social demands that had been pent up
during the dictatorship. These were not only economic demands from the
independent peasant, worker and student organizations, but also political
demands for freedom, justice and the investigation of past crimes and
abuses, pressed by the Church and human rights movement. Businessmen
found this absence of governmental authority inimical to orderly economic
management. The narcotics mafia, already well entrenched during the
Banzer government, stepped up its political and criminal activities and
added to its paramilitary capabilities.

Relatively clean elections were held in July 1979 but produced inconclusive and disputed results. In the presidential contest, Siles officially led Paz, but only by 1,500 votes, with Banzer running a respectable third (Siles 528,700; Paz 527,000; Banzer 218,600). This time the Socialist candidate, Marcelo Quiroga, who had gathered support by denouncing the Banzer regime's crimes, jumped to fourth place with more than 100,000 votes and five deputies, a significant force to the left of Siles's UDP. Since no one candidate had more than 50 per cent of the popular vote, the issue had to pass to the newly elected Congress. But there the idiosyncratic electoral system gave Paz 64 votes to only 46 for Siles, with 73 required for the election of a president. Each of the two front-runners denounced the electoral fraud practised by his rival, but Siles probably had more grounds for complaint. On 16 July 1979 Siles again declared himself president-elect. Congress, however, failed to elect either candidate, and after nine days of humiliating deadlock, the two leading competitors had to compromise, throwing their joint support behind Walter Guevara Arze, the president of the Senate, who was elected for one year pending a fresh poll.

The failure of Bolivia's second presidential election in less than two years to produce a broad-based civilian coalition, or an indisputable victory for one party, left the process of democratization in jeopardy. The Partido Socialista used its representation in Congress to introduce a series of well-documented indictments against the Banzer administration, charging corruption, human rights violations and even treason (the last concerning the negotiations with Chile). In November 1979 the army responded with a coup and the temporary closure of Congress, but in the face of determined popular resistance and U.S. opposition it was forced to retreat to the barracks after sixteen days. It was therefore in a very tense climate that, in July 1980, a third attempt was made to complete the formal democratization process.

The elections of June 1980 resolved the uncertainty over which fragments from the old MNR had retained the greatest popular support during the Banzer dictatorship. Siles, supported by Lechín and the labour Left and in alliance with the MIR, generated more support than Paz, who now unambiguously dissociated himself from any military conspiracy against the emerging democratic regime. Thus, the targets of the August 1971 coup which brought Banzer to power emerged as the victors of the redemocratization process. But to a powerful faction within the armed forces, backed by most of the 'new rich' who had prospered during the Banzer years, this outcome was intolerable.

On 17 July 1980 General Luis García Meza seized power, closed Congress and mounted a campaign of state violence that can best be described as 'Southern Cone' in inspiration. For example, the Socialist leader, Marcelo Quiroga, was brutally murdered. The military had learned from its previous unsuccessful efforts to thwart the democratization process, particularly the short-lived dictatorship of November 1979. This time great violence was needed to break the expectations established by the election and to overcome an aroused resistance. Having waited so long to intervene, and having given their victims the moral support of an election victory, the armed forces had to proceed with unrestrained ferocity. What gave impetus to this assault was not so much fear for the survival of their institution (which, if anything, was threatened more by the proliferation of paramilitary forces than by the Left) or any deep ideological commitment. Rather it was the prospect of illicit enrichment of the officer corps through unrestrained involvement in the narcotics trade.

It may convey something of the flavour of the García Meza regime to note the key role played by Klaus Barbie (the Gestapo's 'butcher of Lyons' during the Second World War).[38] The principle under which García Meza intended to operate was laid down at a meeting in the Ministry of the Interior towards the end of 1980 at which, on the advice of Barbie, the minister (who was related to Roberto Suarez, one of the Big Five drug barons and Barbie's employer) produced a list of the 140 small Santa Cruz dealers who were to be 'suppressed'; none of the Big Five was on the list.[39] In addition to Barbie, García Meza employed Italian neo-Fascists who were responsible for the bombing of Bologna station in October 1980, and he received funds from the Reverend Moon's organization.

The economics of cocaine were spelt out in a December 1980 Bolivian army report:

Even before initiating the campaign of concentration of production, you could collect, without difficulty, around $200 million annually, on the basis of a tax of $2,000 per kilo, which all the exporters were willing to pay, as a single tax. If we

---

[38] Barbie arrived in Bolivia in 1951 and acquired Bolivian nationality (using an assumed name) in 1957. He first rose to public prominence under President Barrientos and was employed as a 'security adviser' after his friend General Banzer seized power in 1971 (teaching the Bolivian military, among other things, the use of electricity in interrogations and the importance of medical supervision if torture is to be conducted efficiently). In 1978 he became security consultant to the cocaine trafficker Roberto Suarez in his rivalry with the Colombian drug mafia. See Magnus Linklater, Isabel Hilton and Neal Ascherson, *The Nazi Legacy: Klaus Barbie and the International Fascist Connection* (New York, 1984), which also traces Barbie's fluctuating relationship with the U.S. military. Barbie was expelled from Bolivia in February 1983 to stand trial in France.

[39] Ibid., p. 289.

can guarantee all the industrial process and the suppression of the intermediaries, without prejudicing the interest of the peasant producers of the leaf, this sum could rise to $600 million annually.[40]

The next twelve months were more damaging to the Bolivian economy, polity and society than any since the Chaco War. In contrast to Banzer's government, the García Meza dictatorship had no attractions for legitimate businessmen, and it soon alienated the support of even those lowland agro-exporters who were cultivating conventional crops. Peasant, worker, student and middle-class opposition was intense and could be contained only by continued resort to violence. The Church and the regional civic committees gained prominence as the main 'tolerated' channels of opposition. Abroad, the regime was viewed as so unsavoury that its strident anti-Communism elicited no response, even from the Reagan administration, and early Argentine support quickly faded. Eventually the armed forces came to realize that they would have to undertake a grudging restoration of civilian rule. To defuse military unrest García Meza promised to stand down on the first anniversary of his coup; when that promise was broken, a new military rebellion forced him to resign. By mid-1981 the Central Bank had run out of dollars, and the government's external credit was exhausted. The departure of García Meza opened the way to a restoration of relations with Washington, but the collapse of public finances and the destruction of public order left the military too weak to resist internal and external pressures for the belated instatement of the government elected in June 1980.

Thus, in October 1982 Hernán Siles returned to the presidency for a second time. Theoretically he was to serve out a four-year term to which he had been elected in 1980, but with a two-year delay so that his government should have ended in 1986. In practice, he presided over a period of political confusion and economic disintegration so severe that he was lucky to complete even a foreshortened three-year term.

The relative economic prosperity of the 1970s was savagely reversed after 1979. In 1980 Bolivia's income per head was already the lowest in Latin America (excluding Haiti). Between 1980 and 1986 per capita income fell by a catastrophic 27 per cent, almost twice as severe a decline as that in the next worst affected republic and four times the fall experienced in Latin America as a whole. The output of the mining sector was almost halved, as was the dollar value of (legally registered) exports. In

---

[40] Quoted in ibid., p. 293.

1985 inflation peaked at well over 10,000 per cent. In short, Bolivia underwent another economic disaster, at least comparable to the impact of the world depression. The multiple causes included a fragile inheritance from the Banzer period; two years of demoralization and insecurity during the attempted return to democracy; twelve months of officially condoned looting under García Meza; the impact of the Latin American debt crisis after 1982; and the disastrous weakness and mismanagement that characterized the second Siles presidency.

In 1982, as in 1956, Siles took office in conditions of great economic difficulty. His fractious coalition lacked a majority in Congress. The tin industry was exhausted and decapitalized, and producer-country attempts to peg the world price were foundering. Natural gas had become Bolivia's leading (legal) export, but it was delivered by pipeline to Argentina, which ran out of hard currency during the South Atlantic conflict. During the preceding two years of military government, ten IMF missions had come and gone without reaching an agreement. The peso had become grossly overvalued, and the fiscal deficit had soared to a record level, without the military making any significant attempt to manage the intensifying economic crisis. Just before Siles re-entered the presidential palace, Mexico ran out of foreign exchange and thus triggered a Latin American– wide debt crisis. Moreover, in 1983 Bolivia's vulnerable agriculture was devastated by the El Niño effect, which brought a disastrous drought to the West and floods to the East.

The Siles government's domestic support came from a loose alliance of democrats and leftists, including the bulk of the labour movement (still headed by Siles's old rival, Lechín), which had suffered repression at the hands of the military and which naturally expected some restitution from a constitutional government. The small PCB held ministerial office, alarming some external elements. The labour movement demanded co-management of the (mostly bankrupt) state mines, and the peasant unions followed suit with demands for a decisive voice in the management of public agencies in the rural areas. These demands were backed up with strikes and the blockade of roads supplying the cities – forms of pressure based on the (realistic) assumption that Siles either would not or could not use the police or the military to reimpose order. Towards the end of his government, the COB called two major general strikes aimed at his ouster. Even so Siles repeatedly attempted economic stabilization (there were six attempts between November 1982 and August 1985, all of which failed), but he succeeded only in antagonizing all of the heterogeneous forces that had temporarily rallied to his banner. There were seven ministers of finance and seven Central Bank presidents in a period of thirty-three months. Among the measures most bitterly resented were the compulsory conversion of dollar bank deposits into the wildly depreciating national currency (which earned the undying hostility of the urban middle class and the financial sector); the purchase of foodstuffs at absurdly low prices from rural producers (effectively requisitioning wage goods for the labour movement but fatally alienating sections of the peasantry in the process); and repeated capitulations to organized groups, which had the effect of discriminating against the self-employed and the vast 'informal' sector of the urban economy. Almost the entire politically active population suffered from the government's inability to restrain inflation, which accelerated from an annual rate of more than 100 per cent in 1982 to more than 1,000 per cent in 1984 and more than 10,000 per cent in 1985. Bolivia's foreign creditors were hit by a mid-1984 decision (made under pressure from the COB) to halt debt service payments, and the ensuing retaliation further crippled the economy. Only the dollar-based cocaine economy continued to function more or less normally. Inevitably the military took advantage of the Siles government's desperate disarray.

It was former President Banzer who crystallized the demand that Siles relinquish office a year early, if he was not to be forcibly unseated. In mid-1984 Banzer demanded the president's resignation on the grounds that Bolivia's non-payment of interest on the external debt was a violation of international treaties and might provoke an economic blockade. Shortly thereafter Siles was briefly kidnapped by a unit of the military, an event which underlined the fragility of his position and reduced the morale of his supporters. With the economy beyond his control and with his two main rivals, Banzer and Paz Estenssoro, converging against him, Siles chose to accept a Church-inspired proposal to bring the next elections forward a year (to June 1985).

In the 1980 election the coalition backing Siles had received 34 per cent of the vote, compared with less than 18 per cent for Paz Estenssoro and less than 15 per cent for Banzer. In 1985 it was only the outgoing vice-president, Jaime Paz Zamora, who salvaged any dignity from the wreckage of the Siles government. His party, now campaigning separately as the MIR, received 8.9 per cent of the vote, far behind Banzer (28.6 per cent) or Paz Estenssoro (26.4 per cent). (The various fragments identified with the Siles administration received only 16 per cent among them.) However, the defeated parties still retained enough support in the new Congress to block General Banzer's hope of return to the presidency. This they did by swinging behind Paz Estenssoro, who returned to the presidency for the fourth time, at the age of seventy-seven. Although he needed the votes of the Left to assume office, Paz Estenssoro soon came to terms with his more natural partners of the Right, with whom he shared the spoils of office under a so-called pact for democracy, which broke down only on the eve of the 1989 elections. After the municipal elections of December 1987 a deradicalized MIR emerged as the principal force of the Left, and when the veteran Paz had served out his four-year term, in August 1989 Jaime Paz succeeded in outmanoeuvring the MNR. He captured the presidency (despite coming third with 21 per cent of the popular vote) thanks to a highly constraining alliance with Banzer's party, which secured most of the key cabinet posts.

These political developments were accompanied by considerable economic, social and ideological transformations. When Paz Estenssoro returned to office in August 1985, the roles played by the two founders of the MNR in the 1950s were in effect reversed. The second time round, Siles had played the radical and Paz the conservative. He introduced a draconian policy of economic austerity and liberalization that at least eliminated inflation, albeit at a severe cost in terms of economic activity. However, the progression of economic disasters was not yet over – within two months of his assumption of office the world tin price truly collapsed, and the following year Argentina announced a severe cut-back in its purchase of Bolivia's other substantial legitimate export, natural gas. (Bolivia had ceased to be a significant oil exporter in the late 1970s.) The only option for the future seemed to be to diversify into non-traditional exports – a herculean task given Bolivia's location and endowments and the region-wide effects of the debt crisis.

Even before the halving of the tin price (which guaranteed the elimination of COMIBOL as a major mining enterprise, with two-thirds of its remaining work-force laid off and a huge exodus from the main mining camps), President Paz Estenssoro had enacted a stabilization decree of great ruthlessness and audacity. Neighbouring republics such as Argentina, Brazil and Peru were in the process of introducing so-called heterodox stabilization plans, but the Bolivian approach was rigorously orthodox. At the time this may have seemed an atavistic strategy, but four years later price-stable Bolivia was singled out for praise by U.S. Secretary of State Baker, while the other three experienced four- or five-digit inflation. Among the distinguishing features of the August 1985 programme was the enforcement of strict fiscal discipline, the sweeping scope of the market liberalization provisions, the pegging of the exchange rate at a generally realistic level with free convertibility and an infusion of foreign exchange. Significant assistance was provided by external creditors. (Bolivia was allowed to 'buy in' much of its external debt at 11 per cent of face value.) Monetary policy was kept quite tight, and although the economy was stabilized it was at a very low level, with little apparent scope for reactivation.

It would be a mistake to assume that the success of the last Paz Estenssoro government was due entirely to its popularity with the privileged Right. In particular the views of the peasant majority should be taken into consideration. Since inflation had signified serious losses and disruption, the return of price stability and market freedom was a considerable relief to rural producers as well as to many in the urban 'informed sector'.

One highly significant development was the departure from the political scene of the three most prominent figures identified with the 1952 revolution. In 1985 Siles left the presidency with more dignity than had his father in 1930, but with no greater residue of political influence. In July 1987 the Seventh Congress of the COB (now a shadow of its former self) dismissed Juan Lechín from the executive secretaryship that he had held continuously for thirty-five years. In August 1989 Paz Estenssoro passed the presidency to his constitutionally selected successor (a distant relative and perhaps an imitator, but in any case of a very different generation and the leader of a rival party). Paz Estenssoro had served a total of three complete and one incomplete presidential terms, making him the most durable political leader since the creation of Bolivia. It will be for history to judge whether his final term (if it should prove to be his final term – he was eighty-two in 1989) was his finest hour or his greatest betrayal.

The 1985–9 government challenged many previous conceptions about Bolivian politics and society. The initial verdict of many external observers was that in a most unpromising context it was remarkably successful in entrenching economic liberalism and political democracy. The paradoxes were startling: the scourge of the tin barons dismantled the state mining enterprise Paz Estenssoro himself had created and reinstated the private mining houses at the economic helm; the nationalist author of South America's most sweeping land reform invited U.S. forces to suppress production of the only crop that was really profitable for small holders; the

alleged Nazi (or *peronista,* or even Nazi–Communist) had consolidated
Bolivia's democratic institutions and presided over a peaceful transfer of
power to his elected opponents; the most extravagant practitioner of populism and deficit finance implemented the most instantly successful anti-
inflation policy in post-debt crisis Latin America. What appeared to unify
these paradoxes was the recognition that by the early 1980s previous
formulae for tackling Bolivia's problems were manifestly bankrupt. The
catastrophic failures of both the García Meza and the Siles administrations
left room for few illusions. The disarticulation of all alternatives opened
the way for a new neo-liberal beginning. Paz Estenssoro had the prestige,
the experience and the will to push through this course, just as in earlier
periods he had maximized the possibilities inherent in some very different
strategies of government.

CONCLUSION

In 1930 the Bolivian economy was essentially structured around the production of tin-ore for delivery to the world market. No major new tin
mines were developed after 1930, and those then in operation steadily
depreciated until finally, when the world price of tin collapsed at the end
of 1985, the traditional tin mining economy of highland Bolivia suffered a
spectacular contraction from which it seems unlikely to recover. Several
other economic activities rose to prominence, although none of them
displayed the strength and durability that would be required to replace tin
permanently as a major export. Cotton, sugar, oil, gas and finally cocaine
all flourished for brief periods, but none of these could be regarded as a
reliable basis for national reconstruction. The crisis of the early 1930s that
resurfaced in the 1950s and then reappeared in an acute form in the mid-
1980s revolved around the possible disappearance of the central economic
activity upon which the Bolivian state had been constructed. If no coherent alternative could be found, the survival of Bolivia as a viable nation
would be in doubt. The major political and economic initiatives taken by
Bolivian governments over the past half-century must all be interpreted in
this light. In many respects Bolivia made impressive progress towards
economic modernization. The population was redistributed in a way that
greatly improved the pattern of territorial occupation; communications
were transformed; the human and physical capital of the nation was radically upgraded. Nevertheless, Bolivia needed to find a secure and rewarding niche in the international division of labour. In 1989 the best estimate

was that the economy was receiving an annual inflow of about U.S. $200 million from illegal exports of cocaine compared with some $600 million from all legal exports.

The political narrative presented in this chapter has inevitably followed the trajectories of a small number of individuals and of a few strategic sectoral groups. Intermittently, at critical junctures, much broader and more diffuse social groups have entered the stage (e.g., the peasantry at the time of the land reform), but no systematic treatment of their evolution has been attempted, and the changing texture of relations between 'elites' and 'masses' has been left beyond the scope of the analysis. The hierarchical structures in place in 1930 were extremely rigid and constraining. The overwhelming majority of the population were rural cultivators, lacking literacy or even much command of spoken Spanish. Their geographical horizons were extremely limited, they were stigmatized by the dominant elites as racially inferior and if they travelled to the urban centres they encountered various forms of ritual humiliation (segregated seating in buses and cinemas, etc.) that underscored their hereditary subordination. Hesitantly during the Chaco War and in the mid-1940s, and then more dramatically after 1952, these rigid barriers were dismantled. Although there was a steady retrogression in terms of national politics from the mid-1950s, at a more subterranean level there was a steady rise in the self-confidence, organizational capacities and in socially recognized entitlement to respect of large sectors of the 'popular classes'. The texture and quality of elite—mass relations was consequently modified by effects that were cumulatively quite profound.

Finally, what balance sheet can be drawn up concerning the underlying process of 'nation-building' in Bolivia from the 1930s to the 1980s? Boundary disputes no longer implied much danger of war, but the encroachment of Brazilian nationals onto the unpopulated lands of the Amazon Basin still carried a potential for territorial dismemberment. Ideological polarization within Bolivia had repeatedly invited external intervention in its internal affairs (e.g., in 1946, 1956, 1967 and 1971), and the potential for future episodes remained considerable. Indeed, in 1967 an international guerrilla force selected Bolivia as the 'weakest link' in the Pentagon's South American line of defence, and in 1971 it was still not unreasonable to fear that Bolivia might be partitioned between its stronger neighbours. The absence of a profitable 'leading sector' of the *legitimate* economy opened the way in the early 1980s to the capture of state power by representatives of the drug mafia, with all the risks that that implied for the national reputation and therefore the security of the republic. In 1986 President Paz gave U.S. drug enforcement officials virtually a free hand to conduct quasi-military operations in certain isolated zones. Finally, of course, in common with other Latin American countries, the Bolivian state appeared virtually insolvent in the 1980s (just as it had been in 1932).

On the other side of the account there were many less visible, but perhaps in the long run more decisive processes at work. Education provides a good example. Only 52,000 children were receiving primary education in Bolivia in 1910, and even in 1952 the total had risen to only 131,000. By 1981, however, 45,000 primary school teachers were responsible for the education of more than 1 million children. On the eve of the national revolution, a brief primary education was generally available only in the urban centres, and even in the main cities one-third of those eligible did not receive it. ('Indian' children were particularly neglected.) By 1981 86 per cent of *all* children between six and thirteen years of age were receiving primary education, and 34 per cent of *all* those aged fourteen to seventeen received secondary education. Inevitably the sense of national community was immensely strengthened by this transformation, and the official Spanish language and rational-legal culture had achieved an irreversible advance. Thus, the next generation of Bolivians will be far better equipped to exercise their rights and carry out their duties as citizens of a modern nation than were their parents, let alone their grandparents.

Almost equally significant was the emergence of a comprehensive system of national transportation and communications. In 1929 virtually the only modern facilities available were the railways and telephone network, both serving a very geographically and socially restricted minority. (There were only 6 commercial aeroplanes in Bolivia in 1929, together with 54 buses, 980 trucks, 1,150 cars and 2,652 telephones.) By 1982 there were several million radios, 400,000 televisions, 160,000 telephones and 70,000 private cars, together with an extensive system of road and air transport. Thus, Bolivia had been transformed from a series of isolated parochial communities with very limited mobility and exchange of information (there were even customs posts at the boundaries between departments) into a national society with a comprehensive and relatively efficient communications system and with considerable ease of internal mobility. Further examples could be given in such areas as electoral registration, military service and the extension of modern property rights. Obviously in all these areas of 'national integration' and 'modernization' there remained huge deficiencies, and the process of advance had been extremely conflict-ridden and uneven. Nevertheless, very powerful processes had been at work during the half-century since 1930. They seemed most likely to continue, and their cumulative effect was to provide the social and material base for the emergence of a modern nation-state and possibly even for a more or less conventional liberal democracy (if such can really be consolidated in conditions of acute scarcity and inequality).

The process of nation-building since 1930 (more particularly since 1950) has, however, been extremely painful, and subject to deviations and setbacks. In order to contain and manage all these strains, harsh forms of social discipline were periodically imposed, and an authoritarian and bureaucratic state system extended its suzerainty. Intermittent periods of relative liberty proved short-lived and chaotic.[41] A fundamental issue of contention in Bolivian society therefore persisted. Which classes, regions, parties or ethnic groups were to be the main beneficiaries of national construction, and which interests had to be sacrificed in the process? For many elements of Bolivian society, probably for a majority of the people, the answers to these questions were distinctly discouraging. Consequently, it remained a formidable task to enlist the co-operation and social support necessary for the rational management of a process that (managed or not) still displayed tremendous forward momentum.

[41] For a more analytical elaboration of this view, see Laurence Whitehead, 'The State and Sectional Interests: The Bolivian Case', *European Journal of Political Research*, 3, no. 2 (1975), pp. 115–46, and Jean-Pierre Lavaud, 'La inestabilidad política de Bolivia' (1975–82) in J. P. Deler and Y. Saint-Geours (eds.), *Estados y naciones en los Andes*, vol. 2 (Lima, 1986).

Part Four

COLOMBIA, ECUADOR AND
VENEZUELA

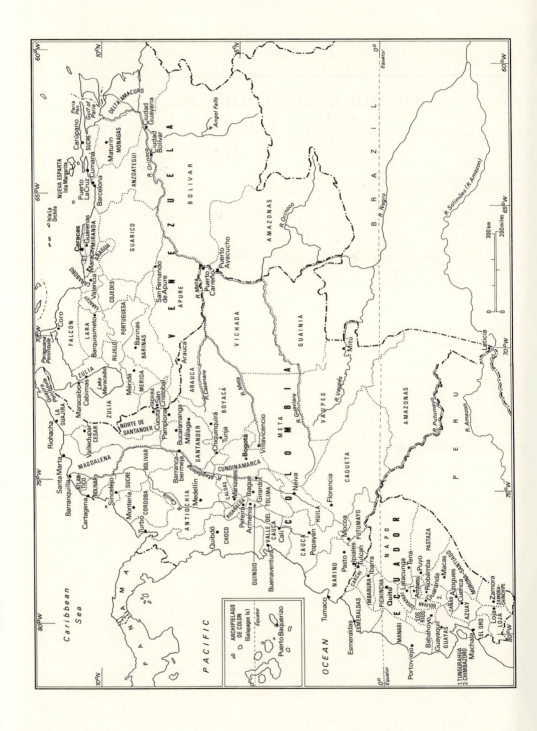

10

COLOMBIA, 1930–58

The consolidation of Colombia as a nation-state has faced a major obstacle in the country's geography, the main topographical feature of which is the Andean mountain range. The central Cordillera of the Andes is separated from the western Cordillera by the Río Magdalena and the Río Cauca. The Pacific coastal plain that extends from Panama to the Ecuadorian frontier is covered by dense jungle, which has prevented the completion of the Pan-American Highway connection between Panama and Colombia. (In contrast, the Caribbean littoral to the north is more open and climatically better favoured.) The eastern plains – the Llanos Orientales – stretch from the foot of the eastern Cordillera south and east to the frontiers with Venezuela, Brazil, Peru and Ecuador. This fragmented landscape contains a wide diversity of altitude and relief, and since temperature depends on altitude rather than season, Colombia is, by convention, divided into 'hot country' (below 3,500 feet above sea-level), 'temperate country' (between 3,500 and 6,500 feet) and 'cold country' (above 6,500 feet).

The obstacles to economic development caused by poor communications can hardly be overestimated. Engineering difficulties and the high cost of construction and maintenance caused by the mountainous terrain impeded the establishment of more than a limited railway network before 1930. Indeed, Bogotá and Medellín had no direct rail connection with the Caribbean coast till the late 1950s. Thus, navigation along the Magdalena remained vital to the country's prosperity. (President Mariano Ospina Pérez in the late 1940s included the level of the Magdalena waters among the daily information that he required.) The completion of the Pacific Railway to the port of Buenaventura in 1914 was welcomed by western interests as an alternative to the Magdalena, but the new port proved insalubrious, congested and disorganized. A transport plan in 1931 envisaged an ambitious transition from export-oriented railway-building to a highway system linking domestic markets. However, its aims were realized only in the 1950s when World Bank financing became available. The difficulties caused by such an antiquated river and rail transportation system were reduced to a degree by the advent of aviation. By 1932 the German airline SCADTA, founded in 1920, operated a service that covered 3,410 miles and made unnecessary both the two-week overland journey from Bogotá to the southernmost departmental capital, Pasto, and the arduous route (including mule-trail) which connected Bogotá and Cúcuta, the capital of Norte de Santander.

For reasons of climate, transport facilities and relative freedom from disease, the Colombian population was heavily concentrated in the Andean region and on the Caribbean coast. The total population, 7.9 million in 1928 according to an unreliable census, grew to 8.4 million in 1938 and 11.6 million in 1951. It was predominantly a population of *mestizos* (persons of mixed race). Indians probably represented less than 2 per cent of the total population in the early 1940s. The surviving unassimilated Indian tribes were located beyond the influence of the state in vast, thinly populated and peripheral areas, designated mission territories by successive concordats with the Vatican, where the tasks of administration, justice and welfare were entrusted to religious orders. Some Indian tribes, like the Motilones of the Goajira region, put up a tenacious resistance to incorporation within a broader culture. Most descendants of black slaves had been absorbed within a broader society and were subject to continuous racial intermixture. In distant locations like the south-western coast, small black settlements survived, carrying on a small trade with the larger Pacific ports and sometimes upriver with Indian tribes in Chocó. European immigrants were usually deterred by Colombia's climate, terrain and poverty. Some 2,300 Spanish republican refugees (perhaps an underestimate) settled in the country in the late 1930s; however, their contribution to the professions and business was disproportionate to their numbers.

It was also a predominantly rural population. The process of urbanization in Colombia was slow until the late 1940s; in 1951, still only 25 per cent of the population lived in towns of more than 10,000 inhabitants (compared with 15 per cent in 1938). The spatial distribution of the urban population was more balanced than in most Latin American countries. Four cities presided over well-defined regional economies: the capital, Bogotá in the Centre-east, Medellín in Antioquia, Cali in Valle del Cauca and Barranquilla on the Caribbean coast. The populations of the four main cities were, according to the censuses of 1938 and 1964, as follows:

	Population (in thousands)	
City	1938	1964
Bogotá	330	1,697
Medellín	168	777
Barranquilla	152	521
Cali	102	813

In an overwhelmingly agricultural economy the coffee sector was dominant. Colombia in 1930 was the world's second coffee producer and the first producer of high-quality 'milds', which consumers distinguished easily from the Brazilian product. Exports had risen steadily from 1 million 60-kilo bags of coffee in 1913 to approximately 3 million in 1930. Despite the world depression and low prices, they continued to rise – to 4 million bags sold in 1937, 5 million in 1943 and more than 6 million in the record harvest of 1953. Colombian entrepreneurs broke into the international market by establishing a network of commission houses, the activities of which were complemented from 1927 by the Federación Nacional de Cafeteros (Fedecafé), which established a more vigorous presence in coffee-producing zones than did the state. Fedecafé fostered export production through campaigns to ensure product quality, improve warehousing and raise the quality of working conditions and agrarian education in coffee-producing localities.

A shift in the main locus of coffee production before 1930 from Cundinamarca and the Santanderes to Antioquia, Caldas and the Quindío region underlined the persistence and competitiveness of peasant production. However, conflicts between rural workers, sharecroppers, tenants and smallholders inhibited effective collective action against large landowners and merchants. Revisionist historiography has challenged the myth of the democratic frontier in the Greater Antioqueño region. Far from promoting an egalitarian society in which the rural poor were converted into small coffee farmers enjoying access to land and a modest prosperity, the prevailing pattern of frontier expansion in the first half of the twentieth century allowed regional elites to raise property values and seize control of coffee processing and marketing.

The intermediate slopes of the Andes, the core region of the economy, yielded cash crops in addition to coffee – maize, beans, yucca, sisal, plantains and citrus fruits. The 'cold country' above produced wheat, barley, potatoes, maize, apples and beans. And the 'hot country' below was suited to rice, cotton, sugar-cane, sesame, cacao, maize, bananas, tobacco and tropical fruits. No other crop, however, challenged the primacy of coffee. And Colombian agriculture remained characterized by underutilization of suitable lands, high levels of land concentration in the most fertile valleys and plains, technological backwardness and low levels of productivity.

In 1930 Colombia was already the fourth most industrialized country in Latin America. Coffee profits were redeployed into incipient industrialization, transport and urban construction, especially in Medellín, from where small quantities of low-quality manufactured goods were distributed to a market of small farmers and urban consumers. Increasingly, the manufacturing ascendancy of Medellín was challenged by Bogotá and, in the 1950s, by Cali. The manufacturing share of gross domestic product (GDP) rose from 7 per cent in 1925 to 14 per cent in 1950. A process of import substitution was evident in a fall in the share of non-durable consumer goods in imports, from 30 per cent in 1930 to 9 per cent in 1940 and then to 3 per cent in 1950. Nonetheless, between 1930 and 1950 industrial development displayed markedly antiquated features: low productivity, small work units and a simple technology. Modern factories were very few, and most manufacturing units consisted of family workshops employing a high proportion of women.

Yet the country possessed considerable mineral and energy resources. Gold, silver, emeralds and platinum were all important. Colombia was also an oil producer, and sometimes self-sufficient. And although they were barely explored in the 1930s, the country possessed large reserves of coal and appreciable potential for hydroelectric power. In fact, Colombia enjoyed the best diversified resource base in Spanish South America; the problem was not lack of resources, but mobilizing abundance.

The 1920s had witnessed the gradual incorporation of Colombia into the commercial, financial and diplomatic orbit of the United States. By 1932 the volume of Colombian trade with the United States was the second largest in South America. Whereas British investment had declined from U.S. $55 million in 1923 to $42 million in 1930, the United States in 1930 held Colombian government bonds worth more than $170 million, and $130 million was directly invested, especially in oil, public utilities and bananas. Economic nationalism was occasionally displayed towards the oil and banana industries, where U.S. investment was greatest. Nationalism over oil was first manifest in 1927 through debate about diversifying sources of foreign investment and proposals to introduce a profit-sharing bill, so that Tropical Oil, based at Barrancabermeja, would not enjoy a monopoly of production and refining. The position in the banana industry was distinct. After the brutal suppression in 1928 of a strike by banana workers on the United Fruit estates near Santa Marta, the banana sector had entered a crisis. Demand was hit by European protection of colonial produce, and supply by crop failures and labour disputes. United Fruit clashed with independent growers over prices, purchases and access to water transport. Xenophobia was, however, unsustained because foreign penetration had been short in duration and shallow in impact in most regions. Henceforth, the language of economic nationalism was used pragmatically to secure the best advantage from incorporation within the international economic system, not in order to withdraw from it.

Revenue from external trade and the funds obtained from the Panama indemnity, part of which served to found the Central Bank along the lines of the Federal Reserve Bank, had combined in the 1920s to invigorate an inefficient and often corrupt state. A small constituency for centralization evolved in Bogotá, but insufficient resources were available to consolidate a central state along Mexican lines, or even to enable it to intervene extensively in regional politics. In the absence of clear urban primacy, decentralizing pressures remained strong and regional government enjoyed much discretion in issues of external borrowing, public order and public works. Meanwhile, regionalism flourished upon memories of arbitrariness and mismanagement at the centre. A small and ill-equipped army with low per capita spending had little influence, and the national police force was only embryonic. Moreover, Bogotá and the surrounding department of Cundinamarca could never dominate Colombian politics as Buenos Aires, city and province, dominated Argentina because they never represented an electoral majority. Nevertheless, the national elite did absorb fragments of regional elites in the 1920s as transport improvements gradually eroded barriers to forming a national market. The predominance of an axis of Bogotá with Antioquia and Caldas became assured, as sectoral and regional interest groups began to overlap, Fedecafé being the first and most pronounced manifestation of this process.

Colombian politics have conventionally been described as oligarchic. There was a consensus within the oligarchy in favour of civilian rule, semi-representative democracy and some limited opportunities for entry by talented members of the middle class into the small circle that negotiated major decisions. In 1930 the two main political parties remained the Conservatives and the Liberals. The tenacity of the two parties was due mainly to their ideological eclecticism and capacity to draw supporters from all regions and classes. Both parties legitimized themselves by reference to heroic episodes of the nineteenth century, the Conservatives invoking the 1886 constitution as a guarantee of prosperity and stability, the Liberals recalling radical experiments in the 1860s and 1870s as episodes of creativity and vitality. The nation-wide operation of both parties was assured by a permanent national and regional press and elaborate networks of party organization. The only other party in 1930 to establish an enduring existence was the small Communist Party, which had emerged out of the agitation of the 1920s. As a result of the prevalence of the smallholder in rural society, limited urban growth and the absence of mass European immigration, the political challenge to the Colombian oligarchy from below was relatively weak.

DEPRESSION AND COALITION, 1930 – 4

Before the economic crisis of the early 1930s Colombia had undergone two decades of export-led growth. Between 1925 and 1929 the growth of exports was particularly impressive; the volume of coffee exports grew 10 per cent annually between 1915–18 and 1930–3. The world depression put an end to this boom, dubbed by the future Liberal president, Alfonso López Pumarejo, the 'dance of the millions'.

The growth of the 1920s had been double-edged. While it stabilized the political system, it destabilized the Conservative Party, which had been in power for half a century, by promoting factionalism, since increased government revenues were insufficient to meet the demands of all Conservative aspirants to power and patronage. President Miguel Abadía Méndez (1926–30), ineffectual in reconciling Conservative factions, also failed to confront a war minister who used isolated incidents of revolutionary agitation and incipient trade union militancy to fabricate a revolutionary scare. Tough repressive legislation, echoing that which preceded the War of the Thousand Days (1899–1902), awakened fears of civil war or a military coup that would usher in a dictatorship like that of Juan Vicente Gómez in Venezuela. The brutal treatment of striking oil and banana workers gave rise to congressional protest and multi-class demonstrations that immobilized an already discredited government. Bitter internal strife, intensified by state corruption, culminated in a succession struggle between two Conservative factions and candidates in the 1930 presidential election campaign.

A new generation of Liberals, too young to have fought in the civil wars at the turn of the century, seized the opportunity provided by Conservative division and demoralization and the economic crisis to weld together a broad-based alliance. Veterans of the War of the Thousand Days and the 1922 election defeat, businessmen excluded from Conservative patronage, progressives from the younger generation, some independent peasants, artisans and urban workers joined in support of the uncontroversial candidacy of Enrique Olaya Herrera on a bipartisan Concentración Nacional ticket. With a programme characterized by an optimistic vision of Colombia's future as an industrializing nation with a work-force benefiting from improvements in public education and hygiene, but a lack of specific policy commitments, Olaya defeated both Conservative candidates. Some Conservative propertied interests, especially in Medellín, then rallied to Olaya in order to restore unity within the ruling class, ensure the continuation of warm relations with Washington and forestall any predatory coup following cuts in military allocations.

Olaya placated the Conservatives, who held a majority in Congress, with a coalition in which they received both ministries and departmental governorships. The president ordered that the secretary of government in each department belong to a party different from that of the governor, that every mayor belong to the majority party of his municipality and that departmental police chiefs be professionals without local roots who came from the national police or army. At the same time, Olaya was careful not to antagonize the metropolitan Church, which, discredited by ill-judged interference in the 1930 presidential campaign, temporarily withdrew from active political participation. This policy smoothed the transition from Conservative to Liberal rule in Bogotá, despite the potential for organized unrest represented by unemployed bureaucrats and artisans protesting against *el gobierno de hambre*.

Elsewhere conflict was fierce. In the *costeño* department of Bolívar, for example, the Conservatives used old registration lists in the mid-term elections of 1931 so effectively to disenfranchise their opponents that local Liberals concluded that it was useless for central government even to mediate. In coffee-producing departments where small properties predominated – Antioquia and Caldas – coffee producers were cushioned from the worst effects of the depression by cultivating subsistence crops, but in the cities of Medellín and Manizales there were not only fierce contests between the parties for public sector jobs (especially on the railways) but also riots and strikes. In the Santanderes and western Boyacá, poorer departments whose main characteristic was agrarian self-sufficiency, family and municipal feuds between Liberals and Conservatives that had been frozen after the presidential election of 1922 were revived in 1930–1, and fraud and violence, exacerbated by police partisanship, were used by both parties in order to secure advantage in the mid-term elections.

Elsewhere in the countryside the 1931–2 crisis produced land invasions and repossessions in the most commercialized agricultural areas – the coffee zones of Sumapaz, Quindío, Huila and northern Valle; the Sinú cattle-ranching area; and the banana zone near Santa Marta. In the coffee-producing regions where large landownership predominated – Tolima and western Cundinamarca – three political groups sought to channel rural grievances: *Unirismo* (from UNIR, Unión Nacional de la Izquierda Revolucionaria), a protest movement led by the radical lawyer Jorge Eliécer Gaitán, had imprecise if ambitious welfare aspirations that included minimum-wage legislation and the right to a pension after twenty years of work; the Communist Party encouraged the formation of self-defence groups that would confront landlords; and a National Agrarian Party was set up, but it never acquired momentum.

The government was under growing pressure to intervene in the countryside, where the consequences of the world depression were compounded by a loss of confidence in the security of property that caused a fall in land values and rural investment. This in turn threatened both production levels and the stability of banks to which estates were mortgaged. Olaya responded by expanding ministerial powers of judicial review and arbitration and by undertaking a policy of parcellization aimed at reassuring banks, landlords and squatters. Peasant militancy was blunted as squatters and rural labourers obtained small properties through parcellization, direct purchase from landlords and government-sponsored colonization. Land judges were responsible for the purchase of estates for subdivision among eleven thousand peasants, mainly in western Cundinamarca and eastern Tolima.

Olaya also made concessions to urban labour. Holding President Abadía responsible for labour unrest in the late 1920s because he had abdicated the role of arbitrator, Olaya recognized unions, introduced the right to strike and strengthened the Labour Office founded in 1924. Nonetheless, from late 1933 there was a wave of strikes in the public sector – among port workers in Barranquilla, river workers on the Magdalena and workers on the Pacific, North-East and Antioquia railways – and in 1934 strike activity spread to the private sector – to the Germania brewery and Fenicia glass-works in Bogotá.

Olaya's cautious strategy for economic recovery aimed to create the conditions in which a new injection of U.S. capital would be possible and would, in conjunction with some domestic capital redeployed to areas of import substitution, bring about renewed growth. From the onset the president was determined to dispel fears of any renewal of the uncontrolled borrowing and wasteful spending of the 1920s by stopping all central funding to departmental public works projects and imposing central responsibility for dealings with foreign companies. Distancing himself from the economic nationalists, Olaya argued that the nationalist oil projects of the late 1920s were impracticable during the depression, when alternative sources of foreign investment did not exist, oil wealth helped support a relatively strong exchange position and coffee prices were unstable. The government hastily introduced legislation granting advantageous conditions to the oil companies in the hope – unfulfilled as it turned out – that they would use their influence with the U.S. banks to extend new credits. In the period from August 1930 to September 1931, an orthodox and monetarist vision prevailed. This was manifest in a set of administrative and economic devices recommended by the second Kemmerer mission of 1931 to reduce aggregate demand and restrict government expenditure by abolishing jobs and lowering wages in the public sector. Fiscal measures aimed specifically at protecting certain industries, such as cotton textiles, were adopted. This policy of general contraction had three main features: the maintenance of the gold standard, unqualified adherence to external debt obligations undertaken in the 1920s and the quest for short-term financing both to alleviate pressures on the capital account and to sustain selected public works schemes, all of which tended to aggravate the crisis. Falling land values and deflation created problems for the banking sector and for debtors, and increasing unemployment in areas of suspended public works projects gave rise to social protest. Meanwhile, the Central Bank's reserves fell by 80 per cent between 1929 and 1931, prompting Olaya to change policy. In September 1931 the government accepted the fiscal deficit, created currency to finance job-creating public works, arranged private debts to the apparent disadvantage of the banks, and imposed stricter exchange restrictions to alleviate import pressures and to curtail a black market in 'coffee dollars'. It also decided to suspend capital payments on the external debt and to cover only the interest on some loans. Tariff increases raised duties on such high-volume, low-price imports as textiles, in which both domestic and U.S. producers were briefly challenged by Japanese competition. Meanwhile, a tax reform provided for Colombia's first income tax and progressive gift and inheritance taxes.

In 1932 the orthodox policies were jettisoned. The gold standard was abandoned; a moratorium on the external debt was declared; exchange restrictions on foreign banks and insurance companies were introduced; gold exports were temporarily suspended; the internal debt and budget deficit were increased; and imports of foodstuffs were restricted. Finally, the exchange rate was adjusted to conform to the pressures of the market, producing a real devaluation of 40 per cent in 1933. The effects of this were immediate: external trade was balanced as coffee exports recovered and the volume of imports shrank. Moreover, devaluation, rather than protection, promoted the growth of industry.

Economic recovery was temporarily threatened by a war with Peru (1932–3) that was precipitated by the Peruvian seizure of disputed territory in the Amazon region at Leticia. However, the war proved convenient to Olaya. Civilian political ascendancy was confirmed by the success of the diplomatic settlement reached with League of Nations assistance; and the failure to achieve a military victory against Peru damaged the prestige of the army, exposing its lack of training for warfare in tropical rain forests and enabling Olaya to reduce Conservative influence by enlarging the officer corps. The government raised a 'patriotic loan' that increased both military expenditure and the generation of employment in the South and West, thus relieving social unrest, alleviating the fiscal crisis and easing deflation.

LÓPEZ AND THE *REVOLUCIÓN EN MARCHA*, 1934–8

The Liberals engaged in the calculated use of patronage and coercion in marginal constituencies to win the congressional elections of 1933, carrying all departments except Antioquia, Caldas and Nariño. Buoyed up by its first majority in fifty years, the party leadership forsook coalition politics and launched the partisan candidacy of Alfonso López Pumarejo for the presidency in 1934.

The first major leader too young to have fought in the civil wars, López was a businessman with little formal education but experience in banking, the coffee business, political management and diplomacy. He had built a national reputation with an iconoclastic critique of Conservative economic policies in the late 1920s and his participation in the 1930 election and in the settlement with Peru. López represented the urban groups that had benefited from the prosperity of the 1920s and that, through witnessing the application of outmoded policies at home, had come to admire experiments in confronting the consequences of the depression in other liberal democracies: the New Deal in the United States and the Second Republic in Spain. He also reflected the consolidation of a national upper class that superseded competing regional elites and included a nucleus of politicians well placed in Bogotá to negotiate between regional and sectoral interests.

Proclaiming a *revolución en marcha*, López offered a broad reformist and welfare programme within the framework of a liberal democracy with increased political participation. This was predicated upon the existence of a law-abiding government and a loyal opposition – conditions that had obtained only irregularly over previous decades. The Liberal candidate gambled upon continued growth making a progressive tax reform to finance an enlarged central state palatable to propertied interests. He sought to stem burgeoning class conflict through greater state intervention. His proposed constitutional reform aimed to reassure those fearful of a reversion to the party's nineteenth-century policies of federalism and laissez-faire as well as to meet the demands of party militants who saw the 1886 constitution as the bulwark of Conservatism and a barrier to institutional change.

Educational reform stood at the centre of the Liberal welfare programme. Convinced that a near monopoly of education by the Church was a major factor in economic backwardness, López tried to attract urban voters with promises to expand the system of lay primary schools and to modernize the Universidad Nacional. Some on the liberal Left wanted to apply to the public sector experiments with curriculum and pedagogic methods that in the 1920s had been confined to innovative private sector establishments, like the Gimnasio Moderno and Universidad Libre. It was generally agreed that education should be reclaimed to serve national purposes.

López also proposed to extend the male vote, and by distributing patronage benefits intelligently, he hoped to secure the support of the newly enfranchised. In addition, the Liberals promised agrarian legislation that would redistribute idle lands on large estates to the landless – a policy ostensibly designed to consolidate Liberal support among a new class of independent peasant farmers, to raise agricultural output and productivity and to stabilise food prices for urban consumers.

A disoriented Conservative Party conducting only a routine opposition and unable to compete with the candidate, programme, organization and control of patronage of the Liberals alleged Liberal gerrymandering over constituency boundaries and abstained in the presidential elections rather than face humiliating defeat. López took office and in August 1934 began to implement his audacious programme.

The management of urban labour presented a major challenge. Despite the urban unemployment caused by the depression, rural–urban migration persisted and the populations of the cities grew steadily – that of Bogotá by 4.3 per cent annually between 1918 and 1938, that of Medellín by 3.7 per cent, that of Cali by 4.2 per cent, that of Barranquilla by 4.4 per cent – so that by 1938 artisans numbered 340,000–370,000, factory workers 80,000–100,000 and transport workers 46,000. A greater tolerance of labour organization was accompanied by competition for influence over labour between the radical wing of the Liberal Party, the Communists and *uniristas,* which gradually rechannelled the disarticulated socialist and anarchist agitation of the 1920s. The liberal Left made headway among railway workers, the Communists in the brewing and construction sectors, *unirismo* in the electric energy, textiles and confectionery sectors in Bogotá.

The López government alarmed sections of the propertied classes by not defending them automatically against an upsurge of strikes among transport, construction, brewing and textile workers in 1934–5 and by supporting some demands for better wages and working conditions. López and his minister of government, Alberto Lleras Camargo, were clearly calculating that, first, by strengthening the machinery of arbitration and conciliation, they would enlarge the interventionist power of the central state; second, by arbitration in favour of selected groups of workers, they would consolidate a permanent *lopista* constituency; and third, by financing the congresses and other activities of a new labour confederation, they might preclude the emergence of an autonomous labour movement that would pose a serious challenge to the state and ruling class. A 'labour aristocracy' was, indeed, being wooed; the relative privilege of a minority of articulate and well-organized workers was being ensured. A loose labour confederation was founded, the Confederación Sindical Colombiana (CSC), renamed the Confederación de Trabajadores de Colombia (CTC) in 1938.

The government had no coherent strategy to confront agrarian problems. It improvised with less success, perhaps because its leadership was less familiar with rural problems, perhaps because they were more intransigent or perhaps because the impact of the state was too restricted. The López administration conserved the practices of conciliation applied by Olaya and endorsed the formation of peasant leagues in western Cundinamarca and Tolima; a similar approach was adopted for the sugar-cane plantations of the Valle del Cauca, where rapid proletarianization in the previous decade was accompanied by conflict between employers and labour.

Olayista agrarian policy had already defused most peasant militancy. Now Law 200 of 1936 attempted to guarantee rural production and reassure both large landowners and *colonos*. Although the law left the system of large estates undisturbed, and effectively legitimized the usurpation of public lands over the past century, it protected *colonos* against dispossession. The government expressed a concern to create family farms (and, indeed, enjoyed electoral support from elements of the peasantry), but it took no significant initiative to break up latifundia. Nor did it obstruct the proletarianization of service tenants and sharecroppers. Defining land use rather than distribution as policy priority, Law 200 stipulated that any property not exploited within a decade of enactment would revert to the public domain.

The multi-class appeal of the *revolución en marcha* did not conceal its broadly pro-entrepreneurial thrust. In the second half of the 1930s manufacturing industry grew at a rate that had no precedent and was never to be repeated – 12.6 per cent annually – as a result of the exceptional opportunities opened up by the world crisis. Domestic investment was complemented by some foreign capital taking advantage of conditions of high profitability, high tariffs and low wages. Industrial growth and initiative were not the direct effect of planned policy but the unintended and fortuitous consequences of measures designed to strengthen the balance of payments, restore public finance and revive domestic foodstuffs production. The 1935 tax reform and López's credit legislation have sometimes been misinterpreted as policies specifically aimed at the industrial sector. Erroneous conclusions about the pro-industrialist aims of economic policy should not be derived from the industrialization of the 1930s and 1940s.

The interventionist and populist language of López has convinced many observers that a progressive industrial bourgeoisie that was opposed to the agro-export and import-trade sector rose to power in the 1930s. Such an assertion has no foundation. As soon as the evidence of recovery was unambiguous, the López administration opted for economic liberalization.

Although a committed interventionist in fiscal, agrarian and labour matters, López was more a free trader than a protectionist, as was clear in the
decision to dismantle exchange controls in 1935. New foreign investments were freed from restrictions on profit remittances and from obligations to sell 15 per cent of their shares at the exchange rate, these measures
favouring renewed investment by the oil and banana companies that possessed blocked funds in pesos and previously had no incentive to expand.

The *revolución en marcha* retreated from the pro-U.S. rhetoric that had
hitherto prevailed. Colombia participated enthusiastically in the League of
Nations, and the first López government tried to diversify external links –
the proportion of coffee exports to countries other than the United States
rose from 8 per cent in 1925–9 to 24 per cent in 1935–9. And a lucrative
trade founded on compensation marks was established with Germany
between 1935 and 1938. Yet in other respects, U.S. economic penetration
gained force and breadth. The financing of external commerce was undertaken by U.S. banks. The 1935 commercial treaty yielded advantages to
the United States in new areas of manufacturing exports – chemicals,
metallurgy, motor cars and lorries – in exchange for the entry of duty-free
coffee into the United States. In the same year more than one-half of
Colombian imports came from the United States. The oil industry remained dominated by U.S. firms, and new legislation in 1936 clarified
their position and reactivated investment when conditions in the world
market were propitious. PanAmerican World Airways took control of the
German-owned pioneer SCADTA, and U.S. capital penetrated public
utilities, principally electric energy. The transition from railway construction to road-building favoured U.S. interests, providing opportunities for
engineering contracts, and expanded markets for U.S. motor car and lorry
manufacturers in a country with one of the lowest indices of railway use in
Latin America.

The one point of friction was the banana sector. A heavily publicized
conflict with United Fruit was astutely exploited by López to project his
credentials as an economic nationalist. When the United Fruit subsidiary
Magdalena Fruit sought to evade legislation that restricted the number of
foreigners on payrolls, the government responded by introducing proposals to extend state control over production and marketing and to make
possible expropriation in the public interest. Yet the independent banana
producers derived little benefit, and the dispute was still unresolved in
1939, when it was frozen by the shipping crisis caused by the Second
World War. The campaign of the State Department to mitigate the ad-

verse public image of United Fruit was successful at least in preventing its reputation from damaging other U.S. companies.

The bold legislative programme of the Liberal administration revitalized the opposition. López's constitutional reform project reunited the Conservative Party, which saw it as a tool to perpetuate Liberalism in power, and reanimated senior churchmen, who interpreted the decision to remove the name of God from the preamble to the constitution as a challenge to the privileged status of the Church. Ecclesiastical conflict was intensified by the educational reform, which was seen as a direct challenge to the Church's influence over education. At a local level parish priests and Conservatives united in their condemnation of the appointment of atheists and socialists as teachers and school inspectors, of co-education and the opening of educational opportunities to women and of the publication of allegedly pornographic materials by the education ministry. Both the secular clergy and religious orders overhauled their systems of primary and secondary schools; and confessional universities were opened in both Bogotá and Medellín as a Church response to secular initiatives. Meanwhile tax and agrarian legislation met with stubborn resistance from the propertied interests in both parties; and Law 200 of 1936 was widely misinterpreted as an assault upon property rights.

The Liberal regime's ham-fisted attempt to draw Fedecafé into the system of state patronage was subject to bipartisan criticism from the coffee sector, which was determined to preserve the neutrality of the pressure group and a measure of autonomy from state intervention. Coffee policy as a whole came under attack, especially from the industry's leading figure, Mariano Ospina Pérez. Against government arguments for an agreement with Brazil that fixed prices and restricted sales while markets were uncertain, Ospina contended to the contrary that demand for Colombian 'milds' was expanding and was unrelated to overproduction in Brazil. A price-fixing agreement with Brazil was eventually reached; and Fedecafé made large purchases of surplus coffee, until it exhausted its funds and, in 1937, was compelled to break the agreement.

Still uncertain of the loyalty of the officer corps, the *revolución en marcha* undertook a military reform designed to raise the technical competence of the army in the event of another confrontation with Peru; and it introduced a police reform to assure the government of armed support if the opposition took to violence. The decision, however, to upgrade the national police force, manned from 1933 by loyal Liberals, into a Chilean-style paramilitary force angered army officers, who were still smarting from the revelation in the Leticia War of the shallowness of their supposed professionalism. A coup attempt by a minority of officers with some Conservative connivance was averted in April 1936 by swift government action and conspiratorial bungling, but it did secure some changes in policy.

The Liberal government absorbed a broad range of individualist and collectivist Liberals, radical anticlericals and a few evolutionary socialists. *Unirismo,* after polling fewer than 4,000 votes against the Liberal party's 477,000 in the 1935 congressional elections, was slowly co-opted by the governing party. The Communist Party was divided by the Comintern decision in 1935 to pursue Popular Front alliances with bourgeois democratic parties against Fascism. Arguing for a Popular Front alliance with capitalists because Colombia stood on the threshold of a 'bourgeois-democratic' stage, the Communist leadership put up little opposition to the one condition for a Popular Front imposed upon it by Lleras Camargo – that the Communist unions apply for judicial recognition and repudiate factory occupations. The Liberal Party was clearly the senior partner in the pact. The limits to the political influence of the Communist Party were demonstrated by its candidate's performance in the 1934 presidential elections (barely 1,000 votes) and by the lack of impact of a nationwide strike of coffee workers called during the harvest of August 1934. Though never institutionalized, the Popular Front had a tangible reality that was visible in joint public demonstrations, in government funding of union congresses (Medellín, 1936; Cali, 1938) and in the decision to impose a model of parliamentary democracy upon the CTC, the executive committee of which was to consist of eight Liberals, four Communists, three Socialists, and one narcho-syndicalist.

Discontent amongst certain sectors of business which felt that the government did not instinctively support them against organized labour led to the establishment of Acción Patriótica Económica Nacional (APEN), which demanded government that ruled explicitly in favour of the private sector and a return to non-interventionist liberalism. However, the principal focus of opposition remained the Conservative Party, which was being revived by Laureano Gómez Castro, who was not connected with the electoral disaster of 1930 and had once been a friend of López. An outstanding orator in Congress and public meetings, Gómez depicted the Conservative ascendancy before 1930 as a period of purposeful restraint and order, and accused the Liberal republic of reckless experimentation that recalled the anarchy of the 1860s and 1870s. Upbraiding his Conservative colleagues for their timidity, he founded a new bogotano newspaper, *El Siglo,* to challenge the prestigious Liberal daily, *El Tiempo,* owned by Eduardo Santos. Gómez tried out new techniques of opposition – mass campaigns of signatures and public demonstrations – in order to sustain public interest and to make inroads into the enlarged electorate. He also fostered links with ultra-montane clerics and provincial elites, promoting anxieties that a 'Sovietizing' government was challenging the sanctity of property and widening urban–rural disparities, so that the mainly Liberal cities might enjoy disproportionately the benefits of economic recovery and thus draw labour – and voters – away from a mainly Conservative countryside. Gómez appealed to Catholic sentiment by denouncing the education minister Dario Echandía as a Freemason, and by condemning school inspectors as crusading atheists who were representatives of the Liberal Party and of central government, rather than education specialists. At an international level, the trend towards Liberal collectivism in the *revolución en marcha* was often compared to the Second Republic in Spain and the New Deal; Colombia would end up 'between Mexico and Russia'.

The use of electoral coercion by some Liberal regional *caciques* like Carlos Barrera Uribe in Caldas, allegations of discrepancies in electoral registration, radio censorship and acts of violence against regional Conservative newspapers encouraged the growth of right-wing youth groups that pulled the Conservative Party in an authoritarian direction. Projecting himself as arbiter between authoritarian and democratic factions within the party, Gómez persuaded Conservatives to abstain from the mid-term elections, perhaps hoping that the absence of a congressional opposition would prompt the Liberal Party to fragment. He also preached non-cooperation and passive opposition along the lines of Gandhi.

Confrontation reached a peak in August 1935 during a demonstration of Catholics at the Eucharistic Congress held in Medellín, the focal point of mass religious commitment. Encouraged by the example of the Right in Spain and irked by local anticlerical provocations, the conservative clergy, led by the archbishop coadjutor of Bogotá, Juan Manuel González Arbeláez, resorted to insurrectionary language in nationally broadcast speeches. Intermittent clashes between a dogmatic clericalism and a doctrinaire laicism threatened to erupt into a civil conflict more general and damaging than the Cristero rebellion in Mexico. The government hastily reached out to the more accommodating elements within the metropolitan Church, led by the archbishop primate Ismael Perdomo, who followed Pope Pius XI's policy of making concessions to Liberals in a world where the main challenges to Roman Catholicism were posed by Communism and Nazism. At the same time, upper-class Conservatives, afraid that political instability would threaten economic recovery, resisted clerical cajolery and exerted a restraining influence upon local-level militants. Thus, political conflict was dampened from the Centre.

By 1937 the *revolución en marcha* had lost its reformist impetus. Caught between the pressures of radical activists and the imperative of securing majorities for legislation in a Congress dominated by the propertied interests, the government was fully exercised by problems of day-to-day survival. The balance of power within the Liberal Party shifted from the reformists to the consolidators led, after Olaya's death in 1937, by Eduardo Santos, who reassured an upper class alarmed by the populist techniques of López and Gómez. Santos insisted on a disciplined party machine, stressed the undisputed ascendancy of the private sector and rejected the Popular Front on the grounds that it divided the Liberal Party and shifted its fulcrum leftwards. Forced on to the defensive by a brief plunge in the price of coffee in 1937, the government opted to consolidate the support of entrepreneurs at the expense of its popular base. The drift of employer–labour policy now favoured the employers. Some reforms were abandoned, others did not complete their passage through Congress and APEN, with no reason for continued existence, was dissolved.

In 1938 the policy of economic liberalization was expanded. Foreign companies were now at liberty to remit profits, earnings and interest on funds brought from abroad; and legislation on gold exports and foreign exchange was eased. Some restrictions on importers and exporters were suspended, and the exchange rate was modified to align with swings in the price of coffee, which had fallen by 30 per cent between 1934 and 1935. The tensions between the state and Fedecafé were resolved by a new compromise, with Fedecafé enjoying influence in exchange policy and coffee diplomacy and the state having a larger role in Fedecafé decisions. The permanence of this relationship was ensured by the state's acceptance of the paramountcy of coffee and by continuity of management in Fedecafé – Manuel Mejía was manager from 1937 to 1957, his successor, Arturo Gómez Jaramillo, from 1957 to 1980 – which successfully avoided bureaucratization and political partisanship.

The main impact of the Olaya and López governments lay in persuading parts of the upper class that development could be achieved without authoritarianism. Sections of the upper class became convinced that the peaceful articulation of grievances, the resolution of disputes through bargaining and compromise, and new practices of political and personnel management were more appropriate to Colombian circumstances than was coercion. At the same time, López, an effective and original communicator, set the tone for the more personalized politics of the mid-1930s to the early 1950s, in which commanding civilian caudillos, Liberal and Conservative, competed to woo mass electorates. A minority of Conservatives might hanker back to the period from 1910 to 1930 as one of authentic democratic restraint; but a larger part of the political nation saw the *revolución en marcha* as the years in which their aspirations received expression within government for the first time, even though they were realized only incompletely.

A language of intervention and arbitration now prevailed. Indeed, the first López administration awakened popular expectations of a state that had an obligation to redistribute wealth among and within classes and a capacity to operate as a mechanism for income distribution. The limits to state intervention, however, were only too finite: government, in many respects, was the junior partner of the private sector, where an ideology of economic liberalism prevailed; public sector investment was low by Mexican or Brazilian standards; and local baronies that embarrassed genuine democrats survived intact. The limits to Liberal reformism were well illustrated by problems in the countryside. In the short term, rural stability was uncertain. In 1938–9 tensions between Indians and cattle ranchers in Cauca, Huila and Tolima, for example, were marked. A temporary peace between the encroaching ranchers and the small surviving pockets of Indian resistance was secured only through the de facto acknowledgement of restored *resguardos* in Ortega and parts of Chaparral. In the longer term, Liberal policy sharpened divisions by creating a problem of differential access to productive resources. *Colonos* were aggrieved that they, unlike the cattle ranchers, had little access to new rural credit facilities; the income gap between the more prosperous peasants and rural labourers broadened; and, owing to inheritance legislation, new small farms created in the 1930s were subdivided into unviable minifundios. The marked problems of the 1930s were compounded by a decision in 1944 to modify Law 200 of 1936 so as to suspend its land use provision indefinitely. The conditions for the post-war *violencia* were taking shape.

In important respects the proponents of the *revolución en marcha* miscalculated. They failed to translate democratic language into reality: Conservative machine politics were replaced by Liberal machine politics; qualities of tolerance and mutual respect could not be imposed on regional bosses. The government misjudged the tenacity of inherited attachments in the localities, and it failed to grasp the local consequences of national policy decisions. The attempt to sustain a multi-class coalition foundered as political decisions were renegotiated within a limited circle, which, on regaining the initiative that seemed lost in 1935–6, outmanoeuvred the radical wings of both traditional parties. In consequence, protest from both Left and Right could not be effectively articulated, and resentment at the failure to satisfy expectations aroused in the 1930s survived into the 1940s.

LIBERALISM IN RETREAT, 1938–46

Eduardo Santos epitomized a cautious brand of Liberalism which was so acceptable to the Conservative propertied classes that they did not field a rival candidate in the 1938 presidential election, although the candidacy of Ospina Pérez was briefly canvassed in the western departments. Santos's claim to the leadership of the Liberal regime was based upon his organization of the revival of the party in 1929–30 and faced little opposition. He sought to engineer consent by carefully cultivating links with Liberal *caciques* and identifying with the career aspirations of the urban middle class. A significant effort was made to reform domestic policy, particularly by the energetic finance minister Carlos Lleras Restrepo. The exemplary electoral behaviour of the administration persuaded the Conservatives to participate in the mid-term elections in 1939. However, they failed to stage a significant recovery, because the Conservative propertied classes were both neutralized by *santista* policies and antagonized by Gómez's bid to sharpen the fading distinction between the parties by stirring up an intransigent *godo* response to isolated incidents of police-instigated violence.

The Santos administration's options were immediately narrowed by the onset of the Second World War. State revenues slumped when European markets were closed. The economy now relied heavily on coffee exports to the U.S. market and on a wide range of manufactured imports from the United States; ideological commitment coincided with export sector interests to make the Santos regime the staunchest supporter of the Allies in Latin America.

The Colombian economy in the late 1930s was enjoying a recovery from the effects of the depression underpinned by good management and an expansion of coffee exports. During the war, the growth of GDP fell slightly as a result of agricultural crisis, restrictions on public works spending and contraction of oil production after 1942. At the same time war-induced isolation encouraged measures to ensure the continuity of the import-substitution process. Exchange controls were improved, and various systems – import licences, classification of merchandise, differential exchange rates, allocations of foreign exchange – were applied in order to restrict imports of finished goods. With the creation of the Instituto de Fomento Industrial (IFI) on the initiative of Carlos Lleras in 1940 the state emerged as an industrial investor in those basic and complementary branches of industry unattractive to private investment because of the initial cost, risk and slow maturation of the investment. Moderate inflation rates – 12 per cent per annum between 1940 and 1950 – provided an appropriate environment for industrial capital accumulation. And there was already a tendency towards concentration. According to the 1945 industrial census, of more than 7,000 industrial establishments, 120 large units represented a paid-up capital of approximately U.S. $550 million; 43.6 per cent of total textiles investment was located in two Medellín companies, Coltejer and Fabricato; 77 per cent of tobacco-processing investment in Coltabaco; and 61 per cent of beverage production in the Bavaria brewery in Bogotá.

The loss of reformist momentum and a descent into mere machine politics signalled the end of the Liberal Republic and the beginning of a Conservative revival. As policy options narrowed, political debate became increasingly personalist. The contrast between the open, candid style of López and the introspective personality of Santos helped the former to secure the Liberal presidential candidacy for the 1942 elections. The Conservatives, still a clear minority, gambled upon an alliance with anti-*lopista* Liberals, whose candidate stood on a programme scarcely distinguishable from that of López. In a violent contest, López won. The new cabinet was dominated by businessmen and professionals who had prospered in the recovery from the depression and was so organized that only one significant concession was made to the Liberal rank and file – the appointment of Jorge Eliécer Gaitán, *alcalde* of Bogotá in the first López government and education minister under Santos, as minister of labour.

Once elected, López was again confronted by Gómez. Reviving the techniques of adversarial politics that had obstructed the *revolución en marcha,* Gómez exploited the shrinkage of the Liberal patronage base and waged campaigns in both Congress and the press against corruption in high places. He seized upon proposals for a reform of the concordat with the Vatican to reconstruct his links with the backwoods clergy. Gómez accused the government of betraying the Catholic susceptibilities of the nation and of using wartime conditions to deny Pope Pius XII information about Colombian opinion. At the same time, Gómez adopted a belligerent international stance with the clear objective of attracting businessmen and small producers who gained little from the U.S. connection and resented privileges granted to the export sector. Reviving dormant memories of the loss of Panama, he accused the United States of using the war to deepen its economic penetration of Latin America and argued that an autonomous poverty was preferable to the cultural degradation and materialism of close ties with the 'Anglo-Saxon' powers. An indirect attack on the new practice of joint ventures between U.S. capital and national manufacturers located mainly in Medellín was intended both to discredit López and to anger *antioqueño* Conservative propertied interests, which were hesitant to endorse *laureanista* policies. Gómez alarmed the Liberals and the Allies by forging links with the Spanish legation, giving space to Francoist journalists in his newspaper and taking part in occasional *falangista* rituals.

Gómez also looked for allies in the officer corps. Concerned about the unreadiness of the army in the event of Latin America becoming a theatre of war, the officer corps was angered by López's ill-disguised preference for the police force, his interference in promotions and his threats that the army would be downgraded to a mere adjunct of the police. The officers also felt isolated from Congress, which ten years before had still contained veterans from the War of the Thousand Days who pressed the military case but now had no such representation. These frustrations culminated in an abortive coup in 1944, when López was briefly kidnapped by dissident soldiers at Pasto and Dario Echandía, temporarily assuming the presidency, declared a state of siege. The evidence of the subsequent courts martial uncovered no direct ecclesiastical or civilian participation in the coup attempt, although it did indicate a nation-wide military conspiracy. The abortive coup exposed the sharp division between the propertied Conservatives who rallied to López out of fear of political instability and the *godos,* who contemplated some hazy plan of armed action. Past incitement to violence provided the Liberals with a pretext for detaining Gómez briefly and closing his newspaper for several months.

The insecure Liberal regime was shored up by congressional support. But as war-induced economic problems became more acute, it became clear that the government could relieve popular discontent, urban and rural, only by taxing the very groups on whose support it depended for survival in Congress. Its failures encouraged the growth of opposition on the Left. The Communists, still tolerated while the Soviet Union and United States were co-belligerents, made advances among trade unionists and enjoyed their greatest ever electoral success between 1943 and 1945. But the leading beneficiary was Gaitán, who, after building a following in Bogotá while *alcalde* and among the labour leadership while labour minister, established a personalist movement within the Liberal Party. Calculating that he could make more impact inside the party than outside it, Gaitán wooed those largely urban elements estranged from the *lopista* and *santista* machines who felt that their radical expectations had been defrauded by Liberal governments.

The willingness of the government to use the army and police against strikers antagonized militant trade unionists. However, a drive towards trade union autonomy failed to acquire any impetus as a result of conflict among Liberal factions and between Liberals and Communists and in the face of government patronage and coercion. At the same time, a right-wing segment of the upper class chose to launch an 'anti-Communist crusade, with the support of the Catholic Church; and fragmentation within the CTC encouraged the Church to promote class collaboration through the formation of Catholic trade unions that further intensified competition for working-class support. The strong Catholic unions in the textile factories of Medellín formed a base of a new Catholic union confederation, the Unión de Trabajadores Colombianos (UTC), founded by the Jesuits in 1946 to challenge the CTC. The *gaitanistas* also toyed with the notion of a rival confederation.

The Liberal press in 1944–5 was not above denouncing the Conservative leadership as crypto-fascist. And, indeed, the *laureanista* arguments that Liberal institutions were outmoded and liberal democracy was a fiction gained plausibility. Corporatist ideas attracted groups which saw parliamentarianism as a sham that masked oligarchic preservation of privilege through cynical bargaining practices. Convinced that the political temperature could be reduced only if the Gómez–López feud were removed from the centre of debate, López resigned in August 1945. He was succeeded by acting president Alberto Lleras Camargo, a prominent minister in both López administrations, who reshaped the cabinet to include three Conservative ministers.

Unable to agree on a single candidate for the 1946 presidential elections, the Liberals put up two – Gaitán and Gabriel Turbay – neither of whom carried the endorsement of López, Santos or *El Tiempo*. The Conservatives hedged their bets. Afraid that the Liberals might resort to civil war if Gómez were elected president, the *laureanistas* decided to confuse their opponents by first backing Gaitán and, then, at the eleventh hour supporting the candidacy of Mariano Ospina Pérez on a bipartisan Unión Nacional ticket. The victory of Ospina, acceptable to the upper class of both main parties, convinced many Liberals, who had held power for a decade and a half that Gómez had finally outwitted them.

COALITION, THE *BOGOTAZO* AND THE BEGINNINGS OF THE *VIOLENCIA*, 1946–50

Mariano Ospina initially reassured the business elites by pursuing policies designed to take advantage of the new possibilities arising from the postwar recovery of the international economy. He won business approval with, for example, measures to increase the generation of electric energy, a cautious monetary policy to slow down inflation and the negotiation of lines of special credit from the Export–Import Bank to promote commercial agriculture. And, recalling the economic successes and political stability of the coalition government of another *antioqueño* businessman, President Carlos E. Restrepo (1910–14), Ospina formed a Unión Nacional cabinet containing both Liberals and Conservatives.

The Unión Nacional coalition not only failed to appeal to the urban lower middle and working classes, it did not even satisfy the local militants of the two main parties. Conservative place-seekers, represented by Guillermo León Valencia, demanded a partisan regime, even though Conservative control of the executive did not extend to Congress or to most departmental assemblies. Claiming that only electoral fraud over more than a decade had ensured a Liberal majority in some departments (Boyacá, Norte de Santander and Nariño), partisan Conservatives worked to displace the Liberals in the mid-term elections, a process hastened by the appointment of Conservative policemen and dismissal of their Liberal counterparts in those departments where coercion and enforced non-registration could most easily influence voting patterns. The first phase (1946–8) of what came to be called the *violencia* thus began in the eastern departments of Boyacá and the Santanderes, with political spoils the main issue. Armed conflict was most marked in municipalities where neither party was clearly dominant. This wave of violence was looked upon wearily by the *bogotano* intelligentsia: it confirmed their stereotypes of the eastern departments and was assumed to be merely ephemeral. Once the coalition government was firmly established, and revenge for Liberal violence in the 1930s was complete, Conservative violence would abate.

The predominantly Liberal populace of Bogotá was increasingly estranged from the government. Lacking oratorical flair, Ospina failed to persuade *bogotano* Liberals of his conciliatory intentions. Social policy palliatives – for example, moves towards establishing a social security system and modest proposals to encourage employee shareholding – did not convince Liberals, who saw them as instruments for forging an urban Conservative clientele. Moreover, even these tentative steps were subject to long delays in a Congress dominated by the propertied classes.

In the aftermath of the presidential elections, the leadership of the Liberal Party, which still had a majority in Congress, was captured by Jorge Eliécer Gaitán. Gaitán had been a nationally known figure since 1928, when he led congressional criticism of the banana zone massacre after investigating grievances in the vicinity of Santa Marta for himself. A man of modest *bogotano* origins, Gaitán's political career had been erratic. His dissolution of *unirismo* and re-entry into the mainstream Liberal Party were surrounded by accusations of opportunism, and his term as mayor of Bogotá was cut short by a strike of taxi-drivers accusing him of authoritarianism. Gaitán's period at the Education Ministry came to an abrupt end when his centralist reform proposals were defeated by a coalition of regional interests in Congress. His record at the Ministry of Labour under López was undistinguished.

In 1946–8, Gaitán did, however, capture the popular mood. A commanding figure, he was an effective orator with a strong sense of theatre and spectacle, attractive to some Conservative peasants and members of the middle class as well as the Liberal rank and file. He enjoyed a powerful reputation as a civilian caudillo in Bogotá, the eastern departments and the Caribbean coast. Unlike the Communists, Gaitán spoke in a comprehensible language of reconquering power and reclaiming lost rights. His assertion that hunger was neither Liberal nor Conservative had an incontrovertibly bipartisan appeal. He also attracted much female political support, although women's suffrage was not introduced until 1957. In his *viernes culturales,* transmitted nationally by radio, Gaitán denounced the 'oligarchy', both Liberal and Conservative, for being parasitic, engendering disorder and undermining the liberal ideal of social harmony. Only when power was recovered by a virtuous *pueblo* would order be restored. Through close self-identification with popular grievances over inflation, wages, job insecurity, unemployment, profiteering from food shortages and urban property speculation, Gaitán built a broad base of support ranging from small businessmen to lottery vendors and market traders. Through a network made as labour minister he also appealed to organized labour, fending off allegations by his Communist rivals that he was a 'social fascist' with counter-accusations of their servility to the oligarchy. And although not anti-American, Gaitán, imitating the tactics used by Gómez against López, shook the Ospina administration with a campaign of exposé and obloquy against ministers who represented export houses, were attorneys of oil companies or clients of U.S. banks.

Never a clearly articulated expression of class politics, *gaitanismo* illustrated the difficulties that confronted populist mobilization in a country where import-substitution industrialization was limited and associated with the established interests. A populist alliance of organized labour, the urban middle class, industrialists and progressive military was not viable. Organized labour was not sufficiently large; the urban middle class was tied to the ruling class through employment; the industrialists were beneficiaries of liberal economic policy; and a progressive military had not evolved. And because rural voters remained an electoral majority, any populist alliance required a substantial rural component to achieve power through elections. Until 1947 this was not available to Gaitán, who did not control the informal network of Liberal *caciques*. At the same time he rejected a violent seizure of power, despite the example of the rise to power in Venezuela of a liberal–radical coalition – Acción Democrática led by Rómulo Betancourt – by means of a coup in October 1945.

For his part, Laureano Gómez resumed his attack on centralized power and metropolitan wealth, and built a counter-alliance of peasants, large landowners outside the export sector, small provincial urban businessmen, Conservative *caciques* and clergy, and place-seekers who had been excluded from the benefits of Liberalism and privileged access to the state. The dominant groups became alarmed at the possibility of a Gómez–Gaitán deal. Ospina tried to restabilize the political system by co-opting Gaitán. In this he was unsuccessful because Gaitán insisted on his accountability to the *pueblo*, not the president. Yet Gaitán's own position was under challenge. Some of his supporters began to question his sincerity; and on becoming *jefe único* of the party he was said to have noticeably less time for the *dirigentes populares*. Meanwhile, the high pitch of political debate among centrist groups reinflamed party competition in the localities; and political violence outside Bogotá was seized upon by each party in the capital as evidence of the incorrigible partisanship of its rival.

Colombia in 1947 was drifting towards ungovernability. Both parties played a part in destabilizing the political order. Liberals, Gaitán included, alternated unpredictably between outright opposition to the government and offers of co-operation in exchange for guarantees. Conservatives used provocative language: the minister of government spoke of defending democratic institutions 'with blood and fire'; Gómez warned of impending civil war. And the Liberal leadership finally withdrew from the governing coalition in protest against electoral irregularities in the mid-term elections.

In April 1948, with the Ninth International Conference of the American States taking place in Bogotá, Colombian politics exploded. Popular discontent, fuelled by inflation, by urban overcrowding made worse by an influx of *boyacense* and *santandereano* refugees from violence and by hostility to conspicuous spending by the government on prestige projects, was channelled by Gaitán into a series of well-disciplined street demonstrations. His 'Plan Gaitán', which included land redistribution and closer state regulation of the banks, met with popular applause and congressional hostility. When on 9 April Gaitán was assassinated on a city street, his death triggered spontaneous urban uprisings in Bogotá and several provincial centres. The crowd assaulted, robbed and razed traditional targets – liquor and jewellery stores, churches, convents, the Education Ministry and the building of *El Siglo,* though not foreign banks and embassies. The social composition of the crowd was diverse; its leadership consisted of *barrio* politicians, radical journalists and Liberal policemen. But the insurrection failed to gather shape and momentum, although fewer than one thousand troops were stationed in Bogotá. Both in Bogotá and other major cities it disintegrated into mere pillaging. However, in smaller cities – Ibagué and Barrancabermeja, for example – the Liberal populace improvised revolutionary juntas following nineteenth-century precedents, and militias of merchants and artisans were formed, only to be disbanded once truces with the local authorities had been reached. And the 9 *de abril* was not exclusively urban: some land invasions took place, for example, in western Cundinamarca and Tolima.

Ospina never lost the support of the military. Rejecting both Gómez's proposal that he be succeeded by an emergency military junta and Liberal moves to replace him with Santos, the first *designado,* Ospina announced his intention to restore the coalition government and invited Echandía, the natural leader of the Liberal Party on Gaitán's death, to be minister of government. Enjoying a more cohesive support base than the *gaitanista* leaders who accused them of betrayal, the official Liberals defused the *bogotazo*. An uneasy calm was restored in the capital after military reinforcements had arrived from Boyacá. And brutal military action put an end to insurrection in Cali, Medellín and elsewhere. There emerged, however, from the martyrdom of Gaitán and the 9 *de abril* a powerful myth which was to have a profound influence upon the new insurrectionary faction of Liberals that took shape in 1949.

The reasons for Gaitán's death are unclear. The identity of the assassin has not been established beyond all doubt; and there remains a strong likelihood that no political group or leader was responsible for the killing. The Ospina government, backed by the leaders of both major parties, blamed the Communists for the insurrection, in spite of clear evidence that they were not ready to seize advantage of it. And after a brief pause in mid-1948, the Conservatives again set out to divide and demobilize the Liberals and the CTC by branding rank-and-file activists as Communists and fellow-travellers. Thus, the 9 *de abril* brought the Cold War to Colombia: Conservatives persecuted Communists; and 'Communist' became as convenient a pejorative for labelling Liberals as 'Fascist' had been for denouncing Conservatives during the Second World War.

The CTC was easily dismantled. A fragile unity was broken by withdrawing funding, by limiting union access to ministers and by using force against militants belonging to the *sindicatos de base*. The government easily exploited divisions among labour, including the rivalries, among official Liberal, *gaitanista*, Communist and Catholic unions, and the abandonment of rural labour by urban-based unions. Workers in the strategic export sector — especially port-, railway- and river-workers — had more combative traditions; artisans, private and public sector service workers (e.g., *bogotano* taxi-drivers) had formed the core of the moderate wing of the CTC since 1938; and factory workers and the unions of Medellín had barely been represented. The Ospina government took advantage of the absence of an insurrectionary tradition among unionists: in 1938 they had been allies of the industrialists; in 1941 union aspirations had been subordinated to the immediate aims of an anti-Fascist front; and the 9 *de abril* had shown conclusively that organized labour was a non-insurrectionary force.

There was cautious optimism when Ospina suspended the state of siege in October 1948, but from January 1949 a sequence of national events culminated in the breakdown of normal relations between the main parties. A revival of the Liberal Party was thwarted by the inability of the official leadership to impose discipline upon radicals demanding direct action, who formed Comandos de Izquierda. A resumption of violence in Boyacá in April preceded the sacking by Ospina of Liberal departmental governors in May, which, in turn, precipitated the withdrawal of Liberal ministers from the coalition cabinet. In the hope of winning or neutralizing Liberal Catholic voters and small property-owners, Conservative newspapers denounced the Liberals as crypto-Communist; the Liberal press replied by denouncing the Conservatives for destroying civil liberties and erecting an authoritarian state. While a clear Liberal victory was achieved in the congressional election of June 1949, the Conservatives made gains, in part because they used central subsidies to apply pressure to the malleable poor departments and marginal constituencies. Then in September an end to *convivencia* between the parties at the national level was symbolized by the assassination in Congress of a Liberal representative by a Conservative. The proclamation of Echandía and Gómez as presidential candidates in October was followed by a decision by the Liberal majority in Congress to begin impeachment proceedings against Ospina. His response in November was to declare a state of siege, close Congress and impose press censorship. Ospina had abandoned attempts at accommodation.

Confrontation at the centre meant that the government could not exercise effective mediation at the local level; the autonomy enjoyed by regional bosses expanded as both central party organizations lost authority. The police were in the sectarian vanguard, frequently in cahoots with the clergy; and heavy concentrations of Conservative policemen pushed militant Liberals in peripheral areas into violence, which they justified by appealing to a tradition of insurrection against arbitrary rule. The army also played a partisan role and was increasingly used by the government to snuff out violence in *municipios* where Liberal activists came to see both central and regional government as exercising an illegitimate dictatorship. While Liberal dissidence in the officer corps was evident in an air force unit in Villavicencio in 1949, the ineffectiveness of the army in reimposing order was reflected by the proliferation of private terror-squads, especially in the Valle del Cauca.

Both party leaderships continued to rationalize the violence of their supporters in terms of the greater excesses of their opponents; and both interpreted any moves towards accommodation as evidence of opportunism. Yet a military coup did not occur. Constitutional traditions were stronger than those of conspiracy in the officer corps. Moreover, Ospina had made generous improvements in military pay, pensions and other benefits. One rationale for not forming a military junta during the 9 *de abril* had been that there were not enough competent military leaders to head both the government and the army. The risk of civil war, however, rose when the assassination of Echandía's brother provoked the Liberal leadership to withdraw the Echandía candidacy and declare mass abstention at the polls. No Liberal presidential candidate would stand again till 1958; Congress would remain closed till 1959; and the state of siege would remain in place for a decade.

An uncontested election in November 1949 enabled Laureano Gómez to assume office in 1950. However, a combination of rigid authoritarianism and failure to halt the violence undermined his support amongst the propertied classes, the military and many Conservatives, and, as we shall see, his government fell in 1953 to a military coup backed by Liberals and *ospinista* Conservatives. Led by General Gustavo Rojas Pinilla, the new military regime promised an end to the *violencia* and a retreat from authoritarianism. Yet as it became more entrenched, the regime antagonized its initial constituency and gave rise to a new wave of violence, some of it instigated by *laureanistas*. A second coup in 1957 led to the restoration of civilian rule and political stability. This, however, could be achieved only after more sophisticated forms of coalition politics, in which all the major Conservative and Liberal factions came to play a part, had been introduced.

LA VIOLENCIA

The Colombian *violencia* in the fifteen years after the Second World War was regarded in Latin America as a unique example of political decomposition, its cases of delinquency, personality disorder and other pathological features nourishing sensational journalism. Yet what was the *violencia?* Why did it occur at all, and then recur? The term *violencia* is itself imprecise. It has become accepted in Colombia because it is amorphous and non-partisan. Widely perceived as a tragedy without rational explanation, the *violencia* had its roots, according to novelists and essayists, in 'hereditary hatreds' among families, clans and parties that originated in the nineteenth century. Party identification was inherited, not chosen. Thus, to defect from the party was to betray the kin group; and to defend the party through violent means was not only justifiable but, in some circumstances, required by honour. Described frequently as an undeclared civil war between Liberal and Conservative peasants, the *violencia* was not, like earlier civil wars, characterized by direct military confrontations between armed bands representing the parties. These seldom occurred. The main pattern of violence consisted of massacre or ambush followed by retaliatory punitive operations that included the razing of cottages, the destruction of crops and equipment, the robbery of cattle and assassination.

In its first phase (1946–8) political spoils were the main issue, and the eastern departments of Boyacá and the Santanders were the locations, as we have seen. A second phase of *violencia* followed the 9 *de abril* and was particularly intense in 1949–50. By 1949 *violencia* was proving to be neither temporary nor containable in the eastern departments, as many had expected. It spread to the western departments, especially Tolima and Caldas, and to the Llanos Orientales. It also spread to the large towns and the small cities. More Liberal militants had joined the guerrillas in the second half of 1948 as a result of the suppression of the CTC and mass dismissals from both the public and the private sector – the sugar-cane *ingenios* of Valle and the oil wells of Barrancabermeja. The ranks of the discontented were swollen further by sacked Liberal railway employees, who had been the beneficiaries of the best employee benefits available to organized labour in the 1930s. For the former *alcalde* of Barrancabermeja, Rafael Rangel, armed resistance was no more than the continuation of union and *gaitanista* struggle by other means.

An insurrectionary faction among Liberals took shape in the Llanos Orientales and Tolima and was swollen by refugees from Boyacá. This group was at odds with the peace faction led by the Directorio Nacional Liberal over the effectiveness and legitimacy of guerrilla activity, but in the Llanos Orientales it succeeded in building a guerrilla force that was financed by taxes imposed on cattle: 10 per cent on herds owned by Liberals, 20 per cent on those owned by Conservatives. Subsequently, the military and guerrillas entered into several cattle truces in an effort to protect the regional economy from devastation.

In mid-1952 there was optimism in the Gómez administration that the *violencia* would soon be ended. The army was overcoming its inexperience in counter-guerrilla operations and launched a combined air, land and river attack on the *llanero* guerrillas. Yet violence now became endemic in some western coffee-producing zones for the first time, with twice-annual bloodshed and robbery accompanying the harvesting and marketing of the crop. The amnesty introduced by the military government of Rojas Pinilla in August 1953 reawakened optimism. Many Liberal guerrillas, notably in the Llanos, trusted the army more than the Conservatives and put down their arms. Others, especially in Tolima, joined the Communists. Yet the *violencia* resumed in 1955–6, and Conservative guerrillas were now formed against the military regime. The Liberal–Conservative coalition of 1958 was intended to solve the *violencia*. Many guerrillas put down their arms during the transition to civilian government. But others, viewing coalition as betrayal, did not recognize the peace formula reached by the official party leaders and prolonged the struggle. Officially the *violencia* was concluded in 1964, but by then it had already merged with a new confrontation between the coalition government and revolutionary guerrillas.

In its first phase the main thrust of *violencia* was political. Intense competition for public office was sharpened by continuous expansion of the electorate and the channelling of state benefits to groups whose partisan loyalties needed consolidation. Conflict was also deepened by the use of the army in a partisan role for ostensibly neutral 'public order' purposes; the partisanship of press, police forces and much of the provincial and local clergy; the fragility and unresponsiveness of local power structures and the judicial system; and the diminishing control of central party machines over provincial constituencies. In 1948–9, sectarian struggle culminated in a breakdown of authority and customary forms of political behaviour, transforming previously limited local tensions into open conflict. In some respects the state collapsed; in others it abdicated functions, devolving powers like policing to private groups, thus encouraging rival groups to evolve self-defence strategies. Access to the state remained vital for small and large entrepreneurs needing credit, tax or import exemptions, police or military support or judicial backing. Yet in important parts of at least six departments and most of the Llanos Orientales, the state had no physical presence for much of the period from 1949 to 1953.

By the early 1950s, the character of *violencia* had changed; it had acquired many of the characteristics of peasant protest. *Colonos* in the 1920s and 1930s had been promised sympathetic treatment by the state in their conflicts amongst themselves and with land entrepreneurs. Yet this was not forthcoming. This grievance was felt strongly in the pioneer zones: southern Tolima, Urabá, the Magdalena Valley, the Macarena, Caquetá and part of the Chocó. Tenant-farmers and sharecroppers were angry at having been denied recognition of their improvements on the land after the 1936 agrarian legislation and at having lost to lawyers their rights to reclaim dispossessed land because they could not pay professional fees. At the same time, the post-war expansion of commercial agriculture increased tensions between landlords, tenant-farmers and sharecroppers competing for control of land and labour, and between rural employers and landless workers competing for control and access to land and water. Thus, violence in parts of Tolima was connected to the repossession of fragmented haciendas by traditional landlords with ambitions to become modern agricultural entrepreneurs and to the undertaking of a counter-offensive to proletarianize the peasantry.

A national economic strategy that disproportionately concentrated the gains from growth at the regional and local levels in the hands of large merchants at the expense of small merchants and of merchants at the expense of producers and wage labourers worsened the position. Rural–rural and rural–urban migration also played a major part. Violence was particularly pronounced in frontiers of recent colonization and in regions of rapid growth such as the Quindío, where competition between rival regional flows of rural–rural migrants combined with the breakdown of relations between local peasants and their political protectors when the latter fled to the towns. The enlargement of floating migrant populations of unemployed that could be enlisted as criminals was complemented by informal relationships forged between guerrillas and sharecroppers over access to agrarian employment.

The inaction of the state explains in part why the *violencia* was so pro-tracted. The prevailing assumption that the state had no arbitration functions – only a role in maintaining public order – intensified violence in Sumapaz and southern Tolima. The Gómez government showed insuffi-cient concern about the *violencia* until it affected the coffee-export-producing regions in 1952, by which time it had acquired an irreversible momentum. However, the oppression exercised by the *chulavita* police in Boyacá and the *pájaro* terror-squads in Valle pointed to a measure of local decision-making independent of the central government. In the Quindío, official tolerance was extended to bandits who were closely connected to informal power-holders. And guerrilla groupings were often sustained by voluntary gifts from politicians and *hacendados,* as well as by forced exactions and pillage in areas where the opposing party predominated.

Guerrillas won peasant co-operation because the state failed to protect them. In Tolima and Caldas, for example, guerrillas took advantage of peasant anger at greater landowner participation in the coffee crop, espe-cially between 1952 and 1954. After the 1954 bonanza, class identifica-tion between guerrillas and the rural population was more secure because more *jefes de banda* were sons of small proprietors and day labourers.

Equally, the military, theoretically the instrument of central government in curbing *violencia,* was not always a neutral actor. Introduced to restore the presence of the state and wean the peasantry away from the *quindiano* guerrillas, some sections of the military, ensnared by local systems of *caciquismo,* were interested mainly in their own survival and enjoyed a cosy coexistence with the guerrillas. This also occurred in parts of eastern Boyacá, where the guerrillas enjoyed periods of immunity in areas free of attack, in which they could regroup before concentrating their strength against Conservative police. Heavy military spending on aircraft and other expensive weaponry inappropriate to a guerrilla war in the mid-1950s was never explained.

The *violencia* was protracted; but at no time did the guerrillas seem likely to defeat the military or even to seize a major departmental capital. The main reason for this was that many guerrillas did not set out to win a national war. Many took up violence to secure remedies to particular grievances. Once these aims and safeguards from military oppression were secured, no further armed action was necessary and re-entry to civilian life took place. Others had only local objectives. Furthermore, the theatre of war was inappropriate for an offensive on central state power. The largest force of guerrillas was located in the Llanos Orientales, which were convenient for absorbing fugitives – disbanded Liberal police, army deserters, agrarian leaders – and adjacent to possible refuge in Venezuela, but provided a poor base for achieving total military victory.

The guerrillas faced considerable difficulties in co-ordinating action over a vast area. Between 1946 and 1949 armed resistance to central government was located mainly in three areas: Tolima, the Llanos Orientales and Barrancabermeja – distant both from Bogotá and from one another. Subsequently, the problem of co-ordination became more pronounced as armed opposition spread to parts of Antioquia, Cundinamarca and Santander. Moreover, the project of building a nationally co-ordinated guerrilla movement was frustrated from its inception in 1952 by personal rivalries, ideological differences and the exclusion of *tolimenses* from debate. Differences between *gaitanistas* and Communists over ideology and strategy were deepened by the close ties of *gaitanistas* with Liberal merchants, landowners and local power brokers. Equally, the government had some success in dissolving pacts among guerrillas by making offers of amnesty and rehabilitation.

Some have seen the industrialists and urban building interests as beneficiaries of *violencia* because it speeded up migration to the city, cheapening labour and stimulating construction activity. Yet there is no evidence that these groups were instigators or practitioners of violence. At the local level, the beneficiaries of violence included rural *fonderos* and urban merchants, enriched by buying cut-price stolen goods, including coffee, and reselling them on the legitimate market. Others who prospered included farm managers and small-town professionals with sufficient liquid wealth to purchase small rural properties when their intimidated owners migrated and property values collapsed. The resale of consolidated properties upon the revival of the market in land gave these groups sufficient capital to migrate to the large cities, where they entered respectable occupations and purchased houses in the residential suburbs. Nevertheless, the structure of rural power remained unchanged. Peasant individualism frustrated collective action, and strategies of communal self-defence were rare. New bosses replaced old, and *caciques* competed to gain access to the control of new government patronage dispensed from the mid-1950s in areas of violence.

Seen from the perspective of the less partisan politics of the National Front after 1958, the role of ideology in the *violencia* can easily be underestimated. There existed among Communist guerrillas in the Llanos a clear revolutionary commitment to overthrowing the capitalist state. In the Quindío, by contrast, such a vision did not prevail. Here *gaitanista* guerrillas fought for the implementation of liberal ideology: the security of property, the restoration of lost rights, the assurance of justice. Guerrillas emphasizing civil liberties and the security of property were relatively easily reincorporated into civilian life.

The study of *violencia* remains in its infancy. No single explanation of its origins and dynamics will suffice. In particular, local circumstances require further attention; no interpretation adequately explains why the *violencia* was more protracted in some localities than in others or why variations in its intensity were so localized. No adequate study exists of a region like the Atlantic coast nor of a *municipio* that was free of violence. Nor is there one that examines a locality little affected by *violencia* in its supposedly classic period but seriously disturbed by agrarian unrest in the late 1960s.

GÓMEZ AND THE *REVOLUCIÓN EN ORDEN*, 1950–3

Laureano Gómez took power in 1950 challenging Liberal assumptions about the status and scope of government authority and advocating the dismantlement of the Liberal state. Inspired by pre-1930 Conservative

regimes and right-wing Iberian experiments, Gómez proclaimed an austere counter-revolution in which the present would be securely anchored
to the past and cherished values of hierarchy, stability and religion would
be reaffirmed. In this vein, he announced a constitutional reform that
would strengthen executive power with a six-year presidency. Congress
was to be replaced by a constituent assembly, the members of which would
be elected on a franchise based upon the family, complemented by appointed representatives of the Church, military, professional bodies and
principal interest groups. Restrictions on non-Catholic religious organizations were to be imposed. The economic policy of Gómez, however, was
barely distinguishable from that of his predecessor Ospina. The government cautiously welcomed the report of a World Bank mission under
Lauchlin Currie that recommended policies emphasizing infrastructural
development in areas of export growth.

More talented and comfortable in opposition than in power, Gómez
failed to recognize that his government lacked the necessary means of
imposing an authoritarian solution on the Liberal opposition. Gómez was
also blind to the incompatibility of his drive to re-create a hierarchical
society with a capitalist growth strategy that dissolved traditional forms;
he cut himself off from those supporters who had voted for him in protest
against policies favouring areas of export growth. The Gómez government
was therefore isolated from its inception. It was distant from the Liberal
bogotano elite and populace and insulated itself through censorship from
sources of information and criticism, with the result that it was more
poorly equipped than its predecessors to assess the impact of its policies in
the localities.

Gómez assumed an unconditional pro-U.S. stance, probably in order to
dispel suspicions among liberal U.S. bureaucrats of his lingering *falangista*
sympathies but also to satisfy those propertied interests which applauded
his authoritarian stance but pressed him to avoid any rupture with the
United States that might threaten trade and investment. Discarding his
past inhibitions about open-door capitalism, he enacted legislation on
foreign investment considered by Washington to be the most favourable in
the continent. The Gómez administration, alone among Latin American
governments, seized the opportunity to send troops (some three thousand
men, about 20 per cent of the army) to the Korean War. This was a
gesture that confirmed his unflinching anti-Communism in the eyes of
Washington, enabled him to move Liberal and politically neutral military
officers abroad and guaranteed a continued supply of military hardware.

Some elements in the army welcomed the diversion from domestic operations and the opportunity to test their professionalism in warfare against men who were not their compatriots.

The Liberals were placed firmly on the defensive. Disagreements with the government could no longer be discussed within a framework of commonly shared references and concepts. Nevertheless, some political leaders, notably López, tried to keep lines of communication open. (The former president went on an unofficial mission to the Llanos to parley with Liberal guerrillas.) Mutual suspicions were so pervasive that no accommodation could be reached. Both Liberals and some *ospinista* Conservatives claimed that the government was couching expediency in a language of high morality and using censorship to conceal blundering and inaction.

In 1952 the government was given a slight reprieve when Gómez stood down owing to ill-health. He was replaced by an interim president, Roberto Urdaneta Arbeláez, an aristocrat with diplomatic and ministerial experience who had served both Conservative and Liberal presidents. However, the change of head of government did not foreshadow any substantial shift in policy. The architect of the anti-Communist crusade of 1945, Urdaneta had one standard response to any form of popular discontent: to perceive it and deal with it as a public order operation.

By 1953 the political stalemate had dangerously reduced the already slender power base of the regime. The propertied interests increasingly distanced themselves from the government as a result of its failure to honour a pledge to lower taxes, the spread of the *violencia* to the coffee-producing departments, and favouritism in the distribution of public works patronage. The government built up no following among the urban working class and distanced itself from Catholic trade unions, which it saw as *ospinista*. Meanwhile, the limitations of the Church as an ally were increasingly evident. Local partisanship in the *violencia* had deprived it of much influence; and a new Primate was more concerned with reuniting the Church, modernizing the parochial structure and maintaining levels of ordination than with propping up an insecure government.

After a brief respite from the tumult of 1949–50, the army was antagonized by a renewal of violence in 1951–2 and official attempts to involve the military in sectarian conflict. The officer corps, increasingly exposed to civilian contact, became conscious of the extent to which the survival of the government depended on its loyalty and came to see the inflexible attitude displayed by Gómez as the main stumbling-block to reconciliation. The officer corps had both long- and short-term grievances. A sense of accumulated humiliation at the hands of the civilian parties over two decades was compounded by anger at official tolerance of private violence and the role assigned to the army in preserving domestic order.

Two events drew together diffuse and uncoordinated opposition to the regime and precipitated the smooth and bloodless coup of June 1953: the full resumption of the presidency by Gómez and his decision to block the ambition of General Gustavo Rojas Pinilla to be war minister.

ROJAS PINILLA AND MILITARY RULE, 1953–7

Entering office on a wave of euphoria reinforced by a high coffee price, the regime of General Rojas Pinilla was endorsed by all sections of the upper class, except the *laureanista* faction, on the understanding that it was merely transitional. The Liberals, relieved that the threat of a *laureanista* hegemony had been averted, tolerated the overwhelmingly Conservative composition of the bureaucracy, and they acquiesced in a moratorium on party politics supported by the *ospinistas*. The Rojas government thus enjoyed a broad base of acquiescence, but not of support; its legitimacy rested on its capacity to curb violence and promote consensus. The coup was welcomed by the United States, because it resolved a crisis in which the political climate for foreign investment was unhealthy and because it brought to power a leader seen as a moderate (unlike Pérez Jiménez in Venezuela) and known for his record as commander-in-chief in the Korean War. Thus, Colombia could enlist U.S. sympathy under the Mutual Assistance Program, becoming the first Latin American country to buy U.S. jets for its air force.

Rojas had no clear strategy except to terminate the *violencia*. Admitting, unlike Gómez, that social and economic grievances were partly responsible for the *violencia,* he launched a welfare programme under the auspices of an Office of Rehabilitation and Assistance, which provided resettlement loans, processed applications for the restoration of properties allegedly lost in illegal seizures, and undertook improvements in regions of *violencia.* Guerrilla leaders were offered an amnesty, which several accepted. Early successes in reducing the *violencia* prolonged the euphoria surrounding the coup.

Yet by 1955 the Rojas regime was under fire. Although the civilian elite perceived it as a makeshift expedient, the president clearly thought otherwise. Assisted by his energetic daughter, María Eugenia Rojas de Moreno Díaz, Rojas founded new patronage institutions, notably Secretaría

Nacional de Asistencia Social y Protección Infantil (SENDAS), in order to cement a civilian power base. Using FAO, CARE and UNICEF resources, SENDAS arranged a programme of food distribution, medical attention and the rehabilitation of victims of the *violencia*. The *rojistas* organized the 'Third Force', which its adherents claimed was essential to overcome a tradition of Liberal–Conservative feuding but which its critics saw as the embryo of an official party. Borrowing a language of *justicialismo* from Argentina, the *rojistas* organized a new trade union confederation, Confederación Nacional de Trabajo (CNT), which was affiliated with the *peronista*-led Asociación de Trabajadores Latino-americanos (ATLAS), while curbing the activities of the CTC and UTC. Rojas employed an anti-oligarchic language that echoed Gaitán and presented his government as the benefactor of the urban lower middle and working classes. This, together with the entry into the regime of Socialists and former *gaitanistas* aiming to radicalize it from within, alarmed the upper class. Industrialists were angered by clumsy attempts to increase direct taxation and to impose wage increases upon them in order to secure working-class support; landowners were concerned by a vacuum in agrarian policy, and private bankers by two new public banks that challenged their position. Conservative and Liberal leaders were suspicious of potentially popular measures, like the opening of the Banco Popular Hipotecario in 1956, intended to provide mortgages for sections of the urban lower middle and working classes. The propertied classes were alarmed at increases in foreign indebtedness to cover public expenditure.

At a local level there was mounting pressure from both Liberals and Conservatives to create an organized opposition. But this was frustrated by the legacy of bitterness between and within the traditional parties, the absence abroad of their most prestigious leaders and the decomposition of their machineries. Moreover, the propertied interests were reluctant to destabilize a regime they disliked while coffee prices remained high. Opposition was therefore led by the media and the Church. The suspension of *El Siglo* was acceptable to all but *laureanistas,* but the closure of *El Tiempo* united the press barons with other propertied interests and foreshadowed a wave of press-orchestrated international revulsion against the regime. Within the Church, moderate elements determined to preserve the separate identities of the Church and the Conservative Party reunited with ultra-montane elements in supporting the condemnation of *justicialismo* by the Primate and making bold criticisms of the regime in Church publications. The Church became a rallying point for opposition, even for anticlericals.

Two events united the opposition: a display of extreme police brutality in the Bogotá bullring in the presence of María Eugenia and her husband and a police attack on the house in Cali of a prominent Conservative, Guillermo León Valencia, which showed that no member of the upper class was immune from official persecution. Mismanagement, the self-enrichment of the Rojas circle and recrudescent violence hastened the downfall of the regime. Erratic shifts between coercion and concession and the government's lack of expertise in policy outside of public works goaded Liberals and *ospinistas* into an opposition campaign of clandestine pamphleteering. As the nature of civilian opposition became clear and a civic movement acquired momentum, it was echoed by rumblings within the armed forces over policy towards the *violencia*. Military discontent was magnified by the practice of promoting officers on grounds of personal loyalty rather than merit. By late 1956 the regime was merely living from day to day; it contained populist features that bore a superficial resemblance to *peronismo* but lacked the resources either to consolidate a support base on *peronista* lines or to undertake the recomposition of the political order.

The breakdown of institutional cohesion in the army culminated in 1957 in a coup against Rojas when a five-man junta (the *pentarquía*) seized power. The junta, led by General Gabriel París, proclaimed an immediate transition from single-man rule to government by the military as an institution and announced a timetable for the restoration of a civilian regime. Shored up by Export–Import Bank credits and a private bank loan that were conditional upon a restoration of civilian rule, the interim junta survived one coup attempt. The right to form political parties was re-established; the date of the presidential elections was announced; and the first steps in dismantling the dictatorship and preparing for the transition to civilian rule were taken.

THE TRANSITION TO CIVILIAN RULE, 1957–8

A wide spectrum of opinion viewed the 1957–8 transition with apprehension. Every government since 1942 had encountered serious problems in simply surviving. Two experiments in seven years in confronting the *violencia* had failed. Having interpreted the consolidation of civilian rule in the 1930s and 1940s as an index of national maturity and a tribute to its own managerial skills, the upper class had lost self-esteem in the crisis of the 1950s. Endemic violence in some localities encouraged a form of cultural pessimism and gave rise to the view that Colombia was ungovernable.

The fantasies of the 1920s of a *Colombia petrolera* displacing Mexico as the first Latin American oil producer had long vanished. Colombia continued to depend on coffee. It enjoyed substantial benefits from international quota arrangements, which, beginning in 1940 as a wartime experiment, acquired a permanent character after the Second World War. But coffee production had stabilized and was perhaps even stagnating in the 1950s.

Colombia lacked a state that was capable of meeting its requirements for economic development and confronting the challenge of presiding over the transition from a predominantly rural to a predominantly urban society. Major welfare issues had been neglected. Health conditions were notoriously defective; a long-term programme by Fedecafé initiated in 1942 to improve the sanitation of rural housing applied only to coffee-producing zones. The position in education was somewhat better. The Instituto Colombiano de la Especialización Técnica al Extranjero (ICETEX), which provided funding for Colombian professionals to train abroad, won support from Medellín industrialists and came to be seen as a model for 'Third World' countries. Levels of literacy were raised by the decision in 1947 to oblige proprietors to open modest schools. The Church, with UNESCO support, experimented through Acción Cultural Popular with radio education from a transmitter at Sutatenza; and perhaps two-thirds of rural parishes were in 1959 promoting a literacy programme controlled by parish priests. Yet the overall achievement in education was patchy.

The ground for elections in 1958 was laid in two meetings between former presidents, Laureano Gómez, Conservative, and Alberto Lleras Camargo, Liberal. The Declaration of Benidorm (1956) established the principle of co-operation between the parties. The historic Pact of Sitges (1957) established that, whatever the result of the election, power would be shared equally between the two parties and that this system of institutionalised *convivencia* would be maintained for sixteen years. Lleras Camargo was selected as the first presidential candidate of the new 'National Front' coalition; not only did he have presidential experience, but, untainted by association with conflict between 1947 and 1953, he was the only figure that could win the allegiance of both the *ospinista* and *laureanista* factions of the Conservatives. Goodwill towards the new civilian coalition government which took power in 1958 was manifest in a plebiscite in which 90 per cent of voters endorsed the new arrangements. But many Colombians doubted the coalition's capacity to survive, even less to bring about the desired combination of political stability, economic development and social change.

11

COLOMBIA SINCE 1958

With a growth in population from 17.5 million in 1964 to 22.3 million in 1973 and 28.6 million in 1985, Colombia was expected to overtake Argentina in the 1990s and resume its nineteenth-century position as the most populous Latin American country after Brazil and Mexico. Between 1951 and 1964 the country had one of the world's highest rates of demographic increase – 3.5 per cent per annum. From 1965 the rate of growth decelerated – in substantial part as a result of a sharp decline in birth-rates (from 40 per thousand in 1960 to 20 per thousand in 1974). By the early 1980s the annual rate had fallen to less than 2 per cent.

This reduced rate of population growth can be associated with urbanization and improved literacy. By the 1980s urban fecundity had fallen to only 55 per cent of the level in the countryside and was in part attributable to explicit policies of birth control, which, despite the power of the Church, had been adopted since the late 1960s. Between 1973 and 1985 the proportion of Colombians under fifteen years of age fell from 43 to 33 per cent. Nevertheless, growth in the under-five age group of 4 per cent per annum, combined with a 4.4 per cent annual increase among five- to fourteen-year-olds, imposed heavy pressures on health, education and housing services during the 1960s and 1970s.

From the 1950s the pattern of internal migration underwent gradual change, the Llanos Orientales, the Amazonian region and the Caribbean coast becoming new migrant destinations. Until mid-century the main flows of migrants were rural–rural; but partly as a consequence of the *violencia,* they became increasingly rural–urban as commercial agriculture, like peasant farming, became saturated with labour from the mid-1960s. At the same time, an itinerant agricultural sub-proletariat took shape as

Christopher Abel alone is responsible for the treatment of the period since 1982.

commercial agriculture benefited from export growth, industrial inputs and the stagnation of the peasant sector producing domestic food crops. This sub-proletariat was composed of working families without land who scoured the countryside for employment in the major harvests – coffee, cotton, sugar-cane, bananas, rice and, in the 1980s, flowers – and during the 'dead period' lived in the poorest *barrios* of the secondary cities. Internal migration was complemented by emigration to Venezuela, the United States and Ecuador. Young, male and skilled workers, in particular, were lost to the United States.

After the Second World War commercial farming was the main beneficiary of the first consistent policies to substitute domestic products for imported agricultural inputs to industry (such as cotton, tobacco and sesame) and to stimulate production of foodstuffs like rice, maize and potatoes for urban consumption. And from 1960 new policies were devised to encourage the export of bananas, beef and, later, cut flowers. These policies ranged from subsidized credits for farmers and diffusion of agricultural technology to an easing of restrictions, between 1950 and 1964, on imports of fertilizers. The government, meanwhile, imposed upon industry an obligation to buy fixed quotas of some agricultural products, like cotton and cacao, especially when international prices were lower than domestic ones. Although the general thrust of policy stressed land use rather than distribution, reformist schemes were introduced in 1961 and 1976. The first, the Ley de Reforma Social Agraria, was to a large extent a consequence of commitments reached in the Alliance for Progress; and the second, the Desarrollo Rural Integral (DRI) was linked with a World Bank loan to arrest the pauperization of minifundia. A relatively modern capitalist agriculture enjoying high productivity per acre and per employee flourished from the 1950s; and the area of cultivated land expanded by an annual average of 2.1 per cent between 1950 and 1975. Yet agrarian entrepreneurs resented the high costs of agricultural inputs from protected industries, like fertilizers, pesticides, agricultural machinery and processed cattle-feed. In order to meet this grievance the state assumed a monopoly on importing agricultural products. Establishing a cocoon around the domestic market for agricultural products, the state imported them only in order to cover production deficits and, at times, to regulate internal prices.

A transition from traditional husbandry to intensive techniques of production in the main coffee zones of the central Cordillera occurred in the 1960s; and better cultivation practices, fertilizer and superior botanical varieties were used in the 1970s. Colombia consolidated its position as the world's second producer. Coffee still represented one-half of export earnings in the early 1980s, but its share continued to decline. The weight of coffee in total agricultural production fluctuated considerably from 1960, fell in the mid-1970s and made some recovery before stagnating in the mid-1980s. Ten commercial crops other than coffee increased their share of total agricultural production – from 10 per cent in 1950–2 to 34 per cent in 1978–80. Agricultural growth and diversification were possible because lands on new frontiers were brought into cultivation while previously idle lands on latifundia in the valleys and plains of Bogotá, Ubaté, Chiquinquirá and Sogamoso were intensively used for the first time. However, 60 per cent of newly exploited lands between 1950 and 1975 were devoted to extensive cattle-raising that generated little employment.

By 1965 a clear dualism existed between the peasant and capitalist sectors in agriculture. The capitalist sector concentrated the best-quality land, credit and modern technology and irrigation; it took advantage of peasant labour, which, compelled by stagnant production and demographic growth, sought seasonal work harvesting commercial crops. And capitalist agriculture responded positively to official initiatives, increasing the proportion of domestic agricultural inputs for industry and, after 1960, generating some exportable surplus. By contrast, per capita production of foodstuffs except for maize, remained stagnant or even declined. *Campesino* operations (e.g., in beans, yucca and potatoes) with a rudimentary technology continued to represent 60 per cent of foodstuffs production as late as 1975; and the expansion of the area of cultivation of peasant crops was insignificant between 1960 and 1985. The value of production of the eight main foodstuffs in the Colombian diet fell as a proportion of total agricultural and livestock production from 78 per cent in 1955–7 to 60 per cent in 1984–6. Thus, high food prices were largely attributable to inefficient production, a failure to meet increasing demand and an inefficient system of marketing.

Urbanization moved apace. The population of Bogotá rose from 1.70 million in 1964 to an estimated 4.21 million in 1985, by which date three other cities possessed more than a million inhabitants: Medellín (2.10 million), Cali (1.65 million) and Barranquilla (1.12 million). Some 85 per cent of total manufacturing was concentrated in these four cities. In the years 1951–73 Bogotá expanded at the fastest rate, attracting a disproportionate share of modern manufacturing industry, physical and social infrastructure and financial and administrative services. Yet there was little question of urban primacy: in the 1970s Bogotá represented about 12 per cent of the total population and in 1985 about 15 per cent. The overall rate of urban population growth was very high, oscillating between 5 and 8 per cent per annum in the period 1950–80. Some cities of intermediate size, defined as containing thirty thousand persons in 1960, grew at 10 to 12 per cent, becoming important foci of exchange and labour and serving as intermediate points in 'stage-migrations' from the countryside to the large cities. Some intermediate cities underwent astonishing growth, like Cúcuta and Ipiales, located on the borders with Venezuela and Ecuador, respectively, and Valledupar, Montería, Villavicencio, Florencia and Apartadó in zones of frontier agriculture. Urbanization also occurred in labour-intensive agricultural areas of high productivity, such as the coffee belt from Manizales to Sevilla and Caicedonia and the sugarcane plantations of the Valle del Cauca.

The growth of a modern manufacturing sector with new industries (metallurgy, petrochemicals, automobiles, paper and electrical goods) appearing after 1958 was accompanied by a decline in some branches of artisan industry, like clothing and furniture. Others, however, both retained their market share and increased their share of employment, competing effectively with the factory sector; in 1970 it was estimated that 60 per cent of employees in the manufacturing sector in the four main cities still worked in workshops. An increasingly diverse service sector grew faster than the manufacturing sector, with an especially pronounced rise in employment in commerce, finance and insurance. Indeed, between 1964 and 1985 the share of the service sector in the total economically active population rose from about 30 to 45 per cent, while that of the primary sector fell from 47 to 34 per cent.

As opportunities for employment in manufacturing failed to keep pace with urban population growth, a large proportion of the population improvized, resorting to urban construction, itinerant vending, domestic service, prostitution and crime. By the 1970s a large informal sector with low income, insecure employment, poor health and a high level of illiteracy represented a bigger proportion of the total urban work-force than was employed in manufacturing industry, transport, formal commerce and construction combined. Barely penetrated by trade union organizations, the informal sector – officially estimated in 1984 as representing 55 per cent of workers in the ten largest cities – lay beyond social security legislation and could register protest only through elections, land invasions, civic strikes and other public demonstrations. Until the 1980s governments treated problems in the informal sector as either public order questions or electoral matters to be met by pragmatic policies aimed at raising levels of income and education. All governments formally committed themselves to urban planning, but the main determinant of urban policy remained market forces – autonomous demographic and economic factors – not state and municipal intervention. In the 1960s and 1970s promises to provide low-cost housing for the urban poor were nullified by a concentration of investment in the residential suburbs of the upper and upper middle classes. This pattern was reinforced by the international agencies' main criteria for borrowing, specifically the effective management of resources and the capacity of the borrower to repay the loan.

Like other Latin American countries, Colombia adopted policies of import substitution and, later, of manufacturing for export. Until 1967, tariff protection was the main explicit component of industrialization policy, being supplemented by such devices as an overvalued peso for imports, subsidized credits and import quotas and licensing. After 1967 exchange policy became the main feature of industrialization strategy, although both entrepreneurs and the unions were able to impede a full reversal of protectionism. Throughout the period, the state played a significant role in industrialization. Special credit lines and the tax reform of 1960 were instrumental in the phase of substitution of intermediate and capital goods that began in the late 1950s, and the state-controlled Instituto de Fomento Industrial (IFI) played a decisive role in launching basic and heavy industries, notably steel and petrochemicals.

Industrial entrepreneurs were nonetheless very cautious. Alert to import competition and wary about crises in the balance of payments, they maintained idle installed capacity and high inventories, which were made possible by intense protectionism and the nearly monopolistic character of factory industry since its inception. Exchange-control policies encouraged a net transfer of funds from coffee to manufacturing; this cheapened capital for industry, and it favoured the tendency towards capital intensity. Thus, the annual rate of growth of industrial employment was disappointing: 4.3 per cent from 1960 to 1975 and then less than 1 per cent between 1975 and 1985, figures lower than the growth of the economically active population and considerably lower than that of urban labour supply.

A high level of protection encouraged an influx of capital from transnational manufacturing enterprises, based mainly in the United States. Indeed, transnational-owned industry was the main beneficiary of export promotion policies contained in the Plan Vallejo (1959), the introduction of tax certificates in 1967 and legislation for Andean integration (1968) which offered fiscal incentives, exchange and credit subsidies and tariff preferences to manufactured exports. Transnational enterprise entered all areas of manufacturing industry, but its contribution to employment was small and the general performance of export manufacturing was disappointing. Although in the 1970s Colombia was the fourth industrialized country of Latin America, it was only the seventh recipient of transnational investment. And of the total transnational investment in 1980, only 8.5 per cent was concentrated in manufacturing; 90 per cent was located in mining and petroleum and 1.5 per cent in banking. Resistance from entrepreneurs and urban labour to the dismantling of policies of industrial protection played a part in slowing down the rate of industrial growth, especially between 1975 and 1984. But other factors explained a marked reduction in the growth rate of the textile industry and of the intermediate and capital goods industries. These included the neoliberal policies espoused by the López Michelsen government (1974–8), a growth in import capacity made possible by the influx of profits from the coffee bonanza (1975–83) and the marijuana and cocaine booms. Other factors included the relative overvaluation of the peso, an increase in domestic interest rates and a rise in food prices which reduced demand for durable consumer goods. Furthermore, the adjustment policies in developed countries played a major part in this manufacturing recession, together with shifts in dollar interest rates and a grave economic crisis in the Andean markets for Colombian manufactures – Venezuela, Ecuador and, to a lesser extent, Peru.

The historic agreement between the Liberals and the Conservatives in 1958 to establish and maintain for sixteen years a 'National Front' was based on two principles, parity and alternation, and enshrined in a new constitution. Liberals and Conservatives were guaranteed an equal share of political power. A Liberal president was to alternate in office with a Conservative and would be accompanied by a Conservative minister of government and a Liberal minister of external affairs, and vice versa. Cabinet posts would be divided on a fifty–fifty basis, with the defence portfolio going to a member of the armed forces. Departmental governors were also chosen by the president according to the two principles and were instructed to apply them rigorously at the departmental and municipal levels. An elective presidency and a bicameral congress were restored, and a mass electorate of both sexes established. Immediate re-election of presidents was unconstitutional, producing a regular turnover of incumbents, all civilian. Executive power, though enhanced by a partial professionalization of the senior civil service and the frequent resort to the state of siege, remained circumscribed by the absence of a permanent and disciplined body of supporters in Congress. Presidents had to work continuously to establish new voting combinations in order to secure the passage of legislation, much of which required a two-thirds majority in Congress. Yet the influence of Congress was less than it was in the 1930s and 1940s, and by the mid-1970s there was pronounced popular unease at the lack of accountability of the executive and the inefficacy of Congress – its inability to initiate legislation, to scrutinize development plans or to question ministers. The vacuum left by an ineffective Congress was filled by ad hoc forums and informal summit negotiations of party leaders and former presidents that had no constitutional existence. Efficiency was also impaired by the constitutional requirement that Congress select both the *procurador* (attorney-general) and the *contralor* (comptroller) from the party opposed to that of the president.

This was a system that functioned at a considerable cost. Parity in the public administration was achieved only by its enlargement to include Liberals, not by the dismissal of Conservatives. Alternation denied the electorate the opportunity to vote for the candidates it preferred. And each government had a contingency existence. In spite of an underlying continuity in economic policy, successive governments behaved as if they were transitional, struggling from day to day to survive. Opposition was curtailed. The most important opposition movement, Alianza Nacional Popular (ANAPO), led by General Rojas Pinilla, was compelled by the 1958 constitution to define its candidates as Liberal or Conservative; they therefore stood as *anapista* Liberals or *anapista* Conservatives. Despite this inhibition ANAPO acquired momentum in the 1960s, posed a major challenge in 1969–72 and fizzled out in the late 1970s. The Communist Party and other left-wing groups made little impact. Hampered by poor leadership and organization, sporadic oppression, inadequate funding and the destruction of popular organizations during the *violencia,* the Communist Party was challenged by short-lived left-wing factions whose main function was to divide the Left and whose influence was usually confined to a fragment of the intelligentsia, the labour leadership and small pockets of rural workers and miners. The restrictive nature of coalition rule and the failure of the democratic Left are important in explaining the appeal and durability of guerrilla organizations. In Colombia, alone in Latin America, these had a continuous existence from 1949.

A transition to competitive politics was looked upon favourably by reformists who saw *bipartidismo* as a brake upon political change. But the transition was slowed by Conservatives, who warned of a return to violence between the parties. Because single-party government was likely to mean the relegation of the Conservative Party to opposition, Gómez insisted in 1957–8 that coalition arrangements last for sixteen years, while Liberals pressed for twelve. In summit negotiations in 1967, Ospina insisted on continued power-sharing. The constitutional reform of 1968 laid down that legislative parity should end at the departmental and municipal levels in 1974 and bureaucratic parity in the executive should last until 1978. Had the Conservatives prevailed, executive power-sharing would probably have survived until 1978 and beyond. In fact, competitive elections for the presidency were restored in 1974 after growing concern over rates of abstention that indicated either apathy towards the coalition or its failure to provide a genuine political choice for voters.

Coalition rule suffocated open debate. As a result major problems, such as the defects of the judicial and policing systems, became more acute for lack of public discussion. Domination of the most powerful media by the party leaders and the practice of self-censorship deepened frustrations. The range of alternatives within the political system was very limited for new groups from the popular sectors. In Colombia the political parties, and not the state, performed the function of incorporating the popular sectors; but the regional leaders of the parties had little incentive to incorporate them. The concern of regional leaders was with sustaining the support of small electorates that were large enough to win electoral majorities through a continuous flow of patronage. Coalition rule did succeed in bringing the *violencia* between the traditional parties to an end in 1964; but by this time violence was acquiring a new class-based form.

The National Front regime was consolidated by the absence of sharp party differences over economic policy. From the 1950s a mild economic nationalism was shared by the parties and manifested in the formation and policies of public enterprises such as the oil company Empresa Colombiana de Petróleos (ECOPETROL) – created when the private De Mares concession held by Tropical Oil expired in 1952 – the iron and steel complex Acerías Paz del Río in Boyacá and the merchant fleet Flota Mercante Grancolombiana, none of which was planned as a state monopoly. Both political parties were slow to learn that such enterprises carry requirements of scale that exceed the limits of the domestic market and are uncompetitive internationally. The lesson was more thoroughly absorbed from another IFI project, Forjas de Colombia, which from the mid-1960s was the leading supplier of foundries for the metallurgical industry. Imbued with the industrialist and statist mentality associated with UN Economic Commission for Latin America (ECLA/CEPAL), both Conservatives and Liberals acquired enthusiasm for planning, and agricultural policy was relegated to second place in their economic priorities except briefly in the late 1960s. At the same time, both Conservatives and Liberals took a generally relaxed attitude towards foreign oil enterprises. Their priority was to assure low internal prices, principally because oil and petroleum products were crucial to both industry and transport in a country where high transport costs restricted growth in the internal market. Coal followed these broad lines, too; and a bipartisan consensus prevailed in tax policy.

The Rojas regime (1953–7) acted as a permanent warning to the civilian elite of the risks of internal decomposition, although the officer corps was not discredited, because the dictatorship had been relatively benign. From 1958 a relatively homogeneous upper class included the military in the governing consensus. Refraining from fomenting inter-service rivalry and avoiding action that precipitated civilian–military confrontation, the coalition also dissolved the problem of military–police feuds by insisting on the seniority of the army, while promoting bipartisanship in the national police and improving its pay, conditions and technology.

Nonetheless, factionalism within the army sometimes surfaced. Officers advocating exclusively repressive remedies to the problems of rural and urban violence clashed with those committed to a joint civic–military approach that included social and economic reforms. Coalition governments rewarded loyalty to the bipartisan solution with job security, improved pay, pensions and fringe benefits and support for the pursuit of greater professionalism – issues that united the officer corps. And civilian governments responded to pressures for enlarged military budgets to tackle guerrilla insurgency, to resist the influence of the Cuban Revolution and to be ready for a possible conflict with Venezuela over maritime oil or illegal Colombian emigration. Military loyalty was further secured through the operation of the state of siege. A flexible instrument that could be applied at a national, departmental or municipal level, this measure empowered the president and cabinet to rule by decree without reference to Congress. Under a state of siege, military justice was imposed together with censorship and restrictions on freedom of speech, assembly and travel. Although frequent resort to the state of siege reassured some soldiers claiming that legal restraints prevented them from curbing violence, some officers expressed alarm that the civilian elite used the state of siege to shunt responsibility for its mismanagement onto the army.

The scale and intensity of military involvement in Colombian politics were not comparable to those in the Southern Cone. This was due partly to the resilience of the civilian system and the strength of constitutional sentiment in the army. But it was also because few pretexts for seizure of total control arose. Left-wing parties were not strong, levels of labour mobilization were low, hyperinflation did not occur, and the private sector was unwilling to jeopardize the benefits gained from the coalition by seeking out alliances with dissident officers.

The National Front coalition permitted a revival of trade unionism. The Confederación de Trabajadores de Colombia (CTC), shorn of its radical wing, was reborn in 1958–9 without alarming the propertied interests; and the progressive laicization of the Unión de Trabajadores Colombianos (UTC) meant that Liberals no longer feared it as a potential clerical militia. The first National Front government, led by Lleras Camargo, made limited concessions to urban labour but also introduced regulations that gave the major confederations little part in wage negotiations and few resources with which to assist affiliated unions. As a result, by 1975 perhaps only 17 per cent of wage-workers belonged to a trade union. Even in the most heavily unionized sectors – manufacturing, the public service and transport – rates of trade union membership did not exceed 40 per cent. This low level was attributable to both the slow growth of an urban proletariat and quite modest inflation: 8 per cent annually between 1950 and 1960; 10 per cent between 1960 and 1970. In the 1970s and 1980s the growth of legitimate unionism was impeded by the size of the informal sector, the impossibility of recruitment in zones of guerrilla warfare, right-wing intimidation and intra-union dissension. Despite inflation in the 1970s, which exceeded 20 per cent per annum, and the depression of real wages, the CTC and UTC failed to attract workers; they were clearly instruments of state management rather than the embodiment of genuine working-class aspirations. New trade union confederations that posed a more combative challenge grew in the 1970s when escalating inflation influenced the number, intensity and duration of strikes. Militancy was most pronounced among public sector workers, in areas of strategic economic activity – like the oil industry – that were geographically isolated, so that a strong correspondence was felt by workers between the workplace and the community. Unions of urban workers and middle-class groups – schoolteachers, bank employees, doctors – became more militant and were active in diverse forms of protest, of which the civic strike (*paro cívico*), precipitated by increases in the tariffs of basic services (water, electricity and transport), was the most important and violent. But, for the most part, owing to union weakness, private employer hostility was focussed on labour legislation, especially the failures of tribunals of binding arbitration established in 1966, rather than labour militancy. Nevertheless, trade union leaders began to speak out more forcefully on a wide range of issues. Limiting their statements in the 1960s to enterprise-level collective bargaining and the content of the labour code, they began in the early 1970s to express views on macro-economic and social policies and on public services, and in the late 1970s entered debate on industrial, financial and external trade policies (but not agrarian and fiscal policies).

Interest groups, especially Federación Nacional de Cafeteros (Fedecafé) and Asociación Nacional de Industriales (ANDI) played a central role within a pragmatic liberal state that absorbed features of Keynesianism and corporatism. The private sector was incorporated through the boards of directors of public banks, the commissions determining monetary and exchange, foreign trade, price and wage policy. Interest groups favoured planning activity in such areas as credit and tax incentives, but not when it meant more intervention. The impact of interest groups throughout the period varied by sector, size, region and level of technical competence. While the period since 1958 witnessed the growth of state enterprise and intervention, along with economic planning and the emergence of a technocratic elite, efficiency continued to be impaired by corruption and a broader bias in favour of powerful interest groups, which brought the state into disrepute. Then, in the 1980s, the crisis of the state became endemic. Indeed, both the efficacy and the legitimacy of the state were thrown into question by the problem of insecurity, arising from the narcotics traffic, guerrilla activity, paramilitary violence and organized criminality. In combination, these undermined the administration of justice and highlighted the absence of a modern system of policing.

Partiality towards producer associations became the subject of sharp attacks from forces outside the National Front, particularly from the early 1970s. However, such movements failed to coalesce for any length of time, the National Front regime and the state system that it evolved proving to be remarkably stable despite their failure to eradicate social and political violence. This was no less characteristic of the 1980s than it was of the 1950s, and as such qualifies any celebration of the endurance of constitutional forms of government during years when most other Latin American countries experienced dictatorial regimes. The maintenance of civilian rule under such conditions may certainly be explained in part by the warm relations that the governing elite enjoyed with Washington, as well as the fact that Colombia possessed a low international profile and produced few strategic commodities. However, neither the absence of external intervention nor the favourable policies of U.S. and multi-lateral economic bodies account for the peculiarities of the country's political trajectory. This was determined primarily by the enduring capacity of the 1958 coalition agreement to fulfil the requirements of the dominant classes and sectors and to overcome a variety of challenges to their social order.

CONSOLIDATION OF THE NATIONAL FRONT COALITION,
1958 – 66

The Lleras Camargo coalition government (1958–62) enjoyed a wider range of options than the coalitions in 1930 and 1946 and succeeded in reducing the level of competition between the parties. However, the National Front also heightened factionalism, since competition was now refocussed on struggles to obtain a majority of posts allocated to each party. Indeed, at its inception the coalition was threatened both by internecine factionalism within the Conservative Party – a minority faction reluctant to forfeit the gains made since 1946 had put up a dissident candidate against Lleras Camargo – and by dissension among the Liberals. The Liberal defectors established the Movimiento de Recuperación Liberal (MRL), which was rebaptized the Movimiento Revolucionario Liberal in enthusiasm for the Cuban Revolution. The MRL was led by the son of President Alfonso López Pumarejo, Alfonso López Michelsen, who drew support with slogans such as 'Pasajeros de la revolución, favor pasar a bordo'. Observing the impact of the Cuban Revolution upon the younger generation, the new organization wooed Liberals hostile to coalition with their former adversaries and adopted a more radical policy – ambiguous in its attitude towards property – than the government. Reaching an apogee of influence in 1962, the MRL (dissolved in 1967) absorbed some guerrilla and bandit leaders into mainstream politics and preserved the Liberal mystique in the face of National Front coalition politics.

The Lleras Camargo government concentrated its initiatives in areas where elite consensus could most easily be achieved. It transformed an advisory planning council, founded in 1949, into a long-range planning department that broadened access to economic information, improved decision-making and mediated with foreign capital and international agencies. The government introduced a coherent programme of colonization, transport and employment in regions of gravest *violencia*. The violence was reduced for a time, but new frustrations were created among those *campesinos* who, on reclaiming their property, encountered inefficient and costly litigation. This engendered further conflict, to which the Lleras Camargo government responded by accelerating plans for a modest agrarian reform administered by a new agency, Instituto Colombiano de Reforma Agraria (INCORA). INCORA aimed to restore rural stability and expand the urban food supply by speeding up the distribution of public lands in zones of colonization and redistributing idle land on large estates, consolidating minifundia in viable units and spreading rural credit through a new co-operative bank. This was an unambitious programme, but it was criticized by the Right as an assault on the sanctity of private property and by the Left as a demagogic half-measure.

The government also sought to pacify the countryside through Acción Comunal (AC), which sponsored self-help community schemes based on local resources and reinforced by national and international funds assembled by the central agencies. AC enabled the coalition to convince the United States of its commitment to an ideology of self-improvement and to consolidate links with municipal elites whose support staved off peasant radicalism. But any benefits from AC that trickled down to the peasantry were strictly modest. Continued peasant dissatisfaction was evident from land invasions organized sometimes by the Left but often by frustrated activists of Federación Agraria Nacional (FANAL), a centrist peasant organization founded in 1946 that was affiliated with the UTC and loosely connected with the Conservatives.

The overall thrust of the Lleras Camargo policy met with the approval of the United States, which courted the coalition as a reformist and democratic government. (During the 1960s Colombia was to rank second in Latin America as a recipient of U.S. economic aid and fifth as a recipient of military aid.) The Lleras Camargo government was the first in Latin America to respond to the Alliance for Progress, unveiling a ten-year development plan for 1961–70 that adhered to U.S. requirements – agrarian reform, fiscal order, monetary stability and adequate instruments of control. Sharing the exuberant liberalism of the Kennedy administration, Lleras welcomed U.S. teams that collaborated with national agencies, and Colombia was vaunted as a showpiece of the Alliance.

By 1962 the coalition had reaped the fruits of a pragmatic impatience with ideology, a willingness to emphasize points of common interest between the parties and a cautious policy of export-led growth combined with increased foreign investment and some manufacturing expansion. The Conservatives dropped a residual Francoist identification, adopting instead a more acceptable Christian Democratic language, and were reconciled to a measure of state-sponsored social change and the use of external aid to promote security objectives. Meanwhile, the Liberal leadership contained radical aspirations within the party and restricted the influence of unions. Thus, the coalition arrangements were sufficiently firm to ensure the transition of power from a Liberal president to a Conservative one.

In 1962 Guillermo León Valencia won the presidential election for the National Front with 1,636,000 votes against 626,000 for the MRL and 309,000 for a dissident Conservative ticket. Valencia pursued much the same policies as Lleras Camargo. Skilled in accommodation, he displayed a mastery of political minutiae that reconciled contending factions. The same talents were not, however, displayed in economic management. A combination of industrial recession, inflation (an 18 per cent increase in the cost of living index for *bogotano* urban workers in the first half of 1963) and rising unemployment prefigured mounting urban agitation and a radicalization of the trade union confederations. Fearful that the urban middle class might defect from the coalition, Valencia decisively crushed a series of strikes. This unexpected ruthlessness threw the trade unions onto the defensive and reassured the propertied interests, which supported a reshuffling of economic ministers and advisers. The producer associations assumed an indispensable role in mediating between interests and reaching a policy consensus that mitigated the shock of a stabilization programme and devaluation.

The main challenge to the coalition government came from Alianza Nacional Popular (ANAPO), an alliance formed in 1961 by former president Rojas Pinilla. Presenting himself as a civilian politician seeking to be elected constitutionally, Rojas reassured the government by distancing himself from military conspiracy. ANAPO attracted both Conservatives and Liberals disenchanted with the National Front. In the 1960s it was more successful in winning Conservative than Liberal votes, both because, as president, Rojas had admitted few Liberals to the bureaucracy and because the dissident Liberals were still being drawn to the MRL. Between 1962 and 1970 ANAPO built an efficient organization with an elaborate network of *barrio* organizations through the sale of membership cards, mass rallies and party training schools. ANAPO even imported a

CARDEX system from the United States to follow the movements of its members and expanded its capacity to present electoral lists from seven departments in 1964 to eighteen in 1970.

Projecting itself as the representative of the dispossessed, ANAPO set about constructing a broad-based coalition united by exclusion from power. It was strikingly successful among youth and the urban lower middle class, to whom it promised opportunities for career advancement. It wooed beneficiaries of *rojista* patronage between 1953 and 1957, small businessmen squeezed by lack of credit, and a wide spectrum of society alarmed that small savings were eroded by inflation. It encompassed critics of the government of diverse social origins: slum-dwellers and migrants from the countryside; schoolteachers, often unpaid for long periods; *costeño* landowners claiming official favouritism of the Andean departments; radical priests and socialist intellectuals from Bogotá, who wanted to push ANAPO towards the Left, and clerical Conservatives from Boyacá, who wanted to pull it to the Right. ANAPO thereby came to be the main rival of the governing coalition by 1966, when one of ANAPO's minor figures gained an impressive 28 per cent of the vote in the presidential election. Subject to local harassment until 1966, ANAPO was treated at a national level with a cautious tolerance, because the National Front was sure that it could be defeated and because its existence was useful in confirming the democratic legitimacy of the regime.

A second challenge was presented by rural guerrillas. Some, founded as self-defence groups during the *violencia,* had laid down their arms after being promised that their grievances would be acknowledged with the restoration of 'normality'. Others remained in existence, arguing that the Liberal–Conservative pact betrayed their ideological commitments and class interests. They did not, however, pose a serious threat to the survival of the government because they suffered from poor financing, geographical fragmentation and internal rivalries. The guerrillas gained only transitory influence in a number of dispersed zones, although permanent control was established in the 'independent republics' of Marquetalia, El Pato, Riochiquito and Guayabeno, which were described by the guerrillas themselves as 'zones of peasant self-defence'. These successes were useful in generating international publicity for their cause, but they also drained limited resources. A campaign by the army to demolish the 'independent republics' and put an end to the 'dismemberment of national sovereignty' culminated in a combined air and ground attack upon Marquetalia by the armed forces in 1964–5.

The response of the Communist Party to guerrilla activity was ambiguous. Rivalry between pro-Soviet and pro-Chinese leaders destroyed attempts to expand its influence, and the Tenth Party Congress (1965) was too preoccupied with the schism in international Communism to take advantage of domestic crises. One faction, afraid of losing Soviet support, upheld the thesis that the conditions for an armed struggle by the urban proletariat had yet to crystallize. But a rival faction sought close links with the guerrillas, because it feared that dissociation denied the party an effective youth movement. After the meeting of Latin American Communist parties in Havana in 1964, the official position of the party shifted to the adoption of 'two simultaneous roads to socialism', the use of all forms of struggle, violent or legal, against the bourgeoisie. Nevertheless, this was seen as inconsistent and opportunistic by some guerrilla leaders, who attacked the party's lack of revolutionary commitment, arguing that its vacillations confused the potentially revolutionary masses and obstructed effective action. Meanwhile, the ruling coalition frequently permitted the party to operate openly, since this allowed it to monitor Communist activities closely, discredited Communist claims of persecution and left the party to squander resources on a newspaper the impact of which was limited to the converted.

A third challenge to the Valencia government came from within the military. Civil—military relations were strained by the choice of General Alfredo Ruiz Novoa as war minister. Senior officers were angry that Valencia broke with precedent by selecting an officer only third in the military hierarchy, and the authoritarian current was hostile to Ruiz's Plan Lazo of 1963, since this incorporated civilian development programmes into the counter-insurgency campaign. Ruiz planned new semi-autonomous offensive units and mobile intelligence groups, which undertook sophisticated information-gathering and analysis and acquired an intimate knowledge of the local terrain before attacking the rebels. Military action was then followed by civic action to ensure peasant support: the distribution of food supplies, the building of roads and schools and the provision of water supplies, medical and other facilities, in which the international charity CARE played a major role.

For his part, Ruiz antagonized segments of the civilian elite by condemning their resistance to structural change, accusing them of exploiting the urban working class and demanding a broader military role in society as a whole. He irritated cabinet colleagues by pressing publicly for an accelerated agrarian reform to reinforce civic—military programmes and oblige large landowners to transfer land from extensive cattle-ranging to intensive foodstuffs production. Convinced that the armed forces possessed technological and managerial skills that were scarce in the civilian domain, Ruiz presented the army as the spearhead of a development programme. These initiatives united the civilian Right, which argued that Ruiz was not pursuing the guerrillas single-mindedly, with progressive Liberals, who thought he posed a threat to the candidacy of Lleras Restrepo in 1966. However, it was only in 1965, when he was driven into personal confrontation with Ruiz for sympathizing publicly with a strike by the UTC, that Valencia extracted Ruiz's resignation amidst rumours of an impending coup.

Lesser problems were posed by student unrest, which took place against a background of rapid university expansion. Resources failed to keep up with the expansion of the student population: between 1945 and 1968 the number matriculating multiplied ninefold, reaching 28,000 in 1968. A fall in the proportion of students attending the Universidad Nacional from 46 per cent in 1939 to 19 per cent in 1968 caused alarm over a trend towards privatization in higher education, the content of teaching at the private universities being more in keeping with development needs, or so it was believed, and thus with remunerative graduate employment. Internal issues – autonomy, *co-gobierno*, admissions policy and curriculum reform – was debated feverishly along with other national questions. Some professors recalled Mariátegui and the university reform movement of the 1920s, in which the Liberal leader Carlos Lleras Restrepo had been prominent. But the students of the 1960s were radicalized more by local activists and contemporary foreign examples, especially the Cuban Revolution and the 1968 events in Paris and Mexico City. At times protest spilled over into violence that was stifled only by the closure of Universidad Nacional for long periods. Student radicalism gained no sustained momentum, because the composition of the student body was constantly changing and because the ultra-leftist vanguardism that prevailed proclaimed a student–worker–peasant alliance that was divorced from reality. In the short term student activism persuaded the political parties to redouble their recruitment efforts. Later the activist graduates of the 1960s put their experience at the service of civic movements.

The government was also troubled by the Frente Unido, a Catholic left-wing group that linked students with the unions and young lay professionals. Amongst its leaders was the charismatic upper-class priest Father Camilo Torres, who was chaplain of the Universidad Nacional and co-founder of its sociology department. His espousal of birth control, divorce and expropriation without compensation preceded a disillusionment with reformist gradualism and his conversion to the view that Marxism and revolutionary violence were Christian imperatives. This decision precipitated his formal 'separation' from the Church by Cardinal Luis Concha, who countered that the Church could take part in revolution only in the event of absolute tyranny. In 1967 Torres was killed in armed action with the revolutionary guerrillas in Santander.

The Church, whose privileged constitutional status was reaffirmed in 1958, tended towards political disengagement (except on particular issues like divorce and contraception) and the promotion of welfare work, in conjunction with such international Catholic charities and relief agencies as CARITAS. Yet the bishops were attacked for supporting the status quo by a vociferous minority of younger clergy, who, influenced by Christian Democracy, the Second Vatican Council and the Cuban Revolution, urged vigorous stands on social and economic issues. Often educated in the social sciences in Europe (especially Louvain) and the United States, these clergy rejected the juridical approach of the Gregorian University and conservative theology that applauded the merits of resignation and class collaboration. Instead, they came to accept that class conflict was necessary to remedy inequalities of wealth contrary to Catholic teaching. Radical priests argued that secularization could be halted only if the Church stood whole-heartedly in the vanguard of social change, entering dialogue with Marxists and ecumenical conversation with Protestants.

Despite their challenge, the conservative bishops remained in an unassailable majority, retained control of the Permanent Secretariat of the Colombian Episcopal Conference, which issued pastoral letters for nation-wide consumption, and exploited new styles of management to make themselves more accessible to the laity. Denying access to the pulpits to international radical leaders like Dom Helder Câmara, archbishop of Recife, the conservative leadership gave its blessing to the expulsion of radical foreign priests and worked to minimize the impact of the radical features of the Second General Conference of Latin American Bishops (Conferencia Episcopal Latinoamericana–CELAM) held at Medellín in 1968. As the Colombian bishops regrouped and assumed the continental vanguard in the conservative counter-offensive that culminated in a right-wing ascendancy at the third CELAM conference at Puebla in 1979, many radical clergy left the Church to enter lay occupations.

REFORM AND RESISTANCE, 1966–74

In the election of 1966 the National Front, whose candidate, Carlos Lleras Restrepo, was the cousin of Lleras Camargo, polled 1,639,000 votes against 519,000 for the *anapista*, 352,000 for the MRL and 334,000 for a dissenting Conservative. Only the second Liberal president since 1946, Lleras Restrepo restored the National Front's impetus with an ambitious programme that combined the pursuit of economic growth with social welfare concessions and broadened political participation. Drawing upon his experience in national and regional politics, coffee, banking and journalism, and adopting a strongly presidential style, Lleras Restrepo broadened the scope of the 'autonomous institutions', insulating some economic policy decisions from partisan politics and enlarging the capacity of the state in planning, regulation and investment, so as to meet the efficiency requirements of the international agencies. In 1968 Lleras introduced a constitutional reform. This gave the executive greater power to shape legislation concerning public expenditure, fiscal exemptions, provision of state-run public services and plans of public works. It also enabled the president to intervene in the Central Bank and in the management of savings and private investments; and it authorized him to decree an 'economic emergency' for up to ninety days per year during which the executive held special powers. The 1968 reform also contained measures to prepare the way for the resumption of competitive politics and to establish a more clearly defined role for the presidency and Congress in economic matters.

Lleras Restrepo gave priority to stabilizing exchange rate policy, which had remained erratic from the mid-1950s to 1967. The 1957 crisis in the balance of payments had prompted the international lending agencies and powerful domestic groups like Fedecafé and private coffee exporters to press for a devaluation. However, both then and subsequently such a response was resisted by ad hoc alliances of importers, industrialists (who exerted pressure through ANDI, Federación de Metalúrgicos – FEDEMETAL – and other interest groups) and, for reasons of prestige, sectors of the government, the opposition, trade unions and other areas of public opinion. The importance of the price of coffee to the national economy ensured that the problem of striking a balance between the interests of exporters, importers and the state was recurrent, not only in terms of economic management but also with respect to the maintenance of political stability.

Decree Law 444 of 1967 adopted the 'crawling peg' as a mechanism to avoid drastic devaluation. Through the administrative manipulation of import controls and a system of multiple rates of exchange for different categories of input, Lleras contrived a concealed devaluation, so that the prestige of his government was unimpaired. Although the importance attached to the decree at the time was somewhat exaggerated, it undoubtedly enabled a more stable exchange management and a reorientation of policy to promote new exports for two principal markets, the United States and the other Andean countries. In the 1970s relative exchange rate stability, monetary control and the recovery of the coffee sector upheld a surplus on capital account and great liquidity. Yet Decree Law 444 alone was not enough to ensure that Colombian exports could reap the benefits of a growth in international trade; Colombia's share, in fact, fell.

The debate about agrarian policy was reopened by Lleras Restrepo because the very limited reform of 1961 and encouragement of peaceful petitioning had failed to halt violence in widely varied agricultural zones. It occurred in areas of recent migration, like Caquetá and the Middle Magdalena, where migrants aiming to restore a peasant economy were confronted with expanding latifundia; and it was evident in the Andean departments, where stable peasant groups demanded backing with credit, prices and marketing assistance, and landless labourers wanted to reconstitute themselves as peasants. Violent conflict was frequent in established areas of latifundismo – some parts of the Caribbean coast and Llanos Orientales – where *hacendados* clashed with rent-paying peasants, fishermen and mobile subsistence agriculturalists, determined to break landowner power when threatened with eviction. Equally affected were areas of agrarian capitalism, such as the fertile lowland plains of Valle del Cauca, Huila, Tolima and other parts of the Caribbean coast, where clashes over wages, working conditions and job security prompted rural workers to seek access to land to reconstitute themselves as peasants.

Arguing that these conflicts showed the urgent need for profound measures, Lleras Restrepo placed heavier stress upon redistribution of land worked by sharecroppers and tenant-farmers than had the reform of 1961. He backed the *via campesina* – the view that agricultural production and productivity would best be raised by encouraging a dynamic sector of small farmers at the expense of a stagnant sector of large landowners. This stress on redistribution was complemented by an emphasis on agrarian diversification, which aimed to reduce imports of foodstuffs, and state promotion of grass-roots peasant organizations. From 1967 these were united in a national organization, Asociación Nacional de Usuarios Campesinos (ANUC), which was designed to divert peasant belligerence to peaceful channels and ensure a flow of information between government and peasantry. By 1970 it was claimed that ANUC had more than 1.5 million members and reached 30 per cent of the rural population, particularly colonists and landless labourers in areas of violence. Field promoters from the Division of Peasant Organization in the Agriculture Ministry used seminars to instruct peasants in land rights, foment a spirit of independence against *gamonales* and encourage resistance to injustices.

For the first time in Colombian history, the landed interests feared social revolution launched by a nation-wide *agrarista* movement. They therefore moved resolutely against Lleras Restrepo's measure and its supporters. The reform precipitated a wave of evictions by large landowners and was resisted by an alliance of right-wing Liberals and Conservatives in Congress. Fedecafé demanded immunity for the coffee sector from what it claimed were the destabilizing effects on export production of land redistribution. Equally, reform was from the start diluted from within the Instituto Colombiano de Reforma Agraria (INCORA), the management of which contained representatives of agrarian groups committed to large landownership – the Sociedad de Agricultores de Colombia (SAC) and Federación de Ganaderos (FEDEGAN). Moreover, INCORA was unequal to the tasks that the president imposed upon it. It had neither the funds nor the competence – sufficient land surveyors, good-quality cadastral surveys, adequate meteorological data, soil studies or statistical information on the volume and value of agricultural production – to perform adequately.

During the Lleras Restrepo presidency a significant programme of industrialization and consolidation of the national market was complemented by proposals to establish a common market containing Venezuela, Colombia, Ecuador, Peru, Bolivia and Chile. The Andean Pact (without Venezuela until 1973) was formed in 1968, with its base at Lima. The principal objective of the pact was the promotion of state-sponsored capitalist development by fostering regional exchange of goods (trade with other Andean countries represented only a small proportion of total foreign trade of each member-country at its inception) and the reassertion of a degree of national economic autonomy by regulations for the screening of foreign investment. Arguing that Colombia stood to benefit from trade expansion with its Andean partners because it enjoyed a regional lead in manufacturing, advocates of the common market stressed the potential for national growth in such areas as petrochemicals and raw materials for man-made fibres. They also claimed that the pact's code contained an effective framework for both the monitoring and regulation of foreign investment (notably Decision 24, by which members were enjoined to buy up majority shareholdings in foreign enterprise gradually) and the promotion of joint enterprise with transnationals that would make possible the import of technology without abrogating national economic control. It was also argued that co-ordinated negotiation by a group of countries was more effective than individual bargaining in negotiation with powerful transnational corporations. Critics of the pact argued that the growth in regional trade predicted by its exponents was not achieved, partly as a result of problems of product variety and partly because the market was still too small to achieve significant economies of scale and efficient levels of output. Some critics went further, contending that the limited growth in trade which was attributed to the pact could have been brought about through bilateral co-operative arrangements without the burden of a costly (and perhaps unaccountable) bureaucracy. In their view the main beneficiaries of the pact were the affiliates and subsidiaries of transnational corporations, which, with greater capital resources and a superior knowledge of the region as a whole than of national enterprise, were able to seize immediate advantage of the lowering of tariff boundaries. Even ardent supporters of the pact conceded that its effectiveness had been reduced by ideological clashes and by differences among members about priorities and the pace of implementation of vital decisions.

Despite their dislike of the more radical of his policies, the upper and middle classes were broadly supportive of Lleras Restrepo. They approved of his tough handling of urban labour unrest, his unaccommodating attitude towards student activism, his demand for high educational requirements among ministers and senior officials, and the imposition of a curfew when urban disturbances reached a peak in 1970, just after the presidential elections.

Nevertheless, the government failed to reckon with the degree of resistance to the reform programme from within the bipartisan state machinery; and while it calculated upon the obstructive effects of inertia at the intermediate levels of public administration by using the expedient of new institutions to bypass local structures, it created new uncertainties about the locus of power and responsibility in the localities. As it lost confidence, the government was shaken by congressional campaigns to expose public immorality, especially in the Agriculture Ministry. The scale of popular dissatisfaction was reflected in substantial *anapista* incursions into the principal city councils in the mid-term elections, a growing *anapista* influence in AC, and the general strike of 1969, which collapsed only because the government skilfully exploited a rift between the UTC and CTC.

ANAPO benefited considerably from the difficulties confronting Lleras Restrepo. Programmatic imprecision was useful to ANAPO, which tailored its appeal to immediate popular needs without being constrained by ideology. A coalition formed around the figure of Rojas and his programme – the 'Decalogue' – which was part radical (profit-sharing schemes for employees, a low-cost urban housing programme and a progressive tax reform) and part conservative (explicit opposition to birth control policies and divorce reform, and agrarian reform proposals less far-reaching than those of Lleras). The absence of a national newspaper was probably advantageous, because *anapista* divisions were not publicly aired and ANAPO, denied advertising by the public sector and pro-government private enterprise, could portray itself as the victim of oligarchic oppression.

The programme presented by Lleras Restrepo was the first in Colombian experience to be based on a careful and extensive assessment of national problems. It could not, however, be effected in the four-year life-span of a coalition government, in which interests hostile to government policies participated in their formulation and execution. Lleras Restrepo was criticized for nearly precipitating the breakdown of the coalition by not making the pursuit of domestic accommodation his overriding aim.

The official National Front candidate for 1970, a Conservative, Misael Pastrana Borrero, confronted two opponents who drew Conservative votes: Rojas Pinilla and Evaristo Sourdis, a powerful *costeño* figure who won a large anti-*bogotano* vote. Despite an expensive campaign that included much use of television, Pastrana was almost defeated, winning by only 41,000 votes out of a total of nearly 4 million cast. In a campaign masterminded by his daughter María Eugenia, Rojas exploited popular dissatisfaction at the failure of *llerista* policies to match the redistributive rhetoric that surrounded them. The margin of electoral defeat was so small that a recount was necessary, after which even opponents of Rojas privately conceded their belief that only fraud at the eleventh hour had secured victory for the overconfident National Front. A group of *anapista* military officers attempted a coup that was rapidly foiled by Lleras, possibly in liaison with Rojas, posturing as a champion of peace who avoided a justifiable civil war by dissuading proponents of a popular uprising.

Pastrana, manager of a leading textile enterprise, was a protégé of President Mariano Ospina Pérez (1946–50) and as a former ambassador in Washington had close connections with the United States. Pastrana was acceptable to the Liberals, partly because he was an experienced administrator who had skilfully piloted the constitutional reform through Congress in 1968 and partly because he was concerned to promote capitalist interests regardless of political affiliation rather than to ensure a Conservative victory in 1974 (when the bipartisan arrangements were due to end). Pastrana was also careful to retain *llerista* reformist rhetoric. The substance of policy, however, shifted considerably. The new president's choice of officials heralded a reduction of state intervention in the private sector and a greater representation of private interests in government. Pastrana did not reverse *llerista* policies, but soft-pedalled them. By appointing senior personnel with slight enthusiasm for the reforms they were supposed to execute, he ensured that the reform programme would lose momentum. After a policy was given time to fail, the appropriate minister announced its termination.

Such a pattern was most conspicuous in agrarian policy. From 1970–2 the strategy of the *via terrateniente* replaced the *via campesina*, by which the state had undertaken a guiding role in agriculture, mobilizing peasant support for a strategy stressing redistribution and passing some of the costs of development on to the large landowners. By contrast, the *via terrateniente* now assigned the responsibility for agrarian growth to large agrarian capitalists, giving the state responsibility for corporatist control of an increasingly organized peasantry through co-option of its more prosperous elements.

From its inception, agrarian reform was weakened by the exclusion of peasants and small producers from decision-making. They might take temporary advantage of differences within the *llerista* alliance; but their bargaining leverage was severely restricted. When the peak of land redistribution was reached, in 1969–71, the industrialist component of the *llerista* alliance defected. It was becoming clear that agrarian modernization could be achieved without redistribution of land as the large landowners increased output and productivity, demonstrating that they did not constitute the obstacle to capitalist growth that reformist bureaucrats claimed. The success of the landowners' counter-offensive was consolidated by the Pact of Chicoral in 1972, in which the reformist bureaucracy capitulated to an alliance of congressmen and landowners.

Radicalized by the failure to implement reform, a more politicized ANUC split into two wings – Línea Armenia, the more conservative, and Línea Sincelejo, the more radical. ANUC Línea Armenia retained the broad position of the *llerista* alliance; but ANUC Línea Sincelejo became the focal point of rural radicalism, mounting land invasions (especially in the latifundia of the Caribbean and Upper Magdalena regions), civic strikes and consumer boycotts, campaigns of civil disobedience, and con-certing pressure with the collaboration of sympathetic clergy and disgruntled INCORA bureaucrats to hasten land redistribution. Subject to hostile media coverage – especially of its 1972 march on Bogotá – and to ritual denunciations that it was a Communist and subversive force, ANUC lost its official subsidies and was denied a part in major negotiations about agrarian policy. Patronage, meanwhile, was channelled via AC, whose funds met basic needs like schools and electrification and were used to fragment the broader peasant movement. Of nearly 22,000 AC juntas that existed in 1978, nearly one-half were created after 1970.

ANUC Línea Sincelejo never recovered its vitality, and the upsurge of peasant militancy lost its momentum. A powerful *agrarista* movement failed to take shape. Probably the most important reason for this was the diversity within ANUC, which precluded a coherent class consciousness. *Colonos,* small rural merchants, wage labourers in large agribusiness enterprises, minifundistas and landless labourers did not have common interests and priorities. The militancy of some was diminished by the partial satisfaction of their demands; that of others was depleted by opportunities to migrate to Venezuela and the marijuana frontiers. Ideological divisions also played a part. Small farmers were antagonized by the doctrinaire vanguardism of Maoist splinter groups, which preached that a carbon copy of the Chinese revolution could be effected immediately in Colombia, and Trotskyists, who lacked worker support but advocated a peasant–worker revolutionary alliance.

The shift in agrarian policy and eventual termination of redistribution of land in 1972 were acceptable to the SAC and the agrarian commodity federations. Militantly resisting the proposals of 1969 for progressive land taxation, the SAC had answered the challenge of the *via campesina* by mod-ernizing itself. It enthusiastically promoted the 'green revolution', with low-interest loans from AID for fertilizers, seeds and tractors supplement-ing local private and public funds. Though obstructed by the inflationary impact of the oil crisis of 1973 upon petroleum-based fertilizer and pesticides essential for new high-yield maize and wheat hybrids, the 'green revolution' enjoyed some successes, especially in rice production. Promoted since 1947 by the Federación de Arroceros, rice producers on the Caribbean coast and in the Llanos responded both to incentives for using machinery and herbicides and to price-support schemes by switching to new varieties and doubling average yield per acre between 1965 and 1975. Rice prices fell substantially relative to the prices of other foodstuffs; and rice came to displace beans in terms of calorific intake in the Colombian diet.

The Pastrana administration proposed one major redistributive reform. This was in urban policy, which had been neglected during the agrarian reform debate. Observing how ANAPO had benefited from defective urban services, the concentration of housing investment in booming upper- and upper-middle-class residential districts and deepening class antagonism, Jorge Valencia, Pastrana's minister of development, drew up an ambitious urban reform as an instrument to relegitimize the National Front coalition. His plan was to rechannel credit to cheap housing for low-income groups, reduce urban rents, eliminate urban land speculation and restrain further expansion of the largest cities through state-sponsored growth of cities of intermediate size. Valencia announced new taxes and regulations intended to redistribute wealth from urban landowners to the poor and to rectify deficiencies in urban services, as well as an increased role for the state in planning and providing housing for medium- and low-income groups. This antagonized the private sector and prompted the coalescence of a new alliance of urban construction and land estate interests with the financial sector. Valencia was ousted.

The Valencia plan was replaced by the 'Cuatro Estrategias' devised by Lauchlin Currie, leader of the World Bank mission more than two decades earlier, which reasserted the primacy of the private sector. Bold and technically impressive, this programme was markedly conservative in effect. Arguing that rural–urban migration should be accelerated in order to enlarge the proportion of the population in productive employment, Currie identified urban construction and export agriculture as the leading growth sectors. Insistent that his overall aim was not the provision of low-cost housing but the expansion of demand through the mobilization and redirection of financial resources towards urban construction, Currie pressed for a construction savings and loans fund with index-linked interest rates. By 1974 the Unidad de Poder Adquisitivo Constante (UPAC) system was operative in Bogotá. It engendered a construction boom and an increase in employment, but also had inflationary consequences, diverted credit from manufacturing to construction, stimulated rural—urban migration, overemphasized urban building and overlooked bottlenecks in the building sector.

The reformism of Lleras Restrepo had pushed the guerrillas onto the defensive. Determined to sharpen the distinction between the evolutionary and revolutionary Left, the president made a permanent trading relationship with the Soviet Union contingent upon Moscow exerting its influence to sever links between the Communist Party and the guerrillas. It was therefore widely assumed that a connection existed between the restoration of Soviet—Colombian diplomatic relations, the rupture between the Ejército de Liberación Nacional (ELN) and the Communist Party and a shift in Communist policy in 1967 to the view that there was now no revolutionary situation in Colombia. Moreover, in the late 1960s the guerrillas underestimated the professionalism of the Colombian army, by now well practised in internal warfare, the problems of maintaining supply lines over the Andes, and the difficulties of winning the permanent goodwill of the peasantry.

The Conservative counter-offensive under Pastrana revived guerrilla activity. Whereas in the early 1940s to take up arms and go to the mountains was considered an obsolete nineteenth-century practice that had no place in a political order where change could be effected democratically, by the early 1970s frustration at *bipartidismo* was so profound that, despite twenty years of slender achievement from armed action, joining the guerrillas was not considered entirely irrational. In fact, four guerrilla groups, differing in ideology, strategy and tactics, subsisted. The largest and most powerful was the Fuerzas Armadas Revolucionarias de Colombia (FARC) led by Manuel Marulanda ('Tirofijo'). Widely believed to be under the aegis of pro-Soviet Communists, the FARC had united scattered groups of guerrillas and bandits from the *violencia* in the mid-1960s and now consisted largely of peasants. The Ejército Popular de Liberación (EPL), a Maoist group smaller than the FARC, was composed principally of young professionals, students and rural wage labourers. The ELN, a Castroite group founded in Cuba in 1963–4, was formed mainly by young professionals and students and advocated the doctrines of *foquismo* popularized by Ernesto 'Che' Guevara; it was as a member of this group that Camilo Torres died in combat in 1967. (The ELN was later to acquire notoriety, making 124 assaults on nationally and internationally owned oil installations in 1985–7 alone.) A fourth group, the Movimiento 19 de abril (M-19), arose from *anapista* outrage at its 'fraudulent' defeat in the 1970 elections and depicted itself as the armed wing of ANAPO, which disowned it. The M-19 carried out spectacular actions, such as the theft of five thousand rifles from an army arsenal and the seizure of the Dominican Republic Embassy during a party attended by the U.S. ambassador and the papal nuncio. Intended to demoralize and damage the prestige of the army, these contributed to the resilience of the guerrilla opposition as a whole, which survived a renewed attack on the 'independent republics' in 1973. The guerrillas' capacity for endurance was indeed remarkable; for much of the 1970s Colombia was the only South American country with active rural guerrilla organizations.

The guerrillas won considerable support from peasants and rural labour, especially in the late 1970s, in the new banana zone of Urabá, for example, as a result of a harsh labour regime; in Arauca, because none of the new oil wealth from the region trickled to the popular sectors; and in the Middle Magdalena, as the consequence of archaic labour relations. But this support was not observed in all areas of guerrilla operations, and visions of a better society soured as violence became more indiscriminate and the romantic notion of the beauty of a youthful death in the armed struggle lost its appeal. Small farmers and their allies were pushed into setting up their own militias, some of which, in western Boyacá, for example, were infiltrated by right-wing death squads in the mid-1980s. By this time some guerrilla organizations were clearly abusing human rights – while mobilizing international opinion to protest human rights abuses committed by the military. As a result, they depended increasingly on violence and the threat of violence, not popular support, to survive.

The aims of the guerrillas were often unclear. Some spoke of revolutionary transformation, others of incorporation and participation in a reformed order. One guerrilla organization showed little interest in more than asserting and conserving control of particular pieces of territory; another proclaimed its determination to defeat foreign firms and their national allies. Thus, the government responded in a confused, even capricious fashion, sometimes denouncing guerrillas as subversives and delinquents and applying the penal code to them, at other times treating them as a regular army with which conversations should be held and truces reached. These ambiguities encouraged some guerrilla organizations to claim international belligerent status on the grounds that they permanently occupied a particular portion of national territory. In the 1980s such claims were at times reinforced by elements in the non-violent Left who argued that guerrilla warfare was justifiable against a 'dissimulated dictatorship'.

The influence of ANAPO peaked in 1970–1, when its share of the presidential poll soared to 35.2 per cent and the movement won all but one of the main city councils in the municipal elections. Overly confident, the movement declared its transformation into a party with Rojas as leader and María Eugenia as national director. However, from 1971 *anapista* support slumped; its share of the vote never exceeded 19 per cent and in 1976 dropped to 4 per cent. No single factor suffices to explain this decline. Certainly, the opportunism of many erstwhile *anapistas* and the tactics of Pastrana played a major part in eroding *anapista* support. The president lured sections of the intermediate leadership with patronage that reduced *anapista* funds (because *anapista* candidates and office-holders were obliged to pay contributions) and undermined the confidence of its following. Pastrana also channelled state resources to departmental governments controlled by Liberals and Conservatives instead of *anapista*-run city councils, thus disappointing the expectations of the *anapista* rank and file.

However, the main cause of *anapista* decline was its lack of organization and programme. ANAPO's national executive, denied influence in decision-making, was appointed and sacked at will by Rojas. An informal triumvirate of Rojas, María Eugenia and her husband, Samuel Moreno de Díaz, made all major policy decisions and arranged appointments to executive bodies and candidates for legislative lists. A shift in the composition of the leadership from a high incidence of retired military officers in the mid-1960s to a predominance of civilians in the early 1970s was not accompanied by a broadening of consultative processes. A high proportion of women in the intermediate leadership in the early 1970s reflected both the power of María Eugenia and the fact that Rojas had introduced women's suffrage. But this was not enough to meet the demands of party workers, angered that influence over policy formulation was possible only through private connections with the triumvirate and that no new generation of leaders was being prepared. Such sentiments were deepened by Rojas's decision in 1974 to appoint María Eugenia as presidential candidate.

The shift of power to María Eugenia accelerated defections. Never as popular as her father, she was unacceptable to some activists on sexist grounds and antagonized the *anapista* Right in key departments – Valle and Antioquia – by endorsing a leftward drift in the party instigated by the *bogotano* intelligentsia. The decision to delegate the task of drafting the programme for 1974 to a Socialist intellectual, Antonio García, fragmented ANAPO. Calculating that a more radical programme was essential to fend off the challenges of both the National Front candidate López Michelsen and the left-wing groups, María Eugenia underestimated the opposition of the *anapista* Right to promises that embodied earlier allusions to *socialismo a la colombiana*. While radicals complained of a lack of democratization, the *anapista* Right expressed dissent over commitments to radical land distribution, the nationalization of foreign-owned banks and profit-sharing schemes for private-sector employees.

The long-term impact of ANAPO was considerable. Its performance in the 1970 presidential elections showed that an opposition could defeat the ruling coalition on its own terms. ANAPO broadened the electorate, and it hastened the erosion of hereditary partisan attachments (especially among rural–urban migrants) by providing a transitional stage for Conservative voters of the 1960s who voted *anapista* in 1970 and then Liberal in 1974, and for Liberal voters who voted *anapista* in 1970 (and perhaps again in 1974) and voted Conservative in 1978.

Although short-lived, the existence of a third party not only affected the level of abstention from elections but also encouraged sections of the electorate to consider voting tactically. Between 1966 and 1974 the abstention rate fell from 65.3 to 46.1 per cent, which suggests that a significant portion of the adult population for the first time found some motive for participating in the political system. Equally, there is evidence to suggest that the strength of hereditary party loyalties underwent some erosion, and support for the two major forces became highly dependent on their policies and record. This development was not, perhaps, of decisive consequence so long as the coalition agreement was in force, but under the 1958 accord it was due to expire in 1974. Both for this reason and because the Communist Party succeeded in grouping various radical organizations behind the candidate of the Unión Nacional de Oposición (UNO), the elections of that year promised to be particularly important.

TOWARDS THE RESUMPTION OF COMPETITIVE
POLITICS, 1974–90

Before the 1974 elections, the Liberals and Conservatives began a lengthy process of consultation aimed at producing a formula that would preserve the stability which the National Front arrangement had provided yet permit a political *apertura* (opening). The coalition partners agreed upon a transition to 'open' competition, in which both Liberals and Conservatives would put up official presidential candidates, but the victor would be obliged to follow the principles of parity, allotting one-half of government posts to the other party. The Liberals put up Alfonso López Michelsen, the Conservatives Alvaro Gómez Hurtado, son of Laureano Gómez.

Arguing that for half a century Colombia had continuously promoted the modern sector of the economy at the expense of the rest, López promised to close the breach between regions and classes by introducing a tax reform that would lessen the income gap between rich and poor. He spoke of a more equitable distribution of public investment and of redistributing wealth among the regions. Identifying with the Socialist International, López Michelsen portrayed himself as a social democrat. By contrast, Gómez Hurtado, angling for the business vote, initially espoused a model similar to that adopted by the Brazilian military after 1964, but he became more tentative as middle-class voters recoiled from Brazilian-style authoritarianism. Meanwhile, the first serious woman contender for presidential office in Latin America, María Eugenia Rojas, entered the contest with a radical redistributionist programme. The number of people who voted was 5.2 million, a turnout double that in 1962 and 1966. In all, 56.2 per cent of voters opted for López, 31.4 per cent for Gómez, 9.4 per cent for María Eugenia and 2.6 per cent for the UNO candidate Echeverry Mejía.

Although López Michelsen won a landslide victory – sometimes attributed to his effectiveness on television – and he was able to claim a *mandato claro,* the new government was one of marked indecisiveness. Though promising radical reform and appearing to opt for a *llerista* strategy emphasizing redistribution and a more efficient state, López resolved the economic policy debate within the upper class in favour of the neo-liberal option, adopting a tight monetary policy in order to counter inflation generated by an unexpected bonanza of foreign exchange. He spoke both of the 'green revolution' and of a radical agrarian reform, which he tried to make palatable to the landed interests by stressing its importance to the counter-insurgency campaign; but he allocated insufficient resources to INCORA for even the most modest proposals and divided it into two weak institutions. López granted legal recognition to two outlawed trade union confederations – the Confederación Sindical de Trabajadores (CSTC) and Confederación General del Trabajo (CGT) – but this move was ambiguous, splintering two trade union confederations, into four and rendering the CSTC and CGT more politically manageable. López, a critic of UPAC, argued that the spread of index-linking from mortgages to life insurance benefits, and informally to wages and prices, overheated the economy and encouraged an inflationary mentality. But his government did not dismantle the UPAC system for fear of offending a powerful coalition of banks, depositors, the construction industry and its suppliers and workers; instead, López reduced indexation to levels below inflation and subjected savings to the capital gains tax.

A thin reformist veneer failed to conceal the absence of radical change. The pressing problem of Colombian migrants resident in Venezuela was left unresolved, and the much-heralded tax reform was obstructed at each stage by delay within branches of the government, back-pedalling, congressional opposition and evasion. Designed to promote equity, the reform increased the burden on the wealthiest by increasing personal income tax and imposing a capital gains tax, but did nothing to reduce the burden on the lower-income groups. It did result in increased revenue – before 1974 the effective tax rate represented 9.0 per cent of gross domestic product (GDP); in 1975 it was up to about 10.5 per cent – but the extent to which this was translated into a net transfer favouring the poor depended upon public expenditure patterns. The limited evidence available suggests that the relative position of low-wage workers, especially in agriculture, declined. Insufficient resources were raised to finance an ambitious Nutrition Plan and a programme of DRI which were, therefore, financed by external borrowing.

The one effective redistributionist reform – the implementation of Decision 24 of the Andean Pact to place international banks under 51 per cent national ownership – assisted domestic capitalists at the expense of international capital. This formed part of a shift towards a more independent foreign and foreign economic policy that was also observed in support for the campaign of General Omar Torrijos to wrest control of the Panama Canal from the United States and in endorsement, albeit lukewarm, of the *sandinista* struggle against the Somoza tyranny in Nicaragua. In 1976 Colombia relinquished U.S. aid for redeployment to needier countries.

The principal thrust of economic policy was to favour large domestic enterprise in the private sector by reducing public expenditure. A doctrinaire monetarist reliance on market forces was qualified by acceptance of the need for the state to promote development; this was not to be achieved by a massive expansion of the public sector, but rather by securing conditions attractive to foreign capital and by slowing down the devaluation of the exchange rate in order to avoid damaging the prospects of minor exports. Impressed by the experiences of Japan, Taiwan and South Korea, the López government spoke of transforming Colombia into the 'Japan of South America'. However, the analogy with the Far East was misplaced. The drive towards rapid industrialization was diminished by two factors: namely, the strength of Colombian agriculture and the erroneous assumption that a reduction in tariffs would automatically bring about a manufacturing sector that was internationally competitive. Since export agriculture competed strongly with industry for capital, labour and infrastructural support, the government was unable to achieve a consensus for industrialization, especially while the coffee price remained high and even the contraband sector was promoting significant agrarian diversification. Moreover, the failure to bring about a 'break-or-bust' industrialization was accompanied by a failure to reduce public expenditure. Continuing growth, made possible by a contraband bonanza that compensated for rising prices of oil and manufactured imports, nullified the argument that prevailing levels of public spending were deterring private initiative. Yet unpopular measures to eliminate a wheat subsidy, increase the sales tax and dismantle price controls were implemented. Prices were de-regulated, but wages remained controlled.

Under these conditions the trade unions acquired unprecedented unity and independence. General strikes in 1965, 1969 and 1971, and a marked increase in the incidence of strikes during the late 1960s, had not laid the basis for a permanent growth of militancy. A reduction in strike activity in the early 1970s had been encouraged by improving the apparatus for arbitration and by state pressure for collective contracts. The UTC and CTC remained part of the system of official patronage, which was reinforced by funds channelled from AID and the American Institute for the Development of Free Trade Unions, advocates of incremental improvement that sought a downgrading of the political component in labour activism.

In the 1970s there was an important shift of allegiance away from the UTC and CTC to the CSTC and CGT confederations and the new independent unions. The CSTC had seceded from the CTC in 1964 and subsequently grew at its expense. Under Communist influence, the CSTC was compelled for lack of legal recognition before 1974 to posture as a set of 'independent' unions when dealing with the government and judiciary.

The CGT was founded in 1970 and also reflected the influence of Marxists. The CSTC-affiliated and independent unions engaged in greater strike activity than did those attached to the UTC and CTC. This was a result not only of their greater autonomy and left-wing orientation but also of the fact that the CTC and UTC unions were concentrated in 'advanced' industries capable of offering better wage increases.

Thus, urban agitation mounted under López. A new peak of strike activity was reached in 1975; further agitation between June 1976 and June 1977 was fuelled by the highest inflation rate in Colombian recorded history – 42 per cent – after six years of continuous erosion of real urban wages that contrasted with the continuous increase observed between 1965 and 1971. Urban protest actions increasingly involved disenchanted sectors of the urban middle class, especially public sector employees, who tried to unite trade union protest at the work-place with popular protest in the *barrio*. A series of actions by doctors and medical workers, schoolteachers, bank and railway employees gave momentum to a general strike in 1976, which no trade union would condemn. All four major trade union confederations united for the first time, and the government miscalculated in its response of demotions and dismissals, which prolonged confrontation and deepened the resolution of public sector employees to secure recognition of their right to strike. The government calculated that militancy would evaporate without a means of expression; but numerous casualties reinforced militancy and in 1978 the number of strikes was the highest for any one year between 1958 and 1981. The initiative of 1976 to resolve disputes among the state, employers and organized labour through a Consejo Nacional de Salarios was aborted by a faction of employers angry because the government rejected the enterprise-level resolution of disputes in favour of national-level arbitration by which it sought to improve its electoral appeal to labour.

The initiative now passed to the military, which was fortified by exposés of civilian corruption that shook the government and Congress. The civilian elite was shocked by an unprecedented public demand by thirty-three generals and admirals for emergency measures to improve internal security and to grant the armed forces new powers, and a rebuke for the judiciary and mass media for attacking the military. An explosion of criminal violence – murders, kidnappings, bank robberies and contraband gangsterism – provided reasons for adopting tougher policing and military tactics against all forms of 'subversion'. Ill-substantiated claims that a general conspiracy threatened national institutions provided the pretext for a Conferencia Nacional de Seguridad in 1975, at which critics of the war minister, General Camacho Leyva, from both main parties argued that the blurring of the distinction between legitimate protest and terrorism both accelerated a drift towards right-wing authoritarianism and assisted terrorism by antagonizing the non-violent opposition.

The assassination of the inspector-general of the armed forces in 1975 united the officer corps, but a widely predicted coup did not occur. Then, between 1975 and 1977, the military itself was divided by revelations of scandal – the local reverberations of the Lockheed aircraft scandal plus alleged pay-offs on the sales of West German rifles and French Mirage jets. Moreover, claims to have finally defeated the rural guerrillas were demonstrably false. In 1975 the military was accused of abandoning its responsibilities in Magdalena and César, allowing armed groups of landowners to persecute remaining ANUC activists and to establish 'independent republics' where the writ of Colombian law did not apply. And with the unmistakeable drift towards what a growing body of public opinion regarded as 'civilian dictatorship', civilian fears that authoritarian factions within the army were using the states of siege to impose local-level dictatorships that might spread to the entire country were echoed by constitutionalist officers.

Large sections of the middle and working classes became increasingly angry that López appeared to be governing on behalf of the transnationals and national big business. The state had been closely associated with a process of 'enterprise conglomeration' that began in the 1960s. In some cases mergers of domestically owned firms occurred through vertical integration, control over enterprises producing inputs to ensure continuity of production; in others, horizontal integration, through the absorption of rival firms; and in still others, as a means of sharing the costs of expensive imported technology. By 1978 economic power was vested in twenty-four conglomerates: twelve 'superconglomerates', four family firms and eight enterprises arising from *grupos financieros,* which financed and increasingly penetrated the industrial sector. Lack of restriction upon big business and the close identification of governments with the financial sector between 1974 and 1982 antagonized small business, especially members of the Asociación Colombiana Popular de Industrias (ACOPI), which in 1979 represented about ten thousand small firms and complained repeatedly about discriminatory lending policies as well as big business's ease of access to government.

A further object of middle-class protest lay in official tolerance of tax evasion by the upper class and complicity in corruption and business irregularities at the highest levels of government. Such discontent was deepened by insensitive handling of protest in the public sector by a government that mistakenly assumed a residual deference among the urban middle class. Thus, López Michelsen underestimated the scale of opposition in the health sector in 1976, when professional anger at the inadequate funding of public health facilities culminated in an occupation of the largest hospital in Bogotá by members of the medical faculty of the Universidad Nacional. Their action was complemented by a strike of Instituto Colombiano de Seguros Sociales (ICSS) employees – doctors and medical workers responsible for medical care for private enterprise. The government, which precipitated the strike by changing the status of ICSS employees to civil servants – a change that deprived them of the right to strike – declared the action illegal but succeeded only in intensifying the strike and expanding its scope. The government thereby entered into outright confrontation with a well organized and influential group that demonstrated the potential of the urban middle class to organize itself autonomously and to sharp effect.

In Cali, urban protest assumed an institutional form in the Movimiento Cívico, founded in 1977 with the primary objective of halting irregularities in public administration. Drawing upon support from members of the traditional parties and apparently independent of them, the Movimiento Cívico was a response to the failure of government to meet the expectations that its rhetoric had raised. Frequently led by professionals – lawyers, architects, economists – who had gained experience from AC and were disillusioned by its ineffectiveness, the movement used the press, radio, public demonstrations and *barrio*-level committees that organized electoral registration and public meetings in order to fight the municipal elections of 1978, when it made an impressive showing, winning 34.9 per cent of the vote.

The Movimiento Cívico reflected broader, nation-wide trends. A growing sense of urban abandonment was evident in frustration at failures to secure improvements in housing, to install adequate services or to establish legal recognition of titles to property. Whereas between 1958 and 1970 there were sixteen civic strikes and between January 1971 and September 1977 there were seventy-two, in the nine months between September 1977 and May 1978 alone there were fifty. Civic strikes occurred not only in the large cities but also in newly expanding industrial satellite towns, like Barbosa near Medellín and Yumbo near Cali, and in small cities like Barrancabermeja and Florencia. The trade unions were not always in the foreground of civic protest, although the CSTC took an active role in preparing the National Civic Strike in the main four cities in September 1977.

It was the civic movements, not the opposition parties, that captured the mood of the mid-1970s. ANAPO had lost most of its force. Selective coercion had prevented the Communist Party from developing a power base in Bogotá working-class *barrios*. (The area of most successful Communist activity was the CSTC.) The Left was fragmented (in 1975–6 at least five left-wing factions competed for working-class support), had no effective leaders and performed weakly. The main mouthpiece of the non-violent left-wing intelligentsia was the periodical *Alternativa,* sponsored by the novelist Gabriel García Márquez, from which grew the Firmes movement, that aimed to unite around a single presidential candidate of the Left.

In the late 1970s a new challenge to democratic institutions was posed by the rise of the *narcotraficantes.* Growing out of the emerald-smuggling tradition and the marijuana bonanza of the 1960s and 1970s, the drug mafia acquired strength in the late 1970s. As cocaine production displaced marijuana cultivation in Colombia – because marijuana was increasingly grown in the United States – the Medellín Cartel asserted its pre-eminence in production and processing in South America, and then in 1978–9 seized control of the distribution of the product in the United States after victory in the 'cocaine war' in south Florida. Cocaine had the attractions of high prices and easy transportation by plane, and the city of Medellín offered an entrepreneurial tradition, as well as a recruiting ground for trained industrial chemists. A vertically integrated and multinational business was gradually built with complex operations that ranged from modern irrigation practices in frontier zones to the use of electronic equipment experts to monitor government surveillance. Industrial recession in the city in the 1980s was to give the Medellín Cartel opportunities to move into small industries. It also diversified into agriculture, posing a challenge to traditional landowners, some of whom resisted business transactions with the Cartel but others of whom were compromised at a time when profits in the legitimate economy were low. The Cartel increasingly exercised a regime of terror in parts of the city, in particular through Muerte a Secuestradores (MAS) – Death to Kidnappers – a group of professional assassins founded in 1981 with the aim of wiping out kidnappers and guerrillas.

By 1978 the main parties seemed ossified and dependent on the protection of artificial constitutional devices. Yet in the elections of that year they abandoned the practice of running joint candidates and engaged in more open competition that both revitalized them and challenged assumptions of Liberal impregnability. The main presidential candidates were Julio César Turbay Ayala (Liberal) and Belisario Betancur (Conservative, but fighting on a National ticket supported by María Eugenia). Turbay had outmanoeuvred Lleras Restrepo for the Liberal candidacy by exploiting his ties with regional *caciques* who had been excluded from most national decision-making by the Lleras government. However, the Liberals faced an unusual challenge from the enlightened candidacy of General Alvaro Valencia Tovar, a reformist and one of the few senior officers to have been a household name thanks to his novel *Uisheda* (1969), in which he had argued forcefully that violence could be resolved only by economic and social change.

Turbay was a professional politician of modest origins, whose experience of managing the Liberal machine was more extensive than that of any rival. His personal power was evident in 1974, when he alone selected López as presidential candidate in preference to Lleras. Closely connected with the major financial groups, especially the Grupo Grancolombiano, Turbay revived the Liberal apparatus and proclaimed a 'crusade against insecurity'. He gained 2,504,000 votes in a close contest against Betancur, who won 2,357,000, including a protest vote from discontented *anapistas* and Liberals. Three left-wing candidates won 2.4 per cent of the vote, and Valencia Tovar 1.3 per cent. Betancur, whose links with the old Conservatives were weak, ran on an effective 'above-party' platform that was generally seen as more progressive than that of Turbay. In Bogotá, which had enjoyed an unbroken tradition of Liberal dominance since the 1930s, the Conservatives won. New electoral possibilities were clearly opening in the cities. However, an abstention rate of 51.9 per cent was an indication of the scale of voter dissatisfaction.

The change of executive heralded shifts in economic policy, most notably in terms of the relationship between the private and public sectors. The Plan de Integración Nacional (PIN) promised extensive decentralization but concealed the government's real purpose of using the state to buttress the power of the Liberal regional bosses, the livestock interests and the large financial conglomerates, which were the main beneficiaries of the 1979 tax law that reversed the progressive features of the 1974 law. Official indifference to recession in the industrial sector so angered indus-

trialists that in 1981 they clashed with the government. Deadlock between them was broken only when the CSTC and CGT called strike
action. A modified programme of Desarrollo Rural Integrado (DRI) in
non-coffee areas was clearly intended to hasten the process of proletarianization and fragmentation of the rural populace by channelling benefits
to the wealthiest 3 per cent of peasants. Concessions to the better-off
peasants and palliatives for the landless and semi-proletarianized completed the process of demobilizing the peasantry that began in 1970–1.
The scope for rural struggle was far narrower in 1979 than in 1969.

Civil–military relations remained substantially unchanged. A new security statute, drawn up in 1978, by which many categories of offence were
transferred from civilian to military courts and media reportage of public
disturbances was restricted, confirmed fears that 'national security' doctrines were being applied in Colombia. There was opposition from lawyers
and local bosses, alarmed that their influence would be eroded by the
military. Opposition crystallized in several human rights organizations, of
which the most active was the Comité de la Defensa de los Presos Políticos,
and in a forum for the preservation of human rights, led by a former
Conservative minister of foreign relations, Alfredo Vásquez Carrizosa, who
asserted that the government was imposing a system of 'dependent fascism'.

Turbay had a long, cordial relationship with the armed forces. He had
been an intermediary between the officer corps and the political parties
during the transitional regime (1957–8); and he had sponsored several
moves in Congress to raise military salaries. On taking office, Turbay fully
endorsed the authoritarian elements of the armed forces and supported
their view that they were the victims of a campaign of defamation. He
approved a reorganization of the military and police that met most institutional demands, including a lifting of restrictions on the campaigns
against terrorists and drug traffickers. Speaking at a meeting of Latin
American military commanders in Bogotá in 1978, Turbay employed a
language reminiscent of the military Right of the Southern Cone, referring to the urgency of international co-operation against domestic subversion by 'supranational mercenaries'. An 'unrestrained offensive' announced
by the war minister was followed by a wave of arrests that included artists
and intellectuals.

The guerrillas responded with a notably audacious offensive. A dramatic
arms seizure in 1979 was followed in 1980 by the M-19's occupation of the
Dominican Republic Embassy during a diplomatic reception. The handling
of the occupation enhanced the reputations of both Turbay, who was praised

for his patience during the crisis and the survival of all hostages, and Vásquez Carrizosa, who was acclaimed for skilful mediation between government and guerrillas. Meanwhile, the M-19 was weakened by the publicity given to internal ideological fissures that came to view during the negotiations. After the occupation, the military launched a combined army–air force operation against guerrillas in eight departments, which revived allegations of assassinations, torture, arbitrary imprisonment and, in Caquetá, search and destroy tactics. From 1978 the conduct of the courts martial against alleged members of the FARC and M-19 prompted human rights groups to publicize numerous violations of normal procedures, including a forced emigration to Neiva of *huilense* peasants. The case of the human rights activists was strengthened by desertions of soldiers protesting against torture and the admission by the military prosecutor in a court martial that confessions had been obtained under torture from alleged FARC members.

The non-violent opposition gained strength. Arguing that authoritarian measures only strengthened the guerrillas, the CTC leadership condemned the refusal of the government to consider dialogue and pressed for the abolition of the security statute and the lifting of the state of siege. Lleras Restrepo spoke of irrefutable evidence of torture by the armed forces whilst the octogenarian former Liberal president Echandía alleged that democratic traditions were threatened by Liberal complicity in military abuses and denounced the war minister, General Camacho Leyva, as a 'dictator'.

Civilian anxieties, deepened by widespread use of weapons and the proliferation of private security agencies, seemed to be confirmed by the failure of the armed forces to take firm action against a right-wing terror squad, the Escuadrón de la Muerte, which threatened draconian measures against guerrillas, left-wing lawyers and journalists. Some elements in the governing elite, impatient because the military lacked a final solution to the 'guerrilla problem', had condoned harassment of the urban middle and working classes and peasantry; they were rudely awakened to their own vulnerability when the president of the Senate was attacked by police. Civilian criticism was compounded by internal military dissent. Noting that the number of guerrilla fronts had multiplied since 1970 in spite of security legislation, that the Security Statute was used to stifle legitimate opposition and that the government had not heeded FARC moves towards a political solution, retired general José Joaquín Matallana demanded a movement towards socialism as the only means of resolving violence. Both the national and international climate now seemed to favour rapprochement. An amnesty bill sent to Congress by Turbay appeared to commit him to a negotiated settlement with guerrillas, as well as being calculated to sharpen divisions among the rebels and to placate the human rights organizations and their allies. The bill was unacceptable to the human rights organizations, which saw it as a mere public relations exercise; to the M-19, which argued that its guarantees were inadequate; and to Camacho Leyva, who argued that the overwhelming priority in the war against the guerrillas was better funding of military intelligence.

An increasingly volatile electorate was clearly ready for a change of political direction by 1982. Belisario Betancur, a Conservative of humble *antioqueño* origins, stood again, this time against Alfonso López Michelsen representing the official Liberal Party. A third figure, Luis Carlos Galán, from the *llerista* wing of the party, campaigned on a 'New Liberalism' ticket for moral purity and a crusade against drug trafficking and corruption. After a 'populist' campaign which included promises of low-cost housing and greater access to higher education, Betancur won by 3,155,000 votes to 2,749,000 for López and 751,000 for Galán. A greatly increased turn-out indicated that many voters believed they were being offered a genuine choice. The success of Betancur was widely attributed to conventionally Liberal urban voters protesting against the unresponsiveness of two successive Liberal governments to their needs by voting Conservative or abstaining. Betancur promised a break with the authoritarian trends of previous years and with the conduct of government in the interests of big business and the *caciques*.

In 1982 the new president took the audacious step of introducing an amnesty decree even before negotiations with the guerrillas began. Offering a truce that promised some concessions in exchange for the reabsorption of guerrillas within legitimate politics, Betancur's initiative was more wide ranging than any of the amnesties, cease-fires and pardons offered since 1953. However, the peace process was hampered by a number of unresolved questions. Was a peace commission with no executive capacity appropriate to conduct negotiations? Was it expedient to exclude the military from negotiations? Could the guerrilla leaders guarantee the compliance of their followers? Would former guerrillas being reabsorbed into civilian life be subject to reprisals by the military or paramilitaries? Were peace negotiations hindering the military in its war against the guerrillas? The officer corps certainly thought so when, in order to assist peace negotiations, the army was instructed to withdraw from an exclusion zone in Yarumillas as it was about to achieve a decisive victory. The majority of the largest guerrilla organization, the FARC, which claimed to operate on twenty-three fronts, did not accept the amnesty until eighteen months after it was decreed. Negotiations with the M-19 were even more complex and a truce was not signed until August 1984. This created a degree of optimism, because it meant that all guerrilla organizations were involved in peace negotiations. However, the process put a considerable strain upon relationships among guerrilla groups, especially when elements in the military broke the truce by taking reprisals against former guerrillas. Betancur's strategy also strained relations between the civil and military wings of government, since the officer corps doubted that a truce with indisciplined guerrillas would last. While both parties vacillated in a Liberal-dominated Congress, Betancur, using his undoubted personal popularity, sustained the peace initiative, even when the M-19 declared that its truce no longer stood. Increasingly bloody confrontations between military and guerrillas, in which there were no captives or wounded, indicated the degree of exasperation on both sides. As violent conflict spread to urban areas, including residential middle-class suburbs of Cali and working-class *barrios* of Cali and Bogotá, the government came under heavy criticism – from supporters who argued that the peace process was mismanaged, from opponents who contended that it strengthened the guerrillas and from military officers convinced that the government was impeding the effective conduct of the war. The military was increasingly estranged from the civilian population, angered by attacks on entire neighbourhoods in Cali, forced migrations of peasants in Valle and the failure of senior generals to take disciplinary action after the *procurador* (attorney-general) implicated soldiers with the MAS.

In November 1985, the M-19 seized the Palace of Justice building in Bogotá, which housed the Supreme Court and the Council of State. The war minister, General Miguel Vega Uribe, ordered a counter-attack. This event shook the nation, dashed the hopes vested in the peace process and raised the spectre of total political decomposition. There were numerous dead, including one-half of the judges of the Supreme Court. The crisis had many reverberations. Betancur took responsibility for the behaviour of the army, but its critics asked whether it had really acted under his instructions. The judiciary and the legal profession, exasperated because the government had refused to negotiate with the occupying guerrillas despite a request from the president of the Supreme Court, were now in direct conflict with the armed forces. The M-19 had underestimated the delicacy of Betancur's position, and having dashed hopes for a settlement, it was now completely discredited in the eyes of the public. National morale was then finally savaged by the first eruption in 140 years of the volcano Nevado del Ruiz, which devastated the town of Armero.

Many Colombians expected the collapse of democratic institutions, but these were resilient enough to survive the battle of the talace of Justice. The fragility of the state was exposed, and the wisdom of Betancur's strategy thrown into doubt. Yet no alternative strategy was publicly acceptable. Former FARC guerrillas did enter legitimate politics, as partners in a new Socialist–Communist coalition, the Unión Patriótica (UP), which won eight congressional seats in 1986, had representation in fifty municipal councils and twenty-two deputies in departmental assemblies, putting up joint lists with reformist Liberals in some constituencies.

The demoralization engendered by political conflict was deepened by a down-turn in economic growth. After two decades of strong growth – an annual average of over 6 per cent between 1960 and 1981 – Colombia recorded only 1 per cent in 1982. Only the construction and mining sectors improved their performance; manufacturing was in absolute decline, caused by the world recession, the contraction of markets in Venezuela and Ecuador, an increase in interest rates precipitated by a tight monetary policy aimed at controlling inflation and a surge in external borrowing. Betancur inherited a total foreign debt of about U.S. $12.5 billion, consisting largely of long-term fixed-interest loans from the international agencies. Budget deficits mushroomed; industrial unemployment grew; small savers were hurt by the collapse of major private banks amidst scandals; and the entire financial sector entered crisis. A government committed to liberalization in foreign trade and investment was compelled to try to restructure the internal debt and nationalize tottering banks that had been overexposed to the pressures of conglomerates of which they were only part and that had entrusted a large share of their portfolios to poorly controlled Panama-based subsidiaries. The 1981 inflation rate of 27.5 per cent would have been treated by many Latin American governments as a major achievement, but it was seen in Colombia as a national humiliation. Meanwhile, the negative features of the contraband drug boom increased; the benefits accruing to the economy from frontier expansion, increased employment and substantial undeclared income were progressively eroded by domestic drug addiction, gangsterism, heavy policing costs, overextension of the banking system, inflation and a decline of investment in non-speculative activities. Manufacturing remained weak. Exports of manufactured goods contracted as a consequence of deteriorating competitiveness and falling demand within the Andean Pact.

Agriculture did not fare as badly, despite complaints from farmers of reductions in state spending in agriculture since the mid-1970s and of increased interest rates. It was expected that Colombia would soon be self-sufficient in foodstuffs. And there was an effort to diversify exports. Bananas were sold to China, cacao and beef to the Caribbean. Counter-trade agreements with Eastern Europe – for example, coffee in exchange for taxi-cabs with Romania – became commonplace. The coffee sector itself remained resilient, but conflicts within this sector culminated in the secession from Fedecafé of the Unión Cafeteros Colombianos (UCC). Representing small and medium-sized producers, the UCC claimed that Fedecafé discriminated in favour of the large producers, applied an unfair pricing system, showed insufficient zeal in pursuing coffee rust and undertook inappropriate policies of crop diversification. The cotton industry, meanwhile, was more healthy than that in any other Latin American country.

Considerable success was achieved in the energy sector, as a consequence of the realization of investments made during the previous decade, changes in the legislative framework and increases in profitability effected by shifts in international prices. Decreasing production of oil was reversed by the exploitation of deposits in the Llanos Orientales and Magdalena Valley; self-sufficiency, with a small surplus for export, was achieved in 1983. New projects in hydroelectric power were announced, with thirteen new stations due to come on stream between 1986 and 1990. But the most spectacular changes occurred in coal, which in 1986 represented 40 per cent of known domestic energy resources. Possessing 38 per cent of proven Latin American resources, mainly at El Cerrejón, Colombia undertook two major new ventures, involving domestic public and private capital and international firms, principally Exxon. The coal sector was due to reach maximum capacity by 1990, at an estimated 10 per cent of world output; but the collapse of the international oil price threw the Cerrejón project into crisis and tempered optimism that was already dampened by doubts about the 'association' contract reached in 1980 between an Exxon subsidiary and the Colombian state coal company CARBOCOL (Carbones de Colombia). The Colombian government had entered negotiations from a position of weakness deriving from bureaucratic rivalries, imprecise knowledge of coal resources, inexperience in handling the accounting methods of transnational firms and ignorance of business practice and terms of concessions elsewhere. A joint venture had been chosen in preference to a parastate enterprise, mainly because the government was handicapped by a serious cash-flow problem and lacked confidence in the managerial skills of Colombians.

After the crisis of 1984 and 'enhanced surveillance', Colombia received a good-behaviour certificate from the International Monetary Fund (IMF) in 1985 as a result of its punctual payment of interest and principal on its foreign debt. Virtually alone in the continent, Colombia obtained a major loan, which was oversubscribed in 1986, but at the cost of an austerity programme of public expenditure cuts, tax hikes and increasing tariffs on public utilities.

The strength of Colombia compared with that of other countries in northern Latin America allowed it to abandon a low-profile approach to hemispheric affairs. In 1983–4 Betancur emerged as principal spokesman for both the Contadora group in Central America and the Latin American debtor nations, calling at a regional meeting in Cartagena for the lifting of U.S. protectionism and the establishment of a link between export earnings and external debt repayments. One central calculation in this shift was that a more independent foreign policy which removed Nicaragua as a possible patron of domestic guerrilla groups would make more likely their incorporation into the political system. Affiliation with the Non-Aligned Movement was predicated on the assumption that national interests would best be served by distancing Colombia from the Reagan administration. By 1985 the constraints upon foreign policy autonomy were more evident. An absence of concerted action among the large Latin American economies, domestic recession and the failure of U.S. economic resurgence to engender Colombian growth combined to undermine Betancur's position. Autonomy in economic policy was reduced by the imposition of IMF-style austerity measures and the alleged surrender of agrarian policy to the World Bank, which demanded a rise in interest rates and the freeing of import restrictions as a condition for a loan. As a result, the Betancur government lost both external bargaining leverage and domestic prestige.

A reunited Liberal Party exploited these factors to secure a clear majority in the 1986 elections in which a turn-out of 7,230,000 demonstrated some success in the efforts made to legitimize the political system. The Liberal candidate, Virgilio Barco, won 4,124,000 votes against 2,536,000 for the Conservative candidate, Alvaro Gómez Hurtado, and 312,000 (4.4 per cent of the votes cast) for the left-wing UP candidate Jaime Pardo Leal.

As President Barco came to power, a gloom pervaded Colombian life that was only partly relieved by the peaceful transfer of power from a president of one party to that of another. Public opinion was shocked by the new dimensions of violence: 49 per cent of the civilians and 58 per cent of the military killed between 1973 and 1986 were killed in 1985–6 alone; 70 per cent of terrorist acts took place in this period. Barco, like Betancur, tackled violence through a dual policy of democratic *apertura* and military and policing methods.

Democratic consolidation was thwarted by institutional and structural problems that pervaded most state agencies. The habit of over-easy accom-modations in a long period of coalition rule had emasculated the system of checks and balances among the executive, Congress and judiciary. The incoming government faced a Congress whose members were so accus-tomed to a cosy coexistence and so immersed in the routines of dispensing patronage that they had never acquired the competence to initiate complex legislation or review effectively the proposals that the executive put before them. The constitutional status of the Supreme Court remained uncertain: a docile, ineffectual body for most of the coalition years, it displayed some independence from the executive from the late 1970s. Beneath the Su-preme Court lay a judicial system that was moribund, handicapped by blocked courts and inefficient litigation and bereft of popular confidence. The legal system was weakened further by an over-supply of lawyers, many of them the products of an uncontrolled growth of poor quality private faculties in the 1970s and 1980s, for whom the main purpose of the practice of law was to delay, not to facilitate.

The party system, too, contained ambiguous and obsolete features that impaired the effective functioning of a modern democracy. The Liberal Party remained notoriously undisciplined and deeply factionalized. On the one hand, it was an instrument of its paymasters among the en-trenched interests that had diluted and left unenforced numerous well-intentioned reform schemes while conceding some popular palliatives. On the other hand, it was still seen as a potential force for radical change by many local activists – often modest professionals and small businessmen – and their allies. The Conservatives, by contrast, rejected the democratic *apertura* and contended that it was a means of camouflaging the ambition of Barco's subalterns to recreate the Liberal hegemony of the 1930s and early 1940s. Arguing both that a democratic *apertura* was inopportune at a time when a united front was needed against terrorism and that coalition government was more broadly representative of the nation than single-party rule, the Conservatives saw a revised version of *bipartidismo* as the only guarantee that they would retain a large slice of patronage. Their

Liberal opponents countered that national interests had been harmed by too long a period of coalition rule.

The consequence of this debate was an unresolved tension between the main parties, which the M-19 sought to aggravate by kidnapping Conservative leaders – first, Andrés Pastrana, son of the former president and candidate for mayor of Bogotá, and then Alvaro Gómez. The Liberal Party continued to govern alone, but the Conservatives sought to influence government policy instead of devising a set of alternative policies; and differences of economic policy – on debt, counter-inflation, exchange rates and balanced budgets – remained matters of nuance that highlighted divisions within the parties rather than matters of substance that united one against the other. Indeed, neither traditional party was ready for a framework of open, competitive politics that combined an accountable government with a loyal opposition. Effective in their established roles as channels of patronage and as election-fighting machines that mobilized captive voters, both were ineffective, moreover, in bringing new popular forces into the electoral arena.

The UP set out to fill this space. Government ministers acknowledged that published voting figures did not indicate the real dimensions of popular support for the UP and that its impact was seriously reduced by the dirty war of the extreme Right, which assassinated several hundred UP activists between 1985 and 1989, including the national leader Pardo Leal, whose successor was Bernardo Jaramillo. Some UP leaders were forced into exile; others rejoined the guerrillas. Strong commitment to the old Communist Party and the FARC was probably the only protection of some UP leaders against the threat of right-wing violence, but it probably also damaged UP hopes of making firm electoral advances. At a national level the real challenge to the status quo lay not with the UP alone but in new alliances between the UP and reforming elements in the main parties that would outmanoeuvre reactionary factions so as to secure the passage and implementation of reforms that had been aborted since the 1960s. At a local level the UP was already in 1987–8 building pragmatic alliances with reformists of other parties, and either alone or in coalitions, it represented an important challenge to the control of rural bosses and their allies in some frontier zones. Preoccupied with survival, electoral and physical, the UP was slow to develop carefully planned alternative policies.

The workings of Colombian democracy were jeopardized by the poor quality of the public administration and its connections with the private sector. After three decades of rhetorical commitment to the professionalization of the civil service, the uppermost consideration of government remained the imperative of rewarding political clients. A small career civil service (13,000 persons), mainly in central government and the diplomatic corps, was demonstrably effective, notably in debt management. But the remainder of the bureaucracy (700,000 strong) was demonstrably ineffective; and specialist institutions established in the 1960s had lost much of their initial impetus and independence. Political, professional and producer groups continued to treat segments of the bureaucracy as private resources to be captured and defended like fortresses. Frequently, the private sector had an interest in conserving a weak public administration and in defying state regulation; in many respects, the state was still the junior partner of the private sector, and the traditional parties its political wing.

The legitimacy of the state was, indeed, at stake. The state lost credibility by devolving initiative in natural disaster relief to the Church, local government and private philanthropists and by devolving public order functions to private companies of vigilantes which grew faster than the official police forces. Barco, following Betancur, aimed at reconciling large sections of the electorate estranged from the state through a bold programme of municipal reform and decentralization, which echoed features of nineteenth-century federalism. Legislation for the popular election of mayors was intended to foster grass-roots participation and accountability; so too was a policy of fiscal decentralization that aimed to reverse a trend of half a century or more towards the concentration of revenues in central government at the expense of local government. City administration in Bogotá and Medellín had the capacity to assume new responsibilities; but many doubts persisted about the consequences of devolving power and resources to numerous poorer municipalities. There remained a question whether new local resources would enhance a democratic challenge to the *caciques* or be appropriated by them.

The strengthening of the democratic order depended in part on economic policy. Private sector critics of the government complained that liberal orthodoxies of a minimalist state that facilitated private enterprise were too often infringed, that the state failed to shape a climate conducive to high levels of sustained private sector growth and, indeed, that the successes of the private sector had been accomplished largely in spite of the state. Colombia's industrialization record compared unfavourably with that of the newly industrializing countries of the Far East; yet by the standards of Latin America, there was cause for cautious optimism about the Colombian economic record even in manufacturing. Colombia never experienced negative growth rates; and in 1986—7 the main debt-related problem confronting Barco was to dissociate Colombia from a stereotyped view among international bankers of Latin America as a credit risk. Colombia had escaped the extremes of hyperinflation, excessive wage increases, unrestrained protection and large fiscal deficits that were associated with populist regimes. It had also avoided the excesses of extreme neo-liberal strategies: the brusque elimination of state subsidies, massive devaluations, brutal wage compression, indiscriminate assaults upon tariffs and a plunge into de-industrialization.

Social policy was equally vital to democratic consolidation. The sacrifice by government of goals of redistribution to the accumulation requirements of capitalists had meant a continuing neglect of social policy. Always under-resourced, social policy was handicapped by a high turnover of ministers, low levels of bureaucratic professionalism and traditions of damaging conflicts – schoolteacher strikes, university closures and confrontations in the hospital sector. For three decades social policy had been the area of greatest inconsistency; the evolution of long-term strategies was sacrificed to the exigencies of short-term accommodations. The most serious failures were recorded in the provision of services in the intermediate cities and small towns; and it was here that crisis was endemic and protest movements flourished most vigorously. In the 1960s governments had claimed plausibly that social policy innovation should be deferred because Colombia was a poor country with a high rate of population growth pressing heavily upon limited resources. By the late 1980s this argument was not persuasive: Colombia enjoyed an intermediate level of wealth; the rate of population growth fell to a manageable 1.8 per cent in 1986. Betancur had lost popularity by finding the funds to prop up mismanaged banks while abandoning urgent social policies. Barco seemed to recognize the importance of social policy in reconciling popular groups to the state: he announced a major overhaul of the social security system and seemed determined to act on his pledge to eradicate absolute poverty. Yet the overall record on social issues was patchy, the accomplishment was limited and in the late 1980s there was little evidence to indicate a rupture with the past.

Human rights issues and the 'dirty war' of the extreme Right continued to exacerbate civil—military tensions. Amnesty International reported that in the first quarter of 1986, 350 UP leaders were assassinated. Most victims of extrajudicial executions carried out by death squads in Cali in 1985—6 came, however, from the urban poor – illegal occupants of vacant lands, prostitutes, beggars, homosexuals and collectors of litter for recycling. Amnesty International also stressed that civilian authorities were not informed of arrests by the armed forces and had no files on military prisoners. The defence ministry protested that human rights agencies, national and international, failed to mention the crimes committed by guerrillas and went on to declare that the armed forces had no connection with the activities of paramilitary groups. Two complaints, in particular, began to stick, however – namely, that some junior officers had committed human rights abuses and that the generals had not always zealously discharged their constitutional responsibility of seeking out offenders. Americas Watch, however, found no evidence of high-command complicity in disappearances and extrajudicial executions. The military, not an unpopular institution in the large cities in the early 1970s, had lost much public esteem. A wide spectrum of civilian opinion was alarmed by the increasingly castelike behaviour of the officer corps, questioned the control of information on public order by the armed forces and their use of disinformation, and accused them of sometimes mounting counter-guerrilla campaigns that were really counter-offensives against the peasantry and rural labour.

The Barco government clearly had a substantial task in reasserting political authority over the armed forces. Admittedly the problem was not on the scale of that of the Southern Cone. The Colombian military had not descended into the lawless and indiscriminate repression seen in Chile and Argentina; direct complicity of the civilian wing of government in the violation of human rights was not proven; and the Betancur and Barco governments were not, as the Pinochet and Videla dictatorships were, regimes that branded human rights activists as subversives and stamped upon the right to dissent. Yet it was necessary to confine military power. One practical course of action was to raise the competence of the national police force and to enlarge its responsibilities. Barco did this in 1988–9 when he chose the national police to spearhead the campaign against drug terrorists. Another possibility was to see to it that the military enjoyed no veto power in the civilian domain. The connections of some officers and retired officers with private militias ('self-defence groups') – legally recognized in specific circumstances since 1965 – became public as evidence of links between drug barons, private militias, right-wing paramilitaries, some military officers and foreign (British and Israeli) mercenaries, especially in the Middle Magdalena, came to light in 1988–9. These exposures prompted the government to ban private militias in 1989.

In 1986 there was much cause for pessimism over the likelihood of the Barco administration's achieving a durable negotiated settlement with the guerrillas. They were now active as protectors of ethnic minorities, like the Amerindians of parts of Cauca; as protagonists of the rights of small farmers, squatters and rural labour in areas of large landownership and absentee management (Sucre, Córdoba, the Middle Magdalena, the new banana zone at Turbó); as spokespersons for the urban poor in depressed industrial areas, like Yumbo, the satellite town of Cali; and as champions of shanty towns without essential public services, like Policarpa Salbarietta on the southern fringe of Bogotá. Yet there were some reasons for optimism in the pursuit of peace. The international climate favoured a peace policy: neither the Soviet Union nor China was sponsoring guerrilla forces in South America; the guerrillas had been successfully reincorporated into civilian life in Venezuela; and the co-operation of Fidel Castro was crucial in securing the release in 1988 of Andrés Pastrana. Nationally, too, there was a change of climate. The public credibility of the guerrillas, already seriously diminished, was dented further by exposure of the contradiction between their pro-democratic rhetoric and the lack of democracy in their internal organization and their behaviour towards the peasantry. And an increasing professionalism of guerrilla operations that was made possible by sophisticated weapons obtained from the international arms market through a short-lived alliance with the drug barons did not bring about a series of major military victories. The ideological armoury of the guerrillas was increasingly shaped by local circumstances rather than by external models. And the stress laid by the M-19 and FARC upon radical Colombian traditions of taking up arms to promote democratic participation and protect small property and rural labour against authoritarian coalitions of local bosses and large landowners was not completely inconsistent with the underlying aims of government policies of decentralization and municipal reform. A shared emphasis upon the need for new structures of local power provided at least a common language and a basis for bargaining with a potential for compromise. The armed forces were wary: they had too often been the direct targets of guerrilla attacks. Nevertheless, no evidence emerged to substantiate allegations that national security doctrines had become entrenched throughout the officer corps.

Peace processes remained fraught with difficulty. There was the problem of who should take part in negotiations. While determined to involve the army because its exclusion by Betancur had created doubts over whether it wanted his peace formula to stick, Barco rejected the Church's offer of mediation on the grounds that negotiations could become unnecessarily confused if there were too many participants. There was also the problem that the guerrillas used the government's willingness to negotiate as evidence that they were a legitimate force with a right to influence policy. Furthermore, the government had to bear in mind the diverse interests intent upon paralyzing peace policies – small-arms dealers, private vigilante firms, land speculators and, above all, narcotics barons, who operated freely as long as the resources of the government were deployed elsewhere. A negotiated settlement with the M-19 in 1989 aroused cautious hopes that the worst of political and social decomposition was past. But old doubts lingered: whether guerrilla leaders were capable of persuading the rank and file of the merits of the settlement; whether guerrillas were ready to return to normal civilian life and would be allowed to do so by paramilitaries; and whether the propertied classes were prepared to underwrite a settlement by paying the taxes necessary to finance far-reaching reforms that would give the urban and rural poor a permanent stake in the political order and encourage them to sever their links with the practitioners of violence.

By 1987 it was clear that the main proponents of violence were the drug terrorists. During the early 1980s the threat of the drug dealers had been underestimated by some sections of the state and the legitimate propertied interests, because the drug mafias, unlike the guerrillas, posed no direct challenge to property as such. The marijuana business had not seriously threatened political and judicial institutions and, though provoking sporadic violence, had not given rise to endemic violence and the professionalization of killing. Coca production, by contrast, transformed the nature of conflict in frontier locations where the failure of the state to establish a consistent presence left a vacuum in which guerrillas and right-wing private armies competed for power. Confrontations over landownership and water and grazing rights were further complicated by the character of coca as a high-profit, speculative, illegal commodity. Police and press investigations uncovered irrefutable evidence of connections between the drug mafias and the paramilitaries of the extreme Right. The Medellín Cartel reinvested profits in areas of rural violence – parts of Córdoba and Sucre, for example – where conflict between squatters and landowners had brought land values down. The Cartel then used paramilitary firepower against guerrillas allied with the squatters and massacred peasants suspected of collaboration with the guerrillas. Betancur had turned down an offer of a truce from the mafia leaders in 1984; and Barco, distinguishing the violence of the guerrillas, which he considered negotiable, from that of the drug terrorists, which he considered non-negotiable, resisted pressure for talks with mafia leaders from former president López, some congressmen and some legitimate propertied interests, notably in Medellín and Cali. Barco followed Betancur in demanding the strengthening of international law against drug contrabandists and rejected proposals to go beyond the rule of law in the domestic struggle against the barons.

Operating in open defiance of the law, the mafias posed an overt challenge to democratic consolidation. Strategies of bribes, intimidation and assassination which were designed to subvert the authority of the state and its institutions and to reduce the media to a feeble compliance encountered ambiguous responses: courageous resistance from some politicians, judges and journalists and other professionals and a temporizing, accommodating stance from others. The decision of the Supreme Court that extradition to the United States was unconstitutional raised public alarm that even Supreme Court members were subject to bribes and intimidation. Prominent *narcotraficantes*, like Pablo Escobar, the Medellín 'kingpin', combined violence with populist politics. To win public support Escobar and his lieutenants projected themselves as nation-builders, folk-heroes, benefactors of the poor and, above all, innovative entrepreneurs who generated employment by seizing the enticing opportunities offered by liberal capitalism. The 'Extraditables' used instant media comment and press communiqués both to identify with provincial traditions of defiance of central government and to depict themselves as nationalist victims of imperialist interference and the human rights abuse of extradition. The military threat posed by the Medellín and Cali cartels became more and more visible: a private army whose most sophisticated branch was the MAS, a training camp operated on military lines, control of squads of professional assassins and patrols of mercenaries that were available for hire by right-wing landowners.

The economic threat was no less profound. A rise in military and policing costs threatened social programmes and economic planning. The statistical basis of economic policy was flawed because the government could not accurately assess the total value of exports and imports. Indeed, all planning was jeopardized by an uncontrolled flow of narco-dollars: counter-inflation policy by their impact on the value of property, goods and services; monetary policy as a result of the growth of the money supply; credit policy by increased rates as the volume of money for legitimate lending contracted; banking policy by threats to the integrity of institutions; tax policy by expanded evasion; the balance of payments by the diversion of land and labour from food crops to narcotics and thus an increase in food imports.

By 1988 it was clear that the government enjoyed certain advantages in the struggle against drug terrorism. Press investigations showed how casually structured were the organizations of the drug barons. Furthermore, the *narcotraficante* leaders were divided between, on the one hand, those determined only to have the same influence within government as Fedecafé had over coffee and, on the other, those with ambitions to seize power. The challenge of the drug terrorists was weakened further by the outbreak of a bloody and prolonged feud between the Medellín and Cali cartels that originated from a battle for control of trade-routes to the United States. Public opinion wanted an end to violence and criminality. In 1989 a demoralized government recovered much prestige and self-confidence by launching a well-coordinated police campaign against the cocaine-processing plants and paramilitary training camps of the drug terrorists. The Extraditables replied by assassinating Luis Carlos Galán, a consistently outspoken enemy of the cartels, who was confidently predicted by the opinion polls to be the front-runner in the presidential contest of 1990. The assassination provided an occasion for Barco to generate a national consensus against the *narcotraficantes* and also to redouble diplomatic efforts to gain international backing for a crusade against them. 'War' was declared by the Medellín Cartel against the government. Ironically, the number of killings declined in the first months of the 'war'; but later in 1989 the national police scored one notable success, the killing in an armed confrontation of the second most notorious of the Extraditables, Rodríguez Gacha. Nevertheless, the difficulties confronting the government seemed almost insuperable. Eradication of the coca crop did not keep pace with expanding cultivation. When government forces destroyed the processing plants of the cocaine barons, they simply shifted to small-scale, mobile operations.

Meanwhile, the Western democracies were lavish with their praise of Colombian efforts but not generous with their assistance. While Western governments pressed for eradication, Western markets demanded more drugs. The second Reagan administration, divided by bureaucratic wrangling and inconsistent leadership, displayed an astonishing permissiveness and complacency. Overstressing the deterrent value of extradition, it conducted a blundering diplomacy the main effect of which was to antagonize many Latin American sympathizers. The exposure of dubious connections between the CIA, the Medellín Cartel, General Manuel Noriega in Panama, dollar-laundering and the financing of the *contra* rebels in Nicaragua damaged the reputation of Washington among Colombian democrats. The record of the countries of the European Economic Community was no better. They did little to answer Colombian requests for help with crop-substitution programmes, for controls on the movement of chemicals used in the processing of coca into cocaine or for improvements in the flow of information between governments. Only after the declaration of 'war' between the government and the Cartels did Britain, Spain and Italy offer some help. Nonetheless, it was difficult to avoid the conclusion that the first European aid packages, like those trumpeted by the incoming Bush administration, were too small to have a serious impact and were designed mainly to reassure constituencies in the aid-donating countries.

Presidential elections were conducted in May 1990 amidst deep gloom. In March, the extreme Right had assassinated the presidential candidate of the UP, Bernardo Jaramillo, and in April, that of the M-19, the former guerrilla leader Carlos Pizarro. These two assassinations demonstrated conclusively that the main challenge to the political order came from the extreme Right and its allies in the Medellín Cartel. The climate of intimidation was a major cause of the low turnout compared with that of 1986; indeed, the UP, 1,051 of whose activists had been killed since 1985, abstained in protest against the lack of guarantees. The youthful Liberal candidate, César Gaviria Trujillo, won by a clear margin in a free contest. He had wooed middle-class voters by campaigning as Galán's heir in the crusade against the drug barons and corruption, but had also made concessions to entrenched groups in order to enlist the support of the party machine. The Conservative Party, divided between two candidates, performed poorly. Less predictably, the eleventh-hour M-19 replacement candidate, Antonio Navarro Wolff, did well to gain 13 per cent of the total vote.

Gaviria was committed to the strengthening of institutions, especially the judiciary, which in much of central Colombia was paralysed by alliances between local interests and drug dealers. His government also inherited a commitment to a new constitution. Gaviria made a bold new peace offer to the FARC, ELN and EPL, namely, representation in the Constituent Assembly if first they laid down their arms. The incoming government promised continuity in economic policy, especially counter-inflation policy, but it placed new emphasis on schemes of privatization and on an opening to the world economy. And new perspectives in social policy were suggested by the audacious choice of Navarro as health minister. This controversial appointment gave the M-19 the opportunity to exploit the lamentable social policy record of the governing parties since 1970 and perhaps also to transform itself into a durable social democratic party. What seemed positive evidence of a democratic opening was welcomed across most of the political spectrum. Yet there was good cause for caution. Optimism about the Constituent Assembly was tempered by fears that it would be hijacked by the traditional parties. The death of the uncompromising FARC leader, Jacobo Arenas, awakened hopes that the principal guerrilla organizations would realign under a joint command that would ease negotiations. But the prospect of closer co-ordination among guerrilla forces also aroused fears that their military strength and political bargaining position would be enhanced. For its part, the extreme right showed no enthusiasm for detente. And the government seemed likely to be successful only in containing the menace of drug terrorism, not in defeating it. There was apprehension about economic policy as well. Few new opportunities for Colombia beckoned in a stagnant world economy. Furthermore, even a non-doctrinaire stress on privatization seemed inappropriate in a country with one of the weakest public sectors in Latin America and where private interests, especially in the regions, treated government as a private resource. New exposures of incompetence and irregularities in public administration deepened frustration; government agencies were palpably incapable of enforcing progressive policies in many regions and localities. The public goodwill that accompanied the Gaviria government as it entered office was unlikely to endure.

On entering the 1990s the Colombian political system possessed undoubted merits. It had survived challenges from the political extremes and embodied aspirations to democratic participation, even if trends towards democratic consolidation were far from irreversible. Political scientists debated where Colombia should be located on a democracy–authoritarianism scale; but their discussion was unsatisfactory, largely because regional and local variations in efficacy of institutions, opportunities for participation, the concentration and dispersion of power, the exercise of responsibility and the practice of accountability impeded fruitful generalization.

An optimistic observer might point to more years of civilian rule after 1930 than in any other country of South America. A framework of democratic institutions and procedures had not in 1990 to be established but to be strengthened. The beginnings of a democratic *apertura* were being accomplished, and oligarchic controls were gradually being loosened. There was a more realistic hope than before that a democratic Left might acquire a permanent significance in Colombian politics. Misgivings about the military were partly dispelled by Barco's exercise of his prerogative of sacking war ministers who broke publicly with him; and concern about the human rights record of the government was partly allayed by the appointment of a presidential adviser on human rights and the openness of civilian ministers in discussing the problem. The ruling elite displayed some flexibility in the face of growing challenges and endorsed, however unenthusiastically, the boldest efforts on the continent to conclude peace settlements with guerrillas. And, above all, the state had demonstrated an elasticity to absorb crisis that nullified apocalyptic predictions. Colombia had also enjoyed modest and sustained growth even in the 1980s: an annual average of 2.3 per cent was recorded between 1980 and 1985 and 4.7 per cent between 1985 and 1988. Thus, it weathered the economic crisis of the 1980s better than many of its neighbours. Major new projects were still being launched even in the troughs of the recession. Productive potential did, indeed, encounter frequent bottlenecks; but tendencies towards saving and investment had been consistently positive. And a powerful private sector had been consolidated, imbued with a pragmatically liberal economic ideology. The growing strength of the domestic economy was indicated by a reduction in the coefficient of exports (share of exports in GDP) from 28 per cent in 1930 to 20 per cent in 1950 and again to 136 per cent in 1986. Some welfare levels had improved: 48 per cent of adult Colombians were illiterate in 1938 compared with 27 per cent in 1973 and 12 per cent in 1985. Meanwhile, between 1950 and 1975 the public health budget multiplied tenfold, and the number of doctors and hospital beds sextupled. In the urban sector infant mortality fell from 40 per thousand in 1955 to 17 per thousand in 1970.

A pessimistic observer might stress that nearly continuous civilian rule for eighty years had failed to convert promises of civil liberties, social justice and the fulfilment of basic needs into a reality for all citizens. Well-intentioned schemes to extend the practice of democracy were thwarted by the failure of committed reformists in central government to build durable, effective alliances with forces pressing in the localities for democratic enhancement. The electoral performance of democratic socialists was still weak, and it remained possible that UP leaders would be co-opted by the traditional parties, be the victims of vengeance killings or rejoin the guerrillas. The armed forces continued to enjoy considerable political autonomy, and proposals by the democratic Left and Left–Centre that a civilian be appointed defence minister had been rejected. Human rights abuses were not curtailed, and the military was alleged to be more concerned with improving its image than with modifying its behaviour. An enlarged democracy required, as President Barco acknowledged, an end to presidentialism and, in particular, to the tradition by which policy continuity was disturbed by each incoming government breaking ostentatiously with the aims of its predecessor and asserting its distinctiveness in policy rhetoric and practice. Meanwhile, the faltering pace of reformist initiative played into the hands of oligarchic interests that showed a tenacity in, for example, their control of the mass media and of the distribution of patronage, which was compounded by an impressive capacity for self-realignment and reassertion in the face of new circumstances. Colombia still exhibited great inequalities in landownership, wealth and income. Various studies show that a process of concentration of rural and urban income that had occurred between 1930 and 1950 was accentuated after 1950, even if the number of beneficiaries expanded to include the new middle classes. There was evidence too of a deterioration in rural living conditions. CEPAL estimated in 1978 that 54 per cent of the rural population and 36 per cent of the urban population were below the line of absolute poverty and that 23 per cent of the rural and 14 per cent of the urban population were below the line of destitution. In 1988 67 per cent of the rural population was below the line of absolute poverty and 25 per cent below that of destitution. Low-income groups, especially in rural areas, continued to be the victims of a regressive bias in public expenditure. Thus, even in prosperity plans constructed during phases of ill-justified euphoria fell apart like castles of playing-cards; and in line with well-established national idiosyncrasy, bonanza did not give rise to optimism but reinforced an entrenched pessimistic vision of Colombian society.

12

ECUADOR SINCE 1930

The consolidation of a nation-state in Ecuador began at the end of the nineteenth century, more than half a century after it won independence from Spain, when an expansion of foreign trade, particularly the export of cacao, accelerated the accumulation of capital and strengthened the country's links with the international market. There emerged within the coastal oligarchy a group of financiers and merchants distinct from the landowners and able to impose its political leadership. This commercial bourgeoisie oversaw the liberal transformation of the country in which the support of the popular sectors was at times of critical importance. Through occasional uprisings the coastal peasantry had for some time challenged the old oligarchic regime. Urban labour and the middle class were also integral to the liberal triumph and responsible for the intermittent emergence of radical ideas. On 5 June 1895, following a popular uprising in Guayaquil, General Eloy Alfaro, the Liberal-radical leader, was appointed *jefe supremo* of the republic. This was the beginning of the Liberal Revolution.

Liberalism was based upon Ecuador's integration into the international economy, national economic integration, most notably by means of the Quito–Guayaquil railway, and the restoration of state authority over the Church. Church and state were separated, the clergy were forcibly deprived of many of their functions and privileges and the Church lost much of its land through expropriation under the so-called Ley de Manos Muertas – measures which constituted a major political and ideological challenge to the traditional order. The initial stages of the Liberal Revolution witnessed new guarantees for certain rights, particularly to education and religious freedom. Nevertheless, the revolution was limited by the nature and interests of its leading social force – the financial and commercial bourgeoisie, which neither needed

687

nor sought, for example, to abolish the structures of latifundism in the Sierra (Andean highlands).

Politically defeated but not economically destroyed, the traditional landlords of the Sierra closed ranks around the Roman Catholic Church. The death in 1912 of General Alfaro coincided with a renewed oligarchic offensive against the Liberal state. The second administration of Leónidas Plaza (1912–16) reached a settlement with the Church by placing limits on anticlerical reform and also secured a truce with the oligarchy by making concessions to the Sierra *latifundistas*. Although the Liberals held power until 1925, both rural violence (e.g., the peasant insurrection in Esmeraldas and Manabí led by Carlos Concha) and urban agitation during this period threatened the regime and presaged its collapse. The middle sectors had expanded through the growth of the state bureaucracy and small-scale commerce and demanded a share of power. The organizations of artisans and workers established early in the century campaigned forcefully for corporate rights, particularly in the 1920s. Such movements acquired particular importance in an ideological climate disturbed not only by the dislocation of a long-standing hierarchical order, but also by the external influence of the First World War and the Russian Revolution.

However, in the coastal zone, and particularly in those areas dedicated to cacao production for export, pre-capitalist relations of production continued to prevail under the system of *sembraduría*, whereby peasants received plots from landlords in exchange for future deliveries of their harvest. Only on a few modern plantations and in two sugar mills did wage labour emerge, and then only gradually. Industry in Guayaquil was also slow to develop, imported goods generally meeting local needs. Moreover, although that proportion of the population living in the coastal region had risen to one-third of the total of 1.5 million in 1930 from one-quarter of a much smaller populace in 1880, Ecuador remained regionally fragmented, and the dominant interests in Guayaquil were unable to impose their stamp on the country as a whole.[1]

In the Sierra, where the majority of the population was concentrated until the middle of the century, the Liberal Revolution had a considerable political and ideological impact, yet the landed class was still able to retain its economic and social power based on the hacienda and servile labour systems. Although coerced labour – *concertaje* – was legally abol-

[1] Alvaro Saenz, 'Problación y migraciones en los ciento cincuenta años de republicana', in *Libro del sesquicentenario* Vol. 1: *Política y sociedad: Ecuador, 1830–1980* (Quito, 1983), p. 102.

ished in 1918, it was not until the second half of the century that the highland *hacendados* began to run their estates in the manner of capitalist enterprises. Equally, whilst artisanal production suffered severely from the expansion of imports, it proved to be remarkably resilient and continued to be an important factor in national manufacturing production.

In the early 1920s the Ecuadorian economy entered a crisis which was to last for almost three decades. The recession which followed the First World War resulted in a rapid contraction of the international cacao market and a subsequent fall in cacao prices. To make matters worse, disease destroyed many cacao plantations. Between 1920 and 1923, the total volume of Ecuadorian cacao exports fell from 20 million U.S. dollars per year to less than half that amount. The collapse of the primary export model shook the political system. As conflicts emerged on the Coast between cacao producers and exporters, the large landowners of the Sierra broke the 'truce' of more than a decade and demanded a greater share of power. Within the bourgeoisie itself, tensions among factions and groups increased. Moreover, a challenge from below aggravated the internal political crisis of the bourgeoisie. On the one hand, sectors of the middle class, hurt by the economic crisis, struggled to find new forms of ideological expression. On the other hand, the popular sectors, which had been directly affected by the economic crisis, came violently onto the political scene. In November 1922, the incipient Ecuadorian working class received its baptism of fire when a strike, begun in the service sector and in certain Guayaquil factories, and to which the unemployed and artisans soon rallied, was cruelly repressed by the Liberal government, with hundreds of deaths.[2]

Political forces regrouped and modern political parties were formed during the 1920s. In 1923 the Liberal Party was reconstructed with a reformulated programme which contained some progressive or radical elements. In 1925 the main representatives of the Sierra landowners reorganized the Conservative Party, strengthening its structure and expanding its programme from old ideological issues, such as support for the Church, to include the new ideas on the 'social question' being raised by the Vatican. The Partido Socialista Ecuatoriano (PSE) was founded in 1926, wracked from the start by internal conflicts that soon developed into a

[2] Amongst the most important studies of this episode are Elias Muñoz V., *El 15 de noviembre de 1922: Su importancia histórica y sus proyecciones* (Guayaquil, 1973); INFOC, *El 15 de noviembre de 1922*, 2 vols. (Quito, 1972).

split. In 1931 a fraction of the Socialist Party founded the Communist Party of Ecuador, as a local section of the Third International.

On 9 July 1925, the government representative of *'liberalismo pluto-crático'* was finally overthrown in a coup d'état staged by young army officers who called themselves 'socialists'. The Movimiento Juliano, however, did not implement any revolutionary changes. Its leaders restricted themselves primarily to establishing mechanisms of state control over the financial system and modernizing certain aspects of the bureaucracy. Nevertheless, the political power of the commercial bourgeoisie was reduced, while the highland and some coastal landowners increased their role in the management of the economy and politics of the country. At the same time, the state bureaucracy was granted increases in salaries and guarantees of social protection, which generally favoured middle-class sectors and strengthened the ties between the military 'radicals' and the reformist movements.

Following the dissolution of several provisional juntas, the army handed over the reigns of government to Dr Isidro Ayora, who became dictator in 1926 and implemented a number of major administrative reforms, such as the creation of a Central Bank. At the same time, measures were adopted to promote the development of industry. In 1928 the Constitutional Assembly issued a new constitution – the thirteenth in Ecuadorian history – which introduced some social guarantees, established the vote for women and elected Dr Ayora constitutional president. As a result of a slight recovery in the country's exports and fiscal reforms, a degree of political stability was restored in the late 1920s. It was not, however, to survive the impact of the world depression.

THE 1930S

The world depression of 1929–32 had devastating consequences for the Ecuadorian economy. Within a few months the prices of exports had been reduced to their lowest levels since 1900 (Table 12.1). By 1933 the value of exports scarcely surpassed 4 million sucres. Commercial establishments were paralysed, business firms and banks went bankrupt and fiscal resources were rapidly depleted. Naturally, the sectors which were directly linked to the world market suffered most, although this in turn had repercussions for the entire national economy.

Successive governments attempted to confront the crisis with timid monetary measures, in particular a strict adherence to the gold standard,

Table 12.1. *Average prices of cacao,*
coffee and rice in the Guayaquil market
(sucres per quintal)

Year	Cacao	Coffee	Rice
1927	68,85	81,33	20,42
1928	53,31	88,25	14,13
1929	56,48	77,42	17,25
1930	51,04	42,54	16,83
1931	38,58	32,33	10,10
1932	30,83	48,92	8,69
1933	35,25	38,15	10,81
1934	50,20	70,70	18,50

Source: *Boletín del Banco Central del Ecuador,*
cited in Luis A. Carbo, *Historia monetaria y*
cambiaria del Ecuador (Quito, 1978).

which was considered the essential feature of the financial system introduced by the U.S. 'money doctor' Edwin Kemmerer in the 1920s.[3] Despite the increasing pressures this generated, the authorities persisted in upholding the standard throughout the harshest period of the crisis; it was not lifted until 1932, following the example of the majority of the world's countries, including Great Britain. As a result, Ecuador lost the impressive sum of more than 2 million sucres from its reserves.[4]

The prolonged recession did not have the same impact on all the regions and social sectors of the country. On the Coast, cacao continued to generate export revenues despite low prices and reduced production, but the high level of unemployment in this sector led many workers to move to Guayaquil, where they began to constitute an urban sub-proletariat. By contrast, in the sugar sector there was an increase in employment, production and export earnings – from 3 million sucres per annum in 1920 to 200 million in the early 1950s. Export earnings from rice also grew – from 340,000 sucres per annum in the 1920s to 127 million in the 1940s – and palm registered some recovery in the 1940s from the contraction of the previous two decades. Between 1926 and 1944 the value of oil

[3] Luis A. Carbo, *Historia monetaria y cambiaria del Ecuador* (Quito, 1941), p. 140. See also Paul W. Drake, *The Money Doctor in the Andes. The Kemmerer Missions, 1923–1933* (Durham, N.C., 1989), chap. 4.

[4] Wilson Miño, 'La crisis en el Ecuador', in *Reseña histórica de la Superintendencia de Bancos* (Quito, 1984), p. 173.

production rose from 2.2 million sucres per annum to 28 million.[5] The cultivation of bananas also expanded significantly. A number of cattle ranches and cereal farms in the northern Sierra underwent some moderniza-tion, and despite contractions in the market for agricultural goods during the 1930s recovery was relatively rapid.[6] In the southern Sierra production of straw hats increased, many small farmers and rural labourers entering this artisanal trade. Thus, the shift away from cacao export, which had dominated the boom years, witnessed not only increased production of other commodities but also a degree of social diversification.

During the 1930s industrial growth, which had begun in the 1920s, was modest but nevertheless appreciable. The industrial sectors that grew most were textiles, food, construction and wood, all of which were already established. At the same time the chemical and pharmaceutical sectors registered their first significant expansion.[7] Most of this growth took place in the Sierra, where manufacturing was permanently protected and had the advantage of a constant labour supply. By contrast, coastal industry, particularly sugar, experienced serious difficulties following the expansion of the late 1920s. External competition reduced both its international and national markets, forcing the closure of several mills. However, there was a marked rise in the production of cane alcohol and liquor, which were state monopolies and, together with matches, became an important source of treasury revenue.

Industrial growth, however, fell off sharply in the 1940s, when primary export production began to recover. Ecuador did not experience a process of import-substitition industrialization on a scale comparable to that of other Latin American countries as a result of the recession of the 1930s and the restrictions on trade caused by the Second World War. This was primarily because of the very limited size of the national market, even for basic goods at low prices. There was no marked improvement in income distribution, and the relations of production, especially in the Sierra, continued to act as a barrier to the expansion of wage labour. This re-flected an economy still under the domination of landlord, commercial and banking groups. Industrial capital lacked the capacity to initiate an autonomous process of growth or form political alliances with the urban masses and petty bourgeoisie in order to encourage industrialization

[5] Juan Maiguashca, *Las clases subalternas en el Ecuador en los años treinta* (Quito, 1988), pp. 5–6.
[6] Osvaldo Barsky and Gustavo Cosse, *Tecnología y cambio social: Las haciendas lecharas del Ecuador* (Quito, 1981), p. 68.
[7] Sabine Fisher, *Estado, clase e industria* (Quito, 1983), p. 140.

through state intervention, which was effectively non-existent.[8] Moreover, the peak years of accumulation had passed. The recession of the 1930s hit Ecuador after its economy had already experienced a decade of crisis and lacked the revenues of the cacao boom that might have been invested in manufacturing industry.

The economic disruption had profound consequences for social and political life. Coastal landowners were hit once again, precisely when foreign trade had seemed to be recovering. Plantation workers' wages were reduced and many of them lost their jobs. The Guayaquil commercial bourgeoisie could no longer resort to traditional 'solutions' such as devaluation and tax reductions, since the *reformas julianas* had taken fiscal and monetary control away from them. Although they themselves were also struck by the crisis, Sierra landowners found that the weakness of their traditional opponents provided them with an opportunity to regain the political power lost as a result of the Liberal Revolution. This they did mainly by mobilizing artisans and groups of small rural producers affected by the recession. Yet while the Guayaquil commercial and banking bourgeoisie had lost supremacy, it still retained sufficient power to block any attempt by Sierra landowners to gain control of the state. As a result of this political impasse between Sierra landowners and the coastal bourgeoisie, the middle class increased its political influence, particularly through the Socialist Party.

The Ayora government was unable to resolve the economic crisis. And the concession of a monopoly in the manufacture of matches to a Swedish company in 1931 triggered a rebellion by the opposition. Following several days of street disturbances and unrest in the barracks, the president resigned in August, handing the office over to Colonel Luis Larrea Alba, the minister of the interior, who was himself unable to maintain control for more than a few weeks. The opposition forced his resignation and replacement by Dr Alfredo Baquerizo Moreno, president of the Senate and a member of the old Guayaquil plutocracy who had served as president between 1916 and 1920. Baquerizo immediately called general elections. While president, he made some changes in economic policy, including the suspension of the gold standard, inconvertibility of the currency, control of exchange rates and the arrangement of loans for the Treasury. The devaluation of the sucre, however, would have to wait another two years.

During the electoral campaign the extent to which the traditional Sierra

[8] Fernando Velasco, *Ecuador: Subdesarrollo y dependencia* (Quito, 1981), pp. 182–3.

landowners had regained much of their lost power was evident. Neftali Bonifaz, their candidate for the presidency, received the support not only of Conservative forces but also of some Liberals and of the Compactación Obrera Nacional, an organization composed primarily of Sierra artisans and controlled by the Church and the landowners. For their part, the Liberals, who represented the interests of the bourgeoisie and their allies, nominated Modesto Larrea Jijón, a highland landowner with progressive tendencies. Larrea was also backed by one Socialist faction, while another supported Lt. Col. Ildefonso Mendoza, a former leader of the Revolución Juliana.

The government was unable to carry out the traditional fraud which had given the Liberals their previous victories, and Bonifaz won by a wide margin. However, the months before the inauguration of the new president were fraught with major disturbances. Finally, in August 1932 the anti-Conservative opposition which had secured a majority in Congress disqualified the president-elect, accusing him of having admitted on several occasions to Peruvian nationality. The Compactación Obrera Nacional, supported by the Quito garrison, rushed to defend Bonifaz and obliged Baquerizo to hand over the government to a *bonifacista*. A large number of troops stationed in the provinces then moved towards the capital. The result was one of the most savagely fought battles of Ecuadorian history, the Four Days' War (28–31 August 1932), which was settled through an arrangement by which Alberto Guerrero Martínez (the president of the Senate) took power and promised to call new elections.

Once again the Liberal old guard was able to employ its traditional methods of control, and Juan de Dios Martínez Mera, a member of the Guayaquil bourgeoisie, was elected president. However, the success of the electoral fraud was only partial since the new president did not obtain a majority in Congress, thus initiating another confrontation between the executive and legislative powers. After several months, during which cabinets collapsed almost daily and during which popular opposition became increasingly fierce, Martínez Mera handed over control of government to his minister of the interior, Abelardo Montalvo.

In elections that took place in December 1933, in which the Liberals did not even present a candidate, José María Velasco Ibarra achieved an easy victory over the Socialist and Communist candidates. Velasco, an intellectual and journalist, had been elected a member of Congress by the supporters of the Conservative Bonifaz. Although he had received a traditional Catholic education and his political programme sought to improve Church–state relations, he called himself a 'liberal'. His main electoral base was the Conservative Party, but his appeal went beyond traditional Conservatism.[9] He assumed in caudillo style the leadership of a conglomerate of forces, especially the popular masses and the petty bourgeoisie that the landed class had been unable to mobilize. Furthermore, Velasco served as the political link between Sierra *latifundismo,* and coastal landowning groups that had abandoned the old Liberalism.

With this electoral victory in 1933 *velasquismo* was born. It was, beyond any doubt, the outstanding phenomenon of twentieth-century Ecuadorian politics. There is little research on and much debate over its nature. It seems clear, however, that *velasquismo* was not a 'populist' movement with all the characteristics that this type of movement has had in other Latin American countries. It might rather be viewed as a typical form of *caudillismo* – an oligarchical alliance formed in order to mobilize the masses. *Velasquismo* did not constitute an organized political force. While Velasco himself, like some of his political followers, remained the same throughout the forty years of his public life, each of the elections in which he participated should be seen in a different context and in terms of the changes in the social composition of each successive expression of *velasquismo*.

Once in office in 1934, Velasco Ibarra led an active but disorganized government, which was orientated fundamentally towards the construction of public works. But he did not manage to last a year in the presidency. In 1935 congressional opposition headed by the Liberal bourgeoisie in alliance with petty bourgeois groups with socialist inclinations broadly defined succeeded in blocking all government activity. When Velasco tried to resolve the impasse by proclaiming himself dictator, the armed forces overthrew him.

The military command supported an interim presidency of Antonio Pons, the minister of the interior. He refused to call elections, arguing that this would be tantamount to handing over the control of the republic to the Conservatives, and preferred to return power to the armed forces, which named Federico Páez dictator in 1936. In the first stage of his administration, Páez declared his intention to govern with socialist ideas, and he even appointed several Socialist ministers. Some monetary and labour reforms were implemented, but when the Socialists pressed for a deepening of the process, the dictator refused and began to persecute left-wing and labour organizations. Páez's dictatorship became notorious as a

[9] See Rafael Quintero, *El mito del populismo en el Ecuador* (Quito, 1978).

result of the issue of the so-called Ley de Seguridad Social, which abolished all political guarantees. Exile, torture and other methods of repression were the order of the day. The Catholic Church and its *latifundista* allies took advantage of the dictatorship's shift to the right, and the government agreed to sign a new agreement between Ecuador and the Vatican by which the Church once more became a legal entity in Ecuador. It was compensated for properties nationalized during the Liberal Revolution, was authorized to acquire new property and was guaranteed control of its educational institutions.

Páez was overthrown in October 1937 by General Alberto Enríquez Gallo, who held power until August 1938. During his short period in office, Enríquez implemented several progressive measures. All of the repressive laws were abolished; the Código de Trabajo was issued, as were complementary laws; ample guarantees were provided for the exercise of political activity; and the privileges of foreign companies were limited. This government's political programme, particularly its most important achievement – the issuing of the Código de Trabajo – signalled a triumph for the Socialists whose influence had grown throughout the decade of the 1930's. This growth, however, was considered increasingly dangerous by the traditional dominant groups, which began to search in earnest for a way to halt the 'socialist advance'.[10]

In 1938 Enríquez handed over the control of government to a Constituent Assembly convoked by him and elected by an unusual procedure: each province was represented equally by Conservatives, Liberals and Socialists. As a result there was no majority party in the legislature. This rendered the decision-making process extremely conflictive, particularly with regard to the election of president of the republic. After prolonged negotiations, Dr Aurelio Mosquera Narváez was called upon to assume office. Mosquera, who had been national director of the Liberal Party, was elected with the support of Socialists. However, from the moment he assumed power he found himself at odds with the Constituent Assembly that had chosen him, particularly with its left wing. The conflict, provoked by an attempt by the Assembly to grant the rank of general to Larrea Alba, provided Mosquera with an opportunity to dissolve the Assembly and declare himself dictator with the support of the armed forces. This time the military did not call a Constituent Assembly to oversee the return to

[10] See Enrique Ayala, *Los partidos políticos en el Ecuador: Síntesis histórica* (Quito, 1986), p. 29; Alejandro Moreano, 'Capitalismo y lucha de clases en la primera mitad del siglo XX', in Leonardo Mejía et al. (eds.), *Ecuador, pasado y presente* (Quito, 1975), pp. 166–206.

constitutional rule. Instead, an arrangement between distinguished Liberals and Conservatives to 'repair' the constitution of 1906 was subsequently legalized by an elected Congress under the control of the dictator. The influence gained by the Socialists and the level of popular agitation were sufficient reason for the 'historic' parties, whose leadership came from the old oligarchy, to put aside their century-old confrontation in order to stop the 'leftist danger'.

During his months as dictator, Mosquera Narváez attacked the entire educational system, particularly the universities, repressed various strikes and handed over an important share of power to the Conservatives. Following a meeting of Congress, various reforms adopted during the presidency of General Enríquez were abolished. In November 1939, however, the president suddenly died, and power was entrusted first to Carlos Arroyo del Río, president of the Senate, one of the most distinguished leaders of the Liberal Party and a prominent lawyer for foreign companies, and then, when Arroyo launched his candidacy for the presidency, to Andrés F. Córdova, the president of the Chamber of Deputies.

FROM *ARROYISMO* TO THE SECOND *VELASQUISMO* 1940−7

Carlos Arroyo del Río was elected president in January 1940 by the usual fraudulent methods, defeating the Conservative candidate Jacinto Jijón y Caamaño and Velasco Ibarra, who had returned from voluntary exile to participate in the elections. There were protests, but these were repressed, and Arroyo del Río took office in September 1940. To consolidate his power he immediately offered cabinet posts to Conservatives, who, despite having vociferously denounced the 'electoral fraud', accepted. Julio Tobar Donoso, one of the most brilliant representatives of the Ecuadorian Right, was appointed minister for foreign affairs − a post he had held some years earlier − whilst the Conservatives retained the control they and their allies had been exercising over the Education Ministry for some time.

Less than a year after Arroyo became president, Ecuador faced a major international crisis. In 1941, following a number of border incidents, the Peruvian armed forces invaded Ecuadorian territory and occupied several frontier areas. The Ecuadorian troops, outnumbered ten to one, were virtually swept off the battlefield and decisively defeated. Since the time when Ecuador had won independence, a vast region in the Amazon Basin had been in dispute between Ecuador and Peru, which had made several attempts at settlement and had entered into a number of armed confrontations. During the 1930s relations between the two countries had deteriorated, Peru choosing a moment when continental attention was focussed on the Second World War to take the disputed territories by force.

Arroyo del Río's government appealed for national unity to confront the external menace. He succeeded in suppressing internal political opposition and in mobilizing men and resources in support of the armed forces. However, Ecuador's military resources were very much weaker than those of Peru. Moreover, conscious of the extent of its unpopularity, the *arroyista* administration was reluctant to hand over weapons to the population. The country's most efficient force, the Cuerpo de Carabineros, an organization of militarized policemen fully trained and endowed with modern equipment, was not even sent to the border but instead continued to defend 'internal order' while a few poorly armed soldiers struggled to defend the southern front without proper leadership.

The state of war lasted for several months, until January 1942, when the Inter-American Conference met in Rio de Janeiro to establish a common front behind the United States, whose entrance into the Second World War had been hastened by the Japanese attack on Pearl Harbor. The war between Peru and Ecuador was a topic of minor importance at Rio, and without even having discussed the matter, the Ecuadorian delegation was forced to sign a Peace, Friendship and Boundary Protocol. In the name of continental unity the country had to renounce 200,000 square kilometres, an area which is only slightly less than the present Ecuadorian territory. Minister Tobar declared that he had no choice but to sign the document, which was later ratified by a majority of *arroyistas* in Congress. Both Liberals and Conservatives finally agreed to abandon a substantial part of the national territory which had belonged to Ecuador for more than a century. The international economic interests at play behind the Rio de Janeiro accord were to re-emerge in the 'petroleum war' some decades later.[11]

Arroyo del Río survived this foreign policy disaster. He established some public works programmes and introduced a systematic fiscal reorganization that produced an increase in Ecuador's reserves and a budget surplus. However, this economic success was achieved at the expense of a deterioration of the living standards of the Ecuadorian population. The effects of the Second World War – a compulsory decrease in imports and

---

[11] See Jaime Galarza, *El festín del petróleo* (Quito, 1966).

increase in exports – did not produce any significant improvement. The favourable economic conditions resulted only in a consolidation of the power of the commercial bourgeoisie, and there was a dramatic increase in domestic prices, while wages and salaries remained virtually unchanged. The Arroyo government responded to increasing popular opposition with repression. The *carabineros* and the official security corps maintained an atmosphere of terror, legalized through the virtually dictatorial authority the government received from Congress. When in 1944, however, Arroyo tried to impose a tame Liberal as his successor, he provoked a popular rebellion. After a number of incidents, on 28 May 1944 the population of Guayaquil, supported by part of the port's military garrison, launched an uprising that in a few hours spread throughout the country.

The popular revolt which brought an end to *arroyismo* was led by Alianza Democrática Ecuatoriana (ADE), a political movement that brought together Socialists, Communists, Conservatives, dissident Liberals and some independents. ADE called upon Velasco Ibarra, the leading opposition figure and living in exile, to take charge of the country. Capitalizing on the reaction against Arroyo and popular aspirations for radical reforms, Velasco declared that 'his heart was on the left' and gave a share of power in his administration to Socialists and Communists. The Left, believing it was possible to control the process of democratization through its presence in the state bureaucracy, supported a caudillo who was able to rally the masses. And by 1945 some democratic and popular organizations had been consolidated, the most important being the Confederación de Trabajadores del Ecuador (CTE), established by the Left in response to the Right's efforts to build union support, evident in the foundation in 1938 of the Confederación Ecuatoriana de Obreros Católicos (CEDOC). However, Velasco did not permit any deepening of the 'Glorious May Revolution'. In fact, he never implemented any important reforms and restricted himself to prosecuting some representatives of the previous government. 'You cannot show me a revolution in the whole world that has been so original as this one', he had declared, '. . . the monk and the communist have shaken hands'.[12] Within a short time, however, Velasco was waging a campaign against leftists and popular organizations.

A Constituent Assembly convened in 1945 had confirmed Velasco as president but enacted a constitution which had a marked socialist tinge. Besides establishing social and labour guarantees, it introduced a number

---

[12] *El 28 de mayo, balance de una revolución popular: Documentos para la historia* (Quito, 1946).

of mechanisms by which Congress could control the executive. Velasco Ibarra's confrontation with the Constituent Assembly, which he attacked as a 'political committee of the left wing', reflected the sharpening of tensions between *velasquismo* and popular organizations. Meanwhile, the government had to devote much of its time to repressing protests against the deterioration of living conditions. Finally, in March 1946, Velasco Ibarra, through the skilful participation of his minister of the interior, Carlos Guevara Moreno, and with support from the Conservatives, staged a coup d'état. The constitution was suspended and the president became dictator once again. Leftist politicians were persecuted and most of their newspapers were closed. In August 1946 a new Constituent Assembly met after an election in which Conservatives and *velasquistas* were virtually the only candidates. This right-wing majority abolished several reforms in the previous constitution, though the Conservatives were not able to dismantle the *estado laico* established more than fifty years earlier.

The Velasco government could not halt the deterioration of the economy. Between 1946 and 1947 prices rose sharply and the fiscal crisis deepened. Political instability and agitation continued. Finally, in August 1947, the defence minister led a successful coup d'état against Velasco, who was once again sent into exile. But the new dictator was unable to maintain himself in power. Within a week he was removed from office by the armed forces. Vice-president Mariano Suárez Veintimilla, a militant Conservative, took control but only on condition that he could convene Congress and then resign. In September an Extraordinary Congress appointed Carlos Julio Arosemena Tola, a banker from Guayaquil, to complete Velasco's presidential term, which had been due to end in 1948.

THE BANANA BOOM, 1948–60

In 1947–8 the turbulence of the preceding two decades gave way to a period of stability, which has been linked with the 'banana boom'. This greatly oversimplifies a very complex process that included many important transformations besides an increase in banana exports. Nevertheless, the elevation of Ecuador to the rank of the leading banana exporter in the world was undoubtedly a vital factor during these years.

In 1942–4, banana exports were approximately 15,000 tons, with an average value of 2 million sucres per year. At the end of the decade of the 1950s, 850,000 tons were exported with a value of more than 600 million sucres. The price per bunch had increased substantially from 3.51 sucres in 1944 to 16.11 sucres in 1950 and 18.46 sucres in 1952. Although other traditional export products, such as coffee and cacao, experienced significant increases as well, in less than ten years, from the late 1940s to the late 1950s, bananas came to represent more than half the total of Ecuador's exports. Such increases cannot be attributed, as is sometimes suggested, to the momentary pause in Central American banana production that forced North American companies which controlled the trade to seek other temporary sources of supply. Although disease and typhoons during these years reduced Central American production, the banana boom in Ecuador was due to the long-term policies of international fruit marketing companies and a significant effort by the Ecuadorian government to favour cultivation and exports.[13]

Whilst cacao was produced primarily on large latifundia, bananas were generally grown on medium-sized and small farms. The huge plantations owned by local landowners or foreign companies produced only 20 per cent of the bananas exported by Ecuador.[14] The traditional agricultural producers were therefore replaced by new social groups (small and medium producers) who cultivated large areas in the inland coastal zone. Government participation in the concession of credits, technical assistance and building of roads and other infrastructures was one of the central factors in this model of agricultural expansion. At the same time, the pre-capitalist relations of the cacao plantations gave way to wage labour, both on large plantations and on smaller farms.

The presence of foreign capital in the direct control of banana production was proportionally reduced, but its domination of the marketing of bananas remained unaffected. Five foreign companies handled 80 per cent of banana exports. Of these, three had their own plantations, but even in these cases most of the exported fruit came from other producers. Although harvesting, transportation and shipping activities were also mainly in local hands, the monopoly by foreign companies of international marketing allowed them to retain 55 per cent of the income from exports, leaving less than 30 per cent for the producer and not much more than 15 per cent for those engaged locally in marketing.[15]

The banana boom meant, therefore, a much tighter integration of

[13] Carlos Larrea, 'Las empresas transnacionales y la economía ecuatoriana durante el período bananero', in *Libro del sesquicentenario*, vol. 3; *Economía: Ecuador, 1830–1890* (Quito, 1982).

[14] Velasco, *Ecuador: Subdesarollo y dependencia*, pp. 195–6.

[15] Junta Nacional de Planificación, *Plan General de Desarrollo Económico y Social*, vol. 1, pt. 1 (Quito, 1963), p. 68.

Ecuador into the international capitalist system and its direct dependence on the international banana cartel. At the same time, domestic control of the production of the fruit strengthened the petit bourgeoisie, not least through the expansion of the government bureaucracy generated by the boom. The increase in exports permitted enormous growth in imports and the consequent strengthening of commercial capital. In the Sierra, the banana boom accelerated the breakdown of the traditional hacienda system and the transition from servile relationships to new forms of production of a capitalist nature. The transfer of the Sierra population to the Coast was of real significance. In 1950 the Coast already contained 40 per cent of the country's population; over the following years it would become the most highly populated area in the country. There were also, however, significant levels of migration within each of the regions and growth of urban populations, some of which, especially in coastal cities, doubled in a few years.

Economic growth in the 1950s was based on a model aimed at the foreign market, but the boom also entailed expansion of the local market and incipient development of import-substitution industries. Albeit erratically, this came to be favoured by the government, which established an institutional system for promoting industry and in 1957 introduced the Ley de Fomento Industrial. However, industrial growth was not autonomous, since it occurred in conditions closely dependent on the international capitalist system.[16]

Ecuador's stabilization in this period cannot be attributed entirely to the banana boom; it reflected the recomposition of social forces resulting from the advance in capitalism as the dominant mode of production in the country. The commercial and financial bourgeoisie was strengthened at the same time that the old landholding class was being transformed into an agricultural bourgeoisie of the modern type. This process not only took place on the Coast, but also extended to certain landholding groups with a modernizing orientation in the Sierra. As a result, the struggles within the dominant class started to shift away from the regional axis of the Sierra and Coast. Equally, the middle sectors experienced changes in social behaviour. Whether based on the bureaucracy, trade or the liberal professions, they progressively participated in the benefits of the banana boom and became active agents in the consolidation of the system. The Ecuadorian working class also became less combative in the face of expectations cre-

---

[16] José Moncada, *La economía ecuatoriana en el siglo XX* (Quito, 1980), p. 47.

ated by the boom. This was not true, however, of the expanding semi-proletarian groups in the cities, especially in Guayaquil, and it was these groups that increasingly led the opposition to the economic model.

Both the economic growth and the transformations in social classes during this period took place within a framework in which the government was assuming important new roles. These extended beyond guaranteeing monetary stability or building roads and other infrastructures to include economic planning, centralized control of basic services and the promotion of investment. This was also a period in which foreign technical missions began to visit Ecuador and to undertake specialized studies. Aid and development contracts with international organizations became a common feature of national life.

The shift in population to the Coast along with the process of accelerated urban growth deprived the Conservatives and the clergy of their control over the majority of the electorate, which in previous decades had been located chiefly in the Andean countryside. Now the liberal bourgeoisie had no problem in accepting, in Agustín Cueva's words, 'the rules of their own game'[17]; it was not necessary to resort to fraud in order to have a good chance in the electoral contest. Hence, the constitutional regime could operate within the framework of stability and continuity. A temporary triumph of the Right did not mean a reverse of the Liberal conquests.

Paradoxically, the loss of control over the electoral majority allowed the Conservative Party to increase its share of power, especially at the local and congressional levels. Throughout the period it had more members in Congress and more municipal governments and provincial councils than any other party. Yet the social forces which supported Conservatism were changing. The old landholding oligarchy was converted into an agricultural bourgeoisie, and the traditional Conservative artisan base was falling apart and losing the power to fight. Within Conservative ranks, divisions opened up, particularly within those sectors that mobilized the party's popular following. The result of these differences was the founding of the Movimiento Social Cristiano, which, in spite of its name, was an elitist group of the extreme Right. Its leader was Camilo Ponce, who came to power in 1956 with Conservative support. Another section of the Right broke off to form a neo-*falangista* type of group called Acción Revoluciona-

---

[17] Agustín Cueva, *El proceso de dominación política en el Ecuador* (Quito, 1981), p. 70.

ria Nacional Ecuatoriana (ARNE), which captured the most brilliant of
several generations of Catholic youth.

The Liberal Party did not hold power during this period, but Liberalism continued to express the interests of the commercial bourgeoisie and
maintained a strong influence over the ideological atmosphere of the day.
Moreover, the Liberal Party became the axis of the Frente Democrático, a
political alliance in defence of laicism which the leftist forces also joined.
The Partido Socialista Ecuatoriano (PSE) cast aside the aggressive positions
it had held in previous decades and accommodated itself to the system,
even participating in the state bureaucracy. This shift reflected the changes
within its major social base: the petty bourgeoisie. Nevertheless, the most
radical sector of the party linked to the working class resisted such moves
and within a few years broke away to form the Partido Socialista
Revolucionario (PSRE). Although the Communist Party maintained stable support in this period, it did not undergo any significant growth and
increasingly diluted its revolutionary strategy in order to permit alliances
with Liberalism and a degree of participation.

The left-wing intelligentsia singularly failed to secure support from the
semi-proletarian urban sectors, products of the accelerated migration of
peasants to the largest cities, especially to Guayaquil. These groups were
mobilized either through *velasquismo* and populist alliances with the oligarchy or through the Concentración de Fuerzas Populares (CFP), another
political movement of the populist type organized under the leadership of
Carlos Guevara Moreno. The CFP, which had its main electoral support in
Guayaquil, where it won the municipality several times, became the most
aggressive force in the opposition. On the streets or in Congress, it confronted all governments during this period.

The 1948 presidential elections were won by Galo Plaza Lasso, who was
the candidate of the Movimiento Cívico Ecuatoriano, an alliance of moderates which united the majority of Liberal voters and even gained some
support from traditional voters of the Right. Plaza, a Sierra landowner with
modernizing tendencies, was the son of an important Liberal president at
the beginning of the century, Leónidas Plaza. He constituted an ideal figure
for the compromise platform which was able to defeat by a narrow margin
the Conservative candidate, Manuel Elicio Flor, and by a wide margin the
official Liberal candidate, General Enríquez (dictator in 1938).

Plaza had good relations with the United States and proved to be highly
capable in directing the modernization process. He reflected and deepened
the country's relationships with foreign capital, especially in the United

States.[18] A few months into his government several foreign technical assistance missions, including one from the International Monetary Fund (IMF), visited the country to advise on new economic policies. The government implemented several development plans, especially for bananas, and provided support with internal and external credit resources. It undertook complementary public works and technical studies, and it provided stability in public sector employment. The Plaza administration held the First National Census in 1950 and met the task of reconstructing a large area of central Ecuador, especially the city of Ambato, which was destroyed by an earthquake in 1949. Plaza rapidly achieved Liberal congressional support and was able to neutralize the Conservative opposition. Thus, he was able to count on relatively solid backing for his political projects. The support for the government was consolidated in 1951, when, after two years in the opposition, the PSE began to co-operate and entered the cabinet, a move which provoked the definitive split in the party. Plaza, however, was not able to suppress the violent opposition of the populist CFP, whose most important bases were in Guayaquil. Several of its leaders, among them Carlos Guevara Moreno, were sentenced to prison for periods of more than a year, which did nothing but consolidate their popularity.

In the 1952 elections *placismo* was decisively rejected, and Velasco once again won the presidency. He was supported by the traditional *empresarios*, by the CFP, by ARNE (shock troops in the campaign) and by a wing of the Conservative Party. His most serious rival was the official Conservative candidate, Ruperto Alarcón. Velasco, however, soon split with CFP and consolidated his political support through an agreement with the traditional Right. Throughout his government, he kept the support of the Conservative Party, ARNE and the Social Christian Movement, whose leader, Camilo Ponce, was the 'strong man' in the regime as minister of the interior. The main emphasis of this administration was on the huge and disorganized proliferation of public works, especially in the fields of communications and education.

The harshly contested 1956 election was won by Camilo Ponce by a small margin on behalf of the unified Right with Velasco's support. His principal opponent was Raúl Clemente Huerta, candidate of the Frente Democrático Nacional, made up of Liberals, Socialists, and other leftist groups. Other candidates in the election were Guevara Moreno, leader of

---

[18] Galo Plaza Lasso was born in New York in 1906. He was educated in the United States and lived there for prolonged periods. Plaza always made public his admiration for the American way of life and actively supported U.S. international policies.

CFP, and José Ricardo Chiriboga, a Liberal dissident. Although the traditional Right triumphed, it had done so with little more than 30 per cent
of the total vote. Ponce was conscious of this and did not attempt, as had
been feared, a drastic reversal of the conquests established by the *estado
laico.* Instead, the Social Christian government took a liberal line, and
Ponce tried to secure a balance of power between the regional oligarchies
of the Sierra and the Coast. The old Sierra landholders and the Catholic
Church continued to hold a share of the power, but they could not undo
the tacit agreement between various sectors of the dominant classes which
derived benefit from the political stability of the 1950s. Despite the
violent opposition of some Liberal, Socialist and Communist groups as
well as the CFP and *velasquismo,* from which Ponce split as soon as he
assumed power, the constitutional regime was never seriously threatened.

The absence of a successful coup d'état did not mean, however, that
'social peace' prevailed in Ecuador, as its leaders proclaimed. The development plan started by Plaza and maintained by his successors could not
overcome the basic contradictions in Ecuadorian society that became increasingly visible from 1955 with the decline in exports. At the end of the
decade the situation became even more difficult, above all for the popular
sectors from Guayaquil. In early June 1959 protests broke out in the main
port, which resulted in acts of vandalism and robbery. The government
responded with indiscriminant repression. At least one thousand deaths
were caused by the military, ordered by the authorities to 'shoot to kill' at
the mobs. This and other acts of violent protest and repression were
symptoms of the termination of the 'democratic stability' of the period
since 1948.

THE 1960S

The crisis of Ecuador's agro-export model began during the late 1950s
and gathered momentum in the 1960s. Exports of tropical products
decreased sharply. Foreign export firms left the country and became
competitors, resulting in the virtual closing of the U.S. market. The
balance-of-payments deficit increased steadily, local currency lost its
value and prices, which in the previous decade had been relatively stable,
increased rapidly and significantly. Several attempts at reform and modernization were made in an effort to rationalize the relations of production in the countryside by reforming the traditional hacienda and at the
same time to develop the industrial sector. The decade of the 1960s was

characterized by agrarian reform and by an impressive take-off of import-substitution industry.

At the beginning of the decade, industrial operations of greater size and with more advanced technology were opened, and there was a significant transfer of capital to the manufacturing sector. While in 1962 the volume of credit granted to industry scarcely reached 572 million sucres, in 1969 the figure had risen to 2,111 million.[19] The financial system was also given a boost. The stock exchanges of Quito and Guayaquil were formed and private financial corporations, banks and other credit institutions were expanded.

The growth of industry occurred under conditions of growing dependence. In effect, the expanding industrial bourgeoisie was not able to formulate a project of autonomous development, but accepted a model of associated development which brought about the increasing denationalization of the economy, and especially of its more dynamic sectors. Over the second half of the decade the flow of foreign capital into the country reached unprecedented levels and within a few years a high proportion of large enterprises were in foreign hands, including several firms which had been established and managed by Ecuadorians over several decades. All these transformations were carried out under conditions in which the state was forced to promote modernization by strengthening its function as entrepreneur.

At the same time, the Cuban Revolution had a major influence on the events of this period. Between the 1960s and the early 1970s there was a significant increase in political mobilization. The struggle of peasants for agrarian reform was intensified; the labour movement recovered its combative power of past decades; and the student movement experienced a general politicization under the control of the Left. Yet whilst the strength of the Left increased, the Communist Party suffered a severe division between sectors linked to the Soviet Union and those supporting the People's Republic of China. The Right, in turn, experienced a radicalization in the face of the Castroist threat. Initially, the Catholic Church played an active role in mobilizing the reactionary forces, but later in the decade groups with progressive positions influenced by the new orientations of the Vatican Council and of the Conference of Latin American Bishops surfaced within the Church.

Velasco Ibarra won the elections in 1960 obtaining roughly the same

[19] Velasco, *Ecuador: Subdesarrollo y dependencia*, p. 210.

number of votes as those obtained by all the other candidates combined. The old leader, playing on popular dissatisfaction and growing anti-Yankee feelings, bitterly attacked his main opponent, former president Galo Plaza, candidate of the Liberal Party and the right wing of the PSE. Velasco was also able to win the votes of traditional Conservatives, whose official candidate was Gonzalo Cordero Crespo, and some of the support of the CFP masses, unhappy with the party's candidate, Antonio Parra, a representative of the Left.

But Velasco's triumph was ephemeral. He could go no further than his nationalistic and anti-oligarchic rhetoric. The economic crisis deepened and the only solution offered by the government was devaluation; speculators made enormous profits. There were repeated denunciations of administrative corruption and serious quarrels in Congress whilst workers and students staged a wave of strikes. This situation became even more complicated as differences grew between Velasco and his vice-president, Carlos Julio Arosemena, who, especially after an official trip to the USSR, appeared to be an admirer of leftist groups.

Although he rapidly lost control of the situation, Velasco managed to stay in power for a while. The strengthening of the Left, especially the student organization Unión Revolucionaria de la Juventud Ecuatoriana (URJE), increased right-wing fears of a government led by Arosemena. Yet when the opposition to Velasco reached a climax in November 1961, the armed forces overthrew him and after some hesitation installed the vice-president in office.

Arosemena tried to lead a progressive government of national conciliation made up of several political forces. Domestically he respected constitutional rights and abroad assumed a more or less independent position with regard to U.S. attempts to reverse the Cuban Revolution. Such a government was far from revolutionary, but it was considered sufficiently dangerous by the Right and U.S. interests for them to seek its overthrow. Concessions were gradually made to the opposition groups, but they urged Arosemena to instigate thoroughgoing repression which the President rejected. The right wing, advised and financed by the CIA, organized a national campaign for the breaking of diplomatic relations with Cuba. The Catholic Church was the most efficient instrument for this mobilization. Right-wing groups linked to the Catholic hierarchy even managed to lead terrorist attacks against religious leaders, and then to blame the Left. The country experienced anti-Communist hysteria, openly fed by the dominant groups.

Faced with right-wing aggression, the Left could do very little beyond defending itself. The government broke off relations with Cuba. Nevertheless, this measure was now considered insufficient, and U.S. agents actively prepared a coup, adding to their campaign personal attacks on the president of the republic. In July 1963 a *junta de gobierno* made up of the four chiefs of the armed forces took power.

The new military government under the presidency of Rear Admiral Ramón Castro Jijón instituted a tough campaign of repression against the Left, while at the same time carrying out various reformist programmes. Its political plan fitted into the U.S. campaign to isolate the Cuban Revolution and to promote structural changes in order to demobilize the popular forces throughout Latin America. The Right welcomed the military coup enthusiastically and tried to exert a decisive influence on the government. However, its political pressure was now shared with that of new groups of professionals and 'development specialists', who gave the administration a heavy technocratic bias. The middle class, virulent opponent of the system in the past, was now the fundamental support of the regime.

The main axis of the military junta's programme was to encourage the expansion of the internal market and the development of import-substitution industries. Organizations were set up to channel investment to industry, and various protectionist laws were passed. At the same time, huge petroleum concessions were made to foreign firms, and under U.S. pressure Ecuador's claim to sovereignty two hundred miles offshore was secretly waived. An Agrarian Reform Law was introduced with the aim of suppressing the 'servile' features of prevailing labour relations in Sierra agriculture. The reform did not bring about any significant change in the landholding structure, but it was the final blow to the traditional hacienda, from which modern agricultural enterprises quickly emerged. The landowners tried to reject the Agrarian Reform Law, but all efforts to stop it were useless. They therefore sought and obtained an increasing influence in the bodies in charge of executing the reform. Many landowners speculated extensively in land prices and transferred their investments to the urban sector. Peasants now encountered unusually favourable conditions for strengthening their organization. The government, however, feared possible agitation and did not seek the support of agricultural worker organizations to implement the reform.

After two years of military government, political groups began to demand a return to a constitutional regime. At the same time that the junta sought to expand its protectionist plans, raising customs tariffs to favour national production, importers in Guayaquil reacted violently and began to conspire openly against the government with the support of the student movement. The military had tried to implement university reform under the aegis of U.S. experts, but this had not curbed the politicization of student organizations. During the first months of 1966, opposition grew rapidly and strikes paralysed the country. The government responded with repression, but when at the end of March it ordered the military occupation of the university, it succeeded only in precipitating its own collapse. A *'junta de notables'* was immediately formed in Quito under the direction of traditional political figures and power entrusted to Clemente Yerovi, a leading member of the Guayaquil oligarchy.

Yerovi headed a government of 'national conciliation', establishing a balance among the traditional political parties. He reversed the tax reforms implemented by the dictatorship and oversaw Ecuador's entry into the Andean Pact for subregional economic integration.[20] Yet Yerovi was not in power long enough to take further measures except to preside over the election of a National Constituent Assembly, which met at the end of 1966 and which soon demonstrated that a return had taken place not only to the legal regime but also to old political formulae. Its members, in their majority the representatives of the traditional interests and corporativist pressure groups – landlords, merchants, bankers – joined together in two 'fronts' of 'right' and 'left' wings, around Conservatism and Liberalism. The fact that neither of the two had a clear majority resulted in the election as president of Otto Arosemena Gómez, another representative of the Guayaquil oligarchy but one who was in alliance with Conservatives and followers of Camilo Ponce Enríquez.

The sixteenth constitution in the country's history came into effect in 1967, and Arosemena was confirmed as president until August 1968. In the elections of that year Velasco Ibarra was once again a candidate, and this time he won by a narrow margin over Andrés F. Córdova, an old Liberal politician. Behind the two front-runners came Camilo Ponce Enríquez, the right-wing candidate; Jorge Crespo Toral, the ARNE representative; and Elías Gallegos, backed by the Communist Party and other left-

[20] Originally the 'Grupo Andino' was formed by Colombia, Ecuador, Peru, Bolivia and Chile. Venezuela joined later. Chile abandoned the group when the Pinochet government refused to follow the common policy of restriction of foreign investment. The best work on the participation of Ecuador in the Andean Pact is Germánico Salgado, *Ecuador y la integración económica de América Latina* (Buenos Aires, 1970).

wing groups. Velasco, who had once more played upon the popular desire for reform, did not 'wipe out the oligarchy in six months' as he promised at the beginning of his government. On the contrary, political power became increasingly concentrated in the hands of the most reactionary groups, and the administration responded to popular protest with repression. Student organizations demonstrated almost daily, maintaining a permanent atmosphere of turmoil. Moreover, opposition came not only from the traditional Marxist Left, but also from the new radical Christian groups committed to socialism. Some of the leaders, including progressive priests, became victims of the fifth *velasquismo*.

In the middle of 1970 Velasco Ibarra suspended the constitution and declared himself dictator with the support of the armed forces, although he announced his willingness to hold elections on schedule in 1972.

As the 1972 elections approached, however, the government could not find an acceptable candidate who had a chance of defeating Assad Bucaram, a former mayor of Guayaquil and leader of the CFP. His image as a populist leader and his anti-oligarchic vocabulary and postures worried not only the Right but also sectors of the middle class and the military as well. As a result, a few months before the announced elections in which Bucaram's success seemed inevitable, the armed forces overthrew Velasco Ibarra and appointed General Guillermo Rodríguez Lara as dictator.

THE OIL BOOM, 1972–8

The new military dictatorship, which lasted from 1972 to 1979 – the longest continuous period of dictatorship in Ecuadorian history – coincided with a period of unprecedented economic prosperity. Ecuador began to export oil extracted from the eastern Amazon fields precisely when international oil prices underwent a rapid rise: from less than U.S. $3 per barrel in 1972 to more than $30 in less than five years. This brought about an unexpected increase in government income, a strengthening of the state and general economic expansion, which in turn led to greater international dependence and medium-term imbalances. One of the most salient characteristics of this period was the acceleration of urban growth. The cities, which in 1950 contained 28.5 per cent of the population, accounted for 42 per cent in 1974.[21] The modernization of farms and the formal imple-

---

[21] Osvaldo Hurtado, 'El proceso político contemporáneo', *Libro del sesquicentenario*, vol. 1: *Política y sociedad, Ecuador, 1830–1980* (Quito, 1980).

mentation of land reform leading to the proliferation of minifundia (small plots of land handed over to the peasants with no credit facilities or technical assistance) brought in their wake not only an exodus from the countryside to the cities by the working population, but also a decrease in agricultural production, particularly in traditional products for the domestic market. Prices of foodstuffs reached record levels. It even became necessary at one point to import maize, the most important crop in the Andean area. In contrast to the depression of the agricultural sector during the decade, industry grew rapidly. Industrial growth was especially favoured by government policies and by the channelling of public and private capital derived from oil exports to the industrial sector. The import-substitution industrial development model reached its peak of influence during the period and found its own limit soon enough. In the first place, the types of goods produced were geared to a very small market of medium- and high-income groups, which did not allow for large-scale production and gave rise to the underutilization of installed capacity. Second, industry could not absorb a substantial number of workers into the growth process, thus failing to relieve the job situation in the cities where most workers remained underemployed.

The growth of industry brought as a corollary the strengthening of the manufacturing bourgeoisie, which now became an important power in economic and political decision-making. This bourgeoisie grew together with − and in no substantial contradiction to − foreign capital, whose rate of penetration also quickened: of the thirty largest corporations of the country in 1976, fourteen belonged to transnational enterprises.[22] Henceforth, this strong presence of foreign capital was matched by a high concentration of capital and technology in highly profitable productive centres that did not absorb a significant amount of manpower. At the same time, many banks and other credit institutions, such as finance and insurance companies, were established or increased their capital. Concentration also increased sharply in this area, to such an extent that it was estimated that in the late 1970s thirty-two people held almost one-half of the country's private bank capital.[23]

Ecuadorian foreign trade underwent substantial changes during the decade. At the beginning of the 1970s, tropical products (mainly bananas, coffee and cocoa) accounted for about 80 per cent of exports, but ten years

[22] José Moncada, *Capitalismo y subdesarrollo ecuatoriano en el Siglo XX* (Quito, 1982) p. 56.
[23] Alberto Acosta, 'Rasgos, dominantes del crecímiento ecuatoriano en las últimas décadas', in Alberto Acasta et al. (eds.), *Ecuador: El mito del desarrollo* (Quito, 1982), pp. 57−8.

later these products barely reached 14 per cent. Petroleum accounted for 60 per cent and industrial products, particularly processed cacao, amounted to 21 per cent of foreign sales.[24] At the same time the expansion of imports included not only industrial equipment, manufactured products and luxury goods, but also mass consumption products such as foodstuffs (wheat and milk among others).

These changes were accompanied by a significant alteration in the role of the state from a typically liberal one, which favoured the long-standing exporting oligarchies, to an openly interventionist stance. This was not only due to the high income accruing to it from oil exports but also because oil production required foreign capital to negotiate directly with the government regarding the conditions of its control of the oil sector. This made it possible for the state to increase its relative autonomy. Equally, it was able to generate the resources to expand the public sector, not only in terms of the bureaucracy (which grew quite significantly) but also through strengthening government enterprises in the service, marketing, credit and banking, transportation and even industrial production sectors.

Despite, and on occasion because of, the growth generated by the oil boom, the domestic economy faced spiralling inflation, the decreasing purchasing power of the local currency and the rapid growth of foreign indebtedness, both government and private. This became particularly evident in the mid-1970s, when the rate of expansion of oil income decreased. It was then that 'aggressive indebtedness' became an official policy of the government and the common practice of local companies.

While notably increasing its economic power, the industrial bourgeoisie continued to be the minor partner in an oligarchical structure of political control, which it showed no signs of intending to break because, it has been argued, 'of ideological-political weakness, . . . of undeniable economic ties, or as a result of the potential development of vertical social contradictions'.[25] This phenomenon was reflected in political organization. The old political fronts of the Right and Left, organized around the Conservative and Liberal parties, broke down completely as new political forces came into play. A new political 'centro' was constituted which also represented an advance in modernization and organization with regard to the old-time oligarchical clientelist parties. At the same time, most of the

---

[24] Iván Fernández, 'Estado y clases sociales en la década del sesenta', in *Ecuador: El mito del desarrollo*, p. 68.
[25] Patricio Moncayo, *Grietas en la dominación* (Quito, 1977), p. 98.

left-wing forces joined together in a broad front, mirroring a process of unification of the different labour organizations of the country. Overcoming doctrinaire disputes, Ecuadorian labour unions worked out a common platform for action which, after several nation-wide strikes, became the basis for the establishment of the Frente Unitario de Trabajadores (FUT).

In February 1972 General Guillermo Rodríguez Lara defined his government as 'revolutionary and nationalistic'. A few weeks later he substantiated this definition in a document entitled 'Philosophy and Plan of Action of the Revolutionary Nationalistic Government of Ecuador'. According to this statement the government was determined to attack the problem of the country's underdevelopment and to increase the living standards of the poorer sectors through land, tax and administrative reforms; it promised a better utilization of natural resources and the creation of jobs in productive activities.[26] It asserted that the assumption of power and the political plan were the institutional responsibility of the armed forces. This implied that all of the factions within the military would share power. But initially, the 'centrist' army officers managed to win the edge over the extreme right-wingers, or 'philosophists'. In addition to the prevailing internal conditions, this balance of forces was influenced by the example of the 'Revolution' currently taking place under the aegis of the military in neighboring Peru.

Bolstered by this conjunction of forces Rodríguez Lara carried out a number of reforms, some of which were openly progressive and almost all of which focussed on oil policy. Concessions granted to foreign companies were revised, and more advantageous conditions established for the country. A gas development contract that was clearly detrimental to the national interest was cancelled. The Corporación Estatal Petrolera Ecuatoriana (CEPE) was established as an official entity involved in prospecting, developing and marketing oil and its derivatives. Construction of a state-owned oil refinery was begun. The government acquired a percentage of the Texaco–Gulf Consortium stocks and provided for the reversion to the state of the Anglo Ecuadorian Oil Fields Co. concessions. These measures advanced by the minister of energy, Admiral Gustavo Jarrín Ampudia, were supplemented by the decision that Ecuador would become a member of the Organization of Petroleum Exporting Countries (OPEC) and by the move towards the establishment of the Organización Latinoamericana de Energía (OLADE).

[26] *Filosofía y plan de acción del gobierno revolucionario y nacionalista del Ecuador* (Quito, 1972).

In agriculture the government tried to accelerate the distribution of land to the peasants. At the same time, it allotted substantial credit to farmers for modernization, guaranteeing that land would not be placed under government control if appropriately cultivated. This initiative, however, met with the aggressive resistance of landowners who, despite having themselves abused government credit, resisted the other reforms, managing first to halt them and then to secure their reversal. The government was much more successful in establishing a state enterprise for the storage and marketing of agricultural products, and another for the distribution of staple foods, though these measures were unable to offset inflation and price increases.

The military dictatorship took a number of steps to encourage industrial development, such as prohibiting certain imports, regulating private credit, channelling government credit to the industrial sector and constructing large infrastructural works of strategic importance. At the same time, it gave firm support to the enforcement of the Andean Subregional Integration Agreement decision, which limited the entry of foreign capital.

After the first two years of the military government, the rate of increase of state revenues declined. Pressure from foreign companies and internal opposition obliged the regime to change its course. By 1975 the initial reformist goals now seemed distant. The entrepreneurial associations, traditionally representing the dominant sectors, intensified their struggle against the government, accusing it of 'statism' and 'underhanded Communism' and of trying to 'destroy private enterprise'. The favourite targets of the attack were the progressively inclined members of the regime. Minister Jarrín Ampudia was removed from office in 1974. Other dismissals and resignations were to follow.

The opposition of economic pressure groups was compounded by the demands of political party leaders for a return to a constitutional form of government. Divided within their ranks and with no capacity for protest during the first years of the dictatorship, by 1975 the parties faced a government which was increasingly vulnerable to pressures for an end to the dictatorship. Nevertheless, several political leaders who headed the campaign were expelled from the country or confined for long periods to the Oriente region, the Upper Amazon.

In 1975 the government decided to decree a 60 per cent increase in export taxes. The immediate reason for this step was to augment state revenues and offset the budget deficit, although it was also clearly intended to encourage the development of national industries. However, when the industrial bourgeoisie failed to rally to the defence of the regime in the ensuing conflict, a group of army officers with contacts in the Chilean Embassy attempted to overthrow Rodríguez Lara. The president managed to stay in power after an armed confrontation, but the collapse of his government had begun.

With the regime severely weakened and the economic situation of the masses deteriorating, the newly united labour movement set out to demand wage increases and the fulfillment of reform promises by staging a general strike on 13 November 1975. Some weeks later peasants moved to demand the implementation of agrarian reform. But General Rodríguez Lara had no intention of meeting such popular demands. In any case, in January 1976 he was replaced by a junta composed of the heads of the three branches of the armed forces.

The Consejo Supremo de Gobierno under the presidency of Admiral Alfredo Poveda Burbano stated that its fundamental goal was to turn government over to civilians. But this time the unconditional and rapid surrender of previous dictatorships was replaced by a step-by-step programme in which the army maintained control over the situation until the new regime took office. Indeed, the military even managed to retain a share of power for the future under constitutional provisions.

The new government intensified the regressive tendencies of its predecessor. Reform principles were left aside; even the label of 'revolutionary and nationalistic' was eliminated. Land reform was brought to a stop, and an Agricultural–Livestock Development Law that guaranteed the property of rural entrepreneurs was enacted. In the oil industry there was a growing dependency on U.S. companies. Although economic policy was handled with notable competence, a general backlash could not be averted as price rises and wage freezes created discontent among the poorer sectors of the population. These movements were met with firm repressive action. The worst act of repression was the massacre of workers at the state-owned sugar mill on 17 October 1977.

In its measures to reconstitutionalize the country, the government responded to pressure by the progressive elements of the armed forces to implement a 'controlled return'. It rejected the traditional device of calling a constituent assembly. Instead, it undertook what was termed the 'juridical restructuring of the state', whereby political and social forces were called to a 'dialogue'; several commissions were subsequently appointed to prepare drafts for a Law of Political Parties; and, finally, two draft constitutions were submitted to a referendum. The most progressively oriented charter was adopted by simple majority vote.

The government adroitly sought the participation of the new political forces in constituting the commissions. The long-standing political fronts centred on the Conservative and Liberal parties had collapsed, and when the progressive wings of the old parties formed separate organizations, the dividing axis between 'Right' and 'Left' shifted from the dispute between Church and the state to differences regarding state intervention in the economy. As a result, both the 'juridical restructuring' and the elections which followed presaged a new political scenario. The Conservatives, Social Christians, Liberals and other minor groups were identified increasingly with the Right. The Centre was composed of the Izquierda Democrática (ID), a splinter from the Liberal Party; Democrácia Popular (DP), formed by the merger of the Christian Democratic Party and 'progressive conservatives', led by Julio César Trujillo; the populist forces of the CFP, led by Bucaram; and the Frente Radical Alfarista (FRA), another Liberal offshoot that had gained strength through populist opposition to the dictatorship. Left-wing organizations and groups temporarily achieved a united platform within the Frente Amplio de Izquierda (FADI), whilst the Maoist movement established the Movimiento Popular Democrático (MPD).

In the first round of the presidential elections held in July 1978 the triumph of the CFP and DP ticket caused a surprise. Jaime Roldós Aguilera, nominated as the CFP candidate because of a legal prohibition preventing party leader Assad Bucaram from participating, won; his running mate was Osvaldo Hurtado Larrea, a former leader of the Christian Democratic Party. Sixto Durán, a candidate of the Right, finished second, and Raúl Clemente Huerta, representative of the Liberals and other right-wing groups, took third place. Rodrigo Borja Cevallos of the Izquierda Democrática, Calderón Muñoz of the FRA and René Mauge of the FADI trailed the field.

The surprising victory of a ticket that carried the slogan *fuerza del cambio* – 'force for change' – upset some of the assumptions of a 'controlled return'. On several occasions before the second round of voting, attempts were made to prevent the transfer of power and permit a continuation of the dictatorship. However, voting finally took place and Roldós won by a landslide. On 10 August 1979 the new constitution came into effect and the Government Council turned power over to Jaime Roldós.

THE 1980S

The constitutional government led by Jaime Roldós encountered difficulties in realizing its programme from the very start. In addition to the
heterogeneity of the ruling alliance, the president had to contend with
growing conflict within the CFP and the opposition of its leader. Roldós
was not prepared to rule according to the dictates of Assad Bucaram and so
rapidly clashed with the CFP leader, thus losing that party's support in
Congress and the ability to command a parliamentary majority. Once he
lost influence over the executive, Bucaram formed an alliance with the
Conservative Party and other right-wing groups that enabled him to be
elected president of Congress. The consequence of this was an enduring
conflict between the presidency and Congress that came to characterize the
pattern of Ecuadorian constitutionalism during the 1980s.

   In an effort to grasp the initiative and secure popular support, Roldós
decided to call for a constitutional referendum, but this was impeded by
the Comisión de Notables, which convinced the president that a referendum would be too dangerous. The conflicts continued, although they lost
some of their intensity as a result of a border crisis with Peru. The division
of the victorious alliance in the 1979 poll, however, was unavoidable. The
president's supporters split from the CFP and founded a new party:
Pueblo, Cambio y Democracia (PCD). In a few years there was a new split
that resulted in the creation of the Partido Roldosista Ecuatoriano (PRE).
This party, led by Abdalá Bucaram, the president's brother-in-law and the
true heir of Assad Bucaram's populist leadership, quickly became the most
powerful political force in Guayaquil. All this served to clarify the balance
of forces as the CFP deepened its ties with the Right and reformist parties
like Izquierda Democrática adopted a position of 'support from a distance'
for the Roldós administration.

   The confrontation with Assad Bucaram almost paralysed the government
and cast the reformist promises of the election campaign in a distinctly sober
light. It proved increasingly difficult to apply the five-year development
plan. However, Roldós was able to make some advances in foreign policy,
upholding an independent stance, supporting the new *sandinista* government in Nicaragua and contributing to the emergent Third World bloc
within the Non-Aligned Movement. However, it proved exceptionally
difficult to retain such positions following the armed conflict with Peru in
the frontier zone early in 1981. Although the president was able to secure
domestic support in confronting the enemy, he was obliged to tone down

his international stance in order to acquire vital political and logistical backing abroad. A further consequence of the clashes with Peru was a substantial drain on the national treasury, particularly for defence spending.

On 24 May 1981 Jaime Roldós was killed in an air crash along with his wife, the minister of defence and the presidential staff. Vice-President Osvaldo Hurtado took over as head of state until the end of the presidential term in 1984, and León Roldós, the late president's brother, was appointed vice-president by Congress. Hurtado succeeded in giving the government greater cohesion, albeit along increasingly moderate and cautious lines. As the economic crisis of the 1980s deepened and social conflict grew, less emphasis was given to reform and more to maintaining social order and reaching compromises with the dominant economic interests.

The economic contraction evident at the start of the constitutional government deepened into a major crisis within a short time. During the 1970s gross domestic product (GDP) had grown at an average rate of 8 per cent; in 1981 the growth rate had fallen to 4 per cent, and by 1984 it was less than 1 per cent, lower even than the level of the 1940s. As industrial production fell a number of important enterprises went bankrupt; agricultural growth rates fell and the expansion of the financial sector slowed markedly. With the exception of maritime products, which rose by 20 per cent, export revenue fell. Although the reduction of banana sales was quite modest, that for cacao was much more serious. The price of a barrel of Ecuadorian petroleum fell from U.S. $40 in January 1981 to less than $25 in 1985.

The scale of the economic crisis was manifest in budget deficits of tens of millions of sucres, an increase in inflation from 15 per cent in 1981 to 63.4 per cent in 1983, a rise in unemployment to 8 per cent in 1984 (when underemployment stood at 40 per cent), constant reductions in real wages and a decline in investment from 36 billion sucres in 1979 to 22.2 billion in 1984 (at 1975 prices).[27]

The expansion begun in the 1970s had been brought to a precipitate halt, and there was widespread acceptance of the fact that the 'petroleum boom' was over. Yet there was much debate concerning the causes and consequences of the slump. The representatives of private capital and their most important spokesman, Deputy León Febres Cordero, declared that the crisis resulted from unnecessary state meddling in the economy, unfair

---

[27] Leonardo Vicuña Izquierdo, 'Tendencias económicas y sociales en 1984', in *Ecuador Debate*, vol. 7 (January, 1985).

tax laws, the 'bureaucratic explosion' set off by the Roldós and Hurtado governments and excessive controls on foreign capital. The trade unions, by contrast, demanded that the government fulfil its commitments to the working class and undertake the structural reforms it had promised in the election campaign.

As rising public expenditure was increasingly funded by external borrowing, the IMF strengthened its influence over policy, and this was enthusiastically supported by business. As a result, the debate over the role of the state in the economy intensified further still. At the same time, the campaign for a devaluation of the sucre grew. Hurtado's government, which sought to accommodate all sectors of business, at first attempted to negotiate the issue. However, it could not resist the pressure, and from 1983 it decreed both 'macro-devaluations' and 'mini-devaluations', which over six hundred days reduced the exchange rate of the sucre to the U.S. dollar from 32:1 to 100:1. Hurtado also introduced the policy of 'sucretization', whereby the private external debt was converted into the national currency, the state taking responsibility for its payment. In a country where some 85 per cent of exports were controlled by only twenty-four economic groups such measures necessarily strengthened those economic groups closely tied to finance capital and the banks, particularly in Guayaquil, the traditional redoubt of the oligarchy. This sector benefited more than any other from the *fuerza del cambio*.[28]

The means by which the government confronted the crisis and the impoverishment caused by these measures, the decline of the oil industry and the natural catastrophe of widespread floods throughout the coastal region provoked a new wave of social protest. The FUT led popular opposition to the devaluations and price increases by staging a series of 'national strikes' that at one point endangered the stability of the regime. However, Hurtado was able to complete his term of office after having played a significant role in the international movement to draw attention to the social costs of the Latin American debt crisis.

In the election of May 1984 the Left and the Centre presented separate candidates, whereas the Right – the Partido Social Cristiano, its traditional ally the Conservative Party, its traditional enemy the Liberal Party and a number of minor groups – united in the Frente de Reconstrucción Nacional behind the candidacy of León Febres Cordero. Rodrigo Borja,

[28] See Enrique Ayala and Rafael Quintero, 'Teorías e ideologías sobre el estado en el Ecuador', in Pablo González Casanova (ed.), *El Estado en América Latina, teoría y práctica* (Mexico, 1990), pp. 383–4.

the candidate of Izquierda Democrática, won the first round of the poll. Yet this success failed to generate sufficient support from voters previously committed to other parties, and Febres Cordero won the second round by a narrow majority. Izquierda Democrática, however, remained the most popular political party in electoral terms. This, together with the growth of Democracia Popular, consolidated the 'Centre' in Ecuadorian politics. The Left also succeeded in strengthening its position. Although the majority of the component parties of FADI subsequently left to join the Communist Party, the FADI increased its vote and congressional representation. And the MPD, the legal front of the Maoists, came fourth in the 1984 poll. The Socialist Party, PSE, reunited and revitalized, also won a significant vote and a seat in Congress as well as expanded its influence within the labour movement, the peasantry and some of the associations of professionals and public sector employees.

León Febres Cordero took office in August 1984 and immediately began to adopt a dictatorial attitude and to apply neo-liberal policies that brought the executive into sharp conflict with other state powers, especially Congress. Some of the economic policies, however, were a continuation of those adopted by the Hurtado administration. Control over foreign exchange was progressively handed over to the private banks and commercial interests, provoking unprecedented increases in the exchange rate. The policy of establishing 'real prices' substantially increased the cost of living and extended the terms of *sucretización,* further benefiting commercial and speculative interests. However, the government's extremely favourable attitude towards foreign capital failed to produce increased investment.

The economic strategy of the government relied on the solid support of the most powerful economic groups of the country as well as the backing of the Reagan administration. Febres Cordero and his economic team obtained important loans and non-refundable credits from the U.S. government, as well as political support in its negotiations with the IMF, the World Bank and private creditors. They managed to renegotiate the external debt in terms widely recognized to be better than those extended to the previous governments. Nevertheless, when in 1987 an earthquake damaged the country's main oil pipe, the *oleoducto transecuatoriano,* and halted oil exports for more than six months, the Febres Cordero government stopped payments on the external debt in an undeclared moratorium.

After several months in office, the administration succeeded in promoting non-oil exports. Coffee, bananas and especially shellfish significantly increased their share of the export market. This export 'boom' primarily benefited the commercial houses and private banks, but it also brought some prosperity to sections of the coastal countryside and Guayaquil, the main exporting port. In this way, Febres Cordero further consolidated his regional support and sharpened the traditional contradiction between Sierra and Coast.

As was predicted during the electoral campaign, the new government immediately entered into violent confrontation with the opposition. Six parties of the opposition from Centre to Left united in Congress as the Bloque Progresista. During the first months of the new administration the Bloque Progresista had a narrow majority in Congress and tried to make appointments to the Supreme Court, Constitutional Tribunal and other state bodies independently of the government. Febres Cordero simply stopped this by sending the police to the Congress and the Supreme Court.[29] For the first time Ecuador was blacklisted by Amnesty International as a country where human rights were systematically violated.

The government claimed that its authoritarian measures were necessary for the country's stability. And in threatening to cancel congressional and municipal elections due in June 1986 the president was said to have the unanimous support of the armed forces. However, the chief of staff of the armed forces, General Frank Vargas Pazzos, demanded the sacking of the minister of defence and the chief of the army for corruption. He seized two air bases and forced an agreement on the president, who subsequently refused to honour it, sending Vargas and some of his supporters to jail. Since Vargas appeared to be a defender of the constitution and the integrity of the armed forces, and was at the same time denouncing the corruption of the government, he immediately became a popular hero, not only in the Sierra, where the government was already unpopular, but also in his native province of Manabí, the second largest and most populated on the Coast. Although the majority of the opposition parties did not openly support Vargas, especially when he attempted to force the resignation of Febres Cordero, they seized the opportunity to renew their attack on the president. The Vargas affair had shown that Febres Cordero could be challenged, that the armed forces were deeply divided and that corruption had reached an exceptionally high level.

In the June 1986 election the government was defeated and, in a referendum held at the same time, the electorate rejected a proposal by the presi-

---

[29] María Arboleda, Raúl Borja and José Steinsleger, *Mi poder en la oposición* (Quito, 1985), pp. 31–8.

dent to change the constitution. When Congress met in August, the opposition had a solid majority. The most controversial decision made by Congress was to grant an amnesty to both General Vargas and Abdalá Bucaram, the former mayor of Guayaquil who had fled the country after being accused of damaging the honour of the armed forces. The government refused to accept the legislative resolution, and Vargas stayed in prison and Bucaram in Panama. Several months later, the president and some members of the cabinet were kidnapped by the garrison of the Taura Air Base during an official visit. Febres Cordero was forced to order the freedom of General Vargas, but the *comandos de Taura* were court martialled and sentenced to several years' imprisonment.[30] As the end of his administration approached, the internal splits widened and Febres Cordero even quarrelled publicly with his vice-president, Blasco Peñaherrera, who joined the opposition and attacked government corruption and abuse of civil rights.[31]

The government could not hold together the Frente de Reconstrucción Nacional for the elections of 1988. Some of its members presented their own slates, but the official candidate was once again Sixto Durán Ballán of the Partido Social Cristiano. The opposition was also divided, Izquierda Democrática and Democracia Popular presenting Rodrigo Borja and Jamil Mahuad, respectively, as their candidates. The PRE, which was certainly the strongest populist force, contested the poll independently with Abdalá Bucaram as its candidate. After prolonged negotiations, the united slate of the Left collapsed and two candidacies were presented: Frank Vargas Pazzos for APRE (Alianza Revolucionaria Popular Ecuatoriana), the PSE and some Communists, and Jaime Hurtado for the two official Communist parties (MPD and FADI). In the first round Borja came first and Bucaram second. In the second round, after a turbulent campaign, Izquierda Democrática finally secured a victory, and on 10 August 1988 Rodrigo Borja became president amidst great expectations.

The electoral victory of Jaime Roldós in 1979 undoubtedly reflected an important shift in national political attitudes and activity. Subsequently much attention was given to the growth and consolidation of 'the Centre' as a newly dominant electoral force. In the early 1980s many considered that in the future political power would be negotiated within the framework of reformism, the Ecuadorian Right having lost its capacity to win elections

[30] See Gonzalo Ortiz Crespo, *Operación Taura* (Quito, 1987).
[31] See Blasco Peñaherrera, *El Viernes Negro: Antes y después de Taura* (Quito, 1988); León Febres Cordero, *Autopsia de una traición* (Quito, 1989).

and its propensity to sponsor military coups. Indeed, so strong was this view that it almost acquired the status of a scientific certainty. However, it was not long before it was shown to be profoundly misconceived.

In reaction to the reformist governments, both military and civilian, the Right had itself undergone significant regroupment and had begun to adopt a new approach that replaced the old confessional and hierarchical politics with an aggressive programme of modernization, very similar in content to the neo-liberal economic strategies adopted by the dictators of the Southern Cone with the support of the United States, combined with the *caudillista* tradition of *velasquismo*. León Febres Cordero, an entrepreneur tied to both foreign capital and the most powerful national companies, took the leadership of this new movement largely through his belligerent activity in Congress. His victory in May 1984 demonstrated that the Right still possessed the ability to win power through elections. It did not, however, necessarily fortify the traditional parties within the Frente de Reconstrucción Nacional, both Liberals and Conservatives continuing to be weakened by divisions. The Febres Cordero administration was, in fact, less the product of political alliance and organization than it was the creation of various sectors of the capitalist class that possessed a long-term socio-economic project for the country — a project expressed and implemented mainly by the Partido Social Cristiano, which had become a strong political force, especially on the Coast, where the Right had never had significant support. *Velasquismo* itself had died with its leader, but populist forces like CFP and PRE survived several splits and electoral setbacks. Although the Coast had been their stronghold, sometimes they were able to secure significant support in the Sierra, as they did in 1979 and even in 1988. At the end of the decade, the PRE, in particular, remained an important political force and, from the oligarchy's point of view, an efficient instrument for the control of the masses.

The political parties of the democratic Centre or Centre Left, Izquierda Democrática and Democracia Popular, succeeded in building considerable political machines throughout the country during the 1980s. Their main support was in the Sierra and Oriente, but they also had backing in the coastal provinces. The social base of both parties was essentially the urban middle class. But it is important to point out that traditional political instruments like *clientelismo* and *patronaje* persisted not only on the Right in the populist parties, but also in the parties of the Centre. And it should also be stressed that although the interests represented by the Centre parties were mainly those of the emerging groups of industrialists and bankers, some powerful members of the traditional oligarchy also became their supporters. In 1988, as we have seen, the candidate of the Izquierda Democrática, Rodrigo Borja, won the presidency. Finally, the Marxist Left, which had been an important actor in Ecuadorian politics since the 1960s, remained a considerable force at the end of the 1980s. In the elections of 1986 and 1988 the three parties – the PSE, FADI (the legal front of the Communist Party) and the Maoist MPD – pooled between 15 and 17 per cent of the vote, their most significant electoral support coming from the Sierra.

All of these political developments took place in the context of persistent economic crisis from the early 1980s. Oil revenue continued to fall, and there was no new source of export earnings to replace it. The external debt rose from U.S. $500 million in 1975 to $11 billion in 1989.[32] On the eve of the final decade of the twentieth century Ecuador, with a population of 10 million, the majority of which lived in urban centres, principally Guayaquil (1.7 million) and Quito (1.2 million), faced deepening social problems, familiar and unfamiliar, and mounting social conflict. Regionalization and the reconstitution of national and ethnic identities presented new challenges. Whilst not as intractible or violent in form as similar challenges in Peru, they undoubtedly placed an additional strain upon the social fabric of the country and its political institutions.

[32] Eduardo Santos Alvite and Mariana Mora Duque, *Ecuador: La decada de los ochenta* (Quito, 1987), pp. 41–8.

13

VENEZUELA SINCE 1930

Venezuela's political, economic and social development in the twentieth century has been unique in Latin America. In 1900, Venezuela was a poor and caudillo-dominated Caribbean country. Export agriculture based on coffee and cacao produced some modest wealth for the planter class, but neither the Andean nor the coastal *hacendados* could be said to constitute a national modernizing elite. Poor communications and regionally based rural economies meant that national loyalties remained weak. Moreover, the nineteenth-century civil wars had played havoc with hopes for economic prosperity, national integration and even political stability as successive regional politico-military cliques came to power in Caracas.

Economic growth accelerated around the turn of the century. Under the dictatorship of the Táchira caudillo Cipriano Castro (1899–1908) foreign companies intensified asphalt exploitation; and from 1914, under the dictatorship of another Táchira caudillo, Juan Vicente Gómez (1908–1935), Venezuela's economy began to undergo a singular transformation with the discovery of rich oil fields in the western province of Zulia and in the eastern coastal region. However, the impact of the oil industry upon Venezuela would not be fully evident until after Gómez's death. Moreover, political life changed little before 1936, except for an expansion of government jobs and a very modest strengthening of central government. Economic patterns and class structure also registered only slight shifts. Many of Gómez's cronies entered the elite by selling concessions to foreign oil companies, and a larger and more affluent middle class arose as Venezuelans found professional employment with the oil companies and in the growing public sector. New capital scorned traditional investment in export agriculture in favour of commerce, services, construction and urban land speculation – a pattern which was to shape development policy for decades after Gómez's death. A few manufacturing industries were

727

established – much later and fewer than in Argentina, Brazil or Mexico – but Venezuelan capital was not drawn to productive industry until the 1940s and 1950s. Arturo Uslar Pietri's demand that the government *'siembre el petróleo'* (sow the petroleum, or rather the petroleum revenues) was visionary but hollow. Venezuela fell easily into the pattern of exchanging oil revenues for imported food and consumer goods.

More visible than industrial entrepreneurs, a small proletariat of oil workers appeared in the 1920s to play a national political role disproportionate to its size. Strikes in the Zulia oil fields in 1925 indicated the emergence of a new ally for the students and military reformers whose protests and attempted coup in 1928 tested the strength of the dictatorship. Some Communist influence was evident in the 1920s unrest, but the conspiring students, workers, young officers and exiled caudillos espoused no programmes to differentiate their efforts from earlier abortive efforts to unseat the dictator. The government outlawed labour unions, and the oil companies easily isolated and dominated the work-force. Jail and exile stifled political opposition from intellectuals and military officers. Many of Gómez's opponents, sensing that the end was near, chose the low-risk tactic of waiting for the ailing and aged caudillo to die.

THE END OF THE GÓMEZ DICTATORSHIP, 1930–5

Gómez had laid out the rules under which the petroleum companies were to operate in Venezuela. His objectives were to concentrate petroleum decisions – and opportunity for graft – in his own hands, to maximize revenues from the companies and to see that they did not so dominate local communities that he would suffer from political backlash. Often criticized by nationalists for having conceded too much to the foreign companies, the old caudillo had few realistic alternatives. In a politically inert and poor nation, Gómez could not mobilize either a strong army or a large, organized population to reduce his vulnerability to the companies. The firms maintained their strength through the sobering example of their withdrawal from Mexico in response to the revolutionary nationalism there, by reducing exploration and production in 1930 at the onset of the depression and by warning that Venezuelan exports were vulnerable to U.S. congressional import tariffs or quotas. The companies therefore seemed to hold all the cards, and Gómez set a precedent by responding in a cautious and conservative fashion.

For both Venezuela and the *gomecistas* the stakes were high. Production rose from 63 million barrels in 1927 to 323 million in 1945. By 1930, Venezuela had more than 107 companies operating in its territory and was the world's largest exporter of petroleum. In that same year, Gómez proudly paid off the entire foreign national debt, only twenty-eight years after default had caused a joint German, British and Italian blockade of the country. The big three companies – Royal Dutch Shell, Gulf and Standard Oil – controlled 98 per cent of the export market. Although Gómez favoured the North Americans, he also encouraged British and Dutch investors, believing that competition would give the nation greater autonomy. (Nonetheless, the Second World War greatly reduced the possibilities of retaining such a balance among the companies, and by the 1940s one U.S. company, Standard Oil through its subsidiary the Creole Petroleum Company, produced more than half of Venezuela's petroleum.)

Between 1930 and 1934 the depression compelled major cut-backs in petroleum production. However, the Gómez government strengthened the currency (bolívar) in 1934 and was able to increase revenue whilst production began to rise again soon thereafter. By 1945 oil contributed 54.2 per cent of government revenues, but for most of the Gómez years customs revenues – the traditional source of Latin American state income – accounted for about half. As was pointed out by Minister of Development Gumersindo Torres, Venezuela *lost* more income from the oil companies' privilege to import goods duty free than it gained from taxes and royalties on petroleum. The importance of commerce, the weakened agricultural export sector (which represented less than 12 per cent of the value of Venezuela's exports after 1932) and the needs of the oil companies contributed to the virtual absence of any call for tariff protection either for industry or for agricultural exports.

Gómez allowed the foreign oil companies considerable autonomy. Lawyers for U.S. oil companies had written the 1922 legislation under which they enjoyed relatively low taxes and royalties, less pressure to initiate exploitation rapidly, no supervision by the Venezuelan Congress and no restriction on the amount of land that one company could hold. Venezuela did not, therefore, drive a hard deal with the companies, but the nation nonetheless received a higher rate of return between 1913 and 1947 than did the Middle Eastern countries.[1]

Although he often tolerated the companies' excesses, Gómez sometimes

[1] B. S. McBeth, *Juan Vicente Gómez and the Oil Companies in Venezuela, 1908–1935* (Cambridge, 1983), p. 65.

issued veiled warnings that foreigners did well to heed. For example, villagers around Lake Maracaibo complained that the rapid and careless oil drilling in the region polluted the lake and spread fire hazards that threatened lives and property; in June 1928 a fire destroyed a good part of the town of Lagunillas, which was partially built on the lake. The local people filed a claim against the offending companies, which agreed under government pressure to pay for some of the damage done; thereafter, the government began timidly to monitor working and living conditions around the lake. In 1931 Minister of Development Torres billed foreign companies for amounts they had deprived the nation of since 1927 through misrepresentation of their costs. Company protests forced Torres' resignation, but the firms, wary of nationalistic attitudes such as those shown in Mexico, may have taken the hint that they should not unduly abuse the nation's hospitality.

The benefits from petroleum exploitation were not widely distributed. The government provided few services even though a mild retreat from laissez-faire began during the depression. A more affluent central state drew rural migrants and middle-class professionals to Caracas to seek jobs in government and on public works projects. Workers had also migrated to the oil-producing regions, but the petroleum industry employed only 1.2 per cent of the national labour force. Foreign companies frequently brought in workers from the Antilles in preference to Venezuelan workers. Moreover, firms freely imported consumer goods to sell in their commissaries, thereby limiting the scope for local businesses.

Oil came to dominate the Venezuelan economy so quickly and at such a critical time that other economic sectors, especially export agriculture, nearly vanished. Farmers complained that they had to compete with both the foreign companies and urban commerce for workers. High production costs fuelled by high interest rates probably hurt the exporters more, and planters contributed to their difficulties by their unwillingness to modernize or invest in improvement of railroads and ports. Venezuelan coffee production had stagnated from 1914 to 1933, although the higher prices of the 1920s partially obscured this fact until the depression dashed the traditional cacao and coffee markets in Europe. The final blow for the reeling farmers came in 1934 when the government raised the value of the bolívar in relation to the dollar; this increased state revenues from petroleum exports, but ended the competitive position of Venezuelan coffee abroad. The government attempted to aid the farmers with subsidies and agricultural credit, but these programmes were poorly administered. Astute planters took advantage of the situation to transfer their capital to commerce or to urban land or public works contracts, where quicker and easier profits were to be had.

Although statistics for this period are few and unreliable it does appear that during the 1930s some small industries – food processing, textiles, construction materials – began to appear despite the high cost of labour, the lack of an experienced entrepreneurial elite, the maintenance of a strong currency and an open market for imported goods. Nevertheless, these few and weak industrialists had even less success than rural capitalists in eliciting sympathy or protection from the *gomecistas*.

In response to the depression, two new government institutions – the Banco Agrícola y Pecuario (BAP) and the Banco Obrero – provided the government with a greater role in the economy. Yet critics charged that the BAP enriched planters without encouraging agriculture since these farmers tended to invest their loans in the cities. At the same time, the Banco Obrero benefited contractors who used the credit to build low-cost housing, which they then sold to workers at inflated prices. Gómez saw no need to provide credit for industrialists.

After the political crisis of 1928–9, Gómez's last years were relatively stable and he allowed Dr Juan Bautista Pérez, a *caraqueño,* to assume the presidency from 1929 to 1931. This alarmed some of his Táchira army colleagues, who mounted a conspiracy to replace Pérez with a more reliable *tachirense* who could protect regional interests after Gómez's death. In mid-1931 Gómez discovered the plot and thwarted it by taking back the presidency. Although a *tachirense* to the core – he was never comfortable in Caracas and refused to live there – Gómez, like most nineteenth-century presidents, had come finally to side with *los doctores* of Caracas. Regional patron–client networks increasingly became one more way of surviving, and advancing, in Caracas rather than a vehicle for serving regional interests.

When the dictator reached the age of seventy-six in 1935, national attention was already focussed on the question of the succession. Would his cousin Eustoquio Gómez continue the clan's hold on the presidency, or would *tachirense* Minister of War Eleazar López Contreras, an ally of Cipriano Castro and Gómez in 1899, be able to seize the prize for himself? López, with a Táchira high school degree in philosophy and letters, proved to have a natural military talent and rose quickly in the army. He then overcame Gómez's initial suspicion that he was too close to Castro and consolidated his position under the new dictatorship. In 1928 as commander of the Caracas garrison, López efficiently suppressed the military cadets' conspiracy with a minimum of bloodshed and imprisoned or exiled the ringleaders. His own twenty-one-year-old son, who had joined the conspiracy against Gómez, enjoyed no special favours and served a jail term before going into exile. Gómez and the Táchira old guard nonetheless criticized López for what they regarded as mild reprisals, and he was banished to the Andes until 1931, when he was appointed minister of war and navy. Although not a military school graduate, López sought to modernize the national army which Gómez had shaped. He travelled to Europe, several Latin American nations and the United States in order to study military organization and training. Within the army, López walked a fine line between the conservative Táchira generals and the impatient younger officers who wanted to combine new equipment, tactics and organization with a stronger, more nationalistic role for the armed forces. López enjoyed some support from civilians, who saw him as more *culto* and reasonable than many of his unschooled Táchira colleagues. After Gómez's long reign, many civilians feared that the absence of a democratic Caesar, as Laureano Vallenilla Lanz had termed Gómez, would allow the social fabric to dissolve, bringing back the conflict and insecurity of the nineteenth century. Even moderates who despised the graft, lack of political freedom and provincial image of the Gómez dictatorship were wary of rapid change. In the absence of any organized political parties – except the clandestine Communist Party – or civilian political institutions, many were prepared to accept López Contreras as president as long as he could maintain order and provide a transition to constitutional rule. When Gómez died, therefore, on 17 December 1935, the Council of Ministers named López provisional president, an 'election' ratified by Congress on 2 January 1936.

THE POST-*GOMECISTA* TRANSITION, 1936–45

López Contreras had no hesitation in calling on the army and police to control the popular demonstrations that erupted in January 1936 as he assumed the presidency. At the same time, he took the unprecedented step of promising a package of social, economic and political reforms which collectively came to be known as the February Programme. Henceforth, the government would formally assume responsibility for economic development and for the welfare and health of its citizens. New economic and social groups – labour, professional, industrialist – saw the possibility of a government that for the first time would answer to their needs. More-over, much like his contemporary, Mexican President Lázaro Cárdenas, López made a point of travelling to all parts of the country, and he was the first Venezuelan president to use the radio effectively to gain support for a national programme. López sought to establish a more open political system, but he believed that fully democratic government could be intro-duced only gradually. The Venezuelan people must first be 'taught' to trust moderate leaders and turn away from demagogues and agitators. López, therefore, continued to share the view that the presidency must be able to manipulate the political system, and he considered competitive politics to be destructive and wasteful. In 1937 the president outlawed open political activity, sent political opponents into exile and backed away from some of the more radical promises of the February Programme. He did not, however, return to the excesses of the Gómez repression, and he allowed the presidential term to be reduced from seven to five years in the 1936 constitution, announcing that he would surrender power in 1941.

López Contreras apparently flirted with the notion of permitting a civilian to succeed him through a direct election. Yet his own natural conservatism, and the protests of his Táchira military colleagues, per-suaded him to take the safer path of designating as his successor the minister of war, General Isaías Medina Angarita. The novelist Rómulo Gallegos provided symbolic opposition in the 'election', in which the Congress voted overwhelmingly for Medina.

Medina Angarita came from a younger generation of Táchira soldiers and had spent most of his adult life in Caracas. He had maintained unswerving loyalty to both Gómez and López and asserted that he had had no political ambitions or interests until López had named him minister of war in 1936. One of the first graduates of the Caracas Military Academy, Medina was more popular with the younger, more professional officers than he was with the old Táchira colleagues of Castro and Gómez, who worried that he was too soft. Indeed, Medina extended López's economic and social initiatives, and went so far as to endorse a modest social security programme through the Instituto de Seguro Social. Under his presidency there was greater political activity in Venezuela than there had been at any time since the late nineteenth century. Unlike López, Medina formed an official government party, the Partido Democrático Venezolano, and he allowed other political parties, including that of the Communists, to operate openly. In line with the Popular Front tactics endorsed by the Comintern from the mid-1930s, many Communists co-operated with a government which was widely respected because it held no political prisoners and displayed a notable even-handedness in its policy and actions.

Both López Contreras and Medina Angarita dealt more firmly with the foreign oil companies. Demonstrations, strikes and arson in the oil camps after Gómez's death in December 1935 indicated that popular nationalism was on the rise. The Mexican oil nationalization in 1938 and the outbreak of the Second World War further strengthened López's hand in revising the petroleum legislation. A new law in 1938 gave the government greater authority to supervise the industry and the right to higher revenues. The companies generally ignored the legislation, but Medina increased the pressure by passing new tax laws in 1942. A year later, he issued a new petroleum law that superseded all previous legislation. It required the oil companies to share profits equally with the nation through higher initial exploitation taxes and higher royalties. It also ended the companies' exemption from customs duties and promoted domestic refining. Since the U.S. State Department was urging hemisphere co-operation during the war, the companies accepted the new legislation in exchange for greater security for their concessions. They received assurances that tariff schedules would be lowered so as not to discourage imports, that the government would drop an investigation into disputed titles and that the concessions due to expire in the 1960s would be extended. The petroleum law of 1943, with minor subsequent revisions, remained in force until the 1976 nationalization of the oil industry. Some of Medina's critics, including members of the newly formed Acción Democrática (AD) party, criticized the 1943 law for not going far enough. Legislation, however, was less important than the government's intention and ability to enforce it. In the conditions of the early 1940s, with few national petroleum experts, the Venezuelan government remained at a disadvantage in dealing with the companies, regardless of the new legislation.

Increased revenues from the oil companies allowed the López and Medina administrations to expand the role of the state in directing the economy, despite the tenacity of laissez-faire beliefs, and in particular to divert oil revenue to other productive activities, particularly agriculture. López announced Venezuela's first three-year development plan in 1938 and created two new cabinet ministries – the Ministry of Agriculture and Livestock and the Ministry of Labour and Communications. A new Banco Industrial provided industrial credit, the Oficina Nacional de Cambios regulated exchange rates and the Banco Central de Venezuela monitored fiscal and monetary policy. Yet Venezuela was still too poor, its population too unskilled, its leaders too inexperienced to be able to dictate the terms of the nation's development and Venezuela's role in the world economic system.

During the depression the Venezuelan government had pursued internal development and provided some jobs by means of large public works expenditures. Gómez took the first major step towards building a modern highway system by ordering construction of the Trans-Andean Highway linking the Andean states with Caracas. (Gómez also recognized the military benefits of a national road system which would allow him to stamp out regional rebellions.) López and Medina gave priority to connecting the oil camps to ports and the camps and provincial cities to Caracas. Most of the new roads led to Caracas, making it a bottleneck through which much transport from the east to the west of the nation had to pass and thus reinforcing its position as the hub of the nation. Air transport, too, was increasingly used to connect the capital with the more distant provinces, and the government invested in a national airline, Aereopostal.

At the time of Gómez's death, Venezuela's population was sparse, rural, largely *mestizo* and concentrated along the coastal corridor and in the Andean states. During the colonial period there had been little to draw Europeans to Venezuela: there existed no large Indian population to provide labour and no precious minerals. The situation had not changed much in the nineteenth century except that the density of population along the northern coast intensified. Small enclaves of indigenous populations existed in the unexplored Far South and the Orinoco Delta. (The Guajiro and the Motilones Indians settled around Lake Maracaibo were subjected to increasing external pressure after the 1920s, but they proved to be tough survivors.) The coastal area from Caracas to Carúpano to the east retained a distinctively Afro-Venezuelan cultural imprint, which was derived from the slaves brought in during the colonial period to work the plantations and the salt mines in the Araya Peninsula. The distribution of population began to change in the early twentieth century as the oil camps and urban construction and commerce drew more peasants into the cities and to Lake Maracaibo. Urbanization gathered pace: the population living in cities larger than 100,000 rose from 313,352 in 1936 to 405,000 in 1946 (and to 1,697,000 in 1958). At the same time, the dominance of Caracas increased as its population grew from 203,342 in 1936 to 495,064 in 1950 (786,863 in 1961).

A trend towards better health began in the decade between Gómez's death and the revolution of 1945. With the new oil wealth, the medical services provided by the oil companies for their workers, scientific advances in the battle against tropical diseases and modest programmes undertaken by the López Contreras and Medina Angarita governments, the incidence of malaria began to decline. Life expectancy was only 38 years in 1936, but it rose to 43.2 years in 1941, 53.9 years in 1950 and 60.9 years in 1961. Meanwhile, the population grew from 2,479,525 in 1920 to 3,364,347 in 1936 to 5,034,838 in 1950 and 7,523,999 in 1961, the growth after 1945 reflecting a considerable influx of European immigrants – Italians, Portuguese and Spaniards.

Women's lives also began to change. In 1936 women's suffrage was demanded by groups like the Agrupación Cultural Femenina, Acción Femenina and the Asociación Venezolana de Mujeres. Women won the right to vote in municipal elections in 1942, but universal suffrage did not come until 1947. Some women participated in protest groups at the jailing of students in 1928, and more joined the student and political activities of the 1930s. The increasing tempo of political organization drew women into the streets, as did new possibilities for employment that accompanied the expansion of the oil industry, government bureaucracy and urban commerce. Rural and urban working-class women had, of course, long formed part of the active labour force since frequently they had to provide the sole support for their children. Insecurity of employment, general poverty and the weakness of the Catholic Church meant that relatively few Venezuelan couples solemnized their unions with legal marriages. Only 24.4 per cent of the population over the age of fifteen was married in 1941. The trend continued upwards in the decades to follow, but still remained low, although marriage statistics indicate nothing, of course, about the stability of consensual unions. The increasing number of marriages, establishment of government and private institutions to protect abandoned children and improved occupational opportunities for women (as well as men) may have contributed to somewhat more stable conditions for children.

The growth of an industrial working class provided the greatest challenge to the rural-based Gómez system. A labour movement had been slow to evolve as a political force both because there was little industry and because successive dictatorships since 1899 had forbidden labour organization as 'Communistic'. Thus, the oil field strikes in 1925 had had no distinguished leaders and no clear goals. The first serious strike by petroleum workers did not occur until 1936. President López Contreras made a number of conciliatory gestures towards labour but outlawed some unions and decreed an end to the strike of December 1936–January 1937 before workers' demands had been met. The unions remained vulnerable to government coercion until after the Second World War, and again during the Pérez Jiménez dictatorship, but from 1936 they clearly had to be taken into account by government. Medina Angarita, although more supportive of labour demands than López, suspended the Second Workers' Congress in March 1944 and cancelled the recognition of some unions, ostensibly because the delegates had expressed support for the Communist Party. The action simultaneously weakened the organized labour movement and strengthened AD, the leading non-Communist influence among the workers. AD also took the lead in organizing rural workers, largely ignored by the Communists. Peasant membership in unions rose from 482 in 1936 to 6,279 in 1945.

Successive governments showed more flexibility towards white-collar workers and business associations. New groups in the 1930s and 1940s followed the example of lawyers, doctors, dentists, pharmacists and engineers who had formed professional associations early in the twentieth century; associations of teachers, journalists and public employees came to life in the decade after Gómez's death. Organizations formed by writers and by students had an impact beyond their numbers, although they experienced more government harassment than did professional groups. The first national convention of the Cámaras y Asociaciones de Comercio y Producción in 1944 brought together existing commercial and industrial associations, and became the forerunner of Fedecámaras.

The expanding middle class was served by new radio programmes, new newspapers such as *El Nacional* and new literary magazines such as *Cultura Venezolana* and *El Morrocoy Azul*. Whereas these organs were managed and written by Venezuelans, foreign publishing chains and news services came to exert a strong influence after the Second World War. Venezuelan novelists like Rómulo Gallegos (*Doña Barbara*, 1929), Ramón Díaz Sánchez (*Mene*, 1936), and Miguel Otero Silva (*Fiebre*, 1939) drew attention to rural problems, the persecution of workers and students and the arrogance of the foreign oil companies. It is significant that not all foreigners, even those associated with the oil companies, suffered at the hands of these writers. Venezuelan literature and political life expressed a common attraction to a multi-class alliance which, with the responsible assistance of foreign capital, would work to reform the traditional political, economic and social structures. But the growing militancy of labour after 1935 helped to confirm the perception that dictators and foreign businessmen had formed an alliance which was not in the best interests of the nation.

López and Medina presided over a cautious foreign policy, albeit one more sensitive to development around the world than had been Gómez's. Venezuela had joined the League of Nations in 1920 and participated actively in the Pan-American Union from the moment of its founding. Gómez, however, believed that some international organizations – notably the International Labour Office – intervened too much in the domestic affairs of nations, and he saw no merit in expanding Venezuela's international role. In 1936 Venezuela withdrew from the League when it was thrown into crisis by the invasion of Ethiopia. Relations with the United States took on greater importance as Washington responded to the challenges of European fascism by encouraging hemispheric co-operation.

Despite their more nationalist attitude towards the oil companies, López and Medina received U.S. approval for avoiding the excesses of the Gómez dictatorship. Venezuela also benefited from the more flexible Latin American policy of President Franklin D. Roosevelt, whose Good Neighbor policy entreated U.S. businesses to 'give them a share' and provided economic advice and loans for agriculture, trade and public works projects. It derived greater benefit still when the U.S. State Department urged the U.S. oil companies to negotiate in good faith with Venezuela on the new oil legislation of 1943.

Negotiation of a new trade treaty with the United States between 1936 and 1939 highlighted the limits of Venezuelan autonomy. The government in Caracas sought a treaty which would carefully limit foreign imports and encourage Venezuelan exports other than oil. Foreign Minister Esteban Gil Borges proposed to exclude petroleum from the agreement altogether, arguing that trade concessions for oil did not benefit Venezuela, but the foreign companies and the Curaçao refineries. However, the proposal for a degree of protectionism ran counter to the U.S. plan to boost its exports through free-trade policies and most favoured nation clauses in commercial agreements. Pressure from the oil companies and threats that the U.S. Congress intended to please domestic suppliers by imposing import quotas on foreign oil caused the Venezuelans to cave in and accept the U.S. draft of the treaty. The absence of a strong industrial class and fears of an interruption of trade in the event of war left them with little choice. The agreement virtually assured U.S. products free entry to the Venezuelan market, lowered income from tariffs, increased dependency on oil exports and inexorably drew Venezuela more firmly into the

U.S. economic orbit. It also limited the implementation of an effective import-substitution policy during the critical period when other Latin American nations began to expand their industrial capacity.

Concern for hemispheric defence and acknowledgement of Venezuela's military vulnerability strengthened political and military ties with the United States. Shortly after Pearl Harbor, Caracas broke relations with the Axis powers but remained technically neutral in order to avoid German attacks. Considerable shock was caused by the loss of Venezuelan lives when a German submarine sank several oil tankers off the coast of the Paraguaná Peninsula in 1942. Venezuela finally declared war in 1945 so as to be eligible to participate in the founding of the United Nations.

The necessities of war encouraged greater national consciousness and a stronger definition and defence of national boundaries. In 1941 a treaty was signed to fix the boundary with Colombia on the Guajira Peninsula, although Venezuela was later to denounce this accord as prejudicial to the national interest. During the war, Medina asserted the country's sole responsibility for the defence of the Gulf of Venezuela. In 1942, Great Britain and Venezuela signed the Gulf of Paría Treaty, which delimited the marine boundaries and shelves between Trinidad and Venezuela.

The wartime emergency and the focus on defence of both strategic resources and national territory increased the importance of the armed forces. Gómez had taken steps towards centralizing and professionalizing the armed forces by opening the Academia Militar in 1910 and by gradually eliminating all other regional caudillos. Yet under Gómez the main role of the military was domestic, checking internal revolts and spying on the dictator's enemies. Professionalism was impeded by Gómez's favouritism towards *tachirenses* in granting promotions and benefits. After 1935 education and training improved, and a number of promising young officers studied abroad in Peru, France and the United States. Influenced by the more grandiose sense of national mission proclaimed by their colleagues in Peru and Argentina and by the general martial atmosphere in Europe, junior officers became impatient with their status in Venezuela. They aspired to a modern political and economic system in which a professional and well-trained armed forces would play a more prominent part. In 1942 younger officers formed a secret military lodge, the Unión Patriótica Militar (UPM). This conspiratorial group grew rapidly under the leadership of Marcos Pérez Jiménez, Martín Márquez Añez, Mario Ricardo Vargas, Julio César Vargas and Carlos Delgado Chalbaud, academic director of the Academia Militar.

At the same time, a civilian political opposition had been developing from its origins in the 1928 student revolt. The jailing and exile of the student leaders began the political education of the generation of Venezuelans who would dominate the nation from the 1940s to the 1980s. Rómulo Betancourt, Raúl Leoni, Ricardo Montilla, Juan Pablo Pérez Alfonzo, Miguel Otero Silva, Juan Bautista Fuenmayor and others went into exile after Gómez released them from jail. Aware of their political ignorance, the young exiles actively read, discussed and corresponded in an effort to understand their national history and to devise an appropriate political system.

Not all of the 1928 rebels came to the same political conclusion. Some, like novelist Miguel Otero Silva and Juan Bautista Fuenmayor, were drawn more strongly to communism. Venezuelan exiles formed or joined Communist parties abroad, and a clandestine national party was established in 1931. The Venezuelan party had ties with the Caribbean Bureau of the Third International, but it failed to function effectively during the dictatorship. Comintern rigidity and dogmatic belief that Latin America would not play a major role in world revolution led the international leaders to undervalue organization in the region.

Initially allied with some of the more traditional of Gómez's opponents, such as José Rafael Pocaterra, Rómulo Betancourt and his friends began to develop a distinct political reform programme. Between 1928 and 1936 they combined elements of Marxism with influences drawn from the Peruvian Alianza Popular Revolucionaria Americana (APRA) and the doctrines of the Mexican Revolution. In 1931 they published the Plan of Barranquilla – a liberal, populist programme designed to appeal to Venezuelan workers and *campesinos* as well as to more traditional liberal exiles. Betancourt then took a turn to the left by working with the Communist Party of Costa Rica between 1932 and 1936. However, by the time he returned to Venezuela in 1936 he had become convinced either that communism was inappropriate for Venezuela or that it would invite reprisals from the oil companies and the U.S. government. He subsequently expressed an unremitting hostility towards Communism.[2]

Opponents of the Gómez–López system briefly united in 1936, but an enduring alliance proved elusive. In May 1936 Conservative Catholic

[2] Betancourt's activities with the Costa Rican Communist Party have been controversial. For two recent studies on this stage in his life, see Alejandro Gómez, *Rómulo Betancourt y el Partido Comunista de Costa Rica: 1931–1935* (Caracas, 1985), and Arturo Sosa A. and Eloi Lengrand, *Del garibaldismo estudiantil a la izquierda criolla* (Caracas, 1981).

students led by Rafael Caldera split with the Federación de Estudiantes de Venezuela (FEV) headed by Jóvito Villaba because of its attacks on the Church. Caldera formed a rival Unión Nacional Estudiantil (UNE), around which gravitated a number of loosely organized political groups. The Catholic Church had never been strong in Venezuela, and President Antonio Guzmán Blanco had dealt it a number of harsh blows in the late nineteenth century. Nevertheless, Catholic schools had played a strong role in the education of Venezuela's elite, with whom church spokesmen were usually in agreement with regard to the dangers of international Communism in general and the young Venezuelan hot-heads who criticized the Church or threatened its educational mission in particular.

The Communist and non-Communist Left continued to collaborate and in October 1936 formed the Partido Democrático Nacional (PDN). Betancourt's allies were suspicious of the Communists but still co-operated with them, openly until López outlawed leftist associations in 1937 and clandestinely for some time thereafter. Foreign affairs also divided the various groups, Betancourt and the Communists supporting the Spanish Republic and Caldera's colleagues endorsing General Francisco Franco. Out of these political associations of the 1930s were to emerge Venezuela's major modern political parties: Betancourt's AD, Gustavo and Eduardo Machado's Partido Comunista de Venezuela (PCV), Caldera's Comité de Organización Política Electoral Independiente (COPEI) and Villaba's Unión Republicana Democrática (URD). Active clandestine organization, especially that of Betancourt's AD, enabled the movements to survive and even grow, until Medina lifted the prohibition on political activity.

In September 1941 AD – tracing its origins through the student movement of 1928, the Plan of Barranquilla, the FEV and the PDN – was founded as a legal political party. Its leaders proved skilful in organizing rural *campesinos* and industrial workers, and they also appealed to the growing professional middle class. When President Medina dissolved the Communist-influenced National Labour Congress in 1944, AD by default came to dominate organized labour. It alone of the parties existing in 1945 had both refused to collaborate with Medina and insisted on liberal political reforms such as the direct election of his successor. Yet even in 1945 AD was undoubtedly a brash and inexperienced minority party. Most Venezuelans supported Medina and his tolerant regime. The most restive and dangerous groups appeared to be the old *gomecistas* and the *lopecistas,* who railed at the unprecedented leftist activity and were far from despairing of a return to power.

Venezuelans continue to debate whether the armed movement which removed President Medina Angarita from office on 18 October 1945 was necessary or deserves the name of 'revolution'. Medina had discussed his chosen successor, Diógenes Escalante, Venezuela's ambassador in Washington, with AD leaders, who believed that he would deepen Medina's reforms and allow direct presidential elections to take place at the conclusion of his term. They therefore endorsed Medina's decision. Unfortunately, Escalante became seriously ill before Congress could elect him, and AD did not trust the man whom Medina had designated to replace Escalante. A succession crisis loomed with the rumour that former President López Contreras planned to lead a military coup and return to power.

The power brokers in 1945 proved to be the young officers of the Unión Patriótica Militar. Impatient with Medina and with the possibility that López Contreras would return to power, they also resented the old *gomecista* generals who blocked their personal ambitions and their ambitions for the nation. Many of the young officers agreed with the civilian reformers that the military and the political spheres of government should be strictly separate. They looked for a civilian group which could join them in their conspiracy, give them more legitimacy than would a barracks rebellion and share power. Since the only party independent of Medina, López and the Communists was AD, Marcos Pérez Jiménez, Carlos Delgado Chalbaud, Luis Felipe Llovera Páez and their companions arranged a meeting to propose such an alliance to the AD leaders. While the Escalante compromise was still a possibility, Betancourt's group rejected these overtures. Subsequently, however, and in spite of Betancourt's suspicions of Pérez Jiménez, AD cast its lot with these officers. This decision was to have a major impact on Venezuelan politics for the next forty years. Participation in the *golpe* provided the party with a 'revolutionary' tradition, not unlike the claim of the Mexican Partido Revolucionario Institucional (PRI) claim to be the party of the revolution. Unlike the Mexican revolutionaries, however, AD brought down the most liberal government that Venezuela had yet seen and did so as the junior partner in a military conspiracy.

The *golpe* itself was something less than dramatic. On 17 October Medina's government discovered the conspiracy and arrested Pérez Jiménez. The arrest triggered the revolt, and Medina put up no resistance. Somewhat to their surprise, the conspirators found themselves ensconced in the presidential office in Miraflores Palace on 18 October trying to form a government. Rómulo Betancourt became provisional president, and AD and other civilians filled all of the cabinet posts except two – Major Carlos Delgado Chalbaud became minister of defence and Captain Mario Vargas took over the Ministry of Communications.

For three years – known as the *trienio* in Venezuelan political history – the armed forces honoured their agreement to let civilians rule. Betancourt served as provisional president until he was replaced in 1948 by Rómulo Gallegos, elected in December 1947. AD captured more than 70 per cent of the vote in the four elections held between October 1946 and May 1948 (Constituent Assembly, Congress, president, municipal councils). The other two major non-Communist parties did not register formally until 1946. Rafael Caldera led the Christian Democratic Party, baptized the Comité de Organización Política Electoral Independiente, and a student leader from 1936, Jóvito Villaba, directed the URD. Hence, AD – and Rómulo Betancourt – claimed most of the credit and received most of the blame for measures taken during the *trienio*.

AD quickly set out to organize its allies and constituents and to implement the political programme developed since 1928. Drawing on the examples of the Peruvian APRA the Mexican PRI, Leninism and their own clandestine experience in the 1930s, the AD leaders believed that the key to success was a disciplined political party. They were determined not to leave a single district or municipality without its AD headquarters. From a membership of about eighty thousand in 1941, the party's rolls grew to nearly half a million by 1948. It became Venezuela's first truly national party; its success virtually eliminated regional parties and precluded, to some extent, the effective political expression of regional interests.

AD also strove to influence and lead the major labour and professional associations. *Adeco* Ramón Quijada founded and led the Federacíon Campesina Venezolana and AD sympathizers dominated the national Confederación de Trabajadores de Venezuela (CTV), which was established in 1947 to bring both urban and rural unions under AD control. Expansion of government and services, especially education, provided jobs and patronage to attract the emerging middle sectors. AD gave women the vote in national elections for the first time and in return received the support of many women.

The new Venezuelan constitution of 1947, although it was soon overthrown, established the framework of a political philosophy which would be revived in the 1961 constitution. (The intervening 1953 constitution echoed the 1945 revision of the 1936 charter.) It guaranteed political freedom, labour and civil rights and committed the government to undertaking measures to promote economic development and social welfare. An element of federalism remained, since residual powers were left to the states, but the central government's new powers generally reduced the states to administrative divisions with little autonomy. The preamble to the charter asserted that Venezuela would be ruled by a democratic system. For the first time voters could choose the president and the members of the two houses of Congress by universal, direct suffrage. Citizens also had the right to education, social security and health. The state imposed limits on individual economic liberty: the government could 'dictate economic measures to plan, rationalize and develop production, and regulate circulation and consumption of wealth, in order to achieve the development of the national economy'.[3] During the *trienio,* however, private capital, domestic and foreign, was invited to help develop the national economy. Only in infrastructure and services (roads, electricity in some regions) or in key sectors such as petroleum refining or when private capital did not respond sufficiently did the state play a direct role in economic development.

Although its rhetoric was nationalist, the *trienio* government did not adopt an aggressive stance towards the oil companies. National control of the petroleum industry was a long-term goal, but AD leaders recognized that Venezuela depended too heavily on petroleum to risk taking over the industry in the 1940s. All other development plans required uninterrupted and increasing petroleum revenues. The AD government announced that the nation would sell no more foreign concessions, but made it clear that existing concessions would be fairly treated. In effect, it updated but did not deviate from the low-risk strategy initiated by Juan Vicente Gómez. The 1943 oil legislation remained in place, but the minister of development, Juan Pablo Pérez Alfonzo, secured an increase in the nation's share of the profits to 50 per cent. Refining more petroleum in Venezuela became a key AD goal. The oil companies had built massive refineries in the Netherlands Antilles off the coast of Venezuela, and in 1945 the three small Venezuelan refineries processed only about 10 per cent of the nation's crude oil. By 1947 expanded capacity meant that the

[3] Allan R. Brewer-Carías, *Las constituciones de Venezuela* (Madrid, 1985), p. 97.

nation would soon be able to double domestic refining and boost both jobs and industrial production.

The Corporación Venezolana de Fomento (CVF) was set up to provide credit and technical assistance for industrial development, especially in targeted areas of basic services and consumer products. AD leaders invited the oil companies to help '*sembrar el petróleo*' in Venezuelan industrial development. Through Betancourt's intercession with Nelson Rockefeller of Standard Oil (Creole of Venezuela), the oil company and the government jointly established the Venezuelan Basic Economy Corporation (VBEC), which supplemented CVF investment, notably in hotels and other tourist services, commerce and rural nutrition projects. The U.S. companies made much of their role in keeping more of the petroleum wealth in the country, but many of the investments in consumer goods and services favoured the foreigners. For example, the Rockefeller chain of supermarkets (CADA) created a new mass market for U.S. processed food products. The planned iron and steel complex in Guayana became the jewel in the crown of the industrialization policy. Subsidiaries of U.S. Steel and Bethlehem Steel, the Venezuelan state and private Venezuelan investors would all participate. Yet since this was a long-term project, the *trienio* itself saw little progress in Guayana. Furthermore, Venezuelan investors were wary of the risk. State and foreign capital played the leading role in this field.

AD did not consider itself a labour party and sought to impede an autonomous labour movement that might challenge the government. The three years of the *trienio* did redistribute national income to the working classes, but the levelling off of benefits in 1948 suggests a weakening of the popular sectors in the multi-class alliance. Labor Minister Raúl Leoni endorsed workers' demands to certain limits only. In February 1948 he forced the petroleum workers to accept a three-year collective contract which provided generous wages and benefits. When real wages dropped by 6 per cent in the first six months of 1948, the commitment of the workers to the contract significantly qualified the gains they had secured in 1946 and 1947. In 1948, President Gallegos ordered striking maritime workers on oil tankers back to work because their strike adversely affected the national economy.

Foreign policy was secondary to domestic concerns, but more aggressive than hitherto and more ideological. Encouraged by the emergence of new democratic governments at the conclusion of the Second World War, Betancourt actively condemned dictators and governments that withheld genuine popular elections. Venezuela broke relations with Franco's Spain and withdrew ambassadors from the dictatorial governments of Anastasio Somoza of Nicaragua and Rafael Trujillo of the Dominican Republic. Relations with the United States were generally good – President Gallegos and his wife visited the United States in July 1948 – but Betancourt still denounced U.S. domination of Puerto Rico as a remnant of colonialism.

All of the AD initiatives aroused some concern among Venezuelan traditionalists and other aspirants to political power. Betancourt and his followers were pictured as lower-class upstarts whose initial actions might be moderate but who could not be trusted in the long run. AD's aggressive partisanship was distrusted, and some suspected that Betancourt intended AD to monopolize political activity as the PRI had in Mexico. *Gomecista* visceral anti-Communism was only a few years in the past, and some Venezuelans persisted in identifying AD programmes with Communism. Critics focussed on three major issues. First, a moderate agrarian reform bill faced angry opposition – more for the *campesino* clientele that it created for AD than for its threat to an agrarian structure which had already been shown to be underproductive. Some predicted that the rise of a well-organized labour–peasant alliance would enable AD to implement an even more radical programme. Second, the 1946 decree which increased state regulation of public and private education aroused fierce opposition from the Church and Catholic educators. The Church was not a strong institution in its own right, but it reinforced and legitimized other conservative opponents of Betancourt's government. Student strikes, congressional opposition and Betancourt's penchant for compromise meant that some of the most objectionable clauses were eliminated from the 1948 education law, but the political damage had been done. Finally, the AD campaign against past administrative corruption caused bitter controversy. In 1946, the government established a Tribunal de Responsabilidad Administrativa, which confiscated the property of those who had held high positions in previous governments and could not satisfactorily explain the sources of their wealth. Many Venezuelans interpreted the trials as vengeful attacks on honourable men such as Arturo Uslar Pietri and Eleazar López Contreras. Betancourt heeded the many protests and allowed some of the property to be returned, but AD passed a law against illicit enrichment to govern the prosecution of corrupt bureaucrats in the future.

By 1948, in an environment of novel press freedom and unhampered political discussion and activity, AD faced constant attacks from all sides. The young officers who had invited AD to power in 1945 deplored the

constant divisions and criticism of the *trienio*. Some – most conspicuously
Marcos Pérez Jiménez – feared that Betancourt intended to strengthen the
party at the expense of the armed forces. Although some officers distrusted
Betancourt more than they did Gallegos, the new president proved less
willing to placate them than Betancourt might have been. Military conspirators presented a list of demands to Gallegos in November 1948, but
he refused to consider them. Warned of a conspiracy, Gallegos failed to
check it by arresting the leaders, who included Minister of Defence Carlos
Delgado Chalbaud. Although Betancourt called on the petroleum workers
to strike in support of the government, his action was too late. On 24
November, Pérez Jiménez, Delgado Chalbaud and their colleagues arrested the president and the other cabinet ministers. Delgado Chalbaud
became president of a military junta which also included Pérez Jiménez
and Luis Felipe Llovera Páez. The three-year experiment with democratic
reform was brought to a sudden halt.

DICTATORSHIP, 1948–58

Many Venezuelans, weary of the agitation and uncertainty of the *trienio,*
welcomed the military *golpe* of 24 November 1948. COPEI and URD
expected that, with the outlawing of AD, they could capture the political
initiative. The Church hoped to secure an independent role in education
and strengthen its role as the moral arbiter of society. Landowners expected to repossess the land which had been confiscated for agrarian reform
or as punishment for corruption. Oil companies looked forward to the
acquisition of new oil concessions and to the relaxation of the stringent tax
laws. Some capitalists wanted the government to subsidize economic
growth without any concessions to labour. The armed forces naturally
expected that they would receive more modern equipment and an important role in national development.

All the political groups wanted to maximize national oil revenues and
to promote rapid economic growth. Since the discovery of petroleum,
most political competition in Venezuela revolved around one question:
who should decide how the oil wealth would be distributed within the
country? Beyond this, there were four unresolved issues critical to the way
in which Venezuela entered the world capitalist system: What economic
model would achieve maximum economic development? What participation should foreign investors have? Which sectors of the Venezuelan population should receive the principal benefits? How strongly should the

government dictate the answers to the other questions? The AD–military coalition had proposed a compromise which would appeal to all. It had chosen capitalist development with foreign investment and had insisted that all social sectors receive some benefits, which, in effect, meant a modest gain for the working class. The state invested directly in human capital but only indirectly in the economy. Delgado Chalbaud, Pérez Jiménez and their allies changed some parts of the formula and made sharper choices than the coalition government had. They channelled benefits principally to the bourgeoisie – domestic and foreign – whilst holding those of labour constant. Moreover, they determined that the state invest directly in some economic activities and only indirectly, if at all, in human capital.

Delgado Chalbaud, as president of the junta, did not immediately set off in this new direction. He seemed satisfied to outlaw some labour unions, AD and the Communist Party, and thus re-establish the superficial calm of the pre-1945 *gomecista* system. And he expressed a willingness to hold elections and return to civilian government as soon as order was restored. He was generally seen as an intelligent and moderate military man with a broad education from his years in France. AD partisans, of course, considered him an opportunist and a traitor, and some of his military colleagues thought him too soft. In November 1950 he was killed in a botched kidnapping attempt. His kidnapper, Rafael Simón Urbina, was killed by his captors, and subsequent investigation never revealed the instigators of the act. Public opinion pointed to Marcos Pérez Jiménez as the most obvious beneficiary. After a decent interval in which a civilian was the titular head of the junta, Pérez became president following a rigged election in 1952, which was probably won by the URD leader and candidate Jóvito Villaba. AD and the Communist Party remained outlawed. With their political hopes dashed, some URD and COPEI political leaders went into exile, although the two parties remained legal if quiescent for the rest of the dictatorship.

Pérez Jiménez's minister of the interior was Laureano Vallenilla Lanz, son of Gomez's apologist and author of *Cesarismo democrático*. He maintained strict press censorship and threatened political opponents with the police, the Seguridad Nacional, headed by Pedro Estrada. The government outlawed or harassed labour and peasant unions. Italian, Spanish and Portuguese immigrant workers willingly replaced any recalcitrant Venezuelan workers. Yet even these measures did not give the government the confidence to hold competitive elections. When Pérez's 'constitutional' term required renewal in 1957, Vallenilla Lanz organized a simple plebiscite in which voters – including foreigners with more than two years of residence in the country – could indicate whether they wished Pérez Jiménez to continue in office. After nearly a decade, Venezuelans were finding the prospect of continuing authoritarian rule less attractive than they had in 1948, but Pérez won the plebiscite.

The foreign vote in the 1957 plebiscite reflected a number of changes about which Venezuelans were ambivalent. Although Venezuela had long tried to attract European immigrants, it was only with the discovery of oil, some limited economic and political modernization and the condition of Europe after the end of the Second World War that the country acquired an appeal to foreigners. After 1945 a flood of Italians, Spaniards and Portuguese (in addition to neighbouring Colombians) entered Venezuela, the percentage of foreigners rising from 1.3 per cent of the population in 1941 to 7 per cent in 1961. Most, as might have been expected, settled in cities, principally Caracas, and took jobs in construction, commerce and services. Some of the more fortunate brought capital with them, or quickly earned it, and purchased their own businesses. Under Pérez Jiménez's dictatorship, a few foreign building contractors became fabulously wealthy. U.S. citizens, while never significant in number, became more visible as they moved from the enclave oil camps into the cities to take advantage of new opportunities for their capital and services. U.S. engineers, accountants, business managers, salesmen and investors probably had more impact on Venezuelan culture than did the Europeans. 'Americanization' deepened as middle-class Venezuelans paid for 'tickets' to *beisbol* games, drank *güiski,* ate *hamburguesas,* read *Selecciones (Readers' Digest)* and *Life,* watched U.S.-made films and took English lessons at the Centro Venezolano-Americano.

Merchants generally welcomed the role the foreigners played in increasing the sales of consumer products. Foreign-owned *abastos* (small grocery stores) and supermarkets catered to the immigrants and middle-class Venezuelans who believed that foreign products were better and cheaper than their own. Industrialists found less to rejoice in as Venezuelan tastes shifted. The *criollo* capitalist Alejandro Hernández complained that the stores refused to stock his canned tomatoes and other products, but the Pérez Jiménez government offered no relief. Although Venezuelan society had rarely exhibited xenophobia, there was a growing sense that the dictator unduly favoured foreigners.

Many businessmen had initially been pleased with the general outlines of the 'New National Ideal', as Pérez termed his development programme. Road construction and port modernization, the dragging of the bar at the entrance to Lake Maracaibo, urban public works and the iron and steel complex in Guayana all improved the national infrastructure and spurred the economy. Industrialization increased dramatically, although commerce, construction and banking continued to dominate. Dissatisfaction grew as the New National Ideal took shape. Foreign investors participated freely in the boom, sometimes edging out Venezuelan capitalists in profitable areas like urban construction. The government retained ownership of major industrial complexes such as steel and petrochemicals – a sore point with those who thought that the state should not compete with the private sector.

Under this relatively open system the industrial boom soon stalled, especially when oil revenues began to decline. Tariffs remained low, profits could easily be repatriated and foreign imports increased. Venezuelan industrialists demanded the revision of the 1939 commercial treaty with the United States in order to protect national production. A new treaty in 1952 continued to allow a virtually open market and highlighted the enduring weakness of the industrial bourgeoisie. The bloated public works budgets barely compensated for this: sixteen firms received the bulk of the contracts between 1948 and 1958, and of those only four lacked close contacts with government insiders. President Pérez Jiménez was a silent partner in several contracting firms and built up his huge personal fortune through commissions and kick-backs. Even those entrepreneurs who were fortunate or well connected enough to secure government contracts disliked being pressured to have projects ready to inaugurate on 2 December, the anniversary of Pérez's election. By 1957, when oil revenues fell, Pérez's government had become so slow in paying the contractors that they suffered serious liquidity problems. Evidence of administrative corruption and mismanagement convinced some entrepreneurs that they would not receive payment at all.

Neither influence peddling nor corruption was new to Venezuela. Moreover, it might be argued that Gómez's 'sharing the wealth' with some of the elite facilitated both political stability and the concentration of investment capital. In fact, capital did move from agriculture to commerce, urban development and construction industries. With an entrepreneurial mentality and government help, the beneficiaries of the favouritism of the 1940s and 1950s might have reinvested their capital in the next step of economic development: industrial expansion. Yet most cautiously kept their capital in the same lucrative, and generally non-productive, sectors of the economy and squandered the excess on imported luxuries and conspicuous consumption. More far-seeing capitalists did reinvest in industry, but they still required government credit and protection to succeed.

Nationalists also attacked Pérez Jiménez for squandering national capital by selling new petroleum concessions to foreign companies in 1955–6. Favouritism towards the foreign firms did not even earn any special consideration in the U.S. market. After the Suez crisis, oil prices declined and independent oil producers in the United States pressed for quotas or restrictions on the importation of foreign oil. Quotas were not imposed during Pérez's government, but the U.S. government entreated companies to limit imports voluntarily. The New National Ideal boom had depended heavily on the sale of new concessions and on petroleum revenues. Stagnation and recession loomed ahead if measures were not taken to diversify the economy.

Workers did reap some benefit at the outset from the creation of new jobs, especially in construction. Yet they too disliked the 2 December construction deadlines since unemployment rose following the completion of public works. They resented the foreign immigrants who took many of the Caracas construction jobs. By 1953, most legal labour union activity had been outlawed, the government closing the unions' headquarters and impounding their funds and property. Pérez Jiménez's feeble efforts to build a government-controlled labour confederation failed, and monumental projects such as the workers' resort of Los Caracas along the Caribbean coast could not mask declining real wages. Resentment accumulated among workers who could recall both the clandestine organization before 1945 and the influence they had enjoyed during the *trienio*.

The Church also began to turn against the dictatorship, not least because of Pope Pius XII's greater concern for social justice and a tempering of the anti-Communist crusade. Catholic education did experience some gains under the dictatorship, especially since many public schools and universities were closed sporadically in response to student protests. The Church and private contributors established a prestigious new private university in Caracas, the Universidad Católica Andrés Bello, run by Jesuits. In 1957, however, overzealousness by Vallenilla Lanz's censorship squad provoked conflict with the Church. Monseñor Rafael Arias published a pastoral letter in May 1957 which indirectly criticized the Pérez Jiménez regime for its lack of social responsibility and pointed to the declining standard of living of the working class. The newspaper *La*

Religión carried a number of editorials attacking the materialism and callousness of the government. Vallenilla either tried to censor the articles or responded fiercely to them in his pseudonymous column in *El Heraldo*. Priests became involved in the clandestine movement against Pérez Jiménez, and several were arrested.

In foreign policy Pérez Jiménez's government was especially close to other military governments of the hemisphere such as those of Juan Perón of Argentina and Manuel Odría of Peru. It restored diplomatic relations with Franco's Spain and eased the tensions that had arisen during the *trienio* between Venezuela and Somoza's Nicaragua and Trujillo's Dominican Republic. Pérez took special pride in hosting the 1954 Inter-American Conference and in co-operating with the efforts of the United States to isolate and overthrow the reformist government of Jacobo Arbenz in Guatemala. Closer contacts with U.S. military missions and the Inter-American Defense Board further expressed his geo-political perception of inevitable alliance with the United States in the struggle against Communism. Pérez Jiménez's relations with the democratic governments of Latin America were less warm. In 1957 Chile broke relations because of Seguridad Nacional's mistreatment of a Chilean citizen, and Argentina severed relations with the nation which granted honour and asylum to Perón after he was overthrown in 1955.

By 1957 even the armed forces had become dissatisfied with Pérez Jiménez's rule, in spite of high military budgets and the construction of an impressive officers' club. Some factions in the armed forces had a firm democratic vocation; others criticized the lack of nationalism in Pérez Jiménez's economic policies. A significant sector of the officer corps feared that the growing clandestine civilian opposition movement – co-ordinated from June 1957 by a *junta patriótica* – could not forever be checked by the arbitrary actions of the Seguridad Nacional, the influence of which also posed an implicit challenge to the armed forces. Even some of Pérez's defenders had resented his growing isolation from the military, his increasing reliance on civilians like Vallenilla Lanz and the open corruption of the regime. Only a small clique of Pérez's favourites shared in the kick-backs and commissions on defence contracts. An abortive military revolt on 1 January 1958 alerted civilians to military discontent. A united military–civilian movement, abetted by uprisings in the Caracas *barrios,* finally caused Pérez and his coterie to flee on 23 January. Admiral Wolfgang Larrazábal assumed leadership of a junta which promised elections, eventually scheduled for 5 December.

Those who tried to ensure that Pérez Jiménez's departure would be only a cosmetic change were the first to suffer in the subsequent struggle for dominance. Moderates and radicals, with the additional pressure of street demonstrations, forced the two officers most closely identified with Pérez Jiménez off the governing junta a few days after Pérez left. In May, they also forced the industrialist Eugenio Mendoza and engineer Blas Lamberti to leave – although not before the so-called Oligarch's Cabinet had seen to the paying of the U.S. $1.4 billion short-term unfunded debt which had so worried businessmen in 1957. The conservatives had been so badly damaged by association with Pérez Jiménez that they could mount no viable effort to retain power alone, either by force or by election.

The Communists initially fared little better despite their heroic participation in the clandestine struggle against the dictatorship, their growing number and their popularity in the *barrios*. Subsequently, many of them thought that they had missed their golden opportunity to come to power at the head of a popular uprising in January 1958.[4] It is unlikely, however, that the armed forces would have permitted an overtly Communist revolution to triumph. The party also lacked electoral strength; it had no candidate with the stature and experience of Betancourt. Seeking legality and national unity, the Communists chose pragmatically to sail in the wake of Admiral Wolfgang Larrazábal, who, in spite of his association with the Pérez Jiménez regime, earned great popularity during his year in office.

Larrazábal bolstered his appeal to the masses with the Emergency Plan, which created jobs and subsidies for workers and suspended rent payments in government housing. Thousands flocked from the countryside to the city to share in this largesse, accentuating urban problems but also providing political support for Larrazábal. The admiral did not waver in his support for open and free elections. He began the process of purging the armed forces of disloyal and undemocratic elements. He also urged the Comisión Investigadora contra el Enriquecimiento Ilícito (CIEI) to initiate investigations and punishment of the *perezjimenistas* who had engaged in administrative corruption. Recognizing the need for administrative reform, he set in motion the Comisión de Administración Pública (CAP) and established the Oficina de Coordinación y Planificación (Cordiplan) to draw up national economic and social plans. Finally, he decreed that the

---

[4] See the series of books edited by Agustín Blanco Muñoz, *Testimonios violentos*, 8 vols. (Caracas, 1980–3).

major oil companies pay higher taxes, the state now receiving nearly 65 per cent of petroleum profits. Larrazábal had little interest in political manoeuvring and, in the event, no political staying power. But he successfully managed a delicate political transition.

AD, COPEI and URD possessed the most experienced leaders and had a head start in the organization of labour and the popular sectors. Having paid the price of their weakness in 1948, they were determined to construct an open, democratic system. The euphoria over having finally defeated the dictatorship fostered a desire to continue the unity of the clandestine movement and obscured some of the differences among the groups.

AD, in particular, was well positioned to dominate the complex political situation. Young *adecos* had worked closely with the Communist leadership in the struggle against Pérez Jiménez while the older AD leaders like Rómulo Betancourt remained abroad in exile. The strategy of Betancourt during 1958 was largely responsible for the unique quality of Venezuelan democracy over the next thirty years. From late 1957 Betancourt held a series of meetings in New York with Jóvito Villaba, Rafael Caldera, business and labour leaders to secure a political truce and field a unity candidate for the first presidential election following the fall of the dictatorship. When the three parties – AD, COPEI and URD – could not agree on a common candidate by October 1958, Betancourt, Caldera and Villaba met at Caldera's home to sign a gentlemen's agreement that they would keep their political competition within the rules of democratic competition. This Pact of Punto Fijo explicitly excluded the Communists and sent a conciliatory signal to businessmen and the United States. On the eve of the election in December 1958, the leaders of the three major parties met again to sign a public confirmation of the pact and to sanction a minimum common political programme. Villaba remained in the pact, although his URD joined the Communists in supporting the Larrazábal candidacy. Betancourt secured victory with 49 per cent of the vote; Larrazábal came second with 35 per cent; Caldera received only 16 per cent.

The election of December 1958 – held under the *perezjimenista* 1953 constitution to avoid another provisional government while a new constitution was written – confirmed both the skills of Rómulo Betancourt and the terms of the Pact of Punto Fijo. However, AD strategists were worried by the fact that their party only came fourth in Caracas; a party with its origins in the rural Venezuela of the 1930s would have to change to accommodate the more modern, urban nation which was increasingly taking shape.

ACCIÓN DEMOCRÁTICA IN POWER, 1959—69

Since the early 1930s when the Gómez regime was crumbling, greatly increased petroleum income, the beginnings of modern transportation and communication systems, industrialization, urbanization, improved literacy and public health and significant foreign immigration in the post-war era had all made their mark on the socio-economic fabric and political culture of Venezuela. Even so, figures for distribution of income indicated the endurance of a traditional social structure: at the outset of the 1960s, half of the population received only 14.3 per cent of the total national income. Governments faced the challenge of providing not only economic growth and political stability but also social justice. Like the *trienio* government, the post-1958 democratic governments tried to juggle the three goals without favouring one unduly, although the voice of the business community, stronger now than it had been thirteen years earlier, almost imperceptibly but inevitably favoured the political and economic objectives.

Rómulo Betancourt and AD, with the co-operation of COPEI and, to a lesser extent, URD, built the foundation for democratic government between 1959 and 1963. In exile during the decade of military rule, Betancourt continued to study, plan and cement ties with other democrats in the Caribbean and in the United States. He synthesized his views on the relationship between dictatorship, petroleum and the social development of the nation in *Venezuela: Política y petróleo,* published in 1956. Elected president at the age of fifty-one, he continued to believe that democratic stability and the ability to implement social and economic reform depended on a highly disciplined, multi-class political party. In a nation where organized labour was relatively weak and where an oligopolistic elite was closely allied with foreign capital, a populist strategy remained the strongest reform option. However, the lesson of the 1948 *golpe* had been that populist reform could not be implemented if the armed forces and the bourgeoisie opposed it.

From the experience of 1945–8 Betancourt had learned two further lessons which guided his strategy in the 1960s. First, the *trienio* government had been weakened by its uncompromising partisanship, which had unleashed fierce attacks on AD by the other political parties. Hence, in 1958 Betancourt rejected all ideas of AD's ruling alone. As agreed under the Pact of Punto Fijo, partisan attacks would be kept within bounds in exchange for a guarantee that the major parties would share influence and patronage. The second principle was more controversial. Betancourt believed that the Gallegos government had fallen in 1948 because the president had not been tough enough to jail or exile conspirators. Betancourt did not intend to repeat that mistake, and he asserted that a democratic government sometimes had to use non-democratic means to survive. He suspended constitutional guarantees, outlawed suspect political parties and authorized the police and the armed forces to take harsh measures if necessary to wipe out the guerrilla threat which emerged in the aftermath of the Cuban Revolution. (Fidel Castro came to power less than a month after the Venezuelan elections.)

Betancourt's system drew both labour and peasant leaders and businessmen into his informal system of agreement, patronage – and coercion. He isolated and attacked those whom he did not trust – the PCV, the younger members of AD who called for more rapid social change after the Cuban model, the implacable 'anti-national' businessmen who refused to cooperate, the *golpistas* in the armed forces who formed conspiracies against him. Although he had been more willing to bargain and negotiate during the *trienio* than his opponents recognized, he now brought political accommodation to a high art. In particular, Betancourt nurtured his alliance with Rafael Caldera of COPEI. (Ironically, the coalition allowed Caldera to develop COPEI and his own presidential ambitions at the expense of the political aspirations of some of Betancourt's AD colleagues – Domingo Alberto Rangel, Raúl Ramos Giménez and later Luis Beltrán Prieto Figueroa.) Betancourt's use of patronage, personalism and co-operation with non-Communist parties adroitly exploited national conditions and succeeded in providing stability. Yet such stability rested on the expectation that oil revenues would continue to grow and that the government could provide some benefits for all economic groups. Any failure to secure a steady increase in government income would seriously strain the populist strategy.

Betancourt used both the carrot and the stick to outmanoeuvre the recalcitrant. The new national police force – Dirección General de Policía (Digepol) – replaced the hated Seguridad Nacional, but on occasion used methods just as arbitrary as those of its predecessor. The government wooed peasants with an agrarian reform bill which redistributed land taken from the *perezjimenistas* to the landless. Nonetheless, Betancourt ordered the Guardia Nacional to eject peasants from rural lands which they had seized without the blessing of the agrarian reform bureaucracy. Military and civilian conspirators were dealt with harshly. In April 1960 Jesús María Castro León led a conservative revolt which was quickly put down, as was another reactionary military uprising in February 1961. In 1960 Dominican dictator Rafael Trujillo backed an effort to assassinate Betancourt, in which the president was badly burned and an aide killed. Betancourt successfully pressed the Organization of American States (OAS) to impose sanctions on Trujillo. Then emerged a new threat in the guerrilla campaign of the Marxist–Cuban-inspired Fuerzas Armadas de Liberación Nacional (FALN). In May 1962 leftists and the Marine Infantry Battalion of Carúpano staged a revolt that the government suppressed with high casualties; constitutional guarantees were suspended and the Movimiento de Izquierda Revolucionaria (MIR) and the PCV were outlawed. A second leftist military revolt took place in Puerto Cabello in June 1962. As international tensions heightened with the Cuban missile crisis in October 1962, Betancourt reiterated his 'shoot first and ask questions later' policy towards presumed subversives. Similarities in the approaches of Trujillo and Castro, the Cold War and the efforts to overthrow the AD government confirmed Betancourt's belief that only democratic governments could be trusted. The combination of circumstances also drew him closer both to the United States and to his own armed forces as indispensable allies.

The Venezuelan armed forces adhered to their professional and non-political role after 1958. They gained both status and experience in the campaign against the guerrillas in the 1960s. Military men on active duty could not vote in national elections, and promotions generally reflected ability rather than political affiliations. Nonetheless, Betancourt and his successors paid careful attention to military opinions. Armed forces officers, both active and retired, intervened most forcefully into the political debate, especially when border problems arose.

Betancourt and his democratic allies waged a less violent, but equally important battle to bind labour and peasant groups to the government and to control the urban poor in the *barrios*. Government patronage – union subsidies, agrarian credit, jobs and services such as piped water and electricity – became preferred weapons. Groups and leaders who refused to accept political discipline found themselves cut off from government support and sometimes had their strikes or their unions declared illegal. Co-operative unions, by contrast, enjoyed all the largesse of government, which, with minor participation by COPEI, dominated the newly reorganized CTV and the Federación Campesina Venezolana. The PCV–URD–MIR leaders were forced out of the CTV in November 1961, the Left then forming a rival Central Unica de Trabajadores de Venezuela (CUTV). An 'unofficial' federation, the CUTV suffered from the same governmental reprisals as did the leftist political leaders. When AD peasant leader Ramón Quijada, impatient with the slow pace of the agrarian reform, moved further to the left, he and his allies were purged from the government-sponsored federation.

The PCV and the MIR enjoyed an initial advantage with the urban poor, with whom they had worked before Pérez Jiménez's fall, and AD's hold on the *barrios* slackened even more when Betancourt cancelled the Emergency Plan in August 1959. When the young *miristas* left AD, the party lost the militants who had the closest contact with the *barrios*. From 1959 to 1962, AD and COPEI simultaneously established a strong police presence in the *barrios* and channelled all patronage or services through AD and COPEI loyalists. The Marxists unwittingly aided the government's strategy when they turned to terrorism. Many of the urban poor lost friends and neighbours to terrorist attacks on policemen and soldiers.

Business associations remained virtually the only significant independent pressure group. Fedecámaras, founded in 1944, included commercial, industrial and agricultural affiliates. In order to limit schisms within the group, Fedecamaras sought to defend the role of the private sector in general rather than measures of specific interest to one sector. The federation resisted having its internal elections politicized along party lines the way the labour and peasant groups had. Betancourt's ally, Alejandro Hernández, president of Fedecámaras from 1958 to 1960, tried to steer the group towards a closer alliance with the government, but he ultimately lost out to those who favoured maintaining an independent role. Hernández and his followers withdrew and joined Pro-Venezuela, which had been founded in 1958 by industrialists who wanted to promote import-substitution policies. This division reflected not only political differences but also the struggle between the industrial and commercial sectors of the business elite. AD recognized in Pro-Venezuela the more nationalistic group and criticized Fedecámaras for its alliance with multinational companies.

The substance of AD policies derived from the original party programme of the 1940s and from recognition of the changed circumstances since then. Betancourt's platform included three principal aims: political freedom and the development of liberal institutions; improvement of health, education and welfare; and diversified economic growth to be achieved through encouragement of import substitution industrialization. However, the economic situation at the end of the 1950s did not augur well for such an ambitious programme. The dictatorship had left a large budget deficit, and capital flight became acute in the uncertain political situation. During Betancourt's term in office, the official unemployment rate averaged 12 per cent. The worst years were 1959–61, and Betancourt's team contracted foreign loans, reduced government appropriations, twice cut government salaries by 10 per cent and imposed exchange controls. AD proposed a devaluation of the bolívar, but the measure was so unpopular with the other political parties – and with importers – that it was not implemented. After 1961, the government financed a number of expansionist construction projects, which provided jobs and boosted the economy, but did nothing significant to alter the economic structure.

Minister of Mines Juan Pablo Pérez Alfonzo held a prominent position in Betancourt's cabinet. He laid the bases for Venezuela's ultimate control of the national petroleum industry, and he implemented an aggressive international petroleum policy. The United States had imposed mandatory import restrictions on foreign oil in the spring of 1959. Pérez Alfonzo protested and pressed for a preference system for Western Hemisphere producers, but to no avail. He had more success in persuading other petroleum-exporting countries of the merits of an international producers' association. In 1959 Pérez Alfonzo attended the First Arab Petroleum Congress in Cairo to outline his ideas for such an organization, but it was only after the sharp drop in oil prices in August 1960 that the Arab nations paid attention to the proposal. In September 1960 Iran, Iraq, Kuwait, Saudi Arabia and Venezuela formed the Organization of Petroleum Exporting Countries (OPEC), which grew to twelve voting members by 1973. The alliance did not immediately live up to Pérez Alfonzo's hopes, since the goal of the Arab nations was to raise revenues, while Venezuela considered it more important to establish greater control over the industry.

Internally, Pérez Alfonzo enforced the December 1958 tax law, which had raised the nation's share of oil profits to approximately 65 per cent of the total. The Corporación Venezolana del Petróleo (CVP) was formed in 1960 and given authority to explore, exploit, refine, transport and market oil as well as to acquire shares in other companies, but the CVP was little more than a training ground for Venezuelans during the first decade of its existence.

Even with the slow start, the national petroleum policy achieved more success and was more coherent than general economic planning or industrial policy. The strength of the multinational oil companies and their Venezuelan allies, the tradition of strong currency and free profit remittances, and the 1952 trade treaty with the United States made it politically difficult to erect real tariff barriers to protect Venezuelan industries. Backing away from an aggressive industrial policy, the AD government did provide credit and encouragement for a number of government and mixed corporations. The CVF assumed primary responsibility for promoting industry. A separate Corporación Venezolana de Guayana (CVG) directed state and private funds into the major iron and steel complex in the area of Ciudad Guayana. Local private investors welcomed the Guayana project, from which they had been excluded by Pérez Jiménez, but in the 1960s few had the capital or inclination to assume more than a minor role in such a huge enterprise. A few entrepreneurs became wealthy, but the new capital-intensive industries provided few new jobs for the expanding Venezuelan labour force. Multinational firms which associated with local capital accounted for a number of the new industrial plants in Venezuela. Many, such as the automobile assembly plants, still remained highly dependent on imported component parts. Thus, Venezuela experienced only very modest industrial growth by the end of the 1960s.

In spite of the agrarian reform programme, agriculture was still unable to feed the population or to provide an adequate income for most rural families. More than 100,000 landless families received land from the government. The agrarian reform programme caused relatively little conflict, since nearly half of the distributed area (2.6 million hectares in 1959–65) was public land, and much of the private land came from exiled *perezjimenistas* or from uncontested purchases. Agricultural production, the total area given to farming and per capita income of people employed in agriculture all rose. Yet by 1965 the per capita annual income of people in agriculture was about one-quarter that of the national average. Administrative and legal problems limited the success of the agrarian reform. By 1966 few of the beneficiaries had received their land titles; land distribution favoured peasant groups near highways and services and overlooked people in more remote areas; and the credit granted by the BAP was poorly administered.

Betancourt's government committed significant resources to education, public health, public water supplies, electricity, rural roads, housing, child care and nutrition, and recreation. The statistical gap between the standard of living in the cities and the countryside remained significant, but narrowed somewhat. These social programmes had the additional benefit of providing jobs for the party faithful of AD and COPEI, and, as critics noted, the laudable goals and tangible advances of reform were qualified by inefficiency and politicization of public administration.

Few accused Betancourt himself of profiting from office, and he attempted to follow the precedent of the *trienio* in punishing administrative corruption. The greatest symbolic success of this campaign was the petition for the extradition of Marcos Pérez Jiménez to stand trial for peculation before the Supreme Court of Venezuela. The courts also tried and seized the property of other *perezjimenistas* for corruption and violation of human rights. The exemplary effect of the Pérez Jiménez trial faded somewhat when AD and COPEI leaders balked at bringing to trial any of their own colleagues who had enriched themselves in public office after 1958. They argued that public denunciation of corruption in the democratic system would weaken confidence in the system. It was difficult to solve the conundrum of how to root out corruption while building a political system which depended heavily on patronage and clientelism.

Some Venezuelans perceived a difference between the corruption of the 1950s and that of the 1960s. Under Pérez Jiménez, the president and a few of his favourites became millionaires and lavished the funds on wasteful private consumption. Under the democratic governments of the 1960s, senior officials were generally honest, but middle- and lower-rank functionaries and *políticos* took some advantage of expanded opportunities to benefit from their positions. The situation did not become as generalized as the famous Mexican *mordida,* but the 'democratization' of influence-peddling was one way of more widely distributing national oil wealth. If kept within bounds, such 'corruption' was tolerable.

Seeking to extend foreign policy beyond the traditional compass determined by the oil industry, Betancourt planned to join the Latin American Free Trade Association (LAFTA), but eventually deferred to the objections of those powerful sectors of the business community tied to foreign capital and imports. An ideological alliance raised fewer objections than an economic one, and Betancourt was able to revive his long-standing idea of a union of democratic governments in the Americas. He called on hemispheric leaders to withhold recognition of de facto governments – a policy that came to be known as the Betancourt Doctrine. Yet, except in the cases of Trujillo and Castro, the American nations resisted Betancourt's argument as unwarranted intervention in the domestic affairs of nations. The sanctions applied against Trujillo and Castro also responded less to the de facto nature of their governments than to their sponsoring subversion or assassination in neighbouring countries.

Betancourt's antipathy towards Fidel Castro was both personal and ideological. From their first meeting in Caracas on 24 January 1959, shortly before Betancourt's inauguration and just after Castro's victory over Batista's forces in Cuba, Betancourt was cool towards him. He disliked the expansive rhetoric and ego of the younger man and sensed in Castro a dangerous competitor for influence in the Americas. A few months later the execution of some of Batista's officials confirmed Betancourt's negative first impression. Venezuela broke diplomatic relations with Cuba in November 1961 before guerrilla war had begun in Venezuela. Betancourt voted in January 1962 for the resolution to expel Cuba from the OAS, and in November 1963 the Venezuelan president asked the OAS to impose sanctions on Cuba because of its support of the FALN guerrillas in Venezuela.

The independence of former British colonies in the Caribbean also drew Venezuela into a more active involvement in regional politics. Caracas denounced the 1899 arbitration decision which had established the boundary with British Guiana near the mouth of the Orinoco River. Venezuela argued that the arbitration tribunal had yielded to British pressure and that the true boundary should be the Essequibo River. The new boundary, if honoured, would award Venezuela approximately three-fifths of independent Guyana's territory. Relations with Trinidad and Tobago were also poor as the newly independent nation defended its fishing rights in the Gulf of Paría and requested that Venezuela abrogate the 30 per cent tariff on Trinidadian goods imported into Venezuela.

Betancourt intended to preside over an orderly, democratic election in 1963, but his own party had been weakened by the guerrilla challenges and two internal divisions. First, Domingo Alberto Rangel, Américo Martín and their allies challenged Betancourt and the AD old guard. Many younger *adecos* who had participated actively alongside the PCV in the clandestine struggle against Pérez Jiménez admired Fidel Castro. They also objected to Betancourt's strong grip on the party and his efforts to please business. When Betancourt forced Rangel, Martín and others out of AD in March 1960, they organized the MIR, which by 1962 had joined the armed struggle to overthrow his government. A further division of AD occurred in January 1962 when Raúl Ramos Giménez tried unsuccessfully to loosen the old guard's control of the party apparatus. Here the issues were more personal than ideological or generational, since Ramos Giménez was seeking the nomination as AD presidential candidate for 1963. Ramos Giménez's group adopted the name AD–ARS (later AD en Oposición), and it continued to field candidates in elections.

The two divisions weakened the party's command of labour, peasant and *barrio* organizations. Betancourt prevented the MIR and the PCV from gaining popular support only when he outlawed the two parties after the 1962 uprising in Carúpano. In 1963 the FALN continued to conduct guerrilla activity and initiated a campaign of urban terrorism to try to prevent the election of December 1963 from taking place. MIR and PCV leaders called on the population to abstain from voting. The election severely tested AD's dominance of the political scene and threatened to end abruptly the democratic experiment.

The AD nominee, Raúl Leoni, drew the support of the labour wing of the party from his tenure as labour minister in the *trienio*. Although Leoni was highly esteemed as part of the AD founding generation, Betancourt had been reluctant to support his candidacy because of the opposition of the COPEI leadership. Fortunately for AD, there were six other presidential candidates, and the Venezuelan population rejected both the guerrilla violence and the tactic of abstention. More than 91 per cent of the registered voters went to the polls. Leoni won 32.8 per cent of the vote, a decline of 16.3 per cent from Betancourt's vote in 1958. Caldera this time came second with 20 per cent, and, rather surprisingly, the novelist and intellectual Arturo Uslar Pietri, who ran on a platform which rejected partisan politics, came fourth with 16 per cent, less than a percentage point behind the third-place candidate, Jóvito Villaba.

Rómulo Betancourt lived in Switzerland during the Leoni government. His successor was less committed to maintaining the coalition with COPEI and tried instead to form a congressional alliance with Jóvito Villaba of URD and Arturo Uslar Pietri of the Frente Nacional Democrática (FND). Congressional co-operation was minimal, but there was more space for manoeuvring as the guerrilla threat waned. Whereas in 1964 there were sixteen active guerrilla groups, by 1968 there were only three. The Left concluded that it had erred badly in believing that Venezuela was ready for a Cuban-style revolution. Nevertheless, terrorism, political assassinations and kidnappings continued, and Leoni suspended constitutional guarantees several times, although less extensively than Betancourt had done. Excesses by the police and army also continued. Professor Alberto Lovera, a member of the PCV, was the most celebrated victim, being arrested by Digepol in 1965, tortured and then wound with chains and tossed into the sea. AD tolerated press and congressional denunciations, but the culprits were not identified, and there was no public house-cleaning at Digepol.

Leoni's two major crises involved the oil companies and Fedecámaras and leftists at the Universidad Central de Venezuela. In 1966 Minister of Mines Manuel Pérez Guerrero announced a revision of the general tax system which would increase personal and corporate income taxes. Venezuelan taxes were among the lowest in the world – only 2.2 per cent on personal income and 16.3 percent on medium-sized corporations. (Comparable rates in Mexico were 8.5 and 44.7 per cent, respectively.) Nonetheless, the companies and the private sector resisted. The oil companies reduced production to the lowest rate in a decade, and Fedecámaras enlisted the aid of banker Pedro Tinoco, Jr., and Arturo Uslar Pietri to lobby for them. Leoni and Pérez Guerrero adroitly used a 'divide and conquer' strategy and by September 1966 were able to settle issues privately with the oil companies. The local opposition then collapsed, since it stood on shakier ground in resisting the modest increments in its own tax rates. The oil companies achieved a short-run truce but in the process betrayed their strongest allies in Venezuela. Fedecámaras and business opposition to regulation of the companies, and even to nationalization, weakened considerably after 1966.

Leoni managed to smooth over most educational conflicts with the Church and COPEI, but those with the Left over university governance at the Universidad Central de Venezuela were intense. Students staged protests against a regulation of 1964 which limited the number of times a student could repeat a course before being dropped by the university. On 14 December 1966 the government sent the armed forces to occupy the university, violating its autonomy, and in 1967 the institution closed because of strikes and violence. The government benefited in its negotiations from a division between the PCV and the MIR in the university. The PCV, in line with the party's decision to return to legal political activity, chose to negotiate and to link student issues more closely with national politics. The MIR, by contrast, supported student strikes, refusal to take exams and violent resistance. Leoni's persistence, and student elections which gave the PCV an edge in 1968, finally brought a wary peace to the nation's foremost university. The issue of university autonomy versus government control remained unresolved.

Leoni sponsored no major initiatives in foreign policy. The UN Conference on the Law of the Sea, which held its initial meeting in Caracas in 1968, increased interest in marine resources and boundaries. Venezuela, conscious of shrinking oil reserves and a costly economic and social development programme, hoped for a new bonanza from the seas. Relations with neighbouring nations became tenser as improved off-shore oil-drilling technology heightened the possibility of spectacular new finds off the Venezuelan coasts. Venezuela and Great Britain signed an agreement in Geneva in 1966 which suspended claims on the Guyana territory while a Venezuelan–Guyanese commission tried to resolve the dispute. However, in 1968 Venezuela violated the spirit of the Geneva agreement by claiming the territorial seas and continental shelf of the disputed territory, a move by which it sought to check the oil concessions that Guyana had made in the zone. Oil claims also disturbed relations with Colombia, which in 1966 awarded exploration concessions in the Gulf of Venezuela to several oil companies. Caracas denounced the concessions as illegal and asserted exclusive sovereignty over the gulf and its shelves. The incidents initiated a long series of boundary negotiations that were exceptionally difficult to resolve. The nationalistic assertion of control of border and disputed territory proved popular with Venezuelans in general and with the armed forces in particular.

The 1968 election, and the manoeuvring that preceded it, affirmed the growing consolidation of the system and marked a turning point. AD experienced a new and more damaging split when the popular founding member Luis Beltrán Prieto Figueroa formed the Movimiento Electoral del Pueblo (MEP) after Betancourt and the old guard used their control of the party machinery to deny him the party's nomination. Betancourt considered his old friend too radical and thought that Gonzalo Barrios, also of the generation of 1928, would be more acceptable to COPEI and the business community. A Betancourt protégé who had been minister of the interior during his presidency, Carlos Andrés Pérez, became secretary-general of the party and worked hard to minimize the effects of the division. In the event, Barrios attracted more voters than had Raúl Leoni in 1963. However, the election of 1968 was narrowly won by Rafael Caldera of COPEI.

Like AD, COPEI had experienced generational and ideological divisions during the ten years of democracy since 1958, but unlike AD it had avoided open splits. The Christian Democrats had gained popular respect, improved their organization and moved away from the doctrinaire conservatism of the 1930s and 1940s. COPEI now displayed no major ideological or programmatic differences from AD. The left wing of the party, centered in the Juventud Revolucionaria Copeyana (JRC), looked for inspiration to the left wing of the Chilean Christian Democratic Party led by Radomiro Tomic. Luis Herrera Campíns argued that the party should show more concern for social justice and less for capitalism, protection of property and anti-Communist rhetoric. Caldera and his allies did not muzzle or expel the dissidents, although a few did leave the party. As 1968 approached, the desire for victory dulled ideological differences, and Caldera adopted a conciliatory campaign strategy, promising amnesty to the leftist guerrillas and visiting poor *barrios* as well as chatting with wealthy matrons in '*café con Caldera*' afternoons. His narrow victory (1,075,375 votes to Barrios' 1,044,081, or barely 2 per cent of the vote) could be attributed to his skilful campaigning and good use of television appearances, as well as to the AD split and some reaction against AD *continuismo*.

Jóvito Villaba of URD had been a force in politics for as long as Betancourt and longer than Caldera. Yet his idiosyncratic and personalist leadership could not place URD within striking range of AD or COPEI. His opportunistic coalition with Uslar Pietri's FND and with Larrazábal behind the candidacy of Miguel Angel Burelli Rivas came in a poor third. Two minor parties represented the simultaneous return to legal politics of the Communists and of Pérez Jiménez. Still suffering from the shattered organization and loss of public sympathy caused by the guerrilla campaign, the Unión Para Avanzar (the legally recognized front for the PCV) won only 2.8 per cent of the national legislative vote. The *perezjimenista* party, the Cruzada Cívica Nacionalista (CCN), fared better: It won 11.1 per cent of the national vote and 26.6 per cent of the Caracas vote and elected Pérez Jiménez to the Senate. The former dictator's trial for peculation had just ended in August 1968, when the Supreme Court found him guilty of minor financial crimes. He was immediately released and took up residence in Spain since he had spent more time in prison during his trial than his sentence called for. Pérez's election to the Senate was, however, nullified on the technicality that he had not registered to vote. (In 1973, the Senate passed a constitutional amendment that prohibited anyone who had been convicted of administrative malfeasance from holding national political office. This was aimed specifically at Pérez and at any attempt he might make to capitalize on discontent with democratic government.)

COPEI IN POWER, 1969–74

Rafael Caldera's modest plurality provided a shaky mandate for what he liked to call '*el cambio*' – the change – and the new president had a difficult time during his first year in office. He wanted an administration which could reflect COPEI's political views, and so he appointed no AD members to his cabinet, and in Congress he formed shifting alliances with the minor political parties. AD leaders adhered to the gentlemen's Pact of Punto Fijo, but their lack of experience in acting as a loyal opposition and their determination to return to power made them defiant. Caldera faced implacable opposition until 1970, when AD and COPEI agreed on limited congressional co-operation. The AD strategists believed that striking a mutually agreeable bargain with Caldera was preferable to allowing Prieto Figueroa's MEP to gain more ground at their expense.

Caldera's ambitious efforts at administrative reform failed to alter the system of political patronage. A civil service law was passed in 1970, and the CAP tried with mixed success to reverse the concentration of wealth and decision-making in Caracas. The CAP, under the leadership of Allan Randolph Brewer-Carías, sponsored a 1969 law which divided the nation into eight economic regions and encouraged the formation of new development corporations such as the Corporación de los Andes to invest funds in the outlying areas. The government also established regional offices of some national ministries and institutes. Brewer-Carías would have gone even further to restore municipal fiscal and political autonomy; he argued that municipal elections should be held separately from national elections and that district representatives should be responsible to their districts rather than to their parties. Caldera, like Betancourt, believed that the national patronage system which supported the two major parties was crucial to the survival of Venezuelan democracy, and he refused to experiment with Brewer-Carías's radical proposal. As long as regional offices were only superimposed on the existing administrative structure, there was no real change – except, of course, the provision of more jobs and patronage for political allies.

The programme of Caldera's 'pure' COPEI government differed little in substance from those of the preceding AD governments. The most striking initiative was a change in foreign policy under the leadership of Foreign Minister Arístides Calvani, who subsequently became a leader of the international Christian Democratic movement. Calvani announced that Venezuela would now follow a path of non-intervention and ideological pluralism in the Americas. Caracas established relations with de facto governments in Panama, Argentina, Peru and Bolivia and with the Communist governments of Hungary (1969) and the Soviet Union (1970). Trade relations with China were initiated, and contacts with Cuba increased. Calvani signed a bilateral anti-hijacking pact with Cuba and pressed the OAS to remove the sanctions which had been imposed on that country. While easing the tensions with Cuba, Caldera projected Venezuela's influence more forcefully into the Caribbean. Caracas joined the Caribbean Development Bank, and Venezuelan private and public investment in the region increased. To play the role of a helpful big neighbour, Venezuela had to temper its dispute with Guyana, the 1970 Protocol of Port of Spain establishing a ten-year moratorium on the dispute over the Essequibo territory.

Caldera's attention to relations with developing nations and his turn towards ideological pluralism accompanied a somewhat cooler relationship with the United States. In 1971 Venezuela denounced the trade treaty with the United States as a preliminary move to joining the Andean Common Market, but the reciprocal trade agreement which replaced the treaty did not seriously alter the trade relationship between Venezuela and the United States. Fate intervened to sweeten relations somewhat as the Middle East crisis in 1973 shut off the Arab oil flow to the United States and the interdependency of the two nations intensified.

Caldera did not change the general petroleum policy set out by the AD administrations. The rising prices after 1970 bolstered national confidence. Talk of nationalization was in the air, but in any case Venezuela could expect to take possession of most of the foreign oil holdings in 1983 when many of the concessions ran out. In anticipation, the Venezuelan Congress nationalized the natural gas industry and required foreign oil companies to post a bond amounting to 10 per cent of the value of their investments to guarantee the good condition of their properties on reversion.

In domestic politics, Caldera's preference for conciliation implicitly widened the Pact of Punto Fijo. As the guerrillas abandoned the armed struggle and returned to legal activity, the Marxist political parties tacitly accepted the rules of the game. The PCV, having resumed legal existence in 1969, divided in 1971 – the dissidents forming the Movimiento al Socialismo (MAS). In 1973, in time for the presidential election, the MIR also returned to legal activity. The trend matched events in the hemisphere, as Salvador Allende's electoral victory in 1970 in Chile encouraged leftist parties to take up the tactic of the '*vía pacífica*'.

The Venezuelan business community, the Church and the armed forces also pressed – peacefully – to increase their influence within the system. Business interests, represented most visibly by Fedecámaras, did not by any means win all of their battles, but they remained a force with which both major parties had to reckon. Caldera disappointed them bitterly with his decision to enter the Andean Common Market. Fedecámaras, confirming its ties to commercial and multinational interests, had argued that the terms of entry into the Andean Pact would discourage investment in Venezuela, cause problems with the U.S. trade agreement, increase local labour costs and import inflation along with the new tariff structure. Caldera, however, saw merit in regional economic agreements and also thought that the union might check Brazilian economic and political expansionism. Venezuela joined the pact in February 1973. A survey taken in 1973 reported that only 38.3 per cent of business association leaders thought that their interests were 'represented' or 'well represented' in public policy. Another survey in the same year, however, showed that Venzuelans in general thought that the fifteen years of democracy had helped powerful economic interests more than the general population.[5]

Caldera faced no problems with military conspiracies, but AD and COPEI still competed for influence within the armed forces. Many officers, proud of their victory over the guerrillas and their enhanced national security mission, objected to the politicization of promotions and appointments. Some officers considered that Caldera had used political rather than military criteria to appoint General Martín García Villasmil as minister of defence. Caldera warned that officers were out of line in publicly criticizing political decisions, and in 1969 the president charged some of his military opponents with conspiracy and had them imprisoned. (García Villasmil tested the political waters further when he retired from active service and ran – unsuccessfully – for the presidency in 1973.) The COPEI leadership thus successfully followed AD's lead in consolidating civilian control over the armed forces.

The Church, the *barrios* and the universities proved more difficult to control. In spite of its Catholic roots and philosophy, COPEI encountered dissent from the Church. The call for social justice that emerged from the Medellín Conference of Latin American Bishops in 1968 also echoed in Venezuela. Some foreign priests criticized the poverty and misery they

---

[5] José Antonio Gil, 'Entrepreneurs and Regime Consolidation', in John Martz and David Myers (eds.), *Venezuela, the Democratic Experience* (New York, 1977), p. 154; Enrique Baloyra, 'Public Attitudes toward the Democratic Regime', in ibid., p. 49.

found in the urban *barrios*. In 1970 Caldera's government expelled a Belgian priest, Padre Francisco Wuytack, for staging an unauthorized demonstration to protest against unemployment and poverty. The Venezuelan Church hierarchy supported the government's action, but younger priests and students denounced the government and defended Padre Wuytack.

The teeming Caracas *barrios* also directly challenged the government to make good its promises of social justice and to check the rising urban crime rate. An undertrained and underpaid police force, inadequate resources and partisan bickering limited Caldera's success. He replaced the much-criticized Digepol with a new national police force, the Dirección de Servicios de Inteligencia y Prevención del Estado (DISIP). An energetic police offensive against urban crime, Operación Vanguardia, began in early 1970 with popular support. Soon, however, police excesses prompted criticism and finally abandonment of the programme. Caldera also attacked the causes of *barrio* crime through improved public services and a low-cost housing programme, inspired by the Chilean Christian Democratic programme. Yet the COPEI programme did not receive enough funds to make a measurable impact, and AD, eager to guard its own political advantage in the *barrios,* further contributed to the weakening of the initiative.

University unrest proved difficult for Caldera to check. Students and faculty protested against the war in Vietnam and against Venezuelan government efforts to control the universities. In 1970 AD and COPEI collaborated on a university reform law which circumscribed university autonomy, defined more strictly who was a regular, voting student and limited the terms of office of university authorities. Student and faculty demonstrations at Universidad Central de Venezuela caused Caldera to order the Guardia Nacional and the Policía Metropolitana to close the institution. Protests spread to Caracas high schools, which the government also closed, and to other national universities. All agreed that the universities suffered from serious educational deficiencies, but many also noted that AD and COPEI displayed a Gómez-like eagerness to destroy independent, autonomous sources of criticism. The government provided its model of an ideal public university when it opened the Universidad Simón Bolívar (USB) in 1970 on the outskirts of Caracas. USB, called the 'university of the future', enforced tougher admissions standards, concentrated on scientific and technical fields and strictly limited student and faculty political activity.

By 1973, after fifteen years of democratic rule, Venezuela had made formidable gains in political institutionalization and economic growth. The GNP had more than doubled in constant dollars between 1958 and 1972. In 1971 per capita GNP had risen to be second only to that of Argentina and within a few years it would be the highest in Latin America. The Venezuelan population was more literate, better fed and healthier, and it lived longer, than in 1958. The number of television sets had risen from 250,000 in 1961 to 822,000 in 1970 – an indicator both of affluence and of the spread of mass media.

Since the 1930s progressive Venezuelans had wanted to *sembrar el petróleo,* to invest oil revenues so that a diversified economy and middle-class population could confidently move into the post-petroleum age. But time was running out. Existing oil reserves had shrunk to only eleven years' supply in 1973. Between 1958 and 1973, there had been only a slight growth in oil revenues. Venezuela's relative position as a primary exporter had slipped as rich North African and Middle Eastern fields came into production. Alaskan, Mexican and North Sea production would shortly glut the market even more.

The democratic governments had not diminished Venezuela's dependence on oil – and on the United States. The value of non-traditional exports and iron-ore exports grew more rapidly than that of petroleum, but provided only a small share of export earnings. The United States was still the market for more than 50 per cent of Venezuelan exports, primarily petroleum, and the supplier of more than 50 per cent of Venezuelan imports. The modest measures intended to encourage industrialization had only slightly changed the items which Venezuela imported; in addition to consumer goods, low or non-existent duties encouraged the purchase of capital goods and heavy machinery for capital-intensive industries. Foreign debt had not been a factor in Venezuela's fiscal history since Gómez had paid off the foreign debt in 1930. But the shortfall left from the debts of the Pérez Jiménez dictatorship, static oil revenues and the costs of government-sponsored industrialization and political patronage led to an increase in the foreign debt from 1,168 million to 8,434 million bolívares between 1958 and 1973. The strength of the Venezuelan currency, tied to the petroleum exports and the U.S. dollar, did not vary and continued to encourage imports over exports.

Income continued to be distributed unevenly both in social terms and among regions. Residents of cities and petroleum zones enjoyed higher incomes than those in the countryside. In 1972, 86 per cent of all earned income went to the cities, where 73.1 per cent of the national population resided. A study in the late 1960s found that in cities of more than 25,000, 57.41 per cent of the families earned less than 1,000 bolívares per month. The figure compared well with the 89.22 per cent of rural families who fell in that category, but did not hold out much optimism for an expansion of the urban middle class.

AD and COPEI had relied heavily on growing petroleum resources and on the assumption that subsidies for industrialists would ultimately provide more jobs and income for the poor. Yet capital-intensive economic development could not absorb the large body of untrained workers. Foreigners were still brought in as consultants and as skilled labour in the steel and petrochemical complexes. The paradox of simultaneous unemployment and labour shortage contributed to a smaller percentage of the national income going to salaried workers and employees. In 1958 workers received 54.5 per cent of the national income, but in 1973 they received only 46.4 per cent. At the same time, income in agriculture was only one-quarter that of the industrial sector, one-sixth that of the trade sector and one-thirteenth that of the petroleum sector.

In the election of 1973 Rómulo Betancourt decided against running again, convinced the AD old guard that it was time to turn over leadership to a new generation and secured the nomination for his protégé, Carlos Andrés Pérez. Although much younger than the founders of his party, Pérez had been active in AD from his teens in the 1940s and had served as minister of the interior under Betancourt, when he earned the hatred of the Left for his unrelenting persecution of student and guerrilla groups. After AD's 1968 election defeat, Pérez had devoted his attention to rebuilding the party organization, trying to minimize the effects of the defection of Prieto and the *mepistas*.

COPEI also experienced some generational strains, but Rafael Caldera secured the nomination for the veteran Lorenzo Fernández, who was loyal but a rather dull candidate. He did not publicly renounce any of Caldera's presidential actions and had trouble wooing those whom Caldera had alienated. The business community disliked Caldera's surprising nationalism and overtures to the Left, and the Left resented his recognition of General Augusto Pinochet shortly after the overthrow and assassination of Salvador Allende in Chile in September 1973.

Other parties put forward candidates, but none effectively challenged the two major parties. They all lacked a strong national organization. Nor could they solve the political programme conundrum: how could a political platform promise more than did the major parties without being perceived as dangerously radical or naïvely unrealistic? Indeed, probably many of the minor presidential candidates ran only to attract a larger congressional vote or to legitimize themselves as 'popular' choices in the unlikely event of a military *golpe*.

By 1973 presidential campaigns had become quinquennial carnivals. Songs, jingles, motorcades, fiestas, banners and beer parties were part of the popular campaigning style. The major parties spent outlandish amounts of money – more per voter than in the United States – for publicity consultants, often foreign, and sophisticated media appeals. Carlos Andrés Pérez, who went all out with the technology and trappings of 'modern' political campaigns, reinforced his youthful image with flashy neckties, sideburns and televised, fast-moving *caminos* through the *barrios* and won a remarkable 48.77 per cent of the vote. The minor parties shrank almost to insignificance as AD and COPEI together pulled in 85 per cent of the vote in the field of twelve candidates; the two leftist candidates attracted only 10 per cent. Analysts noted that the electoral division between Caracas and the rest of the nation had virtually disappeared, the two major parties winning easily in the capital as well as in the rest of the country. Most voters seemed more interested in bread and butter issues – jobs, housing, education, the cost of living, the crime rates – than in more abstract ideological debates. These concerns favoured the major parties, and voters could be satisfied that they were expressing dissatisfaction with one major party when they voted for the other. They did not need to look to 'extremist' candidates to express a protest vote.

THE OIL BOOM AND THE PRESIDENCY OF CARLOS ANDRÉS PÉREZ, 1974–9

The vicissitudes of the petroleum industry and the international market for oil had set the outer limits for Venezuelan development since the 1920s. Half a century later more than 90 per cent of export earnings – and more than 70 per cent of government revenue – still derived from petroleum sales. A U.S. $1 change in the price per barrel of petroleum produced a 2 per cent change in the total government budget. The average price per barrel of oil rose from $2.01 in 1970 to $14.26 in January 1974 and to $29.40 in 1982 (before falling below $13 in 1986).

The Arab oil embargo of 1973 and the unprecedented high prices of oil gave President Carlos Andrés Pérez an opportunity to 'sow the petroleum' more widely and deeply than ever before. Both the new wealth and the perception of it affected all aspects of national life. Foreign policy became more assertive and expansive. Neglected regions of the country received more investment. Massive public development projects reawakened the hope that Venezuela could become economically self-sufficient.

Unfortunately, neither the administrative skills nor the planning apparatus of the state made the same leap as did income. Some Venezuelans had long tolerated a generalized misappropriation of government funds as long as the miscreants did not foolishly and ostentatiously flaunt their new wealth. An unwillingness to separate the civil service from political patronage had further encouraged graft and influence-peddling. The enormous rush of new funds in the 1970s caused a wave of generalized corruption and ill-advised foreign loans. State companies and institutes contracted foreign loans independently, without central government approval and without fiscal overseeing of the distribution of the funds. As long as oil prices continued to climb and interest rates did not, repayment even of the short-term loans posed no problem. An undetermined percentage of the wealth went to finance Miami condominiums, private planes, luxury automobiles, foreign travel and bank accounts. The spiralling national debt appeared in the midst of the grandest party Venezuelans had ever seen. 'Venezuela Saudita' was born, making the Pérez Jiménez 'dance of the millions' look relatively austere by contrast.

High oil prices also made possible the uncontested nationalization of petroleum and other natural resources. The bases for running a nationalized industry had been laid at home with the CVP and internationally with OPEC. Most concessions were due to run out within a decade anyway, and the multinational companies in Venezuela had undertaken virtually no new exploration or offshore drilling. Venezuelans feared that waiting until the reversion date would leave them with little but a pile of rusted machinery, while newer, more productive foreign fields would have stolen the march. Many of the multinational companies' strongest allies in Venezuela had been disappointed with the companies' self-interested compromise on the tax bill of 1966. National control of the petroleum industry promised a new level of independence.

The Venezuelan government took over the iron industry before turning to the petroleum companies. On 1 January 1975, street banners proclaimed '*El hierro es nuestro*' (The iron is ours). In spite of the nationalistic rhetoric, the subsidiaries of U.S. Steel and Bethlehem Steel received generous compensation, and Venezuela agreed to sell iron to the parent companies for up to seven years at the minimum price of 59.89 bolívares per metric ton. Venezuela's iron production had grown from 1.9 metric tons in 1952 to 15.6 million in 1976, of which about 80 per cent was exported. Next to petroleum, iron export earnings were insignificant, but the expansion of the steel industry in Guayana and coal mining in Zulia held out the hope of the development of a Venezuelan Ruhr in the heart of the nation.

The oil nationalization proceeded equally smoothly, although with greater domestic debate. Few disputed the generous U.S. $1,000 million compensation to the foreign companies or the creation of a national holding company (Petroven, later named PDVSA) to co-ordinate the activities of the sixteen subsidiaries of the international companies. Venezuelan critics focussed on Article 5 of the nationalization agreement, a clause which authorized the government to enter into agreements with foreign companies on technical or other matters relating to the industry. Juan Pablo Pérez Alfonzo and other critics thought that Article 5 masked an intention to leave the oil industry in foreign hands, albeit in a new format. President Pérez, supported by Betancourt, countered that the government should retain the utmost flexibility in future development of the oil industry. Pérez won the day, and Venezuela immediately signed contracts with the foreign companies to provide technical assistance, exploration and transportation for Venezuelan oil. The companies probably improved their financial position by exchanging the heavy taxation for service contracts, but Venezuela could not avoid purchasing the services which national companies could not supply.

Nationalization accompanied a major effort to modernize the petroleum industry in Venezuela. Rafael Alfonzo Ravard, head of PDVSA, successfully argued that the holding company must remain free of politics and even of control by the Ministry of Mines. He oversaw the initiation of new exploration to offset the declining reserves and invested in new industry equipment. In 1976 Venezuela's production consisted of 35 per cent light oil, 38 per cent medium and 27 per cent of the least valuable heavy crude oil. The percentage of the cheaper heavy crude continued to rise, and it was hoped that new finds might add to the reserves of the more valuable, lighter oil. Venezuela's least desirable reserves were the tar belt along the northern shore of the Orinoco River. It would take new and expensive technology to recapture usable petroleum from the Orinoco fields, but Caracas banked on the continuing high price of oil and in 1981 began plans for exploitation there. PDVSA also modernized the petroleum-refining and petrochemicals industries. Venezuela's existing refineries, built when there was less heavy crude oil to process, could no longer cope with the domestic demand. Refineries at Amuay, El Palito and Puerto La Cruz were expanded. The petrochemical industry, with the new investments, would have to wait for several years before it showed a profit.

The nationalizations encouraged the rise of a new development strategy. Rather than seeing the iron and steel industries as adjuncts to an industrialization geared to the internal market, the grander strategy concentrated upon possibilities in the international market. The political corollary of this ambitious plan lay in placing a lower priority on fostering a domestic consumer market through redistribution of national income. Politicians faced the risk of protests from that large portion of the population which would indirectly pay the price for the new priorities. Using the nationalized oil to subsidize exports also made the nation doubly vulnerable: to the international petroleum market and to those for steel, petrochemicals and other viable exports. The costs of the high-risk strategy became more obvious when petroleum prices fell and the foreign debt grew in the 1980s.

Carlos Andrés Pérez's impressive electoral victory in 1973 gave him a cushion of support that no previous president had enjoyed. In theory, the Venezuelan Congress had considerable influence, but in practice the political system was strongly presidential, with the role of Congress limited to occasional obstruction. The judicial branch of government was weaker still. Judges, appointed along political lines for limited terms by Congress, presided over an increasingly corrupt and inefficient court system. With an AD majority, Pérez secured congressional approval to govern by decree without congressional or judicial review, and he issued decrees from Miraflores at a dazzling rate.

Pérez's flamboyant style quickly won him enemies. The opposition parties resented his bypassing of Congress and feared that AD, helped by the oil bonanza, would finally achieve a one-party dominance of the political system. Even his mentor Betancourt and much of the AD old guard distrusted Pérez's powerful and idiosyncratic leadership. He appointed to the cabinet younger people who were loyal to Pérez rather than to the party. Although Betancourt himself had always exercised a personal control over AD, he did so for the purpose of developing a disciplined political organization which could dominate both the party faithful and organized interest groups. Pérez's visceral populism ignored the party elders and threatened to go directly to the masses through his skilled and forceful use of the media.

The strongly populist, pro-labour tone of Pérez's first six months in office aggravated the businessmen who favoured the grand strategy of developing export industries. He ordered higher monthly salaries and wages for all people who earned less than 5,000 bolívares per month, and he imposed heavy penalties for unjustified dismissals in an effort to keep unemployment down.

However, Pérez soon reduced his pro-labour stance and shifted towards subsidizing exports by favouring the so-called 'western group' of Maracaibo financiers and entrepreneurs who had bankrolled his campaign. Important members of that group, Enrique Delfino, Ciro Febres Cordero and Pedro Tinoco, were connected with the Banco Hipotecario de Occidente and with the export-led strategy. By 1976, price increases and economic measures which favoured business had cut into workers' living standards. The AD-dominated CTV loyally chose not to challenge the government, but some unions, such as that of the more independent iron miners, occasionally protested against both CTV hegemony and government policies.

An authoritarian tone underlay the superficial populism of Pérez's government. Some guerrilla groups reappeared, and the government responded forcefully. In 1976 Congress passed a Ley Orgánica de Seguridad y Defensa, which created a Consejo Nacional de Seguridad y Defensa with a permanent secretary, standing committees and a national intelligence service. Critics charged that the structure aped the security apparatus so popular with military governments of the Southern Cone. They were troubled by the emphasis on secrecy and the absence of guarantees for citizens' rights. The 1976 kidnapping of William Niehous, general manager of Owens-Illinois of Venezuela, put more pressure on leftists. Nearly four hundred people were detained, and the Trotskyist leader of the Liga Socialista de Venezuela, Jorge Rodríguez, died of a heart attack while undergoing an interrogation by DISIP. In 1978, the investigation of the assassination of a Caracas lawyer revealed that an elite death squad operated within the Policía Técnica Judicial (PTJ).

The erratic combination of populism, authoritarianism and an improved relationship with Cuba confounded the Venezuelan Left. They applauded the presence of former *miristas* like Gumersindo Rodríguez in the administration. Moreover, increased spending for culture – art, films, dance, publishing – indirectly appeased leftist intellectuals, as did the creation of new universities and scholarship programmes. Young Venezuelans competed for Gran Mariscal de Ayacucho scholarships, which financed university study in the United States and Europe. This programme reflected the belief that providing education abroad cost less than starting up new universities and programmes in Venezuela to serve the burgeoning student population. Moreover, the scholarships would transfer some funds out of the overheated Venezuelan economy. By May 1979, more than twenty thousand students had received complete scholarships, and 61 per cent of them studied abroad, which did much to reduce tensions between students and government. Nonetheless, many students returned to Venezuela, frustrated with some of the national flaws they now saw more clearly. Some of them expected to enjoy a U.S. or European middle-class life-style immediately. Yet their ambitions were checked by the political patronage network, which occasionally discriminated against the foreign-trained, and the shrinking job market of the 1980s.

Neither Venezuelan nor foreign universities could supply skilful administrators quickly enough for the 1970s boom. The growth of the bureaucracy and the unprecedented national income strained the patronage-ridden administration beyond its limits. The mushrooming of autonomous state enterprises compounded the problem. In 1980 the Venezuelan state boasted 91 administrative entities, 79 state-owned enterprises and 146 mixed enterprises. Between 1960 and 1975 central-government expenditures nearly quadrupled, but shrank from 54 to 21 per cent of total public expenditures. State companies, by contrast, spent nearly twenty-five times more in 1975 than they had in 1960, and their expenditures represented 62 per cent of public expenditures in 1975, compared with 23 per cent in 1960.

In short, the failure to develop a merit-based and experienced administrative pool in the previous decade and a half ensured that the pressures of rapid growth in the late 1970s would produce greater inefficiency and corruption than the nation had ever seen. Several scandals rocked the administration, but very few cases were brought to the courts since AD and COPEI leaders continued to believe that open trials would shake public confidence in the democratic system. In order to provide an illusion of a public cleansing, the old guard of the two parties agreed on a congressional trial of Carlos Andrés Pérez after his term was completed. In 1979, Congress found him guilty of the unindictable crime of fomenting a climate of political corruption, but exonerated him from 'moral and administrative' responsibility for any specific charges.

Foreign policy under the Pérez administration was controversial and sometimes contradictory. Some AD members disliked the abandonment of earlier anti-Communist attitudes and were suspicious of both the warm relationship with the Socialist International (SI) and the erratic drift to the left. Under Pérez, AD became the largest affiliate of SI and enthusiastically endorsed the Third World overtures encouraged by former West German Chancellor Willy Brandt. Venezuela restored diplomatic relations with Cuba in December 1974 and led an unsuccessful campaign to have the OAS remove sanctions against Fidel Castro's government. Pérez's support for Omar Torrijos during the Panama Canal treaty negotiations and for the *sandinista* guerrillas in Nicaragua further confirmed his activist policy.

In his ambitions to be perceived as an international and Third World leader, Pérez travelled abroad more than any other president; even Moscow was included in one of his itineraries in 1976. Caracas took a prominent role in the North–South economic discussions and the Law of the Sea conferences. Increased economic assistance and diplomatic overtures in the English-speaking Caribbean were clumsy, but usually welcomed by the poorest states. Venezuela signed a pact with other Amazonian nations agreeing to multilateral development of the region. The Venezuelan president also took a more active role in the Andean Pact, with the avowed goal of giving more political substance to the economic union. Such activity reinforced the perception of a 'new Venezuela' as simultaneously a Caribbean, an Andean, an Atlantic and an Amazonian nation.

Pérez's active Third World foreign policy and the oil crisis created some tension with the United States. His government criticized the U.S. Trade Act Amendment of 1974, which denied the benefits of the Generalized System of Preferences to any OPEC nation. The Trade Act was a reprisal for the Arab oil embargo of 1973 and did not acknowledge that Venezuelan oil had continued to flow to the United States during the crisis. In 1976, the United States lifted the discriminatory trade clause, and relations improved somewhat.

Pérez's populist style, his management of the nation's resources and his sometimes contradictory policies became issues of dispute as the presidential elections of 1978 approached. Betancourt had publicly distanced himself from his former friend, who had struck out so strongly on his own. In matters of substance, Betancourt disliked the warmth displayed towards Marxist governments, the Third World stance, the furious spending on monumental projects and the charges of corruption. Betancourt and the traditional AD leadership were therefore determined to freeze Pérez out of the party's decisions, and since Betancourt and his preferred presidential candidate, Luis Piñerúa, retained control of most of the party machinery, Piñerúa won the AD nomination with ease. Pérez defended his own administration but did not openly challenge the party leaders by pressing an alternative candidate.

The existence of numerous minor candidates, including several from the divided Left, and conflict within AD over Pérez's leadership gave COPEI a good chance of winning. Luis Herrera Campíns, identified with the left wing of COPEI, was the clear favourite of his party and received Rafael Caldera's lukewarm endorsement. Herrera had little charisma, but COPEI's media adviser Joseph Garth successfully depicted him as a serious and dignified statesman in contrast to Pérez's flashy capriciousness and Piñerúa's dullness. Herrera livened up his image with some folksy *llano* aphorisms and emerged the winner with 46.6 per cent of the vote. Piñerúa polled 43.4 per cent. Once again, the minor parties could not find the formula to shake the electoral dominance of the two major parties.

THE PRESIDENCY OF LUIS HERRERA CAMPÍNS, 1979–84

Like Carlos Andrés Pérez, Luis Herrera Campíns belonged to a new generation of political leaders. Herrera's climb within COPEI, however, had been less spectacular than that of Pérez in AD. Although he campaigned for Rafael Caldera during the 1940s, Herrera remained somewhat distant from the power centres of the party during the *trienio*. He assumed leadership of the Juventud Revolucionaria Copeyana, a youth group which he helped to found in 1947, and edited the party's newspaper. Unlike many of the COPEI leaders who stayed in Venezuela during the Pérez Jiménez dictatorship, Herrera went into exile in 1952 after he had been jailed briefly for organizing student strikes and denouncing press censorship. In Spain, he studied law at the University of Santiago de Compostela and read extensively in the works of Social Christian theorists like Jacques Maritain and Teilhard de Chardin. When he returned to Venezuela in 1958, he was considered one of the more intellectual members of COPEI. In 1973 COPEI's youth and labour sectors had supported his presidential nomination, but Caldera had been able to impose his associate, Lorenzo Fernández.

Herrera did not get off to a good start. In June 1979 municipal elections were held, the first to be held separately from the presidential and congressional elections. COPEI won these elections, but the extended political campaign made it difficult for Herrera to achieve early momentum. He had trouble naming a cabinet because so many *copeyanos* had already begun to plan for the 1983 presidential election. Only two members of his original cabinet had previously served in government: Interior Minister Rafael Andrés Montes de Oca and Education Minister Enrique Pérez Olivares. The creation of two new ministries disappointed those who wanted Herrera to begin to reduce the swollen public administration. Mercedes Pulido Briceño became minister of state for the participation of women in development, and Luis Alberto Machado took over as minister for the development of intelligence, an office which proposed to expand human intelligence and analytical ability.

Herrera liked to quote from Social Christian theory on themes of communitarian society and commitment to the poor, rhetorically underlining Pérez's lack of attention to social expenditure. Herrera's programmes, however, failed to address the question of structural poverty and did not deliver even the palliatives promised. The poor suffered considerably from the removal of subsidies from many consumer items and the imposition of tariffs on imported goods, including food. The 20 per cent inflation of 1980 was the worst that Venezuelans could remember. A programme to subsidize basic food products for poor families never got off the ground, and Herrera's highly publicized campaign to provide 650,000 new housing units fell far short of the goal. The COPEI president did, however, provide one long-awaited improvement in urban services, a showcase project which had been initiated by Carlos Andrés Pérez. Sections of the remarkable and expensive Caracas metro opened in 1983 to give the traffic-congested capital some relief. Other urban services, however, continued to decay.

As before, a COPEI government encountered more tension with organized labour than did AD. With substantial grievances about rising prices and the government's effort to hold wages steady, labour organizations pressed for greater benefits. In fact, both major parties saw their control of the labour movement eroding as more radical organizers gained a foothold, especially among metal-workers in Guyana, where violence grew as a result of bitterness among rival unions.

Minor guerrilla activities continued to inspire strong reactions from police and the military. William Niehous, the U.S. executive who had been kidnapped in 1976, was found on an abandoned ranch in June 1979, freed in a shoot-out in which two of his captors were killed, and rushed out of the country. Given the general suspicion of the police, many believed that there had been a cover-up to shelter politicians who had had more information on the kidnapping than they had revealed. In late 1982, a surprise army raid in the East resulted in the deaths of twenty-three guerrillas as they shared a meal in camp. Venezuelans were startled at the size of the guerrilla group and the army's inability or unwillingness to take any prisoners.

Herrera scaled down Pérez's grandiose foreign initiatives, but, influenced strongly by Arístides Calvani and sympathy for Christian Democrats, he did not entirely avoid international confrontation. Single-minded support for fellow Christian Democrat José Napoleón Duarte in El Salvador and coolness toward *sandinista* Nicaragua brought Caracas more in line with U.S. initiatives in the region until 1982. Then, disappointed at Washington's lukewarm support of Duarte in the 1982 elections and angered at a joint French–Mexican endorsement of negotiations with the FMLN guerrillas, Herrera urged regional co-operation to lessen tensions in Central America. Established in January 1983, the Contadora group (Colombia, Panama, Venezuela and Mexico) may have helped to limit armed conflict in Central America, but failed to achieve a lasting peace agreement.

Relations with Cuba worsened in the spring of 1980. A number of Cubans sought asylum in the Venezuelan Embassy in Havana, but the Cuban government refused to give them safe-conduct passes out of the country. Fidel Castro and Venezuelan spokesmen exchanged insults, and relations remained cool even after Castro allowed the Cubans to leave, principally for the Unted States. Herrera, who had been wary of Prime Minister Maurice Bishop's leftist government in Grenada and its close relations with Cuba, endorsed the U.S. occupation of the island in 1983. The Venezuelan armed forces believed that the action strengthened regional, and Venezuelan, security. The major deviation from U.S. policy towards Latin America occurred in the spring of 1982 when Herrera supported Argentina in the conflict with Great Britain over the Falklands/ Malvinas Islands. Venezuela was especially interested because of its own boundary conflict with Guyana. If Argentina had succeeded in confirming with arms its legal claim to the Falklands/Malvinas Islands, Venezuela might have been able to do the same with the Essequibo territory.

Nationalization of petroleum in 1976 had allowed Caracas to use petroleum sales directly as an instrument of foreign policy. Pérez had offered petroleum at discount prices to Caribbean countries, contributed larger sums to the Caribbean Development Bank for regional reinvestment and joined with other oil-producing nations to help poorer nations. As with other matters, Herrera scaled back or abandoned these initiatives, in part from disagreement with Pérez's objectives and in part from the growing economic crisis in Venezuela.

Indeed, the shifting economic situation demanded most of Herrera's attention. The debt service was escalating with rising interest rates, oil revenues levelling off and the International Monetary Fund (IMF) pressing for austerity measures that would satisfy Venezuela's foreign creditors. Herrera took a series of unpopular measures which removed or limited government subsidies on numerous consumer items, including gasoline. Herrera's most unpopular measure came on 18 February 1983, a date popularly known as 'Black Friday'. The government devalued the bolívar and established a government-controlled rate of 7.5 bolívares to the dollar in addition to a floating rate. Venezuelans who had foreign debts to be paid in dollars suddenly needed two or three times more bolívares to purchase dollars. The private sector demanded that the government subsidize their exchange dilemma by selling them preferential dollars – or dollars at or near the old rate of 4.3 bolívares to the dollar – to meet their obligations. In gossip-ridden Caracas, nonetheless, the true *vivos* (shrewd people) had spirited their money out of the country and into U.S. banks before the black day of devaluation. There had been a virtual haemorrhage of capital in late 1982 and early 1983.

Herrera established a government agency – RECADI – to review the requests for preferential dollars, but during the election year of 1983 RECADI did virtually nothing. Likewise, Herrera's government began lengthy debt renegotiations with U.S. bankers but refused to make any major commitments during the election campaign, since it wished to avoid the political dangers of making any agreement with the IMF. Caracas insisted on dealing directly with the bankers' representatives. Fiscal controls had been so lax that no one could state with certainty the amount of the foreign debt, but the public sector's debt came close to U.S. $20 billion whilst the private sector owed around $14 billion.

The 1983 devaluation favoured a few heavily capitalized firms, mixed public–private industries such as steel and petrochemicals, and any industries which did not depend upon imported parts or intermediate goods. Commercial sectors which dealt heavily in imported consumer products, small or heavily indebted firms and those which were subsidiaries of or depended upon foreign corporations suffered. Even the industries which had grown under the import-substitution strategy to serve the domestic market could benefit little because unemployment, inflation and a decline in the real standard of living for many caused a stagnation or contraction in the domestic demand for consumer goods. Class consciousness and tensions, which had generally been minimized by populist policies based on expanding oil revenues pursued by both major political parties, began to sharpen.

COPEI did not control Congress during the Herrera presidency and received little co-operation from AD, which was wracked by internal tension aroused by the Pérez presidency. The death of its founder and leader Rómulo Betancourt in September 1981 cast a pall over the party and sharpened the struggles among the younger generation for control. The old-guard senior statesman Gonzalo Barrios, strongly backed by the labour sector, managed to keep the Betancourt alignment intact for the 1983 presidential nomination which was secured by Jaime Lusinchi when he won 75 per cent of the vote in the party's internal primary of January 1982. This represented a rout for Carlos Andrés Pérez, who had urged his allies to endorse David Morales Bello. Nonetheless, Pérez and his followers continued to build support within the party and prepared for another run at the presidency in 1988, when Pérez himself would be eligible again. The constitution stipulated that a president could not succeed himself, but a former president could run again when ten years had passed since his leaving office. As the old guard faded from the scene and second-generation leaders remained bitterly divided over Pérez, the labour wing of the party assumed a new prominence, and for the first time a labour leader, Manuel Peñalver, became the secretary-general of AD.

The Left, disappointed at its poor showing in 1973 and 1978, tried again without success to unite. The surfeit of *presidenciables* seemed as great an obstacle as ideological differences. MAS hoped to benefit from the poor performance of both major parties in the economic crisis and put forward its founder and theorist, Teodoro Petkoff. The other major party of the 'new generation' – MIR – was divided between two founding members and former guerrillas: Américo Martín and Moisés Moleiro. Martín and his followers supported Petkoff, while Moleiro and his allies endorsed a leftist coalition which again nominated José Vicente Rangel.

COPEI now experienced some of the same problems that had afflicted AD in 1978; Herrera's unpopularity had reached such levels that the COPEI candidate had to run against the incumbent of his own party as well as against the AD nominee. A number of second-generation COPEI leaders champed at the bit for their opportunity. Herrera favoured his friend and minister of the interior, Rafael Montes de Oca, but Rafael Caldera still had a strong hold on the machinery and loyalties of COPEI. When he insisted on running again, no other candidate or faction dared to challenge the sixty-seven-year-old former president.

In the election campaign, overshadowed by the state of the economy and the foreign debt, the candidates stressed personal style and party tradition. Caldera played the role of elder statesman, projecting experience and wisdom. Since Lusinchi's political experience had been limited to serving in Congress, he could not challenge Caldera in that area. He concentrated instead on a vague promise to implement a new 'social pact' which would enlarge the political Pact of Punto Fijo and establish a genuine social democracy. In the event, Lusinchi's pleasant smile and his reassuring pediatrician's manner attracted more voters than Caldera's more austere image. He won by the largest margin democratic Venezuela had yet seen: 56.8 per cent of the votes to Caldera's 34 per cent. The leftist parties were frustrated and demoralized at their poor showing during a period of severe economic crisis and apparent popular dissatisfaction with both major parties.

THE PRESIDENCY OF JAIME LUSINCHI, 1984–9

AD's decisive electoral victory in 1983 and the humiliation of the opposition parties, together with a national perception of crisis, gave Jaime Lusinchi considerable political leverage during the first half of his presidency. The AD-controlled Congress allowed him to rule by decree for one year (1984–5) in economic matters. His tripartite commissions, with representation of labour, business and political parties, provided the illusion of a government which consulted widely on proposed economic and political measures, although the commissions met in secrecy. Lusinchi's government was quite reluctant to divulge information to the public – unless the news was good. Figures on unemployment or inflation rates, for example, were delayed and made less accessible. In 1986 it became an open secret that the government had applied pressure to newspapers and television networks in an effort to keep criticism and unfavourable reports from public attention. Although still populist in tone, the government during the economic crisis had become less candid and open.

Lusinchi resumed renegotiation of the debt with the major goal of avoiding the intervention of the IMF. Caracas maintained a discreet distance from other Latin American debtors who wanted to discuss a debtors' cartel. Lusinchi's government signed a draconian debt renegotiation agreement with foreign bankers in February 1986, committing from 30 to 45 per cent of government income to debt service and repayment based on the expectation of receiving from U.S. $20 to $24 per barrel for oil. When oil prices dropped to below $15 per barrel, Venezuela successfully argued for a modest relaxation of the original terms. Nonetheless, hoping to impress foreign bankers and investors by a responsible attitude, Venezuela became the only Latin American nation to repay some principal as well as the interest on its debt. The strategy failed to attract new capital or to improve the negative balance of trade, and in 1988 Caracas requested new foreign loans. The banks refused, leaving Venezuela no alternative but to dip into its international reserves to service the debt.

The foreign bankers' committee had insisted that the government guarantee the private foreign debt. By the end of 1985 virtually all of the private debt had been reviewed by RECADI, and half of it – about U.S. $7 billion – received the preferential exchange rate; this was in effect a public subsidy to the private sector. Rumours circulated that government insiders and friends received millions of bolívares in illegal subsidies. Businessmen protested against the secrecy of the RECADI operations and many of its decisions. They loudly proclaimed a lack of confidence in the government and refused to reinvest in Venezuela the estimated (in 1985) $35 billion they had on deposit in U.S. banks.

After 1982 the Venezuelan economy registered a negative growth rate, and new investment virtually ceased. Lusinchi's government combined an austerity programme and reduced government spending with measures to promote non-traditional exports. In general, the strategy to encourage exports favoured the largest industrial establishments that had been subsidized through low import duties on capital goods. AD spokesmen argued that exports rather than products for the domestic market should be subsidized, because the stagnant economy and declining real income discouraged new investment in consumer industries. Some of Lusinchi's advisers – especially his first director of Cordiplan, Luis Raúl Matos Azócar – counselled a more Keynesian strategy of increased government spending to aid the domestic job market, consumer industries and domestic consumption. Yet Matos Azócar's advice went against both the free-market wisdom of the day and the growing political weight of the export-oriented industrialists. The Cordiplan director was forced to resign.

In a half-hearted move towards privatization, Lusinchi liquidated or offered for sale some of the state corporations. The CVF was abolished, although many of its subsidiaries were simply moved to other agencies or ministries. Investors did not leap at the chance to purchase the loss-making operations, and the government remained reluctant to sell operations which provided basic services or heavy industries which were potentially profitable (e.g., steel and petrochemicals). Lusinchi, like Pérez and Herrera before him, made no effort to reshape the nation's economic structure.

In the context of this economic crisis, petroleum marketing stategy became even more critical. COPEI and AD concurred that Venezuela must find a secure market for its oil through 'internationalization'. In 1982, for example, PDVSA invested in the German Veba Oel refinery and agreed to supply it with 100,000 barrels of oil per day. Veba Oel marketed the product in Europe and paid Venezuela in accordance with the price of the finished product – an agreement which provided some secure sales in the glutted international petroleum market. The Venezuelan company followed up this initiative by making similar arrangements with Swedish and U.S. refineries. Venezuela's long-term economic outlook brightened considerably when major new oil finds in 1987 more than doubled the nation's proven reserves from 26 billion to 55 billion barrels.

In the 1980s, however, a declining petroleum income and the decision to favour exports over the domestic market undermined Lusinchi's promise of a new social order. In late 1985 the average monthly food costs for a family of five (1,700 bolívares) easily exceeded the minimum monthly wage for that same average family (1,500 bolívares). At the same time, the official unemployment rate was 14.5 per cent, affecting professionals as well as unskilled workers. In May 1985, CTV president Juan José Delpino startled the president by publicly denouncing his lack of concern for labour, and in January 1986 Lusinchi awarded wage increases of between 7.5 and 20 per cent for workers who earned 6,000 bolívares a month or less. However, the government then effectively cancelled the effects of the increase by allowing controlled prices of such consumer goods as bread, milk and gasoline to rise. Delpino's open challenges to the government heightened speculation that the AD-controlled CTV was becoming more independent of the party.

The government could ill afford to tolerate mass protests or an outbreak of urban crime. Lusinchi's minister of interior, Octavio Lepage, responded to growing complaints about crime by recruiting more police and improving their training and salaries. Caracas was divided into four zones, with patrolling responsibilities to be shared by three police forces (DISIP, PTJ and Policía Metropolitana) and the Guardia Nacional. Although many *caraqueños* welcomed the measures, they also expressed concern over the large-scale detentions – estimated by Amnesty International in 1986 to be nearly 1 million people in the city of 3 to 4 million. Religious groups and human rights activists denounced some cases of torture and of unexplained 'disappearances' from police custody. The 1986 discovery of bodies in abandoned petroleum wells near Maracaibo and the October 1988 murder by special forces of fourteen unarmed fishermen at El Amparo prompted congressional investigations. The government pressured the news media to minimize accounts of human rights violations, drawing criticism for the attempted censorship. Although the public discussion testified to Venezuela's continuing openness, the economic tensions seemed to have strained the tolerance of the Lusinchi administration.

Faculty and student strikes at the Universidad Central de Venezuela in October 1985 and for five months in 1988 once more highlighted problems with education. Reflecting changing times, the issues were less those of political control of the university than of funding it, cost-of-living pay increases for faculty and employees and the division of funds among the various national universities. The immediate issues might have been resolved without the costly strikes, but Lusinchi's minister of education seemed to relish the confrontations. Some influential businessmen cited the strikes, wastefulness and inefficiency of the public universities as an argument for privatization of national higher education.

Many of the educational conflicts of the democratic era focussed on higher education, but the state also experienced difficulty in managing the burgeoning student population at lower levels. In 1985 the illiteracy rate was 12 per cent of a population of 16 million; the minister of education estimated that more than 2 million children between the ages of four and fifteen were not attending school. In an effort to rectify the general problem, the government launched a major adult literacy campaign in 1985. The goal of better health care also receded somewhat in these years. Public health budgets dropped, and the 1980s witnessed a new outbreak of malaria, which had virtually been eliminated several decades earlier.

Apart from matters related to petroleum and the debt, Lusinchi's administration took no significant foreign policy initiatives. Caracas maintained its quiet participation in the Contadora Group and in the Group of Eight (the Contadora four together with Brazil, Uruguay, Argentina and Peru), which evolved as a high-level consultative body for democratic Latin

American heads of state. Negotiation on Venezuela's two major boundary disputes languished, and other regional relations remained much as Herrera Campíns left them.

Rather surprisingly, Venezuelans seemed not to blame Lusinchi personally for his government's inaction or failures. His continuing popularity gave AD an advantage that the incumbent party had not enjoyed in presidential elections since 1963. Still, AD almost squandered that advantage when its old guard tried to deny the nomination to former president Carlos Andrés Pérez. Pérez used his political skills and populist appeal, however, to court labour and the party's rank and file, and he became the standard bearer in 1988.

COPEI's nomination struggle was even more divisive. Rafael Caldera, convinced that only he could defeat Pérez, wanted the nomination for a fifth time, but the younger Eduardo Fernández wrested the prize from his mentor's grasp. In retaliation, Caldera's followers did little to assist Fernández's campaign. Calling himself *el tigre,* Fernández traded insults and charges with the AD candidate, but his moderate programme differed little from that of AD. Not even the leftist MAS and MIR parties, co-operating to support the presidential candidacy of Teodoro Petkoff, advocated any radical solutions to the nation's economic problems. The first woman presidential candidate, Ismenia Villaba, the wife of URD's ailing founder, provided some novelty in the 1988 campaign. With few issues to distinguish the parties and candidates, Pérez's energetic campaigning and his populist image produced a conclusive AD victory. Pérez received 54.8 per cent of the vote to Fernández's 32.9 per cent, thus becoming on 2 February 1989 the first president in the post-1958 era to assume the presidency for a second term.

The extended fiesta of the electoral campaign, the Christmas holidays and the inauguration ended with Pérez's sober announcement in mid-February of new austerity measures that would most seriously affect the working class and the poor. The decree touched off days of looting and rioting in Caracas in February and March in which hundreds were killed and millions of dollars' worth of property destroyed. Unprecedented in the thirty years of democratic government, the riots shook Venezuelans' confidence in their ability to weather the economic crisis without major social upheavals.

Since the 1920s, oil, the 'devil's excrement', had permitted the growth in Venezuela of a middle class and a strong organized labour movement, an extensive government bureaucracy which both delivered services and provided the patronage that could support a democratic system and a population whose health, literacy and per capita income were among the highest in Latin America. Venezuelan democracy since 1958 had remained rooted in the political centre and had proved to be one of the most successful political systems in modern Latin America. Nevertheless, it had shown signs of distinct strain during fifteen years of wildly fluctuating oil prices since 1973.

Populist reformers hoped that they could *sembrar el petróleo* more widely through government spending and state supervision of the petroleum industry and of the economy in general. The generation of 1928 tended to see control over, or ownership of, the petroleum industry as the critical ingredient of economic independence. They did not propose structural change, and their populist commitment to social justice was gradually eroded. Since the 1930s Venezuela's economic structure and economic dependency had not been substantially altered. The government still depended on the export of petroleum for the major portion of its revenues. These revenues underwrote public and mixed enterprises of petrochemicals, steel and a few manufacturing establishments which were highly vulnerable to external markets and credit. These economic patterns necessarily placed a higher priority on externally generated economic growth than on internal social development. At the end of the 1980s the country was unmistakeably better off, more democratic and more stable than sixty years before. Yet Venezuelans remained uncertain about what their children would reap from the petroleum that was 'sown' after the death of Juan Vicente Gómez.

BIBLIOGRAPHICAL ESSAYS

1. ARGENTINA, 1930–46

Still among the best and liveliest introductions to Argentina in the period between the revolution of 1930 and the rise of Perón (1943–6) are three English-language books published in the early 1940s: John W. White, *Argentina, the Life Story of a Nation* (New York, 1942), which aptly captures the puzzled response among North Americans to the apparently hostile attitudes of Argentines during the late 1930s until 1942; Ysabel Rennie, *The Argentine Republic* (New York, 1945), which remains one of the best general introductions to Argentine history and offers an excellent analysis of the years 1943–5; and Felix Weil, *Argentine Riddle* (New York, 1944). Weil, a member of one of the 'Big Four' grain-exporting families, argued for the type of future association between Argentina and the United States that Pinedo and the liberals had aspired to in 1940, in which the United States would take charge of industrializing Argentina. If the book contains this thread of wishful thinking, it also shows an extremely well informed knowledge of Argentine society and the issues facing the country at this critical juncture. A more recent general introduction, containing several excellent essays, is Mark Falcoff and Ronald H. Dolkart (eds.), *Prologue to Perón: Argentina in Depression and War* (Berkeley, Calif., 1975). See also David Rock, *Argentina, 1516–1987* (Berkeley, Calif., 1987), chap. 6, and for a reinterpretation of the 1940s, Carlos H. Waisman, *The Reversal of Development in Argentina* (Princeton, N.J., 1987).

No single book deals exclusively or quite fully with economic issues in this period. The best introductions are Aldo Ferrer, *La economía argentina: Las etapas de su desarrollo y problemas actuales* (Buenos Aires, 1963); Guido Di Tella and Manuel Zymelman, *Las etapas de desarrollo económico argentino* (Buenos Aires, 1967); Carlos F. Díaz Alejandro, *Essays on the Economic*

History of the Argentine Republic (New Haven, Conn., 1970); and Laura Randall, *An Economic History of Argentina in the Twentieth Century* (New York, 1978). For statistical data, see United Nations, Comisión Económica para América Latina, *El desarrollo económica de la Argentina,* 4 vols. (Mexico City, 1959). On farming, see Carl C. Taylor, *Rural Life in Argentina* (Baton Rouge, La., 1948); Darrell F. Fienup, Russell H. Brannon and Frank A. Fender, *The Agricultural Development of Argentina: A Policy and Development Perspective* (New York, 1969); and Jaime Fuchs, *Argentina: Su desarrollo capitalista* (Buenos Aires, 1965). On industry, see George Wythe, *Industry in Latin Ameria* (New York, 1945); Adolfo Dorfman, *Historia de la industria argentina* (Buenos Aires, 1970); Thomas C. Cochran and Rubén Reina, *Espíritu de empresa en la Argentina* (Buenos Aires, 1965), which examines the career of Torcuato Di Tella, the industrialist; and Miguel Murmis and Juan Carlos Portantiero, 'Crecimiento industrial y alianza de clases en la Argentina (1930–1940)', in Miguel Murmis and Juan Carlos Portantiero, *Estudios sobre los orígenes del peronisno* (Buenos Aires, 1971). An important recent addition to this literature is Paul H. Lewis, *The Crisis of Argentine Capitalism* (Chapel Hill, 1990). The best available studies of population and migration stem from the Centro de Estudios de Población in Buenos Aires headed by Alfredo E. Lattes; for an introduction, see Zulma Recchini de Lattes and Alfredo E. Lattes, *La problación de Argentina* (Buenos Aires, 1975). Foreign investment, foreign debt and many trade issues are discussed in Harold J. Peters, *The Foreign Debt of the Argentine Republic* (Baltimore, 1934); Vernon L. Phelps, *The International Economic Position of Argentina* (Philadelphia, 1938); and Roger Gravil, *The Anglo-Argentine Connection, 1900–1939* (Boulder, Colo., 1985).

The two best general introductions to Argentine politics after 1930 are Robert A. Potash, *The Army and Politics in Argentina, 1928–1945: Yrigoyen to Perón* (Stanford, Calif., 1969), and Alain Rouquié, *Poder Militar y sociedad política en la Argentina,* 2 vols. (Buenos Aires, 1982). See also Alberto Ciria, *Parties and Power in Modern Argentina* (Albany, N.Y., 1974); Carlos Ibarguren, *La historia que he vivido* (Buenos Aires, 1955); Richard J. Walter, *The Province of Buenos Aires and Argentine Politics, 1912–1943* (Cambridge, 1984). For additional information on the 1930 revolution see David Rock, *Politics in Argentina, 1890–1930: The Rise and Fall of Radicalism* (Cambridge, 1975); and Peter H. Smith, 'The Breakdown of Democracy in Argentina, 1916–1930', in Juan J. Linz and Alfred Stepan (eds.), *The Breakdown of Democratic Regimes in Latin America* (Baltimore, 1978), pp. 3–25. For economic policy issues under Justo, see Peter H. Smith, *Politics and Beef in Argentina: Patterns of Conflict and Change* (New York, 1969); Daniel

Drosdoff, *El gobierno de las vacas, 1933–1956: Tratado Roca–Runciman* (Buenos Aires, 1972); Pedro Skupch, 'El deterioro y fin de la hegemonía británica sobre la economía argentina, 1914–1947', in Miguel Murmis and Juan Carlos Portantiero (eds.), *Estudios sobre los orígines del peronismo,* vol. 2 (Buenos Aires, 1973); and Gravil, *The Anglo-Argentine Connection.*

Studies of the political parties during this period are almost non-existent. But see Ciria, *Parties and Power,* and Peter G. Snow, *El radicalismo argentino* (Buenos Aires, 1972). On trade unions, see Hiroschi Matsushita, *Movimiento obrero argentino: Sus proyecciones en la historia del peronismo* (Buenos Aires, 1983); Louise Doyon, 'Organised Labor and Perón: A Study in the Conflictual Dynamics of the Peronist Movement' (Ph. D. dissertation, University of Toronto, 1978); and David Tamarin, *The Argentine Labor Movement, 1930–1945* (Albuquerque, N.M., 1985). Tamarin's work not only deals most informatively with the unions, but provides an excellent account of the workers' role in the events of October 1945. A second outstanding piece is Daniel James, 'October 17th and 18th, 1945: Mass Protest, Peronism and the Argentine Working Class,' *Journal of Social History,* 2 (Spring 1988), pp. 441–61. On the Fuerza de Orientación Radical de la Juventud (FORJA), see Mark Falcoff, 'Argentine Nationalism on the Eve of Perón: The Force of Radical Orientation of Young Argentina and Its Rivals, 1935–45' (Ph.D. dissertation, Princeton University, 1970); Arturo Jauretche, *FORJA y la década infame* (Buenos Aires, 1962). For the *nacionalistas,* see Marysa Navarro Gerassi, *Los nacionalistas* (Buenos Aires, 1969); Enrique Zuleta Alvarez, *El nacionalismo argentino,* 2 vols. (Buenos Aires, 1975); and María Inés Barbero and Fernando Devoto, *Los nacionalistas, 1910–1932* (Buenos Aires, 1983). Federico Ibarguren, *Los orígenes del nacionalismo argentino, 1927–1937* (Buenos Aires, 1969), provides a fascinating glimpse into the *nacionalista* mentality. For *nacionalismo* in the army, see Robert A. Potash (comp.), *Perón y el G.O.U.: Los documentos de una logia secreta* (Buenos Aires, 1984). A work which contains extensive material on this period is David Rock, *Authoritarian Argentina: A History of the Nationalist Movement* (Austin, forthcoming). For an introduction to historical revisionism, see Rodolfo Irazusta and Julio Irazusta, *La Argentina y el imperialismo británico: Los eslabones de una cadena, 1806–1933* (Buenos Aires, 1934).

The past few years have seen the appearance of several high-quality works on the British–Argentine–U.S. triangle in both its economic and political aspects. See Jorge Fodor and Arturo O'Connell, 'La Argentina y la economía atlántica en la primera mitad del siglo veinte', *Desarrollo Económico,* 13, no. 49 (1973), pp. 1–67; Michael J. Francis, *The Limits of*

Hegemony: United States Relations with Argentina and Chile during World War II (Notre Dame, Ind., 1977); Mario Rapoport, *Gran Bretaña, Estados Unidos y las clases dirigentes argentinas* (Buenos Aires, 1981); Carlos Escudé, *Gran Bretaña, Estados Unidos y la declinación argentina, 1942–1949* (Buenos Aires, 1982); R. A. Humphreys, *Latin America and the Second World War*, 2 vols. (London, 1981–2); and C. A. MacDonald, 'The Politics of Intervention: The United States and Argentina, 1941–1946', *Journal of Latin American Studies*, 12, pt. 2 (November 1980), pp. 365–96. For wartime British attitudes towards Argentina, see Sir David Kelly, *The Ruling Few, or The Human Background to Diplomacy* (London, 1953), and for the official line from the United States, Cordell Hull, *The Memoirs*, 2 vols. (New York, 1948). David Green, *The Containment of Latin America: A History of the Myths and Realities of the Good Neighbor Policy* (Chicago, 1971), sheds much light on the attitudes and behaviour of American policy-makers. See also Bryce Wood, *The Dismantling of the Good Neighbor Policy* (Austin, Tex., 1985). A facsimile of the Pinedo Plan appears in *Desarrollo Económico*, 19, no. 75 (1979) pp. 403–26.

On the rise of Perón, the most outstanding works are Potash, *Army and Politics*, and Samuel L. Baily, *Labor, Nationalism and Politics in Argentina* (New Brunswick, N.J., 1967). See also Doyon, 'Organised Labour'; Matsushita, *Movimiento obrero;* Tamarin, *Argentine Labor Movement;* Eldon Kenworthy, 'The Formation of the Peronist Coalition' (Ph.D. dissertation, Yale University, 1970); and Enrique Díaz Araujo, *La conspiración del '43* (Buenos Aires, 1971). For personal details on Perón, see Joseph A. Page, *Perón, a Biography* (New York, 1983). The best accounts of Braden's role in 1945–6 are MacDonald, 'The Politics of Intervention', and Green, *Containment of Latin America*, while the 1946 election has been studied intensively in Manuel Mora y Araujo and Ignacio Llorente (eds.), *El voto peronista: Ensayos de sociología electoral argentina* (Buenos Aires, 1980). Of particular note are essays by Peter H. Smith and Gino Germani. For statistics on the election, see Darío Cantón, *Materiales para el estudio de la sociología política de la Argentina*, 2 vols. (Buenos Aires, 1969).

2. ARGENTINA SINCE 1946

Economy

G. Di Tella and M. Zymelman, *Las etapas del desarrollo económico argentino* (Buenos Aires, 1967), is a general work inspired by W. W. Rostow's stages of growth theory. Aldo Ferrer, *The Argentine Economy* (Berkeley,

Calif., 1967), first published in Spanish in 1964, is a less factual, much more interpretive account that reflects views on development and dependency typical of the late 1950s and early 1960s. Ferrer's *Crisis y alternativas de la política económica* (Buenos Aires, 1977) brings the analysis up to the late 1970s. Carlos Díaz Alejandro, *Essays on the Economic History of the Argentine Republic* (New Haven, Conn., 1970), is a collection of excellent economic analyses of different aspects of Argentine history that has been very influential. Laura Randall, *An Economic History of Argentina in the Twentieth Century* (New York, 1978), tries to interpret Argentina's development as a succession of rather clear-cut economic models; some historians have found it unconvincing. R. Mallon and J. V. Sourruoille, *Economic Policy in a Conflict Society: The Argentine Case* (Cambridge, Mass., 1975), explores economic problems, particularly in the mid-1960s, without excluding political variables. D. Rock, *Argentina, 1516–1987: From Spanish Colonization to Alfonsín* (Berkeley, Calif., 1987), is a comprehensive history that reveals great economic insight; it is the best introduction to the history of Argentina in this period. Gary Wynia, *Argentina in the Post-War Era: Politics and Economic Policy Making in a Divided Society* (Albuquerque, N.M., 1978), concentrates on decision making in the period from 1946 to 1976. Two general essays discuss the main issues in the economic history of the period: G. Di Tella, 'Controversias económicas en la Argentina, 1930–1970', in J. Fogarty, E. Gallo and H. Dieguez (eds.), *Argentina y Australia* (Buenos Aires, 1979), pp. 165–84; and C. Díaz Alejandro, 'No Less Than One Hundred Years of Argentine Economic History Plus Some Comparisons', in G. Ranis, R. L. West, M. W. Leiserson and C. Taft Morris (eds.), *Comparative Development Perspectives: Essays in Honor of Lloyd G. Reynolds* (Boulder, Colo., 1984), pp. 328–58. One of the best and most comprehensive collections of essays on the economic history of post-war Argentina is G. Di Tella and R. Dornbusch (eds.), *The Political Economy of Argentina, 1946–1983* (London, 1989), which analyses the economic policies of every government from Perón's first presidency to the most recent military administration. J. C. de Pablo, *La economía que yo hice* (Buenos Aires, 1980), presents a series of interviews with officials in charge of economic affairs since the 1940s and contains much useful historical information.

Beginning in 1949 the influence of the UN Economic Commission for Latin America (ECLA) under the intellectual leadership of R. Prebisch was widely felt in both political and professional fields. The 1949 ECLA report reflected the post-war spirit in its deep scepticism of the role of foreign trade and its stress on import substitution and industrialization in the internal market. See ECLA, *Economic Development of Latin America and Its Principal Problems* (New York, 1949). The questioning of the ECLA model in the 1960s is reflected in Mario Brodershon (ed.), *Estrategias de industrialización para América Latina* (Buenos Aires, 1967); the contribution by David Félix, 'Más allá de la sustitución de importaciones, un dilema latinoamericano', is a good example of the new perspective. See also Félix's 'The Dilemma of Import Substitution: Argentina', in G. Papanek (ed.), *Development Policy: Theory and Practice* (Cambridge, Mass., 1968), pp. 55–91. M. Diamand, *Doctrinas económicas, desarrollo e independencia económica* (Buenos Aires, 1973), presents an original analysis of the structural imbalance found in the Argentine productive sectors. In the 1970s and 1980s the focus of interest shifted to the causes of Argentine stagnation and decline. A good example of the changing emphasis is the work of J. J. Llach and P. Gerchunoff on the 1964–74 growth experience: 'Capitalismo industrial, desarrollo asociado y distribución del ingreso entre los dos gobiernos peronistas', *Desarrollo Económico*, 15, no. 57 (1975), pp. 3–54, and the subsequent debate in *Desarrollo Económico*, 15, no. 60 (1976), pp. 612–39. The weak economic performance of Argentina and the need for institutional reforms are explored in D. Cavallo and Y. Mundlak, 'Agriculture and Economic Growth: The Case of Argentina', *Research Report 36* (Washington, D.C., 1982); D. Cavallo, *Volver a crecer* (Buenos Aires, 1984); J. J. Llach, *Reconstrucción o estancamiento* (Buenos Aires, 1987); Secretaría de Planificación, *Lineamientos para una estrategia de crecimiento* (Buenos Aires, 1985); and C. A. Rodríguez, 'Estabilización versus cambio estructural: La experiencia argentina', Centro de Estudios Macroeconómicos de Argentina, Documento de Trabajo 62 (1988).

On inflation and stabilization policies in the 1950s and 1960s, see A. Ferrer (ed.), *Los planes de estabilización en Argentina* (Buenos Aires, 1967), with contributions from the editor, M. Brodershon, and E. Eshag and R. Thorp; Eshag and Thorp's article, 'Economic and Social Consequences of Orthodox Policies in Argentina in the Post-War Years', was originally published in *Bulletin of the Oxford Institute of Economics and Statistics* (February 1965), pp. 3–44. See also C. Díaz Alejandro, *Exchange Rate Devaluation in a Semiindustrialized Country: The Experience of Argentina, 1955–1961* (Cambridge, Mass., 1965). Against the conventional wisdom of the time, Díaz Alejandro demonstrated that exchange devaluations may have recessive consequences in a country with an export-oriented agriculture and an inward-oriented industry. This idea had a far-reaching impact. For the period from 1966 to 1973, J. C. de Pablo, 'Relative Prices, Income

Distribution and Stabilization Plans, 1967–1970', *Journal of Development Economics,* 1(1974), pp. 50–78, is an important article; an expanded version is *Politica anti-inflacionaria en Argentina, 1967–1970* (Buenos Aires, 1972). On the same period, see G. Maynard and W. van Ryckeshen, 'Stabilization Policy in an Inflationary Economy', in Papanek (ed.), *Development Policy,* pp. 207–35; G. Di Tella, *Argentina under Perón, 1973–1976* (London, 1983), studies the problems of stabilizing the economy under a labour-based government; see also A. Canitrot, 'La experiencia populista de redistribución de ingresos', *Desarrollo Económico,* 15, no. 59 (1975), pp. 331–51, which underlines the inherent contradictions of the populist model. The stabilization efforts of the military regime between 1976 and 1982 produced very interesting analyses from different perspectives: A. Canitrot, 'Teoría y práctica del liberalismo: Política anti-inflacionaria y apertura económica en la Argentina', *Desarrollo Económico,* 21, no. 82 (1981), pp. 131–89; J. L. Machinea, 'The Use of Exchange Rates as an Anti-inflationary Instrument in a Stabilization-Liberalization Attempt' (Ph. D. dissertation, University of Minnesota, 1983); R. B. Fernández and C. A. Rodríguez (eds.), *Inflación y estabilidad* (Buenos Aires, 1982); and J. Schvarser, *Martínez de Hoz, la lógica política de la política económica* (Buenos Aires, 1983). For conceptual approaches to the theory of inflation, see J. Olivera, 'On Structural Inflation and Latin American Structuralism', *Oxford Economic Papers,* 16 (November 1964), pp. 321–32; idem, 'On Structural Stagflation', *Journal of Development Economics,* 6, no. 4 (1979), pp. 549–55; and A. Canavese, 'The Structuralist Explanation in the Theory of Inflation', *World Development,* 10 (July 1982), pp. 523–9. The monetarist approach is well argued in Fernández and Rodriguez (eds.), *Inflación y estabilidad.* J. J. Llach, 'La megainflación argentina', in N. Botana and P. Waldman (eds.), *El impacto de la inflación* (Buenos Aires, 1988), pp. 75–98, presents an institutional approach. The role of inertial factors in inflation is underlined in R. Frenkel, 'Salarios e inflación: Resultados de investigaciones recientes en Argentina, Brasil Colombia, Costa Rica y Chile', *Desarrollo Económico,* 25, no. 100 (1986), pp. 387–414, the approach of which inspired the Austral Plan launched by the Alfonsín administration in 1985. For the latter experience, see the essays in M. Bruno, G. Di Tella and R. Dorbusch (eds.), *Inflation Stabilization: The Experience of Israel, Argentina, Brazil, Bolivia and Mexico* (Cambridge, Mass., 1988); D. Heyman, *Tres ensayos sobre inflación y políticas de estabilización* (Buenos Aires, 1986); P. Gerchunoff and C. Bozzalla, 'Posibilidades y límites de un programa de estabilización heterodoxo', in J. Villanueva (ed.), *Empleo, inflación y comercio internacional* (Buenos Aires,

1988), pp. 61–105; R. Dornbusch and M. Simonsen, *Inflation Stabilization with Income Policy Support* (Cambridge, Mass., 1986); and R. Frenkel and J. M. Fanelli, *Políticas de estabilización hiperinflación en Argentina* (Buenos Aires, 1990). The account of J. L. Machinea (president of the Central Bank at the time), 'Stabilization under Alfonsín's Government', Centro de Estudios de Estado y Sociedad (CEDES), Documento de Trabajo 42 (1990), must be consulted.

On the evolution of Argentine industry, see A. Dorfman, *Cincuenta años de industrialización argentina, 1930–1980* (Buenos Aires, 1983); J. Katz and B. Kosacoff, *El sector manufacturero argentino: Maduración, retroceso y prospectiva* (Buenos Aires, 1989); and B. Kosacoff and D. Aspiazu, *La industria argentina, desarrollo y cambios estructurales* (Buenos Aires, 1989). On the controversial issue of industrial policies a number of works deserve mention: H. H. Schwartz, 'The Argentine Experience with Industrial Credit and Protection Incentives, 1943–1958' (Ph.D. dissertation, Yale University, 1967), is a pioneer work. See also O. Altimir, H. Santamaria and J. V. Sourrouille, 'Los instrumentos de la promoción industrial en la postguerra', *Desarrollo Económico*, 6, no. 24 (1967), pp. 709–34; J. Berlinski and D. Schydlowsky, 'Incentives for Industrialization in Argentina', in B. Balassa (ed.), *Development Strategies in Semi-industrialized Countries* (Baltimore, 1982), pp. 83–121; J. Berlinski, 'La protección efectiva de actividades seleccionadas de la industria argentina', Instituto Di Tella, CIE, Documento de Trabajo 119 (1985); D. Artana, 'Incentivos fiscales a la inversión industrial', Instituto Di Tella, CIE, Documento de Trabajo 151 (1987); J. Schvarser, 'Promoción industrial Argentina', Centro de Investigaciones Sociales sobre Estado y Administración (CISEA), Documento de Trabajo 90 (1987); S. Teitel and F. Thomi, 'From Import Substitution to Exports: The Recent Experience of Argentina and Brasil', *Economic Development and Cultural Change* (April 1986), pp. 455–90; and J. Nogues, 'Economía política del proteccionismo y la liberalización en Argentina', *Desarrollo Económico*, 28, no. 110 (1988), pp. 159–82.

On agriculture, see C. Díaz Alejandro, 'An Interpretation of Argentine Economic Growth since 1930', *Journal of Development Studies*, pt. 1 (1966), pp. 14–41, pt. 2 (1967), pp. 155–77, is a good example of a negative view of Perón's agricultural policies; J. Fodor gives a different account in 'Perón's Policies for Agricultural Exports, 1946–1948: Dogmatism or Common Sense?' in D. Rock (ed.), *Argentina in the Twentieth Century* (Pittsburgh, Pa., 1975), pp. 135–61. For many years, works in this field focussed on the alleged lack of price elasticity of agricultural production.

L. Reca made a substantial contribution, emphasizing the role of prices, which had previously been underrated, in 'The Price and Production Duality within Argentine Agriculture' (Ph.D. dissertation, University of Chicago, 1967), and further works such as 'Determinantes de la oferta agropecuaria en la Argentina', *Instituto de Investigaciones Económicas de la CGE, Estudios sobre la economia argentina*, 5 (1969), pp. 57–65. Later, E. S. de Obschatko and M. Piñeiro, *Agricultura pampeana: Cambio tecnológico y sector privado* (Buenos Aires, 1986), drew attention to the great technological transformation which took place in agriculture from the 1970s and which led to a great increase in production and productivity.

On the labour market and wages, the following works are recommended: J. J. Llach and C. Sánchez, 'Los determinantes del salario en Argentina', *Estudios*, 7, no. 29 (1984), pp. 1–47; H. Dieguez and P. Gerchunoff, 'Dinámica del mercado laboral urbano en Argentina, 1976–1982', *Desarrollo Económico*, 24, no. 93 (1984), pp. 3–40; A. Marshall, *El mercado del trabajo en el capitalismo periférico* (Santiago de Chile, 1978); L. Beccaria and G. Yoguel, 'Apuntes sobre la evolución del empleo industrial en 1973–1984', *Desarrollo Económico*, 27. no. 1 (1988), pp. 589–606; R. Frenkel, 'Salarios industriales e inflación, 1976–1982', *Desarrollo Económico*, 24, no. 95 (1984), pp. 387–414; and J. L. Llach, *Políticas de ingresos en la década del noventa: Un retorno a la economía política* (Buenos Aires, 1990). The reports produced by Proyecto Argentina PNUD and International Labor Organization entitled *Employment, Human Resources and Wages* and published by the Ministry of Labour between 1984 and 1989 are indispensable.

Little attention was given to the public sector until the mid-1980s; Secretaría de Hacienda, *Política para el cambio estructural en el sector público* (1989), brings together the presidential messages to Congress on the occasion of the passage of the 1986–9 budget laws; particularly useful is the 1989 message, which traces the evolution of the role of the public sector in Argentina since 1930. On the fiscal crisis three works deserve mention: P. Gerchunoff and M. Vicens, *Gasto público, recursos públicos y financiamiento de una economía en crisis: El caso de Argentina* (Buenos Aires, 1989); R. Carciofi, *La desarticulación del Pacto Fiscal: Una interpretación sobre la evolución del sector público argentino en las últimas dos décadas* (Buenos Aires, 1989); and A. Porto, *Federalismo fiscal* (Buenos Aires, 1990). For a different point of view, see Fundación de Investigaciones Económicas Latinoamericanas (FIEL), *El fracaso del estatismo: Una propuesta para la reforma del sector público argentino* (Buenos Aires, 1987).

For the external debt and its repercussions, see E. A. Zalduendo, *La deuda externa* (Buenos Aires, 1988); E. Feldman and J. Sommer, *Crisis financiera y endeudamiento externo en la Argentina* (Buenos Aires, 1986); R. Frenkel, J. M. Fanelli and J. Sommer, 'El proceso del endeudamiento externo argentino', CEDES, Documento de Trabajo 2 (1988); R. Bouzas and S. Keifman, 'Las negociaciones financieras externas de Argentina en el período 1982–1987', in R. Bouzas (ed.), *Entre la heterodoxia y el ajuste* (Buenos Aires, 1988), pp. 27–84; A. García and S. Junco, 'Historia de la renegociación de la deuda externa argentina', *Boletín Informativo Techint*, 245 (1987), pp. 29–58; and J. C. de Pablo and R. Dornbusch, *Deuda externa e inestabilidad macroeconómica en Argentina* (Buenos Aires, 1988).

Politics and society

There are few general works on political and social development over the entire period from 1946 to 1989. The best account available in English is D. Rock, *Argentina, 1516–1987* (Berkeley, Calif., 1987). See also C. Floria and C. García Belsunce, *Historia política de la Argentina contemporánea, 1880–1983* (Madrid, 1988); J. E. Corradi, *The Fitful Republic: Economy, Society and Politics in Argentina* (Boulder, Colo., 1985); G. Wynia, *Argentina: Illusions and Reality* (New York, 1986); and a well-documented chronicle, E. Crawley, *A House Divided: Argentina, 1880–1980* (London, 1985). Although their main subject is the role of the military in politics, R. Potash, *The Army and Politics in Argentina, 1945–1962* (Stanford, Calif., 1980), and A. Rouquié, *Pouvoir militaire et société politique en Republique Argentine* (Paris, 1978), provide general insights for the years up to the 1970s. T. Halperín Donghi, *Argentina, la democracia de masas* (Buenos Aires, 1983), is another valuable contribution. See also M. Peralta Ramos, *Acumulación de capital y crisis políticas en Argentina, 1930–1974* (Mexico, 1978). In a more interpretive vein, several essays deserve mention: G. O'Donnell, 'State and Alliances in Argentina, 1956–1976', *Journal of Development Studies,* 15, no. 1 (1978), pp. 3–33; idem, 'El juego imposible: Competición y coaliciones entre partidos políticos en la Argentina, 1955–1966', which is included in his *Modernization and Bureaucratic Authoritarianism: Studies in South American Politics* (Berkeley, Calif., 1973), pp. 180–213; M. Mora y Araujo, 'El ciclo político argentino', *Desarrollo Económico,* 22, no. 86 (1982), pp. 203–30; idem, 'El estatismo y los problemas políticos desarrollo argentino', in C. Floria (ed.), *Argentina política* (Buenos Aires, 1983), pp. 31–64; and J. C. Portantiero, 'La crisis de un régimen: Una visión retrospectiva', in J. Nun and J. C. Portantiero (eds.), *Ensayos sobre la transición democrática argentina* (Buenos Aires, 1987), pp. 57–80.

On Argentina's social structure, the works of G. Germani, *Estructura social de la Argentina* (Buenos Aires, 1987) and *Política y sociedad en una época de transición* (Buenos Aires, 1965), are of seminal importance. See also ECLA, *Economic Development and Income Distribution in Argentina* (New York, 1969); J. L. Imaz, *Those Who Rule* (Albany, N.Y., 1970); O. Altimir, 'Estimaciones de la distribución del ingreso en Argentina, 1953–1980', *Desarrollo Económico,* 25, no. 100 (1986), pp. 521–66; H. Palomino, 'Cambios ocupacionales y sociales en Argentina, 1947–1985', CISEA, Documento de Trabajo 88 (1987), p. 213; J. Nun, 'Cambios en la estructura social de la Argentina', in Nun and Portantiero (eds.), *La transición democrática argentina,* pp. 117–37; S. Torrado, 'La estructura social de la Argentina, 1945–1983', Centro de Estudios Urbanos, Documento de Trabajo 14 and 15 (1988); Instituto Nacional de Estadísticas y Censos, *La pobreza en Argentina* (Buenos Aires, 1984); idem, *La pobreza en el conurbano bonaerense* (Buenos Aires, 1989). A good bibliography can be found in S. Bagu, *Argentina, 1875–1975: Población, economía y sociedad – Estudio temático y bibliográfico* (Mexico, 1978).

On the military, in addition to the books by Potash and Rouquié already mentioned, see G. O'Donnell, 'Modernization and Military Coups: Theory, Practice and the Argentine Case', in A. Lowenthal (ed.), *Armies and Politics in Latin America* (New York, 1976), pp. 197–243; A. Rouquié, 'Hegemonia militar, estado y dominación social', in A. Rouquié (ed.), *Argentina hoy* (Mexico, 1982); and D. Cantón, *La política de los militares argentinos, 1900–1971* (Buenos Aires, 1971).

On political parties and the Congress, see D. Cantón, *Elecciones y partidos en la Argentina* (Buenos Aires, 1973); P. Snow, *Political Forces in Argentina* (Boston, 1971); D. James, 'The Peronist Left', *Journal of Latin American Studies* 8, no. 2 (1976), pp. 273–96; M. Acuña, *De Frondizi a Alfonsín: La tradición política del radicalismo,* 2 vols. (Buenos Aires, 1984); M. Cavarossi, *Peronismo y radicalismo, transiciones y perspectivas* (Buenos Aires, 1988); D. Cantón, *El Parlamento argentino en épocas de cambio* (Buenos Aires, 1966); M. Goretti and M. Panosyan, 'El personal parlamentario frente a un contexto político cambiante', in *Dos ensayos de ciencia política* (Buenos Aires, 1986); L. de Riz et al., *El parlamento hoy* (Buenos Aires, 1986); and idem, 'Régimen de gobierno y gobernabilidad: Parlamentarismo en Argentina', in D.

Nohlen and A. Solari (eds.), *Reform política y consolidación democrática: Europa y América Latina* (Caracas, 1988), pp. 273–85.

On trade unions, see S. Baily, *Labor, Nationalism and Politics in Argentina* (New Brunswick, N.J., 1967); R. Carri, *Sindicatos y poder en Argentina* (Buenos Aires, 1967); M. Cavarozzi, 'Peronismo, sindicatos y política en la Argentina, 1943–1981', in P. González Casanova (ed.), *Historia del movimiento obrero en América Latina* (México, 1984), pp. 146–99; D. James, *Resistance and Integration: Peronism and the Argentine Working Class, 1946–1976* (Cambridge, 1988); G. Ducatenzeiler, *Syndicats et politique en Argentine, 1955–1973* (Montreal, 1981); R. Rotondaro, *Realidad y dinámica del sindicalismo* (Buenos Aires, 1974); T. Di Tella, *El sistema político argentino y la clase obrera* (Buenos Aires, 1964); R. Zorrilla, *Estructura y dinámica del sindicalismo argentino* (Buenos Aires, 1974); and S. Senen González, *Diez años de sindicalismo, de Perón al proceso* (Buenos Aires, 1984); E. C. Epstein, 'Labor Populism and Hegemonic Crisis in Argentina', in Epstein (ed.), *Labor Autonomy and the State in Latin America* (Boston, 1989), pp. 13–37.

On entrepreneurs, see J. Freels, *El sector industrial en la política nacional* (Buenos Aires, 1970); J. Niosi, *Los empresarios y el estado argentino* (Buenos Aires, 1974); D. Cúneo, *Crisis y comportamiento de la clase empresaria* (Buenos Aires, 1967); M. L. de Palomino, *Tradición y poder: La sociedad rural argentina, 1955–1983* (Buenos Aires, 1988); D. Azpiazu, E. Basualdo and M. Khavisse, *El nuevo poder económico en la Argentina de los años 80* (Buenos Aires, 1986); R. Sidicaro, 'Poder y crisis de la gran burguesía agraria argentina', in A. Rouquié (ed.), *Argentina hoy,* pp. 51–104; and P. Ostiguy, *Los capitanes de la industria* (Buenos Aires, 1990).

On Argentina's foreign relations, see in particular J. A. Lanus, *De Chapultepec al Beagle* (Buenos Aires, 1984); J. S. Tulchin, *Argentina and the United States: A Conflicted Relationship* (Boston, 1990); and C. Escudé, *Gran Bretaña, Estados Unidos y la Declinación Argentina, 1942–1949* (Buenos Aires, 1983).

On Perón's first two terms in office between 1946 and 1955, see the perceptive and colorful historical reconstruction by F. Luna, *Perón y su tiempo,* 3 vols. (Buenos Aires, 1984–6). Profiles of the two major characters of those years can be found in J. Page, *Perón: A Biography* (New York, 1983), and Nicholas Fraser and Marysa Navarro, *Eva Perón* (New York, 1980). The sociological approach is represented by J. Kirkpatrick, *Leader and Vanguard in Mass Society: A Study of Peronist Argentina* (Cambridge, Mass., 1971), and P. Waldman, *El peronismo* (Buenos Aires, 1981). A.

Ciria, *Política y cultura popular, la Argentina peronista, 1946–1955* (Buenos Aires, 1983), deals well with the workings of *peronista* ideology in practice. A useful introductory treatment of a neglected topic is offered by W. Little in 'Party and State in Peronist Argentina', *Hispanic American Historical Review*, 53 (1973), pp. 628–56. L. Doyon, 'Organized Labor and Perón, 1945–1955' (Ph.D. dissertation, University of Toronto, 1978), is indispensable. Some chapters of Doyon's thesis and other valuable contributions are collected in J. C. Torre (ed.), *La formación del sindicalismo peronista* (Buenos Aires, 1988); see also J. C. Torre, *La vieja guardia sindical y Perón* (Buenos Aires, 1990). The relations between Perón and the military are examined in the books already mentioned by R. Potash and A. Rouquié. An informative account of Perón's fall is given in J. Godio, *La caída de Perón* (Buenos Aires, 1973).

On Frondizi's government, see Celia Szusterman, 'Developmentalism and Political Change in Argentina, 1958–1962' (D.Phil. dissertation, Oxford University, 1986); M. Barrera, *Information and Ideology: A Case Study of Arturo Frondizi* (Beverly Hills, Calif., 1973); D. Rodríguez Lamas, *La presidencia de Frondizi* (Buenos Aires, 1984); N. Babini's memoirs, *Frondizi: De la oposición al gobierno* (Buenos Aires, 1984); and E. Kvaternik, *Crisis sin salvataje* (Buenos Aires, 1987). On Illia's presidency see E. Kvaternik, *El péndulo cívico militar, la caída de Illia* (Buenos Aires, 1990). On both presidencies, C. Smulovitz, 'Opposition and Government in Argentina: The Frondizi and Illia Years' (Ph.D. dissertation, Pennsylvania State University, 1990), deserves mention.

The period of military rule between 1966 and 1972 is the subject of a major work by G. O'Donnell, *El estado burocrático autoritario* (Buenos Aires, 1981). See also W. C. Smith, *Authoritarianism and the Crisis of the Argentine Political Economy* (Stanford, Calif., 1989); N. Botana, R. Braun and C. Floria, *El régimen militar, 1966–1972* (Buenos Aires, 1973); F. Delich, *Crisis y protesta social: Córdoba, mayo de 1969* (Buenos Aires, 1970); and R. Perina, *Onganía, Levingston, Lanusse: Los militares en la política argentina* (Buenos Aires, 1983). The memoirs of General Onganía's secretary, Roberto Roth, *Los años de Onganía* (Buenos Aires, 1980), and those of General Agustín Lanusse, *Mi Testimonio* (Buenos Aires, 1977), deserve careful reading.

On Perón's return to power in 1973, see Di Tella, *Argentina under Perón* and L. de Riz, *Retorno y derrumbe: El último gobierno peronista* (México, 1981). The collection of essays compiled by F. Turner and J. E. Miguenz, *Juan Perón and the Reshaping of Argentina* (Pittsburgh, Pa., 1983), contains good analyses of the period. See also M. Mora y Araujo, 'Las bases estructurales del peronismo' and 'Peronismo y desarrollo', in M. Mora y Araujo and I. Lorente (eds.), *El voto peronista* (Buenos Aires, 1980), pp. 397–440. The role of trade unions is studied in J. C. Torre, *Los sindicatos en el gobierno, 1973–1976* (Buenos Aires, 1983). A very illuminating study of Perón's political discourse and its relation to the youth movement is S. Sigal and E. Veron, *Perón o muerte* (Buenos Aires, 1986).

On the military regime of 1976–83 see, for a general view, P. Waldman and E. Garzón Valdez (eds.), *El poder militar en Argentina, 1976–1983* (Frankfurt, 1982); M. Peralta Ramos and C. Waisman (eds.), *From Military Rule to Liberal Democracy in Argentina* (Boulder, Colo., 1987); and Smith, *Authoritarianism,* pp. 224–66. A. Fontana, 'Policy Making by a Military Corporation: Argentina, 1976–1983' (Ph. D. dissertation, University of Texas, 1987), deserves mention. On the guerrilla movement the best study available is R. Gillespie, *Soldiers of Perón: Argentina's Montoneros* (Oxford, 1982). For documents and reports on the human rights issue, see Comisión Nacional sobre la Desaparición de Personas, *Nunca más* (Buenos Aires, 1984; Engl. trans., 1986); and Organization of American States, Inter-American Commission on Human Rights, *Report on the Situation of Human Rights in Argentina* (Washington, D.C., 1980); C. Escude, 'Argentina: The Costs of Contradiction: 1943–1955 and 1976–1983', in A. F. Lowenthal (ed.), *Exporting Democracy: The United States and Latin America* (Baltimore, 1991), sheds light on the contradictions of President Carter's human rights policy. The Malvinas War has been extensively documented; O. Cardozo, R. Kirshbaum and E. Van de Kooy, *Malvinas: La trama secreta* (Buenos Aires, 1983), and M. Hastings and S. Jenkins, *The Battle for the Falklands* (New York, 1983), present both sides of the conflict.

Although a global assessment of Alfonsín's presidency is still lacking, several works deserve mention: M. Mora y Araujo, 'The Nature of the Alfonsín Coalition', and M. Cavarozzi, 'Peronism and Radicalism: Argentina's Transition in Perspective', in P. Drake and E. Silva (eds.), *Elections and Democratization in Latin America* (San Diego, Calif., 1986), pp. 143–88; E. Catterberg, *Los Argentinos frente a la política* (Buenos Aires, 1989); N. Botana et al., *La Argentina electoral* (Buenos Aires, 1985); Nun and Portantiero (eds.), *La transición democrática argentina;* N. Botana and A. M. Mustapic, 'La reforma constitucional frente al régimen político argentino', Instituto Di Tella, Documento de Trabajo 101 (1988); M. Cavarossi and M. Grossi, 'De la reinvención democrática al reflujo político y la hiperinflación', *Consejo Latinoamericano de Ciencias Sociales,* GTPP

12 (1989); J. C. Torre, "Economá ed política nella transizione argentina: Da Alfonsín a Menem', in G. Urbani (ed.), *Le prospettive della democrazia in América Latina* (Bologna, 1990); L. de Riz, M. Cavarossi and J. Feldman, 'El contexto y los dilemas de la concertación en la Argentina actual', in M. dos Santos (ed.), *Concertación politico-social y democratización* (Buenos Aires, 1987), pp. 189–224; C. H. Acuña and L. Golbert, 'Empresarios y política', *Boletín Informativo Techint,* 263 (1990), pp. 33–52; R. Gaudio and A. Thompson, *Sindicalismo peronista y gobierno radical* (Buenos Aires, 1990); A Fontana, 'La política militar en un contexto de transición: Argentina, 1987–1989', CEDES, Documento de Trabajo 34 (1989); R. Fraga, *La cuestión militar argentina, 1987–1989* (Buenos Aires, 1989).

3. URUGUAY SINCE 1930

The literature on Uruguay since 1930 is very uneven in its coverage. The 1930s and 1940s in particular have been neglected, and it was not until the crisis years of the 1960s that a substantial literature developed on Uruguay's contemporary situation and recent past. During the military regime (1973–85), the publication of serious work on recent history and current problems was inhibited, but the position was eased to some extent after 1983. Henry Finch, *Uruguay,* World Bibliographical Series, vol. 102 (Oxford, 1989), is an annotated bibliography of books and articles on all aspects of Uruguayan affairs, the majority of them in English. Among basic source materials, newspapers are a significant source for political developments, but tradition-ally each newspaper represents a political faction and none could be regarded as authoritative. The number of daily newspapers published after 1985 was greatly reduced, and the process of democratization was marked by a prolif-eration of political journals. The weekly *Búsqueda,* published since 1981, comes closer than other papers to being a journal of record. The radical weekly *Marcha,* founded in 1939, is an indispensable source of perceptive analysis and comment on all aspects of the period until its closure in 1974. For basic social and economic data, the *Anuario estadístico* of the Dirección General de Estadística y Censos (DGEC) is central. Population, housing and economic census data are also published by DGEC, as are household survey data on employment and income distribution. Since 1967 the monthly *Boletín estadístico* of the Banco Central del Uruguay (BCU) has been a princi-pal source of economic and financial data; before 1967, the *Suplemento estadístico* of the Banco de la República (BROU) published less complete information. Three compilations of data are Instituto de Economía, *Uruguay: Estadísticas básicas* (1969); Aldo Solari, Néstor Campiglia and Germán Wettstein, *Uruguay en cifras* (1966); and Centro Latinoamericano de Economía Humana (CLAEH), *Uruguay, indicadores básicos* (1983). (Unless otherwise noted, all works in this bibliographical essay were published in Montevideo.)

General works covering most of the period since 1930 include Roque Faraone, *El Uruguay en que vivimos* (1900–1968), 2d ed. (1968) and *De la prosperidad a la ruina* (1987); Martin Weinstein, *Uruguay: The Politics of Failure* (Westport, Conn., 1975), and *Uruguay: Democracy at the Crossroads* (Boulder, Colo., 1988); and M. H. J. Finch, *A Political Economy of Uruguay since 1870* (London, 1981). Important accounts of the early years are Gerardo Caetano and Raúl Jacob, *El nacimiento del terrismo, 1930–33* (1989), Raúl Jacob, *El Uruguay de Terra, 1931–1938* (1984); Ana Frega Mónica Maronna and Yvette Trochon, *Baldomir y la restauración democrática (1938–1946)* (1987); and Germán d'Elía, *El Uruguay neo-batllista, 1946–1958* (1983). The period of the Blanco administrations is reviewed in Rosa Alonso Eloy and Carlos Demasi, *Uruguay, 1958–1968* (1986). The economic development of the period is analysed in Instituto de Economía, *El proceso económico del Uruguay* (1969), and Luis A. Faroppa, *El desarrollo económico del Uruguay* (1965). Russell H. Fitzgibbon, *Uruguay: Portrait of a Democracy* (New Brunswick, N.J., 1954), is well described as an affectionate study of the country. Marvin Alisky, *Uruguay: A Contemporary Survey* (New York, 1969), is not reliable. An informative introduction to Uruguay in the 1960s is Instituto de Estudios Políticos para América Latina (IEPAL), *Uruguay: Un país sin problemas en crisis,* 3d ed. (1967). Luis Benvenuto et al., *Uruguay hoy* (1971), contains five essays on the contemporary situation.

The most detailed account of the functioning of the political system is Philip B. Taylor, *Government and Politics of Uruguay* (New Orleans, La., 1960). Works by Aldo Solari, especially *Estudios sobre la sociedad uruguaya,* 2 vols. (1965), and *El desarrollo social del Uruguay en la postguerra* (1967), contain material on the political system, as well as aspects of social structure and development. 'Bibliografía sobre estratificación y estructura de clases en el Uruguay', in Instituto de Ciencias Sociales, *Uruguay: Poder, ideología y clases sociales* (1970), is comprehensive. Carlos Real de Azua, 'Política, poder y partidos en el Uruguay de hoy', pp. 145–321, and Carlos Martínez Moreno, 'Crepúsculo en arcadia: La institucionalidad y su derrumbe a la uruguaya', pp. 405–55, in *Uruguay hoy* are perceptive accounts of the political situation on the eve of the military coup. See also Howard Handelman, 'Labor–Industrial Conflict and the Collapse of Uruguayan Democracy', *Journal of Interamerican Studies* 23, no. 4 (1981), pp. 371–94. Carlos Real de Azúa, *El impulso y su freno: Tres décadas de batllismo* (1964), is a classic study of the decline of *batllismo,* and there are stimulating reflections in Alberto Methol Ferré, *El Uruguay como problema,* 2d ed. (1971), and Oscar Bruschera, *Los partidos tradicionales y la evolución institucional del Uruguay* (1962). Material on the emergence of the Frente Amplio is provided in *Cuadernos de Marcha,* 46, 47 and 53 (1971). The guerrilla movement is examined in Antonio Mercader and Jorge de Vera, *Tupamaros: Estrategía y acción* (1969); Alain Labrousse, *The Tupamaros* (London, 1973); and Arturo C. Porzecanski, *Uruguay's Tupamaros: The Urban Guerrilla* (New York, 1973). Documents relating to the armed forces' political involvement can be found in Amilcar Vasconcellos, *Febrero amargo* (1973), and *Cuadernos de Marcha,* 68–9 (1973), while the historical background of the military is the subject of Liliana de Riz, 'Ejército y política en Uruguay', in Instituto de Ciencias Sociales, *Uruguay: Poder, ideología y clases sociales.* On the military during and after the dictatorship, see Juan Rial, *Las fuerzas armadas* (1986). A remarkable account of the operations of the CIA in Uruguay during 1964–6 is given by Philip Agee, *Inside the Company: CIA Diary* (London, 1975). The structure and development of the trade union movement are the subject of Alfredo Errandonea and Daniel Costabile, *Sindicato y sociedad en el Uruguay* (1969); Héctor Rodríguez, *Nuestros sindicatos* (1965); and Germán d'Elía, *El movimiento sindical* (Nuestra Tierra 4, 1969).

Important contributions to the history of the industrialization process are Julio Millot, Carlos Silva and Lindor Silva, *El desarrollo industrial del Uruguay: De la crisis de 1929 a la postguerra* (1973), and Luis Bértola, *The Manufacturing Industry of Uruguay, 1913–61* (Gothenburg–Stockholm, 1990). The rural sector is comprehensively analysed in CLAEH-Cinam, *Situación económica y social del Uruguay rural* (1964); Ministerio de Ganadería y Agricultura (MGA)–Comisión de Inversiones y Desarrollo Económico (CIDE), *Estudio económico y social de la agricultura en el Uruguay,* 2 vols. (1967); Aldo Solari, *Sociología rural nacional,* 2d ed. (1958); and Russell H. Brannon, *The Agricultural Development of Uruguay* (New York, 1967). Danilo Astori, *La evolución tecnológica de la ganadería uruguaya, 1930–1977* (1979), addresses an issue of critical importance. Raúl Jacob, *Uruguay, 1929–1938: Depresión ganadera y desarrollo fabril* (1981), is an important source. Survey data on internal migration are presented in

Néstor Campiglia, *Migración interna en el Uruguay* (1968). Recent international emigration is treated in Israel Wonsewer and Ana María Teja, *La emigración uruguaya, 1963–1975* (1985), and César Aguiar, *Uruguay: País de emigración* (1982).

Three accounts of the influence of the International Monetary Fund are Alberto Couriel and Samuel Lichtensztejn, *El FMI y la crisis económica nacional* (1967); Juan Eduardo Azzini, *La reforma cambiaria: Monstruo o mártir?* (1970); and Danilo Astori, Marío Bucheli, Walter Cancela and Luis Faroppa, *El FMI y nosotros* (1983). The pre–national plan diagnosis by Comisión de Inversiones y Desarrollo Económico (CIDE) is made in *Estudio económico del Uruguay: Evolución y perspectivas,* 2 vols. (1963). The two national plans were published as CIDE, *Plan nacional de desarrollo económico y social, 1965–1974,* 5 vols. (1965), and Oficina de Planeamiento y Presupuesto, *Plan nacional de desarrollo, 1973–1977,* 2d ed., 2 vols. (1977). Analysis of the economy in the late 1960s and early 1970s can be found in Instituto de Economía, *Estudios y coyuntura, 1–3,* 3 vols. (1970–3).

The military's own account and documentation of its campaign against the Tupamaros and the early years of the post-1973 regime is given in Junta de Comandantes en Jefe, *Las fuerzas armadas al pueblo oriental,* vol. 1: *La subversión* (1976) and vol. 2: *El proceso político* (1978). Alejandro Végh Villegas, *Economía política: Teoría y acción* (1977), is an important source on the economic policy of the regime. There are extended accounts of recent economic performance in Luis Macadar, *Uruguay, 1974–1980: Un nuevo ensayo de reajuste económico?* (1982); Jorge Notaro, *La política económica en el Uruguay, 1968–1984* (1984); Centro de Investigaciones Económicas (CINVE), *La crisis uruguaya y el problema nacional* (1984); Luis A. Faroppa, *Políticas para una economía disequilibrada: Uruguay, 1958–1981* (1984); and James Hansen and Jaime de Melo, 'The Uruguayan Experience with Liberalization and Stabilization, 1974–81', *Journal of Interamerican Studies,* 25, no. 4 (1983), pp. 477–508. The impact of the regime's policy on manufacturing is analysed in Instituto Alemán de Desarrollo, *Monetarismo en Uruguay: Efectos sobre el sector industrial* (Berlin, 1983), and the position of the rural sector is discussed in M. H. J. Finch, 'The Military Regime and Dominant Class Interests in Uruguay, 1973–82', in P. Cammack and P. O'Brien (eds.), *Generals in Retreat* (Manchester, 1985), pp. 89–114. The social costs of the military regime are clearly established in Juan Pablo Terra and Mabel Hopenhaym, *La infancia en el Uruguay, 1973–1984* (1986), and Rosario Aguirre et al., *El trabajo informal en Montevideo*

(1986). The transition to democratic government is analysed in the sixteen contributions to Charles Gillespie, Louis Goodman, Juan Rial and Peter Winn (eds.), *Uruguay y la democracia* (1985); Carlos Filgueira, *El dilema de la democratización* (1984); Centro de Informaciones y Estudios del Uruguay (CIESU), *7 enfoques sobre la concertación* (1984); and Juan Rial, *Partidos políticos, democracia, y autoritarismo* (1984). The quarterly journal *Cuadernos del Centro Latinoamericano de Economía Humana*, nos. 31 and 32 (1984), contains a number of useful articles. On the issue of electoral reform, see Dieter Nohlen and Juan Rial, *Reforma electoral* (1986), and Angel Cocchi, *Reforma electoral y voluntad política* (1988). The four independent research institutes established in recent years, CINVE, CIESU, CLAEH and Centro Interdisciplinario de Estudios sobre el Desarrollo (CIEDUR), have published a considerable quantity of material, much of it in the form of working papers.

4. PARAGUAY SINCE 1930

Modern Paraguay begins with the Chaco War, which has been studied by many Paraguayan and Bolivian historians, usually in a polemical fashion. An objective study, in English, is David Zook, *The Conduct of the Chaco War* (New Haven, Conn., 1960). Also of interest from the Paraguayan perspective are the memoirs of the victorious commander-in-chief José Félix Estigarribia, *The Epic of the Chaco: Marshal Estigarribia's Memoirs of the Chaco War*, translated and edited by Pablo Max Ynsfrán (Austin, Tex., 1950). On the post-war peace negotiations with Bolivia, see Leslie B. Rout, Jr., *Politics of the Chaco Peace Conference, 1935–1939* (Austin, Tex., 1970).

The February Revolution of 1936 also generated much polemical literature. The essential English-language work on the revolution, and the *febrerista* party that grew out of it, is Paul H. Lewis, *The Politics of Exile* (Chapel Hill, N.C., 1968). The most complete defence of Colonel Franco's government is by his foreign affairs minister, Juan Stefanich, whose four-volume *Capítulos de la Revolución paraguaya* were published while Stefanich was in exile in Buenos Aires during 1945 and 1946. Ruperto Resquín, *La generación paraguaya (1928–1932)* (Buenos Aires, 1978), is also useful for understanding the outlook of the young anti-Liberals who, after fighting in the Chaco War, helped bring about the February Revolution. Perhaps the best critique of the Franco government is Policarpo Artaza, *Ayala, Estigarribia, y el Partido Liberal* (Buenos Aires, 1936).

For the decade from 1937 to 1947, which covers the Paíva, Estigarribia and Morínigo years, the indispensable work is Michael Grow, *The Good Neighbor Policy and Authoritarianism in Paraguay* (Lawrence, Kan., 1981). Grow's study not only sheds interesting light on Paraguay's domestic politics, but also relates them to competition between the United States and Germany for paramountcy in the region. See also General Amancio Pampliega, *Misión cumplida* (Asunción, 1984). Pampliega was a close aide of Estigarribia's and served Morínigo as both minister of defence and minister of interior. On Axis penetration of Paraguay, see Alfredo M. Seiferheld, *Nazismo y fascismo en el Paraguay* (Asunción, 1985). Seiferheld, whose tragic death in 1988 deprived Paraguay of perhaps its most prolific and promising modern historian, also wrote a biography of Marshal Estigarribia: *Estigarribia: Veinte años de política paraguaya* (Asunción, 1982). More polemical, but still worthwhile treatments of this period are Arturo Bray, *Armas y letras,* 3 vols. (Asunción, 1981), which is critical of Estigarribia from an Old Liberal viewpoint, and Leandro Prieto, *El proceso de la dictadura liberal de 1940 (versión documental),* which attacks the Estigarribia government from the Colorado side. Absolutely essential for the whole panorama of Paraguay's politics from the Chaco War to the 1947 civil was is Seiferheld's three-volume *Conversaciones político-militares* (Asunción, 1984–6), which consists of transcribed interviews with leading politicians, soldiers and intellectuals of the period; and Saturnino Ferreira's three-volume *Proceso político del Paraguay: Una visión desde le prensa* (Asunción, 1986–7), which is composed of excerpts from the contemporary press of the era 1936–47. The much-maligned General Morínigo gets his day in court in Augusto Ocampos Caballero, *Testimonios de un presidente* (Asunción, 1983), which is based on interviews with the former president.

The 1947 civil war continues to attract the attention of Paraguayan writers since it is seen as a recent historical watershed. Older works, such as Major Antonio E. González, *La rebelión de Concepción* (Buenos Aires, 1947), and O. Barcena Echeveste, *Concepción 1947* (Asunción, 1948), are frankly pro-Colorado versions. The more recent *La revolución de 1947 y otros recuerdos* (Asunción, 1987) by Colonel Sixto Duré Franco is also by a loyalist soldier and close associate of Stroessner, but has a more dispassionate view of the subject, thanks to the passage of forty years. For the rebel version, see Colonel Afredo Ramos, *Concepción 1947, la revolución derrotada* (Asunción, 1985).

There is still no scholarly work that focusses exclusively on the turbulent period from the end of the civil war to Stroessner's seizure of power. On the *stronato,* the standard work is Paul H. Lewis, *Paraguay Under Stroessner* (Chapel Hill, N.C., 1980), but it is based on research completed in the late 1970s. This is partly remedied in a second study by Lewis, *Socialism, Liberalism, and Dictatorship in Paraguay* (New York, 1982). A new generation of young Paraguayan economists and sociologists has started to produce excellent studies of the contemporary scene. See, for example, the two-volume *Economía del Paraguay contemporáneo* by Carlos Fletschner et al. (Asunción, 1984); Pablo A. Herken Krauer, *Via crucis económico, 1982–86* (Asunción, 1986); and Roberto Luís Céspedes et al., *Paraguay, sociedad, economía, y política* (Asunción, 1988). The issue of Brazil's influence during the *stronato* is thoroughly explored in two excellent articles by R. Andrew Nickson: 'The Brazilian Colonization of the Eastern Border Region of Paraguay', *Journal of Latin American Studies,* 13, no. 1 (1981), pp. 111–31, and 'The Itaipú Hydroelectric Project: The Paraguayan Perspective', *Bulletin of Latin American Research,* 2, no. 2 (1982), pp. 1–20. The Catholic Church's challenge to the regime is summarized in Kenneth Westhues, 'Curses versus Blows: Tactics in Church–State Conflict', *Sociological Analysis,* 36 (1975), pp. 1–16. See also Frederick Hicks, 'Politics, Power, and the Role of the Village Priest', *Journal of Inter-American Studies,* 9, no. 2 (1967), pp. 273–82. Hicks also provides a fine analysis of the hold that traditional party leaders exercised over the peasantry in 'Interpersonal Relationships and Caudillismo in Paraguay', *Journal of Inter-American Studies and World Affairs,* 13, no. 1 (1971), pp. 89–111.

5. CHILE, 1930–58

Most important among the primary sources for this period are newspapers, especially *El Mercurio* and *El Diario Ilustrado* of the Right, the government's *La Nación,* and *La Opinión* and *El Siglo* of the Left. Periodicals such as *Ercilla* and *Zig-Zag* are also useful; see in particular the series of candid interviews with past political actors arranged by Wilfredo Mayorga in *Ercilla* during 1965–8. The tables compiled by Markos Mamalakis, *Historical Statistics of Chile,* 2 vols. (Westport, Conn., 1979, 1980), are an indispensable source of information.

Among the most valuable memoirs are Arturo Alessandri Palma, *Recuerdos de gobierno,* 3 vols. (Santiago, 1952); Claude G. Bowers [U.S. ambassador], *Chile through Embassy Windows* (New York, 1958); Elías Lafertte, *Vida de un comunista* (Santiago, 1961); Arturo Olavarría Bravo, *Chile entre dos Alessandri,* 4 vols. (Santiago, 1962–5); Eudocio Ravines [the disillusioned Comintern agent], *La gran estafa* (Santiago, 1954; and General Carlos Sáez Morales, *Recuerdos de un soldado,* 3 vols. (Santiago, 1934).

The best general history of Chile is Brian Loveman, *Chile: The Legacy of Hispanic Capitalism* (New York, 1979). The most comprehensive history of the period 1932–52 is Paul W. Drake, *Socialism and Populism in Chile, 1932–52* (Urbana, Ill., 1978), wherein a much more extensive bibliography can be found. Other basic works include the collection of articles in Universidad de Chile, *Desarrollo de Chile en la primera mitad del siglo XX,* 2 vols. (Santiago, 1953); Julio César Jobet's revisionist *Ensayo crítico del desarrollo económico-social de Chile* (Santiago, 1955); and Frederick B. Pike, *Chile and the United States, 1880–1962* (Notre Dame, Ind., 1963).

On the political history of the period, the following works by Chileans are important: Ricardo Boizard, *Historia de una derrota* (Santiago, 1941); Fernando Casanueva Valencia and Manuel Fernández Canque, *El Partido Socialista y la lucha de clases en Chile* (Santiago, 1973); César Caviedes, *The Politics of Chile: A Sociogeographical Assessment* (Boulder, Colo., 1979); Luis Correa, *El presidente Ibáñez* (Santiago, 1962); Ricardo Cruz-Coke, *Geografía electoral de Chile* (Santiago, 1952); Ricardo Donoso, *Alessandri, agitador y demoledor,* 2 vols. (Mexico, 1952, 1954); Florencio Durán, *El Partido Radical* (Santiago, 1958); Alberto Edwards Vives and Eduardo Frei Montalva, *Historia de los partidos políticos chilenos* (Santiago, 1949); Juan F. Fernández C., *Pedro Aguirre Cerda y el Frente Popular Chileno* (Santiago, 1938); Marta Infante Barros, *Testigos del treinta y ocho* (Santiago, 1972); Julio César Jobet, *El Partido Socialista de Chile,* 2 vols. (Santiago, 1971); Norbert Lechner, *La democracia en Chile* (Buenos Aires, 1970); and Alfonso Stephens Freire, *El irracionalismo político en Chile* (Santiago, 1957). See also Jordi Fuentes and Lia Cortes, *Diccionario político de Chile* (Santiago, 1967). The most useful political accounts by non-Chileans are Robert J. Alexander's political biography, *Arturo Alessandri,* 2 vols. (Ann Arbor, Mich., 1977); Michael J. Francis, *The Limits of Hegemony: United States Relations with Argentina and Chile during World War II* (Notre, Dame, Ind., 1977); Federico G. Gil, *The Political System of Chile* (Boston, 1966); Ernst Halperin, *Nationalism and Communism in Chile* (Cambridge, 1965); Kalman Silvert, *The Conflict Society* (New Orleans, 1961); John Reese Stevenson, *The Chilean Popular Front* (Philadelphia, 1942); and Donald W. Bray, 'Chilean Politics during the Second Ibáñez Government, 1952–8' (Ph.D. dissertation, Stanford University, 1961).

On the economic history of the period, the starting point is Markos Mamalakis, *The Growth and Structure of the Chilean Economy* (New Haven,

Conn., 1976). Other important works include Jorge Ahumada, *En vez de la miseria* (Santiago, 1965); P. T. Ellsworth, *Chile, an Economy in Transition* (New York, 1945); Ricardo Ffrench-Davis, *Políticas económicas en Chile, 1952–1970* (Santiago, 1973); Albert O. Hirschman, *Journeys toward Progress* (Garden City, N.Y., 1965); Francisco Illanes Benítez, *La economía chilena y el comercio exterior* (Santiago, 1944); Ricardo Lagos Escobar, *La concentración del poder económico* (Santiago, 1961); Markos Mamalakis and Clark Reynolds, *Essays on the Chilean Economy* (New York, 1965); Oscar Muñoz, *Crecimiento industrial de Chile, 1914–65* (Santiago, 1968); Aníbal Pinto Santa Cruz, *Antecedentes sobre el desarrollo de la economía chilena, 1925– 1952* (Santiago, 1954); idem, *Chile, un caso de desarrollo frustrado* (Santiago, 1962); Enrique Sierra, *Tres ensayos de estabilización en Chile* (Santiago, 1970); Universidad de Chile, Instituto de Economía, *Desarrollo económico de Chile, 1940–1956* (Santiago, 1956); and Enrique Zañartu Prieto, *Hambre, miseria e ignorancia* (Santiago, 1938).

Agricultural and labour issues are considered in a number of monographs. On the rural sector, see George M. McBride, *Chile: Land and Society* (New York, 1936); Erico Hott Kinderman, 'Las sociedades agrícolas nacionales y su influencias en la agricultura de Chile' (Dissertation, Universidad de Chile, 1944); Gene Ellis Martin, *La división de la tierra en Chile central* (Santiago, 1960); Brian Loveman, *Struggle in the Countryside* (Bloomington, Ind., 1976); and Thomas C. Wright, *Landowners and Reform in Chile: The Sociedad Nacional de Agricultura, 1919–40* (Urbana, Ill., 1982). The most enlightening books on trade unions are Jorge Barría, *El movimiento obrero en Chile* (Santiago, 1971), and Alan Angell, *Politics and the Labour Movement in Chile* (London, 1972).

The social and cultural-intellectual history of the middle decades of the twentieth century have been neglected. But see Luis Cruz Salas, 'Historia social de Chile: 1931–1945' (Dissertation, Universidad de Chile, 1969); Arturo Torres Ríoseco, *Breve historia de la literatura chilena* (Mexico, 1956); and Raúl Silva Castro, *Historia crítica de la novela chilena, 1843–1956* (Madrid, 1960).

6. CHILE SINCE 1958

For the history of Chile since the late 1950s, reviews and magazines are an important source of information – for example, the invaluable *Mensaje; Panorama Económico* on the economy; *Qué Pasa* for the politics of the Right; the essential weekly news magazine *Ercilla* for the whole period; *Hoy* for the Pinochet era. Amongst the academic publications, *Estudios CIEPLAN* provides excellent critical analyses of the economy; and *Estudios Públicos,* a mixture of economic, political and philosophical analyses from the neoclassical Right. For the Pinochet period, the exile journal *Chile-América* published in Rome is indispensable.

There are few good general accounts of the whole period, but for the years up to 1970, Mariana Aylwin et al., *Chile en el siglo XX* (Santiago, 1985), is valuable. For electoral data, see Germán Urzua, *Historia política electoral de Chile, 1931–1973* (Santiago, 1986). A useful guide to parties and movements is Reinhard Friedman, *1964–1988: La política chilena de la A a la Z* (Santiago, 1988). An excellent interpretation of the politics of the Left is Julio Faúndez, *Marxism and Democracy in Chile: From 1932 to the Fall of Allende* (New Haven, Conn., 1988).

On the economy in this period, there is the excellent technical account of Ricardo Ffrench-Davis, *Políticas económicas en Chile, 1952–1970* (Santiago, 1973). A controversial and stimulating work is Markos Marmalakis, *The Growth and Structure of the Chilean Economy from Independence to Allende* (Washington D.C., 1976). A great deal of useful data are available in the World Bank Report, *Chile: An Economy in Transition* (Washington D.C., 1980). Markos Mamalakis has published five volumes of the indispensable *Historical Statistics of Chile* (London, 1979–86). An interesting comparative study is Barbara Stallings, *Class Conflict and Economic Development in Chile* (Stanford, Calif., 1978). Markos Marmalakis and Clark Reynolds, *Essays on the Chilean Economy* (New York, 1965), is excellent on copper and on public policy. A useful collection of data appears in ODEPLAN, *Antecedentes del desarrollo económico, 1960–1970* (Santiago, 1971). The doctoral thesis of Oscar Landerretche, 'Inflation and Socio-Political Conflicts in Chile, 1955–1970' (Oxford University, 1983) is very perceptive. Industrialization is examined in Oscar Muñoz, *Chile y su industrialización: Pasado, crisis y opiones* (Santiago, 1986); social policy in José Pablo Arellano, *Políticas sociales y desarrollo: Chile, 1924–1984* (Santiago, 1985). The economic policies of the Alessandri and Frei administrations are dealt with in Enrique Sierra, *Tres ensayos de estabilización en Chile* (Santiago, 1969). A very useful collection in the area of political economy is Aníbal Pinto et al., *Chile hoy* (Mexico, 1970). The copper sector in this period is covered in two excellent studies: Theodore Moran, *Multinational Corporations and the Politics of Dependence: Copper in Chile* (Princeton, N.J., 1974); and Ricardo Ffrench-Davis and Ernesto Tironi (eds.), *El cobre en el desarrollo nacional* (Santiago, 1974). See also the earlier but useful studies by Mario

Vera, *La política económica del cobre* (Santiago, 1961), and *Una política definitiva para nuestras riquezas básicas* (Santiago, 1969).

On the politics of this period, Federico Gil, *The Political System of Chile* (Boston, 1966), has stood the test of time as an invaluable reference work. Less valuable is James Petras, *Politics and Social Forces in Chilean Development* (Berkeley, Calif., 1969). Paul Sigmund, *The Overthrow of Allende and the Politics of Chile, 1964–1976* (Pittsburgh, Pa., 1978), is good on the Christian Democrats but somewhat polemical thereafter. Although it focusses on the Allende government, Arturo Valenzuela, *The Breakdown of Democratic Regimes: Chile* (Baltimore, 1978), is full of insights into the structure of Chilean politics. Another book by Valenzuela is of more general interest than its title might suggest: *Political Brokers in Chile: Local Government in a Centralized Policy* (Chapel Hill, N.C., 1977). Social change is examined in Javier Martínez and Eugenio Tironi, *Las clases sociales en Chile: Cambio y estratificación, 1970–1980* (Santiago, 1986).

There is a large literature on the Frei administration. An excellent study of policy-making is Peter Cleaves, *Bureaucratic Politics and Administration in Chile* (Berkeley, Calif., 1974). An insider account supported by academic analysis is given by Sergio Molina, *El proceso de cambio en Chile* (Santiago, 1977). Arturo Olavarria Bravo has written several volumes of opinionated narrative under the title *Chile bajo la Democracia Cristiana* (Santiago, 1966–9). The best overall account is Ricardo Yocelevsky, *La Democracia Cristiana chilena y el gobierno de Eduardo Frei* (Mexico, 1987).

There is a huge literature on the Allende period. For a fascinating account of the origins of the Unidad Popular government, see Eduardo Labarca, *Chile al rojo* (Santiago, 1971). A great deal of sociological data for the period is contained in Manuel Castells, *La lucha de clases en Chile* (Buenos Aires, 1974). Excellent collections of essays are S. Sideri (ed.), *Chile, 1970–1973: Economic Development and Its International Setting* (The Hague, 1979); Arturo Valenzuela and Samuel Valenzuela (eds.), *Chile: Politics and Society* (New Brunswick, N.J., 1976); and Federico Gil, Ricardo Lagos and Henry Landsberger (eds.), *Chile at the Turning Point: Lessons of the Socialist Years, 1970–1973* (Philadelphia, 1979). A valuable account, compiled at the time, is Ann Zammit (ed.), *The Chilean Way to Socialism* (Brighton, 1973); one compiled immediately after the coup is Philip O'Brien (ed.), *Allende's Chile* (London, 1976). The collection edited by Ken Medhurst, *Allende's Chile* (London, 1972), has some interesting essays. A useful recent account of the period is Edy Kaufman, *Crisis in Chile: New Perspectives* (New York, 1988).

A collection of Allende's speeches, *Chile's Road to Socialism* (London, 1973), gives some idea of his policy and aims. Allende's aims are more interestingly explored in Regis Debray, *Conversations with Allende* (London, 1971). At times rather pretentious, but at other times an indispensable source, is the account by Allende's aide, Joan Garcés, *Allende y la experiencia chilena* (Barcelona, 1976). Widely used, though written rather too near the event, is Ian Roxborough, Philip O'Brien and Jackie Roddick, *Chile: the State and Revolution* (London, 1977). Perceptive reflections of a journalist–politician are contained in Luis Maira, *Dos años de Unidad Popular* (Santiago, 1973). Two leading Chilean sociologists provide an interesting interpretation in Manuel A. Garretón and Tomas Moulián, *Análisis coyuntural y proceso político* (Costa Rica, 1978). See also Eduardo Novoa, *Vía legal hacia el socialismo? El caso de Chile, 1970–1973* (Caracas, 1978).

On Allende's economic policy, possibly the best-argued and most informative work is that of a former minister, Sergio Bitar, *Transición, socialismo y democracia: La experiencia chilena* (Mexico, 1979). Another leading economist, Gonzalo Martner, gives his account in *El gobierno de Salvador Allende, 1970–1973: Una evaluación* (Santiago, 1988). An influential early post-mortem can be found in Stefan de Vylder, *Allende's Chile: The Political Economy of the Rise and Fall of the Popular Unity* (Cambridge, 1976). Not very accessible, but of importance, is José Serra and Arturo León, *La redistribución del ingreso en Chile durante el gobierno de la Unidad Popular*, Documento de Trabajo no. 70, Facultad Latinoamericana de Ciencias Sociales (FLACSO) (Santiago, 1978). See also Edward Boorstein, *Allende's Chile: An Inside View* (New York, 1977). Two reports of the Instituto de Económica of the University of Chile are worth consulting: *La economía chilene en 1971* (1972) and *La economía chilena en 1972* (1972).

An interesting case study of the state sector of the economy is Samuel Cogan, 'The Nationalization of Manufacturing Firms in Chile, 1970–1973: A Case Study of the Building Materials Sector' (Dissertation, Oxford University, 1981). A rather optimistic account of the Unidad Popular's economic strategy written before the coup is Sergio Ramos, *Chile: Una economía de transición* (Cuba, 1972). A work that stresses the importance of short-term financial management is Stephany Griffith-Jones, *The Role of Finance in the Transition to Socialism* (London, 1981).

The frantic politics of the period have not been treated as well as the economy. An important article is Atilio Borón, 'La movilización política en Chile', *Foro Internacional* 61 (July–September 1975), pp. 75–121. See also Alan Angell, *Political Mobilization and Class Alliances in Chile, 1970–1973* (Institute for the New Chile, Rotterdam, 1978), which contains extensive references to discussions on *poder popular*. A rather unconvincing account is offered by the left-wing Socialist Carlos Altamirano, *Dialéctica de una derrota* (Mexico, 1977). The work of the French sociologist Alain Touraine, *Vida y muerte del gobierno popular* (Buenos Aires, 1974), is very moving. Problems of ideology and cultural politics are discussed in Manuel Antonio Garretón et al., *Cultura y comunicaciones de masas* (Barcelona, 1975). Relations with the Soviet Union are the theme of Isabel Turrent, *La Unión Soviética en América Latina: El caso de la Unidad Popular Chilena* (Mexico, 1984). The important episode of the educational reform proposal is well treated in Joseph Farrell, *The National Unified School in Allende's Chile* (Vancouver, 1986).

The question of U.S. involvement in the coup first surfaced in the Staff Report of the Select Committe to Study Governmental Intelligence Activities, *Covert Action in Chile, 1963–1973* (U.S. Senate, Washington, D.C., 1975), though a Chilean ambassador, Armando Uribe, had already documented some covert interference in *La livre noir de l'intervention américaine au Chile* (Paris, 1974). See also James Petras and Morris Morley, *The United States and Chile: Imperialism and the Allende Government* (New York, 1975). The account by U.S. Ambassador Nathaniel Davis, *The Last Two Years of Allende* (Cornell, N.Y., 1985) is fascinating. A savage attack on U.S. policy by a leading journalist is contained in Seymour Hersh, *The Price of Power: Kissinger in the White House Years* (Boston, 1980).

There is relatively little on the opposition to Allende. Some suggestive ideas are contained in Paul Drake, 'Corporatism and Functionalism in Modern Chilean Politics', *Journal of Latin American Studies* 10 (May 1978), pp. 83–116; and in the last chapter of the same author's *Socialism and Populism in Chile, 1932–1952* (Chicago, 1978). Pablo Baraona et al., *Chile: A Critical Survey* (Santiago, 1972), contains some interesting essays from the Right.

On the Pinochet period, there are several excellent studies of the economy. See in particular Alejandro Foxley, *Latin American Experiments in Neo-Conservative Economics* (Berkeley, Calif., 1983); the collective work by the economists at CIEPLAN, *Modelo económico chileno: trayectoria de una crítica* (Santiago, 1982); Ricardo Ffrench-Davis, 'The Monetarist Experiment in Chile', *World Development* 11 (November 1983), pp. 905–26; and the chapters on Chile by Fortin in Carlos Fortin and Christian Anglade, *The State and Capital Accumulation in Latin America* (London, 1985). Plans for escaping from the collapse of the boom of the 'Chicago boys' are contained in CIEPLAN, *Reconstrucción económica para la democracia* (Santiago, 1983).

Laurence Whitehead's chapter on Chile in Rosemary Thorp and Laurence Whitehead (eds.), *Inflation and Stabilisation in Latin America* (London, 1979), pp. 117–61, is a perceptive account of the problems of economic stabilization in this period. See also a later account by the same author in Rosemary Thorp and Laurence Whitehead, *Latin American Debt and the Adjustment Crisis* (London, 1987). A study of the process of economic concentration is Fernando Dahse, *El mapa de la extrema riqueza* (Santiago, 1979). An excellent criticism of government policies and alternative recommendations can be found in Alejandro Foxley, *Para una democracia estable* (Santiago, 1985). Alvaro Bardón, Camilo Carrasco and Alvaro Vial, *Una década de cambios económicos: La experiencia chilena, 1973– 1983* (Santiago, 1985), is a defence of free-market policies. See also Sebastián Edwards, and A. C. Edwards, *Monetarism and Liberalism: The Chilean Experiment* (Cambridge, Mass., 1986). A fascinating account of the role of the Chicago boys is given in Arturo Fontaine, *Los economistas y el Presidente Pinochet* (Santiago, 1988). Joaquín Lavin, *La revolución silenciosa* (Santiago, 1987), is a highly publicized eulogy of the free-market experiment. A damaging critique stressing the social costs of the experiment is presented in Eugenio Tironi, *Los silencios de la revolución* (Santiago, 1988). The extent of poverty is documented in Eugenio Ortega and Ernesto Tironi, *Pobreza en Chile* (Santiago, 1988).

The politics of the Pinochet era are briefly discussed in P. O'Brien and J. Roddick, *Chile: The Pinochet Decade* (London, 1983). The constitution of 1980 is examined in detail in Luz Bulnes Aldunate, *Constitución política de la República de Chile* (Santiago, 1981). A set of essays covering events up to 1980 is J. Samuel Valenzuela and Arturo Valenzuela (eds.), *Military Rule in Chile: Dictatorship and Oppositions* (Baltimore, 1986). The role of the press is explored in Fernando Reyes Matta, Carlos Ruiz and Guillermo Sunkel, *Investigaciones sobre la prensa en Chile (1974–1984)* (Santiago, 1986). Cultural policy is lucidly analysed in José Joaquín Brunner, *La cultura autoritaria en Chile* (Santiago, 1981).

The eruption of the military into political life took academics as well as politicians by surprise. There were very few useful accounts of the military, apart from Alain Joxe, *Las fuerzas armadas en el sistema político de Chile* (Santiago, 1970), and Frederick Nunn, *The Military in Chilean History: Essays on Civil–Military Relations, 1810–1973* (Albuquerque, N.M., 1976). A more recent study is Hugo Fruling, Carlos Portales and Augusto

Varas, *Estado y fuerzas armadas* (Santiago, 1982). An early military plotter tells his story in Florencia Varas, *Conversaciones con Viaux* (Santiago, 1972). Carlos Prats tells his own story in *Memorias: Testimonio de un soldado* (Santiago, 1985). Pinochet's account of his involvement in the coup is contained in Augusto Pinochet, *El dia decisivo* (Santiago, 1977). Another military man – now disillusioned – gives his view in Florencia Varas, *Gustavo Leigh: El general disidente* (Santiago, 1979). The best recent accounts are Genaro Arriagada, *La política militar de Pinochet* (Santiago, 1985), and Augusto Varas, *Los militares en el poder: Regimen y gobierno militar en Chile, 1973–1986* (Santiago, 1987).

An impressive attempt to evaluate the politics of Chile since 1970 is Manuel Antonio Garretón, *El proceso político chileno* (Santiago, 1983). The numerous FLASCO publications by Garretón and Tomás Moulián constitute a running commentary on politics and society since 1973. Moulián's constantly stimulating ideas are brought together in his *Democracia y socialismo en Chile* (Santiago, 1983). A useful collection of writings of FLASCO researchers is contained in Manuel Antonio Garretón et al., *Chile 1973–198?* (Santiago, 1983). An influential journalist collects his articles in Genaro Arriagada, *10 años: Visión crítica* (Santiago, 1983). On the first phase of military rule, see Tomás Moulián and Pilar Vergara, 'Estado, ideología y política económica en Chile, 1973–1978', in *Estudios CIEPLAN,* no. 3 (1980), pp. 65–120. A comprehensive account of the ideology of the Pinochet regime is Pilar Vergara, *Auge y caída del neoliberalismo en Chile* (Santiago, 1985). Two lucid and informative articles are Carlos Huneeus, 'La política de la apertura y sus implicancias para la inauguración de la democracia en Chile', and 'Inauguración de la democracia en Chile', in *Revista de Ciencia Política* 7, no. 1, (1985), pp. 25–64, and 8, nos. 1–2 (1986), pp. 22–87. The theme of the transition to democracy is explored with great insight in Manuel Antonio Garretón, *Reconstruír la política: Transición y consolidación democrática en Chile* (Santiago, 1987).

The murky world of state terrorism is, by definition, difficult to examine, but the book by Thomas Hauser, *Missing* (London, 1982), asks some awkward questions – later given wide publicity in an impressive film of the same name. On the assassination of Orlando Letelier, see John Dinges and Saul Landau, *Assassination on Embassy Row* (New York, 1980), and Taylor Branch and Eugene Propper, *Labyrinth* (New York, 1982). An account of domestic brutality is contained in Maximo Pachecho, *Lonquén* (Santiago, 1980). The issue of exile is examined by Alan Angell and Susan

Carstairs, 'The Exile Question in Chilean Politics', *Third World Quarterly* 9 (January 1987), pp. 148–67. Three leading politicians write movingly of their experience of exile, of imprisonment and of their beliefs: Erich Shnacke, *De improviso la nada* (Santiago, 1988); Clodomiro Almeyda, *Reencuentro con mi vida* (Santiago, 1988); and Jorge Arrate, *Exilio: textos de denuncia y esperanza* (Santiago, 1987).

An interesting account of rural conflict, which perhaps over-emphasizes its extent, is provided in Brian Loveman, *Struggle in the Countryside: Politics and Rural Labour in Chile, 1919–1973* (Bloomington, Ind., 1976). The basic source of data is the Comité Interaméricano de Desarrollo Agrícola (CIDA), report, *Chile: Tenencia de la tierra y desarrollo socio-económico del sector agrícola* (Washington, D.C., 1966). See also Luz Eugenia Cereceda and Fernando Dahse, *Dos décadas de cambios en el agro chileno* (Santiago, 1980). For the Partido Demócrata Cristiano (PDC) and Unidad Popular reforms, see Solon Barraclough and Juan Fernández, *Diagnóstico de la reforma agraria chilena* (Buenos Aires, 1974); Kyle Steenland, *Agrarian Reform under Allende: Peasant Revolt in the South* (Albuquerque, N.M., 1978); and Robert Kaufman, *The Politics of Land Reform in Chile, 1950–1970* (Cambridge, Mass., 1973). Jacques Chonchol's work is important; see, for example, the chapter in Pinto (ed.), *Chile hoy;* and 'La reforma agraria en Chile, 1970–1973', in *El trimestre económico,* no. 53 (1976). Post-coup policies are examined in Lovell Jarvis, *Chilean Agriculture under Military Rule* (Berkeley, Calif., 1985); Patricio Silva, *Estado, neoliberalismo y política agraria en Chile, 1973–1981* (Holland, 1987); and José Garrido (ed.), *Historia de la reforma agraria en Chile* (Santiago, 1988).

Urban and mining labour is examined in Alan Angell, *Politics and the Labour Movement in Chile* (Oxford, 1972), for the period up to 1970. An excellent study of labour under Pinochet is Guillermo Campero and José Valenzuela, *El movimiento sindical chileno en el capitalismo autoritario* (Santiago, 1981). A fascinating study at the local level – an altogether too rare example – is Penelope Pollitt, 'Religion and Politics in a Coal Mining Community in Southern Chile' (Dissertation, Cambridge University, 1981). The pioneer of labour studies in Chile, Jorge Barría, has written extensively on the subject; see especially *Trayectoria y estructura del movimiento sindical chileno* (Santiago, 1963) and *Historia de la CUT* (Santiago, 1971). A fascinating study of worker participation under Allende is Manuel Barrera, Gustavo Aranda and Jorge Díaz, *El cambio social en una empresa del APS* (Santiago, 1973). An earlier study of worker attitudes is Torcuato di Tella, Lucien Brahms, Jean-Daniel Reynaud and Alain

Touraine *Huachipato et lota: Etude sur la conscience ouvière dans deux entreprises chilennes* (Paris, 1966).

The role of workers under the Unidad Popular is examined in Juan Espinosa and Andy Zimbalist, *Economic Democracy: Workers' Participation in Chilean Industry, 1970–1973* (New York, 1978), and in two short monographs by Francisco Zapata, *Los mineros de Chuquicamata: Productores o proletarios* (Mexico City, 1975) and *Las relaciones entre el movimiento obrero y el gobierno de Allende* (Mexico, 1974). A brilliant account of a worker takeover is Peter Winn, *Weavers of Revolution: The Yarur Workers and Chile's Road to Socialism* (New York, 1986).

Useful accounts of labour under Pinochet are Gonzalo Falabella, *Labour in Chile under the Junta*, Working Papers no. 4, University of London, Institute of Latin American Studies (1981); the collective publication of Vector, *El movimiento sindical* (Revista de talleres), no. 2 (1981), pp. 49–66; J. Roddick and N. Haworth, 'Labour and Monetarism in Chile', *Bulletin of Latin American Research,* 1, no. 1 (1981), pp. 49–62; and Manuel Barrera, Helia Henríquez and Teresita Selame, *Sindicatos y estado en el Chile actual* (Geneva, 1985). Relatively little has been written on the shanty towns under Pinochet, but see the impressive studies by Rodrigo Baño, *Lo social y lo político* (Santiago, 1985), and Guillermo Campero, *Entre la sobrevivencia y la acción política* (Santiago, 1987). A series of interviews, Patricia Politzer, *La ira de pedro y los otros* (Santiago, 1988), explains the desperation of the youth of the shanty towns.

On the entrepreneurial sector, there is a detailed analysis of the structure of organizations in Genaro Arriagada, *La oligarquía patronal chileno* (Santiago, 1970). A doctoral thesis by Marcelo Cavarozzi, 'The Government and the Industrial Bourgeoisie in Chile, 1938–1964' (University of California, Berkeley, 1975) contains a great deal of useful information. An excellent study of recent entrepreneurial behaviour is Guillermo Campero, *Los gremios empresariales en el período 1970–1983* (Santiago, 1984). A study of the ideology of an important voice of the entrepreneurial sector is Guillermo Sunkel, *'El Mercurio': 10 años de educación político-ideológica* (Santiago, 1983).

Three books begin the task of writing the history of women's involvement in Chilean political life: Julietta Kirkwood, *Ser política en Chile: Las feministas y los partidos* (Santiago, 1985); María Angélica Maza, *La otra mitad de Chile* (Santiago, 1986); and María Elena Valenzuela, *La mujer en el Chile militar* (Santiago, 1987).

Brian Smith, *The Church and Politics in Chile* (Princeton, N.J., 1982), is an impressive study of the Catholic Church. On Protestantism, see Humberto Lagos, *Los Evangélicos en Chile: Una lectura sociológica* (Santiago, 1988). Education is examined in Kathleen Fischer, *Political Ideology and Educational Reform in Chile, 1964–1976* (Los Angeles, 1979), and in Guillermo Labarca, *Educación y sociedad: Chile, 1969–1984* (Amsterdam, 1985).

Political parties have attracted far less attention than their central political role merits. An excellent set of essays, however, is Adolfo Aldunate, et al., *Estudios sobre el sistema de partidos en Chile* (Santiago, 1985). For a general account, see Bernadino Bravo Lira, *Régimen de gobierno y partidos políticos en Chile, 1924–1973* (Santiago, 1978). On the PDC, see George Grayson, *El Partido Demócrata Cristiano Chileno* (Buenos Aires, 1968), and Michael Fleet, *The Rise and Fall of Chilean Christian Democracy* (Princeton, N.J., 1985). On the Socialists, see Fernando Casanueva and Manuel Fernandez, *El Partido Socialista y la lucha de clases en Chile* (Santiago, 1973); and Benny Pollack, Hernán Rosenkranz and Waldino Suárez, *Mobilization and Socialism in Chile* (Liverpool, 1981). Ernst Halperin, *Nationalism and Communism in Chile* (Cambridge, Mass., 1965), remains useful. More recent is Benny Pollack and Hernan Rosenkranz, *Revolutionary Social Democracy: The Chilean Socialist Party* (London, 1986). See also Ignacio Walker, *Del populismo al Leninismo y la 'inevitabilidad del conflicto': El Partido Socialista de Chile (1933–1973)* (CIEPLAN, Santiago, 1986). Three books reconsider Socialist strategies: Jorge Arrate, *La fuerza democrática de la idea socialista* (Santiago, 1985); Jorge Arrate (ed.), *La renovación socialista* (Santiago, 1987); and Ricardo Lagos, *Democracia para Chile: Proposiciones de un Socialista* (Santiago, 1986). On the Communists, see Carmelo Furci, *The Chilean Communist Party and the Road to Socialism* (London, 1984); Eduardo Gobard Labarca, *Corvalán, 27 horas* (Santiago, 1973); and Augusto Varas (ed.), *El Partido Communista en Chile* (Santiago, 1988).

A pioneering study of foreign policy, which touches on the late 1950s and early 1960s, is Frederick Pike, *Chile and the United States, 1880–1962* (Notre Dame, Ind., 1963). A Chilean view covering a longer period can be found in Walter Sánchez and Teresa Pereira, *Ciento cincuenta años de política exterior chilena* (Santiago, 1979). Francisco Orrego Vicuña, *La participación de Chile en el sistema internacional* (Santiago, 1974), is useful. The journal *Estudios Internacionales* (Santiago) carries interesting and well-documented articles on Chilean foreign policy. Manfred Wilhelmy, 'Hacia un análisis de la política exterior Chilena contemporánea', *Estudios Internacionales,* no. 48 (October–December 1979), pp. 440–91, is particularly interesting. The most comprehensive treatment of recent foreign policy is Heraldo Muñoz, *Las relaciones exteriores del gobierno militar chileno* (Santiago, 1986). On relations with the United States see Heraldo Muñoz and Carlos Portales, *Una amistad esquiva: Las relaciones de EE.UU y Chile* (Santiago, 1987).

7. PERU, 1930–60

The best general political history of Peru, with an excellent bibliography, is D. P. Werlich, *Peru: A Short History* (Carbondale, Ill., 1978). The period from 1930 to 1960 is accorded chapters in other general histories such as F. B. Pike, *The Modern History of Peru* (London, 1967); R. B. Marett, *Peru* (London, 1969); H. Dobyns and P. C. Doughty, *Peru: A Cultural History* (New York, 1976); and J. Cotler, *Clases estado y nación en el Perú* (Lima, 1978). Jorge Basadre's massive *Historia de la República del Perú* peters out in 1933, and most Peruvian historical writing on the subsequent three decades is either polemical or takes the form of personal reminiscences by political figures.

D. M. Masterson, 'The Peruvian Armed Forces in Transition, 1939–1963: The Impact of National Politics and Changing Professional Perspectives' (Ph.D. dissertation, Michigan State University, 1976) and 'Soldiers, Sailors and Apristas: Conspiracy and Power Politics in Peru, 1932–1948', in J. F. Bratzel and D. M. Masterson (eds.), *The Underside of Latin American History* (East Lansing, Mich. 1977), provides excellent detailed analyses of political events, focussing on the role of the military. Foreign policy issues, particularly the Leticia case and the war with Ecuador, are covered in R. B. St John, 'The End of Innocence: Peruvian Foreign Policy and the US, 1919–1942', *Journal of Latin American Studies*, 8, no. 2 (1976), pp. 325–44. On the role of the Church, see J. L. Kleiber, *Religion and Revolution in Peru, 1824–1976* (Notre Dame, Ind., 1977), and C. A. Astiz, 'The Catholic Church in Latin American Politics: A Case Study of Peru', in D. H. Pollock, and A. R. M. Ritter (eds.), *Latin American Prospects for the 1970s: What Kinds of Revolution?* (New York, 1973), pp. 131–48. Two analyses of Peruvian class structure and political life written during the 1960s, and typical of conventional thinking in that decade, are C. A. Astiz, *Pressure Groups and Power Elites in Peruvian Politics* (Ithaca, N.Y., 1969), and F. Bourricaud, *Power and Society in Contemporary Peru* (London, 1970).

A general economic history focussing on the modern sectors of the economy is R. Thorp and G. Bertram, *Peru, 1890–1977: Growth and Policy in an Open Economy* (London, 1978), pts. 3 and 4. The pioneering work on quantitative economic history by Shane Hunt appeared in a number of Discussion Papers from the Woodrow Wilson School Research Program in Economic Development, Princeton University; for citations, see Thorp and Bertram, *Peru, 1890–1977*, pp. 436–7. Besides his statistical working papers, Hunt has published 'Distribution, Growth and Government Economic Behaviour in Peru', in G. Ranis (ed.), *Government and Economic Development* (New Haven, Conn., 1972), pp. 375–416; 'Foreign Investment in Peru: New Rules for an Old Game', in A. Lowenthal (ed.), *The Peruvian Experiment: Continuity and Change under Military Rule* (Princeton, N.J., 1975), pp. 302–49; and *Real Wages and Economic Growth in Peru, 1900–1940,* Boston Center for Latin American Development Studies, Discussion Paper no. 25 (1977). On the evolution of real wages through the 1940s and 1950s, see W. Warren, *Inflation and Real Wages in Underdeveloped Countries: India, Peru and Turkey* (London, 1976).

Trends in income distribution during the 1950s are documented by R. C. Webb, *The Distribution of Income in Peru,* Princeton University, Woodrow Wilson School Research Program in Economic Development, Discussion Paper no 26. (Princeton, N.J., 1972) and *Trends in Real Income in Peru,* Princeton University, Woodrow Wilson School Research Program in Economic Development, Discussion Paper no. 41 (Princeton, N.J., 1974); and also by R. Vandendries, 'Income Distribution in Peru After World War II', *Journal of Developing Areas,* 8 (April 1974), pp. 421–36. Similar conclusions on regressive trends in distribution, based on food supply data, were reached in R. Thorp, 'A Note on Food Supplies, the Distribution of Income and National Income Accounting in Peru', *Oxford Bulletin of Economics and Statistics,* 31, no. 4 (November 1969), pp. 229–41.

The role of U.S. capital and the political aspects of foreign investment and aid during the period are discussed in J. C. Carey, *Peru and the United States* (Notre Dame, Ind., 1964). A useful history of the Exxon subsidiary which epitomized foreign capital to most Peruvians is A. J. Pinelo, *The Multinational Corporation as a Force in Latin American Politics: A Case Study of the International Petroleum Company in Peru* (New York, 1973).

The discussion of the evolution of rural society in the Sierra rests heavily on the pioneering research of J. Martinez-Alier, 'Los huachilleros en las haciendas de la Sierra central del Perú desde 1930', in E. Florescano, (ed.), *Haciendas, latifundios y plantaciones en America Latina* (Mexico City, 1975), English trans., and *Haciendas, Plantations and Collec-*

tive Farms (London, 1977). See also C. F. Oman, 'The Formation of Capitalist Society in Peru: "Dualism" and Underdevelopment' (Ph.D. dissertation, University of California, Berkeley, 1978). Florencia E. Mallon, *The Defense of Community in Peru's Central Highlands: Peasant Struggle and Capitalist Transition, 1860–1940* (Princeton, N.J., 1983), has detailed case studies of the Yanamarca Valley and a useful bibliography on the recent literature for the central Sierra. Events in the northern Sierra are described in L. Taylor, 'Main Trends in Agrarian Capitalist Development: Cajamarca, Peru, 1880–1976' (Ph.D. dissertation, University of Liverpool, 1979). The work of T. R. Ford, *Man and Land in Peru* (Gainesville, Fla., 1962), is useful on the situation in the early 1950s, and social mobility in the South is studied in F. Bourricaud, *Changements à Puno* (Paris, 1960). F. L. Tullis, *Lord and Peasant in Peru: A Paradigm of Political and Social Change* (Cambridge Mass., 1970), provides some case studies of rural conflicts in the central Sierra during the 1940s. An overview of agrarian conflicts in both the Sierra and the Coast, with emphasis on the latter, is C. Harding, 'Land Reform and Social Conflict', in A. F. Lowenthal (ed.), *The Peruvian Experiment: Continuity and Change under Military Rule* (Princeton, N.J., 1975), pp. 220–53.

Knowledge of modern Sierra history expanded rapidly during the 1970s, due partly to major field research programmes by anthropologists and sociologists and partly to the opening up of hacienda archives following the 1969 agrarian reform. Examples of the former are B. Roberts, 'The Social History of a Provincial Town: Huancayo, 1890–1972', in R. Miller, C. T. Smith and J. Fisher (eds.), *Social and Economic Change in Modern Peru*, University of Liverpool Centre for Latin American Studies, Monograph Series no. 6 (1976), pp. 130–97; N. Long and B. Roberts, *Peasant Cooperation and Capitalist Expansion in Central Peru* (Austin, Tex., 1978); W. F. Whyte and G. Alberti, *Power, Politics and Social Change in Rural Peru* (New York, 1976); and B. Orlove, *Alpaca, Sheep and Men: The Wool Export Economy in Southern Peru* (New York, 1977). Recent archive-based work by Peruvian historians has focussed on the rise of peasant movements and the crisis of the hacienda; see especially M. Burga and A. Flores Galindo, 'Feudalismo andino y movimientos sociales', in J. Mejía Baca (ed.), *Historia del Peru* (Lima, 1980), vol. 11; A. Flores Galindo, 'Apuntes sobre las ocupaciones de tierra y el sindicalismo agrario: 1945–1964', *Allpanchis* (Cuzco, 1978); W. Kapsoli, *Los movimientos campesinos en Cerro de Pasco, 1800–1963* (Lima, 1975). A survey of events which includes the period 1930–60 is P. Kamman, *Movimientos campesinos en el*

Peru, 1900–1968: Analisis cuantitativo y cualitativo preliminar (Lima, 1982).

Also useful on the rise of peasant movements in mid-century is T. M. Davies, *Indian Integration in Peru: A Half-Century of Experience, 1900–1948* (Lincoln, Neb., 1974). The exceptional peasant movement in the La Convención Valley is discussed in W. W. Craig, *From Hacienda to Community: An Analysis of Solidarity and Social Change in Peru,* Cornell University Latin American Studies Program, Dissertation ser. no. 6 (1967); E. J. Hobsbawm, 'La Convención Peru: A Case of Neo-Feudalism', *Journal of Latin American Studies,* 1, no. 1 (1969), pp. 31–50; and E. Fioravanti, *Latifundio y sindicalismo agrario en el Perú* (Lima, 1976).

A good provincial history of Puno is D. Hazen, 'The Awakening of Puno: Government Policy and the Indian Problem in Southern Peru, 1900–1955' (Ph.D. dissertation, Yale University, 1974). A classic study of social change in the northern Sierra is S. Miller, 'Hacienda to Plantation in Northern Peru: The Process of Proletarianization of a Tenant Farmer Society', in J. Steward (ed.), *Contemporary Change in Traditional Societies* (Urbana Ill., 1967), pp. 133–225. The political role of the Sierra elite in the early twentieth century is covered in R. Miller, 'The Coastal Elite and Peruvian Politics, 1895–1919', *Journal of Latin American Studies,* 14, no. 2 (1982), pp. 97–120.

The Lima *barriadas,* resulting from the rapid rural–urban migration of the 1950s, are described in J. Matos Mar, 'Migration and Urbanization: The Barriadas of Lima, an Example of Integration into Urban Life', in P. M. Hauser (ed.), *Urbanization in Latin America* (New York, 1961), pp. 170–90, and in D. Collier, *Squatters and Oligarchs: Authoritarian Rule and Policy Change in Peru* (Baltimore, 1976). (Chapters 4 and 5 of Collier's book are particularly useful on policy responses during the period from 1945 to 1962.) Discussion of the importance of village-based organization in the Lima *barriadas* is in B. Roberts, 'Urban Migration and Change in Provincial Organisation in the Central Sierras of Peru', University of Manchester mimeo (1974).

Modernization of coastal agriculture is covered in C. Collin-Delavaud, 'Consecuencias de la modernización de la agricultura en las haciendas de la Costa Norte del Peru', in H. Favre (ed.), *La hacienda en el Perú* (Lima, 1967). The history of rural class struggle on the Coast is still patchy; for useful pointers see Harding's essay in Lowenthal (ed.), *The Peruvian Experiment.* Most intensively studied has been the Chancay Valley north of Lima, where a series of projects sponsored by the Instituto de Estudios Peruanos has been conducted; see, e.g., J. Matos Mar, *Yanaconaje y reforma agraria en el Perú* (Lima, 1976). See also M. Burga, *De le encomienda a la hacienda capitalista: El Valle de Jequetepec del siglo XVI al XX* (Lima, 1976), and H. Rodríguez Pastor, *Caquí: Estudio de una hacienda costeña* (Lima, 1969). On the emergence of the sugar-plantation proletariat, see C. Scott, 'Peasants, Proletarianization and Articulation of Modes of Production: The Case of Sugar Cane Cutters in Northern Peru', *Journal of Peasant Studies*, 3, no. 3 (1976), pp. 321–41. An excellent analysis of the emergence and character of the institution of *yanaconaje* is in the appendix to W. Albert, *An Essay on the Peruvian Sugar Industry, 1880–1920* (Norwich, 1976).

The Peruvian oligarchy is described, with three detailed family case studies, in D. Gilbert, *The Oligarchy and the Old Regime in Peru*, Cornell University, Latin American Studies Program Dissertation ser. no. 69 (Ithaca, N.Y., 1977). Further case-study material is in C. Malpica, *Los dueños del Perú* (Lima, 1968), and A. Low, 'Agro-Exporters as Entrepreneurs: Peruvian Sugar and Cotton Producers, 1890–1945' (D.Phil. dissertation, Oxford University, 1979). Reflections on the problems of characterizing the oligarchy are to be found in F. Bourricaud, J. Bravo Bresani, H. Favre and J. Piel, *La oligarquía en el Perú* (Lima, 1969), and in F. Bourricaud, *Power and Society in Contemporary Peru* (London, 1970). Cotler, *Clases, estado y nación*, portrays the oligarchy as perennially compromised by its subservience to foreign capital, locating the roots of its factionalism and weakness in its comprador status. E. V. K. Fitzgerald, *The Political Economy of Peru, 1956–78* (Cambridge, 1979), discusses the relative autonomy of the Peruvian state (chap. 2) and the class structure and political scene of 1960 (chap. 3).

The rise of a national bourgeois industrial fraction is discussed by W. Bollinger, 'The Bourgeois Revolution in Peru: A Conception of Peruvian History', *Latin American Perspectives*, 4, no. 3 (1977), pp. 18–56, but Bollinger's analysis is concerned primarily with the 1960s and 1970s. Similar comments apply to A. Ferner, 'The Dominant Class and Industrial Development in Peru', *Journal of Development Studies*, 15, no. 4 (1979), pp. 268–88, and F. L. M. Wils, 'Agricultural and Industrial Development in Peru: Some Observations on their Interrelationship', *Development and Change*, 5, no. 21 (1973–4), pp. 76–100. An (unconvincing) attempt to document the existence of an industrial fraction of the oligarchy for earlier decades is to be found in two books by B. Caravedo Molinari, *Burguesía e industria en el Perú, 1933–1945* (Lima, 1976), and *Clases, lucha política y gobierno en el Perú, 1919–1930: El oncenio ante la historia – Se puede hablar de*

un período revolucionario? Agro-exportadores versus industriales, el capital impe-
rialista en el Perú (Lima, 1977). The 'industrial groups' of Peruvian and
foreign capital, set up during the later 1950s to dominate the emerging
manufacturing sector, are described in H. Espinoza Uriarte and J. Osorio,
El poder ecónomico en la industria (Lima, 1972).

The characterization of Leguía's *oncenio,* although it lies outside the
period covered here, is important to debates on oligarchic fractions. Por-
traits of Leguía as a leader of the rising middle class against the oligarchy
are M. Capuñay, *Leguía: Vida y obra del constructor del Gran Perú* (Lima,
1951); H. B. Karno, 'Augusto B. Leguía: The Oligarchy and the Modernization of Peru' (Ph.D. dissertation, University of California, Los Angeles,
1970); and G. R. Garrett, 'The Oncenio of Augusto B. Leguía: Middle
Sector Government and Leadership in Peru' (Ph.D. dissertation, University of New Mexico, 1973). The depiction of Leguía as the leader of one
faction within a divided oligarchy and a forerunner of the 'authoritarian
modernizing' regime of Benavides can be found in C. F. Herbold, 'Developments in the Peruvian Administrative System, 1919–1930: Modern
and Traditional Qualities of Authoritarian Regimes' (Ph.D. dissertation,
Yale University, 1973). Similar interpretations are in S. Stein, *Populism in
Peru* (Madison, Wis., 1980), chap. 3; Gilbert, *The Oligarchy and the Old
Regime in Peru;* and Werlich, *A Short History.*

Political factionalism within the oligarchy is discussed in B. Loveday,
Sánchez Cerro and Peruvian Politics, 1930–1933, University of Glasgow
Institute of Latin American Studies, Occasional Paper no. 6 (1973). The
split over the devaluation issue is presented, disguised as a middle-class–
oligarchy split, in M. J. Frankman, 'Export Promotion and Development
Priorities in Peru, 1946–1965' (Ph. D. dissertation, University of Texas,
Austin, 1968). Discussion of the same issue in J. Dragisic, 'Peruvian
Stabilization Policies, 1939–1968' (Ph.D. dissertation, University of Wisconsin, 1971), is distorted by a desire to present the oligarchy as united on
the issue.

B. Caravedo Molinari, *Desarrollo desigual y lucha política en el Perú,
1948–1956: La burgesía arequipeña y el estado peruano* (Lima, 1978), explains Arequipa's activism in largely negative terms, as a reaction against
economic and political centralism. For studies that emphasize the special
character of the Arequipa bourgeoisie, see A. Flores Galindo, *Arequipa y el
sur andino: Ensayo de historia regional, Siglos XVIII–XX* (Lima, 1977), and
A. Flores Galindo, O. Plaza and T. Ore, 'Notas sobre oligarquía y capitalismo en Arequipa, 1870–1940', *Congreso Peruano del Hombre y la Cultura,*

3, no. 4 (1977). The emergence onto the national scene of the Arequipa Catholic constitutionalists is described in J. L. Renique, 'Los decentralistas arequipeños en la crisis del Año 1930', *Allpanchis,* 12 (1979). For a history of the Arequipa labour movement, see V. Colque Valladares, *Dinámica del movimiento sindical en Arequipa: 1900–1968* (Lima, 1976). For self-portraits of three of the leaders of the Arequipa Catholic professionals, see V. A. Belaúnde, *Memorias* (Lima, 1960–2), and *La Crisis Presente, 1914–1939* (Lima, 1940); J. L. Bustamante, *Tres años de lucha por la democracia en el Perú* (Buenos Aires, 1949); and F. Belaúnde Terry, *La conquista del Perú por los peruanos* (Lima, 1964). On Mostajo, see J. G. Carpio Muñoz, 'Francisco Mostajo: Breve historia de un caudillo', *Tarea,* 5 (1981).

Any interpretation of the roots of Alianza Popular Revolucionaria Americana (APRA) and *sánchezcerrismo* must draw heavily on Stein, *Populism in Peru* and 'Populism in Peru: APRA, the Formative Years', in M. L. Conniff (ed.), *Latin American Populism* (Albuquerque, N.M., 1981), pp. 113–34. A good history of APRA is L. M. North, 'The Origins and Development of the Peruvian Aprista Party' (Ph.D. dissertation, University of California, Berkeley, 1973). Víctor Villanueva, prominent in APRA during the 1940s, has written several books on the party: *La sublevación del 48: Tregdía de un pueblo y un partido* (Lima, 1973); *El APRA en busca del poder* (Lima, 1975); and *El APRA y el ejército (1940–50)* (Lima, 1977). A recent addition to the literature is L. A. Sánchez, *Apuntes para una biografía del APRA,* 2 vols. (Lima, 1978–9). A useful bibliography of earlier work on APRA can be found in Werlich, *A Short History,* pp. 400–1.

A debate among leading left-wing thinkers on the competition between APRA and the Communist Party for leadership of the labour movement is presented in M. Lauer et al., *Frente al Perú oligárquico (1928–68): Debate Socialista I* (Lima, 1977). The same issue is tackled, with somewhat more historical substance, in C. R. Balbi, *El Partido Comunista y el APRA en la crisis revolucionaria de los años treinta* (Lima, 1980). On *sánchezcerrismo,* the main source, apart from Stein, *Populism in Peru,* and Loveday, *Sánchez Cerro,* is the work of O. Ciccarelli, 'Sánchez Cerro and the Depression in Peru', *Southern Quarterly,* 9, no. 3 (1971), pp. 231–52; and *Militarism, Aprismo and Violence in Peru: The Presidential Elections of 1931* (Buffalo, N.Y., 1971).

Apart from the contributions by D. M Masterson ('The Peruvian Armed Forces' and 'Soldiers, Sailors and Apristas'), the main historical treatments of the Peruvian military are A. Gerlach, 'Civil–Military Relations in Peru:

1914–1945' (Ph.D. dissertation, University of New Mexico, 1973), and a
series of books by V. Villanueva: *El Militarismo en el Perú* (Lima, 1962), *El
CAEM y la revolución de la fuerza armada* (Lima, 1972) and *100 años del
ejercita peruano: Frustraciones y cambios* (Lima, 1972). The emerging ideology associated with Centro de Altos Estudios Militares (CAEM) in the
1950s is described by L. R. Einaudi and A. C. Stepan, *Latin American
Institutional Development: Changing Military Perspectives in Peru and Brazil*
(Santa Monica, Calif., 1971); by J. Rodríguez Beruff, *Los Militares y el
poder: Un ensayo sobre la doctrina militar en el Perú, 1948–1968* (Lima,
1983); and by G. Philip, *The Rise and Fall of the Peruvian Military Radicals,
1968–1976,* University of London Institute of Latin American Studies,
Monograph no. 9 (1978), who suggests that the CAEM graduates constituted the conservative wing of the military by 1968, having been out-
flanked to the left by Velasco's group.

A sketchy history of the labour movement, but with a useful chronology, is provided by D. Sulmont, *Historia del movimiento obrero peruano
(1890–1977)* (Lima, 1977). The political dimensions of the labour movement are covered in J. Payne, *Labor and Politics in Peru* (New Haven,
Conn., 1965). A general survey of the use of strikes is J. Santistevan and
A. Delgado, *La huelga en el Perú* (Lima, 1981). An excellent historical
treatment of the labour movement, based on the mining unions of the
central Sierra, is J. Laite, 'Miners and National Politics in Peru, 1900–
1974', *Journal of Latin American Studies,* 12, no. 12 (1980), pp. 317–40.

An excellent discussion of the issue of oligarchic hegemony is A. An-
gell, 'The Difficulties of Policy Making and Implementation in Peru',
Bulletin of Latin American Research, 3, no. 1 (1984), pp. 25–43. An earlier
survey of social structure and politics is M. S. Larson and A. E. Bergman,
Social Stratification in Peru, University of California, Berkeley, Institute of
International Studies, Politics of Modernization ser. no. 5 (1969). The
persistent three-way division of the Peruvian electorate is discussed by E.
Chirinos Soto, *Cuenta y balance de las elecciones de 1962* (Lima, 1962), and
data are available in R. Roncagliolo, *Quién ganó? Elecciones, 1931–81*
(Lima, 1980). An analysis of the social composition of Sánchez Cerro's and
Haya's 1931 votes in Lima–Callao, based on rather shaky evidence, is
given in Stein, *Populism in Peru,* pp. 196–7. Comments on changing
hegemonic strategies of the elite are scattered through the literature, e.g,
Herbold, 'Developments in the Peruvian Administrative System'; Bourricaud, *La oligarquía;* and Cotler, *Clases, estado y nación.* The relationship
between economic trends and oligarchic hegemony is discussed in J.

Cotler, 'The Mechanics of Internal Domination and Social Change in Peru', in I. L. Horowitz (ed.), *Masses in Latin America* (New York, 1970), and 'The New Mode of Political Domination in Peru', in A. F. Lowenthal (ed.), *The Peruvian Experiment: Continuity and Change under Military Rule* (Princeton, N.J., 1975), pp. 47–78, although Cotler tends to treat the oligarchy as homogeneous and plays down its internal tensions.

The fall of Leguía and the Sánchez Cerro era are covered in the last volume of G. J. Basadre, *Historia de la República del Perú* (Lima, 1963–64), and in the general histories already listed. A personal reminiscence of 1930 is V. Villanueva, *Así cayó Leguía* (Lima, 1977). Sánchez Cerro's presidency is covered in detail in the works of Stein, *Populism in Peru;* Loveday, *Sánchez Cerro;* Masterson, 'The Peruvian Armed Forces' and O. Ciccarrelli, 'Sánchez Cerro and the Depression in Peru', *Southern Quarterly,* 9, no. 3 (1971), pp. 231–52, and *Militarism, Aprismo and Violence in Peru: The Presidential Election of 1931* (Buffalo, N.Y., 1971). The economic impact of the depression is analysed in Thorp and Bertram, *Peru, 1890–1976,* pt. 2, and in R. Thorp and C. Londoño 'The Effect of the Great Depression on the Economies of Peru and Colombia', in R. Thorp (ed.), *Latin America in the 1930s: The Role of the Periphery in World Crisis* (London, 1984), pp. 81–116.

The 1930 labour upheaval at Cerro de Pasco and the Malpaso massacre are covered in C. M. McArver, 'Mining and Diplomacy: United States Interests at Cerro de Pasco, 1876–1930' (Ph.D. dissertation, University of North Carolina, 1977), and in chap. 7 of A. DeWind, 'Peasants Become Miners: The Evolution of Industrial Mining Systems in Peru' (Ph.D. dissertation, Columbia University, 1977). On the Leticia dispute of 1932, see chap. 5 of R. B. St John, 'Peruvian Foreign Policy, 1919–1930: The Delimitation of Frontiers' (Ph.D. dissertation, University of Denver, 1970). APRA's role in the politics of 1930–1932 is covered, from a rather partisan viewpoint, in chap. 7 of P. F. Klarén, *Modernization, Dislocation, and Aprismo: Origins of the Peruvian Aprista Party, 1870–1932* (Austin, Tex., 1973).

For the Benavides, Prado and Bustamante periods the main specialized sources (as distinct from the general histories) are Masterson, 'The Peruvian Armed Forces'; Gilbert, *The Oligarchy and the Old Regime;* Villanueva, *El APRA y el ejército;* and Caravedo, *Burguesía e industria.* Caravedo chap. 3, contains an extremely useful discussion of the 1936 election campaign. The 1941 war with Ecuador is the subject of D. H. Zook, *Zarumilla–Marañon: The Ecuador–Peru Dispute* (New York, 1964).

The Bustamante presidency is recalled by the president himself in Bustamante, *Tres años de lucha*. The roles of APRA and the military are discussed extensively in Villanueva, *La sublevación del 48* and *El APRA el ejército,* and in Masterson, 'The Peruvian Armed Forces'. The government's problems with stabilization policy are covered in R. Hayn, 'Peruvian Exchange Controls, 1945–1948', *Inter-American Economic Affairs,* 10 (Spring 1957), pp. 47–70; Dragisic, 'Peruvian Stabilization Policies'; M. J. Frankman, 'Export Promotion and Developmental Priorities in Peru, 1946–1965' (Ph.D. dissertation, University of Texas, Austin, 1968); and D. F. Lomax, 'Monetary Control in Peru from 1945 to 1960' (Ph.D. dissertation, Stanford University, 1965). The oligarchic Right's conspiracies of 1948 are dealt with by R. Thorp, 'The Klein Correspondence', mimeo (Oxford, 1974), and in Gilbert, *The Oligarchy and the Old Regime.*

A journalistic but well-informed view of Odría's presidency is provided in T. Szulc, *Twylight of the Tyrants* (New York, 1959). The experiment with floating exchange rates in the 1950s is analysed by S. C. Tsiang, 'An Experiment with Flexible Exchange Rates: Peru, 1950–54', *IMF Staff Papers* (February 1957), pp. 449–76.

8. PERU SINCE 1960

Peruvian economic trends since 1960 are analysed in R. Thorp and G. Bertram, *Peru, 1890–1977: Growth and Policy in an Open Economy* (London, 1978); E. V. K. Fitzgerald, *The Political Economy of Peru, 1965–1978: Economic Development and the Restructuring of Capital* (Cambridge, 1979); and Oscar Dancourt, *Sobre las políticas macro-económicas en el Perú, 1970–1984* (Lima, 1986). A critical bibliographical review of economic writings can be found in Teobaldo Pinzas, *La economía peruana, 1950–1978: Un ensayo bibliográfico* (Lima, 1981).

The economic problems of Belaúnde's first government (1963–8) are analysed in P. P. Kuczynski, *Peruvian Democracy under Economic Stress: An Account of the Belaúnde Administration, 1963–1968* (Princeton, N.J., 1977). On the distribution of income, see R. Webb, *Government Policy and the Distribution of Income in Peru, 1963–1973* (Cambridge, 1977), and Shane Hunt, 'Distribution, Growth and Government: Economic Behavior in Peru', in Gustave Rainis (ed.), *Government and Economic Development* (New Haven, Conn., 1971), pp. 375–416. The problems of industrialization have been treated by M. Beaulne, *Industrialización por sustitución de importaciones, 1958–1969* (Lima, 1975); M. Vega Centeno, *Crecimiento, industrialización y cambio técnico en el Perú, 1955–1980* (Lima, 1983); J. Torres, *Estructura económica de la industria en el Perú* (Lima, 1975). There is an abundant bibliography on agrarian problems. See J. Matos and J. M. Mejía, *La reforma agraria en el Perú* (Lima, 1980); E. Alvarez, *Política económica y agricultura en el Perú, 1969–1979* (Lima, 1983); J. M. Caballero, *Economía agraria de la Sierra peruana: Antes de la reforma agraria de 1969* (Lima, 1981); A. Figueroa, *Capitalist Development and the Peasant Economy in Peru* (Cambridge, 1984); Raúl Hopkins, *Desarrollo desigual y crisis de la agricultura peruana, 1944–1969* (Lima, 1981); E. González, *Economía de la communidad campesina* (Lima, 1984).

On the economic crisis that Peru has been undergoing since the mid-1970s and the different plans for its solution, see J. González I., *Perú, una economía en crisis* (Lima, 1978); *Crisis económica y democracia* (Lima, 1980), by various authors, which discusses the measures adopted by Belaúnde's government in 1980; and D. Carbonetto, M. de Cabellos, O Dancourt and C. Fenon, *El Perú heterodoxo: Un modelo económico* (Lima, 1987), which describes the model García's government tried to install in 1985. E. Gonzáles O. (ed.), *Economía para la democracia* (Lima, 1989), is a compilation of seven lectures from different perspectives. Also by the same author, see *Crisis y democracia* (Lima, 1987), which presents the bases of the crisis and the possibilities for a democratic solution. J. Iguiñiz of the Izquierda Unida (IU) poses the alternatives available to the working and middle classes vis-à-vis the crisis in 'Perspectivas y opciones frente a la crisis', in *Revista Pensamiento Iberoamericano,* no. 4 (1983), pp. 15–44, and 'La crisis peruana actual: Esquema para una interpretación', in H. Bonilla (ed.), *Las crisis económicas en la historia del Perú* (Lima, 1986), pp. 299–364.

In *Libertad, Primer ciclo de conferencias,* 2 vols. (Lima, 1988), several authors belonging to the Movimiento Libertad, headed by Mario Vargas Llosa, diagnose from a neo-liberal perspective the Peruvian crisis and the measures to be taken to achieve a definitive solution. See also R. Thorp, 'The Stabilisation Crisis in Peru, 1975–78', in R. Thorp and L. Whitehead, *Inflation and Stabilisation in Latin America* (London, 1979); G. Pennano, C. Amat y Leon, A. Figueroa and J. Iguiñiz, *Economia peruana: Hacia donde?* (Lima, 1981); O. Ugarteche, *El estado deudor. Economía política de la deuda: Perú y Bolivia, 1968–1984* (Lima, 1986); D. Kisic, *De la corresponsabilidad a la moratoria: El caso de la deuda externa peruana, 1970–1986* (Lima, 1987); R. Webb, 'Deuda interna y ajuste financiero en el Perú', *Revista de la CEPAL* (August 1987), pp. 55–74, which examines the period 1980–5.

Detailed analyses of demographic changes in Peru can be found in Asociación Multidisciplinaria de Estudios de Población, *Problemas poblacionales peruanos,* 2 vols. (Lima, 1986). Changes in social structure and social and political mobilization during the period before the military government installed in 1968 have been examined by F. Bourricaud, *Power and Society in Contemporary Peru* (New York, 1967); F. Bourricaud, J. Bravo, H. Favre and J. Piel, *La oligarquía en el Peru* (Lima, 1969); J. Cotler, 'The Mechanics of Internal Domination and Social Change in Peru', in I. L. Horowitz (ed.), *Masses in Latin America* (New York, 1970), pp. 407–44; J. Cotler, *Clases, estado y nación en el Perú* (Lima, 1978); J. Matos, A. Salazar, A. Escobar and J. Bravo, *Perú: hoy* (Mexico City, 1971); A. Quijano, 'Tendencies in Peruvian Development and Class Structure', in J. Petras and M. Zeitlin (eds.), *Latin America, Reform or Revolution?* (New York, 1968), pp. 289–328.

The roots and patterns of the peasant movement before and after the agrarian reform decreed by the military in 1969 have been analysed by G. Alberti and Rodrigo Sánchez, *Poder y conflicto social en el valle del Mantaro* (Lima, 1974); H. Blanco, *Tierra o muerte: Las luchas campesinas en el Perú* (Mexico City, 1974); Alberto Flores-Galindo, 'Movimientos campesinos en el Perú: Balances y esquema', in R. Ames (ed.), *Las investigaciones en ciencias sociales en el Perú* (Lima, 1979); Diego García Sayan, *Toma de tierras en el Perú* (Lima, 1982); H. Handelman, *Struggle in the Andes: Peasant Political Mobilization in Peru* ((Austin, 1975); W. Kápsoli, *Los movimientos campesinos en el Perú, 1879–1965* (Lima, 1977); H. Neira, *Los Andes: Tierra o muerte* (Madrid, 1968); A. Quijano, *Problema agrario y movimientos campesinos* (Lima, 1979); R. Montoya, *Lucha por la tierra, reformas agrarias y capitalismo en el Perú del siglo XX* (Lima, 1989). On the emergence of the guerrilla movement in the mid-1960s, see H. Bejar, *Perú 1965: Una experiencia guerrillera* (Lima, 1969).

The development of and changes undergone by the workers' movement have been studied by C. R. Balbi, *Identidad clasista en el sindicalismo: Su impacto en las fábricas* (Lima, 1989); J. Parodi, *Ser obrero es algo relativo . . . Obreros, clasismo y política* (Lima, 1986), and 'La desmovilización del sindicalismo industrial peruano en el segundo belaundismo', in E. Ballón (ed.), *Movimientos sociales y crisis: El caso peruano* (Lima, 1986); E. H. Stephens, *The Politics of Workers' Participation: The Peruvian Approach in Comparative Perspective* (New York, 1980); D. Sulmont, *Historia del movimiento obrero peruano (1890–1977)* (Lima, 1977); Y. Yépez del Castillo and J. Bernedo, *La sindicalización en el Perú* (Lima, n.d.).

The military revolution stimulated an intense debate on the country's problems and the military regime's efforts to deal with them. Many of those who present the military revolution in a favourable light served as officials in the regime. Some of their writing can be found in C. Franco (ed.), *El Perú de Velasco,* 3 vols. (Lima, 1983). In addition, advisers to this regime took an active part in explaining and justifying the military revolution. C. Delgado, General Velasco's closest adviser and speech-writer, published several books which are collections of polemical articles: *El proceso revolucionario: Testimonio de lucha* (Mexico, 1972), *Testimonio de lucha* (Lima, 1973), *Revolución y participación* (Lima, 1974), and *Revolución peruana, autonomía y deslindes* (Lima, 1975). See also H. Béjar, *La revolución en la trampa* (Lima, 1974); F. Guerra, *El peruano, un proceso abierto* (Lima, 1975); E. J. Kerbusch (ed.), *Cambios estructurales en el Perú, 1968–1975* (Lima, 1975). For CEPAL's point of view on the changes effected by the military government, see A. Pinto and H. Assael, *La política económica en un proceso de cambio global* (Santiago, 1981).

In M. Lauer (ed.), *El reformismo burgues, 1968–76* (Lima, 1978), representatives of the Left from the 1970s discuss Velasco's government. Essays on the military regime in which different economic and political aspects are analysed from different perspectives can be found in A. F. Lowenthal (ed.), *The Peruvian Experiment: Continuity and Change Under Military Rule* (Princeton, N.J., 1975), and C. McClintock and A. Lowenthal (eds.), *The Peruvian Experiment Reconsidered* (Princeton, N.J., 1983). A Stepan, *The State and Society: Peru in Comparative Perspective* (Princeton, N.J., 1978), is a theoretical reflection on this type of political regime. H. Pease, *El ocaso del poder oligárquico: Lucha política en la escena oficial, 1968–1975* (Lima, 1975) and *Los caminos del poder: Tres años de crisis en la escena política* (Lima, 1979), examines the various courses of action followed by the military government. A. Quijano, *Nationalism and Capitalism in Peru: A Study in Neo-Imperialism* (New York, 1971), examines the military government from a Marxist perspective.

Studies on policies in specific sectors during the military regime can be found in G. Alberti, L. Pasara and J. Santistevan, *Estado y clase: La comunidad industrial en el Perú* (Lima, 1977); D. G. Becker, *The New Bourgeoisie and the Limits of Dependency: Mining, Class and Power in 'Revolutionary' Peru* (Princeton, N.J., 1983); D. Collier, *Squatters and Oligarchs: Authoritarian Rule and Policy Change in Peru* (Baltimore, 1976); Peter Cleaves and Martin J. Scurrah, *Agriculture, Bureaucracy and Military Government in Peru* (Ithaca, N.Y., 1980); and C. McClintock, *Peasant Cooperatives and Political Change in Peru* (Princeton, N.J., 1981). On the redistributive impact of the military's policies, see R. Webb and A. Figueroa, *Distribución del ingreso en el Perú* (Lima, 1975).

The role played by North American business in Peru is examined in C. A. Godsell, *American Corporations and Peruvian Politics* (Cambridge, 1974). The phenomenon of expropriations has been addressed by J. P. Einhorn, *Expropriation Politics* (Lexington, Mass., 1974). On the International Petroleum Company, see A. Pinelo, *The Multinational Corporation as a Force in Latin American Politics: A Case Study of the International Petroleum Company in Peru* (New York, 1973). Relations between the United States and Peru at the moment of the military coup have been examined in D. Sharp (ed.), *U.S. Foreign Policy and Peru* (Austin, Tex., 1972).

Other important sources for the military government are *Velasco, la voz de la revolución: Discursos del Presidente de la República, General de División Juan Velasco Alvarado,* 2 vols. (Lima, 1972); C. Franco, *La revolución participativa* (Lima, 1975); María del Pilar Tello (ed.), *Golpe o revolución? Hablan los militares del 68* (Lima, 1983); Henry Pease and Olga Verme, *Perú, 1968–1973: Cronología política* (Lima, 1974); F. Guerra, *Velasco: Del estado oligarquico al capitalismo de estado* (Lima, 1983).

The political transition from military to civilian government is examined in J. Cotler, 'Military Interventions and Transfer of Power to Civilians in Peru', in Guillermo O'Donnell, Philippe Schmitter and Laurence Whitehead (eds.), *Transitions from Authoritarian Rule:* vol. 2, *Latin America* (Baltimore, 1986), pp. 148–72; L. Abugattas, 'Populism and After: The Peruvian Experience', in J. Malloy and M. Siligson (eds.), *Authoritarians and Democrats: Regime Transition in Latin America* (Pittsburgh, Pa., 1987); L. A. Sánchez, *Testimonio personal: Adios a las armas* (Lima, 1988). Analyses of the constitution of 1980 can be found in E. Chirinos, *La constitución al alcance de todos* (Lima, 1980); Marcial Rubio and E. Bernales, *Constitución y sociedad política* (Lima, 1983); E. Bernales, F. Eguiguren, C. Fernández-Maldonado and D. García Belaúnde, *La constitución: Diez años después* (Lima, 1989).

On political problems during the 1980s, see A. García, *El futuro diferente,* 2d ed. (Lima, 1987); H. Bonilla and Paul W. Drake (eds.), *El Apra de la ideología a la praxis* (Lima, 1989); J. Cotler (ed.), *Para afirmar la democracia* (Lima, 1987), *Clases populares, crisis y democracia en América Latina* (Lima, 1989), and *Estrategias para el desarrollo de la democracia en el Perú y en América Latina* (Lima, 1990). J. Matos, *Desborde popular y crisis del estado: El nuevo rostro del Perú en la década de 1980* (Lima, 1984); L.

Pasara and J. Parodi (eds.), *Democracia, sociedad y gobierno en el Perú* (Lima, 1987).

The 'informal sector' has attracted a great deal of attention. See D. Carbonetto et al., *El sector informal urbano* (Lima, 1988); P. Galin, J. Carrion and O. Castillo, *Asalariados y clases populares en Lima* (Lima, 1986); R. Grompone, *Talleristas y vendedores ambulantes en Lima* (Lima, 1985); H. de Soto, *The Other Path: The Invisible Revolution in the Third World,* 2d ed. (New York, 1989).

On urban social movements, see A. Rodríguez et al., *De invasores a invadidos* (Lima, 1973); M. Barrig, 'The Difficult Equilibrium between Bread and Roses: Women's Organizations and the Transition to Democracy in Peru', in J. Jaquette (ed.), *The Women's Movement in Latin America* (Boston, 1989), pp. 114–48; C. Blondet, *Muchas vidas construyendo una identidad: Mujeres pobladoras de un barrio limeño* (Lima, 1986); C. I. Degregori, C. Blondet and N. Lynch, *Conquistadores de un nuevo mundo: De invasores a ciudadanos en San Martin de Porres* (Lima, 1986); J. Golte and N. Adams, *Los caballos de Troya de los Invasores: Estrategias campesinas en la conquista de la Gran Lima* (Lima, 1987).

Analyses of the changes in the armed forces can be found in L. Einaudi, *The Peruvian Military: A Summary Political Analysis* (Santa Monica, Calif., 1969); L. Einaudi and A. Stepan, *Latin American Institutional Development: Changing Military Perspectives in Peru and Brazil* (Santa Monica, Calif., 1971); Víctor Villanueva, *El CAEM y la revolución de las fuerzas armadas* (Lima, 1972); and *Nueva mentalidad militar en el Perú?* (Lima, 1969); and P. Mauceri, *Militares: Insurgencia y democratización en el Perú, 1980–1988* (Lima, 1989).

Changes in the Church are examined in G. Gutierrez, *A Theology of Liberation* (New York, 1971; the 1988 edition has a new and updated introduction), *We Drink from Our Own Wells: The Spiritual Journey of a People* (New York, 1984), *On Job: God-Talk and the Suffering of the Innocent* (New York, 1987) and *Dios o el oro de las Indias* (Lima, 1989). See also C. R. de Inguiñiz, 'Church, State and Society in Contemporary Peru, 1958–1988: A Process of Liberation' (Ph.D. dissertation, New School for Social Research, 1989); J. Klaiber, *Religion and Revolution in Peru, 1824–1976* (Notre Dame, Ind., 1977); L. Pásara, *Radicalización y conflicto en la Iglesia Peruana* (Lima, 1986); M. G. Mcaullay, 'Ideological Change and Internal Cleavages in the Peruvian Church: Change, Status Quo and the Priest: The Case of ONIS' (Ph.D. dissertation, University of Notre Dame, 1972); and M. Marsal, *La transformación religiosa peruana* (Lima, 1983).

On the emergence and development of Sendero Luminoso, see A. San Martín, C. Rodríguez R., F. Castelnuovo and J. Ansion, *Siete Ensayos sobre la Violencia en el Perú* (Lima, 1985); D. Chavez, *Juventud y terrorismo: Características sociales de los condenados por terrorismo y otros delitos* (Lima, 1989); C. I. Degregori, *Sendero Luminoso: I. Los hondos y mortales desencuentros. II. Lucha armada y utopia autoritaria*, 7th ed. (Lima, 1989), *Qué difícil es ser Dios: Ideología y violencia política en Sendero Luminoso* (Lima, 1989)· and *El nacimiento de Sendero Luminoso: Ayacucho y Huanta en 1969* (Lima, 1990); H. Favre, 'Sentier Lumineux et horizons obscurs', in *Problemes d'Amerique Latine,* no. 72 (1984); A. Flores Galindo, 'La guerra silenciosa', in A. Flores Galindo and N. Manrique (eds.), *Violencia y campesinado* (Lima, 1986), pp. 17–39; C. Harding, 'The Rise of Sendero Luminoso', in R. Miller (ed.), *Region and Class in Modern Peru* (Liverpool, 1986), pp. 179–207; B. J. Isbell, *The Emerging Patterns of Peasants' Responses to Sendero Luminoso* (New York, 1988); N. Manrique, 'Democracia y campesinado indígena en el Perú contemporaneo', in Flores Galindo and Manrique (eds.), *Violencia y campensinado,* pp. 5–15; C. McClintock, 'Why Peasants Rebel: The Case of Peru's Sendero Luminoso', *World Politics* (October 1984), pp. 48–84, and 'Sendero Luminoso: Peru's Maoist Guerrillas', in *Problems of Communism* (September–October 1983), pp. 19–34; Lewis Taylor, *Maoism in the Andes: Sendero Luminoso and the Contemporary Guerrilla Movement in Peru* (Liverpool, 1983); and D. S. Palmer, 'Rebellion in Rural Peru: The Origins and Evolution of Sendero Luminoso', *Comparative Politics,* 18, no. 2 (1986), pp. 127–46. In order to understand the motivations and objectives of this group it is indispensable to study *El Reportaje del Siglo,* presumably an interview with Abimael Guzman, or 'President Gonzalo' (*El Diario* [Lima], 24 July 1988).

On problems of violence and human rights, see the reports issued by Americas Watch and Amnesty International since 1984; Instituto de Defensa Legal, *Perú 1989: En la espiral de la violencia* (Lima, 1989); Comisión de Defensa de los Derechos de la Persona y Construcción de la Paz, *Violencia y democracia* (Lima, 1988); J. Klaiber (ed.), *Violencia y crisis de valores en el Perú* (Lima, 1987); R. Ames (ed.), *Informe al Congreso sobre los sucesos de los Penales* (Lima, 1988); DESCO, *Violencia política en el Perú: 1980–1988* (Lima, 1989); Comisión Especial del Senado sobre las Causas de la Violencia y Alternativas de Pacificación en el Perú, *Violencia y pacificación* (Lima, 1989); and M. P. Tello (ed.), *Sobre el volcán: Diálogo frente a la subversión* (Lima, 1989). On the problem of drug-trafficking, see Diego García Sayan (ed.), *Coca, cocaina y narco-tráfico* (Lima, 1989).

9. BOLIVIA SINCE 1930

The best general account in English of Bolivian politics since the revolution is James Dunkerley, *Rebellion in the Veins: Political Struggle in Bolivia, 1952–82* (London, 1984). James M. Malloy and Eduardo Gamarra, *Revolution and Reaction: Bolivia, 1964–85* (New Brunswick, N.J., 1988), is also valuable. James M. Malloy and Richard S. Thorn (eds.), *Beyond the Revolution: Bolivia since 1952* (Pittsburgh, Pa., 1971), contains a number of essays that are still of value. To a lesser extent it is also worth consulting Jerry R. Ladman (ed.), *Modern-Day Bolivia: Legacy of the Revolution and Prospects for the Future* (Tempe, Ariz., 1982). A standard source for the pre-revolutionary period is still Herbert S. Klein, *Parties and Political Change in Bolivia, 1880–1952* (Cambridge, 1969), which is strong up to the 1930s but peters out thereafter. Klein's more recent survey, *Bolivia: The Evolution of a Multi-Ethnic Society* (Oxford, 1982), pays due attention to the 1940–80 period, although without vindicating its curious subtitle. J. Valerie Fifer, *Bolivia: Land, Location and Politics since 1825* (Cambridge, 1972), gives useful background on the Chaco War but does not develop the implications of Bolivia's location for the post-war period. Other relevant books in English include Jerry W. Knudson, *Bolivia: Press and Revolution, 1932–64* (Larcham, Md., 1986), which contains many nuggets of information, although the analysis is not very sophisticated; Charles F. Geddes, *Patiño: The Tin King* (London, 1972), from a pro-company standpoint; Guillermo Lora, *A History of the Bolivian Labour Movement (1848–1971)* (Cambridge, 1977), by the Trotskyist veteran; Victor Andrade, *My Missions for Revolutionary Bolivia, 1944–62* (Pittsburgh, Pa., 1975), by a long-serving ambassador to Washington; Dwight B. Heath, Charles J. Erasmus and Hans C. Buechler, *Land Reform and Social Revolution in Bolivia* (New York, 1969); William J. McEwen, *Changing Rural Society* (Oxford, 1975); and Jonathan Kelley and Herbert S. Klein, *Revolution and the Rebirth of Inequality: A Theory Applied to the Bolivian National Revolution* (Berkeley, Calif., 1981). George Jackson Eder, *Inflation and Development in Latin America: A Case History of Inflation and Stabilization in Bolivia* (Ann Arbor, Mich., 1968), is a very detailed study of the 1956 counter-inflation plan, which has achieved renewed topicality in the 1980s. Juan Antonio Morales, 'Inflation and Stabilization in Bolivia', describes the 1985 counterpart in Michael Bruno, Guido di Tella, Rudiger Dornbusch and Stanley Fisher (eds.), *Inflation Stabilization: The Experience of Israel, Argentina, Brazil, Bolivia and Mexico* (Cambridge, Mass., 1988), pp. 307–57.

Among the more relevant articles in English, see John Hillman, 'Bolivia and the International Tin Carter', *Journal of Latin American Studies,* 20, no. 1 (1988), pp. 83–110; idem, 'Bolivia and British Tin Policy, 1939–1945', *Journal of Latin American Studies,* 22, no. 2 (1990), pp. 289–315; Cole Blasier, 'The US, Germany, and the Bolivian Revolutionaries', *Hispanic American Historical Review* 52, no. 1 (1972), pp. 26–54; Andrew Pearse, 'Peasants and Revolution: The Case of Bolivia', *Economy and Society,* 1, nos. 3 and 4 (1972); Laurence Whitehead, 'Miners as Voters: The Electoral Process in Bolivia's Mining Camps', *Journal of Latin American Studies* 13, no. 2 (1981), pp. 313–46; Ricardo Godoy, 'Technical and Economic Efficiency of Peasant Miners in Bolivia', *Economic Development and Cultural Change,* 34, no. 1 (1985), pp. 103–20; James Wilkie, 'U.S. Foreign Policy and Economic Assistance in Bolivia, 1948–76', in *Statistical Abstract of Latin America,* no. 22 (Los Angeles, 1983); and Laurence Whitehead, 'Bolivia' in Leslie Bethell and Ian Roxborough (eds.), *Latin America between the Second World War and the Cold War, 1944–48* (Cambridge, forthcoming).

The literature in Spanish is, of course, much larger, although Bolivia has relatively few trained historians and social scientists. The most engagingly written books on Bolivian history (in any language) are by the veteran activist of the Movimiento Nacionalista Revolucionio (MNR), Augusto Céspedes. They are also highly revealing and reasonably accurate, if inevitably partisan. His *Salamanca: O el metafísico del fracaso* (La Paz, 1973), is highly critical and should be read in conjunction with David Alvéstegui, *Salamanca: Su gravitación sobre el destino de Bolivia* (La Paz, 1962). His *El dictador suicida: 40 años de historia de Bolivia* (Santiago, 1956) should be checked against Herbert Klein and Ferrán Gallego, 'Bolivia: Génesis de una revolución: Las experiencias de reformismo militar tras la Guerra del Chaco (1936–39), 3 vols. (Ph.D. dissertation, Universidad Autónoma de Barcelona, 1990). There is as yet no good antidote to Céspedes' best historical contribution, his defence of the MNR's role in the Villarroel government, *El Presidente Colgado* (Buenos Aires, 1966). Other prominent former members of the MNR have also taken up the writing of history to good effect. José Fellmann Velarde, who wrote a hagiographic biography of Víctor Paz Estenssoro in the 1950s, subsequently produced the three-volume *Historia de Bolivia,* of which vol. 3, *La Bolivianidad semi-colonial* (La Paz, 1970), covers the first half of the twentieth century, paying particular attention to the Chaco War. Unfortunately, the author uses no footnotes to document his assertions. Luis Antezana's *Historia secreta del Movimiento Nacionalista Revolucionario,* 6 vols. (La Paz, 1984–7), gives abundant detail, but only limited analysis.

René Zavaleta Mercado provides considerable analysis, but limited detail, in his interpretative essay, 'Consideraciones generales sobre la historia de Bolivia (1932–1971)', in Pablo Gonzáles Casanova (ed.), *América Latina: Historia de medio siglo* (Mexico, 1977), pp. 74–128. A comparable interpretation is offered by Sergio Almaraz, *El poder y la caída* (La Paz, 1969). A good general history of the Chaco War is Roberto Querejazu, *Masamaclay* (La Paz, 1975). For the impact of the 1929 crisis, see Laurence Whitehead, 'La Gran Depresión en Bolivia', *Desarrollo Económico,* 12, no. 45 (1972), pp. 49–50, and Manuel E. Contreras, 'Debts, Taxes, and War: The Political Economy of Bolivia c. 1920–1935', *Journal of Latin American Studies,* 22, pt. 2 (1990), pp. 265–88. Useful on the military is General Gary Prado Salmón, *Poder y fuerzas armadas, 1949–82* (La Paz, 1984). Traditional political history can be found in Porfirio Diaz Machicado, *Historia de Bolivia: Salamanca* (La Paz, 1955), *Toro, Busch, Quintanilla* (La Paz, 1957) and *Pénaranda* (La Paz, 1958). José Luis Roca, *Fisionomía del regionalismo Boliviano* (La Paz, 1980), has made the most sustained effort to develop an interpretation of Bolivian history on the basis of regional interactions, as opposed to the economic determinism and the class or ethnic identities stressed by most non-traditionalists. For another contribution to the regional history of the revolution, see Laurence Whitehead, 'National Power and Local Power: The Case of Santa Cruz de la Sierra, Bolivia', in Francine F. Rabinowitz and Felicity M. Trueblood (eds.), *Latin American Urban Research,* vol. 3 (Beverly Hills., Calif., 1973), pp. 23–46.

A new generation of Bolivian historians and social scientists has begun to reassess the period since 1930. Their main focus has been on agrarian and indigenous history. The founders were Jorge Dandler, *El sindicalismo campesino en Bolivia* (Mexico City, 1969), and Xavier Albó, *Achacachi: Medio siglo de lucha campesina* (La Paz, 1979). The best compilation is Fernando Calderón and Jorge Dandler (eds.), *Bolivia: La fuerza histórica del campesinado* (Geneva 1986), and the best single-author contribution is Silvia Rivera, *Opimidos pero no vencidos* (Geneva, 1986), which is useful for the 1940s. There are two interesting contributions on the Chaco War by René Arze in J. P. Deler and Y. Saint-Geours (eds.), *Estados y naciones en los Andes,* 2 vols. (Lima, 1986). Two 'honorary Bolivians' of British nationality deserve mention here. Chapters 5 and 6 of James Dunkerley, *Orígenes del poder militar en Bolivia: Historia del ejército, 1879–1935* (La Paz, 1987), warrant attention, as does the striking chap. 5 of Tristan Platt, *Estado boliviano y Ayllu andino* (Lima, 1982). On the mining industry there is a useful economic history by Walter Gomez, *La minería en el desarrollo económico de Bolivia* (La Paz, 1978). On the militancy of the mine-workers, see Laurence Whitehead, 'Sobre el radicalismo de los trabajadores mineros de Bolivia', *Revista Mexicana de Sociología*, 42, no. 4 (1980), pp. 1465–96. Several of the contributions in René A. Mayorga (ed.), *Democracia a la deriva* (La Paz, 1987), which is a good introduction to the current state of social science in Bolivia, shed light on the failure of the second Siles government (1982–5). See, in particular, Miguel Urioste, '¿Concertación o hegemonia? La gestión del gobierno UDP'; Jorge Lazarte, 'Co-gestión y participación: Ideología y política del movimiento obrero'; Silvia Rivera, 'Autonomía y dependencia en el movimiento campesino contemporánea'; and Carlos Escobar, 'Las fuerzas armadas y el proceso democrático'.

10 AND 11. COLOMBIA SINCE 1930

There is no dependable one-volume history of Colombia. One useful volume which embodies recent trends in the historiography is Darío Jaramillo Agudelo (comp.), *La nueva historia de Colombia* (Bogotá, 1976). This is complemented by Jaime Jaramillo Uribe et al., *Manual de historia de Colombia*, vol. 3 (Bogotá, 1982), and a contemporary reader, Mario Arrubla et al., *Colombia: hoy*, 2d ed. (Bogotá, 1978).

On the politics of the 1930s and 1940s, see Daniel Pécaut, *L'Ordre et la violence: Evolution socio-politique de la Colombie entre 1930 et 1953* (Paris, 1986); Christopher Abel, *Politica, Iglesia y partidos en Colombia, 1886–1953* (Bogotá, 1987); and Terrance Burns Horgan, 'The Liberals Come to Power, *por Debajo de la Ruana:* A Study of the Enrique Olaya Herrera Administration, 1930–1934' (Ph.D. dissertation, Vanderbilt University, 1983). Alvaro Tirado Mejía, *Aspectos políticos del primer gobierno de Alfonso López Pumarejo, 1934–1938* (Bogotá, 1981), is a valuable introduction from a committed *lopista* perspective. On the economy, there are Rosemary Thorp and Carlos Londoño, 'The Effect of the Great Depression on the Economies of Peru and Colombia', and José Antonio Ocampo, 'The Colombian Economy in the 1930s', both in Rosemary Thorp (ed.), *Latin America in the 1930s: The Role of the Periphery in World Crisis* (London, 1984), pp. 81–143, which should be read with José Antonio Ocampo and Santiago Montenegro, *Crisis mundial, protección e industrialización: Ensayos de historia económica colombiana* (Bogotá, 1984), and Paul W. Drake, *The Money Doctor in the Andes: The Kemmerer Missions, 1923–1933* (Durham, N.C., 1989).

The most useful book on Colombian politics from the late 1940s to the mid-1960s remains Robert H. Dix, *Colombia: Political Dimensions of Change* (New Haven, Conn., 1967), which should be supplemented for the more recent period by the essays – of uneven quality – in R. Albert Berry, Ronald G. Hellman and Mauricio Solaún (eds.), *Politics of Compromise: Coalition Government in Colombia* (New Brunswick, N.J., 1980), and also Francisco Leal Buitrago, *Estado y política en Colombia* (Bogotá, 1984). The interpretation of recent politics by a maverick socialist and one-time *gaitanista,* Antonio García, remains stimulating. See in particular, *Gaitán y el camino de la revolución colombiana: Responsabilidad de las clases, las generaciones y los partidos* (Bogotá, 1974). The somewhat dated accounts of Vernon Lee Fluharty, *Dance of the Millions: Military Rule and the Social Revolution in Colombia, 1930–56* (Pittsburgh, Pa., 1957), and John D. Martz, *Colombia: A Contemporary Political Study* (Chapel Hill, N.C., 1962), still contain useful information. Also valuable is Alexander Wilde, 'Conversations among Gentlemen: Oligarchical Democracy in Colombia', in Juan J. Linz and Alfred Stepan (eds.), *The Breakdown of Democratic Regimes* (Baltimore, 1978), pp. 28–81, which, however, draws an over-easy equation between democracy and the existence of liberal institutions. The book by Jonathan Hartlyn, *Politics of Coalition Rule in Colombia* (Cambridge, 1988), conveniently synthesizes recent political science writings by both Colombian and U.S. authors, while also containing valuable original material on the propertied interests. Hartlyn summarizes his views in 'Colombia: The Politics of Violence and Accommodation', in Larry Diamond, Juan J. Linz and Seymour H. Lipset (eds.), *Democracy in Developing Countries,* vol. 4: *Latin America* (London, 1989), pp. 291–334.

No adequate study of executive power in Colombia exists. Alfredo Vásquez Carrizosa, *El poder presidencial en Colombia: La crisis permanente del derecho constitucional* (Bogotá, 1979), is a stimulating view by a Conservative opposition lawyer and former foreign minister. For congressional behaviour, see Francisco Leal Buitrago, *Estudio del comportamiento legislativo en Colombia,* 2 vols. (Bogotá, 1973–5). The power and composition of the 'oligarchy' and the validity and viability of 'oligarchy' as a concept are treated in James L. Payne, *Patterns of Conflict in Colombia* (New Haven, Conn., 1968), which is trenchantly criticized by Albert O. Hirschman in 'The Search for Paradigms as a Hindrance to Understanding', *World Politics,* 22 (1969–70), pp. 329–43. *Quién es quién en Venezuela, Panama,*

Ecuador, Colombia con datos recopilados hasta el 30 de junio de 1952 (Bogotá, 1952) remains for historians a most valuable guide not only to 'oligarchic' careers but also to those of the professional and business classes. On political parties, Jorge O. Melo (ed.), *Orígenes de los partidos políticos en Colombia* (Bogotá, 1978), is useful for background purposes. For contemporary analysis, see Gabriel Murillo C. and Israel Rivera Ortiz, *Actividades y estructura de poder en los partidos políticos colombianos* (Bogotá, 1973), which moves a long way beyond the subjective and partisan colouration characterizing accounts by political activists of earlier generations. The best examples of previous genres include, for Conservatives, Abel Carbonell, *La quincena política,* 5 vols. (Bogotá, 1952), an opposition view of Liberal reformism in the mid-1930s, and Rafael Azula Barrera, *De la revolución al orden nuevo: Proceso y drama de un pueblo* (Bogotá, 1956), an example of articulate *godo* conservatism of the early 1950s; and for Liberals, a composite apologia for the 1930–46 administrations, Plinio Mendoza N. (ed.), *El liberalismo en el gobierno,* 3 vols. (Bogotá, 1946), Carlos Lleras Restrepo, *De la democracia a la dictadura* (Bogotá, 1955) and idem, *Hacia la restauración democrática y el cambio social,* 2 vols. (Bogotá, 1964). *Gaitanismo* at the national and capital-city levels is best approached by a highly original new monograph, Herbert Braun, *The Assassination of Gaitán: Public Life and Urban Violence in Colombia* (Madison, Wis., 1985), in conjunction with Jorge Eliécer Gaitán, *Gaitán, antología de su pensamiento económico y social* (Bogotá, 1968), and *Los mejores discursos de Gaitán,* 2d ed. (Bogotá, 1968), and popular recollections of the *bogotazo* contained in Arturo Alape, *El bogotazo: Memorias de un olvido* (Havana, 1984). *Gaitanismo* at the regional level can be pursued in Gonzalo Sánchez G., *Los días de la revolución: Gaitanismo y 9 de abril en provincia* (Bogotá, 1983), and Carlos Eduardo Jaramillo, *Ibagué: Conflíctos políticos de 1930 al 9 de abril* (Bogotá, 1983). Few prominent Colombian politicians have written personal memoirs. Notable exceptions include two Liberal presidents, Alberto Lleras Camargo, *Mi gente* (Bogotá, 1976), and Carlos Lleras Restrepo, *Borradores para una historia de la República Liberal,* vol. 1 (Bogotá, 1975), and one eminent Conservative, whose account of the early stages of redemocratization in Colombia in the late 1950s is found in Camilo Vázquez Cobo, *Pro patria El Frente Nacional, su origen y desarrollo: Memorias de Camilo Vázquez Cobo Carrizosa* (Cali, n.d.).

The evolution of political ideas is best approached through Jaime Jaramillo Uribe, *Antología del pensamiento político colombiano,* 2 vols. (Bogotá, 1970), which, for Liberal ideas, can be usefully supplemented by the writing of a Socialist whose intellectual formation was shaped in the Popular Front period, Gerardo Molina, *Las ideas liberales en Colombia,* vol. 2: *1915–1934* (Bogotá, 1974), and Gerardo Molina, *Las ideas liberales en Colombia de 1935 a la iniciación del Frente Nacional* (Bogotá, 1977). There is no comparable work for the study of Conservative ideas, although Laureano Gómez, *Obras completas* (Bogotá, 1984–89) provides a useful introduction to one strand of Conservative thinking and Belisario Betancur, *Colombia: Cara a cara* (Bogotá, 1961), to another.

Opposition parties and movements are studied in Medófilo Medina, *Historia del Partido Comunista de Colombia,* vol. 1 (Bogotá, 1980); Daniel Premo, 'Alianza Nacional Popular: Populism and the Politics of Social Class in Colombia, 1961–70' (Ph.D. dissertation, University of Texas, 1972); and Richard M. Mellman, 'Populist Mass Mobilization in Latin America: ANAPO' (Ph.D. dissertation, Columbia University, 1978). Urban protest is examined further in Jaime Carrillo Bedoya, *Los paros cívicos en Colombia* (Medellín, 1981). See also Marco Palacios, *El populismo en Colombia* (Medellín, 1971).

Long periods of civilian rule have made possible a growth of electoral studies. A most valuable compilation of electoral statistics is found in *Colombia política: Estadísticas, 1935–1970* (Bogotá, 1972). An early example of quantitative analysis is provided by Anita Weiss, *Tendencias de la participación electoral en Colombia, 1935–1966* (Bogotá, 1970). Subsequent psephological studies of increasing technical virtuosity include Rodrigo Losada and Miles Williams, 'El voto presidencial en Bogotá', *Boletín Mensual de Estadística,* 229 (August 1970), pp. xv–xviii; Judith De Campos and John F. McCamant, 'Colombia Política, 1971', *Boletín Mensual de Estadística,* Departmento Administrativo Nacional de Estadistica (DANE), no. 242 (September 1971), pp. 69–128; Rodrigo Losada and Gabriel Murillo, *Análisis de las elecciones de 1972 en Bogotá* (Bogotá, 1973); Fernando Cepeda Ulloa and Claudia González de Lecaros, *Comportamiento del voto urbano en Colombia: Una aproximación* (Bogotá, 1976); Judith De Campos and José Martin, *El comportamiento electoral en 1978* (Cali., 1980), and Mario Latorre, *Política y elecciones* (Bogotá, 1980). For a more descriptive account of electoral practices, consult Mario Latorre, *Elecciones y partidos políticos en Colombia* (Bogotá, 1974).

Several scholars based in the early 1960s at the newly established Department of Sociology at the Universidad Nacional considered a reevaluation and de-mythologization of the political violence of the previous two decades to be a moral imperative. See Germán Guzmán Campos et al.,

La violencia en Colombia: Estudio de un proceso: parte descriptiva, 2 vols. (Bogotá, 1962–4). Also valuable in dispelling influential myths is the work of a political scientist, Paul Oquist, *Violencia, conflicto y política en Colombia* (Bogotá, 1978; Eng. trans., *Violence, Conflict and Politics in Colombia* ([New York, 1980]). Outstanding among recent works on the *Violencia* is a recent monograph by Carlos Miguel Ortiz Sarmiento, *Estado y subversión en Colombia: La violencia en el Quindío años 50* (Bogotá, 1985). Also useful are Gonzalo Sánchez, 'La Violencia en Colombia: New Research, New Questions', *Hispanic American Historical Review,* 65, no. 4 (1985), pp. 789–807; Sánchez and Donny Meertens, *Bandoleros, gamonales y campesinos: El caso de la violencia en Colombia,* 2d ed. (Bogotá, 1985); Sánchez and Ricardo Peñaranda (comps.), *Pasado y presente de la violencia en Colombia* (Bogotá, 1986); various authors, *Once ensayos sobre la violencia* (Bogotá, 1985); Jaime Arocha, 'La violencia in Monteverde, Colombia: Environmental and Economic Determinants of Homicide in a Coffee-Growing Municipio' (Ph.D. dissertation, Columbia University, 1975); and James D. Henderson, *When Colombia Bled: A History of the 'Violencia' in Tolima* (University, Ala., 1985). The violence of the late 1970s and 1980s is considered in two valuable works by journalists, Enrique Santos Calderón, *La guerra por la paz* (Bogotá, 1985), and Germán Hernández, *La justicia en llamas* (Bogotá, 1985); in Malcolm Deas, 'The Troubled Course of Colombian Peacemaking', *Third World Quarterly,* 8 (April 1986), pp. 639–57; and, especially, in Gonzalo Sánchez (co-ordinator), *Colombia: Violencia y democracia – informe presentado al Ministerio de Gobierno* (Bogotá, 1987).

Certain aspects of the military are examined in Francisco Leal Buitrago, *Política e intervención militar en Colombia* (with John Saxe Fernández, Militarismo en América Latina) (Bogotá, n.d.) and Richard Maullin, *Soldiers, Guerrillas and Politics in Colombia* (Lexington, Mass., 1973). On the human rights record of the military in the 1970s and 1980s, see Amnesty International, *Recomendaciones al gobierno colombiano de una misión de Amnesty International a la República de Colombia* (London, 1980); Comité Permanente por la Defensa de los Derechos Humanos, *Represión y tortura en Colombia: Informes internacionales y testimonios nacionales* (Bogotá, 1980); Consejo Regional Indígena del Cauca (CRIC), *Diez años de lucha: Historia y documentos* (Medellín, 1981); and an Americas Watch Report, *Human Rights in Colombia as President Barco Begins* (Washington, D.C., 1986). Official responses can be found in presidential messages and *memorias* of the War Ministry in the same period.

Daniel H. Levine, *Religion and Politics in Latin America: The Catholic*

Church in Venezuela and Colombia (Princeton, N.J., 1981), provides an introduction to the post–Vatican Two Church, which fruitfully pursues a particular line of comparative enquiry but does not fully supersede earlier writings by sociologists of religion like Gustavo Pérez, *El problema sacerdotal en Colombia* (Fribourg, 1963), and Benjamin E. Haddox, *Sociedad y religíon en Colombia* (Bogotá, 1965). The writings of Camilo Torres are conveniently assembled in Camilo Torres Restrepo, *Cristianismo y revolución* (Mexico City, 1970). For a contrasting example of *franquista* Catholicism in Colombia, see Miguel Angel Builes, *Cartas pastorales,* 3 vols. (Medellín/ Bogotá, 1939–57).

The history and sociology of urban labour have been less thoroughly diagnosed in Colombia than elsewhere on the continent. The three principal studies of the 1960s and 1970s are Miguel Urrutia Montoya, *Development of the Colombian Labor Movement* (New Haven, Conn., 1969), which views National Front policies towards organized labour in a broadly favourable light, and Daniel Pécaut, *Política y sindicalismo en Colombia* (Bogotá, 1973), and Edgar Caicedo, *Historia de las luchas sindicales en Colombia,* 2d ed. (Bogotá, 1974), which emobdy dissenting interpretations embracing some Marxist influences. See also Charles Bergquist, *Labor in Latin America: Comparative Essays on Chile, Argentina, Venezuela and Colombia* (Stanford, Calif., 1986); and Guillermo Perry Rubio, Hernando Gómez Buendía and Rocio Londoño Botero, 'Sindicalismo y política económica', *Coyuntura económica,* 12, no. 4 (1982), pp. 174–200. These should be complemented by two valuable essays, Jaime Tenjo, 'Aspectos cuantitativos del movimiento sindical colombiano', *Cuadernos colombianos,* no. 5 (1975), pp. 1–40, and Fernán E. González, 'Pasado y presente del sindicalismo colombiano', *Controversia* (Bogotá), nos. 35–6 (1975), and on a related topic, R. Albert Berry, *Real Wage Trends in Colombian Manufacturing and Construction during the Twentieth Century* (London, Ontario, 1974), and H. Sanín et al., 'El salario real en la industria manufacturera colombiana, 1970–1980'. *Boletín Mensual de Estadística,* 360 (1981), pp. 35–73.

The media have received little scholarly attention, but see Eduardo Ramos, 'Communication in Colombia: Economic and Social Aspects' (Ph.D. dissertation, University of Wisconsin, 1977). The history of primary and secondary education is explored by Aline Helg, *Civiliser le peuple et former les élites: L'éducation en Colombie, 1918–1957* (Paris, 1984), while T. P. Shultz, *Returns in Education in Bogotá, Colombia* (Santa Monica, Calif., 1968), raises issues relating to educational economics. Meanwhile Frank Safford, *The Ideal of the Practical: Colombia's*

Struggle to Form a Technical Elite (Austin, Tex., 1976), broaches some questions regarding technical education but addresses, for the most part, an earlier period.

Relationships between Colombia and the United States are illuminated by German Cavalier, *La política internacional de Colombia,* esp. vol. 3 (Bogotá, 1959); Stephen Randall, *The Diplomacy of Modernization: Colombian–American Relations, 1920–1940* (Toronto, 1977); and David Bushnell, *Eduardo Santos and the Good Neighbor, 1938–1942* (Gainesville, Fla., 1967). The impact of the Spanish civil war, a rewarding subject of study, is reviewed by David Bushnell, 'Colombia', in M. Falcoff and F. Pike (eds.), *The Spanish Civil War: American Hemispheric Perspectives* (Lincoln, Neb., 1982), pp. 159–202. Aspects of U.S.–Colombian relations are examined in U.S. Senate Committee on Foreign Relations, *Survey of the Alliance for Progress – Colombia: A Case Study* (Washington, D.C., 1969), and U.S. House of Representatives, Select Committee, South American Study Mission, August 9–23, 1977, *Report of the Select Committee on Narcotics Abuse and Control,* 95th Congress, 1st Session (Washington, D.C., 1977). Both domestic and foreign policy aspects of the growth of drug-trafficking after 1978 are examined in Bruce M. Bagley, 'Colombia and the War on Drugs', *Foreign Affairs,* 67, no. 1 (Fall 1988), pp. 70–92; Jaime Jaramillo, Leonidas Mora and Fernando Cubides, *Colonización, coca y guerrilla* (Bogotá, 1986); *Journal of Inter-American Studies – World Affairs,* 30, nos. 2 and 3 (1988), special issue (ed. Bruce M. Bagley); and Juan Gabriel Tokatlián, 'National Security and Drugs: Their Impact on Colombian–U.S. Relations', *Journal of Inter-American Studies – World Affairs,* 20, no. 1 (1988), pp. 133–60. On other aspects of recent foreign policy, see Marco Palacios (comp.), *Colombia no alineada* (Bogotá, 1983), and Bruce M. Bagley and Juan Gabriel Tokatlián, 'Colombian Foreign Policy in the 1980s: The Search for Leverage', *Journal of Inter-American Studies-World Affairs,* 27, no. 3 (1985), pp. 27–62. Colombian relationships with the multilateral agencies are best approached through Richard Maullin, *The Colombian–IMF Disagreement of November–December 1966: The Interpretation of Its Place in Colombian Politics* (Santa Monica, Calif., 1967), and two essays of Fernando Cepeda Ulloa, 'Colombia and the World Bank', in International Legal Center, *The Impact of International Organizations on Legal and Institutional Change in the Developing Countries* (New York, 1977), pp. 81–120, and 'Colombia and the International Labour Organization', in ibid., pp. 221–54. On the Andean Pact, see Alicia Puyana de Palacios, *Integración económica entre socios disiguales: El Grupo Andino* (Mexico City, 1983), Carlos Díaz Alejandro, *The Andean Group on the*

Integration Process of Latin America (Stanford, Calif., 1968), and Roberto Junguito, *Situación y perspectivas de la economía colombiana en relación con el proceso de integración andina* (Bogotá, 1974).

Numerous regional and local-level studies clarify political (and related) issues. Perhaps still the most powerful single work by social anthropologists is Gerardo Reichel-Dolmatoff and Alicia Reichel-Dolmatoff, *The People of Aritama* (London, 1961), which examines a settlement in the Sierra Nevada in the north of Colombia. Other studies by scholars from different disciplines and ideological positions include Darío Fajardo, *Luchas sociales y transformaciones en tres regiones del Tolima, 1936–1970* (Medellín, 1977); Michael Taussig, 'The Evolution of Rural Wage Labour in the Cauca Valley of Colombia, 1700–1970', in Kenneth Duncan and Ian Rutledge (eds.), *Land and Labour in Latin America* (Cambridge, 1977); Rolf Knight, *Sugar Plantations and Labour Patterns in the Cauca Valley* (Toronto, 1972); Roberto Pineda Giraldo, *El impacto de la violencia en el Tolima* (Bogotá, 1966); Nathan Whitten, *Black Frontiersmen: A South American Case* (Cambridge, Mass., 1972); Keith Christie, 'Oligarchy and Politics in Caldas, Colombia' (D.Phil. dissertation, Oxford University, 1974), and Shirley Harkness, 'The Elite and the Regional Urban System of Valle, Colombia as a Reflection of Dependency' (Ph.D. dissertation, Cornell University, 1973). To these should be added further works addressing the agrarian sector and peasantry (see later). Local-level politics are cogently diagnosed as well in novels and short stories, most strikingly in Gabriel García Márquez, *Cien años de soledad* (Buenos Aires, 1970; English trans., *One Hundred Years of Solitude* [New York, 1970]), and idem, *El Coronel no tiene quien le escriba* (Buenos Aires, 1976), but also in several writings of another novelist, well known within Colombia but less so outside, Eduardo Caballero Calderón, especially *El cristo de espaldas* (Bogotá, 1962).

The outstanding work of economic history remains the pioneering investigation by Luis Ospina Vásquez, *Industria y protección en Colombia, 1810–1930* (Medellín, 1955), which goes beyond 1930. See also Alvaro Tirado Mejía, *Introducción a la historia económica de Colombia* (Bogotá, 1971), William P. McGreevey, *An Economic History of Colombia, 1845–1930* (Cambridge, 1971), which also contains material on the post-1930 period and which aroused much adverse criticism owing to its heavy reliance on counterfactual statements, and José A. Ocampo (ed.), *Historia economica de Colombia* (Bogotá, 1987). For statistical data, see Miguel Urrutia Montoya and Mario Arrubla (eds.), *Compendio de estadísticas históricas de Colombia* (Bogotá, 1970).

Major development issues are raised in Carlos Díaz Alejandro, *Foreign Trade Regimes and Economic Development: Colombia* (New York, 1976); Fedesarrollo, *Lecturas sobre el desarrollo económico* (Bogotá, 1974) and *Lecturas sobre moneda y banca en Colombia* (Bogotá, 1976); and R. Nelson, T. Schultz and R. Slighton, *Structural Change in a Developing Economy: Colombia's Problems and Prospects* (Princeton, N.J., 1971). For a socialist view, see Mario Arrubla, *Estudios sobre el subdesarrollo colombiano,* 5th ed. (Bogotá, 1971). Since 1949 Colombia has been the subject of a series of reports by international advisory missions. Amongst the most important are International Bank for Reconstruction and Development, *The Basis of a Development Program for Colombia* (Washington, D.C., 1950); Louis Lebret, *Estudio sobre las condiciones del desarrollo en Colombia* (Bogotá, 1958); UN Economic Commission for Latin America, *Analyses and Projections of Economic Development,* vol. 3: *The Economic Development of Colombia* (1957); International Labour Office, *Toward Full Employment* (Geneva, 1970); *Las cuatro estrategias* (Bogotá, 1972); and International Bank for Reconstruction and Development, *Economic Growth of Colombia: Problems and Prospects* (Bogotá, 1976). Valuable light is cast on these reports by Guillermo Perry, *Introducción al estudio de los planes de desarrollo para Colombia* (Bogotá, 1972). Among various case studies, see, for example, Eduardo Wiesner Durán, *Paz de Río: Un Estudio sobre sus origines, su financiación, su experiencia y sus relaciones con el Banco Internacional para la Reconstrucción y Fomento* (Bogotá, 1963); F. Posada and J. de Antonio, *CVC: Un reto al subdesarrollo y al tradicionalismo* (Bogotá, 1966), and Harvey F. Kline, *The Coal of El Cerrejón – Dependent Bargaining and Colombian Policy-Making* (London, 1987). See also Hugo Palacios Mejía, *La economía en el derecho constitucional colombiano* (Bogotá, 1975), and projections for the 1980s from data of the 1970s by such specialists as Miguel Urrutia and Guillermo E. Perry R. in Fedesarrollo, *La economía colombiana en la década de los ochenta* (Bogotá, 1979).

The enlargement of the role of the state in the economy is reflected in diverse monographs and articles. Taxation is approached in R. Bird, *Taxation and Development: Lessons from Colombia* (Cambridge, Mass., 1970), and more recently, Guillermo Perry, 'Las reformas tributarias de 1974 y 1975 en Colombia', *Coyuntura Económica,* 7, no. 3 (1977). The analysis and recommendations contained in R. A. Musgrave and M. Gillis, *Fiscal Reform for Colombia* (Cambridge, Mass., 1971), merit attention. The role of the state in invigilating foreign investment is addressed in both Fernando Cepeda Ulloa and Mauricio Solaún, 'Political and Legal Challenges to Foreign Direct Investment in Colombia', *Journal of Inter-American*

Studies – World Affairs, 15 (September 1973), pp. 77–101, and Francois
J. Lombard, *The Foreign Investment Screening Process in LDCs: The Case of
Colombia, 1967–1975* (Boulder, Colo., 1979). Exchange rate policy and
related matters are unravelled in two works by Eduardo Wiesner Durán,
Política monetaria y cambiaria en Colombia (Bogotá, 1978) and *Devaluación y
mecanismo de ajuste en Colombia* (Bogotá, 1980). On government expenditure, M. Selowsky, *Who Benefits from Government Expenditures? A Case-Study
of Colombia* (Fairlawn, N.J., 1979), should be consulted. See also Carlos
Lleras Restrepo, *La estadística nacional – su organización – sus problemas* (Bogotá, 1938), a pioneering work from an earlier decade that advocated
substantive improvements in parts of the state apparatus.

Income distribution is analysed in R. Albert Berry and Miguel
Urrutia, *Income Distribution in Colombia* (New Haven, Conn., 1976) and
R. Albert Berry and Ronald Soligo (eds.), *Economic Policy and Income
Distribution in Colombia* (Boulder, Colo., 1980). Closely linked questions
of urban policy are explored by Harold Lubell and Douglas McCallum,
Bogotá: Urban Development and Employment (Geneva, 1968); Edgar Reveíz
Roldán et al., *Poder e información: El proceso decisorio en tres casos de política
regional y urbana en Colombia* (Bogotá, 1977); Gabriel Murillo C. and
Elizabeth B. Ungar, *Política, vivienda popular y el proceso de toma de deci-
siones en Colombia* (Bogotá, 1978); and Bruce M. Bagley, 'Political Power,
Public Policy and the State in Colombia: Case Studies of the Urban and
Agrarian Reforms during the National Front, 1958–1974' (Ph.D. dissertation, University of California, Los Angeles, 1979). See also a Marxist
view of urban social structure, J. F. Ocampo, *Dominio de clase en la ciudad
colombiana* (Medellín, 1972), and a recent study by geographers, Alan
Gilbert and Peter M. Ward, *Housing, the State and the Poor: Policy and
Practice in Three Latin American Cities* (Cambridge, 1985), which contains
valuable material on Bogotá.

On industrialization, see Albert Berry (ed.), *Essays on Industrialization in
Colombia* (Tempe, Ariz., 1983); Miguel Urrutia and Clara Elsa Villalba,
'El sector artesanal en el desarrollo económico colombiano', in Miguel
Urrutia, *Cinquenta años de desarrollo colombiano* (Bogotá, 1979), pp. 220–
330; David Chu, *The Great Depression and Industrialization in Colombia*
(Santa Monica, Calif., 1977); G. Ranis, *Challenges and Opportunities Posed
by Asia's Super-exporters: Implications for Manufactured Exports from Latin
America,* Yale University Center Papers 303 (New Haven, Conn., 1981);
and Rhys O. Jenkins, 'Latin America and the New International Division
of Labour: A Critique of Some Recent Views', in Christopher Abel and

Colin M. Lewis (eds.), *Latin America, Economic Imperialism and the State* (London, 1985), pp. 415–29. On trade, see Yesid Castro et al., *El sector comercio en Colombia: Estudio actual y perspectivas* (Bogotá, 1979). Two 'traditional' areas of foreign investment are reviewed in Jorge Villegas, *Petróleo, oligarquía e imperio* (Bogotá, 1969), and Judy White, *Historia de una ignominia: La United Fruit Company en Colombia* (Bogotá, 1978), while more recent penetration by transnational enterprise is considered by Daniel Chudnovsky, *Empresas multinacionales y ganancias monopólicas en una economía latinoamericana,* 3d ed. (Mexico City, 1978). For tendencies towards merger and consolidation of national enterprises, Superintendencia de Sociedades, *Conglomerados de Sociedades en Colombia* (Bogotá, 1978), is highly recommended; and for the participation of interest groups in decision-making, see John J. Bailey, 'Pluralist and Corporatist Dimensions of Interest Representation in Colombia', in James M. Malloy (ed.), *Authoritarianism and Corporatism in Latin America* (Pittsburgh, Pa., 1977), pp. 259–302.

Agrarian history, politics and sociology can be tackled profitably by reading Mario Arrubla (comp.), *La agricultura colombiana en el siglo XX* (Bogotá, 1976), in conjunction with a volume from the 1930s that reflects a tradition of social criticism, Alejandro López, *Problemas colombianos* (Bogotá, n.d.). More recent trends in the social sciences are manifest in Darío Mesa et al., *Colombia: Estructura política y agraria* (Medellín, 1971); Pierre Gilhòdes, *Politique et violence: La question agraire en Colombie, 1958–1971* (Paris, 1974); and Gonzalo Cataño (ed.), *Colombia: Estructura política y agraria* (Medellín, 1975). Catherine LeGrand has made a substantial contribution in *Frontier Expansion and Peasant Protest in Colombia, 1850–1936* (Albuquerque, N.M., 1986), 'Labour Acquisition and Social Conflict on the Colombian Frontier, 1850–1936', *Journal of Latin American Studies,* 16 (May 1984), pp. 27–49, and 'Perspectives for the Historical Study of Rural Politics and the Colombian Case: An Overview', *Latin American Research Review* 12, no. 1 (1977), pp. 7–37. Marco Palacios, *Coffee in Colombia, 1850–1970: An Economic, Social and Political History* (Cambridge, 1980; trans. from Spanish [Bogotá, 1979]), provides a general introduction to coffee history that can be read profitably in conjunction with ECLA/FAO, *Coffee in Latin America: Productivity Problems and Future Prospects,* vol. 1: *Colombia and El Salvador* (1958); Robert Beyer, 'The Coffee Industry in Colombia: Origins and Major Trends 1740–1940' (Ph.D. dissertation, University of Minnestoa, 1947); and B. E. Koffman, 'The National Federation of Coffee-growers of Colombia' (Ph.D. dissertation, University of Virginia, 1969). See also Roberto Junguito, *Un modelo de respuesta en la oferta de café en Colombia* (Bogotá, 1974), and, for the stimulating recollections of an active participant in coffee policy-making, Carlos Lleras Restrepo, *Política cafetera, 1937/1978* (Bogotá, 1980). An early study in agrarian reform policies is available in Albert O. Hirschman, *Journeys towards Progress: Studies of Economic Policy-Making in Latin America* (New York, 1963). On peasant farming, see Sutti Ortiz, *Uncertainties in Peasant Farming: A Colombian Case* (London, 1973). Various features of peasant organization receive attention in Hermes Tovar, *El movimiento campesino en Colombia durante los siglos XIX y XX* (Bogotá, 1972); Ronald Lee Hart, 'The Colombian Acción Comunal Program: A Political Evaluation' (Ph.D. dissertation, University of California, Los Angeles, 1974); and Orlando Fals Borda, *Peasant Society in the Colombia Andes: A Sociological Study of Saucío* (Gainesville, Fla., 1957; Spanish trans. [Bogotá, 1967]). Essential for an understanding of peasant organization in the 1970s is León Zamosc, *The Agrarian Question and the Peasant Movement in Colombia: Struggles of the National Peasant Association, 1967–1981* (Cambridge, 1986).

An early interest in Colombian Indians among national *indigenistas* is observed in Juan Friede, *El indio en la lucha por la tierra* (Bogotá, 1944), and Antonio García, *El problema indígena en Colombia* (Bogotá, 1944). A more recent and contentious study of the treatment by missionaries of Sibundoy Indians is found in Victor Daniel Bonilla, *Siervos de Dios y amos de indios* (Bogotá, 1968; trans. into English [London, 1972] from trans. into French [Paris, 1972]). One example of anthropological writing that sees the study of Indian tribal societies as an urgent necessity before their final disappearance is G. Reichel-Dolmatoff, *Desana: Simbolismo de los indios Tukano del Vaupés* (Bogotá, 1968). One work that has received insufficient scholarly attention in spite of having significance for non-musicologists as well as specialists is George List, *Music and Poetry in a Colombian Village: A Tri-Cultural Heritage* (Bloomington, Ind., 1983), which examines the fusion of Hispanic, Amerindian and African influences in music and dance.

Demographic issues were fruitfully explored in Juan Luis de Lannoy and Gustavo Pérez, *Estructuras demográficas y sociales de Colombia* (Fribourg, 1961). On internal migration, see Centro de Estudios sobre el Desarrollo Económico, *Empleo y desempleo en Colombia* (Bogotá, 1968); T. P. Shultz, *Population Growth and Internal Migration in Colombia* (Santa Monica, Calif., 1969); idem, *Rural–Urban Migration in Colombia* (Santa Monica, Calif., 1970). Colombian migrations to Venezuela receive sensitive journalistic appraisal in Gonzalo Guillén Jiménez, *Los que nunca volvieron: Colombianos en Venezuela* (Bogotá, 1980). The study of kinship, family and oral culture is in its infancy in Colombia. One notable contribution to the subject is Virginia Gutiérrez de Pineda, *Familia y cultura en Colombia: Tipologías, funciones y dinámica de la familia* (Bogotá, 1977).

12. ECUADOR SINCE 1930

Even though in the past fifteen years there has been great progress in social and historical studies in Ecuador, there is still no new general history of the republic in the twentieth century. Best of the older histories written between the 1930s and the 1950s are Oscar Efrén Reyes, *Breve historia general del Ecuador,* 6th ed. (Quito, 1957), and Alfredo Pareja Diezcanseco, *Historia del Ecuador* (Quito, 1954). To these must be added an essay of general historical interpretation by Leopoldo Benitez Vinueza, *Ecuador: Drama y paradoja* (Mexico City, 1950). A collective publication prepared in 1980 which groups short essays on diverse aspects of life in republican Ecuador is *Libro del sesquicentenario,* 4 vols. (Quito, 1980–2). Among the works by the new generation of social scientists, special mention should be made of Agustín Cueva, *El proceso de dominación política en el Ecuador* (Quito, 1982; rev. ed., 1988), an essay of interpretation on political and social development in the country in the twentieth century. See also A. Cueva 'Ecuador, 1925–1975', in *América Latina, historia de medio siglo,* ed. Pablo González Casanova (Mexico City, 1977). Also widely distributed is a reader published by the Instituto de Investigaciones Económicas of the Universidad Central, three articles of which are about the twentieth century: Leonardo Mejía et al., *Ecuador: Pasado y presente* (Quito, 1975). Osvaldo Hurtado, *El poder político en el Ecuador* (Quito, 1977), later translated into English as *Political Power in Ecuador* (Albuquerque, N.M., 1980), emphasizes the socio-political process since 1950. The book also contains an exhaustive bibliography on Ecuador. In English, George Maier, 'Presidental Succession in Ecuador, 1830–1970', *Journal of Inter-American Studies and World Affairs* (July–October 1971), pp. 479–509 is very informative. Finally, a collective work in fifteen volumes, *Nueva historia del Ecuador* (Quito, 1988–90), general editor Enrique Ayala Mora, deserves attention. Volume 10, *El Ecuador entre los veinte y los sesenta,* and vol. 11, *El Ecuador en el último período,* are relevant here. Volumes 12 and 13 contain essays of general interpretation, some with emphasis on the republican epoch. The two final volumes contain a chronology and a documentary appendix.

There is very little new literature on politics in the 1930s, but the origins and nature of *velazquismo* in the 1940s have awakened considerable debate and generated several publications. In addition to the work of Agustín Cueva already mentioned, Rafael Quintero, *El mito del populismo en el Ecuador* (Quito, 1980), deserves attention. George I. Blanksten, *Ecuador: Constitutions and Caudillos* (Berkeley, Calif., 1951), tackles a similar theme. A valuable contemporary course is *El 28 de mayo, balance de una revolución popular* (Quito, 1946). See also *El 28 de mayo de 1944: Testimonio* (Guayaquil, 1984) and Silvia Vega Ugalde, *'La Gloriosa'* (Quito, 1987).

There is little worthy of mention on the politics of the 1950s and 1960s except an unpublished but frequently cited master's thesis by Gonzalo Abad, *El proceso de lucha por el poder en el Ecuador* (Mexico City, 1970); John Fitch, *The Military Coup d' État as a Political Process: Ecuador, 1948–1966* (Baltimore, 1977); and a series of articles by Peter Pyne: 'The Politics of Instability in Ecuador: The Overthrow of the President, 1961', *Journal of Latin American Studies* 7 (1975), pp. 109–33; 'Presidential Caesarism in Latin America: Myth or Reality? A Case Study of the Ecuadorian Executive during the presidency of José María Velasco Ibarra, 1960–1', *Comparative Politics,* 9 (1977), pp. 281–304; 'Legislatures and Development: The Case of Ecuador, 1960–61', *Comparative Political Studies* 9 (1976), pp. 69–72. The lack of literature on the period confers even more importance on a book that caused a worldwide commotion when it was published: *Inside the Company: CIA Diary* (New York, 1975), in which Philip Agee makes revealing statements about his period as a CIA agent in Ecuador.

On the 1970s, a publication that achieved wide distribution was a reader that brought together a number of articles on economics, society, and politics: Gerhard Drekonja et al. (eds.), *Ecuador hoy* (Bogotá, 1978). See also another collection of essays, Alberto Acosta et al. (eds.), *Ecuador: El mito del desarrollo* (Quito, 1982). A valuable study on the period of the military dicatorship is Francisco R. Dávila Aldás, *Las luchas por la hegemonía y la consolidación política de la burguesía en el Ecuador* (Mexico City, 1984). Nelson Argones, *El juego del poder: De Rodríguez Lara a Febres Cordero* (Quito, 1985), focusses with great clarity on the changes in the political scene during a period of more than a decade. Nick D. Mills, *Crisis, conflicto y consenso: Ecuador (1979–1984)* (Quito, 1984), is an assessment of the first constitutional governments after the dictatorship.

The 1980s saw a proliferation of books on the most notable political events of the decade. The military movement led by General Vargas Pazzos against the government of Febres Cordero was, in particular, the topic of a dozen books. Especially worthy of mention are *La hora del general* (Quito, 1986), and *Operación Taura* (Quito, 1987), both by Gonzalo Ortiz Crespo, and John Maldonado, *Taura: Lo que no se ha dicho* (Quito, 1988). A highly publicized polemic between two presidents is Blasco Peñaherrera Padilla, *El viernes negro* (Quito, 1988), and León Febres Cordero, *Autopsia de una traición* (Quito, 1989). Marco Zalamea, *El régimen febrescorderista* (Cuenca, 1988), presents a balanced analytical view of the Febres Cordero administration. Enrique Ayala, *Los partidos políticos en el Ecuador: Síntesis histórica* (Quito, 1986) is a brief overview. Finally, Patricio Moncayo, *Ecuador, grietas en la dominación* (Quito, 1977), H. Handelman, *Ecuador: A New Political Direction* (Hanover, 1979), D. P. Hanson, *Political Decision Making in Ecuador: The Influence of Business Groups* (Ph.D. dissertation, University of Michigan, 1971), and Adrián Carrazco, et al., *Estado, política y democracia en el Ecuador* (Quito, 1988) are worthy of note.

There has been no important demographic study of Ecuador apart from Consejo Nacional de Desarrollo/UNFP, *Población y cambios sociales: Diagnóstico sociodemográfico del Ecuador, 1950–1982* (Quito, 1987). Jean Paul Deler, *Ecuador del espacio al estado nacional* (Quito, 1987), contains important work on the spatial and geographical development of the country. See also Lucas Achig, *El proceso urbano de Quito* (Quito, n.d.), and R. F. Bromley, *Development and Planning in Ecuador* (London, 1977).

There is no general economic history of Ecuador, but a work by Fernando Velasco Abad, *Ecuador: Capitalismo y dependencia* (Quito, 1981), originally a thesis, is a notable effort to outline and analyse the different stages in the socio-economic life of the country. By now it has become a classic. See also José Moncada, *Capitalismo y subdesarrollo ecuatoriano en el siglo XX* (Quito, 1982), and *Capitalismo y neoliberalismo en el Ecuador* (Quito, 1985). Luis A. Carbo, *Historia monetaria y cambiaria del Ecuador* (Quito, 1941; reprinted in 1953 and 1978), contains abundant information and documentation. On the period immediately before the depression of the 1930s, see Banco Central del Ecuador, *Crisis y cambios de la economía ecuatoriana en los años veinte* (Quito, 1987). On public finance in the 1930s, Linda A. Rodríguez, *The Search for Public Policy: Regional Politics and Public Finance in Ecuador, 1930–1940* (Berkeley, Calif., 1985), is an important work. See also Paul W. Drake, *The Money Doctor in the Andes: The Kemmerer Missions, 1923–1933* (Durham, N.C., 1989), chap. 4. José Samaniego, *Crisis económica del Ecuador* (Quito, 1988), treats the periods 1929–33 and 1980–4 in comparative terms. On the economic situation in the late 1980s there has been a great proliferation of books: for example, Pablo Estrella et al., *La crisis de la economía ecuatoriana* (Quito, 1986); Guillermo Landazuria, *El Ecuador en el encrucijada* (Quito, 1987); Louis Lafeber (ed.), *Economía política del Ecuador: Campo, región, nación* (Quito, 1985); Eduardo Santos and Marianita Mora, *Ecuador: La década de los ochenta* (Quito, 1987).

The principal export products of the country have been the topic of specific studies. Particularly worthy of mention is Carlos Larrea et al., *El banano en el Ecuador* (Quito, 1987). In the abundant literature produced on the petroleum question, special notice should be taken of Jaime Galarza, *El festín del petróleo* (Cuenca, 1979), a denunciation. Also noteworthy are Arnaldo Booco, *Auge petrolero, modernización y subdesarrollo: El Ecuador de los años sesenta* (Quito, 1987); Alberto Acosta et al., *Ecuador: Petróleo y crisis* (Quito, 1986); and the study by CEPAL, *Ecuador: Desafíos y logros de la política económica en la fase de expansión petrolera* (Santiago, 1978). Leonardo Vicuña, *Economía ecuatoriana: Problemas, tendencias y proyecciones* (Guayaquil, 1980), analyses various perspectives.

Several works focus on the topic of industrialization: A. Bottomley, 'Imperfect Competition in the Industrialization of Ecuador', *Inter-American Economic Affairs*, 29 (1965); Sabine Fisher, *Estado, clase e industria* (Quito, 1987); and G. Montaño and E. Wygard, *Visión sobre la industria ecuatoriana* (Quito, 1975). But it is the agrarian sector that has seen the most extensive bibliographic production in the past twenty years. A pioneer study is R. Baraona's CIDA (Comité Inter-Americano de Desarrollo Agrícola) report, *Tenencia de la tierra y desarrollo socio-económico del sector agrícola, Ecuador* (Washington, D.C., 1965). Osvaldo Barsky published several works on the agrarian question in the country, which were later synthesized into one book that soon became a basic reference text: *La reforma agraria ecuatoriana* (Quito, 1984). Also worthy of mention are Gustavo Cosse, *Estado y agro en el Ecuador* (Quito, 1984); Andrés Guerrero, *Haciendas, capital y lucha de clases andina* (Quito, 1983); Miguel Murmis (ed.), *Clase y región en el agro ecuatoriano* (Quito, 1986); Luciano Martínez, *La descomposición del campesinado en la Sierra ecuatoriana* (Quito, 1980); and C. Quishpe and V. Piedra, *El proceso de consolidación de la hacienda en el Ecuador* (Cuenca, 1977). FLACSO/ CEPLAES, *Ecuador: Cambios en el agro serrano* (Quito, 1980) was the stimulus for a debate on several agrarian topics. An important recent study is Fausto Jordán, *El minifundio* (Quito, 1988).

Some foreign studies worthy of mention are John Brandl (ed.),

Chimborazo: Life on the Haciendas of Highland Ecuador (London, 1976); Charles S. Blankstein and Clarence Zuvekas, 'Agrarian Reform in Ecuador: An Evaluation of Past Efforts and the Development of a New Approach', *Economic Development and Cultural Change* 22 (1973) pp. 73–94; Howard Handelman, *Ecuadorian Agrarian Reform: The Politics of Limited Change* (Hanover, N.H., 1980); David Lehman, *Share-Cropping and the Capitalist Transition in Agriculture: Some Evidence from Highland Ecuador* (Cambridge, 1982); Miguel Mirmir, *Size of Units, Control of Land and Participation in Production: Some Contextual Material for the Study of Process of Capitalization of Small Producers in Carchi, Ecuador* (Toronto, 1983).

Alongside the agrarian studies, there is a body of work on the indigenous peasant movement and its organization. Fernando Velasco, *Reforma agraria y movimiento campesino indígena en la Sierra* (Quito, 1979), is a valuable study. See also *La movilización campesina antes de la reforma agraria* (Quito, 1979), by Hernán Ibarra, who is also the author of *Bibliografía analítica agraria, 1900–1982* (Quito, 1982).

There has been a substantial development of studies on the indigenous peoples: for example, Oswaldo Albornoz, *Las luchas indígenas en el Ecuador* (Quito, 1971); Gonzalo Rubio Orbe, *Los indios ecuatorianos: Evolución histórica y política indigenistas* (Quito, 1987); Alicia Ibarra, *Los indígenas y el estado en el Ecuador* (Quito, 1987); Norman E. Whitten, Jr., *Sacha Runa: Ethnicity and Adaptation of Ecuadorian Jungle Quichua* (Urbana, Ill., 1976); and José Sánchez Parga, *La trama del poder en la comunidad andina* (Quito, 1986).

On the birth and development of the labour movement, see Pedro Saad, *La CTE y su papel histórico* (Guayaquil, 1974); Patricio Ycaza, *Historia del movimiento obrero ecuatoriano* (Quito, 1983); Iván J. Paz and Miño Cepeda, *La CEDOC en la historia del moviemiento obrero ecuatoriano* (Quito, 1988); and Isabel Robalino Bolle, *El sindicalismo en el Ecuador* (Quito, n.d.). A more general approach is taken in Hernán Ibarra, *La formación del movimiento popular (1925–1936)* (Quito, 1984). But it is the strike and massacre that took place on 15 November 1922 that have attracted most attention: Elías Muñoz Vicuña, *El 15 de noviembre de 1922, su importancia y sus proyecciones* (Guayaquil, 1973); INFOC, *El 15 de noviembre de 1922 y la fundación del socialismo relatados por sus protagonistas*, 2 vols. (Quito, 1982); and Patricio Martínez, *Guayaquil noviembre de 1922* (Quito, 1988).

Another bloody event in labour history which occurred in 1977 is the topic of Víctor Grande, *La masacre de Aztra* (Cuenca, 1979). A general work worthy of mention is Marco Velasco, *Insubordinación y conciencia de clase* (Quito, 1983). There are also several publications in which popular history is discussed in relation to leftist organizations: Manuel Agustín Aguirre, 'El marxismo, la revolución y los partidos socialista y comunista en el Ecuador', in *Carlos Marx Homenaje* (Cuenca, 1983); Alexei Páez, *El anarquismo en el Ecuador* (Quito, 1986); and Leonardo Muñoz, *Testimonio de lucha: Memorias sobre la historia del socialismo en el Ecuador* (Quito, 1988). There is a large quantity of information, although much of it now out of date, in Osvaldo Hurtado and Joachim Herudek, *La organización popular en el Ecuador* (Quito, 1974).

On Ecuadorian culture, especially literature, there are various texts: Benjamín Carrión, *El nuevo relato ecuatoriano* (Quito, 1958); Angel F. Rojas, *La novela ecuatoriana* (Mexico, 1950); Augusto Arias, *Panorama de le literatura ecuatoriana* (Quito, 1956); Antonio Sacoto, *La nueva novela ecuatoriana* (Quito, 1981); Agustín Cueva, *Lecturas y rupturas* (Quito, 1986), and Fernando Tinajero, *De la evasión al desencanto* (Quito, 1987). The richly illustrated *Historia del arte ecuatoriano* (Quito, 1978) offers a broad view of the subject. A general overview of the most recent period can be found in Casa de la Cultura Ecuatoriana, *1969–1979: Diez años de la cultura en el Ecuador* (Quito, 1980). The country's problems of cultural, ethnic and national definition are addressed in Ruth Moya, *Ecuador: Cultura, conflicto y utopía* (Quito, 1987), and *Ecuador multinacional: Conciencia y cultura* (Quito, 1989). The basic reference in the field of the philosophy and history of ideas is a book by Arturo Andrés Roig, *Esquemas para una historia de la filosofía ecuatoriana* (Quito, 1977).

Finally, three bibliographical and research guides should be mentioned: John J. Tepaske (ed.), *Research Guide to Andean History, Bolivia, Chile, Ecuador and Peru,* (Durham, N.C., 1981), in which the section on Ecuador has an introduction by Jaime E. Rodrídguez; Robert E. Norris, *Guia bibliográfica para el estudio de la historia ecuatoriana* (Austin, Tex., 1978), complete and well organized; and a recent volume in the World Bibliographical Series, *Ecuador,* vol. 101 (Oxford, 1989), compiled by David Corkill, which contains a large bibliography in English, classified by topics, but very few titles in Spanish.

13. VENEZUELA SINCE 1930

The best bibliographical guide is John Lombardi et al., *Venezuelan History: A Comprehensive Working Bibliography* (Boston, 1977). Since 1970, the Biblioteca Nacional has irregularly issued the series *Bibliografía venezolana* and *Anuario bibliográfico venezolano.* For historiography, see Germán Carrera Damas, *Historia de la historiografía venezolana: Textos para su estudio* (Caracas, 1961), *Cuestiones de historiografía venezolana* (Caracas, 1964) and *Historiografía marxista venezolana y otros temas* (Venezuela, 1967). A useful chronological guide is A. Arellano Moreno, *Guía de historia de Venezuela,* 3d ed. (Caracas, 1977). The *Diccionario de historia de Venezuela,* 3 vols. (Caracas, 1990), edited by Manuel Pérez Vila and published by the Fundación Polar is invaluable.

Several collections of printed source material have appeared. The most impressive general series is Ramón J. Velásquez, *El pensamiento político venezolano del siglo XX: Documentos para su estudio,* 15 vols. to date (Caracas, 1983–). See also Naudy Suárez Figueroa's *Programas políticos venezolanos de la primera mitad del siglo XX,* 2 vols. (Caracas, 1977). Allan R. Brewer-Carías, *Las constituciones de Venezuela* (Madrid, 1985), discusses and reproduces the texts of all constitutions. José Agustín Catalá has edited and reprinted documents relating to the dictatorship of Pérez Jiménez and the clandestine resistance of the Acción Democrática (AD) – frequently taken from the 1960s trials of *perezjimenistas.* See *Libro negro 1952* (Caracas, 1974); *Documentos para la historia de la resistencia,* 4 vols. (Caracas, 1969); *Los crímenes de Pérez Jiménez* (various subtitles and volumes, Caracas, 1971); *Los jerarcas impunes del perezjimenismo* (various subtitles and volumes, Caracas, 1971). José Rivas Rivas has compiled and reproduced newspaper clippings which cover the period from 1936 to 1958 in *Historia gráfica de Venezuela,* 3 vols. (Caracas, 1961). Economic and statistical sources may be found in the Banco Central de Venezuela, *La economía venezolana en los últimos treinta y cinco años* (Caracas, 1978); Miguel Izard, *Series estadísticas para la historia de Venezuela* (Mérida, 1970); and the official *Anuario Estadístico,* published since 1877 with some interruptions.

Two collections of interviews with public figures provide valuable source material for recent history. Alfredo Peña conducted several lengthy interviews at the time of the 1978 election: *Conversaciones con Douglas Bravo* (Caracas, 1978); *Conversaciones con Luis Herrera Campíns* (Caracas, 1978); *Conversaciones con Américo Martín* (Caracas 1978); *Conversaciones con José Vincente Rangel* (Caracas, 1978); *Conversaciones con Uslar Pietri* (Caracas, 1978); *Conversaciones con Luis Beltrán Prieto* (Caracas, 1979); and *Conversaciones con Carlos Andrés Pérez,* 2 vols. (Caracas, 1979). Agustín Blanco Muñoz's series, *Testimonios violentos,* 8 vols. (Caracas, 1980–3), includes the following titles: *El 23 de enero: Habla la conspiración : La Lucha armada: Hablan 5 jefes; La Lucha armada: Hablan 6 commandantes; La Conspiración civico-*

militar: Guairazo, Barcelonazo, Carupanazo, y Porteñazo; La lqzuierda revo-lucionaria insurge; La Lucha armada: Hablan 3 comandantes de la izquierda revolucionaria; Pedro Estrada habló; Habla el General.

The following general works treat all of Venezuelan history or the period since independence: John V. Lombardi, *Venezuela: The Search for Order, the Dream of Progress* (New York, 1982); Guillermo Morón, *A History of Venezuela* (London, 1976); J. L. Salcedo-Bastardo, *Historia Fundamental de Venezuela* (Caracas, 1979); Mariano Picón Salas, Augusto Mijares and Ramón Díaz Sánchez, *Venezuela independiente: Evolución política y social, 1810–1960* (Caracas, 1975). The most ambitious effort to cover the twentieth century is that of Juan Bautista Fuenmayor, *Historia de la Venezuela política contemporánea, 1899–1960*, 10 vols. to date (1978–). Fuenmayor has written a one-volume survey entitled *1928–1948: Veinte años de política* (Caracas, 1979). Judith Ewell, *Venezuela: A Century of Change* (London, 1984), and Ramón J. Velásquez et al., *Venezuela Moderna: Medio siglo de historia, 1926–1976*, 2d ed. (Caracas, 1979), concentrate on the post-Gómez period.

For economic history, see Federico Brito Figueroa, *Historia económica y social de Venezuela*, 2 vols (Caracas, 1966); Domingo Alberto Rangel, *Capital y desarrollo*, 3 vols. (Caracas, 1969); Loring Allen, *Venezuelan Economic Development: A Politico-Economic Analysis* (Greenwich, Conn., 1977); and Sergio Aranda, *La economía venezolana* (Mexico, 1977). More special-ized studies include M. Ignacio Purroy, *Estado e industrialización en Vene-zuela* (Valencia, 1982); Clemy Machado de Acedo, Elena Plaza and Emilio Pacheco, *Estado y grupos económicos en Venezuela (su análisis a través de la tierra, construcción y banca)* (Caracas, 1981); Janet Kelly de Escobar, *Empresas del estado en América Latina* (Caracas, 1985); Louis E. Heaton, *The Agricultural Development of Venezuela* (New York, 1969); and Gastón Carvallo, *El hato venezolano, 1900–1980* (Caracas, 1985).

For petroleum, see William Sullivan and Winfield J. Burggraaff, *El petróleo en Venezuela: Una bibliografía* (Caracas, 1977). Sullivan and Brian S. McBeth have updated and annotated the guide for the English-speaking audience: *Petroleum in Venezuela: A Partially Annotated Bibliography to 1980* (Boston, 1985). The classic work is still Rómulo Betancourt, *Venezuela: Política y petróleo* (Mexico City, 1956); see also the compilation of Betan-court's essays in *El petróleo de Venezuela* (Barcelona, 1978). Other good studies include Edwin Lieuwen, *Petroleum in Venezuela: A History* (Berkeley, Calif., 1954), and 'The Politics of Energy in Venezuela', in John D. Wirth (ed.), *Latin American Oil Companies and the Politics of Energy* (Lincoln, Neb.,

1985), pp. 189–225; Franklin Tugwell, *The Politics of Oil in Venezuela* (Stanford, Calif., 1975); B. S. McBeth, *Juan Vincente Gómez and the Oil Companies in Venezuela, 1908–1935* (Cambridge, 1983); George Philip, *Oil and Politics in Latin America: Nationalist Movements and State Companies* (Cambridge, 1982); James F. Petras et al., *The Nationalization of Venezuelan Oil* (New York, 1977); Jorge Salazar Carrillo, *Oil in the Economic Development of Venezuela* (New York, 1976); Luis Vallenilla, *Oil: The Making of a New Economic Order – Venezuelan Oil and OPEC* (New York, 1975); and Comisión Ideológica de RUPTURA, *El imperialismo petrolero y la revolución venezolana*, 2 vols. (Caracas, 1977–9). Aníbal Martínez has several useful introductions to the topic, including *Gumersindo Torres* (Caracas, 1980), *Historia petrolera venezolana en 20 jornadas* (Caracas, 1973) and *Cronología del petróleo Venezolano* (Caracas, 1970). Juan Pablo Pérez Alfonzo's writings provide a guide to government policy and his criticisms of it: *Hundiéndonos en el excremento del diablo*, 3d ed. (Caracas, 1976), *El pentágano petrolero* (Caracas, 1967), *Petróleo y dependencia* (Caracas, 1971) and *Política petrolera* (Caracas, 1962).

The literature on the Gómez dictatorship (1908–35) is growing, but little useful material has yet been published on the López and Medina administrations (1936–45). On Gómez, in addition to the old but still useful works of Thomas Rourke [Daniel J. Clinton], *Gomez, Tyrant of the Andes* (New York, 1937), and John Lavin, *A Halo for Gómez* (New York, 1954), see Luis Cipriano Rodríguez, *Gomez: Agricultura, petróleo y dependencia* (Caracas, 1983); Yolanda Segnini, *La consolidación del regimen de Juan Vicente Gómez* (Caracas, 1982); Domingo Alberto Rangel, *Gómez el amo del poder* (Caracas, 1975); Ramón J. Velásquez's fictionalized account, *Confidencias imaginarias de Juan Vicente Gómez* (Caracas, 1979); Elías Pino Iturrieta, *Positivismo y gomecismo* (Caracas, 1978); and Arturo Sosa A., *Ensayos sobre el pensamiento político positivista venezolano* (Caracas, 1985). See also bibliographical essay 18 in Leslie Bethell (ed.), *The Cambridge History of Latin America*, vol. 5 (Cambridge, 1986). On the López Contreras years, see E. López Contreras, *Proceso político social, 1928–1936* (Caracas, 1935), *Páginas para la historia militar de Venezuela* (Caracas, 1945) and *El Triunfo de la verdad* (Mexico, 1949), among his other works; Alfredo Tarre Murzi [Sanin], *López Contreras: De la tiranía a la libertad,* 3rd ed. (Caracas, 1982), a fictionalized account; and Silvia Mijares, *Organizaciones políticas de 1936* (Caracas, 1980). On Medina, see his *Cuatro años de democracia* (Caracas, 1963); Luis Cordero Velázquez, *Betancourt y la conjura militar del 45* (Caracas, 1978); Domingo Alberto Rangel, *Los andinos en el poder* (Caracas, 1975).

Scholars have directed some attention to the democratic *trienio* (1945–8) and the dictatorship of 1948–58. See, for example, Charles D. Ameringer, *The Democratic Life in Exile: The Antidictatorial Struggle in the Caribbean, 1945–59* (Coral Gables, Fla., 1974); Glen L. Kolb, *Democracy and Dicatorship in Venezuela, 1945–1958* (Hamden, Conn., 1974); and Judith Ewell, *The Indictment of a Dictator: The Extradition and Trial of Marcos Perez Jiménez* (College Station, Tex., 1981). Pérez Jiménez's minister of the interior, Laureano Vallenilla Lanz, provides the most interesting of his apologies: *Escrito de memoria* (Caracas, 1967), and *Razones de proscrito* (Caracas, 1967). Andrés Stambouli, *Crisis política: Venezuela, 1945–1958* (Caracas, 1980), is a balanced account, as is Manuel Rodríguez Campos, *Venezuela, 1948–1958: El proceso económico y social de la dictadura* (Caracas, 1983). Three studies competently chronicle Pérez's downfall: Helena Plaza, *El 23 de enero de 1958 y el proceso de consolidación de la democracia representativa en Venezuela* (Caracas, 1978); Philip B. Taylor, Jr., *The Venezuelan Golpe de Estado of 1958: The Fall of Marcos Pérez Jiménez* (Washington, D.C., 1968); and Joseph Doyle, 'Venezuela 1958: Transition from Dictatorship to Democracy' (Ph.D. dissertation, George Washington University, 1967).

Most recent political histories have lauded the development of a viable democracy since 1958 and the role of AD in particular. See, for example, John Martz, *Acción Democrática: Evolution of a Modern Political Party in Venezuela* (Princeton, N.J., 1966); with Enrique Baloyra, *Political Attitudes in Venezuela: Societal Cleavages and Political Opinion* (Austin, Tex., 1979); and with David J. Myers (ed.), *Venezuela, the Democratic Experience* (New York, 1977; rev. ed., 1986). Other standard works are Robert Alexander, *The Venezuelan Democratic Revolution* (New Brunswick, N.J., 1964); Daniel Levine, *Conflict and Political Change in Venezuela* (Princeton, N.J., 1973); idem, 'Venezuela since 1958: The Consolidation of Democratic Politics', in Juan J. Linz and Alfred Stepan (eds.), *The Breakdown of Democratic Regimes* (Baltimore, 1978), pp. 82–109; David Blank, *Politics in Venezuela* (Boston, 1973); idem, *Venezuela: Politics in a Petroleum Republic* (New York, 1984); José Antonio Gil Yepes, *The Challenge of Venezuelan Democracy* (New Brunswick, N.J., 1981); Harrison Sabin Howard, *Rómulo Gallegos y la revolución burguesa en Venezuela* (Caracas, 1976); and Clemy Machado de Acedo, *El positivismo en las ideas políticas de Rómulo Gallegos* (Caracas, 1982). John A. Peeler compares Venezuelan political development with that of two other countries in *Latin American Democracies: Colombia, Costa Rica, Venezuela* (Chapel Hill, N.C., 1985).

Several recent studies have been more critical both of AD and of Venezuelan democracy. See Moisés Moleiro, *El partido del pueblo: Crónica de un fraude,* 2d ed. (Valencia, 1979); José Silva Michelena, *The Illusion of Democracy in Dependent Nations* (Cambridge, Mass., 1971); idem, with Frank Bonilla, *The Failure of Elites* (Cambridge, Mass., 1970); Carlos Rangel, *Del buen salvaje al buen revolucionario* (Caracas, 1976); Daniel Hellinger, 'Populism and Nationalism in Venezuela: New Perspectives on Acción Democrática', *Latin American Perspectives,* 11, no. 4 (1984), pp. 33–59; Terry Karl, 'The Political Economy of Petrodollars: Oil and Democracy in Venezuela' (Ph.D. dissertation, Stanford University, 1982); and nearly all of Domingo Alberto Rangel's monographs.

On Comité de Organización Política Electoral Independiente (COPEI), Rafael Caldera's writings and speeches are valuable; see, for example, *Ideario: La democracia cristiana en América Latina* (Barcelona, 1970) and *Habla el presidente* (Caracas, 1969). See also Donald Herman, *Christian Democracy in Venezuela* (Chapel Hill, N.C., 1980). On other parties, see Robert Alexander, *The Communist Party of Venezuela* (Stanford, Calif., 1980); Steve Ellner, 'The MAS Party in Venezuela', *Latin American Perspectives,* 13 no. 2 (1986), pp. 81–107, and idem, *Venezuela's Movimiento al Socialismo: From Guerrilla Defeat to Innovative Politics* (Durham, N.C., 1988). Manuel Caballero, *Latin America and the Comintern, 1919–1943* (Cambridge, 1986), contains some information on the early history of the Venezuelan Communist Party. Manuel Vicente Magallanes, *Los partidos políticos en la evolución histórica venezolana,* 5th ed. (Caracas, 1983), is indispensable in tracing the rise and fall of many minor parties, as well as the major ones.

The quinquennial elections since 1958 have inspired considerable national self-examination; see, for example, the following compilations from *El Nacional*'s anniversary issues: *Venezuela 1979: Examen y futuro* (Caracas, 1980), and *1984: A donde va Venezuela?* (Caracas, 1984). The excellent *El caso Venezuela: Una ilusión de armonía* (Caracas, 1985), edited by Moisés Naím and Ramón Piñango, does much the same thing from a scholarly perspective.

Rómulo Betancourt is the only major figure who has received extensive attention from political biographers. In addition to Betancourt's own voluminous writings, see Robert Alexander, *Rómulo Betancourt and the Transformation of Venezuela* (New Brunswick, N.J., 1982); Alejandro Gómez, *Rómulo Betancourt y el Partido Comunista de Costa Rica: 1931–1935* (Caracas, 1985); Arturo Sosa A. and Eloi Lengrand in *Del garibaldismo estudiantil a la izquierda criolla: Los origenes marxistas del proyecto de A.D.* (*1928–1935*) (Caracas, 1981); Manuel Caballero, *Rómulo Betancourt* (Caracas, 1979); Ramón J. Velásquez, J. F. Sucre Figarella and Blas Bruni Celli, *Betancourt en la historia de Venezuela del siglo XX* (Caracas, 1980); and the fictionalized biography by Alfredo Tarre Murzi [Sanin], *Rómulo* (Valencia, Venezuela, 1984).

Little has been written on women in politics (or on women in general), and the women who spoke to Fania Petzoldt and Jacinta Bevilacqua for the book *Nosotras también nos jugamos la vida: Testimonios de la mujer venezolana en la lucha clandestina, 1948–1958* (Caracas, 1979) show some bitterness at being overlooked. Angela Zago writes an engaging memoir of her days with the guerrillas in the mid-1960s, *Aquí no ha pasado nada* (Caracas, 1972), and the acrid essays of Elisa Lerner – such as *Crónicas ginecológicas* (Caracas, 1984) – discuss women's roles.

Studies of interest groups and pressure groups have enriched the political literature. See Robert F. Arnove, *Student Alienation: A Venezuelan Study* (New York, 1971); Robert D. Bond, 'Business Associations and Interest Politics in Venezuela: The FEDECAMARAS and the Determination of National Economic Policies' (Ph.D. dissertation, Vanderbilt University, 1975); Samuel Moncada, *Los huevos de la serpiente: FEDECAMARAS por dentro* (Caracas, 1985); John Duncan Powell, *Political Mobilization of the Venezuelan Peasant* (Cambridge, Mass., 1971); and Talton F. Ray, *The Politics of the Barrios of Venezuela* (Berkeley, Calif., 1969). On the military, see Winfield J. Burggraaff, *The Venezuelan Armed Froces in Politics, 1935–1959* (Columbia, Mo., 1972); Angel Ziems, *El gomecismo y la formación del ejército nacional* (Caracas, 1979). And on the Church, see Daniel Levine, *Religion and Politics in Latin America: The Catholic Church in Venezuela and Colombia* (Princeton, N.J., 1981).

The history of the labour movement has received considerable attention. See Charles Bergquist, *Labor in Latin America: Comparative Essays on Chile, Argentina, Venezuela, and Colombia* (Stanford, Calif., 1986); Steve Ellner, *Los partidos políticos y su disputa por el control del movimiento sindical en Venezuela, 1936–1948* (Caracas, 1980); Julio Godio, *El movimiento obrero venezolano, 1850–1980*, 3 vols. (Caracas, 1980); Paul Nehru Tennassee, *Venezuela, los obreros petroleros y la lucha por la democracia* (Caracas, 1979); Mostafa Hassan, *Economic Growth and Employment Problems in Venezuela: An Analysis of an Oil-Based Economy* (New York, 1975); Alberto J. Pla et al., *Clase obrera, partidos y sindicatos en Venezuela, 1936–1950* (Caracas, 1982); Héctor Lucena, *El movimiento obrero y las relaciones laborales* (Carabobo, 1981).

866 *Bibliographical Essays*

Some good studies of social problems have appeared. The best general study of the Venezuelan population is by Chi-Yi Chen and Michel Picouet, *Dinámica de la población: Caso de Venezuela* (Caracas, 1979). See also Chi-Yi Chen, *Movimientos migratorios en Venezuela* (Caracas, 1968); and Susan Berglund and Humberto Hernández Calimán, *Los de afuera: Un estudio analítico del proceso migratorio en Venezuela, 1936–1985* (Caracas, 1985). On national nutritional deficiencies, see George Schuyler, *Hunger in a Land of Plenty* (Cambridge, Mass., 1980); Paulina Dehollain and Irene Pérez Schael, *Venezuela desnutrida* (Caracas, 1978?); and Eleanor Witte Wright, 'The Political Economy of Venezuelan Food Policy, 1958–1978' (Ph.D. dissertation, University of Maryland, 1982). Jeannette Abouhamad provides a profile of Venezuelans in *Los hombres de Venezuela: Sus necesidades, sus aspiraciones* (Caracas, 1970). Agustín Blanco Muñoz deals with class conflict in *Clases sociales y violencia en Venezuela* (Caracas, 1976). See Esteban Emilio Mosonyi, *Identidad nacional y culturas populares* (Caracas, 1982), and Maritza Montero, *Ideología, alienación e identidad nacional* (Caracas, 1984), for a discussion of national psychology and identity.

The multi-volume study undertaken by the Universidad Central de Venezuela, *Estudio de Caracas,* 15 vols. (1967–72), is useful for Caracas's urban problems, and Lloyd Rodman et al., *Planning Urban Growth: The Experience of the Guayana Program of Venezuela* (Cambridge, Mass., 1969), depicts the new city of Ciudad Guayana. People of the *barrios* receive special attention in Luise Margolies (ed.), *The Venezuelan Peasant in Country and City* (Caracas, 1979); Kenneth Karst, Murray Schwartz and Audrey Schwartz, *The Evolution of Law in the Barrios of Caracas* (Los Angeles, 1973); and Lisa Redfield Peattie, *The View from the Barrio* (Ann Arbor, Mich., 1970). For regional issues, see John Friedman, *Regional Development Policy: A Case Study of Venezuela* (Cambridge, Mass., 1966); and Allan R. Brewer-Carías and Norma Izquierdo Corser, *Estudios sobre la regionalización de Venezuela* (Caracas, 1977).

Administrative history has been dominated by the voluminous works of Allan R. Brewer-Carías – for example, *Estudios sobre la reforma administrativa* (Caracas, 1980), *Cambio político y reforma del estado en Venezuela* (Madrid, 1975), *El estado, crisis y reforma* (Caracas, 1984). Roderick Groves, 'Administrative Reform in Venezuela, 1958–1963' (Ph.D. dissertation, University of Wisconsin, 1965), examines the early efforts to streamline the government bureaucracy, and E. Mark Hanson discusses educational administration in *Educational Reform and Administrative Development: The Cases of Colombia and Venezuela* (Stanford, Calif., 1986).

Venezuela's expansionist foreign policy in the 1970s awakened more scholarly interest in this field. See Robert Bond (ed.), *Contemporary Venezuela and Its Role in International Affairs* (New York, 1977); Stephen G. Rabe, *The Road to OPEC: United States Relations with Venezuela, 1919–1976* (Austin, Tex., 1982); Demetrio Boersner, *Venezuela y el Caribe: Presencia cambiante* (Caracas, 1978); Sheldon Liss, *Diplomacy and Dependency: Venezuela, the United States, and the Americas* (Salisbury, N.C., 1978); Fermín Toro Jiménez, *La política de Venezuela en la conferencia inter-Americana de consolidación de la paz: Buenos Aires, 1936* (Caracas, 1977); Freddy Vivas Gallardo, *Venezuela en la sociedad de las naciones, 1920–1939: Descripción y análisis de una actuación diplomática* (Caracas, 1981); Aníbal Romero (ed.), *Seguridad, defensa y democracia en Venezuela* (Caracas, 1980); Andres Serbin (ed.), *Geopolítica de las relaciones de Venezuela con el Caribe* (Caracas, 1983); Julio Portillo, *Venezuela–Cuba, 1902–1980* (Caracas, 1981); Clemy Machado de Acedo and Marisela Padrón Quero, *La diplomacia de López Contreras y el tratado de reciprocidad comercial con Estados Unidos* (Caracas, 1987); Instituto de Estudios Políticos, Universidad Central de Venezuela, *La agenda de la política exterior de Venezuela* (Caracas, 1983). Francisco J. Parra, *Doctrinas de la Cancillería Venezolana: Digesto,* 6 vols. (New York, 1952–64), provides a useful guide to Venezuelan foreign policy since independence.

INDEX